Adobe® Flex™ 2

Training from the Source

Jeff Tapper
James Talbot
Matthew Boles
with Benjamin Elmore and Michael Labriola

Adobe

Adobe® Flex™ 2: Training from the Source

Jeff Tapper / James Talbot / Matthew Boles with Benjamin Elmore and Michael Labriola

Adobe Press books are published by

Peachpit
1249 Eighth Street
Berkeley, CA 94710
510/524-2178
800/283-9444
510/524-2221 (fax)

Find us on the World Wide Web at:
www.peachpit.com
www.adobe.com

To report errors, please send a note to errata@peachpit.com

Copyright © 2007 by Adobe Systems, Inc.

Authors: Jeff Tapper / James Talbot / Matthew Boles with Benjamin Elmore and Michael Labriola
Adobe Press Editor: Victor Gavenda
Editor: Robyn G. Thomas
Technical Editor: Michael Labriola
Production Coordinator: Becky Winter
Copy Editor: Nancy E. Sixsmith
Compositors: Rick Gordon, Emerald Valley Graphics / Debbie Roberti, Espresso Graphics
Indexer: Joy Dean Lee
Cover Design: Peachpit Press
Proofreader: Mark Kozlowski

Printed and bound in the United States of America

ISBN 0-321-42316-X

9 8 7 6 5 4 3 2

*My efforts on this book are dedicated to my wife Lisa
and daughter Kaliope. Everything I do, I do for you two.*

—Jeff Tapper

*My efforts are dedicated to my family and friends as well as the
Adobe Training and Consulting teams for giving me the incredible
opportunities that have allowed this book to come to be.*

—James Talbot

To friends.

*To Sandra, my best friend and wife, who has helped and supported
me in so many ways over the years. Thanks for supporting me even
when I chose to do crazy things, including writing this book.*

*To my siblings, Melissa, Todd, Jody, and Kent (and their wonderful families)
who continue to be better and better friends with each passing year.*

*To Bryan and Colleen, who prove that once built, a solid
friendship can't be diminished with time or distance.*

*To Bob and Connie, who were willing to be friends when I
needed it most, even at the expense of their time.*

*To Sue, Robert, James, Deborah, Tina, Cathrine, Leo, Jon, and Jim, who are not only
my colleagues in Adobe Customer Training, but who have also become great friends.*

—Matthew Boles

*This book is dedicated to my kids Olivia, Haydn, Sydney, Carrington, and Griffen.
It is always hard to take time away from you for such a task as writing.*

—Benjamin Elmore

To my wife Laura; you always make me smile.

—Michael Labriola

Bios

Jeff Tapper is the Chief Technologist and CEO for Tapper, Nimer and Associates, Inc. He has been developing Internet-based applications since 1995 for a myriad of clients including Morgan Stanley, Doctations, Toys R Us, IBM, Dow Jones, American Express, M&T Bank, Verizon, and many others. He has been developing Flex applications since the earliest days of Flex 1. As an Instructor, Jeff is certified to teach all of Adobe's courses on Flex, ColdFusion, and Flash development. He is also a frequent speaker at Adobe Development Conferences and user groups. Jeff Tapper and Mike Nimer formed Tapper, Nimer and Associates provide expert guidance to rich Internet application development and empower clients through mentoring.

James Talbot has been with Adobe (formerly Macromedia) for more than six years, on both the sales engineering and training teams, and has most recently been working with Flex and Flash Lite. He has traveled extensively throughout the world promoting Adobe products and certifying Adobe instructors as well as speaking at conferences. James has been an integral team member on high profile rich Internet application consulting assignments for companies such as AOL / Time Warner, JP Morgan, Fidelity, and TV Guide.

James is actively involved in the Adobe worldwide instructor and developer community, and contributes to developer certification exams as well as organizing and speaking at user groups. James is passionate about Flash on devices as well as rich Internet applications and he believes that both technologies will change the world for the better.

Matthew Boles is the Technical Lead for the Adobe Customer Training group and has been developing and teaching courses on Flex since the 1.0 release. Matthew has a diverse background in web development, computer networking, and teaching in both professional computer classes and the public schools. In addition to this book, Matthew co-authored a version of the *Certified ColdFusion Developer Study Guide*. He has also developed official Allaire/Macromedia/Adobe curricula in both ColdFusion and Flash development content areas.

Benjamin Elmore is the founder and principal partner of Twin Technologies, an enterprise consulting company that specializes in delivering rich Internet applications for Fortune 500 companies. Ben has been working in the RIA/Web 2.0 spaces since its inception and has authored several books on a variety of technologies. Ben founded Twin Technologies with a core principle of embracing a shared knowledge base within the development community. When leading Twin Technologies, Ben travels to Africa and Turkey to speak on leadership on behalf of the EQUIP organization (www.iequip.org), whose goal is to raise a million Christian leaders over five years. A devoted family man, Ben lives with his wife Mary and their five children in upstate New York.

Michael Labriola, who has devoted a decade and a half to Internet technologies, is a Senior Consultant and Project Lead for Digital Primates, Inc. He spends his mornings teaching developers to work with Flex; his afternoons creating rich Internet applications that generate significant ROI for clients; and his nights dreaming up ways to use Flex that its designers never intended.

Acknowledgments

I would like to thank Matt, James, Ben, and Mike for all their hard work, which has helped shape this book. Special thanks go to the team at Adobe/Macromedia, which has made this all possible, especially the efforts of David Mendels, Phil Costa, and Mike Nimer—all of whom have offered invaluable advice during this process. Thanks to Tad Staley of Adobe consulting, who has given me more opportunities than anyone else to work on Flex projects. I would also like to acknowledge Doctations and the IT Reference Data department at Morgan Stanley, clients whose Flex 2 projects coincided with the writing of this book. This book couldn't possibly have been written without the lessons I learned on their projects, nor could their projects have been successfully completed without my work on this book. Thanks to the editorial staff at Adobe Press, who was faced with the Herculean task of making our writings intelligible. Finally, thanks to the 2004 World Series Champion Boston Red Sox.

—Jeff Tapper

This book has consumed many, many hours and sleepless nights, but it is all due to the incredible efforts of Jeff, Matt, Ben, and Michael. I would like to thank each one of them and offer a special thanks to Michael and Robyn. This book could not have been a success without the incredible steadfastness of both Michael and Robyn, who demonstrated incredible eagle eyes and never wavered in their resolve to publish the very best. Thanks to everyone at Adobe, including David Mendels, Sho Kuwamoto, Eric Anderson, Phil Costa, and everyone else on the Flex and Flex Builder teams. I'd like to offer a special thanks to Robert, Sue, Leo, Cathrine, and Jazmine on the Adobe training team, whose efforts allowed me to have time to work on this book.

—James Talbot

Getting this book finished has been a long and arduous road, and I could not have completed the journey without Jeff, James, Mike, Ben, and Robyn. I hope Mike can forgive me for getting him involved in a project that has taken much more time than either of us could have ever imagined. I also hope Robyn can forgive all of the authors for making this such a long project. Josh and the rest of the gang at Digital Primates deserve kudos for the work they have done in testing this book. Thanks also to Dave Mendels, Phil Costa, Sho Kuwamoto, Heidi Williams, and the rest of the Flex and Flex Builder teams for building great products and helping me understand them. Also thanks to Bob Tierney and Kevin Hoyt for giving doses of reality Flex when needed.

—Matthew Boles

I heard someone once say that the best part of writing is when it is over and you get to see the benefit of your labor. My part in this book was a simple one and I would like to acknowledge the great work done by my co-authors who shouldered the largest share. Thank you for the opportunity to assist with the book; it was a pleasure.

At a recent technology get-together I ran into my first mentor, Greg Fisher. My experience in life has shown me that you can either hoard or share your knowledge with those around you. I am grateful for your willingness so many years ago to choose to invest and share with me.

Finally I would like to acknowledge the sacrifice and support of my wife Mary, the object of my eternal affection.

—Benjamin Elmore

I would like to thank Matt, Jeff, James, and Ben for their work and dedication to bringing this project together. Thanks to Robyn for her diligence, understanding and patience during the process. Thanks to Josh, Jim, and Peter of the Digital Primates' team for hours of reading, running code, supporting my half-thought-out ideas, and generally being great friends and colleagues. Thanks to Shirl for her candor and counsel, and specifically for pushing me in this direction. Thanks to Matt for inviting me to join this project and team. Thanks to my family for the encouragement they always provide. Finally, thanks to my wife Laura, who supports my craziest ideas with a smile and a lot of understanding.

—Michael Labriola

Contents

Introduction

It's just a few short years since Macromedia coined the term *rich Internet application*. Back then, the idea felt somewhat futuristic, but all that has changed. rich Internet applications (or RIAs, as we affectionately refer to them) are reality and they are here right now.

Macromedia released Flex a couple of years ago, making it possible for developers to write applications that take advantage of the incredibly prevalent Flash platform. These applications don't just look great; they also are truly portable, can be fully accessible, and (most importantly) dramatically change the end user experience replacing the page request model of the web to something far more elegant and usable. Something richer.

Numerous organizations have discovered the benefits of Flex and have successfully built and deployed applications that run on top of the Flash platform. The highest profile of these is Yahoo!, which created the next generation of Yahoo! Maps in Flex. But despite the early Flex successes, Flex 1 was most definitely not a mass market product. Pricing, tooling, deployment options, and more meant that Flex 1 was targeted specifically for larger and more-complex applications, as well as for more-sophisticated developers and development. But this has now changed.

Now part of the Adobe family, Flex 2 was released mid 2006—a brand new Flex with a new integrated development environment (IDE), new pricing, new deployment options, a new scripting language, and a brand new Flash Player too. Flex 2 is most definitely a mass market product, designed to bring the values and benefits of RIAs to all developers.

Getting started with Flex is pretty easy. MXML tags are easy to learn (especially when Flex Builder writes many of them for you). ActionScript has a steeper learning curve, but developers with prior programming and scripting experience will pick it up easily. But there is more to Flex development than MXML and ActionScript.

There are many things that need to be understood to be a successful Flex developer, including the following:

- How Flex applications should be built (and how they should not)
- Relationships between MXML and ActionScript, and when to use each

- Various ways to interact with back-end data, and the differences between each

- How to use the Flex components, and know how to write their own

- Performance implications of the code they write and how it is written

- Best practices to write code that is scalable and manageable and reusable (there is definitely more to Flex than MXML and ActionScript)

And this is where this book comes in. Matthew Boles, James Talbot, and Jeff Tapper (ably assisted by Benjamin Elmore and Michael Labriola) have distilled their hard-earned Flex expertise into a series of lessons that will jump-start your own Flex development. Starting with the basics and then incrementally introducing additional functionality and know-how, the author team will guide your journey into the exciting world of RIAs, ensuring success at every step of the way.

Flex 2 is powerful, highly capable, fun, and incredibly addictive, too. And *Adobe Flex 2: Training from the Source* is the ideal tour guide on your journey to the next generation of application development.

Enjoy the ride!

Ben Forta
Senior Technical Evangelist
Adobe Systems, Inc.

Prerequisites

To make the most of this course, you should at the very least understand web terminology. This book isn't designed to teach you anything more than Flex, so the better your understanding of the World Wide Web, the better off you'll be. This book is written assuming that you are comfortable working with programming languages and are probably working with a server-side language such as Java, .Net, PHP, ColdFusion, or a similar technology. Although knowledge of server-side technologies is not required to succeed with this book, there are many comparisons and analogies made to server-side web programming. This book is not intended as an introduction to programming or as an introduction to object-oriented programming (OOP). Experience with OOP is not required, although if you have no programming experience at all, you might find the materials too advanced.

Outline

As you'll soon discover, this book mirrors real-world practices as much as possible. Where certain sections of the book depart from what would be considered a real-world practice, every attempt has been made to inform you. The exercises are designed to get you using the tools and the interface quickly so that you can begin to work on projects of your own with as smooth a transition as possible.

This curriculum should take approximately 38–40 hours to complete and includes the following lessons:

Lesson 1:   Understanding Rich Internet Applications
Lesson 2:   Getting Started
Lesson 3:   Laying Out the Interface
Lesson 4:   Using Simple Controls
Lesson 5:   Handling Events and Data Structures
Lesson 6:   Using Remote XML Data with Controls
Lesson 7:   Creating Components with MXML
Lesson 8:   Using Controls and Repeaters with Data Sets
Lesson 9:   Using Custom Events
Lesson 10:   Creating Custom Components with ActionScript 3.0
Lesson 11:   Using DataGrids and Item Renderers
Lesson 12:   Using Drag and Drop
Lesson 13:   Implementing Navigation
Lesson 14:   Using Formatters and Validators
Lesson 15:   Using the History Manager
Lesson 16:   Customizing the Look and Feel of a Flex Application
Lesson 17:   Accessing Server-side Objects
Lesson 18:   Charting Data
Lesson 19:   Introducing Adobe Flex Data Services
Lesson 20:   Pushing Data with Adobe Flex Data Services
Lesson 21:   Synchronizing Data with Adobe Flex Data Services
Lesson 22:   Creating Transitions and Behaviors
Lesson 23:   Printing From Flex
Lesson 24:   Using Shared Objects
Lesson 25:   Debugging Flex Applications
Appendix A: Setup Instructions

Technical Notes

Before getting started, you should follow the setup instructions in the appendix to ensure that you have the environment set up properly for use with this book.

Much of the data for the hands-on tasks is retrieved from www.flexgrocer.com. Of course, you must have an Internet connection to access this site. In lieu of this, you can start the ColdFusion server instance, as detailed in the appendix, "Setup Instructions," and change the URL from http://www.flexgrocer.com/ to http://localhost:8300/ and access the data locally. For example, in Lesson 6, "Using Remote XML Data with Controls," simply replace http://www.flexgrocer.com/units.xml with http://localhost:8300/units.xml to access the same XML data without an Internet connection.

Throughout the book, we use this wording: "Data type the function as void" or "Data type the function as String." This is just to make the instructions simpler; the authors realize the function itself is not data typed—what is really being data typed is the value the function returns.

Who is this Book For?

Macintosh and Windows users of Flex Builder 2 can complete all the exercises in lessons 1-16. Lessons 17-25, however, cover Flex Data Services, which only runs under Windows. Macintosh users can continue with those chapters if they have access to a Flex Data server running on a separate machine. Setting up that server and connecting to it is, alas, beyond the scope of this book.

The Project Application

Adobe Flex 2: Training from the Source includes many comprehensive tutorials designed to show you how to create a complete application using Flex 2. This application is an "online grocery store" that displays data and images and then submits completed orders to the server. It includes an executive Dashboard to enable store managers to view real-time graphs showing sales details, as well as a data-entry application for adding or editing the products sold by the grocery.

By the end of 25 hands-on lessons, you will have built an entire web site using Flex. You will begin by learning the fundamentals of Flex and understanding how Flex Builder can be used to aid in developing applications. In the early lessons, you will make use of Design mode to begin laying out the application, but as you progress through the book and become more comfortable with the languages used by Flex, you will spend more and more time working in Source mode, which gives you the full freedom and flexibility of coding. By the end of the book, you should be fully comfortable working with the Flex languages and can probably work even without Flex Builder by using the freely available Flex 2 SDK and command-line compiler.

Standard Elements in the Book

Each lesson in this book begins by outlining the major focus of the lesson at hand and introducing new features. Learning objectives and the approximate time needed to complete all the exercises are also listed at the beginning of each lesson. The projects are divided into exercises that explain the importance of each skill you learn. Every lesson will build on the concepts and techniques used in the previous lessons.

Tips (▶): Alternative ways to perform tasks and suggestions to consider when applying the skills you are learning.

Notes (✱): Additional background information to expand your knowledge and advanced techniques you can explore to further develop your skills.

Cautions (▼): Information warning you of situations you might encounter that could cause errors, problems, or unexpected results.

Boldface text: Words that appear in **boldface** are terms that you must type while working through the steps in the lessons.

Boldface code: Lines of code that appear in **boldface** within code blocks help you easily identify changes in the block that you are to make in a specific step in a task.

```
<mx:HorizontalList dataProvider="{dp}"
    labelFunction="multiDisplay"
    columnWidth="130"
    width="850"/>
```

Code in text: Code or keywords appear slightly different from the rest of the text so you can identify them.

To help you easily identify ActionScript, XML, and HTML code within the book, the code has been styled in a special font that's unique from the rest of the text. Single lines of code that are longer than the margins of the page allow wrap to the next line. They are designated by an arrow at the beginning of the continuation of a broken line and are indented under the line from which they continue. For example:

```
public function Product (_catID:Number, _prodName:String, _unitID:Number,
    ➡ _cost:Number, _listPrice:Number, _description:String,_isOrganic:Boolean,
    ➡ _isLowFat:Boolean, _imageName:String)
```

Italicized text: Words that appear in *italics* are either for *emphasis* or are *new vocabulary*.

Italics are also used on placeholders, in which the exact entry may change depending upon your situation. For example: *driveroot*:/flex2tfs/flexGrocer, where the *driveroot* is dependent upon your operating system.

Menu commands and keyboard shortcuts: There are often multiple ways to perform the same task in Flash. The different options will be pointed out in each lesson. Menu commands are shown with angle brackets between the menu names and commands: Menu > Command > Subcommand. Keyboard shortcuts are shown with a plus sign between the names of keys to indicate that you should press the keys simultaneously; for example, Shift+Tab means that you should press the Shift and Tab keys at the same time.

Appendix: This book includes one appendix that will guide you through the steps to set up the working environment required to execute the exercises in this book.

CD-ROM: The CD-ROM included with this book includes all the media files, starting files, and completed projects for each of the lessons in the book. These files are located in the assets, start, or complete directories, respectively. Lesson 1, "Understanding Rich Internet Applications," does not include tasks; however, the CD-ROM includes media in the directory Lesson01. This media provides the flexGrocer directory for your project. At any point you need to return to the original source material, you can restore the flexGrocer. Some lessons include an intermediate directory, which contains files in various stages of development in the lesson. Any time you want to reference one of the files being built in a lesson to verify that you are correctly executing the steps in the exercises, you will find the files organized on the CD-ROM under the corresponding lesson. For example, the files for Lesson 4 are located on the CD-ROM in the Lesson04 folder.

The directory structure of the lessons you will be working with is as follows:

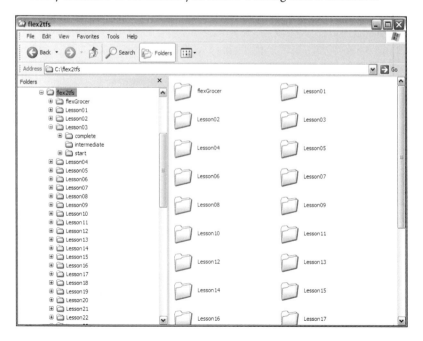

Adobe Training from the Source

The *Adobe Training from the Source* and *Advanced Training from the Source* series are developed in association with Adobe and reviewed by the product support teams. Ideal for active learners, the books in the *Training from the Source* series offer hands-on instruction designed to provide you with a solid grounding in the program's fundamentals. If you learn best by doing, this is the series for you. Each *Training from the Source* title contains hours of instruction on Adobe software products. They are designed to teach the techniques that you need to create sophisticated professional-level projects. Each book includes a CD-ROM that contains all the files used in the lessons, completed projects for comparison, and more.

Adobe Authorized Training and Certification

This book is geared to enable you to study at your own pace with content from the source. Other training options exist through the Adobe Authorized Training Partner program. Get up to speed in a matter of days with task-oriented courses taught by Adobe Certified Instructors. Or learn on your own with interactive online training from Adobe University. All these sources of training will prepare you to become an Adobe Certified Developer.

For more information about authorized training and certification, check out www.adobe.com/training/.

What You Will Learn

You will develop the skills you need to create and maintain your own Flex applications as you work through these lessons.

By the end of the course, you will be able to:

- Use Flex Builder to build Flex applications
- Understand MXML, ActionScript 3.0, and the interactions of the two
- Work with complex sets of data
- Load data from a server using XML, web services, and Remote objects
- Handle events to allow interactivity in an application
- Create your own custom events
- Create your own components, in either MXML or ActionScript 3.0

- Apply styles and skins to customize the look and feel of an application

- Add charts to an application

- And much more…

Minimum System Requirements

Windows

- Intel Pentium 4 processor

- Microsoft Windows XP with Service Pack 2, Windows XP Professional, Windows 2000 Server, Windows 2000 Pro, or Windows Server 2003

- 512MB of RAM (1GB recommended)

- 700MB of available hard-disk space

- Java Virtual Machine: Sun JRE 1.4.2, Sun JRE 1.5, IBM JRE 1.4.2

Macintosh

- Flex Builder for Macintosh is not available at the time this book went to the printers, but is expected shortly.

The Flex line of products is extremely exciting, and we're waiting to be amazed by what you will do with it. With a strong foundation in Flex, you can grow and expand your skillset quickly. Flex is really not too difficult to use for anyone with programming experience. With a little bit of initiative and effort, you can fly through the following lessons and be building your own custom applications and sites in no time.

What You Will Learn

In this lesson, you will:

- Explore alternatives to a page-based architecture
- See the benefits of rich Internet applications (RIAs)
- Compare the RIA technologies available

Approximate Time

This lesson takes approximately 30 minutes to complete.

Lesson Files

Media Files:
   None

Starting Files:
   None

Completed Files:
   None

LESSON 1

Understanding Rich Internet Applications

Computers have been playing a role in the business environment for more than four decades. Throughout that time, the roles of the client and server have been constantly evolving. As businesses and their employees have become more comfortable delegating responsibilities to computers, the look, feel, and architecture of computerized business applications have changed to meet the new demands. This evolving process continues today, as businesses are demanding faster, lighter, and richer Internet applications. In this lesson, you will learn about this evolving nature and understand the business requirements that push us to build rich Internet applications (RIAs).

You will use Flex to build the FlexGrocer application seen here.

Understanding the Evolution of Computer Applications

In the earliest days of computerized business applications, all processing took place on mainframes, with the client having no role other than to display information from the server and accept user input. This was largely dictated by the high cost of processing power. It simply was not affordable to spread powerful clients throughout the enterprise, so all processing was consolidated, and "dumb terminals" provided the user interaction.

As memory and processing power became cheaper, dumb terminals were replaced by micro-computers (or personal computers). With the added power available, more *desktop applications*, such as word processors and spreadsheets, could run *stand-alone*, so no server was necessary. One challenge faced by organizations with microcomputers was a lack of central-ized data. Although the mainframe era had everything centralized, the age of the microcom-puter distributed everything, adding many challenges for centralizing business rules and synchronizing data across the enterprise.

To help resolve this issue, several vendors released platforms that sought to combine the strengths of the microcomputer with those of the mainframe, which led to the birth of cli-ent/server systems. These platforms afforded end users the power and ease of microcomputers while allowing for business logic and data to be stored and accessed from a centralized location—which solved the problems of the day. The new challenge introduced with the client/server systems was distribution. Any time changes needed to be made to client appli-cations, IT departments had to manually reinstall or upgrade the software on every single desktop computer. Many companies found they needed a full-time staff whose primary responsibility was keeping the software on the end users' desktops current.

With the explosive growth of the Internet in the 1990s, a new model for business applications became available. This model worked by having a web browser act as a thin client, whose pri-mary job was to render HTML and send requests back to an application server that dynami-cally composed and delivered *pages* to the client. This is often referred to as a "page-based architecture." This model successfully solved the distribution problem of the client/server days; the application was downloaded from the server each time an end user needed it, so updates could be made in a single centralized place and automatically distributed to the entire user base. This model was and continues to be successful for many applications; however, it also creates significant drawbacks and limitations. In reality, Internet applications bore a great resemblance to mainframe applications, in that all the processing was centralized at the server, and the client only rendered data and captured user feedback. The biggest problems with this surrounded the user interface (UI). Many of the conveniences that end users grew to accept over the previous decade were lost, and the UI was limited by the capabilities of HTML.

For example, desktop software as well as client/server applications frequently use the drag-and-drop feature. However, HTML (Hypertext Markup Language) applications almost never use the feature, due to the complexities and lack of cross-browser support for the DHTML (Dynamic HTML), which it requires to implement in a pure HTML/DHTML solution.

In most cases the overall sophistication of the solutions that could be built and delivered was greatly reduced. Although the web has offered great improvements in the ease and speed of deploying applications, the capabilities of web-based business applications took a big step backward because browser-based applications had to adapt to the limitations of the web architecture: HTML and Hypertext Transport Protocol (HTTP).

Today, the demands for Internet-based applications continue to grow and are often quite different from the demands of the mid-1990s. End users and businesses are demanding more from their investments in Internet technology. The capability to deliver true value to users is forcing many companies to look toward richer models for Internet applications; models that combine the media-rich power of the traditional desktop with the deployment and content-rich nature of web applications.

As Internet applications begin to be used for core business functionality, the maintainability of those applications becomes more crucial. The maintainability of an application is directly related to the application's architecture. Sadly, many web applications were built with little thought about the principles of application architecture, and therefore they are difficult to maintain and extend. Today, it is easier to build a solid architecture for an application by providing a clean separation between the business, data access and presentation areas, with the introduction of elements such as Web Services, *service-oriented architecture* (SOA) became more feasible for web-based applications.

To meet the demands of businesses, RIAs should be able to do the following:

- Provide an efficient, high-performance run time for executing code, content, and communications. In the next section of this lesson, you will explore the limitations of the standard HTML-based applications, and learn that the traditional page-based architectures have a number of performance-related challenges.

- Provide powerful and extensible object models to facilitate interactivity. Web browsers have progressed in recent years in their capability to support interactivity through the Document Object Model (DOM) via JavaScript and DHTML, but they still lack standardized cross-platform and cross-browser support. Building RIAs with these tools so they will work on a variety of browsers and operating systems involves building multiple versions of the same application.

- Enable using server-side objects through using Web Services or other similar technologies. The promise of RIAs includes the capability to cleanly separate presentation logic and user interfaces from the application logic housed on the server.

- Enable use of the applications when "offline." As laptops and other portable devices continue to grow in popularity, one of the serious limitations of Internet applications is the requirement that the machine running the application be connected to the Internet. Although users can be online the vast majority of the time, business travelers know there are times when an Internet connection is not currently possible. A successful RIA should enable users to be productive with or without an active connection.

Breaking away from the Page-based Architecture

For experienced web developers, one of the biggest challenges in building RIAs is breaking away from a page-based architecture. Traditional web applications are centered on the concept of a web page. Regardless which server-side technologies (if any) are used, the flow goes something like this:

1. User opens a browser and requests a page from a web server.

2. Web server receives request.

3. (optional) Web server hands request to an application server to dynamically assemble page or

4. (optional) Web server retrieves static page from file system.

5. Web server sends page (dynamic or static) back to browser.

6. Browser draws page in place of whatever was previously displayed.

Even in situations when most of the content of the previous page is identical to the new page, the entire new page needs to be sent to the browser and rendered. This is one of the inefficiencies of traditional web applications: each user interaction requires a new page loading in the browser. One of the key goals of RIAs is to reduce the amount of extra data transmitted with each request. Rather than download an entire page, why not download only the data that changed and update the page the user is viewing? This is the way standard desktop or client/server applications work.

Although this goal seems simple and is readily accepted by developers taking their first plunge into RIA development, often web developers bring a page-based mindset to RIA applications and struggle to understand how to face the challenges from the page-based world, such as, how to "maintain state." For example, after users log in, how do we know who they are and what they are allowed to do as they navigate around the application?

Maintaining state was a challenge introduced by web-based applications. HTTP was designed as a stateless protocol, in which each request to the server was an atomic unit that knew nothing about previous requests. This stateless nature of the web allowed for greater efficiency and redundancy because a connection did not need to be held open between the browser and server. Each new page request lasted only as long as the server spent retrieving and sending the page, allowing a single server to handle far more simultaneous requests.

The stateless nature of the web added challenges for application developers. Usually, applications need to remember information about the user: login permissions, items added to a shopping cart, and so on. Without the capability to remember this data from one request to the next, true application development would not be possible. To help solve this problem, a series of solutions was implemented; revolving around a unique token being sent back to the server with each request (often as *cookies*, which are small text files containing application specific identifiers for an individual user) and having the server store the user's information.

Unlike traditional web applications, RIAs can bypass many of these problems. Because the application remains in client RAM the entire time it's being used (instead of being loaded and unloaded like a page-based model), variables can be set once and accessed throughout the application's life cycle.

A different approach to handling state is just one of many places in which building applications requires a slightly different mindset than web application development. In reality, web-based RIAs bear more resemblance to client/server applications than they do to web applications.

Identifying the Advantages of Rich Internet Applications

Unlike the dot-com boom days of the mid-to-late 1990s, businesses are no longer investing in Internet technologies, simply because they are "cool." To succeed, a new technology needs to demonstrate real return on investment and truly add value. RIAs achieve this on several levels: they reduce development costs; and add value throughout the organization.

Business Managers

By making it easier for users to work with software, the number of successful transactions is increasing. This increase occurs across many industries and can be quantified by businesses with metrics, such as increased productivity using intranet applications or increased percentage of online shoppers who complete a purchase. More productive employees can drastically reduce labor costs while growing online sales increase revenue and decrease opportunities lost to competitors.

IT Organizations

Breaking away from page-based architectures reduces the load on web servers and reduces the overall network traffic. Rather than transmitting entire pages over and over again, the entire application is downloaded once, and then the only communication back and forth with the server is the data to be presented on the page. By reducing server load and network traffic, infrastructure costs can be noticeably lower. RIAs developed using sound architectural principles and best practices can also greatly increase the maintainability of an application, as well as greatly reduce the development time to build the application.

End Users

End users experience the greatest benefits of RIAs. A well-designed RIA greatly reduces users' frustration levels because they no longer need to navigate several pages to find what they need nor have to wait for a new page to load before continuing to be productive. Additionally, the time users spend learning how to use the application can be greatly reduced, further empowering them. Today, there are a number of excellent applications, which would not be possible without the concepts of an RIA, such as the Harley Davidson Motorcycle Configurator and the Kodak EasyShare Gallery applications. These easy to use applications give an excellent example of the ease of use an RIA can offer an end user.

RIA Technologies

Today, there are several technology choices developers have when they start building RIAs. Among the more popular choices are HTML-based options, such as Ajax (Asynchronous Javascript and XML), as well as plug-in-based options such as Adobe Flash, Adobe Flex, and Laszlo which all run in Flash Player. A new option from Microsoft seems to be on the horizon because the Microsoft channels are abuzz with talk of XAML and the Windows Presentation Foundation.

There are four different run times on which the current RIA landscape is based. Those are Ajax, which is supported by Dojo, OpenRico, Backbase and the Yahoo ToolKit; Flash Player, which is used by Flex and Laszlo; Windows Presentation Foundation (WPF), which is Microsoft's not yet released platform; and Java, which is used by AWT, Swing, and Eclipse RCP. It seems that both the Java and WPF solutions are taking aim at desktop applications, rather than RIAs although they could be used for RIAs as well.

Asynchronous Javascript and XML (Ajax)

One of the easier choices to understand (but not necessarily to implement) is Ajax, which is an acronym for *Asynchronous Javascript and XML*. Ajax is based on tools already familiar to web developers: HTML, DHTML, and JavaScript. The fundamental idea behind Ajax is to use JavaScript to update the page without reloading it. A JavaScript program running in the browser can insert new data into the page or change structure by manipulating the HTML DOM without reloading a new page. Updates may involve new data that is loaded from the server in the background (using XML or other formats) or be in response to a user interaction, such as a click or hover.

The earliest forms used Java applets for remote communication. As browser technologies developed, other means, such as the use of IFrames, replaced the applets. In recent years, XMLHttpRequest was introduced into JavaScript, providing a means to facilitate data transfers without the need for a new page request, applet, or IFrame.

In addition to the benefit of Ajax using elements already familiar to many web application developers, Ajax requires no external plug-in to run. It works purely on the browser's capability to use JavaScript and DHTML. However, the reliance on JavaScript poses one of the new liabilities of Ajax: it fails to work if the user has JavaScript disabled in the browser.

Another issue with Ajax is that it has varying levels of support for DHTML and JavaScript in different browsers on different platforms. For applications in which the target audience can be controlled (such as intranet applications), Ajax can be written to support a single browser on a particular platform (many businesses today have standardized browsers and operating systems). However, when applications are opened to larger audiences (such as extranet and Internet applications), Ajax applications need to be tested (and often modified) to ensure that they run identically in all browsers on all operating systems.

Ajax is not likely to go away any time soon, and each day more and more high-profile Ajax applications are launched with great acclaim (such as Google Maps).

It should be noted that Ajax is not actually a programming model in and of itself. It is really a collection of various JavaScript libraries. Some of these libraries include reusable components designed to make common tasks easier. Although Ajax lacks a centralized vendor, integrating these libraries introduces dependencies on third parties, which assumes a certain amount of risk.

Flash

One of the key competitive run times in the RIA space is Adobe's Flash Platform. The Flash Platform is currently the key competitor to Ajax for RIAs. Originally written as a plug-in to run animations, Flash Player has evolved over the years, with each new version adding new capabilities while still maintaining a very small footprint. Over the past decade, Flash Player has gained near ubiquity, with some version of it installed in more than 97 percent of all web browsers on the Internet. Since 2002, Macromedia (now part of Adobe) began focusing on Flash as more than an animation tool. And with the Flash 6 release, Macromedia began to provide more capabilities for building applications. Macromedia found that with the combination of the ubiquity of the player and the power available from its scripting language (ActionScript), developers could build full browser-based applications and get around the limitations of HTML.

By targeting Flash Player, developers could also break away from browser and platform incompatibilities. One of the many nice features of Flash Player is that content and applications developed for any particular version of Flash Player will (usually) run on any platform/browser that supported that version of the player. With very few exceptions, it remains true today.

Historically, the biggest drawback of building applications for the Flash Player was the authoring environment, which was clearly built as an animation tool for users creating interactive content. Many developers who wanted to build RIAs for Flash Player were thwarted by the unfamiliarity of the tools. This, coupled with the scant materials available in 2002 for learning to use Flash as an application platform, kept many serious developers from successfully building Flash applications.

Although Flash Player remains an excellent platform for RIAs, the introduction of solutions such as Laszlo and Flex have greatly simplified the development process and reduced the number of RIAs developed directly in Flash Studio.

Laszlo

Sensing the need for more developer-friendly tools for building RIAs, Laszlo Systems developed a language and compiler that enabled developers to work with familiar languages from which their compiler could create applications to run in Flash Player.

Just like Ajax, Laszlo applications are built in JavaScript and XML, but they run in Flash Player, so they make available the rich-user experiences of a desktop client along with the deployment benefits of traditional web applications. Flash Player also gives the capability to run on virtually every web browser regardless of the operating system. Unlike Ajax applications, Laszlo uses a compiler that takes the XML and JavaScript and then publishes a Flash SWF file from them. This allows developers freedom from varying levels of JavaScript support across different platforms.

Another way Laszlo is similar to Ajax is that data access is usually done by loading in server-side XML. With the more recent introduction of the OpenLaszlo servlet, Laszlo applications can now also consume Simple Object Access Protocol (SOAP)-based Web Services. In late 2004, the Laszlo platform became open source and therefore free for development and deployment.

At this point, the biggest drawback to Laszlo is one of its early strengths—that it relies on JavaScript. JavaScript is loosely typed; in its current incarnation, it does not support many fundamental object-oriented concepts (such as true classes), which the development community is embracing. A second drawback is that it blocks developers from directly interacting with the rich set of Flash Player APIs, instead requiring you to use APIs that have been exposed through the tags and their corresponding JavaScript API.

As an open-source tool, Laszlo is likely to gain favor among the set of developers who currently tie themselves to the open-source "LAMP" family of products (Linux, Apache, MySQL, and PHP).

The next generation of Laszlo's server is said to have the capability to use the same XML and JavaScript for producing either Flash or Ajax applications. If this proves to be true, the Laszlo toolset could indeed be very valuable.

Flex

For many of the same reasons why Laszlo was developed, Macromedia set forth on its own project to create a more developer-friendly approach for building applications for Flash Player. In 2004, Macromedia released Flex 1.0 (followed by Flex 1.5 and Flex 2.0 in 2005 and 2006, respectively). Architecturally, Flex applications are similar to Ajax applications, in that both are capable of dynamic updates to the user interface, as well as the ability to send and load data in the background.

The Flex 2 product line provides the next generation of developer tools and services that enable developers everywhere to build and deploy RIAs on the Flash platform.

The Flex 2 product line consists of several pieces:

- **ActionScript 3.0** — A powerful object-oriented programming language that pushes forward the capabilities of the Flash platform. ActionScript 3.0 is designed to create a language ideally suited for rapidly building RIAs. Although earlier versions of ActionScript offered the power and flexibility required for creating engaging online experiences, ActionScript 3.0 further advances the language, improving performance and ease of development to facilitate even the most complex applications with large datasets and fully object-oriented, reusable code.

- **Flash Player 9 (FP9)** — Building on Flash Player 8, this next generation of Flash Player focuses on improving script execution. To facilitate this improvement, FP9 includes a brand new, highly optimized ActionScript Virtual Machine (AVM) known as AVM2. AVM2 is built from the ground up to work with ActionScript 3.0, the next generation of the language that powers Flash Player. The new virtual machine is significantly faster, and supports run-time error reporting and greatly improved debugging. Flash Player 9 will also contain AVM1, which executes ActionScript 1.0 and 2.0 code for backward-compatibility with existing and legacy content. Unlike applications built using JavaScript, Flash Player is capable of using a Just In Time (JIT) compilation process, which enables it to run faster and consume less memory.

- **Flex Framework 2** — Using the foundation provided by FP9 and ActionScript 3.0, the framework adds an extensive class library to enable developers to easily use the best practices for building successful RIAs. Flex uses an XML-based language called MXML to allow developers a declarative way to manage the elements of an application. Developers can get access to Flex framework through Flex Builder or the free Flex SDK, which includes a command-line compiler and debugger, allowing developers to use any editor they prefer and still be able to access the compiler or debugger directly.

- **Flex Builder 2** — A brand new tool designed from the ground up with the intention of providing developers with an environment specifically built for building RIAs. Built on top of the industry standard, open-source Eclipse project, Flex Builder 2 provides an excellent coding and debugging environment, is a rich and useful design tool, and promotes best practices in coding and application development. Another benefit of the Eclipse platform is that it provides a rich set of extensibility capabilities, so customizations can easily be written to extend the IDE to meet specific developers' needs and/or preferences.

- **Flex Data Services 2 (FDS2)** — Previous versions of Flex included a set of run-time services to help with data access and integration to existing server infrastructures. Flex Data Services 2 take this idea to the next level by adding to the existing tools a set of message-based services to synchronize data across all tiers of an application. This vastly increases the productivity of developers and the capabilities of RIA. Additionally, FDS2 exposes a robust messaging infrastructure, which enables real-time data streaming, the ability to implement a true server-side push, as well as publish-subscribe messaging. Another set of features available in FDS2 surrounds the capability to rapidly build and deploy occasionally connected applications, so that users can have data available to them, even if they are working without an Internet connection. These services aid in synchronizing the data the next time the user is working with an Internet connection.

Windows Presentation Foundation/XAML/Expression

Microsoft has announced they will launch a set of tools to help developers build RIAs on the Windows platform. The new system consists of the following:

- **WPF** — The Windows Presentation Foundation (formerly code-named Avalon). This is analogous to the Flash Player and Flex frameworks.

- **XAML** — Extensible Application Markup Language. The XML-based language in which you can build WPF applications. XAML is analogous to Flex's MXML language.

- **C#** — The programming language used to build applications for WPF. To follow the Flex 2 analogy, this operates in a similar fashion to ActionScript 3.0 for Flex Applications.

- **Microsoft Expression** — A professional design tool designed to work with XAML and enable interation designers to create the user interface and visual behavior for WPF applications. This is roughly analogous to Flash Studio, as a design tool for WPF applications.

- **Visual Studio** — Microsoft announced plans to make a future version of Visual Studio work with XAML, WinFX, C# and VB.Net.

Using these tools, Microsoft is promoting a workflow in which designers create compelling user interfaces with Expression, and then developers can implement the business and data access logic using Visual Studio.

Because these tools are not publicly available yet, it is impossible to predict the success or market penetration they will have. Microsoft publicly stated they will have support for other platforms (specifically with their WPF/E, which is an abbreviation for Windows Presentation Foundation/Everywhere), but specific information, such as how much of the WPF technologies will be available with WPF/E, has not been forthcoming. It is encouraging to see Microsoft finally promising to provide tools for platforms other than Windows, but it's too soon to see how they will live up to that promise.

Assuming that the cross platform promise is met, WPF may some day offer a very compelling platform, in that they can leverage integration with Visual Studio, which many developers already use, and they have a separate design tool specifically for designers. One potential weakness of WPF is that it is first and foremost designed for building desktop Windows applications, not browser-based ones. The idea is that users will be able to install WPF applications via the browser, but they are likely to be much larger downloads and memory footprints. Also, it is worth noting that it is likely to be a long time before WPF reaches any kind of ubiquity—even on Windows—because of the large download required. Though it has been promised that WPF will work in Windows XP (currently the largest install base of an OS), it's not clear when XP users can really expect it, or what they can expect from it.

What You Will Learn

In this lesson, you will:

- Create a new project and three main application files

- Understand the different parts of the Flex Builder workbench: editors, views, and perspectives

- Code, save, and run application files

- Use some of the features in Flex Builder 2 that make application development faster and easier, such as code hinting and local history

- Work in both Source mode and Design mode

- Use various views, such as Navigator view, Components view, and Flex Properties view

- Understand the process of how the MXML you write is transformed into a SWF file that Flash Player can process at the browser

Approximate Time

This lesson takes approximately 1 hour and 30 minutes to complete.

Lesson Files

Media Files:

None

Starting Files:

None

Completed Files:

Lesson02/complete/DataEntry.mxml
Lesson02/complete/Dashboard.mxml
Lesson02/complete/EComm.mxml

LESSON 2

Getting Started

You're ready to start your adventure of learning Adobe Flex, and the first thing to do is become familiar with the environment in which you will be developing your applications. This environment is Adobe Flex Builder 2, which is based on the Eclipse platform. The Eclipse platform is an open source, integrated development environment (IDE) that can be extended, and Flex Builder 2 has extended and customized Eclipse for building Flex applications.

In this lesson, you become familiar with Adobe Flex Builder 2 by building the main application files of the FlexGrocer application on which you will work throughout this book. By building the three basic files of the FlexGrocer application, you will learn about the Flex Builder 2 interface and how to create, run, and save application files. You will also discover some of the many features Flex Builder 2 offers to make application development easier.

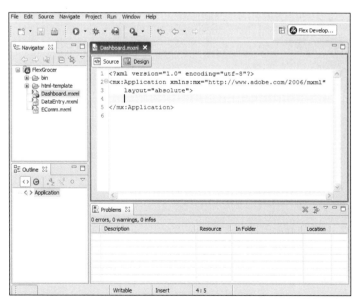

Flex Builder 2 with a file open in Source mode

Getting Started with Flex Application Development

Before a building can be built, the foundation must be laid. This lesson is that foundation for further Flex development. You will leave this lesson knowing that you can manipulate the Flex Builder workbench in ways that make the process of Flex development easier and faster. Along the way you will create the three main application files that define the major sections of the FlexGrocer application.

Part of the study of any new body of knowledge is learning a basic vocabulary, and in this lesson you will learn the basic vocabulary of both Flex development and Flex Builder. You will understand terms such as *view*, *perspective*, and *editor* in relationship to the Flex Builder workbench. You also will understand the terms and processes that transform the text entered in Flex Builder into a file of the type Flash Player can consume at the browser.

Creating a Project and an MXML Application

In this first task, you will be creating a Flex application. To do that, you must first create a project in Flex Builder. A project is nothing more than a collection of files and folders that will help you organize your work. All the files you create for the FlexGrocer application will be in this project. You'll also see that you have two choices when working with an application file. You can be in either Source mode or Design mode. In most cases, the view you choose will be a personal preference, but there are times when some functionality will be available to you only when you are in a particular view.

Also in this task, you will run the Flex application. You'll discover how the MXML code you write is turned into a SWF file that is viewed in a browser.

1 Start Flex Builder 2 by choosing Start > Programs > Adobe > Flex Builder 2.

This is most likely the way you will start Flex Builder. There is a possibility that you had Eclipse already installed on your computer and then added the Flex functionality using the plug-in configuration. In this case, you will need to open Eclipse as you have before.

2 Choose File > New > Flex Project. Select the Basic option; then click Next.

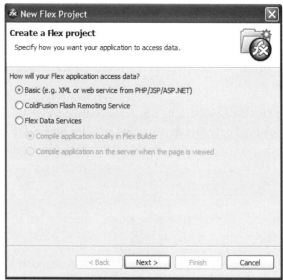

You will be creating only one project for this application, but there are many options from the New menu choice. You'll explore many of these options throughout the book and one of them later in this lesson.

3 For the Project name, enter **FlexGrocer**.

The project name should reflect the files contained in the project. As you continue your work with Flex Builder, you'll soon have many projects, and a project name will be important to remind you which files are in each project.

4 Uncheck the Use default location check box, and for the Folder location enter *driveroot:/***flex2tfs/flexGrocer**. Click Next.

Do not accept the default for this entry. The default uses your My Documents directory and places files very deep in the directory structure. For simplicity's sake, you are putting your working files right on the root drive.

✱ **NOTE:** *driveroot* is a placeholder for the root drive of the operating system you are using, Windows or Mac. Replace *driveroot* with the appropriate path. Also, note that the directory name is case-sensitive.

5 For the Main application file enter **DataEntry.mxml**.

By default, Flex Builder will use an application name that is the same as your project name. You do not want that in this case. Flex Builder automatically creates the main application file for you and includes the basic structure of a Flex application file.

✳ **NOTE:** MXML is a case-sensitive language. So be sure to follow the case of filenames in tags shown in this book. At the end of this lesson, there will be a short discussion on how object-oriented programming affects some of the case usage for filenames, tags, and properties.

6 Click Finish and see the project and application file that were created.

Here you see your first Flex application. Currently the application is displayed in Source mode. Later in this lesson, you will also look at this application in Design mode.

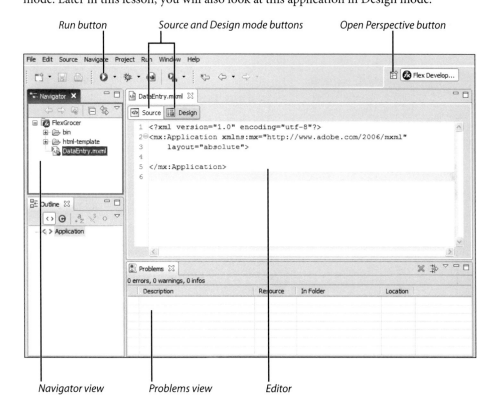

The default application file contains some elements you need to understand. The first line of code (`<?xml version="1.0" encoding="utf-8"?>`) is an XML document type declaration. Because MXML is an XML standard language, the document declaration must be included.

The second line of code (`<mx:Application xmlns:mx="http://www.adobe.com/2006/mxml" layout="absolute">`) defines a Flex main application page. The `<mx:Application>` tag represents the outside container, or holder of all the content in the Flex application. You can have only one `<mx:Application>` tag per Flex application.

Inside the <mx:Application> tag, the attribute/value pair that appears to hold a URL xmlns:mx="http://www.adobe.com/2006/mxml" is defining a namespace for your Flex tags. This code defines the mx prefix to be associated with a set of tags. The value of the attribute that looks like a URL is actually what is referred to as a Universal Resource Identifier (URI) in XML terminology. In a configuration file, flex-config.xml, an association is made between this URI and what is called a manifest file. The manifest file contains all the legal tags that can be used with the mx prefix. In a standard Flex Builder installation, the file is found at this location: *installationdirectory*\Adobe\Flex Builder 2\Flex SDK 2\frameworks\mxml-manifest.xml.

Part of that file is shown in the following example.

```
mxml-manifest.xml  ✕
<?xml version="1.0"?>
<componentPackage>

    <component id="Accordion" class="mx.containers.Accordion"/>
    <component id="AddChildAction" class="mx.effects.AddChildAction"/>
    <component id="AnimateProperty" class="mx.effects.AnimateProperty"/>
    <component id="Application" class="mx.core.Application"/>
    <component id="ApplicationControlBar" class="mx.containers.ApplicationControlBar"/>
    <component id="ArrayCollection" class="mx.collections.ArrayCollection"/>
    <component id="Blur" class="mx.effects.Blur"/>
    <component id="Box" class="mx.containers.Box"/>
    <component id="Button" class="mx.controls.Button"/>
    <component id="ButtonBar" class="mx.controls.ButtonBar"/>
    <component id="Canvas" class="mx.containers.Canvas"/>
    <component id="CheckBox" class="mx.controls.CheckBox"/>
    <component id="ColorPicker" class="mx.controls.ColorPicker"/>
    <component id="ComboBox" class="mx.controls.ComboBox"/>
    <component id="Container" class="mx.core.Container"/>
    <component id="ControlBar" class="mx.containers.ControlBar"/>
    <component id="CurrencyFormatter" class="mx.formatters.CurrencyFormatter"/>
    <component id="CurrencyValidator" class="mx.validators.CurrencyValidator"/>
    <component id="CreditCardValidator" class="mx.validators.CreditCardValidator"/>
    <component id="DataGrid" class="mx.controls.DataGrid"/>
```

Finally, layout="absolute" defines how this application page will lay out its children or what is on the page. With an *absolute* layout you specify *x,y* values to position all children of the application. Other valid choices for the layout's value are vertical and horizontal. A *vertical* layout means all children of the application run vertically down the application's page, and *horizontal* means they run horizontally across the application's page. As you continue to develop in Flex you will use a combination of the layouts to gain the look you want.

Understanding the Flex Builder 2 Workbench

Before you do any more work on your application file, you first should become more familiar with the Flex Builder *workbench*, which is all you see in Flex Builder. There are a number of terms you should become familiar with concerning the interface. For instance, you will learn in this task what *views*, *editors*, and *perspectives* mean in the workbench.

1 Close the current editor by clicking the *x* on the right side of the DataEntry.mxml editor tab. All editors will have a tab on the top left of the editor area.

Whenever you have a file open, it is opened in the workbench in what is called an editor. You just closed the editor containing the DataEntry.mxml file. You can have many editors open at once in the workbench, and each will contain a file with code in it.

2 Open the editor containing the DataEntry.mxml file from the Navigator view by double-clicking the filename.

You can also open the file by right-clicking the filename and choosing Open.

3 Make the editor expand in width and height by double-clicking the editor tab.

There will be times when you want to see as much of your code as possible, especially because Flex Builder does not word wrap. Simply double-clicking the editor tab expands the editor in both width and height, showing as much code as possible.

4 Restore the editor to its previous size by double-clicking the tab again.

As you see, you easily can switch between expanded and non-expanded editors.

5 Click the Design mode button in the editor to view the application in Design mode.

The workbench looks radically different in Design mode, which allows you to drag and drop user interface controls into the application. You will also be able to set property values from Design mode. Obviously, Design mode also lets you see your application more as it will look to an end user.

6 Return to Source mode by clicking the Source button in the editor.

You will be using mostly Source mode in this book, but some tasks are better performed in Design mode.

7 Close the Navigator view by clicking the *x* on the Navigator tab. Just like editors, all views will also have tabs on the top left of the particular view.

In Flex Builder 2, the different sections displaying content are all called *views*.

8 Reopen Navigator view by choosing Window > Project Navigator.

After you close a view you can reopen that view from this menu. There are many views; in fact, if you choose Window > Other Views you'll see a window with many of the views displayed.

9 Click the Open Perspective button just above the top right of the editor, choose the Flex Debugging perspective.

A *perspective* is nothing more than a layout of views that you want to use repeatedly. Flex Builder comes with built-in Flex Development and Flex Debugging perspectives. You can create a layout from your own set of views and save them as a perspective that can be recalled at any time.

10 Return to the Flex Development perspective.

As you can see, it is easy to switch between perspectives. Later in the book, you'll be using the Debugging perspective and discovering its many helpful options.

11 If they are not showing, turn on code line numbers by choosing Window > Preferences. In the dialog box, click the plus signs (+) in front of General and then Editors. Finally click Text Editors and click the check box for Show Line Numbers.

Line numbers are useful because Flex Builder will report errors using line numbers.

TIP: You can also turn on line numbers by right-clicking in the marker bar of the editor and selecting Show Line Numbers. The marker bar is the area just to the left of where the code is displayed in the editor.

Running Your Application

In the first task, you created your project and an application page. Before you got a chance to run the application, the second task took you on a tour of the Flex Builder workbench. You will now get back to your application. You will run it, add code to it, and learn the basics of file manipulation.

1 Open the Project menu. Be sure the Build Automatically option has a check mark in front of it.

When you have Build Automatically checked, Flex continually checks your saved files, compiles them upon a save, and prepares them to run. Syntax errors are flagged even before you run your application, which does not occur if Build Automatically is not checked.

> **TIP:** As your applications grow more complex, you might find that having this setting checked will take too much time, in which case you should uncheck this setting and the build will happen only when you run your application.

2 Run your application by clicking the Run button. You will not see anything in the browser window when it opens.

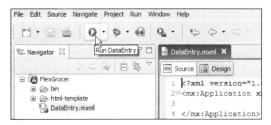

You have now run your first Flex application, and it wasn't that interesting. In this case, the skeleton application contained no tags to display anything in the browser. But you did see the application run and you saw the default browser open and display the results, as uninteresting as it was.

> **NOTE:** What exactly happened when you pushed the Run button? Actually, a number of processes occurred. First, the XML tags in the application file were translated to ActionScript. The ActionScript was then used to generate a SWF file, which is the format Flash Player understands. The SWF file was then sent to Flash Player in the browser.

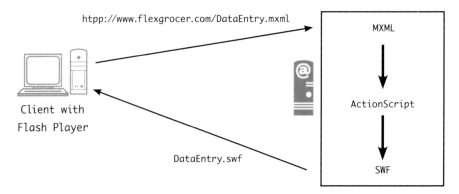

3 Close the browser and return to Flex Builder.

4 Add an `<mx:Label>` tag by placing the cursor between the `<mx:Application>` tags; enter the less-than symbol (**<**) and then enter **mx**, followed by a colon (**:**). You will see a long list of tags. Press the letter *L* (upper or lower case) and select Label by highlighting it and pressing Enter or double-clicking it.

This is an example of code hinting, which is a very helpful feature of Flex Builder that you should take advantage of.

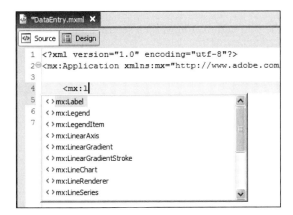

5 Press the spacebar and you'll see a list of options, including properties and methods, which you can use with the `<mx:Label>` tag. Press the letter *t* and then the letter *e*; then select the `text` property.

You can not only select tags with code hinting but you can also choose attributes that belong to those tags.

✳ **NOTE:** In these two cases of using code hinting, both the desired options happened to be at the top of the list. If the option were not at the top, you could either select it by pressing the down arrow key and then pressing Enter or by double-clicking the selection.

6 Enter **My first Flex application** for the value of the text property. Be sure that the text is in the quotes supplied by code hinting.

Proper XML formatting dictates that the value of the attribute be placed in quotes.

7 End the tag with a slash (/) and a greater-than symbol (>).

Check to be sure that your code appears as follows:

```
<?xml version="1.0" encoding="utf-8"?>
<mx:Application xmlns:mx="http://www.adobe.com/2006/mxml"
   layout="absolute">

   <mx:Label text="My first Flex application"/>

</mx:Application>
```

✳ **NOTE:** The code in this example places the *layout="absolute"* attribute=value pair of the Application tag, on a separate indented line. The entire </mx:Application> tag could have been on one line; whether or not to add line breaks to code is a matter of personal preference. Some developers like the look of placing each attribute=value pair on a separate indented line.

Proper XML syntax gives you two ways to terminate a tag. One of them you just used—to place a slash at the end of the tag. The other option is to use the slash in front of the tag name that is completely typed out again, as follows:

```
<mx:Label text="My first Flex application">
</mx:Label>
```

You will usually use the slash at the end of the tag unless there is a reason to place something inside a tag block. For example, if you want to place the </mx:Label> tag inside the <mx:Application> tag block, you have to terminate the </mx:Application> tag on a separate line.

8 Save the file and run it. The "My first Flex application" text appears in your browser.

Finally, you get to see something appear in your new Flex application.

The <mx:Application> tag comes with a default look summarized in this table:

Style	Default
backgroundImage	A gradient controlled by the fillAlphas and fillColors
fillAlphas	[1.0,1.0], a fully opaque background
fillColors	[0x9CB0BA,0x68808C], a gray background slightly darker at the bottom
backgroundSize	100%
paddingTop	24 pixels
paddingLeft	24 pixels
paddingBottom	24 pixels
paddingRight	24 pixels
horizontalAlign	Centered

If you do not want any of these defaults and want to start with the simplest possible look, you can set the styleName equal to plain, as shown here:

```
<mx:Application xmlns:mx="http://www.adobe.com/2006/mxml"
    layout="vertical"
    styleName="plain"/>
```

With the style set to plain, you get the look summarized in this table:

Style	Description
backgroundImage	None
backgroundColor	White
paddingTop	0 pixels
paddingLeft	0 pixels
paddingBottom	0 pixels
paddingRight	0 pixels
horizontalAlign	Left

9 Change the value of the text property from "My first Flex application" to "new text". Save the file and run it.

The next step shows another helpful feature of Flex Builder, but to see this feature you must have at least two saved versions of the file.

10 Right-click in the editor and from the context menu choose Replace With > Local History.

A large dialog box should appear.

11 Compare the current version of your file, which is located on the left side of the dialog box, to the older version on the right. A history of the last 50 versions of your file will be kept at the top of the dialog box. Click Replace to bring back your original text, which reads "My first Flex application".

You will find this feature very helpful when you want to roll back to a previous version of code.

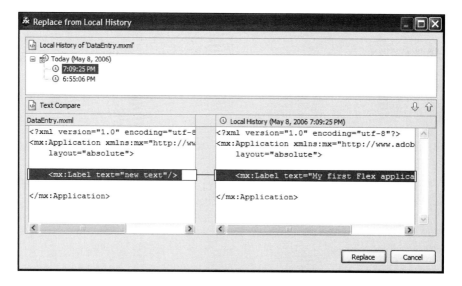

> **TIP:** You can alter the settings for the Local History by choosing Window > Preferences; then from the dialog box choose General > Workspace and click Local History.

12 Purposely introduce an error into the page by changing the <mx:Label> tag to <mx:Labe>, save the file, and then view where the error is reported.

After you save the file, the Build Automatically setting will check your code. The error will be found and reported in two ways. First, a small white x in a red circle will appear next to the line of code in which the coding mistake is located. Also, a listing of the error will appear in Problems view.

TIP: You can place the mouse pointer over the description of the error to see the complete description. You can also double-click the error listed in Problems view, and the cursor will be placed at that line of code in the editor.

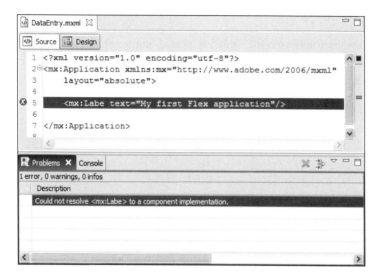

13 Run the application. You will see the following warning, telling you there are errors in your project. In this case, click No so the launch does not continue.

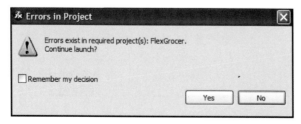

If you click Yes in this dialog box, Flex Builder will run your last successfully compiled version of your application.

14 Correct the error, save the file, and run it to be sure that everything is again working properly. Close the file after it successfully runs.

You are now ready to move on to the next task.

Creating a Second Application Page and Working in Design Mode

Up to this point, you have been working with the file in Source mode. Although you might prefer to look only at the code, there are some tasks that would be much easier in Design mode; for instance, laying out the visual appearance of a page.

1 Choose File > New > MXML Application. In the dialog box that opens, enter the filename **Dashboard**. From the Layout drop-down list, select horizontal. Click Finish.

Flex Builder will remember your last choice for the layout next time you create an application. Remember that with a horizontal layout all the controls you add to the application will appear horizontally across the application.

NOTE: You do not have to enter the .mxml extension; Flex Builder automatically adds the extension.

2 Click the Design mode button in the editor to open the new file in Design mode. Notice that a number of new views opened when you changed to Design mode.

In the following example, examine the diagram to see some of the key views when working in Design mode.

Source and Design mode buttons   States view   Flex Properties view

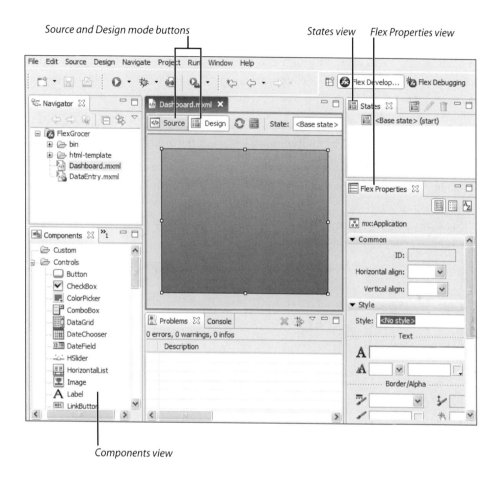

Components view

3 In the Components view, locate the Controls folder. Drag a Text control and position it in the upper portion of the editor. The Text control will center itself because you are in horizontal layout.

The Components view contains the components you will want to use in your Flex applications. This view, which is available only in Design mode, permits you to drag and drop the components into your application. You'll see in a later lesson that you can also position the controls using a constraint-based layout.

4 Locate the States view in the upper right of the editor. Click the minimize icon to minimize the States view.

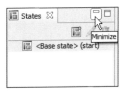

You should focus now on using the Flex Properties view.

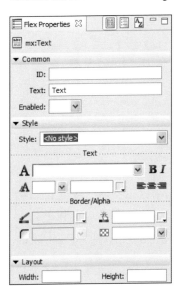

5 Click anywhere in the editor so the Text control is not selected and the application is
selected. The name of the currently selected object will appear at the top of the Flex
Properties view. Be sure it reads mx:Application. Locate the Layout section of the
Flex Properties view. Choose absolute from the Layout drop-down list.

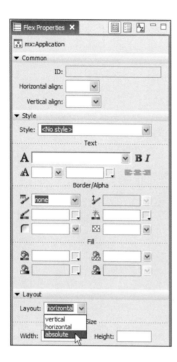

When the layout is horizontal, you cannot specify the position of the Text control using x and y values, which you want to practice here. Absolute layout does allow this.

6 Select the Text control and enter **160** for the x-position value and **180** for the y-position value.

You have now positioned the Text control by setting values in Flex Properties view.

7 Click the Text control and move it to the top left of the screen. Note that the x and y values have changed.

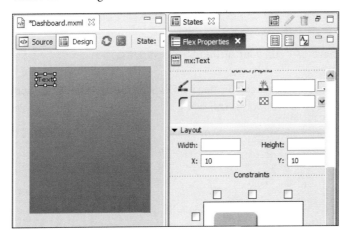

You have now positioned the Text control by dragging and dropping it in Design mode.

8 At the top of the Flex Properties view locate the Common section. For the value of the text property, enter the string **I am using the Flex Properties view**. Press Enter and you will see that the Text control contains the string you just entered.

You have now seen two ways to enter values for properties. In Source mode, you enter the values in quotes following the property name and an equals sign. In Design mode, you select the control to which property values should be supplied and then use the Flex Properties view to enter property values. A third way to change the value of the text displayed is to double-click the control in Design mode and enter or change the text.

✱ **NOTE:** One difference between the Label control and the Text control is that the Text control can contain multiple lines of text. This is not true for the Label control you used in Source mode; it can contain only one line of text.

9 Switch back to Source mode. You see the code that represents what you have done in Design mode. You have a Text control with text, x, and y properties with values that you assigned in Flex Properties view.

You will most likely develop a preference about which mode you work in: Source or Design. You have seen that you can do many of the same things in both views.

10 Run the application by picking Dashboard.mxml from the drop-down list that appears when you click the down arrow next to the Run button. You will see the text from the Text control appear in the browser.

When you run the application it will be positioned in the browser as you positioned it in Design mode.

Congratulations! You have now run your second Flex application.

✳ NOTE: There can be only one <mx:Application> tag per Flex application. At this point, both DataEntry.mxml and Dashboard.mxml contain an <mx:Application> tag. By using multiple <mx:Application> tags, you created two different Flex applications.

11 Back in Flex Builder, remove the Text control in the Dashboard application. Also change the layout back to horizontal.

You need to change this file to ready it for work in later lessons.

Getting Ready for the Next Lesson

The total FlexGrocer application will consist of three Flex application files. You have created two of them: DataEntry.mxml and Dashboard.mxml. The final application, which is called EComm.mxml, will be created in this task.

1 Choose File > New > MXML application. In the dialog box that opens, enter the filename **EComm**. Set the Layout to be absolute. Click the Finish button.

This application will allow customers to order from FlexGrocer. DataEntry.mxml defines where new grocery items will be added to the inventory and quantities updated in the application. Dashboard.mxml defines where product sales can be analyzed.

2 Be sure that all three files contain nothing more than the skeleton code inserted when the file is automatically generated. You will need to remove a Label control from DataEntry. mxml. The layout property of DataEnty.mxml and EComm.mxml should be set to absolute, whereas the layout property of Dashboard.mxml should be set to horizontal.

The only code in all three of the files should be what appears here, with the appropriate value for the layout:

```
<?xml version="1.0" encoding="utf-8"?>
<mx:Application xmlns:mx="http://www.adobe.com/2006/mxml"
    layout="absolute">

</mx:Application>
```

3 Save each file, run it, and then close it to get ready for the next lesson.

You have built the three main application files that you will be working with for the rest of the book.

❇ **NOTE:** Teaching object-oriented programming is not the focus of this book, but to be an effective Flex developer you must have at least a basic understanding of object-oriented terminology and concepts. For instance, the tags you have seen—such as <mx:Application>, <mx:Label>, and <mx:Text>—actually refer to classes. The *Adobe Flex 2 MXML and ActionScript Language Reference* (sometimes referred to as *ASDoc*) is the document that lists these classes, their properties, their methods, and much, much more.

❇ **NOTE:** Object-oriented programming standards have influenced how you named the files in this lesson. Traditionally, class names always start with an uppercase letter, and every class must be stored in a separate file in Flex. The three files you created in this lesson are classes named DataEntry, Dashboard, and EComm, respectively. Each of these classes is a subclass, or child, of the Application class, so they also start with an uppercase letter.

What You Have Learned

In this lesson, you have:

- Created a project to organize your application files (pages 16–20)

- Toured the pieces of the Flex Builder 2 workbench (views, editors, and perspectives) used to create application files (pages 21–23)

- Created and run application files while using code hinting and local history to produce the code for those files (pages 23–29)

- Gained an understanding of the process involved in transforming MXML text into a SWF file that Flash Player at the client can consume (page 24)

- Worked in both Source mode and Design mode in an editor (pages 30–35)

What You Will Learn

In this lesson, you will:

- Use containers
- Lay out an application in Design mode
- Work with constraint-based layouts
- Work with view states
- Control view states
- Lay out an application in Source mode

Approximate Time

This lesson takes approximately 1 hour and 30 minutes to complete.

Lesson Files

Media Files:

None

Starting Files:

Lesson03/start/EComm.mxml
Lesson03/start/Dashboard.mxml

Completed Files:

Lesson03/complete/EComm.mxml
Lesson03/complete/Dashboard.mxml

LESSON 3

Laying Out the Interface

Every application needs a user interface, and one of the strengths of Adobe Flex Builder 2 is that it is simple for developers to use it to lay out the interface for their applications. In this lesson, you will learn about many of the containers in Flex, what differentiates them, and how to use them when laying out your applications. Using states, you can then make the applications dynamically change to react to users!

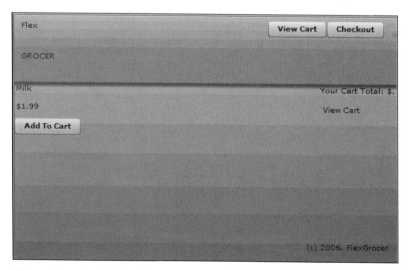

The user interface (UI) for the e-commerce application

Learning About Containers

All layout in Flex is done using containers. In the last lesson, you created three applications; each had an `<mx:Application>` tag, which is in fact a container. Each container has a set of rules, which determines how any child tags will be laid out. The following table shows commonly used containers and the rules they use to lay out their children.

Container	Rule
VBox	Children are laid out vertically; each child is drawn lower on the screen than the previous child.
HBox	Children are laid out horizontally; each child is drawn to the right of the previous child.
Canvas	Children are drawn at the x and y coordinates specified by the developer. If not specified, all children are drawn in the top-left corner of the container. For example, if you add a Button control to a Canvas layout container, and do not specify x and y coordinates, the button is rendered in the top left of the canvas at the default 0,0 position.
Application	Can be set to behave as a VBox, HBox, or Canvas layout container through the use of the `layout` attribute.
Tile	Lays out its children in one or more vertical columns or horizontal rows, starting new rows or columns as necessary. All Tile container cells have the same size. Flex arranges the cells of a Tile container in a square grid, in which each cell holds a single child. The `direction` property is used to determine the layout.
Panel	A subclass of the Box container, a Panel container can act as either an HBox, VBox, or a Canvas container, depending on the `layout` attribute specified (you use `layout="absolute"` to have it behave as a Canvas container, which is the default). In addition to containing its children, the Panel also provides a Title bar area, which can contain a title for the Panel container and a status message.
ControlBar	The ControlBar container is used to dock a toolbar to the bottom of a Panel container or TitleWindow container. The ControlBar container can act as either an HBox container or a VBox container, depending on the direction attribute specified (Horizontal is the default).
ApplicationControlBar	Can act as either an HBox container or a VBox container, depending on the direction attribute specified (Horizontal is the default). The ApplicationControlBar layout container is used to hold components that provide access to elements used throughout an application. If specified as the first child of an `<mx:Application>` tag, and if the dock attribute is set to `true`, the ApplicationControlBar container docks at the top of the application's drawing area, extends the full width of the application, and does not scroll with the application.

Laying Out the E-commerce Application Using Design Mode

The e-commerce application of FlexGrocer is where customers come to shop for groceries. This application has a top region with the store logo as well as links always available to the application. Below that is a series of clickable icons that users can use to browse the various categories of groceries (dairy, meat, fruit, and so on). Below the icons will be an area for displaying products.

1 Open the EComm.mxml file that you created in the previous lesson.

If you didn't complete the previous lesson, you can open EComm.mxml from Lesson03/start and save it in your FlexGrocer directory.

2 Switch FlexBuilder 2 to Design mode.

FlexBuilder 2 has Buttons on top to switch between Design mode and Source mode.

3 In the Components view, open the Layout folder. Drag an ApplicationControlBar container to the top of the Application. Set Dock: to `true`, set the width of the Application-ControlBar container to be 100%, set the height to be 90, and remove any entries for *x* and *y*.

▶ TIP: A blue bar will appear, indicating where you can drop the component.

Once placed, you should see a light gray bar stretching across the top of the page.

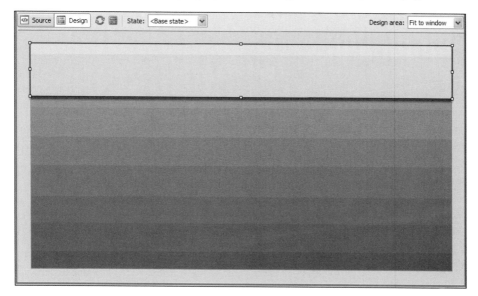

4 From the Components view, drag a Canvas container into the ApplicationControlBar container. In the Flex Properties view, set the canvas width to 100%.

Adding a Canvas container inside the ApplicationControlBar container enables you to specify the exact positioning of the elements within it. By setting the canvas width to 100%, you are telling the canvas to be as wide as the container it is in, which is the ApplicationControlBar container.

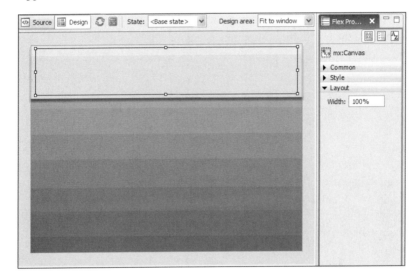

5 In the Components view, open the Controls folder and drag a Label control into the Canvas container in the ApplicationControlBar container. In the Flex Properties view, set the text property for the label to be **Flex** and set the *x* and *y* coordinates to 0.

TIP: Clicking the Show Surrounding Containers button (between the Refresh button and State combo box above the Design area) can help ensure that you place the Label control in the proper container.

This will hold the company name: Flex GROCER.

The company name, Flex GROCER, will be split into two labels. In the next lesson, you will learn that a Label control can hold only a single line of text, and the FlexGrocer logo has the company name split across two lines.

6 From the open Controls folder, drag another Label control into the Canvas; place this one just below the first label. In the Flex Properties view, set the text property for the label to be **GROCER**, set the *x* coordinate to 0, and set the *y* coordinate to 41.

Later in the book, you will apply styles to set the company logo colors and size. For now, you are just placing the text in the appropriate position.

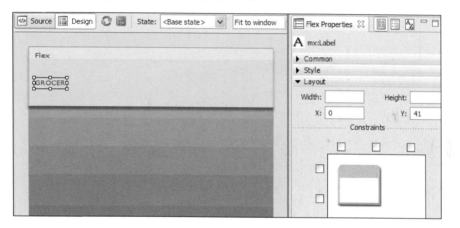

7 With the Controls folder still open, drag a Button control into the Canvas container so it is positioned near the right edge of the container. In the Flex Properties view, give the Button control an ID of btnViewCart and a label of **View Cart**.

Don't worry about the exact placement. Later in this lesson, you will learn how to use a constraint-based layout to position the button so its right edge is always 10 pixels from the right edge of the application.

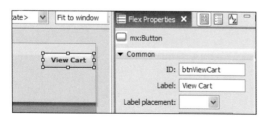

8 Drag a second Button control into the Canvas container, just to the left of the first Button control. In the Flex Properties view, give the Button control an ID of btnCheckout and a label of **Checkout**.

The users will use this button to indicate that they are done shopping and want to complete the purchase of the selected products. Again, the exact placement will happen later in this lesson, when you learn about constraint-based layout.

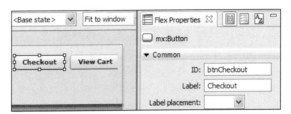

9 Drag a Label control from the Controls folder and place it near the bottom-right edge of the screen. Double-click the label and set the text property to be **(c) 2006, FlexGrocer**.

Much like the buttons you just added, you needn't worry about the exact placement because it will be handled later with constraints.

10 Drag an HBox layout container from the Containers folder and place it in the large area below the ApplicationControlBar container. As you drop it, the Insert HBox dialog box will appear. Set the height and width to be 100% and click OK. In the Flex Properties view, set the *x* and *y* coordinates to 0, and set the ID of the HBox container to be bodyBox.

This HBox container will hold the product details and shopping cart for the application. Remember that an HBox container displays its children horizontally, so you can have products shown on the left and the shopping cart on the right.

11 Drag a VBox layout container from the Layout folder of the Components view and drop it inside the HBox container (you can use the Outline view or the Show Surrounding Containers to verify that you have it in the right container). In the Insert VBox dialog box, assign a height and width of 100% and click OK. In the Flex Properties view, give the VBox container an ID of products.

This VBox container will hold the details for a product.

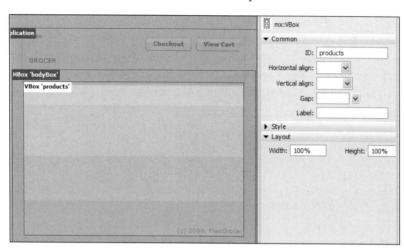

12 Drag a Label control into the new VBox container. Set the ID of the Label control to be prodName and the text to be **Milk**. Drag a second Label control below the first one. Give the second one an ID of price and set **$1.99** as the text.

Because they are children of the VBox container, the product name will appear vertically above the price of the product.

➤ TIP: If you open Outline view, you can see the hierarchy of your application. The root is the `<mx:Application>` tag, which contains an ApplicationControlBar container and an HBox container as children. You can also see the various children of the ApplicationControlBar container. This is a useful view if you want to make a change to a component. It can be difficult to select just the ApplicationControlBar container in Design mode in the Editor. You can easily select it by clicking it in Outline view.

13 Add a Button control below the two labels, with an ID of *add* and the Label **Add To Cart**.

For each product, you will be showing a name of the product and its price. The button gives the user the ability to add that product to their shopping cart. Because those three controls are in a VBox container, they appear one above the other. The functionality for the Button will be added in a later lesson.

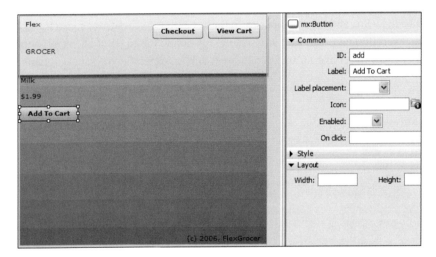

14 Save the file and click Run.

As this runs, you can clearly see the difference between elements in the ApplicationControlBar container and those in the body.

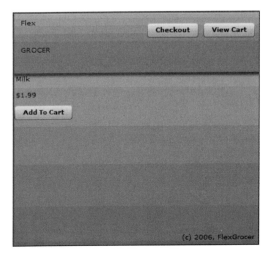

Working with Constraint-based Layouts

Flex supports constraint-based layouts, which enable you to arrange elements of the user interface with the freedom and pixel-point accuracy of absolute positioning while being able to set constraints to stretch or move the components when the user resizes the window.

This is a different way to control the size and position of components from the nested layout containers (like the VBox and HBox containers in the last exercise). The idea of constraint-based layouts is that everything is positioned and sized in relation to the edges of a Canvas container (or a container that can act like a Canvas container, such as Application or Panel container).

The Canvas container requires that elements be positioned to absolute coordinates; however, layout constraints allow it the flexibility to dynamically adjust the layout based on the window size of the browser. For example, if you want a label to always appear in the bottom-right corner of an application, regardless of the browser size, you can anchor the control to the right edges of the Canvas container so its position is always relative to the right edge of the component.

The layout anchors are used to specify how a control should appear relative to the edge of the Canvas container. To ensure that a control is a certain distance from the bottom and right edges, select the check box below and the check box to the right of the control in the Constraints area in the Layout section of the Flex Properties view, and use the text box to specify the number of pixels from the edge to which the control will be constrained.

Flex allows constraints from the Top, Vertical Center, Bottom, Left, Horizontal Center, or Right of a Canvas container.

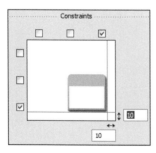

> **TIP:** All constraints are set relative to the edges of the Canvas container (or those that can act as a Canvas container). They cannot be set relative to other controls or containers.

1 Open the EComm.mxml file that you used in the previous exercise.

Alternately, you can open EComm_layout.mxml from Lesson03/intermediate and save it in the FlexGrocer directory as **EComm.mxml**.

2 Find and select the Checkout button. In the Constraints area of the Layout section, add a constraint so the right edge of the button is 10 pixels from the right edge of the container. If you don't set it, the y property will use a default value of 0.

To set a constraint from the right edge, click the rightmost check box above the button icon. In the text box that appears, enter the number of pixels from the edge.

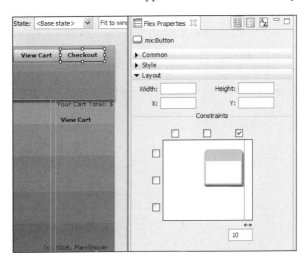

3 Find and select the View Cart button. Add a constraint so the right edge of the button is 90 pixels from the right edge of the container.

If you don't otherwise set it, the y property will use a default value of 0. You now have it set so that regardless of the width of the browser, the two navigation buttons are always anchored relative to the top-right edge of the container.

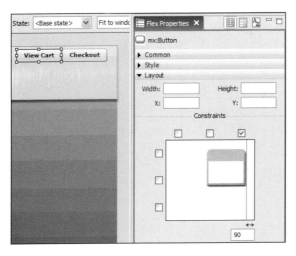

4 Find and select the label with the copyright notice. Constrain this label so that it is 10 pixels above the bottom and 10 pixels off of the right edge of its container.

Because the copyright label is below other containers, it is probably easiest to select it using Outline view. To set the edge constraint, click the check box in the top-right corner of the constraints, and enter **10** in the text box below. Also, click the bottom check box and enter **10** in the text box. These settings ensure that regardless of the width of the Label control its bottom-right edge will always be 10 pixels above and 10 pixels to the left of the bottom-right corner of the Application

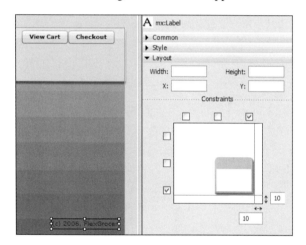

If you switch to Source mode, the whole file should look similar to the following example:

```
<?xml version="1.0" encoding="utf-8"?>
<mx:Application xmlns:mx="http://www.adobe.com/2006/mxml"
    layout="absolute">
    <mx:ApplicationControlBar dock="true" width="100%" height="90">
        <mx:Canvas width="100%" height="100%">
            <mx:Label x="0" y="0" text="Flex"/>
            <mx:Label x="0" y="41" text="GROCER"/>
            <mx:Button label="View Cart" id="btnViewCart" right="90" y="0"/>
            <mx:Button label="Checkout" id="btnCheckout" right="10" y="0"/>
        </mx:Canvas>
    </mx:ApplicationControlBar>
    <mx:Label text="(c) 2006, FlexGrocer" right="10" bottom="10"/>
    <mx:HBox x="0" y="0" width="100%" height="100%" id="bodyBox">
        <mx:VBox width="100%" height="100%" id="products">
            <mx:Label text="Milk" id="prodName"/>
            <mx:Label text="$1.99" id="price"/>
            <mx:Button label="Add To Cart" id="add"/>
        </mx:VBox>
    </mx:HBox>
</mx:Application>
```

Your code may differ slightly, depending on the order you added the items, and the positions to which you dragged the various components. Don't worry, the order is not particularly important in this case. Every container and control that you added in Design mode is represented by a tag in Source mode. When you added elements inside a container, they appear as child tags to the containers tag. Also note that the layout constraints are set as attributes of the related component.

5 Switch back to Design mode and add a second VBox container into the bodyBox HBox container. In the Insert VBox dialog box, leave the width empty and set the height to 100%. Set the ID of the new VBox to cartBox.

If you have difficulty setting the new VBox container inside the HBox container, it might help to turn on Show Surrounding Containers. The Show Surrounding Containers button is located between the Refresh button and the State combo box above the Design area. Then you can click the HBox container and be sure to insert the VBox into the correct container. If you accidentally place it in the wrong container, the easiest fix is to switch to Source mode and move the tags yourself. The code in Source mode should look like this example:

```
<mx:HBox x="0" y="0" width="100%" height="100%" id="bodyBox">
   <mx:VBox width="100%" height="100%" id="products">
      <mx:Label text="Milk" id="prodName"/>
      <mx:Label text="$1.99" id="price"/>
      <mx:Button label="Add To Cart" id="add"/>
   </mx:VBox>
   <mx:VBox height="100%" id="cartBox">
   </mx:VBox>
</mx:HBox>
```

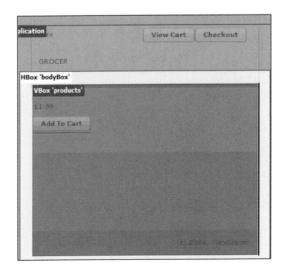

6 Back in Design mode, add a Label control into the new cartBox with the text property set to **Your Cart Total: $**.

To the right of the products, there will always be a summary of the shopping cart, indicating whether there are items in the cart and what the current subtotal is.

7 From the Controls folder of the Components view, drag a LinkButton control below the new Label control and set the label of the link to **View Cart**.

This link will be used to show the user the full contents of their shopping cart.

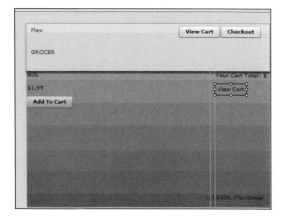

8 Save the file and click Run.

Now, as the application runs you can resize the browser and see that the buttons and bottom text are always properly constrained.

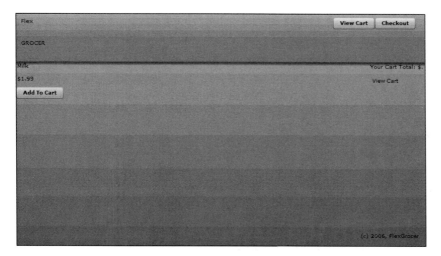

Working with View States

You can use Flex Builder to create applications that change their appearance based on the task the user is performing. For example, the e-commerce application starts by showing users the various products they can buy. When they start adding items to the cart, you want to add something to the view so they can get a feel for what is currently in the cart, such as total cost. Finally, they need a way to view and manage the full contents of the shopping cart.

In Flex, you can add this kind of interactivity with view states. A *view state* is one of several views that you define for an application or a custom component. Every MXML page has at least one state, referred to as the *base view state*, which is represented by the default layout of the file.

Additional states are represented in the MXML as modified versions of the base view state or of other states.

1 Open the EComm.mxml file you used in the previous exercise.

Alternately, you can open EComm_constraint.mxml from Lesson03/intermediate and save it in your FlexGrocer directory as **EComm.mxml**.

2 If it is not already open, open the States view in Flex Builder 2.

If you don't currently see the States view when you look at Flex Builder in Design mode, you can add it to the view by choosing Window > States. Notice that there is already one state created to represent the default layout of the application.

3 Create a new state named cartView, which will be based on <Base state>.

You can create a state by clicking New State at the top of the States view or by right-clicking in the view and selecting the New State option. The cartView state will show users the details of all the items they have added to their cart.

4 With the new cartView state selected, click the products container and set its height and width to 0; then, choose the cartBox container and set its height and width to 100%.

For the cart view, the shopping cart will entirely replace the products in the center of the screen; so, you will resize products to take no space and resize cartBox to take all space available.

5 Still with the cartView state selected, drag a DataGrid control from the Controls folder of the Components view and drop it below the View Cart link. Set the ID of the DataGrid to dgCart and set the DataGrid's width to 100%.

In a later lesson, the DataGrid control will be used to show the user the full contents of the cart.

Be careful and make sure you are adding the DataGrid into the cartBox. Your application and code will look a bit different if you accidently add the DataGrid before the cartBox.

If you look at the file in Source mode, you should see that the following code has been added.

```
<mx:states>
   <mx:State name="cartView">
      <mx:SetProperty target="{products}" name="width" value="0"/>
      <mx:SetProperty target="{products}" name="height" value="0"/>
      <mx:SetProperty target="{cartBox}" name="width" value="100%"/>
      <mx:AddChild relativeTo="{cartBox}" position="lastChild">
         <mx:DataGrid id="dgCart" width="100%">
            <mx:columns>
               <mx:DataGridColumn headerText="Column 1" dataField="col1"/>
               <mx:DataGridColumn headerText="Column 2" dataField="col2"/>
               <mx:DataGridColumn headerText="Column 3" dataField="col3"/>
            </mx:columns>
         </mx:DataGrid>
      </mx:AddChild>
   </mx:State>
</mx:states>
```

6 Save the file.

Testing the file now shouldn't show any differences because you haven't added any ability for the user to toggle between the states. In the next exercise, you will add that navigation.

Controlling View States

Each MXML page has a property called currentState. You can use this property to control which state of the application is shown to a user at any given time.

1 Open the EComm.mxml file that you used in the previous exercise. Switch to Design mode if you are not already there.

Alternately, you can open EComm_states.mxml from Lesson03/intermediate, and save it in your FlexGrocer directory as **EComm.mxml**.

2 If it is not already open, open the States view in Flex Builder 2 and set the chosen state to <Base state> (start).

You will add functionality to the base view state so that users can navigate to the other states of the application.

3 Choose the View Cart LinkButton control from the cartBox container. In Flex Properties view, set its On click: property to this.currentState='cartView'.

Events such as the button click will be explored in detail in Lesson 5, "Handling Events and Data Structures." The important thing to understand now is that when the user clicks the link, the view will change to the cartView state.

CAUTION! The state name is case-sensitive and must exactly match the name as you typed it in the previous exercise. You must use single quotes around the state name when entering it in Design mode.

TIP: You can also enable the View Cart button in the ApplicationControlBar by adding the same code for its click event handler as well.

4 Switch to the cartView state. Add a new LinkButton control below the DataGrid, with the label set to **Continue Shopping** and the click property set to this.currentState=''.

Setting currentState to an empty string resets the application to its initial state.

5 Delete the View Cart link from the cartView state.

When the user is viewing the cart, there is no need for a link to the cart. You can delete the link by selecting it in Design mode and pressing Delete.

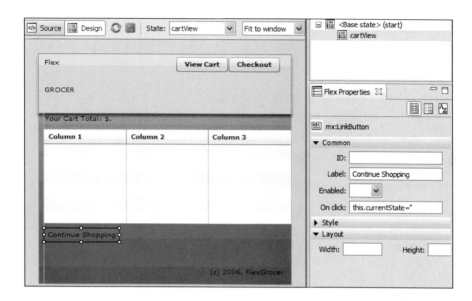

The completed cartView state block of the code in Source mode should read as follows:

```
<mx:states>
   <mx:State name="cartView">
      <mx:SetProperty target="{products}" name="width" value="0"/>
      <mx:SetProperty target="{products}" name="height" value="0"/>
      <mx:SetProperty target="{cartBox}" name="width" value="100%"/>
      <mx:AddChild relativeTo="{cartBox}" position="lastChild">
         <mx:DataGrid id="dgCart" width="100%">
            <mx:columns>
               <mx:DataGridColumn headerText="Column 1" dataField="col1"/>
               <mx:DataGridColumn headerText="Column 2" dataField="col2"/>
               <mx:DataGridColumn headerText="Column 3" dataField="col3"/>
            </mx:columns>
         </mx:DataGrid>
      </mx:AddChild>
      <mx:RemoveChild target="{linkbutton1}"/>
      <mx:AddChild relativeTo="{cartBox}" position="lastChild">
         <mx:LinkButton label="Continue Shopping" click="this.currentState=''"/>
      </mx:AddChild>

   </mx:State>
</mx:states>
```

6 Save and test the application. You can now navigate between the states by clicking the buttons and links to which you added code.

Your file should resemble the code found in Lesson03/complete/EComm.mxml.

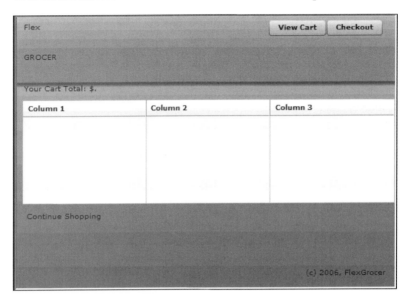

Laying Out an Application in Source Mode

Now that you have seen how to lay out an application with Design mode, you can look a little more deeply at the code and create your second application using Source mode. In this next exercise, you will lay out the Dashboard application, which is designed to give the FlexGrocer executives a quick high-level view of how sales are going for their company.

1 Open the Dashboard.mxml file created in the previous lesson.

Alternately, you can open Dashboard.mxml from Lesson03/start and save it in your flexGrocer directory.

2 Switch FlexBuilder 2 to be in Source mode.

FlexBuilder 2 has buttons on top to switch between Design mode and Source mode.

3 In Source mode, add an <mx:ApplicationControlBar> tag, and set the dock property to true. Add four <mx:LinkButton> tags as children to the ApplicationControlBar container, with labels reading "All", "Sales", "Categories", and "Comparison", respectively.

A bit later in this exercise, you will add code to use these links to toggle between the different states. The completed code should read as follows:

```
<?xml version="1.0" encoding="utf-8"?>
<mx:Application xmlns:mx="http://www.adobe.com/2006/mxml"
    layout="horizontal">
    <mx:ApplicationControlBar dock="true">
      <mx:LinkButton label="All"/>
      <mx:LinkButton label="Sales"/>
      <mx:LinkButton label="Categories"/>
      <mx:LinkButton label="Comparison"/>
    </mx:ApplicationControlBar>
</mx:Application>
```

Remember, you want the `<mx:ApplicationControlBar>` tag to be the first visible child of the `<mx:Application>` tag, so that it will be docked to the top of the application.

4 After the `</mx:ApplicationControlBar>` tag, add a Panel container with an id of sales, a title of Sales Chart, and a height and width of 100%.

By setting the height and width to 100%, this view will use all available space within the application. This will become particularly important as you add states to the application. By setting the height and width of the other items in the Application to 0, the Panel container will use all the space.

```
<mx:Panel id="sales"
    width="100%" height="100%"
    title="Sales Chart">
</mx:Panel>
```

5 Between the open and close `<mx:Panel>` tags, add a ControlBar container. All you need to do is create an opening and closing `<mx:ControlBar>` tag.

The Dashboard will continue to be a work in progress for the next several lessons. In the next lesson, you will add buttons to the control bar. Later, you will add a DataGrid control to view the data for that panel; much later, you will use the graphing controls to show a visual representation of that data.

```
<mx:Panel id="sales"
    width="100%" height="100%"
    title="Sales Chart">
    <mx:ControlBar>
    </mx:ControlBar>
</mx:Panel>
```

6 After the closing tag for the Panel container, add a VBox container with an `id` of `rightCharts`, and width and height each set to 100%. All this requires is the addition of an `<mx:VBox id="rightCharts" width="100%" height="100%"> </mx:VBox>` tag.

```
<mx:Panel id="sales"
   width="100%" height="100%"
   title="Sales Chart">
   <mx:ControlBar>
   </mx:ControlBar>
</mx:Panel>
<mx:VBox id="rightCharts"
   width="100%" height="100%">
</mx:VBox>
```

A VBox container is added so that two items can be shown on the right of the application, one above the other. Because the VBox container is also set to use 100% for its height and width, it will use any space inside the Application not used by the other sales Panel container.

✱ **NOTE:** Flex enables you to assign more than 100 percent total width for a container. In the previous code, you assigned 100 percent width of the bodyBox to both the sales view and the `rightCharts` VBox container. Clearly, an HBox container doesn't have 200 percent width to allocate. The Flex Layout Manager takes this into account and divides the space proportionally based on the requested percentages. Because two times more space was requested than is available, each request for a relative width is divided by 2, so they are each allocated 50 percent. If any elements were assigned a fixed width (that is, a number of pixels instead of a percentage), the fixed size requests will be subtracted from the available space before any relative size requests are allocated.

7 Inside the VBox container add a Panel container with an `id` of `type`, a title of Category Chart, and a height and width each of 100%. Add an empty ControlBar container to that view. After the `type` Panel, but still in the VBox container, add a second Panel container with an ID of `comp`, a title of Comparison Chart, and a height and width each set to 100%.

You now have containers for all the charts that will get added in Lesson 18, "Charting Data."

```
<mx:VBox id="rightCharts"
   width="100%" height="100%" >
   <mx:Panel id="type"
      width="100%" height="100%"
      title="Category Chart">
      <mx:ControlBar>
      </mx:ControlBar>
   </mx:Panel>
   <mx:Panel id="comp"
      width="100%" height="100%"
      title="Comparison Chart">
      <mx:ControlBar>
      </mx:ControlBar>
   </mx:Panel>
</mx:VBox>
```

8 Save and test the application.

You should see the views laid out properly. The next steps are to add states to the application and the ability for users to navigate between the states.

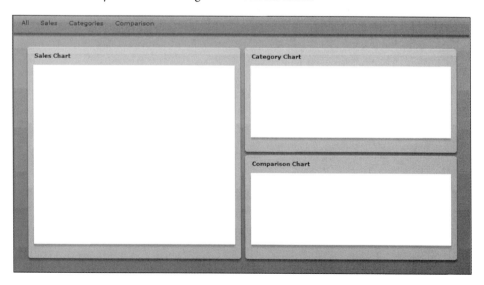

Adding and Controlling View States with MXML

In Flex, states are defined in an `<mx:states>` block. Each state is represented by an `<mx:State>` tag, with attributes indicating the name of the state as well as any other state it might be based on. For example, review the states in the e-commerce layouts earlier in this lesson:

```
<mx:states>
  <mx:State name="cartView">
    <mx:SetProperty target="{products}"
      name="width"
      value="0"/>
    <mx:SetProperty target="{products}"
      name="height"
      value="0"/>
    <mx:SetProperty target="{cartBox}"
      name="width"
      value="100%"/>
    <mx:AddChild relativeTo="{cartBox}"
      position="lastChild">
      <mx:DataGrid id="dgCart"
        width="100%">
        <mx:columns>
          <mx:DataGridColumn headerText="Column 1"
            dataField="col1"/>
          <mx:DataGridColumn headerText="Column 2"
            dataField="col2"/>
          <mx:DataGridColumn headerText="Column 3"
            dataField="col3"/>
        </mx:columns>
      </mx:DataGrid>
    </mx:AddChild>
    <mx:AddChild relativeTo="{cartBox}"
      position="lastChild">
      <mx:LinkButton label="Continue Shopping"
        click="this.currentState=''"/>
    </mx:AddChild>
    <mx:RemoveChild target="{linkbutton1}"/>
  </mx:State>
</mx:states>
```

First, you defined the cartView state that uses the `<mx:SetProperty>` tag four times: once to set the height of the products container to 0; once to set its width to 0; once to set the height of cartBox to 100%; and once more to set the width of cartBox to 100%.

The `<mx:AddChild>` tag is then used to add a DataGrid and link, and the `<mx:RemoveChild>` tag is used to remove a link.

▶ **TIP:** When using the <mx:AddChild> tag, specify the relativeTo and position attributes. The target attribute is the container to which the child will be added; position indicates where in that container the child will be added. Possible values are "before", "after", "firstChild", and "lastChild". The default value is "lastChild". The child to be added is most often specified between the open and closing <mx:AddChild> tags.

1 Open the Dashboard.mxml file that you used in the previous exercise.

Alternately, you can open Dashboard_layout.mxml from the Lesson03/intermediate and save it in your FlexGrocer directory as **Dashboard.mxml**.

2 After the closing <mx:ApplicationControlBar> tag, but before the <mx:Panel id="sales" …> tag, add an <mx:states> tag pair.

Because the <mx:states> tag doesn't represent a visual element in the application, they could really be defined anywhere in the application.

3 Between the open and close <mx:states> tags, add an <mx:State> tag to define a new state named fullSales. Because this will be based on the base view state, there is no need to specify a basedOn attribute.

```
<mx:states>
    <mx:State name="fullSales">
    </mx:State>
</mx:states>
```

4 Use the <mx:SetProperty> tag to define the fullSales state to set the height and width of the rightCharts VBox container to 0.

The body of the Application has only two children, both of which initially requested 100% width. By setting the other child (rightCharts) to use 0 pixels for its width, the first child (the sales view) will expand to fill 100% of the space.

```
<mx:states>
    <mx:State name="fullSales">
        <mx:SetProperty target="{rightCharts}"
            name="width" value="0"/>
        <mx:SetProperty target="{rightCharts}"
            name="height" value="0"/>
    </mx:State>
</mx:states>
```

▶ **TIP:** Remember that the target needs to be specified as a binding; that is, it needs to be the name of the component placed within curly brackets.

5 Define a second state named fullType after the end tag for the fullSales state. The fullType state should use the `<mx:SetProperty>` tag to set the height and width of sales to 0, and the height and width of comp to 0.

When the Dashboard shows the type chart fully, the sales chart and comparison charts both need to be minimized; hence, for the fullType state, you are setting 0 for the height and width of both of the other charts. Because all three charts were initially set up to take 100% for both height and width, when the other two charts no longer use any space, the type chart is free to use the whole screen.

```
<mx:State name="fullType">
   <mx:SetProperty target="{sales}"
      name="width"
      value="0"/>
   <mx:SetProperty target="{sales}"
      name="height"
      value="0"/>
   <mx:SetProperty target="{comp}"
      name="width"
      value="0"/>
   <mx:SetProperty target="{comp}"
      name="height"
      value="0"/>
</mx:State>
```

6 Define a third state named fullComp, which sets the height and width of both sales and type to be 0 pixels.

This directly mirrors the work you did for the fullType state, so that to show the comparison chart fully, you will set the sales and type charts to take up 0 pixels for their height and width. The new fullComp state block should read like this:

```
<mx:State name="fullComp">
   <mx:SetProperty target="{sales}"
      name="width"
      value="0"/>
   <mx:SetProperty target="{sales}"
      name="height"
      value="0"/>
   <mx:SetProperty target="{type}"
      name="width"
      value="0"/>
   <mx:SetProperty target="{type}"
      name="height"
      value="0"/>
</mx:State>
```

7 Add click events for the LinkButton controls in the <mx:ApplicationControlBar> tag to toggle the currentState property.

```
<mx:ApplicationControlBar dock="true">
   <mx:LinkButton label="All"
      click="this.currentState=''"/>
   <mx:LinkButton label="Sales"
      click="this.currentState='fullSales'"/>
   <mx:LinkButton label="Categories"
      click="this.currentState='fullType'"/>
   <mx:LinkButton label="Comparison"
      click="this.currentState='fullComp'"/>
</mx:ApplicationControlBar>
```

8 Save and test the Dashboard. You should be able to control the states from the top links.

You can now navigate and see each of the panels use the full stage to display.

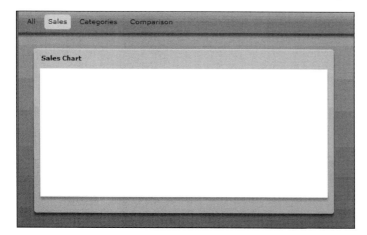

What You Have Learned

In this lesson, you have:

- Used containers (page 40)

- Laid out an application in Design mode (pages 41–46)

- Worked with constraint-based layouts (pages 47–51)

- Worked with view states (pages 52–53)

- Controlled view states (pages 54–56)

- Laid out an application in Source mode (pages 56–63)

What You Will Learn

In this lesson, you will:

- Define the user interface (UI) for the e-commerce application of FlexGrocer
- Use simple controls such as the Image control, text controls, and CheckBox control
- Define the UI for the administrative tool that allows users to update the data
- Use the Form container to lay out the simple controls
- Use data binding to connect the controls to a data model

Approximate Time

This lesson takes approximately 45 minutes to complete.

Lesson Files

Media Files:

Lesson04/start/assets/dairy_milk.jpg

Starting Files:

Lesson04/start/EComm.mxml
Lesson04/start/DataEntry.mxml
Lesson04/start/Dashboard.mxml

Completed Files:

Lesson04/complete/EComm.mxml
Lesson04/complete/DataEntry.mxml
Lesson04/complete/Dashboard.mxml

LESSON 4

Using Simple Controls

In this lesson, you will add user interface elements to enable the end user to work with grocery items. An important part of any application is the user interface, and Adobe Flex contains elements such as buttons, text fields, and radio buttons that make building interfaces easier. Simple controls can display text and images and also gather information from users. You can tie simple controls to underlying data structures, and they will reflect changes in that data structure in real time using data binding. You are ready to start learning about the APIs of specific controls, which are available in both MXML and ActionScript. The APIs are fully documented in the ASDOC, which is available at www.adobe.com/go/flex2_livedocs.

There are many tools within Flex framework that make laying out simple controls easier. All controls are placed within containers (refer to Lesson 3, "Laying Out the Interface"). In this lesson, you will become familiar with simple controls by building the basic user interface of the application you will develop throughout this book. You will also learn about time-saving functionality built into the framework such as data binding, using the Form layout container, and using focus management to optimize the user experience.

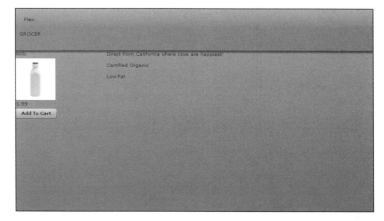

This is what FlexGrocer will look like at the end of this lesson when an Image and Text control bound to a data structure have been added to the e-commerce application.

Introducing Simple Controls

Simple controls are provided as part of the framework and help make rich Internet application (RIA) development easy. Using controls, you can easily define the look and feel of your buttons, text, combo boxes, and much more. You can customize controls to provide your own unique look and feel, and you will learn more about how to do this later in the book. Controls provide a standards-based methodology that makes learning how to use them easy. Controls are the foundation of any RIA.

Flex includes an extensive class library for both simple and complex controls. All these classes can be instantiated via an MXML tag or as a standard ActionScript class, and their APIs (application programming interface) are accessible in both MXML and ActionScript. The class hierarchy also includes other classes that define the new event model, as well as the display attributes that all simple controls share.

You place the visual components of your Flex application inside containers, which provide bounding boxes for text, controls, images, and other media elements (You learned about containers in the last lesson.). All simple controls have events that can be used to respond to user actions, such as clicking a button, or system events, such as drawing another component (Events will be covered in detail in the next lesson.). You will also learn in later lessons how to build your own custom events. Custom events are a fundamental concept used while building easily maintainable applications that reduce the risk of a change to one portion of the application forcing a change in another. This concept is often referred to as building a "loosely coupled" application.

Most applications need to display some sort of text, whether it be static or dynamically driven from a database. Flex has a number of text controls that can be used to display editable or non-editable text. You have already used the Label control to display single lines of text. The Label control cannot be edited by an end user, so if you need that functionality you can use a TextInput control. The TextInput control, like the Label control, is limited to a single line of text. The Text control is used to display multiple lines of text, but is not editable and does not display scroll bars if the real estate is exceeded. The TextArea component is useful for displaying multiple lines of text, either editable or non-editable, with scroll bars if the available text exceeds the screen real estate available. All text controls support HTML 1.0 and a variety of text and font styles.

To populate text fields at run time, you must assign an id to the control. Once you have done that, you can access the control's properties; for example all of the text controls previously mentioned have a `text` property. This property can be used to populate the control with plain text using either an ActionScript function or inline using data binding. The following code demonstrates assigning an id to the label, which enables you to reference the Label control in ActionScript:

```
<mx:Label id="myLabel"/>
```

You can populate any text control at run time using data binding, which is denoted by curly bracket syntax in MXML. The following code will cause your Label control to display the same text as the myLabel control in the previous example:

```
<mx:Label id = "yourLabel" text = "{myLabel.text}"/>
```

Data binding can also be used to bind a simple control to underlying data structures. For example, if you have XML data, which might have come from a server-side dataset, you can use the functionality of data binding to connect a simple control to the data structure. When the underlying data changes, the controls will automatically update to reflect the new data. This provides a powerful tool for the application developer.

Flex framework also provides a powerful container for building forms that will be covered in this lesson. The Form container allows developers to create efficient, good-looking forms with a minimal effort. The heading, spacing, and arrangement of form items are handled automatically by Flex.

Using Flex Explorer to Learn About Simple Controls

Simple controls are the building blocks for creating Flex applications. Flex Explorer contains examples that show you how to execute the basic tasks for building an application. Most importantly, Flex Explorer gives you specific examples of how to use each component.

1 Start Adobe Flex Builder 2, on Windows, by choosing Start > All Programs > Adobe > Adobe Flex Builder 2.

2 Select Help > Flex Start Page.

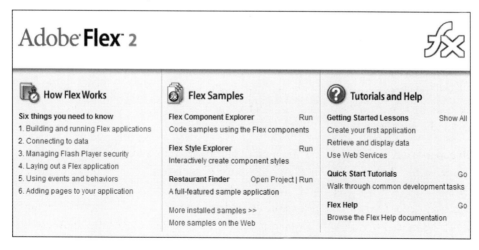

The Flex Start Page, provides a wealth of resources, including sample applications, Tutorials and Help files.

3 Click the Run link next to Flex Component Explorer.

4 Examine the MXML and the result for some of the simple controls by clicking the example links on the left.

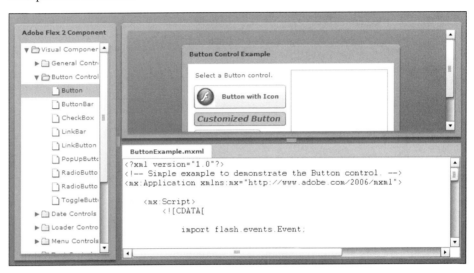

5 Close the web browser and then click the X in the Flex 2 Start Page tab to return to the Flex Builder editors.

Displaying Images

In this task you will be displaying images of grocery products. To do this, you must use the Image control to load images dynamically. The Image control has the capability to load JPG, SVG, GIF, SWF, and PNG files at run time. You also have the ability to use an alpha channel with GIF and PNG files that enable you to create transparencies in images. If you are developing an offline application that does not have access to the Internet, you can use the @Embed directive to include the Image control in the completed SWF file.

1 Open the EComm.mxml file you worked with in the last lesson. If you didn't complete the previous lesson, you can open EComm.mxml from Lesson04/start and save it in your flexGrocer directory.

2 Switch Flex Builder to Design mode by clicking the Design icon.

3 Be sure that the Components view is open. If not, choose Window > Show View > Components.

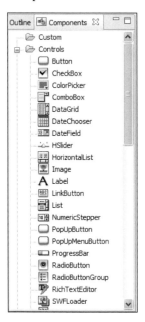

4 Select the Image control and drag and drop the control between the Milk and 1.99 Label controls you already added.

When you drag the Image control from the Components view to the container, Flex Builder automatically adds the MXML to place the Image control on the screen and position it where you indicated when you dropped it.

5 Be sure that the Flex Properties view is open. If not, choose Window > Flex Properties.

The Flex Properties view shows important attributes of the selected component—in this case, the Image control. You can see the Source property, which specifies the path to the Image file. The ID of the Image control is used to reference the instance created from the `<mx:Image>` tag or Image class in ActionScript.

6 Click the Source folder icon and browse to the assets directory. Select the dairy_milk.jpg image and click Open. You will see the image appear in Design mode.

The image you selected in Design mode will display. The `source` property will also be added to the MXML tag.

7 Click the Scale content drop-down list and change the value to `true`.

In an ideal world, all the images that you use in the application would be a perfect size, but this is not always the case. Flex has the capability to set the width and height of images and can scale the image to fit the size of the Image control.

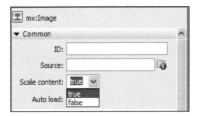

8 Switch back to Source mode and notice that Flex Builder has added an `<mx:Image>` tag as well as the attributes you specified in the Flex Properties window.

As you can see, it is easy to switch between Source mode and Design mode, and each one has its own advantages.

```
            </mx:AddChild>
            <mx:AddChild relativeTo="{cartBox}" position="lastChild">
                <mx:LinkButton label="Continue Shopping" click="this.currentState='
            </mx:AddChild>
            <mx:RemoveChild target="{linkbutton1}"/>
        </mx:State>
    </mx:states>
    <mx:ApplicationControlBar dock="true" width="100%" height="90">
        <mx:Canvas width="100%" height="100%">
            <mx:Label x="0" y="0" text="Flex"/>
            <mx:Label x="0" y="41" text="GROCER"/>
            <mx:Button label="View Cart" id="btnViewCart" right="90" y="0"/>
            <mx:Button label="Checkout" id="btnCheckout" right="10" y="0"/>
        </mx:Canvas>
    </mx:ApplicationControlBar>
    <mx:Label text="(c) 2006, FlexGrocer" right="10" bottom="10"/>
    <mx:HBox x="0" y="0" width="100%" height="100%" id="bodyBox">
        <mx:VBox width="100%" height="100%" id="products">
            <mx:Label text="Milk" id="prodName"/>
            <mx:Image source="assets/dairy_milk.jpg" scaleContent="true"/>
            <mx:Label text="$1.99" id="price"/>
            <mx:Button label="Add To Cart" id="add"/>
        </mx:VBox>
        <mx:VBox height="100%" id="cartBox">
```

9 In the `<mx:Image>` tag that you added, add an `@Embed` directive to the Image control:

```
<mx:Image source="@Embed('assets/dairy_milk.jpg')" scaleContent="true"/>
```

The `@Embed` directive causes the compiler to bake the JPG into the SWF file at compile time. This technique has a couple of advantages over the default of loading the image at run time. First, the image is "preloaded" at the start of the application; so, when the image is actually displayed, the user will have no wait time. Also, it can be useful if you are building offline applications that do not have access to the Internet because the appropriate images will be included in the SWF file and will correctly display. Remember, though, that it will greatly increase the size of your SWF file.

10 Save and compile the application then click Run.

You should see that the Image and Label controls and button fit neatly into the layout container.

Building a Detail View

In this task, you will use a rollover event to display a detailed state of the application. You will explore the use of different simple controls to display text and review how application states work.

1 Be sure that you are still in Source mode in Flex Builder. Locate the `<mx:Image>` tag that displays the image you added in the last section. Add a `mouseOver` event to the tag that will change the `currentState` to expanded.

```
<mx:Image source="@Embed('assets/dairy_milk.jpg')" scaleContent="true"
   mouseOver="this.currentState='expanded'"/>
```

`mouseOver` simply means that when the user rolls the mouse anywhere over the `<mx:Image>` tag, the ActionScript will be executed. In this ActionScript, you are referring to the expanded state, which will be created later in this lesson. You will modify this state so it will display more information about the item the user is interested in purchasing.

2 In the same `<mx:Image>` tag, add a `mouseOut` event that will change the `currentState` back to the default or original state. The beginning view state of the application is expressed as "" or '' inline.

```
<mx:Image source="@Embed('assets/dairy_milk.jpg')" scaleContent="true"
   mouseOver="this.currentState='expanded'"
   mouseOut="this.currentState=''"/>
```

When the user moves the mouse away from this `<mx:Image>` tag, the detailed state will no longer be displayed, and the application will display only the images and labels for the control, which is the default and expressed with an empty String.

3 Switch back to Design mode. Be sure to click the Refresh button to make sure all your changes in code have been applied.

 —— *Refresh button*

4 Be sure that the States view is open. If not, choose Window > States. Click the New State button and create a new state with the name of expanded. Be sure that this state is based on the `<Base state>` state.

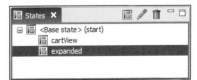

You want the product description to appear when the user rolls over the `<mx:Image>` tag that shows the image associated with each grocery item.

5 Return to Source mode, and locate the expanded state. Add an `<mx:AddChild>` tag and inside of that tag add an `<mx:VBox>` tag. You will see that Flex automatically added the `<mx:State name="expanded"/>` tag, however, it used the single tag syntax described in Chapter 2, "Getting Started." You will need to change this to an open and close tag, as shown:

```
<mx:State name="expanded">
    <mx:AddChild>
        <mx:VBox>

        </mx:VBox>
    </mx:AddChild>
</mx:State>
```

You will place all of the controls to display the item detail inside of a VBox container so that you can position them all at once.

6 Set the x property of the VBox container in the expanded state to 200. Also, set the `width` property to 100%, as follows.

```
<mx:VBox x="200" width="100%">
```

This will place the controls in the `<mx:VBox>` tag in a better position—easier for users to view when they roll over the grocery product.

7 Switch back to Design mode. Ensure that the expanded state is selected in the States view and drag an instance of the Text control from the Controls folder in the Components view, to the VBox container you just modified in the last step.

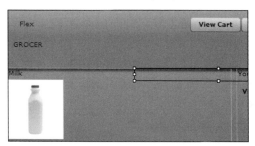

The Text control enables you to display multiple lines of text, which you will do when you display the product description, which will ultimately come from a database. You will use data binding in the next section to make this Text control work. For now, you are just setting up the layout. All the text must use the same styling unless you specify it as HTML text.

8 Drag an instance of the Label control from the Components view to the bottom part of the VBox container you created. Populate the text property with the words **Certified Organic**.

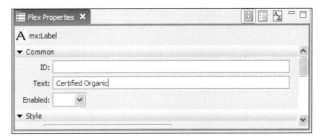

The Label control allows you to display a single line of text. Later on, you will modify the visible property of this component to display only when a grocery item is certified organic.

9 Drag an instance of the Label control from the Components view to the bottom part of the VBox container you created. Populate the text property with the words **Low Fat**.

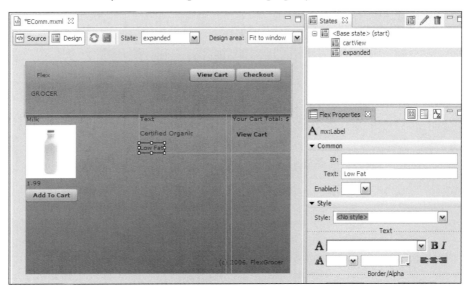

Later, you will set the visible property of this label to true if the grocery item is low fat, or false if it is not.

10 Switch back to Source mode. Notice that Flex Builder has added the Text and two Label controls you added in Design mode.

Note that all of the code created in Design mode is displayed in the code in Source mode.

11 Locate the <mx:Text> tag in the expanded state and set the `width` property of the Text control to 50%.

```
<mx:Text text="Text" width="50%"/>
```

12 Save and run the application.

When you roll over the milk bottle image, you see the Text and Label controls you created in the expanded state.

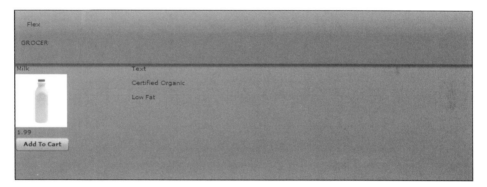

Using Data Binding to Link a Data Structure to a Simple Control

Data binding enables you to connect controls, such as the text controls that you have already worked with, to an underlying data structure. Data binding is incredibly powerful because if the underlying data changes, the changes will be reflected in the control. For example, suppose that you created a text control that displayed the latest sports scores and was connected to a data structure in Flex. When a score changed in that data structure, the changes would also be reflected in the control that the end user views. In this task, you will connect a basic data structure in an <mx:Model> tag to simple UI controls to display the name, image, and price associated with each grocery item. Later in the book, you will learn more about data models, the effective use of a model-view-controller architecture on the client, and how to actually connect these data structures with server-side data.

1 Be sure that EComm.mxml is open and add an `<mx:Model>` tag directly below the `<mx:Application>` tag at the top of the page.

The `<mx:Model>` tag allows you to build a client-side data model. This tag will convert an XML data structure into a format Flex can use.

2 Directly below the opening `<mx:Model>` tag, and before the closing `<mx:Model>` tag, add the following XML data structure. Your `<mx:Model>` tag should look as shown:

```
<mx:Model>
   <groceries>
      <catName>Dairy</catName>
      <prodName>Milk</prodName>
      <imageName>assets/dairy_milk.jpg</imageName>
      <cost>1.20</cost>
      <listPrice>1.99</listPrice>
      <isOrganic>true</isOrganic>
      <isLowFat>true</isLowFat>
      <description>Direct from California where cows are happiest!</description>
   </groceries>
</mx:Model>
```

You have defined a very simple data structure inline inside of an `<mx:Model>` tag.

3 Assign the `<mx:Model>` tag an id of `groceryInventory`. The first line of your `<mx:Model>` tag should look as shown:

```
<mx:Model id="groceryInventory">
```

By assigning an id to the `<mx:Model>` tag, you can reference the data using dot syntax. For example, to access the list price of the item, you could simply say `groceryInventory.listPrice`. In this case, that would resolve to 1.99.

4 Switch Flex Builder to Design mode.

In Design mode, you can easily set up the bindings between the data structure and the controls. You could also set up the bindings in Source mode.

5 Select the Text control in the expanded state and be sure that the Flex Properties view is open. Modify the `text` property to **{groceryInventory.description}**.

The data binding is indicated by the curly brackets {}. Whenever the curly brackets are used, you use ActionScript instead of simple strings. Data binding is extremely powerful because the UI control will be updated if the data structure changes, which will become increasingly important as you begin to work with server-side data.

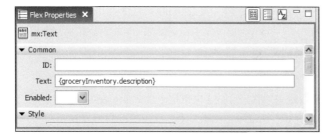

6 Save and run the application.

You should see that the description that you entered in the data model appears when you roll over the grocery item.

Using a Form Layout Container to Lay Out Simple Controls

Forms are important in most applications to collect information from users. You will be using the Form container to enable an administrator to update the inventory for the grocery store. The administrator can add new items, delete old items, and update existing items. The Form container in Flex handles the layout of controls in this Form, automating much of the routine work. With a Form container, you can designate fields as required or optional, handle error messages, and perform data checking and validation to be sure the administrator follows designated guidelines. A Form container uses three separate tags: an <mx:Form> tag, an <mx:FormHeading> tag, and an <mx:FormItem> tag for each item on the form.

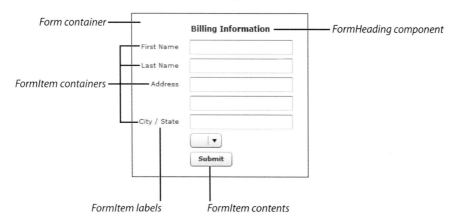

1 Open DataEntry.mxml and switch to Source mode. After the `<mx:Application>` tag, add a new `<mx:Model>` tag, assign it an `id` of `prodModel`, and add the data structure as follows:

```
<mx:Model id="prodModel">
   <groceries>
      <catName>Dairy</catName>
      <prodName>Milk</prodName>
      <imageName>assets/dairy_milk.jpg</imageName>
      <cost>1.20</cost>
      <listPrice>1.99</listPrice>
      <isOrganic>true</isOrganic>
      <isLowFat>true</isLowFat>
      <description>Direct from California where cows are happiest!</description>
   </groceries>
</mx:Model>
```

You will use this application to build an interface so administrators can update and add information in a database. Later in the book, you will use a server-side dataset from an actual database to populate the fields.

2 Below the `<mx:Model>` tag, use the `<mx:Form>` tag to define the outermost container of the form.

```
<mx:Form>
</mx:Form>
```

The Form container, which is the outermost tag of a Flex form, always arranges its children in a vertical fashion and left-aligns them. All your form elements will be defined within this container.

3 Within the Form container, use the `<mx:FormHeading>` tag to define a heading for the current category. Use data binding to set up the binding between the `label` property and the `catName` property of the data model.

```
<mx:FormHeading label="{prodModel.catName}"/>
```

The `<mx:FormHeading>` tag enables you to specify a label for a group of FormItem containers. This is perfect for your application because the user will be updating items from a specific category such as produce or bakery. It is possible to have multiple `<mx:FormHeading>` tags, with the left side of the label in the `<mx:FormHeading>` aligning with the left side of the form.

4 After the FormHeading container, use the <mx:FormItem> tag to define the product name. Inside of the <mx:FormItem> tag, add an <mx:TextInput> tag with an id of product that will be populated with the name of the actual item from the data model. Use data binding to reference the prodName property inside the model.

```
<mx:FormItem label="Product Name">
   <mx:TextInput id="product" text="{prodModel.prodName}"/>
</mx:FormItem>
```

The <mx:FormItem> tag will automatically specify one Label control with one or more form elements, such as TextInput controls. A label displaying 'Product Name' is automatically added with the appropriate spacing and alignment relative to the TextInput control.

5 After the last <mx:FormItem> tag, use another <mx:FormItem> tag, set the label to ProductNameUnit, and specify the direction property as horizontal. Inside the FormItem container, place a ComboBox control and a TextInput control. Leave the ComboBox and TextInput controls blank for now; you will come back to them in a later lesson.

```
<mx:FormItem label="ProductNameUnit" direction="horizontal">
   <mx:ComboBox/>
   <mx:TextInput/>
</mx:FormItem>
```

By default, all the controls in a FormItem are laid out vertically to the right of the Label control. By using the direction attribute in the <mx:FormItem> tag, you can specify that the controls should be laid out horizontally instead of vertically. If the children are laid out horizontally and do not fit into a single row, they are divided into multiple rows with equal-sized columns.

6 After the last <mx:FormItem> tag, add three more <mx:FormItem> tags that define the cost, the list price, and the description of the item. Place TextInput controls with the binding to the text property, inside of each FormItem container:

```
<mx:FormItem label="Cost">
   <mx:TextInput id="cost" text="{prodModel.cost}"/>
</mx:FormItem>
<mx:FormItem label="List Price">
   <mx:TextInput id="listPrice" text="{prodModel.listPrice}"/>
</mx:FormItem>
<mx:FormItem label="Description">
   <mx:TextInput id="Description" text="{prodModel.description}"/>
</mx:FormItem>
```

This process will add more information to the form that the user needs to update, add, or delete a new product.

7 After the last <mx:FormItem> tag, add two more <mx:FormItem> tags that define whether the product is organic or low fat. Use a CheckBox control with the selected attribute and be sure to get this data from the data model tag.

```
<mx:FormItem label="Organic">
   <mx:CheckBox id="isOrganic" selected="{prodModel.isOrganic}"/>
</mx:FormItem>
<mx:FormItem label="Is Low Fat?">
   <mx:CheckBox id="isLowFat" selected="{prodModel.isLowFat}"/>
</mx:FormItem>
```

The CheckBox control can contain a check mark or be left unchecked (empty). When the user clicks the check box, the CheckBox control will change its state from checked to unchecked or vice versa. This is accessed through the selected property, which is a Boolean value (true or false).

8 After the last <mx:FormItem> tag, add another <mx:FormItem> tag that will display two items in a horizontal box: the first is the path of the image in the data model in a TextInput control, and the second is a button that will allow the user to browse for the image.

```
<mx:FormItem label="Image Path">
   <mx:TextInput id="imageName" text="{prodModel.imageName}"/>
   <mx:Button label="Browse"/>
</mx:FormItem>
```

You will add functionality to the Browse button in the next step using the FileReference class, so users can upload data from the client to a server.

9 Add an <mx:Script> block to the top of the application, immediately after the existing <mx:Model> tag. Note that a CDATA tag is automatically added for you by Flex Builder. Import the FileReference class and then create a function with the name of fileBrowse() that instantiates a new instance of the FileReference class and calls the browse() function.

```
<mx:Script>
<![CDATA[
import flash.net.FileReference;
public function fileBrowse():void{
   var myFileRef:FileReferenceList = new FileReferenceList();
   myFileRef.browse();
}
]]>
</mx:Script>
```

The file upload process will be completed in Lesson 17, "Accessing Server-side Objects."

You have used MXML to lay out your application and will now use ActionScript to add functionality and provide logic. The first line of code enables you to make use of the existing FileReference class. The second line of code declares a new function. The void keyword indicates that the function is not expected to return a value to the caller. The first line of the function creates a new object: myFileRef from the FileReference class you imported. It is important to specify the type of all objects that you create. Here you type the object to FileReferenceList. By typing objects, you will receive better error messages to debug your application and get faster performance. The second line in the function calls the browse() method of the FileReference class, which will cause the following window to pop up when the user clicks the Browse button.

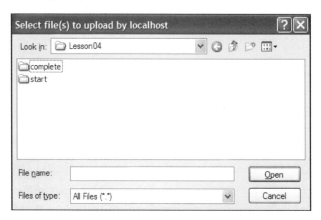

10 Return to the Browse button and add a click event that will call the fileBrowse() you wrote in the last step.

```
<mx:Button label="Browse" click="fileBrowse()"/>
```

This step will call the method that you wrote in the script block and cause the pop-up window to appear. You will learn later in the book how to send the data to a server.

11 After the last <mx:FormItem> tag, add another <mx:FormItem> tag that will display two buttons, one with the label of Update and the other with the label of Delete, in an HBox.

```
<mx:FormItem>
    <mx:HBox>
        <mx:Button label="Update"/>
        <mx:Button label="Delete"/>
    </mx:HBox>
</mx:FormItem>
```

12 Save and run the application.

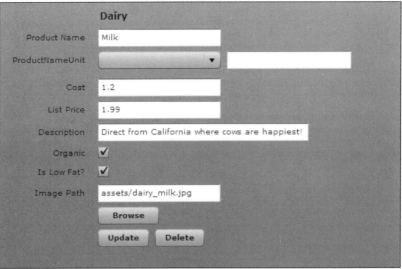

▶ **TIP:** If you tab through the various components of the form, you might wonder whether there is a way to control which components receive the user focus. The form itself (and each top-level container), has a built-in focus manager. The focus manager contains a getFocus() method that will return the component that currently has the focus. You can use the setFocus() method to set the focus to another component. Using the Focus Manager class is the preferred method to control selection in a Flex application.

13 Close the current editor by clicking the X.

Adding Radio Buttons and Date Fields to the Dashboard

Radio buttons in Flex work differently than in HTML. When you have more than one radio button and you want the user to be able to select only one, you must define a RadioButton-Group. Only one radio button in a RadioButtonGroup can be selected at a time. You will define a RadioButtonGroup in the Dashboard application, enabling the user to view data for either gross sales or net sales, but not both.

1 Open Dashboard.mxml and locate the <mx:ApplicationControlBar> tag. Immediately after the comparison <mx:LinkButton> tag (the last one), add an <mx:Spacer> tag and set the width to 100%.

```
<mx:Spacer width="100%"/>
```

This tag will simply add space between the current LinkBar control and the RadioButton controls that you will add.

2 Immediately after the `<mx:Spacer>` tag, add an `<mx:Label>` control, set the `text` property to **Start Date**, and add an `<mx:DateField>` tag with an `id` of `startDate`.

```
<mx:Label text="Start Date"/>
<mx:DateField id="startDate"/>
```

This will create a new date field that the end user can click in, and a calendar date chooser will appear.

3 Add another `<mx:Label>` control and set the `text` property to **End Date**. Add an `<mx:DateField>` tag with an `id` of `endDate`.

```
<mx:Label text="End Date"/>
<mx:DateField id="endDate"/>
```

This will create another new date field that the end user can click in, and a calendar date chooser will appear.

4 Add a new `<mx:RadioButtonGroup>` tag and assign it an `id` of `grossOrNetGroup`.

```
<mx:RadioButtonGroup id="grossOrNetGroup"/>
```

This will define a new RadioButtonGroup. You will add two new radio buttons to this group in the next step. Because they both belong to this group, the user can choose only one radio button.

5 Immediately after the `<mx:RadioButtonGroup>` tag, add a new `<mx:RadioButton>` tag and assign it an `id` of `gross`. Assign the `groupName` property to the `id` of the `RadioButtonGroup` you created, defined previously as `grossOrNetGroup`. Assign it a `label` of Gross Sales, a `data` property of `GROSS`, and set the `selected` property as `true`.

```
<mx:RadioButton id="gross"
    groupName="grossOrNetGroup"
    label="Gross Sales"
    data="GROSS"
    selected="true"/>
```

This creates a new radio button on the screen that belongs to the `grossOrNetGroup`. You have assigned a label of Gross Sales. You can tell which radio button the user has selected through the `data` property. Because you have set the `selected` property to `true`, this radio button will be selected by default.

6 Immediately after the <mx:RadioButton> tag, add a new <mx:RadioButton> tag and assign it an id of net. Assign the groupName property to the id of the RadioButtonGroup you created, defined previously as grossOrNetGroup, and assign it a label of Net Sales. Also, assign the data property as NET.

```
<mx:RadioButton id="net"
    groupName="grossOrNetGroup"
    label="Net Sales"
    data="NET"/>
```

7 Save and run the application.

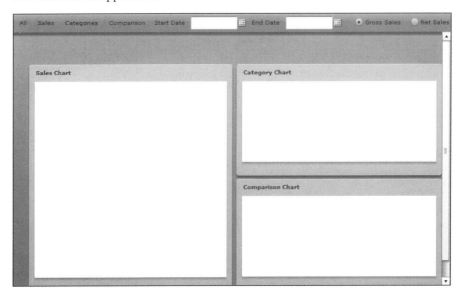

What You Have Learned

In this lesson, you have:

- Learned how to load images at run time with the Image control (pages 68–71)

- Learned how to display blocks of text (pages 72–75)

- Learned how to link simple controls to an underlying data structure with data binding (pages 75–77)

- Learned how to build user forms with a minimum of effort using the Form container (pages 77–82)

- Learned how to use radio buttons (pages 82–84)

What You Will Learn

In this lesson, you will:

- Create an `<mx:Model>` tag that creates a simple client-side data model
- Create a complex client-side data model using an ActionScript class
- Use Flex framework system events
- Implement Flex framework user events
- Examine the event object that is created each time an event is dispatched

Approximate Time

This lesson takes approximately 1 hour and 15 minutes to complete.

Lesson Files

Media Files:

Lesson05/start/assets/inventory.xml

Starting Files:

Lesson05/start/Dashboard.mxml
Lesson05/start/DataEntry.mxml
Lesson05/start/EComm.mxml

Completed Files:

Lesson05/complete/Dashboard.mxml
Lesson05/complete/DataEntry.mxml
Lesson05/complete/EComm.mxml
Lesson05/complete/valueObjects/Product.as
Lesson05/complete/valueObjects/ShoppingCart.as
Lesson05/complete/valueObjects/ShoppingCartItem.as

LESSON 5

Handling Events and Data Structures

An important part of building a rich Internet application (RIA) is building effective client-side architecture. When you use Flash Player to build an application, you have the ability to use an event-based programming model, build rich client-side data models, and create a logical application following good object-oriented best practices. This type of development is very different for web application developers as it does not use a page-based development model. Ultimately, using this client-side, event-based architecture will result in better-performing applications that consume less network traffic because page refreshes are no longer needed. During this lesson, you will receive an introduction to the powerful object-oriented language and event-based programming model of ActionScript 3.0.

```
package valueObjects
{
    [Bindable]
    public class Product
    {
        public var catID:Number;
        public var prodName:String;
        public var unitID:Number;
        public var cost:Number;
        public var listPrice:Number;
        public var description:String;
        public var isOrganic:Boolean;
        public var isLowFat:Boolean;
        public var imageName:String;

        public function Product (_catID:Number, _prodName:String, _unitID:Number, _cost:
            catID = _catID;
            prodName =_prodName;
            unitID =_unitID;
            cost = _cost;
            listPrice = _listPrice;
            description = _description;
            isOrganic = _isOrganic;
            isLowFat =  isLowFat;
```

The finished FlexGrocer data structure built in ActionScript 3.0 and integrated into the application.

Introducing Handling Events and Complex Data Structures

This lesson is where you really start to understand the power of using an event-based, object-oriented programming model. In the tasks that you perform during this lesson, you will see that architecting your application properly will result in a much more scalable, reusable, and maintainable application. You will use proven methodologies to develop client-side data models in both MXML and ActionScript, which is an essential part of using the MVC (model-view-controller) design pattern that will be expanded on later in the book. You will receive an introduction to object-oriented design patterns—specifically, the value object pattern that will make data easier to manage by encapsulating data in one object. This pattern can also help to increase network performance by encapsulating various data structures into a single request, instead of making many separate calls to pass complex data structures. You will use the value object pattern in the application to manage all the client data structures you are building.

In this lesson, you will also use the built-in events of ActionScript 3.0, a powerful event-based programming language available to you in Flash Player. An event can be a simple user action, such as clicking, a system action, such as loading the last byte of data from a server, or a more powerful custom action that can be broadcast throughout an application. To respond to any event you must write an event handler, which is a function (or method) in an <mx:Script> block. This event handler will be called only when the event is broadcast (when a user clicks the button).

To fully understand the event-based programming model of ActionScript 3.0, it is important to understand that each MXML tag that you add to an application represents an object. Objects consist of characteristics that describe them, called properties, and behaviors that describe what they can do or what can be done to them, called methods. Properties are just variables attached to an object and methods are functions attached to an object. For example, a Flex Label object has a property describing the text appearing in the label (the text property). It also has behaviors; for example, the setStyle() method that enables you to change the font of the Label controls.

The concept behind object-oriented programming languages is that computer systems modeled after the real-world environment that they represent are more adaptable. What does this really mean? Hopefully, the concepts of "computer systems," "real-world environment," and "adaptability" are easily understood, but what about the concept of "modeling?" Modeling refers to how a computer system is designed. Thus, a computer system modeled on real-world entities refers to an application that is composed of units with characteristics and behaviors similar to real-world complements.

For example, in a grocery store, an employee is responsible for dealing with product descriptions, categories, list prices, costs, and so on for each product the store sells. Therefore, an object-oriented system to support the store will have an entity representing each grocery item; this entity is called an object. The closer the characteristics and behaviors of this object in the computer system resemble those of a true grocery item, the easier it is to adapt the system to changes in the business.

Objects are created based on a class definition, which is much like an architectural blueprint. A blueprint identifies what a house will look like and what amenities it will have. A blueprint can be used many times to create many houses and it guarantees similarities in all houses built from the blueprint. A blueprint might include details such as the following:

- Number of rooms
- Room dimensions
- Window frames
- Heating dimensions

Collectively, the elements describe the final shape the house takes and how it performs. In object-oriented terms, these are the properties of a house, and would be listed in a class definition.

What if a single architect had to design every element of a new house? Finding an architect who is also a plumbing and heating expert might be a challenge. A better choice would be to have a heating expert design and build the heating system, a plumber to do the plumbing work, and so on. In fact, many of the components of a house are prebuilt. For example, you generally purchase a heating and cooling system, and rarely design your own. Using these prebuilt pieces, the complexity of building a house is greatly reduced.

Object-oriented programming embraces the same methodology, encouraging the use, and reuse, of prebuilt objects, which are tested and guaranteed by experts in the domain. Individual objects can be used interchangeably without redesigning the entire system. As with a home, the complexity of designing and building a new application is greatly reduced by using prebuilt pieces. Continuing with our house metaphor:

- A class definition is like a blueprint; an object, like a house, is what is made from that definition.
- An application, much like a house, is made up of objects interacting with one another.
- Creating a program, much like building a house, involves assembling objects and making them communicate with each other.
- Each object, like each part of a house, has a well-defined role in the system.

In this lesson, you will create custom ActionScript objects to mirror real-world business problems associated with an online grocery store application. You will build custom ActionScript classes that will define each product in inventory and handle customer purchases. You will understand the process for creating objects which are aware of their properties (id, name, description, price, and so on), and you will create methods for interacting with the data. You will learn about and encapsulate data using the value object pattern, which will result in a more maintainable application.

Using the <mx:Model> Tag with a Creation Complete Event

The <mx:Model> tag enables you to store data in ActionScript client-side objects, separating your data structure from the actual user interface controls. The <mx:Model> tag works by including XML structures within the tag. You can either declare properties as child tags or specify an external XML file. This XML is compiled into your application as generic ActionScript objects, which can then be used for data binding. This is most useful for embedding data in an application that will not change; for example, a list of states used to populate a ComboBox control. Because the <mx:Model> tag embeds data into the application during compilation, it can also be useful for offline applications that do not have network access at run time.

There are disadvantages to the <mx:Model> tag: the properties of the object created by the <mx:Model> tag are untyped, which means that the compiler cannot predetermine if the property will hold string or numeric data. This can result in poor performance and severely limits error trapping. The <mx:Model> tag in this lesson is simply serving as a substitute for server-side data, which you will work with extensively in the next lesson. Using an ActionScript class for client-side data structures, which you will learn later in this lesson, solves the problems associated with the <mx:Model> tag.

An event is a type of communication that occurs between objects. Often, events are driven by user actions such as clicking a button. Other times these actions, such as a screen being revealed, are driven by the system. The creationComplete event is a system event, dispatched by the components of Flex framework after elements have been created, drawn on the screen, and are ready for use.

Every component in the framework broadcasts this event; for example, an <mx:Button> tag would broadcast this event once all components of the button, such as any icon or label, are drawn and ready. The <mx:Application> tag also broadcasts this event, but only after all components in the application are ready.

In this task, you will first specify an external XML model for your <mx:Model> tag. You will then use the creationComplete event to call a method, or function that will eventually build individual value objects using a custom ActionScript class.

1 In Flex Builder 2, open the EComm.mxml file you worked with in the last lesson. If you didn't complete the previous lesson, you can open EComm.mxml from Lesson05/start and save it in your FlexGrocer directory

2 Remove the child nodes from the <mx:Model> tag and specify the source attribute of the <mx:Model> tag as "assets/inventory.xml", as follows:

```
<mx:Model id="groceryInventory" source="assets/inventory.xml"/>
```

Instead of defining your data model inline, as you did before, you can specify an external XML file as the source for your <mx:Model> tag. In this case, the inventory.xml file looks as follows:

```
<groceries>
    <catID>1</catID>
    <prodName>Milk</prodName>
    <unitID>2</unitID>
    <cost>1.20</cost>
    <listPrice>1.99</listPrice>
    <description>Direct from California where cows are happiest</description>
    <isOrganic>true</isOrganic>
    <isLowFat>true</isLowFat>
    <imageName>dairy_milk.jpg</imageName>
</groceries>
```

The <mx:Model> tag will automatically parse this XML into a native ActionScript data structure; in this case, an object. In Lesson 6, "Using Remote XML Data with Controls," you will learn about more complex data structures.

3 On the <mx:Application> tag, handle the creationComplete event, as follows:

```
<mx:Application xmlns:mx="http://www.adobe.com/2006/mxml"
    layout="absolute" creationComplete="prodHandler()">
```

The creationComplete event, when it is on the <mx:Application> tag, is dispatched, or fired, only after all the children of that tag have been created, which means it is executed just before the application on the screen is shown to the user. It is useful because it means that everything in the entire application is ready for use. The prodHandler() function called here will reside in a script block.

4 Pass to the prodHandler() the data structure created by the <mx:Model> tag, as follows:

```
<mx:Application xmlns:mx="http://www.adobe.com/2006/mxml"
   layout="absolute" creationComplete="prodHandler(groceryInventory)">
```

The id of your <mx:Model> tag is groceryInventory. The <mx:Model> tag automatically created a simple ActionScript object from the XML file and can be used for data binding.

5 Add an <mx:Script> block immediately after the existing <mx:Model> tag. Note that a CDATA tag is automatically added for you by Flex Builder. At the top of the script block, define a new function with the name of prodHandler(). Be sure to specify the parameter it receives as an object with the name of the Items.

```
<mx:Script>
   <![CDATA[
   private function prodHandler(theItems:Object):void
   {
   }
   ]]>
</mx:Script>
```

This function is called an event handler, which is simply a function that is invoked when an event occurs. You have specified that this function is private, which means it can be accessed only from inside of the class, that it will take a single parameter, of type Object, and it will not return anything because you have specified void as the return type.

6 Inside the prodHandler() function, add two trace statements that will display the name and the price of the items being passed to it.

```
private function prodHandler(theItems:Object):void
{
   trace (theItems.prodName);
   trace (theItems.cost);
}
```

7 Click the debug tool to compile the application.

This will display the results of your trace statements in the console. You should see the product name and the product price displayed in the console. You will need to minimize the browser that pops open and choose Window > Console if the console is not open.

```
Problems  Console  ⊠
EComm [Flex Application] file:/c:/flex2tfs/flexGrocer/bin/EComm-debug.html
[SWF] C:\flex2tfs\flexGrocer\bin\EComm-debug.swf - 716,612 bytes after decompression
Milk
1.2
```

Building a Custom ActionScript Class

In this task, you will build a custom ActionScript class that defines a grocery product. This class enables you to specify each property of the object as a typed property such as String or Number, which will result in better performance and error handling. All of your data for a single grocery item will be encapsulated into one ActionScript object.

Throughout the FlexGrocer application, you will need to manage large amounts of typed data and send this data to other applications. When you have a recurring problem in application design, developing a high-quality solution to this problem is known as developing a design pattern. In this task, you will use a well-known design pattern, the value object pattern, to solve this problem.

1 Create a new ActionScript class file by choosing File > New > ActionScript class. Set the Package to valueObjects, which will cause Flex Builder to automatically create a folder with the same name. Name the class **Product** and leave all other fields with the defaults. Click Finish to create the file.

This process creates a file for you with the basic structure of an ActionScript class. The word package and class are both keywords used in defining this class. Remember this class will be a blueprint for many objects that you will use later to describe each grocery product.

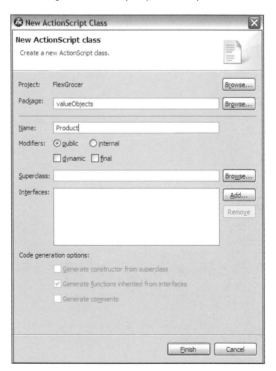

2 Before the class keyword, but after the package keyword, add a [Bindable] metadata tag. Inside of the Product class definition, add a public property with the name of catID and a data type of Number.

```
package valueObjects {
[Bindable]
   public class Product {
      public var catID:Number;
   }
}
```

The [Bindable] metadata tag, when specified in front of the class keyword, means that every property in the class can be bound to controls or other data structures. Metadata is a term used to refer to data that describes other data. In this case, you are using metadata to describe an entire class. When a property is specified as [Bindable], Flex framework will automatically copy the value of the source property to any destination property when the source property changes. Instead of specifying the whole class as [Bindable], you can specify individual properties. In the case of the FlexGrocer application, we want every property to be [Bindable].

3 Create public properties with the names of prodName (String), unitID (Number), cost (Number), listPrice (Number), description (String), isOrganic (Boolean), isLowFat (Boolean), and imageName (String). Your class should look as follows:

```
package valueObjects {
   [Bindable]
   public class Product {
      public var catID:Number;
      public var prodName:String;
      public var unitID:Number;
      public var cost:Number;
      public var listPrice:Number;
      public var description:String;
      public var isOrganic:Boolean;
      public var isLowFat:Boolean;
      public var imageName:String;
   }
}
```

You are creating a data structure to store inventory information for the grocery store. In the top portion of the class, the structure includes all the properties that will be used in the class. This provides a nice separation between the data in the class and the visual UI components, which will display the data.

4 Within the braces for the Product class, after the `imageName` property, define the constructor function of the class and specify the parameters that will be passed to this function. The parameters should match the data type of the properties you already defined, and the names should match but begin with an underscore in order to avoid *name collision* (when the same name could refer to two separate variables) between parameters and properties. Be sure that the name of the function matches the class name and that the constructor is public.

```
public function Product (_catID:Number, _prodName:String, _unitID:Number,
    ➥ _cost:Number, _listPrice:Number, _description:String,_isOrganic:Boolean,
    ➥ _isLowFat:Boolean, _imageName:String){
}
```

The constructor function is automatically called every time an object is created from a class. You can create an object from a class by using the new keyword and passing the class parameters. You will eventually pass the new object elements from your <mx:Model> tag or database, which will result in more-organized data.

5 Inside the constructor function, set each property to the value passed to the constructor function.

```
public function Product (_catID:Number, _prodName:String, _unitID:Number,
    ➥ _cost:Number, _listPrice:Number, _description:String,_isOrganic:Boolean,
    ➥ _isLowFat:Boolean, _imageName:String){

    catID = _catID;
    prodName = _prodName;
    unitID = _unitID;
    cost = _cost;
    listPrice = _listPrice;
    description = _description;
    isOrganic = _isOrganic;
    isLowFat = _isLowFat;
    imageName = _imageName;
}
```

This code will set each property to the value passed when the object is first instantiated using the new keyword.

6 Create a new method directly below the constructor function with the name of toString(), which will return the string [Product] and the name of the product.

```
public function toString():String{
    return "[Product]"+this.prodName;
}
```

This method will return the name of the current product and will be handy for retrieving the name when you need it. Building methods to access properties is good practice because if the property name ever changes, you still call the same function, potentially saving much legacy code. The toString() method is automatically invoked by Flex framework any time an object is traced. This can be very useful for debugging and displaying data structures.

7 Return to the EComm.mxml file and locate the script block at the top of the page. Import the Product class from the valueObjects folder.

```
import valueObjects.Product;
```

To use a custom class, Flex Builder needs an import statement that references the location or package in which the class is located. Flex framework comes with many default classes. However, when you write a custom class, you need to explicitly import a class so it is available to Flex framework. You do this by using the import keyword.

8 Before the prodHandler() function, in the script block, declare the theProduct object as a private property. Add a [Bindable] metadata tag.

```
[Bindable]
private var theProduct:Product;
```

All MXML files ultimately compile to an ActionScript class. You must follow the same conventions when creating an MXML file as when creating an ActionScript class. For example, you must import any classes that are not native to the ActionScript language, such as the Product class you have built, and you must declare any properties that you will use in your MXML file. This is done in a script block. The [Bindable] metadata tag will ensure that the property can be connected to visual controls.

9 Within the prodHandler() function, create a new instance of the Product class with the name of theProduct, and populate and pass the parameter to the constructor function with the information from the <mx:Model> tag, as follows:

```
theProduct = new Product(theItems.catID, theItems.prodName,
    ➥ theItems.unitID, theItems.cost, theItems.listPrice,
    ➥ theItems.description, theItems.isOrganic, theItems.isLowFat,
    ➥ theItems.imageName);
```

This code will place the data from the <mx:Model> tag into a Product value object, allowing for information to be better organized and more accessible. In addition, all of the property values will have datatypes which will result in a faster performing application and more detailed errors.

10 Delete the two `trace` statements from the `prodHandler()` function and add a new `trace` statement that will automatically retrieve the information you specified in the `toString()` method.

```
trace(theProduct);
```

11 Save and debug the MXML file.

You should see `[Product]Milk` in the console window, which indicates that you are using a Product value object to store the data.

Building a Method to Create an Object

In this task, you will build a static method that will accept an object, and return an instance of the Product class.

1 Be sure the Product class in the valueObjects folder is open. Locate the `toString()` method and add the skeleton of a new public static method called `buildProduct()` after the method. Be sure that the return type of the method is set to Product and that it accepts an object parameter, as shown:

```
public static function buildProduct(o:Object):Product{
}
```

A static method can be called without having to first create an object from the class. Instance methods, like those we have used so far, rely on the state of the object they are attached to. Methods that are declared as static need only rely on the class, not on any state of the object. Static methods create behavior that is completely independent of the object. Static methods are useful for utilities such as the `buildObject()` static method you are creating here. You need access to this method without having to create an object first. Used appropriately, static methods can increase performance because you do not have to first create an object that uses space in memory. To reference a static method with the name of `getName()` from the Product class, you would simply write this code:

```
Product.getName();
```

2 Inside the `buildProduct()` method, instantiate an instance of the Product class with the name of p by using the new keyword. Set the `catID`, `prodName`, `unitID`, `cost`, `listPrice`, `description`, `isOrganic`, `isLowFat`, and `imageName` properties as parameters to the con-structor. You will need to cast the `isOrganic` and `isLowFat` variables to Boolean.

```
var p:Product = new Product(o.catID, o.prodName, o.unitID, o.cost,
    ➥ o.listPrice, o.description, Boolean(o.isOrganic),
    ➥ Boolean(o.isLowFat), o.imageName);
```

Casting a variable tells the compiler to treat a given value as a specific type. In this example, we are telling the compiler that you, the developer, know that the `isOrganic` and `isLowFat` properties will contain Boolean data. Casting will be discussed in detail later; however, it is necessary here due to the problems discussed with untyped data and the `<mx:Model>` tag.

3 Return the object you just created by using the return keyword with the name of the object p. Your final `buildProduct()` method should look as follows:

```
public static function buildProduct(o:Object):Product{
    var p:Product = new Product(o.catID, o.prodName, o.unitID,
        ➥ o.cost, o.listPrice, o.description, Boolean(o.isOrganic),
        ➥ Boolean(o.isLowFat), o.imageName);
    return p;
}
```

This code will return the value object created by passing a data structure to the method.

4 Save the Product.as file.

The class file is saved with the new method. No errors should appear in the problems console.

5 Return to EComm.mxml. In the `prodHandler()` method, remove the code that builds `theProduct` and replace it with code that uses the static method to build `theProduct`.

```
theProduct = Product.buildProduct(theItems);
```

This code calls the method that builds an instance of the Product class, which returns a clean, strongly typed value object from a data structure that consisted of objects that were not typed and were loosely organized.

6 Locate the first VBox layout container in the expanded state, which displays the product description, whether the product is organic and whether the product is low fat. Change the text property of `<mx:Text>` tag to reference the theProduct object you created in the `prodHandler()` method. Also, add a `visible` property to both labels, and bind each to the appropriate theProduct object properties, as follows:

```
<mx:VBox width="100%" x="200">
   <mx:Text text="{theProduct.description}"
      width="50%"/>
   <mx:Label
      text="Certified Organic"
      visible="{theProduct.isOrganic}"/>
   <mx:Label
      text="Low Fat"
      visible="{theProduct.isLowFat}"/>
</mx:VBox>
```

You are now referencing the value object you created. Notice that the ActionScript class is self-documenting; because you are using typed properties, they appear as code hints.

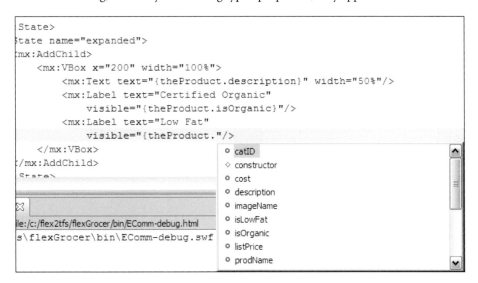

7 Save and debug the application.

You should see the `trace` functions just as before and that the data binding is still working when you roll over the image.

Building Shopping Cart Classes

In this task, you will build a new class for items that are added to the shopping cart. The new class will need to keep track of which product was added and the quantity of product; you will build a method that calculates the subtotal for that item. You will also build the skeleton for a ShoppingCart class that will handle all the logic for the shopping cart, including adding items to the cart.

1 Create a new ActionScript class file by choosing File > New > ActionScript class. Set the Package to valueObjects, which will automatically add this class to the folder you created earlier. Enter **ShoppingCartItem** as the name and leave all other fields with the following default values:

In this class, you will calculate the quantity of each unique item as well as the subtotal.

2 Within the class definition, define a public property with the name of product and a data type of Product, as shown:

```
package valueObjects {
   public class ShoppingCartItem {
      public var product:Product;
   }
}
```

An important piece of the shopping cart is which item has been added. You have already created the Product class to track all this data, so it makes perfect sense to attach an instance of this class to the ShoppingCartItem class.

3 Define a public property with the name of quantity and a data type of uint, as shown:

```
package valueObjects {
   public class ShoppingCartItem {
      public var product:Product;
      public var quantity:uint;
   }
}
```

The uint data type means unsigned integer, which is a non-fractional, non-negative number (0, 1, 2, 3, …). The quantity of an item added to the shopping cart will either be zero or a positive number so it makes sense to type it as a uint.

4 Define a public property with the name of subtotal and a data type of Number, as shown:

```
package valueObjects {
   public class ShoppingCartItem {
      public var product:Product;
      public var quantity:uint;
      public var subtotal:Number;
   }
}
```

Each time a user adds an item to the shopping cart, you will want the subtotal for that item to be updated. Eventually, you will display this data in a visual control.

5 Immediately after the subtotal property, define the constructor function of the class and specify the parameters that will be passed to this function.

The parameters should match the data type of the properties you already defined, and the names should match but begin with the this keyword to avoid name collision. Set the quantity parameter in the function to 1, which is creating a default. Set the subtotal property to equal the `product.listPrice * quantity`. Be sure that the name of the function matches the class name and that the constructor is public. Your constructor function should look as follows:

```
public function ShoppingCartItem(product:Product, quantity:uint=1){
    this.product = product;
    this.quantity = quantity;
    this.subtotal = product.listPrice * quantity;
}
```

The constructor function is automatically called every time an object is created from a class. The constructor will set the properties that are passed in; in this case, an instance of the Product class, and the quantity which is automatically set to 1 as a default. This method will only be used when an item is added to the shopping cart so it makes sense to define the initial quantity as 1.

In this code, we have a variable in the ShoppingCartItem class called `product`, and we have an argument of the constructor called `product`, so we need to tell the compiler specifically which one to use. We use the `this` keyword, to accomplish this goal and avoid something called *name collision*, when the same name could refer to two separate variables. The line 'this.product = product;' tells the compiler to set the `product` variable that resides in the ShoppingCartItem equal to the `product` variable that was passed in as an argument of the constructor. You used a different method, underscores, in the product class to illustrate the same concept. It is not important which strategy you choose to use, just that you are specific so that the compiler understands which variable you intend to modify.

6 Create a public method with the name of `recalc()` that will calculate the subtotal of each item by multiplying the `listPrice` of the product by the `quantity`, as follows:

```
public function recalc():void{
    this.subtotal = product.listPrice * quantity;
}
```

When the user adds items to the shopping cart, you need to perform calculations so that the total can be updated. You also need to check to see whether the item has been added to the cart already; if so, update the quantity. You will learn how to loop through a data structure in the next lesson.

7 Create a new ActionScript class file by choosing File > New > ActionScript class. Set the Package to valueObjects, which will automatically add this class to the valueObjects folder you created earlier. Name the class ShoppingCart and leave all other fields with the defaults, as shown in the following example:

You are creating a new class that will handle the manipulation of the data in the shopping cart. You have already created the visual look and feel of the shopping cart and you will place all your business logic in the ShoppingCart class. This business logic includes adding an item to the cart, deleting an item from the cart, updating an item in the cart, and so on.

8 Add an `import` statement that will allow you to use Flash utilities such as the `trace` statement within the class, as shown:

```
package valueObjects{
    import flash.utils.*
    public class ShoppingCart{
    }
}
```

Just as you have to import your own custom classes for use, you need to import the appropriate classes from the framework to use them. You will be using a `trace()` function and other utilities, which require the import of these classes.

9 Create the skeleton of an `addItem()` method that will accept an instance of the ShoppingCartItem class. Add a `trace` statement that will trace the product added to the cart:

```
package valueObjects{
   import flash.utils.*
   public class ShoppingCart{
      public function addItem(item:ShoppingCartItem):void{
         trace(item.product);
      }
   }
}
```

This is the method in which you will add a new item to the shopping cart. You will add much more business logic to this method in later lessons. For now, you will just trace the name of the item added to the cart. Remember that the `toString()` function you wrote earlier is automatically called whenever an instance of the Product class is traced.

10 Open the EComm.mxml in Flex Builder and locate the script block. Just below the Product `import` statement, import the ShoppingCartItem and ShoppingCart classes from the valueObjects folder, as shown:

```
import valueObjects.ShoppingCartItem;
import valueObjects.ShoppingCart;
```

To use a class, Flex Builder needs an `import` statement that references the location or package in which the class is located.

11 Just below the `import` statements, instantiate a public instance of the ShoppingCart class, name the instance `cart`, and add a `[Bindable]` metadata tag, as follows:

```
[Bindable]
public var cart:ShoppingCart = new ShoppingCart();
```

When the user clicks the Add To Cart button, you want to call the `addItem()` method of the ShoppingCart class you created earlier. You will pass the `addItem()` method an instance of the ShoppingCartItem class. By instantiating the class here, you will ensure that you have access to it throughout the class.

12 Locate the `prodHandler()` method in the `<mx:Script>` block. Immediately after this method, add a skeleton of a new private method with the name of `addToCart()`. Be sure that the method accepts a parameter of product data typed to Product, as shown:

```
private function addToCart(product:Product):void {
}
```

This method will be called when the user clicks Add, and you will pass the Product value object that the user selected. This is a method of the MXML file and will not be called outside of this file. Therefore, you can use the identifier private, which means that the method cannot be accessed from outside the class and helps to provide better data protection.

13 Inside the addToCart() method, create a new instance of the ShoppingCartItem class with the name of sci and pass the constructor the Product class, as shown:

```
var sci:ShoppingCartItem = new ShoppingCartItem(product);
```

14 Inside the addToCart() method, call the addItem() method of the ShoppingCart class. Be sure to pass the method the sci (Instance of the ShoppingCartItem class), as follows:

```
cart.addItem(sci);
```

This code will call the addItem() method of the ShoppingCart class you built earlier. In this next lesson, you will learn how to loop through the data structure to see whether the item is added. For now, this method simply traces the name of the product added to the cart.

15 Add a click event to the Add To Cart button. Call the addToCart() method, passing the method an instance of theProduct:

```
<mx:Button id="add" label="Add To Cart"
    click="addToCart(theProduct)"/>
```

The addToCart() method will create an instance of the ShoppingCartItem and pass it to the addItem() method of the cart class.

16 Save and debug the application.

You should see that the words [Product]Milk appear in the output panel every time you click Add To Cart.

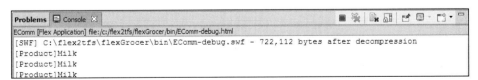

Exploring the Event Object

Every time an event occurs in Flex framework, whether it is a user clicking a button or the creationComplete event signaling that all components are ready for use, an Event object is created. This object is an instance of the Event class and contains important information about what type of event occurred and the object that emitted the event. You have the power to add your own custom events to the Event object. You will work with events much more in future lessons to produce applications that are loosely coupled and follow good object-oriented design.

This procedure defines a project you will use for exploring the event object.

1 Define a new project with the name of **EventTest** and be sure that the EventTest.mxml file is the main application file.

2 Open the EventTest.mxml file and add an <mx:Button> tag. Assign the <mx:Button> tag an id of myButton. Add a click event that will call the myFunction() function and pass it an instance of the Event class, as follows:

```
<mx:Application xmlns:mx="http://www.adobe.com/2006/mxml" xmlns="*"
    layout="absolute">
    <mx:Button id="myButton" click="myFunction(event)"/>
</mx:Application>
```

This very simple application calls a function when the user clicks a button. It passes the function an instance of the Event class, which is created automatically every time any type of event fires. The event object that is created is extremely powerful because the object contains important information about the event that occurred.

3 Above the <mx:Button> tag, add a script block. Inside of this block, define a new function with the name of myFunction(). Specify the parameter as event:Event, as shown:

```
<mx:Application xmlns:mx="http://www.adobe.com/2005/mxml" xmlns="*"
    layout="absolute">
    <mx:Script>
        <![CDATA[
            public function myFunction(event:Event):void{
            }
        ]]>
    </mx:Script>
    <mx:Button id="myButton" click="myFunction(event)"/>
</mx:Application>
```

The function will capture the event when the user clicks the button. In the next step, you will see the useful information that is encapsulated inside this Event object.

4 Inside the myFunction() function, add two trace statements that will trace the currentTarget and the type property:

```
private function myFunction(event:Event):void{
    trace (event.currentTarget);
    trace (event.type);
}
```

Both the currentTarget and type properties are automatically added to every instance of an Event object. The current target is the name of the control that generated the event; in this case, myButton. The type is a simple string of the event itself; in this case, click.

5 Debug the application and click the button.

In the output panel, you should see the fully qualified path to the myButton component that emitted the event and the name of the event that was emitted; in this case, click.

What You Have Learned

In this lesson, you have:

- Learned how to embed external XML files in the <mx:Model> tag (pages 90–91)

- Learned that the creationComplete event is invoked when all controls and data structures are ready for use (pages 90–92)

- Learned class-based development, including how to build methods and properties (pages 93–97)

- Learned about the importance of a constructor function (page 95)

- Learned that a static method does not need an object to be called (pages 97–99)

- Learned how to use a class to manage items in a shopping cart (pages 100–105)

- Learned about the Event object that is generated each time an event occurs (pages 106–107)

What You Will Learn

In this lesson, you will:

- Create an HTTPService object that converts data into an ArrayCollection

- Use an ArrayCollection as a data provider for ComboBox and List controls

- Understand security issues involved with retrieving data into Flash Player

- Create an HTTPService object that converts data into an XMLListCollection

- Use an XMLListCollection to populate a Tree control

- Use ECMAScript for XML (E4X) functionality to manipulate XML

- Create an object and use the object's methods to remove data in an ArrayCollection

Approximate Time

This lesson takes approximately 2 hours and 30 minutes to complete.

Lesson Files

Media Files:

None

Starting Files:

Lesson06/start/EComm.mxml
Lesson06/start/valueObjects/ShoppingCartItem.as
Lesson06/start/valueObjects/ShoppingCart.as
Lesson06/start/valueObjects/Product.as
Lesson06/start/Dashboard.mxml
Lesson06/start/DataEntry.mxml

Completed Files:

Lesson06/complete/EComm.mxml
Lesson06/complete/valueObjects/ShoppingCartItem.as
Lesson06/complete/valueObjects/ShoppingCart.as
Lesson06/complete/valueObjects/Product.as
Lesson06/complete/DataEntry.mxml
Lesson06/complete/Dashboard.mxml

LESSON 6

Using Remote XML Data with Controls

In this lesson, you will begin to connect the grocery applications to remote data. In the e-commerce application, you will access remote XML data and use them to populate the grocery item interface you created in earlier lessons. In the DataEntry application, you will use a Tree control to enable users to easily display details of grocery items. In the Dashboard application, you will dynamically populate a ComboBox control with remote XML data.

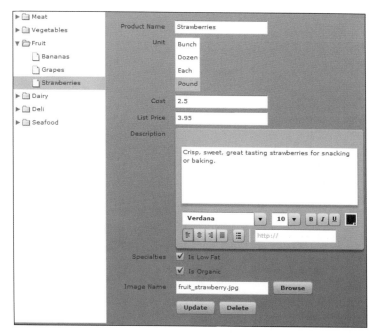

A Tree control populated with remote XML data and used to display details from a particular node of the Tree

109

You will populate the control by using the HTTPService class to load remote XML data. The data could exist on a remote server, or in external files on the same server, but the data is remote to the application. The data will be transmitted through the HTTP protocol. You will work with this XML data in several formats. By default the data is parsed into an ArrayCollection, which is a special featured array, and you will also use functionality from the ECMAScript for XML (E4X) implementation that implements XML as a native data type in ActionScript.

To put this data to actual use, you will use it as a source for controls that take complex data structures as their data provider. These controls enable you to easily display complex data sets and enable the user to navigate these data sets. You will use the List, ComboBox, and Tree data provider controls in this lesson.

Retrieving XML Data with HTTPService

In the last lesson, you embedded XML in a SWF file by specifying the source attribute of the <mx:Model> tag and pointing to an external XML file. This method can be a bad practice because the XML is compiled into the SWF file, increasing the file size. The XML is also not readily updateable; you would have to recompile the SWF every time the data changed. This is not practical for data that will change or for large datasets. In real life, you will rarely embed XML data. It is a much better practice to load the XML at run time using the HTTPService class. When you use the HTTPService class to load the XML dynamically, there will be a small lag as the data is retrieved and loaded because the SWF is actually making an HTTP request using either the GET or POST method.

In this lesson, you will harness the power of XML to connect the e-commerce, Dashboard, and DataEntry applications to XML data using the HTTPService class. This class enables you to make HTTP calls, using GET or POST, at run time directly from a SWF file. You can make asynchronous requests to remote HTTPServices that process the requests and return the data results to the Flex application. The complex data structures can be returned in a number of formats, but in this lesson you will use either an ActionScript XML object or an ActionScript ArrayCollection. You will also use data provider controls that are specifically designed to display this data.

A client-side request/response component, such as HTTPService, can be created in either MXML or ActionScript, and will make an asynchronous call to the URL that you specify; this is one way to access data in a rich Internet application (RIA). The HTTPService object will access either static or dynamically created XML through a URL. This dynamically created XML can be from ColdFusion, .NET, Java, PHP, or any type of server-side technology. After the HTTPService object has executed, the results of the call are sent back to the Flex client and stored in a client-side ActionScript object. You can specify the format of the object using the resultFormat property.

When you call the HTTPService object's send() method, it makes an HTTP or HTTPS, GET or POST request to the specified URL, and an HTTP response is returned. When the last byte of data has been received by the client, a result event is broadcast, and the data is accessible. This is powerful because you can manipulate the data before you start using it. The results of the call are stored in the lastResult property of the HTTPService object and in the result property of the event object created from the ResultEvent class. If you do not specify a resultFormat, Flex will automatically parse the XML data to represent appropriate base ActionScript types.

Using ArrayCollections

By default, complex data structures are returned in an ArrayCollection. Arrays are still very useful in ActionScript, especially for managing large amounts of data. However, collections like the ArrayCollection are a much more robust method of working with data. Arrays do not work well for displaying data visually because they lack the functionality that enables them to work correctly with data bindings. You have worked with data binding in earlier lessons to link an underlying data structure to a visual control, but you have used only very simple data structures. When using complex data structures with controls, you should always use collections instead of Arrays. Collections provide operations that automatically update the visual display when the underlying data changes. They also provide operations that include the retrieval, insertion and deletion of objects, as well as sorting and filtering.

For an example of that functionality, consider the following XML, and assume it was retrieved by an HTTPService object with an id of serviceid.

```
<?xml version="1.0" encoding="utf-8"?>
<allUnits>
    <unit>
        <unitName>Bunch</unitName>
        <unitID>4</unitID>
    </unit>
    <unit>
        <unitName>Dozen</unitName>
        <unitID>2</unitID>
    </unit>
    <unit>
        <unitName>Each</unitName>
        <unitID>1</unitID>
    </unit>
</allUnits>
```

You would retrieve the "Dozen" node outside the result handler using the following code:

```
serviceid.lastResult.allUnits.unit.getItemAt(1)
```

In a result handler, you would retrieve the same node using the following code:

```
private function unitRPCResult(event:ResultEvent):void{
    trace(event.result.allUnits.unit.getItemAt(1));
}
```

Using Collections as Data Providers

There are multiple controls that enable you to display complex data structures using the dataProvider property. The list-based controls, which include List, Tree, DataGrid, TileList and ComboBox, among others, use a dataProvider property.

A data provider is simply a collection of objects, much like an Array or ArrayCollection. You can think of a dataProvider property as a client-side data model and the Flex components as views of the model. You will learn more about this model-view-controller design pattern (MVC) in the next lesson. A data provider control will display a complex data structure to the end user. For example, the dataProvider property of a ComboBox control can be set to an array of objects or an ArrayCollection, which you will work with in this lesson. The labelField property of the data provider controls specify which dataProvider property should be displayed to the end user. The code in the following example would result in a ComboBox displayed with three items: Fruit, Meat and Dairy:

```
<mx:ComboBox id="myCombo" labelField ="type">
  <mx:dataProvider>
    <mx:ArrayCollection>
      <mx:Object type="Fruit" id="zero"/>
      <mx:Object type="Meat" id="one"/>
      <mx:Object type="Dairy" id="two"/>
    </mx:ArrayCollection>
  </mx:dataProvider>
</mx:ComboBox>
```

The data provider controls have multiple advantages. You can populate multiple controls with the same data, you can switch out data providers at run time, and you can modify a data provider so changes in it are reflected by all controls using it.

Understanding Security Issues

Flex is subject to the *security sandbox restrictions* of Flash Player, which means that an application on one domain is prevented from loading data from another domain. To automatically give an application loaded from www.mysite.com access to data on www.yoursite.com, you must use a *cross-domain policy file*. This file, named crossdomain.xml, specifies which domains have access to resources from Flash Player and is placed on the root of the web server that the SWF file is calling. Here is an example of a cross-domain policy file that would enable any SWF to access resources available on the web server where it resides:

```
<cross-domain-policy>
<allow-access-from domain="*"/>
</cross-domain-policy>
```

> ● **TIP:** Browse the URL www.flexgrocer.com/crossdomain.xml to see the cross domain file that allows you to retrieve data from your data source for this book. Also check www.cnn.com/crossdomain.xml to see who CNN allows to syndicate their content using Flash Player.

If you are using Flex Data Services, a built-in proxy is included to overcome this restriction (this will be covered in later lessons). More information about the sandbox restrictions of the Flash Player is available in the tech note on the Adobe site: www.adobe.com/cfusion/knowledgebase/index.cfm?id=tn_14213

Before deploying a cross-domain security file like this to a server, be sure to understand all the ramifications.

Populating a List with Retrieved XML as an ArrayCollection of Objects

In this task, you will use a List control in the form to display the units in which the grocery items are sold, such as pounds or dozens. This data will be dynamically populated from an HTTPService call. You will use an ArrayCollection in the data binding.

1 Open a web browser and browse to the following URL:

www.flexgrocer.com/units.xml

Notice the structure of the XML. Your goal is to populate a List control in the form with this information.

2 Open DataEntry.mxml. In the existing script block, import the following classes:

```
mx.collections.ArrayCollection
mx.rpc.events.ResultEvent
utils.Util
```

You need these classes for the additions you will be making to the DataEntry application in this lesson. The Util class has been custom built for this book.

3 Below the `import` statements, but above the function declaration, add a bindable, private variable named `units` data typed as `ArrayCollection` and set it equal to a new ArrayCollection.

```
[Bindable]
private var units:ArrayCollection=new ArrayCollection();
```

You will be binding an ArrayCollection to the List control. As a best practice, it makes sense to use an ArrayCollection for data binding with a complex data structure because you want it to update when any changes are made to the data structure.

4 Directly below the `<mx:Script>` block, add an `<mx:HTTPService>` tag, assign it an `id` of `unitRPC`, and specify the `url` property to http://www.flexgrocer.com/units.xml. Specify the `result` handler to call `unitRPCResult` handler and be sure to pass the event object, as follows:

```
<mx:HTTPService id="unitRPC"
url="http://www.flexgrocer.com/units.xml"
result="unitRPCResult(event)"/>
```

You are specifying the URL of the HTTPService to point to the XML you examined in step 1. In the next step, you will write a result handler with the name of `unitRPCResult()` that will be called when the data has been retrieved. The `result` event is an event of the HTTPService class that is called when the last byte of data has been retrieved from the remote server. The event will call an ActionScript function when the data has been returned successfully, which enables you to manipulate the returned data.

5 Returning to the script block, add a new private function with the name of `unitRPCResult()`. Be sure to name the parameter event and specify the type as a `ResultEvent`. Populate the units ArrayCollection with the `event.result` property from the event object. Remember from examining the XML that the repeating node is unit.

```
private function unitRPCResult(event:ResultEvent):void{
   units=event.result.allUnits.unit;
}
```

The event object is created when the `result` event is broadcast. This object should be strictly typed to the type of event that is occurring; in this case a `ResultEvent`. All events descend from the Event class in ActionScript. Flex creates one object per event that occurs. The object created contains properties of the standard Event class, but also contains properties unique to the specific type of event that occurred; in this case a

ResultEvent object, referred to as event in a function parameter. One of these properties is the result property, which contains all the returned data in whatever format you specified; in this case the default type converts the XML into an ArrayCollection. You have to understand the structure of the retrieved XML to further specify the actual data, in this case allUnits.unit, is appended to event.result. You must "point" to the repeating node in the XML, which is in this case unit.

6 Move to the top of the application and add a creationComplete event that calls the unitRPC HTTPService using the send() method.

```
<mx:Application xmlns:mx="http://www.adobe.com/2006/mxml"
    layout="absolute"
    creationComplete="unitRPC.send()">
```

The object created from the HTTPService class, with the id of unitRPC, must invoke its send() method to actually make the call to the URL. Most of the controls in the grocery store application depend on the data retrieved from the HTTPService. Therefore, you want to be sure that each control has been initialized and is ready for use. So, it makes sense to call the data service on the creationComplete event of the <mx:Application> tag when each control has been drawn, is initialized, and is ready for use.

7 Locate the ProductNameUnit FormItem and change the label to just Unit and remove the direction="horizontal" property assignment. Locate the ComboBox control. Replace the ComboBox control with a List control and delete the TextInput control. Assign the List control an id of unitID and set the rowCount variable to 4. Specify the dataProvider property to the units ArrayCollection and specify the labelField as unitName. Your <mx:List> tag should look as shown here:

```
<mx:List id="unitID"
    rowCount="4"
    dataProvider="{units}"
    labelField="unitName"/>
```

This will create a List control that will display the units of measurement for the administration tool. You created the units data provider using the ArrayCollection class. From examining the XML, you know that the unitName property is the label you want displayed on the list.

8 Save and run the application.

You should see that the List control is populated with the units, as shown here.

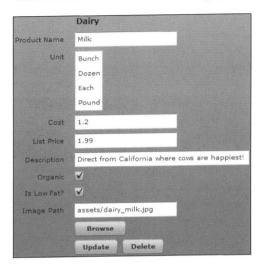

9 Close the file.

You will be working with a different application in the next task.

Populating a ComboBox Control and Programmatically Adding an Option

In this task, you will work on the Dashboard application. You will make a call to an HTTPService that returns all the grocery categories and IDs and uses the returned data to populate a ComboBox control. This task differs from the last in that you will do the common practice of adding an "All" type selection to the ComboBox control. Seldom will the XML or database table contain an "All" type selection for the user interface control that consumes the data. In this case you use the addItemAt() method of the ArrayCollection class to add such an option.

1 Open a web browser and browse to the following URL:

www.flexgrocer.com/category.xml

Notice the structure of the XML. Your goal in this task is to populate a ComboBox control with this information. The XML contains a repeating node, category, which contains the information you will need to populate the ComboBox control.

2 Open up Dashboard.mxml. Add a script block, directly below the mx:Application tag, and two `import` statements that will import the ArrayCollection class from the mx.collections package, as well as the ResultEvent from the mx.rpc.events package. Add a `[Bindable]` ArrayCollection property with the name of `categories`, and set it equal to a new ArrayCollection.

```
<mx:Script>
  <![CDATA[
    import mx.collections.ArrayCollection;
    import mx.rpc.events.ResultEvent;

    [Bindable]
    private var categories:ArrayCollection=new ArrayCollection();
  ]]>
</mx:Script>
```

You will be binding an ArrayCollection to the ComboBox control. As a best practice, it makes sense to use an ArrayCollection for data binding with a complex data structure because you want it to update when any changes are made to the data structure. To use an ArrayCollection, you need to import the class. You will also be using a ResultEvent with the HTTPService class, so you need to import it as well.

3 Directly below the script block, add an `<mx:HTTPService>` tag. Assign it an `id` of `catRPC` and specify the `url` property to http://www.flexgrocer.com/category.xml. Specify the result handler to call `catHandler()` and be sure to pass the event object, as follows:

```
<mx:HTTPService id="catRPC"
  url="http://www.flexgrocer.com/category.xml"
  result="catHandler(event)"/>
```

You are specifying the URL of the HTTPService to point to the XML you examined in step 1. Later you will write a result handler with the name of `catHandler` that will be called when the data has been retrieved. Remember, an event object is created every time a result event occurs.

4 Move to the top of the application and add a `creationComplete` event that calls the `catRPC` HTTPService using the `send()` method.

```
<mx:Application xmlns:mx="http://www.adobe.com/2006/mxml"
  layout="horizontal"
  creationComplete="catRPC.send()">
```

To actually execute the HTTPService call, you must use the `send()` method. Remember, just adding the tag does not execute the call.

5 Returning to the script block, add a new private method with the name of `catHandler()`. Be sure to name the parameter event and specify the type as a `ResultEvent`. Populate the ArrayCollection, categories, with the `event.result.catalog.category` ArrayCollection returned from the HTTPService and stored in the event object.

```
private function catHandler(event:ResultEvent):void{
   categories = event.result.catalog.category;
}
```

As in the first task, you have retrieved data and placed the ArrayCollection that is returned in a variable, in this case `categories`.

6 Now you are going to programmatically add another option to the ComboBox control. Start by creating a new object with the name of catObj just below where you assigned categories a value in `catHandler()`. Set a property as name with the value of All, and set another property as `categoryID` with a value of 0. Your code so far should appear as follows:

```
private function catHandler(event:ResultEvent):void{
   categories = event.result.catalog.category;
   var catObj:Object = new Object();
   catObj.name = "All";
   catObj.categoryID = 0;
}
```

Here you created the Object that will be added to the ArrayCollection, and hence the ComboBox, in the next step.

7 Now add the object to the first index of the ArrayCollection by using the `addItemAt()` method and specifying catObj and the first index, which is 0. Finally, set the `selectedIndex` of the ComboBox to 0 so the new item in the collection is selected at startup. Your code should appear as follows:

```
private function catHandler(event:ResultEvent):void{
   categories = event.result.catalog.category;
   var catObj:Object = new Object();
   catObj.name = "All";
   catObj.categoryID = 0;
   categories.addItemAt(catObj, 0);
   catCombo.selectedIndex = 0;
}
```

Because the data structure from the server does not include an `All` property, you need to add it manually in the result event handler then make it the selected item.

8 Locate the ApplicationControlBar. After the endDate DateField and above the `<mx:RadioButtonGroup>` tag, add a ComboBox control and assign it an id of catCombo. Specify the dataProvider property to the categories ArrayCollection, as follows:

```
<mx:ComboBox id="catCombo"
    dataProvider="{categories}"/>
```

You are specifying the dataProvider for the ComboBox to be the ArrayCollection that you built in the last step.

9 In the `<mx:ComboBox>` tag add a labelField property to the control. Specify the value of name for the property, as follows:

```
<mx:ComboBox id="catCombo"
    dataProvider = "{categories}"
    labelField = "name"/>
```

If you compile the application without adding the labelField property, the ComboBox would not know which property or field to use as the label property. You can specify any of the field names in the data structure as the labelField property. In this case, you specify the name field because you want the name of all the categories to be displayed.

10 Save and run the application.

You should see that the ComboBox has been populated with the XML data you examined in the first step, as well as the word "All" in the first index.

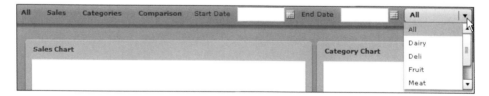

11 Close the file.

Using XML Data with a Tree Control

In this section, you add functionality to the DataEntry application. You will make an HTTPService call to access the data and use this data to populate a Tree control. The Tree control is tailor-made to display XML data. You will use the Tree control to easily navigate the complex data structure and populate the form you created in Lesson 4, "Using Simple Controls."

ActionScript 3.0 contains native XML support in the form of ECMAScript for XML (E4X). This ECMA standard is designed to give ActionScript programmers access to XML in a straight forward way. E4X uses standard ActionScript syntax that you should already be familiar with, plus some new functionality specific to E4X.

▼ **CAUTION!** The XML class in ActionScript 3.0 is not the same as the XML class in ActionScript 2.0. That class has been renamed to XMLDocument, so it does not conflict with the XML class now part of E4X. The old XML document class in ActionScript is not covered in this book. You should not need to use this class except in working with legacy projects.

Understanding E4X operators

In this task and also through the rest of this lesson, you will use E4X functionality. The new E4X specification defines a new set of classes and functionality for working with XML data. These classes and functionality are known collectively as *E4X*.

First, for a very basic, very quick review of XML terminology, examine the XML object as it would be defined in ActionScript:

```
private var groceryXML:XML = new XML();
groceryXML=
<catalog>
   <category name="vegetables">
      <product name="lettuce" cost="1.95">
         <unit>bag</unit>
         <desc>Cleaned and bagged</desc>
      </product>
      <product name="carrots" cost="2.95">
         <unit>pound</unit>
         <desc>Baby carrots, cleaned and peeled</desc>
      </product>
   </category>
   <category name="fruit">
      <product name="apples" cost=".95">
         <unit>each</unit>
         <desc>Sweet Fuji</desc>
      </product>
      <product name="raspberries" cost="2.95">
         <unit>pint</unit>
         <desc>Firm and fresh</desc>
      </product>
   </category>
</catalog>;
```

The following statements describe the XML object, with the XML terminology italicized:

- The *root node* (or element) is catalog.
- There are two category *nodes*.
- The product node has two *child* nodes called unit and desc.
- The product node has two *attributes* name and cost.

Now you have the basic XML terminology understood, you can start using some of the powerful E4X operators. First consider the *dot* (.) operator. You will use these to access data in the XML document. The dot operator behaves much like the dot in `object.property` notation which you are familiar with. You use the dot operator to navigate to child nodes. So the statement

```
groceryXML.category.product.unit
```

would yield the following results:

```
<unit>bag</unit>
<unit>pound</unit>
<unit>each</unit>
<unit>pint</unit>
```

▶ **TIP:** When using E4X notation, the root node, in this case category, is not used in statements.

If you want a specific unit, you would have to employ the *parentheses* [()] operator. The parentheses operator is used to do evaluation in an E4X construct. So the statement

```
groceryXML.category.product.(unit=='pint')
```

would yield the following results:

```
<product name="raspberries" cost="2.95">
   <unit>pint</unit>
   <desc>Firm and fresh</desc>
</product>
```

Notice that E4X, when doing an evaluation with the parentheses, returns the entire node containing the specified unit node, not just the node itself.

You can do the same types of evaluation and searching using the *attribute* (@) operator. To specify an attribute rather than a child node in an evaluation, you use the @ operator. So the statement

```
groceryXML.category.product.(@cost=='2.95')
```

would yield the following results:

```
<product name="carrots" cost="2.95">
   <unit>pound</unit>
   <desc>Baby carrots, cleaned and peeled</desc>
</product>
<product name="raspberries" cost="2.95">
   <unit>pint</unit>
   <desc>Firm and fresh</desc>
</product>
```

Notice because there were two matches of cost attribute matching 2.95, both were returned.

Another very powerful operator in E4X is the *descendant accessor*, represented by two dots (..). This operator navigates to descendant elements of an XML object, no matter how complex the XML's structure. So the statement

```
groceryXML..product
```

would yield the following results:

```
<product name="lettuce" cost="1.95">
   <unit>bag</unit>
   <desc>Cleaned and bagged</desc>
</product>
<product name="carrots" cost="2.95">
   <unit>pound</unit>
   <desc>Baby carrots, cleaned and peeled</desc>
</product>
<product name="apples" cost=".95">
   <unit>each</unit>
   <desc>Sweet Fuji</desc>
</product>
<product name="raspberries" cost="2.95">
   <unit>pint</unit>
   <desc>Firm and fresh</desc>
</product>
```

The descendant accessor operator searched through the entire XML object and returned all the product nodes. The result would have been the same no matter how deeply nested the product nodes were.

You have now seen just a slice of the very powerful E4X implementation in ActionScript 3.0. For more information see Chapter 11: Working with XML in the Programming ActionScript 3.0 documentation that comes with Flex.

Populating a Tree Control with XML Data

Just as you used an ArrayCollection to populate List and ComboBox controls in the last two tasks, you will use an XMLListCollection to populate the Tree control. The XMLListCollection has many of the same characteristics of the ArrayCollection that make it an excellent choice for components that want an XML data provider, like the Tree control.

1 Using a web browser, browse to the following URL:

www.flexgrocer.com/categorizedProducts.xml

The grocery items used for the store inventory are displayed in the XML structure shown in the following example. You see that products are grouped by category. The node displayed shows Broccoli, Vine Ripened Tomatoes, and Yellow Peppers grouped in the Vegetables category.

```
- <catalog>
    + <category name="Meat" catName="Meat" catID="1"></category>
    - <category name="Vegetables" catName="Vegetables" catID="2">
        <product name="Broccoli" prodName="Broccoli" prodID="14" unitName="Pound" cost="2.16"
        listPrice="3.19" imageName="veg_broccoli.jpg" description="Firm and no bitterness" isOrganic="Yes"
        isLowFat="Yes" unitID="3" catName="Vegetables" catID="2"/>
        <product name="Vine Ripened Tomatoes" prodName="Vine Ripened Tomatoes" prodID="3"
        unitName="Pound" cost="1.69" listPrice="3.15" imageName="veg_tomato.jpg" description="Juicy and
        tender tomatoes, ripened on the vine" isOrganic="No" isLowFat="Yes" unitID="3"
        catName="Vegetables" catID="2"/>
        <product name="Yellow Peppers" prodName="Yellow Peppers" prodID="1" unitName="Pound"
        cost="1.25" listPrice="1.99" imageName="veg_pepper_yellow.jpg" description="Yellow Peppers
        cleaned and ready to eat." isOrganic="Yes" isLowFat="Yes" unitID="3" catName="Vegetables"
        catID="2"/>
      </category>
    + <category name="Fruit" catName="Fruit" catID="3"></category>
    + <category name="Dairy" catName="Dairy" catID="4"></category>
    + <category name="Deli" catName="Deli" catID="5"></category>
    + <category name="Seafood" catName="Seafood" catID="6"></category>
  </catalog>
```

This URL displays the XML that you will load at run time. You will parse the XML at the client within Flash Player using the new E4X functionality.

It makes sense to sort the products on the server, instead of at the client. This results in better performance. Sorting can be a processor-intensive task, so if you can do it on the server, you should!

2 Open DataEntry.mxml.

3 Remove the existing `<mx:Model>` tag block.

You will be populating the form with dynamic data from the HTTPService class instead of with static XML data embedded in the SWF file.

4 Directly below the existing HTTPService call, add another <mx:HTTPService> tag, assign it an id of prodByCatRPC, and specify the url property to http://www.flexgrocer.com/categorizedProducts.xml. Specify the resultFormat as e4x.

```
<mx:HTTPService id="prodByCatRPC"
    url="http://www.flexgrocer.com/categorizedProducts.xml"
    resultFormat="e4x"/>
```

The Tree control easily handles E4X data. In this case, you are transforming the XML in the file into ActionScript XML objects. In the next steps you will use this data in the Tree control.

5 Directly after the <mx:HTTPService> tag, add an <mx:XMLListCollection> tag, specify the id as foodColl, and specify the source as prodByCatRPC.lastResult.category.

```
<mx:XMLListCollection id="foodColl"
    source="{prodByCatRPC.lastResult.category}"/>
```

The XMLListCollection is very much like the ArrayCollection except it is used for XML data. This class contains the same hooks for data binding and also contains data manipulation methods. It is a best practice to bind to an XMLListCollection instead of native XML objects. In this case, you are placing the E4X XML data into an XMLListCollection; remember the repeating node is category.

6 Move to the top of the application and add to the existing creationComplete event so it calls the prodByCatRPC HTTPService using the send() method.

```
<mx:Application xmlns:mx=http://www.adobe.com/2006/mxml
    layout = "absolute"
    creationComplete="unitRPC.send();prodByCatRPC.send()">
```

This actually executes the HTTPService call. You need to add a semicolon to separate the two lines of ActionScript code.

7 Scroll to the top of the <mx:Form> tag and remove from the five <mx:TextInput> tags the text properties for each form element. Leave the id properties of the <mx:TextInput> tags as they are, except for the Product Name FormItem, where the id for that TextInput should be changed to prodName to match XML data you will soon be retrieving. Also remove the <mx:FormHeading> tag.

You will be retrieving remote XML data and using it to populate the Form. In this situation, all you need to do is have an instance name, represented by the id of the UI control, for use in a binding.

8 In the Form, change the Description's <mx:TextInput> to an <mx:RichTextEditor>. Set the id to be description and set the height of the control to 200.

```
<mx:FormItem label="Description">
   <mx:RichTextEditor id="description" height="200"/>
</mx:FormItem>
```

The <mx:RichTextEditor> allows users to mark up the text entered into the control. With this control users can change the font family, color, size, and style, and other properties such as text alignment, bullets and URL links of text entered.

9 In the Form, group the isLowFat and isOrganic <mx:CheckBox> tags into one <mx:FormItem> tag with a label of Specialties. Remove the selected properties, and add label properties with the text "Is Low Fat" and "Is Organic."

```
<mx:FormItem label="Specialties">
   <mx:CheckBox id="isLowFat" label="Is Low Fat"/>
   <mx:CheckBox id="isOrganic" label="Is Organic"/>
</mx:FormItem>
```

This is just for aesthetic purposes.

10 In the Form, change the label of the <mx:FormItem> tag which is currently Image Path to Image Name. Also add a direction property set equal to horizontal for this FormItem. Check to be sure your finished Form appears as follows:

```
<mx:Form>
   <mx:FormItem label="Product Name">
      <mx:TextInput id="prodName"/>
   </mx:FormItem>
   <mx:FormItem label="Unit">
      <mx:List id="unitID"
         rowCount="4"
         dataProvider="{units}"
         labelField="unitName"/>
   </mx:FormItem>
   <mx:FormItem label="Cost">
      <mx:TextInput id="cost"/>
   </mx:FormItem>
   <mx:FormItem label="List Price">
      <mx:TextInput id="listPrice" />
   </mx:FormItem>
   <mx:FormItem label="Description">
      <mx:RichTextEditor id="description" height="200"/>
   </mx:FormItem>
   <mx:FormItem label="Specialties">
      <mx:CheckBox id="isLowFat" label="Is Low Fat"/>
      <mx:CheckBox id="isOrganic" label="Is Organic"/>
```

code continues on next page

```
    </mx:FormItem>
    <mx:FormItem label="Image Name" direction="horizontal">
      <mx:TextInput id="imageName"/>
      <mx:Button click="fileBrowse()" label="Browse"/>
    </mx:FormItem>
    <mx:FormItem>
      <mx:HBox>
        <mx:Button label="Update" />
        <mx:Button label="Delete" />
      </mx:HBox>
    </mx:FormItem>
  </mx:Form>
```

You will be populating all this information from the Tree control instead of accessing the data directly, and the changes you made to the Form allow this to happen.

11 Add a Tree control directly above the existing form. Assign it an `id` of `productTree`, a height of 100%, a `dataProvider` of `foodColl`, a `labelField` of `@name`, and a change event of `populateForm`. Be sure to pass the event object that is created.

```
<mx:Tree id="productTree"
    height="100%"
    dataProvider="{foodColl}"
    labelField="@name"
    change="populateForm(event)"/>
```

The Tree control will display complex data structures and enable the end user to easily navigate through them. The user can use the Tree to find the product they are interested in updating or deleting. You are doing all of the categorizing on the server for better performance, which will cause less strain on Flash Player.

12 Surround both the Tree control and the Form container with an HBox so the two elements will be arranged horizontally.

This will make the layout of the application more intuitive.

13 Create the skeleton of a new private function with the name of `populateForm()`, data typed as void. The function should accept a parameter named event data typed as `Event`. Inside of the method, create a variable with the name of `selectedNode` data typed as Object. Set this variable equal to the `selectedItem` of the event.target object, which is the selected node from the Tree control.

```
private function populateForm(event:Event):void{
    var selectedNode:Object=event.target.selectedItem;
}
```

Because you specified that this method would be called on a change event, the `populateForm()` method is called when the user clicks a node in the Tree control.

Because it is an event, an event object is generated, and the `target` is the name of the object that emitted the event; in this case, productTree.

14 Add conditional logic that checks to make sure that the XML attribute `prodName` in that node is defined. Add an `else` statement that will call the `resetForm()` method if there is no `prodName` attribute in the XML data structure.

```
private function populateForm(event:Event):void{
    var selectedNode:Object=event.target.selectedItem;
    if(selectedNode.@prodName != undefined)

    } else {
       resetForm();
    }
}
```

The `selectedItem` property of the Tree control enables you to access the node the user has selected. Once you have that information, you can use E4X notation to get the data located in that node. For example, in each node you have the product name, the cost, the image, and more information that you can access and update using the DataEntry application. The conditional logic checks to make sure that the node you are working with has a `prodName` property; otherwise, you will reset the form. The `prodName` property will not have a value when you click on a category. You will write the `resetForm()` method in an upcoming step.

15 Set the `text` property of the prodName field to the corresponding attribute value of the `selectedNode` using E4X notation. Set the `text` property of the cost field, listPrice, description, and imageName using the same syntax. Set the `selected` property of the isOrganic and isLowFat CheckBoxes to the appropriate value. These are stored in the XML data as yes/no values; you need to use the Util class' yesNoToBoolean() method to convert these values into Booleans. The method should look as follows:

```
private function populateForm(event:Event):void{
    var selectedNode:Object=event.target.selectedItem;
    if(selectedNode.@prodName != undefined){
       prodName.text = selectedNode.@prodName;
       cost.text = selectedNode.@cost;
       listPrice.text = selectedNode.@listPrice;
       description.text = selectedNode.@description;
       isOrganic.selected = Util.yesNoToBoolean(selectedNode.@isOrganic);
       isLowFat.selected = Util.yesNoToBoolean(selectedNode.@isLowFat);
       imageName.text = selectedNode.@imageName;
    } else {
       resetForm();
    }
}
```

This populates the form fields with the data that the user has selected from the Tree control using the attribute (@) E4X notation you are familiar with.

16 As the first line of the if block, use the presetList() method of the Util class to prepopulate the List. Specify the first parameter as unitID, the second parameter as "unitID", and use E4X syntax to obtain the unitID property from the selectedNode.
Your populateForm() method should look as shown:

```
private function populateForm(event:Event):void{
   var selectedNode:Object=event.target.selectedItem;
   if(selectedNode.@prodName != undefined){
      Util.presetList(unitID,"unitID",selectedNode.@unitID);
      prodName.text = selectedNode.@prodName;
      cost.text = selectedNode.@cost;
      listPrice.text = selectedNode.@listPrice;
      description.text = selectedNode.@description;
      isOrganic.selected = Util.yesNoToBoolean(selectedNode.@isOrganic);
      isLowFat.selected = Util.yesNoToBoolean(selectedNode.@isLowFat);
      imageName.text = selectedNode.@imageName;
   } else {
      resetForm();
   }
}
```

You also need to populate the unit List control you created earlier to specify what types of units are displayed. This information is in the data structure stored in the Tree control, but you need to preselect the List with this information. You can use the presetList() method of the Util class to accomplish this. This method will take the data structure from the Tree and populate the List with the appropriate unit elements, enabling the user to select from the List.

17 Build a private resetForm() method that will set all the values back to blank positions if the prodName value is not defined in the Tree data structure.

```
private function resetForm():void{
   prodName.text = "";
   unitID.selectedIndex = -1;
   cost.text="";
   listPrice.text="";
   description.text="";
   isOrganic.selected = false;
   isLowFat.selected = false;
   imageName.text = "";
}
```

If there is no data in the prodName node of the Tree, you should reset all the information in the form. This will occur when the user clicks on a category instead of an actual grocery item.

18 Save and run the application. You should see that the Tree control is populated with data. When you drill down through the data, it is displayed on the form you created earlier.

This provides a great way for the user to navigate a complex data structure and easily find the information they need.

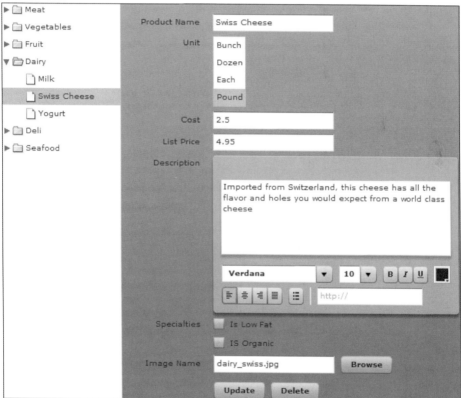

19 Close the file.

Retrieving XML Data and Transforming it into an ArrayCollection of Custom Objects

Once you have gotten the data from the HTTPService you will sometimes need to put this data into a format specific for an application. You will use the new E4X functionality to parse the XML data and place it into an ActionScript array of Product objects so you can use this data structure to display the data. Before the implementation of the E4X functionality, there was no way to work with XML directly in ECMAScript languages. Earlier versions of Action-Script had an XML class, which was not based on the ECMAScript standard, and it was cumbersome and difficult to use because it required complicated looping to obtain the data. The new E4X functionality makes dealing with ActionScript XML objects much easier and more flexible, and uses conventions that should now be familiar to you, such as dot syntax.

After you call the server-side XML using the HTTPService class, you will use E4X functional-ity to loop through the XML and place the data into an ActionScript array. This is incredibly powerful because it enables you to parse through XML without having to build complicated for loops, as you would if you returned the XML directly as base types. For example, if you had an XML file that contained all the support employees at Adobe and you wanted to view only those employees in Flex technical support, you could use E4X to display only those employees in Flex support. This parsing all happens at the client, so the rest of the employees would still be stored in the client-side data structure for later use. With a regular ActionScript array of objects, you would need to build a complicated series of for loops to obtain the same data.

1 Using a web browser, browse to the following URL:

www.flexgrocer.com/categorizedProducts.xml

This is the same categorized grocery item data as used in the last task.

2 Open EComm.mxml.

3 Remove the <mx:Model> tag.

```
<mx:Model id="groceryInventory" source="assets/inventory.xml")/>
```

Instead of defining your data by embedding an external XML file in the SWF file, you will use the HTTPService class to load in XML data at run time. This is an ideal way of connecting to a database. You can write this middle tier using Cold Fusion, ASP, PHP, or other technologies to convert this data into XML, which Flex can then consume.

4 Immediately after the current script block, add an <mx:HTTPService> tag and assign it an id of prodByCatRPC. Specify the URL property as the page that you browsed to in the first step.

```
<mx:HTTPService id="prodByCatRPC"
    url="http://www.flexgrocer.com/categorizedProducts.xml"/>
```

This creates an object with the name of prodByCatRPC from the HTTPService class. When you add this tag, a request is *not* automatically made to the server. You need to actually execute the request, which you will do soon.

5 Specify the result handler of the HTTPService to call the prodHandler() function. Pass the result handler the event object. Specify the resultFormat as e4x. The <mx:HTTPService> tag should now look as follows:

```
<mx:HTTPService id="prodByCatRPC"
    url="http://www.flexgrocer.com/categorizedProducts.xml"
    result="prodHandler(event)"
    resultFormat="e4x"/>
```

You will use ECMAScript E4X functionality to convert the returned XML into an array of Product objects needed in this application. By specifying e4x as the result format, you are returning native ActionScript XML objects. The HTTPService class also gives you the option of performing the XML-to-Object conversion automatically; you have done this in the first two tasks of this lesson. For now, the ActionScript XML objects will give you more flexibility in dealing with the data.

6 In the creationComplete event on the <mx:Application> tag, remove the current call to the prodHandler() method, and invoke the send() method of the prodByCatRPC HTTPService object. The <mx:Application> tag should now look as shown here:

```
<mx:Application xmlns:mx="http://www.adobe.com/2006/mxml"
    layout="absolute"
    creationComplete="prodByCatRPC.send()">
```

Creating the HTTPService object is only the first step in retrieving data, you must also invoke its send() method to actually go and get the data.

7 At the top of the script block, add an import statement that will import the ResultEvent class.

```
import mx.rpc.events.ResultEvent;
```

You need the ResultEvent class to data type the parameter used in the result event handler.

8 In the script block, locate the prodHandler() method. Change the parameter of the prodHandler() method to accept a parameter named event. Be sure to type this to ResultEvent. Remove all the other code in the method and add a trace statement that will display the result property of the event object. The prodHandler() method should look as follows:

```
private function prodHandler(event:ResultEvent):void{
   trace(event.result);
}
```

You changed the function to now be the event handler for the result event of the HTTPService object.

9 Debug the application. You should see the XML in the Console view from the trace statement.

```
<catalog>
  <category name="Meat" catName="Meat" catID="1">
    <product name="Buffalo" prodName="Buffalo" prodID="7" unitName="Pound" cost="4" listPrice="6.5" imageName="mea
    <product name="T Bone Steak" prodName="T Bone Steak" prodID="17" unitName="Pound" cost="6" listPrice="9.98" im
    <product name="Whole Chicken" prodName="Whole Chicken" prodID="6" unitName="Pound" cost="1.5" listPrice="2.99"
  </category>
  <category name="Vegetables" catName="Vegetables" catID="2">
    <product name="Broccoli" prodName="Broccoli" prodID="14" unitName="Pound" cost="2.16" listPrice="3.19" imageNa
    <product name="Vine Ripened Tomatoes" prodName="Vine Ripened Tomatoes" prodID="3" unitName="Pound" cost="1.69"
    <product name="Yellow Peppers" prodName="Yellow Peppers" prodID="1" unitName="Pound" cost="1.25" listPrice="1.
  </category>
  <category name="Fruit" catName="Fruit" catID="3">
    <product name="Bananas" prodName="Bananas" prodID="5" unitName="Bunch" cost="0.95" listPrice="1.98" imageName=
    <product name="Grapes" prodName="Grapes" prodID="4" unitName="Bunch" cost="1.34" listPrice="2.15" imageName="f
    <product name="Strawberries" prodName="Strawberries" prodID="2" unitName="Pound" cost="2.5" listPrice="3.95" i
  </category>
  <category name="Dairy" catName="Dairy" catID="4">
    <product name="Milk" prodName="Milk" prodID="8" unitName="Each" cost="0.99" listPrice="1.59" imageName="dairy_
    <product name="Swiss Cheese" prodName="Swiss Cheese" prodID="15" unitName="Pound" cost="2.5" listPrice="4.95"
    <product name="Yogurt" prodName="Yogurt" prodID="9" unitName="Each" cost="0.99" listPrice="1.19" imageName="da
  </category>
  <category name="Deli" catName="Deli" catID="5">
    <product name="Honey Roasted Ham" prodName="Honey Roasted Ham" prodID="10" unitName="Pound" cost="2.16" listPr
    <product name="Roast Beef" prodName="Roast Beef" prodID="16" unitName="Pound" cost="3.46" listPrice="5.99" ima
    <product name="Roasted Turkey" prodName="Roasted Turkey" prodID="11" unitName="Pound" cost="2" listPrice="3" i
  </category>
  <category name="Seafood" catName="Seafood" catID="6">
    <product name="Alaskan King Crab" prodName="Alaskan King Crab" prodID="18" unitName="Pound" cost="8.5" listPri
    <product name="Maine Lobster" prodName="Maine Lobster" prodID="12" unitName="Pound" cost="8.99" listPrice="18.
    <product name="Salmon Filet" prodName="Salmon Filet" prodID="13" unitName="Each" cost="4.55" listPrice="6.99"
  </category>
</catalog>
```

These are the ActionScript XML objects that are loaded in from the HTTP call. If you had specified object, the Flash Player would have converted the XML into an ArrayCollection automatically. In the next steps you will convert the XML into an array using E4X.

10 In the prodHandler() method, remove the trace statement and create a new instance of an ActionScript array named prodArray. The prodHandler() method should look as follows:

```
private function prodHandler(event:ResultEvent):void{
   var prodArray:Array = new Array();
}
```

The Array class is a native ActionScript data structure that can be used to store complex data. In this case, you will build an array of Product objects, using the value object pattern you worked with in the last lesson. To do this, you will need to build a simple loop that loops through the returned ActionScript XML objects.

11 Still in the `prodHandler()` method, immediately after the Array is declared, build a new `for each..in` loop that iterates through the attributes or properties in the XML objects, as follows:

```
for each (var p:XML in event.result..product){
}
```

The descendant accessor operator represented by a .. provides an easy way for you to access any properties in the XML structure that are stored under the product node, regardless of where the product is in the hierarchical structure. In this case, the product is stored under the category node, but because you are using the descendant accessor (..) operator, you can reference all the information stored in the product node, even though the product node is stored under the category node. It finds the information that you need regardless of where it is in the data structure.

The product node contains all the information that you need to display all the grocery products, including the name, price, image, and so on of each product. You create a new XML object, with the name of p, which stores all the product data for every single node in the XML data structure. It then becomes easy to access the data because the `for each..in` loop iterates over that data.

Remember that the collection represented by `event.result` that you are looping over is comprised of the ActionScript XML objects returned by the HTTPService. You have ActionScript XML objects instead of an ArrayCollection because you specified the `resultType` to be e4x.

12 Within the `for each..in` loop, create a new instance of the Product value object with the name of prod and pass it the attributes of the p XML object that it requires. Be sure to cast each attribute to the appropriate base type. Also note that on the `isOrganic` and `isLowFat` properties you must do a comparison to the string Yes to convert it to a Boolean.

```
var prod:Product = new Product
(
Number(p.@catID),
String(p.@prodName),
Number(p.@unitID),
Number(p.@cost),
Number(p.@listPrice),
String(p.@description),
Boolean(p.@isOrganic=="Yes"),
Boolean(p.@isLowFat=="Yes"),
String(p.@imageName));
```

Because this code is located within the `for each..in` loop that uses the descendant accessor, the attribute sign (@) will display the appropriate attribute for each node of the product XML node. Within the XML there is no mechanism for casting each attribute required by the value object class, so it must be done as the class is being instantiated. The Product class requires typed data, so you must cast each XML attribute as it is coming into the data structure.

✳ **NOTE:** Where you did the comparison to the string Yes in creating the new Product, you could have also used the Util.yesNoToBoolean static method. The method is a bit smarter in that it does not care about the case of the string, but the same outcome is achieved either way; `true` or `false` is placed in the property value instead of Yes or No.

13 Still inside the `for` loop, but outside of the Product object declaration, use the `push()` method of the Array object to add the prod object, which is an instance of the Product class, to the array, as follows:

```
prodArray.push(prod);
```

The `push()` method of the Array object adds an element to the end of the Array. In this case, the Array is empty, so it will push the instance of the Product class into the first index, index 0, of the Array and continue until it is done looping through all the products in the XML file. This simple code gives you a powerful client-side data structure.

14 Immediately after the loop, add a `trace` statement that will trace the `prodArray` data structure you just created. The final `prodHandler()` method should look as follows:

```
private function prodHandler(event:ResultEvent):void{
   var prodArray:Array = new Array();
   for each (var p:XML in event.result..product){
      var prod:Product = new Product(
      Number(p.@catID),
      String(p.@prodName),
      Number(p.@unitID),
      Number(p.@cost),
      Number(p.@listPrice),
      String(p.@description),
      Boolean(p.@isOrganic=="Yes"),
      Boolean(p.@isLowFat=="Yes"),
      String(p.@imageName));
      prodArray.push(prod);
   }
   trace(prodArray);
}
```

15 Save the file and debug the application.

In the Console view, you should see the `toString()` method of the Product class displays the literal text [Product], followed by the name of each product in the Array. A partial display is shown here:

```
[Product]Buffalo,[Product]T Bone Steak,[Product]Whole Chicken,[Product]Broccoli
```

Using Data Binding with Complex Data Structures

In this task, you will display the information from the Array you built from the XML using data binding. For data binding, it is a best practice to use the ArrayCollection class because it will automatically update the visual controls if the underlying data structure changes. A plain old vanilla ActionScript Array does not have this functionality.

1 Return to EComm.mxml. At the top of the script block, add an `import` statement that will import the ArrayCollection class from the mx.collections package.

```
import mx.collections.ArrayCollection;
```

This will give you access to the ArrayCollection class for use in the application.

2 In the `<mx:Script>` block below the `import` statements, declare a bindable, private variable named `groceryInventory` as an ArrayCollection.

```
[Bindable]
private var groceryInventory:ArrayCollection;
```

This declares a private ArrayCollection that you can use throughout the application. You can now use the data binding functionality of the ArrayCollection class, and you will be able to display the data in the visual controls.

3 In the `prodHandler()` method, but outside the `for each..in` loop, on the last line of the method replace the `trace` statement and assign the `groceryInventory` variable a new ArrayCollection object. Pass the `prodArray` as a parameter to the ArrayCollection constructor.

```
groceryInventory=new ArrayCollection(prodArray);
```

This code takes the local array, `prodArray`, and places it in the ArrayCollection with the name of `groceryInventory`. You can now use this for data binding anywhere in the current application.

4 Near the bottom of the file locate the first VBox that displays product information. Modify the code in the VBox to bind the appropriate data to the new ArrayCollection you just created, groceryInventory, rather than displaying static data. Use the getItemAt() method of the ArrayCollection and pass the number 0 to this method, which represents the first index of the Array. When you pass the object to the addToCart() method be sure to cast it as a Product.

```
<mx:VBox id="products" width="100%" height="100%">
  <mx:Label id="prodName" text="{groceryInventory.getItemAt(0).prodName}"/>
  <mx:Image source="{'assets/'+groceryInventory.getItemAt(0).imageName}"
    scaleContent="true"
    mouseOver="this.currentState='expanded'"
    mouseOut="this.currentState=''"/>
  <mx:Label id="price" text="{groceryInventory.getItemAt(0).listPrice}"/>
  <mx:Button id="add" label="Add To Cart"
    click="addToCart(groceryInventory.getItemAt(0) as Product)"/>
</mx:VBox>
```

You have changed all the data binding to use an ArrayCollection. Data binding will now work and display the appropriate controls and images.

The getItemAt() method of collections is defined to return an Object. The addToCart() function is defined to accept a Product as a parameter. If you did not cast the returned Object you would get the "implicit coercion" error. By using "as" to cast the returned item you tell the compiler you understand the difference exists and you want the compiler to ignore it in this case.

5 Within the expanded state, bind the appropriate data to the new ArrayCollection you just created: groceryInventory.

```
<mx:VBox width="100%" x="200">
  <mx:Text text="{groceryInventory.getItemAt(0).description}"
    width="50%"/>
  <mx:Label text="Certified Organic"
    visible="{groceryInventory.getItemAt(0).isOrganic}"/>
  <mx:Label text="Low Fat" x="100" y="60"
    visible="{groceryInventory.getItemAt(0).isLowFat}"/>
</mx:VBox>
```

This code will set up data binding for the product at array position 0 in the ArrayCollection. In a later lesson, you will learn how to dynamically create controls based on an incoming data structure.

6 Save and run the application.

You should see that the data is now bound to the controls. Be sure to roll over the Buffalo item to see the description in the view state.

Sorting and Manipulating Shopping Cart Data

ArrayCollections have methods built in which support sorting, filtering, and manipulating their data. The ability to manipulate the data is done using the concept of a "cursor." A cursor is a position indicator, which allows direct access to any particular item in the collection. This allows for easily manipulating items within the collection. Among the controls you have with a cursor are methods for stepping from one item to the next; finding a particular item; adding, removing, or editing an item; etc. All of this is available natively to the ArrayCollection class, meaning you do not need to write verbose loops to achieve any of these goals.

> ✱ **NOTE:** Cursors are not unique to ArrayCollections, they are available to any of the classes which implement the ICursorView interface. For more information on interfaces, please refer to the About Interfaces section of the Creating and Extending Flex 2 Components documentation.

Before you can use a cursor on an array collection, the data in the collection needs to be sorted. To do this, you will make use of the Sort and SortField classes, and the sort property of the ArrayCollection. Take a look at a simple sort example:

```
var prodSort:Sort = new Sort();
var sortField:SortField = new SortField("prodName");
prodSort.fields=new Array(sortField);
myArrayCollection.sort = prodSort;
myArrayCollection.refresh();
```

Here, you start by creating an instance of the Sort class, in this case, named prodSort. Next, an instance of the SortField class (named sortField) is created. The SortField constructor requires only a single argument, that being which property in the object should the collection be sorted by. Three other optional arguments can also be passed, indicating whether the sort should be case insensitive, should it be a descending sort, and should it be a numeric sort. All three optional arguments have a default value of false. The example sort specifies the collection should be sorted by prodName (the name of the product), and uses the default values for the optional arguments.

A Sort can have several sort fields (for example, you could sort by category then price), which is why the fields property of the Sort class requires that an array of SortFields be specified. If you only want to sort on a single field, create an array with only one SortField within it, as the example does.

Next, the Sort instance is set as the value for the sort property of the ArrayCollection. Lastly, the collections refresh() method is called, which instructs the collection to execute its sort.

> **TIP:** When specifying multiple SortFields, the order in the array is the order in which the sort fields would be applied, so, to sort by category and then price, your code would look like this:

```
var prodSort:Sort = new Sort();
var sortField1:SortField = new SortField("catID");
var sortField2:SortField = new SortField("listPrice");
prodSort.fields=new Array(sortField1, sortField2);
```

In this next exercise, you will write the logic to add items to the users shopping cart. Using a cursor, you will check to see if the item is already in the cart, and if it is, update the quantity, rather than re-adding the item.

1 Open the ShoppingCart.as file in the valueObjects folder.

Alternatively, you can open ShoppingCart.as from your Lesson06/start/valueObjects directory, and save it into your flexGrocer/valueObjects directory. This is the shopping cart class that you built in the last lesson. In this lesson, you will add functionality to the class so the shopping cart e-commerce transactions can be managed.

2 After the existing `import` statement, import the `ArrayCollection` class from the package mx.collections.

```
import mx.collections.ArrayCollection;
```

This enables you to use the ArrayCollection class in the `ShoppingCart` class that you are defining here.

3 Below the last `import` statement, add an `import` statement that will import the IViewCursor interface from the package mx.collections.

```
import mx.collections.IViewCursor;
```

The cursor is available through the use of the `IViewCursor` interface. In order to work with a cursor, you will need to have access to this interface.

4 Right after the `class` keyword, define a [Bindable] public property with the name of *aItems* and a data type of `ArrayCollection`. Use the new keyword to assign a new instance of the ArrayCollection class into your *aItems* property.

```
public class ShoppingCart {
    [Bindable]
    public var aItems:ArrayCollection = new ArrayCollection();
```

This instantiates an ArrayCollection object with the name of *aItems*. You will use this `ArrayCollection` to track all the objects in the shopping cart.

5 Define a [Bindable] public property with the name of total and a data type of Number. It
will be used as the default value for an empty shopping cart, so set the value to 0, as shown:

```
[Bindable]
public var total:Number=0;
```

You will update this variable any time a user adds an item to the cart with the price of the
item. This will enable you to track the total cost of the end user's order.

6 Define a private property with the name of cursor and a data type of IViewCursor. The
ShoppingCart class should look like this so far:

```
public class ShoppingCart {
    [Bindable]
    public var aItems:ArrayCollection = new ArrayCollection();
    [Bindable]
    public var total:Number=0;
    private var cursor:IViewCursor;
    public function addItem(item:ShoppingCartItem):void{
        trace(item.product);
    }
}
```

IViewcursor is an interface available from the collections package, which includes the
ArrayCollection class. By defining a private variable here, you can use the methods of this
interface.

7 Locate the addItem() method of the ShoppingCart class and remove the trace statement.
Use the addItem() method of the ArrayCollection class to add the ShoppingCartItem to
the aItems ArrayCollection:

```
public function addItem(item:ShoppingCartItem):void{
    aItems.addItem(item);
}
```

In the last lesson, you built a ShoppingCartItem class to hold any data associated with
items in a shopping cart. This class has properties to hold the Product (an instance of the
Product class), the quantity (an integer) and the subtotal (a Number derived by multiplying the quantity by the price). When the user clicked the Add To Cart button, you passed
the ShoppingCartItem to this method. The addItem() method is similar to the push()
method you used on the Array class in the last task: it adds the object to the end of the
ArrayCollection.

▶ **TIP:** In the next step you will be asked to locate a specific VBox instance. Use the Outline view
to find named object instances.

8 Switch back to EComm.mxml and locate the `cartBox` VBox. Directly after the LinkButton control, add a List control. Assign the List control an `id` of `cartView`, specify `cart.aItems` as the `dataProvider`, and set the `width` to 100%.

```
<mx:List id="cartView"
   dataProvider="{cart.aItems}"
   width="100%"/>
```

The List control is specifically designed to handle complex data structures. In this case, you are passing the ArrayCollection to the List control. You will see only that a ShoppingCartItem is added to the cart, not which one specifically. This is the default way to display an item. If more than one Product is added, all will be displayed in the List control (the cart).

9 Save and run the application. Click the Add To Cart button for the Buffalo.

You should see the items that you click appear in the cart, as shown in the following example:

Each time you click an item, data binding is fired and the List control is automatically updated. Anytime the underlying data structure changes, the ArrayCollection is "smart" enough to automatically update the display.

The desired behavior is to have only new items added to the cart. If an item is clicked more than once, it should update the quantity of the item. You will use the `IViewCursor` functionality to make this work.

10 Return to the ShoppingCart.as file and locate the `addItem()` method. Delete the existing code inside this method and call the `manageAddItem()` method. Pass the `item` parameter to the `manageAddItem()` method.

```
public function addItem(item:ShoppingCartItem):void{
   manageAddItem(item);
}
```

Each time the user clicks the Add To Cart button, the cart needs to determine if the Product is already in the cart, or not. If the Product isn't already there, the item should be added, but if it is there, the quantity of the ShoppingCartItem the user is trying to add should be added to the existing quantity in the cart for that item.

Rather than having an un-wieldy block of code for all of this logic in the addItem() method, you will instead create a number of smaller methods to implement this logic. The manageAddItem() method will be the gateway into the logical process.

11 Add a new private method with the name of manageAddItem(). The method should accept an argument of type ShoppingCartItem, and return void. Within the method, add conditional logic that tests whether the item is already in the cart. The logic to search through the cart will be implemented in a method you will soon write called isItemInCart(). If the item is not in the cart, call the addItem() method of the ArrayCollection as you had previously done. If it is, call another soon to be written method, called updateItem().

```
private function manageAddItem(item:ShoppingCartItem):void{
   if (isItemInCart(item)){
      updateItem(item);
   }else{
      aItems.addItem(item);
   }
}
```

This demonstrates good architecture, in which you set up different functionality that you will use over and over again in different methods.

12 Create the isItemInCart() method, and be sure it accepts an argument named item as an instance of the ShoppingCartItem class. The method should return a Boolean. Within the method, create a new variable local to the method with the name of sci, which will hold a matched ShoppingCartItem, if there is one.

```
private function isItemInCart(item:ShoppingCartItem):Boolean{
   var sci:ShoppingCartItem = getItemInCart(item);
   if(sci == null){
      return false;
   } else {
      return true;
   }
}
```

When you write the getItemInCart() method, you will build it so that if it finds the item, it returns it; otherwise, it will return null. If the item is not found, sci will be null, so isItemInCart will return a value of false. If something is found, sci will not be null, and therefore the method will return true.

Next, you need to create the getItemInCart() method, which will use a cursor to find an item already in the collection.

13 Create the getItemInCart() method, which takes an argument of type ShoppingCartItem named item, and returns a ShoppingCartItem. Within this method, you will instantiate the cursor property you defined earlier, using the createCursor() method of the ArrayCollection.

```
private function getItemInCart(item:ShoppingCartItem):ShoppingCartItem{
   cursor = aItems.createCursor();
}
```

You need to search through the entire cart to check whether the item the user is adding is already in the cart. The ShoppingCartItem that the user wants to add is being passed to this method; if it is already in the cart, the method will return the item there. As you learned earlier, before a cursor can be used to search through a collection, the collection first needs to be sorted. In the next few steps, you will sort the aItems collection.

14 Within the getItemInCart() method, call the soon to be written sortItems() method. Build a skeleton for this method directly below the getItemInCart() method.

```
private function getItemInCart(item:ShoppingCartItem):ShoppingCartItem{
   cursor = aItems.createCursor();
   sortItems();
}
private function sortItems():void{
}
```

The aItems sort will indicate which field everything should be ordered by. In effect, it tells the cursor how to search through the cart. As you want to verify that the cart only contains one ShoppingCartItem for each product, you will sort on the product property. To facilitate effective reuse, the sorting functionality is encapsulated in its own method.

15 In the sortItems() method, instantiate a new Sort instance with the name of prodSort. Next, instantiate a new SortField instance with the name of sortField, set it equal to a new SortField, and pass the product data field name as a parameter. Finally set the fields property of the prodSort object equal to a new Array passing the SortField as the parameter.

```
private function sortItems():void{
   var prodSort:Sort = new Sort();
   var sortField:SortField = new SortField("product");
   prodSort.fields=new Array(sortField);
}
```

▶ **TIP:** Flex Builder should have automatically imported both the Sort and SortField classes when you created this function. If it did not, be sure to import mx.collections.Sort and mx.collections.SortField.

This sort will be performed on the properties of the shopping cart items in the aItems collection, and enables the cursor to move through this data. The `fields` property specifies an array of fields on which to sort. In this case, you are sorting on a single field, the `product` inside of the `ShoppingCartItem` class. As you learned earlier, there are a number of optional arguments you could pass to the `SortField` constructor, but in this case, the default values are being used, so these can be omitted.

16 Still in the `sortItems()` method, add the Sort to the `sort` property of the aItems ArrayCollection, then call the `refresh()` method of the aItems ArrayCollection. The final `sortItems()` method should look as shown:

```
private function sortItems():void{
    var prodSort:Sort=new Sort();
    var sortField:SortField=new SortField("product");
    prodSort.fields=new Array(sortField);
    aItems.sort=prodSort;
    aItems.refresh();
}
```

When this method is called, it defines how the collection will be sorted, and then executes the sort. As you learned earlier, this is required before a cursor can be used on a collection.

17 Return to the `getItemInCart()` method. Immediately after the call to the `sortItems()` method, pass the `item` parameter to the cursor's `findFirst()` method, and store the results in a Boolean variable named `found`.

```
var found:Boolean = cursor.findFirst(item);
```

In this step, you use the `findFirst()` method of the cursor to search through the collection of ShoppingCartItems looking for a match. The `findFirst()` method requires an object be passed to it. The property within the object is used to determine the name of the property in the item, on which you are looking for a match. The value of the objects property specifies the value to match. In this case, you are instructing the cursor to search through the `product` properties of each ShoppingCartItem, and to find the first Product object whose value matches the Product object in the passed in ShoppingCartItem. If a match is found, the method will return a value of `true`. If no match is found, a value of `false` will be returned. Importantly, the cursor will stop on the matching record.

> **TIP:** In addition to findFirst(), the cursor also has the findAny() and findLast() methods. Any of these three could be used in the code, but because your logic will ultimately prevent more than ShoppingCartItem for each Product from being added, findFirst() seems a logical choice.

18 In the getItemInCart() method add a conditional statement to test if found is true. If true, create a new ShoppingCartItem with the name of sci, which references the current property of the cursor. Add an else statement that will return a value of null. After the conditional, return sci.

```
if(found){
   var sci:ShoppingCartItem = cursor.current as ShoppingCartItem;
}else{
   return null;
}
return sci;
```

The current property of the cursor will return the entire object at the present position of the cursor, which will be the ShoppingCartItem you found using the cursor's findFirst() method. If findFirst() was successful, the cursor will stop on that record, and the current property will remain at that position. Therefore, you can access the ShoppingCartItem at that position and eventually update the quantity for that duplicate item, using cursor. current. The final getItemInCart() method should look like this:

```
private function getItemInCart(item:ShoppingCartItem):ShoppingCartItem{
   cursor = aItems.createCursor();
   sortItems();
   var found:Boolean = cursor.findFirst(item);
   if(found){
      var sci:ShoppingCartItem = cursor.current as ShoppingCartItem;
   }else{
      return null;
   }
   return sci;
}
```

19 Create a skeleton for the updateItem() method, which accepts an argument named item of type ShoppingCartItem. The method will return void. On the first line of the method, define a local variable with the name of sci, data typed to a ShoppingCartItem, which is equal to cursor.current cast as a ShoppingCartItem.

```
private function updateItem(item:ShoppingCartItem):void{
   var sci:ShoppingCartItem = cursor.current as ShoppingCartItem;
}
```

Because the cursor has not been moved since it was used to check if the item was in the cart, cursor.current still refers to the matched item. The sci variable will always be populated because this method is called only if there has already been a match in the cart. If the sci variable is null, this method will not be called, and a new item will be added to the cart using the addItem() method.

The cursor.current object must be cast as a ShoppingCartItem instance because in the ActionScript definition the IViewCursor's current property is data typed as Object.

20 Still in the updateItem() method, update the quantity property of the sci object to its current value plus the value that is located in the existing aItems ArrayCollection.

```
sci.quantity += item.quantity;
```

Remember, whenever a new item is added to the cart, you hard coded the quantity value in the ShoppingCartItem to 1.

21 Still in the updateItem() method and immediately after you set the quantity, call the reCalc() method of the sci ShoppingCartItem class. The final updateItem() method should look like this:

```
private function updateItem(item:ShoppingCartItem):void{
    var sci:ShoppingCartItem = cursor.current as ShoppingCartItem;
    sci.quantity += item.quantity;
    sci.recalc();
}
```

When you first created the ShoppingCartItem class, you added a method with the name of recalc() that created a subtotal property with the price of each product multiplied by each product. When you built the method, you hard coded the quantity to 1. It now makes sense to recalculate that value because you have just updated the quantity property to however many items the user has in their cart.

22 Directly after the updateItem() method, create a skeleton for the calcTotal() method. Set the initial value of the total variable you declared previously to 0.

```
private function calcTotal():void{
    this.total = 0;
}
```

In this method, you will loop over the entire shopping cart and update a total text field with the entire total of the end user's purchases. Initially, you need to set the value of the total variable to 0.

23 Still in the `calcTotal()` method, create a skeleton of a `for` loop that will loop through the `aItems` ArrayCollection. Use the variable `i` as the iterator for the loop and type it to an `int`. Use the `length` property of `aItems` to return the length of the ArrayCollection, and use the `++` operator to increment the iterator.

```
for(var i:int=0;i<aItems.length;i++){
}
```

This builds a simple loop that enables you to loop through the entire shopping cart. The loop will continue to execute as long as `i` (the iterator) is less then the length of the array. Each time the loop executes, the iterator is increased by 1 (`++` is shorthand for this increase).

24 Inside the loop, update the `total` variable with the subtotal of each item stored in the `aItems` array. Be sure to use the `+=` operator so it will add the new value to the existing one. Use the `getItemAt()` method and pass it the value `i` to get a reference to each ShoppingCartItem. Your final `calcTotal()` method should look as follows:

```
private function calcTotal():void{
   this.total = 0;
   for(var i:int=0;i<aItems.length;i++){
      this.total += aItems.getItemAt(i).subtotal;
   }
}
```

This loops through the entire shopping cart, and updates the `total` variable by adding the subtotal (`price * quantity`) of each item in the cart to the current `total`. Now any time you need to calculate the total price of all the items, you can simply call this method.

25 Locate the `addItem()` method and call the `calcTotal()` method you just wrote. The final `addItem()` method should look as follows:

```
public function addItem(item:ShoppingCartItem):void{
   manageAddItem(item);
   calcTotal();
}
```

After a new item is added to the cart, it makes sense to update the `total` field, which is bound to the `total` text field that displays to the end user.

26 Return to EComm.mxml and locate the `cartBox` VBox. Immediately after the Label control that says "Your Cart Total," add another Label control whose `text` property is bound to the `total` property in the cart object. Add an `<mx:HBox>` tag around the two Label controls.

```
<mx:HBox>
   <mx:Label text="Your Cart Total:"/>
   <mx:Label text="{cart.total}"/>
</mx:HBox>
```

This will create another Label control directly above the cart that will display the total cost of the cart, which you set in your calcTotal() method. Remember that you instantiated the ShoppingCart class as the cart in an earlier lesson.

27 Save and run the application. Add Buffalo to the cart and you will see the cart total increases, as well as the item is only added once. Later, you will use a DataGrid to actually display more information (such as price, quantity and subtotal) for each item.

Adding a Remove Button

In this exercise, you will add a Remove button to remove the item from the shopping cart. So far, you have only one item in your store. However, you are building a scaleable application, so you want to be able to handle many different products. Therefore, you will build a method that will search through the entire shopping cart for the item the user wants to remove. In this task, you will see how the architecture of encapsulating the functionality into separate methods, as you did in the previous task makes this task easier. Now you can easily use the search method to search through the entire shopping cart to find the item you wish to delete.

1 Return to EComm.mxml and locate the first VBox that displays the information about the first grocery product. Just after the Add To Cart button, add another button with the label of Remove From Cart and a click event that will call the deleteProd() method. Pass the object at the first index of the groceryInventory ArrayCollection, cast as a Product, as follows.

```
<mx:Button label="Remove from Cart"
    click ="deleteProd(groceryInventory.getItemAt(0) as Product)"/>
```

This will call a method you will soon write in the EComm.mxml file and pass it the product that should be deleted. Be aware, at this point you are hard coding this to only use the first product. In a later lesson, when you are creating all the products dynamically, you will update this so it can delete any product you have in the cart.

2 Still in EComm.mxml, locate the script block, and add a new method with the name of deleteProd(), which takes a single argument, named product and the data type of Product. Set the return type to void. Inside of this method, call the soon to be written removeItem() method from the cart object. The deleteProd() method should look as follows:

```
private function deleteProd(product:Product):void{
    cart.removeItem(product);
}
```

This method asks the cart to remove the specified product.

3 Return to the ShoppingCart class and add a new method with the name of removeItem(), which accepts an argument named prod of the data type Product. Inside this method, create a new ShoppingCartItem variable, with the name of item which contains the prod.

```
public function removeItem(prod:Product):void{
   var item:ShoppingCartItem = new ShoppingCartItem(prod);
}
```

If you remember, you earlier wrote the getItemInCart() method to find any particular Product in the cart, but, it requires that you pass it a ShoppingCartItem, not just a product. To be able to use that method, you are temporarily creating a new ShoppingCartItem, which contains that product.

4 Create a second ShoppingCartItem instance, with the name of sci, and set it equal to the results of a call to your getItemInCart() method. Use an if statement to check if the sci variable is not equal to null. If it is, use the cursor's remove() method to delete the product at that cursor location. Finally, call the calcTotal() method of the cart. Your final removeItem() method should look as follows:

```
public function removeItem(prod:Product):void{
   var item:ShoppingCartItem = new ShoppingCartItem(prod);
   var sci:ShoppingCartItem = getItemInCart(item);
   if(sci != null){
      cursor.remove();
   }
   calcTotal();
}
```

Remember that the getItemInCart() method that you wrote earlier searches the cart for a ShoppingCartItem that contains a particular product and returns that item. When you call that method, the cursor will move to the matching location in the aItems ArrayCollection. Once the cursor is there, you can use the cursor's remove() method to delete the item at that location.

As a best practice, you should verify whether the item being passed in matches the item found in the cart. If the result (sci) of getItemInCart() is null, no product is matched, so it can not be removed. If you omitted this conditional, and clicked the remove button when there were no items in the cart, a run-time error would be thrown. With this conditional logic in place, you are preventing a potential error.

Finally, you need to recalculate all the items in the cart. Call the calcTotal() method, so the interface can continue to show the new correct total.

5 Save and run the application. Add Buffalo to the cart. You should see that you can click the Remove from Cart button to delete Buffalo from the cart and that the `total` field is updated each time you do this.

What You Have Learned

In this lesson, you have:

- Retrieved remote XML data using the `<mx:HTTPService>` tag and used it as a data provider for a List control (pages 110–116)

- Programmatically added an item to an ArrayCollection built from remote XML data and used the ArrayCollection as a data provider for a ComboBox control (pages 116–119)

- Populated a Tree control with XML data (pages 119–129)

- Transformed XML data into an ArrayCollection of custom objects (pages 130–135)

- Used an ArrayCollection of custom objects in data bindings (pages 135–136)

- Implemented shopping cart functionality using a cursor with an ArrayCollection (pages 137–149)

What You Will Learn

In this lesson, you will:

- Understand the need for components and how they can fit into a bigger application architecture scheme

- Understand the class hierarchy used in Flex

- Build both visual and nonvisual components

- Instantiate and use custom components

- Create properties and methods in custom components

- Create a pop-up window and learn how to close it

- Create a value object ActionScript class

Approximate Time

This lesson takes approximately 3 hours to complete.

Lesson Files

Media Files:

Lesson07/assets/AddProduct.mxml

Starting Files:

Lesson07/start/Dashboard.mxml
Lesson07/start/DataEntry.mxml
Lesson07/start/EComm.mxml

Completed Files:

Lesson07/complete/Dashboard.mxml
Lesson07/complete/DataEntry.mxml
Lesson07/complete/EComm.mxml
Lessson07/complete/managers/CategorizedProductManager.mxml
Lesson07/complete/valueObjects/Category.as
Lesson07/complete/views/dashboard/ChartPod.mxml
Lesson07/complete/views/dataEntry/AddProduct.mxml
Lesson07/complete/views/dataEntry/ConfirmScreen.mxml
Lesson07/complete/views/dataEntry/UpdateDeleteProd.mxml

Creating Components with MXML

You have used many components while building the three applications to their current state. Every time you use an MXML tag, you are actually using a component. In fact, Flex is considered to be a component-based development model. In this lesson you'll learn how to create your own components. The custom components you build will either extend functionality of components or group functionality of components.

Up to this point, you do not have a way to break up your application pages. The application would continue to get longer and longer and become more difficult to build, debug, and maintain. It would also be very difficult for a team to work on one large application page. Components let you divide the application into modules, which you can develop and maintain separately. With careful planning, these components can become a reusable suite of application functionality.

A simple component

You will need to learn two things in this lesson. The first is how to build components. You must learn the syntax and rules surrounding how to create and use the custom components you build. Second, is to learn why you'd want to do this and how components can affect your overall application architecture. In the "Introducing MXML Components" section, an overview of how to build components will be given. Then in the tasks throughout the rest of the lesson, you will reinforce your component-building skills and continue to learn more and more details about building custom components. The lesson introduction includes a theoretical discussion of why you would want to use components. The rest of the lesson will use an architectural approach to implementing components.

Introducing MXML Components

All Flex components and all the components you will build are actually ActionScript classes. The base class for the visual components you have been using and the MXML components you will build in this lesson is UIComponent. This means that in a hierarchy of components, UIComponent is at the top, and all the other components inherit from it.

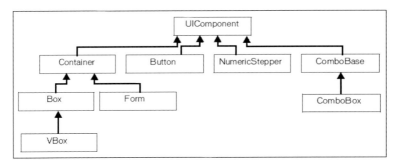

There are general groupings of these classes based on their functionality, such as component, manager and data service classes. Most of the classes you have been using up to this point have been component classes, such as Application, HBox, and TextInput, which have visual representations. You also used the HTTPService tag, which does not descend from UIComponent because it is a nonvisual component—a data service tag.

Package	mx.rpc.http.mxml
Class	public class HTTPService
Inheritance	HTTPService → HTTPService → AbstractInvoker → EventDispatcher → Object
Implements	IMXMLObject, IMXMLSupport

✱ **NOTE:** You can examine a complete description of the class hierarchy in the Flex ActionScript and MXML API reference, referred to as ASDoc.

Understanding the Basics on How to Create a Custom Component

When you build your own component, you basically want to do one of two things: add functionality to a predefined component or group numerous components together.

The basic steps to build a component are as follows:

1. Create a new file with the filename as the name you want for your component. Because this is a class you are building, it should start with an uppercase letter. Also, remember that these names will be case-sensitive, like Flex is in general.

2. Make the first line of code the XML document type definition you have been using for the main application files.

   ```
   <?xml version="1.0" encoding="utf-8"?>
   ```

3. As the first MXML tag, insert the root tag of your component, which will reflect what you want to do in the component. If it is a container, you most likely want to group several components' functionality into one easier-to-use component. If it is not a container, you most likely want to extend the functionality of a predefined component or further extend the functionality of a custom component.

   ```
   <mx:VBox xmlns:mx="http://www.adobe.com/2006/mxml">

   </mx:VBox>
   ```

4. In the body of the component, add the functionality needed. This will vary depending on what functionality you want the component to provide.

5. In the file that will instantiate the component, add an XML namespace so you can access the component. It is considered a best practice to group components in subdirectories according to their purpose. For instance, you will create a directory called views; then under that directory you will add another three subdirectories, one for each of the applications you are building: Dashboard, DataEntry, and EComm. Later in this lesson, you will add a namespace using the letter *v* as the prefix to have access to all the custom components in the views/dataEntry directory. The statement will appear as follows:

   ```
   xmlns:v="views.dataEntry.*"
   ```

6. Instantiate the component as you would a predefined component. For instance, if you created a file component called MyComp.mxml, using the namespace just created, you would instantiate that component as follows:

   ```
   <v:MyComp/>
   ```

Creating a Custom Component Step by Step

Now that you know the general approach to building a component, here is a simple example of adding functionality to a predefined component. Assume that you want to build a List that will automatically have three grocery categories displayed in it. Your component will use `<mx:List>` as its root tag. Up to now, all the MXML pages you've built use the `<mx:Application>` tag as the root tag. Components cannot use the `<mx:Application>` tag as the root tag because it can be used only once per application. Here are the six steps of creating a simple component:

1. Create a file named MyList.mxml. (You don't need to actually do this, just follow along with the logic.)

2. The first line of the component will be the standard XML document declaration
   ```
   <?xml version="1.0" encoding="utf-8"?>.
   ```

3. Because you are extending the functionality of the `<mx:List>`, you will use it as the root tag. Your skeleton component will appear as follows:
   ```
   <?xml version="1.0" encoding="utf-8"?>
   <mx:List xmlns:mx="http://www.adobe.com/2006/mxml">

   </mx:List>
   ```

4. The functionality to add to the body of the component is to display three `<mx:String>` tags in the `<mx:List>`. You know you need to use an `<mx:dataProvider>` tag to supply data to an `<mx:List>`, so here is the finished component:
   ```
   <?xml version="1.0" encoding="utf-8"?>
   <mx:List xmlns:mx="http://www.adobe.com/2006/mxml">

       <mx:dataProvider>
          <mx:String>Dairy</mx:String>
          <mx:String>Produce</mx:String>
          <mx:String>Bakery</mx:String>
       </mx:dataProvider>

   </mx:List>
   ```

5. Assume that a file named CompTest.mxml is created at the root of the project. Also, the component is created in a directory called myComps. Use the letter *c* as the prefix for the components in this folder. Therefore, the XML namespace to add to the `<mx:Application>` tag is `xmlns:c="myComps.*"`.

6. Finally, instantiate the component in the main application file:

```
<?xml version="1.0" encoding="utf-8"?>
<mx:Application xmlns:mx="http://www.adobe.com/2006/mxml"
    xmlns:c="myComps.*">

    <c:MyList/>

</mx:Application>
```

✳ **NOTE:** You will shortly see that Flex Builder makes this process of creating the skeleton of the component very easy.

The CompTest.mxml output would appear as shown here.

Using Custom Components in Application Architecture

You now know the basic mechanics of creating custom components. You might ask yourself, so now what? How does this affect what I have been doing? Why should I use them? How do I use them?

The advantages of components mentioned in the opening pages of this lesson should now be more clear:

- Components make applications easier to build, debug, and maintain.
- Components ease team development.
- With planning, components can lead to a suite of reusable code.

To facilitate the use of components as reusable code, you should make them independent of other code whenever possible. The components should operate as independent pieces of application logic with a clear definition of what data must be passed into them and what data will be returned from them. The object-oriented programming term "loosely coupled" is often applied to this kind of architecture.

Suppose that you have a component that uses an `<mx:List>` to display some information. You later learn of a new component that would actually be a better way to display that data. If built correctly, you should be able to switch the display component used in your custom component and not need to make any other changes. You would have changed the inner workings of the custom component, but the data going into the component and what came out did not change, so no changes to the rest of the application were needed.

Now, you need to think about how components fit into the bigger picture of application architecture. Although this book is not meant to be a discourse on Flex application architectures, it would be negligent not to show how components can fit into the bigger picture. In the applications you are building in this book you will implement a simple form of model-view-controller (MVC) architecture.

MVC is a design pattern or software architecture that separates the application's data, user interface, and control logic into three distinct groupings. The goal is to implement the logic so changes can be made to one portion of the application with a minimal impact to the others. Short definitions of the key terms are as follows:

- **Model:** The data the application uses. It manages data elements, responds to queries about its state, and instructions to change the data.
- **View:** The user interface. It is responsible for presenting model data to the user and gathering information from the user.
- **Controller:** Responds to events—typically user events, but also system events. The events are interpreted and the controller invokes changes on the model and view.

Generally, the flow of MVC is as follows:

1. The user interacts with the user interface (a view), such as clicking a button to add an item to a shopping cart.
2. The controller handles the input event.
3. The controller accesses the model, maybe by retrieving or altering data.
4. A view then uses the model data for appropriate user presentation.

Consider the e-commerce application you are building. Eventually your EComm.mxml main application page will be the controller. There will be views that do the following:

- Display the different grocery item categories
- Display the items in the shopping cart
- Display a detailed view of a particular grocery item
- Display all the grocery items in a particular category

All of these will be fronted by the controller, which in your case is the main application page: EComm.mxml. The model will start as an `<mx:Model>` tag, and by the end of the book transform to data retrieved from a database.

Now the stage is set, and you're ready to get started building components and enhancing the architecture and functionality of the applications you are building.

Creating an Update/Delete Product Component and Instantiating It

This first task will not add any functionality from the user's point of view. The exercise will improve the overall architecture of the DataEntry application. In fact, you'll want the application to appear exactly as it did before you started. What you will do is pull the visual elements of the application into a component, which is a view in terms of MVC architecture. DataEntry.mxml will begin to transform into the controller.

1 Right-click the FlexGrocer project and create a folder named views. Right-click the views folder and create another folder named dataEntry.

It is a best practice to organize your components. In this case, the views folder will contain the views for all three of your application sections. Within the views folder, the dataEntry folder will be where you will be creating your first component.

2 Right-click the dataEntry folder and then choose New > MXML Component. In the New MXML Component dialog box, set the filename to be **UpdateDeleteProd.mxml** and the base component to be an HBox, remove any width and height values, and then click Finish.

In this case, you are using an `<mx:HBox>` as your root tag, which means the children you insert in this component will be aligned beside each other.

3 Insert an `<mx:Script>` block just after the `<mx:HBox>` tag.

You will have a large <mx:Script> block in this component. Some of the code you will copy from the old DataEntry.mxml file, whereas other code you will write new.

4 Import the following three classes at the top of the `<mx:Script>` block:

flash.net.FileReference

utils.Util

mx.collections.ArrayCollection

These are all classes you will be using in this component that you used previously in DataEntry.mxml. Feel free to copy the import statements from the DataEntry.mxml file.

5 From the DataEntry.mxml file, copy the bindable private variable `units` and paste it below the `import` statements in the component. Remove the instantiation of the new ArrayCollection from `units` and change the access modifier from private to public. Create another bindable public variable named `foodColl`, data typed as XMLListCollection.

```
[Bindable]
public var units:ArrayCollection;
[Bindable]
public var foodColl:XMLListCollection;
```

> ✱ **NOTE:** When you data type the `foodColl` variable, Flex Builder will automatically import that class, which is mx.collections.XMLListCollection.

When you copied the variable into the component, and created the second, they actually became properties of the component. Simply by using the `var` statement and defining the variables to be public you create properties of the components that can have data passed into them.

This is no small matter. The basic building blocks of object-oriented programming are objects, properties, and methods. So knowing how to create properties is a very important piece of information.

Later in this lesson, you will add public functions to a component. Just as public variables are properties, public functions are the methods of your components.

6 Copy the three functions `fileBrowse()`, `populateForm()`, and `resetForm()` from the DataEntry.mxml page and paste them in the `<mx:Script>` block below the variable declarations.

You actually could have cut the three functions from the DataEntry.mxml page because they will no longer be needed there after this component is built. But for now, you will leave them there and remove them later.

7 Copy the `<mx:Tree>` tag and the complete Form from the DataEntry.mxml page and paste them below the `<mx:Script>` block but above the closing `<mx:HBox>` tag in the component.

You can see that you are moving the functionality that displayed information in the main application page into this component. In the main application page, the Tree and Form were surrounded by an HBox. That is why an `<mx:HBox>` tag was used as the root tag for your new component.

8 Save the file.

You have now created your first MXML component. Now that the component is built, you will remove code no longer needed in the main application page and then instantiate the new component.

9 Return to the DataEntry.mxml file and remove all the `import` statements except for the following:

```
import mx.collections.ArrayCollection;
import mx.rpc.events.ResultEvent;
```

The removed `import` statements were needed for code that is now placed in the component.

10 After you are sure that they have been copied correctly to the new component, remove the `fileBrowse()`, `populateForm()`, and `resetForm()` functions from the `<mx:Script>` block.

As mentioned earlier, these functions were left in until they had been copied correctly.

11 Remove the Tree and Form and the HBox that contained them.

This is functionality that has been moved into the component.

12 Add a namespace, using the letter *v* as a prefix, which allows you to use the components in the views/dataEntry folder. The code should appear as follows and be placed in the `<mx:Application>` tag:

```
xmlns:v="views.dataEntry.*"
```

There is currently only one component in the dataEntry folder, so you could have specified the name of that one component rather than using the *. Later in this lesson, you will create another component in the dataEntry folder and will want to use it also, and using the * enables use of all components in the directory.

13 Just above the closing `</mx:Application>` tag, instantiate the new component using the prefix defined in the namespace, the letter *v*. The code should appear as follows:

```
<v:UpdateDeleteProd />
```

You have now created and instantiated your first custom MXML component. Notice that the invocation of your custom component looks very similar to instantiating one of the built-in components. You use the prefix (in this case the letter v instead of `mx`) and then the name of the component, followed by `/>`. It is important to remember that the components you build are just as valid as the components that ship with Flex and are used in similar ways.

14 Return to the UpdateDeleteProd.mxml component and note the name of the two properties defined in the component: units and `foodColl`.

These two properties must be passed values for the component to work correctly, which means that in the invocation of the component in the main application page you use these property names and bind values to them.

15 Return to DataEntry.mxml and add two property/value pairs to the instantiation of the component. To the left of the equal signs will be the properties defined in the component, and to the right of the equal signs will be the bindable variables created on this page. In this case, they are intentionally the same:

```
<v:UpdateDeleteProd
   units="{units}"
   foodColl="{foodColl}"/>
```

The property names and the variables bound to them do not have to be named the same, but your coding will be simpler if you do follow this practice.

16 Change the `layout` property in the `<mx:Application>` tag so it is set equal to vertical.

You will be creating another component later in this lesson and will want the two to be displayed vertically.

17 Save the file and check to be sure that your code for that DataEntry.mxml file appears as follows:

```
<?xml version="1.0" encoding="utf-8"?>
<mx:Application xmlns:mx="http://www.adobe.com/2006/mxml"
   layout="vertical"
   creationComplete="unitRPC.send();prodByCatRPC.send()"
   xmlns:v="views.dataEntry.*">

   <mx:Script>
     <![CDATA[
        import mx.collections.ArrayCollection;
        import mx.rpc.events.ResultEvent;

        [Bindable]
        private var units:ArrayCollection =new ArrayCollection();

        private function unitRPCResult(event:ResultEvent):void{
           units = event.result.allUnits.unit;
        }
     ]]>
   </mx:Script>
```

```
    <mx:HTTPService id="unitRPC"
       url="http://www.flexgrocer.com/units.xml"
       result="unitRPCResult(event)"/>

    <mx:HTTPService id="prodByCatRPC"
       url="http://www.flexgrocer.com/categorizedProducts.xml"
       resultFormat="e4x"/>

    <mx:XMLListCollection id="foodColl"
       source="{prodByCatRPC.lastResult.category}"/>

    <v:UpdateDeleteProd
       units="{units}"
       foodColl="{foodColl}"/>

</mx:Application>
```

You see that the main application page is a much smaller than it was and is now acting more like a controller. The main application page is now retrieving model data and instantiating the views.

18 Run the DataEntry.mxml file. You see that the functionality has not changed by creating the component.

The purpose of this first task was not to add functionality to the application but also to rearchitect it. As the functionality of the DataEntry application continued to grow, the main application page would have become much too long and complex. Using components gives you the chance to break it up into manageable application modules.

Popping Up Product Information When Clicking the Update and Delete Buttons

Right now, nothing happens in the DataEntry application when you click the Update/Delete buttons. You will change this now. You will not yet be actually writing data back to the server; that comes in a later lesson. Now you will display in a pop-up window the product information you will later deal with at the server.

You will be creating a *modal* pop-up window. This means that a window will appear with the product information in it, and you will not be able to interact with any other components in the Flex application until you close the pop-up window. To build this functionality, you will use the TitleWindow class for the root tag in your component. You will also use the

PopUpManager class—in particular, the `createPopUp()` and `removePopUp()` methods. Your application will appear as follows with a pop-up window open.

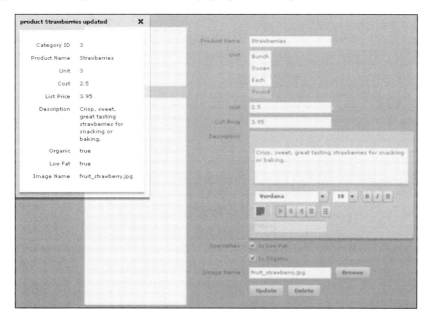

1 Right-click the views/dataEntry folder. Choose New > MXML Component. The filename should be **ConfirmScreen.mxml**, and the base component should be TitleWindow. After you select TitleWindow, set the layout to be vertical, remove any width and height values, and then click Finish.

In this case, you chose the `<mx:TitleWindow>` tag to be the base tag for your component. In the component you built earlier, you chose an `<mx:HBox>`. Your decision for the base tag should be driven by what you want the component to do.

2 Add a `close` event to the `<mx:TitleWindow>` tag. The ActionScript for this `close` event should call the static method of the PopUpManager class `removePopUp()`, in which the argument for the method is `this`. Also set the `showCloseButton` property equal to `true`.

```
<mx:TitleWindow xmlns:mx="http://www.adobe.com/2006/mxml"
    layout="vertical"
    close="PopUpManager.removePopUp(this)"
    showCloseButton="true">
```

The TitleWindow class is well-suited for your use as a pop-up window because you can choose to display a close button, and when the user clicks that button the `close` event will handle that action and close the pop-up window.

Notice that the `removePopUp()` method is used. It is invoked directly from the class name; in this case, PopUpManager. Hence, you know it is must be a static method. You did not have to create an instance of the PopUpManager class to use the `removePopUp()` method.

The argument of the `removePopUp()` method, `this`, refers to the instance of the TitleWindow itself. So in fact you are telling the TitleWindow to close itself.

3 Add an `<mx:Script>` to the block below the `<mx:TitleWindow>` tag. In the `<mx:Script>` block, import two classes: mx.managers.PopUpManager and valueObjects.Product. Also create a bindable public variable named `prod`, data typed as Product.

```
<mx:Script>
    <![CDATA[
        import mx.managers.PopUpManager;
        import valueObjects.Product;

        [Bindable]
        public var prod:Product;
    ]]>
</mx:Script>
```

The PopUpManager must be imported because you have used it in the handler for the `close` event. You will pass a Product object to be displayed in this pop-up window; hence the need for the bindable `prod` variable. And because that variable is of type Product, you must also import that class.

4 Below the `<mx:Script>` block, create an `<mx:Form>` to display all the pertinent data about the product passed to this component, as shown here:

```
<mx:Form>
    <mx:FormItem label="Category ID">
        <mx:Label text="{prod.catID}"/>
    </mx:FormItem>
    <mx:FormItem label="Product Name">
        <mx:Label text="{prod.prodName}"/>
    </mx:FormItem>
    <mx:FormItem label="Unit">
        <mx:Label text="{prod.unitID}"/>
    </mx:FormItem>
    <mx:FormItem label="Cost">
        <mx:Label text="{prod.cost}"/>
    </mx:FormItem>
    <mx:FormItem label="List Price">
        <mx:Label text="{prod.listPrice}"/>
    </mx:FormItem>
    <mx:FormItem label="Description">
        <mx:Text htmlText="{prod.description}"/>
```

code continues on next page

```
    </mx:FormItem>
    <mx:FormItem label="Organic">
      <mx:Label text="{prod.isOrganic}"/>
    </mx:FormItem>
    <mx:FormItem label="Low Fat">
      <mx:Label text="{prod.isLowFat}"/>
    </mx:FormItem>
    <mx:FormItem label="Image Name">
      <mx:Label text="{prod.imageName}"/>
    </mx:FormItem>
  </mx:Form>
```

The purpose of this component is to display the updated or deleted product. The `<mx:Form>` will show the pertinent data in this modal window.

5 Save the file.

You have completed building your second component. You will now return to UpdateDeleteProd.mxml and write the code to instantiate this component when needed. Don't forget that this component is a class, which is a child of the TitleWindow class, which you have now added to your Flex application for use whenever needed.

6 In UpdateDeleteProd.mxml, import mx.managers.PopUpManager and valueObjects.Product. Also declare a private variable named `win`, data typed as ConfirmScreen, the class which your new component creates.

You will need the PopUpManager class to create the pop-up window, and because you will be passing a variable of type Product, you'll also need to import the Product class. The `win` variable will be used in popping up the confirm screen.

7 Just below the `<mx:Script>` block, add an `<mx:Model>` tag with an `id` of `prodModel`. In the body of the `<mx:Model>` tag, create properties for all pertinent information gathered in the Form. The only value not gathered in the form is the `catID`. This value can be retrieved from the selected item from the Tree.

```
<mx:Model id="prodModel">
  <product>
    <catID>{productTree.selectedItem.@catID}</catID>
    <prodName>{prodName.text}</prodName>
    <unitID>{unitID.selectedItem.unitID}</unitID>
    <cost>{Number(cost.text)}</cost>
    <listPrice>{Number(listPrice.text)}</listPrice>
    <description>{description.text}</description>
    <isOrganic>{isOrganic.selected}</isOrganic>
    <isLowFat>{isLowFat.selected}</isLowFat>
    <imageName>{imageName.text}</imageName>
  </product>
</mx:Model>
```

It is a very common practice to bind form data to a Model, which takes the individual pieces of form data gathered in each control and puts them into an object you can more readily use. In this case, you will soon use the prodModel object to build an object of type Product that can be passed to your new component.

> **TIP:** The <mx:Model> tag must have a root node, as <product> is in the Model shown. The name of the root node is not important.

8 Locate the two buttons at the bottom of the Form. Add a click event to the Update button; in the event handler, call a function named doProdUpdate(). Add a click event to the Delete button; in the event handler, call a function named doProdDelete().

```
<mx:Button label="Update" click="doProdUpdate()"/>
<mx:Button label="Delete" click="doProdDelete()"/>
```

You are calling ActionScript functions when an event occurs.

9 At the bottom of the <mx:Script> block, create the skeleton of a private function named showPopUp(), data typed as void. It should accept two parameters: prod, data typed as Product, and title, data typed as String.

```
private function showPopUp(prod:Product,title:String):void{
}
```

You will call this function in both the update and delete functions to display the product that is being acted upon.

10 As the first line of code in the function, set the win variable created earlier (remember that it is data typed as ConfirmScreen) equal to win=ConfirmScreen(PopUpManager. createPopUp(this,ConfirmScreen,true)).

This line of code is a bit tricky and will take some work to understand. First, examine what is inside of the parentheses. Here you are calling the static method createPopUp(). This method accepts three parameters:

- The first parameter is the parent of the pop-up window; in this case, this refers to the current component. The pop-up will appear in front of its parent.

- The second parameter is the class to be created for the pop-up window. Here you are using the component you just built: the ConfirmScreen class.

- The last parameter specifies whether the pop-up window should be modal or not.

If you were not passing data to the component, the code inside the parentheses would display a window, and you would not need any other code to perform the pop-up.

The rest of the code on this line is treating one object as a different type than it actually is. This is sometimes referred to as *casting*, or *coercing*, the object. You need to tell the compiler the expression in the parentheses is a ConfirmScreen object instance. You will now explore what this means and why it is possible.

If you did not cast the object to a ConfirmScreen object you would receive the following error:

```
Implicit coercion of a value with static type mx.core:IFlexDisplayObject to a
possibly unrelated type views.dataEntry:ConfirmScreen
```

In the Adobe Flex 2 Language Refererence (sometimes referred to as ASDoc), it states that the createPopUp() method returns an object of type IFlexDisplayObject. You are trying to assign this object to a variable data typed as a ConfirmScreen, hence the compiler error indicating that they might be possibly unrelated. By surrounding the expression with ConfirmScreen and parentheses, you have told the compiler they can be the same type.

11 When you call the showPopUp() function, you will be passing it two parameters, named prod and title, which hold data to be displayed in the pop-up. As the last two lines of code in the function, assign those parameters to like named properties of the win object.

```
private function showPopUp(prod:Product,title:String):void{
   win=ConfirmScreen(PopUpManager.createPopUp(this,ConfirmScreen,true));
   win.prod=prod;
   win.title=title;
}
```

The reason you worked so hard to create and understand the win variable is because you needed it to pass data to the pop-up window. You can use the prod property you defined when you created the component as one way to pass data to the pop-up window. The title property is part of the TitleWindow class (actually it is a property inherited from the TitleWindow's parent class, Panel).

Now that you have created the showPopUp() function, you will use it in your update and delete functions.

12 At the bottom of the <mx:Script> block, build the skeleton for a private function named doProdUpdate(). Because the function will not return a value, data type it as void.

This is the function that is called when the user clicks the Update button.

13 In the function, use the var statement to create a variable named prod, data typed as Product. This variable should be set equal to an invocation of the static buildProduct() method of the Product class, passing the object built in the <mx:Model> tag, prodModel, as a parameter.

```
var prod:Product=Product.buildProduct(prodModel);
```

The variable created in this statement will be passed as a Product object to be displayed in the showPopUp() function.

14 As the last line of code in the function, call the showPopUp() function you built earlier. The first parameter should be the prod variable. The second parameter should be a concatenated string that displays the word "product," followed by the product name, followed by the word "updated." Your completed function should appear as follows:

```
private function doProdUpdate():void{
    var prod:Product=Product.buildProduct(prodModel);
    showPopUp(prod,"product "+ prod.prodName +" updated");
}
```

Remember that the code in this function will be replaced after you learn how to send data back to the server. At that time, you'll invoke the remote method to actually update the record in the database.

15 Now create a doProdDelete() function. The easiest way to do this is to simply copy the function you just created and change the name of the function as well as the word "updated" in the concatenated string.

```
private function doProdDelete():void{
    var prod:Product = Product.buildProduct(prodModel);
    showPopUp(prod,"product "+ prod.prodName +" deleted");
}
```

With these two functions now created, you're ready for testing.

16 Be sure that the ConfirmScreen and UpdateDeleteProd components, are saved. Run the DataEntry.mxml main application page.

To test the functionality, select a product from one of the categories, and you will see the form filled. Click either the Update or Delete button, and you will see the modal pop-up window appear. Close the pop-up window. Be sure to test both the Update and Delete buttons.

Creating Another Value Object

In this task, you will build a simple value object. Up to this point, you have retrieved only product information; but, as the application continues to grow, it will also be important to retrieve information about the categories in which the products are grouped. For this reason, you need a Category value object that will hold the category name and a category ID, which is the primary key field for the category.

1 Right-click the valueObjects folder. Choose New > ActionScript Class. In the New ActionScript Class dialog box, be sure that the Package Name is valueObjects and supply the Name of the new class to be **Category**. Also, be sure that the only modifier checked is public; then click Finish. You should see the code automatically generated for the class appears as follows:

```
package valueObjects
{
   public class Category
   {
   }
}
```

This creates the skeleton for the new Category value object class.

> ✱ **NOTE:** The positioning of opening braces is purely a style issue. Some developers like the opening brace at the end of the preceding line of code. For instance, the skeleton class code generated by Flex Builder is just as valid with the open braces positioned at the end of the preceding lines of code:

```
package valueObjects{
   public class Category{
   }
}
```

2 Make the class bindable because the two properties in the class both need to be bindable. In the class, create two public properties: the first is catID, data typed as int; the second is catName, data typed as String.

```
package valueObjects{
   [Bindable]
   public class Category{
      public var catID:int;
      public var catName:String;
   }
}
```

When dealing with the categories, there are obviously times when you want to see the category name; hence the need for the catName property. You will also be retrieving products based on category, and that will be done by category ID; hence the reason for the catID property.

3 Below the variable declarations, build the constructor function so it accepts two parameters: the first is id, data typed as int; the second is catName, data typed as String. In the constructor function, assign the catID property the value of the parameter id and the catName property the value of the parameter name.

```
public function Category(id:int,catName:String){
   this.catID=id;
   this.catName=catName;
}
```

When the property names match the parameter names, the class' properties must be preceded by the this prefix when assigning the values in the constructor. So, in this case, only the catName property had to use the this prefix because the name of the property and the name of the parameter are the same.

4 Create a public toString() function data typed as String. In the function, return the word Category in square brackets, followed by a space, and then the category name.

```
public function toString():String{
   return "[Category] "+ catName;
}
```

It is always a good idea to create a toString() function for a value object in case the object is ever used in a trace statement.

5 Check to be sure your completed Category value object appears as follows:

```
package valueObjects{
   [Bindable]
   public class Category{
      public var catID:int;
      public var catName:String;

      public function Category(id:int,catName:String){
         this.catID=id;
         this.catName=catName;
      }
      public function toString():String{
         return "[Category] "+ catName;
      }
   }
}
```

With the category value object now created, you can begin work on the nonvisual data manager component.

Creating a Data Manager Component for All Three Applications

In the first task, you rearchitected part of the application without adding any functionality. In the second task, you added functionality while building more components. This task is like the first, in which you are rearchitecting the application without adding any visible functionality for the user.

All three applications—DataEntry, EComm and Dashboard—share the same data. In this task, you will build an MXML component that can be thought of as a data manager. This component will provide certain types of data to all the applications when they need it. This data manager component will be different from other components you've built in this lesson in that it will not have any visible representation that a user will see. These components are referred to as nonvisual components.

The advantage of building a data manager component is that it will centralize data requests. For instance, rather than having many HTTPService requests on different application pages and components, you can centralize them in this data manager component.

1 Create a new folder named managers under the FlexGrocer project.

Because this new component is neither a value object nor a view, a new folder is needed.

2 Right-click the managers folder and then choose New > MXML Component. In the New MXML Component dialog box, set the filename to be **CategorizedProductManager.mxml** and the base component to be a UIComponent; then click Finish.

The UIComponent is the lightest-weight component you can use when creating an MXML component.

3 Insert an `<mx:Script>` block into the component. Add the following three `import` statements that are needed for this class:

```
import mx.rpc.events.ResultEvent;
import valueObjects.Product;
import valueObjects.Category;
```

These statements are needed because there will be a `result` event from an HTTPService, and you will also be building arrays of Products and Categories.

4 Just below the `import` statements in the `<mx:Script>` block, create three new private variables. The first is named `categorizedProducts`, data typed as Object, and set equal to a new Object. The second is named `aCats`, data typed as an Array, and set equal to a new Array. And the last is named rawData, data typed as XML. It does not have to be set equal to anything.

```
private var categorizedProducts:Object = new Object();
private var aCats:Array = new Array();
private var rawData:XML;
```

5 Open the EComm.mxml file and copy the <mx:HTTPService> tag whose id is prodByCatRPC and paste it under the <mx:Script> block you just created in the CategorizedProductManager component. Change the name of the result event handler from prodHandler to prodByCategoryHandler.

This component is being built to act as a data manager for other components. So, of course, some data will be retrieved in this component.

6 Add to the <mx:UIComponent> tag a creationComplete event and call the send() method of the prodByCatRPC HTTPService.

This is an easy piece of code to forget to add. Remember, setting up the HTTPService does not automatically call the send() method.

7 Again from the EComm.mxml file, copy the entire prodHandler() function and paste it just above the closing <mx:Script> tag in the CategorizedProductManager component. Change the name of the function from prodHandler to prodByCategoryHandler.

With some modifications, the existing function you just copied can supply not only an array of products but also an array of categories and products by category.

8 Remove the following three lines of code from the function:

```
var prodArray:Array=new Array();
prodArray.push(prod);
groceryInventory=new ArrayCollection(prodArray);
```

This code is no longer needed in the new function.

9 As the first line of the function, set the rawData variable equal to event.result and cast it to XML using the 'as' operator as shown:

```
rawData = event.result as XML;
```

When populating the Tree, a function will be called to send back this raw data.

10 Surround the existing `for each..in` loop with another `for each..in` loop. The iterant in the new loop should be a local variable named c, data typed as XML. The loop should look in the event.result XML object for the category nodes. Change the nested `for each..in` loop, so instead of looking in the event.result XML object, it looks in the iterant from the outer loop, c, for product nodes:

```
for each (var c:XML in event.result..category){
   for each (var p:XML in c..product){
      var prod:Product = new Product(
         Number(p.@catID),
         String(p.@prodName),
         Number(p.@unitID),
         Number(p.@cost),
         Number(p.@listPrice),
         String(p.@description),
         Boolean(p.@isOrganic=="Yes"),
         Boolean(p.@isLowFat=="Yes"),
         String(p.@imageName));
   }
}
```

You now have a scenario in which you can build an array of Category objects between the beginnings of the `for each..in` loops.

11 Between the beginnings of the `for each..in` loops, create a variable local to the function named category, data typed as Category. Set that equal to a new Category in which you pass two parameters. The first parameter will be the `catID` attribute of the c iterant, and the second will be the `catName` attribute of the c iterant. The `catID` value will need to be cast as int, and the `catName` value will need to be data typed as String.

```
var category:Category = new Category(int(c.@catID), String(c.@catName));
```

The data types of the parameter values must be data typed because the data is untyped from the XML object.

12 Below the line of code you just created, push the category object onto the `aCats` array:

```
aCats.push(category);
```

The `aCats` array was declared earlier and will be the data returned in a function you will build later in this task. The array holds six Category objects, each containing the `catID` and `catName` properties as shown in the following example from the debugger:

```
⊟ ▪ aCats = Array (@2c52671)
  ⊟ ● [0] = valueObjects.Category (@2d34c41)
      ⌀ catID = 1 [0x1]
      ⌀ catName = "Meat"
  ⊟ ● [1] = valueObjects.Category (@2d34bc1)
      ⌀ catID = 2 [0x2]
      ⌀ catName = "Vegetables"
  ⊞ ● [2] = valueObjects.Category (@2d34b61)
  ⊞ ● [3] = valueObjects.Category (@2d34b41)
  ⊞ ● [4] = valueObjects.Category (@2d34aa1)
  ⊞ ● [5] = valueObjects.Category (@2d34ae1)
      ⌀ length = 6 [0x6]
```

13 Below the line of code you just created, add a new property of the categorizedProducts object using the c iterant's catID attribute in square bracket notation as the property name, and set this equal to a new Array.

```
categorizedProducts[c.@catID] = new Array();
```

You are building a complex data structure here, and depending upon your computer language background, you might understand it as a hashmap, or associative array. In categorizedProducts, there will be a property for each category, identified by its category ID. Each of these properties will hold an array of all the products in that category, as shown in the following example from the debugger.

```
▪ categorizedProducts = Object (@2c3ed21)
⊞ ● [1] = Array (@2cead91)
⊟ ● [2] = Array (@2cea491)
  ⊟ ● [0] = valueObjects.Product (@29e2c11)
      ⌀ catID = 2 [0x2]
      ⌀ cost = 2.16
      ⌀ description = "Firm and no bitterness"
      ⌀ imageName = "veg_broccoli.jpg"
      ⌀ isLowFat = true
      ⌀ isOrganic = true
      ⌀ listPrice = 3.19
      ⌀ prodName = "Broccoli"
      ⌀ unitID = 3 [0x3]
  ⊞ ● [1] = valueObjects.Product (@29e2c59)
  ⊞ ● [2] = valueObjects.Product (@29e2ca1)
      ⌀ length = 3 [0x3]
⊞ ● [3] = Array (@2cea7c1)
⊞ ● [4] = Array (@2cea551)
⊞ ● [5] = Array (@2ceae81)
⊞ ● [6] = Array (@2ceacd1)
```

You must use square bracket notation to create the property. What you are using for the property name contains a dot itself. The compiler would not understand if you used this notation: categorizedProducts.c.@catID.

14 In the inner loop, just after where the Product object is built, push the new prod Product object on to the array you just created.

```
categorizedProducts[c.@catID].push(prod);
```

15 After the close of the two loops, just above the closing brace for the function, insert the following if statement:

```
if(this.parentDocument.categorizedProductDataLoaded != null){
   this.parentDocument.categorizedProductDataLoaded(aCats);
}
```

You need to understand that this if statement code is a bad practice. You are reaching into the parent document and running a function, thus coupling this component to another, which was stated earlier as a bad practice.

That being said, why are you doing this? This checks to be sure that data is loaded from the <mx:HTTPService> tag. You have not yet learned the best practice way to handle this, so for now know that this does the needed job. In a later lesson, you will learn about dispatching custom events, which is the best practice way to handle this situation.

16 Check to be sure that the function you just built appears as follows:

```
private function prodByCategoryHandler(event:ResultEvent):void{
   rawData=event.result as XML;
   for each(var c:XML in event.result..category){
      var category:Category = new Category(int(c.@catID),String(c.@catName));
      aCats.push(category);
      categorizedProducts[c.@catID] = new Array();
      for each (var p:XML in c..product){
         var prod:Product = new Product(Number(p.@catID),
            String(p.@prodName),
            Number(p.@unitID),
            Number(p.@cost),
            Number(p.@listPrice),
            String(p.@description),
            Boolean(p.@isOrganic=="Yes"),
            Boolean(p.@isLowFat=="Yes"),
            String(p.@imageName));
         categorizedProducts[c.@catID].push(prod);
      }
   }
   if(this.parentDocument.categorizedProductDataLoaded != null){
      this.parentDocument.categorizedProductDataLoaded(aCats);
   }
}
```

To be sure that you still have the big picture in mind, here is a recap of the three things that this function has done:

- Built an array named aCats that contains all the category objects.

- Built an object named categorizedProducts that contains a property for each category, and each property contains an array of all the products for that particular category.

- Used a not-best-practice way to be sure data is loaded. This bad practice will be corrected in the lesson on custom events.

17 Just under the variable declarations, create a public function named getProdsForCat(), which is data typed as an Array. It should accept a parameter named catID, data typed as an int.

This is the first of three functions you will build to complete this component. All three of the functions return data to invoking pages. In this case, the function will return a set of products based on the category ID passed to the function.

This is also an example of creating public functions that will be methods that can be called after the component is instantiated on a calling page. For instance, if the component is instantiated as shown here:

```
<m:CategorizedProductManager id="prodMgr"/>
```

you could then invoke the method as follows:

```
prodMgr.getProdsForCat(4);
```

18 As the single line of code in the function, return the categorized products for the catID parameter:

```
public function getProdsForCat(catID:int):Array{
    return categorizedProducts[catID];
}
```

19 Create another public function named getCats(), data typed as an Array. In this function, return the aCats array that was built in the prodByCategoryHandler() function.

```
public function getCats():Array{
    return aCats;
}
```

20 Create another public function named getCategorizedProducts(), data typed as XML. In this function, return the rawData XML object that was built in the prodByCategoryHandler() function.

```
public function getCategorizedProducts():XML{
   return rawData;
}
```

21 Check to be sure that your component appears as follows:

```
<?xml version="1.0" encoding="utf-8"?>
<mx:UIComponent xmlns:mx="http://www.adobe.com/2006/mxml"
   creationComplete="prodByCatRPC.send()">

   <mx:Script>
      <![CDATA[
         import mx.rpc.events.ResultEvent;
         import valueObjects.Product;
         import valueObjects.Category;

         private var categorizedProducts:Object = new Object();
         private var aCats:Array = new Array();
         private var rawData:XML;

         public function getProdsForCat(catID:int):Array{
            return categorizedProducts[catID];
         }
         public function getCats():Array{
            return aCats;
         }
         public function getCategorizedProducts():XML{
            return rawData;
         }
         private function prodByCategoryHandler(event:ResultEvent):void{
            rawData=event.result as XML;
            for each (var c:XML in event.result..category){
               var category:Category=new Category(int(c.@catID),String(c.@catName));
               aCats.push(category);
               categorizedProducts[c.@catID]=new Array();
               for each (var p:XML in c..product){
                  var prod:Product = new Product(
                  Number(p.@catID),
                  String(p.@prodName),
                  Number(p.@unitID),
                  Number(p.@cost),
                  Number(p.@listPrice),
                  String(p.@description),
```

```
                    Boolean(p.@isOrganic=="Yes"),
                    Boolean(p.@isLowFat=="Yes"),
                    String(p.@imageName));
                 categorizedProducts[c.@catID].push(prod);
              }
           }
           if(this.parentDocument.categorizedProductDataLoaded != null){
              this.parentDocument.categorizedProductDataLoaded(aCats);
           }
        }
     }
  ]]>
</mx:Script>

<mx:HTTPService id="prodByCatRPC"
   url="http://www.flexgrocer.com/categorizedProducts.xml"
   result="prodByCategoryHandler(event)"
   resultFormat="e4x"/>

</mx:UIComponent>
```

Now the data manager component is finished, and it's time to put it to use in the next task.

Using the New Data Manager Component

This will be the first of several times you use the new data manager component to retrieve data for an application. In this case, you'll remove the <mx:HTTPService> tag from the main application, DataEntry.mxml, and instead instantiate the new data manager component. With the new data manager component instantiated, you will then use it to get both a list of categories and a list of categorized products. The list of categorized products is used immediately in the UpdateDeleteProd component, and the list of categories will be used later, when you build yet another component in this lesson.

1 Open DataEntry.mxml. Remove the <mx:HTTPService> tag that has the id property of prodByCatRPC. Also remove the invocation of the send() method for this remote procedure call (RPC) in the creationComplete event of the <mx:Application> tag. Finally, remove the <mx:XMLListCollection> tag.

   Here you are removing all the code associated with the <mx:HTTPService> tag that retrieved categorized product information. This will shortly be replaced by instantiating the new data manager component.

2 Check to be sure that your DataEntry.mxml page appears as follows:

```
<?xml version="1.0" encoding="utf-8"?>
<mx:Application xmlns:mx="http://www.adobe.com/2006/mxml"
    layout="vertical"
    creationComplete="unitRPC.send()"
    xmlns:v="views.dataEntry.*">

    <mx:Script>
      <![CDATA[
         import mx.collections.ArrayCollection;
         import mx.rpc.events.ResultEvent;

         [Bindable]
         private var units:ArrayCollection=new ArrayCollection();

         private function unitRPCResult(event:ResultEvent):void{
            units =event.result.allUnits.unit;
         }
      ]]>
    </mx:Script>

    <mx:HTTPService id="unitRPC"
       url="http://www.flexgrocer.com/units.xml"
       result="unitRPCResult(event)"/>

    <v:UpdateDeleteProd
       units="{units}"
       foodColl="{foodColl}"/>

</mx:Application>
```

Make sure that you have a clean base to start with before adding in new code that uses the new data manager component.

3 Add the following namespace definition in the `<mx:Application>` tag:

```
xmlns:m="managers.*"
```

After working so hard to build the new data manager component, this code will allow you to access it.

4 Near the bottom of the file, just above the closing `</mx:Application>` tag, instantiate the new data manager component, named CategorizedProductManager, and assign the `id` property to be `prodMgr`. Remember that you'll need to use the `m:` prefix to instantiate this.

```
<m:CategorizedProductManager id="prodMgr"/>
```

The fruits of your labor are beginning to pay off. You have now instantiated the new component from which you can invoke methods to retrieve data.

5 In the `<mx:Script>` block, add a bindable private variable named `categories`, data typed as an ArrayCollection. Add another bindable private variable named `foodColl`, datayped as an XML.

The `categories` variable will be used to store the array of categories retrieved from the data manager component. The `foodColl` variable will be used to store the grocery items stored by category.

6 Just above the end of the `<mx:Script>` block, create a public function named `categorized ProductDataLoaded()`. Have the function accept a parameter named `aCats`, data typed as an Array, and data type the function itself as void.

```
public function categorizedProductDataLoaded(aCats:Array):void{
}
```

This is the function that is called from the data manager component. Remember that this is a bad practice that will be remedied later.

7 As the first line of code in the function, set the `categories` variable equal to a new ArrayCollection with an argument of `aCats`:

```
categories = new ArrayCollection(aCats);
```

8 Also in the function, set the `foodColl` variable equal to the invocation of the `getCategorizedProducts()` method of the prodMgr component instance.

```
foodColl= prodMgr.getCategorizedProducts();
```

9 Be sure that the main application file DataEntry.mxml appears as follows:

```
<?xml version="1.0" encoding="utf-8"?>
<mx:Application xmlns:mx="http://www.adobe.com/2006/mxml"
   layout="vertical"
   creationComplete="unitRPC.send()"
   xmlns:v="views.dataEntry.*"
   xmlns:m="managers.*">

   <mx:Script>
     <![CDATA[
        import mx.collections.ArrayCollection;
        import mx.rpc.events.ResultEvent;
```

code continues on next page

```
        [Bindable]
        private var units:ArrayCollection=new ArrayCollection();
        [Bindable]
        private var categories:ArrayCollection;
        [Bindable]
        private var foodColl:XML;

        private function unitRPCResult(event:ResultEvent):void{
            units = event.result.allUnits.unit;
        }
        public function categorizedProductDataLoaded(aCats:Array):void{
            categories = new ArrayCollection(aCats);
            foodColl= prodMgr.getCategorizedProducts();
        }
    ]]>
</mx:Script>

<mx:HTTPService id="unitRPC"
    url="http://www.flexgrocer.com/units.xml"
    result="unitRPCResult(event)"/>

<v:UpdateDeleteProd
    units="{units}"
    foodColl="{foodColl}"/>

<m:CategorizedProductManager id="prodMgr"/>

</mx:Application>
```

Now the new data manager component is built and is being used, so it's time for testing.

✱ **NOTE:** When you save DataEntry.mxml, you will be getting an error that is corrected in the next step by changing a data type of a public variable.

10 Open UpdateDeleteProd.mxml and change the data type of the public variable `foodColl` from XMLListCollection to XML. Remove the import of the XMLListCollection class. The variable declaration should appear as follows:

```
public var foodColl:XML;
```

You are now passing XML instead of an XMLListCollection, so this data type must be updated.

✱ **NOTE:** You do not need to import the XML class to replace the XMLListCollection because it is automatically imported as part of the Top Level package. You can see this by looking in ASDoc at the Package information.

11 Locate the instantiation of the Tree component. Add the showRoot property to the Tree and set it equal to false. Also set the width of the Tree equal to 200 pixels.

```
<mx:Tree id="productTree"
    height="100%" width="200"
    dataProvider="{foodColl}"
    labelField="@name"
    change="populateForm(event)"
    showRoot="false"/>
```

The foodColl data used in the dataProvider binding has a root node of catalog which you do not want to be visible. You make the root node not show by setting the showRoot property to false.

12 Run DataEntry.mxml. Select a product from the Tree and you should see that the form fills correctly.

After all the work in the last two tasks, you might be a little disappointed that no new functionality appears to the user. Remember that the last two tasks were for rearchitecting the application, not adding functionality. You now have a component to provide product and category data whenever you need it throughout the three applications.

Implementing Add Product Functionality

If you open the file flex2tfs/Lesson07/assets/AddProduct.mxml, you will see there is nothing in this file that is new to you, so you do not need to spend the time typing the code for the new component. AddProduct.mxml contains the following major sections, all of which you have experience with:

- Building a data model with <mx:Model>

- Creating a form and binding the form data to the model

- Displaying a pop-up on form submission

Now, you will not write the new component, just use it.

1 Copy the AddProduct.mxml component from Lesson07/assets to your flexGrocer/views/dataEntry directory. Open the file and note the two public properties defined named units and cats.

Even though you are not writing this component, you still must have it in the correct location to use it properly.

2 Open the main application file DataEntry.mxml.

This is the file in which you will instantiate the AddProduct.mxml file.

3 Below the instantiation of the UpdateDeleteProd component, instantiate the AddProduct component using the v prefix, which is defined in an XML namespace. You need to bind the `categories` variable to the `cats` property and bind the `units` variable to the `units` property.

```
<v:AddProduct
   cats="{categories}"
   units="{units}"/>
```

You are passing data into the two properties you examined in step 1 of this task. Remember that the categories data is retrieved from the data manager component you built, and the units data is retrieved from the HTTPService call in this file.

4 Run the application DataEntry.mxml. You will see the update/delete product functionality on the top of the page and the add product functionality below that. Fill in the form for the add product functionality and click Add. You should see the new data appear in a pop-up window. Close the pop-up window.

The look of the page is not optimal with the two kinds of functionality appearing on the same page. In a later lesson, you will learn about navigator containers and place these two components in what is called a TabNavigator.

5 Get ready for the next task by closing any open editors.

The next task uses different files than you have been working with up to this point in the lesson.

Creating and Using a Component for the Dashboard Application

In the Dashboard application there are three Panels that currently exist and will eventually display charting data. In this lesson, you abstract those Panels into components. In a later lesson, you will abstract those components even further to add functionality such as maximizing and minimizing.

1 Open Dashboard.mxml and run it.

You will be rearchitecting this application. In the end, you must be sure to have the same results as when you start, so give it a look now to refresh your memory.

2 Create a folder named dashboard under the views folder.

The views for each application will be stored in separate locations.

3 Right-click the dashboard folder and then choose New > MXML Component. In the New MXML Component dialog box, set the filename to be **ChartPod.mxml** and the base component to be a Panel. After you have selected Panel, the layout option appears. Set the layout to be vertical and remove any width and height values; then click Finish.

```
<?xml version="1.0" encoding="utf-8"?>
<mx:Panel xmlns:mx="http://www.adobe.com/2006/mxml" layout="vertical">

</mx:Panel>
```

In this case you are using a Panel as your root tag for this component because it will be used to replace some Panel tags in the main application file.

4 In the new component, insert a `<mx:ControlBar>` tag set.

Because the `<mx:Panel>` tags you are replacing with this component had ControlBars, the component also needs them.

5 Check to be sure that your new component appears as follows:

```
<?xml version="1.0" encoding="utf-8"?>
<mx:Panel xmlns:mx="http://www.adobe.com/2006/mxml"
    layout="vertical">

    <mx:ControlBar>

    </mx:ControlBar>

</mx:Panel>
```

At this time you are just creating the component, not putting any content into it.

6 Return to Dashboard.mxml and insert a new namespace in the `<mx:Application>` tag so the new component can be used. Set the letter *v* to be the prefix:

```
xmlns:v="views.dashboard.*"
```

Remember that you must use the XML namespace so the new component can be located correctly.

7 Locate the three Panels near the bottom of the file. Remove the three sets of `<mx:ControlBar>` tags.

You will replace three instances of the Panel with instances of your new component, which now contains a ControlBar.

8 Replace <mx:Panel> with <v:ChartPod> in the six places you see it. Do not change any other properties or associated values. Both opening and closing tags will be modified:

```
<v:ChartPod id="sales"
   width="100%" height="100%"
   title="Sales Chart">
</v:ChartPod>
<mx:VBox id="rightCharts"
   width="100%" height="100%" >
   <v:ChartPod id="type"
      width="100%" height="100%"
      title="Category Chart">
   </v:ChartPod>
   <v:ChartPod id="comp"
      width="100%" height="100%"
      title="Comparison Chart">
   </v:ChartPod>
</mx:VBox>
```

That finishes up the creation of the component and its use in the Dashboard application.

9 Run the Dashboard.mxml and you should see no difference in the look of the application.

Again, this was a rearchitecting change, with no new functionality added from the user's point of view.

What You Have Learned

In this lesson, you have:

- Gained a theoretical understanding of why components should be used and how they fit into a simple implementation of MVC architecture (pages 152–157)

- Built a component that moved the visual elements from a main application page to the component and then instantiated the component in the main application page (pages 157–161)

- Subclassed the TitleWindow component to create a component that can be used as a pop-up window (pages 161–167)

- Used the UIComponent for the root tag of a nonvisual data manager component that provides category and product information to other applications (pages 170–181)

- Instantiated an AddProduct component that started the implementation of functionality to add new grocery products (pages 181–182)

- Created a now-empty component for the Dashboard application that uses the <mx:Panel> tag as the root tag for the component (pages 182–184)

What You Will Learn

In this lesson, you will:

- Populate a HorizontalList with a data set and display the information using a labelField, labelFunction, and itemRenderer

- Create an MXML component to be used as an itemRenderer

- Loop over a data set using a Repeater component

- Use the currentItem and currentIndex properties and the getRepeaterItem() method with a Repeater

- Reference controls built by a Repeater using array notation

- Instantiate a custom component in a Repeater

Approximate Time

This lesson takes approximately 2 hours to complete.

Lesson Files

Media Files:

None

Starting Files:

Lesson08/start/EComm.mxml

Completed Files:

Lesson08/complete/EComm.mxml
Lesson08/complete/views/ecomm/Cart.mxml
Lesson08/complete/views/ecomm/CategoryView.mxml
Lesson08/complete/views/ecomm/FoodList.mxml
Lesson08/complete/views/ecomm/GroceryDetail.mxml
Lesson08/complete/views/ecomm/TextAndPic.mxml
Lesson08/complete/as/ecomm.as

LESSON 8

Using Controls and Repeaters with Data Sets

In this lesson, you will expand your skill set in working with data sets. You often get a data set from a back-end service in the form of a complex data structure, such as an object, an array, or an array of objects. Up to this point, you have learned few ways to display, manipulate, or loop over these data sets (although you did loop over XML data using a `for each..in` loop).

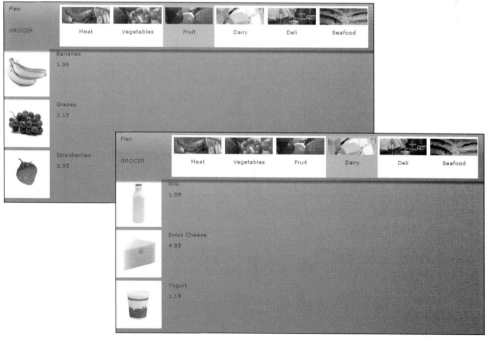

A data set is used with a HorizontalList to display grocery categories and a Repeater to display the grocery items from that category.

One of the focuses in this lesson is to supply a data set to list-based components, especially the HorizontalList and TileList components. These components enable you to display data for each object in the data set in various ways. You will also see that you can override the default behavior of these components, which enables only text to be displayed, by using an **itemRenderer**. This functionality enables you to define a component to display whatever kind of data you choose when using list-based controls.

Another focus of this lesson is using a Repeater component, which enables you to loop over the objects in a data set using MXML. During the looping you can instantiate components, including custom components using data from the data set. For instance, in one of the tasks in this lesson, you will loop over a custom component that displays grocery items from a certain category of groceries.

Introducing Using Data Sets

In this lesson, you will learn two approaches to dealing with data sets. One is to loop over the data using a Repeater in MXML; the other is to use the data set as a `dataProvider` for a special collection of controls. From these basic two approaches you will find many options and learn to decide what your best choice is in different situations.

First, consider the group of list-based controls, which enable a user to scroll though a list of items and select one or more items from the list. All Flex list-based components inherit from the ListBase class and include the following:

- DataGrid
- HorizontalList
- List
- ComboBox
- TileList
- Tree

All these components take a data provider, which in most cases will be a data set. You have already used the Tree and List. In this lesson, HorizontalList and TileList will be discussed. DataGrids will be covered in a later lesson.

Another way to think of these components ties back to the architecture discussion on model-view-controller (MVC) of Lesson 7, "Creating Components with MXML." The components are the view on the model, which is the underlying data, and provides an abstraction between the data and the components used to display that data. This enables you to do the following (among other things):

- Populate multiple components from the same data model

- Switch data providers at run time

- Make a change to a model and have it immediately reflected in all components that use that data

Understanding HorizontalList and TileList Components

Both HorizontalList and TileList components display a list of items; the exact information displayed about each item is controlled by you. HorizontalList displays items horizontally (no surprise there, hopefully) and, if needed, places scroll bars along the bottom of the list to see all the items.

TileList lays out items in dynamically created rows and columns of equal-sized tiles. You can use the direction property to have the items laid out horizontally or vertically. If needed, a scroll bar can be added to one axis to see all the items.

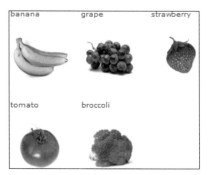

You most likely will be displaying data that comes from an object. The question is, how do you choose what data from the object to display? Looking at some code will help clear this up.

First, assume that you want to display just one property of the object that contains text. To do that, you specify the property `name` in the `labelField` property of HorizontalList.

```
<mx:Script>
   <![CDATA[
      import mx.collections.ArrayCollection;

      private var arrayData:Array=[
         {name:"banana",cat:"fruit",cost:.99},
         {name:"bread",cat:"bakery",cost:1.99},
         {name:"orange",cat:"fruit",cost:.52},
         {name:"donut",cat:"bakery",cost:.33},
         {name:"apple",cat:"fruit",cost:1.05}];

      private var dp:ArrayCollection=new ArrayCollection(arrayData);
   ]]>
</mx:Script>

<mx:HorizontalList dataProvider="{dp}"
   labelField="name"
   columnWidth="100"
   width="600"/>
```

The code would create the display as shown here:

So by specifying the `name` property of the object, you display those property values in the list.

Implementing a labelFunction

Next is the situation in which you want to combine text from a number of the properties to display. To do this, you must write a function that specifies how to format the text and use the `return` statement. Instead of using the `labelField` property, you use the `labelFunction` property. In the function, you accept a parameter of data type Object. This parameter represents the object currently being displayed by the HorizontalList. Convention is to call this parameter `item`, but it is not necessary to use that parameter name. Because the function returns a String, you must data type the function as String. The following code shows an example of a `labelFunction` being used:

```
<mx:Script>
   <![CDATA[
      import mx.collections.ArrayCollection;
```

```
        private var arrayData:Array=[
            {name:"banana",cat:"fruit",cost:.99},
            {name:"bread",cat:"bakery",cost:1.99},
            {name:"orange",cat:"fruit",cost:.52},
            {name:"donut",cat:"bakery",cost:.33},
            {name:"apple",cat:"fruit",cost:1.05}];

        private var dp:ArrayCollection=new ArrayCollection(arrayData);

        private function multiDisplay(item:Object):String{
            return item.cat+": "+item.name+" $"+item.cost;
        }
    ]]>
</mx:Script>

<mx:HorizontalList dataProvider="{dp}"
    labelFunction="multiDisplay"
    columnWidth="130"
    width="850"/>
```

This code would create the display as shown here:

| fruit: banana $0.99 | bakery: bread $1.99 | fruit: orange $0.52 | bakery: donut $0.33 | fruit: apple $1.05 |

For each item in the HorizontalList, the function is called. The current object being displayed is passed to the function, and the string is built and returned from the function and displayed.

✱ NOTE: Even though the function is defined to accept a parameter (`private function multiDisplay(item:Object):String`), you do nothing to pass it in the `labelFunction` property (`labelFunction="multiDisplay"`). Flex automatically passes the correct object to the function.

Implementing an itemRenderer

By default, both HorizontalList and TileList permit only text to be displayed, as you have just seen in the example code. This default can be overridden by using an `itemRenderer` property. For this lesson, you can think of an `itemRenderer` as an MXML file you create to display an item's data in the way you choose, and not have the display limited to text only. For example, it is common to display some text and an image from the HorizontalList.

✱ NOTE: There are actually a number of ways to implement an `itemRenderer`, and you will see more ways in Lesson 11, "Using DataGrids and ItemRenderers."

When using an `itemRenderer` with the HorizontalList or the TileList, you specify an external file in the `itemRenderer` property, which can be either an MXML or AS file. This `itemRenderer` file is then used for each object in the *dataProvider*. For instance, if you have an array of 14 objects as a data provider, the *itemRenderer* would be used 14 times. In the *itemRenderer*, all the particular item's data being rendered is available in a variable called *data*.

In the following code example, the objects hold an image name instead of a price. This first code example contains the HorizontalList control.

```
<mx:Script>
  <![CDATA[
      import mx.collections.ArrayCollection;

      private var arrayData:Array=[
          {name:"banana",cat:"fruit",imgName:"banana.jpg"},
          {name:"grape",cat:"fruit",imgName:"grape.jpg"},
          {name:"strawberry",cat:"fruit",imgName:"strawberry.jpg"},
          {name:"tomato",cat:"vegetable",imgName:"tomato.jpg"},
          {name:"broccoli",cat:"vegetable",imgName:"broccoli.jpg"}];

      private var dp:ArrayCollection=new ArrayCollection(arrayData);
  ]]>
</mx:Script>

<mx:HorizontalList dataProvider="{dp}"
    itemRenderer="Thumbnail"
    width="600"/>
```

The next code example is the *itemRenderer*. The `<mx:VBox>` tag was selected as the root tag of the renderer because the text should appear above the image; but, a renderer need not be a VBox.

```
<?xml version="1.0" encoding="utf-8"?>
<mx:VBox xmlns:mx="http://www.adobe.com/2006/mxml"
    width="100"
    height="120">

    <mx:Label text="{data.name}"/>
    <mx:Image source="{data.imgName}"/>

</mx:VBox>
```

The code would create the display as shown here:

Displaying the Categories Using a HorizontalList and an itemRenderer

In a grocery application, there would be many, many grocery items. So many, in fact, that it would not be reasonable to display minimal information and a thumbnail image for each item without making the user do lots of scrolling to see them. To ease the process, the idea of categories of items will be used.

The first step of getting this functionality to work is to display the categories. In a later task, you will make the categories clickable and display corresponding grocery items; but, for now, you will just get the categories to display. At this point in the application, the categories will be displayed as text and be clickable using a HorizontalList control.

Putting to work what you learned in Lesson 7, you will build a component to display the categories and then instantiate it where you want the categories to be displayed.

1 In the FlexGrocer project, locate the views folder. Create a subfolder named ecomm.

2 Right-click on the ecomm folder and choose New > MXML Component. In the New MXML Component dialog box, set the filename to be **CategoryView.mxml** and the base component to a HorizontalList; then click Finish.

3 Below the <mx:HorizontalList> tag, insert an <mx:Script> block. In the <mx:Script> block, import the mx.collections.ArrayCollection class. Also in the <mx:Script> block, create a bindable public variable named cats, data typed as an ArrayCollection:

```
<mx:Script>
  <![CDATA[
    import mx.collections.ArrayCollection;

    [Bindable]
    public var cats:ArrayCollection;
  ]]>
</mx:Script>
```

To reiterate an important concept from Lesson 7: when you used the var keyword and public access modifier, you created the cats property of the CategoryView class.

4 Add the dataProvider property to the HorizontalList and bind it to the cats ArrayCollection.

```
<mx:HorizontalList xmlns:mx="http://www.adobe.com/2006/mxml"
  dataProvider="{cats}">
```

When you instantiate this component, you will pass to it an ArrayCollection that contains all the category information. This information is the category name, named catName, and that category primary key value, named catID.

5 In the `<mx:HorizontalList>` tag, set the itemRenderer equal to views.ecomm.TextAndPic.

```
<mx:HorizontalList xmlns:mx="http://www.adobe.com/2006/mxml"
   dataProvider="{cats}"
   itemRenderer="views.ecomm.TextAndPic">
```

Remember that when you supply the value for the itemRenderer, you do not include the filename's extension, which could be either .mxml or .as. Include the path to the itemRenderer from the location of the main application file: EComm.mxml.

6 Set the horizontalScrollPolicy to off.

```
<mx:HorizontalList xmlns:mx="http://www.adobe.com/2006/mxml"
   dataProvider="{cats}"
   itemRenderer="views.ecomm.TextAndPic"
   horizontalScrollPolicy="off">
```

The tolerances of the images displayed are tight, and horizontal scroll bars are not needed.

7 Right-click on the ecomm folder and choose New > MXML Component. In the New MXML Component dialog box, set the filename to be **TextAndPic.mxml** and the base component to a VBox. Set the width to 100 pixels and the height to 75 pixels; then click Finish.

```
<?xml version="1.0" encoding="utf-8"?>
<mx:VBox xmlns:mx="http://www.adobe.com/2006/mxml"
   width="100" height="75">

</mx:VBox>
```

This is the skeleton of your itemRenderer.

8 In the `<mx:VBox>` tag, set the horizontalAlign to center.

```
<mx:VBox xmlns:mx="http://www.adobe.com/2006/mxml"
   width="100" height="75"
   horizontalAlign="center">
```

9 In the body of the component, display an image. The image is a JPEG file that is located in the assets folder. The name of the file is the same as the category name with the string nav_ in front of the name and a .jpg extension. Remember that the data passed to this itemRenderer is in an object called data, and the category name is in a property called catName. You need to use string concatenation in the binding for the source property to create the correct path to the image. Also set the height of the image to 31 pixels and the width of the image to 93 pixels.

```
<mx:Image source="{'../assets/nav_'+data.catName+'.jpg'}"
   height="31" width="93"/>
```

> ▶ **TIP:** Adding words together is referred to as *string concatenation*. In ActionScript, you simply use the plus sign (+) to perform string concatenation operations. Notice that when using string concatenation in a binding, the braces surround the entire expression, or alternatively, you could have used the following syntax: source="../assets/nav_{data.catName}.jpg" where the braces are around only the variable name and you do not need the plus signs.

The HorizontalList will use this renderer component once for each category object in the dataProvider, so you will have a unique image displayed for each category.

10 Under the image, use an <mx:Label> tag to display the category name. Again, the data passed to this itemRenderer is an object called data, and the category name is in a property called catName. Set the width of the Label control to 100%.

```
<mx:Label text="{data.catName}" width="100%"/>
```

This is all your renderer file will do: display an image associated with the category and under that display the category name.

11 Open EComm.mxml. Add the following XML namespaces to the <mx:Application> tag so you can use the files you've just built in this lesson, as well as the data manager component built in the last lesson:

```
xmlns:v="views.ecomm.*"
xmlns:m="managers.*"
```

12 Create a bindable private variable named categories, data typed as ArrayCollection.

This variable will store the category information when retrieved from the data manager component.

13 Just above the end of the <mx:Script> block, create a public function named categorizedProductDataLoaded(). Have the function accept a parameter named aCats, data typed as Array, and data type the function itself as void.

```
public function categorizedProductDataLoaded(aCats:Array):void{

}
```

This is the function that is called from the data manager component. Remember that this is a bad practice that will be remedied in the next lesson.

14 As the first line of code in the function, set the `categories` variable created in step 12 equal to a new ArrayCollection with an argument of `aCats`:

```
public function categorizedProductDataLoaded(aCats:Array):void{
   categories=new ArrayCollection(aCats);
}
```

This assigns an array of categories built in the data manager component to your `categories` variable.

15 At the bottom of the page, just above the closing `<mx:Application>` tag, instantiate the data manager component named CategorizedProductManager, and assign the `id` property to be `catProds`. Remember that you'll need to use the `m:` prefix so the component can be located.

```
<m:CategorizedProductManager id="catProds"/>
```

You are now seeing the benefit of building the data manager component in the last lesson. Rather than having to write all the functionality that retrieves the category data, you can just instantiate the data manager component and use data from it.

16 Locate the ApplicationControlBar. Below the two Labels that display the text Flex GROCER, insert the `CategoryView` component. Set the `id` to `catView`, the `width` to 600 pixels, the `left` property to 100 pixels, and bind the `cats` property to the `categories` ArrayCollection.

```
<mx:Label x="0" y="0" text="Flex"/>
<mx:Label x="0" y="41" text="GROCER"/>
<v:CategoryView id="catView"
   width="600"
   left="100"
   cats="{categories}"/>
```

17 In the `<mx:Canvas>` tag that contains the CategoryView, set both the `horizontalScrollPolicy` and `verticalScrollPolicy` to off.

```
<mx:Canvas width="100%" height="100%"
   horizontalScrollPolicy="off"
   verticalScrollPolicy="off">
```

You do not want scroll bars anywhere in the ApplicationControlBar, and this will ensure that none appear.

18 Run your EComm.mxml main application file and you should see the categories being displayed.

Displaying Grocery Products Based on Category Selection

You just passed a data set to a HorizontalList control and had an item displayed for each object in the data set. In addition to this functionality, at some point you will want to loop over the data set. For instance, you might need to loop over the data set and display a radio button or check box for each object in the data set. In this task, you will add functionality— when the category is clicked, appropriate grocery items are displayed.

Using a Repeater to Loop Over a Data Set

You can loop over a data set in MXML using a Repeater component. Just as HorizontalList created one item for each object in the data set, the Repeater will loop once for each object in a data set. You have access to the data in the objects when the Repeater is initially looping and when the user is interacting with the application.

The general syntax for a Repeater is as follows:

```
<mx:Repeater id="instanceName" dataProvider="{data}">
</mx:Repeater>
```

A Repeater loops over a data set and enables you to access each item of that set. Two properties help you access this data while looping. The currentItem property is a reference to the particular piece of data in the set that you are currently processing, and currentIndex is a zero-based counter that specifies this item's order in the data set.

The following code example creates radio buttons for each object in a data set. You will use data from the objects for the radio button label. The code would appear as follows:

```
<mx:Script>
  <![CDATA[
    import mx.collections.ArrayCollection;

      private var arrayData:Array=[
        {name:"banana",cat:"fruit",imgName:"banana.jpg"},
        {name:"grape",cat:"fruit",imgName:"grape.jpg"},
        {name:"strawberry",cat:"fruit",imgName:"strawberry.jpg"},
        {name:"tomato",cat:"vegetable",imgName:"tomato.jpg"},
        {name:"broccoli",cat:"vegetable",imgName:"broccoli.jpg"}];

      private var dp:ArrayCollection=new ArrayCollection(arrayData);

    ]]>
</mx:Script>

<mx:Repeater id="myRepeater" dataProvider="{dp}">
  <mx:RadioButton label="{myRepeater.currentItem.name}"/>
</mx:Repeater>
```

The result of this code would appear as follows:

Note that you use the `name` property from the objects being repeated over for the `label` of the radio buttons. Also notice that there are five objects in the array, and there are five buttons created by the Repeater. The values of the `currentItem` and `currentIndex` properties are meaningful only during the actual looping. For example, after the Repeater has finished looping, `currentIndex` contains the value -1.

Retrieving Data from Repeated Components

The next problem to solve is how to use data from the controls created in the Repeater after the looping is finished. You have already learned that `currentItem` and `currentIndex` will be of no value except during the looping. For example, how can you retrieve costs associated with each grocery item using the preceding example code? Repeated components have a `getRepeaterItem()` method that returns the item in the `dataProvider` property that was used to produce the object. When the Repeater component finishes repeating, you can use the `getRepeaterItem()` method to determine what the event handler should do based on the `currentItem` property.

Assume that you want to expand the code example by filling a Label control with the price of the grocery item when a radio button is selected. You do this by adding a `click` event to the radio button and using the `event.target.getRepeaterItem()` method to get the data. The code would appear as follows:

```
<mx:Script>
    <![CDATA[
        import mx.collections.ArrayCollection;

        private var arrayData:Array=[
            {name:"banana",cat:"fruit",cost:.99},
            {name:"bread",cat:"bakery",cost:1.99},
            {name:"orange",cat:"fruit",cost:.52},
            {name:"donut",cat:"bakery",cost:.33},
            {name:"apple",cat:"fruit",cost:1.05}];

        private var dp:ArrayCollection=new ArrayCollection(arrayData);

    ]]>
</mx:Script>
```

```
<mx:Label id="priceLabel" text="Price Here"/>

<mx:Repeater id="myRepeater" dataProvider="{dp}">
   <mx:RadioButton label="{myRepeater.currentItem.name}"
      click="priceLabel.text=event.target.getRepeaterItem().cost"/>
</mx:Repeater>
```

Although this works, you have learned it is a better practice to call a function on an event. When using a function, the code appears as follows:

```
<mx:Script>
   <![CDATA[
      import mx.collections.ArrayCollection;

      private var arrayData:Array=[
         {name:"banana",cat:"fruit",cost:.99},
         {name:"bread",cat:"bakery",cost:1.99},
         {name:"orange",cat:"fruit",cost:.52},
         {name:"donut",cat:"bakery",cost:.33},
         {name:"apple",cat:"fruit",cost:1.05}];

      private var dp:ArrayCollection=new ArrayCollection(arrayData);

      private function displayCost(repeaterItem:Object):void{
         priceLabel.text=repeaterItem.cost;
      }
   ]]>
</mx:Script>

<mx:Label id="priceLabel" text="Price Here"/>

<mx:Repeater id="myRepeater" dataProvider="{dp}">
   <mx:RadioButton label="{myRepeater.currentItem.name}"
      click="displayCost(event.target.getRepeaterItem())"/>
</mx:Repeater>
```

You pass the object retrieved by event.target.getRepeaterItem() to the function as a parameter and then fill the Label control with the cost property of that object.

The result of this code would appear as follows:

Addressing Components Built by a Repeater

Another issue that needs to be clarified when using a Repeater is how to address the repeated components after they have been instantiated in the loop. Up to this point, you used the id property to uniquely identify each object. When you use an id property on a component within a Repeater, you seemingly would have many components with the same instance name. This is not the case because Flex creates an array of these components when they are repeated over. You actually use array syntax to individually address each of the components. For example, if you repeat it over a check box four times, and that check box had an id of myCheck, you address those four controls as myCheck[0], myCheck[1], myCheck[2], and myCheck[3].

The following code uses this array notation to change the label of radio buttons when the user clicks a button. When the button is clicked, a function is called, and two labels are changed:

```
<mx:Script>
   <![CDATA[
      import mx.collections.ArrayCollection;

      private var arrayData:Array=[
         {name:"banana",cat:"fruit",cost:.99},
         {name:"bread",cat:"bakery",cost:1.99},
         {name:"orange",cat:"fruit",cost:.52},
         {name:"donut",cat:"bakery",cost:.33},
         {name:"apple",cat:"fruit",cost:1.05}];

      private var dp:ArrayCollection=new ArrayCollection(arrayData);

      private function displayCost(repeaterItem:Object):void{
         priceLabel.text=repeaterItem.cost;
      }

      private function changeLabels():void{
         myButtons[0].label="New Banana";
         myButtons[3].label="New Donut";
      }

   ]]>
</mx:Script>

<mx:Label id="priceLabel" text="Price Here"/>

<mx:Repeater id="myRepeater" dataProvider="{dp}">
   <mx:RadioButton id="myButtons"
      label="{myRepeater.currentItem.name}"
      click="displayCost(event.target.getRepeaterItem())"/>
</mx:Repeater>

<mx:Button label="Change Radio Buttons"
   click="changeLabels()"/>
```

The result of this code would appear as follows:

Understanding Performance Differences Between TileList and Repeater

Performance should always be considered when developing an application, and you have a performance decision to make when presenting data in a tiled look. Earlier in the book, you used a Tile container. You could place a Repeater inside the Tile container, and the resulting display would look very much like using the TileList, which you learned about earlier in this lesson. Which is the better option?

Generally speaking, you should probably use the TileList control because TileList control instantiates objects when they are displayed, whereas a Repeater inside of a Tile container instantiates all the objects in the entire data set, whether they are initially displayed or not. Depending on the size of the data set, this could result in a long delay before the page is displayed in Flash Player.

One point to consider in this decision is scrolling. Because the TileList control must instantiate each object as the user is scrolling, you might see better scrolling performance using a Repeater inside of the Tile container when all the objects are initially instantiated.

If the data set is quite small, you will most likely not see any performance difference between the two options.

Displaying Grocery Items Based on Category

In this task, a Repeater will be used to instantiate a custom component numerous times. The data provider of the Repeater will contain all the grocery items that belong to one particular category.

1 In the component CategoryView.mxml in the `<mx:Script>` block, add a bindable public variable named `catSelected`, data typed as `int`.

This variable will be used to store the category ID. That value will then be used to retrieve all the grocery items belonging to that category. Datatyping as int is the best choice because the category ID is always an integer.

2 Also in the <mx:Script> block, create a private function named categorySelect() and data type it as void. In the function, assign the catSelected variable the catID from the selectedItem of the <mx:HorizontalList>, which is the root tag of the component.

```
private function categorySelect():void{
   catSelected=this.selectedItem.catID;
}
```

This will store the category ID value that can later be used to retrieve the corresponding products.

> **TIP:** You cannot assign an id to the root tag of a component, so you could not have added the id property to the <mx:HorizontalList> tag and used the instance name (instead of this) in the code in the function. The function will work correctly without adding the this prefix, but use it if you feel it makes the code more readable.

3 In the <mx:HorizontalList> tag, add a click event to call the categorySelect() function, which will assign the selected category's ID to the catSelected variable.

4 Right-click on the views/ecomm folder and choose New > MXML Component. In the New MXML Component dialog box, set the filename to be **FoodList.mxml**, the base component to a VBox, and remove any width and height values; then click Finish.

5 Add an XML namespace, using the letter v as the prefix, to access components in the views/ecomm folder:

```
xmlns:v="views.ecomm.*"
```

6 In an <mx:Script> block, import mx.collections.ArrayCollection and then create a bindable, public variable named prodByCategory, data typed as ArrayCollection.

```
<mx:Script>
   <![CDATA[
      import mx.collections.ArrayCollection;

      [Bindable]
      public var prodByCategory:ArrayCollection;
   ]]>
</mx:Script>
```

This is the property to which you will pass the products of a certain category.

7 Below the <mx:Script> block, insert an <mx:Repeater> tag block. Set the id to be foodRepeater, and also set the width and height to be 100%. Finally, bind the dataProvider to the prodByCategory property.

```
<mx:Repeater id="foodRepeater"
    width="100%" height="100%"
    dataProvider="{prodByCategory}">

</mx:Repeater>
```

The Repeater will loop once for each product in the result set passed to the component.

8 In the Repeater, instantiate a component named GroceryDetail, which you will begin writing in the next step. Give the component an id of prod and set the width to 80%. Pass the currentItem of the Repeater to a property which you will name groceryItem.

```
<mx:Repeater id="foodRepeater"
    width="100%" height="100%"
    dataProvider="{prodByCategory}">
        <v:GroceryDetail id="prod"
            width="80%"
            groceryItem="{foodRepeater.currentItem}"/>
</mx:Repeater>
```

The GroceryDetail component will be instantiated once for each product looped over in the Repeater.

9 Create another component in the views/ecomm folder named GroceryDetail.mxml and use a Canvas tag as the base tag. Remove any width and height values.

This creates the skeleton of the component that will display grocery items.

10 In the <mx:Canvas> tag, set both the horizontalScrollPolicy and verticalScrollPolicy to off to ensure no scroll bars appear.

11 Add an <mx:Script> block and import valueObjects.Product.

The object passed to this component is a Product, so you need to import this class so you can use it as a data type.

12 Create a bindable public variable named groceryItem, data typed as Product.

```xml
<?xml version="1.0" encoding="utf-8"?>
<mx:Canvas xmlns:mx="http://www.adobe.com/2006/mxml"
   horizontalScrollPolicy="off"
   verticalScrollPolicy="off">

   <mx:Script>
     <![CDATA[
        import valueObjects.Product;

        [Bindable]
        public var groceryItem:Product;
     ]]>
   </mx:Script>

</mx:Canvas>
```

This is the property that accepts an object passed to the component from the currentItem of the Repeater.

13 In the body of the component, insert an `<mx:Image>` tag with an `id` set to `pic` and the source set to the imageName of the groceryItem. Remember that the images are in the assets folder.

```xml
<mx:Image id="pic"
   source="{'../assets/'+groceryItem.imageName}"/>
```

This will display the image of each grocery item in the selected category.

14 Below the image, insert a Label control to display the prodName of the groceryItem. Set the id to prodName, the *x* position to 100, and the *y* position to 0.

```xml
<mx:Label id="prodName"
   text="{groceryItem.prodName}"
   x="100" y="0"/>
```

The product name will appear with the image. It is important to understand that the x and y values supplied here position the Label relative to the top-left corner of the Canvas location, *not* the 0,0 position of the Application. So this Label control will be positioned right 100 pixels and down 0 pixels from the top-left corner of where the Canvas is positioned.

15 Below the first Label, insert another Label control to display the listPrice of the groceryItem. Set the id to price, the *x* position to 100, and the *y* position to 20.

```xml
<mx:Label id="price"
   text="{groceryItem.listPrice}"
   x="100" y="20"/>
```

The product price will be displayed after the product name.

16 Below the Label controls, add a Button with an id of add and a label of Add To Cart. On the click event, call a function named itemAdded(), passing the groceryItem as a parameter. Also, position the Button at *x*, *y* values 100, 40.

```
<mx:Button id="add"
   label="Add To Cart"
   click="itemAdded(groceryItem)"
   x="100" y="40"/>
```

Clicking the button calls the function that will eventually start the process of adding the product to the shopping cart.

17 At the bottom of the <mx:Script> block, create a private function named itemAdded(). The function should accept a parameter named prod, data typed as Product. Because the function does not return a value, data type the function itself as void. In the function, simply trace the prod parameter. The function is highlighted in the completed component:

```
<?xml version="1.0" encoding="utf-8"?>
<mx:Canvas xmlns:mx="http://www.adobe.com/2006/mxml"
   horizontalScrollPolicy="off"
   verticalScrollPolicy="off">

   <mx:Script>
      <![CDATA[
         import valueObjects.Product;

         [Bindable]
         public var groceryItem:Product;

         private function itemAdded(prod:Product):void{
            trace(prod);
         }
      ]]>
   </mx:Script>

   <mx:Image id="pic"
      source="{'../assets/'+groceryItem.imageName}" />
   <mx:Label id="prodName"
      text="{groceryItem.prodName}"
      x="100" y="0"/>
   <mx:Label id="price"
      text="{groceryItem.listPrice}"
      x="100" y="20"/>
   <mx:Button id="add"
      label="Add To Cart"
      click="itemAdded(groceryItem)"
      x="100" y="40"/>

</mx:Canvas>
```

At this point, you will simply trace the product. Later in this lesson, you will add code to the function to place the product in a shopping cart.

> **TIP:** Remember that the Product is an ActionScript value object you built. The reason you can trace it is because you wrote a `toString()` method that displays just the product name.

18 In EComm.mxml, some cleaning up needs to be done. Some functionality then needs to be added to display products by category, which is the whole point of this task. Start by removing the `creationComplete` event from the `<mx:Application>` tag.

You will be retrieving categorized product information from the data manager component, so this HTTPService will not be needed.

19 Remove the bindable private property `groceryInventory`. Don't forget to remove the `[Bindable]` metadata tag with the variable declaration.

This variable was used to store grocery product information. It is no longer needed because this data will now be pulled in from the data manager component.

20 Remove the entire function named `prodHandler()`.

This function-supplied data is now retrieved from the data manager component.

21 Remove the `<mx:HTTPService>` tag with the `id` of `prodByCatRPC`.

The data manager removes the need for this HTTPService.

> **TIP:** In the next step you will be asked to locate a specific VBox instance. Use the Outline view to find named object instances.

22 Locate the VBox with an `id` of products. Remove that VBox and the five children it contains.

The main point of functionality added in this task is to display grocery items based upon product selection. These VBox containers will be replaced by a custom-built component to do just that.

23 In the single remaining State named cartView, locate the two `<mx:SetProperty>` tags.

```
<mx:SetProperty target="{products}" name="width" value="0"/>
<mx:SetProperty target="{products}" name="height" value="0"/>
```

These tags reference the VBox that was removed, so they must be altered.

24 Change the target of the two <mx:SetProperty> tags so they bind to an object named prodTile instead of products.

```
<mx:SetProperty target="{prodTile}" name="width" value="0"/>
<mx:SetProperty target="{prodTile}" name="height" value="0"/>
```

You will create the prodTile object later in this task.

25 Remove the entire <mx:State> block with a name of expanded.

The details that were shown in this State will be added to the GroceryDetail component later in this lesson.

Now, you will start implementing the functionality of displaying grocery items by category.

26 Locate the instantiation of the CategoryView component in ApplicationControlBar. Add a click event and call a function named displayProdByCategory():

```
<v:CategoryView id="catView"
    width="600"
    left="100"
    cats="{categories}"
    click="displayProdByCategory()"/>
```

This will call the function that actually displays the products identified when a user clicks one of the categories.

27 In the <mx:Script> block, create a bindable private variable named prodByCategory, data typed as ArrayCollection.

This variable will store the products grouped by category.

28 At the bottom of the <mx:Script> block, insert a private function named displayProdByCategory(), data typed as void. In the function, create a variable local to the function named prodArray, data typed as Array. Remember that in the component in which you are now working, the data manager component has an instance name of catProds. Assign the prodArray variable the value returned by calling the getProdsForCat() method from the data manager component, passing the catView. catSelected value as a parameter.

```
private function displayProdByCategory():void{
    var prodArray:Array=catProds.getProdsForCat(catView.catSelected);
}
```

This retrieves an array of products based on the category selected from the data manager component and assigns them to a variable.

The parameter is the value from CategoryView component, which holds the category ID of the selected category. What is done here is a bad practice that will be corrected in the next lesson. It is a bad practice because it requires knowledge of the inner workings of the CategoryView component when it is not necessary.

29 As the second line of code in the function, assign the prodByCategory variable a new ArrayCollection object using the prodArray variable as data for the constructor:

```
private function displayProdByCategory():void{
   var prodArray:Array=catProds.getProdsForCat(catView.catSelected);
   prodByCategory=new ArrayCollection(prodArray);
}
```

The prodByCategory variable now holds the array of products of a certain category, based on the category the user clicks. In the next step, you will pass the data out to the FoodList component, which you built earlier.

▶ **TIP:** In the next step you will be asked to locate a specific HBox instance. Use the Outline view to find named object instances.

30 Locate the HBox with an id of bodyBox. It is near the end of the file just below the ApplicationControlBar.

31 As the first child in this HBox, just above the existing VBox, instantiate the FoodList component. Set the id to be prodTile, and the width and height to 100%. Bind the prodByCategory property of FoodList to the prodByCategory variable from this file.

```
<v:FoodList id="prodTile"
   width="100%" height="100%"
   prodByCategory="{prodByCategory}"/>
```

Remember that FoodList in turn calls the GroceryDetail component that actually displays product information, which at this point is nothing more than product name and price.

32 Debug EComm.mxml. Click a category and a list of products should appear. Click one of the Add To Cart buttons and then return to Flex Builder. In your Console view, you should see the trace of the product added to the cart. Be sure to terminate the debugging session by clicking the red box on the top of the Console view.

▶ **TIP:** You must debug the application to see the results of trace statements.

Coding States to Display Detailed Product Information

You have a simple display of the grocery products generated by selecting a category. You will now write code to implement a state that shows detailed product information on a user event.

1 Return to GroceryDetail.mxml.

2 At the bottom of the <mx:Script> block, insert a private function named toggleState(), data typed as void. The function should accept a parameter named state data typed as String. In the function, insert an if..else statement and for the condition check to see whether the parameter state is equal to closed. If the condition is true, set the currentState equal to the empty string, which is the base state. If the condition is false, set the currentState equal to expanded:

```
private function toggleState(state:String):void{
   if(state == "closed"){
      this.currentState = "";
   } else {
      this.currentState = "expanded";
   }
}
```

As you can see from the code, you will create a state named expanded, which shows details of the product. This function will be used to switch the state between the normal view and the product details view based on user interaction.

3 Surround the Image, two Labels, and the Button in an <mx:Canvas> tag block.

You are nesting this <mx:Canvas> tag inside the root tag Canvas to control the mouse events.

4 In the new <mx:Canvas> tag, add a mouseOver event that calls the toggleState() function passing the String open.

```
mouseOver="toggleState('open')"
```

When the user does a mouseOver of product information, the details will be displayed by showing the expanded state.

5 In the new <mx:Canvas> tag, add a mouseOut event that calls the toggleState() function passing the String closed.

```
mouseOut="toggleState('closed')"
```

When the user does a mouseOut of product information, the details will disappear.

6 Above the start of the Canvas block you just inserted (not the base tag), insert an `<mx:states>` block. Set up the basic infrastructure for the state by nesting an `<mx:State>` block inside the `<mx:states>` block, set the name property equal to expanded. Then, nested inside of the `<mx:State>` block, add an `<mx:AddChild>` block. Finally, nested in the `<mx:AddChild>` block, add a VBox container with the width set to 100% and the x property set to 200.

```
<mx:states>
   <mx:State name="expanded">
      <mx:AddChild>
         <mx:VBox width="100%" x="200">
         </mx:VBox>
      </mx:AddChild>
   </mx:State>
</mx:states>
```

As you remember from Lesson 3, "Laying Out the Interface," this is the basic structure for using a VBox in a state.

7 In the VBox, insert an `<mx:Text>` tag. Assign the following properties the associated values to display the product description:

```
text:    {groceryItem.description}
width:   50%
```

```
<mx:Text text="{groceryItem.description}"
   width="50%"/>
```

8 Below the `<mx:Text>` tag, insert an `<mx:Label>` tag. Assign the following properties the associated values:

```
text:    Certified Organic
visible: {groceryItem.isOrganic}
```

```
<mx:Label text="Certified Organic"
   visible="{groceryItem.isOrganic}"/>
```

You use the Boolean value of isOrganic to determine whether the Label should be displayed or not. This way the Label will be displayed only when a product is organic.

9 Insert another `<mx:Label>` to display if the product is low fat. Position this Label at *x, y* values 100, 60.

```
<mx:Label text="Low Fat"
   x="100" y="60"
   visible="{groceryItem.isLowFat}"/>
```

10 In the Add To Cart button, set the `visible` property to `false`.

Initially, you want the Button to not be visible because it will be part of the product details.

11 Just below the closing `<mx:AddChild>` tag and just above the closing `<mx:State>` tag, use an `<mx:SetProperty>` tag to have the Add To Cart Button's `visible` property set to `true`. You set the `target` by binding the Button's instance name of `add`.

```
    </mx:AddChild>
    <mx:SetProperty target="{add}"
        name="visible"
        value="true"/>
</mx:State>
```

This will make the Button visible when the expanded state is active.

12 Run the EComm.mxml application file and test the product details functionality.

When you move the mouse pointer over existing product information, you should see more product details. The text "Certified Organic" and "Low Fat" should appear only for certain products, and no extra space should be left if they are not organic or low fat.

Placing Products in the Shopping Cart

In this task, you improve how the products are placed in the shopping cart. You create a shopping cart component and use that when products are added to the cart.

1 Create another component in the views/ecomm folder named Cart.mxml and use a VBox tag as the base tag. Remove any `width` and `height` values.

This will eventually be your shopping cart display component.

2 In an `<mx:Script>` block, import the following three classes from the valueObjects folder: ShoppingCart, ShoppingCartItem, and Product.

3 Create a bindable public variable named `cart`, data typed as ShoppingCart.

This is the property to which the shopping cart data will be passed.

4 Create a private function named `renderLabel()`, data typed as String. The function should accept a parameter named `item`, data typed as ShoppingCartItem.

This function will create and return a String value that will be added to the List component that is currently the shopping cart display.

5 In the function, return the item quantity, product name and subtotal, concatenated as a single String. There should be a space between the quantity and name, and a colon between the name and subtotal:

```
return String(item.quantity)+" "+item.product.prodName+":"+String(item.subtotal);
```

This will populate the shopping cart as follows:

```
1 Swiss Cheese:4.95
2 T Bone Steak:19.96
```

Because the quantity and subtotal are numeric, you should cast them as Strings to be concatenated, although it is not required.

6 Below the `<mx:Script>` block, insert an `<mx:List>` tag. Give the List an id of `cartView`, bind the `dataProvider` to the `aItems` array of the `cart` property, and set the `labelFunction` property equal to the `renderLabel` function you just created.

```
<mx:List id="cartView"
    dataProvider="{cart.aItems}"
    labelFunction="renderLabel"/>
```

Each time an item is added to the shopping cart, the `cart` property of this component will be updated, causing the `dataProvider` to change; and the List updated.

7 Return to EComm.mxml and locate the `<mx:DataGrid>` tag in the cartView state.

8 Replace the `<mx:DataGrid>` tag with an instantiation of your Cart.mxml component. Set the id equal to `shoppingCart`, set the `width` to 100%, and bind the `cart` property to the cart variable:

```
<v:Cart id="shoppingCart"
    width="100%"
    cart="{cart}"/>
```

Notice the binding. This means that any time the `cart` variable changes on this page (items added or removed from the cart, for instance) the binding will be redone, and changes rippled into your Cart component.

9 In GroceryDetail.mxml, locate the `itemAdded()` function in which you currently trace the product. Replace the `trace` statement with an invocation of the `addToCart()` method of the EComm.mxml application file. Pass the `prod` variable as a parameter. To reference the EComm.mxml file, use the `mx.core.Application.application` property:

```
mx.core.Application.application.addToCart(prod);
```

What you are doing here is not a best practice. You will find in the next lesson a better way to pass the product to the `addToCart()` function.

⬥ **NOTE:** To access properties and methods of the top-level application, you can use the `application` property of the mx.core.Application class. This property provides a reference to the Application object from anywhere in your Flex application. Although this is possible, you should carefully consider its use because it will lead to tightly coupled components and might not be a best practice.

10 In EComm.mxml, change the access modifier of the `addToCart()` function from private to public.

This has to be done because you are accessing the method from outside the file itself.

11 Test the new functionality by running EComm.mxml.

After you add some items to the cart, click the View Cart button to see your shopping cart. You will see two shopping carts, one of which you will remove from a State in the next step.

12 In EComm.mxml, look for an `<mx:RemoveChild>` tag in the State in which the linkbutton1 object is the target. Add another `<mx:RemoveChild>` tag under the existing one in which the `target` removed is `cartView`.

```
<mx:RemoveChild target="{cartView}"/>
```

This prevents the two shopping carts, the one you created in the Cart component and the one in the `bodyBox` HBox near the end of the file, from being displayed at the same time.

13 Create a new folder under the FlexGrocer project named **as**.

14 Right-click on the new as directory and choose New > ActionScript File. In the New ActionScript File dialog box, set the filename to be **ecomm.as**; then click Finish. Remove any comments in the new file.

15 In EComm.mxml, cut all the ActionScript code that is between the character data tags in the `<mx:Script>` block and paste the code into the ecomm.as file.

You have moved this code into a separate file to keep the size of the MXML file more manageable.

⏵ **TIP:** To remove the excess tabs, highlight all the code and press the Shift+Tab key combination three times to move the appropriate code to the left margin.

16 In EComm.mxml, remove the `<mx:Script>` block and replace it with an `<mx:Script>` tag that uses the `source` property to point to the new ActionScript file just created:

```
<mx:Script source="as/ecomm.as"/>
```

Specifying a `source` property to include the ActionScript file is just as if the ActionScript were still in the MXML file. Again, this is not required and is just to make file sizes more manageable.

17 Test EComm.mxml; you should see no differences in functionality after moving the `<mx:Script>` block into a separate ActionScript file.

What You Have Learned

In this lesson, you have:

- Displayed various kinds of data using the HorizontalList (pages 189–192)

- Created a custom component that extends the functionality of the HorizontalList (pages 193–196)

- Built and used an `itemRenderer` (pages 193–196)

- Gained an overall understanding of the Repeater component and details of its use (pages 197–201)

- Used a Repeater to instantiate a custom component multiple times in a loop (pages 201–208)

- Displayed product details using a state (pages 209–211)

- Implemented shopping cart functionality using a custom component (pages 211–214)

What You Will Learn

In this lesson, you will:

- Understand the benefits of a loosely coupled architecture
- Dispatch events
- Declare events for a component
- Identify the need for custom event classes
- Create event subclasses
- Create and use a CategoryEvent class
- Create and use a ProductEvent class
- Use ProductEvent to remove a product from the cart
- Use ProductEvent to add a product to the cart
- Use event bubbling

Approximate Time

This lesson takes approximately 2 hours to complete.

Lesson Files

Media Files:

None

Starting Files:

Lesson09/start/DataEntry.mxml

Lesson09/start/EComm.mxml

Lesson09/start/as/ecomm.as

Lesson09/start/managers/CategorizedProductManager.mxml

Lesson09/start/valueObjects/Category.as

Lesson09/start/valueObjects/Product.as

Lesson09/start/valueObjects/ShoppingCart.as

Lesson09/start/valueObjects/ShoppingCartItem.as

Lesson09/start/views/dataEntry/UpdateDeleteProd.mxml

Lesson09/start/views/dataEntry/AddProduct.mxml

Lesson09/start/views/ecomm/Cart.mxml

Lesson09/start/views/ecomm/CategoryView.mxml

Lesson09/start/views/ecomm/FoodList.mxml

Lesson09/start/views/ecomm/GroceryDetail.mxml

Completed Files:

Lesson09/complete/DataEntry.mxml

Lesson09/complete/EComm.mxml

Lesson09/complete/as/EComm.as

Lesson09/complete/events/CatEvent.as

Lesson09/complete/events/ProductEvent.as

Lesson09/complete/managers/CategorizedProductManager.mxml

Lesson09/complete/utils/Util.as

Lesson09/complete/valueObjects/Category.as

Lesson09/complete/valueObjects/Product.as

Lesson09/complete/valueObjects/ShoppingCart.as

Lesson09/complete/valueObjects/ShoppingCartItem.as

Lesson09/complete/views/dataEntry/UpdateDeleteProd.mxml

Lesson09/complete/views/dataEntry/AddProduct.mxml

Lesson09/complete/views/ecomm/Cart.mxml

Lesson09/complete/views/ecomm/CategoryView.mxml

Lesson09/complete/views/ecomm/FoodList.mxml

Lesson09/complete/views/ecomm/GroceryDetail.mxml

LESSON 9

Using Custom Events

In the last few lessons, you worked with events from built-in objects, such as the click of a Button or the change of a List. As you get deeper into application development, you will often find a need to dispatch your own custom events. In this lesson, you will learn how to create an event object, set the metadata for the object, and dispatch it.

This lesson presents an overview of how to dispatch custom events within your application, and how to create new Event classes by creating a subclass of Event.

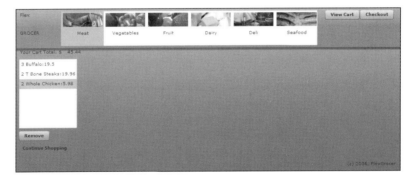

The shopping cart allows you to add and remove items.

Understanding the Benefits of a Loosely Coupled Architecture

At the end of Lesson 7, "Creating Components with MXML," you were left with a bad practice, having the CategorizedProductManager component reach into its parent document to inform the parent that the category data has been loaded. This created a *tightly coupled* application, in that the CategorizedProductManager component can work only if it knows the parent has a certain method. A far better practice—and better object-oriented design—is to use a *loosely coupled* architecture that is made possible by using events to notify other components of changes instead of requiring components to know information about the rest of the application. With a loosely coupled architecture like this, components can be reused across multiple applications without requiring a particular structure to the applications.

Dispatching Events

To broadcast an event from a component, you need to use the `dispatchEvent()` method. This method is defined in the flash.events.EventDispatcher class, which is a superclass in the hierarchy from which UIComponent inherits.

The following is the inheritance hierarchy of the UIComponent class:

```
mx.core.UIComponent extends
flash.display.Sprite extends
flash.display.DisplayObjectContainer extends
flash.display.InteractiveObject extends
flash.display.DisplayObject extends
flash.events.EventDispatcher
```

The `dispatchEvent()` method takes a single argument, which is an event object to be dispatched. When an event is dispatched, anything listening for that event is notified, and the specified event handlers are executed. This offers a much better alternative to tightly coupled architectures.

1 Open CategorizedProductManager.mxml from your flexGrocer/managers directory.

   If you skipped the lesson when this was created, you can open this file from the Lesson09/start/managers directory, and save it in your flexGrocer/managers directory.

2 At the end of the `prodByCategoryHandler()` method, find and delete the lines of code which explicitly call `categorizedProductDataLoaded()` in the parent. The lines to remove are as follows:

```
if(this.parentDocument.categorizedProductDataLoaded != null){
   this.parentDocument.categorizedProductDataLoaded(aCats);
}
```

   Here, you are eliminating the bad practice of tightly coupling this component to its parent.

3 Create a new instance of the event object, with a type `catDataLoaded`.

```
var e:Event = new Event("catDataLoaded");
```

This creates the new event object, which will be used in place of the tight coupling.

4 Just after creating the event object, dispatch it. Save this component.

```
this.dispatchEvent(e);
```

This dispatches the event so that any listening components can hear and respond to it.

5 Open DataEntry.mxml from your flexGrocer directory.

6 Find the instantiation of the CategorizedProductManager component. Listen for the `catDataLoadedEvent` and call the `categorizedProductDataLoaded()` method to handle the event.

```
<m:CategorizedProductManager id="prodMgr"
   catDataLoaded="categorizedProductDataLoaded()"/>
```

Don't be alarmed if you see a problem listed in the Problems panel when you save the file, it will be explained in step 8 and fixed in the next exercise.

7 Find the `categorizedProductDataLoaded()` method in the `<mx:Script>` block. Make the function private and remove the argument from it. Change the line setting of the categories property so that it's set to an ArrayCollection based on `prodMgr.getCats()` instead of on the argument you removed.

```
private function categorizedProductDataLoaded():void{
   categories=new ArrayCollection(prodMgr.getCats());
   foodColl=prodMgr.getCategorizedProducts();
}
```

You are now repurposing the method you wrote in Lesson 8, "Using Controls and Repeaters with Data Sets." You are no longer explicitly calling this method from the data manager; instead, this method is being invoked as a handler for the `catDataLoaded` event. As such, it no longer needs to be public. The array of categories is not passed into this method, so the array collection will be created using the `getCats()` method of the manager.

▶ **TIP:** Following best practices, if a method or property doesn't need to be public, it should not be.

As was mentioned in the previous step, if you save DataEntry.mxml now, you will see an error listed in the Problems panel. This is completely expected, and will be explained in the next step and fixed in the next exercise.

8 Save DataEntry.mxml. Look at the Problems panel and notice that an error exists.

The Problems panel is now showing an error: `Cannot resolve attribute 'catDataLoaded'` `for component type managers.CategorizedProductManager`. This error occurs because you are referring to an attribute of the `CategorizedProductManager` tag named `catDataLoaded`, but the compiler doesn't recognize any properties or events of that component with the name `catDataLoaded`.

For the compiler to know what `catDataLoaded` means, you need to add metadata to the component, specifically declaring any events that the component will dispatch.

Declaring Events for a Component

Every component needs to explicitly declare the events it can dispatch. Components that are subclasses of other components can also dispatch any events that its superclasses have declared. In Flex, events can be declared with metadata tags. This is done with the `[Event]` metadata tag, which is used to declare the event publicly so that the MXML compiler recognizes it. In MXML, an event declaration looks like this:

```
<mx:Metadata>
[Event(name="catDataLoaded",type="flash.events.Event")]
</mx:Metadata>
```

The `<mx:Metadata>` tag declares that the child elements are all metadata. Next, any metadata is declared. Notice that the tags are enclosed within square bracket. Details for these tags are defined within parentheses. In this example, you can see a `catDataLoaded` event declared. This event will be an instance of the flash.events.Event class. In this exercise, you will fix the error from the previous exercise by declaring a custom event for the CategorizedProductManager component.

1 Open CategorizedProductManager.mxml from your flexGrocer/managers directory.

Alternately, you can open CategorizedProductManager_dispatch.mxml from Lesson09/ intermediate/ and save it as **CategorizedProductManager.mxml** in your flexGrocer/ managers directory.

2 Before the `<mx:Script>` block, add a metadata block to declare the `catDataLoaded` event.

```
<mx:Metadata>
    [Event(name="catDataLoaded")]
</mx:Metadata>
```

Because the type has been omitted, the event must be an instance of the flash.events. Event class.

3 Save CategorizedProductManager.mxml. Run the DataEntry application.

The errors should now be gone, and the DataEntry application should run as it always did.

4 Open EComm.mxml from your flexGrocer directory.

5 Find the instantiation of the CategorizedProductManager component. Listen for the `catDataLoadedEvent` and call the `categorizedProductDataLoaded()` method to handle the event.

```
<m:CategorizedProductManager id="catProds"
    catDataLoaded="categorizedProductDataLoaded()" />
```

6 Open ecomm.as from your flexGrocer/as directory.

If you prefer, you can open this file from your Lesson09/start/as directory, and save it in your flexGrocer/as directory. If you recall, in the previous lesson, you moved the ActionScript for EComm.mxml into an external script file.

7 Find the `categorizedProductDataLoaded()` method. Make the function private and remove the argument from it. Change the line setting of the `categories` property so that it's set to an ArrayCollection based on `catProds.getCats()` instead of on the argument you removed.

```
private function categorizedProductDataLoaded():void{
    categories=new ArrayCollection(catProds.getCats());
}
```

8 Save both ecomm.as and EComm.mxml. Run the EComm application.

It should continue to run as it did at the end of the last lesson, although now uses a better, loosely coupled architecture.

Identifying the Need for Custom Event Classes

In the previous exercise, custom events were used to notify other parts of the application about a change in data. In addition to notifications, you sometimes need to pass data around with events. The base flash.events.Event class doesn't support this, but you can create an event subclass that does. The applications you have been building need a few different custom events to function properly. When all is said and done, several user tasks will generate events, for example:

In the DataEntry application:

- Adding a new product
- Updating an existing product
- Deleting a product

In the Ecomm application:

- Browsing for products by category

- Adding a product to a shopping cart

- Removing a product from a shopping cart

If you analyze these events carefully, you will see they all are events that need to pass along data, so the system can react properly (which product to add to the cart, which category to show, and so on). In fact, all these specifically have either a Category or a Product as their data. To facilitate this, you will create two event classes, ProductEvent and CategoryEvent.

So far, all the events you have used are instances of the built-in flash.events.Event class, which does not have a property to enable you to pass data along with an event; it has properties for things such as a type to uniquely identify the event and bubbles, which will be discussed later in this lesson.

As you saw earlier, you can broadcast an event from a component using the dispatchEvent() method.

Considering that dispatchEvent() accepts an event instance as an argument, any custom event classes you create should be a subclass of Event. You can add any methods or properties you need to your event, but you are required to override the clone() method. Overriding a method allows you to redefine a method from the superclass, for your new subclass. This allows you the flexibility to use the functionality you want from the superclass, as well as the ability to define custom functionality for your class. When you override a method, it needs to match the name, access modifier (public, protected, internal, etc.), return type, and argument list of the method from the superclass you are overriding. The clone() method returns a new copy of the Event object with the same values by setting the properties in the clone() method. Typically, you define the clone() method to return an instance of your newly created event class.

Building and Using the CategoryEvent

The first place you will use a custom event is for browsing products by categories. If you remember how the application was left at the end of Lesson 7, there was a tight coupling between the CategoryView component and the e-commerce application. When a user chose a category, this method fired:

```
private function displayProdByCategory():void{
    var prodArray:Array=catProds.getProdsForCat(catView.catSelected);
    prodByCategory=new ArrayCollection(prodArray);
}
```

The bolded code shows the main application file reaching into the CategoryView component to pull out data. Again, this tight coupling is undesirable. A far better solution is for the CategoryView to notify its controller (in this, case the EComm application) that a category had been selected. This event will want to carry an instance of the Category class to indicate which one was selected.

1 Right-click on the flexGrocer project and create a folder named events. Right-click the events folder and create a new ActionScript class. Name the class **CategoryEvent**, and set its superclass to Event.

Filling out the dialog box automatically creates the skeleton of the class seen here.

```
package events{
    import flash.events.Event;
    public class CategoryEvent extends Event {
    }
}
```

2 Inside the class definition, create a public property named cat to hold an instance of the valueObjects.Category class.

```
public var cat:Category;
```

If you use the Code completion feature, the import for the Category class will be automatically added; if not, you need to manually add the following:

```
import valueObjects.Category;
```

3 Create a constructor, which takes a Category and a string, defining the type as arguments. Pass the type to the superclass and set the cat property with the passed-in Category.

```
public function CategoryEvent(cat:Category, type:String){
    super(type);
    this.cat = cat;
}
```

Like all constructors in ActionScript 3.0, this one is also public. The two arguments will be used to populate the event. The cat property will be used to hold the data about the Category on which the event is acting. The type defines what is happening with the Category in this event. Because the constructor of the Event class is defined as accepting an event type as an argument, you can pass the type directly to the superclass to set it.

4 Override the clone() method so it returns a new instance of the CategoryEvent class.

```
public override function clone():Event{
    return new CategoryEvent(cat, type);
}
```

When you override a method in ActionScript 3.0, the method must be defined exactly like the method of the superclass and must include the override keyword. Therefore the clone() method needs to be defined as public override, it must take no arguments, and return an instance of the Event class.

The complete CategoryEvent class should look like the following code block:

```
package events{
    import flash.events.Event;
    import valueObjects.Category;
    public class CategoryEvent extends Event {
        public var cat:Category;
        public function CategoryEvent(cat:Category, type:String){
            super(type);
            this.cat = cat;
        }
        public override function clone():Event{
            return new CategoryEvent(cat, type);
        }
    }
}
```

5 Open CategoryView.mxml from your views/ecomm directory.

Alternatively, you can open it from your Lesson09/start/views/ecomm and save it in your flexGrocer/views/ecomm directory.

6 Inside the <mx:Script> block, find the method called categorySelect(), delete its contents, and write a line that builds a CategoryEvent based on the selectedItem from the HorizontalList, cast as a Category. As a second argument, pass the string categorySelect as the event name.

```
private function categorySelect():void{
   var e:CategoryEvent = new CategoryEvent(this.selectedItem
      ➥ as Category, "categorySelect");
   this.dispatchEvent(e);
}
```

The class definition for the selectedItem of a HorizontalList declares that it is of type Object. You need to tell the compiler that this particular Object is a Category, so that it will accept the value as a valid argument to the CategoryEvent constructor. If you used the code-completion features, imports for both Category and CategoryEvent will automatically be added to your class; otherwise, you will need to manually add imports for both of them.

```
import valueObjects.Category;
import events.CategoryEvent;
```

7 Before the <mx:Script> block, use metadata to declare the new event for the CategoryView component.

```
<mx:Metadata>
   [Event(name="categorySelect",type="events.CategoryEvent")]
</mx:Metadata>
```

Because the event is an instance of events.CategoryEvent, not directly an instance of flash.events.Event, the type declaration of the metadata is required.

Your CategoryView component is now fully equipped to be loosely coupled as it broadcasts an instance of the CategoryEvent class. All that remains to use it is to have the EComm.mxml application listen for and handle this event.

8 Open EComm.mxml from your flexGrocer directory and ecomm.as from your flexGrocer/as directory.

9 Find the instantiation of the CategoryView component. Remove the click handler and replace it with a categorySelect handler, passing the event object to the displayProdByCategory() method.

```
<v:CategoryView id="catView"
   width="600"
   left="100"
   cats="{categories}"
   categorySelect="displayProdByCategory(event)"/>
```

Here you are instructing the EComm application to listen for the `categorySelect` event from CategoryView. When the event is heard, the resulting event object is passed to the `displayProdByCategory()` method.

10 Find the `displayProdByCategory()` method in ecomm.as. Accept an argument containing a CategoryEvent. Remove the reference to `catView.catSelected` and replace it with the `id` of the selected `Category` in the `CategoryEvent`.

```
private function displayProdByCategory(event:CategoryEvent):void{
   var prodArray:Array=catProds.getProdsForCat(event.cat.catID);
   prodByCategory=new ArrayCollection(prodArray);
}
```

If the `import` statement for the CategoryEvent class was not automatically imported, then you will need to explicitly import that class.

```
import events.CategoryEvent;
```

11 Save and run the EComm application. It should run as it did earlier.

Creating and Using the ProductEvent Class

In this next exercise, you will create an event subclass called ProductEvent. ProductEvent will add a single property to the Event class named `product`, which will hold an instance of the Product value object (defined in Lesson 5, "Handling Events and Data Structures"). This procedure will follow the same structure as the CategoryEvent class you created in the last exercise.

1 Right-click the events folder, and create a new ActionScript class. Name the new class ProductEvent, ensure that the Package is set to events, and set Event as the superclass.

The skeleton for your new class should look like this:

```
package events {
   import flash.events.Event;

   public class ProductEvent extends Event {

   }
}
```

2 Create a property of your new class, named `product`, with a data type Product.

If you use code completion and choose the Product class from the list, the `import` statement for valueObjects.Product will automatically be added. If not, you will need to manually import the class.

```
package events {
   import flash.events.Event;
   import valueObjects.Product;

   public class ProductEvent extends Event {
      public var product:Product;
   }
}
```

3 Create a constructor for your class, which takes two arguments. The first argument is an instance of the Product class; the second is a String that indicates the type for the event.

```
public function ProductEvent(prod:Product, type:String){
   super(type);
   product = prod;
}
```

4 Override the base classes clone() method. This method will return a new instance of the ProductEvent class with the same `type` and `product`.

```
public override function clone():Event{
   return new ProductEvent(product, type);
}
```

5 Save the ProductEvent class and verify there are no errors in the Problems panel.

The class should currently look like this:

```
package events {
   import flash.events.Event;
   import valueObjects.Product;
   public class ProductEvent extends Event {
      public var product:Product;
      public function ProductEvent(prod:Product, type:String){
         super(type);
         product = prod;
      }
      public override function clone():Event{
         return new ProductEvent(product, type);
      }
   }
}
```

6 Open UpdateDeleteProd.mxml from your flexGrocer/views/dataEntry directory.

Alternately, you can open this file from the Lesson09/start/views/dataEntry directory, and save it in your flexGrocer/views/dataEntry directory.

7 Add a new private method named `broadcastEvent()`, which takes two arguments: the first an instance of the Product class; the second a String that describe the event type. Inside this method, create a new instance of the ProductEvent class with the two passed-in arguments and dispatch it.

```
private function broadcastEvent(prod:Product, type:String):void{
   var e:ProductEvent = new ProductEvent(prod,type);
   this.dispatchEvent(e);
}
```

Rather than having redundant logic in both `AddProduct` and `UpdateDeleteProduct`, both of which show a pop-up to confirm adding, editing, and deleting a product, both components will dispatch a ProductEvent and use an event type to indicate whether the product is being added, updated, or deleted.

If not automatically added by the code-completion feature, manually add the `import` statement for the ProductEvent class to the top of the `<mx:Script>` block:

```
import events.ProductEvent;
```

8 Find the `doProdUpdate()` method. Remove the call to `showPopUp()`. In its place, call the `broadcastEvent()` method and pass it the product and the string `productUpdate`.

```
broadcastEvent(prod,"productUpdate");
```

9 Find the `doProdDelete()` method. Remove the call to `showPopUp()`. In its place, call `broadcastEvent()` method, and pass it the product and the string `productDelete`.

```
broadcastEvent(prod,"productDelete");
```

10 Add metadata to declare that UpdateDeleteProd.mxml will dispatch events named `productUpdate` and `productDelete`. Declare both events to be of type events. ProductEvent.

```
<mx:Metadata>
   [Event(name="productUpdate",type="events.ProductEvent")]
   [Event(name="productDelete",type="events.ProductEvent")]
</mx:Metadata>
```

11 Open AddProduct.mxml from your flexGrocer/views/dataEntry directory.

Alternately, you can open this file from the Lesson09/start/views/dataEntry directory, and save it in your flexGrocer/views/dataEntry directory.

12 Find the doProdAdd() method. Remove the line calling the showPopUp() method, and instead, create a new instance of the ProductEvent class using the product created on the previous line and the string productAdded.

```
private function doProdAdd():void{
    var prod:Product = Product.buildProduct(prodModel);
    var o:ProductEvent = new ProductEvent(prod;productAdded');
    this.dispatchEvent(o);
}
```

Just as you did with UpdateDeleteProd, you are now preparing AddProduct to dispatch an event using the ProductEvent class.

If not automatically added, you will need to manually add the import statement for the ProductEvent class to the top of the <mx:Script> block:

```
import events.ProductEvent;
```

13 Add metadata to declare that AddProduct.mxml will dispatch an event named productAdded. Declare the event to be of type events.ProductEvent.

```
<mx:Metadata>
    [Event(name="productAdded";type="events.ProductEvent")]
</mx:Metadata>
```

14 Delete the the showPopUp() method from UpdateDeleteProd. Copy and delete the showPopUp() method from AddProduct.

This method will be implemented in DataEntry instead.

15 Open DataEntry.mxml from your flexGrocer directory. After the imports, create a private property named win of type ConfirmScreen.

```
private var win:ConfirmScreen;
```

This will hold the instance of the window that is launched. If you use the code-completion features, the import will automatically be added for you.

16 Inside the <mx:Script> block, paste the showPopUp() method you copied in step 14.

```
private function showPopUp(prod:Product, title:String):void{
    win = ConfirmScreen(PopUpManager.createPopUp(this, ConfirmScreen, true));
    win.prod = prod;
    win.title = title;
}
```

17 At the top of the `<mx:Script>` block, add imports for valueObjects.Product and mx.managers.PopUpManager.

```
import valueObjects.Product;
import mx.managers.PopUpManager;
```

You just added calls to these classes in the previous step. Because you were pasting code, there was no chance to use code completion and have the imports automatically added, so you need to manually import the classes.

18 Call your newly created `showPopUp()` method as the event handler for `productAdded`, `productDelete`, and `productUpdate`.

```
<v:UpdateDeleteProd
    units="{units}"
    foodColl="{foodColl}"
    productUpdate="showPopUp(event.product,'Product Updated')"
    productDelete="showPopUp(event.product,'Product Deleted')"/>
<v:AddProduct
    cats="{categories}"
    units="{units}"
    productAdded="showPopUp(event.product,'Product Added')"/>
```

Now, the DataEntry application is solely responsible for showing confirmation pop-ups. You no longer have to handle it in each child component. If you save and test the application, it will continue to behave as it did in the previous lesson, but it is built in a far more maintainable and reusable manner.

Using ProductEvent to Remove a Product from the Cart

At the end of Lesson 8, you had the ability to add items to your shopping cart, but no means to remove them from the cart. The same ProductEvent class that you wrote for the DataEntry application can be used any time an event needs to carry a Product with it. One such case is when the user decides to remove a product from the shopping cart. In this next exercise, you will use the same ProductEvent class to facilitate removing items from the cart.

1 Open Cart.mxml from flexGrocer/views/ecomm.

Alternatively, you can open the file from Lesson09/start/views/ecomm and save it in your flexGrocer/views/ecomm directory.

2 Add a Button after the List, with a label Remove, and add a `click` event handler that will call a soon-to-be-written method called `removeItem()`.

```
<mx:Button label="Remove"
    click="removeItem();"/>
```

This will allow the user to choose an item in the List and click this button to remove it.

3 Create a new method called removeItem(). This method should use the selectedItem property of the List control to find the ShoppingCartItem, which is selected. Using the ShoppingCartItem, you can find the product for the selected item.

```
private function removeItem():void{
    var item:ShoppingCartItem = cartView.selectedItem as ShoppingCartItem;
    var prod:Product = item.product;
}
```

Currently, this method extracts the product from the selectedItem of the cart List. Knowing the product, you can now create a ProductEvent for it. Remember that if you want to treat the selectedItem as a member of the ShoppingCartItem class, you need to use casting to remind the compiler that the selectedItem of this List is a ShoppingCartItem.

> **TIP:** These two lines:

```
var item:ShoppingCartItem = cartView.selectedItem as ShoppingCartItem;;
var prod:Product = item.product;
```

could be combined into a single line if you prefer:

```
var prod:Product = (cartView.selectedItem as ShoppingCartItem).product;
```

4 At the end of the removeItem() method, create an instance of the ProductEvent class with the selected product and a type of productRemoved. Dispatch the event instance.

```
var e:ProductEvent = new ProductEvent(prod,"productRemoved");
this.dispatchEvent(e);
```

If not automatically added, you will need to specifically add the import statements for the ProductEvent class.

```
import events.ProductEvent;
```

> **TIP:** These two lines:

```
var e:ProductEvent = new ProductEvent(prod, "productRemoved");
this.dispatchEvent(e);
```

could be done as a single line:

```
this.dispatchEvent(new ProductEvent(prod, "productRemoved"));
```

Or you can combine it with the previous tip:

```
this.dispatchEvent(new ProductEvent(ShoppingCartItem(
    cartView.selectedItem).product, "productRemoved");
```

However, it is easier to understand (and therefore maintain), if you leave it as the four lines:

```
var item:ShoppingCartItem = cartView.selectedItem as ShoppingCartItem;
var prod:Product = item.product;
var e:ProductEvent = new ProductEvent(prod,"productRemoved");
this.dispatchEvent(e);
```

5 Add metadata to declare the `productRemoved` event as an instance of the events.ProductEvent class.

```
<mx:Metadata>
   [Event(name="productRemoved",type="events.ProductEvent")]
</mx:Metadata>
```

All that remains is to have the EComm.mxml application listen for this event and remove the product when the event is heard.

6 Open EComm.mxml from your directory. Find the instantiation of `Cart`. Listen for the `productRemoved` event and handle it by passing the event.product object to the deleteProd() method.

```
<v:Cart id="shoppingCart"
   width="100%"
   cart="{cart}"
   productRemoved="deleteProd(event.product)"/>
```

The event that you are receiving here is a ProductEvent, which, as you defined earlier, has a property called `product`. Because the `deleteProd()` method was already written to accept a `product` as an argument, you can reuse the same method without changing it by just passing it the `product` from the event. If you save and run the application, you will find it is still functioning properly, and is built with a much more sound architecture.

▶ **TIP:** If you click the Remove button without selecting an item in the List first, a run-time error will occur. In Lesson 25, "Debugging and Optimizing Flex Applications," you will learn about different strategies for catching and handling this error.

Using ProductEvent to Add a Product to the Cart

The ProductEvent class can also put to use to add products to the shopping cart. At the end of Lesson 8, items were added to the shopping cart from the GroceryDetail component with this line of code:

```
mx.core.Application.application.addToCart(prod);
```

This is tightly coupling the GroceryDetail so that it can be used only in an application that has a method named *addToCart()* in the root application file. A far better practice is for the component to dispatch an event and pass along the product to be added.

1 Open GroceryDetail.mxml from flexGrocer/views/ecomm.

Alternatively, you can open the file from Lesson09/start/views/ecomm and save it in your flexGrocer/views/ecomm directory.

2 Find the `itemAdded()` method and remove the `mx.core.Application.application.`
`addToCart` line. Instead create an instance of the `ProductEvent` class which uses the same product, and has its type set to `itemAdded`. Then dispatch that event.

```
private function itemAdded(prod:Product):void{
    var e:ProductEvent = new ProductEvent(prod,"itemAdded");
    dispatchEvent(e);
}
```

Again, the tightly coupled references are removed and replaced with event-based architecture. Determine if you need to specifically add the import for the ProductEvent class.

```
import events.ProductEvent;
```

3 Add metadata to indicate that GroceryDetail will dispatch an event called `itemAdded()` of type events.ProductEvent.

```
<mx:Metadata>
    [Event(name="itemAdded",type="events.ProductEvent")]
</mx:Metadata>
```

Now that GroceryDetail is dispatching the event, you want its parent, FoodList, to listen for and handle the event.

> ● **TIP:** In the next section, you will see how event bubbling can simplify this process, enabling the event to pass through FoodList without FoodList explicitly redispatching it.

4 Open FoodList.mxml from flexGrocer/views/ecomm.

5 Find where GroceryDetail is instantiated. Add an event handler for the `itemAdded` event and pass the event object to a method you will add shortly named `addItem()`.

```
<v:GroceryDetail id="prod"
    width="80%"
    groceryItem="{foodRepeater.currentItem}"
    itemAdded="addItem(event)"/>
```

Here, you are listening for the itemAdded event and handling it with the addItem() method.

6 Create a new private method called addItem(), which accepts an argument named event as an instance of the ProductEvent class. The method should return void. Inside the function, use the dispatchEvent() method to rebroadcast the event.

```
private function addItem(event:ProductEvent):void{
   this.dispatchEvent(event);
}
```

Determine if you need to add the import statement for the ProductEvent class.

```
import events.ProductEvent
```

7 Add metadata to indicate that this method will dispatch an event called itemAdded that will be an instance of the events.ProductEvent class.

```
<mx:Metadata>
   [Event(name="itemAdded",type="events.ProductEvent")]
</mx:Metadata>
```

You can actually cut and paste this from GroceryDetail if you prefer because it is identical to the definition there.

8 Open EComm.mxml from your directory

Alternatively, you can open EComm_remove.mxml from Lesson09/intermediate and save it as **EComm.mxml** in your directory.

9 Find the instantiation of FoodList. Listen for the itemAdded event and handle it by passing the event.product object to the addToCart() method.

```
<v:FoodList id="prodTile"
   width="100%" height="100%"
   prodByCategory="{prodByCategory}"
   itemAdded="addToCart(event.product)"/>
```

The event that you are receiving here is the ProductEvent you dispatched from the GroceryDetail. Because the addToCart() method was already written to accept a product as an argument, you can reuse the same method without changing it by just passing it the product from the event.

If you save the files and run the EComm application now, it should continue to run as it did.

Understanding Event Flow and Event Bubbling

It might be helpful to understand how Flash Player handles events. Whenever an event occurs, Flash Player dispatches an event. If the event target is not a visible element on the screen, Flash Player can dispatch the event object directly to the designated target. For example, Flash Player dispatches the result event directly to an HTTPService component. However, if the target is a visible element on the screen, Flash Player dispatches the event and it travels from the outermost container (the Application container), down through the target component, and then back up to the Application container.

Event flow is a description of how that event object travels through an application. As you have seen by now, Flex applications are structured in a parent-child hierarchy, with the Application container being the top-level parent. Earlier in this lesson, you saw that flash.events.EventDispatcher is the superclass for all components in Flex. This means that every object in Flex can use events and participate in the event flow; they can all listen for an event with the addEventListener() method, but will hear the event only if the listening object is part of the event flow.

When an event occurs, an event object makes a round trip from the root application, through each of the containers on the way to the component that was responsible for the event (known as the *target* of the event). For example, if a user clicks a Button named button, Flash Player will dispatch an event object whose target is button. Although the target of an event is constant throughout the flow, an event object also has a currentTarget property, which indicates which element in the flow currently has the event object.

The event flow is conceptually divided into three parts:

- The *capture phase* comprises all the containers from the base application to the one containing the event's target.

- The *target phase* consists solely of the target node.

- The *bubbling phase* comprises all the elements encountered on the return trip from the target back to the root application.

The following image describes a branch of an application, in which a Button is contained within an HBox, which is contained by a Panel, which sits in the root Application. For the context of this example, other elements in the application are moot.

| Application |
| Panel |
| HBox |
| Button |

If a user clicks the Button, Flash Player dispatches an event object into the event flow. The object's journey starts at the Application, moves down to the Panel, moves to the HBox and finally gets to the Button. The event object then "bubbles" back up to Application, moving again through the HBox and Panel on its way up.

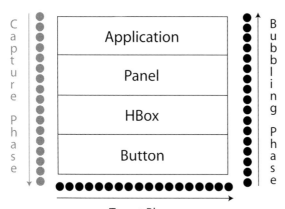

Target Phase

In this example, the capture phase includes the Application, Panel and HBox during the initial downward journey. The target phase comprises the time spent at the Button. The bubbling phase comprises the HBox, Panel, and then Application containers as they are encountered during the return trip.

This event flow offers far more power and flexibility to programmers than the event model of previous versions of ActionScript. Prior to Flex 2, event listeners had to be assigned directly to the object that generated an event. In Flex 2, you can still do this or you can register event listeners on any node along the event flow.

All instances of the Event class have a bubbles property that indicates whether that event object will participate in the bubbling phase of the event flow. You can look to the API documentation to find out whether a particular event type will bubble.

In practicality, this means that an event can occur in a child component and be heard in a parent. Consider this simple example:

```
<?xml version="1.0" encoding="utf-8"?>
<mx:Application xmlns:mx="http://www.adobe.com/2006/mxml"
   click="showAlert(event)" >
   <mx:Script>
      import mx.controls.Alert;
      private function showAlert(event:Event){
         var msg:String = event.target.toString() +" clicked";
         Alert.show(msg);
      }
   </mx:Script>
   <mx:Panel id="panel"
      click="showAlert(event)" >
      <mx:HBox id="hbox"
         click="showAlert(event)" >
         <mx:Button id="button"
            click="showAlert(event)"/>
      </mx:HBox>
   </mx:Panel>
</mx:Application>
```

In this case, there is a Button control inside an HBox, inside a Panel, inside an Application. When the button is clicked, the click event of the Button control is heard from the event handler of the Button, HBox control, Panel, and Application, and as such, four Alert boxes pop up, all saying the following:

```
Application4.panel:Panel.hbox:HBox.button:Button clicked
```

The click event of the Button control can be captured at the Button control itself or in any of the parent containers of the Button instance. This happens because click is a bubbling event. The bubbles property of the Event class is Boolean, which indicates whether an event should bubble. By default, bubbles is set to false on newly created events (although it is preset to true for some built-in events, such as click). When you create event instances or event subclass instances, you can decide whether you want to enable bubbling for the event. If you leave the bubbling to the default false value, the event can be captured only at the source of the event (the Button control in the preceding example). However, if it is set to true, it can be captured by a parent of the dispatching component (such as the HBox, Panel and Application).

In the EComm application, when the itemAdded event is dispatched from the GroceryDetail component, currently you are capturing the event in FoodList and then redispatching it.

However, if the ProductEvent could optionally be set to bubble, there would be no need for the FoodList to capture and rebroadcast the event—it could be handled directly in the EComm application.

1 Open ProductEvent.as from your flexGrocer/events directory.

Alternatively, you can open ProductEvent_initial.as from Lesson09/intermediate and save it in your flexGrocer/events directory as **ProductEvent.as**.

2 Add a third argument to the constructor: bubbles—of data type Boolean with a default value of `false`.

```
public function ProductEvent(prod:Product, type:String, bubbles:Boolean=false){
```

Throughout this lesson, you have been creating instances of the ProductEvent class, which did not bubble. So you don't need to go back to all of them and specifically specify `false` as the third argument to the constructor. A default value of `false` is used. Therefore, when only two values are passed, the bubbles argument comes through as `false`.

3 Inside the constructor, pass the `bubbles` argument to the constructor of the superclass. You should also pass the `bubbles` parameter in the call to create a new ProductEvent in the `clone()` method.

```
package events{
   import flash.events.Event;
   import valueObjects.Product;
   public class ProductEvent extends Event{
      public var product:Product;
      public function ProductEvent(prod:Product, type:String,
         ➥ bubbles:Boolean=false){
         super(type, bubbles);
         product = prod;
      }
      public override function clone():Event{
         return new ProductEvent(product, type, bubbles);
      }

   }
}
```

The flash.events.Event class takes an optional second argument to its constructor that indicates whether the event should bubble. If not provided, the default value of `false` is used.

Save and close ProductEvent.as. It is now ready to creating bubbling instances when requested.

4 Open GroceryDetail.mxml from flexGrocer/views/ecomm.

Alternatively, you can open GroceryDetail_event from Lesson09/intermediate and save it as **GroceryDetail.mxml** in your flexGrocer/views/ecomm directory.

5 Inside the `itemAdded()` method, add `true` as the third argument when creating the ProductEvent instance.

```
private function itemAdded(prod:Product):void{
   var e:ProductEvent = new ProductEvent(prod,"itemAdded",true);
   dispatchEvent(e);
}
```

This one instance of the ProductEvent class is told to bubble. Now you no longer need to capture the event in FoodList; you can instead capture it directly in EComm.

Save and close GroceryDetail.mxml.

6 Open FoodList.mxml from views/ecomm.

Alternatively, you can open FoodList_event from Lesson09/intermediate and save it as **FoodList.mxml** in your views/ecomm directory.

7 Remove the `itemAdded` event handler from the instantiation of the GroceryList component. Also delete the `addItem` method from this file.

The remaining code in FoodList.mxml should look like this:

```
<?xml version="1.0" encoding="utf-8"?>
<mx:VBox xmlns:mx="http://www.adobe.com/2006/mxml"
   xmlns:v="views.ecomm.*">
   <mx:Metadata>
      [Event(name="itemAdded",type="events.ProductEvent")]
   </mx:Metadata>
   <mx:Script>
      <![CDATA[
         import mx.collections.ArrayCollection;
         import events.ProductEvent;
         [Bindable]
         public var prodByCategory:ArrayCollection;
      ]]>
   </mx:Script>
   <mx:Repeater id="foodRepeater"
      width="100%" height="100%"
      dataProvider="{prodByCategory}">
      <v:GroceryDetail id="prod"
         width="80%"
         groceryItem="{foodRepeater.currentItem}"/>
   </mx:Repeater>
</mx:VBox>
```

You no longer need to capture and redispatch the `itemAdded` event here. You do, however, need to have the Event metadata for `itemAdded`, so the compiler will enable EComm to listen to this component for the event.

Save and close FoodList.mxml. Run EComm.mxml and notice that items are still properly added to the cart.

What You Have Learned

In this lesson, you have:

- Understood the benefits of a loosely-coupled architecture (pages 219–221)
- Dispatched events (pages 219–221)
- Declared events for a component (pages 221–222)
- Identified the need for custom event classes (pages 222–223)
- Created and used a CategoryEvent class (pages 223–227)
- Created and used a ProductEvent class (pages 227–231)
- Used ProductEvent to remove a product from the cart (pages 231–233)
- Used ProductEvent to add a product to the cart (pages 233–235)
- Learned about event bubbling (pages 236–241)

What You Will Learn

In this lesson, you will:

- Create a class for your component

- Embed images in ActionScript

- Instantiate Flex components in ActionScript

- Programmatically add components to a Container

- Override the `createChildren()` and `updateDisplayList()` methods

- Understand the `rawChildrenList` property of Containers

Approximate Time

This lesson takes approximately 1 hour and 30 minutes to complete.

Lesson Files

Media Files:

None

Starting Files:

Lesson10/start/Dashboard.mxml
Lesson10/start/views/dashboard/ChartPod.mxml

Completed Files:

Lesson10/complete/Dashboard.mxml
Lesson10/complete/views/Dashboard/ChartPod.mxml
Lesson10/complete/views/MaxRestorePanel.as

Creating Custom Components with ActionScript 3.0

In Lesson 7, "Creating Components with MXML," you learned how to build custom components using MXML. There are times when you will need even more flexibility than MXML can offer you. For these occasions, you can create components in ActionScript 3.0.

In this lesson, you will create a new component called MaxRestorePanel, which extends the Panel component and adds icons to the title bar to enable users to choose to maximize or restore the panel.

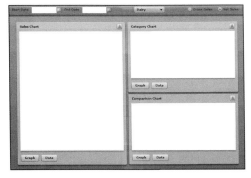

The Dashboard will use your new component instead of the Panel.

Here you see the MaxRestorePanel in its maximized state.

Introducing Building a Component with ActionScript 3.0

In an earlier lesson you learned that any code written in MXML is first translated into Action-Script, before being compiled into a SWF file. In reality, every Flex component that exists is an ActionScript class, regardless of whether it's a UI control, a Container, or some other type of component. Anything you might create in MXML can also be created in ActionScript, and there are things you can do with ActionScript that are not available purely from MXML. This makes it possible to create custom components either in MXML, as you explored in Lesson 7, or you can develop more advanced components purely in ActionScript 3.0, as you will learn in this lesson.

The steps you will take in creating an ActionScript 3.0 component are very similar to the steps you take for building any ActionScript 3.0 class. First, determine what (if any) superclass your new class will extend. Then determine what properties you will need to declare for your class. Next, determine any new methods you might need to implement. You will also need to declare any events your component will dispatch. If your component is a visual class, you will likely need to override createChildren() and updateDisplayList() because they are the methods that Flex components use to create and lay out any child elements of the components.

Creating the Structure of the Class

To create a component with ActionScript 3.0, you will define the component as an ActionScript class. You must decide what superclass you will use for the class. This decision will often be based on the functionality you want for your new component. In the case of the MaxRestorePanel class that you are building here, you want the general look, feel, and behavior of the Panel class, so you can use that as your superclass.

1 In Flex Builder 2, choose File > New > ActionScript Class. Set the package to be views, the name of the class to be MaxRestorePanel, and the superclass to be Panel. Save this file as **FlexGrocer/views/MaxRestorePanel.as**.

This class is created in the views directory because it is not specific to any of the three applications, but can be used by any or all of them. Panel was chosen as a superclass because the intention is to create a component that looks like a Panel, with the addition of a Button for the user to maximize the Panel, or to restore it to its original state.

2 After the package declaration, but before the class declaration, add imports for the flash.events.Event and mx.controls.Button classes.

The import for mx.containers.Panel was automatically added by the wizard when you chose Panel as the superclass. The completed class will need to broadcast events to let a containing MXML file know the user has requested the Panel be maximized or restored, so you will need the Event class. The button, which the user will click to change the state of the Panel, will be an instance of the mx.controls.Button class, so it also needs to be imported.

```
package views {
    import mx.containers.Panel;
    import mx.controls.Button;
    import flash.events.Event;
    public class MaxRestorePanel extends Panel {

    }
}
```

3 Inside the class definition, create a private property named `state`, which will hold a value representing whether the Panel is currently maximized or not. Set its default value to 0.

```
private var state:int = 0;
```

A value of 0 will indicate the Panel is in its normal state; a value of 1 will indicate that it is maximized. Your Panel will start in a normal (non-maximized) state, so the initial value is 0.

▶ **TIP:** Because there will be only two states for the panel, you could use a Boolean property instead; however, in the future you might want to further extend this component with other states, such as minimized, so this is being set as an `int`.

4 Create another private property named `btStateUp` as an instance of the Button class.

```
private var btStateUp: Button;
```

`btStateUp` will be a reference to the button a user can click to request the Panel be maximized.

5 Create one more private property named `btStateDown` as an instance of the Button class.

```
private var btStateDown: Button;
```

`btStateDown` will be a reference to the button a user can click to request the Panel be restored.

Next, you need to embed the images that will be used for the buttons. In Lesson 4, "Using Simple Controls," you learned about the `@Embed` directive for embedding images from MXML. You can use the same strategy, with slightly different syntax, for embedding images in an ActionScript 3.0 class. In ActionScript 3.0, the `[Embed("path to file")]` metadata tag is used to embed an asset. On the line immediately following the `@Embed` directive, a variable should be created (of the type Class) to hold a reference to the embedded asset.

6 After the other property definitions, use an `[Embed]` metadata tag to embed upArrow.gif.

```
[Embed("../assets/upArrow.gif")]
```

When using the [Embed] metadata tag, the path to the file is relative to the component into which the asset is embedded. Many other things you do in Flex (such as defining XML namespaces) are relative to the application's root. The [Embed] tag does not follow this model; it uses a relative reference from the component that is using it.

7 On the next line, create a variable named buttonUpIcon of the type Class.

```
private var buttonUpIcon:Class;
```

By declaring this variable right after the [Embed] tag, the Flex compiler knows to use this variable as a reference to the embedded image.

8 Create another [Embed] metadata tag, this time referencing downArrow.gif. Create a variable for this asset, named buttonDownIcon of the type Class.

```
[Embed("../assets/downArrow.gif")]
private var buttonDownIcon:Class;
```

9 At the top of the class, after the import statements but before the class definition, declare metadata tags for the Maximize and Restore events.

```
[Event(name="restore")]
[Event(name="maximize")]
```

As was discussed in the previous lesson, when a component broadcasts custom events, the events should be explicitly enumerated with metadata. Because these events are both of the default flash.events.Event type, the type attribute of the [Event] metadata tag does not need to be specified.

10 Create a new private method setState(), which takes an int as an argument and returns void. This method will take the argument and set the component instance's state property equal to the value passed in. Then it will check the value and dispatch either a maximize event or restore event, depending on whether the value is 1 or 0, respectively.

```
private function setState(state:int):void{
    this.state=state;
    if (state==0){
        this.dispatchEvent(new Event('restore'));
    } else {
        this.dispatchEvent(new Event('maximize'));
    }
}
```

This method will dispatch the events that you defined, which gives you a single method that is solely responsible for informing any listeners that the user has clicked the Maximize or Restore buttons. When you add the buttons later in this lesson, the event handlers for each of the buttons will call this method to handle the event dispatching.

11 Save your class file.

There is no need to test the class at this point because you haven't yet created any visual elements for your new component. At the end of the next exercise, you will have the ChartPod.mxml component use your new class.

At this point, the class definition for your MaxRestorePanel should read like this:

```
package views{
   import mx.containers.Panel;
   import mx.controls.Button;
   import flash.events.Event;
   [Event(name="restore")]
   [Event(name="maximize")]
   public class MaxRestorePanel extends Panel{
      private var state:int = 0;
      private var btStateUp: Button;
      private var btStateDown: Button;
      [Embed("../assets/upArrow.gif")]
      private var buttonUpIcon:Class;
      [Embed("../assets/downArrow.gif")]
      private var buttonDownIcon:Class;
      private function setState(state:int):void{
         this.state=state;
         if (state==0){
            this.dispatchEvent(new Event('restore'));
         } else {
            this.dispatchEvent(new Event('maximize'));
         }
      }
   }
}
```

Overriding the createChildren() Method

When creating a component in MXML, elements can be added to the component using standard MXML tags. These tags are not available to you when you create components in ActionScript, so to create children of your component, you need to override the createChildren() method of your components superclass. The createChildren() method is automatically called during the initialization sequence of a Flex component.

The initialization sequence is the following:

```
Constructor
createChildren()
commitProperties()
measure()
updateDisplayList()
```

The four methods after the constructor are initially implemented in mx.core.UIObject. Virtually any ActionScript 3.0 component you create will need to override the createChildren() and updateDisplayList() methods, as you will do in the next few exercises. The commitProperties() method needs to be overridden only if you need to set properties dependant on other properties that are already set, or if you want to explicitly pass in properties to be set on newly created components. After all the children of a component are created, commitProperties() is called to set all the properties passed in. By waiting until this method is called, you know that the children have already been successfully instantiated before their properties are set. The measure() method exists to enable you to manually calculate the height and width of all created children, if necessary. This method often needs to be overridden for creation of new containers with unique layout rules. In the case of the MaxRestorePanel, the commitProperties() and measure() methods of the superclass (Panel) are adequate and therefore do not need to be overridden.

Creating a Button in ActionScript

When working with ActionScript 3.0 components, you need a way to instantiate child components. Fortunately, Flex 2 and ActionScript 3.0 enable you to do this just like any other class you instantiate by using the new keyword. To create a new instance of the Button component, you would simply declare the following:

```
import mx.controls.Button;
var myButton:Button = new Button();
```

After you instantiate the Button, you can set any properties on it, just as you would with any other object, such as the following:

```
myButton.label = "click me";
myButton.addEventListener("click",doClick);
myButton.width=150;
```

Using the addChild() Method to Add the Button to your Component

Merely creating a component does not add it to the interface. As you learned earlier, user interface elements in Flex must be shown within a container. To add an element to a container, you need to use the container's addChild() method. The mx.core.Container class implements the addChild() method that will append the new child in the container. Depending on the type of container, this may impact where in the container the child is shown. For example, a VBox shows its children in order vertically, so the first child is shown on top, the next vertically below the first, and so on. So, in the following example, the order in which the children are added dictates the order in which they appear.

```
package {
    import mx.containers.VBox;
    import mx.controls.Label;
    public class Test extends VBox{
        protected override function createChildren(): void {
            var a:Label = new Label();
            a.text = "label one";
            this.addChild(a);
            var b:Label = new Label();
            b.text = "label two";
            this.addChild(b);
            var c:Label = new Label();
            c.text = "label three";
            this.addChild(c);
        }
    }
}
```

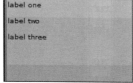

Had this class instead been based on the Canvas class, all three labels would be stacked up on top of each other, as they would all be placed at an *x* and *y* of 0.

> **TIP:** You can explicitly declare where you want a child created by using *addChildAt()* instead of *addChild()*. Both methods are available to all containers.

Understanding chrome and rawChildren

Flex containers have two distinct sections: the layout area, in which their children are drawn; and the chrome, which consists of all the other elements, such as borders, backgrounds, margins, scrollbars, headers, footers, and so on. In the Panel class, the title bar of a panel is implemented as chrome.

The base class flash.display.DisplayObjectContainer does not draw any distinction between child components and chrome—they are all accessible using the getChildAt and numChildren properties. However, the mx.core.Container class (the superclass for all Flex containers) over-rides several methods, including getChildAt() and numChildren(), to give the appearance that the container's only children are the child components. To gain access to all of the elements, you need to use the rawChildren property. Likewise, to add elements to the chrome (as you will do in the next exercise when you add a Maximize and Restore button), they need to be added to the rawChildren property. With a Panel, any children added with addChild() will be rendered below the title bar. If you want to add elements to the title bar, you must use rawChildren.addChild().

Using addChild on rawChildren to Add Elements to the Chrome

In this exercise, you will add two buttons to the chrome of your MaxRestorePanel.

1 Open the MaxRestorePanel.as file you created earlier in this lesson.

This file contains the skeleton of the new class you wrote earlier.

2 Create a new protected function named createChildren(), which overrides the function from the superclass.

```
protected override function createChildren(): void {
}
```

As was mentioned in Lesson 9, "Using Custom Events," any method overriding a method from a superclass must have exactly the same signature; therefore, your createChildren() method must be protected and must have the same argument list (in this case, none), and the same return type: void.

3 Inside the new function, call the superclass' createChildren() method.

```
super.createChildren();
```

You still need the rest of the Panel's chrome to be created, so you should explicitly invoke the createChildren() method of the superclass, so those elements will still be created.

4 Create the new btStateUp button.

```
btStateUp = new Button();
```

In the property definitions at the top of the class, you declared variables for two buttons: btStateUp and btStateDown. This is instantiating a button into the first of these two.

5 Create the new btStateDown button

```
btStateDown = new Button();
```

6 Set event listeners on each button. Clicking btStateUp should fire a soon-to-be-written method called doMaximize(); clicking btStateDown should fire a soon-to-be-written method called doRestore().

```
btStateUp.addEventListener("click",doMaximize);
btStateDown.addEventListener("click",doRestore);
```

7 Use the buttons' `setStyle()` methods to set the embedded graphics as the icons for the buttons.

```
btStateUp.setStyle("overIcon",buttonUpIcon);
btStateUp.setStyle("downIcon",buttonUpIcon);
btStateUp.setStyle("upIcon",buttonUpIcon);
btStateDown.setStyle("overIcon",buttonDownIcon);
btStateDown.setStyle("downIcon",buttonDownIcon);
btStateDown.setStyle("upIcon",buttonDownIcon);
```

You will learn about the `setStyle()` method in detail in Lesson 16, "Customizing the Look and Feel of a Flex Application." For now, it's worthwhile to understand that you can use the `setStyle()` method to specify an icon to use for each of the states. The up state is the normal default appearance; the over state is how the button appears when the mouse is over it; the down state is how the button appears when the mouse is clicked on the button. For now, you are setting all three states to be the same, so the button will not change its appearance when the user moves their mouse over it or clicks it.

8 Set the initial visibility of the buttons so that `btStateUp` is visible and `btStateDown` is not when the application starts.

```
btStateUp.visible =true;
btStateDown.visible =false;
```

In a few steps, you will add code to ensure that only one button is seen whenever it's clicked. The previous line ensures that the MaxRestorePanel starts with only a single button visible as well.

9 Add the newly created buttons to the `rawChildren` property.

```
rawChildren.addChild(btStateUp);
rawChildren.addChild(btStateDown);
```

At this point, the `createChildren()` method should look like this:

```
protected override function createChildren(): void {
    super.createChildren();
    btStateUp = new Button();
    btStateDown = new Button();
    btStateUp.addEventListener("click",doMaximize);
    btStateDown.addEventListener("click",doRestore);
    btStateUp.setStyle("overIcon",buttonUpIcon);
    btStateUp.setStyle("downIcon",buttonUpIcon);
    btStateUp.setStyle("upIcon",buttonUpIcon);
    btStateDown.setStyle("overIcon",buttonDownIcon);
    btStateDown.setStyle("downIcon",buttonDownIcon);
```

code continues on next page

```
btStateDown.setStyle("upIcon",buttonDownIcon);
btStateUp.visible =true;
btStateDown.visible =false;
rawChildren.addChild(btStateUp);
rawChildren.addChild(btStateDown);
}
```

10 Create a doMaximize() method, which will set the state property to 1; toggle the visibility of the buttons, so that btStateDown is visible and btStateUp is not.

```
private function doMaximize(event:Event) :void{
   setState(1);
   btStateUp.visible = false;
   btStateDown.visible = true;
}
```

This method will call the setState() method you wrote earlier, and pass it the value 1. This tells your Panel it should become maximized. When you set the state to maximized, the btStateUp button is hidden, and the btStateDown button is shown.

11 Create a doRestore() method to set the current state to 0; toggle the visibility of the buttons, so that btStateUp is visible and btStateDown is not.

```
private function doRestore(event:Event) :void{
   setState(0);
   btStateUp.visible = true;
   btStateDown.visible = false;
}
```

This method will call the setState() method you wrote earlier and pass it the value 0. This tells your Panel that it should be restored to its initial state. When you set the state to restored, the btStateUp button is shown, and the btStateDown button is hidden.

12 Open the ChartPod.mxml file from /views/dashboard.

13 Set the ControlBar id to controls. Add two buttons inside the <mx:ControlBar> tag. One with an id of btGraph and a label of Graph and the other with the id of btData and the label set to Data.

```
<mx:ControlBar id="controls">
   <mx:Button id="btGraph"
      label="Graph" />
   <mx:Button id="btData"
      label="Data" />
</mx:ControlBar>
```

14 Change the root node of ChartPod from <mx:Panel> to <v:MaxRestorePanel>, and add an XML namespace to relate v: to the views directory.

```
<?xml version="1.0" encoding="utf-8"?>
<v:MaxRestorePanel
    xmlns:mx="http://www.adobe.com/2006/mxml"
    xmlns:v="views.*"
    layout="vertical">
    <mx:ControlBar id="controls">
        <mx:Button id="btGraph"
            label="Graph" />
        <mx:Button id="btData"
            label="Data" />
    </mx:ControlBar>
</v:MaxRestorePanel>
```

15 Save ChartPod.mxml. Test the Dashboard application.

As the Dashboard application runs, you should see the up and down arrows placed on top of each other in the top-left corner of each Panel. As you click the buttons in the corner, it will toggle them so only one of the two is visible. You might notice that the button is not showing a border or background, like buttons normally do; in the next exercise, you will set the size of the button so it can render itself properly with borders and background. In that exercise, you will also position the buttons appropriately.

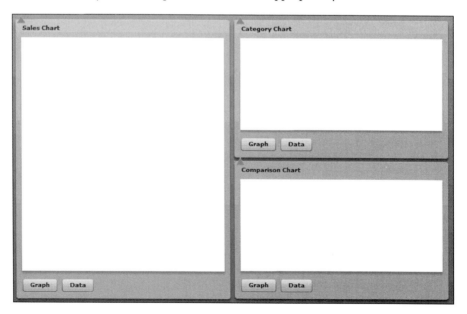

Overriding the updateDisplayList() Method

At this point, you have created the bulk of the ActionScript 3.0 component. You defined the class, instantiated the children, and added them to the chrome. All that remains is to position them appropriately. For this, you will override the updateDisplayList() method. This method is automatically invoked each time the component is redrawn, such as when it changes size or when the browser is resized. When you override this method, you should first call the super.updateDisplayList() method to ensure that the Panel's layout is also done properly. Each time this method is called, it is passed two attributes, unscaledHeight and unscaledWidth, which are the actual height and width of the component regardless of any scaling that may have been applied.

1 Open the MaxRestorePanel.as file you created in the previous exercise.

This file contains the class you created earlier in this lesson, with the buttons added to the chrome of the Panel.

2 Override the updateDisplayList() function, which will accept two numeric arguments (call them unscaledWidth and unscaledHeight), and return void.

```
protected override function updateDisplayList(unscaledWidth: Number,
    ➥ unscaledHeight:Number):void {
}
```

3 As the first line inside updateDisplayList(), call updateDisplayList() in the superclass and pass in the same two arguments received by your function.

```
super.updateDisplayList(unscaledWidth, unscaledHeight);
```

To ensure that the updateDisplayList() method of the superclass (Panel), is run properly, you need to explicitly call it in your override method. The unscaledWidth and unscaledHeight attributes tell the function the exact pixel width and height of your MaxRestorePanel. Because you want to place the buttons near the top-right corner of the Panel, knowing the actual width is required, so the button can be placed relative to the right side.

4 Add a conditional statement to set the component's visible property to true if the unscaledWidth parameter is greater than 0. Add an else block to set the visible property to false when it isn't.

```
if(unscaledWidth > 0){
    this.visible = true;
} else {
    this.visible = false;
}
```

When one of your panels is maximized, you'll set the height and width of the other panels to 0. This conditional statement enables you to determine whether the instance of the component has a nonzero size. If so, you will add all the necessary logic to render the component; otherwise, you will simply hide it.

5 Just after the conditional statement added in the previous step, create a handle on the graphics used for btStateUp and btStateDown by using the buttons' getChildByName() method.

```
var upAsset:DisplayObject = btStateUp.getChildByName("upIcon");
var downAsset:DisplayObject = btStateDown.getChildByName("upIcon");
```

The getChildByName() method of a component is specified as an instance of the DisplayObjectclass. This class is a superclass of all Flex components, and implements the properties height and width, amongst others. Because this is the first time you are using the DisplayObject class, you should add it to the imports at the beginning of the class, if it wasn't automatically added when you created the variable.

```
package views {
    import flash.events.Event;
    import mx.containers.Panel;
    import mx.controls.Button;
    import flash.display.DisplayObject;
```

6 Just after the variable declarations for upAsset and downAsset, create a variable named margin, of data type int, with a value of 4.

```
var margin:int = 4;
```

The margin variable enables you to have a few pixels between the icon and border of the button. Here, the value of 4 allows for 2 pixels on each side of the button.

7 Call the setActualSize() method for both buttons, passing in the width and height of the icons plus the margin.

```
btStateUp.setActualSize(upAsset.width+margin, upAsset.height+margin);
btStateDown.setActualSize(downAsset.width+margin, downAsset.height+margin);
```

Because the assets you are using are 14 by 14, this will set the size of the buttons to be 18 by 18—giving a 2-pixel border to the top, left, right, and bottom of the button. This allows room for the border to be drawn and to show some area for a background.

8 Save the component and run Dashboard.mxml.

The buttons are now appropriately sized. Now, you need to position them.

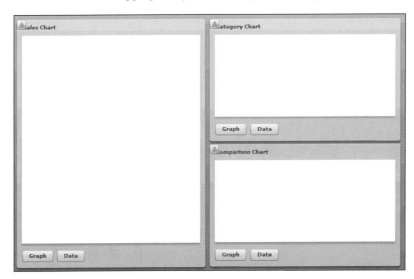

9 Just after the two setActualSize() calls, define variables to indicate the width of the button and the distance which it should be rendered from the top and right edges.

```
var pixelsFromTop:int = 5;
var pixelsFromRight:int = 10;
var buttonWidth:int=btStateUp.width;
```

Because both buttons have the same width, it isn't necessary to create a different variable for each button's width. If you were building a system in which each button might have a different width, you would need to explicitly capture each button's width. If you hadn't set the size of the component in the earlier step, btState.width would be equal to 0 (which would not work as you expect).

10 Create a variable which will compute the *x* coordinate for the buttons by subtracting the unscaledWidth from the buttonWidth; then subtract the pixelsFromRight variable.

```
var x:Number = unscaledWidth - buttonWidth - pixelsFromRight;
```

This sets the button's position relative to the right edge of the Panel. Because the *x* coordinate indicates the left edge of the button, subtract the width of the panel (unscaledWidth) from the button's width and then subtract the pixelsFromRight to offset the button from the edge of the Panel.

11 Create a variable *y* equal to the pixelsFromTop variable.

```
var y:Number = pixelsFromTop;
```

12 Move both buttons to the newly computed *x* and *y* coordinates.

```
btStateDown.move(x, y);
btStateUp.move(x, y);
```

Both buttons are set to the same coordinate because only one of the two will be seen at any given time.

13 Save **MaxRestorePanel.as**. Run Dashboard.mxml.

As this runs, you should see that the buttons are rendered in the correct place and properly toggle when clicked. All that remains to make this functional is to have the main application (Dashboard.mxml) listen to each of the components for the maximize or restore events and to toggle the states appropriately.

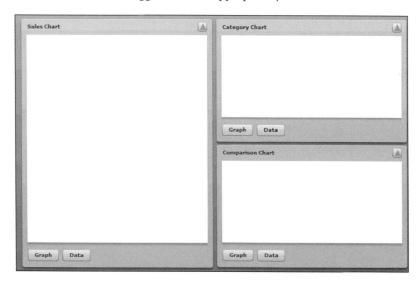

Your completed updateDisplayList() method should read like this:

```
protected override function updateDisplayList(unscaledWidth: Number,
    ➥ unscaledHeight:Number):void {
    super.updateDisplayList(unscaledWidth, unscaledHeight);
    if(unscaledWidth > 0){
        this.visible = true;
    } else {
        this.visible = false;
    }
    var upAsset:DisplayObject = btStateUp.getChildByName("upIcon");
    var downAsset:DisplayObject = btStateDown.getChildByName("upIcon");
    var margin:int = 4;
```

code continues on next page

```
btStateUp.setActualSize(upAsset.width+margin, upAsset.height+margin);
btStateDown.setActualSize(downAsset.width+margin, downAsset.height+margin);
var pixelsFromTop:int = 5;
var pixelsFromRight:int = 10;
var buttonWidth:int=btStateUp.width;
var x:Number = unscaledWidth - buttonWidth - pixelsFromRight;
var y:Number = pixelsFromTop;
btStateDown.move(x, y);
btStateUp.move(x, y);
}
```

14 Open the Dashboard.mxml file.

You can also copy Lesson10/start/Dashboard.mxml to your flexGrocer directory if you choose.

15 Remove the four LinkButton controls and the Spacer control from the ApplicationControlBar. Add two new `<mx:Spacer>` tags, one between the endDate DateField and the ComboBox, and another between the ComboBox and the RadioButtonGroup, to force the remaining controls to occupy the entire ApplicationControlBar.

```
<mx:ApplicationControlBar dock="true">
   <mx:Label text="Start Date"/>
   <mx:DateField id="startDate"/>
   <mx:Label text="End Date"/>
   <mx:DateField id="endDate"/>
   <mx:Spacer width="100%"/>
   <mx:ComboBox id="catCombo"
      dataProvider="{categories}"
      labelField = "name"/>
   <mx:Spacer width="100%"/>
   <mx:RadioButtonGroup id="grossOrNetGroup"/>
   <mx:RadioButton id="gross"
      groupName="grossOrNetGroup"
      label="Gross Sales"
      data="GROSS"
      selected="true"/>
   <mx:RadioButton id="net"
      groupName="grossOrNetGroup"
      label="Net Sales"
      data="NET"/>
</mx:ApplicationControlBar>
```

You no longer need the links, as each panel now has a button you can use to maximize it.

16 Add an attribute to the first `<mx:ChartPod>` tag, which will set the currentState to fullSales when the maximize event occurs. Add another attribute to reset the currentState when the restore event occurs.

```
<v:ChartPod id="sales"
    width="100%" height="100%"
    title="Sales Chart"
    maximize="this.currentState='fullSales'"
    restore="this.currentState=''">
```

Remember, your MaxRestorePanel is the base class for ChartPod, so ChartPod will broadcast the maximize and restore events that you defined in MaxRestorePanel.

17 Handle the maximize and restore events for the other two ChartPods. The restore event handler will be identical for all three, the maximize event handler for the type pod will set the currentState to fullType, and the maximize event handler for the comp pod will set the currentState to fullComp.

```
<v:ChartPod id="type"
    width="100%" height="100%"
    title="Category Chart"
    maximize="this.currentState='fullType'"
    restore="this.currentState=''">
</v:ChartPod>
<v:ChartPod id="comp"
    width="100%" height="100%"
    title=" Comparison Chart"
    maximize="this.currentState='fullComp'"
    restore="this.currentState=''">
</v:ChartPod>
```

18 Save and run Dashboard.mxml. You should now be able to maximize or restore any of the three pods.

What You Have Learned

In this lesson, you have:

- Created a class for your component (pages 244–247)

- Embedded images in ActionScript (pages 245–246)

- Instantiated Flex components in ActionScript (page 248)

- Programmatically added components to a container (pages 248–249)

- Used the rawChildren property of Containers (pages 249–253)

- Overridden the createChildren() method (pages 250–251)

- Overridden the updateDisplayList() method (pages 254–259)

What You Will Learn

In this lesson, you will:

- Define the viewable columns of a DataGrid through DataGridColumn

- Use a `labelFunction` and an itemRendererDisplay to display DataGridColumn information

- Create an MXML component to be used as an item renderer

- Create an inline custom item renderer for a DataGridColumn

- Raise events from inside an item renderer to the container MXML file of the DataGrid using `outerDocument`

Approximate Time

This lesson takes approximately 1 hour and 30 minutes to complete.

Lesson Files

Media Files:

None

Starting Files:

Lesson11/start/Dashboard.mxml
Lesson11/start/views/dashboard/ChartPod.mxml
Lesson11/start/views/ecomm/Cart.mxml
Lesson11/start/valueObjects/ShoppingCartItem.as

Completed Files:

Lesson11/complete/Dashboard.mxml
Lesson11/complete/views/dashboard/ChartPod.mxml
Lesson11/complete/views/ecomm/Cart.mxml
Lesson11/complete/valueObjects/ShoppingCartItem.as
Lesson11/complete/renderers/ecomm/ProductName.mxml

LESSON 11

Using DataGrids and Item Renderers

In Lesson 8, "Using Controls and Repeaters with Data Sets," you learned about working with data sets and some controls that could be used to show the data. In this lesson, you will build upon that set of base controls and be introduced to the primary MXML component used to display and manipulate large data sets.

In this lesson, you will learn how to use the DataGrid component to display a data set in an interactive way using rows and columns. Aside from using the DataGrid in its simplest form, you will learn how to override the default behavior of a particular column in the DataGrid by implementing a custom item renderer; do a custom sort of the data for a column; and change the editing controls, which manage underlining data.

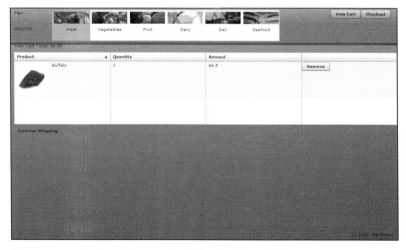

Here, you see the shopping cart displaying in a DataGrid.

Introducing DataGrids and Item Renderers

Using a DataGrid as a way to display the data of your application will provide the largest possible number of options for your users to interact with the data. At the simplest level, the DataGrid organizes the data in a column-by-row format and presents this to the user. From there, the DataGrid can be configured to allow you to modify the data it contains.

In this lesson, you will make modifications to two of the applications. The first is the Dashboard application, in which you will look to use the DataGrid for purely display purposes. The second is the EComm application, in which the DataGrid will give you a view of the cart and the ability to both update and remove items from the cart.

> **TIP:** Although the DataGrid does provide the most versatile manner of interacting with the data of your application, it does come with additional overhead (performance and size). It is wise to consider what you expect the user to do with the data/control before you automatically choose to use a DataGrid.

Adding a Generic DataGrid to ChartPod

This task will have you extending the current ChartPod.mxml, created in Lesson 10, "Creating Custom Components with ActionScript 3.0," in two ways. The first is to add a DataGrid, in which you can view sales data that is passed in. The second is to add a property to the component to allow the containing MXML file to pass in the data set that the component should use when displaying the data in the DataGrid. This task will focus on the base usage of the DataGrid, which allows for the DataGrid to get the definition of which columns it will use from the data set.

1 Open the ChartPod.mxml file.

   If you didn't complete Lesson 10 or if you were unhappy with the state of the application after that lesson, you can copy Lesson11/start/views/dashboard/ChartPod.mxml to your flexGrocer directory.

2 Below the beginning `<mx:MaxRestorePanel>` tag, place an `<mx:Script>` block to enable you to declare attributes that can be passed into the component.

```
<mx:Script>
    <![CDATA[
    ]]>
</mx:Script>
```

   This is needed to allow you to import classes and declare functions and properties for the ChartPod.

3 Inside of the script block, add an import for the mx.collections.ICollectionView class.

```
import mx.collections.ICollectionView;
```

The attribute passed into the component will be of type ICollectionView, so you need the import to data type the attribute.

4 Below the import, declare a public variable, named dp, which will hold the reference of the data passed into the component. Make it of type ICollectionView and make it [Bindable] so that the DataGrid can update its data as the property value changes.

```
[Bindable]
public var dp:ICollectionView = null;
```

A value of null is used to act as the initial state of the property until a value is passed in. The [Bindable] metadata is used to tell the compiler that this property is being watched by another part of the application.

5 Below the script block, insert an <mx:DataGrid> tag.

```
<mx:DataGrid />
```

It is not necessary for you to always define columns for a DataGrid. By not defining any columns in the DataGrid definition, the DataGrid will implicitly create a column for each column of the data set that is assigned to it. Also, you don't need to worry about how the DataGrid is positioning relative to the ControlBar because of the ControlBar's behavior of placing itself at the bottom of the component.

6 In the <mx:DataGrid> tag, set the width and height to 100%.

```
<mx:DataGrid width="100%" height="100%" />
```

This means that the DataGrid should fill 100% of the width and height of its parent.

7 Bind the dataProvider attribute of the <mx:DataGrid> tag to dp.

```
<mx:DataGrid dataProvider="{dp}" width="100%" height="100%" />
```

This will set the data set for the DataGrid to whatever is passed into the component.

8 Save the ChartPod.mxml file.

There is no need to test this component at this point because you don't have data being passed to it yet.

Adding HTTPService Calls to Dashboard

These next tasks have you returning to the Dashboard.mxml file, modifying it to retrieve the data from a HTTPService, and passing it to the modified ChartPod.mxml component. The data currently resides in static XML files that you will pull into the application to fill the DataGrids in your Dashboard. The data is already presorted.

1 Open the Dashboard.mxml file.

You can also copy Lesson11/start/Dashboard.mxml to your flexGrocer directory if you choose.

2 Insert three `<mx:HTTPService>` tags to retrieve sales information for the three pods in the Dashboard. Place them just below the script block.

```
<mx:HTTPService id="salesRPC"
    url="http://www.flexgrocer.com/rawSalesData.xml"
    result="salesRPCResult(event)"
    fault="showFault(event)"/>

<mx:HTTPService id="typeRPC"
    url="http://www.flexgrocer.com/categorySalesData.xml"
    result="typeRPCResult(event)"
    fault="showFault(event)"/>

<mx:HTTPService id="compRPC"
    url="http://www.flexgrocer.com/salesData.xml"
    result="compRPCResult(event)"
    fault="showFault(event)"/>
```

In Lesson 6, "Using Remote XML Data with Controls," it was discussed in detail how to use the `<mx:HTTPService>` tag and how to use the result handlers of the tag. Each tag has its own specific result handle method but uses one shared fault handle method.

3 In the script block at the top of the file, create a private `salesRPCResult()` method. This method will handle the result from the HTTPService that gets the sales data by taking the result and passing it along to the sales pod.

```
private function salesRPCResult(event:ResultEvent):void{
    sales.dp = event.result.salesData.dailySales;
}
```

This function takes the `ResultEvent` event passed in and assigns it to the sales component through the `dp` attribute that you defined earlier in the lesson.

4 Just like the last step, create a private typeRPCResult() method in the script block. This method will handle the result from the HTTPService that gets the sales type data by taking the result and passing it along to the type pod.

```
private function typeRPCResult(event:ResultEvent):void{
   type.dp = event.result.categorySalesData.categorySales;
}
```

This function takes the ResultEvent event passed in and assigns it to the type component through the dp attribute.

5 In the script block at the top of the file, create a private compRPCResult() method. This method will handle the result from the HTTPService that gets the sales type data by taking the result passing it along to the comp pod.

```
private function compRPCResult(event:ResultEvent):void{
   comp.dp = event.result.salesData.dailySales;
}
```

This function takes the ResultEvent event passed in and assigns it to the comp component through the dp attribute.

6 Inside the script block, add an import for the mx.rpc.events.FaultEvent class.

```
import mx.rpc.events.FaultEvent;
```

You need this class to be able to capture errors that were made during your request for the xml files.

7 In the script block, create a private showFault() method. This method will trace out the fault codes that occur in the HTTPService call.

```
private function showFault(event:FaultEvent):void{
   trace(event.fault.faultCode+":"+event.fault.faultString);
}
```

8 Create a private method called getData(). It accepts no arguments and returns void.

```
private function getData():void{
}
```

This function will be called at application startup to fetch the data for the drop-down list and the three pods. In a later lesson, this function will be called when the filter criteria changes, which will request data from the server using the values the user specifies.

9 In the getData() method, call the three HTTPServices through their send() methods to fetch the data.

```
private function getData():void{
   salesRPC.send();
   typeRPC.send();
   compRPC.send();
}
```

As you may remember from an earlier lesson, we created a single method, called getData(), where the data is requested for the whole Dashboard Application. Because you have three different outbound requests, you will need to call them all from inside this method.

10 Create a private method called init(). It accepts no arguments and returns void.

```
private function init():void{
}
```

This function will hold your initialization routine for the first time the application is started.

11 Inside the init() method, initialize the startDate DateField control to have a selectedDate of 4/1/2006 and the endDate DateField control to have a selectedDate of 5/1/2006.

```
private function init():void{
   startDate.selectedDate = new Date(2006,3,1);
   endDate.selectedDate = new Date(2006,4,1);
}
```

This will default the start and end date of your date filter controls. You will use these in Lesson 17, "Accessing Server-side Objects," when you start to interact with the server to get the data dynamically.

✱ **NOTE:** The constructor for the Date object allows you to quickly build a new date by specifying values such as the Year, Month and Day. However, in Flex, months are 0 based, meaning 0 represents January and 11 represents December. Specifying 2006, 3, and 1 to the constructor means April 1, 2006.

12 Move the HTTPService call responsible for getting the categories from the creationComplete event of the <mx:Application> tag to inside the init() method.

```
private function init():void{
   startDate.selectedDate = new Date(2006,3,1);
   endDate.selectedDate = new Date(2006,4,1);
   catRPC.send();
}
```

13 Make a call to the getData() method inside the init() method.

```
private function init():void{
   startDate.selectedDate = new Date(2006,3,1);
   endDate.selectedDate = new Date(2006,4,1);
   catRPC.send();
   getData();
}
```

This will retrieve the data for the Dashboard—to be made available at the startup of the application.

14 In the creationComplete event of the <mx:Application> tag, call the init() method.

```
<mx:Application xmlns:mx="http://www.adobe.com/2006/mxml"
   layout="horizontal"
   creationComplete="init();"
   xmlns:v="views.dashboard.*">
```

This sets the defaults for the filter controls and then initially loads the Dashboard data after the whole application is loaded.

15 Save and run your Dashboard.mxml and see the data populated in the pods on the dashboard.

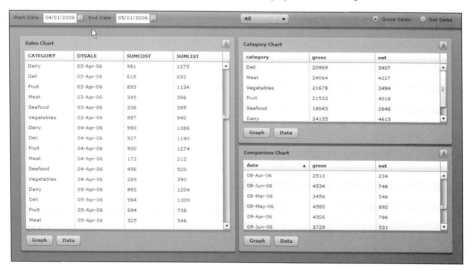

✱ NOTE: Sorting the data is part of the default behavior of the DataGrid. The data came back from the XML file already presorted, so there was no need to sort the data upon receipt. Lesson 17 will demonstrate how to pragmatically sort the data of a DataGrid.

Displaying the Shopping Cart with a DataGrid

When you left off in Lesson 8, you had the contents of your cart displayed in a List control with the ability to remove the current item you were viewing from the cart via a Remove button. You will switch this over to use a DataGrid to display the contents of the cart. The DataGrid control supports the syntax to allow for you to specify the columns explicitly through the DataGridColumn. This is done with the following syntax:

```
<mx:DataGrid … >
   <mx:columns>
      <mx:DataGridColumn dataField=""…>
      <mx:DataGridColumn…>
      <mx:DataGridColumn…>
   </mx:columns>
</mx:DataGrid>
```

The dataField is used to map the column in the data set to a given column. The order in which the DataGridColumns are listed is the order you will see the columns from left to right in the DataGrid. This is useful when you need to specify a different order to the columns than specified in the data set. Each DataGridColumn supports a large number of attributes that affect the DataGrid's rendering and interaction with the given column.

1 Open Cart.mxml from the flexGrocer/views/ecomm directory.

If you prefer, you can copy this file from the Lesson11/start/views/ecomm directory to your flexGrocer/views/ecomm directory.

2 Replace the `<mx:List>` tag with an `<mx:DataGrid>` tag. Set the width and height to 100%, set draggableColumns to false, and set editable to true.

```
<mx:DataGrid
   id="cartView"
   dataProvider="{cart.aItems}" width="100%" height="100%"
   editable="true" draggableColumns="false">
   <mx:columns>
   </mx:columns>
</mx:DataGrid>
```

You are specifying the editable as true because you will allow one of the columns to be changed by the user. If it is set to false, the whole DataGrid becomes read-only. You no longer need the labelFunction attribute for data formatting on the base control because it is the DataGridColumns that will specify how each piece of data is shown. For now, leave the code in the script block that defined the label function; you will return to it in a few steps. The DataGrid will remain bound to the same data set as before (cart.aItems). You also had to set the draggableColumns attribute to false because the default value is true, and you don't want the columns to be able to be moved around.

3 Define an <mx:DataGridColumn> for the product name and place it at the top of the column list. Set dataField to product, editable to false, and headerText to Product.

```
<mx:DataGridColumn dataField="product" headerText="Product"
   editable="false" />
```

The headerText attribute will specify the text of the DataGridColumn header. If you don't specify this, it will take the value of the dataField attribute.

> **TIP:** You could have optionally set the dataField attribute to product.prodName because the product field is actually a complex object available as a property of ShoppingCartItem. The DataGridColumn can resolve property.property references.

Because the editable attribute is set to true on the <mx:DataGrid> tag, you need to set it to false for each column you don't want to use for editing.

4 Define an <mx:DataGridColumn> for displaying the quantity and place it after the last <mx:DataGridColumn>. Set dataField to quantity and headerText to Quantity.

```
<mx:DataGridColumn dataField="quantity" headerText="Quantity" />
```

This column will be used to allow users to change the quantity of a specific product they want to buy.

5 Define an <mx:DataGridColumn> for displaying subtotals for each item and place it after the last <mx:DataGridColumn>. Set dataField to subtotal, editable to false, and headerText to Amount.

```
<mx:DataGridColumn dataField="subtotal" headerText="Amount"
   editable="false" />
```

The column will show the cost for this specific product. You don't want the customer to be able to change this amount, so you are setting the editable attribute to false.

6 Save Cart.mxml. Run the EComm Application, add the Buffalo product to the shopping cart and click on 'View Cart'.

You can see the cart shown in a DataGrid. A small note is that the Product column is showing up as text in the DataGrid, even though it is a complex attribute in the data set because there is a toString() function declared on the Product value object. If this wasn't defined, you would see [Object Product]. You will look at how to better display a complex object in a second. For now, this is what you should see:

Add Inline Editing Control for DataGridColumn

In a DataGrid, you have the ability to specify that a column of the data shown can be changed by the user when focus is brought to the cell. This is done by setting the editable attribute to true. The default editing control for the column is a text field. It is possible to specify the editor to use when managing the data via the itemEditor attribute and the editorDataField, which specifies the attribute of the editor control used to manage changing of the value for the cell and which attribute on that control the data set should look at to get the changed value. The following are the built-in controls you can specify (full package names are needed unless imported into the containing page):

- Button
- CheckBox
- ComboBox
- DateField
- Image
- Label
- NumericStepper
- Text (Default)
- TextArea
- TextInput

▶ TIP: You can also specify your own control if you desire, as long as it implements the IDropInListItemRenderer interface in its class definition.

1 Open the Cart.mxml you created in the previous exercise.

If you didn't finish the previous exercise, you can open Cart_1.mxml from Lesson11/intermediate and save it as **Cart.mxml** in your flexGrocer/views/ecomm directory.

2 In the `<mx:DataGridColumn>` tag that maps to the quantity, set the `itemEditor` to `mx.controls.NumericStepper`, `editorDataField` to value, and editable to true.

```
<mx:DataGridColumn dataField="quantity"
    itemEditor="mx.controls.NumericStepper"
    editorDataField="value" editable="true" headerText="Quantity" />
```

This now has the Quantity column being edited as a Numeric Stepper. The underlying value of the column is bound to the `value` attribute of the Numeric Stepper.

3 Save Cart.mxml. Run the EComm Application, add the Buffalo product to the shopping cart, and click 'View Cart'.

When you click in the Quantity column, you will notice that it doesn't open up as a free-form text field, but rather as a NumericStepper control.

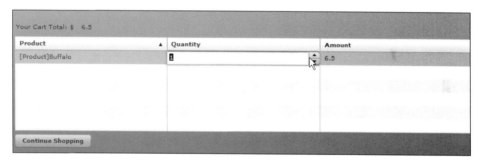

Create an MXML Item Renderer for Displaying the Product

The default behavior of the DataGrid is to convert every value of the data set that is being shown into a String and then display it. However, when you are dealing with a complex object that is stored in the data set, another alternative is to create a custom item renderer that shows more information about the column. In this case, you are going to create a simple item renderer that shows the product's name and image.

When working with item renderers, you will find that there is an implicit public variable available to you in the item renderer called `data`, which represents the data of the row itself. You can use the data to bind your controls without having to worry about what column you are working with. When the DataGrid creates a column that has a custom item renderer associated with it, it creates a single instance of the cell renderer per row, so you don't have to worry about scoping between rows.

1 Create a new folder under the FlexGrocer project named renderer and one under that called ecomm.

2 Right-click on the ecomm folder you just created and choose New > MXML Component. In the New MXML Component dialog box, set the filename to **ProductName.mxml**, the base component to an HBox, and remove any width and height values and then click Finish.

This MXML file will define the layout of a given cell in the DataGrid. You are creating it in a separate file so that, if needed, it can be used on multiple DataGrid columns and/or multiple DataGrids.

3 Open ProductName.mxml.

The file should already be open in your Flex Builder workspace; if not, the file is located in your flexGrocer/renderer/ecomm directory.

4 In the <mx:HBox>, set the verticalScrollPolicy and horizontalScrollPolicy attributes to off.

```
<mx:HBox xmlns:mx="http://www.adobe.com/2006/mxml"
    verticalScrollPolicy="off" horizontalScrollPolicy="off">
```

This will keep the cell renderer from having scroll bars if the DataGrid is resized too small.

5 Place an <mx:Image> tag inside of the <mx:HBox> to display the product's thumbnail image. You will need to set the source attribute to a hard coded directory location, but the filename should be bound to the imageName of the product. That will make it look like assets/{data.product.imageName}.

```
<mx:Image source="{'assets/' +data.product.imageName}"/>
```

You do not need to specify the height or width of the image because it will resize the column to fit the image.

▶ **TIP:** The image location used is relative to the location where the main application is loaded from, not the location of the file that contains the <mx:Image> tag.

6 Place an <mx:Text> tag for product name in the <mx:HBox> below the <mx:Image> tag. Bind the text attribute to data.product.prodName. Set the height and width to 100%.

```
<mx:Text text="{data.product.prodName}" width="100%" height="100%"/>
```

7 Save the ProductName.mxml file.

There is no need to test this component at this point because it is not assigned to the DataGrid yet.

8 Open the Cart.mxml you created in the previous exercise.

Alternately, you can open Cart_2.mxml from Lesson11/intermediate and save it as **Cart. mxml** in your flexGrocer/views/ecomm directory.

9 Update the <mx:DataGridColumn> with a dataField of product with a new attribute, itemRenderer, set to renderer.ecomm.ProductName.

```
<mx:DataGridColumn dataField="product" headerText="Product"
   itemRenderer="renderer.ecomm.ProductName" editable="false"/>
```

With the use of the itemRenderer attribute, you are overriding the default TextInput editor. You need to use the fully qualified class name to set your item renderer unless you have imported the class package that it exists in.

10 Update the <mx:DataGrid> with a new attribute variableRowHeight set to true.

```
<mx:DataGrid
   id="cartView"
   dataProvider="{cart.aItems}" width="100%" height="100%"
   editable="true" draggableColumns="false"
   variableRowHeight="true">
```

It is necessary for you to set the variableRowHeight to true, so that Flex will resize the row's height to accommodate the thumbnail image.

▶ **TIP:** This attribute can be used to allow for exploding details inside a DataGrid row. In this case, you can have summary data in one cell that if you click on an icon or button, the cell expands to show the new details.

11 Save Cart.mxml. Run the EComm Application, add the Buffalo product to the shopping cart and click on 'View Cart'.

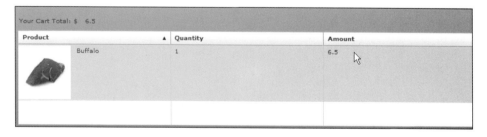

Create an Inline MXML Item Renderer for Displaying the Remove Button

Another option for creating an item renderer is through the `<mx:itemRenderer>` tag, which allows you to declare and create the item renderer inline with the DataGridColumns. From a compiler perspective, doing an inline item renderer is the equivalent of building it in an external file (it actually compiles the code of the inline item renderer as a separate file internally). Inside the `<mx:cellRenderer>` tag, you will place an `<mx:Component>` tag, which defines the boundaries of the inline item renderer file from the rest of the page. Thus, the inside of the `<mx:Component>` tag will have its own scope that you will need to do imports, function declarations, and the like.

> **TIP:** Although this will be very efficient from a coding perspective to build inline item renderers, it does not allow you to reuse the item renderers for other DataGrids. Good candidates are item renderers that are specific to one DataGrid only, such as action item controls.

Just like the item renderer you just created, this one will have access to the `data` variable, which will hold the reference to the row. In addition, you will also be able to talk out of the inline cell editor back into the page through the `outerDocument` scope. Note, however, that all functions and variables in the containing page that you want to reference must be declared as `public`, because it is really a component talking to another component.

For this example, you will look to replace the Remove button that is outside of the DataGrid with a Remove button inside of each row.

1 Open the Cart.mxml you created in the previous exercise.

   Altermately, you can open Cart_3.mxml from Lesson11/intermediate and save it as **Cart.mxml** in your flexGrocer/views/ecomm directory.

2 Create a new `<mx:DataGridColumn>` to hold a Remove button at the bottom of the DataGrid column list. Set `editable` to `false`; otherwise, the cell would be able to receive focus. You also do not need to specify `dataField`, because there is no data you are mapping directly to.

```
<mx:DataGridColumn editable="false">
</mx:DataGridColumn>
```

   This will create the placeholder column in the DataGrid. We used a start and end `<mx:DataGridColumn>` tag because the item renderer definition will be placed inside it.

3 Place the `<mx:itemRenderer>` and `<mx:Component>` tags inside the `<mx:DataGridColumn>` tag.

```
<mx:itemRenderer>
   <mx:Component>
   </mx:Component>
</mx:itemRenderer>
```

4 Place an <mx:VBox> tag inside the <mx:Component> tag to provide a container for the Remove button.

```
<mx:itemRenderer>
   <mx:Component>
      <mx:VBox>
      </mx:VBox>
   </mx:Component>
</mx:itemRenderer>
```

When creating this inline item renderer we want to use the VBox to help us be able to center the button in the DataGrid no matter the size of the cell.

5 Place an <mx:Button> tag inside the VBox. Set the label to Remove and set the click event to call the removeItem() function on the containing page. You will need to use the outerDocument reference to call the function.

```
<mx:VBox>
   <mx:Button
      label="Remove"
      click="outerDocument.removeItem(valueObjects.ShoppingCartItem(data));"/>
</mx:VBox>
```

In prior lessons, you used the Remove Button that was outside of the List to remove an item from the shopping cart. The remove function could simply look at the selectedItem in the List to determine which product to remove. Because you are building an inline item renderer you will need to change the method signature of the removeItem() function to accept a ShoppingCartItem instance that the row is pointing to. It is necessary for you to do this because the DataGrid will not always have a concept of a selected row that the code can remove.

You need to fully qualify the casting of the data property into the ShoppingCartItem because the import statements made at the top of the file are in a different scope than the inline item renderer.

▶ **TIP:** As an alternative to the 'as' operator, you can convert an object instance from one type to another (as long as they are compatible) by simply wrapping the desired object instance in the ClassNameToConvertTo(object) syntax.

6 Change the method signature of removeItem to accept a ShoppingCartItem as an argument. Also, change the method to public.

```
public function removeItem(cartItem:ShoppingCartItem):void{
```

When the button is clicked, the item renderer will pass the cart item of the row it is on, so we need to add an argument to accept this cart item. We need to make this method public so that the code running inside the inline cell renderer can access it.

7 Change the first two lines of the `removeItem()` function, so that the Product to be removed from the cart is set equal to the argument passed in.

```
var prod:Product = cartItem.product;
```

The whole function should now look like this:

```
public function removeItem(cartItem:ShoppingCartItem):void{
   var prod:Product = cartItem.product;
   var e:ProductEvent = new ProductEvent(prod,"productRemoved");
   this.dispatchEvent(e);
}
```

You no longer need to build the product item from the selected row because the row is now calling this method and passes in the specific cart item.

8 Inside the script block, add an `import` for the mx.controls.dataGridClasses.DataGrid-Column class.

```
import mx.controls.dataGridClasses.DataGridColumn;
```

You need to update the `labelFunction` that you had for the List control so that it will work with a DataGrid. The method signature for `labelFunction`s on DataGrids are `labelFunctionName(item:Object, dataField:DataGridColumn)`.

> ▶ **TIP:** In the Flex Builder integrated development environment (IDE), if you choose DataGridColumn from the list of classes that are presented after the : of your argument, the IDE will automatically import the class for you if it is not already present.

9 Add an argument to the end of the `renderLabel()` function to call `dataField` of type DataGridColumn.

```
private function renderLabel(item:ShoppingCartItem,
   ➥ dataField:DataGridColumn):String{
```

Because the DataGrid has multiple columns that can each have its own `labelFunction`, as well as share the same `labelFunction`, the additional argument is used to distinguish between which `labelFunction` is being used. If you know that your function will only be used on just one column, you can ignore this argument in your code.

10 Update the `renderLabel()` function to just return the subtotal of the item with a $ on the front. Change the name to `renderPriceLabel()`.

For now, you want to put a simple mask on the price to represent the number as a dollar figure. The signature and functionality of the labelFunction is the same on the DataGrid as it is on the List.

```
private function renderPriceLabel(item:ShoppingCartItem,
  ➥ dataField:String):String{
    return "$"+String(item.subtotal);
}
```

11 Update the <mx:DataGridColumn> with a dataField of subtotal with a new attribute of labelFunction set to renderPriceLabel.

```
<mx:DataGridColumn dataField="subtotal" headerText="Amount"
  labelFunction="renderPriceLabel" editable="false"/>
```

This will have the subtotal column use renderPriceLabel on each of the rows in the DataGrid.

12 Remove the old <mx:Button> that called the remove logic outside the DataGrid.

The final code for the Cart.mxml should look like the following:

```
<?xml version="1.0" encoding="utf-8"?>
<mx:VBox xmlns:mx="http://www.adobe.com/2006/mxml">
  <mx:Metadata>
    [Event(name="productRemoved",type="events.ProductEvent")]
  </mx:Metadata>

  <mx:Script>
    <![CDATA[
      import mx.controls.dataGridClasses.DataGridColumn;
      import events.ProductEvent;
      import valueObjects.ShoppingCart;
      import valueObjects.ShoppingCartItem;
      import valueObjects.Product;

      [Bindable]
      public var cart:ShoppingCart;

      private function renderPriceLabel(item:ShoppingCartItem, dataField:
      ➥ DataGridColumn):String{
        return "$"+String(item.subtotal);
      }

      public function removeItem(cartItem:ShoppingCartItem):void{
        var prod:Product = cartItem.product;
        var e:ProductEvent = new ProductEvent(prod,"productRemoved");
        this.dispatchEvent(e);
      }
    ]]>
  </mx:Script>
```

code continues on next page

```
<mx:DataGrid
   id="cartView"
   dataProvider="{cart.aItems}" width="100%" height="100%"
   editable="true" draggableColumns="false"
   variableRowHeight="true">
   <mx:columns>
      <mx:DataGridColumn dataField="product" headerText="Product"
         itemRenderer="renderer.ecomm.ProductName" editable="false"/>
      <mx:DataGridColumn dataField="quantity"
         itemEditor="mx.controls.NumericStepper"
         editorDataField="value" editable="true" headerText="Quantity"/>
      <mx:DataGridColumn dataField="subtotal" headerText="Amount"
         editable="false" labelFunction="renderPriceLabel"/>
      <mx:DataGridColumn editable="false">
         <mx:itemRenderer>
            <mx:Component>
               <mx:VBox>
                  <mx:Button
                     label="Remove"
                     click="outerDocument.removeItem(valueObjects.
                     ➥ ShoppingCartItem(data));"/>
               </mx:VBox>
            </mx:Component>
         </mx:itemRenderer>
      </mx:DataGridColumn>
   </mx:columns>
</mx:DataGrid>

</mx:VBox>
```

13 Save Cart.mxml. Run the EComm.mxml Application, add the Buffalo product to the
shopping cart and click on 'View Cart'. Notice both the formatting on the Amount column and the Remove button in the shopping cart.

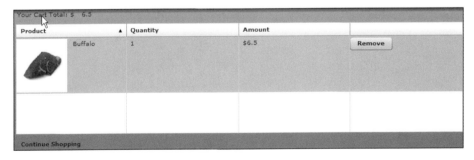

Update ShoppingCartItem with Set and Get Functions

One thing you might have noticed when you took the shopping cart out for a test run was that when you changed the quantity of the cart, the pricing didn't update. This is because changes to either price or quantity are not triggering the recalc() function you created on the ShoppingCartItem class.

ActionScript enables you to declare some behind-the-scenes functions that will fire whenever you attempt to access a property of a class. These are called custom set and get functions. In the function, you will place the keyword of either get or set in your function declaration that has the same name as the property you are trying to mask. Also, you will change the property to be a private variable that is named differently than before. It is recommended that you prefix it with an underscore. The three parts will follow this brief structure:

```
private var _insVar:uint;
public function set insVar(qty:uint):Void
public function get insVar():uint
```

1 Open ShoppingCartItem.as from your flexGrocer/valueObjects directory.

If you prefer, you can copy this file from the Lesson11/start/valueObjects to your flexGrocer/valueObjects directory.

2 Change the quantity property declaration to have a prefix of _ and to be private.

```
private var _quantity:uint;
```

We changed this property to be private so that no one can directly access this property outside the class itself.

3 Add a set quantity() function declaration and have it call the recalc() function.

```
public function set quantity(qty:uint):void{
   _quantity = qty;
   recalc();
}
```

This will be called every time something changes quantity. This is where you want to call the recalc() function.

4 Add the get quantity() function declaration.

```
public function get quantity():uint{
   return _quantity;
}
```

5 Add a public function called `toString()`, which will return type String. Have the function return a concatenation of the `ShoppingCartItem` quantity and its product's name.

```
public function toString():String{
return this.quantity.toString() + ": " + this.product.prodName;
}
```

This function will be used if Flex is asked to display the contents of the ShoppingCartItem. Currently this is done on the small cart view off the main product page.

6 Save ShoppingCartItem.as. Run EComm.mxml application, add the Buffalo product to the shopping cart and click on 'View Cart'. Change the quantity of the Buffalo item in your cart and see the subtotal change.

When you change the quantity of a cart item, you will see the updating of the price after you leave the column because the DataGrid is watching for changes to the data set to which it is assigned. The reason that you need to leave the column is that the updating of the data that DataGrid is managing does not happen until after you are finished working with the column. This is to avoid constant broadcasting of every change made to the column until the user is finished editing the value. Be aware that the cart total above the cart does not change just the price of the individual items in the cart. You will be updating the cart in a later lesson.

What You Have Learned

In this lesson, you have:

- Displayed a data set via a DataGrid (pages 262–267)
- Defined the viewable columns of a DataGrid through DataGridColumn (pages 268–270)
- Displayed information from a DataGridColumn using a `labelFunction` and an item renderer (pages 271–273, 276–277)
- Changed the default editing control of a DataGridColumn using an `editorClass` (pages 270–271)
- Created an MXML component to be used as an item renderer (pages 271–273)
- Created an inline custom item renderer for a DataGridColumn (pages 274–278)
- Learned how to raise events from inside an item renderer to the containing MXML file of the DataGrid using `outerDocument` (pages 274–275)
- Learned how to create custom set and get functions on a class (pages 279–280)

What You Will Learn

In this lesson, you will:

- Learn the terminology associated with drag-and-drop operations in Flex
- Understand that the list-based components in Flex have enhanced drag-and-drop support built in
- Implement drag and drop on drag-enabled components
- Use various drag events
- Implement various methods of the DragSource and DragManager classes to implement drag and drop on nondrag-enabled components
- Use formats to allow dropping of drag proxy objects

Approximate Time

This lesson takes approximately 1 hour and 30 minutes to complete.

Lesson Files

Media Files:

None

Starting Files

Lesson12/start/EComm.mxml
Lesson12/start/as/ecomm.as
Lesson12/start/views/ecomm/GroceryDetail.mxml
Lesson12/dragDrop/start/Task1_DG_to_DG.mxml
Lesson12/dragDrop/start/Task2_DG_to_List.mxml
Lesson12/dragDrop/start/Task3_Label_to_List.mxml

Completed Files

Lesson12/complete/EComm.mxml
Lesson12/complete/as/ecomm.as
Lesson12/complete/views/ecomm/GroceryDetail.mxml
Lesson12/dragDrop/complete/Task1_DG_to_DG.mxml
Lesson12/dragDrop/complete/Task2_DG_to_List.mxml
Lesson12/dragDrop/complete/Task3_Label_to_List.mxml

LESSON 12

Using Drag and Drop

Drag and drop is a common user interface technique in desktop applications. Not so, however, in web applications until the idea and implementation of rich Internet applications (RIAs) came along. Flex and Flash Player permit you as a web developer to use drag and drop just as a desktop developer does.

Implementing drag and drop in a Flex application utilizes the Drag and Drop Manager and the tools it provides. The Drag and Drop Manager enables you to write a Flex application in which users can select an object, drag it over another, and drop it on the second object. All Flex components support drag-and-drop operations, and a subset has additional drag-and-drop functionality, in which implementation is little more than adding a single property.

In this lesson you will implement drag and drop in your e-commerce application so a user can click on a product, drag it to the shopping cart, and drop it to add it to the shopping cart.

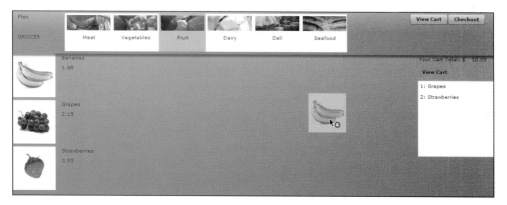

Dragging a grocery item to the shopping cart

Introducing the Drag and Drop Manager

The first step in understanding the Drag and Drop Manager is to learn the terminology surrounding it. The terminology is summarized in the following table.

Term	Definition
Drag initiator	Component or item from a component being dragged from
Drag source	Data being dragged
Format	Property of the DragSource that allows an object to be dropped, or not, on another object; the data in the DragSource is also associated with the format; the data type of the formats are simple strings
Drag proxy	Image displayed during the dragging process
Drop target	Component the drag proxy is over

The following figure gives you a visual representation of the terminology:

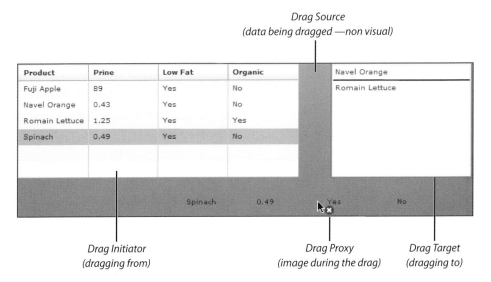

Drag Source
(data being dragged —non visual)

Drag Initiator
(dragging from)

Drag Proxy
(image during the drag)

Drag Target
(dragging to)

There are three phases to a drag-and-drop operation:

1. Initiating: A user clicks a Flex component or an item in a Flex component and then begins to move the component or item while holding down the mouse. The component or item is the drag initiator.

2. Dragging: While holding down the mouse button, the user moves the mouse around the screen. Flex displays an image called a drag proxy, and the associated nonvisual object called the drag source holds the data associated with the component or item being dragged.

3. Dropping: When the user moves over another component that will allow it, the item can be dropped onto a drop target. The data is then inserted into the new component in some way.

Flex components fall into two groups when it comes to drag-and-drop support, those with enhanced drag-and-drop functionality and those without it. The following list-based controls have enhanced support for drag and drop:

- DataGrid
- PrintDataGrid
- Tree
- Menu
- List
- HorizontalList
- TileList

What this means to you as a developer is that your life will be a little bit easier when implementing drag and drop with those controls that have enhanced support. In fact, in many cases it might be no more than setting a single property value for each of the controls involved in the drag-and-drop operation.

Dragging and Dropping Between Two DataGrids

Your first foray into implementing drag-and-drop operations in Flex will be between two DataGrids. Because they are list-based components and have enhanced drag-and-drop support, this will require the least amount of coding on your part to make work.

Two properties are important in this first phase: `dragEnabled` and `dropEnabled`. Here are their descriptions:

- `dragEnabled`: Assigned a Boolean value to specify whether the control is allowed to act as a drag initiator (defaults to `false`). When `true`, the user can drag items from the component.

- dropEnabled: Assigned a Boolean value to specify whether the control is allowed to act as a drop target (defaults to false). When true, the user can drop items onto the control using the default drop behavior.

Stated most simply, you set the dragEnabled property in the component from which you are dragging to true, and set the dropEnabled property in the component on which you are dropping true.

So now you will put your drag-and-drop knowledge to use by implementing drag and drop from one DataGrid to another DataGrid.

1 Select File > New > Flex Project. Select Basic and then click Next.

You do not need FDS or ColdFusion support for this project.

2 Make the project name **flex2tfs_DragDrop** and use your flex2tfs/Lesson12/dragDrop/ start folder. Click Next.

The directory contains starter files you will use for your exploration of drag and drop.

3 Click the Browse button next to the Main application file option and select the file Task1_DG_to_DG.mxml. Click OK and then click Finish.

You are creating a new project because some of the work in this lesson will not be directly involved with any of the three applications you are working on from the FlexGrocer site.

4 Examine the code in the Task1_DG_to_DG.mxml file, and then run it.

Note that the existing code does not use any concepts you have not already learned in this book. The file uses an HTTPService remote procedure call (RPC) to get back grocery info. It then uses a result handler to place the data into an ArrayCollection and is then used as a dataProvider in a DataGrid. When you run the application you see you have a DataGrid populated with grocery product info and another DataGrid below it. Try to drag and drop between the DataGrids; you will see that this functionality is not yet working.

5 In the first DataGrid set the dragEnabled property to true. Run the application; you can click one of the rows in the DataGrid and drag the drag proxy around the screen.

Setting this property did two obvious things: it enabled dragging and created the drag proxy, the image attached to the mouse pointer when dragging. Another nonvisual event occurred at the same time, and that is a DragSource object was created to hold the data. The data is associated with a format named items, as the following screenshot from the debugger shows:

DragSource object

Actual data here

6 In the `<mx:Script>` block below the existing variable declaration, create a bindable private variable named `targetGridDP` of data type ArrayCollection and set it equal to a new ArrayCollection. Then bind this variable as the `dataProvider` of the second DataGrid, whose id is `targetGrid`.

These two steps initialize the `dataProvider` of the drop target DataGrid. This means it tells the control what the data type is of the data it will be dealing with. If you do not do this, you will get run-time errors.

7 In the second DataGrid, set the `dropEnabled` property to `true`. Your second DataGrid should appear as follows:

```
<mx:DataGrid id="targetGrid"
  dataProvider="{targetGridDP}"
  dropEnabled="true">
  <mx:columns>
    <mx:DataGridColumn dataField="name"
      headerText="Product"/>
    <mx:DataGridColumn dataField="category"
      headerText="Category"/>
  </mx:columns>
</mx:DataGrid>
```

You've done three basic steps so far to drag-and-drop–enable the application:

- Added the `dragEnabled` property to the drag initiator
- Initialized the drop target's `dataProvider`
- Added the `dropEnabled` property to the drop target

Now you're ready to test.

8 Run the application and drag from the first DataGrid and drop into the second.

Notice that the entire set of data for the row is dragged, not just the visible properties in the DataGrid. The `category` column is not displayed in the first DataGrid, but when dropped, that column is displayed in the second DataGrid. This shows you that all the data for the row is in the DragSource, not just the rows that happen to be displayed.

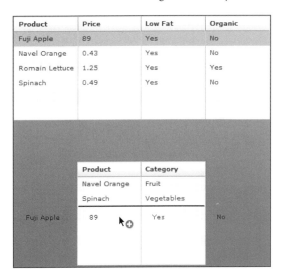

Dragging and Dropping Between a DataGrid and a List

In the last task in describing the `dropEnabled` property the following sentence was used, "When true, the user can drop items onto the control using the default drop behavior." So what is this "default drop behavior"? Basically it means that Flex will try to figure out what should be dropped and do what it thinks is best, but that might not be what you want. In the last task it was clear to Flex that when dragging from one DataGrid to another, the columns in the drop target DataGrid should be filled with like-named properties from the DragSource data.

In this task you will drag from a DataGrid to a List component. In this case the "default drop behavior" won't know what data to drop into the List and will dump the whole object into the List, which is not what you want.

In this case, you have to use a drag event to get the data that you want into the List. Here is a summary of the events for both the drag initiator and the drop target:

Drag Events for the Drag Initiator	Description
mouseDown and mouseMove (MouseEvent class)	Although not drag events, these MouseEvent class events are used to start the drag-and-drop process when not using dragEnabled components. The mouseDown event is broadcast when the user selects a control with the mouse and holds down the mouse button. The mouseMove event is broadcast when the mouse moves.
dragComplete event (DragEvent class)	Broadcast when a drag operation completes, either when the drag data drops onto a drop target or when the drag-and-drop operation ends without performing a drop operation.

Drag Events for the Drop Target (all events of the DragEvent class)	Description
dragEnter	Broadcast when a drag proxy moves over the target from outside the target.
dragOver	Broadcast while the user moves the mouse over the target, after the dragEnter event.
dragDrop	Broadcast when the mouse is released over the target.
dragExit	Broadcast when the user drags outside the drop target, but does not drop the data onto the target.

Now it is time to get to work.

1 Examine the code in the Task2_DG_to_List.mxml file and then run it. Drag from the DataGrid to the List; you will see [object Object] appear in the List.

The default drop behavior did not know what data you wanted placed in the List, so it dropped the whole data object in. Because the List cannot display the entire object, it lets you know what has happened by displaying [object Object]. The following example shows the default behavior when dragging from DataGrid to the List.

Product	Prine	Low Fat	Organic		[object Object]
Fuji Apple	89	Yes	No		
Navel Orange	0.43	Yes	No		
Romain Lettuce	1.25	Yes	Yes		
Spinach	0.49	Yes	No		

2 Add a `dragDrop` event listener to the List, and call a function named `doDragDrop()` in the ActionScript executed when the event is broadcast. Pass the event object as a parameter to the function.

```
<mx:List id="targetList"
    width="200"
    dropEnabled="true"
    dataProvider="{targetListDP}"
    dragDrop="doDragDrop(event)"/>
```

The event is named `dragDrop`, and you have no control over that. The function name `doDragDrop()` is a good choice for the function name, but it can be named whatever you choose.

3 At the bottom of the `<mx:Script>` block, create a private function named `doDragDrop()` data typed as void. The function should accept a parameter named event data typed as `DragEvent`. Also import the class `mx.events.DragEvent`.

This function will be called when the user drops the drag proxy onto the List, which is the drop target in this application. Later in this task, you will write code in this function to display just the name of the product in the List.

4 As the first line of code in the function, create a variable local to the function named `dgRow` data typed as Object and set equal to a new Object.

```
var dgRow:Object=new Object();
```

This variable will be used to store information about the row dragged from the DataGrid and stored in the DataSource object.

5 As the second line of code in the function, set the `dgRow` variable equal to the data in the DragSource object associated with the `items` format. Use the `dataForFormat()` method.

```
dgRow=event.dragSource.dataForFormat("items");
```

The dataForFormat() method is a method of the DragSource class. It retrieves from the DragSource object the data associated with the particular format—in this case, items.

✱ **NOTE:** Remember that the format name associated with data in a DataGrid is always items.

6 Set a breakpoint at the closing brace of the doDragDrop() function. You do this by double-clicking in the marker bar just to the left of the line numbers in the editor. You will see a small blue dot appear to indicate the breakpoint was set.

The breakpoint will cause Flex Builder to halt execution at the marked line of code, and you will be able to check values of variables. You will learn more about the debugger in Lesson 25, "Debugging and Optimizing Flex Applications."

7 Debug the application and drag a row to the List. When you drop the drag proxy, the process flow will return to Flex Builder and then you should view the Debugging perspective. Examine the dgRow variable value in the Variables view. You should then see that the variable contains all the data from that DataGrid row.

The following example shows the row of data being dragged.

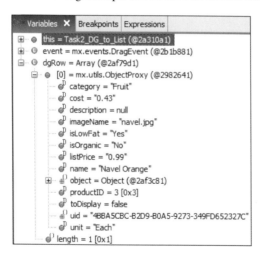

Notice that the variable contains an array of length 1, which means you have only 1 index, which is 0. Also note that the name property contains the name of the product.

▶ **TIP:** If you want to allow the user to drag multiple rows of data, set the DataGrid multipleSelection property equal to true.

8 Terminate the debugging session by clicking the red box in either the Debug or Console views. Return to the Development perspective by clicking on the chevron (>>) in the upper-right corner of Builder and selecting that perspective.

Normally, the Development perspective is best to work in because you can see so much more of your code.

9 As the third line of code in the function, add the name of the product to the List by using the addItem() method of the List's dataProvider. Remember that the dgRow variable contained an array of length 1, so use dgRow[0].name to reference the name.

```
targetList.dataProvider.addItem(dgRow[0].name);
```

This is a case in which viewing how the data is stored using the debugger is very helpful in retrieving the information.

10 Run the application and drag from the DataGrid to the List. You should see the product being placed in the List, but [object Object] also appears.

The event continued to do what it was supposed to do, even though you displayed some different data; hence you still see the reference to the object.

Product	Prine	Low Fat	Organic		[object Object]
Fuji Apple	89	Yes	No		Fuji Apple
Navel Orange	0.43	Yes	No		
Romain Lettuce	1.25	Yes	Yes		
Spinach	0.49	Yes	No		

11 As the last line in the function, use the event class' preventDefault() method to cancel the event default behavior.

```
event.preventDefault();
```

In this case, you can cancel the default behavior. Not all events can be canceled; you must check the documentation for definitive answers on an event-by-event basis. By cancelling this event, you prevent the display of [object Object] in the List.

12 Run the application. When you drag from DataGrid to List, only the name of the product appears in the List.

This wraps up our second task in this lesson on drag and drop.

Using a Nondrag–Enabled Component in a Drag-and-Drop Operation

So far, you have been taking advantage of enhanced functionality in list-based components when it concerns drag and drop. Now it is time to learn how to implement drag and drop on non-enhanced components. In this particular task, the use case is very simple: you want to drag a Label to a List. Because the Label does not have enhanced drag-and-drop functionality, there is more of a burden on you as the developer in implementation.

Understanding what the list-based components did for you is a good place to start when having to write all the implementation yourself. Here is a list of mechanisms, hidden from you when using the list-based components, which you will need to do when implementing drag and drop without the help of the enhanced components:

- Assign the data to the DragSource object.
- Check to see whether the formats allow dropping into the drop target.
- Use the data in the drop target (although in the second task you did some of this manually).
- Permit the component to be dragged.
- Actually accept the drop.

Although you have been using the DragSource class up to now in this lesson, you will need to dig deeper into the class when implementing all the functionality yourself. In this task, you use the following methods of the DragSource class:

Method of DragSource Class	Description
addData(data:*,format:String):void	Adds data to the associated format in the DragSource object; the * denotes the data can be of any data type.
hasFormat(format:String):Boolean	Returns true if the DataSource object contains a matching format of the drop target; otherwise, it returns false.
dataForFormat(format:String):Array of *	Retrieves the data for the specified format added by the addData() method; returns an Array of objects containing the data in the requested format; a single item is returned in a one item Array.

These methods allow you to implement the first three hidden mechanisms. To accomplish the last two, you need to use methods of the DragManager class:.

Method of DragManager Class	Description
doDrag(initiator:Component, ➥ dragSource:DragSource, ➥ mouseEvent:MouseEvent):void	Enables the initiator component to be initially dragged; often in an event handler for mouseDown or mouseMove.
acceptDragDrop(target:Component):void	Call this method in your dragEnter handler; often used in an if statement where the condition uses the hasFormat() method.

> ▶ **TIP:** The doDrag() method has a number of optional parameters to control the look of the drag proxy.

Now you're ready to start coding this task.

1 Examine the code in the Task3_Label_to_List.mxml file and then run it.

   You see you have a Label with the text "Drag me" in it and an empty List below it. At this point, there is no drag-and-drop functionality working.

2 Import the four classes shown here that you will need in the application:

```
import mx.core.DragSource;
import mx.managers.DragManager;
import mx.events.DragEvent;
import mx.core.IUIComponent;
```

   You could have also just used these classes as data types, and Flex Builder would have imported them for you automatically.

3 In the Label, add a mouseDown event and have the event call a function named dragIt().
The function call should pass four parameters; the first is the drag initiator, which in this
case is the instance name of the Label: myLabel. The second parameter is the data you
will later place in the DragSource object. In this case, just pass a String of "My data here".
The third parameter is the event, which of course is just event. The last parameter is the
format that will be associated with this data. In this task, use myFormat.

```
mouseDown="dragIt(myLabel,'My data here',event,'myFormat')"
```

This is the function that will be called to initiate the drag-and-drop operation. You need
to pass the parameters because they are all needed in the function to allow:

- Dragging to start

- Placing the data in the DragSource object associated with the format

4 At the bottom of the <mx:Script> block, create a private function named dragIt(), data
typed as void. The function should accept four parameters that, of course, correspond to
the data passed to the function. Use the names and data types shown here:

```
initiator:Label
dsData:String
event:MouseEvent
format:String
```

Of these parameters, the initiator could be any kind of component, and the dsData
could be nearly any kind of data you want to be dragged from one component to another.
The event will often be the mouseDown MouseEvent or the mouseMove event, but that would
not change either the event parameter name nor the data type used here. The format will
always be a String.

5 As the first line of code in the function, create a variable local to the function named ds
data typed as DragSource and set it equal to a new DragSource object.

```
var ds:DragSource=new DragSource();
```

This creates the DragSource object that will have data added to it.

6 Next in the function, use the addData() method of the ds DragSource object to add the
data passed in the dsData parameter to the ds object. Associate it with the format passed
in the format parameter.

```
ds.addData(dsData,format);
```

An important point here is that you can store data associated with multiple formats,
which means you can use multiple addData() methods on the same DragSource object.

You might want to do this if you have multiple drop targets and want to drop different data in each drop target. The different drop targets would use different arguments in the `dataForFormat()` method to get the appropriate data.

7 As the last line of code in the function, permit the Label to be dragged by calling the static `doDrag()` method of the DragManager class. You pass it the three parameters `initiator`, `ds`, and `event`. Check to make sure that your completed function appears as shown here:

```
private function dragIt(initiator:Label,dsData:String,event:MouseEvent,
   ➥ format:String):void{
   var ds:DragSource=new DragSource();
   ds.addData(dsData,format);
   DragManager.doDrag(initiator,ds,event);
}
```

Remember that a static method is one you can invoke directly from the class without first instantiating it.

8 Run the application and drag the Label. At this point there is no drop target that will accept the Label.

You now move on to coding the List to accept the drop of the Label and displaying the data passed in the DragSource in the List.

9 In the List, add a `dragEnter` event and have it call a function named `doDragEnter()`. The function should pass two parameters. The first is the event, and the second is the format—which in this case should match the format used earlier: `myFormat`.

```
dragEnter="doDragEnter(event,'myFormat')"
```

You are passing data to the function that allows the initiator, the Label, to be dropped on the drop target, the List.

10 At the bottom of the `<mx:Script>` block, create a private function named `doDragEnter()`, data typed as void. The function should accept two parameters. Name the first parameter event, data typed as DragEvent, and the second parameter `format`, data typed as String.

Both these parameter values are needed to allow the dropping of the initiator.

11 Insert into the function an `if` statement that checks to see whether the formats of the two objects match. Use the `hasFormat()` method of the dragSource object, which is contained in the event object. The argument of the `hasFormat()` method should be the `format` parameter passed to the function.

```
if(event.dragSource.hasFormat(format)){
}
```

What is occurring is that the List is looking in the DragSource object and seeing whether a format exists that matches the formats it is allowed to accept. The hasFormat() function will return either true or false.

12 If the hasFormat() function returns true, use the DragManager's static function acceptDragDrop() method to allow the dropping. The argument of the function should be the List itself, which is best referred to in this case as event.target.

```
DragManager.acceptDragDrop(event.target);
```

You could have actually replaced event.target with the instance name of the List, myList, and the function would have had the same result. The advantage of using the more generic event.target is that it makes this function more reusable. You can use the function for any dragEnter result handler—it will work correctly.

13 The acceptDragDrop() method is defined to accept an object of type IUIComponent. For this reason you need to cast event.target as an IUIComponent to satisfy the compiler.

The IUIComponent class defines the basic set of APIs that must implemented to be a child of a Flex container or list.

14 Be sure that the new function appears as follows and then run the application.

```
private function doDragEnter(event:DragEvent,format:String):void{
    if(event.dragSource.hasFormat(format)){
        DragManager.acceptDragDrop(IUIComponent(event.target));
    }
}
```

You should now be able to drag the Label. When it moves over the List, the red X disappears, and you can drop the drag proxy. At this point, nothing happens when you do the drop.

15 In the List, add a dragDrop event and have it call a function named doDragDrop(). The function should pass two parameters, the event and the format, which in this case should match the format used earlier: myFormat.

```
dragDrop="doDragDrop(event,'myFormat')"
```

You are passing the data needed to have the data retrieved from the DragSource and have it displayed in the List.

16 At the bottom of the `<mx:Script>` block, create a private function named `doDragDrop()`, data typed as void. The function should accept two parameters. Name the first parameter event, data typed as DragEvent, and the second parameter `format`, data typed as String.

You need the event object in this function because it contains the DragSource object, and that is where the data is stored. Remember that you stored the String `"My data here"` in the DragSource object in steps 3–6 of this task. The format is needed because that is how you pull data from the DragSource object using the `dataForFormat()` method.

17 As the first line of code in the new function, create a variable local to the function named `myLabelData`, data typed as Object, and set it equal to a new Object.

```
var myLabelData:Object=new Object();
```

This is a temporary variable to hold the data when extracted form the DragSource object.

18 Use the `dataForFormat()` function to retrieve the data from the `dragSource` property of the event object. The argument of the function should be the `format` parameter passed to the function.

```
myLabelData=event.dragSource.dataForFormat(format);
```

Remember that you can store data associated with multiple formats, so you must specify which format's data to retrieve when retrieving data.

19 Display the data just retrieved in the List. You need to use the `addItem()` method on the List's `dataProvider` property to do this.

```
myList.dataProvider.addItem(myLabelData);
```

You have achieved your goal of moving the Label's data into the List.

20 Be sure that the new function appears as follows and then run the application.

```
private function doDragDrop(event:DragEvent,format:String):void{
   var myLabelData:Object=new Object();
   myLabelData=event.dragSource.dataForFormat(format);
   myList.dataProvider.addItem(myLabelData);
}
```

Now when you drag and drop the Label onto the List, you will see that the data from the Label, the String `"My data here"`, is displayed in the List. The following example shows the List after successfully dropping the Label data.

Now that you have a solid background in drag and drop, you will implement drag-and-drop functionality in the e-commerce application of FlexGrocer.

Dragging a Grocery Item to the Shopping Cart

The culmination of your work in this lesson is to implement dragging a grocery item into the shopping cart, which you will do in this task. The tasks you have performed so far in this lesson have prepared you well for this last task; in fact, some of the code you have already written will be copied and pasted for use in this task.

In this task, you will permit the user to click the grocery item, drag it to the small shopping cart, and then drop it in. The grocery item is displayed in a Canvas, and the shopping cart is a List. Because the Canvas is not a drag-and-drop–enhanced component, you will have to pattern your code here after what you just wrote in the section, "Using a Nondrag–Enabled Component in a Drag-and-Drop Operation."

1 Open the file views/ecomm/GroceryDetail.mxml.

This is the component in which the grocery data is displayed, so this is where you will have to permit the data to be dragged.

▶ **TIP:** At first, you will drag all the data to the shopping cart and then write the code so that just the image of the item acts as the drag proxy.

2 In the <mx:Canvas> which is the root tag of the component, add a mouseMove event and have the event call a function named dragIt(). The function call should pass four parameters. The first is the drag initiator, which in this case is the component itself, which you reference as this. The second parameter is the data you will later place in the DragSource object. In this case, it is the instance of the Product class named groceryItem. The third parameter is the event, which is named event. The last parameter is the format that will be associated with this data. In this task, use cartFormat.

```
mouseMove="dragIt(this,groceryItem,event,'cartFormat')"
```

By placing the mouseMove event on the root container tag of the component it will enable the user to start the drag process by clicking any information about the grocery item.

3 Open the file Task3_Label_to_List.mxml and copy the dragIt() function from the <mx:Script> block of that file to the bottom of the <mx:Script> block of GroceryDetail.mxml. Change the data type of the first parameter, initiator, from Label to Canvas. Change the data type of the second parameter, dsData, from String to Product.

```
private function dragIt(
   ➥ initiator:Canvas,dsData:Product,event:MouseEvent,format:String):void{
   var ds:DragSource=new DragSource();
   ds.addData(dsData,format);
   DragManager.doDrag(initiator,ds,event);
}
```

The way in which you built this function in the previous section enabled you to bring it into this task almost unchanged. Because the initiator is a Canvas instead of a Label, and because the data you passed to it is an instance of a Product instead of a String, you had to change those data types and nothing else.

Recall that this function has two main purposes: to get data into the object being dragged and to permit the component to be dragged. The first line of code creates a new DragSource object; then the second line places the Product object passed to the function into the DragSource object and associates it with the format passed to the function. The third line of code actually enables the Canvas that contains the grocery item information to be dragged.

4 At the top of the <mx:Script> block, import the mx.managers.DragManager and mx.core.DragSource classes.

These classes are used in the function you just copied into the file.

5 Run the EComm.mxml application. You should be able to drag the grocery item data.

You see the drag proxy is the outline of the Canvas, or a big rectangular box. Later in this task, you will change the drag proxy to the image of the grocery item.

At this point there is no drop target, so you cannot drop the data anywhere.

6 Open the file EComm.mxml.

This file contains the List that is your shopping cart to which grocery items are dragged.

7 Locate the List with the id of `cartView` and add a *dragEnter* event to the List. In the ActionScript the event executes, call a `doDragEnter()` function and pass it two parameters: event and the String `cartFormat`.

```
dragEnter="doDragEnter(event,cartFormat')"
```

You pass the information to this function that will permit the drag initiator to be dropped on the List.

8 Open the file as/ecomm.as.

Remember that this file is actually what would be in the `<mx:Script>` block in EComm.mxml, but it was pulled out and placed in an external file.

9 From the file Task3_Label_to_List.mxml, copy the `doDragEnter()` function from the `<mx:Script>` block and paste it to the bottom of the ecomm.as file.

```
private function doDragEnter(event:DragEvent,format:String):void{
   if(event.dragSource.hasFormat(format)){
      DragManager.acceptDragDrop(IUIComponent(event.target));
   }
}
```

Because you wrote the function generically using only the parameters passed to the function, no changes need to be made in this function.

This function has only one purpose: to check whether formats enable the drag initiator to be dropped. The `if` statement determines whether there are matching formats; then the `acceptDragDrop()` method allows the actual dropping to take place.

10 At the top of the `file`, import the mx.managers.DragManager, mx.events.DragEvent and mx.core.IUIComponent classes.

These classes are used in the function you just copied into the file.

11 Run the EComm.mxml application. You should be able to drag the grocery item data; when you drag over the shopping cart List, you should see the red X disappear and you can drop the drag proxy.

At this point, nothing happens when you drop the drag proxy.

12 In EComm.mxml, locate the List with the id of `cartView` and add a *dragDrop* event to the List. In the ActionScript, the event calls a `doDragDrop()` function and passes it two parameters: event and the String `cartFormat`.

```
dragDrop="doDragDrop(event,cartFormat')"
```

You pass the information to this function which will place data in the shopping cart.

13 In the file Task3_Label_to_List.mxml, copy the doDragDrop() function from the <mx:Script> block of that file to the bottom of the ecomm.as file. Remove the code in the body of the function so you are left with just the skeleton of the function.

```
private function doDragDrop(event:DragEvent,format:String):void{

}
```

In this case, the code in the function will completely change. You previously placed a String in a Label; now you will be adding a ShoppingCartItem to a shopping cart, so none of the existing code is applicable except the signature of the function.

▶ **TIP:** Open the file valueObjects/ShoppingCartItem.as and review that the constructor's parameters are a Product object and an optional quantity.

14 As the first line of code in the function, create a variable local to the function named prodObj, data typed as Product. Use the static buildProduct() method of the Product class to set prodObj equal to a new Product object. The argument of the buildProduct() method should be the object in the DragSource. Retrieve it using the dataForFormat() method.

```
var prodObj:Product=Product.buildProduct(
    ➥ event.dragSource.dataForFormat(format));
```

This Product object is needed to create a ShoppingCartItem in the next step of the task.

15 Next in the function, create a variable local to the function named sci, data typed as ShoppingCartItem. Set that variable equal to a new ShoppingCartItem. The argument of the ShoppingCartItem constructor should be the Product object created in the last step.

```
var sci:ShoppingCartItem = new ShoppingCartItem(prodObj);
```

Here is a quick review of how the Product object got in the DragSource:

- In steps 2 and 3 of this task you passed a Product object to the dragIt() function.

- The function placed the product object into the DragSource object using the addData() method and associated it with the cartFormat format.

- In this function you retrieved that same Product and will now place it in the shopping cart.

16 As the last line of code in the function, invoke the addItem() method of the cart ShoppingCart object and pass the sci ShoppingCartItem variable as a parameter. Check to be sure your function appears as shown here.

```
private function doDragDrop(event:DragEvent,format:String):void{
   var prodObj:Product=
     ➥ Product.buildProduct(event.dragSource.dataForFormat(format));
   var sci:ShoppingCartItem = new ShoppingCartItem(prodObj);
   cart.addItem(sci);
}
```

The method invocation actually places the ShoppingCartItem object in the shopping cart.

17 As of Flex 2, there is a bug in the drop target's location. As a work around for the bug add the following code to the bottom of ecomm.as:

```
override public function localToContent(point:Point):Point {
   return point;
}
```

18 Run the application. You can now drag and drop grocery items into the shopping cart.

You see that the drag-and-drop operation is working, but the drag proxy is the whole container that surrounds the grocery item data. In the next step you add code so the drag proxy becomes just the image of the grocery item.

19 Return to GroceryDetail.mxml and locate the dragIt() function in the <mx:Script> block. At the top of the function create a new Image object local to the function named imageProxy. Use the load() method of the Image class to assign the current imageName in the groceryItem to the Image object. You can find the correct path for the image by finding it in the existing <mx:Image> tag currently displaying the grocery item. Finally, set both the height and width of the new Image object to 80.

```
var imageProxy:Image=new Image();
imageProxy.load("../assets/"+groceryItem.imageName);
imageProxy.height=80;
imageProxy.width=80;
```

The reason you must create a new Image object is because by default the drag-and-drop operation removes the drag proxy from its source. You could have simply given the image being displayed an instance name and used it as the drag proxy, but after dragging and dropping the image would no longer be shown with the other grocery item data. Also, the default width and height are 0 by default when you create a new Image object in ActionScript, so you must set those property values for the image to be visible.

20 In the `DragManager.doDrag()` method invocation, add a fourth parameter of `imageProxy`.

`DragManager.doDrag(initiator,ds,event,imageProxy);`

This fourth parameter represents the `dragImage`. Instead of the outline of the container of the grocery item data being the drag proxy, you have now specified that only the image of the item should be displayed when dragging is taking place.

21 Check to be sure that your `dragIt()` function appears as follows; then run the application. You should be able to drag the image of the grocery item and drop it in the cart.

```
private function dragIt(initiator:Canvas,dsData:Product,event:MouseEvent,format:
String):void{
    var imageProxy:Image=new Image();
    imageProxy.load("../assets/"+groceryItem.imageName);
    imageProxy.height=80;
    imageProxy.width=80;
    var ds:DragSource=new DragSource();
    ds.addData(dsData,format);
    DragManager.doDrag(initiator,ds,event,imageProxy);
}
```

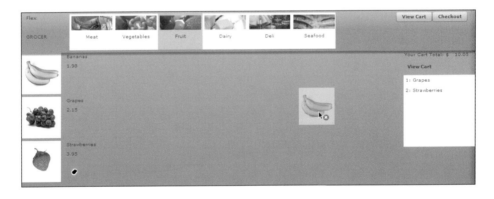

This completes the last task of the lesson.

What You Have Learned

In this lesson, you have:

- Implemented drag-and-drop operations between two drag-enabled components and used the default drop process (pages 285–288)

- Implemented drag-and-drop operation between two drag-enabled components and customized the drop process to use the data stored in the DragSource object (pages 288–292)

- Implemented drag-and-drop operations between nondrag-enabled components (pages 293–299)

- Implemented drag-and-drop operations between nondrag-enabled components and used a custom `dragImage` (pages 299–304)

What You Will Learn

In this lesson, you will:

- Use the ViewStack class as the basis for implementing navigation
- Use the ViewStack selectedIndex and selectedChild properties for navigation
- Use built-in tools to control a ViewStack and normal Button controls
- Use the TabNavigator to place two different kinds of application functionality on different tabs
- Use and manipulate a date control and the Date class

Approximate Time

This lesson takes approximately 1 hour and 30 minutes to complete.

Lesson Files

Media Files:

Lesson13/assets/CCInfo.mxml
Lesson13/assets/HomePage.mxml

Starting Files:

Lesson13/start/DataEntry.mxml
Lesson13/start/EComm.mxml
Lesson13/start/as/ecomm.as

Completed Files:

Lesson13/complete/DataEntry.mxml
Lesson13/complete/EComm.mxml
Lesson13/complete/as/ecomm.as
Lesson13/complete/events/ObjectDataEvent.as
Lesson13/complete/valueObjects/OrderInfo.as
Lesson13/complete/views/ecomm/BillingInfo.mxml
Lesson13/complete/views/ecomm/CCInfo.mxml
Lesson13/complete/views/ecomm/Checkout.mxml
Lesson13/complete/views/ecomm/HomePage.mxml
Lesson13/complete/views/ecomm/OrderConf.mxml

LESSON 13

Implementing Navigation

Imperative to any application is a navigation system. You want the user to be able to easily move around your application and locate the needed functionality. In technical terms, Flex implements navigation by using a special set of containers, called navigator containers, that control user movement through a group of child containers (for example, VBox, HBox, Canvas, and even other navigator containers).

Some navigation will be completely at the user's discretion, such as clicking a button to move to the home page or the checkout process. Other navigation can be tightly controlled by you, the developer—for example, a checkout process in which users cannot proceed to the next screen until certain conditions are met on an existing screen. In this lesson you will implement both types of navigation.

The checkout process will be controlled by a ViewStack, one of Flex's navigator containers.

Introducing Navigation

Navigation enables users to move through your application and (just as important) enables you to control user movement through the application. For an example of letting the user choose where to move in an application, you will add navigation to the data-entry application so the user can choose between adding a product and updating/deleting a product. Right now, functionality for both processes share the same crowded screen. There are also times when you want to control the user's movement through an application. You will do this in this lesson when you implement a checkout process to the e-commerce application. During this process, you need to control which screens the user sees and when. Both approaches are easily implemented using Flex's navigator containers.

Navigator containers control user movement through the application by controlling which containers are displayed. You've used many containers so far (for example, Canvas, VBox, HBox, and Form); they enable you to add functionality to move among them. Here is a list of Flex's navigator components displayed in the Components panel:

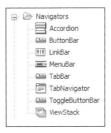

At the heart of navigation in Flex is the ViewStack class, which is a Flex container component. The ViewStack is a collection of other containers, or children, that are stacked on top of each other so only one is visible at a time. You then add functionality to control which child is visible at any one time. The ViewStack can have only other containers as children, including other navigator containers. If you use a noncontainer as a child of a ViewStack a run-time error is produced. So this is a valid ViewStack because it contains only containers:

```
<mx:ViewStack id="myNav" height="100%" width="100%">
    <mx:HBox id="child0" label="Child 0">
        <mx:Label text="Zeroth child label 1" fontSize="40"/>
        <mx:Label text="Zeroth child label 2" fontSize="40"/>
    </mx:HBox>
    <mx:VBox id="child1" label="Child 1">
        <mx:Label text="First child label 1" fontSize="40"/>
        <mx:Label text="First child label 2" fontSize="40"/>
    </mx:VBox>
</mx:ViewStack>
```

The following would generate a run-time error because the ViewStack contains a Label component that is not a container:

```
<mx:ViewStack id="myNav" height="100%" width="100%">
    <mx:HBox id="child0" label="Child 0">
        <mx:Label text="Zeroth child label 1" fontSize="40"/>
        <mx:Label text="Zeroth child label 2" fontSize="40"/>
    </mx:HBox>
    <mx:VBox id="child1" label="Child 1">
        <mx:Label text="First child label 1" fontSize="40"/>
        <mx:Label text="First child label 2" fontSize="40"/>
    </mx:VBox>
    <mx:Label text="This will not work here"/>
</mx:ViewStack>
```

Although the ViewStack is the key element to implementing navigation in Flex, it does not intrinsically have a way to switch which child is visible; that must be done using another tool. You can use built-in tools to control the ViewStack or build your own.

An example built-in component to control the ViewStack is the LinkBar. If you set the dataProvider of the LinkBar to be the ViewStack, a link will appear for each child. Displayed on the link will be the label of the child container. For instance, code using a ViewStack and LinkBar is shown as follows, followed by its result when run. In the result, the middle link displaying the VBox container has been clicked.

```
<mx:LinkBar dataProvider="{myNav}" fontSize="30"/>
<mx:ViewStack id="myNav" height="100%" width="100%">
    <mx:HBox id="child0" label="Child 0">
        <mx:Label text="Zeroth child label 1" fontSize="20"/>
        <mx:Label text="Zeroth child label 2" fontSize="20"/>
    </mx:HBox>
    <mx:VBox id="child1" label="Child 1">
        <mx:Label text="First child label 1" fontSize="20"/>
        <mx:Label text="First child label 2" fontSize="20"/>
    </mx:VBox>
    <mx:HBox id="child2" label="Child 2">
        <mx:Label text="Second child label 1" fontSize="20"/>
        <mx:Label text="Second child label 2" fontSize="20"/>
    </mx:HBox>
</mx:ViewStack>
```

The following example is of a ViewStack being used with a LinkBar (with the middle link selected).

```
Child 0  Child 1  Child 2
First child label 1
First child label 2
```

You might want to control navigation by implementing your own process, such as by using Buttons. If you do this, two properties of the ViewStack are very important: `selectedIndex` and `selectedChild`. You use the `selectedIndex` to choose which child of the ViewStack should be displayed.

> ✳ **NOTE:** The ViewStack is zero-indexed, so the "first" child is numerated 0 in human terms.

Use the `selectedChild` property if you would rather indicate which child of the ViewStack should be displayed by a logical name rather than numeric index. The `selectedChild` property will display the appropriate container in the ViewStack based on the instance name provided in the `id` property. The following example shows how to use plain Button components to control which child of the ViewStack is displayed using both the `selectedChild` and `selectedIndex`:

```
<mx:HBox>
    <mx:Button label="Child 0" click="myNav.selectedIndex=0"/>
    <mx:Button label="Child 1" click="myNav.selectedChild=child1"/>
    <mx:Button label="Child 2" click="myNav.selectedIndex=2"/>
</mx:HBox>
<mx:ViewStack id="myNav" height="100%" width="100%">
    <mx:HBox id="child0">
        <mx:Label text="Zeroth child label 1" fontSize="20"/>
        <mx:Label text="Zeroth child label 2" fontSize="20"/>
    </mx:HBox>
    <mx:VBox id="child1">
        <mx:Label text="First child label 1" fontSize="20"/>
        <mx:Label text="First child label 2" fontSize="20"/>
    </mx:VBox>
    <mx:HBox id="child2">
        <mx:Label text="Second child label 1" fontSize="20"/>
        <mx:Label text="Second child label 2" fontSize="20"/>
    </mx:HBox>
</mx:ViewStack>
```

This would create a result as shown here when run (with the middle Button clicked). The following example is of a ViewStack being used with Buttons:

With this brief overview of the navigator containers, you are now ready to implement navigation in your applications.

Using a TabNavigator in the Data-entry Application

The ViewStack class has no built-in mechanism to control which child container is displayed or made active. A number of tools are supplied by Flex to control this—one of them is the TabNavigator. This class, which extends the ViewStack, builds tabs for each child container and uses the label property of the container to determine what should be displayed on each tab. When you click a tab, the content in the corresponding container will be displayed or made active. You simply replace the <mx:ViewStack> tags with <mx:TabNavigator> tags to use this navigator container, as shown here:

```
<mx:TabNavigator id="myNav" height="200" width="450">
  <mx:HBox label="Child 0">
    <mx:Label text="Zeroth child label 1" fontSize="20"/>
    <mx:Label text="Zeroth child label 2" fontSize="20"/>
  </mx:HBox>
  <mx:VBox label="Child 1">
    <mx:Label text="First child label 1" fontSize="20"/>
    <mx:Label text="First child label 2" fontSize="20"/>
  </mx:VBox>
  <mx:HBox label="Child 2">
    <mx:Label text="Second child label 1" fontSize="20"/>
    <mx:Label text="Second child label 2" fontSize="20"/>
  </mx:HBox>
</mx:TabNavigator>
```

This code generates the following when run (with the last tab clicked):

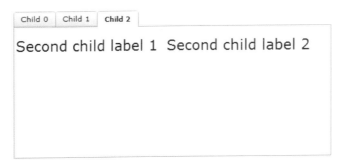

You will now use a TabNavigator component to place the two pieces of functionality in the data-entry application, updating/deleting products and adding products, onto different tabs.

1 Open DataEntry.mxml.

In this file you instantiate two custom components: one to update/delete products and one to add products. Remember that UpdateDeleteProd.mxml subclasses the HBox class, and that AddProduct.mxml subclasses the VBox class. This is important because to use the TabNavigator with these custom components, they must be containers.

2 Locate the instantiation of the two custom components near the bottom of the file.

```
<v:UpdateDeleteProd units="{units}"
   foodColl="{foodColl}"
   productUpdate="showPopUp(event.product,'Product Updated')"
   productDelete="showPopUp(event.product,'Product Deleted')"/>

<v:AddProduct
   cats="{categories}"
   units="{units}"
   productAdded="showPopUp(event.product,'Product Added')"/>
```

The two implementations of functionality currently appear on the same page.

3 Surround both component instantiations with a `<mx:TabNavigator>` tag set. Set the `width` to 700 and the `height` to 600.

```
<mx:TabNavigator width="700" height="600">
   <v:UpdateDeleteProd units="{units}"
      foodColl="{foodColl}"
      productUpdate="showPopUp(event.product,'Product Updated')"
      productDelete="showPopUp(event.product,'Product Deleted')"/>
```

```
    <v:AddProduct
        cats="{categories}"
        units="{units}"
        productAdded="showPopUp(event.product;'Product Added')"/>
</mx:TabNavigator>
```

4 Run DataEntry.mxml.

You now see two tabs of the TabNavigator appear; you can click each tab to see the application functionality separated. Also note that because no `label` properties are set on the custom components, the tabs have no text on them.

5 Add a `label` property to the UpdateDeleteProd custom component with a value of Update/Delete Product. Add a `label` property to the AddProd custom component with a value of Add Product. Run the DataEntry.mxml application again; the label text is now displayed on the tabs.

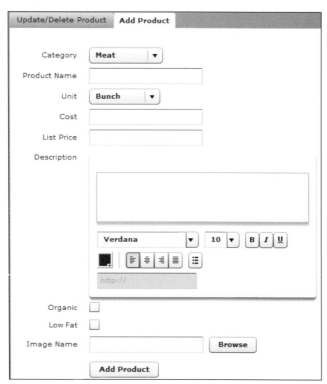

Adding a Home Page and Checkout Page in the E-commerce Application

Up to this point the only functionality available in the e-commerce application was selecting products and adding them to the shopping cart, which is all implemented by using states. You will now add a home page and a checkout process. You will build a ViewStack and Buttons to navigate between the home page, product selection, and checkout screens.

1 Copy the file HomePage.mxml from Lesson13/assets to your flexGrocer/views/ecomm folder.

Feel free to open this file and see that it contains no code that you haven't already worked with.

2 Open EComm.mxml and locate near the bottom of the file the HBox with the id of bodyBox.

You will add two more containers to this HBox in a ViewStack.

3 Just above the bodyBox HBox, instantiate the new HomePage.mxml component. Give it an id of homePage.

```
<v:HomePage id="homePage"/>
```

Because this will be the first child in the ViewStack, it will be the page displayed by default.

4 Create a new MXML component in the views/ecomm folder named Checkout.mxml and use a VBox as the base tag. Remove any width and height values.

This is the page that will control the checkout process.

5 In the component, use a Label to display the text "In the checkout component".

This is just temporary to test the navigation. Later in this lesson you will complete the checkout process.

6 In EComm.mxml (just below the closing tag for the bodyBox HBox and just above the instantiation of the CategorizedProductManager), instantiate the new Checkout.mxml component. Give it an id of checkout. Also set the width and height to 100%.

```
<v:Checkout id="checkout" width="100%" height="100%"/>
```

Later in this lesson this component will turn out to be a controller for the checkout process.

7 Run EComm.mxml and select a grocery category. You should see the home page, products, and text from the checkout component all stacked up on each other.

This mess will soon be cured with navigation.

8 Surround the HomePage, bodyBox HBox, and Checkout containers with an `<mx:ViewStack>` tag block and give the ViewStack an id of ecommNav. Set the `width` and `height` to 100%, and the `creationPolicy` to `all`. Run EComm.mxml; only the home page is now displayed.

```
<mx:ViewStack id="ecommNav"
   width="100%" height="100%" creationPolicy="all">
   <v:HomePage id="homePage"/>
   <mx:HBox x="0" y="0" width="100%" height="100%" id="bodyBox">
      <v:FoodList id="prodTile"
         width="100%" height="100%"
         prodByCategory="{prodByCategory}"
         itemAdded="addToCart(event.product)"/>
      <mx:VBox height="100%" id="cartBox">
         <mx:HBox>
            <mx:Label text="Your Cart Total: $"/>
            <mx:Label text="{cart.total}"/>
         </mx:HBox>
         <mx:LinkButton label="View Cart" click="this.currentState='cartView'"
            id="linkbutton1"/>
         <mx:List id="cartView"
            dataProvider="{cart.aItems}"
            width="100%"
            dragEnter="doDragEnter(event,cartFormat')"
            dragDrop="doDragDrop(event,cartFormat')"/>
      </mx:VBox>
   </mx:HBox>
   <v:Checkout id="checkout" width="100%" height="100%"/>
</mx:ViewStack>
```

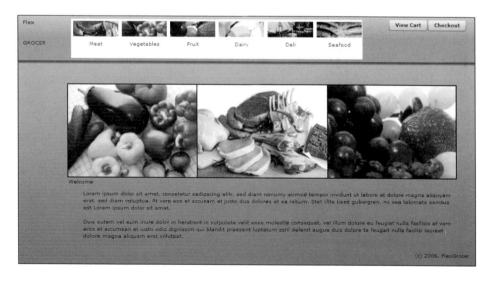

By default, the first container in a ViewStack is displayed and the others are hidden, so you will now see just the home page. Flex normally creates visual elements as they are needed. The home page would be created immediately, however bodyBox and Checkout would be created only when the ViewStack changes the visible child. As you have not yet implemented any way to change which child of the ViewStack is displayed, Flex would only create the home page. By setting the creationPolicy to all, you are instructing Flex to create all of the children at the same time it creates the ViewStack. The decision to modify this property is normally made to optimize performance of specific application areas; here you are setting the property to simplify the remaining steps.

9 Move the <mx:Label> tag that contains the FlexGrocer copyright information from directly above the newly added ViewStack to just below it and above the CategorizedProductManager.

As was demonstrated in step 7, Flex allows child tags and containers to occupy the same x and y coordinates on the page. Each child occupies a different depth (their place on the z axis) initially determined by the order they are declared in MXML. Previous to this step, the <mx:Label> tag was placed on the screen and then the <mx:ViewStack>. Because they were not occupying the same x and y coordinates, they never formed the mess in step 7; however, as you continue to develop the application, there will be times when these two occupy the same space. By moving the declaration for the <mx:Label> tag below the <mx:ViewStack> we are ensuring that the label will be at a higher depth, and always seen.

10 Add a click event to both Labels in the ApplicationControlBar to display the home page. Use the id, the selectedChild property of the TabNavigator, and the id of the HomePage component to accomplish this.

```
<mx:Label x="0" y="0" text="Flex"
    click="ecommNav.selectedChild=homePage"/>
<mx:Label x="0" y="41" text="GROCER"
    click="ecommNav.selectedChild=homePage"/>
```

This follows the convention that is used in many web applications of clicking the site name at the top of the page to return to the home page.

11 Add a click event to the Checkout Button in the ApplicationControlBar to display the Checkout custom component when this Button is clicked.

```
<mx:Button label="Checkout"
    id="btnCheckout"
    right="10" y="0"
    click="ecommNav.selectedChild=checkout"/>
```

This will make Checkout component the active child of the ViewStack.

12 Add a click event to the View Cart Button in the ApplicationControlBar. Have the event call a function named showCart().

```
<mx:Button label="View Cart"
    id="btnViewCart"
    right="90" y="0"
    click="showCart()"/>
```

You will follow the best practice of creating a function and calling it when you have multiple lines of code for an event handler.

13 Open ecomm.as and at the bottom of the file insert a private function named showCart() data typed as void with the code needed to control the view state and navigation.

```
private function showCart():void{
    ecommNav.selectedChild=bodyBox;
    this.currentState='cartView';
}
```

Remember that you could have used the selectedIndex property instead of placing ids on the containers and using the selectedChild property.

❄ **NOTE:** The selectedChild property has at least two advantages over selectedIndex. First, it is probably more intuitive for you to display the child of the ViewStack by name rather than number. Second, if you ever add a container anywhere except as the last child into the ViewStack, you do not have to renumber references to the children.

14 In EComm.mxml add a click event to the instantiation of the CategoryView component to call a function named showProducts().

```
<v:CategoryView id="catView"
    width="600"
    left="100"
    cats="{categories}"
    categorySelect="displayProdByCategory(event)"
    click="showProducts()"/>
```

This ensures that when the user clicks the categories HorizontalList, the products will be displayed.

15 Open ecomm.as and at the bottom of the file insert a private function named showProducts() data typed as void with the code needed to control the view state and navigation.

```
private function showProducts():void{
    ecommNav.selectedChild=bodyBox;
    currentState='';
}
```

This function will ensure that the products are displayed when a user clicks a product category in the ApplicationToolbar.

16 Run EComm.mxml and navigate around the application to be sure that you are seeing the correct child of the ViewStack displayed as you click each button.

Creating the First Step of the Checkout Process Displayed by a ViewStack

After users have all the groceries they want in their shopping cart, they need to check out. You just implemented the mechanism to get to a checkout page, and in this task you will create a ViewStack that controls the steps the user will follow to check out.

The basic process is as follows:

- The user clicks a button to proceed to the checkout page (already done in the last task).
- The user fills in a form that supplies basic billing/shipping information such as name, address, and so on.
- The user clicks a button on the basic billing information page and is then taken to a credit card information form.
- The user fills in a form supplying credit card information.
- The user clicks a button to purchase the groceries and is then taken to an order confirmation page.

✱ **NOTE:** A button will exist on the order confirmation page to print the order confirmation. This functionality will be implemented in a later lesson.

1 Create a value object by right-clicking the valueObjects folder and selecting New > ActionScript Class. The name of the class should be **OrderInfo**. Click Finish.

This class will hold all the information about the order, including billing information about the user.

2 In the class create the following public properties, using the data types shown. Mark the entire class as bindable.

- billingName:String
- cardType:String
- billingAddress:String
- cardNumber:Number
- billingCity:String
- cardExpirationMonth:Number
- billingState:String
- cardExpirationYear:Number
- billingZip:String
- deliveryDate:Date

You will later add to the property list a property for the actual shopping cart that holds the grocery items that were purchased.

✱ **NOTE:** The Date class is used here. The class hierarchy of the Date class is very simple; it has only the Object class as a parent. The Date class has many properties that hold date and time information, and many methods to get and set those properties. In this lesson, the key properties will be date, month, and fullYear.

3 Check to be sure that your complete class appears as follows:

```
package valueObjects{
    [Bindable]
    public class OrderInfo{
        public var billingName:String;
        public var billingAddress:String;
        public var billingCity:String;
        public var billingState:String;
        public var billingZip:String;
        public var cardType:String;
        public var cardNumber:Number;
        public var cardExpirationMonth:Number;
        public var cardExpirationYear:Number;
        public var deliveryDate:Date;
    }
}
```

This class looks very different from other classes you have built earlier because this class has no constructor. In actuality, it does have a constructor because ActionScript will automatically create a constructor for you if one is not written.

There is a reason to build the class this way. Because the property values will be gathered from different components, it is easy to instantiate an OrderInfo object. Whenever values are gathered from the user, you can simply assign them by using dot notation. If you wrote a constructor that needed all 10 parameters at one time it would be more difficult to populate the object in this particular case.

4 Open Checkout.mxml from the views/ecomm folder and remove the Label inserted in the last task.

The Label was used only temporarily to be sure the ViewStack implemented in the last task was working.

5 Insert an `<mx:ViewStack>` tag block with an `id` of `checkoutNav` and the `width` and `height` set to 100%.

You will have three components instantiated in this ViewStack that correspond to the steps of 1) gathering user info, 2) gathering credit card info, and 3) displaying a confirmation page.

6 Create a new MXML component in the views/ecomm folder named BillingInfo and use an HBox as the base tag. Remove the width and height values.

This is the form to gather user information such as name, address, and so on.

7 Add the following to gather user information:

```
<mx:VBox>
   <mx:Form>
      <mx:Label text="Checkout Page 1 of 3"/>
      <mx:FormHeading label="Customer Information"/>
      <mx:FormItem label="Name">
         <mx:TextInput id="billingName"/>
      </mx:FormItem>
      <mx:FormItem label="Address">
         <mx:TextArea id="billingAddress" width="160"/>
      </mx:FormItem>
      <mx:FormItem label="City">
         <mx:TextInput id="billingCity"/>
      </mx:FormItem>
      <mx:FormItem label="State">
         <mx:TextInput id="billingState" maxChars="2"/>
      </mx:FormItem>
      <mx:FormItem label="Zip">
         <mx:TextInput id="billingZip"/>
      </mx:FormItem>
   </mx:Form>
```

```
   </mx:VBox>
   <mx:VBox>
      <mx:Spacer height="40"/>
      <mx:Form>
         <mx:FormItem label="Delivery Date">
            <mx:DateChooser id="deliveryDate"/>
         </mx:FormItem>
         <mx:FormItem>
            <mx:Button label="Continue"/>
         </mx:FormItem>
      </mx:Form>
   </mx:VBox>
```

The DateChooser control is used here for the first time in the book. It presents a calendar to the user—who can choose both a particular month and day. The DateChooser `selectedDate` property then holds the date value selected. The data type of the `selectedDate` is Date, a class discussed earlier in this lesson.

▶ **TIP:** Flex has another date selection control called DateField. This control has what appears to the user to be an empty TextInput box with a calendar icon beside it. The user can click the icon, and a calendar appears for date selection. After the selection, the date appears in the TextInput box.

8 Create the following Model just below the opening `<mx:HBox>` tag to group the form information into a single data structure:

```
<mx:Model id="checkoutInfo">
   <custInfo>
      <billingName>{billingName.text}</billingName>
      <billingAddress>{billingAddress.text}</billingAddress>
      <billingCity>{billingCity.text}</billingCity>
      <billingState>{billingState.text}</billingState>
      <billingZip>{billingZip.text}</billingZip>
      <deliveryDate>{deliveryDate.selectedDate}</deliveryDate>
   </custInfo>
</mx:Model>
```

As you have done before, you gather the form information into a Model. You will pass the Model information back to the Checkout page later in this task.

9 Above the Model, use an `<mx:Metadata>` tag to create a custom event named `billingInfoReturn` of type `ObjectDataEvent`, which you will write in a following step.

```
<mx:Metadata>
   [Event(name="billingInfoReturn",type="events.ObjectDataEvent")]
</mx:Metadata>
```

What you will do in this component is gather up the user information in the form, place that data in an object, and then dispatch a custom event containing that data. Here you create the name of the custom event.

10 Insert an `<mx:Script>` block under the `<mx:Metadata>` tag block and import the events.ObjectDataEvent custom event class.

```
import events.ObjectDataEvent;
```

You will build this class in the next step.

11 Right-click the events folder and select New > ActionScript class. Give it the name **ObjectDataEvent** and set the superclass to flash.events.Event. The custom class will have only one property, an Object named `data`, which will be passed into the custom event object as the second parameter of the constructor. Inside the constructor, pass the type to the superclass and set the `data` property with the passed-in object. Override the clone method to use your new constructor and your class should appear as follows:

```
package events {
   import flash.events.Event;
   public class ObjectDataEvent extends Event{
      public var data:Object;
      public function ObjectDataEvent(type:String,data:Object){
         super(type);
         this.data = data;
      }
      override public function clone():Event {
         return new ObjectDataEvent(type, data);
      }
   }
}
```

This is a generic custom event class. You can use it whenever you want to use a custom event to pass a generic Object in the custom event object.

12 Back in BillingInfo.mxml, add a `click` event to the Continue Button at the bottom of the Form and call a function named `process()`.

This function will eventually dispatch the custom event, along with the event object that contains the form data.

13 At the bottom of the `<mx:Script>` block, create the skeleton for a private function named process(), and data type the function itself as void. In the function create a variable local to the function named o, data typed as ObjectDataEvent and set it equal to a new ObjectDataEvent.

```
var o:ObjectDataEvent=new ObjectDataEvent();
```

You are building the custom event object that will be dispatched and handled in the Checkout component. You still have to add the event name and data to the object.

14 As parameters in the new ObjectDataEvent, pass the name of the custom component, the String billingInfoReturn, and the data to be returned, which is stored in the Model whose instance name is checkOutInfo.

```
var o:ObjectDataEvent=new ObjectDataEvent("billingInfoReturn",checkoutInfo);
```

The correct object is now created and ready for dispatching.

15 As the second—and last—line of code in the function, dispatch the ObjectDataEvent object just built. Check to be sure that your function appears as follows:

```
private function process():void{
   var o:ObjectDataEvent=new ObjectDataEvent("billingInfoReturn",checkoutInfo);
   dispatchEvent(o);
}
```

This completes the BillingInfo component. You will now move back to the Checkout component and instantiate the new BillingInfo component. You will also handle the custom event and use the data sent back in the event object.

16 Return to Checkout.mxml. Add an XML namespace to the `<mx:VBox>` tag so you can use components in the views/ecomm folder. Use the letter v as the prefix.

```
xmlns:v="views.ecomm.*"
```

This permits you to use the BillingInfo component you just created.

17 In the `<mx:ViewStack>` block, instantiate the BillingInfo component. Give it an instance name of billingInfo, and set the width and height to 100%.

```
<v:BillingInfo id="billingInfo"
   width="100%" height="100%"/>
```

This is the first of three containers that will be in this ViewStack.

18 Handle the custom `billingInfoReturn` event in the component. In the ActionScript for the event, call a function named `doBillingInfoReturn()`. Pass the event object as a parameter.

```
billingInfoReturn="doBillingInfoReturn(event)"
```

If you happen to save at this point you will get an error because the custom event class is not yet imported.

19 Insert an `<mx:Script>` block and import the classes valueObjects.OrderInfo and events.ObjectDataEvent. Also create a public variable named `orderInfo`, data typed as OrderInfo and set equal to a new OrderInfo object.

```
import valueObjects.OrderInfo;
import events.ObjectDataEvent;
[Bindable]
public var orderInfo:OrderInfo=new OrderInfo();
```

The whole point of the checkout process is to build an OrderInfo object to be sent to the back end for processing, so obviously you need that class and an instance of that class to place data in. An event object instance of the class ObjectDataEvent is passed to the function, so you need this class for data typing.

20 At the bottom of the `<mx:Script>` block, create a private function named `doBillingInfoReturn()` and data type the function as void. The function should accept a parameter named event data typed as ObjectDataEvent. In the function, assign the six properties passed in the custom event object to the orderInfo object instance, using the same property names.

```
private function doBillingInfoReturn(event:ObjectDataEvent):void{
    orderInfo.billingName=event.data.billingName;
    orderInfo.billingAddress=event.data.billingAddress;
    orderInfo.billingCity=event.data.billingCity;
    orderInfo.billingState=event.data.billingState;
    orderInfo.billingZip=event.data.billingZip;
    orderInfo.deliveryDate=event.data.deliveryDate;
}
```

> **TIP:** A great way to check to be sure that the data coming from the component is valid is to use the debugger. For instance, before you added the six lines of code to assign property values, you could have marked a breakpoint in the empty function and then debugged the application. After you submitted the form, you would have seen in the Variables pane the data passed in correctly, as well as the exact object path to get to the data.

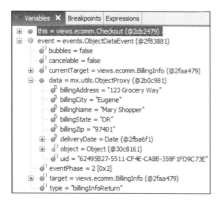

The data passed in the event object is stored in the data property because that is how it is named in the custom event class.

This concludes this task, and you now have the personal information from the user in the OrderInfo object. Next you will use a component to get credit card information.

Completing the Checkout Process Using the ViewStack

In this task, your goal is to get credit card information into the OrderInfo object in the Checkout component and then display this information in a confirmation screen. In this case, you will use a component that is already built because it is identical in logic to the BillingInfo component you just built. In the task, you will open the CCInfo component and examine its logic to see the similarities. You will then instantiate the component and manipulate the ViewStack to get it to appear. Finally, you will take all the order information and display it on an order confirmation screen.

1 Copy the file CCInfo.mxml from Lesson13/assets to your FlexGrocer/views/ecomm folder. Open the file and examine the code.

As you look at the code, you will see that the logic is the same as in the BillingInfo component you just built. Note that the custom event name is ccInfoReturn. You will need this name to use the component correctly. Also note the property names of the data gathered in the Model:

- cardType

- cardNumber

- cardExpirationMonth

- cardExpirationYear

2 Open Checkout.mxml. In the `<mx:ViewStack>` block, under the BillingInfo component, instantiate the CCInfo component. Give it an instance name of `ccInfo`, and set the `width` and `height` to `100%`.

This is the second of three containers that will be in the ViewStack.

3 Handle the custom `ccInfoReturn` event in the component. In the ActionScript for the event, call a function named `doCCInfoReturn()`. Pass the event object as a parameter, which must be data typed as ObjectDataEvent. Also handle the `back` custom event. In the ActionScript for the event, set the `selectedChild` of the `checkoutNav` ViewStack to `billingInfo`. Be sure that your instantiation appears as follows:

```
<v:CCInfo id="ccInfo"
    width="100%" height="100%"
    ccInfoReturn="doCCInfoReturn(event)"
    back="checkoutNav.selectedChild=billingInfo"/>
```

Review the CCInfo custom component to confirm what these two custom events do.

4 At the bottom of the `<mx:Script>` block, create a private function named `doCCInfoReturn()` and data type the function as void. The function should accept a parameter named event data typed as ObjectDataEvent. In the function, assign the four properties passed in the custom event object to the `orderInfo` object instance, using the same property names.

```
private function doCCInfoReturn(event:ObjectDataEvent):void{
    orderInfo.cardType=event.data.cardType;
    orderInfo.cardNumber=event.data.cardNumber;
    orderInfo.cardExpirationMonth=event.data.cardExpirationMonth;
    orderInfo.cardExpirationYear=event.data.cardExpirationYear;
}
```

At this point, your OrderInfo object should contain all the billing and credit card information collected from the user in the two custom components.

5 As the last line of code in the `doBillingInfoReturn()` function, make the ccInfo component displayed in the ViewStack.

```
checkoutNav.selectedChild=ccInfo;
```

Until you add this code, there was no way to get to the CCInfo component. What happens now is when the user clicks the button in the billing information screen, the event is dispatched, the data is written into the OrderInfo object, and then the CCInfo component is displayed.

6 Run EComm.mxml. Click the Checkout button and fill in the billing information form. Click the Continue button and you will be shown the credit card information form. Fill in this form and click the Continue button. At this point, nothing happens. The Back button will take you back to the Customer Information screen.

You now have the customer information and credit card information in the single Order-Info object.

> ▶ **TIP:** Use the debugger to confirm that all the data is in the orderInfo object. To do this, set a breakpoint at the end of the doCCInfoReturn() function and run EComm.mxml. Upon return to the Flex Builder debugger, add orderInfo as a Watched Expression in the Expressions pane.

7 Create a new MXML component in the views/ecomm folder named OrderConf, use a VBox as the base tag and remove any width and height values.

This component will display the order information.

8 Insert an `<mx:Script>` block and import the OrderInfo value object. Also, create a bind-able public variable named orderInfo data typed as OrderInfo.

```
import valueObjects.OrderInfo;
[Bindable]
public var orderInfo:OrderInfo;
```

This creates a property in the class. Order information will be passed to this property when the component is instantiated in the Checkout.mxml page.

9 Below the `<mx:Script>` block, insert the following form to display the order information to the user.

```
<mx:Form>
<mx:Label text="Checkout Page 3 of 3"/>
   <mx:FormHeading label="Billing Information"/>
   <mx:HBox>
     <mx:VBox>
       <mx:FormItem >
         <mx:Label text="{orderInfo.billingName}"/>
       </mx:FormItem>
       <mx:FormItem >
         <mx:Label text="{orderInfo.billingAddress}"/>
       </mx:FormItem>
```

code continues on next page

```
      <mx:FormItem >
         <mx:Label text="{orderInfo.billingCity}"/>
      </mx:FormItem>
      <mx:FormItem >
         <mx:Label text="{orderInfo.billingState}"/>
      </mx:FormItem>
      <mx:FormItem >
         <mx:Label text="{orderInfo.billingZip}"/>
      </mx:FormItem>
   </mx:VBox>
   <mx:VBox>
      <mx:FormItem label="Delivery Date">
         <mx:Label text="{orderInfo.deliveryDate.month+1}/
            {orderInfo.deliveryDate.date}/{orderInfo.deliveryDate.fullYear}"/>
      </mx:FormItem>
   </mx:VBox>
   </mx:HBox>
</mx:Form>
```

Note that you are displaying three properties of the Date class in the Delivery Date section. Because the month count is zero index (January being 0) you must add 1 to the month value to make it meaningful for humans.

10 Below the form, insert the following Buttons: Label and Spacer.

```
<mx:Button label="Complete Order"/>
<mx:Label text="* Clicking this button will bill your credit card and complete
   this order"/>
<mx:Spacer height="20"/>
<mx:Button label="Edit Information" click="back()"/>
```

Functionality for the Complete Order button will be implemented in a later lesson. The event handler for the Edit Information button will be implemented in the next step.

11 Add an `<mx:Metadata>` block just under the opening `<mx:VBox>` tag and add a custom event named back.

```
<mx:Metadata>
   [Event(name="back")]
</mx:Metadata>
```

In this case, you do not have to supply the type because the default type for an event is the Event class.

12 At the bottom of the `<mx:Script>` block, create a private function named back, data typed as void. Create an object named o, data typed as Event and set it equal to a new Event object passing as a parameter the string back. Dispatch the o object in the second line of the function.

```
private function back():void{
    var o:Event=new Event("back");
    dispatchEvent(o);
}
```

In this case, because you are NOT dispatching data in the custom event object, you did not need to create a custom event class.

13 Return to Checkout.mxml. At the bottom of the ViewStack, instantiate the newly created OrderConf component, and set the width and height to 100%. Set the orderInfo property equal to a binding of the like named variable from the Checkout component. Finally, handle the back event by setting the selectedChild of the checkoutNav ViewStack to billingInfo.

```
<v:OrderConf id="orderConf"
    width="100%" height="100%"
    orderInfo="{orderInfo}"
    back="checkoutNav.selectedChild=billingInfo"/>
```

This is the third and final component used in this ViewStack. At this point, the user has no way to see this component, which will be remedied in the next step.

14 As the last line of code in the doCCInfoReturn() function, make the orderConf component displayed in the ViewStack.

```
checkoutNav.selectedChild=orderConf;
```

In this checkout process, you control when the different containers are displayed. The user cannot click nor do anything else to jump between these different screens. In a later lesson, you will see how validation ties into this navigation scheme to not let users move to the next step until the form is filled out correctly.

✱ NOTE: You will be getting warnings that data binding will not be able to detect assignments to the date, fullYear, and month items. You will correct this in the next lesson using a DateFormatter.

15 Run EComm.mxml and click the Checkout button. After you fill in the customer informa-tion screen and click the Continue button, you will be taken to the credit card information form. After filling in this form and clicking the Continue button, you will be shown the order confirmation screen with the data entered in earlier forms now displayed.

Your checkout process should mimic the one shown here. At this point, the Complete Order button is not functional. Following are the three steps of the checkout process. In a later lesson, you will format the left margins of the form.

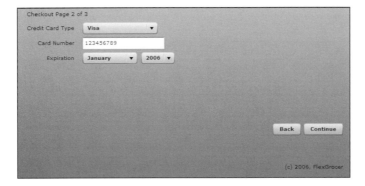

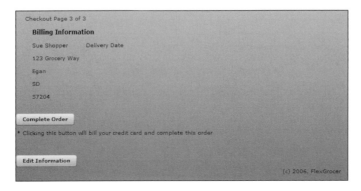

What You Have Learned

In this lesson, you have:

- Gained a general understanding of how Flex implements navigation and how the ViewStack is at the heart of this process (pages 308–311)

- Used a TabNavigator control to separate functionality from two components onto different tabs of the TabNavigator (pages 311–318)

- Implemented a checkout process using a ViewStack to control user progression through the process (pages 318–330)

What You Will Learn

In this lesson, you will:

- Create a new validator object on the client machine
- Use the validator to check and see if the data is in a valid format
- Create a new formatter object on the client machine
- Use the formatter to format data

Approximate Time

This lesson takes approximately 1 hour and 30 minutes to complete.

Lesson Files

Media Files:

None

Starting Files:

Lesson14/start/EComm.mxml
Lesson14/start/views/dataEntry/AddProduct.mxml
Lesson14/start/views/ecomm/BillingInfo.mxml
Lesson14/start/views/ecomm/CCInfo.mxml
Lesson14/start/views/ecomm/GroceryDetail.mxml
Lesson14/start/views/ecomm/OrderConf.mxml

Completed Files:

Lesson14/complete/EComm.mxml
Lesson14/complete/utils/AddressValidator.as
Lesson14/complete/views/dataEntry/AddProduct.mxml
Lesson14/complete/views/ecomm/BillingInfo.mxml
Lesson14/complete/views/ecomm/CCInfo.mxml
Lesson14/complete/views/ecomm/GroceryDetail.mxml
Lesson14/complete/views/ecomm/OrderConf.mxml

LESSON 14

Using Formatters and Validators

Flex provides many types of built-in Validators and Formatters that enable you to validate many types of user-defined supplied data such as dates, numbers, and currencies. Using the built-in data Validators on the client side, you can make your application perform better by reducing calls to the server. You can also save development time by using the built-in Formatters to automate the often repetitive process of formatting data.

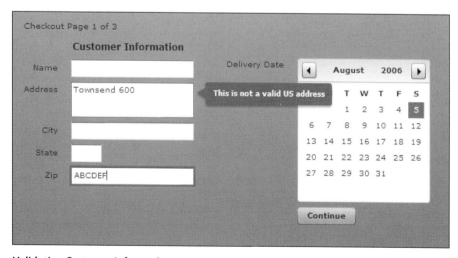

Validating Customer Information

Introducing Formatters and Validators

Data validation is used to ensure that data meets specific criteria before the application uses it. Flex has a set of Validator classes that can be used to check and make sure that data has been entered correctly. You can use Validator classes either as MXML tags or instantiate them directly in ActionScript. With Flex framework, it is possible to use validators to perform this checking at the client instead of when the data is submitted to the server. This is advantageous because it reduces the amount of data transmitted between the client and the server, which can result in a better-performing application. Of course, some types of secure data validation are best performed at the server, but using Validator classes at the client improve performance by offloading some validation to Flash Player.

All validators subclass the Validator class. Some of the validators available as part of Flex framework include the following:

- CreditCardValidator
- DateValidator
- EmailValidator
- NumberValidator
- PhoneNumberValidator
- SocialSecurityValidator
- StringValidator
- ZipCodeValidator

You often need to perform data validation outside the scope of built-in Validator classes, so Flex enables you to use the functionality of the Validator classes to build your own custom validators. For example, you might want to be sure that a user attaches a valid type of file to be uploaded. Or you might want to display only files to the user that have the word "Flex" in them. By subclassing the Validator classes, you can build a custom validator for any situation that might arise using a minimum of code.

Flex also has a set of Formatter classes that can format raw data into a customized string. You can use the Formatter classes with data binding to automate data binding tasks and be able to apply the formatting to multiple fields simultaneously.

All formatters subclass the Formatter class; some of the formatters available include these:

- mx.formatters.CurrencyFormatter
- mx.formatters.DateFormatter
- mx.formatters.NumberFormatter
- mx.formatters.PhoneFormatter
- mx.formatters.ZipCodeFormatter

Using a Formatter Class to Display Currency Information in the E-commerce Application

In this task, you will apply a CurrencyFormatter class so all the price selections are displayed as U.S. dollars in the e-commerce application. There are multiple places in which prices are displayed in the application, including these:

- The list of grocery products displayed

- The total of the shopping cart

- The subtotal and list prices in the DataGrid that is the user's shopping cart

The CurrencyFormatter adjusts the decimal rounding and precision, and sets the thousands separator and the negative sign. You can specify the type and placement of the currency symbol used, which can contain multiple characters including blank spaces. The first step of using the CurrencyFormatter involves instantiating the Formatter class by using either MXML or ActionScript; the second step is calling the format method of the object, passing the number to be formatted to the method.

1 Open the GroceryDetail.mxml from the views/ecomm folder.

This is the component that is duplicated using the repeater control based on the grocery information retrieved from the server. All the information about each grocery product is displayed in this component.

2 Immediately after the script block, add an `<mx:CurrencyFormatter>` tag. Assign the tag an id of `curFormat` and specify the `currencySymbol` attribute as a dollar sign (*$*) and a precision of 2, as follows:

```
<mx:CurrencyFormatter id="curFormat"
    currencySymbol="$"
    precision="2"/>
```

The decimal rounding, the thousands separator, and the negative sign are properties that can be specified on the CurrencyFormatter; we have left these at their defaults. You specified a precision of 2, meaning that two decimal places will always be displayed, and that a dollar sign be added to the formatted number. You could have specified any other character, for example, the character string Yen, for the currency symbol, including an empty space to be added between the symbol and the formatted number.

3 Locate the Label control a few lines down that displays the list price. Inside of the data binding for the text property, call the format() method of the curFormat object, and pass the groceryItem.listPrice to the method, as follows:

```
<mx:Label id="price"
    text="{curFormat.format(groceryItem.listPrice)}"
    x="100"
    y="20"/>
```

The format() method takes the value and applies all the parameters you specified in the <mx:CurrencyFormatter> MXML tag. In this case, you are adding a dollar sign and specifying the precision, so two digits to the right of the decimal point will always be maintained.

4 Save the changes to GroceryDetail.mxml and run the application. Select some grocery items.

You should see that all the grocery items display formatted list prices, as shown.

5 Open the EComm.mxml file.

EComm is where the total of the end user's shopping cart is displayed. You will apply a currency formatter to this field.

6 Immediately after the script tag, add an <mx:CurrencyFormatter> tag. Assign the tag an id of cartFormat, specify the currencySymbol as a dollar sign ($), and the precision as 2, as follows:

```
<mx:CurrencyFormatter id="cartFormat"
    currencySymbol="$"
    precision="2"/>
```

7 Locate the Label control (on approximately line 66) that displays "Your Cart Total". In place of the existing dollar sign, call the `format()` method of the cartFormat Currency-Format object, and pass the `cart.total` to the method. Remove the second Label control, which currently displays the `cart.total`, and delete the HBox that surrounds them both. The code for the remaining Label control should look as shown here:

```
<mx:Label text="Your Cart Total: {cartFormat.format(cart.total)}"/>
```

The `format()` method will format the cart.total according to the parameters you specified in the `cartFormat` object.

8 Save and run the application. Add some grocery items to the cart.

The total text field describing the contents of the shopping cart is displayed as currency with a dollar sign.

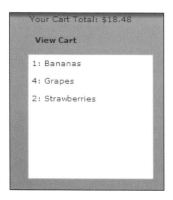

9 Open the OrderConf.mxml file from the views/ecomm directory.

In the last lesson, you concatenated portions of the date, (month, day and year) to format the delivery date for orders. Flex provides a built-in DateFormatter class. In this exercise, you will apply a DateFormatter to your class.

10 Directly below the existing `<mx:Script>` add an `<mx:DateFormatter>` tag. Assign the tag an id of orderFormat.

```
<mx:DateFormatter id="orderFormat"/>
```

A new object with the name of `orderFormat` is created. You can use this Formatter class to format dates throughout the application. Because you have not specified any properties, the default format is used, `"MM/DD/YYYY"`. You can customize it by setting the `formatString` property.

11 Still in OrderConf.mxml, locate the Delivery Date form item, and change the `<mx:Label>` so the `text` property calls the `format()` method of the `orderFormat` DateFormatter on the `deliveryDate` property of the orderInfo data structure. Be sure to remove manual date formatting from the last lesson. The `<mx:Label>` should look as shown here:

```
<mx:Label text="{orderFormat.format(orderInfo.deliveryDate)}"/>
```

This applies the DateFormatter object to the `deliveryDate` property and displays the date in the format "MM/DD/YYYY".

12 Save and run the application. Fill in the customer information fields and be sure to choose a delivery date. Note that the warnings are gone in the Problems section. Browse to the order confirmation section.

Note that the delivery date is formatted as shown in the following example.

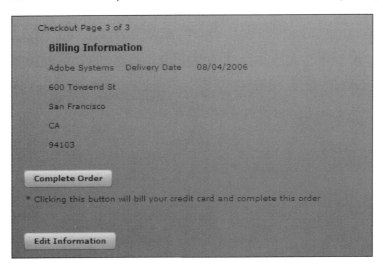

Using Validator Classes

In this task, you will use a ZipCodeValidator class to check whether a postal code is a valid U.S. ZIP code or Canadian postal code. Using a CreditCardValidator, you will also check whether a credit card number is valid during the checkout process.

1 Open BillingInfo.mxml from the views/ecomm directory.

This is the file that displays the billing information for the end user. It includes their name, address and postal code.

2 Immediately after the `<mx:Model>` tag, add an `<mx:ZipCodeValidator>` tag, and assign it an `id` of `zipV`. Set up a binding to the `source` property as the `billingZip` input text box. Specify the property as `text` and specify the `domain` attribute as the US or Canada.

```
<mx:ZipCodeValidator id="zipV" source="{billingZip}"
   property="text" domain="US or Canada"/>
```

The `<mx:ZipCodeValidator>` validates that a string has the correct length for a five-digit ZIP code, a five digit + four digit U.S. ZIP code, or a Canadian postal code. The `source` attribute is simply the name of the control being validated and where the error message will appear. The `property` attribute is where the actual information that should be validated is stored.

3 Save and compile the application.

Click the Checkout button; enter some letters for the ZIP code in the billing information screen. When you exit the field, you should see a red highlight around the text field; when you hover the mouse cursor over the text field, you will see the default error message appear.

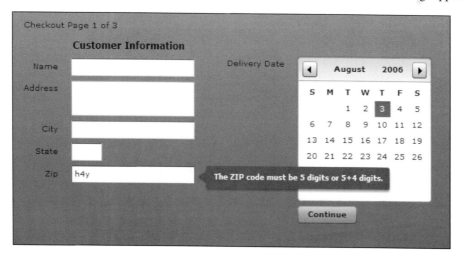

4 Open CCInfo.mxml from the views/ecomm directory.

This is the next step of the billing process: the user enters credit card information after filling out billing information.

5 Modify the `dataProvider` for the `cardType` ComboBox control. Change the `data` property of the `dataProvider` items to "American Express", "Diners Club", "Discover", "MasterCard", "Visa".

```
<mx:ComboBox id="cardType">
   <mx:dataProvider>
      <mx:Object label="American Express"
         data="American Express"/>
      <mx:Object label="Diners Club" data="Diners Club"/>
      <mx:Object label="Discover" data="Discover"/>
      <mx:Object label="MasterCard" data="MasterCard"/>
      <mx:Object label="Visa" data="Visa"/>
   </mx:dataProvider>
</mx:ComboBox>
```

These constants that you have assigned indicate the type of credit card to be validated. In the next step, you will access these constants from the Validator, which indicate which algorithm should be applied when using the Validator.

6 Immediately after the `<mx:Model>` tag, add an `<mx:CreditCardValidator>` tag and assign it an `id` of ccV. Set up a binding between the `CardTypeSource` property and the `cardType.selectedItem` of the ComboBox control. Also specify the `cardTypeProperty` as data.

```
<mx:CreditCardValidator id="ccV"
   cardTypeSource="{cardType.selectedItem}" cardTypeProperty="data"/>
```

The type of card is being stored in a ComboBox control in the `data` property of the `selectedItem`. You specify the control in which the object is being stored by using the `cardTypeSource` property. In the last step, you specified that the information is being stored in the `data` property.

7 Still in the `<mx:CreditCardValidator>` tag, add another property with the name of cardNumberSource and set up a binding to the cardNumber text field. Specify the cardNumberProperty attribute as text. The final CreditCardValidator class should look as follows:

```
<mx:CreditCardValidator id="ccV"
   cardTypeSource="{cardType.selectedItem}"
   cardTypeProperty="data"
   cardNumberSource="{cardNumber}"
   cardNumberProperty="text"/>
```

The `cardNumberSource` property is the input text field in which the user has typed in the credit card number. The number is stored in the `text` property of the input text field, which is why you specify the `cardNumberProperty` attribute.

8 In the <mx:Script> block, import the mx.events.ValidationResultEvent and declare a variable with the name of vResult as a ValidationResultEvent.

```
import mx.events.ValidationResultEvent;
private var vResult:ValidationResultEvent;
```

ValidationResultEvent will return either valid or not for the CreditCardValidator class. You must import these events to use them. If the credit card is valid, you want the user to continue with the checkout process. If it is not valid, you want the user to enter the appropriate credit card number.

9 In the <mx:Script> block, immediately inside the process() method, assign vResult to the value returned from the validate() method on the ccV validator. Surround the current code in the process() method with conditional logic that checks to see whether the vResult.type property is equal to the ValidationResultEvent.VALID. If it does match, place the code that continues the checkout process within the if statement. Add an else statement that will do nothing if the condition is not met.

```
vResult = ccV.validate();
if (vResult.type==ValidationResultEvent.VALID){
    ➥ var o:ObjectDataEvent=new ObjectDataEvent("ccInfoReturn",checkoutInfo);
    ➥ dispatchEvent(o);
} else {

}
```

The validate() method, which is part of the CreditCardValidator class, executes an algorithm that checks if a valid credit card number has been entered. The algorithm checks only that a valid card number was entered, not whether that card is actually active. After the validation is done, the method will return a ValidationResultEvent with a property of type set to the constant ValidationResultEvent.VALID if it looks like a credit card number. (You are adding logic that will test for this.) If so, continue with the checkout process; otherwise, do not continue.

10 Save and compile the application.

Click the Checkout button. Click the Continue button in the billing information screen to advance to the credit card section. Enter some letters into the credit card field and click the Continue button. You will see the text field display a red outline; roll over the text field and note the error message.

Using Regular Expressions to Validate Data (Part 1)

Regular expressions enable you to easily search through a text string without having to build complicated looping structures. Regular expressions are simply patterns that enable you to search and match other strings. They are created by using a special language—the regular expression language—which you will get a taste of in this task. Flex framework has support for this language built in.

In this task, you will use regular expressions to build a custom validator to verify an image name the user has attached by dragging and dropping. You will check the file name to ensure that there is at least one character before the dot, and that the image they are attaching is a GIF file. There are lots of considerations that will make your search more complicated. For example, you will have to consider all case possibilities when searching for the GIF string: GiF, gif, and even giF are all valid. You also need to search for the string GIF only at the end of the filename, after the dot. For example, you would not want a file with the name of gift.jpg to register as valid.

1 Open AddProduct.mxml from the views/dataEntry directory.

2 On the first line of the doProdAdd() method, create a new RegExp object with the name of pattern, as follows:

```
var pattern:RegExp = new RegExp();
```

The RegExp class is used to write regular expressions that can search and replace through text strings. The object will store the pattern that you use to search through these strings. The next step will take you through the syntax of the pattern.

3 Inside the parentheses for the RegExp() class, define the first character of the string as a period.

```
var pattern:RegExp = new RegExp(".");
```

The constructor for the RegExp class accepts a String to define the search pattern. The first step to defining your filename search is to ensure that at least one character appears directly before the period in the filename. In regular expressions syntax, a single valid character, also referred to as a wildcard, is represented by a period.

4 After defining the first period, define a literal search for a period using two backslashes and a period.

```
var pattern:RegExp = new RegExp(".\\.");
```

In step 3, you learned that a period represents any character in regular expressions. To make your search for an appropriate file type work, you need to be able to literally search for a period as well. This is accomplished using an escape character, which is a double backslash in Flex. The escape character tells the regular expression that you literally mean a period, and not another wildcard character.

5 After the defining the search for the literal period, add searches for uppercase G, lowercase g, uppercase I, lowercase i, uppercase F, or lowercase f. To express this in a regular expression, you would surround each of the upper/lowercase character combinations in square brackets.

```
var pattern:RegExp = new RegExp(".\\.[Gg][Ii][Ff]");
```

This will check that the string ends with any variation of the capitalization of "GIF".

6 Immediately after defining the pattern object, surround the rest of the method with conditional logic. Within the conditional logic, use the search() method of the String class to search the string located in prodModel.imageName with the RegExp pattern you completed in the last step. If the value is not equal to -1, execute the code.

```
if(prodModel.imageName.search(pattern) != -1){
   var prod:Product = Product.buildProduct(prodModel);
   var o:ProductEvent = new ProductEvent(prod,'productAdded');
   this.dispatchEvent(o);
}
```

The search() method of the String class will search the prodModel.imageName string for the regular expression that you defined in the pattern. It will look for a character before a period; for a period; and for the character G, I, or F in any case. If the string matching the pattern you defined is not found in the imageName, -1 will be returned. If the string is found, the search method will return the position where the pattern begins in imageName.

7 Add an else statement that will display an Alert box if -1 one is returned. The final doProdAdd() method should look as follows:

```
private function doProdAdd():void{
   var pattern:RegExp = new RegExp(".\\.[Gg][Ii][Ff]");
   if(prodModel.imageName.search(pattern) != -1){
      var prod:Product = Product.buildProduct(prodModel);
      var o:ProductEvent = new ProductEvent(prod,'productAdded');
      this.dispatchEvent(o);
   }else{
      mx.controls.Alert.show("Please attach a GIF file");
   }
}
```

If the user has not attached a file with the extension gif, an Alert box will display, asking the user to attach a GIF file.

8 Save this file and run the DataEntry application. Click the Add Product tab and attempt to add a new image by typing some different combinations into the image field. Then click the Add Product button.

You should see only those combinations that have at least one character in front, a period, and the extension GIF add properly.

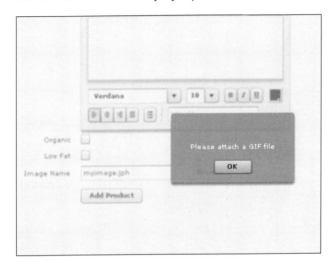

Using Regular Expressions to Validate Data (Part 2)

In this task, you will continue to use regular expressions and delve into some more complicated syntax. You will use regular expressions to be sure that an end user in the e-commerce application has entered a valid address. In reality, validating an address is difficult, there are many possible combinations; in this example you will verify that a street address starts with a number, contains a space, and then contains some more characters. This will work for the vast majority of the U.S. addresses.

1 Open BillingInfo.mxml in the views/ecomm directory.

2 On the first line of the process() method, create a new RegExp object with the name of pattern, as follows:

```
var pattern:RegExp = new RegExp();
```

This creates a new pattern object that can store regular expression strings for searching.

3 Inside the constructor for the RegExp() object, define the search pattern as two back-slashes and a d+.

```
var pattern:RegExp = new RegExp("\\d+");
```

The d indicates to search for a single digit. The + sign is referred to as a Quantifier; it works with the d to indicate that you will accept one or more digits as a match.

4 After defining the expression that searches for the beginning digits, add an escape character, the set of double backslashes, and add an x20 character that represents a space.

```
var pattern:RegExp = new RegExp("\\d+\\x20");
```

This indicates that a space is required between the digits and the letters of the address.

5 In brackets, check for all lowercase and all uppercase letters using A-Z and a-z. Add a plus sign after the brackets to allow for any length of those letters.

```
var pattern:RegExp = new RegExp("\\d+\\x20[A-Za-z]+");
```

This searches for any length of letters, in any case directly after the space. You have now built a pattern that will check for valid addresses!

6 Immediately after defining the pattern object, surround the rest of the method with conditional logic. Within the conditional logic, use the search() method of the String class to search the checkoutInfo.billingAddress with the regular expression pattern you defined in the last step. If the value is not equal to -1, execute the code.

```
if(checkoutInfo.billingAddress.search(pattern) != -1){
    var o:ObjectDataEvent =
      ➥ new ObjectDataEvent ("billingInfoReturn",checkoutInfo);
    dispatchEvent(o);
}
```

The search() method of the String class will search the entire checkoutInfo.billingAddress string for the regular expression that you defined earlier.

7 Add an else statement that will display an Alert box if -1 is returned. The final process() method should look as follows:

```
private function process():void{
   var pattern:RegExp = new RegExp("\\d+\\x20[A-Za-z]+");
   if(checkoutInfo.billingAddress.search(pattern) != -1){
      var o:ObjectDataEvent =
         ➥ new ObjectDataEvent("billingInfoReturn",checkoutInfo);
      dispatchEvent(o);
   }else{
      mx.controls.Alert.show("Please enter a valid US address");
   }
}
```

8 Save and run the EComm application.

Type in some different combinations into the Address field. You should see that only those combinations that begin with numbers, have a space, and then a sequence of letters are accepted.

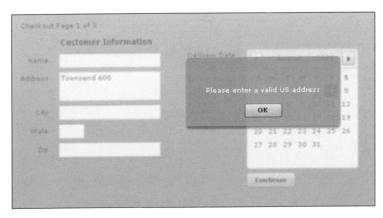

Building a Custom Validator Class

In this task, you will build a custom Validator class that can check for U.S. address formatting. In the last task you built the logic that can check whether a U.S. address is valid by using regular expressions. If the user types in a bad address, an Alert box displays. However, you do not take advantage of any of the built-in Validator class functionality. With the Validator class, you can offer the user visual cues to where the error is as well as display customized error messages. Flex framework offers the ability to extend all the Validator classes and to add your own functionality.

1 Create a new ActionScript class by right-clicking the utils folder and selecting New > ActionScript Class. The name of the class should be **AddressValidator**, ensure the package name is utils, and specify a superclass of mx.validators.Validator as shown.

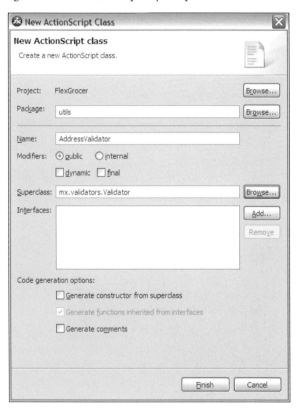

This will be a new custom Validator class that will use the regular expression functionality you built in the last task.

2 Import the mx.validators.ValidationResult class.

```
package utils {
    import mx.validators.Validator;
    import mx.validators.ValidationResult;
```

The ValidationResult class contains several properties that enable you to record information about any validation properties, such as the error messages and codes that are generated from a failure.

3 Immediately inside of the class definition, declare the private results array.

```
public class AddressValidator extends Validator{
   private var results:Array;
```

The results array will be returned from the doValidation() method that you will override.

4 Declare a public constructor with the name AddressValidator and call the base class constructor using super().

```
public class AddressValidator extends Validator{
   private var results:Array;
   public function AddressValidator(){
      super();
   }
```

The public constructor function invokes super() of the base Validator class. The base class can perform the check to ensure that data was entered into a required field.

5 Override the protected function doValidation() method and set the parameter of the method to Object. The method will return an array.

```
override protected function doValidation(value:Object):Array{
}
```

The method on the AddressValidator class is now overriding the existing Validator class method, and you are defining a new doValidation() method. The doValidation() method will return an array of ValidationResult objects.

❋ **NOTE:** Public methods and properties are available to any object in the system. Private methods and properties are only available inside the class where they are defined. Protected methods and properties are available inside the same class and all derived classes, or subclasses.

6 Inside the method, clear the results array and call the base class doValidation() method, passing it the value from our doValidation() method. Return the results array at the end of the method.

```
override protected function doValidation(value:Object):Array{
   results = [];
   results = super.doValidation(value);
   return results;
}
```

The results array is simply an array of ValidationResult objects, one for each field examined by the Validator. If the validation is successful, the results array will remain empty. If the validation is not successful, one ValidationResult per each field will be returned whether the validation of the individual field is successful or not. The isError property of the ValidationResult can be examined to determine whether the field passed or failed validation.

7 Immediately after calling the super.doValidation() method, add conditional logic to test if the value object passed into the AddressValidator doValidation() method is null.

```
override protected function doValidation(value:Object):Array{
   results = [];
   results = super.doValidation(value);
   if(value!=null){
   }
   return results;
}
```

You are about to search this value with your regular expression, but only if the value contains some data.

8 Return to the BillingInfo.mxml file and locate the process() method. Inside this method, remove the conditional logic and cut the definition of the pattern regular expression to the clipboard. Save the BillingInfo.mxml file. The final process() method should look as follows:

```
private function process():void{
   var o:ObjectDataEvent =
      ➥ new ObjectDataEvent("billingInfoReturn",checkoutInfo);
   dispatchEvent(o);
}
```

You will place this logic inside of the new AddressValidator class that you are creating. You can still make sure that the user enters a valid U.S. address and you will have all of the functionality of the Validator class.

9 Return to the AddressValidator class. Inside the conditional logic, paste the definition of the pattern regular expression. Add conditional logic that uses the search method of the String class to search value for the pattern and tests for -1, as follows:

```
if(value!=null){
   var pattern:RegExp = new RegExp("\\d+\\x20[A-Za-z]+", "");
   if(value.search(pattern) == -1){
   }
}
```

You have defined the same regular expression that will search for valid U.S. addresses, except now it is part of a new class subclass of Validator. If a valid U.S. address is not found, the search method will return -1, and you will need to inform the user that the validation failed.

10 Inside the conditional logic that searches for the regular expression, push a new ValidationResult with the parameters: true, null, "notAddress", and "You must enter a valid US address" into the results array. Save the file. The final doValidation() method should appear as follows:

```
override protected function doValidation(value:Object):Array{
   results = [];
   results = super.doValidation(value);
   if(value!=null){
      var pattern:RegExp = new RegExp("\\d+\\x20[A-Za-z]+", "");
      if(value.search(pattern) == -1){
         results.push(new ValidationResult
            ➥ (true, null, "notAddress", "This is not a valid US address"));
      }
   }
   return results;
}
```

If the regular expression is not found in the string the user entered, a new ValidationResult error will be added to the results array. Remember that this is how the Validator class works: it displays error messages from the results array in the field that the user mouses over. You can have more than one error message so it needs to be an array. In this case, if the user entered a non–U.S. address, the error message "This is not a valid US address" will display.

11 Return to BillingInfo.mxml. Add a new namespace to the <mx:HBox> tag at the top of the page, with the name u, that will reference all files in the utils.* directory.

```
<mx:HBox xmlns:mx="http://www.adobe.com/2006/mxml"
   xmlns:u="utils.*">
```

This will enable you to reference the new customized AddressValidator class you created by using the namespace u.

12 Directly below the existing ZipCodeValidator class, add a new <u:AddressValidator> tag. Specify the id as addressV, the required property as true, the source as a binding to the billingAddress field, and the property as text.

```
<u:AddressValidator id="addressV" required="true"
   source="{billingAddress}" property="text"/>
```

This creates an instance of the new Validator class you have created. Because it is subclassing the existing Validator class, the properties are exactly the same as before.

13 Save and run the application.

Click the Checkout button and enter an address that begins with a letter (which is not valid in the United States). Tab off the field; the field is now highlighted in red, and you should see the error message you specified earlier when you roll over the field.

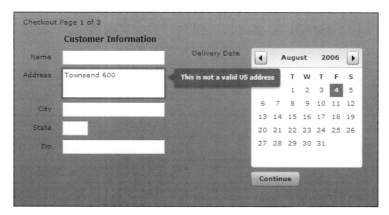

What You Have Learned

In this lesson, you have:

- Learned how to apply a Formatter to incoming text (pages 335–338)
- Learned how to apply a Validator to outgoing data (pages 338–341)
- Learned how to use regular expressions for validation of text (pages 342–351)

What You Will Learn

In this lesson, you will:

- Use standard history management
- Import the HistoryManagement classes
- Build a custom HistoryManager class for the CategoryView component

Approximate Time

This lesson takes approximately 45 minutes to complete.

Lesson Files

Media Files:

None

Starting Files:

Lesson15/start/as/ecomm.as
Lesson15/start/DataEntry.mxml
Lesson15/start/views/ecomm/CategoryView.mxml

Completed Files:

Lesson15/complete/as/ecomm.as
Lesson15/complete/views/ecomm/CategoryView.mxml

LESSON 15

Using the History Manager

An important part of most rich Internet applications (RIAs) is the capability to use the back and forward buttons in the browser. Most users of RIAs are accustomed to navigating through web pages by using these buttons, and it makes sense to implement the same functionality in your Flex applications.

The navigational components that you learned about in the Lesson 13, "Implementing Navigation," have this functionality automatically built in—including the Accordion, TabNavigator, and TabBar containers—and components that descend from the ViewStack container. You can also add this functionality to your own components by using the HistoryManager class. In this lesson, you will enable the back and forward buttons in the FlexGrocer application using the HistoryManager class in a custom component.

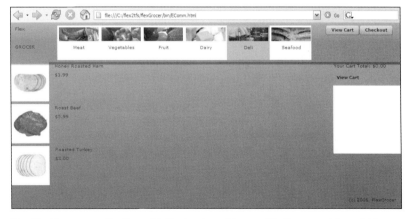

The FlexGrocer application with the back and forward buttons working within the browser

Introducing History Management

Using history management, the user can navigate through an application using the browser's back and forward buttons. For example, a user can click a tab in a TabNavigator or Accordion container and then move to the previous tab by clicking the back button in the browser.

Flex automatically supports history management for any navigator container without using any additional MXML or ActionScript tags. It is enabled by default for the Accordion and TabNavigator containers. If you want to turn history management off for these containers you simply specify the attribute `historyManagementEnabled` and set it to `false`, as follows:

```
<mx:TabNavigator historyManagementEnabled="false">
```

History management is disabled by default for the ViewStack container. You can turn history management on for the ViewStack container by specifying `historyManagementEnabled` and setting that attribute to `true` as follows:

```
<mx:ViewStack historyManagementEnabled="true">
```

When history management is turned on, as the user moves from state to state within the application, each navigation state is saved. When the browser's back or forward button is selected, the History Manager will load and display the next navigation state that was saved previously. Only the state of the actual navigator container is saved; if the navigator has any children, the states of these components are *not* saved, unless history management is enabled for that container.

History management actually saves each state of the application by using the Adobe Flash Player `navigateToURL()` function. This function loads an invisible HTML frame into the current browser window. All the states of the Flex application are encoded into the URL parameters for the invisible HTML frame. A SWF file called history.swf, which is located in the invisible frame, decodes the query parameters and sends the navigation state information back to the HistoryManager class in Flex—where the saved data is displayed.

You can add history management to any custom component in which it is appropriate. For example, in the FlexGrocer application, you will add history management to the CategoryView component so the user can use the back and forward buttons in the browser to navigate between different food categories, as shown here:

There are six steps to implementing history management with a component that does not implement it by default:

1. Specify that your component will implement the IHistoryManagerClient interface.

2. Register the component with the HistoryManager class in Flex.

3. Implement the loadState() method in the custom component.

4. Implement the saveState() method in the custom component.

5. Implement the toString() method in the custom component.

6. Call the static methods of the HistoryManager class in Flex.

To implement the IHistoryManagerClient interface on a custom component, you add an implements property to the root node of your component and specify the interface name, in this case mx.managers.IHistoryManagerClient. Specifying that a component implements a specific interface is like making a contract with the compiler. You are guaranteeing that your custom component will implement every method required by the interface, in this case loadState(), saveState() and toString(). This contract tells the HistoryManager that it is safe to work with the component as the proper functionality is guaranteed to be in place.

To register a component with the HistoryManager class, you call the static register() method of the HistoryManager class and pass a reference to the component instance. This tells the HistoryManager that your component needs to know when the user navigates using the forward or back buttons on the browser. To fulfill your contract with the HistoryManager your component must implement three methods of the mx.managers.IHistoryManagerClient interface in your component—saveState(), loadState() and toString() —with the following signature:

```
public function saveState():Object
public function loadState(state:Object):void
public function toString():String
```

The saveState() method returns an object that contains name-value pairs that represent the current navigational state of the component. These name-value pairs are limited by the maximum URL size supported by the user's browser, for example Internet Explorer only supports 2083 characters. Because the space available is limited, you should try to write the least amount of data possible.

The loadState() method of the component is activated when the user clicks the forward and the back buttons in the web browser. The HistoryManager class passes a parameter to this method, which is identical to the object created by the saveState() method. Components that use the history management functionality must also implement the toString() method, but there is a default implementation of this method in the UIComponent class, meaning that if the component descends from UIComponent, it already has a default `toString()` method. However, as you learned in previous lesson, it is still a good idea to write your own `toString()` method, specific to your class, as it helps significantly in debugging.

If you are using history management in a custom HTML page (one not generated by Flex Builder), you must manually set up that HTML to support history management. This code is written for you, if you are using Flex builder to automatically generate the HTML.

You must include this HTML at the top of the page:

```
<script language='javascript' charset='utf-8'
    src='/flex/flex-internal?action=history_js'></script>
```

You then need to add the `historyURL` and `iconId` parameters to the `flashVars` variable in JavaScript as shown:

```
document.write("flashvars = 'historyUrl=
    ➥ %2Fflex%2Fflex%2Dinternal%3Faction%3Dhistory%5F html&Iconid=
    ➥ " + lc_id +"&versionChecked=true'");
```

Add the history `iframe`, as shown here:

```
<iframe src='/flex/flex-internal?action=history_html' name='_history'
    frameborder='0' scrolling='no' width='22' height='0'></iframe>
```

Implementing History Management within a Navigator Container

Due to security constraints, users of Microsoft Internet Explorer will not be able to build and preview the examples in this lesson as they have so far. History management does not work in Internet Explorer *when previewing a local file*, meaning that it does not work when previewing local files on your hard drive; however, it will work if the file is on a web server or accessed through a HTTP URL as opposed to the file:/// URL that is used during normal development. If you are using Internet Explorer you will need to preview these files from a web server. History Management does work in Firefox and Netscape browsers when previewing a local file.

In this task, you will examine how standard history management is implemented in the DataEntry application.

1 Open DataEntry.mxml and run the application. Navigate between the two tabs on the tab navigator on the first page. Note that the back and forward buttons are working within the browser.

By default, history management is turned on for the TabNavigator and Accordion components. Unless you want to turn off history management, you need to use the `historyManagementEnabled` property. If your navigation system uses a regular ViewStack component, then you need to explicitly turn on history management using this property. Notice that the back button is enabled because history management is automatically turned on.

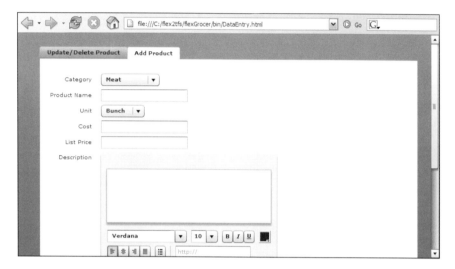

2 Locate the TabNavigator component and add a `historyManagementEnabled` attribute to the tag and set it to `false`. Save and run the application.

Note that the back and forward buttons in the browser are no longer working when you move between the Update/Delete Product and Add Product tabs.

3 Locate the TabNavigator component and remove the `historyManagementEnabled` attribute.

If you save and run the application, the browser back and forward buttons will work again.

Building a Custom History Manager

In this task, you will implement history management in the CategoryView.mxml component so that users can navigate between categories using the back and forward buttons on the browser.

1 Open CategoryView.mxml from the views/ecomm directory.

You will implement history management inside of this component. When users click a category, they can return to the previous category by clicking the back button or move to the next category by clicking the forward button.

2 Run the application from EComm.mxml and click on the HorizontalList that contains the categories of food.

Notice that neither the back nor forward buttons are enabled. You will enable these buttons in the next steps.

3 Return to CategoryView.mxml; inside the `<mx:Script>` block, import the mx.managers.IHistoryManagerClient interface and the mx.managers.HistoryManager class.

```
import mx.managers.IHistoryManagerClient;
import mx.managers.HistoryManager;
```

These classes are needed to use history management in Flex. These classes interpret the information sent from the history.swf file, which decodes the URL parameters that have been saved in an invisible frame of the HTML document. When the user moves back and forth using the browser buttons, the HistoryManager will also save this information to the invisible frame.

4 On the `<mx:HorizontalList>` tag at the top of the file, add an `implements` attribute that references the mx.managers.IHistoryManagerClient interface.

```
<mx:HorizontalList xmlns:mx="http://www.adobe.com/2006/mxml"
    dataProvider="{cats}"
    itemRenderer="views.ecomm.TextAndPic"
    horizontalScrollPolicy="off"
    click="categorySelect()"
    implements="mx.managers.IHistoryManagerClient">
```

Implementing the IHistoryManagerClient interface specifies that you will create two methods in this component, with the names `loadState()` and `saveState()`.

If you tried to compile the application at this point, you would receive an error because neither the `loadState()` method nor the `saveState()` method have been implemented. You will implement them in the next steps.

5 Call a new new method with the name of `registerWithHistoryManager()`, on the creationComplete event of the HorizontalList control.

```
<mx:HorizontalList xmlns:mx="http://www.adobe.com/2006/mxml"
    dataProvider="{cats}"
    itemRenderer="views.ecomm.TextAndPic"
    horizontalScrollPolicy="off"
    click="categorySelect()"
    implements="mx.managers.IHistoryManagerClient"
    creationComplete="registerWithHistoryManager()">
```

You need to register this component with the HistoryManager to receive notice when the user clicks the back or forward buttons on the browser. Encapsulating the work to register the component into a separate method, `registerWithHistoryManager()`, is a good design practice.

6 In the `<mx:Script>` block, create a new private method with the name of `registerWithHistoryManager()`that returns `void`. Inside the method, call the static `register` method of the HistoryManager and pass it a reference to the component, as shown.

```
private function registerWithHistoryManager():void{
    HistoryManager.register(this);
}
```

This code will register the CategoryView component with the HistoryManager, and enable the forward and back buttons in the browser. The CategoryView component is referenced from the `this` keyword.

7 Remaining in the `registerWithHistoryManager()` method, save the current state in the HistoryManager using the static `save()` method. The final `registerWithHistoryManager()` method should look like this:

```
private function registerWithHistoryManager():void{
    HistoryManager.register(this);
    HistoryManager.save();
}
```

The `save()` method of the HistoryManager saves the current state of the component. When you first register a component, you must explicitly call this `save()` method.

8 Change the name of the `categorySelect()` method to `broadcastCategoryEvent()`. The new `broadcastCategoryEvent()` method should look as follows:

```
private function broadcastCategoryEvent():void{
    var e:CategoryEvent = new CategoryEvent(this.selectedItem as
    ➥ Category, "categorySelect");
    this.dispatchEvent(e);
}
```

Remember that the `categorySelect` event is called when the user clicks a category in the HorizontalList control. You are moving the functionality of broadcasting an event into a separate method.

9 Create a new private method with the name of `categorySelect()` that returns `void`. On the first line of the method, call the static `save()` method of the HistoryManager class. On the second line, call the `broadCastCategoryEvent()` method you created in the last step to dispatch the event.

```
private function categorySelect():void{
    HistoryManager.save();
    broadcastCategoryEvent();
}
```

When the user clicks a category, this method saves the current state in the HistoryManager and broadcasts the event.

10 Remaining in the `<mx:Script>` block, create a new public method with the name of `saveState()` that returns an `Object`. Inside the method, create a new local object with the name of state. Create a `selectedIndex` item property of the state object and set this property to the `selectedIndex` property of the component. Return the state object from the method. The method should look as follows:

```
public function saveState():Object{
   var state:Object = new Object();
   state.selectedIndex = this.selectedIndex;
   return state;
}
```

The HistoryManager class's save() method collects the state object returned by the saveState() method for each registered component. This method is required and saves the current selectedIndex of the HorizontalList control so you can easily come back to it later.

❋ NOTE: In previous lessons you were told that selectedItem is preferable to selectedIndex when working with controls. The selectedChild refers to the actual item selected while the selectedIndex refers to the order of that item in the list, which can change if you reorder the elements. However, when working with history management, you can only store a limited amount of data. Storing a single number that indicates the position takes less storage space than the name of the selected child. Storing the index is a common practice in this scenario.

11 Remaining in the `<mx:Script>` block, create a new public method with the name of `loadState()`. The method should accept a parameter of state data typed as `Object`. Be sure that the method returns a type of void. On the first line of the method, declare a new variable named newIndex data typed as an int. Next, add conditional logic that checks for the existence of the state object. If it exists, set the value of the newIndex variable to the selectedIndex of the state object, cast as an int. Remember, the state object is the object that you created in the saveState() method.

```
public function loadState(state:Object):void{
   var newIndex:int;
   if (state) {
      newIndex = int( state.selectedIndex );
   }
}
```

This code resets the selectedIndex of the HorizontalList to the index that was saved earlier. The loadState() method is automatically called by the HistoryManager when the back and forward buttons on the browser are selected. The categorySelect event will fire when the previous state is selected.

12 Remaining in the loadState() method, add an else statement that will set the value of newIndex to -1. After the closing brace of the previous conditional logic, use another if statement to check whether the value of the newIndex variable is different than the selectedIndex variable. If so, set the value of the selectedIndex variable to the value of the newIndex variable and call broadcastCategoryEvent(). Your final loadState() method should appear as follows:

```
public function loadState(state:Object):void{
    var newIndex:int;
    if (state) {
        newIndex = int( state.selectedIndex );
    }else{
        newIndex = -1;
    }
    if(newIndex != selectedIndex){
        selectedIndex = newIndex;
        broadcastCategoryEvent();
    }
}
```

The if statement, which checks if the state object is null, catches the case where you have selected only one category and then clicked the back button. In this case, you have set the newIndex variable equal to -1, which removes any selection from the HorizontalList. If the newIndex variable is not equal to the current selectedIndex, you set the HorizontalList control to display the previous category the user selected. You then call the broadcastCategoryEvent() method to inform other areas of the application that the category has changed. Remember, the loadState() method is called only when the back or forward buttons on the browser are selected.

13 Open ecomm.as from the as directory.

You need to make a change in ecomm.as to support the case when a category is not selected.

14 Find the `displayProdByCategory()` method. Add conditional logic around the existing contents of the method to check if `event.cat` is not equal to `null`. Add an `else` clause to the condition logic, and set the `prodByCategory` variable equal to a new ArrayCollection. Your `displayProdByCategory()` method should look as follows:

```
private function displayProdByCategory(event:CategoryEvent):void{
   if (event.cat != null){
      var prodArray:Array=
         ➥ catProds.getProdsForCat(event.cat.catID);
      prodByCategory=new ArrayCollection(prodArray);
   }else{
      prodByCategory=new ArrayCollection();
   }
}
```

If the category information passed to this method is not valid, the `prodByCategory` variable will be set to an empty ArrayCollection, which will cause the FoodList component to not display any items. If a user selects only one category, and then clicks the back button, we will now also have correct behavior.

15 Save and run the application. Click on different categories and navigate throughout the application using the back and forward buttons on the browser.

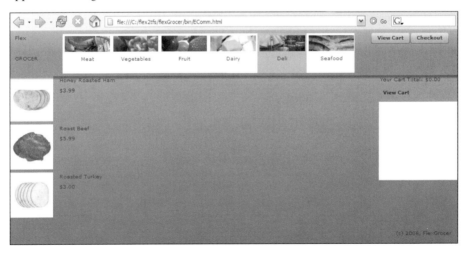

You should see that the back and forward buttons are enabled as you move through the application using the history management functionality.

What You Have Learned

In this lesson, you have:

- Turned history management on and off for the ViewStack components (pages 354–356)
- Turned history management on and off for the TabNavigator (pages 356–357)
- Used the History Manager in a custom component (pages 357–362)

What You Will Learn

In this lesson, you will:

- Learn how Flex applications are styled

- Set styles via tag attributes

- Learn about inheritable style properties

- Set styles via the `<mx:Style>` tag

- Set styles via CSS files

- Create a custom skin for components

Approximate Time

This lesson takes approximately 1 hour and 30 minutes to complete.

Lesson Files

Media Files:

Lesson16/assets/flexGrocer.css

Starting Files:

Lesson16/start/EComm.mxml
Lesson16/start/views/ecomm/BillingInfo.mxml
Lesson16/start/views/ecomm/Cart.mxml
Lesson16/start/views/ecomm/CCInfo.mxml
Lesson16/start/views/ecomm/GroceryDetail.mxml
Lesson16/start/views/ecomm/Homepage.mxml
Lesson16/start/views/ecomm/OrderConf.mxml
Lesson16/start/views/ecomm/TextAndPic.mxml

Completed Files:

Lesson16/complete/EComm.mxml
Lesson16/complete/flexGrocer.css
Lesson16/complete/skins/OrangeOval.as
Lesson16/complete/views/ecomm/BillingInfo.mxml
Lesson16/complete/views/ecomm/Cart.mxml
Lesson16/complete/views/ecomm/CCInfo.mxml
Lesson16/complete/views/ecomm/GroceryDetail.mxml
Lesson16/complete/views/ecomm/Homepage.mxml
Lesson16/complete/views/ecomm/OrderConf.mxml
Lesson16/complete/views/ecomm/TextAndPic.mxml

Customizing the Look and Feel of a Flex Application

Out of the box, Flex provides a lot of functionality, but a rather generic look to applications. In this lesson, you will explore how to apply a design to a Flex application, both through the use of styles and by creating entirely new looks with skins.

The FlexGrocer e-commerce application you have been building all along gets a face-lift with styles and skins.

Applying a Design with Styles and Skins

There are two different approaches you can use to apply a design to your Flex applications: styles and skins.

You can modify the appearance of any Flex components through the use of *style* properties, which can be used for setting the font size, background color, and many other predefined style properties. In this lesson, you will explore the use of styles, learn about style inheritance, and see several different ways to apply styles to your application.

The other option for customizing the look of a Flex application is by using *skins*, which are graphical elements (provided as files or drawn with ActionScript) that can be used to replace the default appearance of the varying states of a component. Although skinning is inherently more complex than applying styles, you will learn why you might need to do it, and how.

Applying Styles

As you have seen so far in your explorations, Flex development is done in a number of standards-based languages, such as MXML (based on XML) and ActionScript 3.0 (based on ECMAScript). It should be no surprise to learn that styles are also applied in a standards-based way through the use of Cascading Style Sheets (CSS). There are several different ways to apply a style: by setting a single style on a particular component; by using CSS class selectors to set several styles together, which can then be applied to various components; or by using a type selector to specify that all components of a particular type should use a set of styles.

In the next several exercises, you will have a chance to apply styles in all these different ways.

Regardless of which way a style is being applied, you need to know the style property that will effect the changes you want. ASDoc, also known as the *Adobe Flex 2 Language Reference* (which ships with Flex), has a complete listing of all styles available for every built-in component in Flex.

For example, any component showing text has the following styles:

Style Property	Description
Color	Color of text in the component, specified as a hexadecimal number. The default value is 0x0B333C.
disabledColor	Color of the component if it is disabled, specified as a hexadecimal number. The default value is 0xAAB3B3.
fontFamily	Name of the font to use specified as a String. Any font family name can be used. If you specify a generic font name (such as _sans), it will be converted to an appropriate device font. The default value is Verdana.
fontSize	Height of the text specified as a number of pixels. The default value is 10.
fontStyle	String indicating whether or not the text is italicized. Recognized values are normal and italic. The default is normal.
fontWeight	String indicating whether or not the text is boldfaced. Recognized values are normal and bold. The default is normal.
marginLeft	Number of pixels between the container's left border and the left edge of its content area. The default value for Text controls is 0, but different defaults apply to other components.
marginRight	Number of pixels between the container's right border and the right edge of its content area. The default value for Text controls is 0, but different defaults apply to other components.
textAlign	String indicating the alignment of text within its container or control. Recognized values are "left", "right", or "center". The default value is "left".
textDecoration	String indicating whether or not the text is underlined. Recognized values are "none" and "underline". The default value is "none".
textIndent	Offset of first line of text from the left side of the container, specified as a number of pixels. The default value is 0.

Although these style properties are available for any component that has text, each component has its own unique list of style properties available, such as the selectionColor or rollOverColor (used in ComboBox, List, DataGrid, and so on), which accepts a color as a hexadecimal value, to indicate the color of the bar around an item when it is selected or has the mouse positioned over it.

Setting Styles Inline with Tag Attributes

Styles can be applied to individual instances of a component by setting an attribute of the tag of the component with the name of the style property you want to set and the value to be set; for example, to make a label have a larger font size, you could specify the following:

```
<mx:Label text="Only a Test" fontSize="40"/>
```

In this exercise, you will set the rollOverColor and selectionColor for a ComboBox control in the second screen of the Checkout process (CCInfo.mxml).

1 Open CCInfo.mxml from your views/ecomm directory.

If you skipped the lesson when this was created, you can open this file from the Lesson16/start/views/ecomm directory and save it in your views/ecomm directory.

2 Find the declaration for the first ComboBox control with the id of cardType at about line 51. Add an attribute of the tag to specify the rollOverColor to be #AAAAAA.

```
<mx:ComboBox id="cardType" rollOverColor="#AAAAAA">
    <mx:dataProvider>
        <mx:Object label="American Express" data="AmericanExpress"/>
        <mx:Object label="Diners Club" data="DinersClub"/>
        <mx:Object label="Discover" data="Discover"/>
        <mx:Object label="MasterCard" data="MasterCard"/>
        <mx:Object label="Visa" data="Visa"/>
    </mx:dataProvider>
</mx:ComboBox>
```

It should be noted that letters used as part of a hexadecimal number (such as #AAAAAA) are not case-sensitive; #aaaaaa works just as well.

3 Add another attribute to the same tag to specify the selectionColor as #EA800C.

```
<mx:ComboBox id="cardType" rollOverColor="#AAAAAA" selectionColor="#EA800C">
```

You are now telling this one ComboBox control that when a user puts the mouse over one of the items, its color should be a pale gray (#AAAAAA) instead of the pale cyan (#0EFFD6), which it uses as a default.

4 Save CCInfo.mxml. Open and run EComm.mxml. Click Checkout in the upper-right corner. On the Customer Information form, click the Continue button. Click the Credit Cart Type ComboBox and notice the color of selected and rolled-over items.

You can easily compare this with the default look of the ComboBox control because you have changed only one of the three on this screen. Open either of the other two to see the default selectionColor and rollOverColor.

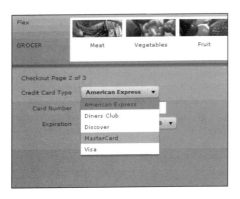

> ▶ **TIP:** It is also possible to set styles on individual instances in ActionScript using the setStyle() method. For example, the same style could have been applied with this code:

```
cardType.setStyle("selectionColor",0xEA800C);
cardType.setStyle("rollOverColor",0xAAAAAA);
```

> ✱ **NOTE:** When using setStyle(), colors are prefixed with 0x, which is the ECMAScript standard prefix for hexadecimal numbers. When applying a style in an attribute or <mx:Style> tag (as you will soon see), you can use a pound sign (#) instead of 0x. When set through ActionScript, numeric values (even those that are hexadecimal) do not have quotes around them.
>
> Although setStyle() is useful for times when styles need to change at run time, it should be used sparingly because it is a processor-intensive operation.

Understanding Style Inheritance

As you look at the ASDocs on various components, you can see that each style has a yes or no property for something called CSS inheritance.

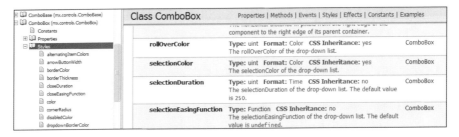

For example, here you see a few styles of the ComboBox control—selectionColor and rolloverColor—do allow CSS inheritance, whereas selectionDuration does not. What this means is that if a parent container of a ComboBox control has a value for selectionColor, and the ComboBox control itself does not, the container's value will be used. However, because selectionDuration does not support inheritance, even if a parent container had a value set for selectionDuration, the ComboBox control would use the default value because it does not inherit the value.

Setting Styles with the <mx:Style> Tag

Many of you use CSS in web pages you have built. You can also use many of the same CSS styles in your Flex applications. One way to do this is to add an <mx:Style> tag pair to any MXML document; you can write standard CSS style declarations between the open and close tags.

Standard CSS tends to have style properties whose names are all lowercase and uses hyphens as a separator between words:

```
background-color : #FFFFFF;
```

In the last exercise, you used multiword styles by declaring them with camel case syntax; that is, the style declaration started with a lowercase letter and each subsequent word started with an uppercase letter, with no spaces or hyphens used:

```
<mx:ComboBox rollOverColor="#AAAAAA"/>
```

The reason for the difference is that a hyphen is not a valid character for an XML attribute, and MXML tags are all XML tags. To work around this, when style names are set via attributes, they must be set with the ActionScript equivalent of the style name, so you use backgroundColor instead of background-color. The lowercase hyphenated versions of style properties are available only for properties that exist within traditional CSS. Any styles created specifically for Flex (such as rollOverColor) are available only in camel case. When you specify a style within an <mx:Style> tag, you can use either syntax, and it will be applied properly.

```
<mx:Style>
.customCombo{
   background-color: #AAAAAA;
   selectionColor: #EA800C;
}
</mx:Style>
```

Another choice you have when using CSS styles is the type of selector to use. Flex supports the use of CSS class selectors or CSS type (or Element) selectors.

A class selector defines a set of style properties as a single style class, which can then be applied to one or more components through the use of the component's styleName property.

```
<mx:Style>
.customCombo{
   color: #FF0000;
   selectionColor: #EA800C;
}
</mx:Style>
<mx:ComboBox styleName="customCombo"/>
```

> ● **TIP:** Unlike CSS for HTML, Flex does not support ID selectors.

Here, the ComboBox control is using the customCombo style class, which sets both the text color as well as the selectionColor.

A type selector enables you to specify a set of styles that will be applied to all instances of a type of component. In HTML applications, you can do this to define the look of an <H1> tag for your site. The same syntactic structure works to define a set of styles to be applied to all instances of a type of Flex control, as in the following:

```
<mx:Style>
ComboBox {
   color: #FF0000;
   selectionColor: #EA800C;
}
</mx:Style>
<mx:ComboBox id="stateProvenceCombo"/>
<mx:ComboBox id="countryCombo"/>
```

In this example, the color and selectionColor style properties are being applied to all ComboBox control instances.

> ● **TIP:** The terms *type* and *class selector* might seem counterintuitive if you didn't previously work with CSS. These terms come from CSS standards. The confusion is that a type selector is what you would use to affect all instances of an ActionScript class; a class selector has no relation to any ActionScript class, but instead defines a style class that can be used on several elements.

In this next task, you will build a class selector and apply it to an <mx:Form> tag in CCInfo.mxml. This will not only showcase the use of a class selector, but you will also see style inheritance in use because the style will be inherited by all of the ComboBox controls in that form.

1 Open CCInfo.mxml from the previous exercise.

If you didn't finish the previous exercise, you can open CCInfo_inline.mxml from Lesson16/intermediate and save it as **CCInfo.mxml** in your views/ecomm directory.

2 Just after the root <mx:Canvas> tag, create an <mx:Style> tag pair.

```
<mx:Canvas xmlns:mx="http://www.adobe.com/2006/mxml">
   <mx:Style>
   </mx:Style>
   <mx:Metadata>
```

You now have an <mx:Style> block, in which you can create type or class selectors.

3 Inside the <mx:Style>block, create a class selector called customCombo that specifies a rollOverColor of #AAAAAA and a selectionColor of #EA800C.

```
<mx:Style>
   .customCombo{
      selectionColor:#EA800C;
      rollOverColor:#AAAAAA;
   }
</mx:Style>
```

Like traditional CSS, but unlike style properties set as attributes, no quotes are used around the values of the style properties.

4 Remove the rollOverColor and selectionColor attributes of the ComboBox control. Instead, specify a styleName="customCombo" as an attribute on that ComboBox control.

```
<mx:ComboBox id="cardType" styleName="customCombo"/>
```

If you save and test the application, the one ComboBox control should behave as it did before—with custom colors—whereas the other two show the default colors.

5 Cut the styleName="customCombo" from the ComboBox and instead paste it as an attribute of the <mx:Form> tag.

```
<mx:Form width="100%" styleName="customCombo">
```

Because the form contains three ComboBox controls, applying these cascading styles to the form affect all the ComboBox controls within the form.

6 Save and run the application.

Verify that the style is now applied to all three ComboBox controls in the form.

Setting Styles with CSS files

You can use an `<mx:Script>` tag to either define a block of code inline on the MXML document or you can use its `source` attribute to specify an external file to be compiled into the application. The `<mx:Style>` tag works in a similar way. Used as a tag pair, you can specify a series of styles inline in your MXML documents or you can use the `source` attribute to specify an external file.

```
<mx:Style source="path/to/file.css"/>
```

One great advantage of using an external file is that you can share CSS files between multiple Flex applications, or even between Flex and HTML applications. This is possible because CSS parsers in both Flex and HTML are smart enough to ignore any declarations they don't understand. So even if Flex supports only a subset of standard CSS, and in fact creates a number of its own custom declarations, neither your HTML nor your Flex applications will be hurt by declarations they cannot understand.

In this exercise, you will make use of a prebuilt CSS file to style the FlexGrocer application.

1 Copy flexGrocer.css from Lesson16/assets to your flexGrocer directory.

Open up the file, and you will see a series of style definitions, some as type selectors (such as `Application`, `DateChooser`, and so on) and a number of class selectors (`.formPage1`, `.borderBox`, and so on). Styles that match traditional HTML styles (such as `background-color`, `font-family`, and so on) are all lowercase so they can work in both HTML and Flex applications, whereas any Flex-specific styles (`headerColors`, `hGridLines`, `alternatingRowColors`, and so on) are in only camel case.

2 Open the CCInfo.mxml file you worked on in the previous task and remove the `<mx:Style>` block you added.

As a best practice, all styles for the application are defined in a single style sheet. This way, if you want to change the look and feel of the application at a later time, you don't need to dig through the code to find all the places where styles were applied; instead, you can restyle the application by changing only one file!

3 Open EComm.mxml from your flexGrocer directory.

Alternatively, you can open this file from Lesson16/start and save it in your flexGrocer directory.

4 Just after the `<mx:Application>` tag, use an `<mx:Style>` tag with the `source` attribute to read in the CSS file.

```
<mx:Style source="flexGrocer.css"/>
```

This instructs the Flex compiler to read in the CSS file, making all those type and class declarations available to you.

5 Save the file and run the application.

Notice right away that any of the type selectors are automatically applied. This will become readily apparent as you notice that every ComboBox, DataGrid, List, and DateChooser control has the selectionColor and rollOverColor applied as they are specified in the Application type selector. This is because these two style properties are inheritable and they are applied at the topmost container (Application), so they will cascade to everything else within the application.

```
Application{
    font-family: Arial, Helvetica, sans-serif;
    background-color: #333333;
    selectionColor: #EA800C;
    rollOverColor: #CECECE;
}
```

Of course, more work needs to be done to the application because the default dark blue/green text on a dark gray background is nearly impossible to read. Don't worry—you will apply the other styles in the application to rectify it.

6 Still in EComm.mxml, find the labels for the logo in the ApplicationControlBar (at about lines 35 and 38). Set a styleName attribute of the first label to be logoTop and the second logo to be logoBottom.

```
<mx:Label x="0" y="0"
    text="Flex"
    styleName="logoTop"
    click="ecommNav.selectedChild=homePage"/>
<mx:Label x="0" y="41"
    text="GROCER"
    styleName="logoBottom"
    click="ecommNav.selectedChild=homePage"/>
```

The logoTop class selector specifies 40 point bold text with a #EA800C (orange) color. The logoBottom has the same color and bold, but with 19 point text instead.

7 Still in EComm.mxml, find the <mx:ViewStack> tag with an id of ecommNav (at about line 60). Set a styleName attribute of this tag to be whiteBg.

```
<mx:ViewStack id="ecommNav"
    width="100%" height="100%"
    creationPolicy="all"
    styleName="whiteBg">
```

This sets a white (#FFFFFF) background for the body of the application. Because the ViewStack container is the outermost container for everything in the body, setting its background color to white will also create a white background for all its children.

8 Still in EComm.mxml, find the <mx:Label> that has the bottom branding (at about line 81). Set its styleName property to be bottomBranding.

```
<mx:Label text="©2006 flexGROCER. All rights reserved."
    right="10" bottom="10"
    styleName="bottomBranding"/>
```

The bottom text is set to be black, so it contrasts nicely with the white background.

9 Save and test the application.

You should see a white background on the body, the orange logo, and the properly sized and colored bottom branding. After you have seen and tested it, you can close EComm. mxml. The rest of the styles you will be applying will be in child components.

10 Open Homepage.mxml from your views/ecomm directory.

Alternatively, you can open this file from the Lesson16/start/views/ecomm directory and save it in your views/ecomm directory.

11 Find the Label control with an id of welcome. Assign it a styleName of homePageTitle.

```
<mx:Label id="welcome"
     text="Welcome"
     left="{image.x}"
     top="{image.height+image.y}"
     styleName="homePageTitle"/>
```

The homePageTitle style class makes this label orange (#EA800C) with 90 point text, so it is very large.

12 Find the <mx:Text> tag with an id of homePageText. Assign it a styleName of homePageText.

```
<mx:Text width="{image.width-30}"
     left="{image.x+30}"
     top="{welcome.y + (welcome.height/2)}"
     styleName="homePageText">
```

The homePageText style class makes this text gray (#333333) with 13 point text.

13 Save Homepage.mxml and run the application.

You should now see the home page text styled properly. Notice that the labels under the category navigation are still too dark to read against the dark gray background. In the next set of steps, you will fix it.

After you see this rendering properly, you can save and close Homepage.mxml.

14 Open TextAndPic.mxml from your views/ecomm directory.

Alternatively, you can open this file from the Lesson16/start/views/ecomm directory and save it in your views/ecomm directory.

15 Find the <mx:Label> tag. Assign it a styleName of categoryText.

```
<mx:Label text="{data.catName}"
    width="100%"
    styleName="categoryText"/>
```

The categoryText style class makes this label white (#FFFFFF), 14 point, bold, and centered.

16 Save TextAndPic.mxml and run the application.

The category names should now be bigger, bolder, and white to make them visible against the dark background. However, if you click any of the categories, you will find that the text by each product seems very small, rendering in the default size of 10 point. You will address it next.

17 Open GroceryDetail.mxml from your views/ecomm directory.

Alternatively, you can open this file from the Lesson16/start/views/ecomm directory and save it in your flexGrocer directory.

18 Find the <mx:Label> tag with an id of prodName (at about line 71). Assign it a styleName of standardOrange.

```
<mx:Label id="prodName"
    text="{groceryItem.prodName}"
    x="100" y="0"
    styleName="standardOrange"/>
```

The standardOrange style class will be used throughout the application when orange (#EA800C), nonbold, 12-point text is desired. When you finish the styling, GroceryDetail is one of four files that will use this style.

19 Find the <mx:Label> tag with an id of price (at about line 75). Assign it a styleName of standardBlackBold.

```
<mx:Label id="price"
    text="{curFormat.format(groceryItem.listPrice)}"
    x="100" y="20"
    styleName="standardBlackBold"/>
```

The standardBlackBold style class will be used throughout the application when black (#333333), bold, 12-point text is desired. This same style will also be used once in the BillingInfo component.

20 Find the <mx:VBox> tag added for the expanded state (at about line 51). Assign it a styleName of standardBlack.

```
<mx:states>
   <mx:State name="expanded">
      <mx:AddChild>
         <mx:VBox width="100%"
            x="200"
            styleName="standardBlack">
            …
         </mx:VBox>
      </mx:AddChild>
      …
   </mx:State>
</mx:states>
```

By applying the standardBlack (#333333, 12 point) style to the VBox, all the text contained by the VBox will use this style.

The last thing to do in GroceryDetail is to add a black border around the item when it is in its expanded state.

21 After the closing </mx:AddChild> tag that adds the <mx:VBox>, and before the <mx:SetProperty> tag that toggles the visibility of the Add button, add a new <mx:SetStyle> tag that will set the styleName property of the component to borderBox.

```
<mx:SetStyle
   name="styleName"
   value="borderBox"/>
```

Now, whenever the user moves the mouse over a product, in addition to showing the details, the borderBox style is also applied; it sets a dark gray (#333333) border around the entire component.

22 Save GroceryDetail.mxml and run the application.

As you run the application, clicking any of the categories should show all the styles now applied to the grocery details.

23 Open Cart.mxml from your views/ecomm directory.

Alternatively, you can open this file from the Lesson16/start/views/ecomm directory and save it in your views/ecomm directory. If you navigated to the fullCart state, the default look and feel of the DataGrid control feels a bit flat compared with the rest of the styled application. In these next steps, you will make the DataGrid control feel more like the rest of the application.

24 Find the <mx:DataGrid> tag. Assign this a styleName of cartGrid.

```
<mx:DataGrid
   id="cartView"
   dataProvider="{cart.aItems}"
   width="100%" height="100%"
   editable="true"
   draggableColumns="false"
   variableRowHeight="true"
   styleName="cartGrid">
```

Looking back to the stylesheet, you can see that the cartGrid style class sets the header colors to fade between white (#FFFFFF) and orange (#EA800C). Take a closer look at how the fade was specified.

```
.cartGrid{
   header-colors: #FFFFFF, #EA800C;
   horizontal-grid-lines: false;
   alternating-item-colors:#FFFFFF,#FFFFFF;
   vertical-grid-lines: false;
}
```

Notice that two of the styles (header-colors and alternating-item-colors) have comma-delimited lists of values specified. If you look to ASDocs for the definitions of these styles, you will see that they are both built to accept an array. Because CSS is not a programming language, nor really part of the ActionScript language, you can't use traditional approaches for creating an array (such as square brackets or the new Array() command). Instead, you specify an array in a CSS by providing a comma-delimited list of the elements. Another important thing to note is that alternating-item-colors needs at least two elements, even if they are the same. If this were defined only as alternating-item-colors: #EAEAEA; a run-time error would be thrown because Flash Player is looking to find an array and instead is finding only a single number.

▶ **TIP:** Elements that take an array, such as alternating-item-colors, are not limited to only two colors; you can usually specify several colors, and it will alternate between each of them.

25 Save Cart.mxml and run the application.

Choose a category, click the Add To Cart button for a few products, and then click the View Cart button. You should now see the Shopping Cart DataGrid control looking more like it belongs to this application.

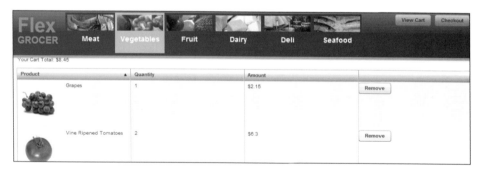

All that remains to have styles from the stylesheets applied to them are the pages of the checkout process.

26 Open BillingInfo.mxml from your views/ecomm directory.

Alternatively, you can open this file from the Lesson16/start/views/ecomm directory and save it in your views/ecomm directory.

27 On the root node of this document (an <mx:HBox> tag), apply a styleName of formPage1.

```
<mx:HBox xmlns:mx="http://www.adobe.com/2006/mxml"
    xmlns:u="utils.*"
    styleName="formPage1">
```

The formPage1 style sets a labelWidth for all the form elements, so they now line up nicely and look less ragged than before. This also sets the indicatorGap style, which determines the space between the right edge of the label and the left edge of the controls.

28 Find the <mx:Label> tag, which tells the user they are on "Checkout Page 1 of 3", and apply a styleName attribute of standardOrangeBold to it.

```
<mx:Label text="Checkout Page 1 of 3"
    styleName="standardOrangeBold"/>
```

The standardOrangeBold style is the orange (#EA800C) version of the standardBlackBold style you applied to the price label in the GroceryDetail component.

29 On the next line, apply a styleName of standardBlackBold to the <mx:FormHeading> tag.

```
<mx:FormHeading label="Customer Information"
    styleName="standardBlackBold"/>
```

As was mentioned earlier, this style class sets black, 12-point bold text.

30 Save BillingInfo.mxml and run the application.

While running the application, click the Checkout button in the top-right corner of the screen. You should see the form items line up nicely, and have bold orange text for the step numbers, and bold black text for the form heading. The <mx:DateChooser> control has had styles applied to it, too (There is a type selector in the CSS file that sets the DateChooser control header colors, and it is inheriting the selectionColor and rollOverColor styles from the application.).

31 Open CCInfo.mxml from your views/ecomm directory.

Alternatively, you can open this file from the Lesson16/start/views/ecomm directory and save it in your views/ecomm directory.

32 Find the <mx:Form> tag (at about line 47). Replace the styleName attribute you set earlier (customCombo) with the value formPage2.

```
<mx:Form width="100%"
    styleName="formPage2">
```

The formPage2 style is similar to the formPage1 style you used in the previous document, except that it needs a larger labelWidth to accommodate longer text.

33 On the next line, set the styleName of the <mx:Label> to be standardOrangeBold.

```
<mx:Label text="Checkout Page 2 of 3"
    styleName="standardOrangeBold"/>
```

Because you want to keep a consistent look and feel across the checkout process, the same style is used on the text to tell users where they are in the process.

34 Save CCinfo.mxml and run the application.

35 Open OrderConf.mxml from your views/ecomm directory.

Alternatively, you can open this file from the Lesson16/start/views/ecomm directory and save it in your flexGrocer directory.

36 Find the <mx:Form> tag (at about line 23). Set its styleName attribute to be formPage1.

```
<mx:Form styleName="formPage1">
```

This form, like the first, uses shorter labels, so the formPage1 style is more appropriate for it.

Because you want to keep a consistent look and feel across the checkout process, in the next few steps you will add the same style to similar elements on the different pages to help the users know where they are in the process.

37 On the next line set the `styleName` of the `<mx:Label>` to be `standardOrangeBold`.

```
<mx:Label text="Checkout Page 3 of 3"
    styleName="standardOrangeBold"/>
```

38 On the next line, set the `styleName` of the `<mx:FormHeading>` to be `standardBlackBold`.

```
<mx:FormHeading label="Billing Information"
    styleName="standardBlackBold"/>
```

39 On the next line, set the `styleName` of the `<mx:HBox>` to be `formHBox`.

```
<mx:HBox styleName="formHBox">
```

This style sets only the `horizontalGap` of the HBox. On this page, it represents the distance between the first and second columns of data.

40 Save OrderConf.mxml and run the application.

Styles have now been consistently applied throughout the application.

Skinning Components

There are times when you might need to apply a design to a Flex application, for which no style will easily fit your needs. In these cases, you need to use *skinning*.

Skinning is used to change the appearance of a component by modifying or replacing its visual elements. Unlike styles, which change values of the existing skins for a component, skinning enables you to actually replace the elements used. This can be done graphically with images and SWF files, or programmatically with class files and the drawing API.

Each component is made of several skins to represent the different visual looks of the component. For example, a button has a separate skin for its normal appearance (upSkin), for how it appears when the mouse is over it (overSkin), for when it is pressed (downSkin), and when it is disabled (disabledSkin). Each of the available skins for a component can be found in the styles section of that components entry in ASDocs.

Graphical Skins

One way to apply skins to a component is to specify new graphical elements to be used in place of the default skins. If you are working with designers who have very specific graphic needs for the look and feel of components, you can use their graphical assets (JPG, GIF, PNG or SWF files) as a replacement skin for any state of any component. Skins are actually applied as a style, they can be done inline, in a <mx:Style> block or CSS file, or via the setStyle() method. For example:

- Inline:

```
<mx:Button upSkin="@Embed('../assets/myFancyUpSkin.gif')"/>
```

- <mx:Style> block or CSS file:

```
<mx:Style>
   Button {
      overSkin: Embed("../assets/images/myFancyOverSkin.gif");
   }
</mx:Style>
```

- setStyle() method:

```
<mx:Script>
   [Embed("assets/myFancyDownSkin.gif")]
   var ds:Class;
   function initApp(){
      myButton.setStyle("downSkin",ds);
   }
</mx:Script>
```

Programmatic Skins

Rather than use graphical assets for skins, it is also possible to use the drawing API of Flash Player (mostly found in the flash.display.Graphics class) to programmatically draw your own skins. To do this, you create a class file that will define the skin.

The main reason why you might choose to use a programmatic skin instead of a graphical one is that you can have much more control over them when they are done programmatically. Instead of embedding graphics of a fixed size, programmatic skins can easily be built to resize themselves, whereas a graphical skin does not resize so elegantly. Programmatic skins also tend to use less memory as they contain no external graphic files.

By drawing a skin programmatically, you have access to more flexibility than you would normally have by using styles. For example, a button has styles to allow a gradient fill by using the fillColors style property; however, you can't control the ratio of the fill. Imagine a gradient that was 20 percent red and 80 percent blue. The fillColors property applies an equal amount of each color, whereas the drawing API provides a beginGradientFill() method that not only allows you to specify the array of colors but also the percentages of each (as well as a matrix) to determine the direction of the fade.

To create a programmatic skin, you first need to choose a superclass for your new skin class. Flex provides three classes that you can choose from:

Superclass	Description
ProgrammaticSkin	The ProgrammaticSkin class implements the IFlexDisplayObject, ILayoutClient, and IStyleable interfaces. This is the lightest weight class that can be used as the superclass for a skin.
Border	The Border class extends the ProgrammaticSkin class and adds support for the borderMetrics property. If you are looking to implement a skin with a border that doesn't use a background image, this is the choice for you.
RectBorder	The RectBorder class extends the Border class and adds support for the backgroundImage style.

The bulk of the work you will do to write a programmatic skin is to override the updateDisplayList() method. If you recall, during Lesson 10, "Creating Custom Components with ActionScript 3.0," you overrode this method when creating the MaxRestorePanel. This method is what is used to draw the visual elements of any class, so to create a new look for a skin, this method will need to be overridden.

If you choose to use one of the bordered classes (Border or RectBorder) as a superclass, you will also want to override the getter method for the borderMetrics property, so it returns your custom metrics instead of the default values.

In this task, you will create a custom skin for the Button controls in your application. This skin will use an ellipse instead of the default rectangle as the shape for the skin.

1 In Flex Builder, create a new directory named skins as a subdirectory of your flexGrocer directory.

If you followed the default locations for your project, this new directory would be in your flexGrocer directory.

2 Create a new ActionScript class named **OrangeOval** in the skins package. The superclass for your skin should be mx.skins.ProgrammaticSkin.

```
package skins{
   import mx.skins.ProgrammaticSkin;

   public class OrangeOval extends ProgrammaticSkin{
   }
}
```

Because you don't need a border around your button, the ProgrammaticSkin class is an appropriate superclass for you.

3 Create the skeleton for your overridden updateDisplayList() method.

```
protected override function updateDisplayList(w:Number, h:Number):void{
}
```

Remember that an overridden method needs to exactly match the signature of the method in the superclass. Looking at ASDocs, you can find that this is a protected method, returning void, which accepts two numeric arguments.

4 Inside the updateDisplayList() method, create two local variables: An int named lineThickness with a value of 4 and a Number named backgroundFillColor.

```
var lineThickness:int=4;
var backgroundFillColor:Number;
```

When you draw the shape, these variables will be used with the drawing API.

5 Create a switch statement to determine which skin is being drawn. Assign the backgroundFillColor the appropriate value from the following table for each version of the skin.

Skin	Color
upSkin	0xEA800C
overSkin	0xF8B872
downSkin	0xB06109
disabledSkin	0xCCCCCC

```
switch (name) {
   case "upSkin":
      backgroundFillColor = 0xEA800C;
      break;
   case "overSkin":
      backgroundFillColor = 0xF8B872;
      break;
   case "downSkin":
      backgroundFillColor = 0xB06109;
      break;
   case "disabledSkin":
      backgroundFillColor = 0xCCCCCC;
      break;
}
```

The name property used in the switch statement is the current name of the skin. For a programmatic skin of a Button control, the name property could be any of the skin states. This method will automatically be called each time the button is redrawn (such as when the Button control changes state), and Flex automatically updates the value of the name property.

6 Use the drawing API to clear any previously drawn elements.

```
graphics.clear();
```

The ProgrammaticSkin class has a property called graphics, which is an instance of the flash.display.Graphics class. This is the class that contains the drawing API. Because this same updateDisplayList() will be used to draw all four states, you want to remove the previously drawn elements before drawing the current state.

7 Use the beginFill() method of the Graphics class to set the background color to be drawn.

```
graphics.beginFill(backgroundFillColor);
```

When the shape for the skin is drawn, this will now fill the shape with the appropriate color determined from the switch statement.

8 Use the drawEllipse() method to draw the skin.

```
graphics.drawEllipse(0, 0, w, h);
```

This line does the actual drawing and creates an ellipse from the component's top left (0,0) to the height and width, as specified by the arguments automatically provided to the updateDisplayList() method.

9 End the fill.

```
graphics.endFill();
```

Flash Player waits until the endFill() method is called before actually drawing the fill on the screen.

10 Save and close OrangeOval.as.

The completed class file should read like this:

```
package skins{
    import mx.skins.ProgrammaticSkin;
    public class OrangeOval extends ProgrammaticSkin{
        protected override function updateDisplayList(w:Number,
            ➥ h:Number):void{
            var lineThickness:int=4;
            var backgroundFillColor:Number;
            switch (name) {
                case "upSkin":
                    backgroundFillColor = 0xEA800C;
                    break;
                case "overSkin":
                    backgroundFillColor = 0xF8B872;
                    break;
                case "downSkin":
                    backgroundFillColor = 0xB06109;
                    break;
                case "disabledSkin":
                    backgroundFillColor = 0xCCCCCC;
                    break;
            }
            graphics.clear();
            graphics.beginFill(backgroundFillColor);
            graphics.drawEllipse(0, 0, w, h);
            graphics.endFill();
        }
    }
}
```

11 Open flexGrocer.css.

If you didn't copy this file over earlier in the lesson, you can find it in the Lesson16/assets directory. Save it in your root directory.

12 At the bottom of the file, create a type selector for the Button class, which sets the upSkin, downSkin, overSkin and disabledSkin style properties to use ClassReference('skins.OrangeOval');.

```
Button {
   upSkin:ClassReference('skins.OrangeOval');
   downSkin:ClassReference('skins.OrangeOval');
   overSkin:ClassReference('skins.OrangeOval');
   disabledSkin:ClassReference('skins.OrangeOval');
}
```

Programmatic skins can be applied in a CSS file by using the ClassReference directive. This directive takes a class name as the argument.

It tells all buttons to use your new skin class for all four states.

13 Still in the Button type selector, add one more style declaration, setting the color property to white (#FFFFFF);

```
Button {
   upSkin:ClassReference('skins.OrangeOval');
   downSkin:ClassReference('skins.OrangeOval');
   overSkin:ClassReference('skins.OrangeOval');
   disabledSkin:ClassReference('skins.OrangeOval');
   color:#ffffff;
}
```

The white text makes the button easier to read.

14 Save the stylesheet and run the application.

All the Button controls in the application are rendered with the OrangeOval skin.

What You Have Learned

In this lesson, you have:

- Learned how Flex applications are styled (pages 367–368)
- Set styles via tag attributes (pages 369–370)
- Learned about inheritable style properties (pages 370–371)
- Set styles via the `<mx:Style>` tag (pages 371–373)
- Set styles via CSS files (pages 374–384)
- Created a custom skin for components (pages 384–390)

What You Will Learn

In this lesson, you will:

- Use the `<mx:WebService>` tag to retrieve data from the server

- Sort the collection returned from the server as result of the Web Service call

- Declare the specific operations on the `<mx:WebService>` tag

- Bind specific parameters to a Web Service operation

- Upload a file to the server

- Use the WebService ActionScript object to update data on the server

- Implement a DataManager ActionScript class to centralize all your Web Service calls

- Use the `<mx:RemoteObject>` tag to place an order on the server

- Map a server object to an ActionScript class for data transfer between client and server

Approximate Time

This lesson takes approximately 2 hours to complete.

Lesson Files

Media:

Lesson17/assets/DataManager.as

Starting Files:

Lesson17/start/Dashboard.mxml
Lesson17/start/DataEntry.mxml
Lesson17/start/valueObjects/Product.as
Lesson17/start/valueObjects/OrderInfo.as
Lesson17/start/views/dataEntry/AddProduct.mxml
Lesson17/start/views/dataEntry/UpdateDeleteProd.mxml
Lesson17/start/managers/CategorizedProductManager.mxml
Lesson17/start/EComm.mxml
Lesson17/start/views/ecomm/Checkout.mxml
Lesson17/start/views/ecomm/OrderConf.mxml

Completed Files:

Lesson17/complete/Dashboard.mxml
Lesson17/complete/DataEntry.mxml
Lesson17/complete/valueObjects/Product.as
Lesson17/complete/valueObjects/OrderInfo.as
Lesson17/complete/views/dataEntry/AddProduct.mxml
Lesson17/complete/views/dataEntry/FileUpload.mxml
Lesson17/complete/views/dataEntry/UpdateDeleteProd.mxml
Lesson17/complete/managers/CategorizedProductManager.mxml
Lesson17/complete/EComm.mxml
Lesson17/complete/views/ecomm/Checkout.mxml
Lesson17/complete/views/ecomm/OrderConf.mxml
Lesson17/complete/managers/DataManager.as
Lesson17/complete/events/DataManagerResultEvent.as

Accessing Server-side Objects

Until now, the data that you have been displaying (available products, categories, sales data, and so on) has come from XML feeds or written into the application via MXML/ActionScript. In the real world, every application that you write will have three logic areas: the client, the business logic (logic that implements the requirement of the system), and the data it runs on. Although Adobe Flex is a great platform for developing your rich-client interface and can also be used to write business logic, from an architectural standpoint it is sometimes best to put your core business logic outside of your Flex application. For example, have the process that does a real-time evaluation of a checked-out state on a piece of data reside on the server and be called by the client before using access data to make sure it can still be used. In this example, you see it is best to implement the central business rules and data access in a location in which all the users accessing the system will have access. This best practice can be implemented in a variety of technologies and accessed from Flex in several different ways.

Confirmation screen after adding a new product

In this lesson, you will initially learn how to access code (server-side objects) written on the server to retrieve data to feed the Dashboard, update product information, and place an order. Then you will learn how the `<mx:WebService>` and `<mx:RemoteObject>` tags enable you to use both an industry standard and an open binary protocol to call this Server object. Because the data that defines a product is its picture, you will implement the ability to upload a file. Finally, you will write some high-level architectural features to assist you with centralizing your server access and passing data between the client and server tiers. The previous example shows the confirmation screen after a new product is added.

From this lesson going forward, all external access from the application will be using the local ColdFusion instance. Please refer to the appendix, "Setup Instructions," to learn how to install, set up, and run the ColdFusion server instance and application.

Introducing Server-side Objects

When discussing any communication with the server, it makes sense to discuss the origins a bit to better understand the two primary ways in which you access the server. The way you access the server determines the manner in which events are handled by Flex on these remote calls and the difference between push/pull server communications.

The need for clients to make calls to a server for business processing came the first time multiple users could access the same system at the same time. The original calls were done over custom defined protocols dubbed remote procedure calls (RPCs). The first RPCs were primarily designed to work within a specific vendor's platform and product. They typically had a specific format for the data being passed (binary, encryption, what bit position referred to what piece of data, and so on). Today, the term *RPC* describes the most basic call between a client and a server instead of a specific protocol or message format.

The need for an enterprise to share the business logic written in one application with another quickly drove the need to standardize the way one application talks with another one. The emergence of Common Object Request Broker Architecture (CORBA) as an industry-maintained standard for exposing the middle-tier server objects was a big step forward in the capability to share logic between applications. The big drawback was the difference in each vendor's implementation of CORBA and the mapping of data between different systems.

Java introduced Remote Method Invocation (RMI) as a more refined way of calling remote objects and the passing of data between the client and server tier. However, because of its complexity to implement, RMI was not heavily used by developers outside the Java world.

The latest way to interface between the client and the server, Web Services, leverages XML (text-based) to describe how the server objects are used as well as the format in which the communication is done. This results in a human readable description of an object and the call to the server. However, this strength is also a weakness because it is a departure from binary communication between the client and the server and hence not as efficient.

In Flash MX, Flash Remoting was introduced as a way to provide binary communication between the Flash client and the server. Flash Remoting is based on an open protocol called Action Message Format (AMF) that enables you to communicate with a variety of server technologies including Java, PHP, and ColdFusion.

Using the Event Model Remote Server Calls

When making calls via `<mx:WebService>` or `<mx:RemoteObject>`, you are calling logic that resides outside of Flex. Just like the `<mx:HTTPService>` tag discussed in Lesson 6, "Using Remote XML Data with Controls," you do not have control over when the server will finish executing the request you made. Therefore, you need to use events and event listeners to capture when the server is finished with the request.

There are two ways in which the client can receive data/events from the server. The first is in response to a call initiated by the client and is known as *synchronous communication*. In the second method (which is known as *asynchronous communication* and is discussed in detail in Lesson 19, "Introducing Flex Data Services"), the server pushes data down to the client because of some change in the data (DataService) or event (Publisher) on the server. For the scope of this lesson, you will focus on just calling the server and receiving events from those calls.

Configuring an Application to Work Locally

From this lesson forward, you will be using the local ColdFusion server for all data and remote objects that the application will use. With ColdFusion started and running, the next set of steps will have you update the application to point all the `<mx:HTTPService>` tags to the local ColdFusion server.

✱ **NOTE:** See the appendix, "Setup Instructions," for instructions on how to install and start the ColdFusion server. The instructions will have you configure ColdFusion to receive requests from Flex to retrieve, add, and update data. You must have ColdFusion set up from this point forward to run the lessons.

1 If you have not done so already, start your local ColdFusion server.

If your ColdFusion server is installed according to the "Setup Instructions" in the appendix, you can start the server by executing the command "jrun -start cfusion" from a command prompt in the *driveroot*\cfusionFlexTFS\bin directory. If you are using Windows, be sure to leave the command prompt open, but minimized, while using the server.

2 Open Dashboard.mxml.

Alternately, you can open Dashboard.mxml from your Lesson17/start directory and save it to your flexGrocer directory.

3 Replace each incidence of http://www.flexgrocer.com/ in the url attribute of each <mx:HTTPService> tag with http://localhost:8300/flexGrocer/xml/.

```
<mx:HTTPService id="salesRPC"
    url="http://localhost:8300/flexGrocer/xml/rawSalesData.xml"
    result="salesRPCResult(event)"
    fault="showFault(event)"/>

<mx:HTTPService id="typeRPC"
    url="http://localhost:8300/flexGrocer/xml/categorySalesData.xml"
    result="typeRPCResult(event)"
    fault="showFault(event)"/>

<mx:HTTPService id="compRPC"
    url="http://localhost:8300/flexGrocer/xml/salesData.xml"
    result="compRPCResult(event)"
    fault="showFault(event)"/>

<mx:HTTPService id="catRPC"
    url="http://localhost:8300/flexGrocer/xml/category.xml"
    result="catHandler(event)"/>
```

4 Open DataEntry.mxml.

Alternately, you can open DataEntry.mxml from your Lesson17/start directory and save it to your flexGrocer directory.

5 Replace each incidence of http://www.flexgrocer.com/ in the url attribute of each <mx:HTTPService> tag with http://localhost:8300/flexGrocer/xml/.

```
<mx:HTTPService id="unitRPC"
    url="http://localhost:8300/flexGrocer/xml/units.xml"
    result="unitRPCResult(event)"/>
```

6 Open CategorizedProductManager.mxml from your managers directory.

Alternately, you can open CategorizedProductManager.mxml from your Lesson17/start/ managers directory and save it to your flexGrocer/managers directory.

7 Replace each incidence of http://www.flexgrocer.com/ in the url attribute of each `<mx:HTTPService>` tag with http://localhost:8300/flexGrocer/xml/.

```
<mx:HTTPService id="prodByCatRPC"
   url="http://localhost:8300/flexGrocer/xml/categorizedProducts.xml"
   result="prodByCategoryHandler(event)"
   resultFormat="e4x"/>
```

8 Run the Dashboard, Data Entry, and Ecommerce applications. You should notice no difference in their functionality from what you saw at the end of Lesson 16.

Using a Web Service in the Dashboard

In this task, you will replace the three `<mx:HTTPService>` tags with a single `<mx:WebService>` tag for retrieving the data for the Dashboard. The `<mx:WebService>` tag is pointing to a Server object that has three different methods to retrieve the data that is needed.

There are two ways to call a Web Service in Flex. The first is tag-based; the other is via ActionScript. You will use the `<mx:WebService>` tag in this task to create a WebService object against which you can call your methods.

1 If you have not done so already, start your local ColdFusion server.

2 Open Dashboard.mxml.

3 Below the script block, locate the first three `<mx:HTTPService>` tags (salesRPC, typeRPC and compRPC) that get the XML data for the Dashboard and replace them with a single `<mx:WebService>` tag. Set the id attribute to dashboardWS. Set the wsdl attribute to http://localhost:8300/flexGrocer/cfcs/aggregate.cfc?wsdl. Finally, leave the fault handler the same as what the `<mx:HTTPService>` used.

```
<mx:WebService
   id="dashboardWS"
   wsdl="http://localhost:8300/flexGrocer/cfcs/aggregate.cfc?wsdl"
   fault="showFault(event)">
</mx:WebService>
```

The technology that you are using here is a ColdFusion Web Service. By specifying the wsdl attribute of the tag, you are telling Flex to fetch the definition Web Service Description Language (WSDL) of the Web Service on the first request to the Web Service. You can trap an event called load, which fires when the WSDL file loads successfully.

In Flex, you can use the methods on a Web Service in three ways:

- **Undeclared Method:** You use the `<mx:WebService>` with the `id` attribute. Flex looks at the loaded WSDL for the method and arguments based on how you call the `<mx:WebService>` in your ActionScript.

- **Declared Method:** You define the operation as a child of the `<mx:WebService>` tag via the `<mx:operation>` tag. Arguments are validated by looking into the WSLD.

- **Fully Declared Method:** You define the operation and its arguments as a child of the `<mx:WebService>` tag via the `<mx:operation>` and `<mx:request>` tags.

> **TIP:** The data returned from a WebService call is captured via the `fault` or `result` event. One of the benefits of declaring the methods/operations on a WebService is that you can apply specific event handlers to each operation.

4 Create a child `<mx:operation>` tag inside the `<mx:WebService>` tag. Give it a `name` of `getTypeSalesData` and point the `result` handler to the `typeRPCResult()` function, passing the event object as the only parameter.

```
<mx:operation name="getTypeSalesData" result="typeRPCResult(event)">
</mx:operation>
```

This created a method that will return the sales data summarized for each category of food sold. You had a previously defined function `typeRPCResult()` that was set up to deal with the result (passed in as a variable called event) from the `<mx:HTTPService>`. You will modify this function later to handle the new format in which the data is returned.

5 In between the `<mx:operation>` tags, create an `<mx:request>` pair.

```
<mx:operation name="getTypeSalesData" result="typeRPCResult(event)">
   <mx:request>
   </mx:request>
</mx:operation>
```

6 Specify a tag for `startDate` that binds to `startDate.selectedDate` and a tag for `endDate` that binds to `endDate.selectedDate`.

```
<mx:request>
   <startDate>{startDate.selectedDate}</startDate>
   <endDate>{endDate.selectedDate}</endDate>
</mx:request>
```

What this does is preset the `getTypeSalesData()` method to always have the arguments containing the right values. Using binding updates the `startDate` and `endDate` with the latest selected date from the user.

> ▶ **TIP:** Specifying the arguments of the WebService (or RemoteObject) method and then having the values updating via binding can be a very nice way to simplify your calls.

7 In the script block at the top of the file, add a public variable called `selectedType` of type String. Default it to `All`.

```
[Bindable]
public var selectedType:String = "All";
```

This variable will be used to store the category selected in the ComboBox. It is defaulted to `All`, which is the initial selection criteria. You will update this value later in the lesson.

8 Create another child `<mx:operation>` tag, under the close of the last `<mx:operation>` tag inside the `<mx:WebService>` tag. Give it a `name` of `getSalesData` and point the `result` handler to the `salesRPCResult()` function, passing it the event object.

```
<mx:operation name="getSalesData" result="salesRPCResult(event)">
</mx:operation>
```

This method will return the sales data summarized by each day for the selected category of food sold. You had a previously defined the function `salesRPCResult()` that was setup to deal with the result from the `<mx:HTTPService>`. You will modify this function later to handle the new format in which the data is returned. This operation will provide data for two of the ChartPods in the Dashboard, both the sales and comparison ones. In the next lesson, you will use this data uniquely when you do the charting.

9 In between the `<mx:operation>` tags, create a `<mx:request>` pair.

```
<mx:operation name="getSalesData" result="salesRPCResult(event)">
    <mx:request>
    </mx:request>
</mx:operation>
```

10 In between the `<mx:request>` tags, specify a tag for `startDate` that binds to `startDate.selectedDate`, a tag for `endDate` that binds to `endDate.selectedDate`, and a `category` that binds to the public `selectedType` variable.

```
<mx:request>
    <startDate>{startDate.selectedDate}</startDate>
    <endDate>{endDate.selectedDate}</endDate>
    <category>{selectedType}</category>
</mx:request>
```

What this does is preset the `getSalesData()` method to always have the arguments containing the right values. Using binding updates the `startDate` and `endDate` with the latest date the user selected. It also uses the category selected in the ComboBox as the value to filter on (as you will see in the `setCat()` function you will create later).

Handling Web Service Results

Because the Web Service requests are made external to the Flex application, you need to "listen" for the result back from the server. The WebService class enables you to listen for the result at the WebService object itself or at the individual method definitions via the result event. The event class that is returned to these methods is mx.rpc.events.ResultEvent. Because the server is not returning the sales data presorted, you need to create a sort function that sorts the results before it assigns it into the data provider of the ChartPod.

1 Still in the Dashboard.mxml, create a private function called sortByDateField that returns an ArrayCollection. The first argument is called aSales of type ArrayCollection, the second argument is called colName and is of type String.

```
private function sortByDateField(aSales:ArrayCollection, colName:String):
    ➥ ArrayCollection{
}
```

The first argument contains the results passed back from the Web Service. The second argument tells the function which field in the result to do the date sort on. You need to provide the second argument because it this will give you the flexibility of sorting on different columns, depending upon which result is returned.

2 Create a local ArrayCollection variable called salesData and assign it the passed in argument aSales.

```
private function sortByDateField
    ➥ (aSales:ArrayCollection, colName:String):ArrayCollection{
    var salesData:ArrayCollection = aSales;
}
```

This is used as a pointer to the ArrayCollection passed into the function.

3 Inside the script block, add an import for the mx.collections.Sort class.

```
import mx.collections.Sort;
```

4 Inside the sortByDateField method, create a local Sort variable called sort.

```
private function sortByDateField
    ➥ (aSales:ArrayCollection, colName:String):ArrayCollection{
    var salesData:ArrayCollection = aSales;
    var sort:Sort = new Sort();
}
```

You will use this variable to setup the sort definition for your local ArrayCollection.

5 Inside the script block, add an import for the mx.collections.SortField class.

```
import mx.collections.SortField;
```

6 Back inside the sortByDate method, set the `fields` property of sort as an array with the first entry a new `SortField` with two arguments passed to its constructor. The first is `colName` which will specify the field name for the sort and the second is `true`, which will make the sort case-sensitive.

```
private function sortByDateField
    ➥ (aSales:ArrayCollection, colName:String):ArrayCollection{
    var salesData:ArrayCollection = aSales;
    var sort:Sort = new Sort();
    sort.fields = new Array(new SortField(colName,true));
}
```

For each data set that you use, you should specify the field name on which you are sorting.

7 Assign the local sort variable to the sort property of `salesData` and refresh the `salesData` ArrayCollection.

```
private function sortByDateField
    ➥ (aSales:ArrayCollection, colName:String):ArrayCollection{
    var salesData:ArrayCollection = aSales;
    var sort:Sort = new Sort();
    sort.fields = new Array(new SortField(colName,true));
    salesData.sort = sort;
    salesData.refresh();
}
```

8 Return the sorted `salesData` ArrayCollection from the function.

```
private function sortByDateField
    ➥ (aSales:ArrayCollection, colName:String):ArrayCollection{
    var salesData:ArrayCollection = aSales;
    var sort:Sort = new Sort();
    sort.fields = new Array(new SortField(colName,true));
    salesData.sort = sort;
    salesData.refresh();
    return salesData;
}
```

9 Go to the salesRPCResult() function. Use the sortByDateField() function to sort `event.result` on the DTSALE field and assign the result to `sales.dp`. You will need to cast `event.result` into an ArrayCollection before you pass it into the function.

```
private function salesRPCResult(event:ResultEvent):void{
    sales.dp = this.sortByDateField(event.result as ArrayCollection,"DTSALE");
}
```

The call to the ColdFusion Web Service returns the sales data as an ArrayCollection, but the result property on the event object is cast as a generic object. To use it in your function, you need to cast it to an ArrayCollection. By doing sorting here, you are making sure that the data is sorted before you pass it to the component. This handler is mapped to the result event of the WebService's method.

10 Go to the typeRPCResult() function. Cast the event.result value in an ArrayCollection.

```
private function typeRPCResult(event:ResultEvent):void{
    type.dp = (event.result as ArrayCollection);
}
```

The call to the ColdFusion Web Service returns the sales data as an ArrayCollection, but the result property on the event object is cast as a generic object. To use the result, you need to cast it as an ArrayCollection. This handler is mapped to the result event of the WebService's method.

11 Remove the compRPCResult() function. You will add this functionality to the salesRPCResult() function because both sales.dp and comp.dp now use the same data. Assign comp.dp to the same sorted results as is used to set sales.dp.

```
private function salesRPCResult(event:ResultEvent):void{
    sales.dp = this.sortByDateField(event.result as ArrayCollection,"DTSALE");
    comp.dp = this.sortByDateField(event.result as ArrayCollection,"DTSALE");
}
```

Because you no longer need the additional Web Service call to get the data for the Sales ChartPod, it makes sense to collapse the setting of the dp properties of the components in one method.

Calling Web Service Methods

You call a Web Service a bit differently then you do an HTTPService, especially based upon how you have defined the WebService. Instead of a standard send() function on the HTTPService, you call the actual send() function on the method reference on the WebService using the wsId.methodName.send() format. In these tasks, you create this WebService with its operations and arguments defined. You are not worried about passing data to the method because the binding is keeping the arguments always current with the right data.

You will need to update your getData() function to now call the WebService. Currently, you have getData() being called on the initialization of the Dashboard. You have configured your Web Service to use a start date, an end date, and a category name as a filter to the data. As these values change, you will want to call the getData() function again.

1 Still in Dashboard.mxml, go to the getData() function. Replace the call to the three HTTPService send() functions with the calls to the Web Services' getTypeSalesData.send() and getSalesData.send() methods.

```
private function getData():void{
   dashboardWS.getTypeSalesData.send();
   dashboardWS.getSalesData.send();
}
```

2 Create a private function called setCat() that returns void. Have it accept one argument called event of type Event.

```
private function setCat(event:Event):void{
}
```

This function will capture any selection change in the ComboBox, set the selected category, and refresh the data of the Dashboard.

3 Set the public variable selectedType to the current category name, which is found in ComboBox(event.currentTarget).selectedItem.name. Then call the getData() function to refresh the data.

```
private function setCat(event:Event):void{
   selectedType = ComboBox(event.currentTarget).selectedItem.name;
   getData();
}
```

You need to first cast event.currentTarget into a ComboBox so that you can access the text property. In the text property you will find the name of the current category name selected by the user.

4 On the change event of the catCombo ComboBox, call the setCat() function passing along the event argument.

```
<mx:ComboBox id="catCombo"
   dataProvider="{categories}"
   change="setCat(event)"
   labelField="name"/>
```

5 On the startDate and endDate DateFields call the getData() function on their change events.

```
<mx:Label text="Start Date"/>
<mx:DateField id="startDate" change="getData()"/>
<mx:Label text="End Date"/>
<mx:DateField id="endDate" change="getData()"/>
```

Because you have bound the arguments of the methods on the WebService to the selected dates of these controls, you only need to call the `getData()` function because the binding has already updated the method call with the new date values.

6 Save and run Dashboard.mxml. Notice that the data loads at startup. Select a different Start Date and see how the data refreshes. Do the same for the Category ComboBox and notice that the Type Pod changes (It is located in the bottom-right part of the screen.).

Playing with the controls, you can see how your leverage of binding on the method arguments enabled you to simply call the method in one place without having to worry about getting the data to pass to the server.

When you run the Dashboard with a filter on Category, you should see the following example.

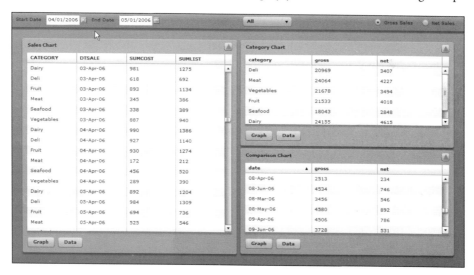

Using a Web Service in the DataEntry Application

This next set of tasks has you going to the DataEntry.mxml file and using a Web Service to create a new product through ActionScript rather then via the `<mx:WebService>` tag. When creating a workflow to work with data you need to plan for three pieces of your application:

- The data or value object that is to be changed
- How that data is displayed (to be selected)
- How data is changed and saved

In the DataEntry application, the existing data is shown via a Tree control and is edited through various controls. You select the data to change by selecting the product via its category in the tree.

You need to pass the product information back to the server. To uniquely identify each product, you need to add an attribute that acts as its ID or primary key. You will also need to update everything in the code that makes reference to the product.

1 If you have not done so already, start your local ColdFusion server.

2 Open Product.as from your valueObject directory.

You can also copy Lesson17/start/valueObjects/Product.as to your flexGrocer/valueObjects directory if you choose.

3 Add a public attribute called `prodID` that is a Number.

```
public var prodID:Number;
```

From this point forward, you can use the `prodID` to unique identify the product.

4 Add a `_prodID` argument to the `product()` constructor and set the product's `prodID` attribute with it.

```
public function Product(
    _prodID:Number,
    _catID:Number,
    _prodName:String,
    _unitID:Number,
    _cost:Number,
    _listPrice:Number,
    _description:String,
    _isOrganic:Boolean,
    _isLowFat:Boolean,
    _imageName:String){
        prodID = _prodID;
        catID = _catID;
        prodName = _prodName;
        unitID = _unitID;
        cost = _cost;
        listPrice = _listPrice;
        description = _description;
        isOrganic = _isOrganic;
        isLowFat = _isLowFat;
        imageName = _imageName;
    }
```

You currently have the constructor set up to accept one argument per attribute so that by adding the _prodID, you can now create a new product and set the prodID via a new Product(..) statement.

> **TIP:** Refactoring occurs when you introduce a change to a method signature and have to make the change everywhere.

5 Update the buildProduct() function to look for o.prodID and pass it into the new Product() method call.

```
public static function buildProduct(o:Object):Product{
   var p:Product = new Product(
      o.prodID,
      o.catID,
      o.prodName,
      o.unitID,
      o.cost,
      o.listPrice,
      o.description,
      Boolean(o.isOrganic),
      Boolean(o.isLowFat),
      o.imageName);
   return p;
}
```

6 Save the Product.as file.

7 Open CategorizedProductManager.mxml from your managers directory.

You can also copy Lesson17/intermediate/managers/CategorizedProductManager.mxml to your flexGrocer/managers directory if you choose.

As you remember, the CategorizedProductManager.mxml file deals with the retrieval of the product data and the categories that they are assigned to. You need to update this file to make sure that it creates its products with the new prodID and you need to make sure that you can tell the manager to refresh its data on every add, update, or delete of the products.

8 In the `prodByCategoryHandler()` function, locate where you are creating a new product. Add a new argument using the XML variable `p.@prodID`. Make sure it is a `Number`.

```
for each (var p:XML in c..product){
   var prod:Product = new Product(
      Number(p.@prodID),
      Number(p.@catID),
      String(p.@prodName),
      Number(p.@unitID),
      Number(p.@cost),
      Number(p.@listPrice),
      String(p.@description),
      Boolean(p.@isOrganic=="Yes"),
      Boolean(p.@isLowFat=="Yes"),
      String(p.@imageName));
   …
}
```

9 Create a public function called `refreshData()` that returns void. In this function have it make a call to the HTTPService `prodByCatRPC` to refetch the XML data.

```
public function refetchData():void{
   prodByCatRPC.send();
}
```

You can now call the `refetchData()` method to refresh the data from outside this file.

10 Replace the url attribute of the `<mx:HTTPService>` tag at the bottom of the page with `http://localhost:8300/flexGrocer/xml/categorizedProducts.cfm`.

```
<mx:HTTPService id="prodByCatRPC"
   url="http://localhost:8300/flexGrocer/xml/categorizedProducts.cfm"
   result="prodByCategoryHandler(event)"
   resultFormat="e4x"/>
```

Because you will be adding, updating and deleting products, the XML feed will no longer get static and to avoid any browser caching issues that would arise from updating the xml document directly, you will want to have the xml dynamically generated using ColdFusion.

11 Save the CategorizedProductManager.mxml file.

12 Open DataEntry.mxml.

You can also copy Lesson17/intermediate/DataEntry.mxml to your flexGrocer directory if you choose.

13 Inside the script block, add an import for the `mx.rpc.soap.WebService` class.

```
import mx.rpc.soap.WebService;
```

14 Create a new private function called addProduct(). Have it pass in one argument called product of type Product. This function does not return anything.

```
private function addProduct(product:Product):void{
}
```

15 Declare a local variable called ws of type WebService and set it equal to new WebService(). Set the wsdl attribute to http://localhost:8300/flexGrocer/cfcs/ProductManager.cfc?wsdl.

```
var ws:WebService = new WebService();
ws.wsdl = "http://localhost:8300/flexGrocer/cfcs/ProductManager.cfc?wsdl";
```

You created a WebService object through the use of the WebService class instead of the <mx:WebService> tag. There is no difference in the way the WebService is internally handled.

16 Call the loadWSDL() function on the WebService object.

```
ws.loadWSDL();
```

Before you can call any methods on the WebService, you must load the WSDL file so that the WebService knows what methods it can call, which arguments to pass the method, and what is returned. The WebService uses this information to make requests to the Web Service correctly. You cannot call any method on the WebService without having this loaded.

▶ **TIP:** You can use the canLoadWSDL() function on the WebService object to see whether it could load the WSDL.

17 Assign a listener on the WebService object that listens for the result event and maps it to the addProductResult() method. Add another listener to the WebService object that listens to the fault event and maps it to the addProductFault() method.

```
ws.addEventListener("result", addProductResult);
ws.addEventListener("fault", addProductFault);
```

You will be creating the addProductResult() and the addProductFault() methods next to handle the results.

18 Create a new private function called addProductResult(). Have it pass in one argument called event of type ResultEvent. This function does not return anything.

```
private function addProductResult(event:ResultEvent):void{
}
```

19 Show a pop-up window with the results using the showPopUp() function. You need to use the Product.buildProduct() method to take the result of the call to the server and create a new Product from the event.result.

```
showPopUp(Product.buildProduct(event.result),'Product Added');
```

The result from the Web Service is an `Object` that you pass to the `buildProduct()` function. It will create a new product with the data returned. The `Object` return type is defined by the WSDL file.

20 Call the `refetchData()` function on `prodMgr` to have it go to the server to get the updated XML file.

```
prodMgr.refetchData();
```

There are several ways to deal with updating the list of products that populates the Tree component. Instead of adding this product to the collection (which is one option), you will simply recall the method to refetch the data from the server. This was chosen for simplicity rather then a best practice.

21 Create a new private function called `addProductFault()`. Have it pass in one argument called event of type `FaultEvent`. This function does not return anything.

```
private function addProductFault(event:FaultEvent):void{
}
```

Ensure that the `import` statement for `mx.rpc.events.FaultEvent` was added by Flex Builder or add it manually to the top of the script block.

22 Add a `trace` statement to this function which sends the contents of the variable `event.fault.message` to the console in the event of a fault.

```
trace( event.fault.message );
```

If a problem occurs accessing the ColdFusion CFC, a fault message will be printed in your Flex Builder console.

23 In the `addProduct()` function, call the `ws.addProduct()` method at the bottom and pass in an argument called `product`.

```
ws.addProduct(product);
```

Earlier you learned how to call a `WebService` when the methods are declared as part of the WebService's definition. When you are using a WebService ActionScript object, you will want to use the wsObject.methodName (arg1, arg2, …) format because the method names and signatures are not known.

This calls the `addProduct()` function on the Web Service. The `product` argument passed in will be translated into an Object to be passed to the Web Service.

24 Look for the included AddProduct component. Change the productAdded event to call the addProduct() function, passing into it event.product.

```
<v:AddProduct cats="{categories}"
   units="{units}"
   productAdded="addProduct(event.product)"/>
```

25 Save DataEntry.mxml and run the application. Fill out the new product section. Notice the category you specified in the ComboBox and click Add Product. You will notice a pop-up window confirming that the new product was added. Go to the Edit/Delete tab to see the new product in the Tree component.

When you run the DataEntry and add a product to the Meat category, you should see the following after you expand the Tree component:

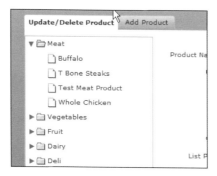

Uploading Files to the Server

When you add a product, it is possible that the image you want to represent the product in the cart is not on the server. You will then need to use the File Upload capabilities in Flex to upload the file to the server. Because you have two types of management screens, new and existing products, it makes sense for you to make a file upload component for reuse.

1 Right-click the view/dataEntry folder and select New > MXML Component. In the New MXML Component dialog box, set the filename to be **FileUpload.mxml**, set the base component to a Canvas, clear the Height and Width boxes, and then click Finish.

The component will be very basic. You will simply put in a button and the logic for uploading the file.

2 At the top of the file, place an `<mx:Script>` block to hold variables and functions.

```
<mx:Script>
   <![CDATA[
   ]]>
</mx:Script>
```

3 Inside of the script block, add an `import` for `flash.net.FileReference`.

```
import flash.net.FileReference;
```

The FileReference class is used to both browse for a specific file as well as upload a file to a specified location.

4 Create a private variable called `fileRef`, of type `FileReference`.

```
private var fileRef:FileReference;
```

5 Create a private function called `fileBrowse()` and have it return `void`.

```
private function fileBrowse():void{
}
```

6 Inside the function, set the `fileRef` variable to a new `FileReference` instance.

```
private function fileBrowse():void{
   this.fileRef = new FileReference();
}
```

7 Add an event listener on the `fileRef` object that listens for the `Event.Select` event. Have it assigned to the `selectHandler` function.

```
private function fileBrowse():void{
   this.fileRef = new FileReference();
   fileRef.addEventListener(Event.SELECT, selectHandler);
}
```

The FileReference class contains many different events pertaining to choosing and uploading files. The `Event.Select` event fires after the user has selected the file in the dialog box and chooses OK. When working with built-in Flex components, it is a standard practice to use the event names stored as variables within the event class instead of a string value, when you assign your event listeners through `addEventListener`. In this case, instead of passing in the string value of 'select' you use the variable `Event.SELECT` to listen to the selection of the file from the file picker. While they both evaluate to the same thing, by using the variable you don't have to worry about any change to the underlining event name affecting your code and the Flex compiler can throw an error at compile time if the event you are trying to access does not exist in the class.

8 Call the browse() method on the fileRef object, which will open up the dialog box to select the file to upload.

```
private function fileBrowse():void{
   this.fileRef = new FileReference();
   fileRef.addEventListener(Event.SELECT, selectHandler);
   fileRef.browse();
}
```

9 Create a private function called selectHandler() that accepts one argument called event of type Event. Have it return void.

```
private function selectHandler(event:Event):void {
}
```

You will use this function to initiate the uploading of the file to the server.

10 Inside the function, create a local variable called request of type URLRequest. URLRequest accepts a valid URL as its argument in its constructor. Set it to http://localhost:8300/ flexGrocer/cfcs/fileUpload.cfm.

```
private function selectHandler(event:Event):void {
   var request:URLRequest = new URLRequest
      ➥ ("http://localhost:8300/flexGrocer/cfcs/fileUpload.cfm");
}
```

This location holds the location to the ColdFusion page that will upload the file.

✳ NOTE: When you upload a file via Flex, the file is uploaded as a form value with the name of Filedata.

11 Call the upload() method of the fileRef object, passing in the local request object as its only argument.

```
private function selectHandler(event:Event):void {
   var request:URLRequest = new URLRequest
      ➥ ("http://localhost:8300/flexGrocer/cfcs/fileUpload.cfm");
   fileRef.upload(request);
}
```

12 Create a Button to enable the user to start the upload process. Set the label to Browse and on the click event handler, have it call the fileBrowse() function.

```
<mx:Button click="fileBrowse()" label="Browse"/>
```

13 Save FileUpload.mxml.

14 Open AddProduct.mxml from your views/dataEntry directory.

The file is located in the flexGrocer\view\dataEntry\ directory.

15 In the base VBox that wraps the file, create namespace v and point it to `views.dataEntry.*`.

```
<mx:VBox xmlns:mx=
    "http://www.adobe.com/2006/mxml" xmlns:v="views.dataEntry.*">
```

You now have a namespace to reference the FileUpload component.

16 Toward the bottom of the page, replace the button labeled Browse with your new FileUpload component. Prefix the component name with v.

```
<v:FileUpload />
```

You removed the old button and are calling your component instead.

17 Remove the `import` statement for `flash.net.FileReference` and the `fileBrowse()` function.

Because this code has been moved to the FileUpload component, it is a good practice to remove it from this file, even though leaving it here would not affect anything.

18 Save AddProduct.mxml.

19 Open UpdateDeleteProd.mxml from your views/dataEntry directory.

The file is located in the flexGrocer\view\dataEntry\ directory.

20 In the base HBox that wraps the file, create namespace v and point it to `views.dataEntry.*`.

```
<mx:HBox xmlns:mx=
    "http://www.adobe.com/2006/mxml" xmlns:v="views.dataEntry.*">
```

21 Toward the bottom of the page, replace the button labeled Browse with your new FileUpload component. Prefix the component name with v.

```
<v:FileUpload />
```

You removed the old button and are calling your component instead.

22 Remove the `import` statement for `flash.net.FileReference` and the `fileBrowse()` function.

Because this code has been moved to the FileUpload component, it is a good practice to remove it from this file even though leaving it here would not affect anything.

23 Save UpdateDeleteProduct.mxml.

24 Open and run the DataEntry.mxml file. On either the Add or Update tab, click the Browse button. Select a file and go to the file system to see the image uploaded.

When you click the Browse button, you should see a dialog box similar to the following pop-up window. The uploaded file should be in your flexGrocer/assets directory.

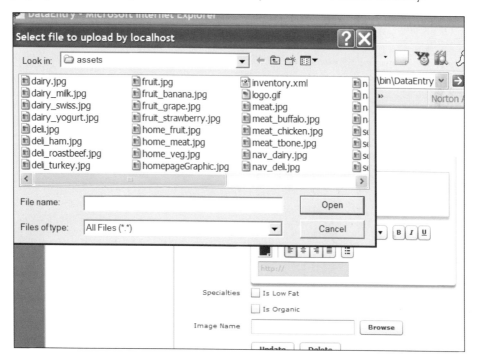

Centralizing Web Service Access

In these next tasks you will create an ActionScript class that will act as a central point in which you can mange all your Web Service calls in the DataEntry application. You will go back to the DataEntry.mxml and use a new Management class to enable you to update and delete a product.

The DataManager simplifies the interaction with the <mx:WebService> tag by giving you one class that you can get a WebService object to call your methods against. By having your code in one place that creates the Web Services, you can guarantee that every object is created the same. Be aware that this section is a brief review of some advanced functionality of Flex. Because many topics will be new, do not worry if you need some real life project to work with in order to fully understand how this works. That being said you may want to use the DataManager in the real life applications you build.

1 If you have not done so already, start your local ColdFusion server.

2 Copy DataManager.as into the managers directory.

The file to copy is located in the Lesson17/assets directory.

3 Open DataManager.as and review.

4 Review the `DataManager()` constructor.

```
public function DataManager(pri:PrivateClass, wsdl:String){
   this.ws = new WebService();
   ws.wsdl = wsdl;
   ws.loadWSDL();
}
```

This function is responsible for creating the `WebService` object that the DataManager uses. It has a public attribute called ws that holds the reference to the `WebService` object it created. The constructor expects a WSDL file to be passed in along with a `PrivateClass` object. This PrivateClass definition is located at the bottom of the file with the following definition:

```
/* PrivateClass is used to make DataManager constructor private */
class PrivateClass{
   public function PrivateClass(){}
}
```

> **TIP:** This PrivateClass class is defined at the bottom of the DataManager file and is marked as private. This is a quick technique to make sure that each DataManager created must be done via a static method on the DataManager. That is the only area of the application that can access the private class due to Flex's scoping rules. This is the key way to force a Singleton pattern in Flex.

5 Review the static function `getDataManager()`.

```
public static function getDataManager(wsdl:String):DataManager{
   if(DataManager.instanceMap[wsdl] == null){
      DataManager.instanceMap[wsdl] = new DataManager(new PrivateClass(),wsdl);
   }
   var dm:DataManager = DataManager.instanceMap[wsdl];
   if(dm.ws.canLoadWSDL())
      {return dm;}
   else
      {throw new Error("BAD WSDL:"+wsdl);}
}
```

This function acts as the only way that you can create new DataManager objects. You will create one DataManager object per unique Web Service by using the WSDL filename as the unique key into the static `instanceMap` object. Because `instanceMap` is a static variable on the class itself, there will be only one variable for the whole application. This means that every time this `getDataManager()` is called, it will check to see whether there was ever a `WebService` with that WSDL file called before. If so, it will use that instance.

6 Review the `makeRemoteCall()` function.

```
public function makeRemoteCall(methodName:String,eventName:String,
    ➥ args:Object):void{
    trace("DataManager.makeRemoteCall("+methodName+","+eventName+","+args+")");
    var op:mx.rpc.AbstractOperation = ws[methodName];
    ws.addEventListener("result",doResults);
    ws.addEventListener("fault",doFault);

    if (args){
        op.arguments = args;
    }

    var token:AsyncToken = op.send();
    token.eventName = eventName;
}
```

This method uses the `argument` property of the `AbstractOperation` to generically pass arguments to a operation on the Web Service. These generic arguments are in an object structure with the key names equal to the parameter names specified by the Web Service. The function is called on the DataManager object to initiate a call to the method, specified by `methodName`, on the Web Service and raises an event on the `DataManager`, specified by `eventName`, upon the successful call to the Web Service. The raised event is of type `DataManagerResultEvent` event. Effectively, it will call whatever method you specify, passing it the parameters in the accompanying object and raising the specified event when successful.

7 Copy DataManagerResultEvent.as into the events directory.

The file is copy is located in the Lesson17/assets directory.

8 Open DataManagerResultEvent.as and review.

9 Review the `DataManagerResultEvent()` constructor.

```
public function DataManagerResultEvent(type:String,result:Object){
    super(type);
    this.result = result;
}
```

This event class has only one attribute on it: result. This is used as a pass through of what the result was from the original Web Service call. The constructor first specifies the event name to raise via the type argument and then the result that came back from the Web Service.

10 Open the views/dataEntry/UpdateDeleteProd.mxml file.

The file is located in the flexGrocer/views/dataEntry directory.

11 Below the import, declare a public variable named prodID that will hold the reference of the identity of the product used by the component. Make it of type int and make it Bindable.

```
[Bindable]
public var prodID:int;
```

Earlier, you added a prodID attribute to the Product value object. You need to update the UpdateDeleteProd component to be aware of the prodID of the Product value object it is working with.

12 In the populateForm() function, set the prodID attribute from the node using selectedNode.@prodID. Do this right after you check to make sure that the selectedNode.@prodName is not undefined.

```
if(selectedNode.@prodName != undefined){
   prodID = int(selectedNode.@prodID);
```

13 Add a new tag to the prodModel model called prodID. Bind the value equal to public variable prodID.

```
<mx:Model id="prodModel">
   <prodID>{this.prodID}</prodID>
```

The model is built into a Product value object before it is passed out of the component through a ProductEvent. By adding this tag, you will set the prodID of the value object.

14 Save the UpdateDeleteProd.mxml file.

15 Open the DataEntry.mxml file.

The file is located in flexGrocer directory.

16 Inside the script block, add an import for the managers.DataManager and events.DataManagerResultEvent classes.

```
import managers.DataManager;
import events.DataManagerResultEvent;
```

17 Create a private function called updateProduct(). Have it accept one argument called product of type Product.

```
private function updateProduct(product:Product):void{
}
```

18 Create a local variable called dm of type DataManager. Set it equal to a new DataManager that is created through the static method DataManager.getDataManager(). Use http://localhost:8300/flexGrocer/cfcs/ProductManager.cfc?wsdl as the wsdl to get the Web Service.

```
private function updateProduct(product:Product):void{
var dm:DataManager = DataManager.getDataManager
  ➥ ("http://localhost:8300/flexGrocer/cfcs/ProductManager.cfc?wsdl");
}
```

This will be the instance of the DataManager that you call the method on which to update the product.

19 Assign an event listener on dm object that listens for the updateProductResult event. Have it call the updateProductResult() function.

```
private function updateProduct(product:Product):void{
var dm:DataManager = DataManager.getDataManager(
  ➥ "http://localhost:8300/flexGrocer/cfcs/ProductManager.cfc?wsdl");
  dm.addEventListener("updateProductResult", updateProductResult);
}
```

20 On dm, call the makeRemoteCall() method. For the first argument pass in a string of updateProduct, which specifies the appropriate method to call on the Web Service. Next, pass in a string of updateProductResult, which will cause the DataManager to raise an event of the same name upon success. Lastly pass in a new object, created inline, which contains the product argument passed into the updateProduct method as a property called aProduct.

```
private function updateProduct(product:Product):void{
var dm:DataManager =
  ➥ DataManager.getDataManager("http://localhost:8300/flexGrocer/cfcs/
ProductManager.cfc?wsdl");
  dm.addEventListener("updateProductResult", updateProductResult);
  dm.makeRemoteCall("updateProduct", "updateProductResult", {aProduct:product});
}
```

21 Create a private function called updateProductResult() that accepts one argument called event, of type DataManagerResultEvent.

```
private function updateProductResult(event:DataManagerResultEvent):void{
}
```

22 Show the pop-up window with results using the showPopUp() function. You will need to use the Product.buildProduct() method to take the result of the call to the server and create a new Product from the event.result.

```
private function updateProductResult(event:DataManagerResultEvent):void{
    showPopUp(Product.buildProduct(event.result),'Product Updated');
}
```

The result from the Web Service is an Object that you pass to the buildProduct() function. It will create a new product with the data returned.

23 Call the refetchData() function on prodMgr to have it go to the server to get the updated XML file.

```
private function updateProductResult(event:DataManagerResultEvent):void{
    showPopup(Product.buildProduct(event.result),'Product Updated');
    prodMgr.refetchData();
}
```

Once again, you will just refresh the Tree component by going back to the server to get the latest XML of the products.

24 On the UpdateDeleteProd component, change the productUpdate event to call the updateProduct() function. Have it pass the event.product it receives along to this function as the argument.

```
productUpdate="updateProduct(event.product)"
```

25 Create a private function called deleteProduct(). Have it accept one argument called product of type Product.

```
private function deleteProduct(product:Product):void{
}
```

26 Create a local variable called dm of type DataManager. Set it equal to a new DataManager that is was created through the static method of DataManager.getDataManager(). Use http://localhost:8300/flexGrocer/cfcs/ProductManager.cfc?wsdl as the wsdl to get the WebService.

```
private function deleteProduct(product:Product):void{
var dm:DataManager = DataManager.getDataManager(
    ➥ "http://localhost:8300/flexGrocer/cfcs/ProductManager.cfc?wsdl");
}
```

This will be the instance of the DataManager class that you will use to update the product.

27 Assign an event listener to dm that listens for the deleteProductResult event. Have it call the deleteProductResult() function.

```
private function deleteProduct(product:Product):void{
var dm:DataManager = DataManager.getDataManager(
    ➥ "http://localhost:8300/flexGrocer/cfcs/ProductManager.cfc?wsdl");
    dm.addEventListener("deleteProductResult", deleteProductResult);
}
```

28 On dm, call the makeRemoteCall() method. For the first argument pass in a string of deleteProduct, which specifies the appropriate method to call on the Web Service. Next, pass in a string of deleteProductResult, which will cause the DataManager to raise an event of the same name upon success. Lastly, pass in a new object, created inline, which contains the product argument passed into the updateProduct method as a property called aProduct.

```
private function deleteProduct(product:Product):void{
var dm:DataManager = DataManager.getDataManager(
    ➥ "http://localhost:8300/flexGrocer/cfcs/ProductManager.cfc?wsdl");
    dm.addEventListener("deleteProductResult", deleteProductResult);
    dm.makeRemoteCall("deleteProduct", "deleteProductResult", {aProduct:product});
}
```

29 Create a private function called deleteProductResult() that accepts one argument, called event, of type DataManagerResultEvent.

```
private function deleteProductResult(event:DataManagerResultEvent):void{
}
```

30 Show a popup window with the results using the showPopUp() function. You will need to use the Product.buildProduct() method to take the result of the call to the server and create a new Product from the event.result.

```
private function deleteProductResult(event:DataManagerResultEvent):void{
    showPopUp(Product.buildProduct(event.result),'Product Deleted');
}
```

The result from the Web Service is an Object that you pass to the buildProduct()function that will create a new product with the data returned.

31 Call the refetchData() function on prodMgr to have it go to the server to get the updated XML file.

```
private function deleteProductResult(event:DataManagerResultEvent):void{
    showPopup(Product.buildProduct(event.result),'Product Deleted');
    prodMgr.refetchData();
}
```

Once again you will just refresh the Tree component by going back to the server to get the latest XML of the products.

32 On the UpdateDeleteProd component, change the `productDelete` event to call the `updateProduct()` function. Have it pass the `event.product` it receives along to this function as the argument.

```
productDelete="deleteProduct(event.product)"
```

33 Save DataEntry.mxml and run the application. Click a product from the Tree component. Change the name of the product and press Update. You will see the new product name in the Tree component.

When you run the DataEntry and update a product's name, you should see the following figure after you expand the Tree component.

Using Remote Object to Save an Order

In these next tasks you will modify the EComm.mxml to place an order using the `<mx:RemoteObject>` tag after the user has finished going through the checkout process. RemoteObject is different from Web Services on several points:

- RemoteObject uses the serialized binary protocol AMF instead of XML-based Simple Object Access Protocol (SOAP).

- RemoteObject requires a configuration file that is compiled with the application to determine the location of the remote service.

- RemoteObject enables you to map a defined ActionScript class; for example, the `Product` value object, to a server class of the same definition.

Both RemoteObject and WebServices enable you to talk to multiple server technologies. Over Web Services, the WSDL file defines what the SOAP message should look like, and the WSDL on the server is used by the server technology to translate the SOAP message into the specific technology. RemoteObject, or Remoting (a slang term of the use of RemoteObjects) doesn't work that way. There is a configuration file, services-config.xml, that Remoting uses to determine how to make the calls to the server. This file acts much like the WSDL file does for WebService. To use Remoting in your stand-alone version, you need to make sure it is in your compiler commands in Flex Builder.

It is necessary for you to specify the following sections via the configuration file:

- **Technology Adapter:** This is the specific class that translates the generic AMF message into the specific technology. In the following snippet, you see an adapter, referenced by the `id` of `cf-object`, which points to an adapter that handles ColdFusion requests. It is also marked as `default="true"`, which means that this adapter is to be used for each destination defined that has no specific adapter noted.

```
<adapters>
   <adapter-definition id="cf-object"
      class="coldfusion.flash.messaging.ColdFusionAdapter" default="true"/>
</adapters>
```

- **Channels:** This defines the location in which the server with the remote services exists and what the technology is that the server is using. You will be using only AMF, but it is possible to use other types of channels in a Flex application as well. You should also note two things from the following snippet of code. First is that the gateway used by Flex 2 is `/flex2gateway`, which is using the AMF 3.0 specification. Flex version 1.5 uses a different one. Second, note the `<instantiate-types>` tag, which must be set to `false` when connecting to ColdFusion.

```
<channel-definition id="my-cfamf" class="mx.messaging.channels.AMFChannel">
   <endpoint uri= "http://localhost:8300/flex2gateway/"
      class="flex.messaging.endpoints.AMFEndpoint"/>
   <properties>
      <polling-enabled>false</polling-enabled>
         <serialization>
            <instantiate-types>false</instantiate-types>
         </serialization>
   </properties>
</channel-definition>
```

- **Destination Handles:** These are the grouping of adapters, channels, and custom properties that Flex will reference by the `id`, that are needed to make the connection and request to the remote service using Remoting. When dealing with Remoting, the key tag to look at in the following code is the `<source>` tag. This can be used to restrict which class directories the Remoting can make the request to or specify the exact class that the destination is referencing. If you specify an exact class in the `<source>` tag, you will not need to pass in a source attribute in the `<mx:RemoteObject>` tag.

```
<destination id="ColdFusion">
  <channels>
    <channel ref="my-cfamf"/>
  </channels>
  <properties>
    <source>*</source>
  </properties>
</destination>
```

Update Flex Compiler Command

As noted, in order to have the stand-alone Flex Builder configuration work with RemoteObjects, you need to specify to the Flex Compiler which services-config.xml to use. The configuration file will store the location of your RemoteObjects.

> **TIP:** You will have to compile with different configuration files if the final server location is different than your development or staging environment as each configuration file (when dealing with Standalone Deployments) will have a specific location in it. For ease of managing, it is best if you create a unique configuration file, as was done for this book, rather then modify the default one provided.

1 Go to Projects > Properties > Flex Compiler screen. Enter **-services "*driveroot*\flex2tfs\ flexGrocer\assets\FlexGrocer_CF_Services.xml"** into the Additional Compiler Arguments box after any existing items in this field.

   Assuming that you have installed the ColdFusion as per the setup instructions (if not then the directory structure will be different), you should see the following before you click OK:

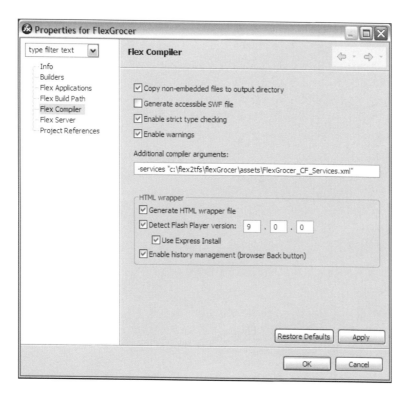

2 Click OK to close the window.

Raise Order Confirmed Event in the Checkout Process

Now you need to provide a way to confirm an order so the checkout process knows it can place the order.

1 Open OrderConf.mxml from the views/ecomm directory.

2 Define an event named orderConfirmed. This will be a generic event, so you don't need to specify a specific event type in the event definition. Place it between the <mx:Metadata> tags at the top of the page.

```
[Event(name="orderConfirmed")]
```

You will dispatch this event when the order is confirmed to let the checkout process know that it can now place the order.

3 Create a private function called orderConfirm() that returns void.

```
private function orderConfirm():void{

}
```

This function will be called when the order is confirmed and then dispatch the orderConfirmed event.

4 Create a local variable, called o, of type Event. Set it equal to a new event with an event name of orderConfirmed.

```
private function orderConfirm():void{
    var o:Event = new Event("orderConfirmed");
}
```

The simplest way of raising an event on a component is to use the Event class. This event only holds an event name and is used only to note that the event occurred instead of passing data around.

5 Dispatch the locally created event, called o, via this.dispatchEvent() passing in o.

```
private function orderConfirm():void{
    var o:Event = new Event("orderConfirmed");
    this.dispatchEvent(o);
}
```

6 Call the orderConfirm() function from the Complete Order button's click handler.

```
<mx:Button label="Complete Order" click="orderConfirm()"/>
```

Create and Call Remote Object

In this task, you will configure the Checkout component to send order information directly to a ColdFusion component. You will also create and dispatch an event to notify other areas of the application that the user has completed their order successfully.

1 Open Checkout.mxml from the views/ecomm directory.

2 Inside the script block, add an import for the valueObjects.ShoppingCart class.

```
import valueObjects.ShoppingCart;
```

3 Below the imports, declare a public variable named cart, which will hold the reference of the shopping cart of the application. Make it of type ShoppingCart.

```
public var cart:ShoppingCart = null;
```

The cart will be set by the component being included in the main application. This is a reference to the whole shopping cart.

4 Insert a `<mx:MetaData>` pair above the `<mx:Script>` block.

```
<mx:Metadata>
</mx:Metadata>
```

5 Define an event named `checkOutComplete`. This will be a generic event, so you don't need to specify a specific event type in the event definition.

```
<mx:Metadata>
    [Event(name="checkOutComplete")]
</mx:Metadata>
```

Upon the completion of the checkout, you will want to raise an event that you successfully completed the checkout.

6 Below the `<mx:Script>` tags put a `<mx:RemoteObject>` tag. Set the `id` attribute to srv, set the `destination` attribute to `ColdFusion`, set source to `FlexGrocer.cfcs.Order`, and set `showBusyCursor` to true. Finally set the default result handler `result` to `saveOrderResult`, passing along the event.

```
<mx:RemoteObject
    id="svc"
    destination="ColdFusion"
    source="FlexGrocer.cfcs.Order"
    result="saveOrderResult(event)"
    showBusyCursor="true"/>
```

This creates a RemoteObject component with the `id` of svc, which points to the Order ColdFusion component on the server. You know it is ColdFusion not by the destination called ColdFusion but also by looking in the services-config.xml file to see which technology the destination of ColdFusion pointed to. The `showBusyCursor` attribute equal to true is used to turn the cursor to a busy icon. It does not restrict the user from clicking buttons or using the application; it is just visual.

Because the RemoteObject requests are made external to the Flex application, you need to "listen" for the result back from the server. The RemoteObject class enables you to listen for the result at the RemoteObject itself via the `result` event. The event class that is returned to these methods is `mx.rpc.events.ResultEvent`.

> **TIP:** You can also define your operations on your RemoteObject just as you could with the `<mx:WebService>` tag. It follows the same rules.

7 Inside the script block, add an import for the `mx.collections.ArrayCollection` class.

```
import mx.collections.ArrayCollection;
```

You need this to reset the item's `ShoppingCart` value object.

8 Inside the script block, add an `import` for the `mx.rpc.events.ResultEvent` class.

```
import mx.rpc.events.ResultEvent;
```

9 Inside the script block, add an `import` for the `mx.controls.Alert` class.

```
import mx.controls.Alert;
```

You need this to be able to show an alert window to the user on order placement.

10 Create a private function called `saveOrderResult()`. Have it pass in one argument called event of type `ResultEvent`. This function does not return anything.

```
private function saveOrderResult(event:ResultEvent):void{
}
```

11 Clear the items in the `ShoppingCart`, stored on `cart.aItems`, by setting the variable to a new `ArrayCollection()`.

```
private function saveOrderResult(event:ResultEvent):void{
   this.cart.aItems = new ArrayCollection();
}
```

12 You want to show a MessageBox, or Alert, with the order number generated for this new order. You will need to raise the alert window with `Alert.show()` and pass it a single string argument. You will pass in a message using the `orderNum` property of the `event.result` object.

```
private function saveOrderResult(event:ResultEvent):void{
   this.cart.aItems = new ArrayCollection();
   Alert.show("New Order Num: " + event.result.orderNum);
}
```

If you need to create a simple alert window, you can call the static `show()` method on the Alert class. The `event.result` holds the result of the call to the server. In this case, the server returns a result that is an Object. It has all the same properties as an `OrderInfo` value object plus the `orderNum`, which holds the Order Number created.

13 Create a local variable, called o, of type `Event`. Set it equal to a new Event with an event name of `checkOutComplete`.

```
private function saveOrderResult(event:ResultEvent):void{
    this.cart.aItems = new ArrayCollection();
    Alert.show("New Order Num: " + event.result.orderNum);
    var o:Event = new Event("checkOutComplete");
}
```

The simplest way of raising an event on a component is to use the Event class. This event only holds an event name and is used only to note that the event occurred rather than passing data around.

14 Dispatch the locally created event, called o, that was created via `this.dispatchEvent()` passing in o.

```
private function saveOrderResult(event:ResultEvent):void{
    this.cart.aItems = new ArrayCollection();
    Alert.show("New Order Num: " + event.result.orderNum);
    var o:Event = new Event("checkOutComplete");
    this.dispatchEvent(o);
}
```

15 Set the ViewStack for the checkout process, `checkoutNav`, to display the billingInfo view.

```
private function saveOrderResult(event:ResultEvent):void{
    this.cart.aItems = new ArrayCollection();
    Alert.show("New Order Num: " + event.result.orderNum);
    var o:Event = new Event("checkOutComplete");
    this.dispatchEvent(o);
    checkoutNav.selectedChild=billingInfo;
}
```

You need to set the process back to the beginning, so the next time you check out it will start from the beginning.

16 Create a private function called `completeCheckOut()` that will call the RemoteObject. Have it return void.

```
private function completeCheckOut():void{
}
```

This function will be called when the user confirms that the order is correct.

17 In `completeCheckOut()` function, make a call to the `saveOrder()` method on the RemoteObject svc. Pass in `orderInfo` and `cart.aItems`.

```
private function completeCheckOut():void{
   svc.saveOrder(orderInfo, cart.aItems);
}
```

Calling a method on RemoteObject is the same as you did with WebService. You call the actual method name on the RemoteObject you want to call using the remoteObject.methodName (arg1, arg2, etc) format.

The Checkout component acts as a wizard in that it collects the order information, address, and credit card data and puts it into an `OrderInfo` value object called `orderInfo`. You need to pass that information and the items in the shopping cart to the remote service.

18 Call the `completeCheckOut()` function from the OrderConf component's `orderConfirmed` event handler.

```
<v:OrderConf id="orderConf"
width="100%" height="100%"
   orderInfo="{orderInfo}"
   back="checkoutNav.selectedChild=billingInfo"
   orderConfirmed="completeCheckOut()"/>
```

19 Save the Checkout.mxml file.

Pass in ShoppingCart into Checkout Component

Your new Checkout component needs a reference to the user's shopping cart. You will now add that information to the component in EComm.

1 Open the EComm.mxml file.

The file is located in flexGrocer/ directory.

2 In the Checkout component, add an attribute of `cart` that is bound to the public variable of `cart`.

```
<v:Checkout id="checkout" cart="{cart}" width="100%" height="100%"/>
```

Change State of the Application Back to Welcome

Once the user has completed the ordering process, we need to return them to the welcome screen. You will now use the event previously created to facilitate this change.

1 If you have not done so already, start your local ColdFusion server.

2 Capture the `checkOutComplete` event on the `Checkout` component and have it set the `selectedChild` on the `ecommNave` ViewStack equal to `homePage`.

```
<v:Checkout
    id="checkout"
        checkOutComplete="ecommNav.selectedChild=homePage"
        cart="{cart}" width="100%" height="100%"/>
```

This will cause the EComm application to show the home page upon successful completion of the order.

3 Save EComm.mxml and run the application.

When you run the EComm application and check out, you should get an alert at the end noting that the order was placed. You should see the following:

Mapping ActionScript Objects to Server Objects

This task shows you how you can map an ActionScript class to a Server object and pass an instance of that class between the two of them. This is done through the [`RemoteObject()`] metadata descriptor in your value object class and relies on the server and client objects having the same properties (names and number of). There are several benefits of this approach. For starters, you save the need to translate the result for a Remoting call into a specific value object. A good example of this is that the need you have for the `buildProduct()` function on the Product class. This would not be necessary if you could pass ActionScript objects via Web Services, which is only supported by Remoting. The second benefit is that it allows you to start using the results of the Remoting call right away; you can have methods on the value object that use the properties. This is immediately available. You can simply say event.result. someMethod(), assuming that event is the argument that is used to capture the result of a Remoting call. It is important to realize that this is not a requirement to pass data between Flex and the server via ActionScripts objects, but instead just a possibility for you to use when developing your applications.

> **TIP:** This is especially helpful to do when you have all the data in your application stored in ActionScript classes (ValueObjects).

1 If you have not done so already, start your local ColdFusion server.

2 Open OrderInfo.as from the valueObjects directory.

The file is located in the flexGrocer\valueObjects directory.

3 Right above the class declaration, add a [RemoteClass] metadata attribute. Set the alias to FlexGrocer.cfcs.OrderInfo.

```
[RemoteClass(alias="FlexGrocer.cfcs.OrderInfo")]
public class OrderInfo {
```

The RemoteClass metadata attribute points to the server object that the ActionScript class maps to via the alias argument. This is case-sensitive where the server object is located (class path). For the mapping to occur, Flex requires that there be an exact match in properties on the ActionScript class and the server object.

> **TIP:** Be aware that when you are mapping ActionScript classes to server objects, you must keep the definitions in sync. Any change on the server object that is not exactly matched on the client will have Flex simply translate the server object returned as an Object. That said, the best patterns to use this feature with are Proxy, Domain, or ValueObject.

4 At the bottom of the other property declarations, declare a public variable named createDate, which will hold the date that the order was created. Make it of type Date.

```
public var createDate:Date;
```

As previously stressed, it is important to have an exact property match between the ActionScript class and the server object to which it is associated.

5 At the bottom of the other property declarations, declare a public variable named orderNum that will hold the Order Number, which was created when the order was placed, to uniquely reference it. Make it of type String.

```
public var orderNum:String;
```

6 Below all the property declarations, create a public function called getOrderInfoHeader(), which will return a message containing the order number and the date it was created. It will receive no arguments, using the value object properties instead, and will return a String.

```
public function getOrderInfoHeader():String{
   return "Order '" + orderNum + "' was created on " + createDate;
}
```

You will use this method to give a message to users about the details of the order they just placed.

7 Save the OrderInfo.as file.

8 Open Checkout.mxml from the views/ecomm directory.

9 In the completeCheckOut() function, switch to call the saveOrderWithVO() function on the RemoteObject, svc, passing in the same arguments as before.

```
private function completeCheckOut(){
   svc.saveOrderWithVO(orderInfo, cart.aItems);
}
```

The method saveOrderWithVO() is already written on the RemoteObject. It is configured to accept a ValueObject rather then an Object.

10 In the saveOrderResult() function, change the text being passed into the Alert.show() function to be returned from getOrderInfoHeader() method called directly on the event.result.

```
private function saveOrderResult(event:ResultEvent):void{
   this.cart.aItems = new ArrayCollection();
   Alert.show(event.result.getOrderInfoHeader());
   var o:Event = new Event("checkOutComplete");
   this.dispatchEvent(o);
   checkoutNav.selectedChild=billingInfo;
}
```

The remote service is returning an OrderInfo value object from the server. This means that event.result is of type OrderInfo rather than Object. As a result, you can call the getOrderInfoHeader() method you created to get a formatted description of the order.

11 Save the Checkout.mxml file.

12 Run EComm.mxml.

When you run the EComm application and check out, you should get an alert at the end noting that the order was placed using the new header message. You should see the following:

What You Have Learned

In this lesson, you have:

- Used the <mx:WebService> tag to retrieve data from the server (pages 398–400)

- Declared the specific operations on the <mx:WebService> tag (pages 398–400)

- Sorted the collection returned from the server as result of the Web Service call (pages 401–403)

- Bound specific parameters to a Web Service operation (pages 403–405)

- Used a WebService ActionScript object to update data on the server (pages 405–411)

- Upload a file to the server (pages 411–415)

- Implemented a DataManager ActionScript class to centralize all your Web Service calls (pages 415–422)

- Used the <mx:RemoteObject> tag to place an order on the server (pages 422–431)

- Mapped a Server object to an ActionScript class for data transfer between client and server (pages 431–434)

What You Will Learn

In this lesson, you will:

- Work with the pie, column, and line charts

- Learn how to provide data to charts

- Specify chart axes

- Handle chart events

- Animate charts when data is set

- Apply styles to charts

Approximate Time

This lesson takes approximately 1 hour and 30 minutes to complete.

Lesson Files

Media Files:

> Lesson18/assets/TypeChart.mxml
> Lesson18/assets/ComparisonChart.mxml
> Lesson18/assets/SalesChart.mxml

Starting Files:

> Lesson18/start/Dashboard.mxml

Completed Files:

> Lesson18/complete/Dashboard.mxml
> Lesson18/complete/views/dashboard/ComparisonChart.mxml
> Lesson18/complete/views/dashboard/SalesChart.mxml
> Lesson18/complete/views/dashboard/TypeChart.mxml

LESSON 18

Charting Data

Displaying data in a chart or graph can make data interpretation much easier for users of the applications you develop with the Adobe Flex 2 product line. Instead of presenting a simple table of numeric data, you can display a bar, pie, line, or other type of chart using colors, captions, and a two-dimensional representation of your data.

Data visualization enables you to present information in a way that simplifies data interpretation and data relationships. Charting is one type of data visualization in which you create two-dimensional representations of your data. Flex supports some of the most commons types of two-dimensional charts—such as bar, column, and pie charts—and provides you with a great deal of control over the appearance of charts.

A simple chart shows a single data series, in which a series is a group of related data points. For example, a data series might be monthly sales revenues or daily occupancy rates for a hotel. The following chart shows a single data series that corresponds to sales over several months:

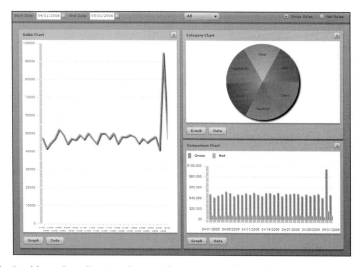

The Dashboard application shows rich interactive charts about the company's sales.

Exploring Flex Charting Components

Among the many powerful tools available with Flex framework is a robust set of Charting components. The Flex Charting components enable you to create some of the most common chart types and also give you a great deal of control over the appearance of your charts. After you understand the API for the charts, it becomes easy to add rich interactive charts to any application. Throughout this lesson, you will be adding charts to the Dashboard application, enabling users to better visualize how sales are going for the FlexGrocer company.

Available Charts

Flex provides a number of different types of charts, including the following:

- Area
- Bar
- Bubble
- Candlestick
- Column
- HighLowOpenClose
- Line
- Plot

You can see the various types of charts being used in the Charting section of Adobe's Flex 2 Component Explorer: http://examples.adobe.com/flex2/inproduct/sdk/explorer/explorer.html.

Chart Packaging

Although the Flex Charting components are available for all versions of Flex Builder, they are not included free of charge. The standard install of Flex Builder includes a limited trial of the Charting components; there is a separate version of Flex Builder available that includes these components and another package that makes these components available for developers using the Flex SDK.

Parts of a Chart

All Flex Charting components have a similar API, so after you learn to work with one type of chart, it should be pretty easy to pick up any of the others.

There are a number of different tags you need to use to define a particular chart, but in general, most charts follow this structure:

```
<ChartType>
  <mx:series>
    <mx:SeriesName/>
  </mx:series>
```

```
    <!-- Define the axes. -->
    <mx:horizontalAxis>
        <mx:AxisType/>
    </mx:horizontalAxis>
    <mx:verticalAxis>
        <mx:AxisType/>
    </mx:verticalAxis>

    <!-- Style the axes and ticks. -->
    <mx:horizontalAxisRenderer/>
    <mx:verticalAxisRenderer/>

    <!-- Add grid lines and other elements to the chart. -->
    <mx:annotationElements/>
    <mx:backgroundElements/>
</mx:ChartType>
<mx:Legend/>
```

In the pseudo code, you can see that a chart can contain a chart type, one or more series, one or more axes, renderers, and other elements.

The `<ChartType>` tag is the root tag for each chart. It is required and is used to determine what kind of chart will be used (such as LineChart, ColumnChart, PieChart, and so on). This tag can also be used to customize elements of the chart, such as the data to render, whether ToolTips should be shown as elements are moused over, and so on.

The series defines an array of Series classes, which are used to specify data to render in a chart. For each series of data, specific styles (such as fill, stroke, and so on) can be used to customize how that data is rendered. Because an array of Series is provided, a chart can contain multiple sets of data, such as you will implement in the comparison chart later in this lesson—graphing both Net and Gross sales. Every chart must have a series defined before any data will be rendered. Each chart type has its own Series class that can be used; for example, the series for an `<mx:ColumnChart>` is an `<mx:ColumnSeries>`, whereas the series for an `<mx:PieChart>` is an `<mx:PieSeries>`.

The Axis class is required for any of the rectangular two-dimensional charts (known as Cartesian charts), because it specifies what data should be rendered for the horizontal and vertical axes of the chart. There are Axis subclasses that enable you to specify whether the Axis is numeric (`LinearAxis`) or string-based (`CategoryAxis`).

An AxisRenderer can optionally be used to describe how the horizontal and vertical axes of a chart should be shown. For example, an axis is responsible for rendering the labels, tick marks, and title along the axis. Among the items that can be specified with an AxisRenderer are Cascading Style Sheets (CSS), text properties, label rotation, and spacing (such as the capability to drop labels to make the axis fit better).

Other chart elements, which can also be provided, include annotationElements and back-groundElements, both of which are subclasses of the ChartElement class. The background-Elements subclass enables you to add things such as background images, whereas the annotationElements subclass enables you to add items to further describe the chart, such as gridLines.

Laying Out the Initial Charts

In this first exercise, you will use the Charting components to lay out the basics of three chart types: type chart, sales chart and comparison chart. The skeleton files for the three charts are provided for you in the Lesson18/assets directory.

Up to this point, each skeleton file only contains a DataGrid component with data relating to products sold. You will now start to add charts to visualize this data as well.

1 Open TypeChart.mxml from the Lesson18/assets directory and save it to your flexGrocer/views/dashboard directory.

2 Inside the first `<mx:VBox>` within the `<mx:ViewStack>` add an `<mx:PieChart>`, with a height and width of 100% and a dataProvider bound to dp.

```
<mx:ViewStack id="chartStack"
    width="100%" height="100%">
    <mx:VBox width="100%" height="100%">
       <mx:PieChart id="chart"
          width="100%" height="100%"
          dataProvider="{dp}">
       </mx:PieChart>
    </mx:VBox>
    <mx:VBox width="100%" height="100%">
       <mx:DataGrid id="chartData" dataProvider="{dp}">
    …
</mx:ViewStack>
```

This is the skeleton of a pie chart, which requires that you specify one or more series before it will be rendered. You will do this in a later exercise.

3 Save TypeChart.mxml.

As was mentioned earlier, there are several elements necessary before a chart will render. If you run the application now, no chart will appear. We need to provide more infor-mation, which you will do in the next exercise. The file at this point should resemble TypeChart_initial in the intermediate directory.

4 Open SalesChart.mxml from the Lesson18/assets directory and save it to your flexGrocer/views/dashboard directory.

5 Inside the first `<mx:VBox>` tag within the `<mx:ViewStack>` tag, add an `<mx:LineChart>` tag with a *dataProvider* bound to *dp*, and a *height* and *width* of 100%.

```
<mx:VBox width="100%" height="100%">
   <mx:LineChart id="chart"
      dataProvider="{dp}"
      height="100%" width="100%"/>
</mx:VBox>
```

This is the skeleton of a line chart. Before it works properly, a line chart requires one or more series, as well as its axis. You will do this in a later exercise.

6 Save SalesChart.mxml.

The file at this point should resemble SalesChart_initial in the intermediate directory.

7 Open ComparisonChart.mxml from the Lesson18/assets directory and save it to your flexGrocer/views/dashboard directory.

8 Inside the first `<mx:VBox>` tag within the `<mx:ViewStack>` tag, add an `<mx:ColumnChart>` tag with a *height* and *width* of 100% and a *dataProvider* bound to *dp*.

```
<mx:VBox>
   <mx:ColumnChart id="chart"
      dataProvider="{dp}"
      width="100%" height="100%"/>
</mx:VBox>
```

This is the skeleton of the column chart, which requires you to specify one or more series, as well as a vertical axis, before it will work. You will do so in a later exercise.

9 Save ComparisonChart.mxml.

If you run the application now, no chart will appear because you need to provide more information, such as the series and axis data. The file at this point should resemble ComparisonChart_initial in the intermediate directory.

Populating Charts

Depending on the type of chart you are using, there are one or more steps necessary before a chart will be drawn. All charts, regardless of type, require that you specify one or more series of data for the charts. Any of the Cartesian charts also require that you specify the horizontal and/or vertical axes.

A series is a set of data provided to a chart. Depending on the type of chart you are using, there are different Series classes to use.

Series Class Name	Description
AreaSeries	The AreaSeries class defines a data series for an AreaChart control.
AreaSet	AreaSet is a grouping set that can be used to stack AreaSeries in any arbitrary chart.
BarSeries	The BarSeries class defines a data series for a BarChart control.
BarSet	BarSet is a grouping set that can be used to stack or cluster BarSeries in any arbitrary chart.
BubbleSeries	The BubbleSeries class defines a data series for a BubbleChart control.
CandleStickSeries	The CandleStickSeries class represents financial data as a series of candlesticks representing the high, low, opening, and closing values of a data series.
ColumnSeries	The ColumnSeries class defines a data series for a ColumnChart control.
ColumnSet	ColumnSet is a grouping set that can be used to stack or cluster ColumnSeries in any arbitrary chart.
HLOCSeries	The HLOCSeries class represents financial data as a series of elements representing the high, low, closing, and optionally opening values of a data series.
LineSeries	The LineSeries class defines a data series for a LineChart control.
PieSeries	The PieSeries class defines the data series for a PieChart control.
PlotSeries	The PlotSeries class defines a data series for a PlotChart control.

Although it's not as common a use case, many charts allow you to mix and match different series within the same chart, so it is possible to overlay a line chart above a column chart, for example.

Specifying the Charts Series

In this next section, you will make the charts functional by adding the required series elements.

1 Open Dashboard.mxml and change the `<v:ChartPod id="sales">` to use `<v:SalesChart id="sales ">` instead. Change the `<v:ChartPod id="type">` tag to use `<v:TypeChart id="type">`, and change `<v:ChartPod id="comp">` to use `<v:ComparisonChart id="comp">`. Leave the rest of the attributes exactly as they were.

```
<v:SalesChart id="sales"
   width="100%" height="100%"
   title="Sales Chart"
   maximize="this.currentState='fullSales'"
   restore="this.currentState=''">
```

```
    </v:SalesChart>
    <mx:VBox id="rightCharts" width="100%" height="100%">
      <v:TypeChart id="type"
        width="100%" height="100%"
        title="Category Chart"
        maximize="this.currentState='fullType'"
        restore="this.currentState=''">
      </v:TypeChart>
      <v:ComparisonChart id="comp"
        width="100%" height="100%"
        title="Comparison Chart"
        maximize="this.currentState='fullComp'"
        restore="this.currentState=''">
      </v:ComparisonChart>
    </mx:VBox>
```

You will start to make the charts functional, but you will need to call them from the Dashboard application to see it function.

2 Add a new attribute to both the <v:SalesChart> and <v:TypeChart> tags, binding the selection.data of the grossOrNetGroup to the grossOrNet property.

```
<v:SalesChart id="sales"
    width="100%" height="100%"
    title="Sales Chart"
    grossOrNet="{grossOrNetGroup.selection.data}"
    maximize="this.currentState='fullSales'"
    restore="this.currentState=''">
</v:SalesChart>
<mx:VBox id="rightCharts" width="100%" height="100%">
    <v:TypeChart id="type"
        width="100%" height="100%"
        title="Category Chart"
        grossOrNet="{grossOrNetGroup.selection.data}"
        maximize="this.currentState='fullType'"
        restore="this.currentState=''">
    </v:TypeChart>
    …
</mx:VBox>
```

This will pass the string GROSS or NET, whichever value the user selects from the radio buttons into the SalesChart and TypeChart components. You don't need to pass this string to the ComparisonChart because it will ultimately show both net and gross sales at once.

3 Open TypeChart.mxml from the flexGrocer/views/dashboard directory.

Alternately, you can open TypeChart_initial from the intermediate directory and save it as **TypeChart.mxml** in your flexGrocer/views/dashboard directory.

4 Between the open and close <mx:PieChart> tags, add an <mx:series> tag pair. Inside
the <mx:series> tag, create an <mx:PieSeries> tag with the field attribute bound to
grossOrNet.

```
<mx:PieChart id="chart"
   width="100%" height="100%"
   dataProvider="{dp}">
   <mx:series>
      <mx:PieSeries field="{grossOrNet}">
      </mx:PieSeries>
   </mx:series>
</mx:PieChart>
```

When using the <mx:PieSeries>, you need to specify which property to render in the
chart. By binding that property to grossOrNet, the chart will show either the gross or net
sales, based on which radio button the user selected in the main application.

Save and test the Dashboard application. At this point, the pie chart should be functional.

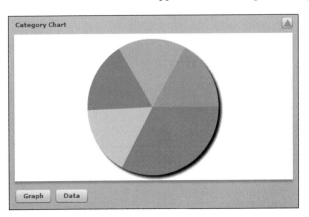

5 Add a labelPosition attribute to the <mx:PieSeries> tag, specifying insideWithCallout as
the value.

```
<mx:PieSeries
   labelPosition="insideWithCallout"
   field="{grossOrNet}">
```

The label position specifies how to render labels. The valid values are as follows:

- **"none"**—Do not draw labels. This is the default.

- **"outside"**—Draw labels around the boundary of the pie.

- **"callout"**—Draw labels in two vertical stacks on either side of the pie. The pie shrinks
  if necessary to make room for the labels.

- **"inside"**—Draw labels inside the chart, centered approximately ⁷⁄₁₀ of the way along each wedge. Shrink labels to ensure that they do not interfere with each other. If labels shrink below the `calloutPointSize` property, Flex removes them. When two labels overlap, Flex gives priority to labels for larger slices.

- **"insideWithCallout"**—Draw labels inside the pie, but if labels shrink below a legible size, Flex converts them to callouts.

Save and test the application again. Notice that the labels are showing the value, but not the category name, as might be expected.

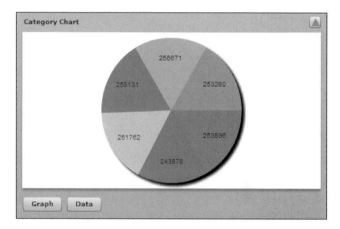

6 In the `<mx:Script>` block, create a new function called `renderLabel()`, which takes four arguments, and returns a String. The function should return `item.CATEGORY`.

```
private function renderLabel(item:Object, field:String, index:int,
   ➥ pct:Number):String{
   return item.CATEGORY;
}
```

You will use this label function to tell the chart which field to render as its label. For a PieSeries, the label function is automatically passed four arguments:

- **item**—contains the object being graphed. In your pie chart, to show the category name, you want to return the `item.CATEGORY`.

- **field**—a string that contains the field (NET or GROSS in your app), which is being graphed.

- **index**—the item number being graphed.

- **pct**—the percentage of the pie for this item.

7 Specify the labelFunction attribute of the <mx:PieSeries> to be renderLabel.

```
<mx:PieSeries labelPosition="insideWithCallout"
   field="{grossOrNet}"
   labelFunction="renderLabel">
```

Save and test the application. You should now see the labels rendering properly. This file should resemble TypeChart_labels.mxml in the intermediate directory.

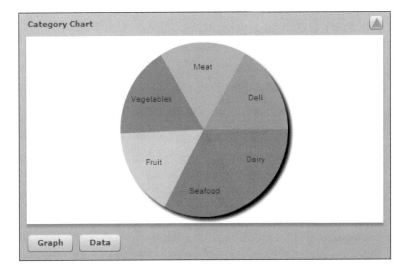

8 Open SalesChart.mxml from your flexGrocer/views/dashboard directory.

Alternately, you can open SalesChart_initial.mxml from the intermediate directory and save it as **SalesChart.mxml** in your flexGrocer/views/dashboard directory.

9 After the opening <mx:LineChart> tag, add an <mx:series> tag; within the <mx:series>, add an <mx:LineSeries> tag with the yField attribute bound to grossOrNet.

```
<mx:LineChart id="chart"
   dataProvider="{dp}"
   height="100%" width="100%">
   <mx:series>
     <mx:LineSeries yField="{grossOrNet}">
     </mx:LineSeries>
   </mx:series>
</mx:LineChart>
```

You are telling the LineChart that the selected property (either gross or net) will be the field that defines the value for the y-axis.

10 Save SalesChart.mxml and run the application.

The chart is now rendering. Notice, however, that the labels along the axis have no bearing on the data they represent. You will fix this in the next exercise when you specify the horizontal and vertical axes. This file should resemble SalesChart_labels.mxml in the intermediate directory.

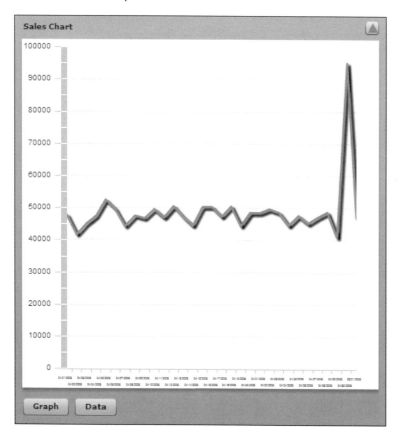

11 Open ComparisonChart.mxml from your flexGrocer/views/dashboard directory.

Alternately, you can open ComparisonChart_initial.mxml from the intermediate directory and save it as **ComparisonChart.mxml** in your flexGrocer/views/dashboard directory.

12 Specify two column series—one for the yField set to GROSS and one with a yField set to NET.

```
<mx:ColumnChart id="chart"
    dataProvider="{dp}"
    width="100%" height="100%">
    <mx:series>
        <mx:ColumnSeries yField="GROSS">
        </mx:ColumnSeries>
        <mx:ColumnSeries yField="NET">
        </mx:ColumnSeries>
    </mx:series>
</mx:ColumnChart>
```

This chart takes two different Series—one to plot a day's gross sales; the other to show the day's profit (net sales).

13 Save ComparisonChart.mxml and run the application.

The column chart is now rendering, showing columns for both gross and net sales. Notice, however, that the labels along the horizontal axis are index numbers, not the dates you would expect. You will fix this in the next exercise when you specify the horizontal axis. This file should resemble ComparisonChart_labels.mxml in the intermediate directory.

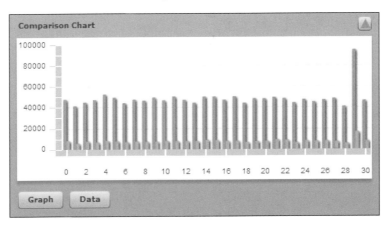

Adding Horizontal and Vertical Axes to Line and Column Charts

After data has been provided to the charts, you can refine how the axis labels are rendered by using the <mx:horizontalAxis> and <mx:verticalAxis> tags. These tags can be used to specify valid ranges for the chart and also to map the data on the chart.

There are four supported Axis types in Flex:

- **CategoryAxis**—Maps a particular property of the objects in the chart to the axis. For example, a chart showing the total enrollment of a school based on the students' demographics could use a CategoryAxis to map the students' race property to the horizontal axis.

- **LinearAxis**—Maps numeric data to the points on an axis. This can allow for easily specifying valid numeric ranges, numbers to skip, and so on.

- **LogAxis**—Maps logarithmic data to an axis. To facilitate this, the Log axis has labels for each power of 10 (1, 10, 100, 1000, and so on).

- **DateTimeAxis**—Maps time-based values to an axis. This can also be used to set the format for the labels.

Flex assumes that any axis not specifically defined is mapping a numeric field to the axis. This is why, in the previous exercise, the horizontal axis was showing the index number of the item instead of the date.

1 Open SalesChart.mxml from your flexGrocer/views/dashboard directory.

Alternately, you can open SalesChart_labels.mxml from the intermediate directory and save it as **SalesChart.mxml** in your flexGrocer/views/dashboard directory.

2 Add an `<mx:horizontalAxis>` tag pair inside the `<mx:LineChart>` tag. Within the `<mx:HorizontalAxis>` tags, add an `<mx:CategoryAxis>` with the `categoryField` attribute set to DTSALE.

```
<mx:LineChart id="chart"
    dataProvider="{dp}"
    height="100%" width="100%">
    <mx:horizontalAxis>
        <mx:CategoryAxis categoryField="DTSALE"/>
    </mx:horizontalAxis>
    <mx:series>
        <mx:LineSeries yField="{grossOrNet}">
        </mx:LineSeries>
    </mx:series>
</mx:LineChart>
```

You are now telling the chart what data to plot along the horizontal axis. By specifying a CategoryAxis with a `categoryField` of DTSALE, you are mapping the DTSALE property across the x-axis. It would also be possible to use a DateTimeAxis instead of a CategoryAxis; if you had a situation in which you had more day data than you wanted to graph, you could use DataTimeAxis and specify a start and end date. In this case, you want to graph any data returned by the server, so a CategoryAxis is more appropriate.

3 Save SalesChart.mxml and run the application.

The dates are now showing across the bottom of the chart. Notice that it is showing too many to effectively read the labels. If you change the dates in the ApplicationControlBar (at the top of the Dashboard application) to limit the search to only one week's worth of data, you can more clearly see that part of the problem is that the labels are too long and not particularly user-friendly.

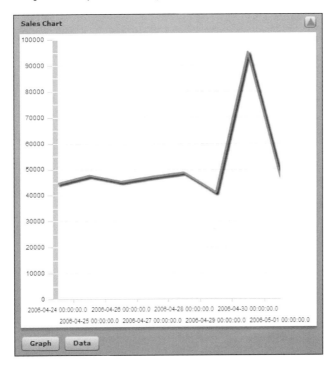

4 In the <mx:Script> block, add a function called renderDate(), which will format the labels on the horizontal axis as dates.

```
private function renderDate(value:Object, previousValue:Object,
    ➥ axis:CategoryAxis, item:Object):String{
    return mmddyyyy.format(value);
}
```

A label function for a CategoryAxis is automatically passed four arguments:

- **value**—the value of the property for the object being rendered. In this case, that value is the DTSALE property, which contains the date.

- **previousValue**—the value of the property for the previous column.

- **axis**—a reference to the axis.

- **item**—the whole data object.

In your case, all you need to do is return the formatted version of the date as a String. You can use the DateFormatter named mmddyyyy, which is already present in this file.

If you use the code completion feature, the import for CategoryAxis will automatically be added; otherwise, you will need to explicitly add it:

```
import mx.charts.CategoryAxis;
```

5 Specify renderDate as the labelFunction for the CategoryAxis.

```
<mx:CategoryAxis categoryField="DTSALE" labelFunction="renderDate"/>
```

This tells the axis to use the renderDate() function when creating labels.

6 Save SalesChart.mxml and run the application.

You can now see the dates rendered properly. There are still too many dates shown at once; you will fix that soon, when you learn about AxisRenderers. This file should resemble SalesChart_labelFunction.mxml in the intermediate directory.

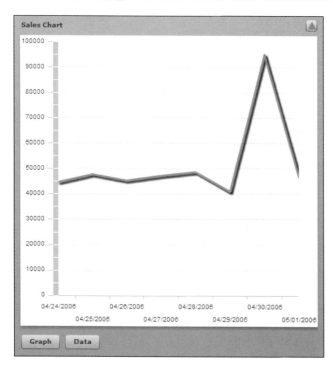

7 Open ComparisonChart.mxml from your flexGrocer/views/dashboard directory.

Alternately, you can open ComparisonChart_labels.mxml from the intermediate directory and save it as **ComparisonChart.mxml** in your flexGrocer/views/dashboard directory.

8 Add an `<mx:horizontalAxis>` tag pair inside the `<mx:ColumnChart>` tag. Within the `<mx:horizontalAxis>` tags, add an `<mx:CategoryAxis>` with the `categoryField` attribute set to DTSALE.

```
<mx:ColumnChart id="chart"
   dataProvider="{dp}"
   width="100%" height="100%">
   <mx:horizontalAxis>
      <mx:CategoryAxis categoryField="DTSALE" />
   </mx:horizontalAxis>

   ...
</mx:ColumnChart>
```

Just like the line chart, the column chart will use DTSALE as its field on the horizontal axis. You already discovered the need for a label function, so next you will add a label function for the horizontal axis.

9 In the `<mx:Script>` block, add a function called `renderDate()`, which will format the labels on the horizontal axis as dates.

```
private function renderDate(value:Object, previousValue:Object,
   ➥ axis:CategoryAxis, item:Object):String{
   return mmddyyyy.format(value);
}
```

Just like the line chart, you are using this function to format DTSALE as a date. If you use the code completion feature, the `import` for CategoryAxis will automatically be added; otherwise, you will need to explicitly add it.

10 Specify `renderDate` as the `labelFunction` for the CategoryAxis.

```
<mx:CategoryAxis categoryField="DTSALE"
   labelFunction="renderDate"/>
```

This tells the axis to use the `renderDate()` function when creating labels.

11 Save ComparisonChart.mxml and run the application.

The comparison chart now shows the dates correctly. Next, you will add a `labelFunction` for the vertical axis as well.

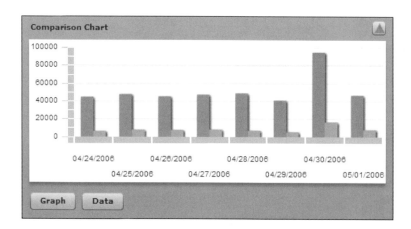

12 Just after the </mx:horizontalAxis> tag, add an <mx:verticalAxis> tag pair. Inside the vertical axis pair, add an <mx:LinearAxis> tag, to specify a labelFunction called renderDollars.

```
<mx:horizontalAxis>
    <mx:CategoryAxis dataProvider="{dp}"
    categoryField="DTSALE" labelFunction="renderDate"/>
</mx:horizontalAxis>
<mx:verticalAxis>
    <mx:LinearAxis labelFunction="renderDollars"/>
</mx:verticalAxis>
```

A LinearAxis will work fine for the vertical column because the values are all numeric. In the next step, you will create the renderDollars() function.

13 In the <mx:Script> block, create a function called renderDollars(), which accepts three arguments: value, previousValue and Axis.

```
private function renderDollars(value:Number, previousValue:Number,
    ➥ axis:LinearAxis):String{
    return dollars.format(value);
}
```

The labelFunction for a LinearAxis is automatically passed thee arguments: the value, the previous value, and a reference to the axis. If you use the code completion feature, the import for LinearAxis will automatically be added; otherwise, you will need to explicitly add it.

14 Save ComparisonChart.mxml and run the application.

The comparison chart now shows the dates and dollars correctly. The current file should resemble ComparisonChart_labelFunctions.mxml in the intermediate directory.

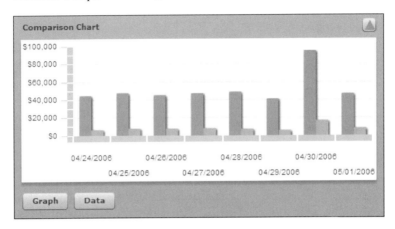

Adding Legends to the Charts

Adding a legend to a Flex chart is incredibly easy. The <mx:Legend> tag requires only one argument, dataProvider, which is bound to the chart. There are several other attributes you can use to further customize the legend, a couple of the commonly used ones are as follows:

- labelPlacement—Just like the labelPlacement of a check box or radio button, this indicates if the label should be left, right, top, or bottom as compared with the colored square that identifies the data.

- direction—Indicates if the items in the legend should be laid out vertically or horizontally.

1 Open ComparisonChart.mxml from your flexGrocer/views/dashboard directory.

Alternately, you can open ComparisonChart_labelFunctions.mxml from the intermediate directory and save it as **ComparisonChart.mxml** in your flexGrocer/views/dashboard directory.

2 Inside the <mx:VBox>, before the <mx:ColumnChart> tag, add an <mx:Legend> tag with the direction set to horizontal and the dataProvider bound to chart.

```
<mx:VBox>
   <mx:Legend direction="horizontal" dataProvider="{chart}"/>
   <mx:ColumnChart id="chart"
      dataProvider="{dp}"
      width="100%" height="100%">
      ...
</mx:VBox>
```

This should create a legend placed horizontally which appears before the chart inside the <mx:VBox>.

3 Find the <mx:ColumnSeries> tag for the GROSS column. Add a displayName attribute with the value Gross. Find the <mx:ColumnSeries> tag for the NET column. Add a displayName attribute with the value of Net.

```
<mx:series>
   <mx:ColumnSeries yField="GROSS" displayName="Gross">
   </mx:ColumnSeries>
   <mx:ColumnSeries yField="NET" displayName="Net">
   </mx:ColumnSeries>
</mx:series>
```

The displayName indicates what should be shown in the legend.

4 Save and run the application.

You should see a legend appear above the comparison chart. The current file should resemble ComparisonChart_legend.mxml in the intermediate directory.

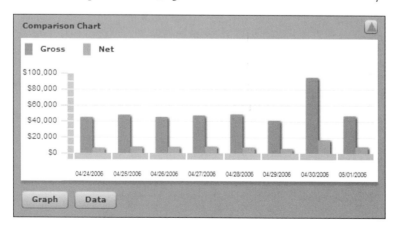

Limiting the Labels Shown on an Axis

When graphing large data sets, there is often too much data for every item to get its own label on the axis. To help you, there is a AxisRenderer that you can use to customize the rendering of the axis.

The syntax for an AxisRenderer looks like this:

```
<mx:horizontalAxisRenderer>
   <mx:AxisRenderer
   canDropLabels="true|false"
   canStagger="true|false"
   showLabels="true|false"
   showLine="true|false"
   tickLength="Default depends on axis"
   tickPlacement="inside|outside|cross|none"
   title="No default"/>
</mx:horizontalAxisRenderer>
```

> ✴ **NOTE:** This is only a subset of the elements that can be set on an AxisRenderer.

1 Open ComparisonChart.mxml from your flexGrocer/views/dashboard directory.

Alternately, you can open ComparisonChart_legend from the intermediate directory and save it as **ComparisonChart.mxml** in your flexGrocer/views/dashboard directory.

2 Between the open `<mx:ColumnChart>` tag and the first `<mx:horizontalAxis>` tag, add an `<mx:horizontalAxisRenderer>` tag pair. Inside the pair, add an `<mx:AxisRenderer>` tag, setting the `canDropLabels` attribute to true.

```
<mx:ColumnChart id="chart"
   dataProvider="{dp}"
   width="100%" height="100%">
   <mx:horizontalAxisRenderer>
      <mx:AxisRenderer canDropLabels="true"/>
   </mx:horizontalAxisRenderer>
   <mx:horizontalAxis>
      <mx:CategoryAxis dataProvider="{dp}" categoryField="DTSALE"
labelFunction="renderDate"/>
   </mx:horizontalAxis>
   ...
</mx:ColumnChart>
```

This tells the horizontal axis that if there is not room for every label, it is okay to render the labels that fit. Labels will be rendered at regular intervals (such as every other item, every third item, and so on).

3 Save and test the application.

You should now see that regardless how many days, weeks, or months of data you are viewing, the labels are always rendered legibly.

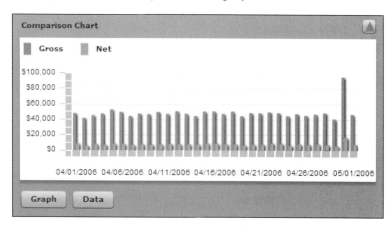

Interacting with Charts

Like all elements in Flash Player, charts have a rich set of interactions that can be easily integrated into an application. Among the elements easily implemented are showing data tips as users mouse over elements of the charts, as well as enabling users to click elements in the chart to effect other changes throughout the application.

Mouse Over Events

Mouse over events are incredibly useful and simple to implement. All charts inherently support a property called showDataTips. By setting this to true for a chart, a ToolTip-type element will appear, showing more data about the element the user is mousing over.

Click Events

Another easy to implement interaction is by handling a click event. In this next exercise, you will add data tips to the type and sales charts, and enable users to filter the type and comparison charts by category when the user clicks a slice of the pie chart.

Adding Chart Events

Using events, you will make your charts more interactive.

1 Open SalesChart.mxml from your flexGrocer/views/dashboard directory.

Alternately, you can open SalesChart_labelFunction.mxml from the intermediate directory and save it as **SalesChart.mxml** in your flexGrocer/views/dashboard directory.

2 Set the showDataTips attribute of the <mx:LineChart> tag to true and specify the dataTipFunction attribute equal to renderTips.

```
<mx:LineChart id="chart"
    dataProvider="{dp}"
    height="100%" width="100%"
    showDataTips="true"
    dataTipFunction="renderTips">
```

This tells the chart to show data tips when any element is moused over and to use the function renderTips() to determine what to show. You create renderTips() in the next step.

3 In the <mx:Script> block, create a function named renderTips(), which takes a single argument, called hd of type HitData, and returns a String.

```
private function renderTips(hd:HitData):String {
    var item:Object = hd.item;
    return "<b>"+mmddyyyy.format(item.DTSALE)+"</b><br>" +
        ➥ dollars.format(item[grossOrNet]);
}
```

If you use the code completion feature, the import for HitData will automatically be added; otherwise, you will need to explicitly add it.

4 Save and test the application.

Notice that as you mouse over elements in the line chart, nicely formatted data tips are now available. The completed file should look like SalesChart_dataTips.mxml in the intermediate directory.

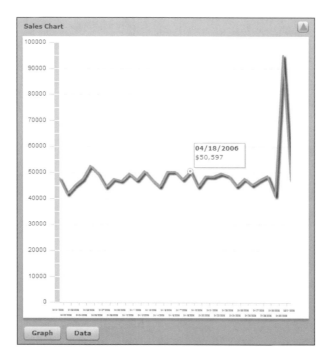

5 Open TypeChart.mxml from your flexGrocer/views/dashboard directory.

Alternately, you can open TypeChart_labels.mxml from the intermediate directory and save it as **TypeChart.mxml** in your flexGrocer/views/dashboard directory.

6 Set the showDataTips attribute of the <mx:PieChart> tag to true; specify the dataTipFunction attribute equal to renderTips().

```
<mx:PieChart id="chart"
   dataProvider="{dp}"
   height="100%" width="100%"
   showDataTips="true"
   dataTipFunction="renderTips">
```

You create renderTips() in the next step.

7 In the <mx:Script> block, create a function named renderTips(), which takes a single argument, called data of type HitData, and returns a String.

```
private function renderTips(data:HitData):String{
   var gross:Number = data.item.GROSS;
   var net:Number = data.item.NET;
   return "Total Sales: " + dollars.format(gross)+ '\n' +
      ➥ "Total Profit: " + dollars.format(net);
}
```

Remember, you may need to explicitly import the mx.charts.HitData class, unless it was automatically imported for you.

Here, the renderTips() function takes a HitData object, finds the value for the gross and net properties, and builds a string formatting them before returning it.

8   Save and test the application.

Notice that as you mouse over elements in the pie chart, nicely formatted data tips are now available. Next you will react to click events in the pie chart.

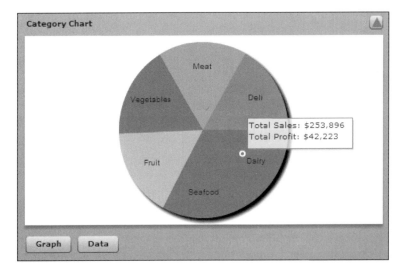

9   In the <mx:PieChart> tag, specify an itemClick attribute to call a function named broadcastTypeChange() and pass it event.hitData.item as an argument.

```
<mx:PieChart id="chart"
    width="100%" height="100%"
    dataProvider="{dp}"
    showDataTips="true"
    dataTipFunction="renderTip"
    itemClick="broadcastTypeChange(event.hitData.item)">
```

itemClick is invoked when the user clicks an item in the chart. When this happens, a ChartItemEvent object is created, which has a property called hitData. The hitData property is an object describing the click. The item property of hitData contains a reference to the item on which the user clicked. In the next step, you will write the broadcastTypeChange() function, so an event is dispatched back to the main application when the user clicks a category on this chart.

10 In the `<mx:Script>` block, create a function called `broadcastTypeChange()`, which takes an argument called `item` of type Object, and returns void. This function will create an instance of the ObjectDataEvent class and dispatch it.

```
private function broadcastTypeChange(item:Object):void{
   var o:ObjectDataEvent= new ObjectDataEvent("typeChange", item.CATEGORY);
   this.dispatchEvent(o);
}
```

`ObjectDataEvent` is an event written earlier, which has a custom property called `data` that is of type Object.

11 Declare an event named `typeChange` of type `events.ObjectDataEvent` in an `<mx:MetaData>` tag at the top of the TypeChart.mxml component.

```
<v:MaxRestorePanel
   xmlns:mx="http://www.adobe.com/2006/mxml"
   xmlns:v="views.*">
   <mx:Metadata>
      [Event(name="typeChange", type="events.ObjectDataEvent")]
   </mx:Metadata>

   ...
</v:MaxRestorePanel>
```

12 Save TypeChart.mxml.

You need to make a change to Dashboard.mxml before you can test this latest change. TypeChart.mxml should now resemble TypeChart_events.mxml in the intermediate directory.

13 Open Dashboard.mxml from your flexGrocer directory.

This is the application that instantiates all three charts.

14 Find where TypeChart is instantiated. Add an attribute to handle the `typeChange` event and call a soon-to-be-written function called `doTypeChange()`.

```
<v:TypeChart id="type"
   width="100%" height="100%"
   title="Sales By Type"
   grossOrNet="{grossOrNet}"
   typeChange="doTypeChange(event)"
   maximize="this.currentState='fullType'"
   restore="this.currentState=''"/>
```

When TypeChart dispatches a type change, you want the rest of the application to react and update itself accordingly.

15 In the <mx:Script> block, create a function called doTypeChange(), which takes an argument of type ObjectDataEvent. This function should use the Util classes static presetCombo() method to set the ComboBox control in the ApplicationControlBar container. Next, the selectedType property should be set to event.data.toString(). Finally, the function should send the dashboardWS.getSalesData web service.

```
private function doTypeChange(event:ObjectDataEvent):void{
   Util.presetCombo(catCombo,"name",event.data.toString());
   selectedType = event.data.toString();
   dashboardWS.getSalesData.send();
}
```

When a ObjectDataEvent is broadcast, you want to have the ApplicationControlBar reflect the currently selected type, so you can use the presetCombo() function you saw earlier. If you recall from Lesson 17, "Accessing Server-side Objects," the getSalesData web service method takes three arguments: startDate, endDate, and selectedType. So the service will return the right data, you will first set selectedType and then send the service.

Don't forget, both the utils.Util and events.ObjectDataEvent classes need to be imported.

16 Save and run the application.

After the charts are drawn, if you click a slice of the pie in the type chart, the ComboBox is updated, and new data is loaded from the server, showing only the sales for that type of product.

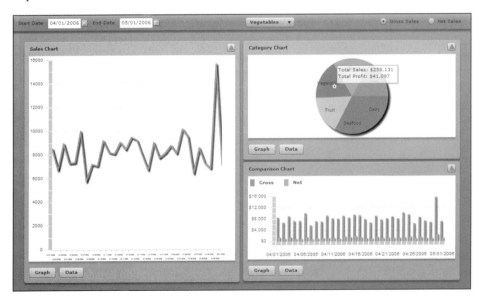

Adding Animations to the Charts

The customizations that can be applied to the charts in Flex are nearly limitless. Among the myriad of customizations you can make include the ability to have data animate into the chart or to apply colors, gradients, and so on to the elements of a chart.

There are three types of built-in animations that can be easily applied to charts. They are all built as subclasses of the mx.charts.effects.SeriesEffect class. These classes can be used with a series `showDataEffect` or `hideDataEffect` attribute. The classes are the following:

- **SeriesInterpolate**—The SeriesInterpolate effect moves the graphics that represent the existing data in a series to the new points. Instead of clearing the chart and then repopulating it, it creates a nice smooth animation between the original data points and the new ones. You use the SeriesInterpolate effect only with a showDataEffect effect trigger. It has no effect if set with a hideDataEffect.

- **SeriesSlide**—The SeriesSlide effect slides a data series into and out of the chart's boundaries. The direction property specifies the location from which the series slides. If you use SeriesSlide with a hideDataEffect effect trigger, the series slides from the current position onscreen to a position off the screen in the indicated direction. If you use SeriesSlide as a showDataEffect, the series slides from offscreen to a position onto the screen, in the indicated direction.

- **SeriesZoom**—The SeriesZoom effect implodes and explodes chart data into and out of the focal point that you specify. As with the SeriesSlide effect, whether the effect is zooming to or from this point depends on whether it is assigned to the `showDataEffect` or `hideDataEffect` effect triggers.

1 Open TypeChart.mxml from your flexGrocer/views/dashboard directory.

Alternately, you can open TypeChart_events.mxml from the intermediate directory and save it as **TypeChart.mxml** in your flexGrocer/views/dashboard directory.

2 Right before the `<mx:ViewStack>` tag, add an `<mx:SeriesInterpolate>` tag with an id attribute of `interpolate` and an `elementOffset` of 5.

```
<mx:SeriesInterpolate id="interpolate" elementOffset="5"/>
```

The `elementOffset` attribute specifies a number of milliseconds to delay before starting the effect.

3 Find the <mx:PieSeries> tag and add an attribute showDataEffect="interpolate".

```
<mx:PieSeries field="{grossOrNet}"
   labelPosition="insideWithCallout"
   labelFunction="renderLabel"
   showDataEffect="interpolate" >
```

This attribute instructs the series to animate the data when it is added to the chart.

4 Save and run the application.

Notice the effects as data is rendered in the pie chart or any time the data changes. The completed file should closely resemble TypeChart_interpolate.mxml in the intermediate directory.

Customizing the Look of Charts with Styles

There are a number of different elements that can be styled in a chart, such as line colors, fill colors, fill gradients, alphas, and so on. One place they are often set are for each Series in a chart. As you have seen throughout this lesson, without setting any styles at all, the elements are automatically assigned colors and render. However, if you want more control over the color choices, you can specify Series colors to whatever degree you need.

Specifying fill colors for a Series has this structure:

```
<mx:ColumnSeries displayName="net" yField="NET">
   <mx:fill>
      <mx:LinearGradient>
         <mx:entries>
            <mx:GradientEntry color="#0000FF"
               ratio="0" alpha="1"/>
            <mx:GradientEntry color="#0000DD"
               ratio=".1" alpha="1"/>
            <mx:GradientEntry color="#000022"
               ratio=".9" alpha="1"/>
            <mx:GradientEntry color="#000000"
               ratio="1" alpha="1"/>
         </mx:entries>
      </mx:LinearGradient>
   </mx:fill>
</mx:ColumnSeries>
```

Here, you see a four-color gradient fill being applied to a series of columns in a column chart. Notice that a gradient fill takes an array of GradientEntries, each with a color, ratio, and alpha, called entries. In this next exercise, you will apply a gradient fill to the pie chart.

1 Open TypeChart.mxml from your flexGrocer/views/dashboard directory.

Alternately, you can open TypeChart_interpolate.mxml from the intermediate directory and save it as **TypeChart.mxml** in your flexGrocer/views/dashboard directory.

2 Between the open and close `<mx:PieSeries>` tags, add an `<mx:fills>` tag.

```
<mx:PieSeries field="{grossOrNet}"
    labelPosition="insideWithCallout"
    labelFunction="renderLabel"
    showDataEffect="interpolate" >
    <mx:fills>
    </mx:fills>
    ...
</mx:PieSeries>
```

In the next step, you will specify six different gradients to use for the data in the pie chart.

3 Inside the `<mx:fills>` tags you just created, specify six radial gradients, each with two colors. The first has a ratio of 0, and the second has a ratio of 1, as indicated in the following table.

First Color	First Color Ratio	Second Color	Second Color Ratio
#EF7651	0	#994C34	1
#E9C836	0	#AA9127	1
#6FB35F	0	#497B54	1
#A1AECF	0	#47447A	1
#996666	0	#999966	1
#339933	0	#339999	1

```
<mx:fills>
    <mx:RadialGradient>
        <mx:entries>
            <mx:GradientEntry color="#EF7651" ratio="0"/>
            <mx:GradientEntry color="#994C34" ratio="1"/>
        </mx:entries>
    </mx:RadialGradient>
    <mx:RadialGradient>
        <mx:entries>
            <mx:GradientEntry color="#E9C836" ratio="0"/>
            <mx:GradientEntry color="#AA9127" ratio="1"/>
        </mx:entries>
    </mx:RadialGradient>
```

code continues on next page

```
<mx:RadialGradient>
   <mx:entries>
      <mx:GradientEntry color="#6FB35F" ratio="0"/>
      <mx:GradientEntry color="#497B54" ratio="1"/>
   </mx:entries>
</mx:RadialGradient>
<mx:RadialGradient>
   <mx:entries>
      <mx:GradientEntry color="#A1AECF" ratio="0"/>
      <mx:GradientEntry color="#47447A" ratio="1"/>
   </mx:entries>
</mx:RadialGradient>
<mx:RadialGradient>
   <mx:entries>
      <mx:GradientEntry color="#996666" ratio="0"/>
      <mx:GradientEntry color="#999966" ratio="1"/>
   </mx:entries>
</mx:RadialGradient>
<mx:RadialGradient>
   <mx:entries>
      <mx:GradientEntry color="#339933" ratio="0"/>
      <mx:GradientEntry color="#339999" ratio="1"/>
   </mx:entries>
</mx:RadialGradient>
</mx:fills>
```

Feel free to experiment and find colors that work best for you. You can add as many colors to the array as you want. Experiment switching between radial gradients and linear gradients to get a feel for how they each work.

4 Save and run the application.

Notice the subtle gradient in each slice of the pie.

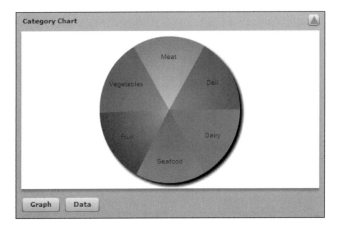

What You Have Learned

In this lesson, you have:

- Worked with the pie, column and line charts (pages 438–441)

- Learned how to provide data to charts (pages 441–448)

- Specified chart axes (pages 448–457)

- Handled chart events (pages 457–462)

- Animated charts when data is set (pages 463–464)

- Styled charts (pages 464–466)

What You Will Learn

In this lesson, you will:

- Understand what FDS is and how it works

- Install FDS

- Build a simple Flex application for use with the FDS

Approximate Time

This lesson takes approximately 1 hour and 30 minutes to complete.

Lesson Files

Media Files:

None

Starting Files:

None

Completed Files:

Lesson19/complete/ proxy-config.xml
Lesson19/complete/TfsDataServices.mxml

Introducing Adobe Flex Data Services

Flex Data Services (FDS) is the J2EE server software that enables you to access and synchronize data across one or more applications built with Flex framework. In this lesson, you will learn about FDS and its configuration. You will install FDS and build a simple application that can be used with FDS and understand the server compilation process as well as some of the features of FDS.

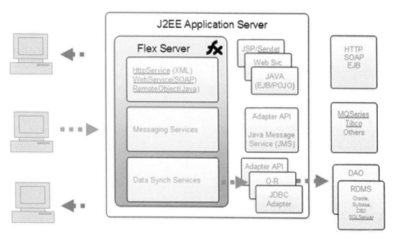

The different pieces of the Adobe Flex Data Services and how they can integrate with the enterprise

Introducing Flex Data Services (FDS)

FDS enables you to create real-time, data-driven applications that have been built with the Flex framework. FDS itself is a server-side Java application that is designed to work with most Java application servers, including JRun, JBoss, WebLogic, WebSphere, Oracle 10g, and Tomcat. There are four different parts to FDS, which include the following:

- Flex Message Service (FMS)

- Flex Data Management Service

- Flex Proxy Service (FPS)

- Remoting Service

Following is a diagram of the FDS basic architecture and an explanation of the functionality of the different elements:

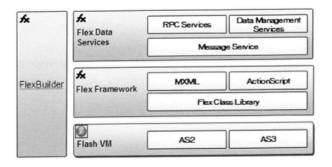

The *Flex Message Service (FMS)* enables you to build applications that support real-time chat and collaboration. A client application in Flash Player uses a client-side API to send and receive messages from a server-side destination. Messages are sent via a special protocol. You can build applications that allow collaboration, such as Adobe Breeze, which enables the synchronization of desktops. Using the FMS, you also can push data out from the server. For example, using FMS, you could build an application that updates sports scores or stock data on the fly. The application data in Flash Player would update whenever the server-side data changed.

The *Flex Data Management Service* provides tools for managing distributed data in Flex applications. The service consists of both server- and client-side components. On the server side, there are adaptors for common data persistence frameworks. On the client side, there are components that automate synchronization of an application's client and server tiers. You can use the Data Management Service to create applications that might be occasionally connected, as well as performing data synchronization and replication. You can manage large sets of data by paging through that data. Using the Data Management Service, you can also manage nested data relationships such as one-to-one and one-to-many relationships.

For security reasons, a Flex application is not permitted to access data from another domain unless a cross-domain security file has been installed on that remote server. The *Flex Proxy Service (FPS)* is designed to overcome the *sandbox security restrictions* of Flash Player when you try to retrieve data or other assets at run time from remote servers. The Proxy Service relays HTTP and web service requests from the Flex application in Flash Player to the server that is hosting the remote service. The communication with the remote server now occurs from FDS instead of Flash Player. This means that when you use the server-side proxy, the security sandbox error will no longer appear.

Remoting Service is similar to web service, but communication between the application and the server is done in Action Message Format (AMF), which is a binary format that is faster than a textual protocol such as SOAP or XML. Java classes that are used as remote objects are hosted by an application server that is compatible with version 3 of the AMF protocol. FDS can host Plain old Java objects (POJOs) as well as ColdFusion 7 applications built with Cold-Fusion components.

You can install FDS on an integrated JRun server or as a J2EE web application. You should use the integrated JRun server only for testing because it is not designed for production environments. For production environments, you can select the J2EE web application option to create an installable .war file, which can then be deployed on a J2EE server.

FDS uses a directory structure that follows the standard model for all J2EE web applications. The application root is known in J2EE as the context root; under this directory, there is a WEB-INF subdirectory that contains all the directories and files that configure the behavior of a J2EE web application. In this lesson, you will install the FDS and learn about the capabilities by building a simple application.

Flex projects built with FDS have the added benefit of being able to generate or compile SWF files on the server. Up until now, all the SWF files you have created have been compiled on the client by default in a directory called bin. FDS has the capability to generate SWF files dynamically based on a browser request. The browser will request a SWF file from FDS, and data services (on the server) will generate a SWF file along with the required HTML and JavaScript code that will detect Flash Player. The server will then send the generated SWF back to the client. After the SWF file has been generated, it will be cached in the server memory. The process looks as shown in the following example:

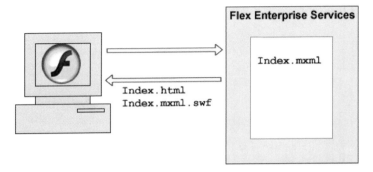

It is also possible to configure FDS to compile an application locally. The compiled Flex application does not need to reside in the root directory of FDS. However, the application must be delivered to the web browser from a web root directory that is in the same domain as the installation of the FDS. When you build a project in Flex Builder, there is an option for choosing local compilation of the file. Also, you can use the command-line compiler (mxmlc) to compile the application, which is included with FDS.

With FDS, you have a very powerful way to increase the personalization and customization of your applications. Using FDS, you can create applications that can communicate even more efficiently with Flash Player, resulting in a best of breed-rich Internet application. The Remoting Service speeds up data transfer using the AMF protocol, the messaging service can push data from the server into Flash Player. The Flex Data Management Service enables you to efficiently synchronize data between the client and the server. The FPS solves the security sandbox issues that might have frustrated you up until this point. FDS will run on a variety of industry-standard J2EE application servers so they can fit into many production environments and offer solutions for all applications.

Installing the Adobe FDS

In this task, you will install the FDS on the Adobe JRun server.

1 Install FDS with the integrated JRun server option using all the default settings. Double click the Flex Data Services installation file, FDS-win2.exe.

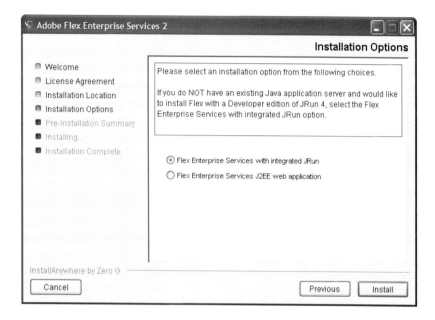

Accept the license agreement. Specify which browser to install the Flash player into. FDS, running on a stand-alone JRun server, enables you to have access to all the data services.

2 Open Windows Explorer (or if you are working on another operating system, any type of file management utility) and navigate to the Flex context root. The default directory location for the Windows installation is the following:

c:\fds2\jrun4\servers\default\flex

This path refers to the application root, also known as the context root, which is where all the files you will use for the data services are installed. Note that underneath this directory, there is a subdirectory called WEB-INF, which contains all the directories and files that configure the behavior of a J2EE web application. Adobe Flex Data Services is available for Windows 2000 Server, Windows XP professional Server 2003, Red Hat Enterprise Server 4 or the SUSE Linux enterprise server from Novell.

3 Open the WEB-INF directory within the context root and examine the files in this directory.

The web.xml file contains instructions for processing requests from the Flex client application. The flex subdirectory contains all libraries and configuration files required by FDS, and the classes subdirectory is the preferred location for compiled Java classes that will be called by the FDS at run time. There is also a lib subdirectory, which is the preferred location for JAR files that contain compiled Java classes that will be called by the FDS at run time.

4 Open a command window by clicking the Windows Start menu. Select the Run option, enter **cmd**, and click OK.

Because you installed the stand-alone version of JRun, you must start the server to use the FDS. In the first step, you installed the FDS as an application rather than a service, which means you must keep the command window open to keep the server running.

5 Still in the command window, switch to the bin subdirectory of the integrated JRun server by using the change directory. Enter **cd /fds2/jrun4/bin at the prompt**. The bin directory is under the data services root, and this is where you start the FDS service.

6 Enter this command:

```
jrun -start default
```

You should see the JRun server start in the command window. FDS is now ready to use.

Creating a Flex Builder Project with FDS

In this task, you will create a new Flex project in Flex Builder that will use the FDS. You will also create a simple application and browse and compile that application.

1 Open Flex Builder 2 and be sure that FDS is running. From the menu, choose File > New > Flex Project. Select Flex Data Services. Also, select the Compile application on the server when the page is viewed radio button.

This will set up a project that uses the FDS and generate the SWF files on the server when the page is viewed instead of compiling the SWF files on the client. This offers many advantages for customization and personalization of applications. In addition, the FDS server has the capability to cache these SWF files for later use.

2 Click Next. Uncheck the Use default location for local Flex Data Services server check box and select the following location as the Flex context root you want to use for your Flex project:

c:\fds2\jrun4\servers\default\flex

The Flex development server location defaults to the integrated server's Flex context root. If you want to use a different context root, uncheck the default location option and make the appropriate changes.

3 Click Next, assign the project a name of **TfsDataServices**, and leave all the defaults.

This creates a new folder underneath the FDS context root with the name of TfsDataServices. A new MXML file that will serve as your application root is also created, again with the name of TfsDataServices. Of course, you can change all these names by unchecking the Use default location check box.

4 Click Finish, and note the [source path] user_classes folder as well as the html-template folder, and the flex-config.xml that have been created for you.

When you click Finish, you should see that your new project has been created and that the main application file is ready for editing. The [source path] user-classes folder that has been created for you is simply a link to the WEB-INF/flex/user_classes directory in the installation of the FDS. Any ActionScript classes that are placed in this directory are part of the application's classpath. The html-template file is a directory that contains the model for the HTML and Flash Player detection code that will be generated and sent to the browser. You can customize the HTML by making changes to the included index. template.html file. The flex-config.xml is a link to this file in the WEB-INF directory, in which you can modify configuration settings.

5 From the Flex Builder menu, choose File > New > File. Click the Advanced button to display more options and click the Link to file in the file system check box. Click Browse and navigate to the WEB-INF/flex directory under the Flex context root and select the file services-config.xml file. Enter the filename **services-config.xml** as an alias in the filename text box. Be sure not to include any directory information. Click Finish.

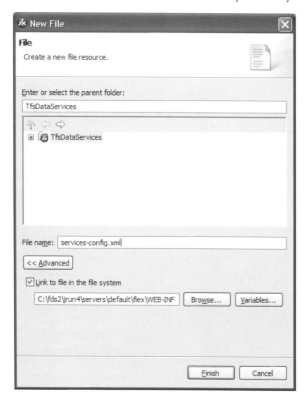

You should now see the linked file in the Navigator window. This will create a link to the external default FDS configuration file in Flex Builder that you can access. This is a file that you will access many times, and it is handy to have a link to it in Flex Builder. You could also use any text editor to modify this file as well but it will make it much easier for you if you can access it directly from Flex Builder.

Using the Flex Proxy Service

In this task, you will use the Proxy Service to overcome the security restrictions of Flash Player that apply when you try to retrieve data or other assets from remote servers at run time.

1 Open Flex Builder 2 and be sure FDS is running. Be sure the TfsDataServices file is open, and add an `<mx:HTTPService>` tag. Assign the tag an `id` of `myHTTPCall`, and specify the URL as http://www.flexgrocer.com/categorizedProducts.xml. Specify the `resultFormat` as e4x, as follows:

```
<mx:HTTPService id="myHTTPCall"
   url ="http://www.flexgrocer.com/categorizedProducts.xml"
   resultFormat="e4x"/>
```

This will make an HTTP call to the flexgrocer.com server to access the XML file. If a cross-domain file is installed at the web root of the server, this will work fine without the use of the FPS.

2 Add a `creationComplete` event to the `<mx:Application>` tag and call the `send()` method of the `myHTTPCall` HTTPService tag, as follows:

```
<mx:Application
   xmlns:mx= "http://www.adobe.com/2006/mxml"
   layout= "absolute" creationComplete="myHTTPCall.send();">
```

This will actually execute the HTTPService call when all the controls have been built within the application.

3 After the `<mx:HTTPService>`tag, add a Tree control to the application and specify the `dataProvider` as `myHTTPCall.lastResult.category`. Set the `labelField` property to `@name` and set `showRoot` to `false`. Run the application.

```
<mx:Tree dataProvider="{myHTTPCall.lastResult.category}"
   labelField="@name"
   showRoot="false"/>
```

The Tree control is populated with the data from the HTTPService call because a cross-domain security file has been installed at the web root of the flexgrocer.com server, and any SWF file can access the URL without violating the security sandbox restrictions of Flash Player.

4 Modify the `<mx:HTTPService>` tag so that the URL property is pointing to the http://www.flex2.net/categorizedProducts.xml server and then run the application.

```
<mx:HTTPService id="myHTTPCall"
   url="http://www.flex2.net/categorizedProducts.xml"
   resultFormat="e4x"/>
```

You should see that the Tree control is no longer populated, and the following run-time error should appear:

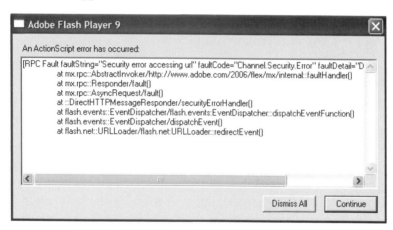

This error appears because no cross-domain security file is installed at the flex2.net server, and the security sandbox restriction in Flash Player is violated. In the next steps, you will use the proxy service of the FDS to access this URL and bypass the sandbox restrictions.

5 From the Flex Builder menu, choose File > New > File. Click the Advanced button to display more options and click the Link to file in the file system check box. Click Browse and navigate to the WEB-INF/flex directory under the Flex context root and select the file proxy-config.xml file. Enter the file name, **proxy-config.xml**, in the filename text box.

You should now see the linked file in the Navigator view, which creates a link to the external default Proxy Service configuration file in Flex Builder that you can access. The Proxy Service relays HTTP and web service requests from the Flex application in the browser to the server that's hosting the remote service. Because the communication with the remote server now comes from the FDS instead of directly from Flash Player, you no longer need to create a cross-domain security file. In the proxy-config.xml file, you can configure which servers the proxy can access.

6 In the proxy-config.xml file, locate the DefaultHTTP <destination> tag. Add a properties tag pair inside of the destination. Then, add a dynamic-url tag pair inside of properties. Add the string http://www.flex2.net/* inside of the dynamic-url tag, as shown following:

```
<destination id="DefaultHTTP">
   <properties>
      <dynamic-url>
         http://www.flex2.net/*
      </dynamic-url>
   </properties>
</destination>
```

When setting up a Proxy Service destination, you choose between the default destination and a specially named destination. The default destination always has an id of DefaultHTTP. Within the properties element, you can create one or more <dynamic-url> elements. Each element represents a URL that has permission to use the Proxy Service to communicate with the remote server. Each URL is essentially a whitelist for addresses that are acceptable to use with the Proxy Service.

7 Return to the TfsDataServices.mxml file and locate the <mx:HTTPService> tag. Add a useProxy attribute to the tag and set the value to true, as shown here.

```
<mx:HTTPService id="myHTTPCall"
    url= "http://www.flex2.net/categorizedProducts.xml"
    resultFormat="e4x" useProxy="true"/>
```

The request will use the default destination because the url property matches one of the default destination's dynamic URL patterns specified in the proxy-config.xml file.

8 Save and run the application.

You should see the application load and the data display correctly.

Creating a Named Proxy Service Destination

In this task, you will use a named Proxy Service instead of the default destination. It can be very useful to reference a name instead of a URL. A URL can change. If it does, you need to change the URL in all of your code. If you reference a named object, you would need to change the URL only in the configuration file.

1 In the proxy-config.xml file, just above the closing service tag, add a new <destination> tag with the id of categorizedProducts, as follows:

```
<destination id="categorizedProducts">
</destination>
```

When you set up a destination in the proxy configuration file, you can reference the name of the URL instead of specifying the actual URL. In this case, you have set up a categorizedProducts destination. In your application, in the <mx:HTTPSerice> tag, you can reference the name of categorizedProducts.

2 Within the destination tag node, add a new <properties> tag and as a node of that, specify a URL property pointing to the http://www.flex2.net/categorizedProducts.xml URL that you are accessing the data from, as follows. Save the changes to the file.

```
<destination id="categorizedProducts">
<properties>
   <url>
      http://www.flex2.net/categorizedProducts.xml
   </url>
</properties>
</destination>
```

From now on, you will reference the name categorizedProducts every time you need to make a call to this URL.

3 Return to the TfsDataServices.mxml file and locate the <mx:HTTPService>tag, and remove the url property from the tag. Add a destination attribute to the tag and specify the name of categorizedProducts, as follows:

```
<mx:HTTPService id="myHTTPCall"
   destination="categorizedProducts"
   resultFormat="e4x" useProxy="true"/>
```

4 Save and run the application.

You should see that it works just like it did before.

What You Have Learned

In this lesson, you have:

- Installed the Flex Data Services (FDS) (pages 472–474)

- Configured the Flex Data Services (FDS) (pages 474–477)

- Used the Flex Proxy Service (FPS) (pages 478–481)

- Learned how and why to use named destinations (pages 481–482)

What You Will Learn

In this lesson, you will:

- Learn more about the Flex Message Service (FMS)
- Configure Flex Builder to run your application through Flex Data Services (FDS)
- Configure the FMS destination
- Use the <mx:Consumer> tag
- Push data from an application server to the Flex client

Approximate Time

This lesson takes approximately 2 hours to complete.

Lesson Files

Media Files:

Lesson20/assets/typeSalesGateway.xml

Starting Files:

Lesson20/start/Dashboard.mxml
Lesson20/start/EComm.mxml
Lesson20/start/views/ecomm/Checkout.mxml

Completed Files:

Lesson20/complete/Dashboard.mxml
Lesson20/complete/EComm.mxml
Lesson20/complete/views/ecomm/Checkout.mxml

Pushing Data with Adobe Flex Data Services

In the last lessons, you got an overview of the features available from Flex Data Services (FDS) and learned how FDS can be used with your Flex applications to provide greater functionality. In this lesson, you will explore how a Flex application can register itself as a listener for new data pushed from the server, which makes it possible to have the server asynchronously send updates to the clients. You will use this to automatically update the Dashboard charts to reflect new sales in real time!

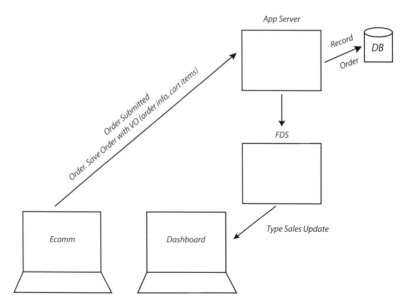

When a user completes an order, the Application server sends a gateway message to the FDS server, which sends an update to the Dashboard application in real time. The charts are updated to always display current information.

Understanding Flex Message Services

One of the most useful features of Adobe Flex Data Services 2 (FDS) is the capability to have a server update the connected clients in real time. This can be useful in many situations, such as updating inventory so clients can know what is in stock while they are still shopping, facilitating collaboration between disparate clients or even keeping sales dashboards updated to show completed sales as they happen. These features, and countless more, can now be easily integrated into your applications through the use of the Flex Message Services (FMS) of FDS.

Push technology is the capability for a server to send a message to the client without the client specifically requesting it. This makes it possible to have the client application automatically notified of updates as they happen. Over the years, this has been very difficult to implement for web-based applications. Developers have tried various solutions to "push" data from a server to a web client. They usually take the form of a "scheduled pull," so that on a set interval (maybe every 30 seconds or so) the client makes an HTTP request to the server asking for updated data. If anything new is available, the server returns it in its response. A classic example can be seen with gmail.com. When you have a web browser open to a logged-in gmail account, every 30 seconds the browser makes an HTTP request to the server, asking for new messages. Although this emulates "push" technology, it really is a scheduled pull, with the server responding only to a request. With Flash Media Server or XML sockets it has been possible to build push applications for Flash Player, although they have often not been trivial to implement.

One of the great features of FDS is the capability to easily register an application to listen for a type of notification from the server. Whenever the server broadcasts a message of that type, the Flex client responds and can be updated instantly with the new data. Imagine the possibilities of having a web portal instantly notify users of severe weather alerts, incoming e-mail, real-time scores of their favorite sports teams, or up-to-the-second stock quotes.

Creating a New Project in Flex Builder

Up to this point, you have been working with Flex Builder in a stand-alone fashion. Flex Builder has acted as the development environment and compiler, which created stand-alone SWF files that you could deploy to your web server. To take advantage of the features of FDS, you need to create a separate project in Flex Builder. The new project will be associated with FDS, so that it can be automatically deployed to the server when it is compiled.

Because the tasks in this lesson use both FDS and ColdFusion, the first thing you will do is start both of them in consoles.

1 Start FDS by opening a console window (DOS prompt), moving to the *driveroot:*/fds2/ jrun4/bin directory and entering **jrun –start default**. Be sure that FDS starts with no errors being shown. To stop the service, press Ctrl+C or close the console window. To restart the service, if you are still in the console, just press the up arrow; you will be returned again to the prompt.

You need to leave the console window open when you are using FDS because it runs only while the console window is open.

2 Start the configured ColdFusion by opening another console window (DOS prompt), moving to the *driveroot:*/cfusionFlexTFS/bin directory and entering **jrun –start cfusion**. Be sure that ColdFusion starts with no errors being shown. To stop the service, press Ctrl+C or close the console window. To restart the service, if you are still in the console, just press the up arrow; you will be returned again to the prompt.

You need to leave the console window open when you are using ColdFusion.

3 Find your FDS flex directory (*driveroot:*/fds2/jrun4/servers/default/flex on Windows) and create a new subdirectory called flexGrocer.

Having the files in a subdirectory with the FDS server enables the application to run through FDS.

4 Copy the files from the flexGrocer directory you have been using up to now into the new flexGrocer directory in your FDS server.

Alternatively, you can copy the files from the Lesson20/start directory into the FDS flexGrocer directory.

5 In FlexBuilder, create a new Flex Project by using FDS, compiled locally in Flex Builder.

You could also choose to compile the application on the server as the page is viewed, but it is more efficient to place precompiled applications onto the server rather than have the user wait for the application to be compiled when it is first requested.

6 Click Next. Ensure that the Use default location for local Flex Data Services server check box is checked.

If you installed the Flex Server to a different location, you can specify that location and URL here instead of accepting the default.

7 Click Next. Give the project a unique name (such as FlexGrocer-FDS) and then specify the directory you created in step 3 for the Project Contents.

The process to create this Flex project is almost identical to the one you followed in Lesson 2, "Getting Started." In both situations you are telling Flex Builder where to find the files for your project. The only difference is that this time the files are located within a subdirectory of your FDS server.

8 Click Next. Specify EComm.mxml as your Main application file and bin as your Output folder. Then click Finish.

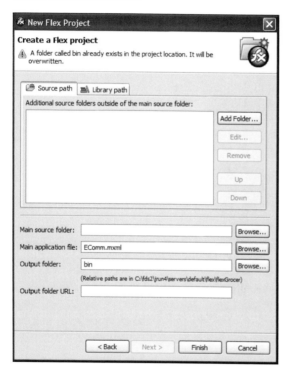

You should now be set to run the application through FDS. However, you still need to adjust the code in one file to allow the checkout process to work. This will be explained in the next few steps.

Understanding How the Flex Message Service Works

The FMS provides both a client API and a server-side service for creating messaging applications. The core purpose of these services is to enable messages to be asynchronously exchanged between Flex clients and the Flex server. There are a number of different places these messages could originate, such as the following:

- Java Message Service (JMS)
- ColdFusion event gateways
- Other Flex clients using the `<mx:Producer>` tag (not covered in this book)

There are a few important terms you should understand when working with FMS:

Message—A piece of data sent from a message producer through the messaging service to a consumer. A message consists of a header that describes the message and a body that contains the data for the message.

Consumer—An application that makes use of messages. By the end of this lesson, your Dashboard application will be a consumer.

Producer—The sender of a message.

Destination—An identifier for a place to which a producer sends a message. The FMS will route the message appropriately, based on its destination. This architecture makes it possible for the producers and consumers to be entirely *decoupled*, knowing nothing about each other.

Channel—A gateway to a message destination. Producers use channels to connect to the destination within FDS, and FDS uses channels to connect to the listening consumers.

Adapter—Elements that translate messages between the FDS and external messaging services. FDS ships with adapters for JMS, ColdFusion Gateways, and the ActionScript adapter, which is used to send messages to the Flash clients.

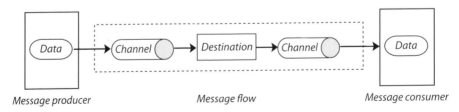

Message producer   Message flow   Message consumer

Enabling RemoteObject Calls to a ColdFusion Server

When using RemoteObject to communicate with a server in an application served by the FDS, the RemoteObject is inherently looking to communicate back to the FDS server. If you followed the setup directions in the appendix, "Setup Instructions," you have installed the FDS server and the ColdFusion server to run as two separate servers. This setup can greatly simplify configuration issues with the servers, but it unfortunately requires a bit of extra work to enable the application to retrieve data from the ColdFusion server instead of the FDS server. Normally, Flex applications served by the FDS server will use channels as defined in the server's services-config.xml file. This file lacks the necessary information to connect to your ColdFusion server, so you can dynamically add a custom channel to your `<mx:RemoteObject>` instance instead. Here, you can see a sample of the ActionScript 3.0 code to create a custom channel:

```
// Create a ChannelSet.
private var cs:ChannelSet = new ChannelSet();
// Create a Channel.
var customChannel:Channel = new AMFChannel("newAMF", URLtoGateway);
// Add the Channel to the ChannelSet.
cs.addChannel(customChannel);
// Assign the ChannelSet to a RemoteObject instance.
svc.channelSet = cs;
...
<mx:RemoteObject id="svc" ... />
```

To create a new channel, you first need to create an instance of the mx.messaging.ChannelSet class. A ChannelSet is a group of channels that are used to tell RemoteObject calls how to find their destination. Each ChannelSet can contain one or more *channels* (instances of classes in the mx.messaging.Channel package). In the example code, a new channel called customChannel is defined as a new AMFChannel; that is, a channel that would communicate over the Action Message Format (AMF) protocol. The constructor takes two arguments: a name for the channel and a URL to the Remoting Gateway. If you want to create a channel to talk to your local ColdFusion server, you can replace the URLtoGateway reference with **http://localhost:8300/flex2gateway/**. The customChannel is then added to the ChannelSet by using the ChannelSet's addChannel() method. Finally, the `<mx:RemoteObject>` tag has its channelSet specified with the newly created ChannelSet.

In this next exercise, you will create a custom channel to allow the EComm application to continue to leverage the ColdFusion server, even though it is running through your FDS server.

1 Open Checkout.mxml from the views/ecomm directory of your newly created flexGrocer directory.

Be sure to open the file located in the FDS root because the version of the file you have in the old flexGrocer directory does not need to have it specified.

2 Create a new private property within the script block in Checkout.mxml named cs of type ChannelSet, which contains an instance of a new ChannelSet.

```
private var cs:ChannelSet = new ChannelSet();
```

If you used the code-completion features of Flex Builder, the ChannelSet class was automatically imported for you; otherwise, you need to manually add the following:

```
import mx.messaging.ChannelSet;
```

3 Create a new method called initApp(), which returns void. As the first line of this method, create a local variable named customChannel of datatype Channel, which contains a new AMFChannel with an ID of my-cfamf and a destination of http://localhost:8300/flex2gateway/.

```
var customChannel:Channel = new AMFChannel("my-cfamf",
    ➥ "http://localhost:8300/flex2gateway/");
```

If the imports for both the Channel and AMFChannel classes were not automatically imported for you, you need to manually add those imports to your file.

```
import mx.messaging.Channel;
import mx.messaging.channels.AMFChannel;
```

4 Still in the initApp() method, add the new customChannel variable to your cs ChannelSet, using the addChannel() method.

```
cs.addChannel(customChannel);
```

By adding the new AMFChannel to the ChannelSet, any elements using this ChannelSet now know how to communicate with your ColdFusion server.

5 Still in the initApp() method, set the channelSet property of the RemoteObject named svc to be cs.

```
svc.channelSet = cs;
```

This should complete the loop and inform your RemoteObject how to communicate with your separate ColdFusion server.

6 Add a `creationComplete` event handler to the root `<mx:VBox>` tag for the Checkout component. Specify `initApp()` as the method to be called when the `creationComplete` Event occurs.

```
<mx:VBox xmlns:mx="http://www.adobe.com/2006/mxml"
    xmlns:v="views.ecomm.*"
    creationComplete="initApp()">
```

If you save and test your FDS version of the EComm application, it should continue to run as it did in previous lessons. An order number will be sent back upon order completion because it again knows how to communicate with the ColdFusion server.

Configuring a Message Destination

To begin working with messaging in a Flex application, you need to configure FDS to recognize the incoming messages. This configuration will be done in the messaging-config.xml file.

Here, you can see a sample messaging-config.xml file:

```
<?xml version="1.0" encoding="UTF-8"?>
<service id="message-service"
    class="flex.messaging.services.MessageService"
    messageTypes="flex.messaging.messages.AsyncMessage">
    <adapters>
        <adapter-definition id="actionscript"
            class="flex.messaging.services.messaging.adapters.ActionScriptAdapter"
                default="true"/>
        <adapter-definition id="jms"
            class="flex.messaging.services.messaging.adapters.JMSAdapter"/>
        <adapter-definition id="cfgateway"
            class="coldfusion.flex.CFEventGatewayAdapter"/>
    </adapters>
    <destination id="TypeSalesUpdate">
        <adapter ref="cfgateway"/>
        <properties>
            <gatewayid>*</gatewayid>
        </properties>
        <channels>
            <channel ref="my-rtmp"/>
            <channel ref="my-polling-amf"/>
        </channels>
    </destination>
</service>
```

Notice that the file has two main sections. First, adapters are defined that list the various types of system FDS to which Flex can send and receive messages. The three default adapters are listed here. If any custom adapters are written for the project, they also would be referenced in the adapters section.

Next, a destination is defined. The destination has an id, which is the name you will use in the MXML tags. (You'll see this in use in the next section.) This is followed by a reference to the proper adapter for the destination. In this example, the message is coming from a ColdFusion event gateway, so the cfgateway adapter is used. Any specific properties, which need to be set, are then added in the properties node. This example uses the gatewayid property of *, which enables the message to define a specific gateway, as opposed to restricting it to a specific event gateway from the server. Finally, the channels that this destination can use are specified. They reference channel-definition nodes in the services-config.xml file.

1 Open messaging-config.xml from your FDS server (the default directory is *driveroot*:/fds2/jrun4/servers/default/flex/WEB-INF/flex on Windows). Make a copy of the file before you start because the FDS server does not start if there are errors in this file. Add an adapter definition with an id of cfgateway and a class of coldfusion.flex.CFEventGatewayAdapter.

```
<adapter-definition id="cfgateway"
   class="coldfusion.flex.CFEventGatewayAdapter"/>
```

With this addition, the completed file should read as follows:

```
<?xml version="1.0" encoding="UTF-8"?>
<service id="message-service"
   class="flex.messaging.services.MessageService"
   messageTypes="flex.messaging.messages.AsyncMessage">
   <adapters>
   <adapter-definition id="actionscript"
      class="flex.messaging.services.messaging.adapters.ActionScriptAdapter"
      default="true" />
   <adapter-definition id="jms"
      class="flex.messaging.services.messaging.adapters.JMSAdapter"/>
   <adapter-definition id="cfgateway"
      class="coldfusion.flex.CFEventGatewayAdapter"/>
   </adapters>

</service>
```

2 Open typeSalesGateway.xml from the Lesson20/assets folder and copy all the text to the clipboard. Paste this code just after the closing adapter's node of the messaging-config.xml file:

```xml
<?xml version="1.0" encoding="UTF-8"?>
<service id="message-service"
   class="flex.messaging.services.MessageService"
   messageTypes="flex.messaging.messages.AsyncMessage">
   <adapters>
      <adapter-definition id="actionscript"
      class="flex.messaging.services.messaging.adapters.ActionScriptAdapter"
      default="true"/>
      <adapter-definition id="jms"
      class="flex.messaging.services.messaging.adapters.JMSAdapter"/>
      <adapter-definition id="cfgateway"
      class="coldfusion.flex.CFEventGatewayAdapter"/>
   </adapters>
   <destination id="TypeSalesUpdate">
      <adapter ref="cfgateway"/>
      <properties>
         <gatewayid>*</gatewayid>
      </properties>
      <channels>
         <channel ref="my-rtmp"/>
         <channel ref="my-polling-amf"/>
      </channels>
   </destination>
</service>
```

❋ **NOTE:** The code you copied in has several comments, which have been omitted here.

This defines a destination to enable the ColdFusion server to notify your Flex application of changes to sales.

3 Save and close messaging-config.xml.

4 Restart the Flex server and verify that there are no errors.

Using the <mx:Consumer> Tag

For your Flex application to make use of messages from the FDS, you use the <mx:Consumer> tag. This tag specifies which destination the Flex application will listen to. The following is an example of the syntax of the <mx:Consumer> tag:

```
<mx:Consumer id="some id"
   destination="destination name"
   message="event handler"
   fault="event handler"/>
```

With this simple syntax, you can specify an identifier for the tag, the name of the destination, and event handlers for the message or fault events. Whenever an incoming message is heard, the message event is fired, containing an mx.messaging.events.MessageEvent object. The body of the message can be referenced by the event.message.body property.

In addition to adding the tag, one more step is required to register a consumer: to call the subscribe() method of the consumer.

1 Open Dashboard.mxml from your flexGrocer directory.

Alternatively, you can open this file from the Lesson20/start directory and save it in the new flexGrocer directory.

2 Just after the opening <mx:Application> tag, add an <mx:Consumer> tag with an id of consumer, a destination of TypeSalesUpdate, and event handlers for the message and fault events.

```
<mx:Consumer id="consumer"
    destination="TypeSalesUpdate"
    message="messageHandler(event)"
    fault="faultHandler(event)"/>
```

The destination is set to match the destination id you specified in the messaging-config.xml file.

3 In the script block, add a faultHandler() function, which takes an argument of type MessageFaultEvent. The body of this method should use an Alert to display the event.faultString.

```
private function faultHandler(event:MessageFaultEvent):void{
    Alert.show(event.faultString);
}
```

If the import for the MessageFaultEvent was not automatically added, you need to manually add that import statement. The same is true for the Alert class.

```
import mx.messaging.events.MessageFaultEvent;
import mx.controls.Alert;
```

If any issues arise in messaging, you will see the error in an Alert box. Otherwise, you might not be aware of any issues.

4 Still in the script block, add a messageHandler() function, which takes an argument of type messageEvent.

```
private function messageHandler(event:MessageEvent):void{
    type.dp = new ArrayCollection(event.message.body.ATYPESALES as Array);
    startDate.selectedDate = event.message.body.STARTDATE;
    endDate.selectedDate = event.message.body.ENDDATE;
    dashboardWS.getSalesData.send();
}
```

If the import for the MessageEvent was not automatically added, you need to manually add that import statement.

```
import mx.messaging.events.MessageEvent;
```

The data coming back from the FDS via the ColdFusion gateway is an object with an array of Sales data called ATYPESALES, and STARTDATE and ENDDATE properties. The sales data is passed into the type chart, so it can be graphed; then the start and end dates are used to update the interface. Finally, the getSalesData service is used to retrieve the latest data for the other two charts as well.

5 Find the init() method. Just before the end of the method, add consumer.subscribe(), to subscribe to the TypeSalesUpdate destination.

```
private function init():void{
    startDate.selectedDate = new Date(2006,3,1);
    endDate.selectedDate = new Date(2006,4,1);
    catRPC.send();
    getData();
    consumer.subscribe();
}
```

Subscribing to a destination enables you to receive the messages that the destination sends.

6 In two separate browsers, run the EComm and Dashboard applications. In the EComm application, add a product to the cart, check out, and complete the checkout process.

When the sale is completed, the pie chart automatically updates itself to reflect the latest sales data.

7 Save and close Dashboard.mxml.

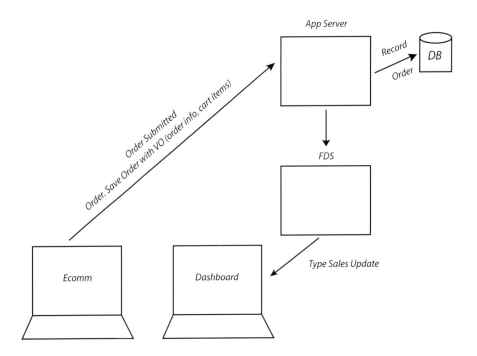

You have now reconfigured your application to receive real-time updates to the Dashboard data when a new order is placed. When you place an order from the e-commerce application, it calls a method in Order.cfc on the ColdFusion server. The order is recorded in the system. Order.cfc sends a message to the event gateway. The consumer in the Dashboard application has subscribed to receive any messages from the gateway. So, when this new message arrives from the ColdFusion server, the Dashboard application is immediately notified and uses the new data to update its model. Using data binding, the charts respond to the change in this model and update the screen display.

What You Have Learned

In this lesson, you have:

- Learned about the FMS (pages 486–490)

- Set up a Flex Builder Project to use FDS (pages 486–489)

- Enabled RemoteObject calls (pages 491–493)

- Configured a Flex destination (pages 493–495)

- Used an <mx:Consumer> tag (pages 495–498)

What You Will Learn

In this lesson, you will:

- Conceptually understand how the Data Management Service functions
- Configure the Data Management Service to work with a destination that uses ColdFusion components
- Use a Flex Builder 2 wizard to create ColdFusion components that implement Data Management Service functionality
- Retrieve data from a database using the Data Management Service
- Use an editable DataGrid and have the changes synchronized with the server tier data store
- Create an add and delete application using the Data Management Service

Approximate Time

This lesson takes approximately 1 hour and 30 minutes to complete.

Lesson Files

Media Files:

None

Starting Files:

Lesson21/start/DMS_2.mxml

Completed Files:

Lesson21/complete/DMS_1.mxml
Lesson21/complete/DMS_2.mxml
Lesson21/complete/valueObjects/SmallProduct.as (created by Flex Builder CFC Wizard)
Lesson21/complete/flex2tfs/dmsCFCs/SmallProduct.cfc (created by Flex Builder CFC Wizard)
Lesson21/complete/flex2tfs/dmsCFCs/SmallProductAssembler.cfc (created by Flex Builder CFC Wizard)
Lesson21/complete/flex2tfs/dmsCFCs/SmallProductDAO.cfc (created by Flex Builder CFC Wizard)

LESSON 21

Synchronizing Data with Adobe Flex Data Services

This lesson will introduce you to the Flex Data Services' Data Management Service, and explain how to use it to synchronize data between client and server. Keep in mind that this is an introduction only—it would take many times the number of pages in this lesson to fully explore all the amazing features of the Data Management Service. In the few pages in this lesson, you will see how to harness some of the powerful features when using Flex Data Services 2 and ColdFusion together.

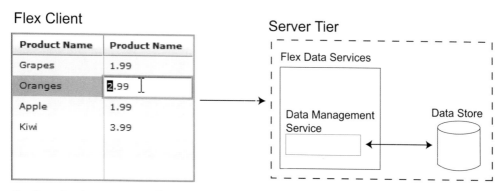

Flex Data Services automatically propagates a changed DataGrid control to edit the remote data store.

Introducing the Data Management Service

Adobe Flex Data Services 2 (FDS) provides the Data Management Service that assists in data synchronization and data replication between the Flex front end and your back end. The back end could be written in Java or ColdFusion, for example. In this lesson, you will use ColdFusion and take advantage of some wizards built into Flex Builder that automatically create the required ColdFusion components needed for the Data Management Service.

The Data Management Service greatly eases your work when you're creating applications that use distributed data. A client-side DataService component, instantiated in MXML or ActionScript, calls methods on a server-side destination to perform such activities as providing data to client-side data collections and synchronizing changes at the client to the server. Notice the sentence said the "DataService component," not "you the developer writing code," calls methods. The DataService component manages data at the client, and the Data Management Service manages the distribution of data among multiple clients and the server-side data resources.

A key factor in successfully implementing the Data Management Service is proper configuration. To configure the service properly, you need to know the vocabulary involved with the technology.

The first term to understand is a *destination*. A destination is an endpoint for a message (data) where the message will be acted upon. Destinations are configurable in the data-management-config.xml file. When configuring a simple ColdFusion destination, you specify, among other things, a destination name, the ColdFusion component (CFC) where method requests are sent, and the primary key value of the database table the CFC is working with.

Another item specified in the destination is the message channel that the destination should use to communicate. The message channels are part of the overall Flex messaging service. Possible channels to use are Action Message Format (AMF), HTTP, secure AMF, secure HTTP, and Real-Time Messaging Protocol (RTMP). The basic communication model of the Data Management Service is shown in the following example:

When a message hits the destination on the client side, it is processed. On the server side, the Data Management Service often interacts with a data store.

The data adapter controls how Flex Data Services works with a particular interface, like a CFC or Java object. The data adapter updates the persistent data store. By default, three adapters are included with Flex Data Services: the Java adapter, the ActionScript adapter, and the Hibernate adapter. A ColdFusion adapter can be used simply by inserting it in a configuration file, which you will do in the first task in this lesson.

Once configured, you can then use methods of the DataService object to synchronize data between the Flex client and the back end.

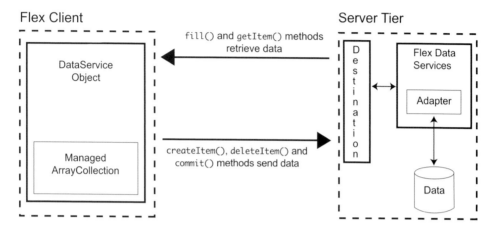

Configuring Data Management Services

The following configuration instructions assume you have installed the following software according to the setup instructions included in the Appendix, "Setup Instructions":

- Flex Builder 2
- Flex Data Services
- ColdFusion
- ColdFusion Extensions for Flex Builder 2

You will make changes to two files to configure Flex Data Services to work with the Data Management Service using ColdFusion as the back end.

▼ **CAUTION!** You must be very careful when making changes to these files. One mistake or comment in the wrong place can cause Flex Data Services to not start.

Flex Data Services provides the exact code, or at least a template, for you to use during configuration. The files containing the configuration help are in the directory *driveroot*/fds2/resources/config. In this task, you will be copying data from files in this directory and pasting it into the actual configuration files in the folder *driveroot*/fds2/jrun4/servers/default/flex/WEB-INF/flex.

1 Locate the *driveroot*/fds2/jrun4/servers/default/flex/WEB-INF/flex directory. Make copies of the following files:

- services-config.xml

- data-management-config.xml

By making copies of the two files you will be modifying in the next steps of this task, you have the originals to refer to if something should go wrong.

2 Be sure that Flex Data Services is not running. Open the file services-config.xml located in *driveroot*/fds2/resources/config. Locate the two channel definitions from lines 137–160 that are commented as ColdFusion specific RTMP channel and ColdFusion specific HTTP channel. Copy this block of code:

```
<!-- ColdFusion specific RTMP channel -->
<channel-definition id="cf-dataservice-rtmp"
   class="mx.messaging.channels.RTMPChannel">
   <endpoint uri="rtmp://{server.name}:2048"
      class="flex.messaging.endpoints.RTMPEndpoint"/>
   <properties>
      <idle-timeout-minutes>20</idle-timeout-minutes>
      <serialization>
      <!-- This must be turned off for any CF channel -->
         <instantiate-types>false</instantiate-types>
      </serialization>
   </properties>
</channel-definition>

<!-- ColdFusion specific HTTP channel -->
<channel-definition id="cf-polling-amf"
   class="mx.messaging.channels.AMFChannel">
   <endpoint uri="http://{server.name}:
      {server.port}/{context.root}/messagebroker/cfamfpolling"
      class="flex.messaging.endpoints.AMFEndpoint"/>
   <properties>
      <serialization>
      <!-- This must be turned off for any CF channel -->
         <instantiate-types>false</instantiate-types>
      </serialization>
      <polling-enabled>true</polling-enabled>
      <polling-interval-seconds>8</polling-interval-seconds>
   </properties>
</channel-definition>
```

This XML enables these message channels that will be used when configuring ColdFusion destinations.

3 Open the file services-config.xml from the *driveroot*/fds2/jrun4/servers/default/flex/
WEB-INF/flex directory. Locate the tag that ENDS the channels node of the XML,
`</channels>`. Paste the copied block of code just ABOVE the closing `</channels>` tag.

You have moved the channel configurations you need from the "helper" file to the actual
configuration file.

4 Open the file data-management-config.xml from the *driveroot*/fds2/jrun4/servers/
default/flex/WEB-INF/flex directory. You will see an `<adapters>` node. Add the following
as the last line of XML in the node:

```
<adapter-definition id="coldfusion-dao"
   class="coldfusion.flex.CFDataServicesAdapter"/>
```

This defines the adapter that will be used with ColdFusion.

5 Be sure your adapters node appears as follows:

```
<adapters>
   <adapter-definition id="actionscript"
      class="flex.data.adapters.ASObjectAdapter" default="true"/>
   <adapter-definition id="java-dao"
      class="flex.data.adapters.JavaAdapter"/>
   <adapter-definition id="coldfusion-dao"
      class="coldfusion.flex.CFDataServicesAdapter"/>
</adapters>
```

This enables the adapter that you will use with ColdFusion.

6 Open the file data-management-config.xml from the directory *driveroot*/fds2/resources/
config. Locate the destination definition from lines 288–395 that is commented as
ColdFusion Sample - Contact sample application. Copy this block of code. Be sure you
get the entire destination definition marked by the `<destination id="cfcontact">` and
`</destination>` tags.

This defines a destination for a sample application, but not for what you need. After you
paste the code into the correct location, you will modify the XML for the application you
are building in this lesson.

7 Open the data-management-config.xml file from the *driveroot*/fds2/jrun4/servers/
default/flex/WEB-INF/flex directory (you added an adapter definition to this file in step
4). Paste the destination definition you just copied BELOW the closing `</adapters>` and
ABOVE the closing `</service>` tag.

You have moved a destination definition you need from the "helper" file to the actual
configuration file. You will now edit the destination definition so it contains the information for the application you are building in this lesson.

8 Change the comment at the top of the definition as shown:

```
<!-- ========================================= -->
<!-- flex2tfs Lesson 21 application-->
<!-- ========================================= -->
```

The comment now reflects the use of the destination.

9 Just below the comment, change the id of the destination so it is equal to flex2tfs:

```
<destination id="flex2tfs">
```

When you create a DataService object in your MXML, you will use this id value.

10 In the properties node, change the component value to flex2tfs.dmsCFCs.smallProductAssembler:

```
<component>flex2tfs.dmsCFCs.smallProductAssembler</component>
```

The CFC indicated will be created automatically by a wizard and acts as the front end to code that will update the data store.

11 Locate the metadata node, and change the property attribute's value to prodID.

```
<metadata>
    <identity property="prodID"/>
</metadata>
```

This defines the primary key value of the database table.

12 Save both the data-management-config.xml and services-config.xml files, and then close them.

These configuration files will be used when you start FDS.

13 Start Flex Data Services by opening a console window (DOS prompt) and moving to the *driveroot*/fds2/jrun4/bin directory. Then enter **jrun –start default**. Be sure FDS starts with no errors being shown. To stop the service, use the Ctrl+C key combination, or close the console window. To restart the service, if you are still in the console, just press the up arrow and it will bring back to the prompt what you previously typed.

You will need to leave the console window open when you are using FDS as FDS will only be running while the console window is open.

14 Start the configured ColdFusion by opening another console window (DOS prompt) and moving to the *driveroot*/cfusion/bin directory. Then enter **jrun –start cfusion**. Be sure ColdFusion starts with no errors being shown. To stop the service use the Ctrl+C key com-bination, or close the console window. To restart the service, if you are still in the console, just press the up arrow and it will bring back to the prompt what you previously typed.

You will need to leave the console window open when you are using ColdFusion.

Creating the Data Management CFCs

The Data Management Service requires a set of CFCs that implement three design patterns:

- **data transfer object**—A single object instance, or value object, which you can think of as a single row of data from the database table

- **data access object**—The code that reads and writes to the data store

- **transfer object assembler**—The code that manages communication between Flex Data Services and the data access object

> **TIP:** Data transfer object is Sun's new name for value object, which you may be more familiar with.

Luckily, you do not have to write those three CFCs for every database table you want to have as a data store for a Flex application. A wizard is available that creates these CFCs for you automatically. Not only that, the wizard also creates an ActionScript class that is the value object needed in the Flex application.

1 Create a Flex project that will use Flex Data Services. Select the option to compile the application on the server. Click Next.

When an application will use Flex Data Services you must state that when creating the project.

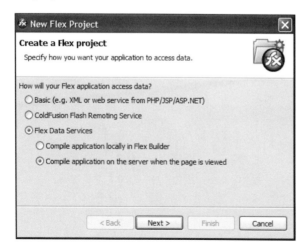

2 You can use the default location for the Flex Data Services server. Click Next.

If you do not use the default Flex Data Services installation and change this path, then FDS remembers the new path the next time you create a project that uses FDS.

3 Supply the Project name of **DMS**, set the Project location to ***driveroot*/fds2/jrun4/ servers/default/flex/flex2tfs**, and specify the Main application file as **DMS_1.mxml**. Click Finish to create the project and main application file.

▶ **TIP:** The complete path does not exist, so you will need to create a directory. Either just type in the complete path and Flex Builder will create the directory, or click the Make New Folder button after you click Browse.

You now have the project set up to create MXML applications that will run under Flex Data Services.

4 Right-click on the DMS project and choose New > Folder. Create a folder named valueObjects.

The valueObjects folder will be the destination for the value object automatically created in the wizard.

5 From the main menu, choose File > New > Other. Open the Simple folder and select Project. Click Next. Make the Project name **dmsCFCs**. Uncheck the Use default option and specify the path as ***driveroot*\cfusionFlexTFS\servers\cfusion\cfusion-ear\ cfusion-war\flex2tfs\dmsCFCs**. Click Finish.

> **TIP:** The complete path does not exist, so you will need to create two directories. Either just type in the complete path and Flex Builder will create the directories, or click the Make New Folder button after you click Browse.

This creates the project and directory where the CFCs will be created in the wizard. The path to the web root of the ColdFusion server may not be familiar to you. This is the web root when ColdFusion is installed with the multiserver option.

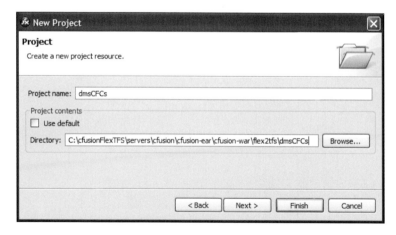

> **TIP:** If you will be using Flex Builder with ColdFusion files, you would be well served to install CFEclipse to get tag help and other features for ColdFusion files. Go to www.cfeclipse.org/ for more information and plug-in installation instructions.

6 Show the Remote Development Services (RDS) view by selecting Window > Other Views, then open the ColdFusion folder and select RDS Dataview. Click OK.

This displays the view that exposes DSNs you have access to through RDS.

7 Alter the RDS configuration by selecting Window > Preferences and then checking the RDS Configuration option. Click on the localhost RDS server so you can alter its configuration. Change the Port Number option to 8300, and uncheck the Prompt for Password option. Click OK.

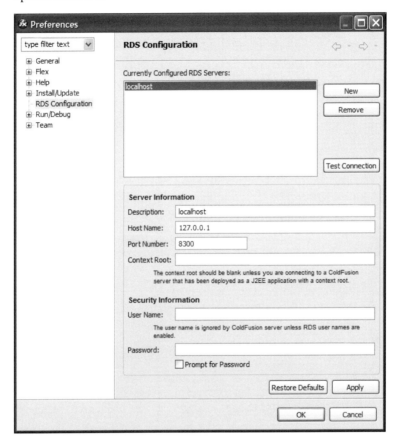

These changes match the configured ColdFusion instance you are using, which runs on port 8300 and has no password for RDS.

8 In the RDS Dataview view, click the plus sign in front of localhost, then flex2, then Tables, until you see the SmallProduct table. Right-click on SmallProduct and choose ColdFusion Wizards > Create CFC.

You are selecting a database table from which to create a set of CFCs.

This will open the dialog box where you will create the needed CFCs and ActionScript value object.

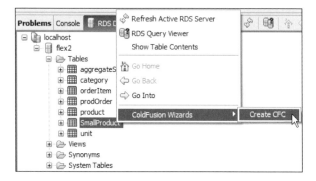

9 Provide the following values in the dialog box (leave all other entries as default):

CFC Folder: /dmsCFCs

CFC Type: Flex Data Service Assembler CFCs

Check the Create an ActionScript value object in addition to the CFC(s) checkbox

AS Folder: /DMS/valueObjects

AS Package Name: valueObjects

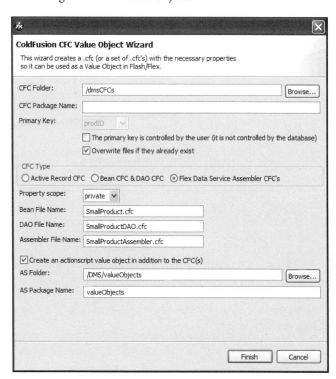

10 Click Finish.

You will see the four files created in different editors. Check to see that all the files are in the specified directories.

Using Data Management Service Data in an MXML Application

Finally, the preliminaries are done and you can write a Flex application that uses Flex Data Services' Data Management Service. In this case, you will create a DataGrid that is populated with data from FDS, and then make the DataGrid editable and see that the changes to the DataGrid are automatically sent back to the data store—in this case, an Access database.

1 Return to the file DMS_1.mxml, add a `creationComplete` event to the `<mx:Application>` tag, and have the event handler call a function named `initApp()`.

You will use the `initApp()` function to initialize key variables for the application.

2 Insert an `<mx:Script>` block just below the Application tag. In the block, import the following classes:

```
import mx.data.DataService;
import mx.collections.ArrayCollection;
import valueObjects.SmallProduct;
```

These three classes are going to do an amazing amount of work for you. The DataService class is how you will associate your DataService object to the destination you defined earlier. You've used the ArrayCollection class many times, but this time you will take advantage of the fact that changes to it can be tracked by Flex Data Services, and those changes can be automatically transmitted back to the data store. The SmallProduct class is the value object created by the wizard and will be used to represent the rows of the database.

3 Below the `import` statements, create the following three private variables of the data type indicated. Make the `products` variable bindable.

```
private var ds:DataService;
private var temp:SmallProduct;
[Bindable]
private var products:ArrayCollection;
```

You will need the ds object and the products object later in the lesson. The `temp` variable is needed only so the SmallProduct class is compiled into the SWF.

4 Open the SmallProduct.as file and note the metadata that reads `[RemoteClass(alias= "SmallProduct")]`. Then close the SmallProduct.as value object class definition.

This metadata is what ties the ActionScript value object to the CFC value object created from the database table, as indicated by the [RemoteClass] metadata.

▼ **CAUTION!** If you do not create a variable of the type SmallProduct, as done in step 3, you will get neither a compile nor a run-time error. The application will fail silently as it sends untyped objects back to the server, and the CFCs will not know what to do with them.

5 Below the variable declarations, create a private function named initApp() of the data type void. In the function, set the products variable equal to a new ArrayCollection. Set the ds variable equal to a new DataService object, passing the string flex2tfs as an argument. Finally, use the fill() method of the DataService object to populate the products ArrayCollection object.

The argument passed to the DataService constructor is the id given to the destination created in the first task of this lesson. The id was defined in the XML that you pasted into the data-management-config.xml configuration file, and then edited.

The fill() method uses the DataService object created to go to the database table associated with this particular destination, retrieve all the records, and place them into the products ArrayCollection object.

▶ **TIP:** If you want to retrieve just one row from the database, use the getItem() method.

6 Check to be sure your application so far appears as follows:

```
<?xml version="1.0" encoding="utf-8"?>
<mx:Application xmlns:mx="http://www.adobe.com/2006/mxml"
    layout="absolute"
    creationComplete="initApp()">

    <mx:Script>
        <![CDATA[
            import mx.data.DataService;
            import mx.collections.ArrayCollection;
            import valueObjects.SmallProduct;

            private var ds:DataService;
            private var temp:SmallProduct;
            [Bindable]
            private var products:ArrayCollection;

            private function initApp():void{
                products=new ArrayCollection();
                ds=new DataService("flex2tfs");
                ds.fill(products);
            }
        ]]>
    </mx:Script>
</mx:Application>
```

In this lesson, you have completed the following tasks in preparation for displaying data retrieved by Flex Data Services' Data Management Service:

- Configured the Data Management Service—in particular, you created a destination associated with CFCs that work with a particular database table.

- Used a wizard to create three CFCs and a value object needed to work with the Data Management Service.

- Wrote the code to retrieve data into an ArrayCollection.

7 Below the script block, insert an `<mx:DataGrid>` tag with an id of `prodGrid` and a `dataProvider` bound to the `products` ArrayCollection.

```
<mx:DataGrid id="productGrid" dataProvider="{products}"/>
```

The DataGrid displays the data retrieved by the DataService object.

8 Run the application. You should see the DataGrid display three columns of data for four products.

When this example runs correctly, you know you have configured Flex Data Services properly and used the Data Management Service CFC wizard correctly. If the application does not run correctly, you should check in the configuration files you edited in task 1, "Configuring Data Management Services," of this lesson. Very carefully walk through the configuration file edits again.

9 Change the `<mx:DataGrid>` tag into a tag set with opening and closing DataGrid tags. Nest an `<mx:columns>` tag set in the DataGrid tags. Nested in the columns tag set, insert an `<mx:DataGridColumn>` tag with the `dataField` set equal to `prodName` and the `headerText` set equal to Product Name. Insert another `<mx:DataGridColumn>` tag with the `dataField` set equal to cost and the `headerText` set equal to Cost.

```
<mx:DataGrid id="prodGrid"
   dataProvider="{products}">
   <mx:columns>
      <mx:DataGridColumn dataField="prodName" headerText="Product Name"/>
      <mx:DataGridColumn dataField="cost" headerText="Cost"/>
   </mx:columns>
</mx:DataGrid>
```

You will soon make the DataGrid editable. You do not want to be able to edit the prodID field, however, which is the primary key field of the database table you are working with. By specifying these two DataGridColumns, the prodID field will not be visible in the DataGrid.

10 Open the SmallProduct.as value object class definition. Note the [Managed] metadata. Close the value object file.

Because this value object is marked as managed, any changes to objects of this value object class will automatically be sent back to the data store.

11 In the DataGrid, set the editable property equal to true.

12 Run the application and make a couple of changes to the data in the DataGrid. Refresh the page to be sure you are reading the data from the server side.

▶ **TIP:** At this point every keystroke is being sent back to the server for updating. Of course you would not want this in a production environment. Read more about the commit() method to control this.

Creating and Deleting with the Data Management Service

You have seen how to retrieve data using the fill() method, and how to update data with an editable DataGrid. You will now create a small application to create and delete products.

1 Copy the file DMS_2.mxml from your Lesson21/start directory to *driveroot*/fds2/jrun4/servers/default/flex/flex2tfs. Return to Flex Builder, open that file, then run the DMS_2.mxml application.

Click on one of the products in the DataGrid, and you see that it populates the form and enables the Delete button.

This is the starting file for creating and deleting data with the Data Management Service. The file contains nothing you haven't already done in this book; the only FDS functionality used is the fill() method.

2 Locate the deleteProduct() function. As the first line of code in the function, use the deleteItem() method of the ds DataService object to delete the selectedItem from the DataGrid.

```
ds.deleteItem(prodGrid.selectedItem);
```

3 As the second line of code in the function, call the resetForm() method.

4 Run the application. Select a product and click the Delete button.

You see that the product is removed from the DataGrid. Refresh the page to be sure it is removed from the data store.

The product disappeared from the DataGrid upon deletion because the product was part of the ArrayCollection: it was removed from the ArrayCollection, and the DataGrid's `dataProvider` uses a binding to the DataGrid; hence, the DataGrid shows the latest and greatest data.

5 Locate the `createProduct()` function. As the first lines of code in the function, assign the product name and cost values from the form to the `product` variable. You will have to use the `Number()` function to convert the text gathered in the cost TextInput control to be able to assign it to the Number typed cost variable from the SmallProduct value object.

```
product.prodName=productNameInput.text;
product.cost=Number(costInput.text);
```

This builds a new SmallProduct object to be inserted into the data store via the Data Management Service.

6 Use the `createItem()` method of the ds DataService object to create the `product` item in the data store.

```
ds.createItem(product);
```

This will insert the new product in the products ArrayCollection, as well as send the new product to the server side to be inserted into the data store.

7 As the last line of code in the function, call the `resetForm()` method. Also, check to be sure your completed `createProduct()` function appears as shown.

The `resetForm()` method simply clears the form and resets the application to its beginning state.

```
private function createProduct():void{
    product.prodName=productNameInput.text;
    product.cost=Number(costInput.text);
    ds.createItem(product);
    resetForm();
}
```

8 Run the application. Input new data for a product and click the Add button.

You see that the new product is added to the DataGrid. Refresh the page to be sure it was also added to the data store.

Where to Go from Here

As mentioned in the introduction to this lesson, you have only begun to scratch the surface of the power of the Data Management Service. Many topics still need your attention to fully grasp the power of this service. They include:

- Working with the DataService with autoCommit turned off. This is when you decide data should be sent back to the data store instead of letting FDS make the decision.

- Using the AsyncToken class. This permits you to store data with messages returned from data interactions.

- Working with database tables that have joins. This permits you to work with more complicated database tables. This is referred to as "hierarchical data" in the Flex Data Services documentation.

- Securing destinations. This permits you to add security to a configured destination.

- Clustering Flex Data Services. This gives information on using FDS in a clustered environment.

- Resolving data synchronization conflicts. What happens if two or more users try to update the same piece of data? There is actually a conflict resolution API to assist implementation.

What You Have Learned

In this lesson, you have:

- Developed a conceptual understanding of the Data Management Service (pages 502–503)

- Configured the Data Management Service (pages 503–506)

- Created the ColdFusion components needed by the Data Management Service (pages 507–512)

- Written two applications that synchronize data using the Data Management Service (pages 512–516)

What Will You Learn

In this lesson, you will:

- Use prebuilt behaviors in Flex to fade in the display of a component

- Use prebuilt transitions in Flex to smooth out the change from one state to another

Approximate Time

This lesson takes approximately 45 minutes to complete.

Lesson Files

Media Files:

None

Starting Files:

Lesson22/start/EComm.mxml
Lesson22/start/as/ecomm.as
Lesson22/start/views/ecomm/GroceryDetail.mxml

Completed Files:

Lesson22/complete/EComm.mxml
Lesson22/complete/as/ecomm.as
Lesson22/complete/views/ecomm/GroceryDetail.mxml

LESSON 22

Creating Transitions and Behaviors

You can apply dynamic effects to your application using behaviors and transitions that can include animation and/or sounds. These effects can be based on application or user triggers, which cause behavior or transition to occur. Content is the most important consideration, but animations and sound can also greatly enhance the user experience—especially in dynamic presentation interfaces.

Behaviors are dynamic effects that can be applied directly to Flex components, whereas transitions are dynamic effects applied to view states. Animations can often enhance the user's experience when navigating throughout an application. In this lesson, you will modify the FlexGrocer application so that the transitions between states are smoother and components are displayed using a fade-in effect.

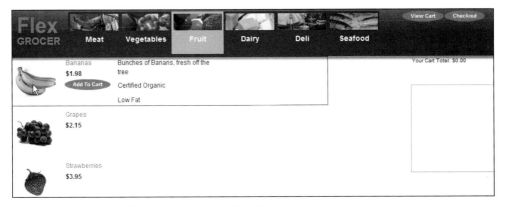

Grocery item details will be displayed using a WipeRight transition.

Introducing Behaviors and Transitions

Behaviors and transitions enable you to add animation and sound to objects in your Flex application.

Using Behaviors on Components

Behaviors are prebuilt animations and sounds that can be applied directly to components, including user-defined components. Transitions are simply effects that are applied to application states used within an application. Some examples of effects that can be applied to components or application states include the following:

- Fading in/fading out
- Dissolving in/dissolving out
- Moving or resizing a component
- Rotating a component
- Zooming
- Wiping left/right/up/down
- Using other visual effects such as glow and iris
- Using sound effects

Content is, of course, the most important part of the FlexGrocer application, and at first glance it may seem that adding animation is not necessary. However, animation can greatly enhance the user experience. In the current FlexGrocer application you have built to this point, many of the transitions between components and application states are not optimal and appear jerky and sudden. Animation in the FlexGrocer application will serve many useful purposes, including these:

- Drawing the users' attention to items changing on the screen and giving visual cues about where their attention should be focused
- Enhancing the user experience using movement and animation
- Using effects to suggest to the user which elements of an application are interactive

When you click a grocery category in the FlexGrocer application, the appropriate component just appears. In this lesson, you will use a prebuilt fade-in effect to smooth out the display of the custom component and to draw the end users' attention to the right place.

When applied to components, behaviors have two parts:

- **Trigger**—An action such as a user clicking a button, a component coming into focus, or a component becoming visible

- **Effect**—A visible or audible change to the component that occurs over a period of time

Components have triggers, but they do not do anything until you associate them with an action. The trigger is *not* an event. A button has both a mouseDownEventEffect trigger and a regular mouseDown event. The trigger itself is what causes the event to fire, whereas events specify a specific custom event handler that fires when the event occurs. When you use a mouseDownEventEffect trigger, you do not specify an event handler; you specify the behavior that you want to occur. It is possible to specify multiple effects when a trigger is fired. For example, when a user presses the mouse button, you could have a window resize and fade out. The triggers you can use with behaviors include the following:

- focusInEffect

- focusOutEffect

- hideEffect

- mouseDownEffect

- mouseUpEffect

- rolloutEffect

- rolloverEffect

- showEffect

To apply an effect to a component, you set the trigger name property equal to the name of the Effect class. You can declare only one effect when you define the trigger inline in the component, and you cannot customize the effect in any way. Here is an example of applying an effect to a List control when it is first displayed:

```
<mx:List id="myList" showEffect="Fade"/>
```

If you want to customize the event, you can define a reusable tag and specify the available property, in this case duration, which instructs Flex to perform the effect over a duration of milliseconds, as follows:

```
<mx:Dissolve id="myDissolve" duration="2000"/>
```

You can then apply the customized effect to the targets by using data binding, as follows:

```
<mx:Button id="sendButton" mouseDownEffect="{myDissolve}"/>
```

You can apply multiple effects (with the same trigger) to a component by using the <mx:Parallel> and the <mx:Sequence> tags. The <mx:Parallel> tag specifies that the effects will occur all at the same time, whereas the <mx:Sequentce> tag specifies that the events will occur in order. It is possible to nest <mx:Parallel> and <mx:Sequence> tags within one another to generate more complex animations. You will use these tags to build complex effects later in this lesson.

Using Transitions on View States

Transitions enable you to apply effects to view states, which then enable you to vary the content and appearance of a component in response to a user interaction. Transitions are great for creating much smoother changes between states. Transitions are different from behaviors; they apply to application states, whereas behaviors apply to components. You can apply one or more effects to one or more components in a view state, and you are not limited to the same effects when expanding or collapsing a state. The following properties are available in the Transition class:

- **fromState**—A string that specifies the view state you are changing from when you apply the transition.

- **toState**—A string that specifies the view state you are in when you apply the transition.

- **Effect**—The Effect object you want to play when you apply the transition. You can use an <mx:Parallel> tag or an <mx:Sequence> tag to define multiple effects.

To use transitions, you must surround one or more <mx:Transition> tags with an <mx:transitions> tag block, in lowercase. The reason for the case difference is that the <mx:transitions> tag represents a property of the Application, which can then contain one or more Transition objects.

```
<mx:transitions>
<mx:Transition id="myTransition1"
   fromState="state2" toState="state3">
      <mx:Dissolve duration="800"/>
</mx:Transition>
```

```
<mx:Transition id="myTransition2"
    fromState="*" toState="*">
[…]
</mx:Transition>
<mx:Transition id="myTransition3"
    fromState="state1"
    toState="state2">
[…]
</mx:Transition>
</mx:transitions>
```

By using the `<mx:transitions>` tag, you can have multiple `<mx:Transition>` tags applied.

If you define multiple effects within a specific Transition object, you must use the `<mx:Parallel>` or `<mx:Sequence>` tags. You can use the `targets` property of the `<mx:Parallel>` or `<mx:Sequence>` tags to apply these effects to multiple components within a state. Parallel effects trigger at the same time, whereas sequence effects trigger in order. You can be more specific about which components you want the effect to apply to by using the `targets` property, as shown here:

```
<mx:transitions>
<mx:Transition id="myTransition1"
    fromState="state1
    toState="state2">
    <mx:Sequence targets="{[VBox1, VBox2, VBox3]}">
        <mx:Move targets="{[VBox1, VBOX2]}"
            duration="400" />
        <mx:Dissolve duration="800"/>
    </mx:Sequence>
</mx:Transition>
<mx:Transition id="myTransition2"
    fromState="state2"
    toState="state3">
    […]
</mx:Transition>
<mx:Transition id="myTransition3"
    fromState="*"
    toState="*">
    <mx:Parallel targets="{[VBox1, VBox2, VBox3]}">
        <mx:Iris duration="400" />
        <mx:Move duration="400" />
    </mx:Parallel>
</mx:Transition>
</mx:transitions>
```

After you have set up the transition, you can trigger it by setting the `currentState` property in a `click` event. When a view state is triggered, Flex searches for and runs the Transition object that matches the current and destination view state. If more than one transition matches, Flex will use the first transition defined in the `<mx:Transitions>` tag.

Implementing Effects on a Component

In this task, you will add a dissolve behavior that smoothes the transition when the user clicks the grocery category to display the list of items in that category.

1 Be sure to go back to work with your regular FlexGrocer project, not the FlexGrocer-FDS project. Also, be sure that ColdFusion is running in a console window as application data is now dynamically retrieved. As a reminder, go to the cfusionFlexTFS/bin folder in a console window and enter **jrun –start cfusion**.

You will be working with the code you finished in Lesson 18, "Charting Data," which is what is in your FlexGrocer project.

2 Open EComm.mxml and run the application. Click a grocery category.

The file is located in your flexGrocer directory. If you skipped Lesson 18, when this version was created, you can open this file from Lesson22/start and save it in your flexGrocer directory.

Notice that the transition from the home page to the list of grocery products is immediate and appears rather jerky. You will add a dissolve behavior that will greatly improve the user experience.

3 In EComm.mxml, directly below the `<mx:CurrencyFormatter>` tag, add an `<mx:Dissolve>` tag, assign it an id of `bodyDissolve`, and set the `duration` attribute to 2000, as follows:

```
<mx:Dissolve id="bodyDissolve" duration="2000"/>
```

This creates an effect that you can later reference from a trigger on a component. As you learned earlier, the triggers that you can use are `focusInEffect`, `focusOutEffect`, `hideEffect`, `mouseDownEffect`, `mouseUpEffect`, `rolloutEffect`, `rolloverEffect`, and `showEffect`.

4 Locate the invocation of the custom FoodList component that you built earlier. Add a showEffect trigger and set up a binding to the bodyDissolve behavior you created in the last step. Your final invocation of the <mx:FoodList> component should look as follows:

```
<v:FoodList id="prodTile"
    width="100%" height="100%"
    prodByCategory="{prodByCategory}"
    itemAdded="addToCart(event.product)"
    showEffect="{bodyDissolve}"/>
```

FoodList is where the list of grocery items are displayed based upon the category the user clicks. You want to apply a dissolve behavior here that will create a better transition for the user. The FoodList component changes when the user clicks an item in the category. You want the dissolve effect to display when the FoodList component changes. The showEffect trigger is fired only when the visible property of a component is changed. In this case, you need to manually set the visible property.

5 Open up the ecomm.as file in the as folder and locate the displayProdByCategory() method. Modify the method so the first line sets the visible property of the prodTile container to false. Then set the visible property of the prodTile container to true as the last line of the method. Your final displayProdByCategory() function should look as follows:

```
private function displayProdByCategory(event:CategoryEvent):void{
    prodTile.visible=false;
    if ( event.cat != null ){
        var prodArray:Array=catProds.getProdsForCat(event.cat.catID);
        prodByCategory=new ArrayCollection(prodArray);
    }else{
        prodByCategory=new ArrayCollection();
    }
    prodTile.visible=true;
}
```

By manually setting the visible property of the FoodList component—which has an id of prodTile—from false to true, you will fire the showEffect trigger you added in the last step. This will cause the dissolve effect to be used each time a new category is selected, which is exactly the behavior you want!

6 Run the EComm application.

You should see the dissolve effect display when you click a category.

Adding Effects to View States

In this task, you will add a transition that will be applied when a view state within a component is displayed. In this case, you will add the transition when the user rolls over the food item to display the details.

1 Open GroceryDetail.mxml in views/ecomm.

The file is located in your flexGrocer/views/ecomm directory. If you skipped Lesson 18, when this version was created, you can open this file from Lesson22/start/views/ecomm and save it in your flexGrocer/views/ecomm directory.

This is the component that contains all the view states that are displayed when the user rolls over a food item.

2 Below the `<mx:Script>` tag, add an `<mx:transitions>` tag block. Inside of that tag, nest an `<mx:Transition>` tag block. Assign the `<mx:Transition>` tag an id of `foodTransition`. Specify the `fromState` attribute as an asterisk (*) and the `toState` attribute as an asterisk (*). Your code should appear as follows:

```
<mx:transitions>
   <mx:Transition id="foodTransition"
      fromState="*"
      toState="*">
   </mx:Transition>
</mx:transitions>
```

The `fromState` is simply a string that specifies the view state that you are changing from when the transition is applied. In this case, you specify an asterisk (*) which means any view state. The `toState` is a string that specifies the view state that you are changing to when the transition is applied. In this case, you specify an asterisk (*), which means any view state.

3 Within the `<mx:Transition>` tag block, nest an `<mx:WipeRight>` effect and specify the `duration` property as 500. Also, add the `target` to be bound to `foodBox`.

```
<mx:transitions>
   <mx:Transition id="foodTransition"
      fromState="*"
      toState="*">
        <mx:WipeRight duration="500" target="{foodBox}"/>
   </mx:Transition>
</mx:transitions>
```

Remember that the <mx:Transition> tag defines the effects that make up a transition. You can specify the duration of the WipeRight effect so the text will gradually "roll in" when the end user rolls over the appropriate grocery item.

4 Locate the <mx:VBox> tag in the <mx:AddChild> tag in the expanded view state. Give this VBox an id set equal to foodBox.

```
<mx:VBox id="foodBox"
    width="100%"
    x="200"
    styleName="standardBlack">
    …
</mx:VBox>
```

This is the target you bound to in the WipeRight effect.

5 Run the EComm application. Select a category from the horizontal list and roll over a grocery item.

When you roll over each item, you should see the item description and other item information displayed from left to right.

What You Have Learned

In this lesson, you have:

- Learned what different effects are available (pages 520–524)
- Learned how to apply behaviors to components (pages 524–526)
- Learned how to apply transitions to view states (pages 526–527)

What You Will Learn

In this lesson, you will:

- Instantiate a FlexPrintJob object and then use the start(), addObject() and send() methods to produce printed output

- Implement code to gracefully exit the printing process if the user cancels the print job at the operating-system level

- Use the PrintDataGrid control for printing data from a DataGrid

- Create a container that is not visible on the screen and is used for formatting printed output

- Create a custom component that is not visible on the screen and is used for formatting printed output

- Scale printed output on a page using static constants of the FlexPrintJobScaleType class

Approximate Time

This lesson takes approximately 2 hours to complete.

Lesson Files

Media Files:

None

Starting Files:

Lesson23/printing/start/PrintingTask1.mxml
Lesson23/printing/start/PrintingTask2.mxml
Lesson23/printing/start/PrintingTask3.mxml
Lesson23/printing/start/PrintingTask4.mxml
Lesson23/start/views/ecomm/OrderConf.mxml

Completed Files:

Lesson23/printing/complete/PrintingTask1.mxml
Lesson23/printing/complete/PrintingTask2.mxml
Lesson23/printing/complete/PrintingTask3.mxml
Lesson23/printing/complete/PrintingTask4.mxml
Lesson23/printing/complete/views/PrintView.mxml
Lesson23/complete/views/ecomm/OrderConf.mxml
Lesson23/complete/views/ecomm/PrintReceipt.mxml

Printing From Flex

In many (if not most) cases, you will not want your printed output to look exactly like the screen display. Adobe Flex gives you functionality to build containers and components to format printed output that does not have to resemble the screen display at all. Two classes, FlexPrintJob and PrintDataGrid, are key to implementing printing.

No longer do web applications have to print receipts and itineraries that are poor resemblances of the real things.

A printed receipt from the checkout process

Introducing Flex Printing

Printing from web applications has often been problematic in the past. A user would have to print from the browser and see a replica of the screen with odd page breaks and formatting. Now with Flex you have the power to build containers and components that will print exactly as you would like and do not have to be visible on the screen display at any time. The printed output does not have to be related to the screen display in any way.

Two classes are key to implementing this functionality:

- **FlexPrintJob**—A class that you instantiate and then can print one or more objects. The objects can be containers or custom components that you build specifically for displaying printed material. The class will also automatically split large objects over multiple pages and scale output to fit on a particular page size.

- **PrintDataGrid**—A subclass of the DataGrid control with appearance and functionality better suited for printing. The PrintDataGrid class has properties and methods that support printing grids that contain multiple pages of data.

The basic process for printing in Flex is as follows:

1. Instantiate an object from the FlexPrintJob class.

2. Start the print job using the FlexPrintJob's `start()` method.

3. Add an object or objects to be printed using the FlexPrintJob's `addObject()` method.

4. Send the job to the printer using the FlexPrintJob's `send()` method.

5. Clean up objects no longer needed after printing.

Printing for the First Time from Flex

In this task you will print for the first time from Flex. In this case you will focus on the steps needed to enable printing; what you print will be of lesser importance. You will print a VBox container that contains a Label and a Button control.

1 Choose File > New > Flex Project. Select Basic and then click Next.

You do not need FDS or ColdFusion support for this project.

2 Make the project name **flex2tfs_Printing** and use the folder flex2tfs/Lesson23/printing/start. Click Next.

The directory contains starter files you will use for your exploration of drag and drop.

3 Click the Browse button next to the Main application file option and select the file PrintingTask1.mxml. Click OK and then click Finish.

You are creating a new project because some of the work in this lesson will not be directly involved with any of the three applications you are working on from the FlexGrocer site.

Notice that this file has a VBox that contains a Label and a Button control. The Button has a click event that calls a function named doPrint(). The skeleton of the doPrint() function is supplied in a script block.

4 At the top of the script block, import the mx.printing.FlexPrintJob class.

Remember that you could have skipped this step; when you used the class for data typing a variable, it would have been automatically imported for you.

5 As the first line of code in the function, create a variable local to the function named pj, data typed as FlexPrintJob, and set it equal to a new FlexPrintJob.

```
var pj:FlexPrintJob=new FlexPrintJob();
```

This instance of the FlexPrintJob class will be where all the printing will center around.

6 On the pj FlexPrintJob object instance, invoke the start() method.

```
pj.start();
```

This initializes the FlexPrintJob object and causes the underlying operating system to display a print dialog box.

7 On the pj object, invoke the addObject() method passing the id of the VBox, printContainer, as a parameter.

```
pj.addObject(printContainer);
```

This adds the VBox to the list of objects to be printed.

8 On the pj object, invoke the send() method.

```
pj.send();
```

This sends the added objects to the printer to start printing.

> **TIP:** The send() method is synchronous, so the code that follows it can assume that the call completed successfully.

9 Ensure that your function appears as follows:

```
private function doPrint():void{
    var pj:FlexPrintJob=new FlexPrintJob();
    pj.start();
    pj.addObject(printContainer);
    pj.send();
}
```

Between the calls to the start() and send() methods, a print job is spooled to the under-lying operating system. You should limit the code between these calls to only print-specific methods. For instance, there should not be user interaction between those two methods.

10 Run the application. Click the Button labeled Print Page in the Flex application to print the contents of the VBox.

You have now implemented the simplest print job in Flex.

11 Run the application again. Click the print Button and this time cancel the print job. (Depending on your environment, you might have to be very quick to cancel the print job.)

Notice that the screen clears when you do this. You need to gracefully handle when the user cancels the print job.

12 In the function, wrap the invocation of the start() method in an if statement. Check to see whether the value returned from the invocation is not equal to true. If the condition is true, simply return from the function. Your code should appear as follows:

```
private function doPrint():void{
    var pj:FlexPrintJob=new FlexPrintJob();
    if(pj.start() != true){
        return;
    }
    pj.addObject(printContainer);
    pj.send();
}
```

This causes Flex to gracefully exit back to the application page if the user cancels the print job.

13 Run the application again and cancel the print job after clicking the print button.

You should see that the application remains visible this time.

Using the PrintDataGrid in a Nonvisible Container

As mentioned in the lesson introduction, sometimes what the screen displays is not what you want printed. The layout will be for the computer monitor, wider than it is long, when the printed page is usually longer than it is wide. You can build a container that is not visible to the user on the monitor, but is printed when the user asks for a hard copy. The PrintDataGrid class is often used in this case because it is tailored to have a better printed appearance than the normal DataGrid, as well as print across multiple pages instead of displaying scroll bars like the normal DataGrid.

The normal DataGrid appears on the left of the following figure, and the PrintDataGrid appears on the right.

Price	Product	Price	Product
1.98	Bananas	1.98	Bananas
3.95	Stawberries	3.95	Stawberries
4.95	Swiss Cheese	4.95	Swiss Cheese
1.19	Yogurt	1.19	Yogurt

1 Open the file PrintingTask2.mxml from the flex2tfs_Printing project. Run the application.

Notice that this file contains a Form with some default information in the TextInput controls, followed by a DataGrid. Your goal in this task is to display the name and e-mail address above the DataGrid when printed. Of course, you will not display the exact Form, but place the user information in a Label control and display it above the PrintDataGrid container with the same data as the normal DataGrid.

2 Below the Form, insert a VBox that will be used as the print container. It should have the following properties and associated values:

```
id:                 printVBox
backgroundColor:    #FFFFFF
width:              450
height:             250
paddingTop:         50
paddingLeft:        50
paddingRight:       50
visible:            false
```

The VBox property values are special in two ways. First, the backgroundColor and padding have the values they do for better appearance when printing. The white background is best for printing, and the large amount of padding will keep the output from getting too close to the edges of the paper.

Second, at application startup this VBox will not be visible. Although setting the VBox visible property to false makes the VBox disappear, the VBox will still occupy space on the screen, which will just look like blank space at the end of the page.

3 In the VBox, insert an <mx:Label> with an id of contact.

This is where you will bind the user name and e-mail address gathered in the form.

4 Following the Label control, insert a <mx:PrintDataGrid> tag with an id of myPrintDG and a width and height of 100%.

You will tie the dataProvider of the normal DataGrid to this one.

5 Check to be sure that your VBox appears as follows:

```
<mx:VBox id="printVBox"
    backgroundColor="#FFFFFF"
    height="250" width="450"
    paddingTop="50" paddingLeft="50" paddingRight="50"
    visible="false">

    <mx:Label id="contact"/>
    <mx:PrintDataGrid id="myPrintDG"
        width="100%"
        height="100%"/>
</mx:VBox>
```

In a function that is called on the Button click, you will dynamically modify this VBox and content with values you want displayed when printing.

6 In the script block, import the mx.printing.FlexPrintJob class.

Remember that you could have skipped this step; when you used the class for data typing a variable, it would have been automatically imported for you.

7 At the bottom of the script block, create a private function named doPrint() data typed as void. In the function, create a new FlexPrintJob object local to the function named pj. Also insert an if statement that gracefully handles the situation if the user cancels the print job, which you learned in the last task. At this point, your function should appear as follows:

```
private function doPrint():void{
    var pj:FlexPrintJob = new FlexPrintJob();
    if(pj.start() != true)
    {
        return;
    }
}
```

In most circumstances you can assume that the start of functions you build to do printing will start in this way.

8 Fill the contact Label from the VBox with the customer name and customer e-mail concatenated together with the literal text Contact: preceding them.

```
contact.text="Contact: " + custName.text + " " + custEmail.text;
```

Here you are taking information gathered from the Form and reformatting it for the printed output.

9 Set the `dataProvider` of the PrintDataGrid equal to the `dataProvider` of the normal DataGrid.

```
myPrintDG.dataProvider=prodInfo.dataProvider;
```

You want to display the same data in the PrintDataGrid as the data in normal DataGrid, and making them use the same `dataProvider` is a sure way to make that happen.

10 Add the VBox to the print job using the `addObject()` method and then send the print job to the printer using the `send()` method.

```
pj.addObject(printVBox);
pj.send();
```

11 Check to be sure that your function appears as follows:

```
private function doPrint():void{
   var pj:FlexPrintJob = new FlexPrintJob();
   if(pj.start() != true)
   {
      return;
   }
   contact.text =
      ➥ "Contact: " + custName.text + " " + custEmail.text;
   myPrintDG.dataProvider = prodInfo.dataProvider;
   pj.addObject(printVBox);
   pj.send();
}
```

You now have a function that can print your VBox.

12 Add a `click` event that calls the `doPrint()` function to the Button in the Form with the label Print.

```
<mx:Button id="myButton"
   label="Print"
   click="doPrint()"/>
```

This provides functionality to the user to print when wanted.

13 Run the application. Click the Button labeled Print in the Flex application.

You should be able to both print and cancel the print job. When you print, you will see the VBox printed with the appropriate properties' values and content.

cost	listPrice	name	unitName
6	9.98	T Bone Steak	pound
0.99	1.59	Milk	each
0.99	1.19	Yogurt	each
2.5	3.95	Grapes	pound
1.25	1.99	Bell Peppers	each
1.09	1.95	Bananas	bunch

Contact: Sally Shopper sally@shopper.com

Building the Printable View in a Separate Component

In the last task, a separate container (a VBox) was used on the main application page that was configured especially for printing. If the printing configuration was very long and complex, it would probably not be a workable solution; a separate custom component would be better. In this task, you will do just that: build a custom component whose job is to hold the printable version of whatever data you want the user to print. Just like the previous task, the component will not be visible on the screen. However, this component will not create extra blank space on the screen; it will be built just for printing.

1 Right-click the views folder in the flex2tfs_Printing project and choose New > MXML Component. Set the Filename to be **PrintView.mxml**, and the Based On component should be a VBox. Set the width to 450 and the height to 250. Click Finish.

This is the skeleton of the custom component that will be used just for printing.

2 Set the following properties for the VBox:

```
backgroundColor:   #FFFFFF
paddingTop:        50
paddingLeft:       50
paddingRight:      50
```

3 In the VBox, insert an `<mx:Label>` with an id of `contact`.

This is where you will bind the user name and e-mail address gathered in the Form.

4 Following the Label control, insert an `<mx:PrintDataGrid>` tag with an id of `myPrintDG` and a `width` and `height` of 100%.

You will tie the `dataProvider` of the normal DataGrid to this PrintDataGrid.

5 Check to be sure that your custom component appears as follows:

```
<?xml version="1.0" encoding="utf-8"?>
<mx:VBox xmlns:mx="http://www.adobe.com/2006/mxml"
    height="250" width="450"
    backgroundColor="#FFFFFF"
    paddingTop="50" paddingLeft="50" paddingRight="50">

    <mx:Label id="contact"/>
    <mx:PrintDataGrid id="myPrintDG"
        width="100%" height="100%"/>
</mx:VBox>
```

Of course, the custom component could be as complex as needed to meet your printing needs.

6 Open the file PrintingTask3.mxml from the flex2tfs_Printing project.

Note that this application file has the Form used in PrintingTask2, as well as the skeleton of the `doPrint()` function created.

7 In the `doPrint()` function, create a new FlexPrintJob object local to the function named `pj`. Insert an `if` statement that gracefully handles the situation if the user cancels the print job. At this point, your function should appear as follows:

```
private function doPrint():void{
    var pj:FlexPrintJob = new FlexPrintJob();
    if(pj.start() != true)
    {
        return;
    }
}
```

Flex Builder will automatically add the import for `mx.printing.FlexPrintJob` to the file when you specify the type of the variable `pj`. You can also import it manually by adding it to the top of the script block.

8 At the top of the script block, import the custom component you built earlier in this task.

```
import views.PrintView;
```

You will instantiate an instance of this class shortly, so you must import it.

9 In the function just below the if block, create an instance local to the function of the PrintView custom component class named myPrintView.

```
var myPrintView:PrintView=new PrintView();
```

This is the instance of the custom component you will use for printing.

10 Use the addChild() method to add the newly created myPrintView object as a DisplayObject of the Application.

```
this.addChild(myPrintView);
```

The addChild() method is a method of the mx.core.Container class, which is the parent of the Application class. The method adds a child DisplayObject object to the specified container.

> **TIP:** Remember that you cannot give an instance name to the Application (or any tag used as a base tag of a component), so you refer to the Application by using the keyword this.

11 Fill the contact Label from the PrintView component with the customer name and customer e-mail concatenated together with the literal text Contact: preceding them. Remember that you must reference the Label through the myPrintView object.

```
myPrintView.contact.text = "Contact: " + custName.text + " " + custEmail.text;
```

12 Set the dataProvider of the PrintDataGrid equal to the dataProvider of the normal DataGrid. Remember that you must reference the PrintDataGrid through the myPrintView object.

```
myPrintView.myPrintDG.dataProvider = prodInfo.dataProvider;
```

13 Add the myPrintView object to the print job using the addObject() method and then send the print job to the printer using the send() method.

```
pj.addObject(myPrintView);
pj.send();
```

14 To "clean up" after printing, remove the myPrintView object.

```
removeChild(myPrintView);
```

15 Check to be sure that your function appears as follows:

```
private function doPrint():void{
   var pj:FlexPrintJob = new FlexPrintJob();
   if(pj.start() != true)
   {
      return;
   }
   var myPrintView:PrintView=new PrintView();
   this.addChild(myPrintView);
   myPrintView.contact.text = "Contact: " + custName.text + " " + custEmail.text;
   myPrintView.myPrintDG.dataProvider = prodInfo.dataProvider;
   pj.addObject(myPrintView);
   pj.send();
   removeChild(myPrintView);
}
```

Just to reiterate, this function instantiates the custom component, adds it as a display object to the Application (even though it is not actually displayed to the screen), sets the data values, prints, and finally cleans up after itself.

16 Run the application. Click the Button labeled Print in the Flex application.

You should be able to both print and cancel the print job. When you print, you will see the custom component with the appropriate properties' values and content.

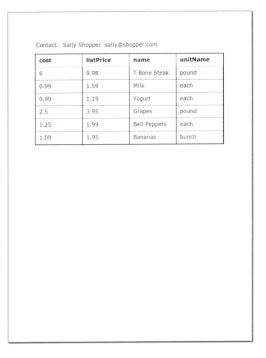

cost	listPrice	name	unitName
6	9.98	T Bone Steak	pound
0.99	1.59	Milk	each
0.99	1.19	Yogurt	each
2.5	3.95	Grapes	pound
1.25	1.99	Bell Peppers	each
1.09	1.95	Bananas	bunch

Contact: Sally Shopper sally@shopper.com

Scaling the Printed Output

You might want to scale the output to fill a certain dimension of the printed page, or pages. You have five dimension-formatting choices when adding an object to the print job with the addObject() method. All your options are static constants from the FlexPrintJobScaleType class. This means that to use them, you import the class and then use the constant in the form FlexPrintJobScaleType.CONSTANT. The options are as follows:

- **MATCH_WIDTH**: Scales the printed object to fill the page width. If the height exceeds the width, the output will span multiple pages. This is the default setting.

- **MATCH_HEIGHT**: Scales the printed object to fill the page height. If the width exceeds the height, the output will span multiple pages.

- **SHOW_ALL**: Scales the printed object to fit on a single page, filling one dimension. It selects the smaller of the MATCH_WIDTH or MATCH_HEIGHT and then fills that dimension.

- **FILL_PAGE**: Scales the printed object to fill at least one page. It selects the larger of the MATCH_WIDTH or MATCH_HEIGHT scale types.

- **NONE**: Does not scale the printed object. The printed page has the same dimensions as the object on the screen.

1 Open PrintView2.mxml from the flex2tfs_Printing/project/views folder. Notice that only two columns of the PrintDataGrid are displayed, and the width and height of 100% is removed from the previous PrintView custom component.

  These changes are made so they don't interfere with the scaling.

2 Open the file PrintingTask4.mxml from the flex2tfs_Printing project.

  This file should be identical to the one you left off with in the last task.

3 Run the Application. Click the Button labeled Print from the Flex application to print the page.

  This will give you a baseline to which to compare other printouts.

4 In the script block, import the class mx.printing.FlexPrintJobScaleType.

  You must import this class to use its static constants.

5 In the addObject() method, pass a second parameter of FlexPrintJobScaleType.MATCH_WIDTH. Run the application and click the Print Button in the Flex application to print the page.

```
pj.addObject(myPrintView, FlexPrintJobScaleType.MATCH_WIDTH);
```

You see there is no difference between the first and second printouts, confirming that MATCH_WIDTH is the default setting.

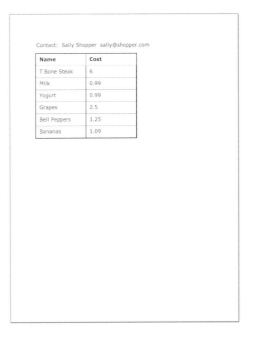

6 Change the scale to FlexPrintJobScaleType.MATCH_HEIGHT in the addObject() method. Run the application and click the Print Button in the Flex application to print the page.

Because the MATCH_HEIGHT was specified to scale to, and the width of the object was greater than the height, the output was spread over multiple pages.

Contact: Sally Shopper sal ly@shopper.com		
Name	**Cost**	
T Bone Steak	6	
Milk	0.99	
Yogurt	0.99	
Grapes	2.5	
Bell Peppers	1.25	
Bananas	1.09	

7 Change the scale to `FlexPrintJobScaleType.NONE` in the `addObject()` method. Run the application and click the Print Button in the Flex application to print the page.

Because `NONE` was specified, the printed output matches the screen, and the output is smaller than your baseline printing from step 3.

The `NONE` value produced the smaller printed output on the right in the following figure.

Printing a Receipt from the Checkout Process

In this task, you will put your new knowledge about printing to work in the EComm application. You will add a Button to the order confirmation page to give the customer an option to print a receipt. In this case, you will create a custom component to print the receipt.

1 Back in the normal FlexGrocer project, open views/ecomm/OrderConf.mxml.

This is the page in which you will add the print receipt Button.

2 Add a Button control beneath the last Button on the page with a `label` of Print Receipt and add a `click` event that calls a method named `doPrint()`.

```
<mx:Button label="Print Receipt" click="doPrint()"/>
```

This printing process will be similar to what you did in the previous task in this lesson.

3 At the bottom of the script block, create a private function named doPrint() data typed as void. In the function, create a new FlexPrintJob object local to the function named pj. Also insert an if statement that gracefully handles the situation if the user cancels the print job. Your function should appear as follows:

```
private function doPrint():void{
   var pj:FlexPrintJob = new FlexPrintJob();
   if(pj.start() != true)
   {
      return;
   }
}
```

This is the standard way to start printing functions. The FlexPrintJob class was automatically imported when you created the pj instance; otherwise, add an import for mx.printing.FlexPrintJob to your script block.

4 At the top of the script block, import a custom component you will build later in this task named PrintReceipt, which will be created in the views/ecomm folder.

```
import views.ecomm.PrintReceipt;
```

You will instantiate an instance of this class, so you must import it.

5 In the doPrint() function just below the if block, create an instance local to the function of the PrintReceipt custom component class named theReceipt.

```
var theReceipt:PrintReceipt=new PrintReceipt();
```

This is the instance of the custom component you will use for printing.

6 Use the addChild() method to add the newly created theReceipt object as a DisplayObject of the current file.

```
this.addChild(theReceipt);
```

This adds an instance of the PrintReceipt class, which you will develop shortly, to the current container.

7 Assign the orderInfo variable to a like named property you will create in the theReceipt object.

```
theReceipt.orderInfo=orderInfo;
```

Here you are taking information gathered from the billing information Form and assigning it a property of the custom component. You will display some of this information on the receipt.

8 Add the theReceipt object to the print job using the addObject() method and then send the print job to the printer using the send() method.

```
pj.addObject(theReceipt);
pj.send();
```

9 To "clean up" after printing, remove the myPrintView object.

```
this.removeChild(theReceipt);
```

10 Check to be sure that your function appears as follows:

```
private function doPrint():void{
   var pj:FlexPrintJob = new FlexPrintJob();
   if(pj.start() != true){
      return;
   }
   var theReceipt:PrintReceipt=new PrintReceipt();
   this.addChild(theReceipt);
   theReceipt.orderInfo=orderInfo;
   pj.addObject(theReceipt);
   pj.send();
   this.removeChild(theReceipt);
}
```

This completes the code needed on the OrderConf.mxml page. Now, you need to build the custom component used. From the code you have written, you know that the custom component must be called PrintReceipt.mxml and it must have a property named orderInfo. You also will display whatever you want the printed receipt to contain.

11 Right-click the views.ecomm folder in the FlexGrocer project and choose New > MXML Component. Set the Filename to be **PrintReceipt.mxml**. and the Based On component should be a VBox. Set the width and height to be 450. Click Finish.

This is the skeleton of the custom component that will be used just for printing.

12 Set the following properties for the VBox:

```
backgroundColor: #FFFFFF
paddingTop:      50
paddingLeft:     50
paddingRight:    50
```

13 Insert a script block and import the valueObjects.OrderInfo class.

This is the datatype that will be used for the property you are about to create.

14 In the script block, create a bindable, public variable name `orderInfo`, data typed as OrderInfo.

This is the property that was assigned a value in the printing function.

15 Following the script block, insert a Label with the `text` set equal to the literal text Flex Grocer Thanks You!, a `fontSize` of 20 and a `width` of 100%.

This will be printed at the top of the receipt.

16 Next, copy the complete Form block from the OrderConf.mxml page and paste it below the Label. Remove the Label from this new copy of the Form that reads Checkout Page 3 of 3.

Remember that what you print does not have to match what the screen looks like. In this case, the Label that indicates where you are in the checkout process makes no sense to be printed, while the rest of the information from the Form should be part of the printed receipt.

17 Also copy the `<mx:DateFormatter>` tag from OrderConf.mxml and paste it just below the script block.

This is used to format the date in the Form.

18 Run the EComm.mxml application. Go through the ordering process. On the last page, click the Print Receipt Button.

▶ **TIP:** Remember that you must have the ColdFusion instance started for EComm to function correctly.

You will see that the receipt prints.

Flex Grocer Thanks You!

Billing Information

Arthur Customer   Delivery Date   08/22/2006

600 Townsend St.

San Francisco

CA

94103

What You Have Learned

In this lesson, you have:

- Printed a container that is contained on the main application page that is specifically formatted for printed output (pages 531–533)

- Printed data from the PrintDataGrid control for better appearance (pages 534–537)

- Printed data from a custom component that is specifically formatted for printed output (pages 537–540)

- Scaled printed output in multiple ways to fit on a page (pages 541–543)

- Printed a receipt at the end of the checkout process (pages 543–547)

What You Will Learn

In this lesson, you will:

- Create a new shared object on the client machine

- Write a complex data structure to the shared object

- Read data from an existing shared object

- Use data from an existing shared object to populate form controls

Approximate Time

This lesson takes approximately 45 minutes to complete.

Lesson Files

Media Files:

None

Starting Files:

Lesson24/start/views/ecomm/Cart.mxml
Lesson24/start/views/ecomm/Checkout.mxml
Lesson24/start/valueObjects/ShoppingCart.as

Completed Files:

Lesson24/complete/views/ecomm/Cart.mxml
Lesson24/complete/views/ecomm/Checkout.mxml
Lesson24/complete/valueObjects/ShoppingCart.as

LESSON 24

Using Shared Objects

An important part of most applications is the capability to persist data, such as remembering information about a specific user. Persisting user data can be done at the server by associating a user with a login ID and then passing specific information back to a server. The information is then written to a database and can be loaded back into the application when needed.

Using Adobe Flex, it is also possible to persist data on the client side, actually within Flash Player using the SharedObject class. Shared objects are similar to HTTP cookies, but are much more powerful because you can store complex data structures within them. In this lesson, you will use the SharedObject class to store information about which grocery items a user is interested in purchasing.

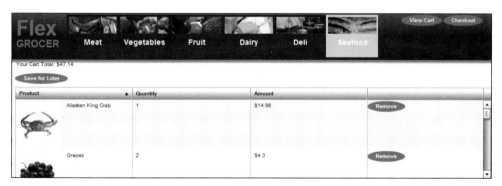

The Save For Later button writes items in the shopping cart into a shared object on the local machine for later retrieval.

Introducing Shared Objects

Whether you decide to persist data on the client or on the server depends largely on the type of data you have and its purpose. Data that needs to be stored permanently for business reasons, such as contact information for a customer, should be stored on the server. Information that is persisted primarily as a convenience for users, such as application preferences or a shopping cart the user wants to save for later, should be stored on the client to save the overhead of transmitting the data back to the server and putting it in a database.

Shared objects are the Flex equivalent of web cookies, but are much more powerful. Using ActionScript, you can write code to store data as a shared object on a user's machine. Properties assigned to a shared object are stored in the file as soon as the SWF file is removed from Flash Player by exiting the browser or moving onto a different web page or application. It is also possible to manually store the information at run time; for example, when an event occurs.

Data in a local shared object can be referenced from within the Flex application just like any other object.

Shared objects have the following characteristics:

- They are stored on the end user's machine in a location that varies depending on the platform.

- They have the extension .sol.

- By default, they can be up to 100 KB in size. The user can adjust the size limit and can deny or approve storage of larger objects.

- They can contain complex data structures.

- They cannot contain methods or functions.

- The end user must manually delete them or write code to delete them programmatically. Clearing cookies from the browser does not delete Flex shared objects.

- Like cookies, shared objects cannot be read from different domains. Flash Player has the capability of reading shared objects only if the shared object was created from the same domain as the SWF file.

✱ NOTE: When you test applications within the Flex Builder authoring environment, you can access only shared objects created by the same application because testing an application opens it as a local file and does not establish a domain.

Creating Shared Objects

The static `getLocal()` method of the SharedObject class retrieves an existing shared object; if a shared object does not exist, it creates a new one. All shared objects are written as soon as the SWF file is removed from Flash Player. If you need to write a shared object sooner, you can use the static `flush()` method.

The following ActionScript code creates a shared object:

```
var soMy:SharedObject = SharedObject.getLocal("myCookie");
```

A file called myCookie.sol is created on the user's machine. The shared object is manipulated in ActionScript as soMy.

To populate the shared object with data, you assign your variables as properties of the `data` property of the shared object. This is the shared object's only built-in property. The following ActionScript code stores the user Jeff in a shared object:

```
soMy.data.user = "Jeff";
```

To store complex data structures in a shared object, that object must be instantiated within the shared object. The following code creates an array inside a shared object and places an existing and populated array, `employees`, into that object:

```
soMy.data.aUsers = new Array();
soMy.data.aUsers = employees;
```

Although shared objects are automatically written as soon as the SWF file is removed from Flash Player, you can write shared objects to disk at other times; for example, using the `flush()` method in response to an event such as a user clicking a button. The syntax is as follows:

```
mySharedObject.flush(minimumDiskSpace);
```

The `minimumDiskSpace` parameter specifies the size of the .sol file to be created, instead of simply letting the file size be set by the actual size of the data being written. Using this technique to create an .sol file larger than the current data being written builds in the flexibility for the data size of the shared object to fluctuate without the user being prompted for approval at every slight change.

For example, if a shared object is currently 100 bytes but you expect it to grow to a maximum size of 500 bytes, create it with a value of 500 for the `minimumDiskSpace` parameter:

```
soMy.flush(500);
```

After the user responds to the dialog box, this method is called again and returns either `true` or `false`.

Because local objects are persisted on the client, you need to consider disk space constraints. By default, Flex can save shared objects up to 100 KB in size. Each application can have an unlimited number of shared objects, and the 100 KB limit is per shared object. When you try to save a larger object, Flash Player displays the Local Storage dialog box, which enables the user to allow or deny storage for the domain that is requesting access.

The user can also specify permanent local storage settings for a particular domain. Although Flash Player application is playing, right-click, choose Settings, and then open the Local Storage panel. The panel that opens is shown here.

Additionally, if the user selects a value that is less than the amount of disk space currently being used for locally persistent data, Flash Player warns the user that any locally saved shared objects will be deleted.

Reading Shared Objects

When Flash Player tries to read the shared object, one of two possible outcomes occurs:

- A new shared object is created if one with the same name does not already exist (from the same domain).
- If the shared object does exist, the contents are read into the *data* property of the shared object.

Just as with cookies, it is a best practice to test for the existence of a shared object before referencing it. The following code snippet shows how to test for the existence of a user property:

```
if (soMy.data.user != undefined){
   //statements
}
```

After you know that the object exists, you can reference its properties as you can those of any other object in ActionScript. For example, to populate a Text control with the ID of txtUserName from a shared object, you can use the following code:

```
var soMy = sharedObject.getLocal("myCookie");
if (soMy.data.user != undefined){
    txtUserName.text = soMy.data.user;
}
```

All object properties can be referenced from a shared object just as you can do with any other object. However, you cannot store methods in a shared object. For example, to reference the length property of the Array object contained in the shared object, you can use the following code:

```
for (var i:int = 0; i < soCart.data.aCart.length; i++){
    //statements
}
```

Building a SharedObject to Store Shopping Cart Data

In this task, you will add a new button that, when clicked, will read the data from the end user's shopping cart and write that information to a shared object on their client machine. This will enable users to access their shopping cart data any time before they have actually gone through the purchasing process. You will also examine the resulting .sol file on the client machine.

1 From the FlexGrocer project, open the file views/ecomm/Cart.mxml.

In this file, you will add a Save For Later button. When clicked, this button will read the shopping cart data and write this data to a shared object on the client machine.

2 Immediately after the <mx:Script> block, add a <mx:Button> tag with the label of Save for Later.

```
<mx:Button label="Save for Later"/>
```

This code displays a Button with the label of Save for Later immediately below the current DataGrid.

3 Add a click event to the <mx:Button> tag that will call the saveCart() method of the cart object.

```
<mx:Button label="Save for Later" click="cart.saveCart()"/>
```

The cart object, an instance of the ShoppingCart class, has already been created in the script block. You will add a saveCart() method to this class, which will read the data from the user's shopping cart and write this data to a shared object.

4 Save the changes to Cart.mxml and open up the valueObjects/ShoppingCart.as file.

It makes sense to place the saveCart() method in the ShoppingCart class because this is where the shopping cart data, aItems, that will be written to the shared object is stored.

5 At the top of the class, add an import statement that will import the flash.net.SharedObject class. Within the class, declare a new, public, bindable shared object with the name of soCart. At the end of the ShoppingCart class, add the skeleton of a new public() method with the name of saveCart() data typed as void.

```
import flash.net.SharedObject;
public class ShoppingCart {
   [Bindable]
   public var soCart:SharedObject;
   public function saveCart():void{
   }
   ...
}
```

You will be using the data structure written to the client machine, the shared object, to populate the DataGrid when the application first starts. Therefore, it is important to declare the shared object itself as Bindable.

6 In the saveCart() method, using the static getLocal() method of the SharedObject class, declare a new shared object with the name of soCart. Pass the parameter of cartInfo to the getLocal() method.

```
public function saveCart():void{
   this.soCart = SharedObject.getLocal("cartInfo");
}
```

This will create a new shared object and write a file to the end user's machine with the name of cartInfo. The extension of the file created will be .sol.

7 In the saveCart() method, declare a new Array with the name of aCart in the data property of the SharedObject.

```
public function saveCart():void{
   this.soCart = SharedObject.getLocal("cartInfo");
   this.soCart.data.aCart = new Array();
}
```

To assign data to a shared object, you must use the data property. This is the only property of the shared object class and how all data can be set and retrieved. If you are storing complex data structures in the shared object, the object itself must be instantiated within the object.

8 Immediately after declaring the Array, create a new variable with the name of `len` that will obtain the length of the `aItems` ArrayCollection and build the skeleton of a `for` loop that will loop through the `aItems` ArrayCollection:

```
var len:int = aItems.length;
for (var i:int = 0;i < len;i++){
}
```

Remember that the current contents of the shopping cart are stored in the `aItems` Array-Collection. You are building a `for` loop to loop through the `aItems` array and populate the client-side shared object with that information.

9 Inside of the `for` loop, populate the `soCart.data.aCart` array, inside the SharedObject with the `aItems` ArrayCollection. Use the `getItemAt()` method to access the data in the ArrayCollection. The final `saveCart()` method should look as follows:

```
public function saveCart():void{
    this.soCart = SharedObject.getLocal("cartInfo");
    this.soCart.data.aCart = new Array();
    var len:int = aItems.length;
    for (var i:int = 0;i < len;i++){
        this.soCart.data.aCart[i] = this.aItems.getItemAt(i);
    }
}
```

This will place the values from the ArrayCollection into the shared object. The SharedObject class can store only native ActionScript data structures such as an array of objects. An ArrayCollection cannot be stored in a shared object, nor can objects created using the value object pattern. These data structures will be converted to arrays of objects.

10 Run the EComm application. Add some items to the shopping cart and view the cart. Click the Save for Later button.

When you click the Save For Later button, you will write a .sol file to the client machine. When you call the `SharedObject.flush()` method or simply close your browser, all the information in the shopping cart will be written to this file.

11 The storage location of Local Shared Objects is operating system–dependent. If you are using Windows, browse to *driveroot:*/Documents and Settings/{*username*}/Application-Data/Macromedia/Flash Player/#Shared Objects. From this point, search for cartInfo.sol.

12 Save ShoppingCart.as.

▶ **TIP:** The path might include some odd directory names because you are not browsing the MXML file, but running it from Flex Builder.

> **TIP:** On Macintosh OSX, shared objects are stored in /Users/{*username*}/Library/Preferences/ Macromedia/Flash Player.

Inside the .sol file you will see the data structure of the shopping cart. This is the file that Flash Player can read and use to populate controls.

Reading Data from an Existing Shared Object

In this task, you will read the information from the existing shared object and use this information to populate the DataGrid control that is displaying the information.

1 Open views/ecomm/Cart.mxml.

You will populate the DataGrid, located in Cart.mxml, from the shared object that has already been written to the client machine.

2 At the top of Cart.mxml, locate the `<VBox>` root tag and add a `creationComplete` event that will call the `loadCart()` method from the cart object.

```
<mx:VBox xmlns:mx="http://www.adobe.com/2006/mxml"
    creationComplete="cart.loadCart()">
```

It makes sense to call the method that will populate the DataGrid on the `creationComplete` event to be sure that the DataGrid is available for use.

3 Save Cart.mxml and open valueObjects/ShoppingCart.as.

You will write the `loadCart()` method in the ShoppingCart class because the `aItems` ArrayCollection that populates all the controls is built in this class. You will build the ArrayCollection from the data structure stored in the shared object.

4 At the end of the class, add a skeleton of the `loadCart()` method, data typed as void, and use the `getLocal()` static method of the SharedObject class to read the existing cartInfo SharedObject. Store the shared object in a variable with the name of `soCart`.

```
public function loadCart():void{
    this.soCart = SharedObject.getLocal("cartInfo");
}
```

5 Add conditional logic that ensures that the `aCart` variable is not undefined.

```
if ( this.soCart.data.aCart != undefined ){
}
```

The `data` property of a new shared object does not contain any properties until you add them. Before you attempt to use the `aCart` data that might be stored in the shared object, you need to ensure that it exists.

6 Within the conditional logic, create a new local variable with the name of `len` and obtain the length of the `aCart` array stored in the `data` property of the `soCart` SharedObject, as follows:

```
var len:int = this.soCart.data.aCart.length;
```

`data` is the only property of the SharedObject class and is where all the data stored in the shared object is accessed. You are accessing the array in this case and can use all Array properties and methods.

7 Next, set up a looping structure that will loop through the `aCart` array stored in the `soCart` shared object.

```
for (var i:int=0;i<len;i++){
}
```

This will loop through the `aCart` array stored in the shared object. You will loop through this data structure and place the resulting data structure in the `aItems` ArrayCollection, which has already been bound to all the controls. Data stored in shared objects can be only native ActionScript data structures, so you will need to convert these objects into the value objects that `aItems` is expecting.

8 Create a new instance of the Product class using the static `buildProduct()` method. Pass the method the Product object stored inside of the `aCart` array.

```
var myProduct:Product = Product.buildProduct (this.soCart.data.aCart[i].product);
```

The `buildProduct()` method will build a new Product value object based on the Product class you wrote earlier. You must do this because all value objects stored in a shared object are automatically converted into native data structures. Unless you convert these objects back into the appropriate value objects, you will receive a type coercion error when you try to place the objects into the `aItems` array, which is linked to the visual controls.

9 After building the Product, define a new quantity of type `int` from the `quantity` property stored in the shared object.

```
var myQuantity:int = this.soCart.data.aCart[i].quantity;
```

To define a new ShoppingCartItem, you must define a Product object, which you did in the previous step. You also must define a quantity, which is stored in the shared object. The quantity property in the shared object is untyped, and the ShoppingCartItem requires a variable that has the type of `int`, so you must define it again here.

10 Define a new ShoppingCartItem and pass the constructor the myProduct Product object you created in the previous two steps.

```
var myItem:ShoppingCartItem = new ShoppingCartItem(myProduct, myQuantity);
```

The aItems array is an ArrayCollection of ShoppingCartItem value objects, and you must re-create these value objects to avoid type coercion errors because these value objects are not stored as value objects in the shared object. They are stored as a native ActionScript array of objects.

11 Still within the for loop, call the addItem() method on the class you are currently working-ing on and pass it the myItem ShoppingCartItem. The final loadCart() method should look as follows:

```
public function loadCart():void{
   this.soCart = SharedObject.getLocal("cartInfo");
   if ( this.soCart.data.aCart != undefined ){
      var len:int = this.soCart.data.aCart.length;
      for (var i:int=0;i<len;i++){
         var myProduct:Product =
            ➥ Product.buildProduct(this.soCart.data.aCart[i].product);
         var myQuantity:int = this.soCart.data.aCart[i].quantity;
         var myItem:ShoppingCartItem =
            ➥ new ShoppingCartItem(myProduct, myQuantity);
         this.addItem(myItem);
      }
   }
}
```

To build the aItems ArrayCollection, you will use the addItem() method of the ShoppingCart. This method checks to see whether the item is already in the cart, manages the quantity of each item, and updates the subtotals of each item.

12 At the end of the class, add a skeleton of the clearCart() method data typed as void. Within the method, call the aItems.removeAll() method, the soCart.clear() method, and the calcTotal() method of this class.

```
public function clearCart():void{
   aItems.removeAll()
   soCart.clear();
   calcTotal();
}
```

This method empties all the items from the aItems ArrayCollection, clears the contents of the soCart shared object, and forces the shopping cart to recalculate the total. You will call this method when the user finishes the ordering process.

13 Open views/ecomm/Checkout.mxml.

You will change the saveOrderResult() method to use your new clearCart() method.

14 Find the saveOrderResult() method. Change the first line, which currently sets the cart.aItems to a new ArrayCollection, to call your clearCart() method on the cart object instead. The final saveOrderResult() method should look as follows:

```
private function saveOrderResult(event:ResultEvent):void{
   this.cart.clearCart();
   Alert.show(event.result.getOrderInfoHeader());
   var o:Event = new Event("checkOutComplete");
   this.dispatchEvent(o);
   checkoutNav.selectedChild=billingInfo;
}
```

15 Save all open files. Run the EComm application. Add some items to the shopping cart and view the cart. Click the Save For Later button. Close the browser, restart the application, and view the cart again. Finally, complete the order process.

When you restart the application and view the shopping cart, you should see that the shared object has been read and has populated the DataGrid with the items previously in the shopping cart. This information was written to the client machine in the shared object. When you complete the checkout process, the shopping cart and the shared object are both cleared. If you view the cart again, the items will be gone.

What You Have Learned

In this lesson, you have:

- Learned how to create and read shared objects using the SharedObject class (pages 550–553)

- Saved shopping cart data into a shared object (pages 553–556)

- Read shopping cart data from a shared object (pages 556–559)

What You Will Learn

In this lesson, you will:

- Learn how to use the `<mx:TraceTarget>` tag to view server-client communication

- Use the debugger in Flex Builder in new ways

- Handle errors using the `try-catch-finally` statements

Approximate Time

This lesson takes approximately 1 hour and 30 minutes to complete.

Lesson Files

Media Files:

   None

Starting Files:

   Lesson25/start/DataEntry.mxml
   Lesson25/start/EComm.mxml
   Lesson25/start/as/ecomm.as

Completed Files:

   Lesson25/complete/DataEntry.mxml
   Lesson25/complete/EComm.mxml
   Lesson25/complete/as/ecomm.as

LESSON 25

Debugging Flex Applications

Bugs will occur when developing your applications. In this lesson, you will take two approaches to these bugs. The first part of the lesson gives you insight into how to find bugs and apply what you have learned in the rest of the book to correct them. In the rest of the lesson, you learn how to handle bugs that slip by and programmatically catch them at run time using error handling with the **try-catch-finally** statements.

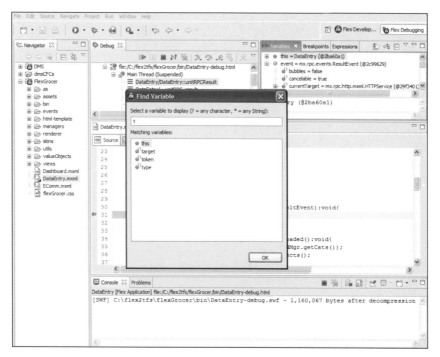

Using the debugger to search for properties beginning with the letter "t."

Introducing Debugging Techniques

Finding and correcting bugs is part of application development. This lesson will give you additional tools to do just that. This lesson is different from other lessons in that you will not write code, but instead use debugging tools with existing code to learn about ways to help you debug your applications.

In the first section of the lesson, you will use the `<mx:StackTrace>` tag to give you insight into what communication is happening between the client and server when using functionality that accesses server-side data such as RemoteObject, HTTPService, and Flex Data Services (FDS).

Next, you will see some new ways to use the debugger that you have not yet explored in this book. You will also get some more explanation and vocabulary about the Flex Builder's built-in debugger.

Finally, you will learn how to handle errors that occur during run time. Most likely, you will not be able to correct every bug and anticipate every way a user will interact with your application, so it is possible that run-time errors could occur. To handle these run-time errors, you will learn how to use `try-catch-finally` statements to gracefully catch and recover from run-time errors.

✱ **NOTE:** You need to have both FDS and ColdFusion running in console windows for the following tasks.

Watching Server-Client Data Exchange

One of the most frustrating debugging tasks can occur when dealing with data exchange on the server side. In some cases, you will not be able to tell if the problem exists in how you are handling the data once it has been received at the client or you simply are not getting the expected data back. The `<mx:TraceTarget>` tag and debugging your application will give you a wealth of information about the traffic passing between client and server.

 1 From the FlexGrocer project, open EComm.mxml. Just after the opening the
    `<mx:Application>` tag, insert an `<mx:TraceTarget/>` tag. Debug the EComm application
    by selecting it from the debug menu.

➤ **TIP:** You might want to insert the <mx:TraceTarget> tags on the far left margin, ignoring best practice indentation. Because you do not want this debugging tag in your production code, it is easy to locate and remove when it is sitting on the left margin.

2 Return to Flex Builder and double-click the Console view. Notice the HTTPService information in the Console view.

```
[SWF] C:\flex2tfs\flexGrocer\bin\EComm-debug.swf - 1,231,127 bytes after decompression
'0C43236E-46E3-E632-438D-3573BDC724AF' producer set destination to 'ColdFusion'.
'63C5E353-518F-1463-C894-3573BE15DD03' producer set destination to 'DefaultHTTP'.
'direct_http_channel' channel endpoint set to http:
'63C5E353-518F-1463-C894-3573BE15DD03' producer sending message
  ➥ 'A5E7E4ED-6D21-40C1-C45F-3573BF5D1C27'
'direct_http_channel' channel sending message:
(mx.messaging.messages::HTTPRequestMessage)#0
  body = (Object)#1
  clientId = (null)
  contentType = "application/x-www-form-urlencoded"
  destination = "DefaultHTTP"
  headers = (Object)#2
  httpHeaders = (Object)#3
  messageId = "A5E7E4ED-6D21-40C1-C45F-3573BF5D1C27"
  method = "GET"
  recordHeaders = false
  timestamp = 0
  timeToLive = 0
  url = "http://localhost:8300/flexGrocer/xml/categorizedProducts.cfm"
'63C5E353-518F-1463-C894-3573BE15DD03' producer connected.
'63C5E353-518F-1463-C894-3573BE15DD03' producer acknowledge of
  ➥ 'A5E7E4ED-6D21-40C1-C45F-3573BF5D1C27'.
```

This information can give you a confirmation of the HTTPService request information.

3 Terminate the current debugging session by clicking the red square in the Console view. Double-click the Console view to restore the normal debugging perspective. Remove the <mx:TraceTarget> tag and save the EComm.mxml application.

4 From the DMS project you created in Lesson 21, "Synchronizing Data with Adobe Flex Data Services," open DMS_1.mxml. Just below the <mx:Application> tag, insert an <mx:TraceTarget/> tag. Debug the application. Change the price of grapes to 10.99. In the Console view, examine the wealth of information provided about the work Flex Data Services did. Note that you can see the data sent back to the server in part of that information.

```
body=(Array)#0
  [0] (Array)#1
    [0] "cost"
  [1] (valueObjects::SmallProduct)#2
    cost = 1.99
    prodID = 1
    prodName = "Grapes"
    uid = "1"
  [2] (valueObjects::SmallProduct)#3
    cost = 10.99
    prodID = 1
    prodName = "Grapes"
    uid = "1"
```

You can use this information to confirm that you have received data back to the client, and if a problem exists, it is most likely in the handling of the data at the client.

5 From the DMS project, open DMS_2.mxml. Insert an <mx:TraceTarget/> tag just below the <mx:Application> tag. Debug the application. To see the information about a particular interaction, clear the console view by clicking the Clear Console button.

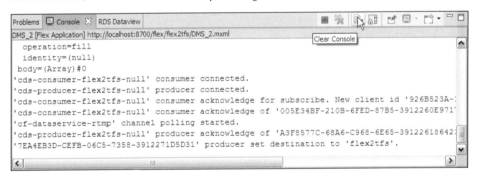

You have seen how much data is placed in the console. If you want to eliminate all the data except for a particular server interaction, clear the Console view by clicking the button indicated in the example figure.

6 Now return to your browser and add a new product. Examine the data in the Console view.

When adding a new product, the new primary key value (in this case prodID) is automatically sent back to the client and synchronized.

7 Remove all the <mx:TraceTarget> tags from your code and save the files.

The TraceTarget is for debugging and should not be left in your production code.

Learning More About the Debugger

So far in this book you've used the debugger built into Flex Builder in a limited way on a number of occasions. In this task, you will learn more about the debugger and how it can help you find errors in your application and more fully understand your application.

Learning More Details About Setting Breakpoints

In earlier lessons, you created breakpoints by double-clicking in the marker bar (next to the line numbers in an editor) to toggle breakpoints on and off. Here are more details about creating breakpoints:

- You can add breakpoints only on executable lines of ActionScript code. This means you can set breakpoints on lines that contain the following:

  - MXML tags that contain an event handler. For example,

    ```
    <mx:Button click="clickHandler()"/>
    ```

  - ActionScript code enclosed in an `<mx:Script>` block.

  - Executable ActionScript in an ActionScript file.

- If you set a breakpoint on a line that does not meet one of the listed criteria, Flex Builder will automatically scan down 10 lines to try and find a valid line to place a breakpoint. If it does, the breakpoint will be moved. If it cannot find a valid line for a breakpoint within 10 lines, the breakpoint will be ignored when debugging.

- The moving of the breakpoints will happen when you start your debugging session; if you set another breakpoint during a debugging session, it will be moved immediately.

After you hit a breakpoint and are in Flex Builder in the Flex Debugging perspective, you have a number of options for controlling application flow and breakpoint manipulation. On top of the Debug view, you see options for controlling your debugging session.

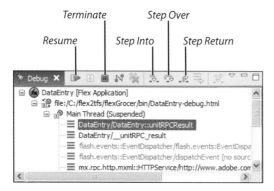

Here are the most common commands:

- **Resume**—Resumes execution of an application that has been interrupted by a debugging session. You can either run the application to completion or to another breakpoint set in the editor.

- **Terminate**—Stops the debugging session.

- **Step Into**—Steps into the called function and stops at the first line of the function.

- **Step Over**—Executes the current line of the function and then stops at the next line of the function.

- **Step Return**—Continues execution until the current function has returned to its caller or until another breakpoint is reached.

Inspecting Variables and Their Associated Values in the Debugger

After you have hit a breakpoint, you have a number of ways to inspect values of variables at the current state of the application. In a previous lesson, you used the Variables view to check the value of a variable. In the Variables view, you can check the values of the current object context, located in the this variable. If you happen to be in a function, you can also check the variables defined in that function by inspecting the variables labeled with an L in the circle in front of the variable. The following figure shows a debugging session stopped in an event handler where the event is passed to the function as a parameter, and hence scoped local to the function.

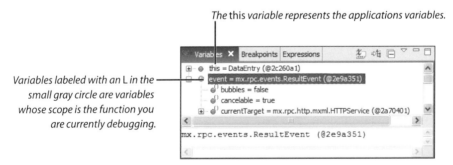

The this variable represents the applications variables.

Variables labeled with an L in the small gray circle are variables whose scope is the function you are currently debugging.

In the Variables view, there can be hundreds of variables to inspect. There is a feature in Flex Builder to help you find a variable from that long list: the Find Variable option. You can use either Ctrl+F or right-click in the Variables view and select Find Variable to bring up the interface. As you type in the data-entry section, the variables matching your entry will be listed. You can then click on the variable you want to be highlighted in the Variables view.

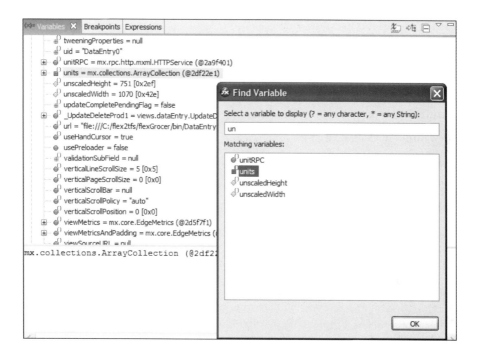

If you are watching one variable or a small set of variables, a better option is to use the Expressions view. In the Expressions view, you can enter variables (or expressions) to watch; when debugging, the values of the variables will then appear in the Expressions view. You don't have to search for them in a long list of values in the Variables view.

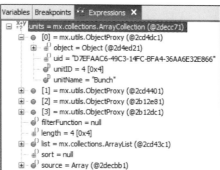

1 From the FlexGrocer project, open DataEntry.mxml. Locate the `unitRPCResult()` event handler, which is called when the HTTPService successfully returns unit information. Place a breakpoint on the line of code that assigns the `unit` variable a value from the event object by double-clicking in the gray column to the left of the line numbers.

```
30              private function unitRPCResult(event:ResultEvent):void{
31                  units=event.result.allUnits.unit;
32              }
```

2 Debug the DataEntry.mxml application. Be sure that you are viewing the Flex Debugging perspective in Flex Builder.

You will either be automatically taken back to Flex Builder after you debug the application, or else you might have to click the blinking Flex Builder icon in the Task Manager to get back to Flex Builder. If you are prompted to go into the Flex Debugging perspective, click OK.

3 Assume that you want to check the value of the `units` variable to be sure that the values are properly assigned. The first thing to do is to be sure that the event object contains the correct data. Use the Variables view and drill into the event object to see that the data is returned correctly.

In this case, the path to the XML data returned by the HTTPService is event→result→allUnits→object→unit. There you see the ArrayCollection returned.

4 Now you know that the data is being retrieved correctly. Next, you want to be sure it is assigned to the units variable. Click the Expressions view tab and then right-click in the Expressions view and select Add Watch Expression. Enter **units** and then click OK. Notice that the variable is defined because it is declared as an ArrayCollection in the application. Drill down into the variable; you will see it does not have any values.

The reason why the units variable has no values yet is because the breakpoint stops execution before the line is executed. So you must run the line of code before the assignment is made.

5 In the Debug view, click the Step Over button; you will see that the debugging session is now sitting on the closing brace of the function and that units now has the correct values.

✶ **NOTE:** Do not terminate the debugging session because you will shortly see that you can add breakpoints during an active debugging session.

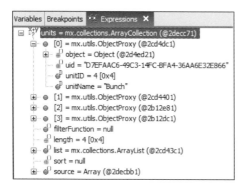

6 Now assume that you want to be sure the data returned from the Data Manager is also correct, which retrieves data for the variables categories and foodColl. Place a breakpoint on the closing brace of the categorizedProductDataLoaded() method.

```
34        private function categorizedProductDataLoaded():void{
35            categories = new ArrayCollection(prodMgr.getCats());
36            foodColl= prodMgr.getCategorizedProducts();
37        }
```

7 Be sure that you have not terminated the debugging session and then click the Resume command. You will see that the debugging session has now highlighted where you set the second breakpoint. Double-click the Variables tab to make it full screen.

Because there are so many properties in the Variables view, it is often helpful to make it full screen when looking for variables and their associated values.

8 In the Variables view, be sure to expand the variable to see all the variables within the scope. Right-click in the Variables view and select Find Variable. Start typing **categories** until you can see that variable highlighted in the Variables view. Click OK to close the Find Variable window, and then check to be sure the correct data stored in an ArrayCollection is in categories. Right-click in the Variables view again and select Find Variable. Start typing **foodColl** until you can see that variable highlighted in the Variables view. Click OK to close the Find Variable window and then ensure that the correct XML data is in foodColl.

Notice that you can see the values of the variable selected in the Variables view in the Detail Pane. When you select foodColl, you can see the actual XML in the Detail Pane—either to the right of or below the variable display.

You can change the location of the Detail Pane by choosing the option from the Variables view menu (a downward-facing triangle) and selecting the Orientation option of your choice.

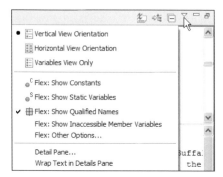

9 Be sure you are still in a debugging session, and assume that you want to be sure that correct data is being returned from a component that updates a product. Set a third breakpoint on the first line of code in the updateProduct() function.

```
62              private function updateProduct(product:Product):void{
63                  var dm:DataManager = DataManager.getDataManager("http://localhost
64                  dm.addEventListener("updateProductResult", updateProductResult);
65                  dm.makeRemoteCall("updateProduct", "updateProductResult", {aProdu
66              }
```

This breakpoint will behave a bit differently from the second one you set. When you resumed the application to continue to the second breakpoint, you did not have to interact with the application, loading data happened on startup. When you resume, you will have to interact with the application for the third breakpoint to be hit.

10 Select the Resume command from the Debug view. Return to the browser where the application is running and select a product from the Tree on the Update/Delete Product tab. Make a change to the product information and then click Update. Be sure that you are viewing the Flex Debugging perspective in Flex Builder. In the Variables view, check to be sure that Product has your new value.

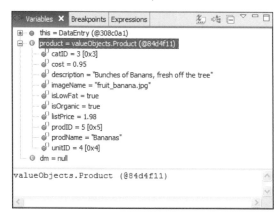

> **TIP:** Of course you could have terminated the debugging session, cleared the first two break-points, and then set a single breakpoint on the updateProduct() function. But by following that procedure, you would not have seen that you can select Resume, return to the application and get to the next breakpoint in a single debugging session.

11 Terminate the debugging session and close any open files.

You will be working with a different main application in the next task.

Handling Errors with try-catch

No matter how careful you are when developing your applications, there will be times when run-time errors will occur. You might make a mistake in development, or perhaps users will use your application in a way that you never anticipated. It is considered a poor practice to allow those errors to be seen by users. Instead, you should anticipate where a run-time error could occur and handle those using try-catch statements. Run-time errors, also called exceptions, can be caught, and you can choose what should happen—depending on the type of exception caught and the situation. Exception handling gives your applications the chance to recover gracefully from run-time errors instead of having the user have the error pop up when using your application.

The new ActionScript 3.0 compiler reports syntactical errors to you in Flex Builder and prevents your application from being built. These types of errors are not the type to be dealt with using try-catch. Run-time errors occur when a user is running your application and represent errors caused during playback of the SWF file.

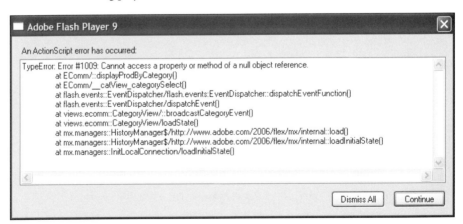

In earlier versions of Flash Player, more often than not, Flash Player failed silently. This was not a good situation for you as the developer because you were not given a clue about why the application did not work, you just knew it did not. So run-time errors are a good thing for you as a developer, but you should not let the users of the application see them.

Using the try-catch Syntax

The general syntax for using try-catch is the following:

```
try{
    //possible error producing code;
}
catch (e:ErrorType){
    //code to execute when error is caught;
}
```

A simple example designed to guarantee an error is as follows:

```
<mx:Script>
    <![CDATA[
        import mx.collections.ArrayCollection;
        private var newAC:ArrayCollection=new ArrayCollection();
        private function test():void{
            try{
                var myVar:Object=newAC.getItemAt(10);
            }
            catch (e:Error){
                errorLabel.text="error caught";
            }
        }
    ]]>
</mx:Script>
<mx:Label id="errorLabel" text="error Label"/>
<mx:Button label="Cause a Problem" click="test()"/>
```

In this case, when the Button is clicked, the Label would display **error caught**, and no exception error would be displayed in the browser running the application.

You can also access properties and methods of the error object, stored in the e variable in the previous code example, in the catch statement. Those available properties and methods are as follows:

- **message** (property)—Contains the message associated with the Error object.

- **name** (property)—Contains the name of the Error object.

- **getStackTrace()** (method)—For debugger versions of the Flash Player, only; this method returns the call stack for an error as a string at the time of the error's construction.

- **toString()** (method)—Returns the string "Error" by default or the value contained in Error.message, if defined.

By using the trace() statement in the catch block, you can see what appears in the Console view for each property and method:

```
catch (e:Error){
    trace(e.message);
    trace(e.name);
    trace(e.getStackTrace());
    trace(e.toString());
}
```

NOTE: Remember that when using the trace() statement you must Debug, not Run, your application to see the results in the Console view.

Understanding the Error Types

So far, both code examples use the Error class, which is the base class for all error classes in ActionScript. There are number of error classes. One set is defined by ECMAScript, and the others are ActionScript specific:

ECMAScript Errors	ActionScript Specific Errors
Error	ArgumentError
EvalError	SecurityError
RangeError	VerifyError
ReferenceError	EOFError
SyntaxError	IllegalOperationError
TypeError	IOError
URIError	MemoryError
	ScriptTimeOutError
	StackOverFlowError

Using Multiple catch Blocks

You can use these error types with a single catch block or you can have multiple catch blocks associated with a single try statement. So if you have a piece of code that might throw different kinds of errors, and you want to handle the different errors with different code, you can use multiple catch blocks. Here are some rules to remember it you are doing this:

- The first catch block with a matching error type will be executed.

- Only one catch block will be executed.

- Never place a catch block with the type Error before other catch blocks. Because Error will match all errors, you guarantee that the other catch blocks will never be used.

Here are a few examples to further clarify the rules to remember:

Example Using Only One catch Block

```
<mx:Script>
  <![CDATA[
      import mx.collections.ArrayCollection;
      private var newAC:ArrayCollection=new ArrayCollection();
      private function test():void{
        try{
          var myVar:Object=newAC.getItemAt(10);
        }
        catch (e:EvalError){
          errorLabel.text="EvalError class";
        }
```

code continues on next page

```
        catch (e:RangeError){
            errorLabel.text="RangeError class";
        }
        catch (e:Error){
            errorLabel.text="Error base class";
        }
    }
    ]]>
</mx:Script>
<mx:Label id="errorLabel" text="error Label"/>
<mx:Button label="Cause a Problem" click="test()"/>
```

When the Button is clicked, the Label would display the RangeError class. The code in the try block would cause the error. The first catch block is looking for an EvalError, which would not be a match so processing would continue. The second catch block is a RangeError, which is a match, so the corresponding string would be displayed. The third catch block with the base Error class is also a match, but because a previous catch block was used, the Error catch block is skipped.

Example Showing Bad Practice of Using the Error Base Class in the First catch Block

```
<mx:Script>
    <![CDATA[
        import mx.collections.ArrayCollection;
        private var newAC:ArrayCollection=new ArrayCollection();
        private function test():void{
            try{
                var myVar:Object=newAC.getItemAt(10);
            }
            catch (e:Error){
                errorLabel.text="Error base class";
            }
            catch (e:EvalError){
                errorLabel.text="EvalError class";
            }
            catch (e:RangeError){
                errorLabel.text="RangeError class";
            }
        }
    ]]>
</mx:Script>
<mx:Label id="errorLabel" text="error Label"/>
<mx:Button label="Cause a Problem" click="test()"/>
```

When testing this code, the Label would display the Error base class. The code in the try block would cause the error. The first catch block is looking for the Error base class, which would match any kind of error, so the corresponding string would be displayed. Because the first catch block is executed, the second and third catch blocks are ignored. This demonstrates the rule that you should never place a catch block with the type Error before other catch blocks. In this example, the specific error type, RangeError, was used to show that it was never evaluated because of order of the catch blocks.

Using the finally Statement

ActionScript, like many languages that implement some kind of try-catch syntax, offers a finally statement. The finally statement should be placed after all of your catch blocks, and the code it contains will be executed whether an error occurs in the try statement or not. In the example code shown, the errorLabel would display the RangeError class, and the finallyLabel would display "finally executed".

```
<mx:Script>
  <![CDATA[
      import mx.collections.ArrayCollection;
      private var newAC:ArrayCollection=new ArrayCollection();
      private function test():void{
        try{
          var myVar:Object=newAC.getItemAt(10);
        }
        catch (e:RangeError){
          errorLabel.text="RangeError class";
        }
        finally{
          finallyLabel.text="finally executed";
        }
      }
  ]]>
</mx:Script>
<mx:Label id="errorLabel" text="error Label"/>
<mx:Label id="finallyLabel" text="finally Label"/>
<mx:Button label="Cause a Problem" click="test()"/>
```

In this example, even if you commented the assignment statement in the try statement, and no error occurred, the finally statement would still be executed, and the finallyLabel would display the corresponding text.

Using the throw Statement

There might be times when you want to manually generate an error. This means that something has occurred in your application that although it is not a run-time error, you want to raise an exception so it can be handled in your normal exception handling scheme. For instance, you might have a situation in which the number of products ordered is less than those in stock. You could programmatically take care of the situation, but might also want to handle the problem by raising an exception.

One approach would be to use an existing error class and put in a message you could later examine to check what the error was. In the following code example, in the try statement the throw statement is used to raise an exception of type Error, and the error is then caught and the custom message is displayed.

```
<mx:Script>
  <![CDATA[
        import mx.collections.ArrayCollection;
        private var newAC:ArrayCollection=new ArrayCollection();
        private function test():void{
           try{
              throw new Error("This is a custom message on a throw statement");
           }
           catch (e:Error){
              errorLabel.text=e.message;
           }
        }
  ]]>
</mx:Script>
<mx:Label id="errorLabel" text="error Label"/>
<mx:Button label="Cause a Problem" click="test()"/>
```

In this code example the errorLabel would display "This is a custom message on a throw statement".

Creating Your Own Error Classes

When wanting to throw an error, the next step would be to throw an error of a class you have created. Perhaps you will look for that specific class in your catch and/or it will contain a special code to alert you of a particular exception. The following ActionScript class defines a custom error class that extends the base Error class. You add an instance variable named customCode that will hold the error code that will be generated in a specific situation you have defined. By the package name, errorClasses, you see that this class was saved in a directory named errorClasses.

```
package errorClasses {
   public class CustomError extends Error {
      public var customCode:int;
      public function CustomError(message:String,customCode:int){
         super(message);
         this.customCode=customCode;
      }//end constructor
   }//end class
}//end package
```

To use this custom class, you'll need to import the class and then throw it when a certain condition occurs. When you instantiate it, you'll need to pass both a custom message as the first parameter and a custom integer code as a second parameter. The following code example shows just that:

```
<mx:Script>
   <![CDATA[
         import errorClasses.CustomError;
         private function test():void{
            try{
               throw new CustomError("Custom message",123);
            }
            catch (e:CustomError){
               errorLabel.text=e.message;
               codeLabel.text=String(e.customCode);
            }
         }
   ]]>
</mx:Script>
<mx:Label id="errorLabel" text="error Label"/>
<mx:Label id="codeLabel" text="code Label"/>
<mx:Button label="Cause a Problem" click="test()"/>
```

When the Button is clicked, the errorLabel displays "Custom message", and the codeLabel displays 123, both of which are arbitrary example values.

✱ **NOTE:** Because of security constraints, users of Microsoft Internet Explorer cannot build and preview this next task. History Management is used and does not work in Internet Explorer when previewing a local file, meaning that it does not work when previewing local files on your hard drive. However, it will work if the file is on a web server or accessed through an HTTP URL as opposed to the file:// URL that is used during normal development. If you are using Internet Explorer, you will need to preview these files from a web server. History Management does work in Firefox and Netscape browsers when previewing a local file.

1 From the FlexGrocer project, open the file as/ecomm.as. Locate the displayProdByCategory() method and remove all if statement logic so it appears as follows:

```
private function displayProdByCategory(event:CategoryEvent):void{
   prodTile.visible=false;
   var prodArray:Array=catProds.getProdsForCat(event.cat.catID);
   prodByCategory=new ArrayCollection(prodArray);
   prodTile.visible=true;
}
```

You are removing the logic that prevents a run-time error from occurring. You will replace the if logic with try-catch-finally.

2 Run the EComm.mxml application. Click one of the categories, and then click the browser's Back button to get the run-time error to appear.

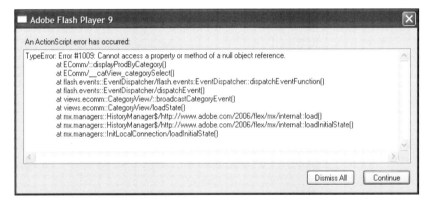

3 In the function, surround the four lines of code with a try block; then trace the message property of the error in a catch block. Debug the application. Click one of the categories and then click the browser's Back button.

```
private function displayProdByCategory(event:CategoryEvent):void{
   try{
      prodTile.visible=false;
      var prodArray:Array=catProds.getProdsForCat(event.cat.catID);
      prodByCategory=new ArrayCollection(prodArray);
      prodTile.visible=true;
   }catch(e:Error){
      trace(e.message);
   }
}
```

You should see in the Console view that the trace statement displays the same message as in the first line of the run-time error.

4 Remove the trace statement.

Even though the trace statement will display only information when debugging an application, there is no need to leave the code in the function.

5 Move the code that sets the prodTile's visible property to false above the try block. Just below this line of code, create a variable local to the function named prodArray and data type it as Array. Alter the existing code, as shown in the following example, and implement the logic of the try-catch-finally code with the newly created prodArray variable.

```
private function displayProdByCategory(event:CategoryEvent):void{
   prodTile.visible=false;
   var prodArray:Array;
   try{
      prodArray=catProds.getProdsForCat(event.cat.catID);
   }catch( err:Error ){
      prodArray=new Array();
   }finally{
      prodByCategory=new ArrayCollection(prodArray);
   }
   prodTile.visible=true;
}
```

This will catch the error and just set the ArrayCollection to an empty array if the user presses the back button too many times. So, instead of an error being thrown and the application crashing, the application is ready to use.

6 Save ecomm.as and run the Ecomm.mxml application. Click one of the categories and then click the browser's back button.

Rather than an error being displayed, the area below the toolbar is blank.

What You Have Learned

In this lesson, you have:

- Used the <mx:StackTrace> tag to watch data passed between client and server (pages 562–564)

- Learned new details about Flex Builder's built-in debugger (pages 565–572)

- Handled run-time exceptions using the try-catch-finally statements (pages 572–581)

This appendix contains the requirements and instructions for you to complete the exercises in this book. It covers the following:

- Hardware requirements
- Software requirements
- Software installation

Hardware Requirements

Windows

- Intel® Pentium® 4 processor or equivalent
- 512 MB RAM (1GB of RAM recommended)
- 700 MB of available hard disk space

Macintosh

- Flex Builder for Macintosh is not available at the time this book went to the printers, but is expected shortly.

Software Requirements

- Microsoft Windows XP with Service Pack 2, Windows XP Professional, Windows 2000 Server, Windows 2000 Pro or Windows Server 2003

- Java Virtual Machine: Sun JRE 1.4.2, Sun JRE 1.5, IBM® JRE 1.4.2

- For the Flex Builder plug-in, Eclipse 3.1.1 or 3.1.2 is required (Eclipse 3.2 is not currently supported.)

- A recent version of one of the following browsers:

  - Internet Explorer

  - Mozilla Firefox

  - Netscape Navigator

  - Opera

✱ NOTE: Due to security constraints, History Management does not work in Internet Explorer when previewing a local file, meaning that it does not work when previewing local files on your hard drive. However, it will work if the file is on a web server or accessed through an HTTP URL as opposed to the file:// URL that is used during normal development. If you are using Internet Explorer you will need to preview these files from a web server. History Management does work in Firefox and Netscape browsers when previewing a local file.

- The latest version of Adobe Flash Player, or at least version 9 (During the installation of Flex Builder 2 your Flash Player will be upgraded to version 9.)

► TIP: To check your Flash Player version, go to www.adobe.com, right-click the main ad banner, and select About Macromedia Flash Player; or go to www.adobe.com/software/flash/about.

Software Installation

There are three phases of the installation:

- Installing Flex products

- Installing lesson files

- Installing the ColdFusion Extensions for Adobe Flex Builder 2

APPENDIX A

Setup Instructions

Be sure to complete the installation of all required files before working through the lessons within the book.

Installing Flex Products

If you do not yet have Flex Builder 2 and Flex Data Services (FDS) installed, step through the following directions to install them.

1 Browse to the URL www.adobe.com/products/flex and click the Download Now link; download both the following:

- Flex Builder 2

- Flex Data Services 2

2 Install Flex Builder 2, accepting all the default options. The trial period on Flex Builder 2 is 25 days.

3 Install Flex Data Services 2, accepting all the default options.

When asked for a serial number, *leave it blank*. This installs the Express version that does not time out.

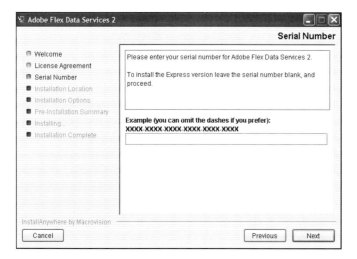

Installing Lesson Files

Once again, it is important that all the required files are in place before working though the lessons within the book.

1 From the CD included with your book, copy the flex2tfs directory to the root of your drive.

In this directory there is a subdirectory named flexGrocer, in which you will be doing most of your work. Also included are directories for each lesson in the book with starting code and completed code for the work you do in the lesson.

2 From the CD included with your book unzip the cfusionFlexTFS.zip file to the root of your drive.

All files are unzipped to a directory named cfusionFlexTFS. This is a fully configured version of ColdFusion Developer Edition. The files directly related to this book are located in *driveroot*:/cfusionFlexTFS/servers/cfusion/cfusion-ear/cfusion-war/flexGrocer.

❈ NOTE: The server code for this book relies upon the files and directory structure created during the installation process described. If you install the files in a location other than the default, you must update the path information of two files within the ColdFusion server: fileUpload.cfm on line 2 and ProductManager.cfc on line 125, both originally located at /cfusionFlexTFS/servers/cfusion/cfusion-ear/cfusion-war/flexGrocer/cfcs, with your modified installation directories.

Installing the ColdFusion Extensions for Adobe Flex Builder 2

1 Start Flex Builder; then select Help > Software Updates > Find and Install.

2 Select the Search For New Features To Install option and click Next.

3 Click the New Archived Site button.

4 Select the CF_FB_Extensions.zip file, and click Open. The default location for this file in Windows is C:\WINDOWS\Downloaded Installations\Adobe Flex Builder 2\ColdFusion Extensions for Flex Builder\CF_FB_Extensions.zip.

The location of this file is where you directed the install files to be unzipped when first starting the installation of Flex Builder.

5 When the Edit Local Site dialog box appears, click OK.

6 Ensure that the CF_FB_Extensions.zip is checked and click Finish.

7 In the Updates window, select the check box next to CF_FB_Extensions.zip, and click Next.

8 Select the I Accept The Terms In The License Agreement option and click Next.

9 Click Finish.

10 Click Install All.

11 When the installation is complete, click Yes to restart Flex Builder.

Starting Flex Data Services and ColdFusion

1 To ensure that the installation worked correctly, start Flex Data Services by opening a console window (DOS prompt), moving to the *driveroot:*/fds2/jrun4/bin directory, and entering **jrun –start default**. Be sure that FDS starts with no errors being shown. To stop the service, press Ctrl+C or close the console window. To restart the service, if you are still in the console, just press the up arrow and it will bring back to the prompt the previously typed entries.

2 To ensure that the installation worked correctly, start the configured ColdFusion by opening another console window (DOS prompt), moving to the *driveroot:*/cfusionFlexTFS/bin directory, and entering **jrun –start cfusion**. Be sure that ColdFusion starts with no errors being shown. To stop the service, press Ctrl+C or close the console window. To restart the service, if you are still in the console, just press the up arrow and it will bring back to the prompt the previously typed entries.

Starting in Lesson 17, "Accessing Server-side Objects," both ColdFusion and FDS need to be running in console windows to complete the exercises in the lessons.

Installing Flash Debug Player

At various times in the book, you will be using features of Flash Debug Player. If you happen to get a notice saying you do not have Flash Debug Player installed, follow these steps to install it:

1 Locate the directory *installDirectory*/Flex Builder 2/Player/debug.

✱ **NOTE:** In a default Windows installation this directory would be C:/Program Files/Adobe/Flex Builder 2/Player/debug.

2 To install Flash Debug Player for Internet Explorer, run the program Install Flash Player 9 AX.exe. For other versions of web browsers, run the program Install Flash Player 9.exe.

▶ **TIP:** In rare instances, you might run the appropriate installer and still get the message that you don't have the debug version of the player. In this case, uninstall the version you currently have by using the information located at this URL: www.adobe.com/cfusion/knowledgebase/index.cfm?id=tn_1415.

Index

Middle and Secondary Classroom Management

THIRD EDITION

MIDDLE AND SECONDARY CLASSROOM MANAGEMENT

Lessons from Research and Practice

CAROL SIMON WEINSTEIN

Rutgers, the State University of New Jersey

Boston   Burr Ridge, IL   Dubuque, IA   Madison, WI   New York   San Francisco   St. Louis
Bangkok   Bogotá   Caracas   Kuala Lumpur   Lisbon   London   Madrid   Mexico City
Milan   Montreal   New Delhi   Santiago   Seoul   Singapore   Sydney   Taipei   Toronto

Higher Education

MIDDLE AND SECONDARY CLASSROOM MANAGEMENT: LESSONS FROM RESEARCH AND PRACTICE
Published by McGraw-Hill, a business unit of The McGraw-Hill Companies, Inc., 1221 Avenue of
the Americas, New York, NY 10020. Copyright © 2007, 2003, 1996 by The McGraw-Hill Companies,
Inc. All rights reserved. No part of this publication may be reproduced or distributed in any form
or by any means, or stored in a database or retrieval system, without the prior written consent of
The McGraw-Hill Companies, Inc., including, but not limited to, in any network or other electronic
storage or transmission, or broadcast for distance learning. Some ancillaries, including electronic
and print components, may not be available to customers outside the United States.

This book is printed on acid-free paper.

3 4 5 6 7 8 9 0 FGR/FGR 0 9 8

ISBN-13: 978-0-07-301039-7
ISBN-10:   0-07-301039-1

Vice President and Editor-in-Chief: *Emily Barrosse*
Publisher: *Beth Mejia*
Executive Editor: *David Patterson*
Developmental Editor: *Beth Kaufman*
Freelance Permissions Coordinator: *Connie Dowcett*
Marketing Manager: *Melissa S. Caughlin*
Managing Editor: *Jean Dal Porto*
Senior Project Manager: *Becky Komro*
Art Director: *Jeanne Schreiber*
Interior Designer: *Kay Fulton*
Cover Designer: *Marianna Kinigakis*
Cover Credit: © *BananaStock/SuperStock*
Interior Photographs: *Suzanne Karp Krebs*
Senior Production Supervisor: *Carol A. Bielski*
Composition: *10/12 Garamond by Interactive Composition Corporation*
Printing: *45# New Era Matte, Quebecor World*

Library of Congress Cataloging-in-Publication Data

Weinstein, Carol Simon.
    Middle and secondary classroom management : lessons from research and
practice / Carol Simon Weinstein.—3rd. ed.
        p. cm.
    Rev. ed. of: Secondary classroom management. c2003.
    Includes bibliographical references and indexes.
    ISBN-13: 978-0-07-301039-7 (softcover : acid-free paper)
    ISBN-10: 0-07-301039-1 (softcover : acid-free paper)
1. Classroom management. 2. Education, Secondary. 3. Education,
Elementary. 4. Classroom environment. I. Weinstein, Carol Simon.
Secondary classroom management. II. Title.
LB3013.W46 2007
373.1102′4—dc22

                                                                    2006046207

The Internet addresses listed in the text were accurate at the time of publication. The inclusion of a Web site does not
indicate an endorsement by the authors or McGraw-Hill, and McGraw-Hill does not guarantee the accuracy of the
information presented at these sites.

www.mhhe.com

ABOUT THE AUTHOR

Carol Simon Weinstein is professor emerita in the Department of Learning and Teaching at Rutgers Graduate School of Education. She received her bachelor's degree in psychology from Clark University in Worcester, Massachusetts, and her master's and doctoral degrees from Harvard Graduate School of Education. Dr. Weinstein began her research career by studying the impact of classroom design on students' behavior and attitudes. She pursued this topic for many years, writing about the ways that classroom environments can be designed to facilitate teachers' goals and to foster children's learning and development. Eventually, her interest in organizing classroom space expanded to include classroom organization and management in general. She is the author (with Andrew J. Mignano, Jr.) of *Elementary Classroom Management: Lessons from Research and Practice* (McGraw-Hill, 2007), as well as numerous chapters and articles on classroom management and teacher education students' beliefs and expectations. In 2000, Dr. Weinstein was recognized by the American Federation of Teachers for "Bridging the Gap between Theory and Practice in Effective Classroom Management." Most recently, Dr. Weinstein co-edited (with Carolyn Evertson) the first *Handbook of Classroom Management: Research, Practice, and Contemporary Issues* (Lawrence Erlbaum Associates, Inc., 2006), a compendium of 47 chapters written by scholars from around the world.

DEDICATION

To Fred, Donnie, Sandy, and Christina—You have taught me
so much and inspired so many.

BRIEF CONTENTS

PART IV   COPING WITH THE CHALLENGES   311

Contents

PART III ORGANIZING AND MANAGING INSTRUCTION 185

Preface

"Don't smile until Christmas."

When I went through my own teacher education program in the late 1960s, that was all I learned about preventing inappropriate behavior. The field of "classroom management" had not yet been defined, and teachers had to rely on instinct, tricks of the trade, and luck. Fortunately, that is no longer the case. A substantial knowledge base for classroom management now exists, and beginning teachers can learn research-based principles, concepts, and practices for creating orderly classrooms. Indeed, as Jere Brophy (2006) has written, "The work on classroom management can be counted among the major success stories of educational research in the 20th century" (p. 39).

Goals for the Third Edition

As in the earlier editions, my goal for the third edition of *Middle and Secondary Classroom Management* has been to use this research base to provide readers with clear, practical suggestions for organizing and managing classrooms. Chapters within the book address the ongoing management tasks that teachers face—from organizing physical space, creating community, and teaching behavioral norms to motivating students, organizing instruction, and responding to inappropriate behavior. Throughout the text, I have tried to convey my belief that *classroom management is fundamentally about interpersonal relationships*—about connecting with students, conveying a sense of caring, and building community. For sure, there are specific management strategies to be learned and implemented, but at its core, successful classroom management requires positive teacher–student and student–student relationships. As a reader of an earlier edition wrote in an e-mail: "One thing that I took from the book is that you can have every management strategy out there memorized, but if you can't communicate to your students that you care about their success, you're going to have a hard time."

PROFILES OF REAL TEACHERS: A UNIQUE FEATURE OF THE TEXT

The full title of this book is *Middle and Secondary Classroom Management: Lessons from Research and Practice.* As the subtitle indicates, I have integrated what research has to say about effective classroom management with knowledge culled from practice. This is done by highlighting the thinking and the actual management practices of four real secondary teachers: Fred Cerequas (social studies), Donnie Collins (mathematics), Sandra Krupinski (chemistry), and Christina Lugo Vreeland (English). Readers will come to know these four teachers—to hear their thinking on various aspects of classroom management and to see the ways they establish relationships with students and parents. Their stories provide real-life examples of the concepts and principles derived from research.

These four teachers not only teach different subjects, they also work in school districts that differ substantially in terms of race, ethnicity, and socioeconomic status. For example, Fred's suburban district is predominantly European American (64 percent) and Asian American (20 percent), and only 12 percent of the students are eligible for the federal free or reduced-price lunch program. In contrast, Donnie's urban district is 54 percent Latino and 41 percent African American, and 80 percent of the students are eligible for the federal lunch program. Donnie and Christina teach basic skills classes, while Sandy teaches an advanced placement course, and Fred teaches an elective entitled "Institute for Political and Legal Education." Because of differences like these, their ways of managing their classrooms often look very different. But all of the teachers are able to build caring relationships with students, and all of the teachers enact the same basic principles of classroom management.

One point about the structure of the book needs to be made explicit. The portraits of Fred, Donnie, Sandy, and Christina are composites derived from material that I started collecting for the first edition in 1994. In other words, I have created a portrait of each teacher by describing incidents that occurred in different years with different students as though they had all occurred in the same academic year with the same class. Christina and Sandy are still working in their schools, so they were able to contribute to this new edition; however, Fred and Donnie retired several years ago.

THE THIRD EDITION: AN OVERVIEW

Beginning teachers frequently contend that their teacher preparation programs inadequately prepared them for the real-life challenges of classroom management. In particular, they call for more preparation in areas such as communicating with parents; responding to inappropriate behavior; working in diverse, multicultural settings; and teaching students with disabilities. They crave "real life stories on how to resolve classroom management issues" (Jones, 2006, p. 889) and complain about courses that are too theoretical and removed from the realities of managing a classroom.

In similar fashion, leading teacher educators have also called for more extensive preparation focused on a limited number of key classroom management skills. Lasley (1994), for example, recommends that preservice teachers focus on three general skill areas: (1) developing and implementing classroom rules, (2) dealing with misbehavior, and (3) working with parents when dealing with chronic misbehavior. Similarly, Jones (2006) has argued that preservice teachers need to develop the skills to (1) base management decisions on students' personal and cultural needs; (2) create positive teacher–student, student–student, and teacher–parent relationships; (3) implement motivating instructional methods; (4) develop behavior standards and routine procedures that ensure a safe, supportive classroom environment; and (5) respond effectively to student misbehavior. He suggests that this approach is far more fruitful than exposing preservice teachers to "a limited number of theorists" or focusing "on one or a few specific models (e.g., Glasser, Canter, Dreikurs)" (p. 893).

In revising this edition, I have tried to heed the concerns of beginning teachers and the recommendations of these teacher educators. Like the earlier editions, the third edition of *Middle and Secondary Classroom Management* is grounded in the real world of the secondary classroom. I address topics that are often omitted in classroom management texts but that seem crucial—such as working with families and using time effectively. I also discuss strategies for motivating students and managing the instructional formats commonly used in middle and secondary classrooms (e.g., independent work, groupwork, recitations, and discussions), topics more commonly found in general methods books. On the other hand, I have *not* included a discussion of the various models of classroom management (e.g., Canter's Assertive Discipline; Glasser's Reality Therapy), although I sometimes refer to them in the context of other issues. As always I have tried to balance the need for breadth and depth of coverage with the need for a book that is easy to use and reasonable in length. I have also tried to maintain a writing style that is clear, lively, conversational, and engaging. Readers of previous editions have told me that the book is unlike any textbook they have read, and I take that as a compliment.

NEW TO THE THIRD EDITION

During this revision process, I have focused on the following specific areas for expansion and improvement:

- IMPORTANT CONTENT ADDITIONS—The third edition has been thoroughly updated to reflect recent scholarship and current concerns. Based on reviewer feedback and recent trends within the classroom management field, I have placed much greater emphasis on the following key topics:
  - *Increased Coverage of Classroom Management at the Middle School Level*—As noted by the new book title, I have slightly expanded the scope of the Third Edition to better address the issues and concerns of those who will be teaching middle school students. Wherever possible, I have included content about particular classroom management issues that may arise at the middle school level.

- *Building caring, respectful relationships with students.* This topic is not only the focus of Chapter 3 (formerly Chapter 5), it is echoed throughout the entire book. It reflects my belief (stated earlier) that classroom management is fundamentally a matter of teacher–student relationships. In addition, research consistently demonstrates that when students view their teachers as being caring and supportive, they are more likely to engage in academic activities and to exhibit responsible, prosocial behavior.

- *Issues related to cultural diversity.* A key assumption of the book (discussed in Chapter 1) is that teachers must be "culturally responsive classroom managers," and this theme is addressed in every chapter of the book. A new marginal icon spotlights the specific places in the text where this coverage can be found.

- *Students with disabilities and teaching in inclusive classrooms.* In addition to the description of attention-deficit/hyperactivity disorder included in the last edition, Chapter 12 (Helping Students with Special Needs) now examines the characteristics of children with a variety of special needs, such as learning disabilities, emotional/behavior disorders, autism, and Asperger Syndrome. Chapter 12 also contains a discussion of co-teaching and collaborating with special educators and paraprofessionals, as well as a section on "functional behavioral analysis," the process of understanding *why* students engage in specific problem behaviors.

- *Motivating disaffected and alienated students.* Discussion of this crucial topic has been expanded and focuses on the need to establish positive teacher–student relationships and to hold high expectations. Recommendations have been taken directly from reports of inner-city adolescents who talk honestly about the kind of teachers who can help them succeed.

- *Coverage of hot topics affecting educators today.* I have also added content on a variety of current issues, such as: cyber-bullying, discipline and students' First Amendment rights, the debate over ebonics, holding class meetings, and involving parents in interactive homework assignments.

- NEW PEDAGOGICAL FEATURES TO IMPROVE STUDENT LEARNING—In addition to these substantive content changes, this edition contains several new pedagogical features that both students and instructors will find useful:

  - Each chapter now includes several *Pause and Reflect* boxes to encourage student reflection and promote comprehension of key chapter concepts.

  - The text now uses a *marginal diversity icon* to highlight important multicultural coverage that appears within each chapter.

  - Useful, applied classroom management strategies are now presented in *Practical Tips* boxes so that they stand out and can be easily accessed by readers.

  - For instructors' ease of use, *Activities for Skill Building and Reflection* (at the end of each chapter) have been expanded and divided into three discrete sections: "In Class," "On Your Own," and "For Your Portfolio."

  - The *For Further Reading* feature has been greatly improved by adding more detailed annotations.

ELEMENTARY CLASSROOM MANAGEMENT: A COMPANION TEXT

This edition of *Middle and Secondary Classroom Management* parallels the fourth edition of *Elementary Classroom Management: Lessons from Research and Practice* (Weinstein & Mignano, 2007) so that instructors teaching courses with both elementary and secondary teacher education students can use the two books as a package. While the principles and concepts discussed are the same, the teachers on which the companion book is based all work at the elementary level, and the "lessons from research" are based largely on studies conducted in kindergarten through sixth grade.

ACKNOWLEDGMENTS

Once again, I express my gratitude to the four teachers featured in this book. They allowed me to observe in their classrooms and shared their wisdom, frustrations, and celebrations during countless hours of interviews. I am also grateful to the district administrators who agreed to this project and to the school counselors who took the time to speak with me and shared their perspectives. To my students, many thanks for allowing me to use your journal entries and for providing me with feedback on everything from confusing content to printing errors. It should be noted that in some cases, details from the journals have been changed to avoid embarrassment to anyone, and at times, composite entries have been created.*

I am also extremely grateful to Joyce Epstein from the Center on School, Family, and Community Partnerships at Johns Hopkins University, who carefully reviewed the chapter on working with families and provided me with insightful comments and up-to-date references. Thanks also to Margie Boudreau, a sensitive special educator who read the previous edition and gave me suggestions about where to include additional material on students with special needs. I also thank Leslie Soodak of Pace University for her expert help with the section on inclusion and Ruth Moscovitch who generously talked with me about the legal issues involved in discipline. I also acknowledge the contribution of Delia Cruz Fernandez, a talented Spanish teacher who allowed me to observe in her classroom, to interview her students, and to question her about why she did what she did. (She even taught me some Spanish!) I would have loved to have included her as a fifth teacher in the book, but she moved more than halfway across the country before we were done.

I express deep appreciation to the individuals who reviewed the earlier edition: Eileen Austin, University of South Florida; Robert Gates, Bloomsburg University; Laurel Gibbons, University of Alabama; Dr. Gerald McGregor, University of Texas at Tyler; Chris Melby-Codling, Mississippi State University; Heidi Pellett, Minnesota State University, Mankato; Harry Weisenberger, Minnesota State University; Amy White, University of South Carolina, Charlotte; and Tom Williams, West Virginia Wesleyan College. If there are any errors or misstatements, the fault is entirely my own.

*A special thank you goes to Mary Marcos for allowing me to use her case study on reframing.

I feel fortunate to have had the opportunity to work with Beth Kaufman, an outstanding consulting editor whose expertise, enthusiasm, and energy always helped to cheer me on. I am also very grateful for the unflagging support and patience of Cara Harvey Labell and David Patterson at McGraw-Hill. To Becky Komro, my thanks for being such a conscientious, efficient project manager. Finally, a special thank you to Neil, who agreed to work one more semester so I could retire and devote full-time to the revisions.

Carol Simon Weinstein

References

Brophy, J. (2006). History of research on classroom management. In C. M. Evertson & C. S. Weinstein (Eds.), *Handbook of classroom management: Research, practice, and contemporary issues.* Mahwah, NJ: Lawrence Erlbaum Associates, Inc.

Jones, V. (2006). How do teachers learn to be effective classroom managers? In C. M. Evertson & C. S. Weinstein (Eds.), *Handbook of classroom management: Research, practice, and contemporary issues.* Mahwah, NJ: Lawrence Erlbaum Associates, Inc.

Lasley, T. (1994). Teacher technicians: A "new" metaphor for new teachers. *Action in Teacher Education, 16*(1), 11–19.

OTHER COMPANION TEXTS THAT ARE AVAILABLE FROM MCGRAW-HILL

Middle and Secondary Classroom Management can also be supplemented with any of the following McGraw-Hill texts. Contact your local McGraw-Hill sales representative for packaging information:

A Guide to Observation, Participation, and Reflection in the Classroom with Forms for Field Use CD-ROM, 5th Edition by Arthea Reed and Verna Bergemann, ISBN 0-07-298553-4.

This complete, hands-on guide to classroom observations provides detailed guides for observing the dynamics of the classroom, participating with the classroom teacher, and then reflecting on the experience. It also includes more than 50 practical blank forms that cover all aspects of observation, participation, and reflection, from the structured observation of a lesson to a checklist for determining teaching styles to reflections on small-group teaching.

Understanding Children: An Interview and Observation Guide for Educators, 1st Edition by Denise Daniels, Lorrie Beaumont, and Carol Doolin, ISBN 0-07-248185-4.

This hands-on book is a guide for interviewing and observing children in educational settings. It includes practical tips for interviewing and observing children as a way to understand their behavior, learning, and development; makes connections to the work of major developmental theorists and educational researchers; and discusses the analysis of observational data and its uses for guiding educational practices (e.g., instruction, cooperative grouping, and parent conferences).

Teaching Portfolios: Presenting Your Professional Best, 2nd Edition by Patricia Rieman and Jeanne Okrasinski, ISBN 0-07-287684-0.

This portfolio handbook includes authentic, student-generated artifacts as well as insights from administrators, teachers, and parents. Issues of classroom management, diversity, communication, planning, standards-based education, and reflection are all addressed in the context of how to approach these important aspects within a teaching portfolio and during interviews. The materials are designed for continued use as the students become in-service educators.

Case Studies for Teacher Problem Solving, by Rita Silverman, William Welty, and Sally Lyon.

Choose from an online menu of 80 cases addressing core curriculum areas in teacher education—development, classroom management, leadership, special education, diversity, teaching methods, educational psychology, and more. Visit www.mhhe.com/primis to preview the cases, then order a printed and bound copy for your consideration. If you like your case book, placing an order is easy. If you don't, make changes—there is no obligation.

***Taking Sides: Clashing Views on Controversial Issues in Classroom Management,* by Robert G. Harrington and Leticia Holub; ISBN 0-07-352718-1.**

Presenting current controversial issues in a debate-style format designed to stimulate student interest and develop critical thinking skills, *Taking Sides: Classroom Management* frames each issue with a thoughtful summary, an introduction, and a postscript.

***McGraw-Hill's Praxis I & II Exam,* by Laurie Rozakis; ISBN 0-07-144085-2.**

Written by a test designer and reader at ETS, McGraw-Hill's Praxis I & II is a complete insider's guide, offering a full-spectrum preparation for the two most important sections of the Praxis: Praxis I: Academic Skills Assessment and Praxis II: Subject Assessments.

Middle and Secondary Classroom Management

PART I

INTRODUCTION

Characteristics and Contradictions of the Middle and High School Classroom

For many prospective and beginning teachers, entering a middle or high school classroom is like returning home after a brief absence. So little has changed: desks with oversized arms are still arranged in straggly rows; bells still signal the end of classes; and bulletin boards still display faded copies of bell schedules and fire drill instructions. The familiarity of these sights and sounds makes us feel comfortable and at ease; in fact, it may lead us to conclude that the transition from student to teacher will be relatively easy. Yet, ironically, this very familiarity can be a trap; it can make it difficult to appreciate what a curious and demanding place the middle or secondary school classroom really is. Looking at the classroom as if we have never seen one before may help us recognize some of its strange characteristics and contradictions.

Viewed from a fresh perspective, the classroom turns out to be an extremely crowded place. It is more like a subway or a bus than a place designed for learning,

"I expect you all to be independent, innovative, critical thinkers who will do exactly as I say."

Figure 1.1   Students are urged to be independent and responsible, yet they are also expected to show complete obedience to the teacher.
Source: Reprinted by permission of Warren.

and it is hard to think of another setting (except prison, perhaps) where such large groups of individuals are packed so closely together for so many hours. Nonetheless, amid this crowdedness, students are often not permitted to interact. As Philip Jackson (1968) has noted, "students must try to behave as if they were in solitude, when in point of fact they are not. . . . These young people, if they are to become successful students, must learn how to be alone in a crowd" (p. 16).

There are other contradictions in this curious place. Middle and high school students are expected to work together in harmony, yet they may be strangers—even rivals—and may come from very different cultural backgrounds. Students are urged to help one another, but they are also told to keep their eyes on their own papers. They are encouraged to cooperate, but they are often in competition. They are lectured about being independent and responsible, yet they are also expected to show complete, unquestioning obedience to the teacher's dictates. (This peculiar situation is captured in the cartoon that appears in Figure 1.1.) They are urged to work slowly and carefully, but they are often reminded that 42- (or even 84-) minute periods require adherence to a rigid time schedule.

In addition to these contradictions, Walter Doyle (1986, 2006) has pointed out six features of the classroom setting that make it even more complex. First, classrooms are characterized by *multidimensionality.* Unlike a post office or a restaurant, places devoted to a single activity, the classroom is the setting for a broad range of events. Within its boundaries, students read, write, and discuss. They work on projects, view DVDs, and listen to lectures. They also form friendships, argue, and evaluate last Saturday's basketball game. Teachers lead whole-class discussions, coordinate small-group activities, and administer tests. They also take attendance, settle disputes, and counsel students with problems. Somehow, the classroom environment must be able to accommodate all these activities.

Second, many of these activities take place at the same time. This *simultaneity* makes the classroom a bit like a three-ring circus. Secondary teachers tend to use whole-group instruction more than their elementary counterparts; nonetheless, it is not uncommon to see a cluster of students working on a project while a few individuals write at their desks or on computers and a small group meets with the teacher about materials to include in their portfolios. Still other students may be passing notes about yesterday's soccer game. It is this simultaneity—this three-ring circus quality—that makes having "eyes in the back of your head" so valuable to teachers.

A third characteristic of classrooms is the rapid pace at which things happen. Classroom events occur with an *immediacy* that makes it impossible to think through every action ahead of time. An argument erupts over a perceived insult; a student complains that a neighbor is copying; a normally silent student makes a serious, but irrelevant, comment during a group discussion. Each of these incidents requires a quick response, an on-the-spot decision about how to proceed. Furthermore, classroom incidents like these cannot always be anticipated, despite the most careful planning. This *unpredictability* is a fourth characteristic of classrooms. It ensures that being a teacher is rarely boring, but unpredictability can also be exhausting.

A fifth characteristic of classrooms is the *lack of privacy*. Classrooms are remarkably public places. Within their four walls, each person's behavior can be observed by many others. Teachers talk of feeling as though they are always "on stage" or living in a "fishbowl" (Lortie, 1975). Their feelings are understandable. With 20 or 30 pairs of eyes watching, it is difficult to find a moment for a private chuckle or an unobserved groan. But the scrutiny goes two ways: Teachers constantly monitor students' behavior as well. And in response to this sometimes unwelcome surveillance, students develop an "active underlife" (Hatch, 1986) in which to pursue their own personal agendas. With skills that increase as they progress from grade to grade, students learn to pass notes, comb their hair, and do homework for another class, all—they hope—without the teacher's ever noticing. Yet, even if they avoid the teacher's eyes, there are always peers watching. It is difficult for students to have a private interaction with the teacher, to conceal a grade on a test, or to make a mistake without someone noticing.

Finally, over the course of the academic year, classes construct a joint *history*. This sixth characteristic means that classes, like families, remember past events—both positive and negative. They remember who got yelled at, who got away with being late to class, and what the teacher said about homework assignments. They remember who was going to have only "one more chance" before getting detention, and if the teacher didn't follow through, they remember that too. The class memory means that what happens today affects what happens tomorrow. It also means that teachers must work to shape a history of shared experiences that will support, rather than frustrate, future activities.

Calvin and Hobbes   by Bill Watterson

Figure 1.2   Calvin is captive.
Source: Calvin and Hobbes © Watterson. Reprinted with permission of Universal Press Syndicate. All rights reserved.

Crowded, competitive, contradictory, multidimensional, fast-paced, unpredictable, public—this portrait of the classroom highlights characteristics that we often overlook. I have begun the book with this portrait because I believe that *effective organization and management require an understanding of the unique features of the classroom.* Many of the management problems encountered by beginning teachers can be traced back to their failure to understand the complex setting in which they work.

Past experiences with children and adolescents may also mislead beginning teachers. For example, you may have tutored an individual student who was having academic difficulties, or perhaps you have been a camp counselor or a swim-club instructor. Although these are valuable experiences, they are very different from teaching in classrooms. Teachers do not work one-on-one with students in a private room; they seldom lead recreational activities that participants have themselves selected. Teachers do not even work with people who have chosen to be present. (See Figure 1.2 for Calvin's perspective on compulsory attendance.) Instead, *teachers work with captive groups of students, on academic agendas that students have not helped to set, in a crowded, public setting.* Within this setting, you must gain the cooperation of students and get them involved in educational activities. This is not a simple task. As Tracy Kidder (1989) has noted:

> The problem is fundamental. Put twenty or more children of roughly the same age in a little room, confine them to desks, make them wait in lines, make them behave. It is as if a secret committee, now lost to history, had made a study of children and, having figured out what the greatest number were least disposed to do, declared that all of them should do it. (p. 115)

Middle and Secondary Classroom Management is designed to help prospective and beginning teachers understand the special characteristics of the classroom setting and their implications for organization and management. I hope to provide concepts and principles that you can use to think about the managerial tasks you will encounter as a teacher. For example, once you recognize that students are a captive audience, you are better able to see why it's necessary to stimulate interest in lessons. Comprehending the norms of the traditional classroom leads you to appreciate the difficulty that students have in cooperative learning situations. Being aware of the crowded, public nature of classrooms helps you understand the importance of dealing with behavior problems in an unobtrusive way. A group of strangers can become a cohesive learning community if you know how to foster an atmosphere of caring and mutual support.

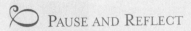

PAUSE AND REFLECT

Before going any further, jot down the words that come to mind when you hear the phrase "classroom management." Then write the answer to this question: "What is the goal of classroom management?" After reading the next section, compare your goals statement with the statement in the book. Are they similar? Different?

GUIDING ASSUMPTIONS

Sometimes, we become so preoccupied with basic management issues (like getting everyone to sit down), we forget that *classroom management is not about achieving order for order's sake; it's about achieving order so that learning can occur.* Indeed, classroom management has two distinct purposes: It not only seeks to establish and sustain an orderly environment so students can engage in meaningful academic learning, it also aims to enhance students' social and emotional growth. From this perspective, *how* a teacher achieves order is as important as *whether* a teacher achieves order (Evertson & Weinstein, 2006). Keeping this in mind, let us consider seven underlying assumptions that guide the content and organization of this book. (These are summarized in Table 1.1.)

The first assumption is that *successful classroom management fosters self-discipline and personal responsibility.* Let's be honest: Every teacher's worst fear is the prospect of losing control—of being helpless and ineffectual in the face of

---

TABLE 1.1   Guiding Assumptions about Classroom Management

1. Successful classroom management fosters self-discipline and personal responsibility.
2. Most problems of disorder in classrooms can be avoided if teachers foster positive student–teacher relationships, implement engaging instruction, and use good preventive management strategies.
3. The way teachers think about management strongly influences what they do. Teachers who view classroom management as a process of guiding and structuring classroom events tend to be more effective than teachers who stress their disciplinary role or who see classroom management as a product of personal charm.
4. The need for order must not supersede the need for meaningful instruction.
5. The tasks of classroom management vary across different classroom situations.
6. Managing today's diverse classrooms requires the knowledge, skills, and predispositions to work with students from diverse racial, ethnic, language, and social class backgrounds. In other words, teachers must become "culturally responsive classroom managers."
7. Becoming an effective classroom manager requires reflection, hard work, and time.

unruly, anarchic classes. Given this nightmare, it's tempting to create a coercive, top-down management system that relies heavily on the use of rewards and penalties to gain obedience. Yet, such an approach does little to teach students to make good choices about how to act. Furthermore, as Mary McCaslin and Tom Good (1998) point out, "the success of a compliance model depends upon constant monitoring (if the teacher turns her or his back, students misbehave . . .)" (p. 170). An emphasis on external control is also inconsistent with current thinking about curriculum and instruction (McCaslin & Good, 1992, 1998). It doesn't make sense to design learning activities that encourage independence, problem solving, and critical thinking, and then use managerial strategies that encourage dependence on points, popcorn parties, and punishment. This is not to discount the importance of teachers' authority; clearly, in order to be effective, you must be willing to set limits and guide students' behavior. Nonetheless, what you are aiming toward is an environment in which students behave appropriately, not out of fear of punishment or desire for reward, but out of a sense of personal responsibility.

The second assumption is that *most problems of disorder in classrooms can be avoided if teachers foster positive student–teacher relationships, implement engaging instruction, and use good preventive management strategies.* Let's look at each of these components in order. Extensive research demonstrates that when students perceive their teachers to be supportive and caring, they are more likely to engage in cooperative, responsible behavior and adhere to classroom rules and norms (Woolfolk Hoy & Weinstein, 2006). Similarly, when students find academic activities meaningful, engrossing, and stimulating, they are less inclined to daydream or disrupt. Finally, a pivotal study by Jacob Kounin (1970) documented the fact that orderly classes are more the result of a teacher's ability to *manage the activities of the group* than of particular ways of handling student misconduct. As a result of Kounin's work, we now distinguish between *discipline*—responding to inappropriate behavior—and *classroom management*—ways of creating a caring, respectful environment that supports learning.

A third assumption is that *the way teachers think about management strongly influences what they do.* Research has provided some fascinating examples of the links between teachers' beliefs about management and their behavior. Consider Sarah, for example, a first-year teacher who was having difficulty managing her class (Ulerick & Tobin, 1989). Sarah's behavior in the classroom seemed to reflect her belief that effective teachers should use charm and humor to engage students in learning and gain their cooperation. In short, her thinking about management reflected a metaphor of "teacher as comedian." Eventually, Sarah reconceptualized the role of teacher, discarding the comedian metaphor and adopting a metaphor of teacher as "social director." As "social director," the teacher's job was to "invite students to appropriate, interesting, and meaningful learning activities" (p. 12) and to assist students in directing their own learning activities. This change in Sarah's thinking about classroom management led to changes in her behavior and to dramatic improvements in the atmosphere of her classes.

In a similar study, Carter (1985) reviewed narrative descriptions of life in the classrooms of an effective and an ineffective classroom manager. Carter's analysis led her to conclude that the two teachers thought about classroom management in very different ways. The effective manager saw her managerial role as "a driver navigating a complex and often treacherous route" (p. 89). From this perspective, her responsibility was to guide classroom events smoothly and efficiently; she emphasized the academic tasks that students needed to accomplish and did not allow minor misbehaviors and interruptions to get her off course. In contrast, the ineffective manager seemed to see her role as "defender of a territory." Constantly vigilant for threats to order, she was careful to catch all misbehaviors whenever they occurred and used reprimands and appeals to authority in order to control inappropriate behavior.

Taken together, these studies suggest that teachers who view classroom management as a process of guiding and structuring classroom events tend to be more effective than teachers who stress their disciplinary role or who see classroom management as a product of personal charm (Brophy, 1988). This perspective on classroom management is also consistent with an emphasis on prevention.

Fourth, *the need for order must not supersede the need for meaningful instruction.* Although instruction cannot take place in an environment that is chaotic and disorderly, an excessive focus on management can sometimes *hinder* instruction (Doyle, 1986, 2006). For example, a teacher may wish to divide the class into small groups for a cooperative learning activity. Yet her anxiety about the noise level and her fear that students may not work well together could make her abandon the small-group project and substitute an individual worksheet assignment. Academic work that is more intellectually and socially challenging may also be more challenging from a managerial perspective. Yet, it is crucial that teachers not sacrifice the curriculum in order to achieve an orderly classroom. As Doyle (1985) comments, "A well-run lesson that teaches nothing is just as useless as a chaotic lesson in which no academic work is possible" (p. 33). The solution is to anticipate the specific managerial "hazards" that can arise in different situations (Carter, 1985) and try to prevent them from occurring.

The fifth assumption is that *the tasks of classroom management vary across different classroom situations.* Ecological psychologists remind us that the classroom is not a "homogenized glob" (Kounin & Sherman, 1979, p. 150). Rather, it is composed of distinct "subsettings"—teacher presentations, whole-class discussions, transition times, small-group activities, laboratory investigations—and what constitutes order may be different in each of these subsettings. For example, "calling out" may be a problem during a teacher-directed question-and-answer session (often referred to as recitation), but it may be perfectly acceptable in a more student-centered discussion. Similarly, students may be prohibited from helping one another during an independent writing assignment, but they may be encouraged to work together during a cooperative learning activity. Students have the right to know what is expected of them in these different classroom situations. This means that teachers must think about the behavior that is appropriate in each classroom subsetting and make a point of teaching students how they need to behave.

The sixth assumption is that *managing today's diverse classrooms requires the knowledge, skills, and predispositions to work with students from diverse racial, ethnic, language, and social class backgrounds.* In other words, *teachers must become "culturally responsive classroom managers"* (Weinstein, Curran, &

Tomlinson-Clarke, 2003; Weinstein, Tomlinson-Clarke, & Curran, 2004). Sometimes, a desire to treat students fairly leads teachers to strive for "color-blindness" (Nieto, 2002), and educators are often reluctant to talk about cultural characteristics for fear of stereotyping. But definitions and expectations of appropriate behavior are culturally influenced, and conflicts are likely to occur if we ignore our students' cultural backgrounds. Geneva Gay (2006) provides a telling example of what can happen when there is a "cultural gap" between teachers and students. She notes that African Americans frequently use "evocative vocabulary" and "inject high energy, exuberance, and passion" into their verbal communication (p. 355). European-American teachers may interpret such speech as rude or vulgar and feel compelled to chastise the students or even impose a punishment. Because the students see nothing wrong with what they said, they may resent and resist the teacher's response. As Gay notes: "The result is a cultural conflict that can quickly escalate into disciplinary sanctions in the classroom or referrals for administrative action" (p. 355).

To avoid situations like this, we need to become aware of our own culturally based assumptions, biases, and values, and reflect on how these influence our expectations for behavior and our interactions with students. By bringing our cultural biases to a conscious level, we are less likely to misinterpret the behaviors of our culturally different students and treat them inequitably. In addition, we must acquire cultural content knowledge. We must learn, for example, about our students' family backgrounds and their culture's norms for interpersonal relationships. Obviously, this knowledge must not be used to categorize or stereotype, and it is critical that we recognize the significant individual differences that exist among members of the same cultural group. Nonetheless, cultural content knowledge can be useful in developing *hypotheses* about students' behavior (Weiner, 1999).

The final assumption is that *becoming an effective classroom manager requires reflection, hard work, and time.* Classroom management cannot be reduced to a set of recipes or a list of "how-to's." As we have seen, the classroom environment is crowded, multidimensional, fast-paced, unpredictable, and public. In this complex setting, pat answers just won't work. Similarly, well-managed classrooms are not achieved by following "gut instinct" or doing "what feels right." Classroom management is a *learned craft.* That means that you must become familiar with the knowledge base that undergirds effective management. You must also be ready and willing to anticipate problems, analyze situations, generate solutions, make thoughtful decisions—and learn from your mistakes.

PLAN OF THE BOOK

Middle and Secondary Classroom Management focuses first on ways of creating a classroom environment that supports learning and self-regulation, such as designing an appropriate physical setting, building an atmosphere of caring and respect, developing standards for behavior, and using time wisely. It then moves to the managerial tasks directly related to instruction—for example, motivating students to learn, organizing groupwork, and managing student-centered discussions. Finally, the book examines the inevitable challenges associated with classroom management, such as responding to inappropriate behavior, helping students with special needs, and preventing and coping with violence.

Throughout the book, concepts and principles derived from research are woven together with the wisdom and experiences of four real secondary teachers. You learn about the classes they teach and about the physical constraints of their rooms; you hear them reflect on their rules and routines and watch as they teach them to students. You listen as they talk about motivating students and fostering cooperation, and as they discuss appropriate ways to deal with misbehavior. In sum, *this book focuses on real decisions made by real teachers as they manage the complex environment of the classroom.* By sharing their stories, I do not mean to suggest that their ways of managing classrooms are the only effective ways. Rather, my goal is to illustrate how four reflective, caring, and very different individuals approach the tasks involved in classroom management. And now, let's meet the teachers (in alphabetical order) and learn about the contexts in which they teach.

MEETING THE TEACHERS

Fred Cerequas

Fred Cerequas ("Ser-a-kwas") works in a school district that has a reputation for innovation. Four of its 11 schools have been designated "Blue Ribbon Schools" by national review panels assembled by the United States Department of Education, and

Fred Cerequas

three have received "Star School" status in the state. This well-regarded school district currently has about 7,500 students and is gaining more than 400 a year. The student population is also becoming increasingly diverse; it is now 64 percent European American, 20 percent Asian American, 10 percent African American, and 6 percent Latino. More than 50 different first languages are spoken—in particular, Spanish, Gujarati, Hindi, Cantonese, and Arabic—and the socioeconomic range is striking. Although people think of the community as middle- to upper-middle-class, a sizable number of its children live in low-cost mobile home parks. About 12 percent are eligible for the federal free or reduced-price lunch program.

A 58-year-old father of three, Fred is a member of the 10-person social studies department at the high school. The building is only three years old—a sleek, modern facility with state-of-the-art laboratories, an auditorium with 1,000 seats, and wide, spacious hallways. It currently houses 1,800 students (up from 1,200 only five years ago), but an addition is already needed because of the continuing population growth.

Fred's route to teaching was circuitous. As the son of factory workers who had to leave school for economic reasons, Fred went into the United States Army after high school. He worked as an information specialist in Alaska, where he had a radio and television show, narrated troop information films, and wrote for several army newspapers. When he was discharged, he began to work his way through college by driving a school bus for high school students. It was then that he discovered he was able to "connect with kids" and decided to earn a teaching certificate "just in case." A successful and gratifying student teaching experience led him to decide that this was the career he wanted to pursue. He's taught in the same district for his entire career—a total of 34 years. Far from being burned out, Fred still believes he learns as much from his students as they do from him. In fact, he proclaims that last year was the most interesting and exciting of his career—and that this one looks even better.

Fred currently teaches five classes: two sections of U.S. History I (honors); one section of the Institute for Political and Legal Education (IPLE), a practicum in law, government, and politics for a heterogeneous group of seniors; and two sections of Contemporary World Issues, a non–Western history course for seniors (one honors and one "regular"). It is the Contemporary World Issues course that excites Fred the most; here, students study non–Western cultures and examine the impact—positive and negative—of Western influence.

Fred articulates his goals for his students by telling the story of Tanida, a senior he had in class last year. After learning about the problems of women and children in the third world, Tanida organized her classmates to sponsor a little girl in Africa through *Save the Children*—all without prompting from the teacher. To Fred, Tanida's efforts represent a combination of knowledge and compassion, and it is this combination that he strives for in his classes. He tells us:

I believe *real* teachers are cultivators. They nurture the seeds of wisdom in their students by helping them become independent, eager learners who combine experience and knowledge with the genuine concern for others that gives life its meaning.

Fred admits that his goals are not easily achieved in today's typical high school, where an "Industrial Revolution mentality" dominates:

> **Buildings like factories; seats in rows; rigid schedules; production quotas; quality controls. . . . The whole system seems geared to efficiency rather than humanity. At times, it seems to me that schools as they are designed actually inhibit education.**

Despite the obstacles to learning that he sees in our current system of schooling, Fred is energetic and optimistic, and he continually seeks better and more interesting ways to teach. Several years ago, he participated in a summer institute at the National Humanities Center in North Carolina, along with 20 other outstanding teachers from around the country. He was also named a Dodge Foundation Fellow and received a grant from the National Endowment for the Humanities to study ways of integrating literature more effectively into a history curriculum. He regularly works with student teachers.

Professional activities like these fuel his determination to connect with kids and to "nurture wisdom." Early in the fall, for example, Fred led a discussion in Contemporary World Issues on the social institutions common to all cultures. Although students were generally cooperative, about one-half of the class wasn't fully engaged—a fact that did not escape his notice. Fred stopped the lesson and addressed the students' apathy in his characteristically direct, down-to-earth manner:

> **Listen, we don't study junk in here. What we're doing in here is trying to understand processes of change. This *affects* us; this stuff can make a *difference in your life*. And if you can be more than just bored seniors, we can do some really important stuff in here.**

After class, Fred sat in the teachers' room reflecting on the students' resistance. He reviewed the class roster, noting which youngsters had participated and which had remained silent. He spoke of the skepticism and detachment frequently displayed by students, particularly seniors; he acknowledged the difficulty of convincing them that what they were studying held meaning for their lives. Nonetheless, he vowed to "convert" them, and looked ahead to the day when he would actually have to chase them out after class. Given Fred's commitment and passion for teaching, there was little doubt that he would succeed. After all, according to Fred, "*Teacher* is not a word that describes what I do for a living; rather, it defines who I am."

Donnie Collins

Donnie teaches in a mid-sized urban district that serves 6,500 students in 10 schools; 54 percent of the students are Latino and 41 percent are African American. Many of the children come from poor or low-income families, evidenced by the fact that 80 percent of the students qualify for the federal free or reduced-price lunch program. The socioeconomic conditions breed other problems—drugs, transiency, homelessness, teenage pregnancy, physical abuse.

Donnie Collins

The high school is a few miles from the heart of downtown, a low brick building set back from the street on a wide expanse of lawn. Built in the 1960s, the school currently accommodates 788 students in grades 9 through 12. A large sign just inside the main entrance proclaims "Care and Excellence—Our #1 Goal," and fancifully painted murals honor the school's mascot, the zebra. The long hallways are lined with metal lockers in banks of red, green, blue, orange, and yellow. On the walls are posters advertising school clubs and activities; one announces a meeting of WWF—Working With Fathers—an organization for adolescent fathers.

On the second floor, in a corner classroom opposite the math department office, we find Donnie, a 9th- through 12th-grade mathematics teacher. A 56-year-old mother of one, Donnie began teaching math in Birmingham, Alabama, and then moved to her current district; she's been teaching there ever since, first on the junior high level and then at the high school. This year, since the high school is now on block scheduling (a topic we will discuss in Chapter 6), Donnie teaches two 80-minute classes at the high school—Algebra I and "SRA," a special review course for students who have failed the mathematics portion of the state exam required for graduation. She then drives to a nearby elementary school, where she teaches mathematics to eighth-graders in the gifted and talented program.

Being a teacher was Donnie's childhood dream. "As a child I always wanted to play school," she recalls, "and I always wanted to be the teacher, never one of the pupils." Reflecting on this early dream, Donnie acknowledges the influence of her grandmother, who had been an elementary teacher before she opened a beauty school and shop. Although Donnie's parents were farmers, they recognized that farming was not for her. As Donnie puts it, "My calling was to be a teacher."

Donnie was influenced not only by her grandmother but also by two of her own teachers. Her fifth-grade teacher, Mrs. Poole, was intimidating at first, but Donnie soon realized that she needn't be frightened. Mrs. Poole wasn't mean; she was just concerned about students' achievement and well-being. "From Mrs. Poole, I learned about the importance of maintaining discipline, about the need to be firm and fair, and the value of keeping in touch with parents." Later, in high school, Donnie encountered Miss Anchrum, a young math teacher fresh out of college, with lots of new ideas about how to make math exciting: "Miss Anchrum made math real, and she would accept nothing less than our best." From her, Donnie learned the importance of motivating students and holding high expectations.

Donnie eventually earned both a bachelor's degree and a master's degree in mathematics, along with certification to teach. But the impact of Mrs. Poole and Miss Anchrum has stayed with her, and her teaching reflects the lessons she learned from them. When asked about her goals, she answers without hesitation:

I want the same things my teachers wanted. I want my students to become creative, independent thinkers; I want them to be able to function effectively in our everyday world; I want them to make a positive contribution to society. I continually stress that there is always more than one way to solve a problem and I encourage them to find alternative solutions. I believe strongly in the importance of groupwork and peer tutoring so that students can learn to work together and to take constructive criticism. When students say, "Oh, Ms. Collins, I don't need to know this; all I need to know is how to count my money," I tell them: "But first you have to *make* the money, and once you've made your money, you have to *keep* it. And you have to know math to do that."

Donnie's goals are not achieved easily. She is frustrated by those students "who can't see beyond today," who cause disruption, and who create problems for those who do want to learn. She is also concerned about a lack of parental involvement (a topic we will discuss in Chapter 5), and the problems that her students face. As she puts it, "Education is just not a priority for many of my students. *Survival* is the priority." Sometimes she has to forgo a math lesson in order to discuss the more immediate problems of her students: conflicts with families, pregnancy, parenting (the high school has a day care center for the children of its students), running away from home, violence in the community, drugs. With a certain amount of resignation, Donnie comments:

If you try to go ahead with a math lesson when they're all riled up about something that has happened at home or in the neighborhood, you're doomed. There's just no point to it. It's better to put away the quadratic equations and *talk*.

In a continuing effort to meet the needs of her students, Donnie has served as a trainer in the school's Peer Leadership Program. During a week-long retreat, 15 to 20 high school seniors are taught interpersonal, communication, and problem-solving skills so that they can then help freshmen make the adjustment from eighth grade to high school. Donnie is also committed to her own professional development—she frequently attends workshops and courses on a variety of topics, such as classroom management, dealing with diverse students, sensitivity training, even teaching the Holocaust. But it is the daily help provided by her colleagues for which she is most grateful: "It's important to know that you're not alone in dealing with a student. I am lucky to have colleagues I can go to for advice and support."

Despite the difficulties of teaching in an urban district, Donnie is still enthusiastic and optimistic about her chosen career. One of the major satisfactions is the fact that each day brings something new. Another is "seeing the light come on," and knowing that a student suddenly understands what the lesson is all about. Particularly satisfying is sharing the successes of former students—and knowing that she played a part:

> I was recently given a surprise birthday party, and one of my former students was invited. He's currently working for the General Electric Corporation, and there he was at my party, talking about having had me in eighth grade and the impact I had on his life. That's the real reward of teaching.

Listening to Donnie Collins speak about the goals she has for her students and the satisfactions she derives from teaching, it is obvious that the legacy of Mrs. Poole and Miss Anchrum lives on in this secondary mathematics teacher.

Sandra Krupinski

Sandy Krupinski teaches in a small, extremely diverse community. The district's three schools serve children who live in homes valued at $600,000 as well as those from low-income apartment complexes. The student population of 1,650 is 53 percent European American, 17 percent African American, 14 percent Latino, and 16 percent Asian American. About 26 percent of the children qualify for the federal free or reduced-price lunch program. The high school currently houses 650 students in grades 7 through 12. Built in 1925, the building was recently renovated and expanded, thanks to the passage of a $15-million-dollar bond referendum that allowed the district to make long-overdue capital improvements.

In the science wing on the second floor is the chemistry classroom where Sandra Krupinski, a 50-year-old mother of two, teaches three classes of chemistry—two college prep and one advanced placement. This year, Sandy's classes are larger and more diverse than in previous years. In her sixth-period class, for example, there are 25 students, including five African Americans, one Latino, one Asian American, and one whose family has come from India. The class also includes a student classified as emotionally disturbed.

Sandy Krupinski

Sandy's love of science was awakened when she herself was a student at the very same high school, and teaching seemed like the obvious, logical career. "At that time," Sandy remembers, "women just weren't encouraged to consider other options. It was either teaching or nursing." Her father, a construction worker, and her mother, an office manager for an insurance company, applauded the decision to be a teacher, proud that Sandy would be the first in her family to attend college.

Although Sandy recognizes that becoming a teacher was not the result of thoughtful deliberation, she is confident that she pursued the right course. After 22 years of teaching, she still doesn't regard it as "just a job." Even in the summer, after only a few weeks of vacation, she finds herself gravitating back to school so she can begin to prepare for classes.

Sandy is very clear about what she is trying to achieve with her students. She sees chemistry as a vehicle for helping students develop problem-solving skills, self-discipline ("a new experience for some"), and self-confidence:

 Chemistry is seen as a difficult subject, and some students begin the year thinking they'll never be able to master it. They'll come up to me with a blank paper and say, "I couldn't do this, Mrs. K." I can't stand

that. My hope is that by the end of the year these students will have the confidence to attack problems and the ability to develop appropriate strategies. That's much more important to me than getting the right answers.

In order to achieve this goal, Sandy tries hard to create an accepting, non-threatening atmosphere in her class. On the first day of school, for example, she gives her students an index card and asks them to answer four questions: (1) How do you learn best? (2) What do you expect to be excited about in chemistry? (3) What do you expect to be nervous about? and (4) What can I do to help? Their responses are revealing, particularly to the third and fourth questions. One student shares his fear of talking in front of the class and asks her not to call on him. Several confide that they are anxious about the difficulty of the course, particularly the mathematics and the need to memorize "lots of itsy, bitsy facts"; they ask her to be patient and to take extra time. One girl who is learning English as a second language writes about the fact that her "language is not good," and asks Sandy to speak slowly and to "sometimes explain something for me."

When students return on the second day of class, Sandy addresses each concern that has been raised (telling students that these are the fears expressed by "two or more students"). She thanks them for sharing information that will help her to help them and reassures them that she will be patient, that they will proceed slowly, and that she will always be available for extra help outside of class. Afterwards, thinking about why she takes the time to do this, Sandy comments:

As I talk about each fear they've expressed, I can actually see their shoulders drop, and I can feel the anxiety level in the class go down. Doing this also gives me information that I can use to help them. For example, take the boy who's afraid of speaking in front of the class. Today, students were putting problems on the board that they had done for homework. Normally, I don't particularly want people with the right answers to put the problems up on the board, because I want them to see that what's important is developing a strategy, not just getting the correct answer. In this case, however, it was important for him to feel confident about going up to the board. So, as I walked around the room, I glanced at his paper and saw that he had a particular problem correct. I told him he had done a good job with it and asked him to put it on the board. Instead of getting anxious, he smiled at me! This couldn't have happened if I hadn't asked students to share their concerns with me.

Sandy may be sensitive to students' anxieties about chemistry, but she still communicates high expectations and a no-nonsense attitude. This year, during an unexpectedly long "vacation" brought about by a fierce blizzard, Sandy called all of her Advanced Placement students to give them an assignment "so they wouldn't fall behind." Her students weren't surprised; one of them told her, "Oh, Mrs. K., we just *knew* you'd call!"

Sandy's no-nonsense attitude is also apparent in an incident that occurred during very different weather many months earlier. Last year, on a hot spring day when temperatures in the chemistry lab hovered around 100° Fahrenheit, Sandy glanced out the window and saw one of her students lying on the lawn. The girl was blatantly cutting class. Sandy called the vice principal and asked her to bring the student to the classroom. "Are you sure you don't want me to take her to the detention room?" asked the vice principal. "Of course not," Sandy told her. "I want her in here, where I can teach her something!"

Sandy is troubled by incidents like this; it is hard for her to accept the fact that she doesn't succeed with every student, and she continually takes courses and workshops to find ways to reach even the least motivated youngster. Yet, it is incidents like this that have helped to build Sandy Krupinski's reputation as a teacher who is passionate about chemistry and fiercely committed to students' learning—a teacher who manages to be both demanding and caring.

Christina Lugo Vreeland

With 24 schools and 12,900 students, Christina's district is the largest of our four districts. The high school, built in 1963 (and one of three in the district), is a two-story, yellow brick building tucked away—almost hidden—behind a residential development of small one-story houses. It serves almost 900 students from 10 different towns. In addition, the high school houses the district's English as a Second Language (ESL) program, providing instruction for 80 students who have recently arrived from non–English-speaking countries. The student body is predominantly European American (61 percent), but the racial and ethnic diversity is steadily

Christina Lugo Vreeland

increasing (African American, 8 percent; Latino, 10 percent; Asian American, 20 percent; Native American, 1 percent), and 13 percent of the students qualify for the federal free or reduced-price lunch program.

In the English wing on the second floor, we find Christina Lugo Vreeland—24 years old, newly married, and in her second year of teaching English and journalism. Christina grew up in the community, the daughter of a truck driver whose family emigrated from Puerto Rico when he was three, and an office worker raised in a nearby community. She attended the state university, where she majored in English and minored in Spanish. After receiving her bachelor's degree, Christina continued on for a master's degree and certification in English Education. Her academic achievements were impressive: In addition to being elected to Phi Beta Kappa, Christina received a James Dickson Carr Scholarship and a Martin Luther King, Jr., Scholarship, highly prestigious awards for outstanding minority students.

Like Donnie and Sandy, Christina never really considered a career other than teaching (except for a time in eighth grade when she wanted to be a fashion designer). Even as a little girl, Christina "always had to be the teacher and tell everyone else what to do." But it wasn't until her junior year in high school that Christina began to think seriously about the kind of teacher she wanted to be:

 I had an excellent teacher, Helaine Rasmussen. She was very strict, and we were afraid of her before we actually had her, but then we got to like her. She really enjoyed what she was doing. I have one vision of her teaching *The Great Gatsby*. She was sitting on the window sill, and she was describing a scene in the novel where there are two girls sitting in flowing dresses. She was acting it out, showing how their flowing dresses would look. It was so exciting. I had read the novel, but I hadn't pictured it. She made it real for me. . . .

We also had to do a big term paper that year. . . . We knew from 10th grade that we were going to have to do this. It seemed insurmountable—20 pages! But Mrs. Rasmussen had former students come in and talk about how they had done the project, and she took us through it step by step, so that . . . everything just seemed to fall into place. We were able to compose this paper we had never thought we would be able to do.

Then in my senior year, I had Angela Korodan for honors English. She started off by meeting with us at the end of junior year to give us the summer reading assignment. She gave us her address and opened the lines of communication. We had to mail her one of our assignments over the summer. She started teaching before she had to. And then the first two or three days of school, we sat in a circle, and talked about ourselves. These were people I had known for a long time, but I still learned things. She did the same; she told us about how she became a teacher, and how she had been a nun.

From Mrs. Rasmussen, Christina learned the importance of making literature vivid for students and being rigorous, yet systematic, when teaching research skills. From Mrs. Korodan, she learned about the value of building communication and a sense of community. These are lessons that Christina tries hard to remember now that she is on the other side of the desk.

Like Donnie's high school, Christina's school uses block scheduling, so Christina meets three 84-minute classes a day, with one professional or "prep" period. Given the double periods, "year-long" classes last for half a year; this means that Christina gets new students and new courses every January. Her current schedule calls for two 10th-grade English classes, one with 29 students and one with 25 students, and one basic skills class for 11 students who have failed the state test required for graduation.

One of Christina's major goals is to help her students "make a place for reading and writing in their everyday lives." She explains:

 I think that lots of times English teachers are so passionate about literature and analysis of literature that we forget that our students are not preparing to be English teachers. . . . The way I read and the way my students read is different, and that's okay. What I need to do is foster the kind of reading and writing that will be useful for them and to create the *desire* to read and write.

To promote students' fluency in writing, Christina begins every class period with journal writing. As soon as the bell rings, students glance at the journal topic on the chalkboard, take out their journals, and begin writing. Sometimes journal entries serve as a lead-in to the day's lesson; for example, when students were about to discuss Antigone's decision to bury her brother, they wrote on a journal topic related to civil disobedience: "If you believed that what you were doing was right, would you break a law knowing that the penalty would be five years in jail?" Sometimes, journal entries are intended to stimulate thinking about the character traits we value in people ("Whom do you admire and why?" "What is patience, and who is the most patient person you know?"); sometimes, they're responses to music ("Describe the music you're listening to.").

In addition to teaching, Christina is a coadvisor for the school's newspaper, *The Torch*. Only five students were consistently involved when Christina and a colleague in the English Department took on the challenge of advising; now there are about 50, and the increased participation is a source of great satisfaction. Christina also likes the fact that she's "involved in something extracurricular that shows the fruits of what I teach—writing, editing skills, thinking skills." Christina is also active in the school's "Learn and Serve" program, which integrates community service with the life and curriculum of the school. The school has been recognized at both state and national levels as a "Learn and Serve Leader School." This means that Christina and her students are involved in a variety of service learning projects, such as the construction of a neighborhood playground for toddlers and an interdisciplinary project to create, dramatize, and donate children's books to a local elementary school.

One day in midwinter, Christina reminisced about her first year and a half of teaching. She was recovering from a bout of flu, and she was feeling upset about having missed several school days right at the beginning of the new term. She talked about feeling overwhelmed by the stacks of ungraded essays, the service learning project, and the classes that were larger than usual. With an embarrassed smile, Christina expressed some of the doubts she had recently been feeling:

For the last few days, I've been questioning, "Why do I want to be here? Why do I say I enjoy this?" And then today, we had a great discussion about *Ethan Frome*. The kids really understood things. They really got into it; they got excited about it. I had kids making important points—I didn't have to ask the leading questions each time. And they had the *desire* to discuss with each other and to read more. . . . At the end of the class [in the English Department office], the other teachers looked at me and saw me smiling. They knew I'd been feeling overwhelmed. And one of them asked, "Why are you so happy?" And I told them, "I just had an experience that renewed my faith in my ability to do this for the rest of my life."

 PAUSE AND REFLECT

Now that you've met the teachers, take a minute to think about their personalities and approaches to classroom management. Do you feel a special kinship with any of the four teachers? If your answer is yes, why do you feel this way?

Next, reflect on your own secondary school experiences. Were there any teachers that you would characterize as especially effective classroom managers? What did they do that made them especially effective? Are there any similarities between these teachers and the teachers you've just read about?

WHAT DO THE STUDENTS SAY?

While working with these four teachers, I became curious about the perceptions of the students in their classrooms. In particular, I was interested in why they thought students were cooperative and well behaved in some classes and uncooperative and ill behaved in others, as well as their views of the particular classes I was observing. In each class, the teacher left the room so that the students and I could talk more comfortably. I explained that I wanted the "student perspective" on classroom management and asked them to explain in writing "why kids behave in some classes," "why kids misbehave in some classes," and "how kids generally behave in this class and why." After students had a chance to write down their thoughts, they shared their responses.

Across classes, students demonstrated extraordinary consistency. Whether students were 8th-graders or 12th-graders, basic skills or honors students, their responses reflected three main themes. First, students stressed the importance of teachers' *relating to students with caring and respect.* They talked about teachers who "can relate to our teenage lifestyle," who "try to get to know us and understand us," who "create trust," who "help you and explain what they want," and "who work with you not against you." A student in one of Fred's classes put it this way: "When a teacher takes some time to get to know students and shows some humor or shares a bit of their personal life, students may relate to them better." In Sandy's classes, students also echoed the importance of relationships: "The teacher must relate to the students. Understand when there is a problem and try to solve it. When the students see a teacher doing his/her best to make them feel comfortable with what they're learning, they behave well." And one of Christina's students wrote this:

> I want to cooperate in this class because she is not all serious, she can laugh, have fun, and still get all the work done. Students can tell when a teacher wants to help you and teach you, and when they just do it because they have to.

Clearly, not all teachers relate to students in this way. Students wrote about teachers "who put students down" and treat them like "little kids," about teachers who "don't care," and about teachers who are "beyond strict and just don't want to hear what we have to say." As one student wrote:

> Sometimes, if a teacher really demands the respect from day one, instead of earning it, a disliking developes [sic]. If a teacher doesn't think about what the students are feeling, they won't like him/her. Students can always detect those sort of things. Dislike = misbehave.

Many students used the word *respect* in both their written and oral comments, and I pressed them to tell me what "respecting students" looks like. They didn't have difficulty: Teachers respect students when they give them their grades privately, when they come prepared for class, when they don't tell students a question is dumb, when they "scold a student quietly instead of in class in front of others," when they take time to help kids who are confused, when they allow students to give their own opinions, when they make sure that students treat each other well (e.g., they don't allow kids to talk when another kid is talking), and when they show students that they *care*.

A second theme that students discussed was the need for teachers to "*set the rules and follow them*." This was expressed in a number of different ways: "Teachers need to be a strong authority figure"; "teachers need to tell kids what they expect and give no second tries"; "teachers need to show strength"; "teachers need to be strict (but not mean)"; "teachers need to come off as someone who has control." (See Figure 1.3 for related research.) What is clearly conveyed by these responses is students' lack of respect for teachers who are too permissive, who are "too cowardly to take charge," and who "let kids run all over them." One student wrote: "Kids misbehave when the teacher lets them pretty much do whatever they want. If they're disrupting class the teacher will try to go on with her class by maybe trying to speak above the person disrupting the class or ignoring it." This view was reiterated in another student's response: "Usually misbehavior happens in classes when teachers are too lenient. Every class needs to have some time to relax and fool around, but the teacher should know the limit." Still another summed it up this way:

> Some teachers seem very insecure about misbehaving students. They tend to say "stop or I'll send you to the office" too much. When a teacher first meets his/her class they need to set down guidelines and go over them confidently and be sure of what he/she is doing.

The final theme to emerge from students' comments was the importance of *teaching in a way that is motivating and interesting*. One of Donnie's students

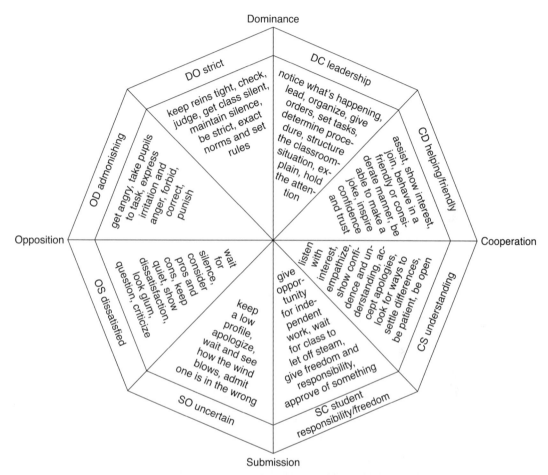

Figure 1.3   Students' Perceptions of Teacher Interpersonal Behavior

The first two themes emerging from students' comments echo the results of an extensive research program investigating teacher-student relationships in secondary classrooms (Wubbels, Brekelmans, van Tartwijk, & den Brok, 2006). Developed by Theo Wubbels and his colleagues in the Netherlands, the research has now spread to other countries, including Australia, Canada, Israel, Turkey, Korea, Taiwan, and the United States. In this research, teacher interpersonal behavior is described in terms of two dimensions: cooperation-opposition and dominance-submission. When these two dimensions are arranged as two axes, they create eight types of teacher behavior, as shown in the diagram. Each type is labeled by two initials (e.g., DC, CD, CS, SO) indicating the particular combination of the two dimensions. For example, DC ("leadership") indicates a teacher who is high in both dominance and cooperation, but the dominance aspect is stronger than the cooperation. CD ("helping/friendly") is also characterized by dominance and cooperation, but here, cooperation prevails over dominance. OS ("dissatisfied") describes a teacher who is oppositional and submissive (or low in dominance).

In general, studies examining the relationship between students' attitudes towards class and their perceptions of teachers' behavior demonstrate that students prefer teachers who are both dominant and cooperative. In other words, they prefer teachers in the DC and CD sections of the diagram. As you can see, this preference describes the same kind of teacher the students in our four teachers' classes preferred—a teacher who is not only caring and respectful, but is also a strong authority figure.

captured this widely shared perspective:

> Teachers have to make the class fun, but organized. Have a lot of interaction between students and challenge them. . . . Sometimes teachers are boring. The class drags on and the students lose attention span towards the teacher and the class. If the teacher teaches in an old-fashion [sic] style, the kids become frustrated.

These ideas were expressed in a number of ways: Teachers need to be knowledgeable and to *love* what they do ("kids can tell"); teachers need to teach in creative ways—not just out of the book; they need to get the whole class involved; they need to relate the material to students' lives. Although a lot of people used the word *fun,* one of Fred's students wrote, "Not everything can be fun; it doesn't have to be fun, but there are ways teachers can make it more interesting and more challenging." For Christina's students, the "cool things Mrs. Vreeland picks for us to do" were especially important, since their classes are 84 minutes long. They clearly appreciated the fact that class sessions are "not just lectures and question and answer" and that Christina "uses different ways to teach us as opposed to 'open your book, read questions 1 to 5 and answer them.'"

These themes—*relating to students with caring and respect, setting limits and enforcing them, and teaching in a way that is motivating and interesting—* characterize the behavior of the four teachers featured in this book. As I watched them teach, I was repeatedly struck by the caring and sensitivity they showed to students, by their authoritative, "no-nonsense" attitudes, and by their efforts to stimulate students' interest and engagement in lessons. The ability to combine these three characteristics is clearly recognized and appreciated by students.

We will address these themes in the three sections of the book that follow.

Pause and Reflect

After listening to these students discuss the characteristics of effective classroom managers—caring and respect, firmness (the ability to set and enforce limits), and teaching in a way that is motivating and engaging—take a moment to reflect on your own strengths and weaknesses in these three areas. What do you think will be your greatest challenge?

Concluding Comments

Fred, Donnie, Sandy, and Christina teach different subjects in different settings. Grade levels range from 8th to 12th. Sandy, Fred, and Christina teach classes that are predominantly White (although still quite diverse), while Donnie's classes are predominantly African American and Latino. Fred and Christina work in districts where about 10 percent of the children are eligible for free or reduced-price lunch, compared with the 26 percent figure in Sandy's district, and the 80 percent figure in Donnie's district. Sandy teaches an advanced placement class, while Donnie and Christina teach basic skills classes for students who have failed portions of the state test required for graduation. Donnie and Christina teach in schools that have adopted block scheduling, while Fred and Sandy's classes are about 45 minutes. All four teachers follow district curricula that reflect state standards, but Fred and Sandy have more flexibility than Donnie and Christina in terms of implementation and choice of materials. In order to be effective, our four teachers must be sensitive and responsive to these differences in age, race, culture, socioeconomic conditions, achievement levels, and district policies.

Despite these differences, Fred, Donnie, Sandy, and Christina are alike in many ways. Obvious similarities emerge when they talk about the tasks of classroom management. Earlier in this chapter, I cited research suggesting that teachers who view classroom management as a process of guiding and structuring classroom events tend to be more effective than teachers who stress their disciplinary role. Interestingly, when Fred, Donnie, Sandy, and Christina speak about classroom management, they rarely use the words *discipline* or *punishment, confrontation* or *penalty.* Instead, they emphasize mutual respect; they talk about the importance of being organized and well prepared; they stress the need to develop a "caring community," in which all individuals are contributing, valued members (Schaps, 2003; Watson & Battistich, 2006); they speak about involving students and helping them to achieve.

It's important to remember that Fred, Donnie, Sandy, and Christina are real human beings working in the complex, uncertain environment of the secondary classroom. Christina is only in her second year of teaching, and as she herself admits, she is "a novice when it comes to knowing what works." Fred, Donnie, and Sandy are experienced, skillful teachers who are extremely effective at preventing misbehavior, but even their classrooms are not free of problems. (In fact, Chapter 11 focuses specifically on the ways all four teachers deal with misbehavior.) Like all of us, these teachers make mistakes; they become frustrated and impatient; they sometimes fail to live up to their own images of the ideal teacher. By their own testimony, they are all still learning how to run more effective classrooms.

It is also important to remember that these four teachers do not follow recipes or prescriptions for classroom management, so their ways of interacting with students often look very different. Nonetheless, underlying the differences in behavior, it is often possible to detect the same guiding principles. The chapters that follow will try to convey the ways these four excellent teachers tailor the principles to fit their own particular contexts.

Finally, it is necessary to point out that these teachers do not work in schools where conditions are so bad that classes have to be held in stairwells or storage closets, where windows remain broken for years, and where 40 students in a class have to share a handful of books. Nor do they teach in schools that have installed metal detectors, where students regularly carry weapons, and where gang activity is common. In recent years, the districts in which the teachers work have all experienced an increase in serious problems, but violence is certainly not an everyday occurrence. Whether the strategies discussed here are generalizable to severely troubled schools is not clear. Nevertheless, I hope that *Middle and Secondary Classroom Management* will prove to be a useful starting point for teachers everywhere.

Summary

This chapter examined some of the contradictions and special characteristics of classrooms. It argued that effective management requires an understanding of the unique features of the classroom environment and stressed the fact that teachers work with captive groups of students on academic agendas that students have not helped to set. It then discussed seven assumptions that guided the content and organization of the book.

Contradictions of the Classroom Environment

- Classrooms are crowded, yet students are often not allowed to interact.
- Students are expected to work together harmoniously, yet they may not know or like each other.
- Students are urged to cooperate, yet they often work in individual or competitive situations.
- Students are encouraged to be independent, yet they are also expected to conform to the teacher's dictates.
- Students are instructed to work slowly and carefully, but they have to be aware of the "press of time" in a 42- (or an 84-) minute period.

Characteristics of the Classroom Environment

- Multidimensionality
- Simultaneity
- Immediacy
- Unpredictability
- Lack of privacy
- History

Guiding Assumptions of the Book

The ultimate goal of classroom management is to promote learning and social–emotional growth.

- Successful classroom management promotes self-regulation.
- Most problems of disorder can be avoided if teachers foster positive teacher–student relationships, implement engaging instruction, and use good preventive management strategies.
- The way teachers think about management influences the way they behave.
- The need for order must not supersede the need for meaningful instruction.
- Behavioral expectations vary across different subsettings of the classroom.
- Teachers must be "culturally responsive classroom managers."
- Becoming an effective classroom manager requires reflection, hard work, and time.

Meeting the Teachers

This chapter introduced the four teachers whose thinking and experiences will be described throughout the rest of the book.

- **Donnie Collins** (middle and high school mathematics) teaches in an urban district of 6,500 students (54 percent Latino and 41 percent African American); 80 percent of the students qualify for the federal free or reduced-price lunch program.
- **Sandra Krupinski** (high school chemistry) teaches in a small district of 1,650 students (53 percent European American, 17 percent African American, 14 percent Latino, and

16 percent Asian American); about 26 percent of the students qualify for the federal free or reduced-price lunch program.

- **Fred Cerequas** (high school social studies) teaches in a district of about 7,500 students and growing fast; student population is 64 percent European American, 20 percent Asian American, 10 percent African American, and 6 percent Latino; about 12 percent of the students are eligible for the federal free or reduced-price lunch program.
- **Christina Vreeland** (high school English) teaches in a district of 12,900 students in 24 schools (61 percent European American, 20 percent Asian American, 10 percent Latino, 8 percent African American); about 13 percent of the students qualify for the federal free or reduced-price lunch program.

Although these four teachers teach different subjects in very different settings, they are alike in many ways. In particular, they speak about classroom management in very similar terms: They emphasize the prevention of behavior problems, mutual respect, involving students in learning activities, and the importance of being organized and well prepared.

What Do the Students Say?

The four teachers' views of effective classroom management mirror their students' conceptions. When asked why they behave well in certain classes and not in others, students consistently voiced three themes: relating to students with caring and respect; setting limits and enforcing them; and teaching in a way that is motivating and interesting. We will return to these three themes in subsequent chapters.

ACTIVITIES FOR SKILL BUILDING AND REFLECTION

In Class

1. In a group, discuss the six characteristics of classroom environments and share your ideas about how these characteristics will affect you as a classroom teacher.

2. Reflect on your past experiences with children and adolescents (e.g., tutoring, being a camp counselor). What did you learn from those experiences that might help you in the classroom?

3. Review the biographies of each teacher. Identify three or four major ways in which the teachers are similar.

On Your Own

Think about the questions that Christina was pondering: "*Why do I want to be here? Why do I say I enjoy this?*" What is it that *you* want in your classes? What do *you* find enjoyable (or *think* you will find enjoyable) about teaching? Then consider the implications for classroom organization and management. In other words, if you want students to participate enthusiastically, what will you have to do to encourage their participation? If you want them to treat one another with respect and kindness, what will you have to do to create that kind of atmosphere?

For Your Portfolio

Pretend you are a teacher being featured in this book. What is *your* story? Think about what motivated you to choose a career in teaching and what your goals are. Write down some of the key points you would want included in your own introduction. (This piece of writing can be a useful document to review before interviewing and can serve as inspiration during the often difficult first year of teaching.)

FOR FURTHER READING

Charney, R. S. (2002). *Teaching children to care: Classroom management for ethical and academic growth, K-8.* Greenfield, MA: Northeast Foundation for Children.

This book provides a lively, practical guide to creating a respectful, friendly, academically rigorous classroom. Based on Charney's experiences as a teacher and informed by work on the *Responsive Classroom* approach (Northeast Foundation for Children), the book illustrates ways of managing classrooms to nurture students' social and intellectual growth. Although the book is geared to elementary school, it is also appropriate for teachers in middle school and junior high.

Weinstein, C. S. (Ed.) (2003). Classroom management in a diverse society, *Theory Into Practice, 42*(4).

The articles in this special theme issue of *TIP* address different aspects of classroom management in a diverse society, but all of them reflect the idea that the fundamental task of classroom management is to create an inclusive, supportive, and caring environment. All the authors view classroom management in terms of human relationships—relationships between teachers and students and among students themselves. Some of the articles that appear in the special issue are listed below.

Brown, D. F. Urban teachers' use of culturally responsive management strategies, pp. 277-282.

Curran, M. E. Linguistic diversity and classroom management, pp. 334-340.

Delpit, L., & White-Bradley, P. Educating or imprisoning the spirit: Lessons from ancient Egypt, pp. 283-288.

McCarthy, J., & Benally, J. Classroom management in a Navajo middle school, pp. 297-304.

Norris, J. A. Looking at classroom management through a social and emotional learning lens, pp. 313-318.

Weinstein, C. S., Curran, M., & Tomlinson-Clarke, S. Culturally responsive classroom management: Awareness into action, pp. 269-276.

REFERENCES

Brophy, J. (1988). Educating teachers about managing classrooms and students. *Teaching and Teacher Education, 4*(1), 1-18.

Carter, K. (March-April 1985). Teacher comprehension of classroom processes: An emerging direction in classroom management research. Paper presented at the annual meeting of the American Educational Research Association, Chicago.

Doyle, W. (1985). Recent research on classroom management: Implications for teacher preparation. *Journal of Teacher Education, 36*(3), 31–35.

Doyle, W. (1986). Classroom organization and management. In M. C. Wittrock (Ed.), *Handbook of research on teaching.* New York: Macmillan, pp. 392–431.

Doyle, W. (2006). Ecological approaches to classroom management. In C. M. Evertson & C. S. Weinstein (Eds.), *Handbook of classroom management: Research, practice and contemporary issues.* Mahwah, NJ: Lawrence Erlbaum Associates, Inc.

Evertson, C. M., & Weinstein, C. S. Classroom management as a field of inquiry. In C. M. Evertson & C. S. Weinstein (Eds.), *Handbook of classroom management: Research, practice, and contemporary issues.* Mahwah, NJ: Lawrence Erlbaum Associates, Inc.

Gay, G. (2006). Connections between classroom management and culturally responsive teaching. In C. M. Evertson & C. S. Weinstein (Eds.), *Handbook of classroom management: Research, practice and contemporary issues.* Mahwah, NJ: Lawrence Erlbaum Associates, Inc.

Hatch, J. A. (March 1986). Alone in a crowd: Analysis of covert interactions in a kindergarten. Presented at the annual meeting of the American Educational Research Association, San Francisco. ERIC Document Reproduction Service No. ED 272 278.

Jackson, P. (1968). *Life in classrooms.* New York: Holt, Rinehart & Winston.

Kidder, T. (1989). *Among schoolchildren.* Boston: Houghton Mifflin.

Kounin, J. S. (1970). *Discipline and group management in classrooms.* New York: Holt, Rinehart & Winston.

Kounin, J. S., & Sherman, L. (1979). School environments as behavior settings. *Theory Into Practice, 14,* 145–151.

Lortie, D. (1975). *Schoolteacher.* Chicago: University of Chicago Press.

McCaslin, M., & Good, T. L. (1992). Compliant cognition: The misalliance of management and instructional goals in current school reform. *Educational Researcher, 21*(3), 4–17.

McCaslin, M., & Good, T. L. (1998). Moving beyond management as sheer compliance: Helping students to develop goal coordination strategies. *Educational Horizons,* Summer, 169–176.

Nieto, S. (2002). *Language, culture, and teaching: Critical perspectives for a new century.* Mahwah, NJ: Lawrence Erlbaum Associates, Inc.

Schaps, E. (2003). Creating a school community. *Educational Leadership, 60*(60), 31–33.

Ulerick, S. L., & Tobin, K. (March 1989). The influence of a teacher's beliefs on classroom management. Paper presented at the annual meeting of the American Educational Research Association, San Francisco.

Watson, M., & Battistich, V. (2006). Building and sustaining caring communities. In C. M. Evertson and C. S. Weinstein (Eds.), *Handbook of classroom management: Research, practice, and contemporary issues.* Mahwah, NJ: Lawrence Erlbaum Associates, Inc.

Weiner, L. (1999). *Urban teaching: The essentials.* NY: Teachers College Press.

Weinstein, C. S., Curran, M., & Tomlinson-Clarke, S. (2003). Culturally responsive classroom management: Awareness into action. *Theory Into Practice, 42*(4), 269–276.

Weinstein, C. S., Tomlinson-Clarke, S., & Curran, M. (2004). Toward a conception of culturally responsive classroom management. *Journal of Teacher Education, 55*(1), 25–38.

Woolfolk Hoy, A., & Weinstein, C. S. (2006). Student and teacher perspectives on classroom management. In C. M. Evertson and C. S. Weinstein (Eds.), *Handbook of classroom management: Research, practice, and contemporary issues.* Mahwah, NJ: Lawrence Erlbaum Associates, Inc.

Wubbels, T., Brekelmans, M., van Tartwijk, J., & den Brok, P. (2006). An interpersonal perspective on classroom management in secondary classrooms in the Netherlands. In C. M. Evertson & C. S. Weinstein (Eds.), *Handbook of classroom management: Research, practice, and contemporary issues.* Mahwah, NJ: Lawrence Erlbaum Associates, Inc.

PART II

Establishing an Environment for Learning

DESIGNING THE PHYSICAL ENVIRONMENT

Discussions of organization and management often neglect the physical character-istics of the classroom. Unless it becomes too hot, too cold, too crowded, or too noisy, we tend to think of the classroom setting as an unimportant backdrop for in-teraction. This general tendency to ignore the physical environment is especially prevalent in middle and secondary schools, where many teachers are like nomads, moving from room to room throughout the day. In this unfortunate situation, it is difficult to create a classroom setting that is more than simply adequate. Nonethe-less, it is important to recognize that the *physical environment can influence the way teachers and students feel, think, and behave.* Careful planning of this environment—within the constraints of your daily schedule—is an integral part of good classroom management. Moreover, *creating a comfortable, functional class-room is one way of showing your students that you care about them.*

Environmental psychologists point out that the effects of the classroom setting can be both *direct* and *indirect* (Proshansky & Wolfe, 1974). For example, if stu-dents seated in straight rows are unable to carry on a class discussion because they can't hear one another, the *environment is directly hindering their participation.* Students might also be affected *indirectly* if they infer from the seating arrangement that the teacher does not really want them to interact. In this case, the arrangement of the desks is sending a message to the students about how they are supposed to behave. Their reading of this message would be accurate if the teacher had deliberately arranged the seats to inhibit discussion. More likely, however, the teacher genuinely desires class participation but has never thought about the link between the classroom environment and student behavior.

This chapter is intended to help you develop *environmental competence* (Steele, 1973; Martin, 2002): awareness of the physical environment and its impact and the ability to use that environment to meet your goals. Even when they share space or move from room to room, environmentally competent teachers are sensitive to the messages communicated by the physical setting. They plan spatial arrangements that support their instructional plans. They know how to evaluate the effectiveness of a classroom environment. They are alert to the possibility that physical factors might contribute to behavioral problems, and they modify at least some aspects of the classroom environment when the need arises.

As you read this chapter, remember that classroom management is not simply a matter of dealing with misbehavior. As I stressed in the first chapter, successful managers *promote students' involvement in educational activities, foster self-regulation, prevent disruption, and relate to students with care and respect.* My discussion of the classroom environment reflects this perspective: I am concerned not only with reducing distraction and minimizing congestion through good environmental design but also with ways the environment can promote students' security, increase their comfort, and stimulate their interest in learning tasks.

Throughout this chapter, I will illustrate major points with examples from the classrooms of the four teachers you have just met. Interestingly, Donnie, Fred, and Sandy happen to teach their classes in one room this year, although they share their room with other teachers. For Donnie and Fred, teaching in one room is a substantial improvement from past years, when they had to move from room to room. Last year was particularly difficult for Fred: He taught his five classes in four different rooms! This year, it is Christina who has to move; another English teacher uses her room during the first two blocks of the day, when Christina has prep period and then teaches her state test class in another room.

> ## Pause and Reflect
>
> Think about your favorite place to shop. What physical characteristics, such as store layout, accessibility of products, and attractiveness, make the shopping experience an enjoyable one? Now think about a negative shopping experience or a store that you do not like to frequent. Are there any elements of the physical design that deter you from shopping in that store?
>
> Reflect on whether the positive and negative characteristics you identified apply to classroom environments. As you read this chapter keep in mind the way environments can shape your feelings and the ease with which you can accomplish your tasks—whether shopping or learning!

Five Functions of the Classroom Setting

Fred Steele (1973), a consultant in the field of organizational development, has suggested that all physical settings serve a number of basic functions. Five of Steele's functions—security and shelter, social contact, symbolic identification, task instrumentality, and pleasure—provide a useful framework for thinking about the physical environment of the middle and secondary classroom. They make it clear that designing the physical setting is far more than decorating a few bulletin boards.

Security and Shelter

This is the most fundamental function of all built environments. Like homes, office buildings, and stores, classrooms should provide protection from bad weather, noise, extreme heat or cold, and noxious odors. Sadly, even this most basic function is sometimes not fulfilled, and teachers and students must battle highway noise, broken windows, and leaky roofs. In situations like this, it is difficult for any of the other functions to be met. Physical security is a *precondition* that must be satisfied, at least to some extent, before the environment can serve students' and teachers' other, higher-level needs.

Physical security is a particularly important issue in classes such as science, home economics, woodworking, and art, where students come into contact with potentially dangerous supplies and equipment. It is essential that teachers of these subjects know about their state's safety guidelines regarding proper handling, storage, and labeling. Sandy goes even further; she tries to anticipate where accidents might occur and to arrange supplies in a way that minimizes risk. For example, when her students are doing a lab that involves two chemicals that are harmful together, she sets one chemical out and keeps one under her control. In this way, students have to ask her for it ("I'm ready for my nitric acid"), and she can double-check that they are following correct lab procedures.

Physical security is also a matter of special concern if you have students in wheelchairs, with leg braces, on crutches, or with unsteady gaits (e.g., from muscular dystrophy). Navigating through crowded classrooms can be a formidable and dangerous task. Be sensitive to the need for wide aisles and space to store walkers and crutches when not in use. The physical or occupational therapists working in your school can provide consultation and advice.

Often, school environments provide *physical* security but fail to offer *psychological* security—the feeling that this is a good, comfortable place to be. Psychological security is becoming increasingly crucial as more and more youngsters live in impoverished, unstable, and sometimes unsafe home environments. For them, in particular, schools must serve as a haven.

One way of enhancing psychological security is to make sure your classroom contains some "softness." With their linoleum floors, concrete block walls, and formica desks, classrooms tend to be "hard" places. But youngsters (and adults) tend to feel more secure and comfortable in environments that contain items that are soft or responsive to their touch. In elementary classrooms, we sometimes find small animals, pillows, plants, beanbag chairs, and area rugs, but these are generally absent in middle and secondary classrooms. If you are lucky enough to have your own classroom, think about ways that you can incorporate elements of softness into the environment. Also keep in mind that warm colors, bright accents, and varying textures (e.g., burlap, wood, and felt) can help to create an atmosphere of security and comfort.

Another way of increasing psychological security is to arrange classroom space so that students have as much freedom from interference as possible. In the crowded environment of the classroom, it is easy to become distracted. You need to make sure that students' desks are not too near areas of heavy traffic (e.g., the pencil sharpener, the bookcase, the front door). This is particularly important for students with attention-deficit/hyperactivity disorder (ADHD), a neurobiological disability that interferes with an individual's ability to sustain attention. Students with ADHD have difficulty focusing attention, concentrating, listening, following instructions, and organizing tasks. They may also exhibit behaviors associated with hyperactivity: difficulty staying seated, fidgeting, impulsivity, lack of self-control. (See Chapter 12 for additional information on ADHD.) You can help students with ADHD by seating them away from noisy, high-traffic areas, near well-focused students, and as close to you as possible so that it's easy to make eye contact (Carbone, 2001). Although many teachers seat distractible students in the center-front (given a traditional row arrangement), Perlmutter (1994) suggests that the *second* seat from the front in the end rows may be more effective in limiting distractible stimuli.

You can also enhance psychological security by allowing students to select their own seats. Often, students want to sit near their friends, but some individuals have definite spatial preferences as well (e.g., they prefer to sit in a corner, near the window, or in the front row). Donnie, Sandy, and Fred all allow students to sit where they wish—as long as they behave appropriately, of course (and Fred advises his students to "sit next to someone smart"). If you have your own room, you might also set up a few cubicles where students who want more enclosure can work alone, or provide folding cardboard dividers (three pieces of heavy cardboard bound together) that they can place on their desks. All of us need to "get away from it all" at times, but research suggests that opportunities for privacy are particularly important for youngsters who are distractible or have difficulty relating to their peers (Weinstein, 1982).

Social Contact

Interaction among Students

As you plan the arrangement of students' desks, you need to think carefully about how much interaction you want among students. Clusters of desks promote social contact since individuals are close together and can have direct eye contact with those across from them. In clusters, students can work together on activities, share materials, have small-group discussions, and help each other with assignments. This arrangement is most appropriate if you plan to emphasize collaboration and cooperative learning activities. But it is unwise—even inhumane—to seat students in clusters and then forbid them to interact. If you do that, students receive two contradictory messages: The seating arrangement is communicating that it's okay to interact, while your verbal message is just the opposite!

As a beginning teacher, you may want to place desks in rows facing the front of the room until you are confident about your ability as a classroom manager. Rows of desks reduce interaction among students and make it easier for them to

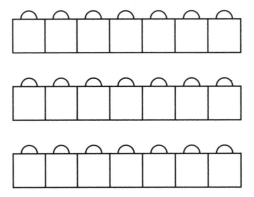

Figure 2.1   A Horizontal Arrangement

concentrate on individual assignments (Axelrod, Hall, & Tams, 1979; Bennett & Blundell, 1983; Wheldall, Morris, Vaughan, & Ng, 1981). This appears particularly true for students who have behavior and learning disabilities. Wheldall and Lam (1987) found that on-task behavior dropped by half and disruptive behavior increased by three times when "behaviourally troublesome" adolescents with moderate learning problems moved from rows to tables.

Rows direct students' attention toward the teacher, so they are particularly appropriate for teacher-centered instruction. But there are a number of variations on this theme. For example, you might consider putting desks in horizontal rows. (See Figure 2.1.) This arrangement still orients students toward the teacher, but provides them with close "neighbors" on each side. Another variation is shown in Figure 2.2.

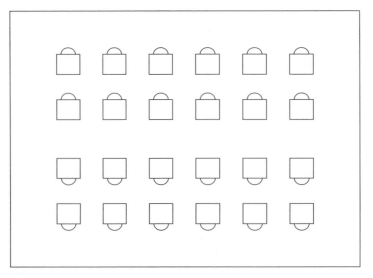

Figure 2.2   Rows Facing Each Other

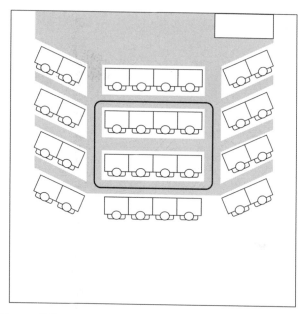

Figure 2.3 **Fredric Jones's Interior Loop Arrangement.**
An interior loop allows you to work the crowd
with the fewest steps.

Here, desks are arranged two-deep in rows that face each other, with a wide aisle down the middle of the classroom. Since this arrangement allows students to see each other and to interact more easily, it is particularly useful in subjects like world language. Still another row option, advocated by Frederic Jones (2000), is shown in Figure 2.3. Here, an "interior loop" allows you to "work the crowd with the fewest steps" (p. 34).

Figures 2.4 to 2.7 illustrate the way Sandy, Fred, and Christina have arranged their classrooms. As you can see, Sandy's classroom is divided into whole-group in-structional areas and laboratory or work areas. For presentations and homework re-view, students sit in a horizontal row arrangement. An aisle separates clusters of two and three trapezoidal desks (which Sandy hates because they take up so much room). Although she is unhappy that students are packed so closely together, Sandy wants to get as many students as possible in a row, so that all students are rel-atively close to the front of the room.

Fred and Christina have chosen to arrange their desks in rows; however, both teachers regularly have students move into other configurations when appropri-ate. As Christina explains:

 I don't like them in rows . . . but it's a functional place to start, espe-cially since I share the room. My philosophy is that I move them based on the activity. [Having the desks in rows] is a good starting point for

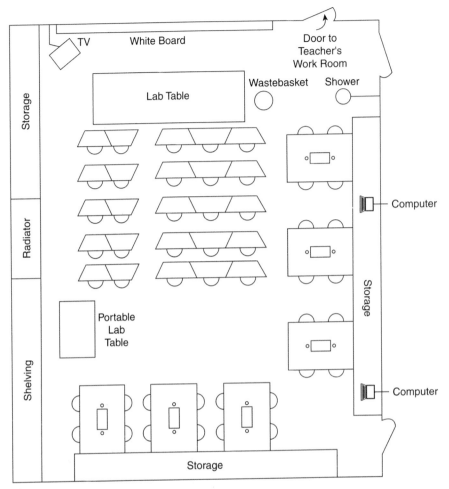

Figure 2.4   Sandy's Room Arrangement

journal writing, attendance, and whole-group presentations, and then I move them when I want to.

Both Fred and Christina have students rearrange their desks into clusters for small group work and—when classes are small enough—into a circle for class discussions. This year Christina's large classes have led to experimentation with a new arrangement for discussion (see Figure 2.7):

 When we're going to have discussions, I stand in the center of the room, and I tell all the kids to turn their desks to a 45-degree angle, so that they're all facing the center. Then I sit outside the circle; it helps me to keep my mouth shut.

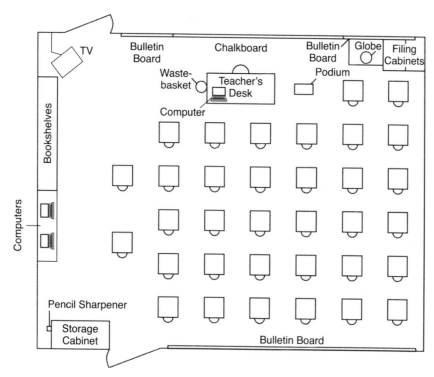

Figure 2.5   Fred's Room Arrangement

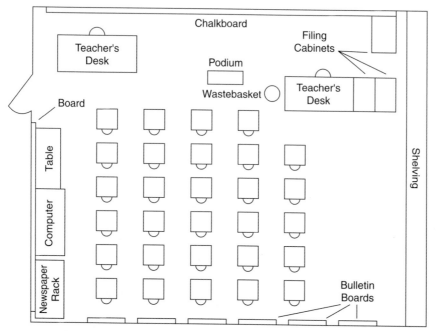

Figure 2.6   Christina's Room Arrangement

Christina's arrangement for class discussions

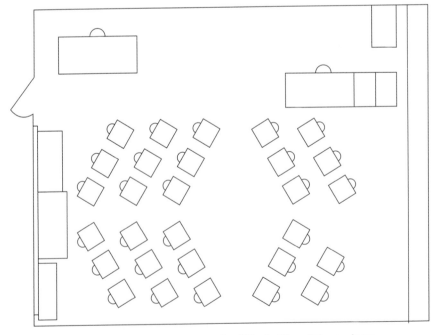

Figure 2.7   Christina's Arrangement for Whole-Class Discussions

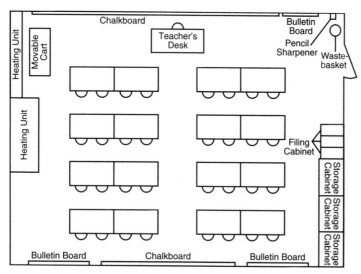

Figure 2.8   Donnie's Initial Arrangement

In Donnie's classroom, the two-person tables are new this year. She has arranged them in groups of two, forming horizontal rows, but continues to try other arrangements (see Figures 2.8 and 2.9). She even allows individual students to move their tables into configurations that they feel are more comfortable. Interestingly, although Donnie's tables are attractive and facilitate small-group work, she actually prefers desks, which are easier to arrange in a horseshoe.

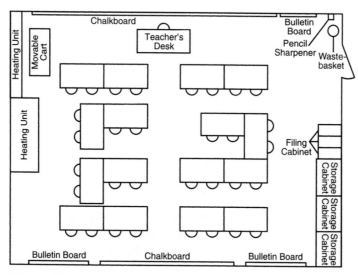

Figure 2.9   Donnie's Rearrangement

Interaction between the Teacher and the Students

The way students are arranged can also affect the interaction between teacher and students. A number of studies have found that in classrooms where desks are arranged in rows, the teacher interacts mostly with students seated in the front and center of the classroom. Students in this "action zone" (Adams & Biddle, 1970) participate more in class discussions and initiate more questions and comments.

Educational researchers have tried to tease out the reasons for this phenomenon. Do students who are more interested and more eager to participate select seats in the front, or does a front seating position somehow produce these attitudes and behaviors? This issue has not yet been fully resolved, but the weight of the evidence indicates that a front-center seat does encourage participation, while a seat in the back makes it more difficult to participate and easier to "tune out." During a discussion with students in one of Sandy's classes, it was clear that they were aware of this phenomenon. As one student said, "When we're all so close to the front, you know that the teacher can see you real easily. That helps keep you awake!"

Christina is also well aware of the influence that seating can have on participation and involvement. On the first day of school, she assigns seats alphabetically. A few weeks later, however, she reassigns seats to maximize students' engagement and participation:

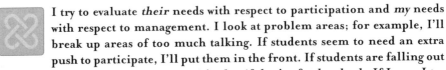

I try to evaluate *their* needs with respect to participation and *my* needs with respect to management. I look at problem areas; for example, I'll break up areas of too much talking. If students seem to need an extra push to participate, I'll put them in the front. If students are falling out of their chairs trying to participate, it's okay if they're farther back. If I can, I try to avoid seating people in the back corners; that's where they can get lost. But in my class of 29 students, *someone* has to be in the back corners. I try to remedy this by changing seats every few weeks and by having students reconfigure the seating arrangements for different activities.

Although research on the action zone has only examined row arrangements, it is easy to imagine that the same phenomenon would occur whenever teachers direct most of their comments and questions to the students who are closest to them. Keep this in mind and take steps to ensure that the action zone encompasses your whole class. Some suggestions are to (1) move around the room whenever possible; (2) establish eye contact with students seated farther away from you; (3) direct comments to students seated in the rear and on the sides; and (4) periodically change students' seats (or allow students to select new seats) so that all students have an opportunity to be up front.

Symbolic Identification

This term refers to the information provided by a setting about the people who spend time there. The key questions are these: What does this room tell us about the students—their classroom activities, backgrounds, accomplishments, and preferences? And what does the classroom tell us about the teacher's goals, values, views of the content area, and beliefs about education?

Too often, classrooms resemble motel rooms. They are pleasant but impersonal, revealing nothing about the people who use the space—or even about the subject that is studied there. This "anonymity" is exacerbated in middle and secondary school where six or seven classes may use a space during the day (and then an adult class uses it in the evening, as in Fred's situation!). Nonetheless, it's important to think about ways of personalizing your classroom setting. Before using wall space or bulletin boards, however, be sure to negotiate "property rights" with the other teachers who are using the room.

All four teachers attempt to personalize their classrooms, within the constraints of their individual circumstances. In Christina's classroom, mobiles of drama masks and literary genres hang from the ceiling. Five brightly colored bulletin boards across the back wall are devoted to various aspects of English. The two nearest the windows contain photographs of famous writers at their desks; quotations describe the ways they approach—and conquer—the agonies of writing. Donnie has the use of only two bulletin boards, but she tries to have them reflect her students' activities and accomplishments. She watches the newspaper and regularly posts stories about her current and former students. One bulletin board is usually devoted to a "Math Honor Roll" (students who have received As or Bs for the marking period). Sometimes, she even takes photographs of the students in her classes and displays them in honor of special events (e.g., when a student does particularly fine work, when a student has had outstanding attendance, etc.).

Sandy also posts photographs of her students conducting laboratory investigations, although never without explicit permission. Occasionally, Sandy also displays students' outstanding work, but she offers words of caution:

> High school students often don't want their work posted on the bulletin board, because they don't want to "stand out" from their peers in any way. If I do put work up, I make sure to put their names on the *back* of the paper.

You can also personalize classroom space by displaying materials that reflect the cultural backgrounds of the students in your class, especially as they relate to your subject matter (Weinstein, Curran, & Tomlinson-Clarke, 2003). For example, an art classroom could exhibit work by artists from your students' native countries, while a science classroom could display posters of scientists from around the world who have made significant contributions to scientific progress. In a math classroom, "ethnomathematical" displays could explore concepts such as number, graphs, topology, probability, and symmetry in the context of non–Western cultures (e.g., Africa, China, India, the Incas, the Mayans).

Finally, consider ways you can use the environment to communicate something about your *own* cultural background, experiences, and idiosyncrasies. You might want to hang your favorite art prints, display pictures of your family, or exhibit your collections of "precious objects." Over Christina's desk is a mobile of wooden apples that she made during the summer before her first year of teaching. A teddy bear represents the collection of bears she has at home. On the front chalkboard, a framed poem, written by a former student, begins this way: "This is a poem/about the one who tried to teach us/Though sometimes we all were stubborn/She still managed to reach us."

Task Instrumentality

This function concerns the many ways the environment helps us to carry out the tasks we need to accomplish. Think about the tasks and activities that will be carried out in your classroom. Will students work alone at their desks on writing assignments? Will they work cooperatively on activities and projects? Will you instruct the whole class from the chalkboard? Will you work with small lab groups? Will students do research using the Internet?

For each of these tasks, you need to consider the physical design requirements. For example, if you plan to give whole-group instruction before students work independently (e.g., at centers), think about where to locate the instructional area vis-á-vis the work area. Do you want it near a chalkboard or a bulletin board? In any case, its location should allow all students to see and hear your presentations without being cramped. You also want the work areas to be organized well so that individuals or small groups do not interfere with one another.

If you have one or more computers in your classroom, you also need to think carefully about where to create your computer workstation (although the placement may be dictated by the location of electrical outlets and wiring for Internet access). If students are going to work in pairs or in small groups, place the station in an area where clusters of students can gather round without creating traffic congestion and distraction. Also be sure to keep the computers away from water and from chalkboards because dust can cause a problem.

Whatever tasks will occur in your classroom, there are a few general guidelines you need to keep in mind. These are presented in the Practical Tips box.

Pleasure

The important question here is whether students and teachers find the classroom attractive and pleasing. To the already overworked teacher preoccupied with covering the curriculum, raising test scores, and maintaining order, aesthetic concerns may seem irrelevant and insignificant (at least until parent conferences draw near). Yet given the amount of time that you and your students spend in your classroom, it is worth thinking about ways to create a pleasing environment. It is sad when students associate education with sterile, uncomfortable, unpleasant places.

The classic study on environmental attractiveness was conducted by Maslow and Mintz (1956). These experimenters compared interviews that took place in an "ugly" room with those that took place in a "beautiful" room. Neither the interviewer nor the subject knew that the real purpose of the study was to assess the impact of the environment on their behavior. Maslow and Mintz found that interviewers assigned to the ugly room complained of headaches, fatigue, and discomfort. Furthermore, the interviews *finished more quickly* in the ugly rooms. Apparently, people in the ugly room tried to finish their task as quickly as possible in order to escape from the unpleasant setting.

PRACTICAL TIPS FOR

ARRANGING A FUNCTIONAL CLASSROOM

- *Frequently used classroom materials should be accessible to students.* Materials like calculators, scissors, dictionaries, textbooks, and rulers should be easy to reach. This will minimize the time spent preparing for activities and cleaning up. Decide which materials will be kept in locked or closed cabinets and which will be kept on open shelves. Think about whether materials are accessible to students in wheelchairs or with crutches or walkers.

- *Shelves and storage areas should be well organized so that it is clear where materials and equipment belong.* It is useful to label shelves so that everyone knows where things go. This will make it easier to obtain materials and to return them. You should also have some sort of a system for the distribution and collection of students' work (e.g., in-out boxes).

- *Pathways throughout the room should be designed carefully to avoid congestion and distraction.* Paths to the pencil sharpener, supply closet, and trash can should be clearly visible and unobstructed. These high-traffic areas should be as far from students' desks as possible. Are pathways wide enough for students in wheelchairs?

- *The seating arrangement should allow students to have a clear view of instructional presentations.* If possible, students should be able to see instructional presentations without turning their desks or chairs around.

- *The location of the teacher's desk depends on where you will be spending your time.* If you will be constantly moving about the room, your desk can be out of the way, in a corner perhaps. If you will use your desk as a conference area or as workstation, then it needs to be more centrally located. But be careful: With a central location, you may be tempted to remain at your desk for long periods of time, and this cuts down your ability to monitor students' work and behavior. Moreover, if your desk is in a central location, holding student conferences there may be distracting to other students.

- *Decide where to store your own personal teaching aids and supplies.* If you move from room to room, arrange to have a desk drawer or a shelf in a storage cabinet for your own personal use. At the very least, you will probably need storage for pens and markers, paper clips, a stapler, rubber bands, chalk, tape, tissues, attendance forms, and file folders. An alternative strategy is to carry your personal supplies with you, perhaps in one of the plastic carrying bins often used for home cleaning supplies. Some teachers even use a movable cart.

Additional studies have also demonstrated that aesthetically pleasing environments can influence behavior. For example, two college-level studies have indicated that attractive classrooms have a positive effect on attendance and feelings of group cohesion (Horowitz & Otto, 1973) and on participation in class discussions (Sommer & Olson, 1980). The classrooms in these studies had specially designed seating, soft lighting, plants, warm colors, and carpeting, hardly the kinds of aesthetic improvements that can be implemented by most secondary school teachers. Nonetheless, it is worth thinking about the kinds of environmental modifications that *are* possible, especially if you have your own room. Try to be as creative as Roberta Jocius, a high school English teacher in Portage, Indiana, who is passionate about creating an attractive, homey classroom (Schmollinger, Opaleski, Chapman,

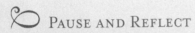

PAUSE AND REFLECT

I have heard middle and high school teachers comment that the five functions of the classroom setting are interesting, but more applicable to the elementary classroom. I disagree. Think about how a secondary teacher can use the five functions of the classroom in planning and setting up an environment that is developmentally appropriate for the 6th through 12th grade student.

Jocius, & Bell, 2002). In one corner of Jocius's classroom is a rocking chair with an afghan and reading lamp, right next to a display of young adult novels. Lace curtains and an artificial fireplace with an electric log also enhance the feeling of warmth and hominess, along with a set of china teacups and teapots that she uses in conjunction with her students' study of *Great Expectations*!

THE TEACHER AS ENVIRONMENTAL DESIGNER

Steele's functions give you a way of thinking about the environment, but they don't provide you with an architectural blueprint. If you think about the various roles that settings play, you will realize that the functions not only overlap, they may actually conflict. Seating that is good for social contact may be bad for testing, as Donnie can attest: She often prepares two to three versions of a test, since students are sitting so close to one another! Similarly, room arrangements that provide students with privacy may be poor for monitoring and maintaining order. As you think about your room and your own priorities, you will have to determine which functions will take precedence over others. You also need to think about what is possible for you to achieve if you are a "nomad" who must move from room to room or share space with other teachers. This section of the chapter describes a process that you can follow as you design your classroom.

Think about the Activities the Room Will Accommodate

The first step in designing a classroom is to reflect on activities your room is to accommodate. For example, if you are teaching a lab science, you may need to accommodate whole-group instruction, "hands-on" lab work, media presentations, and testing. If you are teaching history, you may want to have small-group research projects, debates, simulations, and role-plays in addition to the standard lecture, recitation, discussion, and seatwork formats. If you are teaching a world language, you may want to facilitate conversation among students. List these activities in a column, and next to each activity, note if it poses any special physical requirements. For example, computers need to be near electrical outlets and away from chalkboards. For access to the Internet, the location of the computer will also be dictated by hard wiring.

Next, consider which of these activities will *predominate* in your classroom and reflect on the physical arrangement that will be most suitable for the majority of the time. Will students most often be participating in whole-class discussion? If so, you may want to arrange the desks in a large circle. Will you generally be doing presentations and demonstrations at the board? If your answer is yes, then some sort of row arrangement may be best. In addition, consider how the furniture can be rearranged to accommodate the *other* activities you will be conducting. For example, Christina has desks arranged in rows, but as soon as students are done with journal writing (the first activity of every period), they move into clusters of four or five to carry out small-group tasks.

Think about Whether the Students in Your Classroom Have Special Needs That Require Environmental Modifications

Also think about the characteristics of the students who will be using the room and whether you need to make any environmental modifications so the classroom is safe and comfortable. Will any students have orthopedic problems that require wide aisles or special equipment and furniture? (For example, Sandy has a portable lab table to accommodate a student in a wheelchair.) Will any of your students have full-time aides who accompany them from room to room? If so, the aide may need a desk or chair also, perhaps in close proximity to the student. If any students have hearing impairments, it's desirable to minimize noise by placing felt or rubber caps on chair and table legs. (Tennis balls work well!) Covering table surfaces with fabric and lining study carrels with acoustical tile or corkboard can also help cut down on noise (Mamlin & Dodd-Murphy, 2002).

Also think about special needs when assigning students their seats. Will you have any students with attention difficulties who may need seats away from distractions? If you have students with learning disabilities, make sure that they can easily see what you are writing on the board; in other words, don't block their line of sight. Similarly, if you have students with a hearing impairment who need to lip-read, locate their seats so they can see you at all times.

Draw a Floor Plan

Before actually moving any furniture, draw a number of different floor plans and select the one that seems most workable. (Figure 2.10 depicts symbols that

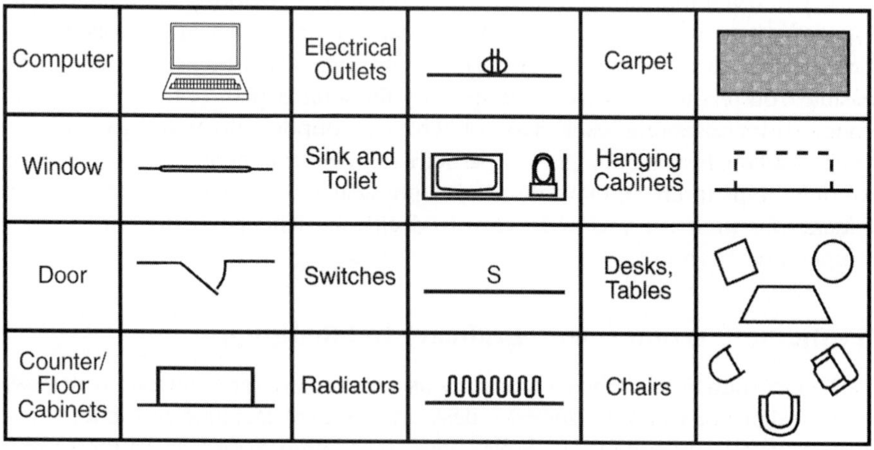

Figure 2.10   Drawing a Floor Plan: Some Useful Symbols

may be useful.) In order to decide where furniture and equipment should be placed, consider the special requirements noted on your list of activities, as well as the room's "givens"—the location of the outlets, the chalkboard, the windows, the built-in shelves, computer wiring, cabinets, or lab tables. Also keep in mind our discussion of psychological security, social contact, and task instrumentality.

It may be helpful to begin by deciding where you will conduct whole-group instruction and the way students will be seated during this time. Think about where the teacher's desk should be, whether frequently used materials stored on shelves or in cabinets are accessible to you and your students, and whether pathways are clear. Remember, there is no one right way to design your classroom. The important thing is to make sure that your spatial arrangement supports the teaching strategies that you will use and the kinds of behaviors you want from your students.

Involve Students in Environmental Decisions

Although a great deal can be done before the start of school, it is a good idea to leave some things undone, so your students can be involved in the design process. Although their suggestions are occasionally beyond the means of the normal public school—planetarium-type ceilings and rope ladders (Hill, 1968)—it is likely that many of their ideas will be reasonable. Listen to Arthur, a student at an inner-city junior high, speaking of his ideal classroom (Coles, 1969):

> *I'd like comfortable chairs, like ones that had cushions so your back doesn't hurt and your bottom either. I'd like us sitting around—you know, looking at each other, not in a line, not lined up. I'd like a sink, where you could get some water to drink, and you wouldn't have to ask the teacher to go down the hall....There'd be a table and it would be a lot nicer homeroom than it is now. (pp. 49-51)*

If you teach four or five classes in one room, it is obviously impossible to involve everyone in all environmental decisions; however, you might solicit ideas for room design from your various classes, and then select those that seem most feasible. You might also rotate responsibility for some aspect of the environment among your classes (e.g., each class could have an opportunity to design a bulletin board display). Inviting students to participate in environmental decision making not only helps to create more responsive physical arrangements, it also prepares students for their roles as active, involved citizens who possess environmental competence.

Try the New Arrangement, Evaluate, and Redesign

Use Steele's functions of the environment as a framework for evaluating your classroom design. For example, does the desk arrangement facilitate or hinder social contact among students? Do displays communicate information about the subject matter and students' work? Are frequently used materials accessible to students? Does the room provide pleasure?

As you evaluate the effectiveness of the classroom setting, stay alert for behavioral problems that might be caused by the physical arrangement. For example, if a student suddenly becomes inattentive when his desk is moved next to the pencil sharpener, it is likely that an environmental change is in order, rather than detention. If the classroom floor is constantly littered despite your appeals for neatness, the underlying problem may be an inadequate number of trash cans.

Improving your room does not have to be tedious and time consuming. In fact, small modifications can bring about gratifying changes in behavior. This was demonstrated by Krantz & Risley (1972), who found that when kindergartners crowded around a teacher who was reading a story, they were inattentive and disruptive. Just spreading the children out in a semicircle markedly improved their attentiveness. In fact, this simple environmental modification was as successful as a complicated system of rewards and privileges that the experimenters had devised!

SOME THOUGHTS ON HAVING TO SHARE ROOMS

When we sat down as a group to discuss the role of the physical environment in classroom management, it became clear that all of the teachers feel frustrated by the need to share classrooms. Christina was blunt about having to teach in two different rooms: "I hate it!" Sandy emphasized the difficulties that are created when access to the classroom is limited:

> When *I'm* not in my room, someone *else* is; that means that I can't get into the room during the school day to prepare labs—and we do six labs a week. I have to prepare labs before or after school, and that's also when I carry out the other responsibilities associated with being a chemistry teacher, like organizing materials, disposing of old chemicals, making sure all the equipment is in working order, and of course, working with kids who are having trouble. Although I'd like to pay attention to creating a more attractive environment, that's got to be a lower priority.

The teachers also expressed irritation over other common problems—for example, inadequate storage space (Christina likes to "hoard" things), inappropriate furniture, and insufficient numbers of desks. They traded war stories about materials that disappear (Fred's gone through three staplers this year) and the lack of personal work areas (it took Sandy three years to get a desk where she could sit during free periods to plan lessons and grade papers; when she finally got one, it was in a storage closet!). They also talked about the problems that arise when the other teachers sharing the room are inconsiderate "roommates" who fail to clean up adequately. Since this was a topic that clearly raised their blood pressure, it seems important to share a few of the lessons they have learned.

Being a Good Roommate

During our discussion, Donnie shared an anecdote that illustrates the kinds of problems that can occur when teachers have to share rooms.

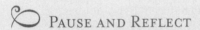

I share the room with a long-term substitute who's supposed to monitor a study hall in my room during second period. He thinks he doesn't really have to watch the kids, so they sit there and write all over the desks. Finally, I couldn't stand it anymore; I took a sponge and cleanser and cleaned all the tables before school began. I taught first period and then turned the room over to him. When I came back third period, the desks were covered with writing again! I was furious!

Given the other teacher's status as a long-term substitute coming in the middle of the year, Donnie's situation was particularly difficult. In general, however, it is helpful to work out an explicit agreement at the very beginning of the year about how the room is to be left. You and your roommate might agree that desks are to be returned to their standard places, boards are to be erased, the floor is to be cleaned, no food is to be in the room, and (of course) no writing is to be on the desks. You also need to agree on a procedure to follow if the agreement is violated, so you don't have to suffer in silence. As Sandy tells us, "It's not enough to have an agreement; you have to follow through. My roommate and I have agreed to hold the kids accountable for the condition of the room. If I come in and find a problem, I tell her about it, and she deals with it the next time she sees those students."

PAUSE AND REFLECT

Think about the problems that arise when teachers have to share rooms. If you are in that situation, what specific items would you want to include in an agreement about how the room is to be left? What procedure would you want to have in place if the agreement is violated?

CONCLUDING COMMENTS

Despite the constraints imposed by sharing rooms, all four teachers agreed on the importance of thinking about the physical environment. As Fred commented:

Some of the ideas—like the action zone, for example—are important for teachers to know about even if they move from room to room and have little control over the classroom. On the other hand, some of the ideas—like psychological security—are hard to put into practice if you're a nomad like I was. But that's okay; thinking about these issues is important anyway. We need to say to new teachers, "Listen folks, you're going to have to be clever in dealing with this. If you can't add soft, warm fuzzies to your room, then you're going to have to compensate. You're going to have to find other ways of providing psychological security, like making sure your kids feel safe in your classroom because they know they're not going to get hammered."

As Fred's comments suggest, it is not easy for secondary teachers to create their ideal classroom settings. Nonetheless, I hope this chapter has given you a greater awareness of the physical environment and its impact, along with a realistic sense of how you can use the environment to meet your goals.

SUMMARY

This chapter discussed how the physical environment of the classroom influences the way teachers and students feel, think, and behave. It stressed the need for teachers to be aware of the direct and indirect effects of the physical environment. This awareness is the first step to developing "environmental competence." The chapter suggested ways to design a classroom that will support your instructional goals, using Steele's five functions of the environment as a framework for discussion.

Security and Shelter

- Be aware of and implement safety guidelines for dangerous supplies and equipment.
- Be sensitive to the needs of students with physical disabilities and attentional problems.
- Add elements of softness.
- Arrange space for freedom from interference.
- Create opportunities for privacy by adding cubicles or folding cardboard dividers.

Social Contact

- Consider how much interaction you want among students.
- Think about whether you are making contact with *all* of your students; avoid a small action zone.

Symbolic Identification

- Personalize your classroom space so that it communicates information about you, your students, and your subject matter.

Task Instrumentality

- Make sure frequently used materials are accessible to students.
- Make it clear where things belong.
- Plan pathways to avoid congestion and distraction.
- Arrange seats for a clear view of presentations.
- Locate your desk in an appropriate place (off to the side helps to ensure that you will circulate).

Pleasure

- Create an aesthetically pleasing environment through the use of plants, color, and bulletin board displays.

Careful planning of the physical environment is an integral part of good classroom management. When you begin to design your room, think about the activities it will accommodate; if possible, invite your students to participate in the design process. Also reflect on whether any of your students have special needs that require environmental modifications. Try your arrangement, evaluate it, and redesign as necessary. If you are sharing your room with other teachers, be sure to work out an explicit agreement about how the room is to be left at the end of the period.

ACTIVITIES FOR SKILL BUILDING AND REFLECTION

In Class

In small groups, consider the following seating arrangements. For each one, think about the types of instructional strategies for which it is appropriate or inappropriate. The first one has been done as an example.

Arrangement	Instructional Strategies for Which This Arrangement Is Appropriate	Instructional Strategies for Which This Arrangement Is Inappropriate
Rows	*Teacher or student presentations; audio-visual presentations; testing*	*Student-centered discussions; small-group work*
Horizontal rows		
Horseshoe		
Small clusters		
Circle		

On Your Own

Visit a middle school or high school classroom, draw a classroom map, and evaluate the physical layout in terms of Steele's five functions of the environment. The following questions, adapted from Bruther (1991), may be helpful.

Security and Shelter

1. Does the classroom feel like a safe, comfortable place to be?
2. Does it contain furnishings and materials that are soft or inviting?
3. Do students have freedom from intrusion and interference?
4. Is there any opportunity for privacy?

Social Contact

5. Does desk arrangement facilitate or hinder social contact among students? Is this compatible with the explicit objectives?

students view public humiliation as an *unacceptable* form of discipline (Woolfolk Hoy & Weinstein, 2006). Moreover, students consider it a very *severe* intervention—not something to be shrugged off lightly. In a study of 300 junior high school students in Israel, Zeidner (1988) found that students viewed *"shaming or personally insulting student" as severe as "permanent suspension from school,"* and more severe than detention, student–teacher conferences, reporting to the principal's office, and verbal reprimands. Students also rated public humiliation as significantly more severe than teachers did. Clearly, public humiliation can poison your relationship with students.

In order to preserve that relationship, Donnie approaches misbehaving students quietly and sets up a time to meet:

 I'll tell them, "I don't want to take up class time and I don't want to embarrass you. Stop by after school so we can talk privately." If that's not possible, we'll meet during lunch or before school. It means giving up some of my own time, but it's much more effective than talking during class in front of everyone.

Sensitivity also means understanding that students' energy levels ebb and flow, and dramatic mood changes from day to day are not uncommon. Football games, Valentine's Day, food fights, and special events can all affect "student weather," and "telling students it makes no difference that the prom is the next day is whistling in the wind" (Gordon, 1997, p. 58).

On an individual level, it's important to notice if someone looks especially edgy, depressed, or angry, and privately communicate your concern. As Donnie puts it:

 Sometimes a student will come in and they just don't have the same *glow*. I'll go over and say, "Is everything OK?" And sometimes they'll say, "No, Miss, I'm having problems at home" or "I'm having trouble with my boyfriend." If they tell me that, I try to respect that and give them some space. I'll go a little easier on them that day, like I won't call on them as much.

It's also important to take students' concerns seriously if they choose to confide in you. From your adult vantage point, breaking up with a girlfriend, having to be home by 1:00 A.M. on a Saturday night, or not making the track team might not be sufficient cause for depression. But Christina emphasizes how important it is to acknowledge the legitimacy of students' concerns:

 One of my eleventh-grade students was absent for two days, and when he came back, he was falling asleep, wouldn't talk with anyone, was real cranky. I called him out in the hall while other students were working in small groups and asked him what the problem was. Of course he said, "Nothing." But I told him I was really concerned, and, eventually, he told me his girlfriend had broken up with him. Later that day, I arranged for him to see the guidance counselor. She let him stay there, gave him tea. It really meant a lot to him. We can't just blow these things off, even if they don't seem that

earth-shattering to us. He needed to know that we noticed and cared about how he was feeling.

Finally, be sensitive to anxiety or difficulty your students may be experiencing with course material or requirements. During a visit to Sandy's class after a severe blizzard that had closed school for several days, I watched students resume a lab activity they had begun before the "vacation." It required them to use pipettes, a new piece of equipment, and several students expressed concern about having forgotten how to use the pipettes.

Sandy acknowledges their concerns: "I know that some of you are worried that you don't remember how to use the equipment. That's a valid concern, since it's been such a long time since you practiced. But don't worry. See if you remember, and if not, just call me over and I'll help you out." Later, when two students express confusion about the lab procedure, she comments: "Your confusion is understandable, because this is the first time we're doing this procedure. Next time we do it you'll know what to do. Remember when we were learning to use the balance, and you were so confused? The first time is always a challenge." At the end of the period, the students express anxiety over an upcoming test: "What if it snows again tomorrow and we don't have a chance to finish the lab, and we're supposed to have the test the next day?" Sandy is reassuring: "If we are in school tomorrow [a Wednesday], then the test will be on Thursday as scheduled. But if we have a delayed opening or no school tomorrow, the test will be on Friday. You've got to see my face for a whole period before the test!

Welcome Students' Input

Allow students to voice their suggestions and opinions about lessons, assignments, or grouping decisions. Interestingly, all four teachers begin the school year by asking students to talk or write about their expectations for the class. As we saw in Chapter 1, Sandy begins the school year by asking her students to write answers to four questions: (1) How do you learn best? (2) What do you expect to be excited about in chemistry? (3) What do you expect to be nervous about? and (4) What can I do to help? In similar fashion, Donnie also solicits students' expectations. On the first day of school, she has students write her a letter, focusing on their attitudes and feelings about mathematics, about the kinds of teaching and managerial strategies they like or dislike, and about their own responsibility in making the classroom a good place to be.

Christina not only asks students to write about their expectations, she also invites their continuing suggestions and feedback on the class:

"I want you to know that I really welcome your input. I'm sure you have good ideas, and I'm interested in hearing your suggestions for things we can do. Also, if you think something didn't work very well, I welcome your criticism too. For example, you might say, 'I know that you were trying to have a good discussion today, but a lot of people weren't responding because . . .' That kind of feedback would be very helpful." Christina points out her e-mail address and encourages students to use it.

There is an interesting postscript to my first-day observations of Christina's request for suggestions and criticism. Several months later, it became clear that a few students were disgruntled by the amount of work they had been assigned. Christina tells it this way:

It was right after spring break, and there were a couple of kids who seemed upset and complaining about work. So, wondering how widespread it was, I opened up a discussion. It was like opening Pandora's box. Out came all these complaints about how I was giving too much homework, and some of it was too difficult for them to do by themselves—they wanted partners. They kept saying it was like college work, and that they were only 15!

I was floored at first, but after everyone had their say, I tried to address their concerns. We made some changes. I postponed some assignments and promised to give them in-class time to work in groups on some of them. I explained why I was giving them challenging work, and I made it clear that I am here every day to work with anybody who needs help. But I also told them that what was most upsetting to me was the fact that they hadn't come to me about all this sooner.

Since the discussion, a lot of kids have been coming in for help, and things really seem to be better. But what I learned is that even if you invite kids to provide input, you still have to go back and check that it's working. You have to teach them that it's really okay to come to teachers and talk about these things. I just assumed my invitation was enough, but it wasn't.

Be Fair

It seems obvious that caring teachers must strive for fairness. For example, issues of fairness often arise in relationship to evaluation and grading. Jeffrey Smith, a colleague who specializes in assessment, emphasizes the need for communication:

If you know the criteria for good work, tell your students. Don't make them guess. Don't withhold information about how you're going to grade, and then play "gotcha." If you're going to count participation and effort as part of the grade, tell students that too, and tell them what you mean by participation.

Christina earnestly follows Jeff's advice. Since she counts participation as one-third of students' grades, she provides her classes with a weekly "participation check-sheet" that lists the behaviors she expects, and she spends considerable time explaining how it works. (See Figure 3.2.) During one interview, she shared her reasoning:

Most teachers don't use participation as an actual portion of the grade; they use it as a tie-breaker (like if you're trying to decide between an A and a B). But I think it's one of the most important things. Participation is not just raising your hand and speaking out. It's also having your work

Weekly Participation			
Name _____			
Week # ____ Beginning Date _____ Ending Date _____			
	Pts.	**Points Assigned**	
Criteria	**Avail.**		**Total**
Attentive to directions	15		
Attentive to class discussion	10		
Contributes to class discussion	15		
Prepared for class	10		
Begins assigned tasks immediately	10		
Completes assigned tasks	10		
Uses time efficiently	15		
Respectful to others	15		
Total for Positive Behaviors	**100**		
Verbally disruptive	-10		
Physically disruptive	-10		
Inappropriate language	-10		
Disrespectful	-10		
Late for class	-10		
Total for Negative Behaviors	**-50**		
Final Weekly Score	**100**		
Grade			

Figure 3.2   Christina's Participation Checksheet

done, being prepared for class, being engaged, staying on task. I know some kids are going to be more verbal and more confident, but everyone can make some contribution to class.

In these instances, caring and fairness seem to go hand in hand. But it's not always so simple. Indeed, teachers who are trying to treat students well often experience a tension between two moral orientations (M. S. Katz, 1999). Being fair generally involves "making judgments of students' conduct and academic performances without prejudice or partiality" (M. S. Katz, 1999, p. 61). In terms of classroom management, this translates into ensuring that rules apply to everyone, no matter what. On the other hand, being fair can also imply a recognition that people may need different, personalized treatment, and being caring certainly seems to demand that we acknowledge students' individuality. From this perspective, treating everyone the same is *unfair.* So what is a teacher to do?

Even experienced, masterful teachers who care deeply about students' well-being may have conflicting positions on this fundamental dilemma. Consider Sandy and Fred. Sandy observes:

> **You can't have community in the classroom unless everyone feels that they'll be treated fairly, whether they're the student congress president or not. You're better off having a class with very few rules that apply to everyone, rather than a lot of rules that apply to only some people.**

Sandy demonstrated this principle not too long ago, when three of her students, including a boy classified as having an emotional disorder, didn't have their homework and asked for permission to turn it in the next day:

> **My answer was no. I don't accept late homework, and they know it. I want them to learn how to budget their time and to prepare. This was a 20-point homework assignment, due on Monday. I reminded them all week, and made a big point of it on Friday. Then they walk in on Monday without it. I said, "I believe you did it; your integrity is not in question. But it's not here." To my horror, Billy (the boy classified as emotionally disturbed) started to cry in front of the whole class. I got him out of the room and talked with him. I told him I understood that other things can interfere with doing homework, but the rule applies to everyone. I know this seems harsh, but I think this was a really significant event. It was important for Billy—and the rest of the class—to see that he has to meet the same expectations.**

From Sandy's perspective, having the rules apply to everyone is both fair *and* caring. But Fred takes a somewhat different position:

> **I try to treat kids fairly in that my decision is always based on what is best for the kid. At times that means you treat everyone the same, and that's the right decision. Other times you may treat everyone differently, and *that's* the right decision. There's no recipe for being fair that we can all follow. We have to constantly examine our decisions and ask, "Is this in the best interest of the kid?"**
>
> **I gain some things by not always treating everyone the same. I have more flexibility this way. I can say, "This kid is having a really hard time, and I'm not going to give him a zero for the day, no matter what the rule says." I'm just going to throw out that rule. And I've never had a kid say "That's not fair." But I lose some things too—namely, the consistency that comes when everyone knows exactly what's going to happen. So you have people who push the envelope. I have to be more on guard; I have to watch for people who are trying to take advantage.**

In sum, being fair is certainly an essential component of being caring, but it's not always obvious what this means in terms of actual practice. Teaching is messy and uncertain, and we often don't know what the right decisions are until after we've made them. What *is* certain, however, is that teachers need to engage in ongoing reflection about these complex moral issues. (We will return to these issues in Chapter 11 when we discuss fairness and consistency in dealing with inappropriate behavior.)

Be a Real Person (Not Just a Teacher)

On the first day of school, Donnie takes a few minutes to explain how she got the name Donnie, that her husband is the principal of a nearby elementary school, and that they have a daughter who "is one year short of a quarter of a century." (When students look at her questioningly, she laughs and tells them, "Do your math!") Within the first few minutes of the very first class meeting, she has already communicated an important message: In addition to being a teacher, Donnie Collins is a real person with a life outside of school.

Beginning teachers often puzzle over the extent to which they should share information about their personal lives. I remember having teachers who refused to reveal their first names—as if that would somehow blur the boundary between teacher and student and diminish their authority. On the other hand, there are teachers who are extremely open. In an article on "Building Community from Chaos" (1994), Linda Christensen, a high school English teacher in Portland, Oregon, writes:

> Students have told me that my willingness to share stories about my life—my father's alcoholism, my family's lack of education, my poor test scores, and many others, opened the way for them to tell their stories. Students have written about rape, sexual abuse, divorce, drug and alcohol abuse. And through their sharing, they make openings to each other. Sometimes a small break. A crack. A passage from one world to the other. And these openings allow the class to become a community. (p. 55)

As a new teacher, it's probably wise to find a happy medium between these two extremes and to discuss limited aspects of your out-of-school life (Jones & Jones, 1998), such as trips and vacations, cultural and athletic activities, hobbies, or pets. As Chapter 2 discussed, you can also use the physical environment to convey information about your family, cultural background, experiences, and idiosyncrasies. You might want to hang a poster of your favorite music group, display photographs of your family or pets, or exhibit a collection. (I've seen giraffes, penguins, kaleidoscopes, even hubcaps!) All of these "artifacts" communicate the fact that you are a *person* and create opportunities for you to interact with students on a more personal level.

As you gain experience and confidence, you can decide if you want to follow Linda Christensen's example and share more information about your personal life. During an early visit to Christina's classroom, for example, I watched as she introduced a writing assignment on identity. She began by distributing copies of her own identity essay. In it, she reflects on her Puerto Rican father, her "all-American" mother (unable to "recount all of her various nationalities"), her "Asian eyes" (with eyelids that "kept escaping" the blue eyeshadow she tried to use), and the "curious ambiguity" of her skin. Four months later, near the end of the school year, Christina talked about her students' reactions to the essay:

I think it helped to build connections with the students. It stimulated all kinds of questions: What do you do for this holiday? Do you go to the Puerto Rican Day parade? They were able to see me as a real person. Just today, it came up again and led to a good discussion about the most appropriate terms for various ethnic and racial groups. It clearly made an impact on them.

Another way of showing your humanity is to admit when you don't know something. Teachers sometimes feel that they have to be the "sage on the stage," but it can be beneficial for students to see that even "experts" don't know all the answers all the time. The best way to encourage students to take risks in the process of learning is to take risks yourself.

It's also important to admit when you make a mistake and to acknowledge that you are fallible. I recently visited a Spanish I class taught by a native Spanish speaker who told students that she would "give two points to the student who wins the *more*." When a boy corrected her in a respectful way ("It should be wins the *most*"), the teacher thanked him for helping her with her English. Her willingness to admit her mistake and to learn from a student certainly reinforced the lesson that she tries so hard to teach. As she told me later, "I constantly stress the fact that it's okay to make mistakes when you are talking and learning another language, and you don't have to be afraid of that."

Become Aware of Adolescent Culture

Positive relationships with students can be facilitated if you have what Robin Gordon (1997) calls "social insight"—knowledge of popular music, styles of dress, current movies, and other aspects of adolescent culture. Donnie also finds it helpful to sit quietly and listen to students' chatter right before homeroom:

That's when I learn all about the concerts they've attended or the deejays they like. We talk about today's music; I tell them I don't know what the groups are saying these days, and they explain. They also like to hear about the things that I did "back in the old days" and compare it with the things they're doing now.

In particular, teachers need to be aware of the digital media that are so much a part of students' lives. Today's teenagers have been dubbed the *DIG Generation* for "digital immediate gratification" (Renard, 2005). They download information, songs, and movies from the Internet; take photographs with digital cameras and share their pictures online; communicate through e-mail and instant messaging; and disclose their thoughts and experiences on blogs. Not only do you need to understand how digital technologies have changed the way adolescents live and think, you need to harness the excitement about technology to make academic activities more relevant and motivating. For example, you can design a "WebQuest," an inquiry-oriented activity that asks students to explore a set of high-quality online information sources to complete a specific task. (WebQuests for all content areas and grade levels, as well as training for teachers interested in designing such activities, can be found at www.WebQuest.org.) In addition, teachers can create a class blog on which students reflect on assignments, exchange comments about one another's work, share resources, and submit homework. (See the University of Houston's Blogs in Education Web page [http://awd.cl.uh.edu/blog] for information and examples.) As Renard (2005) comments, "Students may perceive writing for the audiences they reach through blogs as more 'real' than writing for the teacher or even for a class workshop" (p. 46).

Promote Autonomy by Sharing Responsibility

Visiting kindergarten classes, I'm always struck by how much more choice and control they have over their day than secondary students do. I see kindergartners making decisions about what they want to do and with whom they want to do it. Ironically, as students advance through the grades, becoming more capable of making decisions and more concerned about having autonomy, we offer fewer opportunities for choice and involvement in decision making (Nucci, 2006). At the junior high level, research has documented the declines in intrinsic motivation and interest in school that result from this mismatch between adolescents' increasing desire for greater autonomy and the schools' increasing emphasis on teacher control (e.g., Eccles, Wigfield, & Schiefele, 1998).

Angela Vaughan (2005) is a high school math teacher who recognized that this mismatch was causing problems in her Algebra I class. Students were bored because the work was too easy or frustrated because it was too difficult; they rarely completed homework, showed no interest in learning the content, and created constant discipline problems. Vaughan decided to redesign the course so that it would be entirely self-paced. First, she spent several weeks teaching her students the skills they would need to become successful, autonomous learners (e.g., how to take notes, how to decide which activities would be the most helpful, how to plan their work). Students then began working their way through a set of modules. They began each module with a pretest and, based on the results, planned their learning activities and decided when they would take the exam on that module. Although colleagues, administrators, and parents predicted disaster, Vaughan reports that her freshmen "far exceeded" her expectations. Achievement increased and misbehavior decreased; students assigned themselves more homework than she ever did; and they paid close attention to teacher presentations.

Although few beginning teachers are inclined to undertake the radical restructuring that Angela Vaughan did, you can certainly find ways of providing opportunities for students to exercise some autonomy and to make decisions about their own behavior and class events. For example, you might sometimes allow students to choose their own groups for cooperative learning activities. You might give students responsibility for creating assignments, constructing questions for class discussions and tests, leading class activities, and evaluating their own progress and behavior (Ridley & Walther, 1995).

You might also assign "block homework assignments" that require students to develop their own timeline for completion. For example, Sandy usually assigns a certain amount of reading and 25 to 30 problems that are due in a week or so. She recommends that students do four or five problems a night, but she does not require them to show her their work on a daily basis. She realizes that this means some students will wait until the last night to do all the problems:

 High school teachers have to remember that students want to be treated like young adults, not like babies. It's important to give them some responsibility for their own behavior. They might make the wrong decisions and "fall and scrape their knees," but then they can see the consequences. I think they're more likely to take responsibility for their mistakes if teachers don't dictate everything.

Sharing decision making can be difficult for teachers. When you're feeling pressured to cover the curriculum and to maximize learning time, it's easier to make the decisions by yourself. For example, assigning topics for a term paper is faster than allowing students to decide on their own topic; giving students a particular kind of paper and three paint colors is simpler than helping them to decide on the paper and colors they want to use. Involving students can be messy and time-consuming, and allowing students to make decisions about their own behavior means that they'll sometimes make the wrong decisions. Nonetheless, a "short-term investment of time" can lead to "a long-term gain in decision-making ability and self-esteem" (Dowd, 1997).

Be Inclusive

In recent years, *inclusive education* has been used to refer to the practice of placing students with disabilities in general education classrooms rather than segregating them in special classrooms or schools. But the term can also be used more broadly, to describe classes in which differences related not only to disability, but also to race, class, ethnicity, gender, cultural and linguistic background, religion, and sexual orientation are acknowledged, understood, and respected. As Mara Sapon-Shevin (1999) asserts:

> The goal of having an inclusive classroom is *not* to homogenize those differences, pretending that they are not there or do not have an impact on students or their lives. The goal is to acknowledge those differences and create a classroom community that works with those differences (and sometimes around those differences) so that every student can feel a sense of connection and belonging. (pp. 63–64)

This, of course, is easier said than done. Before we can "create a classroom community that works with differences," we need to recognize that we are often afraid and suspicious of those differences. As I mentioned in Chapter 1, sometimes we deny even *seeing* differences. It is not uncommon, for example, for my European-American teacher education students to pride themselves on being color-blind, assuming that "to be color-blind is to be fair, impartial, and objective" (Nieto, 1996, p. 136). Yet, to deny cultural or racial differences is to deny an essential aspect of people's identity—and recognizing those differences does not make us racist. During one conversation, Fred spoke passionately about these issues:

> So many times I hear teachers say things like, "I don't think of kids as Black or Hispanic or Asian—just as kids." But being Black or Hispanic or Asian is part of who those kids are—just like being Polish and Russian is part of who I am. . . . A part of the whole community-building thing is acknowledging that these differences exist. We're not all the same . . . To build community we also need to face the fact that racism and bias are part of the real world. People don't want to admit it's there. But it's everywhere; it's part of all of us. The question is not "Are you a racist?" but "How much of a racist are you, and how can you become less so?"

In addition to *acknowledging* differences, creating inclusive classrooms means learning about disabilities, or cultures, or races, or religions that we've never before encountered. For example, you can't acknowledge, understand, and respect behaviors that have cultural origins if you have no idea that the behaviors are rooted in culture. Teachers may be shocked when Southeast Asian students smile while being scolded if they are unaware that the smiles are meant not as disrespect but as an admission of culpability and an effort to show that there is no grudge (Trueba, Cheng, & Ima, 1993). Similarly, teachers who are not cognizant of the fact that Pacific Islanders value interpersonal harmony and the well-being of the group may conclude that these students are lazy when they are reluctant to participate in competitive activities (Sileo & Prater, 1998). Teachers who are unaware that the culture of most American Indians tends to emphasize deliberate thought may become impatient when those students take longer to respond to questions (Nieto, 1996).

A particularly heated debate about students' use of Ebonics or Black English illustrates the problems that occur when teachers are unaware of the cultural origins of language and styles of discourse. Ernie Smith (2002), an African American linguist, notes that during his years of schooling teachers often equated the use of Ebonics with deficiency:

> Teachers and other school officials often used such terms as "talking flat," "sloven speech," "corrupt speech," "broken English," "verbal cripple," "verbally destitute," "linguistically handicapped," and "linguistically deprived" to describe the language behavior of my Black classmates and me. They suggested that our language differences were deficiencies that were related to physical and/or mental abnormalities. Often during Parent-Teacher Conferences or at Open House Conferences, my teachers were not hesitant to suggest to my parents, and to parents of other children, that we should be assigned to the school speech clinic for speech therapy or to the school psychologist for a diagnostic examination, and treatment for possible congenital mental disorders. (pp. 17–18).

Not surprisingly, this negative reaction to children's home language frequently leads to alienation from school. As Lisa Delpit argues in *The Skin That We Speak* (2002), "language is one of the most intimate expressions of identity" so "to reject a person's language can only feel as if we are rejecting him" (p. 47). Rejection like this has no place in an inclusive classroom; instead, inclusive teachers honor students' home language while teaching them the importance of learning to speak Standard English—what Delpit (1995) calls the "language of the culture of power." In other words, our goal is to enable students to "code switch" according to the norms of the setting.

It's unrealistic to expect beginning teachers (or even experienced ones!) to have familiarity with all of the cultures that might be represented in their extremely diverse classrooms. Certainly, developing this kind of "cultural literacy" takes time and effort. Some specific suggestions are listed in the Practical Tips box. Meanwhile, when you encounter behaviors that seem inappropriate and inexplicable, ask yourself whether these behaviors might, in fact, be culturally grounded. In addition, think about how you can use your students as a resource. Listen to Fred:

If I have kids from other countries in my class, I'll ask about customs there, and how they compare with customs here. Not only do I learn something I didn't know before, but I can just see the "little lights go on." It's like, "Hey, here's someone who's interested in my experiences." We don't have to be intrusive about it, but it's important that classrooms be a place where we can learn about one another. I can use my classroom like a textbook.

PRACTICAL TIPS FOR

DEVELOPING CULTURAL LITERACY

- **Explore students' family backgrounds.** Where did the student come from? Was it a rural or urban setting? Why did the family move? How long has the student been in this country? How many people are in the family? What are the lines of authority? What responsibilities does the student have at home? What are parents' beliefs with respect to involvement in the school and in their child's education? Do they consider teachers to be experts and therefore refrain from expressing differences of opinion? Is learning English considered a high priority?

- **Explore students' educational background.** If students are new to this country, how much previous schooling have they had? What kinds of instructional strategies are they used to? In their former schools, was there an emphasis on large group instruction, memorization, and recitation? In students' former schools, what were the expectations for appropriate behavior? Were students expected to be active or passive? independent or dependent? peer-oriented or teacher-oriented? cooperative or competitive?

- **Be sensitive to cultural differences and how they may lead to miscommunication.** How do students think about time? Is punctuality expected or is time considered to be flexible? Do students nod their heads to be polite or to indicate understanding? Do students question or obey authority figures? Do students put their needs and desires before those of the group or vice versa? Are expressions of emotion and feelings emphasized or hidden?

- **Use photographs to communicate without words.** Take pictures of the students engaged in various activities to take home to parents; display photographs around the room; invite students to bring in pictures of themselves and their families; use photographs for get-acquainted activities.

Sources: Kottler, 1994; Sileo & Prater, 1998.

Just as we must learn to acknowledge and respect racial and cultural diversity, we must also learn to create an accepting classroom environment for other, less visible kinds of differences. Several years ago, *Newsweek* magazine featured a special report on "Gay today: How the battle for acceptance has moved to schools, churches, marriage, and the workplace." The article on the schools (Peyser & Lorch, 2000) described the efforts of two 17-year-olds, Leslie-Claire Spillman and Martin Pfeiffer, to establish a Gay–Straight Alliance in their Baton Rouge, Louisiana, high school. Like other gays and lesbians, Spillman and Pfeiffer had suffered through years of harassment and hatred. As a result, Pfeiffer had once been suicidal; Spillman had dropped out of school, become addicted to heroin, and spent five weeks in "detox." Such problems are all too common among homosexual youth; indeed, some researchers have found that gay and lesbian adolescents are two to three times more likely to attempt suicide than their heterosexual peers; they are also at increased risk for poor school performance, truancy, and dropping out (Nichols, 1999). It is essential that teachers work to create an atmosphere of tolerance for what Anderson (1997) calls the "forgotten children"—those "whose needs have been ignored, whose existence has been whispered about, and whose pain is just beginning to surface" (p. 65). You can take a step toward creating that atmosphere by making it clear that homophobic name-calling is absolutely unacceptable, by respectfully using the words *gay, lesbian,* and *bisexual,* and by referring to spouses or partners rather than husbands or wives (Edwards, 1997).

Search for Students' Strengths

We often think of teaching as a search for deficits—find out what students don't know or can't do, and then try to fix the problems. Certainly, responsible teaching does involve the identification of gaps, misconceptions, and weaknesses. But responsible teaching also involves a search for strengths. In *Teaching to Change the World* (1999), Jeannie Oakes and Martin Lipton argue that when teachers and students have a caring relationship, they work together to find competence: "The student's search is his own discovery of what he knows and how he knows it. The teacher's search—an act of care and respect—is also discovering what the student knows and how he knows it" (p. 252).

I thought of this perspective on caring during one meeting with the teachers, when Sandy talked about her conviction that "everyone needs their 15 minutes of fame":

 Chemistry lends itself to a variety of talents—the math problems, the writing, the spatial relations, the mechanical ability. So I can give different people a chance to shine. Take Adam. He's really good at spatial relationships so I know that I can call on him to do diagrams.

When we have student presentations, I always try to think who I want to call on so I can showcase kids' different strengths. For example, I told the class that I was going to randomly choose a lab group to present the lab to the rest of the class. Everyone had to think about how to teach this and to be prepared. It was a nice safe situation—a great opportunity to get these two quiet girls to shine. I knew they had done a good job on the lab. So I wrote their names 12 times and put the slips in a beaker, and had someone pull out a slip. Of course their presentation went very well. But it was important for the girls—and everyone else—to think it was a risky situation, that they had just gotten chosen by chance. When they got a great evaluation, they felt terrific.

Pause and Reflect

At the beginning of this chapter, I stressed the fact that students are more likely to cooperate with teachers who are perceived to be caring. Since a big part of showing care is being a good listener, it's important to think about exactly what that means. Before reading the next section on communication skills, think about a time when someone *really listened well* to a problem you were relating. What kinds of behaviors did this person display? How did you know they were *really* listening?

Develop Communication Skills

Another way of showing students that you care is by being a good listener. Sandy puts it this way:

> How come there are only certain teachers in the school that kids will go to [when they have a problem]? After all, most kids have six teachers a day. It's all about listening. When you're a high school teacher, you have to listen seriously to problems that might not be problems to you, but they are to them. And that's a way of gaining their trust. A kid is not going to come to you and say I want to commit suicide if three weeks earlier you said, "Oh grow up, you'll get over her."

Being a good listener means being attentive, trying to understand students' feelings and concerns, asking appropriate questions, and helping students solve their own problems. Let's briefly examine each of these.

Attending and Acknowledging

Giving a student your complete, undivided attention is the first and most basic task in being helpful (Kottler & Kottler, 1993). It is rare that individuals are fully attentive to one another. Have you ever tried to talk with someone who was simultaneously organizing papers, posting notices on the bulletin board, or straightening rows of desks? Divided attention like this communicates that the person doesn't really have time for you and is not fully paying attention.

Attending and acknowledging involve both verbal and nonverbal behaviors. Even without saying a word, you can convey that you are totally tuned in by orienting your body toward the student, establishing eye contact, nodding, leaning forward, smiling, or frowning. In addition, you can use verbal cues. Thomas Gordon (1974) recommends "empathic grunting"—the little "uh-huhs" and phrases (e.g., "Oh," "I see," "Mmmmm") that communicate, "I'm really listening." Sometimes, when a student needs additional encouragement to talk more, you can use an explicit invitation, what Gordon calls a "door opener": "Tell me more," "Would you like to say more about that?" "Do you want to talk about it?" "Want to go on?"

One of the hardest ideas for teachers to accept is that a person can help another simply by listening. But Kottler and Kottler (1993) remind us that attending can be a powerful helping tool:

> You would be truly amazed at how healing this simple act can be—giving another person your full attention. Children, in particular, are often so used to being devalued by adults that attending behaviors instantly tell them something is different about this interaction:"Here is a person who seems to care about me and what I have to say." (p. 40)

Active Listening

Attending and acknowledging communicate that you are totally engaged, but they do not convey if you really *understand*. Active listening takes the interaction one step further by having you reflect back what you think you heard. This feedback allows you to check out whether you are right or wrong. If you're right, the student knows that you have truly understood. If you're off target, the student can correct you, and the communication can continue. Examples of active listening appear in Table 3.1.

If you're new to active listening, you may find it useful to use the phrase, "You feel . . ." when you reflect back what you heard. Sometimes, novices feel stupid, as if they're simply parroting back what the person just said. (In fact, when I was first learning to do active listening, a student became really annoyed and demanded to know why I kept repeating what he had said!) As you gain more skill, however, you are able to *paraphrase* what you hear, and the interaction becomes far more subtle.

You can also use active listening to respond to the nonverbal messages contained in students' facial expressions and body language. For example, if you see that a student entering the room looks really angry, you might be able to ward off problems by recognizing that something is wrong. Here is a recent journal entry from a student teacher who did this without even knowing about active listening:

> *I was writing the "Do Now" on the marker board when all of a sudden I heard a loud crash behind me—the sound of a backpack crammed full of books hitting the floor. I turned around, and there was John sulking in the seat directly behind me. Obviously, I could not let this slide, so I quickly finished writing the "Do Now" for the rest of the class to begin while I attended to John. I came up to him, squatted down to his level, and asked, "What's wrong? You seem really upset"—not knowing at the time this was a communication strategy called Active Listening. His immediate response was, "Nothing." I paused, trying to come up with something "teacher-y" to say and in that pause of 10 seconds, John spoke! The problem was that he was mad at his parents. He had broken his book bag the day before, and since he had to use the same broken bag the next day, he was extremely embarrassed. We talked about his anger and he started to work once he had vented. The next day he came into class with a different book bag—an old one, but a functional one. I took notice, and even though he was mad that it was an old one, he was glad I paid attention to him and his problem.*

Active listening is not always this easy. Student teachers with whom I work often want to reject it out of hand; many find it unnatural and awkward, and they

TABLE 3.1 Examples of Active Listening

STUDENT: Wait till my mom sees this test grade. She's gonna flip out.

TEACHER: You think she'll be really mad at you, huh?

STUDENT: Yeah, she expects me to come home with all As.

TEACHER: Sounds like you're feeling really pressured.

STUDENT: Well, I am. You'd think that getting a B was like failing. My mom just doesn't understand how hard this is for me.

TEACHER: So you think a B is an okay grade in a tough course like this, but she thinks that you can do better.

STUDENT: Yeah, she has this thing that if I come home with a B, I'm just not working.

TEACHER: That's rough. I can see how that would make you feel like she doesn't appreciate the efforts you're making.

STUDENT: I can't believe I have to be home at 12:00! It's crazy! All my friends have a later curfew—or they don't have any curfew at all!

TEACHER: So you think your parents are a lot stricter than the other kids' parents.

STUDENT: Well, they are! I mean, I know it's 'cause they care about me, but it's really a pain to have to be home earlier than everyone else. I feel like a dork. And besides, I think I'm responsible enough to have a later curfew.

TEACHER: So you're not just embarrassed, you're mad because they don't realize how responsible you are.

STUDENT: All along my boyfriend's been telling me how he'll stick by me if I get pregnant, and then it happens, and he's gone.

TEACHER: You feel really abandoned.

STUDENT: I don't want to go to School-Base [for mental health counseling]. Only crazy kids go to School-Base!

TEACHER: Going to School-Base is kind of embarrassing . . .

STUDENT: Yeah. My friends are gonna give me a really hard time.

TEACHER: You think they're going to say you're crazy.

STUDENT: Yeah. I wanna go, but I don't want people to make fun of me.

TEACHER: I can understand that. It's really rough when people make fun of you.

STUDENT: I had the worst nightmare last night! I mean, I know it was just a dream, but I just can't get it out of my head. This bloody guy with a knife was chasing me down this alley, and I couldn't get away.

TEACHER: Nightmares can be so scary.

STUDENT: Yeah, and I know it's babyish, but I just can't shake the feeling.

TEACHER: Sometimes a bad feeling from a nightmare stays with you a long time . . .

would much prefer to give advice, not simply communicate that they understand. But knowing that someone really understands can be profoundly important, especially to teenagers who so often feel misunderstood. In addition, active listening provides an opportunity for students to express their feelings and to clarify their problems. It can also help to defuse strong feelings without taking the responsibility away from the student for solving the problem.

Questioning

When people tell us their problems, we often want to ask them questions in order to find out more information. Kottler and Kottler (1993) caution teachers to be careful about this practice:

> The problem with questions, as natural as they may come to mind, is that they often put the child in a "one down" position in which you are the interrogator and expert problem solver. "Tell me what the situation is and I will fix it." For that reason, questions are used only when you can't get the student to reveal information in other ways. (p. 42)

Sandy also warns beginning teachers about the use of questions:

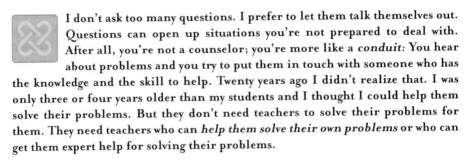

I don't ask too many questions. I prefer to let them talk themselves out. Questions can open up situations you're not prepared to deal with. After all, you're not a counselor; you're more like a *conduit:* You hear about problems and you try to put them in touch with someone who has the knowledge and the skill to help. Twenty years ago I didn't realize that. I was only three or four years older than my students and I thought I could help them solve their problems. But they don't need teachers to solve their problems for them. They need teachers who can *help them solve their own problems* or who can get them expert help for solving their problems.

If you must ask questions, they should be open-ended—requiring more than a one-word response. Like active listening, open-ended questions invite further exploration and communication, whereas close-ended questions cut off communication. Compare these questions:

"What are you feeling right now?" versus "Are you feeling angry?"

"What do you want to do?" versus "Do you want to tell your boyfriend?"

Kottler and Kottler point out one notable exception to the rule of avoiding questions whenever possible: that is, when it is important to get very specific information in a potentially dangerous situation, such as when a student is discussing suicide. Then it would be appropriate to ask specific questions: Have you actually tried this? Will you promise not to do anything until we can get you some help?

Problem Solving

Instead of trying to solve students' problems, you can guide them through a process that helps them to solve their *own* problems. In problem solving, students define their problem, specify their goals, develop alternative solutions that might be constructive, narrow the choices to those that seem most realistic, and put the plan into action (Kottler & Kottler, 1993).

Not too long ago, Donnie used a problem-solving approach when a female student told her she was pregnant and asked if she should get an abortion.

First, the student needed to clarify the situation: Was her boyfriend available or not available? Were her parents supportive or not supportive? Was she using drugs or not using? Also, she needed to think about what resources were available to her. All of these factors play a role in making a decision about what to do.

Then, she needed to figure out what her values and priorities were—does she want to go to college? How does she feel about giving the baby up for adoption? Finally, I tried to help her figure out the alternatives—adoption, abortion, staying single and keeping the baby, getting married and keeping the baby.

I don't give advice in situations like this—I wouldn't know what kind of advice to give. But I *can* try to help kids clarify the situation. They're confused, and as an outside party who can think clearly, I can help them to see alternatives they haven't thought of, to talk about the resources that are available to them. My goal is to help them make the best possible decision for themselves.

A Note about Touching

In recent years, the fear of being accused of sexual harassment and physical abuse has made teachers wary of showing students any physical affection. This is a particularly salient issue for males (King, 1998). Indeed, one of my male student teachers recently wrote this entry in his journal:

> *I had occasion to talk to a student who had a death in the family. She was pretty upset. After explaining that she needn't worry about her class work for that day, I tried my best to comfort her. It's funny, under any other circumstances I would have put an arm around a person in that state, but in this case, I wasn't sure if that would be right.*

This student is not alone in his concern. Hansen and Mulholland (2005) interviewed male teacher education students about to begin their teaching careers. The men experienced a tension between their natural inclinations to be warm, caring, and affectionate to children and the fear that their behavior would be misconstrued as sexual. As one participant in the study commented:

> It annoys and frustrates me that you can't be yourself.... I mean, when you see the female teachers being able to be affectionate [with the children] at times ... it frustrates you when maybe a child needs to be comforted or something and you just feel as though you can't really do it. (p. 125)

According to Hansen and Mulholland, the anxiety about showing physical affection decreased somewhat as the teachers became more experienced. The young male teachers also found other ways of expressing their affection—for example, by talking and listening with empathy.

Although our four teachers have all been told to avoid touching students, they do not want to forgo all physical contact. Listen to Fred:

I have colleagues who say they'll never touch a kid at all. I understand, but I think you have to touch people if you're going to be a teacher. There have to be rules, of course. I would never be alone with a kid, because of the appearance of impropriety, but I'll hug kids. . . . It doesn't have to be any big demonstrative thing, but just touching somebody's hand or shoulder can mean a lot. If someone's getting antsy, I'll put my hand on their shoulder, and they'll settle down. If they're hurting, and they need a hug, I'll give them one. What kind of community is it if you can't give someone who's hurting a hug?

Delia Cruz Fernandez, a junior high teacher from Puerto Rico, agrees with Fred. She also emphasizes the fact that there are differences in cultural norms about touching that teachers need to keep in mind:

> *We Hispanic people, we talk with our hands, we use a lot of body language, we get closer when we talk with other people, and we use a lot of touch on shoulders or arms. When I first started teaching, I tried not to touch any students and to respect their space, but as the years passed, I started touching more on shoulders or arms. If a student says, "Don't touch me," I touch the desk, but I had that only once; the rest of the students react positively. They seem to feel more comfortable if there's some touching, like "she really cares about me, I'm important to her."*

It's important to point out that both Fred and Delia have been in their districts for many years and have a solid reputation. As a new teacher, you are in a very different situation. Speak with your colleagues about the policy in effect in your school; some schools actually direct teachers to "teach but don't touch." Even if there is no explicit prohibition against touching students, you need to be cautious so that your actions are not misconstrued. Give your hugs in front of others. Give "high fives" instead of hugs (Jones & Jones, 1998). When a student stays after school, keep the door open, or make sure that other students or teachers are around.

BUILDING CARING RELATIONSHIPS AMONG STUDENTS

A great deal has recently been written on ways of fostering supportive, trusting relationships among students. Unfortunately, much of the advice focuses on elementary classrooms, where teachers generally work with the same group of children for the entire day and there's more opportunity to build a sense of connectedness. The challenge of creating a safe, caring community is certainly more daunting when you teach three or four or five groups of students a day, for 42 or 45 or even 84 minutes. What can secondary teachers possibly do in the limited amount of time—especially when there's so much pressure to cover the curriculum? I posed this question to our four teachers. Here are some of their suggestions, along with others from educational writers interested in students' social and emotional learning.

Ask the Students

In *Beyond Discipline: From Compliance to Community* (1996), Alfie Kohn suggests that teachers begin the school year by asking students about ways of building feelings of safety:

> A teacher might say, "Look, it's really important to me that you feel free to say things, to come up with ideas that may sound weird, to make mistakes—and not to be afraid that other people are going to laugh at you. In fact, I want everyone in here to feel that way. What do you think we can do to make sure that happens?"

It's also a good idea to ask students to provide you with feedback about their perceptions of the classroom environment. "*What Is Happening in This Class?*" is a questionnaire developed by Fraser, McRobbie, and Fisher (1996) to assess a variety of classroom dimensions, including student cohesiveness, teacher support, involvement, cooperation, and equity. Some of the items from the questionnaire appear in Table 3.2. As you can see, they are scored from 1 ("almost never") to 5 ("almost always"), so a higher score means that students perceive the environment more positively. If you periodically administer some of the items listed in Table 3.2, you can get a sense of how students are feeling about your classroom environment.

TABLE 3.2 Items from the *What Is Happening in This Class?* Questionnaire

Student Cohesiveness:

I know other students in this class.	①	②	③	④	⑤
Members of the class are my friends.	①	②	③	④	⑤
I work well with other class members.	①	②	③	④	⑤
In this class, I get help from other students.	①	②	③	④	⑤

Teacher Support:

The teacher takes a personal interest in me.	①	②	③	④	⑤
The teacher considers my feelings.	①	②	③	④	⑤
The teacher helps me when I have trouble with the work.	①	②	③	④	⑤
The teacher talks with me.	①	②	③	④	⑤
The teacher is interested in my problems.	①	②	③	④	⑤

Involvement:

My ideas and suggestions are used during classroom discussions.	①	②	③	④	⑤
I ask the teacher questions.	①	②	③	④	⑤
I explain my ideas to other students.	①	②	③	④	⑤
I am asked to explain how I solve problems.	①	②	③	④	⑤

Cooperation:

I cooperate with other students when doing assignment work.	①	②	③	④	⑤
When I work in groups in this class, there is teamwork.	①	②	③	④	⑤
I learn from other students in this class.	①	②	③	④	⑤
Students work with me to achieve class goals.	①	②	③	④	⑤

Equity:

The teacher gives as much attention to my questions as to other students' questions.	①	②	③	④	⑤
I have the same amount of say in this class as other students.	①	②	③	④	⑤
I am treated the same as other students in this class.	①	②	③	④	⑤
I receive the same encouragement from the teacher as other students do.	①	②	③	④	⑤

Note: Items are scored 1, 2, 3, 4, and 5, respectively, for the responses *almost never, seldom, sometimes, often,* and *almost always.*

Source: Fraser, McRobbie, & Fisher, 1996.

Model the Traits You Want Students to Have

I once knew a professor of educational psychology who taught about motivation in his courses; he also announced grades while he returned tests—in descending order. Apparently, the professor had not taken to heart the material he taught.

Teachers frequently exhort students to treat one another with respect. Yet exhortation is unlikely to be effective unless teachers themselves are respectful. As Mary Williams (1993) tells us, "'Do as I say, not as I do' clearly does not work" (p. 22). Williams was interested in learning how respect was taught and learned by students in middle school classrooms (grades 6 through 8). She found that respect was best taught through modeling. According to students, teachers "have to follow the values themselves" (p. 22). Students resented teachers who told them to be kind and to respect others, yet exhibited favoritism, treated students "like babies," didn't listen, and gave "busywork."

I thought a lot about the importance of modeling respect during a discussion I recently had with a teacher about her treatment of a "troublemaker" named Serena:

> *Serena was late to class today. She said it was because another student had been bullying her in the hallway on the way to class. I told her to go to the office to report it. When I told another teacher about the incident, she said, "You believe her?!" She looked at me like I was crazy. But I don't like the way Serena and some of the other kids are stereotyped. It's true, they're often troublemakers, but I wasn't in the hallway, so I don't know what happened. I want to treat Serena with the same respect I show to other students. I want to give her the benefit of the doubt. Kids shouldn't have to live the whole year with the same label and not have their improvements recognized.*

As this anecdote illustrates, teachers sometimes categorize students as troublemakers (or criminals, gang members, thieves, and prostitutes [S. R. Katz, 1999]) and fail to accord them the respect that they as teachers demand. But students are unlikely to be respectful of teachers who treat them in demeaning ways. This is certainly a case of "Do unto others. . . ."

Provide Opportunities for Students to Get to Know One Another

On the first day of school, Christina distributes a handout entitled "Find Someone Who." Students must find one person in the class who fits each of the 36 descriptions (e.g., someone who "has read at least three Stephen King novels," someone who "has the same favorite television show as you do," someone who "is a procrastinator," and someone who "would rather work alone than in groups") and have the person sign his or her name next to the appropriate statement. Students are allowed to sign their names only once per sheet, even if more than one item applies.

"Find Someone Who" can be especially useful if you include items relating to race, cultural and linguistic background, and disability and solicit information in addition to a signature. Consider these examples (Sapon-Shevin, 1995):

> Find someone who grew up with an older relative. What's one thing that person learned from the older relative?

Christina's students get to know one another by completing "Find Someone Who."

Find someone whose parents come from another country. What's one tradition
  or custom that person has learned from his or her parents?
Find someone who has a family member with a disability. What's something
  that person has learned by interacting with the person with a disability?

In order to build community, we have to create opportunities for students to
learn about one another and to discover the ways in which they are both different
and similar. There are numerous getting-acquainted activities like the one Christina
chose that teachers can use. Some of these are listed in the Practical Tips box.

It's important to note that one or two activities at the start of school are not
sufficient to enable students to get to know one another, let alone to build community. As Sapon-Shevin (1995) reminds us:

> Communities don't just happen. No teacher, no matter how skilled or well inten-
> tioned, can enter a new classroom and announce, "We are a community." Commu-
> nities are built over time, through shared experience, and by providing multiple
> opportunities for students to know themselves, know one another, and interact in
> positive and supportive ways. (p. 111)

Christina learned this lesson halfway through the school year:

 **Since my basic skills class only has 11 kids I figured that they had all got-
ten to know one another, especially since I had done getting-to-know-
you activities at the beginning of school. But one day, when they were
working in small groups, I found out that some kids didn't know other**

PRACTICAL TIPS FOR

HELPING YOUR STUDENTS TO GET ACQUAINTED

- **Guess Who?** Have students write a brief autobiographical statement (family background, hobbies, extracurricular activities, etc.), which they do not sign. Collect the statements, read each description, and ask students to write the name of the individual they believe wrote the description. (You can participate too.) After all the descriptions have been read, reread them and ask the authors to identify themselves. Ask students to indicate how many classmates they correctly identified. (Jones & Jones, 1998)

- **Two Truths and a Lie** (or **Two Facts and a Fiction**). Have students write down and then share three statements about themselves, two of which are true and one of which is a lie. For example, I might write, "I once played the princess in *Once Upon the Mattress,* and one night during a performance I fell from the top of 15 mattresses and herniated a disk in my back," "I won third prize in the All-Alaska Logging Championship for the rolling pin toss," and "I trekked through Nepal on my honeymoon." Students guess which one is the lie, and then I tell the truth. (I didn't trek through Nepal; I backpacked through Colorado and Wyoming.) The activity can be done as a whole class or in small groups. In either case, since the activity allows students to select what to disclose about themselves, there is little chance of embarrassment. It also provides opportunities for students to discover common interests and experiences and to test assumptions and stereotypes. (No one looking at me today, for example, would ever guess that I had camped on my honeymoon!) (Sapon-Shevin, 1999)

- **Little-Known Facts about Me.** This is a variation of the previous activity. Students write a statement about themselves that they think others won't know. The papers are folded, collected, put in a box, and shaken. Students take turns drawing a paper and reading the statement aloud. Everyone guesses who wrote the little-known fact. (Sapon-Shevin, 1999)

- **Lifelines.** Each student draws a line on a piece of paper and then marks six to ten points representing important events in their lives that they are willing to share (e.g., the birth of a sibling, the death of a close family member, the time they starred in the school play, when they moved to this school). Students then get into pairs and share their life stories. Members of each pair could also introduce each other to the rest of the class, referring to points on the lifeline. (Sapon-Shevin, 1999)

- **Your Inspiration.** Have students bring in pictures of people or things that inspire them, along with an accompanying quotation. Post them on a bulletin board. (Schmollinger, Opaleski, Chapman, Jocius, & Bell, 2002)

- **What Are You Most Proud of Yourself For?** Have students write their individual responses to this question on paper in the shape of a footprint. Post these on a bulletin board in the shape of a path labeled "success." (Schmollinger, Opaleski, Chapman, Jocius, & Bell, 2002)

kids' names. I was astounded. The class was a combination of English language learners and native English speakers who were very low achieving, and I realized that these two groups of kids had never really gotten to know one another. Obviously, I should have done more team building throughout the year; once or twice at the beginning of school was just not enough.

Sometimes, the curriculum itself provides opportunities for students to learn about their classmates and to develop empathy. For example, Linda Christensen (1994), a high school English teacher, had her students read literature that forced them to look beyond their own world and reflect on the experiences of "others." In conjunction with the reading, Christensen paired her native English speakers with students who had emigrated from another country—Vietnam, Laos, Cambodia, Eritrea, Mexico, Guatemala, and Ghana. They interviewed their partner and wrote a profile of the student to share in class. Christensen describes her class's reactions:

> Students were moved by their partners' stories. One student whose brother had been killed at the beginning of the year was paired with a student whose sister was killed fighting in Eritrea. He connected to her loss and was amazed at her strength. Others were appalled at how these students had been mistreated at their school. Many students later used the lives of their partners in their essays on immigration. . . . Besides making immigration a contemporary rather than a historical topic, students heard the sorrow their fellow students felt at leaving "home." In our "curriculum of empathy," we forced our class to see these students as individuals rather than the ESL [English-as-a-Second Language] students or "Chinese" students, or an undifferentiated mass of Mexicans. (p. 53)

Hold Class Meetings

During advisory or homeroom periods, middle school teachers can implement a type of class meeting called "Circle of Power and Respect" or "CPR" (Kriete, 2002). CPR is the middle school version of "Morning Meetings," with which many elementary teachers begin the day, and it contains the same four components. Sitting in a circle, students first *greet one another;* the greeting can be simple—a simple hello, a handshake, or a high-five. As students become more comfortable, the teacher can introduce variations (e.g., greeting one another in different languages). *Sharing* comes next; during this phase of CPR, a few students present news they wish to share, and others ask questions and comment. Sometimes teachers can generate a question for a "focused sharing" (e.g., "What's one accomplishment you feel proud of?" "If you could change one thing about school, what would you change and why?" "What person do you most admire? Why?"). After sharing, the class engages in a *group activity* to build team spirit and to encourage cooperation, participation, and inclusion. Group activities can include games (e.g., Twenty Questions, Charades, Telephone), puzzles, and choral readings of poems. Finally, students focus on a chart containing *news and announcements;* typically, the chart tells them about class and school events and presents an "academic challenge" to develop and reinforce language, math, and other academic skills. (See Figure 3.3.)

Ideally, CPR should be done at least three times a week at the beginning of the day, although schedules do not always allow that. Implemented regularly, CPR allows middle school students to learn CARES—cooperation (rather than competition), assertion (rather than aggression), responsibility (rather than apathy), empathy (rather than self-absorption), and self-control (rather than lack of control). For detailed information about this type of class meeting, see Kriete (2002).

November 21, 2005

Good Morning, Everyone!

Today there will be an assembly program at 11:15 honoring Rosa Parks, who died last month. Ms. Parks is known as the "mother of the civil rights movement." In 1955, she changed the course of American history by refusing to give up her seat on a bus for a white man.

Write something you know about Rosa Parks here:

Figure 3.3   **An Example of a News and Announcements Chart**

Curb Peer Harassment

"Boys call me cow." "Boys call one girl popcorn because she has zits." "One time a kid missed the ball . . . , and they called him a f—ing fag." According to Shakeshaft and her colleagues (1997), verbal assaults like these permeate junior and senior high school. Shakeshaft's research team spent three years interviewing more than 1,000 Long Island, New York, students from eight different schools and from all socioeconomic levels. Everywhere they went, they found that "kids made fun of other kids" (p. 22). The primary targets were girls who were unattractive, unstylish, or physically mature and boys who didn't fit the "stereotypic male mold" (p. 23). A 2002 survey of 760 teens (ages 12–17) by the National Mental Health Association reinforces Shakeshaft's findings. Survey results indicate that students who are overweight, those who dress differently, and those who are gay or thought to be gay are prime targets for teasing and bullying. And more recently, a survey of school climate in America (Harris Interactive and GLSEN, 2005) found that 90 percent of lesbian, gay, bisexual, and transgender teens (LGBT) report being verbally or physically harassed or assaulted during the past year, compared with 62 percent of non-LGBT teens. In addition, almost 70 percent of teens frequently hear students say "that's so gay" or "you're so gay," where "gay" means something bad or devalued.

Such pervasive, hurtful peer harassment is certainly disturbing, but what is also disturbing is the fact that teachers often fail to intervene, leading students to conclude that teachers just didn't care. For example, one girl in Shakeshaft's study reported that "in science class, the boys snap our bras. The [male] teacher doesn't . . . say anything. . . . The boys just laugh" (p. 24). According to Shakeshaft, when teachers did intervene, their responses were minimal. As one student commented,

For name-calling, they'll [teachers] just say, "I don't want to hear that," and then that's it. They really don't do anything else. . . . I wish teachers would stop it right away; even if they hear only one thing. (p. 25)

Another put it this way:

> *They [teachers] don't take as much control as they should. They say, "Don't do it next time." And when they [the harassers] do it the next time, they [the teachers] keep on saying the same thing. They don't take control. (p. 25)*

Shakeshaft and her colleagues contend that adults must take the lead in putting a stop to peer harassment. They recommend that teachers use reflective activities in order to raise awareness. In literature classes, for example, students can read fiction that relates to the topic of harassment and bullying; in math classes, students can conduct surveys and analyze the results; in art classes, students can depict their feelings about name-calling and put-downs. In addition, students and faculty can work together to define the behaviors that are appropriate to inclusive, caring schools.

Taking peer harassment seriously is crucial if teachers are to build safer, more caring classrooms. Stephen Wessler, Director of the Center for the Prevention of Hate Violence at the University of Southern Maine, urges teachers to respond immediately to degrading language in the classroom and to send a clear message that disrespect is unacceptable. He writes:

> When I ask students what they want adults to do when slurs and put-downs occur, the students generally tell me the same thing, whether they are in the 3rd, 7th, or 11th grade: "Say something." Silence sends an unintended but powerfully destructive message. By speaking up, we take an important step toward creating respectful classrooms and schools. (2005, p. 43)

Note that teasing and peer harassment are also discussed in Chapter 13, "Preventing and Responding to Violence."

Be Alert for Student-to-Student Sexual Harassment

On the way out of your classroom, a boy pats a girl on her bottom. She gives him an annoyed look and tells him to "quit it." Another girl comes to you in tears because a boy in the class is spreading stories about what they did on a date last weekend. You hear two girls in your class laughing and teasing a boy about what a "stud" he is. Are these instances of sexual harassment? And should you do anything about them?

Sexual harassment is generally defined as *unwanted and unwelcome sexual attention*. This includes a wide range of behaviors:

> leering, pinching, grabbing, suggestive verbal comments, pressure for sexual activity, spreading sexual rumors, making sexual or sexist jokes, pulling at another student's clothing, cornering or brushing up against a student in a sexual way, insulting comments referring to students' sexual orientation, date rape, sexual graffiti about a student, or engaging in other actions of a sexual manner that might create a hostile learning environment. (Hyman, 1997, p. 318)

Several studies (AAUW, 1993; Lee, Croninger, Linn, & Chen, 1996; National Council for Research on Women, 1994) have documented the fact that sexual harassment is an all too common occurrence in American high schools. Lee, Croninger, Linn, and Chen (1996), for example, found that 83 percent of girls and 60 percent of boys report unwanted sexual attention in school. Their results also indicate that it's not a simple case of some students being perpetrators while others are victims: Over half of the students report that they have harassed their classmates *and* been harassed themselves.

It can sometimes be difficult for you—and your students—to distinguish between harmless flirting and sexual harassment. When you're faced with this situation, it's helpful to keep in mind the fact that whether harassment has occurred is truly in the "eye of the beholder." In other words, the determining factor is "how the person on the receiving end is affected by the behavior, not with what the other person means by the behavior" (Strauss & Espeland, 1992, p. 15). Kissing, touching, and flirting that the recipient likes or wants is *not* sexual harassment (although it may be inappropriate in school!).

Our four teachers stress the importance of responding seriously when students complain that other students are making them feel "uncomfortable." Donnie tells about a first-year teacher in her school who failed to take action when a girl in his class complained that the boy sitting behind her kept touching her hair and "bothering" her:

 Her complaint was vague (I think she didn't want to spell out what was happening), and so even though she kept asking to be moved, he didn't do anything. He just kept saying she should ignore the boy or tell him to stop. Finally, the girl's mother e-mailed him, with a copy to the principal and the superintendent, saying that repeated requests to be moved had been ignored. It was a mess, but the teacher learned a good lesson: If kids are complaining that someone is bothering them, you have to take it seriously. People need to feel comfortable in your classroom and they need to feel that they can trust you to keep them safe.

Given the importance of the recipient's feelings in determining whether sexual harassment has occurred, people can be nervous about whether signs of affection and compliments will be misunderstood. You can suggest that students ask themselves a few simple questions to guide their behavior (Strauss & Espeland, 1992):

Would I want my comments or behavior to appear in the newspaper or on TV?

Is this something I would say or do if my mother or father, girlfriend or boyfriend, sister or brother were present?

Is this something I would want someone else to say or do to my mother or father, girlfriend or boyfriend, sister or brother?

Is there a difference in power between me and the other person (e.g., in size or social status)?

In recent years, an increasing number of districts have written and distributed sexual harassment policies for both students and school personnel. These generally define sexual harassment, outline the procedures to follow when you learn about an incident of sexual harassment, and spell out the consequences. It's important that you obtain a copy of this policy and follow the specified procedures. Keep in mind that the Supreme Court has ruled that school districts can be found liable if they are "deliberately indifferent" to information about "severe, pervasive, and objectively offensive" harassment among students (Walsh, 1999).

Use Cooperative Learning Groups

Research suggests that there are few opportunities for interaction among students during the school day (Osterman, 2000). These findings are disturbing in light of innumerable studies attesting to the power of cooperative learning to promote the development of positive peer relations. More specifically, cooperative learning facilitates interaction and friendship among students who differ in terms of achievement, sex, cultural and linguistic background, and race; fosters acceptance of students with disabilities; increases positive attitudes toward the class; and promotes empathy (Good & Brophy, 2000).

David and Roger Johnson (1999), two prominent researchers in the field of cooperative learning, distinguish among three types of cooperative learning. In *formal cooperative learning,* teachers assign students to small heterogeneous groups that work together on carefully structured tasks; groups may stay together for one class period up to several weeks. In *informal cooperative learning,* students work together in "temporary, ad-hoc groups" that might last from a few minutes to a whole period (Johnson & Johnson, 1999, p. 128). For example, during a whole-class presentation, Donnie frequently tells her students to "turn to your neighbor and talk about how you'd tackle this problem." Finally, *cooperative base groups* are long-term, heterogeneous groups in which students support one another's academic progress and emotional well-being. Members of the base group can collect assignments for absent students and provide assistance when they return, tutor students who are having problems with the course material, check homework assignments, and provide study groups for tests. According to Jones and Jones (1998), it's helpful to have base groups meet several times a week for 5 to 15 minutes: "At the very least, the base group provides a setting in which at least three members of the class are concerned about each student's learning" (p. 133). (See Chapter 9, "Managing Groupwork," for a more detailed discussion of cooperative learning.)

A Cautionary Tale

Building a caring classroom community is not an easy task, especially for secondary teachers who see students for such a limited amount of time. This lesson was brought home to me during a meeting in which Sandy ruefully described an incident that had just occurred in her classroom. I relate the incident here, not to discourage you, but to acknowledge the reality that building community is challenging work.

My kids were going over homework, and they were in groups of three. I picked the groups. In one group, I had a girl who happens to be an honors student and a boy who had to be convinced to take chemistry. They finished reviewing the homework pretty quickly. Another group was in need of assistance, so I suggested that they get help from the first group. Mitchell, one of the kids in the second group, called over to the girl—the honors student—to come and help them. So Ryan—the kid who had to be convinced to take chemistry—says, "Wait a minute. Why did you just ask her, not us? Do you think we're stupid?" Then he turns around to me and says, "See, Mrs. K., that's why I didn't want to take chemistry. Because all the smart kids know who they are and they know who's stupid. They think that kids who haven't done well in school could never do well in chemistry."

I'm standing there thinking, "How do I get out of *this* one? What do I say?" I had watched it all unfold in front of me. And 24 pairs of eyes are looking at me. Finally I said, "Well, I guess you certainly fooled them." I wish you could have seen it. Ryan's chest puffed up, and he says to Mitchell, "Lucy's not going to help you; I'm going to help you."

Here I thought that we had created a cohesive community, and then I find out there are all these little subgroups. The kids have these perceptions of one another, and they become barriers between them. Mitchell's perception was that Lucy would be best at explaining. Ryan's perception was that Mitchell thinks I'm stupid. I'm always trying to demonstrate that people have multiple intelligences, multiple talents. I have them working in all these cooperative learning groups, and still, there are these barriers. But I'll just keep trying to knock them down.

CONCLUDING COMMENTS

Alfie Kohn (1996) suggests that it would be helpful if we all reflected on "what makes school awful sometimes" (p. 114). Then we might be more inclined to make sure that those kinds of experiences and situations don't happen for students in our classrooms. I recently followed his advice. I thought back to my sophomore year in high school, when Friday gym classes were devoted to ballroom dancing. All the boys lined up on one side of the gym, while girls lined up on the other. When the physical education teacher said "OK, go!" the boys rushed across the gym floor to get a dance partner. I tried hard to pretend that I didn't care as more popular, more attractive girls were asked to dance, and I was left standing there. But it was hard to pretend on the one occasion when I was the very last girl standing in line. There was also one boy left, and he was obviously unhappy about having to pair up with me. The teacher approached. The conversation went something like this: "Ask her to dance." "No." "I said, 'Ask her to dance.'" "No!" "Ask her to dance or you get a zero for the day!" He asked me to dance.

I've shared this story with my students—along with my feelings of humiliation—and I've asked them to think about similar experiences. Here are some of their responses to the question, "When was school awful for you?"

As a high school junior, I took Algebra II and Trigonometry. Although I was a good student, the teacher and I did not hit it off for some reason. . . . Midyear, we had an exam on logarithms. I thought I understood it, but I made the same mistake reading the log charts for every problem and I failed the test. I came into class the next day thinking I had done OK on the test. The teacher held up my exam in front of the class and gloated that he had failed me. I hated going to that class for the rest of the year, and I hated that teacher for humiliating me.

When I was a sophomore in high school, one of the girls would follow me around and torment me, call me names, and threaten to hurt me. . . . None of my teachers or any authority figure ever helped. I'm still curious why she hated me so much.

The worst was in junior high. . . . I was made fun of by the other girls, girls with whom I had been friends the year before. . . . I was tormented for not having money or clothes and for having a conscience (and by that I mean not breaking the law or hurting other people's feelings). It was the first year I didn't like going to school.

School was awful for me when I was switched from second track to first track in Spanish. . . . I wanted to be in that class because I wanted those students to like me and not think I was a dork. However, the guidance counselor went behind my back and called my parents. He did not inform them that I did not want to switch so they said it was OK. I did not even get a chance to talk to them before they switched my schedule. I felt powerless and betrayed.

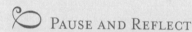

PAUSE AND REFLECT

For too many students, school is a place where they feel humiliated, threatened, ridiculed, tormented, teased, powerless, and betrayed. Think about when school was awful for *you*. If you can keep those times in mind and try to ensure that they never happen to your students, you will be well on your way to creating a safer, more caring community.

SUMMARY

This chapter began by discussing the tension that novice teachers often feel between wanting to care and needing to achieve order. It stressed the fact that caring and order are not irreconcilable goals and concluded that it is possible to create a classroom that is not only relaxed and comfortable but also orderly and productive. The chapter then considered ways of showing students that you care about them and ways of building caring relationships among students.

Ways of Showing Care

- Be welcoming.
- Be sensitive.
- Welcome students' input.
- Be fair.
- Be a real person (not just a teacher).
- Become aware of adolescent culture.
- Promote autonomy by sharing responsibility.

- Be inclusive.
- Search for students' strengths.
- Develop communication skills.

Building Caring Relationships among Students

- Ask the students.
- Model the traits you want students to have.
- Provide opportunities for students to get to know one another.
- Hold class meetings
- Curb peer harassment.
- Be alert for student-to-student sexual harassment.
- Use cooperative learning groups.

For too many students, school is a place where they feel humiliated, threatened, ridiculed, tormented, teased, powerless, and betrayed. Teachers who can "remember when school was awful" are better able to create a safe, caring community for their students.

ACTIVITIES FOR SKILL BUILDING AND REFLECTION

In Class

1. Think about the teachers you had in middle school and high school. Select one teacher who showed caring to students and one teacher who did not. Write a paragraph on each teacher, providing details and examples to illustrate what each teacher actually did. Share these in small groups.

2. In the following bits of conversation, students have confided in teachers about problems they are experiencing, and the teachers have responded in ways *not* suggested in this chapter. Provide a new response for each case, using the communication skills discussed in this chapter: acknowledging, active listening, asking open-ended questions, and problem solving.

> STUDENT: My parents won't allow me to go visit my boyfriend at college for the weekend. They say they trust me, but then they don't show it!
>
> TEACHER: Well, I'm sure they have your best interests at heart. You know, you really shouldn't gripe. After all, a lot of kids don't have parents who care about them. I see a lot of kids whose parents let them do anything they want. Maybe you think you'd like that, but I'm sure you wouldn't . . .
>
> STUDENT: I can't stand my stepmother. She's always criticizing me and making me come home right after school to watch my sister, and making me feel really stupid.
>
> TEACHER: Oh, come on now, Cinderella. I'm sure it's not that bad.
>
> STUDENT: My parents want me to go to college, but I really want to join the Marines. What do you think I should do?
>
> TEACHER: Do what your folks say. Go to college. You can always join the Marines later.

On Your Own

1. Interview a few middle or secondary students about their definitions of caring teachers. Ask them to identify the ways in which teachers show caring to students.

2. Do some planning for the first week of school. First, plan a way of showing students that you welcome their input. (Will you have students verbally share their suggestions and opinions about rules, lessons, assignments, or grouping? Write a letter to you? Answer specific questions?) Second, plan an introductory activity designed to help students become acquainted.

For Your Portfolio

Document the ways in which you work (or will work) to create a caring, safe classroom community. Include artifacts such as welcoming letters to students, lesson plans on peacemaking, conflict resolution, and teasing, getting-to-know-you activities, etc.

FOR FURTHER READING

Building classroom relationships. (2003). *Educational Leadership, 61*(1).

>   The entire September 2003 issue is devoted to this very important topic. Issues addressed include how to win students' hearts and minds (Steven Wolk), giving students what they need (Jonathan C. Erwin), personalizing schools (Dan Hoffman and Barbara A. Levak), practicing democracy in high school (Sheldon H. Berman), degrading talk (Stephen L. Wessler), and building relationships with challenging children (Philip S. Hall and Nancy D. Hall).

Gordon, J. A. (1998). Caring through control: Reaching urban African American youth. *Journal for a Just and Caring Education, 4*(4), 418–440.

>   Gordon discusses the fears of African American parents that White, middle-class teachers will not understand the difference between discipline designed to assist children's growth ("tough love") and discipline that "breaks their spirit." The article examines the ways that African American educators in two alternative educational programs for African American urban youth work to balance caring and control. What comes through clearly is that "intervention and interruption of unacceptable behavior were seen by the informants as a sign of caring."

Rodriguez, L. F. (2005). Yo, Mister! *Educational Leadership, 62*(7), 78–80.

>   Written by a teacher in an alternative urban high school, this article emphasizes the importance of positive teacher–student relationships. Rodriguez shows how he tries to acknowledge students as people, legitimize their knowledge and experiences, and engage with them personally and intellectually.

Building community in our schools. (Fall 2004). Special "Best of" issue of *Teaching Tolerance.*

>   This free magazine, available from the Southern Poverty Law Center, features articles on the tragedy at Columbine High School five years later, as well as a special section containing six "all-time favorite stories" on ways to build and strengthen school communities. Articles discuss the teasing and bullying faced by GLBT students and those who are overweight, sexual harassment, and antiracist education. (www.teachingtolerance.org)

Valenzuela, A. (1999). *Subtractive schooling: U. S.-Mexican youth and the politics of caring.* Albany: State University of New York Press.

 This book reports a three-year ethnographic study of immigrant Mexican and Mexican-American students attending an inner-city high school in Houston. Valenzuela argues that the school actually *subtracts* resources from students by ignoring and denigrating their language, culture, and community, leaving them vulnerable to academic failure. She probes the question of what it means to care about children in a cultural and political context, and argues that these students need to feel *cared for* before they can *care about* school.

ORGANIZATIONAL RESOURCES

The Anti-Defamation League (ADL), 823 United Nations Plaza, NY, NY 10017 (www.adl.org; 1-800-343-5540). Dedicated to combating anti-Semitism, hate crime, and bigotry through programs, services, and materials. (The *ADL Material Resource Catalog* is a wealth of resources, including lesson plans, curriculum guides, and lists of children's books.)

The Southern Poverty Law Center, 400 Washington Avenue, Montgomery, AL 36104 (www.teachingtolerance.org). The Teaching Tolerance project provides teachers at all levels with ideas and free resources for building community, fighting bias, and celebrating diversity.

Collaborative for Academic, Social, and Emotional Learning (CASEL), Department of Psychology (M/C 285), University of Illinois at Chicago, 1007 West Harrison St., Chicago, IL 60607 (312-413-1008; www.casel.org). Dedicated to the development of children's social and emotional competencies and the capacity of schools, parents, and communities to support that development. CASEL's mission is to establish integrated, evidence-based social and emotional learning (SEL) from preschool through high school.

REFERENCES

American Association of University Women [AAUW]. (1993). *Hostile hallways: The AAUW survey on sexual harassment in America's schools.* Washington, D.C.: AAUW.

Battistich, V., Watson, M., Solomon, D., Lewis, C., & Schaps, E. (1999). Beyond the three R's: A broader agenda for school reform. *The Elementary School Journal, 99*(5), 415–432.

Charles, C. M. (2000). *The synergetic classroom: Joyful teaching and gentle discipline.* New York: Longman.

Christensen, L. (1994). Building community from chaos. In B. Bigelow, L. Christensen, S. Karp, B. Miner, & B. Peterson (Eds.), *Rethinking our classrooms: Teaching for equity and justice.* Milwaukee, WI: Rethinking Schools Limited, pp. 50–55.

Cothran, D. J., Kulinna, P. H., & Garrahy, D. A. (2003). "This is kind of giving a secret away…": Students' perspectives on effective class management. *Teaching and Teacher Education, 19,* 435–444.

Delpit, L. (2002). No kinda sense. In L. Delpit & J. K. Dowdy (Eds.), *The skin that we speak: Thoughts on language and culture in the classroom.* New York: The New Press.

Dowd, J. (1997). Refusing to play the blame game. *Educational Leadership, 54*(8), 67–69.

Eccles, J. S., Wigfield, A., & Schiefele, U. (1998). Motivation to succeed. In W. Damon (Ed.), *Handbook of child psychology*, 5th ed., Vol. 3, N. Eisenberg (Vol. Ed.), *Social, emotional, and personality development*, 1017–1095. New York: John Wiley.

Edwards, A. T. (1997). Let's stop ignoring our gay and lesbian youth. *Educational Leadership, 54*(7), 68–70.

Fraser, B. J., McRobbie, C. J., & Fisher, D. L. (1996, April). Development, validation and use of personal and class forms of a new classroom environment instrument. Paper presented at the annual meeting of the American Educational Research Association, New York.

Good, T. L., & Brophy, J. E. (2000). *Looking in classrooms,* 8th ed. New York: Longman.

Gordon, J. A. (1998). Caring through control: Reaching urban African American youth. *Journal for a Just and Caring Education, 4*(4), 418–440.

Gordon, R. L. (1997). How novice teachers can succeed with adolescents. *Educational Leadership, 54*(7), 56–58.

Gordon, T. (1974). *T. E. T.—Teacher effectiveness training.* New York: Peter H. Wyden.

Hansen, P., & Mulholland, J. A. (2005). Caring and elementary teaching: The concerns of male beginning teachers. *Journal of Teacher Education, 56*(2), 119–131.

Harris Interactive and GLSEN (2005). *From teasing to torment: School climate in America: A survey of students and teachers.* New York: GLSEN.

Hyman, I. A. (1997). *School discipline and school violence: The teacher variance approach.* Boston: Allyn and Bacon.

Irvine, J. J. (2002). *In search of wholeness: African American teachers and their culturally specific classroom practices.* New York: PALGRAVE.

Johnson, D. W., & Johnson, R. T. (1999). The three Cs of school and classroom management. In H. J. Freiberg (Ed.), *Beyond behaviorism: Changing the classroom management paradigm.* Boston: Allyn & Bacon, pp. 119–144.

Jones, V. F., & Jones, L. S. (1998). *Comprehensive classroom management: Creating communities of support and solving problems.* Boston: Allyn & Bacon.

Katz, M. S. (1999). Teaching about caring and fairness: May Sarton's *The small room.* In M. S. Katz, N. Noddings, K. A. Strike (Eds.), *Justice and caring: The search for common ground in education.* New York: Teachers College Press, pp. 59–73.

Katz, S. R. (1999). Teaching in tensions: Latino immigrant youth, their teachers, and the structures of schooling. *Teachers College Record, 100*(4), 809–840.

King, J. R. (1998). *Uncommon caring: Learning from men who teach young children.* New York: Teachers College Press.

Kohn, A. (1996). *Beyond discipline: From compliance to community.* Alexandria, VA: Association for Supervision and Curriculum Development.

Kottler, E. (1994). *Children with limited English: Teaching strategies for the regular classroom.* Thousand Oaks, CA: Corwin Press.

Kottler, J. A., & Kottler, E. (1993). *Teacher as counselor: Developing the helping skills you need.* Newbury Park, CA: Corwin Press.

Kriete, R. (2002). *The morning meeting book,* 2nd ed. Greenfield, MA: Northeast Foundation for Children.

Lee, V. E., Croninger, R. G., Linn, E., & Chen, X. (1996). The culture of sexual harassment in secondary schools. *American Educational Research Journal, 33*(2), 383–417.

McLaughlin, H. J. (1991). Reconciling care and control: Authority in classroom relationships. *Journal of Teacher Education, 42*(3), 182–195.

Milner, H. R. (2006). Classroom management in urban classrooms. In C. M. Evertson & C. S. Weinstein (Eds.), *Handbook of classroom management: Research, practice, and contemporary issues.* Mahwah, NJ: Lawrence Erlbaum Associates, Inc.

National Council for Research on Women. (1994). Teen-on-teen sexual harassment. *Issues Quarterly, 1*(1), 1–6.

National Mental Health Association (2002). What does gay mean? Teen Survey Executive Summary. (Downloaded from http://www.nmha.org/newsroom/surveys.cfm).

Nichols, S. (1999). Gay, lesbian, and bisexual youth: Understanding diversity and promoting tolerance in schools. *The Elementary School Journal, 99*(5), 505–519.

Nieto, S. (1996). *Affirming diversity: The sociopolitical context of multicultural education,* 2nd ed. White Plains, NY: Longman.

Nucci, L. (2006). Classroom management for moral and social development. In C. M. Evertson & C. S. Weinstein (Eds.), *Handbook of classroom management: Research, practice, and contemporary issues.* Mahwah, NJ: Lawrence Erlbaum Associates, Inc.

Oakes, J., & Lipton, M. (1999). *Teaching to change the world.* Boston: McGraw-Hill.

Obidah, J. E., & Teel, K. M. (2001). *Because of the kids: Facing racial and cultural differences in schools.* New York: Teachers College Press.

Osterman, K. F. (2000). Students' need for belonging in the school community. *Review of Educational Research, 70*(3), 323–367.

Peyser, M., & Lorch, D. (March 20, 2000). Gay today: The schools. High school controversial. *Newsweek,* 55–56.

Renard, L. (2005). Teaching the DIG generation. *Educational Leadership, 62*(7), 44–47.

Ridley, D. S., & Walther, B. (1995). *Creating responsible learners: The role of a positive classroom environment.* Washington, D. C.: American Psychological Association.

Rodriguez, L. F. (2005). Yo, Mister! *Educational Leadership, 62*(7), 78–80.

Roeser, R. W., Eccles, J. S., & Sameroff, A. J. (2000). School as a context of early adolescents' academic and social–emotional development: A summary of research findings. *The Elementary School Journal, 100*(5), 443–471.

Sapon-Shevin, M. (1995). Building a safe community for learning. In W. Ayers (Ed.), *To become a teacher: Making a difference in children's lives.* New York: Teachers College Press.

Sapon-Shevin, M. (1999). *Because we can change the world: A practical guide to building cooperative, inclusive classroom communities.* Boston: Allyn & Bacon.

Schmollinger, C. S., Opaleski, K. A., Chapman, M. L., Jocius, R., & Bell, S. (2002). How do you make your classroom an inviting place for students to come back to each year? *English Journal, 91*(6), 20–22.

Shakeshaft, C., Mandel, L., Johnson, Y. M., Sawyer, J., Hergenroter, M. A., & Barber, E. (1997). Boys call me cow. *Educational Leadership, 55*(2), 22–25.

Sheets, R. H. (1996). Urban classroom conflict: Student–teacher perception: Ethnic integrity, solidarity, and resistance. *Urban Review, 28*(2), 165–183.

Sileo, T. W., & Prater, M. A. (1998). Creating classroom environments that address the linguistic and cultural backgrounds of students with disabilities: An Asian Pacific American perspective. *Remedial and Special Education, 19*(6), 323–337.

Smith, E. (2002). Ebonics: A case history. In L. Delpit & J. K. Dowdy (Eds.), *The skin that we speak: Thoughts on language and culture in the classroom.* New York: The New Press.

Strauss, S., with Espeland, P. (1992). *Sexual harassment and teens: A program for positive change.* Minneapolis, MN: Free Spirit.

Trueba, H. T., Cheng, L. R. L., & Ima, K. (1993). *Myth or reality: Adaptive strategies of Asian Americans in California.* Washington, D.C.: Falmer Press.

Valenzuela, A. (1999). *Subtractive schooling: U. S.-Mexican youth and the politics of caring.* Albany: State University of New York Press.

Vaughan, A. L. (2005). The self-paced student. *Educational Leadership, 62*(7), 69-73.

Walsh, M. (June 2, 1999). Harassment ruling poses challenges. *Education Week, 18*(38), 1, 22.

Watson, M., & Battstich, V. (2006). Building and sustaining caring communities. In C. M. Evertson & C. S. Weinstein (Eds.), *Handbook of classroom management: Research, practice, and contemporary issues.* Mahwah, NJ: Lawrence Erlbaum Associates, Inc.

Weinstein, C. S. (1998). "I want to be nice, but I have to be mean": Exploring prospective teachers' conceptions of caring and order. *Teaching and Teacher Education, 14*(2), 153-163.

Wessler, S. L. (2003). It's hard to learn when you're scared. *Educational Leadership, 61*(1), 40-43.

Williams, M. (1993). Actions speak louder than words: What students think. *Educational Leadership, 51*(3), 22-23.

Woolfolk Hoy, A., & Weinstein, C. S. (2006). Student and teacher perspectives about classroom management. In C. M. Evertson & C. S. Weinstein (Eds.), *Handbook of classroom management: Research, practice, and contemporary issues.* Mahwah, NJ: Lawrence Erlbaum Associates, Inc.

Zeidner, M. (1988). The relative severity of common classroom strategies: The student's perspective. *British Journal of Educational Psychology, 58,* 69-77.

ESTABLISHING NORMS FOR BEHAVIOR

Middle and high school teachers sometimes contend that their students know how to behave, since they've been in school for many years. The argument goes like this:

> My kids aren't babies. By junior or senior high school, students know the importance of coming to class on time, doing homework, respecting other people's property, and raising their hands to make a comment. Besides, there's so much material to cover, I can't waste time teaching rules to kids who should already know all this stuff.

This reasoning has a certain appeal, particularly for teachers who are enthusiastic about their content area and eager to get started. Yet it's important to recognize that although your students have general notions about appropriate school behavior, they do not know *your specific expectations.* Furthermore, your students probably see five different teachers each day, and specific expectations vary from class to class. A student's first-period teacher may not mind if everyone is milling around the room when the bell rings, while the second-period teacher insists that students be in their seats. In third period, the teacher wants students to put homework in the upper right-hand corner of their desks, but the fourth-period teacher has students drop homework in a basket at the front of the room.

What will *you* expect with regard to basic classroom routines like these—and how will your students know what to do if you don't tell them? It is unfair to keep students guessing about the behaviors you expect. Not knowing the norms for appropriate behavior causes insecurity and misunderstandings, even among "school smart" adolescents. In contrast, *clearly defined classroom rules and routines help to create an environment that is predictable and comprehensible.*

Clear expectations for behavior have another major benefit. As Chapter 1 emphasized, classes are crowded, public, unpredictable places in which individuals engage in a variety of activities, often within the time constraints of a 42- or 45-minute period. *Clear rules and routines minimize confusion and prevent the loss of instructional time.* They enable you to carry out "housekeeping" tasks (e.g., taking attendance, distributing materials) smoothly and efficiently, almost automatically. They free you and your students to concentrate on the real tasks of teaching and learning.

This chapter describes research that demonstrates the importance of rules and routines. We then consider some principles to guide you in establishing rules for your own classrooms. We'll also learn how Donnie, Christina, Sandy, and Fred introduce rules and routines to their students and what they think about this central task of classroom management.

RESEARCH ON EFFECTIVE CLASSROOM MANAGEMENT

Prior to 1970, teacher preparation programs could offer only limited advice about classroom management to beginning teachers. Teacher educators shared useful "tricks of the trade" (e.g., flick the lights on and off for quiet), stressed the importance of firmness and consistency, and warned prospective teachers not to smile until Christmas. But research identifying the behaviors of effective managers was unavailable, and it was simply not clear why some classrooms function smoothly and others are chaotic.

That situation began to change in 1970, with the publication of Jacob Kounin's study of orderly and disorderly classrooms. In an effort to explain the differences, Kounin (1970) set out to compare teachers' methods of responding to misbehavior. To his surprise, he found that the reactions of good classroom managers were not substantially different from the reactions of poor classroom managers. What *did* differ were the strategies that teachers used to *prevent* misbehavior. Effective classroom managers constantly monitored students' behavior. They displayed what Kounin called "withitness": They were aware of what was happening in all parts of the room, and they communicated this awareness to students. They also exhibited an ability to "overlap"—to do more than one thing at a time—certainly a desirable skill in a setting where so many events occur simultaneously! Furthermore, effective managers kept lessons moving at a brisk pace so that there was little opportunity for students to become inattentive and disruptive.

Kounin's work led researchers to wonder how effective managers began the school year. In the late 1970s, a series of studies was launched at the Research and Development Center for Teacher Education, located at the University of Texas at Austin. One project (Evertson & Emmer, 1982) involved observations of 26 mathematics teachers and 25 English teachers in junior high schools in an urban district.

Each teacher was observed teaching two different classes. During the first three weeks of school, researchers observed extensively in each classroom and kept detailed records of what occurred. During the rest of the academic year, each teacher was observed once every three to four weeks (in both of his or her classrooms). On the basis of these latter data, the researchers identified six more and six less effective managers in mathematics and seven more and seven less effective managers in English. They then went back to the information collected at the beginning of the year and compared what the teachers had done during the first three weeks of school. Striking differences were apparent—even on the very first day of school!

Among the major differences documented by Evertson and Emmer was the way teachers handled rules and procedures. Although all of the teachers had expectations for behavior, and they all took time to present or discuss these with students, the more effective managers were more successful in *teaching* the rules and procedures. For example, the more effective teachers were more likely to distribute handouts stating their behavioral expectations or to have students copy them into their notebooks. They were also clearer and much more explicit about behaviors that are likely to cause problems—namely, those that occur frequently and that may vary from teacher to teacher (e.g., call-outs, movement through the room, student–student interaction, hand raising). Interestingly, for behaviors that occur infrequently per period (e.g., tardiness, bringing materials) and are fairly straightforward, no differences between the two groups of teachers were apparent.

Subsequent research has confirmed the importance of explicitly teaching students your expectations for their behavior. Douglas Brooks (1985), for example, videotaped two experienced and two inexperienced junior high school teachers (two in math and two in science) as they met with their classes for the very first time. The contrast between the experienced and inexperienced math teachers is especially vivid.

The experienced math teacher, perceived by students and administrators as exceptionally clear and organized, began her presentation of behavioral expectations by distributing a copy of class rules that students were to keep in their folders. She first discussed schoolwide policies, but spent most of the time on classroom standards—how to enter the class, how to use materials, how to interact with the teacher and other students, what to do in the case of an emergency, and how to exit the class. In general, *she stated a rule, explained the rationale, provided an example of an appropriate behavior, and concluded with the consequences for noncompliance.* Interestingly, she rarely smiled during her presentation of rules and procedures (although she smiled a lot during her later introduction to the course). She spoke in a businesslike tone and continually scanned the classroom; no instances of disruption were observed during her presentation.

In contrast, the inexperienced math teacher was rambling and disorganized. Students were not given a copy of the rules, nor were they encouraged to write them down. Even as the teacher presented rules and procedures about talking in class, she tolerated students talking to each other. In addition, she repeatedly smiled during her presentation of the consequences for misbehavior, a nonverbal behavior that seems incompatible with a discussion of detention and calling home (and might have sent the message that she was not serious about imposing these consequences).

As the following excerpt from the transcript illustrates, the inexperienced math teacher provided few examples or rationales. In fact, she *never* used the experienced teacher's sequence of rule-rationale-example-consequence. Although many of the rules resembled those of the experienced math teacher, she presented rules she could not enforce (wanting students to respect all teachers), and she omitted discussion of some fundamental rules (listening while the teacher is talking). Furthermore, the rules did not appear to be prioritized or organized in any way:

> OK. I'm just going to tell you a few of my classroom rules. And, ah, so that you'll know these. The first thing I want you to know is I want, that I expect every student will obey any school policies that there are. . . . OK, all the school policies, if you haven't gotten it as of yet you will get it, this yellow sheet. It's got all the school policies on it. It explains everything to you. These apply in school and around school. . . . OK, another thing when you come in that door I expect you to walk through that door being prepared to start class. When you come in don't plan on going back out to get something out of your locker. . . . OK, when you come in you'll have a pencil, your paper, your folders, and a book. . . . OK, if you're fast at working you might bring something extra to do after you finish your work so that you can have something to keep you busy because I don't want any talking. . . . OK, and all times we'll use pencil . . . I don't want any ink on your homework papers or test papers. It should all be done in pencil . . . OK, we'll also have a folder that we'll do and I'll tell you about it later . . . OK, another thing is I expect you to be respectful. First, I want you to respect yourself, at all times respect yourself and then your classmates and also the teachers. Any teacher in the building should be respected by you and each student and if you see one anything they say goes. (pp. 67–68)

Reading this transcript, it's impossible not to feel sympathy for this inexperienced teacher. After all, most beginning teachers, particularly those being observed, are nervous on the first day of school. But it is precisely *because* of this nervousness that you must (1) think about your expectations ahead of time and (2) plan the way you will present them to your students. Let's look at each of these steps separately.

Defining Your Expectations for Behavior

Before the first student enters your classroom, you need to think about your expectations for behavior. Not only do you need to decide on *rules for students' general conduct,* you also need to identify the *behavioral routines or procedures* that you and your students will follow in specific situations. For example, when students arrive at your classroom door, are they to go immediately to their seats, or may they congregate in small groups and socialize until you tell them to be seated? May they go to the storage cabinet and get the projects they've been working on, or should they wait for you to give out the projects one by one? When students need paper or rulers or protractors for an assignment, will they get them by themselves, will you have students distribute the materials, or will you distribute them yourself? If students have to leave your classroom to go to their lockers or to the library, must they have a pass? When students are working at their seats, may they help one another or must they work individually?

Because these seem like such trivial, mundane issues, it is easy to underestimate their contribution to classroom order. But lessons can fall apart while you try to decide how to distribute paper, and students feel anxious if they're unsure whether answering a classmate's question during an in-class assignment is helping or cheating. As we will see, rules and routines may vary from class to class, but no class can function smoothly without them.

Planning Rules for General Conduct

Rules describe the behaviors that are necessary if your classroom is to be a good place in which to live and work—for example, "come prepared," "follow directions," and "respect others." In Christina's class, the norms for general conduct are contained in a "newspaper" that Christina writes and distributes on the first day of class. Here are some of her basic rules:

- Respect every member of the class by using appropriate language, by paying attention when another person is speaking, and by raising [your] hand to speak.
- Complete all assignments on time and to the best of your ability.
- Bring a pencil and any other required materials (as assigned by the teacher) to class each day.

As you reflect on rules for your own classroom, there are four principles to keep in mind. These are summarized in Table 4.1 (and violated in the cartoon in

TABLE 4.1 Four Principles for Planning Classroom Rules

Principle	Questions to Think About
1. Rules should be reasonable and necessary.	What rules are appropriate for this grade level? Is there a good reason for this rule?
2. Rules need to be clear and understandable.	Is the rule too abstract for students to comprehend? To what extent do I want my students to participate in the decision-making process?
3. Rules should be consistent with instructional goals and with what we know about how people learn.	Will this rule facilitate or hinder my students' learning?
4. Classroom rules need to be consistent with school rules.	What are the school rules? Are particular behaviors required in the halls, during assemblies, in the cafeteria, etc.?

Mrs. Mutner liked to go over a few of her rules
on the first day of school.

Figure 4.1   Teaching rules on the first day of school.

Source: Close to Home ® 1993 John McPherson. Reprinted with
permission of Universal Press Syndicate. All rights reserved.

Figure 4.1). First, *rules should be reasonable and necessary.* Think about the age
and characteristics of the students you are teaching, and ask yourself what rules are
appropriate for them. For example, it would be unreasonable to expect students to
enter the classroom without greeting one another and chatting. Given adolescents'
irresistible desire to interact, creating such a rule would only result in resentment,
frustration, and subterfuge. It's far more sensible to establish a rule like "talk quietly," which specifies *how* the talk is to occur.

Also ask yourself whether each rule is necessary. Is there a compelling
reason for it? Will it make the classroom a more pleasant place to be? Will it increase students' opportunity to learn? Can you explain the rationale to students,
and will they accept it? Sandy stresses the importance of this principle when she
comments:

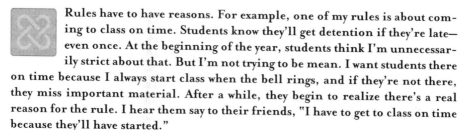

Rules have to have reasons. For example, one of my rules is about coming to class on time. Students know they'll get detention if they're late—
even once. At the beginning of the year, students think I'm unnecessarily strict about that. But I'm not trying to be mean. I want students there
on time because I always start class when the bell rings, and if they're not there,
they miss important material. After a while, they begin to realize there's a real
reason for the rule. I hear them say to their friends, "I have to get to class on time
because they'll have started."

Contrast this situation with that of a biology teacher I know who insists that
students take notes in black pen only. Although the teacher is able to enforce the
rule, she's unable to explain it with any conviction, and her classes perceive it as arbitrary and ridiculous. Similarly, an English teacher insists that students use cursive

writing during spelling and vocabulary tests. Even to her student teacher, this seems like an unreasonable rule:

> *Being a printer myself whose cursive has not improved beyond the third grade, I am not a fan of mandated cursive writing. In the real world whenever I have filled out a form, I have been required to print so the words are legible to the reader. The only time cursive is required is when I sign my name and for vocabulary tests in my cooperating teacher's class. I can see why students are sometimes annoyed with our rules.*

It's easier to demonstrate that a rule is reasonable and necessary if it applies to *you* as well as your students. Although some rules may be intended only for students (e.g., raise your hand to speak), others are relevant for everyone (e.g., show respect for other people and their property). Sandy tells us, "If a rule is important for kids, it's important for you too. For example, I make sure that I get to class on time, and if I'm late, I owe them an explanation." Fred echoes this idea when he observes, "I try to make it clear to my students that we *all* have to follow the rules. After all, rules are not about power; they're what make civilized life possible."

Second, *rules need to be clear and understandable.* Because rules are often stated in very general terms ("be polite"), they may be too abstract to have much meaning. When planning your rules, you need to think of specific examples to discuss with students. For example, one of Donnie's basic rules is "Be prepared." She makes sure that "preparation" is spelled out in precise, concrete behaviors: "Class preparation consists of having your homework, notebook, pen or pencil, and a covered textbook with you each day."

Some teachers believe that rules are more understandable and more meaningful when students are allowed to participate in the decision-making process. Participation, especially at higher grade levels, may increase students' willingness to "buy into" the rules, may make them more invested in seeing that rules are followed, and may help to prepare students for adult life. At the middle-school level, some teachers begin by asking students what their "hopes and dreams" are for that class (e.g., "What are your most important hopes and dreams for math this year? What would you really like to accomplish?"). Students then reflect on what they will need—from others as well as from themselves—in order to fulfill these hopes and dreams. Generating ideas for rules comes next. (For detailed information on this approach, see *Rules in School* by Brady, Forton, Porter, & Wood, 2003.)

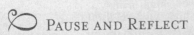

PAUSE AND REFLECT

Take a moment to reflect on the idea of having students generate the rules. Did any of your own secondary teachers ever use this approach? What do you see as the benefits? If you were to do this, what would you have to keep in mind and what pitfalls might you need to plan for?

As a beginning teacher, you may feel more comfortable presenting rules you have developed yourself. In fact, despite their many years of experience, neither Donnie, Sandy, nor Fred allows students to create classroom rules. They do, however, discuss the rationales for the rules they have established, and they solicit examples from students.

A third principle to keep in mind is that *rules should be consistent with instructional goals and with what we know about how people learn.* The first chapter discussed the assumptions underlying this book. One assumption was that the need for order should not supersede the need for meaningful instruction. As you develop rules for your classroom, think about whether they will *facilitate or hinder the learning process.* For example, in the pursuit of order, some teachers prohibit talking during in-class assignments, and others refrain from using cooperative learning activities for fear that students will be too rowdy. Obviously, such restrictions are necessary at times (e.g., you may want students to work alone on a particular assignment so you can assess each student's comprehension of the material). It would be sad, however, if restrictions like this became the status quo. Educational psychologists who study the ways children learn stress the importance of their interaction. Much of this thinking is based on the work of the Soviet psychologist Lev Vygotsky, who believed that children's intellectual growth is fostered through collaboration with adults who serve as coaches and tutors and with more capable peers (Wertsch, 1985). Interestingly, research on the use of small groups indicates that these interactions benefit the *tutor* as well as the person being tutored. Noreen Webb (1985), for example, found that junior high school students who provided explanations for their peers showed increased achievement themselves. Given the important role that interaction plays in young people's learning and cognitive development, it seems sensible not to eliminate interaction, but to spend time teaching students how to interact in ways that are appropriate. (This topic will be addressed more fully in Chapter 9.)

Finally, *classroom rules need to be consistent with school rules.* The importance of this principle can be illustrated by an excerpt from a student teacher's recent journal entry:

> *The first week of school I ejected a student from the room and told him he couldn't come back into the class until he had a note from his parents. Not only was the student back in class the next day without a note, but I was informed that (1) I was in violation of the school code when I ejected the student, and (2) only homeroom teachers communicate directly with the parents.*

Your school may hold an orientation meeting for new teachers where school rules, policies, and procedures are explained. In particular, find out about behaviors that are expected during assemblies, in the cafeteria and library, and in the hallways. You should also learn about the administrative tasks for which you are responsible (e.g., taking attendance, collecting field trip money, supervising fire drills, recording tardiness). If there is a school handbook, be sure to get a copy and use it as a guide for establishing your own rules and routines.

You also need to know if you are supposed to review the handbook with students. For example, Fred's students receive a booklet explaining the school's "Rules, Regulations, and Policies," and teachers go over it with their first-period class. The handbook addresses topics such as lateness, absenteeism, smoking, substance abuse, leaving school grounds, bias incidents, use of beepers, pagers, and cell phones, fighting and physical assault, and possession of weapons. After reviewing the handbook, students sign a statement indicating that they agree to abide by the rules. The statement is then returned to the main office.

Reviewing the handbook with his students allows Fred to explain how his classroom rules and routines jibe with those of the school:

 OK, as you can see, the school rule is that you have to bring a note when you return to school after an absence. Let's talk about this a little more. When you're absent, it's *your* responsibility to call someone in class and make up the activity. So before you leave school today, get someone's phone number. [He smiles.] Try to get someone who is as smart or smarter than you. [The students laugh. He continues.] Now the school rule is that if you're out for three days, you have that many days to make up the work. I tend to be a little more lenient than that, but you need to come see me and ask for additional time. Any questions? [There are none.] OK. With respect to lateness, the school rule is "Don't be late." If you're late three times, there's a penalty. I watch the lates pretty carefully, so I'll warn you if I think you're getting in trouble. Now, about cutting. You cut, I'll ask for you to leave my class. Jason, what did I say? [Jason repeats the comment.] Right! I can't teach you if you're not in my class. [He speaks slowly and with emphasis.] *If you cut my class, I take it personally.* Now I'm a human being. I realize there are times when you need to not be here; you have to go to the bathroom or the library. But you need to come and ask and get a pass. If you don't, that's a cut. *And I'm death on that one.* So don't cut.

Planning Routines for Specific Situations

So many different activities occur in classrooms that trying to define behavior for specific situations can be daunting. Researchers at the Learning Research and Development Center at the University of Pittsburgh observed the behavior of effective classroom managers and categorized the routines they used (Leinhardt, Weidman, & Hammond, 1987). I have adapted their three-category system to provide you with a way of thinking about routines for your own classroom.

Class-Running Routines

These are *nonacademic routines* that enable you to keep the classroom running smoothly. This category of routines includes *administrative duties* (taking attendance, recording tardiness, distributing school notices), *procedures for student movement* (entering the room at the beginning of the period; leaving the room at the end of the period; leaving the room to go to the nurse, the library, or lockers; fire drills; moving around the room to sharpen pencils or get materials), and *housekeeping routines* (cleaning lab tables, watering plants, maintaining storage for materials used by everyone).

Without clear, specific class-running routines, these activities can consume a significant part of the school day. Research on the way time is used in fifth-grade classrooms has indicated that, on the average, these activities (transition, waiting, housekeeping) consume almost 20 percent of the time spent in the classroom—more than the amount of time spent in mathematics instruction (Rosenshine, 1980). This figure is undoubtedly higher in classrooms that are not well managed.

By defining how students are to behave in these specific situations, you can save precious minutes for instruction. You also enable students to carry out many of these routines without your direct supervision, freeing you to concentrate on instruction or other tasks. For example, Christina's students begin each class period by writing in their journals while Christina silently takes attendance. Students know that as soon as they enter the room, they are to get their journals, copy the journal topic from the board, and write silently for the allotted time. On the first day of school, Christina laid the groundwork for the smooth functioning of this activity. In the following vignette, we see her introduce the journals to her basic skills class.

Before we start going over what this class is going to be about, I want to give you your journals, which you will keep on a daily basis. . . . Write your name on the cover—but open the journals first so you [can see which way is up and you] won't write your name upside down, which is often a problem. Then write English 3T, Block 2, then my name. [Points to her name on the board.] Open up your journals and write the date on the first page. I'm going to write a journal topic on the board, and I want you to copy it down, and then write a response to that topic. [Writes: *What do you expect from this class?*] When we do journals, you write until I say to stop writing, five to ten minutes. Don't say you don't have anything to write about or that you can't think of anything else to say. If you run out of things to say about the topic I have given you, write about something else. OK, begin now.

Lesson-Running Routines

These routines directly support instruction *by specifying the behaviors that are necessary for teaching and learning to take place.* They allow lessons to proceed briskly and eliminate the need for students to ask questions like "Do I have to use a pen?" "Should we number from 1 to 20?" and "What do I do if I'm finished?"

Lesson-running routines describe what items students are to have on hand when a lesson begins, how materials and equipment are to be distributed and collected, what kind of paper or writing instrument is to be used, and what should be done with the paper (e.g., folded into eight boxes; numbered from 1 to 10 along the left margin; headed with name, date, and subject). In addition, lesson-running routines specify the behaviors that students are to engage in at the beginning of the lesson (e.g., have books open to the relevant page, silently sit and wait for instructions from the teacher) and what they are to do if they finish early or if they are unable to finish the assignment by the end of the time period.

Clear lesson-running routines are especially important in classroom situations that are potentially dangerous, such as woodworking, auto mechanics, and cooking. When Sandy introduces chemistry labs, for example, she is very careful to specify the special safety procedures:

There are some special safety procedures for this lab. First, before working with the Bunsen burners, make certain that your hair is tied back. Second, make certain that your goggles are on. Third, I'll have a beaker on my desk where you can discard the metals. Everything else you

can throw away in the sink. Finally, after you're finished, go to your seat and write the equations. There are reference books up here to help you. You may find that you have to go back and redo part of the lab. That's OK.

Homework procedures can also be included among lesson-running routines, since the pace and content of a lesson often depends on whether students have done their homework assignments. You need to establish routines for determining quickly which students have their homework and which do not, as well as routines for checking and collecting assignments. You also need to have routines for providing assignments for students who have been absent.

Interaction Routines

These routines refer to the *rules for talk*—talk between teachers and students and talk among students themselves. Interaction routines specify *when talk is permitted and how it is to occur.* For example, during whole-class discussions, students need to know what to do if they want to respond to a question or contribute a comment. All four of our teachers, like many others, usually require students to raise their hands and wait to be called on, rather than simply calling out. In this way, the teachers can distribute opportunities to participate throughout the class and can ensure that the conversation is not dominated by a few overly eager individuals. The teachers can also check on how well the class understands the lesson by calling on students who do not raise their hands.

Often it's hard to keep track of which students have had an opportunity to speak. In order to avoid this problem, Donnie sometimes creates a pattern for calling on students, one that is more subtle than simply going up and down rows:

> I may start at the back corner of the room and call on students in a diagonal line. Or I might use the alphabetical list of students in my grade book, and alternate between students at the beginning of the list and those at the end. I try not to be obvious, but sometimes students figure out the pattern, and they'll say to me, "You missed so-and-so," or "I didn't get a question," so we'll go back and make sure that person has a turn.

Another way to keep track of which individuals have had a turn is to use the "popsicle stick system." Delia Cruz Fernandez, a junior high school Spanish teacher, has a plastic glass for each of her classes; each glass contains popsicle sticks labeled with students' names. Delia gives the glass to a student who shakes it, pulls out a name, and then places the popsicle stick on the side until everyone has had a turn. Delia explains why she uses this approach:

> *Sometimes kids are really afraid to talk in a language class; they look down at the floor and try to get real small, hoping that I won't notice them. But this course has been designed as a "proficiency development" course, where students learn how to use Spanish in "real world"*

*situations. If they don't speak, they don't learn. Using the popsicle sticks
is my way of making sure that I don't miss anyone.*

During some lessons, you may want students to respond chorally rather than
individually. A simple signal can be used to indicate that the rules for talk have
changed. For example, Donnie nods and extends her hands, palms up, in a gesture
of invitation. Fred, with a background in music, literally conducts the group as if it
were a chorus.

Sandy also suspends the normal rules for talk at times, but she adds words of
caution for beginning teachers:

 **If I'm at the board, with my back turned to the class, and a student
wants to ask a question, I don't mind if he or she just calls out, "Mrs.
K., I don't understand . . ." Or sometimes, during a whole-class
discussion, someone will ask a question, and I'll ask other kids to help
out. They'll turn to one another and start asking and answering questions as if I
weren't even there. I can just stand aside and watch. It's great to see this kind of
student–student interaction. But beginning teachers need to be careful about
this. If things start to get unruly, I can just say, "Hey guys, use hands," and
things settle right down, but I've seen situations like this get out of hand for
beginning teachers.**

Interaction routines also include *procedures that students and teachers use to
gain each other's attention.* For example, if students are busy working, and you
need to give additional instructions, how will you signal that you want their attention? Will you flick the lights, hold up your arm, or say, "Excuse me," the way Donnie does? Conversely, if you are busy working with a small group or an individual,
and students need your assistance, how will they communicate that to you? Will
they be allowed to call out your name or leave their seats and approach you?

Finally, you need to think about the rules that will govern *talk among students.* When 20 to 30 students sit so close to one another, it's only natural for them
to talk. You must decide when it's all
right for students to talk about the television show they saw last night (e.g., before the bell rings) and when their talk
must be about academic work (e.g., during cooperative learning activities). You
also need to think about times when
students may talk quietly (e.g., during
in-class assignments), and when you
need to have absolute silence (e.g.,
when you are giving instruction or during a test).

Table 4.2 summarizes the three types
of routines we have just discussed.

PAUSE AND REFLECT

I have distinguished between norms for general conduct
(*rules*) and the procedures that students will follow in
specific situations (*routines*). In order to make sure that you
grasp the distinction, consider the following expectations.
For each one, decide if it is a rule or a routine: (1) At the end
of the period, students are to wait until you tell them class is
over before beginning to pack up. (2) Students are to be
courteous. (3) Listen respectfully when people are talking.
(4) When students enter the classroom, they are to take their
seat and begin the "do now." (5) When you need to go to the
restroom, you must sign out and take the pass.

TABLE 4.2 Summary of Classroom Routines

CLASS-RUNNING ROUTINES: Nonacademic routines that enable the classroom to run smoothly

Administrative routines
    Taking attendance
    Recording tardiness
    Distributing school notices

Routines for student movement
    Entering the room at the beginning of the period
    Leaving the room at the end of the period
    Going to the restroom
    Going to the nurse
    Going to the library
    Fire drills
    Sharpening pencils
    Using computers or other equipment
    Getting materials

Housekeeping routines
    Cleaning chalkboards
    Watering plants
    Storing personal items (book bags)
    Maintaining common storage areas

LESSON-RUNNING ROUTINES: Routines that directly support instruction by specifying the behaviors that are necessary for teaching and learning to take place
    What to bring to class
    Collecting homework

    Recording who has done homework
    Returning homework
    Distributing materials
    Preparing paper for assignment (heading, margins, type of writing instrument)
    Collecting in-class assignments
    What to do when assignments have been completed

INTERACTION ROUTINES: Routines that specify when talk is permitted and how it is to occur

Talk between teacher and students
    During whole-class lessons
    When the teacher is working with a small group
    When the teacher needs the class's attention
    When students need the teacher's attention

Talk among students
    During independent assignments
    Before the bell rings
    During transitions
    During loudspeaker announcements
    During cooperative learning activities
    During peer conferencing
    When a visitor comes to speak with the teacher

The First Few Days of School: Teaching Students about the Norms

In order to minimize confusion, you need to *teach students the rules for general conduct*, defining terms clearly, providing examples, and discussing rationales. As I indicated earlier in this chapter, Evertson and Emmer's (1982) research indicates that this is crucial for behaviors that are likely to occur frequently and where the appropriate behavior may be ambiguous (e.g., talking during an independent assignment). You also need to *teach the routines* you want students to follow for specific situations. Such thoroughness is particularly important in new situations, like chemistry laboratories, wood shop, keyboarding, or ceramics studios, where students have had little prior experience.

    Let's see what this looks like in action. On the morning of the first day of school, Donnie begins by introducing herself to her students and asking them to introduce themselves. Afterwards, she introduces the topic of "ground rules." Note that she also provides information on topics that are sure to be on students' minds—homework, notebooks, grading, and extra help:

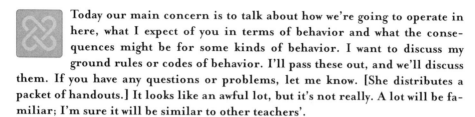

Today our main concern is to talk about how we're going to operate in here, what I expect of you in terms of behavior and what the consequences might be for some kinds of behavior. I want to discuss my ground rules or codes of behavior. I'll pass these out, and we'll discuss them. If you have any questions or problems, let me know. [She distributes a packet of handouts.] It looks like an awful lot, but it's not really. A lot will be familiar; I'm sure it will be similar to other teachers'.

OK, let's look at the first page. Here we have my ground rules. The first item on the page deals with general class procedures. *I expect you to be in your seat when the bell rings.* [She says this slowly and firmly. Her tone is serious but pleasant.] Today several people were tardy. I can understand that. I recognize that today is the first day and you're running around, maybe lost. [She smiles.] But I anticipate that *there will be no late arrivals after this.* I'll talk about what happens for tardiness in a few minutes.

Donnie continues to elaborate on the printed statements, answering questions and inviting comments. She reviews the ground rules for notebooks, homework, extra help, paper headings, and participation, and goes on to explain the grading system. She then goes over an assignment sheet that students may use to record assignments and due dates, and elaborates on a checklist she will use to evaluate notebooks.

As this example illustrates, teaching students the rules for conduct doesn't have to be unpleasant or oppressive. In fact, some teachers don't even use the word rules. Sandy, for example, prefers to talk about "chemistry classroom guidelines" (see Figure 4.2), but like Donnie, she makes sure her expectations for behavior are explicit. Sandy defines terms ("Late means not being in the room when the bell rings"), provides examples wherever necessary, and stresses the reasons for each guideline. She explains why it's important for textbooks to be covered ("so they don't get chemicals on them"); why she has a "disclaimer" in her guidelines reserving the right to give unannounced quizzes ("That's there in case I see you're not doing the reading. But I really don't like to do this; I want kids to do well on tests"); why hats cannot be worn in class (for safety reasons); why she insists on promptness ("I start when the bell rings"); and why she lets them leave when the bell rings—even if she's in the middle of a sentence ("I will not keep you, because you'd be late to the next class and that's not fair to you or to the next teacher. But don't pack up books before the bell rings"). Sandy also discusses course requirements. In particular, she explains how grades are calculated and how homework is assigned and evaluated:

OK, people, let's talk about homework. Homework is assigned a point value of 10. I always write the homework assignments in this corner of the chalkboard and they're always given as block assignments with stated due dates. For example, your very first assignment is to do pages 3–29, with all the problem numbers. This averages out to five pages plus five problems a night. It's in your best interest to do some every night, instead of waiting until the very end.

1. Always be prepared for class. You MUST bring the following items with you each class period.
   a. notebook
   b. pen or pencil
   c. your COVERED textbook
   d. a scientific calculator

2. Be prompt to class. Tardiness will not be tolerated. You are considered late to class if you enter the room after the bell rings.
   a. 1st late 10 minutes after school (with me)
   b. 2nd late 20 minutes after school (with me)
   c. 3rd late 30 minutes after school (with me)
   d. 4th late 7:15 A.M. detention

3. Grades are calculated according to a point system. Every assignment (labs, homework, classwork) and exams (tests and quizzes) are assigned points. Your grade is the number of points received compared to the total number of possible points.

4. Tests and quizzes are based on the information received through class discussions, textbook readings, and lab work. It is imperative that you take notes during class discussions. All tests (with the exception of the midterm and final) are assigned a value of 100 points. Quizzes range in point value from 25–50. A quiz does not have to be announced.

5. Homework is assigned a point value of 10. Homework is always given as a block assignment with a stated due date. Any written work that is assigned will be collected on the stated due date. NO LATE HOMEWORK WILL BE ACCEPTED.

6. If you are absent, it is YOUR responsibility to find out what was missed. Any lab missed due to an absence must be made up within one week of the absence. EXCEPTIONS: (a) If you are absent 3 days or more, more time will be allowed for make-up; (b) If you are absent the day of a test or quiz and you were in class the day before, you will be required to make up that test the day you return to school.

7. THERE WILL BE NO CUTTING!!!!

8. Hats may not be worn in class.

9. NO EXTRA CREDIT POINTS ARE GIVEN IN THIS CLASS!!!

Figure 4.2   Chemistry Classroom Guidelines (Mrs. Krupinski)

Please keep in mind that I will not accept late homework. It doesn't all have to be in the same pen; it doesn't all have to be in the same color. I don't care if you start in blue and finish in black. But it does have to be in at the beginning of the period on the day it's due. Part of the assignment is to get it in on time. I'll give you a reminder when you come in that homework is due, but if you don't hear and then you remember halfway through I don't want it. It's also important for you to understand that homework is not graded based on how correct it is. It's graded on the basis of your effort. Homework is not useless in my class. We go over every single item.

Finally, Sandy stresses the need to come to class (in terms that are amazingly similar to Fred's):

OK, Number 7 is pretty clear ("There will be no cutting"); I don't really think this needs to be discussed. I want you here. I expect you to be here. *And I take it personally if you're not.*

In addition to going over her own class rules, Sandy also reviews the school's academic integrity policy. With an extremely serious demeanor, she explains the distinction between cooperating and cheating ("the ultimate disrespectful behavior"). She talks about the numerous behaviors that constitute cheating (e.g., giving or receiving test information, using "unauthorized written aids" or information from electronic devices during tests, claiming sole credit for work completed with other students, copying work that was supposed to be done independently, and fabricating laboratory data). She also gives students strategies for resisting peer pressure to cheat: "If someone asks you what was on the test, just tell them, 'Oh, you know Mrs. K! You have to know everything!'" Sandy also spends a lot of time talking about plagiarism. She tells students that "plagiarism is like someone behind you reaching into your backpack and taking your cell phone. Ideas belong to people, just like cell phones."

Like Sandy, Christina also talks about "guidelines" for behavior. On the first day of school she distributes a newspaper that she creates for each class she teaches. Each newspaper begins with a "Letter from the Editor," welcoming students and inviting them to contact her at an e-mail address she has set up specifically for her classes. In addition to listing the "guidelines for student conduct," the newspaper enumerates course objectives, grading policies, penalties for late work and missed assignments, and essential routines regarding notebooks, portfolios, and paper headings. (See Figure 4.3.) Listen as Christina introduces the newspaper to English 10R:

Here's a page of information about this course. On the front page, there's a letter from the editor. That's me; I'm the editor. Read that silently, please. [She gives students a few minutes to read the letter.]

There are a couple of things I want to point out. Let's look at the objectives for this class. [She goes over the objectives, clarifying terms and talking about some of the activities they'll be doing to fulfill the objectives.] OK, let's look at the "Guidelines for Student Conduct." [She goes through the list commenting on some of the bulleted points.] We're all working together to make this a positive, comfortable class. I can't do it by myself. There are 29 of you and only one of me. So you have to contribute to the environment—being nice to each other, not using put-downs, using appropriate language. You won't hear me using inappropriate language, so I don't expect you to use it either; I'm very strict about that. . . . "Obtain and complete make-up work." I expect you to be vigilant, to find out what you missed. You have two days to get the work in. "Come to class on time." On time means in your seat, not by someone else's desk. If you need to use the restroom, come to class first, put your books away, and let me know you're here. Then you can go. That way if you're 10 or 20 seconds late, I'll know where you are. Remember that coats, scarves, hats, food, and drink are not allowed in class; that's a school rule so you should all be familiar with that.

[She turns the page over.] Let me point out the penalty box: You get one warning for disruptive behavior and then you're removed from the classroom. Take a minute to look over the texts we'll be using and the grading policy.... Read over the section on paper headings carefully.

OK, to make sure that we're all on the same page about rules and procedures, read this paper and then sign it. [She gives out the "Dear Student and Parent/Guardian" page.] Your first homework assignment is to take this home and get your parents to sign it too.

English 10 R

Reading
Writing
Speaking
Listening
Viewing

January—June   Mrs. C. Vreeland

A letter from the Editor:

Dear Students,

Welcome to tenth grade English. I hope you had a pleasant first semester and are ready for some exciting educational experiences. I am looking forward to working with you this semester.

I have been working hard to plan this course for you and I think you will learn a great deal and have some fun this semester. In order to make this class successful, I must ask for your cooperation. I will ask for your input frequently and if you have any ideas, you may feel free to share them at any time.

Please raise any questions or comments at an appropriate time during class or check my schedule on the classroom door to reach me during the school day. In addition, you can reach me through e-mail if you have access at home. My e-mail address is: **Celvreeland@aol.com** and this address is designated for student use only, so feel free to use it whenever you wish.

However, please note that I cannot guarantee immediate response to your e-mail. Therefore, questions or comments that require immediate attention should be addressed before you leave school. "You didn't answer my question on e-mail" is not a valid excuse for not doing your homework!

Please read the rest of this introductory handout carefully and share it with your parents, as it will provide you with an overview of the course. You will learn about rules, procedures, grading policies, and course objectives; all of which will be helpful to you throughout the semester.

I wish you much success this semester and I know that you will achieve your goals and mine if you approach this class with enthusiasm and dedication.

Sincerely,
Mrs. C. Vreeland

Objectives

After successfully completing this course, students will be able to:

1. Recognize the act and importance of listening.
2. Organize, prepare, and present a spoken presentation clearly and expressively.
3. Collaborate by sharing ideas, examples, and insights productively and respectfully.
4. Recognize that reading has many purposes and demonstrate an ability to choose an approach appropriate to the text and purpose.
5. Experience and respond to print and non-print media.
6. Use research skills to access, interpret, and apply information from a variety of print and non-print sources.
7. Compose a variety of written responses for different purposes and audiences.
8. Use a variety of technologies as a tool for learning.
9. Use their language arts skills for decision making, negotiating, and problem solving.
10. Develop a better understanding of themselves, of others, and of the world through literature and through language.
11. Read and respond to a broad range of literature.

Guidelines for Student Conduct

The student will be responsible to:

- Create a positive, comfortable learning environment in the classroom.
- Respect every member of the class, by using appropriate language, by paying attention when another person is speaking, and by raising his/her hand to speak.
- Complete all assignments on time and to the best of his/her ability.
- Obtain and complete make-up work on time — two days for each day absent.
- Listen to and follow all directions given by the teacher, asking for clarification if he/she does not understand the directions. (NOTE: Refusal to follow directions constitutes interference with the educational process and will result in disciplinary action.)
- Come to class on time and be in his/her seat when the bell rings.
- Bring his/her textbook, notebook, a writing implement, a pen AND pencil, and any other required materials (as assigned by the teacher) to class each day.
- Leave ALL food, drink, and outerwear in his/her locker.
- LEARN and THINK independently as well as cooperatively.

Figure 4.3   Christina's Introductory Newspaper

Penalty Box

Students who do not listen to directions or obtain make-up work will receive a "double F" for all missed assignments. Late work will not be accepted.

Students who are not in their seats when the bell rings will be marked late(three lates equal one cut).

Students who disrupt the learning of others or refuse to follow directions given by the teacher will lose participation credit. If disruption or refusal persists, students will be removed from the classroom. Appropriate disciplinary action will follow.

Texts

- Selected poetry, short stories, and nonfiction
- <u>A Separate Peace</u> by John Knowles, a novel
- <u>Of Mice and Men</u> by John Steinbeck, a novel
- <u>Ethan Frome</u> by Edith Wharton, a novel
- Selections from *The Legend of King Arthur*
- Sophocles' *Antigone*, a drama
- Shakespeare's *Julius Caesar*, a drama
- Woodbridge Township Research Paper Guide
- Media Center Materials

Grading Policy

There will be three components to your grade at the end of each marking period. Each of the three will be worth one third of your final grade.

<u>Tests</u> — Includes traditional end of unit tests as well as large projects or papers. If an assignment is going to count as a test grade, it will be announced when the assignment is given.

<u>Homework/Classwork/ Quizzes</u> — Includes all assignments that receive a letter grade and are completed for homework, classwork, or as a quiz. This may

include groupwork. Quizzes may be announced or unannounced.

<u>Participation</u> — Includes a variety of different activities/assignments that are important for you to complete to understand the material or to learn/practice a specific skill that cannot be rated in a traditional A-F format. Participation grades will be assigned weekly and participation will be scored according to a rubric. You will see your participation rubric each week.

Procedures

Notebooks

Notebooks must be maintained. Your notebook must be clearly labeled with your name, your homeroom number, the title of the course, block, classroom number, and my name. A <u>three-ring binder</u> type notebook is recommended, as it will accommodate calendars and other handouts that students will be expected to keep at all times.

Notebooks must be divided into the following sections:

- Calendar Section
- Vocabulary Section—daily SAT vocabulary words and vocabulary from literature
- Daily Journal Section—dated with journal topic noted
- Literature Notes Section
- Miscellaneous Section—notes on writing and research as well as project handouts

Journals

Students will maintain daily journals in their notebooks. Journal topics will be provided and students will be expected to begin writing as soon as they enter the classroom. They will continue writing until the teacher signals the end of the journal session. Journal sessions will last approximately 5-10 minutes.

Portfolios

Students will create and maintain portfolios. Portfolios are integral to the class and will receive two test grades each semester (total = four test grades). Details about the portfolio will follow.

Paper Headings & Presentation

Students will be expected to write proper headings on all of their papers. Headings will be written neatly on the right-hand side of the top margin. Headings will include the following:

- Student's Full Name
- Course and Block
- Teacher's Name
- Date

Work will be submitted on clean paper without ragged edges. Work will be written in blue or black ink. Assignments will be clearly labeled on the top line of the paper, noting the title of the assignment and other relevant information, including page numbers. Work that does not meet these minimum requirements will not be accepted.

Figure 4.3   (*continued*)

In contrast to Donnie, Sandy, and Christina, Fred introduces rules and routines in a relatively informal way. As we saw earlier, when he reviews the school handbook with his first-period class of sophomores, he uses the school rules as a jumping-off point for a presentation of his class rules. Even here, however, he distributes no handouts, nor does he post rules, and he interjects a degree of humor:

> [Fred finishes reviewing the handbook and has students sign the page acknowledging receipt and agreement. He then continues with his own rules for the class.] Do you know what an acronym is? It's letters that form a word and each letter stands for a word. PITA is an acronym. And it's the main rule we have in here: *Don't be a PITA.* What's a PITA, Suzanne? [She shakes her head.] You don't know? [He looks around to see if anyone else knows. There's silence.] A PITA is a . . . pain . . . in . . . the . . . neck! [There's some laughter as the class catches on.] I want you to inscribe PITA across your forehead. Don't forget: Don't be a PITA. Now, I have one rule for me, too: I must make you laugh once every day. If I don't, I go home in a suicidal mood. [Students laugh.] OK, let's talk about what you'll be learning in U.S. History I.

With his seniors, Fred prefers an even less systematic approach. On the first day of class, he introduces himself, takes attendance, and immediately launches into a description of the course. During the period, he explicitly teaches his students routines for specific situations that arise (e.g., how to pass in papers), but he does not teach rules for general conduct. Instead, he monitors the class carefully and immediately informs students about behavior he finds unacceptable. His interactions with individual students are watched carefully by the rest—and they quickly learn what he expects. When Fred asks one student to takes off his baseball cap, for example, another hears and takes off his own hat. To a student wearing sunglasses, Fred asks, "Is there is a medical reason for those glasses?" and the student immediately removes them. Later on, when the same student yawns loudly and conspicuously, Fred turns to him and speaks firmly:

> FRED: James, please don't do that.
> STUDENT: I was just yawning.
> FRED: If you have to do that, please transfer to a different class. OK?
> STUDENT: OK. [Fred moves closer to James and continues the discussion.]

At the end of the period, Fred asks James to stay for a minute, a request that is obviously noted by the other students. They speak privately, and then James leaves for his next class. Afterwards, Fred shares what happened:

> That was clearly a test, but I think I passed it. I told him that yawning like that was clearly inappropriate and that if he couldn't demonstrate the same respect for me that I showed him, then he'd have to find another place to be. I can't operate in an atmosphere of "me against you." He said it was because he hadn't had a cup of coffee. I told him there are no excuses, that it just won't happen in here, that he can't be here if he acts inappropriately. He said OK, and we agreed to chalk it up to a mistake and forget about it. But I'll have to watch him.

As this incident illustrates, Fred communicates expectations for conduct to older students primarily by providing clear, immediate feedback when behavior is unacceptable. He recognizes that one reason this approach works for him is the reputation he has established during his years at the high school. Reflecting on this reputation, Barry Bachenheimer, Fred's student teacher, observes:

> *Everyone knows that he plays the "dumb old man," but that he's not. He has this incredible relationship with the kids; he knew everyone's name within two days. He works them hard, but he projects warmth, and the kids know he really cares. I've never seen a kid give him lip. One look is enough.*

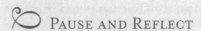

PAUSE AND REFLECT

You have listened in on each of our four teachers as they set up rules and procedures in their classrooms. Which teacher has an outlook most like yours? Is there a particular style that resonates with you, or will you borrow an idea from Donnie and add one from Fred? As you develop your own management style, keep in mind the ways these teachers approached their classrooms and use their thoughts to grow your own ideas.

CONCLUDING COMMENTS

Donnie, Christina, Sandy, and Fred all have well-defined expectations for student behavior, and they make these expectations absolutely clear. Nonetheless, the four teachers have somewhat different expectations, and they introduce rules and routines in different ways. These differences reflect their beliefs about what works best for their own particular students in their own particular contexts. Donnie, Christina, and Sandy teach rules and routines in a systematic, explicit fashion; they all spend considerable time explaining what they expect, and they distribute written copies of the rules for students to keep in their notebooks. Christina goes further: She requires her students to sign a statement that they have read and understood the information about student conduct, penalties, grading policies, and expected class procedures and to obtain their parents' signatures as well. In contrast, Fred is much more informal. With his sophomores, Fred explicitly teaches rules, but he neither posts them nor distributes copies. With his seniors, he teaches specific routines, but relies primarily on monitoring and feedback to communicate what he expects in terms of general conduct.

As a beginning teacher, you would be wise to adopt a deliberate, thorough approach to teaching rules and routines. Once you've gained experience—and a reputation—you might try a less formal approach with your older students. Also keep in mind that rules and routines are not invented in a single year, polished and fully developed. Instead, they will evolve over time, products of your experience and creative efforts.

SUMMARY

This chapter discussed two important functions of rules and routines in the classroom: (1) to provide a structure and predictability that help students to feel more comfortable; and (2) to reduce the complexity of classroom life, allowing you and your students to concentrate on teaching and learning. It then outlined two broad categories of behavioral expectations—rules for general conduct and routines for specific situations—and emphasized the need to teach these explicitly.

When Deciding on Rules for General Conduct, Make Sure They Are:

- Reasonable and necessary.
- Clear and understandable.
- Consistent with instructional goals and with what we know about how people learn.
- Consistent with school rules.

Plan Routines for Specific Situations:

- Class-running routines.
    - Administrative duties.
    - Procedures for student movement.
    - Housekeeping responsibilities.
- Lesson-running routines.
    - Routines governing use and distribution of materials.
    - Routines for paper headings, homework procedures, what to do if you finish early.
- Interaction routines.
    - Routines specifying when talk is permitted and how it is to occur.
    - Routines for students and teachers to use to get each other's attention.

Teach Rules Explicitly:

- Define terms.
- Discuss rationales.
- Provide examples.

Remember, developing good rules and routines is only the first step. For rules and routines to be effective, you must actively teach them to your students. Time spent on rules and routines at the beginning of school will pay off in increased instructional time throughout the year.

ACTIVITIES FOR SKILL BUILDING AND REFLECTION

In Class

1. Thinking about rules: Working together in small groups, develop a set of rules for your classroom. About five rules should be sufficient. For each rule, list a rationale and examples that you will discuss with students to make the rules more meaningful. Think about which rules are most important to you and why.

2. Thinking about routines: In a small group, refer to Table 4.2, which lists the areas for which you will need specific behavioral routines. First, share your ideas about the actual routines you might use in each category (e.g., what kind of routine can you establish for taking attendance in an efficient way?). Then, think about which routines need to be taught on the first day. In other words, decide on priorities so that you can teach a routine when it is most appropriate (and most likely to be remembered).

On Your Own

If you are teaching or student teaching, keep a reflective journal on developing and teaching rules and routines. Using the routines listed in Table 4.2, note which routines cause the most problems, the nature of the problems, and how you might respond to those problems. Also note which routines work particularly well.

For Your Portfolio

Write a brief statement on the rules that will guide behavior in your classroom. Will you develop and distribute them yourself? If so, what rules will you create? Will you generate rules with students? If so, how will you do this? Describe the specific approach you will take.

FOR FURTHER READING

Bicard, D. F. (2000). Using classroom rules to construct behavior. *Middle School Journal, 31*(5), 37-45.

> Arguing that "rules are one of the most cost-effective forms of classroom management available to teachers," Bicard reviews the characteristics of positive, negative, and vague rules and discusses the keys to developing and implementing positive rules in classrooms. The article also discusses what to do when students violate rules.

Brady, K., Forton, M. B., Porter, D., & Wood, C. (2003). *Rules in school.* Greenfield, MA: Northeast Foundation for Children.

> One of the Strategies for Teachers Series, this book provides practical suggestions for involving K through 8 students in generating classroom rules that grow out of their hopes and dreams. Chapter 6 focuses specifically on middle school (grades 6 through 8) and includes a discussion of logical consequences to ensure accountability.

Marzano, R. J., with Marzano, J. S., & Pickering, D. J. (2003). *Classroom management that works: Research-based strategies for every teacher.* Alexandria, VA: Association for Supervision and Curriculum Development.

> Chapter 2 focuses on rules and procedures. The authors first discuss research confirming the importance of classroom norms. They then outline a series of "Action Steps" that teachers can take to identify appropriate rules and procedures and to involve students in their design.

REFERENCES

Brooks, D. M., (1985). The teacher's communicative competence: The first day of school. *Theory Into Practice, 24*(1), 63-70.

Evertson, C. M., & Emmer, E. T. (1982). Effective management at the beginning of the school year in junior high classes. *Journal of Educational Psychology, 74*(4), 485-498.

Kounin, J. S. (1970). *Discipline and group management in classrooms.* New York: Holt, Rinehart and Winston.

Leinhardt, G., Weidman, C., & Hammond, K. M. (1987). Introduction and integration of classroom routines by expert teachers. *Curriculum Inquiry, 17*(2), 135–175.

Rosenshine, B. (1980). How time is spent in elementary classrooms. In C. Denham and A. Lieberman (Eds.), *Time to learn.* Washington, D.C.: U.S. Department of Education.

Webb, N. M. (1985). Student interaction and learning in small groups: A research summary. In R. E. Slavin, S. Sharan, S. Kagan, R. Hertz-Lazarowitz, C. Webb, & R. Schmuck (Eds.), *Learning to cooperate, cooperating to learn.* New York: Plenum.

Wertsch, J. V. (1985). *Vygotsky and the social formation of mind.* Cambridge, MA: Harvard University Press.

WORKING WITH FAMILIES

"I had no idea his mother lost her job and his father hasn't been around for a month. No wonder he's been so belligerent!"

"Her grandmother has been so good about making sure she's doing her homework. She's really working with me on this."

"His father has offered to chaperone the eighth-grade cookout and to organize the softball game! It will be terrific to have him along!"

Comments like these can be heard in teachers' rooms all across the country. They reflect some of the benefits that accrue when teachers and families establish positive, productive relationships. First, *knowing about a student's home situation provides insight into the student's classroom behavior.* Listen to Donnie:

> It was the very first day of school—when everyone is still being really good—but this one girl was really loud and hyperactive. It was clear that everyone disliked her. She seemed completely unable to control herself.
> I checked into her home situation as soon as I had a free period. I found out that her mother had kicked her out of the house; she said she couldn't handle all the kids. The girl had tried to commit suicide, but now she was really trying to get her act together. She had gotten a part-time job, and she was living with an

aunt. This girl had really been thrown out into the world, and school is her haven. Actually, when I think about what she's facing, I'm really impressed by how well she's doing.

As Donnie's example illustrates, it's easier to understand why Johnny sits with his head down on his desk if you're aware that he spent the night in a homeless shelter; Carla's apathy makes sense if you know that her mother is going through chemotherapy; and Jana's anxiety about getting all As is understandable if you appreciate how much her parents pressure her to succeed. Furthermore, insights like these can help you decide what course of action to take when dealing with a student's problems. You're better able to judge if a suggestion that a parent proofread term papers is inappropriate because the parent can't read, or if a note home will lead to benefits or to beatings.

Second, *when families understand what you are trying to achieve, they can provide valuable support and assistance.* Most parents want their children to succeed in school and will do what they can to help. But they can't work in a vacuum. They need to know what you are trying to achieve and how you expect children to behave in your classroom. Familiarizing parents with your curriculum, routines, and policies minimizes confusion, misinterpretations, and conflict. For this reason, Christina requires parents to sign an acknowledgment form at the beginning of the course, indicating that they have read and understood the "newspaper" she sends home describing course objectives, policies, and procedures.

Third, *families can help to develop and implement strategies to change students' behavior.* Working together, parents and teachers can bring about improvements in students' behavior that would be impossible working alone. Fred shares this example:

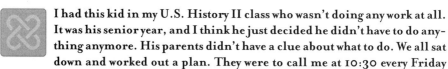

I had this kid in my U.S. History II class who wasn't doing any work at all. It was his senior year, and I think he just decided he didn't have to do anything anymore. His parents didn't have a clue about what to do. We all sat down and worked out a plan. They were to call me at 10:30 every Friday morning. If the report on their son was good, he got the car keys, got to go out with his friends, got to go to the ball game. If the report was bad, the weekend did not exist. We told him, "We really care about you and if this is what we have to do to get you through senior year, then so be it." The kid tested the plan once, and there was no weekend for him. After that, he really started to perform and ended up with a B for the year. Plus, there was an additional payoff. His parents were able to give him all kinds of good strokes because he started taking responsibility.

Finally, *parent volunteers can provide needed assistance in the classroom and the school.* Since schools are almost always short-staffed, parents can provide an extra pair of hands: They can work in libraries, computer centers, and homework programs; help make school safe by greeting visitors; accompany students on field trips; make phone calls to other parents; and join with school personnel to create, manage, and deliver special programs. They can also enrich the curriculum by sharing information about their hobbies, careers, travels, and ethnic backgrounds.

Despite the obvious benefits of close communication and collaboration, parents and teachers are often at odds with one another. Sometimes the relationship is detached and distant; sometimes it's distrustful and adversarial. What causes this adversarial relationship and what can teachers do to avoid it? In this chapter, we examine three challenges to close working relationships—teacher reluctance to involve parents, parent reluctance to become involved, and the changing nature of families. We then turn to our teachers and to the literature on parent involvement in order to suggest ways that families and schools can work together to *overcome* the challenges.

 PAUSE AND REFLECT

Before reading on, think of three possible answers to each of the following questions:

* Why would teachers sometimes be reluctant to involve parents in their youngster's schooling?
* Why would parents sometimes be reluctant to become involved?
* How does the changing nature of the family affect parent-teacher collaboration?

CHALLENGES TO FAMILY–TEACHER COOPERATION

Teacher Reluctance to Involve Families in Schooling

A primary reason for teachers' reluctance to work with families is the *extra time and energy that are required.* Teaching is physically and emotionally exhausting, and reaching out to parents is sometimes viewed as one more burdensome task. Epstein and Becker (1982) remind us how much time it takes to make just one call home: "If a teacher telephones 30 parents and talks for 10 minutes to each, the teacher spends 5 hours voluntarily on the telephone with parents" (p. 103). And that's for just one class! Since this is obviously in addition to the normal workload, it's understandable if teachers wonder whether the extra time required is worth the trouble. Furthermore, there are few external rewards to encourage teachers to spend time working with parents (Epstein & Becker, 1982), and teachers often lament the lack of support from their principals or other teachers. For new teachers, the task of reaching out to parents may seem even more onerous. As Christina admits, "I'm always preparing materials and lessons, grading, or commenting on student papers. It takes time to be creative and effective—and that means there's less time for parent contact than I would like."

In addition, *teachers' perceptions of families* undoubtedly contribute to the reluctance to seek greater parental involvement. Many teachers recognize that time is often a scarce commodity for parents, limited by responsibilities at work, household chores, and caring for other family members. These teachers question whether it is fair to ask already burdened parents to spend time working with their teenage children on academic activities or assisting with behavior problems. As Sandy told us:

 Some parents are just overwhelmed. One poor, single mother I know just doesn't have the time or energy to become more involved. She's worried about keeping her job and making ends meet. Her plate is just too full; she can't handle anything else. It's not that she doesn't care. But

PARENTALAPATHY ? I DON'T KNOW - WE HAVEN'T THOUGHT MUCH ABOUT IT ONE WAY OR THE OTHER !

Figure 5.1   Parental apathy is sometimes viewed as a problem.
Source: Reproduced by permission of Luci Meighan.

the fact that her kid is not doing his homework is just not her highest priority right now. Knowing this is important. Once you know you're not going to get parent involvement, you can figure out another approach.

Other teachers may see parents as too "ignorant" to be a resource (Eccles & Harold, 1993), while still others have been burned by encounters with angry, irresponsible, or apathetic parents. (See Figure 5.1 for a perspective on parental apathy.) They would tend to agree with Anne Walde and Keith Baker (1990), who contend that "far too many parents—and not just disadvantaged ones—simply don't give a damn. For them, school is a free babysitting service" (p. 322). Walde and Baker argue that many parents are not concerned with their child's education, do not want to be involved, or lack the skills needed to support their children. They describe numerous encounters with parents to support their assertion. Here is one example:

TEACHER: John isn't doing his homework.
PARENT: I know he isn't. He watches TV all the time and doesn't do his homework. I just don't know what to do.
TEACHER: Why don't you turn the TV off?
PARENT: Oh, he'd never let me do that!

Teachers may also worry that parents may not understand their role in the classroom. Some parent volunteers intervene when they shouldn't (e.g., imposing their own punishments for inappropriate behavior instead of consulting the teacher); they may instruct students in ways that contradict what the teacher has demonstrated; or they may violate confidentiality by sharing student records and relating sensitive information. When situations like these occur, teachers may wonder if parent volunteers are more of a hindrance than a help.

Finally, teachers may be reluctant to involve parents in schooling because they want to protect their "turf." As public servents, teachers are often exposed to criticism. Parents may blame them for children's problems or question their professional competence. Sara Lawrence Lightfoot (1978) writes:

> The only sphere of influence in which the teacher feels that her authority is ultimate and uncompromising seems to be with what happens *inside* the classroom. Behind the classroom door, teachers experience some measure of autonomy and relief from parental scrutiny. (p. 26)

Lightfoot concludes that teachers who are "more confident of their skills, expertise, and abilities" (p. 30) will be more likely to reach out to parents, and research supports her contention. In a study of factors that facilitate parent involvement, Hoover-Dempsey, Bassler, and Brissie (1987) found that *teacher efficacy* (teachers' beliefs that they can teach and that their students can learn) was the factor most strongly related to parent involvement.

Parent Reluctance to Become Involved in Schooling

It is well recognized that family involvement in schools declines as students move from elementary to middle school and junior high, and that by high school, it has practically disappeared (Rioux & Berla, 1993). During one conversation with Donnie, she explained the decline in parent involvement this way:

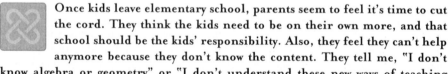

> Once kids leave elementary school, parents seem to feel it's time to cut the cord. They think the kids need to be on their own more, and that school should be the kids' responsibility. Also, they feel they can't help anymore because they don't know the content. They tell me, "I don't know algebra or geometry" or "I don't understand these new ways of teaching math." They're scared off by the content and feel they can't offer assistance.

In addition to this general, pervasive trend, there are more specific reasons why families may resist involvement. Griffith (1998), for example, found that lower socioeconomic status was associated with lower parent participation in schooling. Among the most obvious reasons for this association are the competing demands of work. Low-income households are more likely to have two parents who work full-time, parents who have two or more jobs, parents who have to work evenings and nights, and parents who have jobs with inflexible or unpredictable hours.

Since mothers have traditionally assumed much of the responsibility for raising children and being involved in their education, it is not surprising that maternal employment has generally been shown to have a negative impact on involvement in schooling. However, recent research on low-income mothers' involvement in their children's education (Weiss and colleagues, 2003) has revealed an unexpected pattern. Although mothers who worked or attended school *full-time* were less involved than other mothers, mothers who worked or attended school *part-time* were *more* involved than other mothers—including those who didn't work or attend school at all. In explanation, Weiss and her colleagues speculate that part-time working mothers are not only less likely to experience the time constraints of full-time work, they are also less likely to experience the mental health risks (such as depression) associated with unemployment. In any case, their study clearly demonstrates the ingenuity required to negotiate the competing demands of work and involvement in schooling. The mothers in this study had to become expert at multitasking, doing things at odd times, and arranging their own work or school schedule to coincide with their children's. One mother, for example, took her lunch hour in mid-afternoon so that she could escort her children home from the bus stop, which was near the deli where she worked. Another waited on tables and volunteered in her son's classroom between shifts in order to spend time with him.

In addition to the difficulties imposed by work, there are more subtle reasons for parental reluctance to become involved. Some adults have *unhappy memories* of their own experiences as students. Listen to this father describe his reasons for not participating more fully in his son's schooling:

> They expect me to go to school so they can tell me my kid is stupid or crazy. They've been telling me that for three years, so why should I go and hear it again? They don't do anything. They just tell me my kid is bad. . . . See, I've been there. I know. And it scares me. They called me a boy in trouble but I was a troubled boy. Nobody helped me because they liked it when I didn't show up. If I was gone for the semester, fine with them. I dropped out nine times. They wanted me gone. (Finders & Lewis, 1994, p. 51)

Some families *feel guilty* when their teenage children have difficulties in school. They may become defensive and uncooperative when teachers try to discuss their youngster's problem or may be too embarrassed to disclose troubles they are having at home. Rather than deal with the child's problem, these families may try to deny what is occurring and to avoid communication with the teacher.

Other families *are unnerved by the "threatening monolith" we call school* (Lightfoot, 1978, p. 36). This is particularly so when parents are poor, uneducated, or have limited proficiency in English. Some may find teachers and administrators unresponsive to their requests (Gutman & McLoyd, 2000); others may even fear teachers, viewing them as authority figures who must not be questioned (Lindeman, 2001). Immigrant parents may be confused by educational practices that are different from their own; they may not know the words (e.g., "standards," "student-centered," "cum file," "grade equivalence") that would allow them to have a meaningful exchange.

Chrispeels and Rivero (2000) interviewed 11 Latino families about family involvement in schooling. They report that 9 of the 11 felt they had little influence on what happened at school and left decisions in the hands of the teacher. Mrs. Andres was typical:

> My daughter's report card from fourth grade arrived with all Bs. In third grade she came out with excellence and an A. We waited for the next report card and

again she got all Bs. . . . She told me, "My teacher says that she will not give any As because that will make the children who get an F feel bad." My daughter said that in that case she would not try hard because she was not going to get an A. (p. 22)

Although Mrs. Andres felt this was unfair she did not ask the teacher for an explanation: "In a way I felt the teacher could say 'Well, who tells you that your daughter deserves an A?' My fear of that comment kept me from going to ask" (p. 22).

Still other families simply *do not see involvement in schooling to be part of their role as parents* (Hoover-Dempsey & Sandler, 1997). They may believe that schooling should be left to the professionals or that they are showing their support for teachers by not interfering. Beliefs like these may be culturally influenced. Asian American families, for example, generally hold high expectations for their children's academic success; nonetheless, they tend to view educational matters as the province of the school (Fuller & Olsen, 1998). Similarly, Latinos typically perceive their role as ensuring their children's attendance; instilling respect for the teacher; encouraging good behavior in school; meeting their obligations to provide clothing, food, and shelter; and socializing children to their family responsibilities (Chrispeels & Rivero, 2000; Trumbull, Rothstein-Fisch, Greenfield, & Quiroz, 2001). Becoming involved in school is *not* a key component of this role.

A good example of how both the demands of work and parents' role-definition can affect involvement comes from Lopez (2001), who studied the Padillas, an immigrant, migrant family whose children were all very successful in school. Their parental involvement, however, took the form of exposing their children to their hard work in the fields and teaching them that without an education they might end up in the same situation. Here is an excerpt from one interview:

INTERVIEWER: Now I want to know if you or your wife are involved in the schools in one way or another? For example, like volunteers or in the Parent's Committee.

MR. PADILLA: No sir. . . .

INTERVIEWER: Hmmm. Haven't you gone to a parents' meeting or something like that?

MR. PADILLA: No. Not really. It's just that we're always busy with work. We rarely go to the school.

INTERVIEWER: Not even to a conference with the teachers?

MR. PADILLA: Well, maybe once in a while. But it's really difficult. There's a lot of work.

INTERVIEWER: So how are you involved in your children's education?

MR. PADILLA: Well, I have shown them what work is and how hard it is. So they know that if they don't focus in their studies, that is the type of work they'll end up doing. I've opened their eyes to that reality. (p. 427)

As Lopez points out, if the Padillas' "involvement" were defined by bake sales and back-to-school nights, they would appear to be uninvolved in their children's education. Yet they were *highly* involved in fostering their children's positive attitudes toward school. Clearly, we need to be cautious about assuming that parents who are uninvolved in "traditionally sanctioned ways" are unconcerned and uncaring (p. 435).

The Changing Nature of the Family

In 1955, 60 percent of American households consisted of a working father, a homemaker mother, and two or more school-age children (Hodgkinson, 1985). Teachers sent letters home addressed to "Dear Parents," reasonably confident that two parents would read them, and schools scheduled "Parent Conferences" with the expectation that parents were the primary caregivers of their children.

Times have changed. Consider this entry from the journal of a sixth-grade student teacher:

> *One boy in my class is very bright . . . but he never turned in assignments or participated in class discussions. He tended to annoy the students around him by doing strange things.*
>
> *Two weeks ago he missed two days of school. Last week he missed four. Some students saw him playing outside over the weekend, but he wasn't in school at all this week. There were no phone calls, and the social worker had to look into it.*
>
> *His uncle came to school today and told us that the father dropped him off with the grandparents Monday and hasn't been heard from since. He is officially a "missing person." The mother lives in another state and doesn't want the boy. His parents apparently went through a very messy divorce. Now this boy is tossed around with no one who wants him. And we as teachers were concerned that he didn't do his spelling homework!*

Stories like this have become all too common. The typical family of the 1950s now represents less than 10 percent of our households (Cushner, McClelland, & Safford, 2000). Today, almost half of all marriages end in divorce (Heuveline, 2005), and 50 percent of our children will live in a single-parent family at some point during their childhood (Children's Defense Fund, 2004). In 2003, 30 percent of children were not living with two parents (*Kids Count Data Book,* 2005). Most are growing up with a single parent, but for some, the significant adults in their lives are not their parents at all, but grandparents, aunts, uncles, brothers, sisters, or neighbors. The "stay-at-home" mother is vanishing; indeed, 60 percent of all preschoolers have a mother in the workforce (Children's Defense Fund, 2004). With a surge in immigration from Central and Latin America, the Middle East, Southeast Asia and the Pacific, and Russia and Eastern Europe, many students come from homes where a language other than English is spoken, and their families are unfamiliar with schools in the United States.

The changing nature of the American family has made communication and collaboration more difficult than ever. Nonetheless, research has found that *teachers' attitudes and practices—not the educational level, marital status, or workplace of parents—determine whether families become productively involved in their children's schooling* (Epstein, 2001; Griffith, 1998). In other words, it's the teacher that makes the difference. For this reason, you must not only understand the challenges to parent involvement, you must also be aware of the ways that families and schools can work together.

OVERCOMING THE CHALLENGES: FOSTERING COLLABORATION BETWEEN FAMILIES AND SCHOOLS

Joyce Epstein and her colleagues at Johns Hopkins University have studied comprehensive parent involvement programs and have identified six different types of family–school collaboration (Epstein, 2001; Sanders & Lewis, 2005; Simon, 2004). These are summarized in Table 5.1. The first four of Epstein's categories provide a framework for our discussion. (For more information and to learn about the last two categories—including families as participants in school decision making and collaborating with the community—see Epstein and colleagues, 2002; Chapter 6 is specifically devoted to "Strengthening Partnership Programs in Middle and High Schools.")

Helping Families to Fulfill Their Basic Obligations

This category refers to the family's responsibility to provide for children's health and safety, to supervise and guide children at each age level, and to build positive home conditions that support school learning and behavior (Epstein & Dauber, 1991). Schools can assist families in carrying out these basic obligations by providing workshops on parenting skills; establishing parent support groups; holding programs on teenage problems (e.g., drug and alcohol abuse, eating disorders); communicating with families through newsletters, videotapes, and home visits; and referring families to community and state agencies when necessary.

Asking teachers to assume responsibilities for the education of *families,* in addition to the education of *children,* may seem onerous and unfair. Not surprisingly, some teachers hesitate to become "social workers," a role for which they are untrained. Others feel resentful and angry at parents who do not provide adequate home environments. Although these attitudes are understandable, you need to remember that your students' home environments shape their chances for school success. As the number of distressed families grows, assisting families to carry out their basic obligations becomes increasingly critical.

What can you, as a teacher, realistically do to assist families in carrying out their basic obligations? Although you will probably not be directly involved in planning parent education workshops, writing newsletters, or creating videotapes, you can play an important, *indirect* role. You can let families know about available materials, motivate and encourage them to attend programs, bring transportation problems to the attention of appropriate school personnel, and help families to arrange car pools (Greenwood & Hickman, 1991).

In Sandy's and Fred's districts, parent support groups are available through Effective Parenting Information for Children (EPIC) (Hayes, Lipsky, McCully, Rickard,

TABLE 5.1 Epstein's Six Types of Involvement for Comprehensive Programs of Partnership

Type	Examples
1. Helping families to fulfill their basic parenting obligations	Provide suggestions for home conditions that support learning at each grade level.
	Provide parent education workshops and other courses of training for parents.
	Provide family support programs to assist families with health, nutrition, and other services.
2. Communicating with families	Design effective forms of school-to-home and home-to-school communications about school programs and children's progress.
	Hold conferences at least once a year, with follow-ups as needed.
	Provide language translators to assist families.
	Have parent–student pickup of report cards, with conferences on improving grades.
	Have a regular schedule of useful notices, memos, phone calls, newsletters, etc.
	Provide clear information on all school policies and programs.
3. Family involvement in school (volunteering)	Recruit and organize parent help and support.
	Provide parent room or family center for volunteer work, meetings, and resources for families.
	Send an annual postcard survey to identify all available talents, times, and locations of volunteers.
	Have parent patrols to aid safety of school programs.
4. Family involvement in learning activities at home	Provide information to families about how to help students at home with homework.
	Provide family math, science, and reading activities at school.
	Allow family participation in setting student goals each year.
5. Family involvement in school decision making	Maintain active PTA/PTO or other parent organizations, advisory councils, or committees.
	Maintain district-level councils and committees for family and community involvement.
	Provide information on school or local elections for school representatives.
6. Collaborating with the community	Identify and integrate resources and services from the community to strengthen school programs and family practices.
	Provide information on community activities that link to learning.
	Provide service to the community by students, families, and schools.
	Establish partnerships involving school, community agencies and organizations, and businesses.

Source: Epstein, Sanders, Simon, Salinas, Jansorn, & Van Voorhis, 2002.

Sipson, & Wicker, 1985). EPIC provides parents, teachers, and school support staff with training in ways to help children become responsible adults. It also offers opportunities for families to get together to share concerns and to discuss topics like communicating with adolescents, discipline, resisting peer pressure, and home/school cooperation. A similar program, the Parent Involvement Corps (PIC), was established at Donnie's school some years ago. Designed for parents of ninth-grade students, the program was intended to welcome parents to school, to help them feel comfortable there, to teach parenting skills, and to inform parents of their rights. Although PIC was a one-year, grant-funded program, it led to the creation of a permanent Parent–Teacher Association, which the high school had sorely needed. If programs like EPIC and PIC exist in your school, you can make sure families are aware of them, even if you are not directly involved; if you see a family with special needs, you can alert school personnel involved in these programs about the situation.

You can also educate families about relevant community and state agencies. Donnie, for example, advises families who have no health insurance where they can obtain medical and dental attention. When it became clear that one of her students was bulimic (at prom time!), Donnie worked with the family to find an agency that could provide the necessary psychological and medical assistance.

In addition to playing this indirect assistance role, there are times when it may be appropriate to work *directly* with families. Fred reports that he often needs to provide parents with some perspective on "this unique creature called 'teenager'": "They haven't had 150 kids, and it's often a revelation for them to learn that they're not the only parents having problems." Similarly, Sandy tells us that a lot of her interactions with parents involve helping them to communicate more effectively with their teenage children:

Many times, I find that my discussions with parents begin with the problems their children are having in chemistry class, but move on to more general problems. You start talking about grades, and the next thing you know you're talking about curfews and dating. Many of the parents have no control over their 15- and 16-year-olds. They'll say to me, "I just don't know what to do. He or she is the same way at home. I'm at a loss." I acknowledge their frustration and the difficulty of working with teenagers. (It helps that I have teenagers too!) I tell them, "You're not alone. Many 15- and 16-year-olds behave this way, and many parents feel this way." I try to provide some perspective and give them some tips about communication. I try to encourage them to set some limits. I find that a lot of parents don't like to set limits; they don't want confrontations with their kids, and they need encouragement to monitor what their kids are doing.

Sometimes I encounter overbearing parents who put too much pressure on their kids. Their expectations are unrealistic. Ninety-five on a test is not good enough; they want their child to have the highest test grade in the class. I tell them, "Wait a minute, we both want what's best for your child; we want him to work to his utmost ability, but utmost ability is not perfection on every test." I remember one situation, where a girl in my class was putting out very little effort. She got a 79 on the first test, which was far below her ability. After I spoke with her, she started working a lot harder, and her grade on the next test was 89. I told her how proud I was of her, and said something like, "Your parents must have been delighted." She got this funny look on her face, and I knew something was wrong. I found out that they had made only one comment: "Why wasn't it an A?" They didn't give her any praise at all. I decided I needed to speak with them about the situation. I told them, "Look, your daughter went from doing no work and getting a 79 to working hard and getting an 89, and you didn't even acknowledge the improvement. She's going to figure out that she might as well do no work and get 79s, since working hard and getting 89s doesn't get her any approval." Parents like this need to understand the importance of acknowledging improvement, instead of holding out for the perfect grade.

If you have students whose families have recently immigrated to this country, you might also help them to understand the expectations and norms of American secondary schools. For example, immigrant parents sometimes view extracurricular activities as distractions from serious study and family responsibilities. A colleague shares this story:

> *My parents, who emigrated from the Ukraine, did not permit me to work on the school paper or yearbook. They did not give my brother permission to play soccer (although he signed the permission slip himself and played).... If someone had told my parents that extracurricular activities are really part of the holistic education of their children, I think they would have responded positively.*

 As you reflect on how to help families with parenting responsibilites, keep in mind that there are cultural differences in beliefs about child-rearing, and these differences may lead to cultural clashes between home and school—with students caught in the middle. Parents from collectivistic cultures, for example, may emphasize respect, obedience, helpfulness, and responsibility to the family, while teachers from individualistic cultures stress individual achievement, independence, and self-expression (Trumbull, Rothstein-Fisch, Greenfield, & Quiroz, 2001). Tonia Moore, a Student Assistance Counselor at Sandy's school, provides additional examples of cultural clashes:

> *I see so many students who are caught between two cultures. At home, they're expected to follow a set of traditional values, but at school they really want to be American teenagers. It's so hard. We hold dances, but we have kids who are going to have arranged marriages. An Indian father wouldn't let his daughter go to Project Graduation [a boat trip the school organizes after graduation so that students will be in a safe, confined space without alcohol or drugs]. He said she couldn't stay out all night. An Iranian girl couldn't go to the prom; her father didn't believe in it. An Asian girl who just got 1400 on her SATs has to spend the summer taking review courses for college achievement tests. Her parents stress the need to achieve, while mainstream American culture stresses the importance of being well-rounded.*

When families express values and goals that are different from those of the school, it is all too easy to dismiss them as "out-of-touch," "narrow-minded," or just plain "wrong." But attitudes like this only increase parents' resentment and suspicion. Awareness and respect are the keys to reaching cross-cultural understanding. As Trumbull, Rothstein-Fisch, Greenfield, & Quiroz (2001) stress, "When both teachers and parents are aware of their somewhat different orientations, they have a greater chance of forging alliances and discovering *shared goals* for children" (p. 27).

Fulfilling the Basic Obligations of Schools—Communicating with Families

Epstein's second category of family–school involvement refers to the school's obligation *to communicate about school programs and children's progress.* Communications include report cards and progress reports, notes and e-mail messages, open houses and parent–teacher conferences, and phone calls. This is certainly the most commonly accepted way to work with parents, and there is no doubt that these communications are essential. The crucial question, however, is not only whether these communications occur, but *when they occur, whether they are being understood, and whether they lead to feelings of trust and respect or alienation and resentment.*

All of the teachers stress the importance of communicating with parents in a way that promotes a feeling of partnership. Donnie comments:

> Sometimes I see parents in the market, or in church, or downtown. When I do, I acknowledge them, and I invite them to call and talk about their children. I tell them, "We've got to work together. We're partners."

Fred echoes Donnie's message:

> Sometimes teachers don't invite contact. They'll only call if there is a problem. But some parents need that initial encouragement. If you can make that initial contact, then the parent will usually continue the contact. It's important to make parents understand that you're both working in the best interests of the kid. When you make that clear, even the most irate parent turns into a pussycat. I tell them, "Listen, everything I do is designed to be the best for your kid. But if you're concerned about something, let me know. Feel free to call." I tell my parents: "We need to work together as a team. And your kids need to know we're working together."

Research on family–school communication supports the importance of partnership. A study by Lindle (1989), for example, indicates that maintaining a professional, businesslike manner is not the best way to gain the respect and support of parents. In fact, parents view "professionalism" as *undesirable*; they express dissatisfaction with school personnel who are "too businesslike," "patronizing," or who "talk down to us." Rather than a professional–client relationship, parents prefer an equal partnership, characterized by a "personal touch." (Sometimes, partnership is

FRANK AND ERNEST®   **By BOB THAVES**

Figure 5.2   The use of educational jargon sometimes impedes communication.
Source: Frank and Ernest reprinted by permission of NEA, Inc.

threatened by the use of educational jargon that parents may find difficult to understand; see Figure 5.2.)

It is clear that Donnie, Sandy, Christina, and Fred are able to establish productive partnerships with families, and the next few sections of this chapter describe some of the ways they do this. In addition, the Practical Tips box lists some suggestions for communicating with parents who are particularly hard to reach.

Phone Calls

Given the hectic lives that people lead, one of the main problems about telephone calls is making the connection! At the beginning of the school year, all four teachers find out when and how to contact the families of their students. Some businesses have strict policies about employees' receiving phone messages, and a call during work hours may result in a reprimand. Some parents work at night, and a call in the morning will interrupt much-needed sleep; others may not have a phone at all, and you'll need to send a note home asking them to call you. (Donnie and Sandy both send notes home in plain, white envelopes—without the school's return address. This way there is less chance that a wary teenager will remove the letter from the pile of mail before the parent ever sees it!) All of the teachers also let parents know when they can receive telephone calls during the school day. Donnie even gives parents her home phone number; she says that no parent has ever abused the information.

To get the information she needs, Sandy has her students fill out a card with their parents' home and work numbers on the first day of school. She also asks students to indicate if their parents are permitted to get telephone calls at work. In addition, when Sandy has to call a parent, she'll often make a "precall," asking when it would be a convenient time to call and reassuring the parent that there's no earth-shattering problem. She's especially careful about checking the school personnel records to see which parent should be contacted:

 A majority of my students come from divorced homes. If the parents are not sharing joint custody, you cannot talk to the noncustodial parent. If the parents are sharing custody, then the record tells which parent the student is residing with, and I call that parent. Sometimes, the records will indicate if calls are to be made to both parents or if written communications are to be done in duplicate for both parents.

PRACTICAL TIPS FOR

REACHING "HARD TO REACH" PARENTS

Step 1: Try to figure out why parents are hard to reach. Ask yourself (or someone in the school or community who would know):

- Do parents speak English?

- Do parents come from cultures that do not identify parent involvement as a priority? Do they come from cultures that believe schooling should be left to the educators?

- Do parents have work schedules that conflict with conferences?

- Do parents live far from the school? Do they have transportation?

- Do parents have other children who would require babysitting during parent-teacher meetings?

- Do parents know where the school is?

- Are the parents homeless (and therefore have no good address for receiving written communications from school)?

Step 2: Develop outreach strategies to address the underlying issue. For example:

- Make sure that parents receive messages in their native language.

- Make sure that written communications are easy to read, warm, and friendly.

- Figure out how to get messages to parents who are homeless.

- Schedule conferences at flexible times to accommodate parents with conflicting work schedules.

- Provide child care for meetings, conferences, and events.

- See if neighbors or friends can be used as a liaison.

- Determine if meetings can be held in a more convenient, more familiar, more neutral location.

- Arrange for home visits (with appropriate security).

- Make it clear that you value the language, culture, knowledge, and expertise of parents and family members.

Source: Adapted from Swap, 1993.

Before calling a parent about an academic or behavior problem, Sandy always gives her students notice:

I say something like, "I know you want to be treated like an adult, but sometimes we need to work together with mom or dad to ensure your success. We need some help here. We can't solve this alone." I never use the telephone call as a threat or punishment. And I always wait 24 hours before calling. That way, the student can tell the parent that the call is coming (or about how the 75 they said they got on the test was really a 55!). When I talk with parents, I'm really careful about how I phrase things, so that I don't promote a negative reaction. Instead of saying, "Your son is disrupting the class," I'll say something like "We have to help your son control his behavior so that he can learn some chemistry." If the kid is disrespectful, I'll say, "I'm calling you about this because I know you wouldn't approve of this. I know you'd want to hear." In this way, you're conveying the idea that the parent will be supportive of you and that you don't think the kid comes from a family that would approve of such behavior.

During one meeting, I asked the four teachers to share some of the ideas they have for ensuring that telephone contacts with parents are productive. Their responses are listed in the Practical Tips box.

A few additional words of caution are in order. Although it's important to contact parents about serious problems, frequent phone calls about minor misbehaviors can be annoying. Furthermore, the practice can convey the message to both parents and children that the school can't deal with problems that arise; it's like saying, "Wait till your parents find out!"

PRACTICAL TIPS FOR

MAKING PRODUCTIVE TELEPHONE CONTACTS WITH PARENTS

- When the office receives a telephone call for you from a parent, and you're in class, have the secretary ask when would be a good time to call back.

- Even if a call comes during your free period, have the office take the message and say you'll call back. That gives you time to shift gears and prepare for the call. You can check your record book so that you are familiar with the student's progress.

- If a parent is calling with a complaint, try very hard not to get defensive. Listen and try to understand the parent's frustration. Respond by expressing your concern and assuring the parent that you are really committed to finding a solution.

- If a parent calls to complain that a child is upset about something ("He says you're picking on him" or "She says you're embarrassing her in front of the class"), acknowledge the student's perception. Convey your regret that the student has that perception. For example: "Gee, I'm really sorry that she has that perception. What specifically has she said, so that I can figure out what's going on? Help me to understand, because I don't want her to feel that way." Don't start out defensively: "I don't pick on kids."

- For chronic callers (parents who call three times a week) make it clear that it's important for you and the child to work the problem out. Explain that the frequent calls are embarrassing the student.

- If the telephone call is difficult, and there's a danger of your becoming defensive, have another person in the room to help monitor your tone of voice. He or she can tap you on the shoulder or make a face if you begin to get hostile or defensive.

- If a parent is out of control, suggest that you talk again at a later time, so that you both have a chance to calm down.

- If parents ask you to call every week with a report on their child's progress, suggest that they call you instead. (After all, you may have 150 students to think about, while they have only one!) Designate a day and time for them to call (e.g., on Fridays, during your prep period).

It's also important to emphasize that phone calls should not be reserved for problems. As Donnie reminds us:

 Teachers shouldn't just call when there's something bad. It's really important to call parents to give good news, to say "Your kid is really doing well," to tell them about something terrific that happened. Sometimes, when I do that, the student will come in the next day and say, "You called my house! And you didn't say anything bad about me!" And I'll tell them, "I had nothing bad to say!" I'll also let parents know what's coming up, the things that are going on. If you do that, then you've laid the foundation for a good relationship, and parents are more open later on. If you do have to call about a problem, they're less likely to be hostile or defensive.

E-mails and Web Sites

In recent years, more and more teachers have begun using electronic mail and the Internet to facilitate communication with parents. For example, a class Web site can list assignments and due dates, the subject for the week, dates of quizzes and tests, news about current and upcoming events, and requests for supplies or assistance. A Web site can also provide links to related sites that might help students to complete assignments.

Although Sandy doesn't have a class Web site, she does use "ParentConnect," software that allows parents and guardians to visit a password-protected, read-only site to view their children's grades in her online grade book. (Note that parents have access for their child only.) Having grades online makes it easier for parents to track their children's academic progress, but teachers can't assume that all parents have Internet access (or that they use it even if they have it). As Sandy emphasizes, "Teachers still have to take responsibility for calling parents if their kid is not doing well in class."

Sandy and Christina also communicate with parents and students via e-mail. Again, a few words of caution based on their experiences are in order. First, e-mail seems to encourage sloppiness and inaccuracy, so be sure to edit your e-mails for misspellings or grammatical errors. Second, be careful about using e-mail to discuss sensitive issues or problems. E-mail doesn't allow you to convey your message in a calm, quiet tone of voice or to "soften" it with smiles, gestures, or body language; nor can you see or hear parents' reactions. For this reason, e-mail may be more likely to lead to misinterpretations than face-to-face interactions or even phone calls. On the other hand, written messages (whether e-mail or snail mail) enable you to choose your words carefully and deliberately, an advantage you may not have when you're interacting with parents in "real time." Third, don't fire off an e-mail in anger. Wait until you've calmed down and have thought carefully about what you want to say.

This last caution deserves some additional comment. Be prepared for the fact that parents will not always follow this advice and will e-mail you when they are angry or upset about something their child has told them about school. The message may sound angry or even abusive. Understand that the parent sent the message in anger and try not to let the tone detract from dealing with the issue.

Report Cards

Report cards have been the traditional way of communicating with families about a child's progress in school. Unfortunately, they are often not very informative. What exactly does it mean when a student receives a C in Spanish? Is she having problems with vocabulary, with comprehension, or with conversation? Is another student's D in mathematics due to difficulties with problem solving, or is it merely a result of careless computational errors? Because many high schools use computerized report cards, it is not always possible for the teacher to elaborate on grades with a personalized narrative. Donnie tells us:

On our report cards, you can pick from nine little statements, like "the student is disruptive," "comes late," "is doing well," "is working at or above grade level," "has missed tests." But you're only allowed to check two! And they're so impersonal, I'm not sure that they really communicate much of anything.

Another common problem with report cards is timeliness. If you rely solely on report cards to communicate with parents about a student's progress, two months might pass from the time a problem first appears until parents learn about it. In order to avoid this problem, some schools require teachers to send out progress reports midway through each marking period. Specific policies vary from district to district. Sandy explains what happens at her high school:

Progress reports have to be sent out mid–marking period for all seventh- and eighth-graders. In grades 9 through 12, we only have to send home a progress report if a student is in danger of receiving a D or an F for the marking period, but I send them out for other reasons too, like attendance or behavior or for commendable progress. I also tell students that I'm sending a progress report home, and I show it to them. I believe that they have the right to know.

Sometimes, showing students the progress reports encourages them to clean up their act. For example, Edward had a 75 average because he had two assignments missing. When I told him I was sending home a progress report, he asked me to just report the 75 average and leave off the part about the two missing assignments. He said his mother "would kill" him if she found out he wasn't doing his homework consistently. He promised he'd never miss another assignment. I decided he was serious, and so I agreed, but I told him that if she asked, I'd have to tell her. He never missed another assignment.

Although Sandy is conscientious about sending home progress reports, she also believes that any serious problem should be dealt with sooner:

Teachers should not rely on progress reports to tell parents about serious problems. Teachers need to contact parents if a problem develops. All of my students' parents know if their child has a D or an F before progress reports. I send progress reports because I have to, but my parents already know. Relying on progress reports is not very smart, since probably 50 percent of the kids take them out of the mail before their parents ever see them!

Back-to-School Night

For many parents, open house or back-to-school night is the first opportunity to meet you and to see the classroom. It's also the first opportunity *you* have to show parents all the great things you've been doing and to tell them about the plans you have for the future. As Fred says,

> I feel good about what happens in my room, and I want the parents to feel good about what's happening, too. I outline my objectives and the course syllabus; I describe my expectations for kids and for parents, and I talk about what they can expect from me. I usually talk about why I teach history; I give a little propaganda speech about what I'm trying to accomplish and how they can help. But it's always been a fun night. I believe that the parents have to laugh, just like the kids. The bell always rings when I'm halfway through; there's never enough time, but I talk with the parents at the coffee hour afterwards.

If you don't feel quite as enthusiastic as Fred, don't feel bad. Even teachers as experienced as Sandy sometimes feel nervous about back-to-school night. In fact, Sandy tells us:

> I hate back-to-school night! The one good thing is that I always get so nervous that I talk really fast and finish early. That leaves plenty of time for people to ask questions.

As these comments suggest, back-to-school night usually involves a brief presentation to groups of parents who move from room to room, following their children's schedules. This is not always the case, however. In Christina's school, for example, teachers remain in their assigned rooms for 90 minutes, while parents visit teachers in any order they wish for brief, individual conferences. Since the time with each parent is so limited, Christina's goals are simply to attach a face to a name, to give parents a general sense of their children's progress, and to invite them to set up a longer conference. She also displays current class projects, so parents can look them over while they are waiting to see her.

Whatever format your school uses, keep in mind that first impressions *do* matter, so you need to think carefully about how you will orchestrate this event. The Practical Tips box on page 138 contains some guidelines that emerged during my discussions with Sandy, Fred, Donnie, and Christina. (Obviously, some of them apply only if you are giving group presentations.)

Parent–Teacher Conferences

Schools generally schedule one or two formal parent-teacher conferences during the school year. (See Figure 5.3 for Calvin's reaction to the prospect of such a conference.) Interestingly, these meetings are often a source of frustration to both

PRACTICAL TIPS FOR

BACK-TO-SCHOOL NIGHT

- Greet people at the door, introduce yourself, and find out who they are. *Do not assume that the student's last name is the same as the parents' last name, or that both parents have the same last name.*

- Make sure your presentation is succinct and well organized. Parents want to hear about your goals, plans, and philosophy, as well as the curriculum and policies about homework and absences.

- If parents raise issues that are unique to their child, let them know in a sensitive way that the purpose of open house is to describe the general program. Indicate that you're more than happy to discuss their concerns during a private conference. You may want to have a sign-up sheet available for this purpose.

- Listen carefully to questions that parents have. Provide an opportunity for parents to talk about *their* goals and expectations for their children in the coming school year. This can begin the two-way communication that is so crucial for family–school collaboration.

- Provide a sign-up sheet for parents who are able to participate in classroom activities (e.g., as a guest speaker or chaperone on field trips).

- Display the books and materials that are used in your courses.

- If refreshments are being served after the class meetings, go down and join in conversations with parents. Clustering with the other teachers separates you from parents and conveys the idea that there is a professional barrier.

- PREPARE!

teachers and parents. Parents resent the formality of the situation (Lindle, 1989) and find the limited conference period frustrating. As one mother puts it, "Ten minutes is ridiculous, especially when other parents are waiting right outside the door. I need time to tell the teacher about how my child is at home, too" (Lindle, 1989, p. 14).

Calvin and Hobbes   by Bill Watterson

Figure 5.3   Parent–teacher conferences provide a way of communicating with families.

Teachers, too, are sometimes unhappy with these formal conferences. They agree with parents that the brief time allotted often precludes meaningful exchange. Furthermore, teachers complain about the lack of attendance: "The parents you *don't* need to see show up, while the ones you desperately *want* to talk with don't come." Interestingly, Donnie doesn't mind that the parents of good students come to parent conferences:

> If there's a real problem, I've already contacted the parents by the time parent conferences come along. We've already met. So I think it's nice to see the ones whose kids are doing well. It's nice to be able to give positive reports. And parents want reassurance that all is going well.

Before a conference, it's important to prepare carefully. For example, Sandy looks over each student's grades, prints out a student progress sheet using a computerized grading program, notes any trends in academic performance or behavior, and jots down a few key words to use when she's talking to parents. It's also useful to have a few samples of students' work to show parents.

Conferences can be tense—especially if you're meeting with family members for the first time—so our four teachers begin by trying to put parents at ease. They suggest leading with something positive: "Your son is a delight to have in class" or "Your daughter appears to be really interested in the topics we've been studying." You should be aware, however, that immigrant Latino parents (and others from collectivistic cultures) may be uncomfortable hearing extended praise of their children, since praise singles a person out from the group (Trumbull, Rothstein-Fisch, Greenfield, & Quiroz, 2001).

Next, problems or weaknesses can be broached—not as character flaws ("She's lazy"), but as problems that need to be solved ("She's having difficulty getting her assignments in on time. What can we do about this?"). Donnie puts it this way:

> I might tell parents, "We have a problem. Your son's performance is going down. Can you help me to understand? Is there anything going on that I should know about?" I stress that we have to work together. I explain that if I understand more about the home situation, then I'll know better how to approach the student. Maybe there's been a death in the family, or the father moved out, or a move is imminent. All this helps me to be more effective.

Sandy also tries to enlist parents' assistance in dealing with problems; however, she cautions teachers not to make demands that are impossible for parents to carry out:

> Don't say things like, "You have to get your child to participate more in class." Be reasonable. If you're talking about a 17-year-old senior, what are the chances that a parent can do that? On the other hand, you *can* say, "Joanne is very quiet in class. Is this her normal behavior?"

Although they try to provide parents with substantive information, our teachers emphasize the need *to listen*. All four teachers always allow time for parents to ask questions and to express their concerns, and they solicit parents' suggestions. A conference should be a two-way conversation, not a monologue. *It's also critical not to assume that poor parents, uneducated parents, or parents with limited English proficiency have nothing of value to offer.* One mother in the study by Finders and Lewis (1994) expressed her frustration this way:

> Whenever I go to school, they want to tell me what to do at home. They want to tell me how to raise my kid. They never ask what I think. They never ask me anything.

Kottler (1994) stresses the importance of encouraging families whose first language is not English to help you understand their children's educational and cultural background. For example, you might ask about past educational experiences, if their son or daughter is experiencing any cultural conflicts, what their educational goals for their child are, whether English is used at home, and if there are any special needs or customs you need to take into consideration.

You also need to be sensitive to cultural differences in communication styles. Cultures shape the nature of verbal interaction, providing norms for who can initiate conversation, whether it's all right to interrupt, and how long to pause between a question and its answer (Swap, 1993). If these norms are not shared, participants may feel uncomfortable. The following example of conversation between Athabaskan Indians and whites in Alaska illustrates how misunderstanding can arise because of different communication styles:

> [A] white speaker often will ask a question, then pause, waiting for the Indian speaker to reply; then, when it appears the listener has nothing to say, the white speaker will speak again. The Indian, who wishes to reply, but is accustomed to longer pauses between speakers, is not given an adequate opportunity to speak.
>
> On the other hand, when Indian speakers do have the floor, they are interrupted frequently because they take what are perceived by whites to be "lengthy" pauses between thoughts. As an Athabaskan woman said to one of us, "While you're thinking about what you're going to say, they're already talking." Hence, Indian speakers often say very little and white speakers seem to do all the talking. (Nelson-Barber & Meier, 1990, p. 3, as cited in Swap, 1993, p. 91)

In addition, you need to recognize that different cultures hold different views about appropriate classroom behavior. For example, a European-American teacher may encourage students to participate actively in classroom discussions, to voice their opinions, and to ask questions. In contrast, some Latino and Asian-American parents may expect their children to be quiet and obedient and not to contradict the teacher or ask questions (Scarcella, 1990).

It's also important to understand that Latino immigrant parents may be primarily interested in the child's social and moral development. As Trumbull, Rothstein-Fisch, Greenfield, and Quiroz (2001) explain:

> [A] dominant (although not always welcome) theme these parents introduce into parent–teacher conferences is children's behavior. . . . [They ask], "Como se porta mi hijo/a?" ("How is my son/daughter behaving?") The teacher may try to direct the conversation toward the child's academic achievement, only to be asked again

about the child's behavior. Teachers may encounter similar questions from Vietnamese-American or Japanese-American parents.... (pp. 17–18)

Finally, our teachers stress the importance of not closing doors to further communication. If a conference is not going well, you might suggest another meeting, perhaps with the department supervisor or a guidance counselor on hand to mediate the discussion.

Some schools have started to experiment with three-way conferences that include the teacher, the parent or guardian, and the student (Bailey & Guskey, 2001). First, all participants, beginning with the student, share their perceptions of the strengths demonstrated in the student's work. They then discuss two areas on which the student needs to work, outline goals for the future, and agree on the kinds of support that each party will provide. Finally, the teacher answers questions and summarizes agreements.

Recent research indicates that the three-way conference has distinct advantages over the traditional parent–teacher conference. A study by Minke and Anderson (2003), for example, compared traditional parent–teacher conferences with conferences that included students as participants ("family–school conferences"). Families chosen to participate in the project had children with mild learning or behavior problems. Two primary findings emerged with respect to traditional conferences. First, both teachers and parents agreed that conferences are important opportunities for an exchange of information; second, both groups approached conferences with trepidation. Parents used words like worried, nervous, overwhelmed, angry, and apprehensive to describe their emotions, and teachers described their feelings of "exhaustion and relief" when conference days were over (p. 59). In contrast, both parents and teachers felt that the family–school conference model increased trust and communication and provided greater opportunities to learn about each other and the child. Adults were particularly impressed by students' "unexpectedly mature behavior" and their "honest, insightful comments about their own learning" (p. 60). Indeed, "Teachers often noted that the child was the first one to bring up 'bad news,' which teachers saw as relieving them of a worrisome burden and greatly reducing parental defensiveness" (p. 60). Evidence also suggested that family–school conferences can be conducted in the same 15–20 minutes usually allotted to routine, two-party conferences. It should be noted, however, that three-way conferences like this require training and careful preparation. (See Bailey and Guskey, 2001, for practical strategies and suggestions.)

PAUSE AND REFLECT

Teachers often complain about the fact that the parents you don't need to see are the ones who come to Back-to-School Night and to parent-teacher conferences, while the parents you really do need to see are the ones who don't show up. Review the possible reasons for parents' absences at these events. Then think of three specific actions you might take to reach "hard-to-reach" parents.

Family Involvement in School

At the middle and high school level, most family involvement in school consists of attendance at student performances, athletic events, or other programs. Family involvement may also take place "behind-the-scenes"; for example, parents may engage in fund-raising activities, interview prospective teachers and administrators, prepare breakfast on "Teacher Appreciation Day," participate on committees developing discipline and attendance policies, and chaperone social events.

Participation in classroom activities is far less common, but involving even a few parents can provide considerable support and enrich the curriculum. When Fred's Contemporary World Cultures classes study religions, for example, parents of different faiths come in to explain their religious beliefs; in his Institute for Political and Legal Education (IPLE) class, parents who are lawyers sometimes share their expertise; and his history classes may be visited by survivors of Nazi concentration camps. In Sandy's chemistry classes, parents speak on scientific or environmental issues and parents who are faculty members at a nearby university have set up tours of the chemistry labs there. Donnie holds a "mini-career day," when successful former students share their career experiences and communicate the message, "You can do this too." In Christina's journalism classes, parents, friends of parents, former students, and local contacts speak about their careers as journalists.

If you decide to invite parents to participate in your classroom, you need to think carefully about how to recruit them. Sometimes parents don't volunteer simply because they're not sure what would be expected or how they could contribute. Back-to-school night offers a good opportunity to make a direct, in-person appeal and to explain the various ways parents can assist.

If you're teaching in a district where there has been little parent involvement in school, special efforts will be needed to change the situation. At Donnie's high school, a committee has been established to consider ways of making the school more "parent-friendly." As a result of the committee's efforts, teams of teachers have visited neighborhood churches on Sunday mornings to invite parents to the high school. As Donnie puts it,

Parents were complaining that they don't feel welcome. Well, the point of these trips is to say, "We want you to visit. This is *your* school; come in and see what's going on. If you can, volunteer, work in the library, help kids with homework. We welcome you.

Parents of Youngsters with Special Needs

Since 1975, when Congress enacted Public Law 94-142 mandating that "all handicapped children have available to them . . . a free appropriate public education which emphasizes special education and related services," parents of children with disabilities have had a legal mandate to participate in the planning of their children's educational program. Since then, P. L. 94-142 has been amended and renamed the Individuals with Disabilities Education Act (IDEA), but the essence of the law remains the same. Under IDEA, parents are required to be members of the team that creates the student's Individualized Education Program (IEP), specifying *educational goals, services to be provided* (e.g., physical, occupational, or speech therapy, transportation, counseling), and *placement* (e.g., special school, self-contained special education class in the neighborhood school, general education class, etc.). Parents also have the right to see their children's records, to be informed prior to any change in placement or services, to initiate a due process hearing in the case of a disagreement with the school, and to appeal decisions through the court system.

The IDEA requires children with disabilities to be educated in the "least restrictive environment"—meaning that, whenever possible, they should be in classrooms with their nondisabled peers. In recent years, this principle has gained tremendous momentum. Advocates for "inclusion" have argued that the regular classroom benefits children with disabilities academically because they are held to higher expectations and are exposed to more stimulating content. Advocates also point to the social benefits that occur when students with disabilities can make friends with youngsters from their own neighborhoods and can observe peers behaving in a socially appropriate manner. (See Chapter 12 for additional information on inclusion.)

Given the increase in inclusion and the fact that the IDEA mandates parental participation, you are likely to have contact with parents of children with disabilities and, possibly, to be involved in the annual IEP meetings (at which a teacher must be present). But Sandy, who has an emotionally disturbed student in her class this year, cautions teachers not to wait for the formal, mandated meetings, or even for the regularly scheduled parent conferences:

> Anytime I have a student with an IEP, I go to the case manager right away and say, "Tell me about this kid." Then I ask them to set up a time for us to meet with the parents, usually in the first week and a half of school.
>
> This shows parents that you're aware of the IEP; it gives them a sense of relief and confidence. They know that the IEP isn't just a piece of paper, that the teacher is already thinking about how to modify the course for the student. It starts you off on the right track, establishes the right tone.
>
> At our initial meeting, we talk a lot about the IEP. You've got to remember that IEPs are open to interpretation, and that needs to be discussed. For example, an IEP may say that the student can have more time for tests. What does that mean? Is that an indefinite amount of time? Ten minutes? What?
>
> I also want parents to educate me about their kid. This year, with an emotionally disturbed boy, it was important for me to know what sets him off. What will be stressful for him that might result in an outburst? Every kid is different, and I don't like surprises if I can avoid them. Sometimes it's as simple as "don't pair him with another male."

In addition to a meeting like this early in the year, Sandy keeps in close contact with parents throughout the year. Sometimes parents want a weekly report, and Sandy is happy to comply; however, she asks them to take the responsibility for calling or e-mailing: "With so many kids, it's just too hard for me to remember."

Family Involvement in Learning Activities at Home

Epstein's fourth type of involvement refers to the ways families can assist their children's learning at home. At the secondary level, this kind of involvement often creates considerable anxiety for parents. As Donnie mentioned earlier, some parents are scared off by the subject matter. Sandy agrees:

> At the elementary level, parents often help with homework, read to their children, and monitor their studying. But at the high school level, the first thing out of a parent's mouth is "I can't do calculus. I can't do chemistry. There's no way I can help."

Parents are not the only ones who wonder how they can help with their teenagers' homework assignments. Some teachers also question whether parents can really be useful, given their "highly variable instructional skills" (Becker & Epstein, 1982, p. 86). Indeed, in a survey of teachers' attitudes toward parental involvement in learning activities at home (Becker & Epstein, 1982) about half of the 3,700 respondents had serious doubts about the success of such efforts. Furthermore, some teachers believe that it's unfair to ask already overworked parents to assume teaching responsibilities.

Although our four teachers acknowledge that parents may not have familiarity with the subject matter, they are convinced that parents can play an extremely important role by monitoring their children's schoolwork, providing support and encouragement, and setting limits. Fred tells us:

> I find that parents really want to help their kids, but they often don't have a clue about what to do. They're really receptive to suggestions. Sometimes I suggest that parents help by checking the spelling on their kids' papers. Maybe I'll suggest that they check that the kid has done the homework. Maybe I'll explain the requirements for a research paper, and suggest they check to see the requirements are met. I'll suggest they ask to see the kid's papers. A lot of times kids put their papers in the garbage and never show them to their parents.

Similarly, Sandy tells parents not to worry if they don't know chemistry; they can still help to structure their child's environment:

> If a kid is having trouble with chemistry, 99 percent of the time, the problem is not with the *subject,* but with the *time spent* on the subject. Parents can monitor the time spent on homework. They can say, "Doing chemistry in front of the TV is not working." They can say, "You have to do your homework before you go out." They can suggest that their child call a friend if they're having trouble. They can make sure that their child comes in for help after school. I'll tell them, "I want your child in here two days a week so I can help with the chemistry. But you have to see that they get here."

Some recent research reinforces the importance of parents monitoring their children's schoolwork and setting limits. A survey of middle school students' homework practices (Xu & Corno, 2003) found that family members were especially helpful in arranging the environment (e.g., finding a quiet area, creating space for the child to work, turning off the television) and assisting children to control their emotions (e.g., calming a frustrated youngster, providing encouragement when a child is upset). Interestingly, the homework helper's educational level was unrelated to effective homework assistance. As Xu and Corno conclude,

> Our study suggests that the kind of direction parents or family members give to children matters more than if the parents or family members have higher education. . . . Families of all kinds can play a role in promoting responsible completion of homework by children through and beyond the elementary years. (p. 515)

It is important to recognize that this view of the parental role may conflict with some families' beliefs about the importance of independence and self-sufficiency. A mother in the study by Finders and Lewis (1994) explains why she stays out of her daughter's schooling:

> It's her education, not mine. I've had to teach her to take care of herself. I work nights, so she's had to get up and get herself ready for school. I'm not going to be there all the time. She's gotta do it. She's a tough cookie. . . . She's almost an adult, and I get the impression that they want me to walk her through her work. And it's not that I don't care either. I really do. I think it's important, but I don't think it's my place. (p. 52)

As Finders and Lewis (1994) comment, "This mother does not lack concern for her child. In her view, independence is essential for her daughter's success" (p. 52).

A program called "Teachers Involve Parents in Schoolwork" (TIPS), developed by Joyce Epstein, colleagues, and teachers (1995), features homework assignments that require students to involve family members with specific conversations or other interactions. For example, in math, middle school students might have to ask family members for their shoe sizes or height and then compute the averages; in science, students might conduct a simple experiment using liquids of different thickness and then discuss the results with a family partner. TIPS assignments are assigned once a week or twice a month; students are given several days to complete the activity (to allow time to involve family); and parents are expected to provide feedback about the activity's effectiveness. Although there is limited research on the impact of TIPS on family involvement and achievement, results are encouraging. For example, Van Voorhis (2003) found that sixth- and eighth-grade students completing TIPS interactive assignments in science reported significantly higher levels of family involvement and turned in more accurate assignments than students completing noninteractive assignments. TIPS students also earned significantly higher science report card grades.

An example of a literacy assignment appears in Figure 5.4. Additional examples can be found on the Web site for the National Network of Partnership Schools. (See the list of organizational resources at the end of the chapter.) Another new and useful resource on TIPS is a CD that includes over 500 activities for the elementary and middle grades, with prototype assignments in math, language art, and science (Van Voorhis & Epstein, 2002).

 PAUSE AND REFLECT

Homework is a controversial subject. For example, in *The End of Homework: How Homework Disrupts Families, Overburdens Children, and Limits Learning,* Etta Kralovec and John Buell argue that homework actually promotes discrimination. Children who are able to get support and assistance from their families (the "haves") can surge ahead while those who come from families that are unable to help them (the "have-nots") fall further and further behind. What do you think about this issue?

Student's Name_____ Date_____

TIPS: Hairy Tales

Dear Family Partner,
In language arts I am working on using information gathered from others to write explanations. For this assignment, I am comparing today's hairstyles with those of the past. I hope that you enjoy this activitiy with me. This assignment is due _____.

Sincerely,

_____
Student's signature

Family Interview

FIND A FAMILY MEMBER TO INTERVIEW.
Who is it?
Ask:
1) In what decade were you born? (1960s, 1970s, etc.)_____

2) What is one hairstyle that was popular when you were my age?

For boys:_____

For girls:_____

3) What hairstyle did you have when you were my age?_____

4) Did your family agree with your choice of hairstyle?_____

5) What is your favorite current hairstyle and why?_____

6) What is your least favorite current hairstyle and why? _____

_____

First Draft
Use the information from your interview to write a paragraph about hairstyles. Remember to:
• Give a paragraph a title.
• Be sure all of your sentences related to your topic.
• Use descriptive words to help explain the ideas.
• If you compare hairstyles, tell how they are alike and how they are different.

Ask your family member to show you a picture of a hairstyle from the past. Draw a picture of the hairstyle here.

Write your paragraph here

Title:_____

_____
_____
_____
_____
_____
_____
_____

Read your paragraph aloud to your family partner. Revise or add sentences, as needed.

Extension Activity

Select another topic for comparison—for example, clothing styles, ways to have fun, or rules at home or school. What topic did you choose?_____

Next to each "Q" line, write a questions about your topic. Use your questions to interview a family member. Write the family member's answer next to each "A" line.
1. Q: _____
   A: _____
2. Q: _____
   A: _____
3. Q: _____
   A: _____

Home-to-School Connection

Dear Parent/Guardian,
Your comments about your child's work in this activity are important. Please write YES or NO for each statement:
___My child understood the homework and was able to discuss it.
___My child and I enjoyed this activity.
___This assignment helps me understand what my child is learning in language arts..
Other comments:_____
_____
_____

Epstein, J.L., Salinas, K.C., Jackson, V., & Van Voorhis, F.E. (revised 2000). Teachers Involve Parents in Schoolwork (TIPS) Interactive Homework for the Middle Grades. Baltimore: Center on School, Family, and Community Partnerships, Johns Hopkins University. (Adapted for the elementary grades.)

Figure 5.4   TIPS Literacy Homework Activity for the Middle Grades

CONCLUDING COMMENTS

This chapter has described different ways that teachers can reach out to families. The suggestions vary considerably in terms of how common they are and how much time and energy they demand. As you get to know your students and their family situations, you will be able to decide which practices are most appropriate and most feasible. Of course, you need to be realistic: As a beginning teacher, you may have to delay major efforts to facilitate communication and collaboration with families.

Nonetheless, you need to remember that family involvement is key to students' success. This is an age of single parents, of mothers who work outside of the home, of grandparents, aunts, and neighbors who care for children, of increasing numbers of families whose cultural backgrounds differ from that of most teachers. Family–school collaboration has never been more difficult—but it has never been more essential.

SUMMARY

This chapter began by discussing the benefits to working closely with families. It then outlined the challenges to family–teacher cooperation and stressed that teachers' attitudes and practices—not the educational level, marital status, or workplace of parents—determine whether families become productively involved in their children's schooling. Finally, the chapter presented strategies for overcoming the challenges and for fostering collaboration between families and schools.

Benefits of Working Closely with Families

- Knowing about a student's home situation provides insight into the student's classroom behavior.
- When families understand what you are trying to achieve, they can provide valuable support and assistance.
- Families can help to develop and implement strategies for changing behavior.
- Parent volunteers can provide assistance in the classroom and school.

Challenges to Family–Teacher Cooperation

- Teachers are sometimes reluctant to involve families in schooling because of
    The extra time and energy that are required.
    Their perceptions that families are too overburdened, apathetic, and irresponsible or that they lack the skills needed.
    A desire to protect their "turf" and avoid parental scrutiny.
- Parents are sometimes reluctant to become involved in schooling because
    They are overburdened by the demands of work.
    They have unhappy memories of school.
    They believe schooling should be left to the experts.
    They feel guilty if their children are having problems.
    They find schools intimidating and threatening places.
    They do not see involvement in school as part of their parental role.
- The changing nature of the family means that
    The number of single-parent families has increased.
    The "stay-at-home" mother is vanishing.
    The significant adults in children's lives may not be parents, but grandparents, neighbors, aunts, or uncles.
    Many children come from non–English-speaking homes.

Fostering Collaboration between Families and Schools

- Schools can assist families in carrying out their basic obligations by providing parent education, establishing parent support groups, and referring families to community and state agencies.

- Teachers need to communicate about school programs and students' progress through phone calls, Web sites and e-mails, report cards, progress reports, and face-to-face interactions (e.g., back-to-school night, parent conferences).
- Family members can serve as volunteers in classrooms and schools.
- Families can assist their children at home on learning activities:
  Supervising homework.
  Providing encouragement and support.
  Setting limits.

As a beginning teacher, you have to decide what you can realistically accomplish with respect to communication and collaboration with parents. Nonetheless, you need to remember that family involvement is critical to students' success. In this age of single parents, mothers who work outside the home, and students who come from diverse cultural backgrounds, meaningful family–school collaboration has never been more difficult, but it has never been more essential.

ACTIVITIES FOR SKILL BUILDING AND REFLECTION

In Class

Working in small groups, read the following vignettes (one per group) and do the following:

- Discuss the information provided in the vignette.
- Make a list of other information you might like to get and how you might get it.
- Make a list of possible ways you might address the issue aside from talking to the parent/guardian/family. What might some underlying issues be?
- Think about what you will do to prepare for the conference.
- Decide how you will structure the meeting so that you can state your information in a productive way without being defensive.
- Role-play the conversation that you might have with the family member about this issue.

Vignette 1

You have stressed that research scientists work in teams, and you use a lot of cooperative learning activities in your seventh-grade general science class. Although students sit in rows, their seats are assigned so that they can quickly turn their desks around to form four-person "research groups" that are heterogeneous in terms of race, ethnicity, gender, and achievement level. At parent conferences, the father of a Pakistani girl in your class requests that you place his daughter in an all-girl group. As he explains, his culture frowns upon girls and boys sitting together, and he was extremely unhappy when he learned about his daughter's seat assignment and the composition of her research team.

Vignette 2

Last week you conducted a parent conference with Mrs. Lewis, Joey's mother. During the conference you described his disruptive behaviors and what you've done to deal with them. You also explained that he is in danger of failing your class because he rarely does homework and has gotten poor grades on most quizzes and tests. Mrs. Lewis seemed to accept and understand the information; however, the next day, an irate *Mr.* Lewis called. He told you that he had never seen his wife so upset and that he wants another conference as soon as possible to get to the bottom of the problem. He also intimated that the problem might be due to a personality conflict between you and his son. Although the phone call caught you off-guard, you scheduled the conference for two days later.

Vignette 3

You have a student in your tenth-grade class who is failing to complete her homework. She is an academically competent student in class; she does most of her class work and is friendly and easygoing. You have asked the student repeatedly to do her homework, yet she comes in almost daily with little or none of it complete. When you ask her why she has not done the work, she answers by saying, "I don't know." You have sent two letters home, and left one phone message for her family. Her mother shows up unexpectedly at the end of a school day, demands to speak with you, and tells you that her daughter is complaining that you are picking on her and do not like her.

Vignette 4

Paul is an African American student in your sixth-grade class. You know his mother is very active on the PTA and is quite involved in school and district politics. Unfortunately, Paul is not doing well in class. He is an excellent reader and writer and he is quite intelligent, but you have documented his lack of class work, and you have anecdotal notes referring to his negative comments about the kinds of assignments you assign the class. He is getting more and more disengaged and disrespectful of you. You feel well prepared for the parent conference, because you have very thorough records and notes. When Paul's parents come to the conference, you carefully lay out your case. His father responds by explaining that in their home they encourage their children to question what they are taught and not to believe information just because it is presented in class. He explains that many students of color disengage from school because they are not represented in the Eurocentric curriculum. Paul's mother then suggests that in order to fully engage your students you need to learn about their history and culture. She even goes on to suggest that as a European American teacher you should listen to Paul's criticisms of your assignments and use that as a way to examine and evaluate what is essentially a biased curriculum.

On Your Own

1. In getting ready for the school year, you have decided to send a letter to the family of each student in your classes. The point of the letter is to introduce yourself, describe the curriculum, highlight a few upcoming projects, and explain your expectations in terms of homework, behavior, and attendance.

    Select a subject that you might actually teach (e.g., American History, Algebra I, Spanish, Home Economics I, World Literature, Physical Education, etc.), and write such a letter. As you write, think about the need to create a warm tone, to be clear and organized, to avoid educational jargon, and to stimulate interest about school.

2. Anita is extremely "forgetful" about doing homework assignments. She has received innumerable zeros and regularly has to stay for detention to make up the work. You have called her mother to report on this behavior and to ask for assistance, but her mother does not want to get involved. As she puts it, "I've got all I can do to handle her at home. What she does with school work is your responsibility!"

    Interview two experienced teachers about what they would do in a case like this, and then formulate your own course of action based on what you learn.

For Your Portfolio

Demonstrate your capacity to communicate with families by including two or three artifacts (e.g., newsletters; interactive homework; requests for parental help with homework; invitations to class events; student award certificates; checksheets to be used at parent conferences).

FOR FURTHER READING

Bailey, J. M., & Guskey, T. R. (2001). *Implementing student-led conferences.* Thousand Oaks, CA: Corwin Press, Inc.

    In a student-led conference, students take the responsibility of communicating their progress, while teachers serve as facilitators. This very helpful book provides suggestions for preparing, conducting, and evaluating student-led conferences. It includes sample conference announcements and formats, portfolio planners, reproducible letters, and parent and student response forms.

Delgado-Gaitan, C. (2004). *Involving Latino families in schools: Raising student achievement through home-school partnerships.* Thousand Oaks, CA: Corwin Press.

    Concha Delgado-Gaitan provides strategies for including Latino parents in the goal of increasing student achievement. She stresses three conditions of increased parental participation: connecting to families, sharing information with parents, and supporting continued parental involvement. Among the topics examined are Latino families' aspirations for their children; the communication systems needed between schools and Latino families; and techniques to foster Latino parent involvement.

Epstein, J., Sanders, M. G., Simon, B. S., Salinas, K. C., Jansorn, N. R., Van Voorhis, F. L. (2002). *School, family, and community partnerships: Your handbook for action,* 2nd ed. Thousand Oaks, CA: Corwin Press, Inc.

    This handbook provides a wealth of information on the six types of involvement, with "stories from the field" to show how schools are actually using the framework to implement partnership programs. It stresses the importance of taking an Action Team Approach and provides practical strategies for conducting workshops and presentations, implementing interactive homework, organizing volunteers, and strengthening and evaluating partnership programs.

Trumbull, E., Rothstein-Fisch, C., Greenfield, P. M., & Quiroz, B. (2001). *Bridging cultures between home and school: A guide for teachers.* Mahwah, NJ: Lawrence Erlbaum Associates.

    Researchers and teachers involved in the Bridging Cultures Project explain the ways that the individualistic values of American schools can conflict with the more collectivistic values of Latino students' home cultures. They provide research-based strategies for improving home–school relationships with immigrant Latino families.

ORGANIZATIONAL RESOURCES

The National Network of Partnership Schools (Johns Hopkins University, Center on School, Family, and Community Partnerships, 3003 North Charles Street, Baltimore, MD 21218).

NPPS provides information on implementing comprehensive, goal-oriented programs of school, family, and community partnerships. Check out the interactive homework assignments (TIPS) and the collections of "Promising Partnership Practices" at their Web site (www.partnershipschools.org).

REFERENCES

Bailey, J. M., & Guskey, T. R. (2001). *Implementing student-led conferences.* Thousand Oaks, CA: Corwin Press, Inc.

Becher, R. M. (1984). *Parent involvement: A review of research and principles of successful practice.* Washington, D.C.: National Institute of Education.

Becker, H. J., & Epstein, J. L. (1982). Parent involvement: A survey of teacher practices. *The Elementary School Journal, 83*(2), 85–102.

Children's Defense Fund (2004). *The state of America's children yearbook.* Washington, D.C.: Children's Defense Fund.

Chrispeels, J. H. & Rivero, E. (April 2000). Engaging Latino families for student success: Understanding the process and impact of providing training to parents. Paper presented at the Annual Meeting of the American Educational Research Association, New Orleans.

Cushner, K., McClelland, A., & Safford, P. (2000). *Human diversity in education: An integrative approach,* 3rd ed. Boston: McGraw-Hill.

Davies, A., Cameron, C., Politano, C., & Gregory, K. (1992). *Together is better: Collaborative assessment, evaluation and reporting.* Winnipeg, MB, Canada: Peguis Publishers.

Delgado-Gaitan, C. (1992). School matters in the Mexican-American home: Socializing children to education. *American Educational Research Journal, 29*(3), 495–513.

Eccles, J. S., & Harold, R. D. (1993). Parent–school involvement during the early adolescent years. *Teachers College Record, 94*(3), 568–587.

Epstein, J. (1984). *Effects on parents of teacher practices in parent involvement.* Baltimore: Johns Hopkins University, Center for Social Organization of Schools.

Epstein, J. L. (1988). How do we improve programs for parent involvement? *Educational Horizons,* 58–59.

Epstein, J. (2001). *School, family, and community partnerships: Preparing educators and improving schools.* Boulder, Co: Westview Press.

Epstein, J. L., & Becker, H. J. (1982). Teachers' reported practices of parent involvement: Problems and possibilities. *The Elementary School Journal, 83*(2), 103–113.

Epstein, J. L., & Dauber, S. L. (1991). School programs and teacher practices of parent involvement in inner-city elementary and middle schools. *The Elementary School Journal, 91*(3), 289–305.

Epstein, J. L., & Van Voorhis, F. L. (2001). More than minutes: Teachers' roles in designing homework. *Educational Psychologist, 36,* 181–194.

Epstein, J. L., Sanders, M. G., Simon, B. S., Salinas, K. C., Jansorn, N. R., & Van Voorhis, F. L. (2002). *School, family, and community partnerships: Your handbook for action,* 2nd ed. Thousand Oaks, CA: Corwin Press.

Finders, M., & Lewis, C. (1994). Why some parents don't come to school. *Educational Leadership, 51*(8), 50–54.

Fuller, M. L., & Olsen, G. (1998). *Home–school relations: Working successfully with parents and families.* Boston: Allyn and Bacon.

Greenwood, G. E., & Hickman, C. W. (1991). Research and practice in parent involvement: Implications for teacher education. *The Elementary School Journal, 91*(3), 279–288.

Griffith, J. (1998). The relation of school structure and social environment to parent involvement in elementary schools. *The Elementary School Journal, 99*(1), 53–80.

Gutman, L. M., & McLoyd, V. G. (2000). Parents' management of their children's education within the home, at school, and in the community: An examination of African-American families living in poverty. *The Urban Review, 32*(1), 2000.

Hayes, T. F., Lipsky, C., McCully, T., Rickard, D., Sipson, P., & Wicker, K. (1985). *EPIC—Effective parenting information for children.* Buffalo, NY: EPIC.

Haynes, N. M., Comer, J. P., & Hamilton-Lee, M. (1989). School climate enhancement through parent involvement. *Journal of School Psychology, 27,* 87–90.

Henderson, A. T., & Berla, N. (Eds.) (1996). *A new generation of evidence: The family is critical to student achievement.* Washington, D.C.: National Committee for Citizens in Education. Eric Document Reproduction Service No. ED 375 968.

Heuveline, P. (2005). *Estimating the proportion of marriages that end in divorce.* A research brief prepared for the Council on Contemporary Families. (Available online at www.contemporaryfamilies.org.)

Hodgkinson, H. (1985). *All one system: Demographics of education, kindergarten through graduate school.* Washington, D.C.: Institute for Educational Leadership.

Hoover-Dempsey, K. V., Bassler, O. T., & Brissie, J. S. (1987). Parent involvement: Contributions of teacher efficacy, school socioeconomic status, and other school characteristics. *American Educational Research Journal, 24*(3), 417–435.

Hoover-Dempsey, K. V., & Sandler, H. M. (1997). Why do parents become involved in their children's education? *Review of Educational Research, 67*(1), 3–42.

Kids Count Data Book. (2005). Baltimore, MD: Annie E. Casey Foundation. (Available online at www.aecf.org/kidscount/kc_pubs.htm.)

Kottler, E. (1994). *Children with limited English: Teaching strategies for the regular classroom.* Thousand Oaks, CA: Corwin Press.

Kralovec, E., & Buell, J. (2000). *The end of homework: How homework disrupts families, overburdens children, and limits learning.* Boston: Beacon Press.

Lemlech, J. K. (1988). *Classroom management: Methods and techniques for elementary and secondary teachers.* New York: Longman.

Lightfoot, S. L. (1978). *Worlds apart: Relationships between families and schools.* New York: Basic Books.

Lindeman, B. (2001). Reaching out to immigrant parents. *Educational Leadership, 58*(6), 62–66.

Lindle, J. C. (1989). What do parents want from principals and teachers? *Educational Leadership, 47*(2), 12–14.

Lopez, G. R. (2001). The value of hard work: Lessons on parent involvement from an (im)migrant household. *Harvard Educational Review, 71*(3), 416–437.

Minke, K. M., & Anderson, K. J. (2003). Restructuring routine parent-teacher conferences: The family-school conference model. *The Elementary School Journal, 104*(6), 49–69.

Nelson-Barber, S., & Meier, T. (1990, Spring). Multicultural context a key factor in teaching. *Academic Connections,* Office of Academic Affairs, The College Board, 1–5, 9–11.

Rioux, J. W., & Berla, N. (1993). *Innovations in parent and family involvement.* Princeton Junction, NJ: Eye on Education.

Sanders, M. G., & Lewis, K. C. (2005). Building bridges toward excellence: Community involvement in high school. *High School Journal, 88*(3), 1-9.

Scarcella, R. (1990). *Teaching language minority students in the multicultural classroom.* Upper Saddle River, NJ: Prentice Hall Regents.

Simon, B. S. (2004). High school outreach and family involvement. *Social Psychology of Education, 7,* 185-209.

Swap, S. M. (1993). *Developing home-school partnerships: From concepts to practice.* New York: Teachers College Press.

Trumbull, E., Rothstein-Fisch, C., Greenfield, P. M., & Quiroz, B. (2001). *Bridging cultures between home and school: A guide for teachers.* Mahwah, NJ: Lawrence Erlbaum Associates.

Van Voorhis, F. L. (2003). Interactive homework in middle school: Effects on family involvement and science achievement. *Journal of Educational Research, 96*(6), 323-338.

Van Voorhis, F. L., & Epstein, J. L. (2002). *Teachers involve parents in schoolwork: Interactive homework CD.* Baltimore: Johns Hopkins University Center on School, Family, and Community Partnerships.

Walde, A. C., & Baker, K. (1990). How teachers view the parents' role in education. *Phi Delta Kappan, 72*(4), 319-320, 322.

Weiss, H. B., Mayer, E., Kreider, H., Vaughan, M., Dearing, E., Hencke, R., & Pinto, K. (2003). Making it work: Low-income working mothers' involvement in their children's education. *American Educational Research Journal, 40*(4), 879-901.

Xu, J., & Corno, L. (2003). Family help and homework management reported by middle school students. *The Elementary School Journal, 103*(5), 503-517.

Making the Most of Classroom Time

On the first day of school, the academic year seems to stretch out endlessly. If you're a beginning teacher, you may wonder how you'll ever fill all the hours of school that lie ahead—especially if you're not even certain what you're going to do *tomorrow.* And yet, as the days go by, you may begin to feel that there's never enough time to accomplish all you need to do. With assemblies, fire drills, announcements over the intercom, standardized testing, snow days, holidays, and clerical tasks, the hours available for instruction seem far fewer than they did at first. Indeed, by the end of the year, you may view time as a precious resource—not something that has to be filled (or killed), but something that must be conserved and used wisely. (Of course, your students may not share this view—as Figure 6.1 illustrates!)

This chapter discusses issues of time and time management. Guiding the chapter is the premise that the wise use of time will maximize opportunities for learning and minimize opportunities for disruption. First, we look at the amount of school time that is actually available for teaching and learning. Then we consider

Calvin and Hobbes

by Bill Watterson

Figure 6.1   Calvin doesn't agree that time passes quickly in classrooms.
Source: Calvin and Hobbes © Watterson. Reprinted with permission of
Universal Press Syndicate. All rights reserved.

strategies for using classroom time efficiently, focusing on three complementary approaches—maintaining activity flow, minimizing transition time, and holding students accountable. Finally, we examine block scheduling, a reform effort that replaces the traditional 42- or 50-minute period with fewer, longer classes of 85 to 90 minutes.

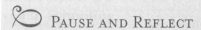 PAUSE AND REFLECT

Keeping in mind that the average student spends 1,080 hours per year in school (180 days × 6 hours per day), estimate either the number of hours or the percent of time that students are actually involved in productive learning (i.e., they are engaging in meaningful, appropriate academic tasks). Then read on to see what researchers have calculated and find out if you are on target.

HOW MUCH TIME IS THERE, ANYWAY?

Although this seems like a straightforward question, the answer is not so simple. In fact, the answer depends on the kind of time you're talking about (Karweit, 1989). Most states mandate a school year of approximately 180 days. Let's suppose that you're teaching in a school that has divided each of these days into 42-minute periods. This amounts to 126 hours of *mandated time* for each of your classes. But students are absent, and special assembly programs are scheduled; snowstorms cause delayed openings, and parent conferences require early closings. Factors like these immediately reduce the time you have for teaching, so the *time available for instruction* can be substantially less than mandated time. Listen to the reflections of a student teacher who has learned to deal with the constant interruptions and cancelations:

> *"Well, at least you're learning to be flexible!" If I heard that once, I heard it a million times. I believe every teacher that I've had contact with this semester has made this statement to me. A record snowfall, proficiency testing, marine biology field trips, half-day inservice days, pep rallies, assemblies.... The actual amount of time I have had a full class of students ... for more than two consecutive days is minimal. Nowhere is the realization that I must be flexible more evident than in my lesson plan book. When I began student teaching, my lesson plans were typed and*

clipped into a binder [and labeled "Monday," "Tuesday," etc.]. A short time later I began calling each day "Day One," "Day Two," "Day Three," and so on. A short time after that I began writing the lessons in a plan book in pencil. About halfway through my student teaching experience, I began doing my lessons on Post-it paper which I could arrange as needed. I only transferred the lesson to the blocks in the book as I became absolutely sure that they would not be disrupted. I have continued to use this practice with great success and have actually started one of my cooperating teachers on the same method.

Even when school is in session, students are present, and you have your class for the full 42 minutes, some portion of the available class time must be spent in noninstructional activities. This means that only part of the 42-minute period actually constitutes *instructional time.* In *A Place Called School* (1984), John Goodlad reports that the senior high school teachers he studied generally spent about 76 percent of available class time on instruction, 20 percent on routines, and 1.3 percent on behavior control; the remaining 2.2 percent was spent on socializing. Interestingly, the figures varied by subject area: Foreign language classes ranked first in terms of time spent on instruction (83 percent at the senior high level), while English ranked last (73 percent). School-to-school differences were also apparent, with instructional time varying from 68 percent to 84 percent at the senior high level. There was similar variation at the junior high level. At Crestview Junior High, for example, teachers spent 69 percent of class time on instruction and 25 percent on routines, while Fairfield Junior High teachers spent 87 percent on instruction and only 9 percent on routines.

Even within a school and a subject area, there can be considerable variation from teacher to teacher. In some classes, settling in at the beginning of the period, taking attendance, distributing materials, collecting homework, and reprimanding misbehaving students consume an inordinate amount of time. Karweit (1989) describes a "one-hour" math class, for example, in which the first 10 minutes were typically used to collect lunch money, and the last 10 were used to line up the students for lunch—leaving only 40 minutes for actual instruction.

Situations like this are not unusual in the classrooms of teachers who lack efficient strategies for carrying out routine, noninstructional tasks. Leinhardt and Greeno (1986) provide us with a glimpse into the difficulties encountered by one beginning teacher, Ms. Twain, as she attempted to check homework at the beginning of math class. Ms. Twain had two goals: to identify who had done the homework and to correct it orally. She began by asking, "Who doesn't have their homework?" In response, students did one of three things: They held up their completed work, called out that they didn't have it, or walked over to the teacher and told her whether they had done it or not. Ms. Twain then talked about the importance of homework and marked the results of this check on a posted sheet of paper.

Next, Ms. Twain chose students to give the correct answers to the homework problems:

She called out a set of problem numbers (1–10) and assigned a child to call out the answers as she called the problem number. The student slowly called out the answers in order. (The first child chosen was the lowest in the class, did not have her work done, and was doing the problems in her head.) Thus, for the first 10 problem answers, the teacher lost control of pace *and* correctness of answer; however, it was only when the child failed on the sixth problem that Twain realized the student had not done her homework. (p. 87)

Ms. Twain continued to call on students to give the answers, while the rest of the class checked their work. The last student chosen went through the sequence of problems quickly, but gave both the problem number and the answer, a situation that caused some confusion (e.g., "24, 27; 25, 64"). Ms. Twain's entire homework check took six minutes—and it was clear to the observers that she was never certain which students had done their homework.

In contrast, Leinhardt and Greeno describe a homework check conducted by Ms. Longbranch, a successful, experienced teacher. Ms. Longbranch first gave a cue, "Okay, set 43," and then began to call the students' names. Those who had done the homework simply responded, "yes." Those who hadn't done the work got up and wrote their names on the chalkboard. In 30 seconds—with a minimum of fuss— Ms. Longbranch was able to determine who had completed the assignment.

The next goal was to correct the work:

The students took colored pencils out and responded chorally with the correct answer, a fraction in lowest terms. As the teacher called the problem, "1/12 + 1/12," they responded "2/12 or 1/6." Time to complete was 106 seconds. (p. 85)

Ms. Longbranch's homework check is not presented as a model to be copied in your classroom; indeed, her procedure may not be appropriate for your particular class. The important point is that Ms. Longbranch has established a routine that enables her to check homework efficiently, almost automatically, while Ms. Twain does not yet have a workable strategy. Although the difference in the time used by the two teachers is only about four minutes, it is probably symptomatic of the ways they managed class time in general.

As you can see, the answer to the question, "How much time is there, anyway?" depends on whether we are talking about the number of hours mandated by the state and district (mandated time), the number of hours your class is actually in session and students are in attendance (available time), or the time actually used for instructional activities. Indeed, a recent study of time use in second, fifth, and eighth grades in an urban school district vividly demonstrates that there can be staggering disparities among these kinds of time. (See Figure 6.2.) But even when teachers are actually teaching, students are not necessarily paying attention. We must consider still another kind of time—*engaged time* or *time-on-task.*

Let's suppose that while you are teaching, some of your students choose to pass notes about last Saturday night's party, do their homework for the next period, comb their hair, or stare out the window. In this case, the amount of time you are devoting to instruction is greater than the amount of time students are directly engaged in learning. This is not an atypical situation. Research documents the fact that students tend to be "on-task" about 70 percent of the time (Rosenshine, 1980). Again, there are sizable variations from class to class. A study of 30 middle and high school science teachers (McGarity & Butts, 1984) found that some classes had an engagement rate of 54 percent (i.e., the average student was attentive about one-half of the time), while in other classes the engagement rate was 75 percent.

BetsAnn Smith set out to find out how much instructional time was actually delivered to elementary students in a large urban district during the course of one year. Researchers visited eight typical schools and observed more than 300 periods of instruction in language arts, mathematics, and social studies in Grades 2, 5, and 8. They examined *allocated instructional time* (time formally scheduled for daily and annual instruction), *enacted instructional time* (time actually used for teaching curriculum), and *noninstructional time* (time spent on classroom management, waiting, doing nothing, etc.).

Out of a 330-minute school day, 300 minutes were supposed to be devoted to instruction (in both academic and nonacademic areas such as art, music, health, physical education, library, and computers). But noninstructional time consumed about 23 percent of the time. There was a great deal of variation in this figure, depending on the managerial effectiveness of the teacher. About half of the observed teachers were very effective managers, and in their classrooms, noninstructional time was only 14 percent. But in the other half, the average rate of noninstructional time was as much as 30 percent. In these rooms, observation records revealed "the usual suspects: long settling-in routines, repeated directions, false starts, low expectations for output, and down time" (Smith, 2000). In these classes, students received less than 200 minutes of instructional time daily—*only two-thirds of the district's official mandate.*

An example from an observer's log illustrates the problems that were observed:

9:00 a.m. Students are straggling in from the rain. As they enter, the teacher directs them to get out of their coats and to their desks. The kids chatter with one another as their classmates enter. At 9:15 a.m., after they stand to say the pledge of allegiance, the teacher begins to take attendance and to collect money from a candy sale. There is confusion about what has and has not been turned in yet. She then hands out some worksheets and asks students to get out their language arts books, but several students do not have their books. There is a short lecture about this and an emotional explanation from one upset student. Students move around to buddy up so everyone has a book. The attendance officer comes to collect paperwork. At 9:30 a.m., they settle in and begin work on a vocabulary assignment. . . . (Smith, 1998, p. 9)

In addition, Smith observed that a growing number of "special days" further eroded learning time. In one school, for example, third-grade students had at least 37 days when part or all of the day was given over to a special activity of one kind or another, such as Halloween parades, field trips, student council conventions, science fairs, assemblies, spelling bees, picture day, dental screening, and standardized testing.

Taking all the factors that detract from instructional time into account, Smith calculated that students in this urban district actually received only 40 to 60 percent of the district's goal.

Figure 6.2   The Use of Time in One Large Urban District
Source: Smith, B. (1998 and 2000).

To a large extent, variations like these reflect teachers' ability to manage classroom events and to get students involved in learning activities. But other factors also come into play—students' attitudes toward school and subject matter (Marks, 2000), time of day, and day of week. And some teachers insist that attention falls off (and misbehavior increases) when there is a full moon!

There are also substantial differences in engagement from activity to activity. In a recent study by Shernoff, Csikszentmihalyi, Schneider, and Shernoff (2003), for example, high school students reported higher engagement (defined as interest, concentration, and enjoyment) during groupwork and individual work than while listening to lectures or watching television and videos. It seems clear that instructional strategies requiring students to be active are more engaging than those in which students are passive. Students also reported more engagement when they perceived the task at hand to be relevant and appropriately challenging—which brings us to a final type of time.

This last type of time is the *amount of time students spend on work that is meaningful and appropriate.* We sometimes get so caught up in trying to increase students' time-on-task that we overlook the tasks themselves. I once saw students in a ninth-grade general science class spend 15 minutes coloring a worksheet that showed diagrams of flower parts. The students seemed absorbed; indeed, an observer coding time-on-task would have recorded a high engagement rate. But what was the purpose of the activity? In first grade, coloring may be useful for developing children's fine motor skills, but it is hard to imagine why it would be worthwhile in high school. Coloring flower parts is not science, and in this case, one-third of the science period was allocated to a nonscientific activity.

It also makes no sense to have students spend time working on tasks they don't understand and are unable to complete successfully. This was vividly demonstrated in the Beginning Teacher Evaluation Study (BTES), an influential project that examined the use of time in schools (Fisher, Berliner, Filby, Marliave, Cahen, & Dishaw, 1980). BTES researchers created the term *academic learning time* (ALT) to refer to the proportion of engaged time in which students are performing academic tasks with a high degree of success. When students can accomplish a task with relatively few errors, it suggests that the task is appropriately matched to their level of achievement and that the teacher has provided sufficient preparation. (It is important to note, of course, that the BTES focused on the performance of straightforward, routine tasks, not complex, problem-solving tasks.)

This chapter began by asking, "How much time is there, anyway?" Figure 6.3 depicts the answer to this question. The bar at the far left shows the number of

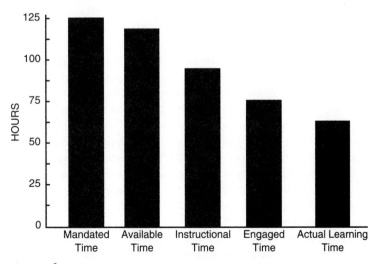

Figure 6.3 How Much Time Is There, Anyway?

hours that a typical 42-minute class would meet in the typical mandated school year—126 (180 days × 42 minutes). For the sake of argument, let's assume that student absences and assembly programs reduce this figure by 10 days or seven hours (10 days × 42 minutes). Thus, the second bar indicates that available time is 119 hours. To be consistent with Goodlad's (1984) findings on the use of available class time, let's also assume that clerical and administrative tasks consume 20 percent of each class, leaving only 34 minutes each day for actual instruction. This yields 96 hours (bar 3). If students pay attention 80 percent of that time (an optimistic estimate), engaged time is 77 hours (bar 4). And assuming that students work on meaningful, appropriate tasks for 80 percent of the time they are engaged, we see that actual learning time is only 62 hours—*about one-half of the "mandated" school time for this typical secondary class* (bar 5).

Obviously, these figures are estimates. As I have stressed, there are substantial variations from subject to subject, school to school, and classroom to classroom. Nonetheless, the graph illustrates the fundamental point: *The hours available for learning are far more limited than they initially appear.*

Pause and Reflect

Most teachers are surprised when they see how little time is actually spent in productive learning. What are some practices that erode the amount of time? What are some practices that you could use to maximize the opportunity for productive learning? Keep both of these in mind as you read the next section of the chapter.

Increasing Opportunity to Learn

In addition to contributing the concept of ALT, the Beginning Teacher Evaluation Study (BTES) also demonstrated the relationship between time and achievement. The findings are not surprising. *As allocated time, engaged time, and academic learning time increase, so does student learning;* of the three, academic learning time is the best predictor of achievement.

The BTES data made time a popular topic for reform-minded educators. In 1983, for example, the National Commission on Excellence in Education declared that we were "a nation at risk" because of "a rising tide of mediocrity" in our educational system. The report advocated a variety of reforms, including recommendations to extend the school day to seven hours and to lengthen the school year to 200 or 220 days. A decade later, the National Education Commission on Time and Learning (1994) also argued the need for more time. The Commission characterized teachers and students as "prisoners of time" and paraphrased Oliver Hazard Perry's dispatch from the War of 1812: "We have met the enemy and they are [h]ours." Acknowledging the "new work of the schools"—education about personal safety, AIDS, family life, driver education, consumer affairs—the Commission asserted the need to relegate the six-hour, 180-day school year to museums, "an exhibit from our education past" (p. 5).

Most recently, an education task force established by the Center for American Progress and the Institute for America's Future reached the same conclusions about the need for more time. In a report entitled "Getting Smarter, Becoming Fairer"

KIPP, an acronym for the Knowledge Is Power Program, began in 1994 when teachers Dave Levin and Mike Feinberg completed their Teach for America commitment and launched a program for fifth-graders in a public school in inner-city Houston, Texas. KIPP has since grown to a national network of almost 40 charter schools, serving fifth- through eighth-graders in high-need communities in 15 states and the District of Columbia. Three-quarters of KIPP students receive free or reduced-price lunches, and 90 percent are students of color.

At KIPP schools, the school day typically begins at 7:30 a.m. and ends at 5 p.m. Half-day classes are also held on Saturdays, and students attend a summer session of two to four weeks. On average, KIPP students spend 62 percent more time in school each year than other students.

Research on KIPP schools has demonstrated improved outcomes for students at risk for academic failure. For example, Gaston College Preparatory (GCP) is a KIPP school in Gaston, North Carolina. Although fewer than half of incoming fifth-graders were performing at grade level when they entered GCP, more than 90 percent of them were doing so by the end of their first year in school. Out of North Carolina's 2,219 schools in 2002–2003, GCP was the sixth-highest performing school in the state. Although many factors—rigorous curriculum, a commitment to high-quality instruction, and high expectations—all contribute to GCP's success and to that of KIPP schools elsewhere, the schools' extended time appears to be a key component.

Figure 6.4   The Knowledge Is Power Program (KIPP)

> *Source:* "Getting Smarter, Becoming Fairer," the report of Renewing Our Schools, Securing Our Future: A National Task Force on Public Education (2005), and the KIPP Web site, www.kipp.org.

(2005), the task force observed that "the allocation and use of time today is still tied to an agrarian economy…, where children were needed to help in the fields during the after-school hours and summer months" (p. 15) and asserted that "abruptly thrusting American children out of the classroom door in the middle of the afternoon is a wasted opportunity" (p. 18). The first recommendation of the task force is to increase the amount of time that students spend in school by lengthening the school day and, in the case of low-performing schools, the school year.

Despite the cogency of the Commissions' reports, the six-hour, 180-day school year is still the norm in the United States. (See Figure 6.4 for a description of one program that has substantially extended allocated time.) Thus, it is critical for teachers to manage the limited time available with skill and efficiency. The next sections of this chapter will discuss three strategies for increasing students' productive learning time: *maintaining activity flow, minimizing transition time, and holding students accountable.* (See the Practical Tips box on the next page for a summary.) Of course, these strategies not only maximize time for learning, they also help to create and maintain classroom order.

Maintaining Activity Flow

Good and Brophy (2003) observe that "four things can happen" when students must wait with nothing to do, and "three of them are bad: (1) Students may remain interested and attentive; (2) they may become bored or fatigued, losing the ability

PRACTICAL TIPS FOR

INCREASING STUDENTS' LEARNING TIME

- *Maintain activity flow*
  Avoid flip-flopping.
  Avoid "stimulus-bounded events" (being pulled away from the ongoing activity by an event or object that doesn't really need attention).
  Avoid overdwelling and fragmentation.

- *Minimize transition time*
  Prepare students for upcoming transitions.
  Establish clear routines.
  Have clear beginnings and endings: bring first activity to a halt, announce the transition, monitor the transition, make sure everyone is attentive, begin second activity.

- *Hold students accountable*
  Communicate assignments clearly.
  Monitor students' progress.

to concentrate; (3) they may become distracted or start daydreaming; or (4) they may actively misbehave" (p. 122). Given the three-to-one odds that waiting will result in undesirable behavior and a loss of valuable learning opportunities, it's essential for teachers to learn how to maintain the flow of classroom activities.

Once again, we turn for guidance to the work of Jacob Kounin (1970). Kounin investigated differences in teachers' ability to initiate and maintain activity flow in classrooms. He then looked for relationships between activity flow and students' engagement and misbehavior.

Kounin's research identified many differences in the ways teachers orchestrated classroom activities. In some classrooms, activities flowed smoothly and briskly, while in others, activities were "jerky" and slow. Kounin even developed a special vocabulary to describe the problems he observed. For instance, he found that some ineffective managers would terminate an activity, start another, and then return to the first activity. Kounin called this *flip-flopping.* It is illustrated by the following situation: A foreign language teacher finishes reviewing homework with the class and tells students to turn to the next chapter in their textbook. She then stops and says, "Wait a minute. How many got all the homework problems right? . . . Very good . . . Okay, now let's talk about the imperfect tense."

Kounin also observed *stimulus-bounded events,* situations in which teachers are "pulled away" from the ongoing activity by a stimulus (an event or an object) that really doesn't need attention. Kounin describes the case of a teacher who is explaining a math problem at the board when she notices that a student is leaning on his left elbow as he works the problem. She leaves the board, instructs him to sit up straight, comments on his improved posture, and then returns to the board.

Sometimes, teachers slow down the pace of activity by *overdwelling*—continuing to explain when students already understand or preaching at length about appropriate behavior. Another type of slowdown is produced when a teacher breaks an activity into components even though the activity could be performed as a single unit—what Kounin called *fragmentation:*

> The teacher was making a transition from spelling to arithmetic as follows: "All right everybody, I want you to close your spelling books. Put away your red pencils. Now close your spelling books. Put your spelling books in your desks. Keep them out of the way." [There's a pause.] "All right now. Take out your arithmetic books and put them on your desks in front of you. That's right, let's keep everything off your desks except your arithmetic books. And let's sit up straight. We don't want any lazy-bones do we? That's fine. Now get your black pencils and open your books to page sixteen." (p. 106)

Flip-flops, stimulus-boundedness, overdwelling, fragmentation—these are all threats to the flow of classroom activities. Not only do they result in lost learning time, they can have a significant impact on students' behavior. When activities proceed smoothly and briskly, students are *more involved in work and less apt to misbehave.* Indeed, as Kounin concluded two decades ago, *activity flow plays a greater role in classroom order than the specific techniques that teachers use to handle misbehavior.*

During one visit to Sandy's classroom, I watched the skillful way she maintained the flow of activity in her class. It was the end of October, and students were in the middle of a very intriguing lab that involved the production of silver. As you read the vignette, note how Sandy ensures that there will be no "down time" by preparing the board for the homework review before class begins, by starting class promptly, by having students put homework problems on the board during the lab activity, and by ensuring that students will have something to do if they finish the lab before others.

11:21   Sandy writes the numbers 4 through 11 on the chalkboard, evenly spacing them across the entire width.

11:22   She positions herself by the classroom door to greet students as they enter the room.

11:23   The bell rings. Sandy moves from the door to the front of the room. "Hats off, please. We have a lot to do today. First, we have to finish the lab. You need not wear your goggles. Second, I want to review the chemical equation sheet you did. You'll put the final balanced equations on the board. And third, you'll learn to solve problems associated with the balanced equations. So let's get going."

11:24   The students move to lab tables, get their equipment, and begin working. While students are doing the lab, Sandy moves around the room, assisting, questioning, and monitoring. The atmosphere is very relaxed. Sandy smiles, laughs, and jokes with students about the silver they're producing. While she circulates, she also notes which students are just about done with the lab and selects them to put the homework problems on the board: "Joe, are you finished? You have all your data? Okay, put number four up. Kim, you're done? Please put number five on the board." They leave their lab tables, get their homework, and put their assigned problems on the board. By the time the lab is over, numbers 4 through 11 are up on the chalkboard.

11:33   Sandy notices that students are nearing the end of the lab. She tells them: "When you're finished, take your seats so I know you're finished." One by one, students begin to move back to their seats; they take out their homework and begin to compare their answers to the work on the chalkboard.

11:37   The equipment is all put away, the lab tables have been cleaned, and the class is all seated.

11:38   Sandy introduces the problems on the chalkboard: "OK, let's turn to the equations on the board. Let me preface this by saying that you should not panic if you're having trouble writing formulas. You don't have to be able to write formulas until December. But what you do need to know now is how to balance the equations. All right, let's look at the first one." She turns to the first problem written on the board and begins the review.

12:00   All the problems have been discussed, and Sandy moves to the third activity of the morning. "Now I want you to listen very carefully. Do not take notes. I know this sounds strange, but I want you to be able to watch and listen and think. I'm going to show you a new type of problem." She writes a chemical equation on the board and challenges them to think about it. The students are stuck. Sandy lets them ponder the problem; she asks some easier questions to help them get started, and suggests they use paper if they want to. She walks around the room to see how they're doing, commenting on their efforts, encouraging them to consult with one another.

12:07   The bell rings. Students are still involved in trying to solve the problems. Sandy tells the class, "Think about this tonight, and come back with your ideas tomorrow."

Later, Sandy reflected on the day's lesson and talked about her very deliberate attempts to maintain the flow of activities:

 Some people would regard this as obsessive. Many teachers have kids finish the lab, sit down, and *then* put all the problems on the board. But what do you do when students are sitting there and others are putting things on the board? Even during labs, if they have to boil something for 10 minutes, I'll give them a problem to do. Kids can't just sit and watch something boil for 10 minutes. That's when they'll start squirting water bottles. Maybe I'm strange, but I just can't stand any down time. There's so much to accomplish and so little time.

Minimizing Transition Time

From the perspective of time management, transitions between activities can be very problematic. An analysis by Paul Gump (1982, 1987) helps us to understand the reasons. First, Gump observes, there may be difficulty "closing out" the first activity—especially if students are deeply engaged. (Ironically, the very involvement that teachers strive to achieve makes it more difficult to get students to switch activities!) Second, transitions are more loosely structured than activities themselves (Ross, 1985). Since there's usually more leeway in terms of socializing and moving around the room, there is also more opportunity for disruption. In fact, in a study of 50 classes taught by student teachers, Marshall Arlin (1979) found that there was almost twice as much disruption during transitions (e.g., hitting, yelling, obscene gestures) as during nontransition time.

Third, students sometimes "save up" problems or tensions and deal with them during the transition time. They may seek out the teacher to complain about a grade, ask for permission to retrieve a book from a locker, or dump out the contents of their bookbags in search of a lost homework assignment. Although these behaviors are legitimate—and help to protect the adjacent activities from disturbance—they also make transitions more difficult to manage. Finally, there may be delays in getting students started on the second activity. Students may have difficulty settling down, or teachers may be held up because they are dealing with individual students' concerns or are busy assembling needed materials.

Gump's analysis suggests that teachers can reduce the potential for chaos *by preparing students for upcoming transitions, by establishing efficient transition routines,* and *by clearly defining the boundaries of lessons* (Ross, 1985). These guidelines are especially important for students with attention-deficit/hyperactivity disorder (ADHD) and those with autism, who have particular difficulty with transitions and changes in routine (McIntosh, Herman, Sanford, McGraw, & Florence, 2004).

Advance Preparation

Marshall Arlin's (1979) research revealed that transitions were far more chaotic when student teachers failed to warn students about the imminent change of activity. This often occurred at the end of the period because student teachers didn't even realize that time was up:

> The lesson was still continuing when the bell would ring. Not having reached any closure, the teacher, with some degree of desperation, would say something like "OK, you can go," and pupils would charge out of the room, often knocking each other over. (Sometimes, pupils did not even wait for the signal from the teacher.) The teacher might then remember an announcement and interject to the dispersing mob, "Don't forget to bring back money for the trip!" (p. 50)

In contrast, other student teachers in Arlin's study were able to prepare students for the upcoming transition. If they were about to dismiss the class, they made sure that desks were in order and that students were quiet and ready to leave. They made announcements while students were still seated and then made sure students left the room in an orderly fashion.

Our four teachers are very diligent "clock watchers." They take care to monitor time and to inform students when the class period is drawing to a close. This is not as easy as it sounds, even for the three very experienced teachers. During one visit to

Donnie's class, I watched both teacher and students get caught up in the lesson and lose track of time. When the bell rang, one girl actually blurted out, "Dang! That went fast!" Donnie laughingly agreed, broke off the lesson, and gave the homework assignment. Fortunately, she had taught her students early in the year that *she*, not the bell, dismissed them, so students stayed seated and attentive until she was finished.

In addition to warning students about the end of the period, it's also helpful to prepare them for changes in class activities during the period. In the following example, we see Fred explain to students what they will be doing that day and remind them periodically about how much time is left before they will be changing activities.

The bell rings. Fred tells his students to take out paper and pencil while he distributes an article from *Newsweek* magazine regarding human rights and China. "While I meet with people one by one to go over grades, you will read and take notes on this article. You'll have about 12 minutes. At the end of that time, we will discuss these questions: What is the problem we're trying to solve between China and the United States? And is this just a case of Western arrogance? Take good notes—I'm going to collect them—and I will ask you to give an oral presentation of your views."

As students settle down to read, Fred gets out his grade book and sits at his desk. He quietly signals for individuals to come up to discuss their marking quarter grades. A few minutes later, he checks his watch. "Ladies and gentlemen, you have about seven more minutes to finish reading and taking notes."

Later, he issues another warning about the time: "About two more minutes, so you should be finishing up." At the end of 12 minutes, he gets up from his desk. "Okay, you've had enough time now to read the article and take some notes. At the bottom of the paper, please summarize in 25 words or less what the basic problem is between China and the United States."

The Use of Routines

Chapter 4 talked about the importance of having clear, specific routines in order to keep the classroom running smoothly. At no time is the use of routines more important than during transitions. Well-established routines provide a structure to transitions that helps to prevent confusion and lost time.

In Christina's class, the routine for entering the room is very clear. Her students come in, take their seats, take out their journals, and begin writing on the journal topic posted on the board. According to Christina, using the journal achieves a number of objectives:

Using this routine allows me to have students engaged in a meaningful activity while I'm taking attendance, checking homework, etc. The journal is a timed writing exercise that encourages fluency in writing. I make it clear that students are not allowed to stop writing until I signal that time is up. . . . It's difficult in the beginning for them to understand that they can't be "finished" with this assignment—that it's timed! However, after a few days of prompting, they get the hang of it. Also, the journal entries are often related to the literature we're studying so they help to introduce or extend the reading. And having a daily journal assignment creates a nice, quiet atmosphere in which I can give instructions for the next activity.

Similarly, Donnie begins every period with a "Do Now" activity that helps get students settled and gives her a few moments to take attendance. She stresses that the "Do Now" is not busy work that is disconnected from the lesson; rather, it assesses students' understanding of material covered the day before or provides a "kick off" for the current lesson.

 It's period 6 geometry. As students enter the room, they see the "Do Now" assignment on the board—Pages 57–58, #10–13. Instead of heading for their desks, most of the students go over to the side of the room and get calculators and workbooks. Donnie stands at the side of the room, watching silently. The stragglers notice her standing there; they glance at the board, and then get their materials. When everyone has settled down, Donnie announces, "OK, you have four or five minutes to finish those problems. Then we'll talk about them." While students are working, she takes attendance silently. Then she begins to circulate.

In many classrooms, the transition routines are *implicit,* and students are expected to figure out what to do by picking up on subtle cues. This may be fine for the majority of students, but those with ADHD, autism, or other disorders may have trouble and end up getting reprimanded. If you have students like this in your classes, it is essential (and only fair) to spend time teaching them how to make efficient, orderly transitions. McIntosh, Herman, Sanford, McGraw, and Florence (2004) suggest that you teach routines explicitly, provide "precorrections" and positive reinforcement, and actively supervise. These techniques are described more fully in the Practical Tips box on page 168.

Clear Beginnings and Endings

Arlin's (1979) study demonstrated that transitions proceed more smoothly if teachers bring the first activity to a halt, announce the transition, allow time to make sure that everyone is attentive, and then begin the second activity. In other words, smooth transitions are characterized by well-defined boundaries.

In the following vignette, we see Christina implement a transition with well-defined boundaries. Watch the way she prepares her students for the transition from small-group work to a whole-class activity.

 Students are seated in clusters of four or five, working on the poetry lessons they are creating for the rest of the class. Christina is circulating. She checks the clock and then moves to the front of the room. "May I have your attention please? We are ready to move to the next part of the lesson. Please listen carefully to all of my instructions and do not move until I tell you to. First, you will have one member of your group hand in your assignment. This person will check to make sure each person's name is on the paper.

PRACTICAL TIPS FOR

TEACHING TRANSITIONS

- Think about the transitions that occur during the period, such as the following:
    Entering and leaving the classroom.
    Putting materials away and preparing for the next task.
    Cleaning up a work area.
    Moving from group to independent work.
    Turning in homework.
    Choosing partners for small-group activities.
- Explicitly teach the expected transition behavior:
    Model the behavior using both correct and incorrect examples.
    Provide opportunities for students to practice.
    Provide feedback.
    Reteach if needed.
- Provide precorrections (reminders of the expected behavior *before* the transition begins).
- Provide positive reinforcement for efficient, orderly transitions:
    Give specific praise or special privileges and activities.
    Use tangible rewards (such as food) if necessary.
- Actively supervise the transition:
    Scan the room, looking for both appropriate and inappropriate behavior.
    Walk around the room, using proximity to encourage students to engage in the appropriate behavior.
    Interact with students during the transition, providing reminders and specific praise.

Source: McIntosh, Herman, Sanford, McGraw, & Florence, 2004.

Then you will return to your regular seats, take out your notebooks and textbooks, and open your books to page 295. Also, have a pen out and on your desk. When you are settled, please begin reading the brief introduction on page 295. Are there any questions? Good. You may move now."

Later, when I commented on how quickly and efficiently her students had made the transition, Christina observed that it was sometimes difficult to get students to wait patiently for instructions:

What I mean is, if the transition will require a series of movements, they want to move as soon as you give them the first direction. If you allow them to do this, they won't hear the *rest* of the directions. The transition time will actually be longer, since you'll have to spend time repeating everything. I've learned to tell them, "Don't move until I'm finished."

Holding Students Accountable

Walter Doyle (1983) has commented that students tend to take assignments seriously only if they are held accountable for them. Your own school experiences probably testify to the truth of this statement. Even as adults, it takes a good deal of self-discipline and maturity to put your best effort into work that will never be seen by anyone. And middle and high school students are *adolescents*. Unless they know that they will have to account for their performance, it is unlikely that they'll make the best use of class time.

Furthermore, students are *unable* to make good use of their time if they are confused about what they're supposed to be doing. Teachers sometimes tell students to "get to work" and are immediately bombarded by questions: "Can I use pen?" "Do I have to write down the questions or can I just put the answers?" "Do we have to show all our work?" "Can I work at the lab table?" When this happens, precious class time has to be spent clarifying the original instructions.

In order to help students use their time wisely, teachers must *communicate assignments and requirements clearly and monitor students' progress* (Emmer, Evertson, & Worsham, 2000). These practices minimize students' confusion and convey the message that schoolwork is important. Let's see what our teachers and the research have to say about these two practices.

Communicating Assignments and Requirements

One finding of the BTES study (Fisher et al., 1980) was that students were more likely to have success on assignments when teachers provided clear, thorough directions. Interestingly, the number of explanations given *in response to students' questions was negatively associated with high student success.* What could account for this curious finding? One possibility is that when many students have to ask about an assignment, their teachers failed to provide sufficient preparation. In other words, the original instructions were not clear or thorough enough.

Before students begin to work, it's a good idea to explain what they'll be doing and why, how to get help, what to do with completed work, what to do when they're finished, and how long they'll be spending on the task. You also need to make sure that students are familiar with your work standards—for example, what kind of paper to use, whether they should use pencil or pen, how to number the page, whether or not erasures are allowed, and what it means to "show all their work." Once you've given your instructions, it's also a good idea to have students explain what they will be doing in their own words and to give students a chance to ask questions. Asking "Does everyone understand?" rarely yields useful information.

Sometimes, in an effort to maintain activity flow, teachers rush into instructions and activities without checking that students are "with them." Arlin (1979) writes: "Several times I noticed over 15 children continuing the previous activity while the teacher was giving directions for the new activity" (p. 50). Needless to say, those teachers then became exasperated when students asked questions about what to do.

On the other hand, Paul Gump (1982) warns that waiting *too* long can cause a loss of momentum. He writes: "Waiting for absolute and universal attention can sometimes lead to unnecessarily extended transition times" (p. 112). Gump reminds us that by keeping the instructional program going, teachers can often "pull in" students whose attention has momentarily wandered.

This lesson was brought home to me on a lovely day in April as I watched Fred's Contemporary World Cultures class. As soon as the bell rang, Fred scanned the room and then announced that he was going to divide the class into six groups of four or five each (by having students count off). Once students had moved into their groups, Fred distributed paper and atlases, appointed a chairperson for each group, and gave students the following instructions: "Put your name at the top of the page. Turn to page 81 in your atlas—the map of Africa. Your first task is to find the country of Burkina Faso and to write down the names of the countries that surround it." Students immediately started working, and I sat at the side of the room wondering why Fred had not explained why they were doing this and what they would be doing for the rest of the period. Only when students had finished this first task did Fred provide more elaborate instructions:

Ladies and gentlemen, give me your attention so you'll know what we're doing today. You'll remember that after we saw the film on Africa, we talked about how the problems seem so big, so paralyzing. What can an ordinary person do? The situation is just too overwhelming. Well, I found some readings about two ordinary people, Minata in Burkina Faso and Keko in Tanzania. Today, you'll read about these two people and the problems they face. Then I want you to think about the best thing for them to do. What would *you* do if you were in their shoes? [He distributes the readings.]

Here's how you're going to do it. First read the articles and jot down your own notes to the questions. Then share your reactions in your small group. Then each of you will write out final answers that represent the thinking of the whole group. The chairperson will turn in the notes and the final answers at the end of the period. You already did the first question when you found the countries surrounding Burkina Faso. You'll do the same thing for Tanzania when you read about Keko. Any questions about what you're going to do? [There are a few questions, and he answers them.] This is worth eight points.

Later, I asked Fred why he had started students on the activity *before* explaining what they would be doing for the period and giving general instructions (clearly a departure from "standard operating procedure"). He answered without hesitation:

Look, it's spring, and they're juniors and seniors suffering from spring fever. If I had tried to give instructions when they first came in, half of them wouldn't have been listening, and I would have had to say everything all over again. This way, I got them into groups and got them going on an easy task—finding the countries surrounding Burkina Faso. They got focused, and *then* I could give instructions and they'd all be listening.

In addition to providing explicit directions for in-class activities, teachers need to communicate homework assignments in a clear, organized manner. This is particularly important if you are working with students who have difficulty remembering what they are supposed to do. Sandy has devised a routine for assigning

homework that she first developed to help students with learning disabilities. She
soon realized, however, that the routine was helpful for everyone:

> When I first write a homework assignment on the board, I write it really
> big in the middle of the board and tell students to copy it down *now*.
> Then I move it to the left-hand corner of the board where it remains
> until the due date. Periodically, I remind students about it. I'm also re-
> ally clear about the numbers of the problems that students have to do. For exam-
> ple, if the assignment is to do numbers 1 through 5, and then 7, 9, 11, and 13
> through 16, I'll write out 1, 2, 3, 4, and 5, because some kids (especially my learn-
> ing disabled students) don't see the difference between the comma and the dash.

Christina is also very diligent about writing out assignments and directions, especially for big projects. Sometimes, she provides a printed handout with detailed
instructions. Other times, she'll have students copy the directions from the board
or an overhead projector.

> Students have been conducting research on various careers. As part of
> the research, they have conducted interviews and done library research.
> On Wednesday they will be giving "informative speeches" lasting two to
> four minutes. Christina reminds them that they are to pretend they
> work for Career Services; their job is to inform college students about the careers
> they've researched. Today she reviews the research materials that are due on
> Wednesday. She turns on the overhead projector; on a transparency are listed the
> components they are to hand in:

> 5 source cards (4 from library; 1 from interview)
> 16 note cards (12 from library sources, 4 from interviews)
> list of 10+ interview questions
> record of interview (tape, video, written record)
> a works-cited page
> outline of speech

Christina reviews each component and answers questions that students have
about the interviews ("What if your interviewee doesn't want to give her last
name?"), the speeches, and the written work ("What do we do if there's no author
listed?"). When students have no more questions, she tells students to put away
their materials so they can begin the next activity.

After class, Christina and I talked about how explicit her directions had been:

> Not only does this help to alleviate the number of questions I need to
> answer—over and over again—it also makes students accountable for the
> details of the assignment. They can't say, "You didn't tell us we needed
> five sources" if they've copied it down from the overhead, or "You didn't
> say to use textual evidence to support our answers" if the written handout states
> this requirement. I've also learned that doing this is useful for meeting with
> parents because you have every assignment documented. I save all my handouts

and overhead transparencies with the directions. This way, I can prove I stated the requirements to students (and to parents on the rare occasions when I'm questioned). And I also save myself from rewriting directions when I'm using an assignment again.

Monitoring Student Progress

Once you've given directions for an assignment and your class gets to work, it's important to monitor how students are doing. The BTES study found that teachers with high-achieving classes circulated around the room while students were working at their seats (Fisher, Berliner, Filby, Marliave, Cahen, & Dishaw, 1980). This practice enables you to keep track of students' progress, to identify and help with problems, and to verify that assignments are matched to students' ability. Circulating also helps to ensure that students are using their time well.

Observations of our four teachers revealed that they rarely sit down, unless they're working with a small group.

Donnie's class is working with rulers and protractors to discover the properties of parallelograms. As students work, Donnie continually circulates. She keeps up a steady stream of comments, questions, and praise: "Very good, Veronica." "Everybody finished with that first question?" "Answer the questions as you go, so you'll have all the answers when you finish." "Anyone need help?" "What does *consecutive* mean, José?" "Is there anyone who's having problems with the protractor?"

After class, Donnie talked about the fact that she is constantly on the move:

I don't see how a person can teach math and sit down. I just wouldn't feel comfortable sitting down. You have to write on the board, you have to guide students through the problems, you have to see they're on the right track. By walking around the room, I can catch mistakes. I can ask, "What were you doing here? Explain your reasoning." I can talk them through the problem. I have to be up and moving when I'm teaching.

In addition to circulating while students are working, it's essential to monitor whether students are regularly completing assignments. This requires you to *establish routines for collecting and checking class work and homework.* For example, at the beginning of class, Donnie has students take out their homework and put it on their tables. While they review the assignment, she circulates around the room and notes in her grade book who has done the homework. The whole procedure takes just a few minutes and there's no loss of instructional time, since the class is simultaneously going over the homework problems.

Sandy uses a different system. She has a folder for each class that she keeps on the front table. Homework assignments are to be placed in the folder at the very beginning of class. She gives a "last call for homework," and then closes the folder. Sometime during the period, Sandy checks the papers to see if any assignments are missing. This allows her to verify immediately that she does not have an assignment from a particular student and to find out what happened. As she puts it, "This way I can avoid the situation where a student says, 'But I *did* do the homework. You must have lost it.' "

It's especially important to *keep track of students' progress on long-term homework assignments.* By establishing intermediate check points, you can help students develop a "plan of attack." For example, if they are writing a research paper, you can set due dates on which they have to submit each stage of the assignment (e.g., the topic; preliminary notes; a list of references; the first draft; the final draft). Not only does this allow you to monitor students' progress, it also helps to lessen the anxiety that adolescents sometimes feel when faced with a large assignment.

Fred tells an ironic story that points out the value of this approach:

 Last year, my students did a long research paper. I had them turn in each piece to show me how they were coming along—a working outline, a bibliography, their notes, a rough draft, and then the final copy. I used a point system. The first four parts of the assignment were worth 10 points each; the final copy was worth 60 points.

This year, I decided it was babyish to do this, so I didn't do it. I told my classes, "I'm going to treat you like adults," and they said, "Great. We can do it." Well, they didn't get their papers in. They told me, "We messed up. We let it go, we procrastinated." They asked me to do what I had done last year! I trusted them to be mature, and they said, "We're not."

Finally, you need to *maintain records of what students are accomplishing.* In some districts, teachers can develop their own system for recording students' progress; others require teachers to follow a prescribed format. For example, Donnie's grade book has to reflect her weekly lessons plans and the "quarterly topic plans" she has to submit four times a year; following the district's objectives for her courses, these plans describe what she will be teaching day by day. For each marking period, Donnie must have two grades per week for homework and at least one test grade per objective. If five objectives are to be covered during a particular marking period, then Donnie would have to have at least five test grades.

In contrast, Fred is allowed to develop his own record-keeping system. Fred doesn't even have a regular grade book; instead he records his students' grades on the computer. Nonetheless, like Donnie, he is careful to keep up-to-date records of students' progress. He explained his record-keeping system to students at the very beginning of the year:

I want to take a minute or two to discuss grades with you. I don't have a grade book. I keep your grades on the computer. We can go anytime after school and check out your grades. What I use is homework, class work, projects, tests, and quizzes. Each in-class assignment is about four points. A big exam would be worth about five in-class assignments—about 20 points. The total point value for the marking period is 120–130 points. You can always find out what your point total is, what your grade is at any time. . . . It's important to me that everyone in here passes this class and does well. If you need me to get on your case, so you'll do okay in here, let me know. Remember, the grades are yours. You can see them at any time.

Checking or grading all the work that students do each day is an arduous, time-consuming task. One student teacher in English recently wrote about "the looming mountain of paperwork that a teacher must perpetually climb":

> *Sometimes I'm not sure if I'm a teacher or a certified [public] accoun-*
> *tant! However, my experience ... has enabled me to find ways to reckon*
> *with the ponderous load. Simple things like color-coordinated folders for*
> *each class, or writing the names of absent students on quiz sheets to*
> *keep track of makeup work, are "tricks" that I am extremely grateful to*
> *have been shown along the way.*

Like this student teacher, you need to find ways to "make a molehill out of a mountain" (Shalaway, 1989). I asked Sandy, Donnie, Christina, and Fred how they handle the paperwork. Their ideas are listed in the Practical Tips box.

THE USE OF BLOCK SCHEDULING

Many secondary schools have moved to block scheduling in an effort to maximize time for learning, to encourage the use of varied instructional strategies, and to allow teachers and students to explore topics in depth. There are two common scheduling configurations. On the *4 × 4 block schedule,* four 80- or 90-minute instructional blocks are scheduled each day, instead of the traditional six or seven. Since classes meet every day, a course that would normally last a year is completed in one semester or 90 days, and students take only four courses at a time. The *A-B or alternating day schedule* also offers four extended periods each day, but classes meet every other day for the entire school year. This means that students still take six or seven courses at one time.

Although one 80- or 90-minute block does not actually provide more contact time with students than two 42- or 50-minute periods, advocates of block scheduling contend that the extended class provides more *usable instructional time* (Fleming, Olenn, Schoenstein, & Eineder, 1997). Since classes meet half as many times, the time spent in routine tasks at the beginning of the period (e.g., taking attendance, getting students settled in, distributing materials) and at the end (e.g., talking about homework, getting packed up) is also halved. More importantly, instructional time is less fragmented. As Roger Schoenstein, a Latin and English teacher in Colorado Springs, observes:

> *[On the old 50-minute schedule,] I'd just get the point across, just get them*
> *ready to do something with what we had been learning, ... and the bell*
> *would ring. "Hang onto this stuff, don't forget it, tomorrow we'll practice*
> *it—tomorrow we'll do something with it." I said that day after day as they*
> *scrambled out the door. When "tomorrow" came, I'd spend 10 to 20 min-*
> *utes reteaching the same material as the day before, trying to catch my*
> *students back up to the point where they were when the bell rang. On the*
> *4 × 4 block I find those minutes given back to me day after day. The*

PRACTICAL TIPS FOR

HANDLING PAPERWORK

FRED: Check that students do in-class assignments and routine homework, but don't spend a lot of time reading and grading these. Develop a simple system for keeping track of students' routine assignments (e.g., four points for full-credit; 3.5 points for an almost-completed assignment, etc.).

Spend your time on the assignments that require higher-level thinking. These are harder to grade!

On tests, create "structured essay" questions. Construct your own answer to the essay. (Know what the essay is "supposed to say.") Look for key words when grading.

Refuse to grade papers that contain more than three technical errors (spelling, punctuation, etc.). I tell students, "I have 100 of these to grade; it's not fair for me to sit here and correct your spelling mistakes. I'm not here to proofread.... Have someone who's good at this proofread your papers before you turn them in."

SANDY: With homework, grade on attempt/effort, not whether it's right or wrong.

For the first few assignments, read *everything* really carefully. Go over lab reports with a fine-tooth comb. That way, students come to see that you have really high expectations and that they have to be clear and thorough. Then, later, you can skim the first few pages (objectives, procedures, materials), and spend the bulk of your time on the data section.

Sometimes, in long labs, have students present their data in table form.

DONNIE: Review homework every day, but have students check their own work. In your gradebook, enter a check (as opposed to a grade) to show who has done the assignment.

Have students grade one homework assignment each week that you record in your grade book.

Collect one homework assignment each week to grade yourself.

CHRISTINA: Think of "time-spent-grading" as part of your lesson plans. Carefully plan activities and due dates to allow you enough time to grade assignments. For example, after I collect research papers, I plan for students to be primarily engaged in classwork assignments that I can monitor without collecting very much paperwork. This allows me to spend the majority of my grading time on the research papers.

Use rubrics to provide detailed feedback without having to write the same comments over and over again.

Instruct students in proper editing, revision, and response procedures so they can provide feedback to one another. For example, I provide a detailed response on the first draft of the first section of a long research paper. Then students use a checklist with marking instructions to provide feedback to one another on the second and third sections of the paper.

students can go right from instruction to application, ...right from my lecture to cooperative groups to do something with what they've encountered. (Fleming, Olenn, Schoenstein, & Eineder, 1997, p. 14)

At this point, research examining the effects of block scheduling on achievement is inconsistent. For example, a study of three high schools using 4×4 block scheduling showed an increase in average standardized test scores, a higher percentage of students on the honor roll, and decreased failure rates (Evans, Tokarczyk, Rice, & McCray, 2002). Similarly, a study of five high schools (Nichols, 2005) found a positive (albeit small) effect on students' achievement in language arts and English. Positive effects have also been shown on the middle school level (Mattox, Hancock, & Queen, 2005), where mathematics achievement increased significantly after the first year of implementation. On the other hand, some studies have found no difference (e.g., Bottge, Gugerty, Serlin, & Moon, 2003) and some have found negative effects for block scheduling (e.g., Gruber & Onwuegbuzie, 2001).

Although the achievement findings are inconsistent, block scheduling does seem to generally lead to a more relaxed school climate and a decline in discipline problems—possibly because it cuts down on hallway traffic (Shortt & Thayer, 1998/9). On the 4×4 schedule, teachers have an additional benefit: They generally teach only *three* classes a day instead of four or five, so they are responsible for approximately 75–90 students at a time, rather than 125 or 150. Undoubtedly, this makes it easier to develop more attentive, caring relationships with students.

Despite these advantages, it is clear that block scheduling does not always result in the kind of innovative, varied instruction that proponents had envisioned (Queen, 2000). Richard Elmore (2002), an expert on school restructuring, reports that he once asked a high school social studies teacher what he thought of block scheduling. The teacher replied that it was the best thing that had ever happened in his teaching career. When Elmore asked why, the teacher explained: "Now we can show the whole movie."

As this anecdote suggests, changing the *structure* of time doesn't always change the *use* of time. This was clearly documented in an observational study by Bush and Johnstone (2000), which found a predominance of traditional teacher-centered instruction in 48 extended classes (12 each in algebra, biology, English, and U.S. History). Teachers in all subject areas spent the majority of time presenting content and monitoring seatwork, while students primarily listened to the teacher, responded to teacher questions, and completed seatwork. There was little individualization of instruction and little groupwork. These findings underscore the comments of one high school senior who observed that an 80-minute class does not necessarily lead to more active learning:

Rather, it will simply create more time for students to daydream, scribble in their notebooks, or catch up on sleep. A student who is bored in a 40-minute class will not suddenly become interested if the length of the class is doubled. (Shanley, 1999)

Although Christina recognizes the truth of this comment, she is an enthusiastic advocate of her school's 4×4 block schedule. During my visits to her classroom, I was able to observe the effective way she takes advantage of the 84-minute periods. During one class, Christina typically uses a variety of instructional formats—whole-group presentation, small-group work, student-led discussion, writing, student presentations—in order to maintain students' engagement and promote active participation. She may also include a variety of the content areas that comprise "English class." In the following excerpt, we see a class in which students write individually in their journals, work on reading strategy development in small groups, learn the format for a reference or "works cited" page in a mini-lesson, and act out a play they have been reading:

11:35 Students enter, take their seats, read the journal entry written on the board, and begin to write on the day's topic: "Write about how your life would have been changed if one day in your past had come out differently. What actually happened that day?" While students write, Christina silently takes attendance.

11:45 Christina hands out the checksheets with students' participation grades for the previous week. She tells them to fill out the page for the coming week. "You should be up to week 14, 12/20 to 12/23." After a few minutes, Christina instructs them to pass the pages forward.

11:50 Christina gives the agenda for the class: "First you're going to meet in your groups to practice making inferences. Then we'll have a mini-lesson on creating a works-cited page. On Wednesday, you'll be giving your speeches. I'll collect all the written components before you give your speeches, so I want to review what you'll need to turn in. Finally, we'll finish reading *Antigone.*"

11:52 Students get into their small groups to practice making inferences. Christina circulates and assists.

12:18 Christina announces that the groups have two more minutes to work.

12:20 Students move the chairs back into rows and return to their regular seats. Christina tells them to take out their notebooks and turn to the section on doing research. She moves the overhead projector to the front-center of the room, pulls down the shades, and announces that she wants to explain how to do the "works-cited" page for their research papers. She puts an overhead transparency on the projector and reviews the required format. Students are very attentive, taking notes and asking questions.

12:40 "Okay, guys, let's form the Greek Theater so we can finish reading *Antigone.*" Students get into a new configuration, roughly a circle, with the "chorus" at one end and an opening for the entrance to the "stage." "We left off on page 337. Chorus, take your places." Christina reads the stage directions, and students begin acting out *Antigone,* ending with the Queen's death. A boy reads the last speech of the play.

12:58 "All right, everyone, move your desks back to where they belong and listen to what you're going to do next." After students are back in their regular seats, Christina announces the final activity of the period: "Open your

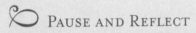 PAUSE AND REFLECT

Would you prefer to teach on a block schedule or a traditional schedule? What are your reasons? Do you think the difference in the length of the period would make a difference in your instruction?

journals and open your book. You have four minutes. Write about the last speech you just heard. What does it mean? Why is it important? Do you agree with it?"

1:02   Students finish their journal entries. The bell rings.

CONCLUDING COMMENTS

Tracy Kidder's book, *Among Schoolchildren* (1989), describes one year in the life of Chris Zajac, an elementary teacher who's feisty, demanding, blunt, fair, funny, and hard working. At the very end of the book, Kidder describes Chris's thoughts on the last day of school. Although she is convinced that she belongs "among schoolchildren," Chris laments the fact that she hadn't been able to help all her students—at least not enough:

> Again this year, some had needed more help than she could provide. There were many problems that she hadn't solved. But it wasn't for lack of trying. She hadn't given up. She had run out of time.

Like Chris, we all run out of time. The end of the year comes much too quickly, and some students' needs are much too great. Hopefully, the concepts and guidelines presented in this chapter will help you to make good use of the limited time you have.

SUMMARY

This chapter described time as a "precious resource." First, it considered the amount of school time that is actually available for teaching and learning. Then it described three strategies for increasing students' academic learning time—maintaining activity flow, minimizing transition time, and holding students accountable. The last section of the chapter examined the use of block scheduling.

Types of Time

- *Mandated time:* the time the state requires school to be in session.
- *Available time:* mandated time minus the time lost to absences, special events, half-days.
- *Instructional time:* the time that is actually used for instruction.
- *Engaged time:* the time a student spends working attentively on academic tasks.
- *Academic learning time (ALT):* the proportion of engaged time in which students are performing academic tasks with a high degree of success.

The Relationship between Time and Learning

- As allocated, engaged, and academic learning time increase, so does student learning.
- Of the three, ALT is the best predictor of achievement.

How to Increase Hours for Learning

- Maintain activity flow by avoiding
    - Flip-flopping.
    - Stimulus-bounded events.
    - Overdwelling.
    - Fragmentation.
- Minimize transition time by
    - Preparing students for transitions.
    - Establishing routines.
    - Defining boundaries to lessons.
- Hold students accountable by:
    - Communicating assignments and requirements clearly.
    - Monitoring students' progress.
    - Establishing routines for collecting and checking classwork and homework.
    - Maintaining good records.

Block Scheduling

- Types of block scheduling
    - 4×4 block schedule: four 80- or 90-minute instructional blocks scheduled each day for one semester or 90 days; students take four classes at a time.
    - A-B or alternating day schedule: 80- or 90-minute instructional periods every other day for the entire school year; students take six or seven courses at a time.
- Advantages
    - More usable instructional time.
    - Less fragmented instructional time.
    - More relaxed school climate.
    - Decrease in hallway traffic.
    - Opportunities for the use of varied instructional strategies.
- Problems
    - Block scheduling does not always result in the innovative, varied instruction that proponents envision.

By using time wisely, you can maximize opportunities for learning and minimize occasions for disruption in your classroom. Think about how much time is being spent on meaningful and appropriate work in your room, and how much is being eaten up by business and clerical tasks. Be aware that the hours available for instruction are much fewer than they first appear.

ACTIVITIES FOR SKILL BUILDING AND REFLECTION

In Class

Read the following vignette and identify the factors that threaten the activity flow of the lesson. Once you have identified the problems, rewrite the vignette so that activity flow is maintained OR explain how you would avoid the problems if you were the teacher.

Mrs. P. waits while her sophomore "A" level students take out the 10 mixed number addition problems she had them do for homework last night. Jack raises his hand. "I brought the wrong book by mistake, Mrs. P. My locker is right across the hall. Can I get my math book?"

"Be quick, Jack. We have 10 problems to go over, and the period is only 50 minutes long." Jack leaves, and Mrs. P. turns back to the class. "OK, this is what I want you to do. Switch papers with your neighbor." She waits while students figure out who will be partners with whom. She scans the room, trying to make sure that everyone has a partner. "OK, now write your name at the bottom of the page, on the right-hand side, to show that you're the checker. When I collect these papers, I want to know who the checkers were, so I can see who did a really accurate, responsible job of checking." She circulates while students write their names at the bottom of the page. "Ariadis, I said the right-hand side." Ariadis erases her name and rewrites it on the right side. "OK, now let's go over the answers. If your neighbor didn't get the right answer, put a circle around the problem and try to figure out what they did wrong so you can explain it to them. OK, number one, what's the right answer?" A student in the rear of the class raises his hand. "Billy?"

"I don't have a partner, Mrs. P. Can I go to the bathroom?"

"Jack will be right back, and then you'll have a partner. Just wait until we finish going over the homework." Jack returns. "Take a seat near Billy, Jack, and exchange homework papers with him."

Jack looks sheepishly at Mrs. P. "It's not in my book, Mrs. P. I must have left it on my desk last night. I was working on it pretty late."

"Class, go over the answers to problems one and two with your neighbors. See if you agree, and if you did the problems the same way. Jack, step outside."

Billy waves his hand again. "Mrs. P., can I *please* go to the bathroom now?"

"Yes, Billy. Fill out a pass, and I'll sign it. Just get back quickly." Leaving the door open so she can keep an eye on the other students, Mrs. P. follows Jack out of class. "You haven't had your homework done three times in the last two weeks, Jack. What's the problem?"

"Well, Mrs. P., my mother's been ... " The office intercom phone buzzes.

"Want me to get that, Mrs. P.?" a student calls from the class.

"Yes, tell them I'll be right there."

"They said to just tell you that Billy has to go to the office if he's not doing anything right now."

"Go take your seat, Jack. I'll talk to you after class." Mrs. P. moves to the front of the room again. "I'm sorry, class, let's begin again. Did you all do numbers one and two?" The class murmurs assent. "OK, number three. Let's start with problem three. Joan?"

Joan gives the correct answer. Mrs. P. gets responses and explanations for three more homework problems. As the class reviews the homework, Mrs. P. wanders up and down the rows. As she passes Tanya's desk, she notices a pink slip of paper. "Class, I almost forgot to collect the slips for the Academic Fair. This fair is a chance for us to show how much progress we've made this year in math. How many of you remembered to fill out the slip, describing the project you're going to do?" Students proceed to hunt through their backpacks and flip through their math books. Those who find their pink slips give them to Mrs. P. She reminds the others to return them tomorrow. "OK, let's get back to problem . . . six, no, seven. We were on seven, right? Shakia." Shakia begins to respond. Then Billy returns. A student in a seat by the door reminds Mrs. P. that Billy has to go to the office. "Billy, go to Mr. Wilkins's office."

"Why, Mrs. P.? All I did was go to the john."

"I don't know, Billy. Just go and make it quick. We're trying to have a class." Billy leaves, and Mrs. P. turns to the class. "Pass your papers to the front. I'll check the rest for you and give you credit for your homework. We need to move on to subtraction with fractions. Who can think of a real life problem where you would need to subtract fractions? Missy?"

"Can I go to the nurse, Mrs. P.? I don't feel good."

On Your Own

1. While you are visiting a class, carefully observe the way the teacher uses the time. Keep an accurate record for a complete period, noting how much of the available time is actually used for *instructional purposes.* For example, let's suppose you elect to observe a 50-minute mathematics class. The *available time* is 50 minutes. But while you are observing, you note that the first five minutes of the period are spent checking to see who does or does not have the homework (a clerical job). In the middle of the period, the teacher asks students to get into groups of four, and moving into groups takes up another five minutes that is not actually spent in instruction. Then an announcement comes over the loudspeaker, and the class discusses the announcement for another three minutes. Finally, the teacher wraps up class five minutes before the end of the period and gives everyone free time. *Conclusion: Out of 50 minutes of available time, 18 minutes were spent on nonacademic or noninstructional activities, leaving 32 minutes of actual instructional time*

2. Observe a class that is on a block schedule. How is the extended time used? What instructional strategies are used (e.g. lecture, cooperative learning, discussion, simulations, etc.)? How long does each instructional strategy last? Does the teacher make use of the entire period? Do students seem able to sustain attention and involvement?

For Your Portfolio

Develop a routine or transition activity for each of the following situations. Remember, your goal is to use time wisely.

    a. Beginning class each day.
    b. Taking attendance.
    c. Checking homework.
    d. Collecting papers.
    e. Returning papers.
    f. Moving from the whole group into small groups.
    g. Ending class each day.
    h. Leaving class at the end of the period.

FOR FURTHER READING

Adelman, N. E., Haslam, M. B., & Pringle, B. A. (1996). *The uses of time for teaching and learning. Volume I: Findings and conclusions.* Washington, D.C.: U. S. Department of Education, Office of Educational Research and Improvement. (Available online at www.ed.gov/pubs/SER/UsesOfTime.)

    This report summarizes findings from a three-year study of 14 schools and programs that have adopted innovative approaches to the uses of time for teaching and learning.

The investigators examined the quantity and quality of time in schools as well as the use of out-of-school time. One conclusion is that simply adding more classroom time to the school year or the school day is a "weak reform strategy."

Gettinger, M., & Seibert, J. K. (1995). Best practices for increasing academic learning time. In A. Thomas & J. Grimes (Eds.), *Best practice in school psychology-III,* pp. 943-954. Washington, D.C.: National Association of School Psychologists.

> This chapter reviews the findings on the relationship between academic learning time (ALT) and student achievement. Gettinger and Seibert suggest ways to assess time use and identify areas for improvement in order to maximize learning time. Although the chapter is intended for school psychologists, it should be helpful to teachers themselves.

Intrator, S. M. (2004). The engaged classroom. *Educational Leadership, 62*(1), 20-24.

> Sam Intrator, a college professor, spent 130 days shadowing students in a diverse California high school in order to understand the "experiential terrain of students' class time." In this article he describes the different kinds of time that students experience: slow time, lost time, fake time, worry time, play time, and engaged time.

Shernoff, D. J., Csikszentmihalyi, M., Schneider, B., & Shernoff, E. S. (2003). Student engagement in high school classrooms from the perspective of flow theory. *School Psychology Quarterly, 18*(2), 158-176.

> This study investigated how 526 high school students spent their time in school and the conditions under which they reported being engaged. Participants experienced higher engagement when the perceived challenge of the task and their own skills were high and in balance, when instruction was relevant, and when the learning environment was under their control. Participants were also more engaged in individual and groupwork versus listening to lectures, watching videos, or taking exams.

Smith, B. (2000). Quantity matters: Annual instructional time in an urban school system. *Educational Administration Quarterly, 36*(5), 652-682.

> The official time policy of the Chicago public elementary schools is to provide students with 300 minutes of instruction per day for 180 school days per year. This adds up to 900 hours on instruction annually. But based on classroom observation records, field notes, teacher interviews, school calendars, and other documents, this report concludes that nearly half of Chicago students may be receiving only 40 percent to 50 percent of the recommended hours. The reasons for this erosion of instructional time are discussed, and recommendations are outlined.

REFERENCES

Arlin, M. (1979). Teacher transitions can disrupt time flow in classrooms. *American Educational Research Journal, 16,* 42-56.

Bottge, B. J., Gugerty, J. J., Serlin, R., & Moon, K. (2003). Block and traditional schedules: Effects on students with and without disabilities in high school. *NASSP Bulletin, 87,* 2-14.

Bush, M. J., & Johnstone, W. G. (2000, April). An observation evaluation of high school A/B block classes: Variety or monotony? Paper presented at the Annual Meeting of the American Educational Research Association, New Orleans.

Doyle, W. (1983). Academic work. *Review of Educational Research, 53*(2), 159-200.

Elmore, R. F. (2002). The limits of "change." *Harvard Education Letter.* Downloaded from www.edletter.org/past/issues/2002-jf/limitsofchange.shtml.

Emmer, E. T., Evertson, C. M., & Worsham, M. E. (2000). *Classroom management for secondary teachers.* Boston: Allyn and Bacon.

Evans, W., Tokarczyk, J., Rice, S., & McCray, A. (2002). Block scheduling: An evaluation of outcomes and impact. *The Clearing House, 75*(6), 319-323.

Fisher, C. W., Berliner, D. C., Filby, N. N., Marliave, R., Cahen, L. S., & Dishaw, M. M. (1980). Teaching behaviors, academic learning time, and student achievement: An overview. In C. Denham & A. Lieberman (Eds.), *Time to learn.* Washington, D.C., U. S. Department of Education, pp. 7-32.

Fleming, D. S., Olenn, V., Schoenstein, R., & Eineder, D. (1997). *Moving to the block: Getting ready to teach in extended periods of learning time.* (An NEA Professional Library Publication.) Washington D.C.: National Education Association.

Good, T. L., & Brophy, J. E. (2003). *Looking in classrooms.* 9th ed. New York: Addison Wesley Longman.

Goodlad, J. I. (1984). *A place called school.* New York: McGraw-Hill.

Gruber, C. D., & Onwuegbuzie, A. J. (2001). Effects of block scheduling on academic achievement among high school sudents. *The High School Journal, 84*(4), 32-42.

Gump, P. (1982). School settings and their keeping. In D. L. Duke (Ed.), *Helping teachers manage classrooms.* Alexandria, VA: Association for Supervision and Curriculum Development, pp. 98-114.

Gump, P. V. (1987). School and classroom environments. In D. Stokols & I. Altman (Eds.), *Handbook of environmental psychology.* New York: John Wiley & Sons, pp. 691-732.

Karweit, N. (1989). Time and learning: A review. In R. E. Slavin (Ed.), *School and classroom organization.* Hillsdale, NJ: Lawrence Erlbaum.

Kidder, T. (1989). *Among schoolchildren.* Boston: Houghton Mifflin.

Kounin, J. (1970). *Discipline and group management in classrooms.* New York: Holt, Rinehart and Winston.

Leinhardt, G., & Greeno, J. G. (1986). The cognitive skill of teaching. *Journal of Educational Psychology, 78*(2), 75-95.

Marks, H. M. (2000). Student engagement in instructional activity: Patterns in the elementary, middle, and high school years. *American Educational Research Journal, 37*(1), 153-184.

Mattox, K., Hancock, D. R., & Queen, J. A. (2005). The effect of block scheduling on middle school students' mathematics achievement. *NASSP Bulletin, 89,* 3-13.

McGarity, Jr., J. R., & Butts, D. P. (1984). The relationship among teacher classroom management behavior, student engagement and student achievement of middle and high school science students of varying aptitude. *Journal of Research in Science Teaching, 21*(1), 55-61.

McIntosh, K., Herman, K., Sanford, A., McGraw, K., & Florence, K. (2004). Teaching transitions: Techniques for promoting success *between* lessons. *Teaching Exceptional Children, 37*(1), 32-38.

National Commission on Excellence in Education (1983). *A nation at risk: The imperative for educational reform.* Washington, D.C.: Government Printing Office.

National Education Commission on Time and Learning (1994). *Prisoner of time.* Washington, D.C.: Government Printing Office.

Nichols, J. D. (2005). Block-scheduled high schools: Impact on achievement in English and language arts. *The Journal of Educational Research, 98*(5), 299–309.

Queen, J. A. (2000). Block scheduling revised. *Phi Delta Kappan, 82*(3), 214–222.

Renewing Our Schools, Securing Our Future: A National Task Force on Public Education (2005). Getting smarter, becoming fairer [online]. (Available at http://www.ourfuture.org/docUploads/gsbf_popup.html.)

Rosenshine, B. (1980). How time is spent in elementary classrooms. In C. Denham & A. Lieberman (Eds.), *Time to learn.* Washington, D.C.: U.S. Department of Education.

Ross, R. P. (1985). Elementary school activity segments and the transitions between them: Responsibilities of teachers and student teachers. Unpublished doctoral dissertation, University of Kansas.

Shalaway, L. (1989). *Learning to teach . . . not just for beginners.* Cleveland, OH: Instructor Books, Edgell Communications.

Shanley, M. (October 22, 1999). Letter to the Editor. *The New York Times,* A26.

Shernoff, D. J., Czikszentmihalyi, M., Schneider, B., & Shernoff, E. S. (2003). Student engagement in high school classrooms from the perspective of flow theory. *School Psychology Quarterly, 18*(2), 158–176.

Shortt, T. L., & Thayer, Y. V. (1998/99). Block scheduling can enhance school climate. *Educational Leadership, 56*(4), 76–81.

Smith, B. (1998). *It's about time: Opportunities to learn in Chicago's elementary schools.* Chicago: Consortium on Chicago School Research. (Available online at www.ncrel.org/sdrs/areas/issues/envrnmnt/go/go61k10.htm.)

Smith, B. (2000). Quantity matters: Annual instructional time in an urban school system. *Educational Administration Quarterly, 36*(5), 652–682.

PART III

ORGANIZING AND MANAGING INSTRUCTION

ENHANCING STUDENTS' MOTIVATION

Sitting in the teachers' room of a large suburban high school, I overheard a conversation among members of the foreign language department. One ninth-grade teacher was complaining loudly about his third-period class:"These kids don't care about school. I'm not going to waste my time trying to get them motivated. If they can't be responsible for their own learning by now, it's just too bad."As I reflected on the teacher's statement, it seemed to me he was suggesting that motivation is entirely the student's responsibility; to be successful in school, students must arrive motivated, just as they must arrive with notebooks and pens. The statement also suggests that motivation is a stable characteristic, like eye color. From this perspective, some individuals come to school wanting to learn, and some don't. This can be a comforting point of view: If motivation is an innate or unchangeable characteristic, then we don't have to spend time and energy figuring out ways to motivate students.

On the other hand, some educators argue that motivation is an acquired disposition that is amenable to change. It can also be situation-specific, varying with the nature of the particular activity. Thus, students in foreign language classes can be enthusiastic about role-playing a visit to a restaurant but can appear bored and uninterested when it's time to conjugate verbs.

According to this latter perspective, teachers are responsible for stimulating students' engagement in learning activities. It may be gratifying (and a lot easier) when students come to school already excited about learning; however, when this is not the case, teachers must redouble their efforts to create a classroom context that fosters students' involvement and interest. This year, for example, one of Fred's Contemporary World Issues classes has a large proportion of students who, according to Fred, are "just marking time." During one conversation, Fred shared both his frustration and his determination:

 These kids are a constant struggle—the toughest kind of kids to work with. They're not dumb; they're not bad; they're just not intrinsically motivated when it comes to school. And they're used to taking it easy; for the last three years of high school, they've found that passive resistance works. They're so passive that teachers just leave them alone. But I refuse to give up on them. I look them in the face and say, "Tell me you want to stay home and be a slug and I'll leave you alone." And nobody's told me that. Actually, I think they're finally getting resigned to the fact that they can't coast in my class. And they can't even be mad at me, because they know that I'm on their side.

As Fred's comment indicates, stimulating students' motivation is easier said than done, especially when dealing with adolescents. The downturn in motivation during the transition years from elementary to secondary school is well documented (Anderman & Maehr, 1994)—and it is often dismaying to beginning teachers, particularly those who are passionate about their subject fields. Consider this entry taken from the journal of a student teacher in English:

I began my student teaching with all of these grand ideas about how I was going to enlighten students to the beauty of literature and unlock all the insight and talent that had been buried.... I gave serious, complicated lectures and multitudes of homework assignments, sure that my students would all be grateful when they witnessed the emergence of their intellectual prowess. Somewhere in the middle of the third week, however, the truth came rearing its ugly head: Most of my students did not, and probably never would, approach literature with [as much] enthusiasm [as they feel for] a new computer game.

To assist teachers who find themselves in this all too familiar situation, this chapter focuses on ways to enhance students' motivation. We begin by reflecting on what is realistic and appropriate with respect to motivating middle and secondary students. We then examine the factors that give rise to motivation. Finally, we consider a variety of motivational strategies drawn from research, theory, and the practice of our four teachers.

 PAUSE AND REFLECT

Think of a time when you were extremely motivated to learn. It might have been in preparation for your driver's license or the winter you learned to ski. Why were you motivated to learn? What supported you in your learning? What made it a successful experience? Try to relate your experiences to what you will be doing every day in your classroom.

What Is Realistic? What Is Appropriate?

Many of the teacher education students with whom I've worked believe that teachers motivate students *by making learning fun.* In fact, they frequently mention the ability to design activities that are enjoyable and entertaining as one of the defining characteristics of the "good teacher." Yet, as Jere Brophy (1998) reminds us, "schools are not day camps or recreational centers" (p. xviii), and teachers are not counselors or recreational directors. Given compulsory attendance, required curricula, class sizes that inhibit individualization, and the specter of high-stakes standardized testing, trying to ensure that learning is always fun is unreasonable and unrealistic. Bill Ayers (1993), a professor of education who has taught preschool through graduate school, is even more blunt. Characterizing the idea that good teachers make learning fun as one of the common myths that plague teaching, Ayers writes:

> Fun is distracting, amusing. Clowns are fun. Jokes can be fun. Learning can be engaging, engrossing, amazing, disorienting, involving, and often *deeply pleasurable.* If it's fun, fine. But it doesn't need to be fun. (p. 13)

Probably all of us can remember situations in which we were motivated to accomplish an academic task that was not fun, but that nonetheless seemed worthwhile and meaningful. The example that immediately comes to my own mind is learning French. I have never been very good at languages, and I was anxious and self-conscious whenever I had to speak in French class. I found conversation and oral exercises painful; role-plays were excruciating. Yet, I took three years of French in high school and two more in college, determined to communicate as fluently as possible when I finally got to visit France.

Brophy (1998) refers to this kind of drive as *motivation to learn*—the "tendency to find academic activities meaningful and worthwhile and to try to get the intended learning benefits from them" (p. 12). He distinguishes motivation to learn from *intrinsic motivation,* in which individuals pursue academic activities because they find them pleasurable. At times, of course, you may be able to capitalize on students' intrinsic interests so that the learning activities will be perceived as fun. But it's unlikely that this will always be the case. For this reason, teachers need to consider ways of developing and maintaining students' motivation to learn.

An Expectancy × Value Framework

It is helpful to think about stimulating motivation to learn in terms of an expectancy × value (or expectancy-times-value) model (Brophy, 1998; Feather, 1982; Wigfield & Eccles, 1992). This model posits that motivation depends on *students' expectation of success* and *the value they place on the task* (or the rewards that it may bring—such as being able to speak fluent French). The two factors work together like a multiplication equation (expectancy × value): If either one is missing (i.e., zero), there will be no motivation.

The expectancy-times-value model suggests that you have two major responsibilities with respect to motivation. First, you need to ensure that students can perform the task at hand successfully if they expend the effort. This means creating assignments that are well suited to students' achievement levels. This may also mean helping students to recognize their ability to perform successfully. Consider the case of Hopeless Hannah (Stipek, 1993). During math class, Hannah frequently sits at her desk doing nothing. If the teacher urges Hannah to try one of the problems she is supposed to be doing, she claims she can't. When the teacher walks her through a problem step by step, Hannah answers most of the questions correctly, but she insists that she was only guessing. Hannah considers herself incompetent, and she interprets her teacher's frustration as proof of her incompetence. She is a classic example of a student with "failure syndrome" problems (Brophy, 1998).

Fortunately, extreme cases like Hannah's are uncommon (Stipek, 1993). But we've probably all encountered situations where anticipation of failure has led to avoidance or paralysis. A lengthy term paper assignment is overwhelming, so we procrastinate until it's too late to do it really well. Calculus is daunting, so we take general mathematics instead. If failure is inevitable, there's no point in trying. And if we rarely try, we rarely succeed.

A second responsibility of teachers is to help students recognize the value of the academic work at hand. For example, Satisfied Sam (Stipek, 1993) is the class clown. He earns grades of C+ and B−, although he's clearly capable of earning As. At home, Sam spends hours at his computer, reads every book he can find on space, loves science fiction, and has even written a short novel. But he displays little interest in schoolwork. If assignments coincide with his personal interests, he exerts effort; otherwise, he simply sees no point in doing them.

In order to help students like Sam, you need to communicate the value of class activities or the value of the rewards that successful completion or mastery will bring. For example, students may see little value in learning biology, but still recognize that a passing grade is required for college admission.

In accordance with the expectancy-times-value model, Brophy (1987, 1998) has reviewed relevant theory and research and derived a set of strategies that teachers can use to enhance students' motivation. The following sections of this chapter are based on Brophy's work. (See Table 7.1.) We begin with strategies that focus on the first variable in the model—students' expectations of success.

As you read, keep in mind *that none of these strategies will be very effective if you have not worked to create and sustain a safe, caring classroom environment* (Chapter 3). Before students can become motivated, they must feel safe from humiliation, understand that it's all right to take risks and make mistakes, and know that they are accepted, respected members of the class (Ryan & Patrick, 2001). In fact, Brophy considers a supportive environment to be an "essential precondition" for the successful use of motivational strategies (Good & Brophy, 2000, p. 221).

 PAUSE AND REFLECT

Now that you have read about the expectancy × value model, reflect on its implications for teachers. How would you use this model to motivate a disinterested student in a topic in your content area?

TABLE 7.1 Brophy's Strategies for Enhancing Motivation to Learn

Strategies for Increasing Expectation of Success

- Provide opportunities for success.
- Teach students to set reasonable goals and to assess their own performance.
- Help students recognize the relationship between effort and outcome.
- Provide informative feedback.
- Provide special motivational support to discouraged students.

Strategies for Increasing Perceived Value

- Relate lessons to students' own lives.
- Provide opportunities for choice.
- Model interest in learning and express enthusiasm for the material.
- Include novelty/variety elements.
- Provide opportunities for students to respond actively.
- Allow students to create finished products.
- Provide opportunities for students to interact with peers.
- Provide extrinsic rewards.

STRATEGIES FOR INCREASING EXPECTATIONS OF SUCCESS

Provide Opportunities for Success

If tasks appear too difficult, students may be afraid to tackle them. You may have to modify assignments for different students, make assignments open-ended so that a variety of responses can be acceptable, provide additional instruction, divide lengthy projects into shorter, more "doable" parts, or allow extra time. Fred calls this the "slanty rope theory" of class work: "If we set a rope across a room at four feet, some kids can get over it and some can't. But if we slant the rope, then everyone can find their way over at some point." According to Fred, "success is a better motivator than anything else I know. If I can get kids to feel success, then maybe I'll be able to get through to them."

When Christina teaches her students to write research papers, she tries to guarantee success by breaking the assignment into small sections—taking notes, constructing a bibliography, creating an outline, writing the introductory paragraph, using parenthetical documentation—and having students turn in each part before writing the final paper. This not only makes the task seem less overwhelming, it also enables Christina to correct mistakes and set students on the right course before it's too late.

Sometimes, it's necessary to go back and reteach material rather than simply plowing ahead. For example, during one class period when Donnie was explaining how to construct and bisect congruent angles, it became apparent that most youngsters were lost. As students labored over their papers, frustrated comments began to be heard from all corners of the room: "I can't do it; you told me not to change the compass, but I had to"; "I need an eraser"; "Huh?"; "How you do this?";

"I don't get this." Circulating around the room, Donnie tried to help individuals who were having trouble. Finally, she moved to the front and center of the room and addressed the class: "Okay, let's start again. I see a lot of people are out in left field." She began to explain the procedure again, very slowly. After every step, she asked, "Does everyone have this?" before moving on to the next step. Students began to respond more positively: "Yeah"; "Uh-huh"; "Okay, we got it." One girl, who had been having particular difficulty, called out, "C'mere, Miss Collins, I wanna show you what I got." Donnie checked her work; it was correct. The girl turned to her neighbor and announced loudly, "You see, all I needed was a little help. Sometimes I gotta work step by step. I got it. I got it."

Sometimes, providing opportunities for success requires differentiated assignments for students of varying achievement levels. Consider this example from Tomlinson (1999):

> Seniors in Mr. Yin's government class are conducting research in groups of three to five. Their goal is to understand how the Bill of Rights has expanded over time and its impact on various groups in society.
>
> Mr. Yin has placed students in groups of somewhat similar readiness (e.g., struggling readers to grade-level readers, or grade-level readers to advanced readers). All research groups must examine an issue such as (1) how one or more amendments in the Bill of Rights became more inclusive over time; (2) societal events that prompted reinterpretation of one or more amendments in the Bill of Rights; (3) court decisions that redefined one or more of the amendments; (4) current interpretations and applications of one or more of the amendments.
>
> Students have a common rubric for the structure and content of appropriate writing, and they will be asked individually to develop a written piece that stems from what they have learned from their group's research. A wide range of print, computer, video, and audio resources are available to all groups.
>
> Mr. Yin has differentiated the work in two major ways. Some research groups will investigate society groups that are more familiar to them, areas where issues are more clearly defined, or areas where there is more information available on a basic reading level. Other groups will examine unfamiliar society groups, issues that are less defined, or issues where the library resources are more complex. In addition, students may choose to write an essay, parody, or dialogue to reflect their understandings. (Tomlinson, 1999, pp. 54–55)

Another way of enhancing the probability of success is to vary instructional approaches so that students who learn differently have equal access to instruction. Numerous schools have developed programs based on Howard Gardner's (1993, 1995) theory of "multiple intelligences" (MI). According to Gardner, people have at least eight types of intellectual capacities. (These are listed in Table 7.2.) Schools have traditionally emphasized the development of linguistic and logical-mathematical intelligences (and have favored those who are relatively strong in these), while they have neglected and undervalued the other intelligences. Although Gardner does not advocate one "right way" to implement a multiple intelligences education, he does recommend that teachers approach topics in a variety of ways, so that more students will be reached and more can experience "what it is like to be an expert" (1995, p. 208). For example, when teaching about photosynthesis, you might not

TABLE 7.2 Gardner's Multiple Intelligences

Type of Intelligence	Description
Linguistic	Capacity to use language to express and appreciate complex meanings; sensitivity to the sounds, rhythms, and meanings of words
Logical-mathematical	Capacity to reason and recognize logical and numerical patterns; to calculate, quantify, consider propositions and hypotheses
Spatial	Capacity to perceive the visual world accurately; to think in three-dimensional ways; to navigate oneself through space; to produce and understand graphic information
Musical	Sensitivity to pitch, melody, rhythm, and tone; to produce and appreciate different forms of musical expression
Bodily-kinesthetic	Capacity to use the body and to handle objects skillfully
Interpersonal	Capacity to understand and interact effectively with others; to discern accurately the moods and emotions of others
Intrapersonal	Capacity to understand oneself; perceptiveness about one's own moods, emotions, desires, motivations
Naturalist	Capacity to understand nature and to observe patterns; sensitivity to features of the natural world

Sources: Arends, 2004; Campbell, Campbell, & Dickinson, 1999.

only have students read the section of their textbook describing photosynthesis (linguistic intelligence), you might also have students do activities that tap different intelligences: paint the process of photosynthesis with watercolors (visual-spatial); write a journal entry that reflects on a personally transformative experience and compare it to photosynthesis (intrapersonal); create a time line of the steps of photosynthesis (logical-mathematical); role-play the "characters" involved in the process of photosynthesis (bodily-kinesthetic); or compare seedlings grown in sufficient light to those growing without adequate light (naturalist) (Campbell, Campbell, & Dickinson, 1999).

Obviously, in the real world of 42-minute periods and high-stakes standardized testing, incorporating all the intelligences into every topic is impossible. Nonetheless, the theory of MI can suggest varied ways of having students engage with academic content. By routinely integrating two or three different intelligences into your planning, you can provide students with greater opportunities for success.

Teach Students to Set Reasonable Goals and to Assess Their Own Performance

Some students think anything less than 100 on a test is a failure, while others are content with a barely passing grade. You may have to help students set goals that are reasonable and obtainable. At the very beginning of each course, Christina has students set the goals they hope to reach. (See Figure 7.1.) Then, based on these

Goals

Your individual goals should represent what you wish to accomplish in this course. Choose goals that are directly relevant to your expectations for the course. For example, while it is valid to say that you want to be a millionaire, that goal is not specifically relevant to English class. Choose a more specific shorter-term goal.

Once you have chosen your goals, explain your reasons for selecting them on the lines provided. Then, list 2 ways that you think you can reach these goals.

Complete Goals #1–5 at this time. Do not complete the Goal Revisions and Additions sections until you are instructed to do so.

Goal #1 _____
Reason for selection of this goal
_____
_____

2 things you can do to help you reach your goal
#1 _____
#2 _____

Goal #2 _____
Reason for selection of this goal
_____
_____

2 things you can do to help you reach your goal
#1 _____
#2 _____

Goal #3 _____
Reason for selection of this goal
_____
_____

2 things you can do to help you reach your goal
#1 _____
#2 _____

Goal #4 _____
Reason for selection of this goal
_____
_____

2 things you can do to help you reach your goal
#1 _____
#2 _____

Goal #5 _____
Reason for selection of this goal
_____
_____

2 things you can do to help you reach your goal
#1 _____
#2 _____

Figure 7.1　Christina's Goal-Setting Handout

Goal Revision/Addition #1

Reason for selection of this goal

2 things you can do to help you reach your goal
#1 _____
#2 _____

Goal Revision/Addition #2

Reason for selection of this goal

2 things you can do to help you reach your goal
#1 _____
#2 _____

Figure 7.1   (*continued*)

goals, students decide the criteria they will use to evaluate their work. They have to include four specific items that Christina requires and eight more that they devise for themselves. Throughout the marking period, students keep their work in a "collection folder," from which they then select work representing their progress in meeting the goals they set. For each selection, students also complete a "reflection sheet," which asks them to explain which goals and criteria the piece represents. The selected work, along with its reflection sheet, gets moved into a portfolio that both they and Christina assess.

Christina also gives her students a rubric that details how each major project will be scored and requires students to score their work before turning it in: "This way, students are aware of the score they will be receiving, and they can make a choice about whether they're happy with that or want to do more." Interestingly, Christina finds that students' self-evaluations are usually within a few points of her own assessments of their work.

I observed another example of helping students set goals when one of Fred's eleventh-grade students turned in an appalling essay at the beginning of the year. Not only was it short, superficial, and vague, but both the handwriting and spelling were atrocious. When Fred investigated, he found out that the student had a learning disability; nonetheless, he told the student in no uncertain terms that his performance was inadequate: "Look, you can't write, you can't even print, and you can't spell. But you're not stupid. So what are you going to do to get better? Let's set some goals." With the assistance of the resource room teacher, they devised a plan for the student to learn keyboarding and to use a spell checker. When the next writing assignment was due, the student came to Fred complaining that it was too hard. Fred was sympathetic and supportive—but adamant that the student complete it. He did, and although it was far from adequate, it was a definite improvement over the first assignment. Reflecting on the student's problems, Fred comments:

 We can all feel sorry for him, but he can't go around like this; he has to be pushed to overcome his deficits. People have allowed him to stay a baby, but it's time for him to grow up. There are ways he can improve. My job is to teach him to set some reasonable goals and then work to achieve them.

Help Students Recognize the Relationship between Effort and Outcome

Like Hopeless Hannah, some youngsters proclaim defeat before they've even attempted a task. When they don't do well on an assignment, they attribute their failure to lack of ability, not realizing that achievement is often a function of effort. Other students may be overconfident—even cocky—and think they can do well without exerting much effort. In either situation, you have to make the relationship between effort and outcome explicit. Whenever possible, point out students' improvement and help them to see the role of effort: "See, you did all your math homework this week, and it really paid off. Look at how well you did on the quiz!"

The relationship between effort and outcome became painfully clear to a student in Sandy's class who refused to take notes during class. When Sandy first noticed that he wasn't taking notes, she told him to take out his notebook and open it. He did, murmuring, "I'll open my notebook, but you can't force me to take notes." Later, he told Sandy he didn't need to take notes like the other kids, because he had a good memory. She explained that her years of experience had shown her that taking notes in chemistry was absolutely necessary; she suggested he keep his notebook out and open "just in case." When the first test was given, the boy's grade was 40. Sandy told him: "I know it's not because you're unable to do the work. So what do you think? What conclusion do you draw from this?" The boy responded, "I guess I gotta take notes."

Provide Informative Feedback

Sometimes turning in work to a teacher is like dropping it down a black hole. Assignments pile up in huge mounds on the teacher's desk, and students know that their papers will never be returned—graded or ungraded. From a student's perspective, it's infuriating to work hard on an assignment, turn it in, and then receive no feedback from the teacher. But a lack of academic feedback is not simply infuriating. It is also detrimental to students' motivation and achievement. The Beginning Teacher Evaluation Study (Fisher et al., 1980) documented the importance of providing feedback to students:

> One particularly important teaching activity is providing academic feedback to students (letting them know whether their answers are right or wrong, or giving

them the right answer). Academic feedback should be provided as often as possible to students. When more frequent feedback is offered, students pay attention more and learn more. Academic feedback was more strongly and consistently related to achievement than any of the other teaching behaviors. (p. 27)

If you circulate while students are working on assignments, you can provide them with immediate feedback about their performance. You can catch errors, assist with problems, and affirm correct, thoughtful work. In the following vignette, we see Sandy help two girls having problems pouring a solution into a funnel. Only a clear, colorless solution was supposed to come out into the beaker, but the solution was yellow and had particles of the solid in it.

SANDY: Why did this happen?

TANYA: Because I poured too fast and too much.

SANDY: Right. [She calls all the students over to see the problem that the two girls had.] So what happened?

LISA: The yellow stuff got over the filter paper, behind the fold.

SANDY: Okay, so what can you do?

TANYA: Pour it back in, but we're going to lose some.

SANDY: [To the other students] Can they pour it back in?

STUDENT: Yeah.

SANDY: Sure. It was good you washed the beaker.

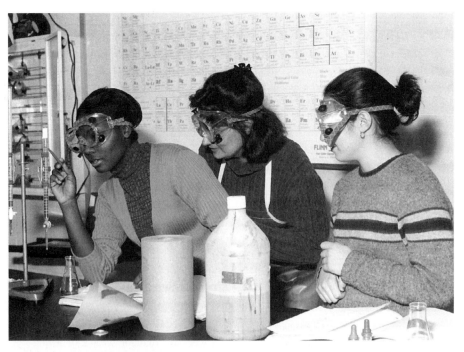

Sandy monitors the activity of lab groups.

Sometimes you're unable to monitor work while it's being done. In this case, you need to check assignments once they've been submitted and return them to students as soon as possible. You might also decide to allow your students to check their own work. Donnie believes this has numerous educational benefits:

> I like to go over the homework in class and have students check their own work. This gives them the chance to see how they're doing, where they're confused. If I just had them turn in the work and I graded it, they'd know which problems were right and which were wrong, but they wouldn't know why. Once a week, though, I do collect the homework and go over it myself. That way I can see for myself how students are doing.

As an English teacher, Christina finds that having students evaluate their own work and that of their peers is not only educational, it also allows them to receive feedback more quickly:

> I used to think it was an easy way out to have students grade their own papers or do peer editing, but experienced teachers told me it wasn't so, and I've come to agree. I couldn't have a writing-based classroom if I had to give all the feedback myself. My students write many drafts of their papers, and I simply cannot read them all quickly enough. . . . So I teach them to self- and peer-evaluate before revising. . . . They learn a lot when they do peer editing, and they can get instant feedback.

Whether you correct work while it's being done, at home over a cup of coffee, or together with your students, the important point is that students *need to know how they are progressing*. It's also important to give feedback in terms of *absolute standards or students' own past performance rather than peers' performance* (Brophy, 1998). Thus, instead of saying, "Congratulations! You received the sixth highest grade in the class," you could say, "Congratulations! You went from a 79 on your last quiz to an 87 on this quiz." Similarly, you can point out strengths and weaknesses and add a note of encouragement for further effort ("You've demonstrated a firm grasp of the perspectives of the slaveholders and the abolitionists, but not the slaves themselves. Check the chapter again, and add a paragraph to round out your presentation.")

Provide Special Motivational Support to Discouraged Students

For students with limited ability or learning disabilities, school may be a constant struggle to keep up with classmates and to maintain a sense of enthusiasm and motivation. Such students not only require instructional assistance (e.g., individualized activities, extra academic help, well-structured assignments, extra time), they may also need special encouragement and motivational support. For example, Donnie constantly exhorts students not to get discouraged if they're having trouble and reminds them that people work and learn at different paces. Often, she pairs low-achieving students with those she knows will be patient and helpful and encourages peer assistance and peer tutoring. Similarly, Sandy frequently reassures her students that they're in this together:

 So many of my students are afraid of taking chemistry, and they find it harder than any subject they've taken. I spend the first five or six weeks of school reassuring them—"You're not alone, there's support, I'm here to help you, we'll do this slowly and systematically. . . . you don't have to learn it in three or four days; it may be a long haul but that's OK. If I can get them to trust me, and I believe they can do it, then eventually they develop more confidence and a sense of well-being.

Sandy also makes sure that she expresses concern and surprise when students don't do well on a test or assignment. She'll ask, "What happened here?" or "What's the problem?" so that students know she's not writing them off:

 Too many times teachers will say "good job" to the person who's gotten the A, but nothing to the kid who got the D or F. But if you don't ask what happened, they think you expected it. Sometimes what you don't say is more powerful than what you do say.

Christina finds that students who have failed the standardized test required for high school graduation are particularly discouraged and anxious. Like Sandy, she makes it clear that she expects them to pass the next time around; at the very least, they will improve their scores. She cheers them on as they take numerous practice tests and analyze their performances. Then she has them think of one thing they will do differently when they take the test again. Responses vary—"I won't fall asleep"; "I'm going to read *all* the answer choices before I choose one"; "I'm going to figure out what kind of text I'm reading and mark it up"—but simply having a plan seems to help students to be more optimistic. Christina also gives her students granola bars and other healthful snacks the day before the test, an attempt to get them to go to bed early and eat a good breakfast!

Unfortunately, teachers sometimes develop counterproductive behavior patterns that communicate low expectations and reinforce students' perceptions of themselves as failures. Table 7.3 lists some of the behaviors that have been identified.

As Brophy (1998) points out, some of these differences are due to the behavior of the students. For example, if students' contributions to discussions are irrelevant or incorrect, it is difficult for teachers to accept and use their ideas. Moreover, the boundary between *appropriate differentiated instruction and inappropriate differential treatment* is often fuzzy. Asking low achievers easier, nonanalytic questions may make instructional sense. Nonetheless, it's important to monitor the extent to which you engage in these behaviors and to reflect on the messages you are sending to your low-achieving or learning disabled students. If you find that you are engaging in a lot of the behaviors listed in Table 7.3, you may be "merely going through the motions of instructing low achievers, without seriously working to help them achieve their potential" (Brophy, 1998, p. 85).

TABLE 7.3 Ways That Teachers May Communicate Low Expectations

1. Waiting less time for low achievers to answer a question before giving the answer or calling on someone else.
2. Giving answers to low achievers or calling on someone else rather than helping the students to improve their responses by giving clues or rephrasing questions.
3. Rewarding inappropriate behaviors or incorrect answers.
4. Criticizing low achievers more often for failure.
5. Praising low achievers less often for success.
6. Paying less attention to low achievers.
7. Seating low achievers farther away from the teacher.
8. Demanding less from low achievers than they are capable of learning.
9. Being less friendly in interactions with low achievers; showing less attention and responsiveness; making less eye contact.
10. Providing briefer and less informative answers to their questions.
11. Showing less acceptance and use of low achievers' ideas.
12. Limiting low achievers to low-level, repetitive curriculum with an emphasis on drill and practice tasks.

Source: Brophy, 1998.

ENHANCING THE VALUE OF THE TASK

Recall that when I asked the students in the classes of our four teachers "why kids behave in some classes and not others," they stressed the importance of teaching in a way that is stimulating. As one student wrote, "Not everything can be fun . . . , but there are ways teachers can make [material] more interesting and more challenging." (See Chapter 1.) This student intuitively understands that motivation to learn depends not only on success expectations, but also on students' perceptions of the value of the task or the rewards that successful completion or mastery will bring. Remember Satisfied Sam? Seeing no value in his course assignments, he invests little effort in them, even though he knows he could be successful. Since students like Sam are unlikely to respond to their teachers' exhortations to work harder, the challenge is to find ways to convince them that the work has (1) *intrinsic value* (doing it will provide enjoyment), (2) *utility value* (doing it will advance their personal goals), or (3) *attainment value* (doing it will affirm their self-concept or fulfill their needs for achievement, understanding, skill mastery, and prestige) (Brophy, 1998; Eccles & Wigfield, 1985). Let's consider some of the strategies that teachers can use to enhance the perception of value.

Relate Lessons to Students' Own Lives

A study by Newby (1991) of the motivational strategies of first-year teachers demonstrated that students are more engaged in classrooms where teachers provide reasons for doing tasks and relate lessons to students' personal experiences. Unfortunately, *he also found that first-year teachers use these "relevance strategies" only occasionally.* (See Figure 7.2.)

SHOE   **By JEFF MACNELLY**

Figure 7.2   It's important to point out the relevance of learning activities.

I thought about Newby's study as I read a vignette about a seventh-grade teacher attempting to explain why an oxygen atom attracts two hydrogen atoms (Gordon, 1997). Jesse, a boy in the class, did not find this particularly engaging. However, by phrasing the concept in terms of the fact that two seventh-grade girls were attracted to him, the teacher was able to spark his involvement. As Gordon wryly observes, "metaphors involving sex immediately pique adolescents' interest" and can be particularly useful in generating attention and involvement—"as long as the metaphors do not cross the invisible boundary of propriety" (p. 58).

When students are not from the dominant culture, teachers must make a special effort to relate academic content to referents from the students' own culture. This practice not only helps to bridge the gap between the two cultures, it also allows the study of cultural referents in their own right (Ladson-Billings, 1994). Morrell and Duncan-Andrade (2002, 2004), English teachers in a large multicultural, urban school in California, provide a compelling example. Reasoning that hip-hop music could be used "as a bridge linking the seemingly vast span between the streets and the world of academics" (2002, p. 89), Morrell and Duncan-Andrade used hip-hop to develop the critical and analytical skills of their underachieving twelfth-grade students. First, the teachers paired "canonical poetry" with rap songs (e.g., Coleridge's "Kubla Khan" with "If I Ruled the World" by Nas; Eliot's "Love Song of J. Alfred Prufrock" with "The Message" by Grand Master Flash). They then divided their class into small groups and assigned one pair of texts to each group. Students were to interpret their poem and song and analyze the links between them. One group, for example, talked about how both Grand Master Flash and T. S. Eliot view their rapidly deteriorating societies as a "wasteland." Another group pointed out that both John Donne and Refuge Camp use a relationship with a lover to symbolize the agony they feel for society. The curriculum unit that Morrell and Duncan-Andrade designed illustrates the power of what Gloria Ladson-Billings (1994) calls *culturally relevant teaching.*

Our four teachers are well aware of the need to relate academic tasks to youngsters' lives. When Donnie teaches percents, for example, she has students do a project entitled "Buying Your First Car." Students work in small groups to determine how much a car they select will actually cost—a task that involves knowing and using compound interest formulas, calculating depreciation, learning about base prices and shipping fees, and figuring out if monthly payments will fit in their budgets. When Fred's students study the Bill of Rights, they debate whether wearing a T-shirt with an obscene slogan is protected free speech. Reflecting on the need for relevance, he comments:

 You don't have to do it every day, but little bits and pieces help. Teachers always have to ask, "So what? What does this material have to do with me?" My brother always said, "If it doesn't make me richer or poorer, then don't bother me with it." My brother was not a good student. So whenever I teach anything, I use "my brother Bob test." I ask myself, "So what? How will it make my kids richer or poorer in some way?"

Provide Opportunities for Choice

One of the most obvious ways to ensure that learning activities connect to individuals' personal interests is to provide opportunities for choice. Moreover, research has shown that when students experience a sense of autonomy and self-determination, they are more likely to be intrinsically motivated (Ryan & Deci, 2000) and to "bond" with school (Roeser, Eccles, & Sameroff, 2000). Mandated curricula and high-stakes standardized testing thwart opportunities for choice, but there are usually alternative ways for students to accomplish requirements. Think about whether students might (1) participate in the design of the academic task; (2) decide how the task is to be completed; and/or (3) decide when the task is to be completed (Stipek, 1993).

Flowerday and Schraw (2000) asked 36 teachers about the types of instructional choices they gave to their students. Although types of choices varied as a function of content areas and grade levels, all teachers agreed on six main types of choice: (1) topics of study (for research papers, in-class projects, and presentations); (2) reading materials (type of genre, choice of authors); (3) methods of assessment (exam versus final project); (4) activities (book report or diorama); (5) social arrangements (whether to work in pairs or small groups, choice of group members); and (6) procedural choices (when to take tests, what order to study prescribed topics, and when assignments were due). Teachers also expressed the belief that choice has a positive effect on students' motivation by increasing their sense of ownership and self-determination, interest, and enthusiasm.

Despite this belief, teachers tended to use choice as a *reward* for effort and good behavior, rather than as a *strategy for fostering* effort and good behavior. Thus, teachers were most likely to give choices to students who were already self-regulated. It's easy to understand why teachers would provide choice to students who have previously shown that they are responsible, motivated, and well-behaved. (It certainly seems safer!) But if we think of choice as a motivational strategy rather than a reward, we can see that it might be useful to motivate students like Satisfied Sam.

There are many ways to build choice into the curriculum. To prepare for the state's high school graduation test, Christina's students have to complete various writing tasks, such as a persuasive letter or essay on a controversial topic, a cause/effect essay, and a problem/solution essay, but students often choose their own topics for all of these. When Fred's classes report on a historical figure, they are instructed to choose the figure who seems most like them (or whom they'd like to be like). Donnie encourages students to "put their heads together" in small groups to identify the homework problems that caused the most difficulty; those are the ones they then review. And all four teachers sometimes allow students to choose their own groups for collaborative work.

Model Interest in Learning and Express Enthusiasm for the Material

When Fred is about to introduce a difficult concept, he announces: "Now please listen to this. Most Americans don't understand this at all; they don't have a clue. But it's really important, and I want you to understand it." Christina often refers to her love of reading and the fact that she writes poetry. When Donnie gives students complex problems that involve a lot of skills and steps, she tells them, "I love problems like this! This is so much fun!" In similar fashion, Sandy frequently exclaims, "This is my favorite part of chemistry," a statement that usually causes students to roll their eyes and respond, "Oh, Mrs. K., *everything* is your favorite part!"

Include Novelty/Variety Elements

During a visit to Donnie's class, I watched as she introduced the "challenge problem of the day." Donnie distributed a xeroxed copy of a dollar bill and told students to figure out how many $1 bills would be needed to make one mile if they were lined up end to end. The enthusiasm generated by the copies of the dollar was palpable. Fred also used money during one observation to make a point about choosing a more difficult, but more ethical course of action. He moved up an aisle and dropped a $5 bill on an empty chair. Turning to the girl sitting in the next seat, he commented, "You could just stick that in your pocket, walk out the door, and go to McDonald's, right? Take the money and run. That would certainly be possible, but would it be right?"

In Christina's basic skills class, I watched as students read and discussed *The Martian Chronicles* by Ray Bradbury. Then Christina explained how they were to create small illustrations of key incidents, which would then be assembled in sequential order on large pieces of butcher paper and mounted in the library. As she assigned the incidents ("Andrew, pages 78 and 79, when Tomas is speaking to Pop at the gas station"; "Natal, pages 92 to 94, when the men take up the collection so he can go on the rocket"), it was clear that incorporating this art activity not only reinforced students' understanding of the story but also generated a great deal of enthusiasm.

Provide Opportunities for Students to Respond Actively

So often the teacher talks and moves, while students sit passively and listen. In contrast, our four teachers structure lessons so that students must be actively involved.

Fred and his students plan a mock trial.

When Fred's Institute for Political and Legal Education (IPLE) class studies the judicial system, students engage in a mock trial. In Christina's classes, where many students voice an entrenched dislike of poetry, Christina works hard to have students experience poetry in a way that is memorable and personal. She divides the class into groups to design a poetry lesson that requires each student in the class (1) to write a poem that uses a particular literary device (e.g., allusion, metaphor, simile, irony, alliteration, consonance, etc.) and (2) to study a poem. Instructing the groups to use as a model Mr. Keating (the Robin Williams character) from *Dead Poets Society,* Christina encourages students to design lessons that "appeal to the senses," that "are like games or sports with a lot of poetry added in," and that require students "to get up and move around." One group, for example, designed an impossible scavenger hunt for the class to attempt and then explained how the hunt related to Poe's poem "El Dorado."

Allow Students to Create Finished Products

Too much school time is devoted to exercises, drills, and practice. Students practice writing, but rarely write. They practice reading skills, but rarely read. They practice mathematical procedures, but rarely do real mathematics. Yet, creating a finished product gives meaning and purpose to assignments and increases students' motivation to learn.

After a fierce winter blizzard that closed school for seven days and left administrators trying to figure out how to make up the lost time, Fred's students wrote letters to state legislators offering various proposals. Since the task was *real,* the letters had to be suitable for mailing; motivation was far greater than it would have been if the task had been a workbook exercise on writing business letters. Similarly, Sandy's labs are not simply exercises in following a prescribed set of steps leading to a foregone conclusion. They are real investigations into real problems.

As an introduction to a multigenre project, Christina's students wrote children's books. First, a parenting-class teacher spoke with the class about writing for young children (e.g., how many characters would be appropriate; whether fantasy themes or something closer to children's own experiences would be most suitable; the importance of using simple vocabulary). Then students wrote their books, engaging in peer editing and revision. They read each others' books and chose six from each class. These were sent to the art classes, where they were illustrated and bound. Drama classes also got involved: They chose four of the books to act out to first-graders who came to the high school.

Provide Opportunities for Students to Interact with Peers

All four teachers firmly believe that motivation (and learning) are enhanced if students are allowed to work with one another. They provide numerous opportunities for peer interaction (a topic that will be explored further in Chapter 9).

Sometimes, groups are carefully planned; at other times, they are formed more casually. For example, one day I saw Donnie shuffle a deck of cards (admitting that she never learned how to do this really well) and then walk around the room, asking each student to pick a card. She then told students to get up and find the person or persons with the same number or face card that they had. Once students had found their partners, she proceeded to explain the group task.

Provide Extrinsic Rewards

Some effective managers find it useful to provide students with rewards for engaging in the behaviors that support learning (such as paying attention and participating) and for academic achievement. The use of rewards in classrooms is based on the psychological principle of *positive reinforcement:* Behavior that is rewarded is strengthened and is therefore likely to be repeated. Although rewards do not increase the perceived value of the behavior or the task, they link performance of the behavior or successful completion of the task to attractive, desirable consequences.

Rewards can be divided into three categories: social rewards, activity rewards, and tangible rewards. *Social rewards* are verbal and nonverbal indications that you recognize and appreciate students' behavior or achievements. A pat on the back, a smile, a thumbs-up signal—these are commonly used social rewards that are low in cost and readily available.

Praise can also function as a social reward. In order to be effective, however, praise must be *specific and sincere.* Instead of "Good paper," you can try something like this: "Your paper shows a firm grasp of the distinction between metaphor and similes." Instead of "You were great this morning," try, "The way you came into the room, took off your baseball caps, and immediately got out your notebooks was terrific." Being specific will make your praise more informative; it will also help you to avoid using the same tired, old phrases week after week, phrases that quickly lose any impact (e.g., "good job"). If praise is to serve as a reinforcer, it also needs to be *contingent on the behavior you are trying to strengthen.* In other words, it should be given only when that behavior occurs so that students understand exactly what evoked the praise.

 Donnie distributes a lab worksheet that asks students to draw a parallelogram and then work through five activities to discover the figure's properties. She stresses that students should write down their observations after each activity and then draw some final conclusions. As students work on the problems, she circulates through the room. When she sees Shaneika's paper, she tells her: "Shaneika, you are really following directions. You're writing the answers as you go along."

In addition to pats on the back and verbal praise, some teachers institute more formal ways of recognizing accomplishment, improvement, or cooperation. For example, they may display student work, provide award certificates, nominate students for school awards given at the end of the year, or select "Students of the Week." Whichever approach you use, be careful that this strategy of public recognition doesn't backfire by causing students embarrassment. As Sandy reminded us in Chapter 3, secondary students generally do not want to stand out from their peers. Moreover, individual public recognition may be upsetting to students whose cultures value the collective over individual achievement (Trumbull, Rothstein-Fisch, Greenfield, & Quiroz, 2001).

In addition to social rewards, teachers sometimes use *special activities* as rewards for good behavior or achievement. In middle and high school, watching a DVD, listening to music, having free time, or having a night of no homework can be very reinforcing. One way of determining which activities should be used as rewards is to listen carefully to students' requests. If they ask you for the opportunity to listen to music or have a popcorn party, you can be confident that those activities will be reinforcing (at least for those particular students). It's also helpful to observe what activities students engage in when they have free time (e.g., do they read magazines? talk with friends? draw?)

Finally, teachers can use *tangible, material rewards* for good behavior—cookies, candy, key chains, pencils—although such rewards are used less in high school than in elementary school. For example, Donnie goes to a discount supermarket and buys a big supply of candy that she keeps in a back closet; when students have been especially cooperative, she'll break out the Twizzlers for an unexpected treat. Similarly, Fred sometimes gives prizes when students have to review factual information for tests, a task they usually find boring. He may have students play vocabulary bingo, telling them: "I have two prizes in my pocket for the winner—two tickets for an all-expense-paid trip to Hawaii or a piece of candy. You get whichever one I pull out of my pocket first." Every now and then, Fred also uses candy to show his appreciation for good behavior. In his words,

> If someone has never given me grief, I may be moved to a spontaneous act of generosity. I'll say, "Here take this," and give them a Sugar Daddy or package of Sweet Tarts. It's amazing; kids go crazy over a little piece of candy.

Problems with Rewards

The practice of providing extrinsic rewards has been the focus of considerable controversy. One objection is that giving students tangible rewards in exchange for good behavior or academic performance is tantamount to bribery. Proponents of this position argue that students should engage in appropriate behavior and activities for their own sake: They should be quiet during in-class assignments because that is the socially responsible thing to do; they should do their homework so that they can practice skills taught during class; they should learn verb conjugations in Spanish because they need to know them. Other educators acknowledge the desirability of such intrinsic motivation, but believe that the use of rewards is inevitable in situations where people are not completely free to follow their own inclinations. Even Ryan and Deci (2000), two psychologists who strongly endorse the importance of self-determination and autonomy, acknowledge that teachers "cannot always rely on intrinsic motivation to foster learning" since "many of the tasks that educators want their students to perform are not inherently interesting or enjoyable" (p. 55).

Another objection to the use of rewards is the fact that they are attempts to control and manipulate people. When we dispense rewards, we are essentially saying, "Do this, and you'll get that"—an approach not unlike the way we train our pets. Indeed, Alfie Kohn, author of *Punished by Rewards: The Trouble with Gold Stars, Incentive Plans, A's, Praise, and Other Bribes* (1993), contends that rewards and punishments are "two sides of the same coin" (p. 50). Although rewards are certainly more pleasurable, they are "every bit as controlling as punishments, even if they control by seduction" (p. 51). According to Kohn, if we want youngsters to become self-regulating, responsible, caring individuals, we must abandon attempts at external control and provide students with opportunities to develop competence, connection, and autonomy in caring classroom communities.

Another major concern is that rewarding students for behaving in certain ways actually *undermines their intrinsic motivation to engage in those behaviors.* This question was explored in an influential study conducted by Lepper, Greene, and Nisbett (1973). First, the researchers identified preschoolers who showed interest in a particular drawing activity during free play. Then they met with the children individually. Some children were simply invited to draw with the materials (the "no-reward" subjects). Others were told they could receive a "good-player" award, which they received for drawing (the "expected-reward" subjects). Still others were invited to draw and were then given an unexpected reward at the end (the "unexpected-reward" subjects). Subsequent observations during free play revealed that the children who had been promised a reward ahead of time engaged in the art activity half as much as they had initially. Children in the other two groups showed no change.

The study by Lepper, Greene, and Nisbett stimulated a great deal of research on the potentially detrimental effects of external rewards. Although the results were not always consistent, this research led educators to conclude that *rewarding people for doing something that is inherently pleasurable decreases their interest in continuing that behavior.* A common explanation for this effect is the *overjustification hypothesis.* It appears to work like this: Individuals being rewarded reason that the task must not be very interesting or engaging, since they have to be rewarded (i.e., provided with extra justification) for undertaking it. In other words, what was previously considered "play" is now seen as "work" (Reeve, 2006). Another explanation focuses on the possibility that external rewards conflict with people's need for autonomy and self-determination. This explanation argues that interest in a task decreases if individuals perceive rewards as attempts to control their behavior.

The detrimental effect of extrinsic reward on intrinsic motivation has been—and continues to be—hotly debated. In fact, reviews of the research (Cameron, 2001; Cameron & Pierce, 1994; Cameron, Banko, & Pierce, 2001; Deci, Koestner, & Ryan, 1999, 2001) have reached contradictory conclusions about the effects of expected tangible rewards. According to Cameron (2001), it's all right to say, "If you complete the assignment with at least 80 percent accuracy, you'll get a coupon for something at the school store at the end of the period" (expected reward contingent on completion and level of performance), but it's *not* all right to say, "Work on the assignment and you'll get a coupon for something at the school store at the end of the period" (noncontingent reward). In contrast, Deci, Koestner, and Ryan (1999, 2001) contend that expected "tangible rewards offered for engaging in, completing, or doing well at a task" are *all* deleterious to intrinsic motivation (1999, p. 656). With respect to verbal rewards and unexpected tangible rewards, the reviews are more consistent: Both sets of researchers conclude that verbal praise can enhance intrinsic motivation and that unexpected tangible rewards have no detrimental effect.

At the present time, caution in the use of external rewards is clearly in order. As you contemplate a system of rewards for your classroom, keep in mind the suggestions listed in the Practical Tips box.

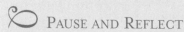

PAUSE AND REFLECT

Galvanized by No Child Left Behind, schools across the country are trying to improve attendance by offering students the chance to win cars, computers, iPods, shopping sprees, groceries—even a month's rent (Belluck, 2006). Having just read the section on providing extrinsic rewards, what do you think about this practice? Do you think such rewards are likely to bring about an increase in attendance?

MOTIVATING UNDERACHIEVING AND DISAFFECTED STUDENTS

In "Building Community from Chaos" (1994), Linda Christensen, a high school teacher in Portland, Oregon, vividly portrays the challenge of motivating the academically unmotivated. Christensen writes about her fourth block senior English class, a tracked class where most of the students were short on credits to graduate

PRACTICAL TIPS FOR

USING REWARDS

- *Use verbal rewards to increase intrinsic motivation for academic tasks.* It seems clear that praise can have a positive impact on students' intrinsic motivation. But remember that individual public praise may be embarrassing to teenagers and to those from cultures that value the collective over individual achievement. In order to be reinforcing, praise should be specific, sincere, and contingent on the behavior you are trying to strengthen.

- *Save tangible rewards for activities that students find unattractive.* When students already enjoy doing a task, there's no need to provide tangible rewards. Save tangible rewards for activities that students tend to find boring and aversive.

- *If you're using tangible rewards, provide them unexpectedly, after the task performance.* In this way, students are more likely to view the rewards as information about their performance and as an expression of the teacher's pleasure rather than as an attempt to control their behavior.

- *Be extremely careful about using expected tangible rewards.* If you choose to use them, be sure to make them contingent upon completion of a task or achieving a specific level of performance. If you reward students simply for engaging in a task, regardless of their performance, they are likely to spend less time on the task once the reward is removed.

- *Make sure that you select rewards that students like.* You may think that animal stickers are really neat, but if your high school students do not find them rewarding, their behavior will not be reinforced.

- *Keep your program of rewards simple.* An elaborate system of rewards is impossible to maintain in the complex world of the classroom. The fancier your system, the more likely that you will abandon it. Moreover, if rewards become too salient, they overshadow more intrinsic reasons for behaving in certain ways. Students become so preoccupied with collecting, counting, and comparing that they lose sight of why the behavior is necessary or valuable.

but long on anger and attitude. Convinced that English class was a waste of time, her students made it clear that they didn't want "worksheets, sentence combining, reading novels and discussing them, writing about 'stuff we don't care about'" (p. 51). Christensen knew she needed to engage them "because they were loud, unruly, and out of control" (p. 51), but she didn't know how. She eventually decided to use the novel, *Thousand Pieces of Gold,* by Ruthann Lum McCunn, a book normally read by her college-level course in Contemporary Literature and Society:

> *Students weren't thrilled with the book; in fact they weren't reading it. I'd plan a 90-minute lesson around the reading and dialogue journal they were supposed to be keeping, but only a few students were prepared. Most didn't even attempt to lie about the fact that they weren't reading and clearly weren't planning on it.*
>
> *In an attempt to get them involved in the novel, I read aloud an evocative passage about the unemployed peasants sweeping through the*

Chinese countryside pillaging, raping, and grabbing what was denied them through legal employment. Suddenly students saw their own lives reflected back at them through Chen whose anger at losing his job and ultimately his family led him to become an outlaw. Chen created a new family with this group of bandits. Students could relate: Chen was a gang member. I had stumbled on a way to interest my class. The violence created a contact point between the literature and the students' lives.

This connection, this reverberation across cultures, time, and gender challenged the students' previous notion that reading and talking about novels didn't have relevance for them. They could empathize with the Chinese but also explore those issues in their own lives. (pp. 51-52)

As Christensen's story illustrates, finding ways to enhance students' motivation is particularly daunting when students are disaffected, apathetic, or resistant. Such students find academic tasks relatively meaningless and resist engaging in them—even when they know they could be successful. Some may also be fearful that school learning "will make them into something that they do not want to become" (p. 205). This fear is apparent in some African Americans and other students of color who equate academic achievement with "acting White." In a seminal paper published two decades ago, Fordham and Ogbu (1986) describe how bright Black students may "put brakes" on their academic achievement by not studying or doing homework, cutting class, being late, and not participating in class. Not surprisingly, the existence of "acting White" has been the subject of heated debate ever since, but a recent study (Fryer, 2006) provides empirical evidence to support this phenomenon.

Motivating resistant, underachieving, or apathetic students requires "resocialization" (Brophy, 1998, p. 203). This means using the strategies described in this chapter in more sustained, systematic, and personalized ways. Extrinsic rewards may be especially useful in this regard (Hidi & Harackiewicz, 2000). By triggering engagement in tasks that students initially view as boring or irrelevant, "there is at least a chance" that real interest will develop (p. 159).

Resocialization also means combining high expectations for students with the encouragement and support needed to achieve those expectations—in short, showing students that you care about them as students and as people. As I mentioned in Chapter 3, a substantial body of research exists on students' perceptions of school and teachers (see Woolfolk Hoy & Weinstein, 2006). This research consistently demonstrates that when students perceive their teachers as caring and supportive, they are more likely to be academically motivated, to engage in classroom activities, and to behave in prosocial, responsible ways (e.g., Wentzel, 1997, 1998; Murdock & Miller, 2003; Ryan & Patrick, 2001).

Perceiving that teachers care appears to be especially important for students who are alienated and marginalized and those who are at risk of school failure. Davidson (1999), for example, interviewed 49 adolescents representing diverse socioeconomic, cultural, and academic backgrounds. Data revealed not only students' appreciation and preference for teachers who communicated interest in their well-being, but also students' willingness to reciprocate by being attentive and conscientious. This was particularly evident in the responses of "stigmatized" students who faced "social borders"—divisions between their academic and social worlds. Describing Wendy Ashton, a teacher who prodded students to achieve, one student commented, "She won't put you down, she'll talk to you and she'll go, 'Yeah, you know I love you. You know I want you to make something out of yourself, so stop messing around in class'" (p. 361). Davidson speculates that students who do not face social borders might be more accepting of teachers who are relatively distant and impersonal, because the students basically trust school as an institution; however, when students face the social divisions that can lead to alienation and marginalization, it is essential for teachers to be attentive, supportive, and respectful.

As the comment about Wendy Ashton suggests, this kind of caring is less about being "warm and fuzzy" and more about being a "warm demander"—someone who provides a "tough-minded, no-nonsense, structured, and disciplined classroom environment for kids whom society has psychologically and physically abandoned" (Irvine & Fraser, 1998, p. 56). Corbett, Wilson, and Williams (2005) identified a small group of teachers like this during a three-year study in two urban districts that served diverse student populations. Both districts were desperately trying to find ways to close the achievement gap that existed between lower- and higher-income students. The researchers interviewed parents, students, teachers, and administrators and visited the classrooms of a sample of teachers from each grade level in each school. Their observations and interviews enabled them to identify a set of teachers who *simply refused to let students fail.* One of the teachers was Mrs. Franklin, an African American sixth-grade teacher whose school served mostly students of color. Mrs. Franklin believed that too many teachers had given up on students and didn't expect very much. As she put it: "Kids aren't the problem; adults are the ones finding the excuses" (p. 9). Mrs. Franklin didn't give her students an excuse not to do well. Her grading policy required any student work earning a grade lower than a C to be done over. Interestingly, interviews with students revealed that rather than resenting the strict grading policy, they appreciated it. As one student reported: "My teacher never let people settle for D or E; she don't let people get away with it. She give us an education. Other teachers don't care what you do. They pass you to be passing. Here, I pass my own self" (p. 10). And another explained why Mrs. Franklin was a good teacher:

INTERVIEWER: What's a good teacher?

    STUDENT: They make sure all kids get the work done. If the kids don't get good grades, let 'em do it over. Like our teacher.

INTERVIEWER: What does your teacher do?

    STUDENT: My teacher's strict.

INTERVIEWER: What do you mean by "strict"?

    STUDENT: She wants you to get your work done. If you don't, you stay until you get it done.

INTERVIEWER: What do you think of that?

    STUDENT: I like it.

INTERVIEWER: Why?

    STUDENT: Because I want to pass and not get stuck in this grade another year, or I'll be driving to class. (p. 10)

Significantly, in addition to being demanding, Mrs. Franklin made sure that students knew she cared about whether they were learning and that she would help them:

> *I have some students who say, "I don't want a C." Then we stay after school. I say, "I can stay all night." On Friday, when the building empties out fast, we are the only ones left here. I also make house calls and show up on the porch with a book in my hand. My key phrase is, "I'm like one of your family." I just don't accept mediocrity. The world is too demanding, too competitive. (p. 10)*

CONCLUDING COMMENTS

A while back, a professor of educational psychology told me that learning about classroom management would be unnecessary if prospective teachers understood how to enhance students' motivation. Although I thought his argument was naive and unrealistic, I understood—and agreed with—its underlying premise: *namely, that students who are interested and involved in the academic work at hand are less likely to daydream, disrupt, and defy.* In other words, management and motivation are inextricably linked.

As you contemplate ways to increase your students' expectations for success and the value they place on academic tasks, remember that motivating students doesn't happen accidentally. Fred emphasizes this point when he contends that "how I will motivate my students" should be an integral component of every lesson plan. Fortunately, the motivational strategies discussed in this chapter are consistent with current thinking about good instruction, which emphasizes students' active participation, collaborative groupwork, and the use of varying assessments (Brophy, 1998).

Finally, remember the suggestions in Chapter 3 for creating a safer, more caring classroom. As I have stressed, students are more motivated when they perceive that teachers care about them. In Brophy's (1998) words: "You can become your own most powerful motivational tool by establishing productive relationships with each of your students" (p. 254).

SUMMARY

Although teachers are responsible for enhancing motivation, this chapter began by questioning the belief that "good teachers should make learning fun." Such a goal seems unrealistic and inappropriate given the constraints of the middle and high school classroom—compulsory attendance, required curricula, class sizes that inhibit individualization, and the specter of high-stakes standardized testing. A more appropriate, realistic goal is to stimulate students' *motivation to learn,* whereby students pursue academic activities because they find them meaningful and worthwhile.

An Expectancy–Times–Value Framework

- Motivation depends on (1) students' expectation of success and (2) the value they place on the task (or the rewards that it may bring).
- If either factor is missing, there will be no motivation.

Strategies for Increasing Expectations of Success

- Provide opportunities for success.
- Teach students to set reasonable goals and to evaluate their own performance.
- Help students recognize the relationship between effort and outcome.
- Provide informative feedback.
- Provide special motivational support to discouraged students.

Strategies for Enhancing the Value of the Task

- Relate lessons to students' own lives.
- Provide opportunities for choice.
- Model interest in learning and express enthusiasm for the material.
- Include novelty/variety elements.
- Provide opportunities for students to respond actively.
- Allow students to create finished products.
- Provide opportunities for students to interact with peers.
- Provide extrinsic rewards:
    Keep in mind the different types of rewards: social rewards, special activities, tangible rewards.
    Be aware that rewarding people for doing something they already like to do may decrease their interest in continuing that behavior.
    Think carefully about when and how to use rewards:
        Use verbal rewards to increase intrinsic motivation for academic tasks.
        Save tangible rewards for activities that students find unattractive.
        Provide tangible rewards unexpectedly (after the task performance).
        Provide expected tangible rewards only for completion of a task or for achieving a specific level of performance.
        Select rewards that your students like.
        Keep your reward program simple.

By working to ensure that students are engaged in learning activities, you can avoid many of the managerial problems that arise when students are bored and frustrated. Management and motivation are closely intertwined.

ACTIVITIES FOR SKILL BUILDING AND REFLECTION

In Class

1. In the following two vignettes, the teachers have directed the activity. In a small group, discuss ways they could have involved students in the planning, directing, creating, or evaluating.

a. Mrs. Peters felt that the unit her seventh-grade class completed on folk tales would lend itself to a class play. She chose Paul Bunyan and Pecos Bill as the stories to dramatize. The students were excited as Mrs. Peters gave out parts and assigned students to paint scenery. Mrs. Peters wrote a script and sent it home for the students to memorize. She asked parents to help make the costumes. After three weeks of practice, the play was performed for the elementary classes and the parents.

b. Mr. Wilkins wanted his tenth-grade World Civilization class to develop an understanding about ancient civilizations. He assigned a five-part project. Students had to research four civilizations (Egyptian, Mesopotamian, Indus Valley, and Shang); write a biography of Howard Carter, a famous archaeologist; describe three pyramids (step, Great Pyramid, Pyramid of Sesostris II); outline the reigns of five kings (Hammurabi, Thutmose III, Ramses II, David, and Nebuchadnezzar); and make a model of a pyramid. He gave the class four weeks to complete the projects and then collected them, graded them, and displayed them in the school library.

2. Working in small groups that are homogeneous in terms of discipline (i.e., English, world language, math, science), select a topic in your content area and design a lesson or activity that incorporates at least two of the strategies for enhancing perceived value. For example, you might relate the material to students' lives, provide opportunities for choice, allow students to work with peers, or produce a final product.

On Your Own

Interview an experienced, effective teacher about the motivational strategies he or she finds particularly effective with disaffected, resistant students.

For Your Portfolio

Design a "slanty rope assignment" in your content area that will enable students of varying achievement levels to experience success. For example, the task might vary in complexity; it might be open-ended, allowing a variety of acceptable responses; it might require the use of different reference materials; or it might allow students to choose the format in which they demonstrate their understanding (e.g., a report, poster, or role-play). (Use the example of Mr. Yin in this chapter as an example.)

FOR FURTHER READING

Brewster, C., & Fager, J. (2000). *Increasing student engagement and motivation: From time-on-task to homework.* Portland, OR: Northwest Regional Educational Laboratory (NWREL). Downloaded from http://www.nwrel.org/request/oct00/textonly.html.

    This booklet, the 14th in a series of "hot topic" reports from the Northwest Regional Educational Laboratory, reviews research on motivation, provides strategies for motivating students to engage in class activities and to complete homework, and provides descriptions of three school systems that have made notable efforts to involve students. Included for each location is contact information, a description of the program, and observed outcomes.

Instrator, S. M. (2003). *Tuned in and fired up: How teaching can inspire real learning in the classroom.* New Haven: Yale University Press.

    Sam Intrator spent a year in Mr. Quinn's academically and ethnically diverse fourth-period English class. He observed and recorded class sessions, repeatedly interviewed the teacher and students, and collected student writing, including "experience journals" where students recorded the "peaks and valleys" of the school day. His goal: to capture "treasured moments" when teenagers "become immersed in their work" and experience a sense of energy and vitality. This book is about those moments of inspired learning.

Kohn, A. (1993). *Punished by rewards: The trouble with gold stars, incentive plans, A's, praise, and other bribes.* Boston: Houghton Mifflin Company.

Kohn argues that our basic strategy for motivating students ("Do this and you'll get that") works only in the short run and actually does lasting harm. Instead of rewards, Kohn suggests that teachers provide the "three Cs"—collaboration, content (things worth knowing), and choice. The result, he posits, will be "good kids without goodies."

Tomlinson, C. A. (2001). *How to differentiate instruction in mixed ability classrooms.* 2nd ed. Alexandria, VA: Association for Supervision and Curriculum Development.

Tomlinson explains what differentiated instruction is (and isn't), provides a look inside some differentiated classrooms, presents the "how-to's" of planning lessons differentiated by readiness, interest, and learning styles, and discusses the complex issues of grading and record-keeping. An appendix provides a useful summary of instructional and managerial strategies for differentiated, mixed-ability classrooms.

References

Anderman, E. M., & Maehr, M. L. (1994). Motivation and schooling in the middle grades. *Review of Educational Research, 64*(2), 287–309.

Arends, R. I. (2004). *Learning to teach.* 6th ed. Boston: McGraw-Hill.

Ayers, W. (1993). *To teach: The journey of a teacher.* New York: Teachers College Press.

Belluck, P. (Feb. 5, 2006). And for perfect attendance, Johnny gets a car. *The New York Times, 1,* 20.

Brophy, J. (1998). *Motivating students to learn.* Boston: McGraw-Hill.

Brophy, J. (1987). Synthesis of research on strategies for motivating students to learn. *Educational Leadership, 45,* 40–48.

Cameron, J. (2001). Negative effects of reward on intrinsic motivation—A limited phenomenon: Comment on Deci, Koestner, and Ryan (2001). *Review of Educational Research, 71*(1), 29–42.

Cameron, J., & Pierce, W. D. (1994). Reinforcement, reward, and intrinsic motivation: A meta-analysis. *Review of Educational Research, 64,* 363–423.

Cameron, J., Banko, K. M., & Pierce, W. O. (2001). Pervasive negative effects of rewards on intrinsic motivation: The myth continues. *The Behavior Analyst, 24*(1), 1–44.

Campbell, L., Campbell, B., & Dickinson, D. (1999). *Teaching and learning through multiple intelligences.* 2nd ed. Boston: Allyn & Bacon.

Christensen, L. (1994). Building community from chaos. In B. Bigelow, L. Christensen, S. Karp, B. Miner, & B. Peterson (Eds.), *Rethinking our Classrooms: Teaching for Equity and Justice* (A special edition of *Rethinking Schools*). Milwaukee, WI: Rethinking Schools.

Corbett, D., Wilson, B., & Williams, B. (2005). No choice but success. *Educational Leadership, 62*(6), 8–12.

Davidson, A. L. (1999). Negotiating social differences: Youths' assessments of educators' strategies. *Urban Education, 34*(3), 338–369.

Deci, E. L., Koestner, R., & Ryan, R. M. (2001). Extrinsic rewards and intrinsic motivation in education: Reconsidered once again. *Review of Educational Research, 71*(1), 1–27.

Deci, E. L., Koestner, R., & Ryan, R. M. (1999). A meta-analytic review of experiments examining the effects of extrinsic rewards on intrinsic motivation. *Psychological Bulletin, 125*(6), 627–668.

Eccles, J., & Wigfield, A. (1985). Teacher expectations and student motivation. In J. Dusek (Ed.), *Teacher expectancies* (pp. 185–226). Hillsdale, NJ: Lawrence Erlbaum Associates, Inc.

Feather, N. (Ed.) (1982). *Expectations and actions.* Hillsdale, NJ: Erlbaum.

Fisher, C. W., Berliner, D. C., Filby, N. N., Marliave, R., Cahen, L. S., & Dishaw, M. M. (1980). Teaching behaviors, academic learning time, and student achievement: An overview. In C. Denham & A. Lieberman (Eds.), *Time to learn.* Washington, D.C.: U. S. Department of Education, pp. 7–32.

Flowerday, T., & Schraw, G. (2000). Teacher beliefs about instructional choice: A phenomenological study. *Journal of Educational Psychology, 92*(4), 634–645.

Fordham, S., & Ogbu, J. U. (1986). Black students' school success: Coping with the "burden of 'acting white.'" *The Urban Review, 18*(3), 176–206.

Fryer, R. G., Jr. (2006, Winter). "Acting white." *Education Next,* 52–59.

Gardner, H. (1993). *Multiple intelligences: The theory in practice.* New York: Basic Books.

Gardner, H. (1995). Reflections on multiple intelligences: Myths and messages. *Phi Delta Kappan, 77*(3), 200–209.

Good, T. L., & Brophy, J. E. (2000). *Looking in classrooms.* 8th ed. New York: Addison Wesley Longman.

Gordon, R. L. (1997). How novice teachers can succeed with adolescents. *Educational Leadership, 54*(7), 56–58.

Hidi, S., & Harackiewicz, J. M. (2000). Motivating the academically unmotivated: A critical issue for the 21st century. *Review of Educational Research, 70*(2), 151–179.

Irvine, J. J., & Fraser, J. (May 13, 1998). Warm demanders: Do national certification standards leave room for the culturally responsive pedagogy of African-American teachers? *Education Week, 17*(35), p. 56.

Kohn, A. (1993). *Punished by rewards: The trouble with gold stars, incentive plans, A's, praise, and other bribes.* Boston: Houghton Mifflin.

Ladson-Billings, G. (1994). *The dreamkeepers: Successful teachers of African American children.* San Francisco: Jossey-Bass.

Lepper, M., Greene, D., & Nisbett, R. E. (1973). Undermining children's intrinsic interest with extrinsic rewards: A test of the "overjustification" hypothesis. *Journal of Personality and Social Psychology, 28,* 129–137.

Morrell, E., & Duncan-Andrade, J. M. R. (2002). Promoting academic literacy with urban youth through engaging hip-hop culture. *English Journal, 91*(6), 88–92.

Morrell, E., & Duncan-Andrade, J. (2004). What they do learn in school: Using hip-hop as a bridge between youth culture and canonical poetry texts. In J. Mahiri (Ed.), *What they don't learn in school: Literacy in the lives of urban youth.* New York: Peter Lang.

Murdock, T. B., & Miller, A. (2003). Teachers as sources of middle school students' motivational identity: Variable-centered and person-centered analytic approaches. *The Elementary School Journal, 103*(4), 383–399.

Newby, T. (1991). Classroom motivation: Strategies of first-year teachers. *Journal of Educational Psychology, 83,* 195–200.

Reeve, J. (2006). Extrinsic rewards and inner motivation. In C. M. Evertson & C. S. Weinstein (Eds.), *Handbook of classroom management: Research, practice, and contemporary issues.* Mahwah, NJ: Lawrence Erlbaum Associates, Inc.

Roeser, R. W., Eccles, J. S., & Sameroff, A. J. (2000). School as a context of early adolescents' academic and social–emotional development: A summary of research findings. *The Elementary School Journal, 100*(5), 443–471.

Rogers, S., & Renard, L. (1999). Relationship-driven teaching. *Educational Leadership, 57*(1), 34–37.

Ryan, R. M., & Deci. E. L. (2000). Intrinsic and extrinsic motivations: Classic definitions and new directions. *Contemporary Educational Psychology, 25,* 54–67.

Ryan, A., & Patrick, H. (2001). The classroom social environment and changes in adolescents' motivation and engagement during middle school. *American Educational Research Journal, 38*(2), 437–460.

Stipek, D. J. (1993). *Motivation to learn: From theory to practice.* 2nd ed. Boston: Allyn and Bacon.

Tomlinson, C. A. (1999). *The differentiated classroom: Responding to the needs of all learners.* Alexandria, VA: Association for Supervision and Curriculum Development.

Trumbull, E., Rothstein-Fisch, C., Greenfield, P. M., & Quiroz, B. (2001). *Bridging cultures between home and school: A guide for teachers.* Mahwah, NJ: Lawrence Erlbaum Associates, Inc.

Wentzel, K. R. (1997). Student motivation in middle school: The role of perceived pedagogical caring. *Journal of Educational Psychology, 89*(3), 411–419.

Wentzel, K. R. (1998). Social relationships and motivation in middle school: The role of parents, teachers, and peers. *Journal of Educational Psychology, 90*(2), 202–209.

Wigfield, A., & Eccles, J. (1992). The development of achievement task values: A theoretical analysis. *Developmental Review, 12,* 265–310.

Woolfolk Hoy, A., & Weinstein, C. S. (2006). Student and teacher perspectives on classroom management. In C. M. Evertson and C. S. Weinstein (Eds.), *Handbook of classroom management: Research, practice, and contemporary issues.* Mahwah, NJ: Lawrence Erlbaum Associates, Inc.

MANAGING INDEPENDENT WORK

Chapter 1 discussed the assumption that the tasks of classroom management vary across different classroom situations. I pointed out that the classroom is not a "homogenized glob" (Kounin & Sherman, 1979) but is composed of numerous "subsettings" such as opening routines, homework routines, teacher presentations, transitions, and whole-class discussions. How order is defined in each of these subsettings is likely to vary. For example, during transitions students may be allowed to sharpen pencils and talk with friends, but these same behaviors may be prohibited during a whole-group discussion or a teacher presentation.

Variations in behavioral expectations are understandable, given the fact that subsettings have different goals and pose different challenges in terms of establishing and maintaining order. To be an effective manager, you must consider the unique characteristics of your classroom's subsettings and decide how your students need to behave in each one in order to maximize opportunities for learning.

This chapter focuses on the subsetting known as *independent work,* the situation in which students are assigned to work at their desks with their own materials, while the teacher is free to monitor the total class—to observe students' performance, provide support and feedback, engage in miniconferences, and prepare students for homework assignments. Independent work is often used to provide students with the chance to practice or review previously presented material. For example, in "direct instruction" or "explicit teaching" (Rosenshine, 1986), the teacher reviews previous material, presents new material in small steps, and then gives students the opportunity to practice, first under supervision ("guided practice") and then independently ("independent practice").

To be honest, this chapter almost didn't get written. Independent work is also referred to as *seatwork,* and this term has very negative connotations, particularly among educators who promote students' active participation and collaboration. Indeed, when I sat down with Donnie, Sandy, Fred, and Christina to discuss their views, I found heated differences of opinion on this particular subsetting. On one hand, Fred argued that seatwork could be a valuable activity:

I use seatwork to give kids the opportunity to practice skills like making predictions, valid inferences, generalizations. . . . Intellectual skills like these benefit from practice just like a backhand stroke in tennis. If I have 27 kids doing an assignment in class, I can walk around, see immediately what they're doing, give individual critiques, catch them if they're having a problem. I can't give that individual, immediate feedback if the work is done as homework.

On the other hand, Sandy was vehemently negative: "I hate seatwork," she told us. "As far as I'm concerned, it's just a way of killing time." Similarly, Donnie claimed that she never used seatwork. I pointed out that I had frequently observed her using a pattern of direct instruction, beginning class with a review of the homework, then introducing a small segment of the new lesson, and having students do one or two problems at their seats while she circulated throughout the room. Donnie readily acknowledged her use of "guided practice," but argued that this was not seatwork:

It's not like elementary school, where you have different reading groups, and you have to find a way for kids to be busy for long periods of time while you're working with a small group. Most of my instruction is done with the whole group, so there's no need for all the kids to be sitting there quietly working on worksheets.

Finally, Christina admitted some ambivalence. She acknowledged that whenever she heard the word *seatwork,* she immediately thought of "bad teachers who sit at their desks grading papers, writing lesson plans, or even reading the newspaper, while their students do boring work designed to keep them in their seats and quiet." But she also recognized that independent work was sometimes useful:

Realistically, there are times when I need to confer with individuals, so I need the rest of the class to be meaningfully occupied. Or I might want students to do something in class so I don't have to give them additional homework (especially if they're already working on a long-term assignment). Or I might want the work to be preceded by some instruction and to be followed by an interactive activity. This necessarily situates the seatwork in the middle of the class period, rather than for homework. But because I'm so leery about seatwork, I always try to ask myself, "Does this work need to be done in the classroom, or should it be done as homework?"

We debated, we moralized, and we shared anecdotes about the awfulness or the usefulness of seatwork. Eventually, we came to realize that there was no fundamental difference of opinion among us. We all agreed that teachers sometimes need to assign work for students to do on their own but in class, with or without close teacher supervision. We also agreed that seatwork didn't have to mean silence; in fact, all the teachers felt strongly that students should generally be allowed to help one another. But we also agreed that seatwork is too often busywork, that it frequently goes on for too long, and that too many teachers use it as a substitute for active teaching. As Donnie put it:

> **Some teachers think of seatwork as "give them something to do all period so I can do something else." They'll teach for 10 minutes, then give their students 30 minutes of seatwork, and sit down. That's not seatwork—that's a free period.**

This chapter begins by discussing the problems that occur when independent work is misused—when teachers do not reflect on ways to organize the work so that it is appropriate and meaningful for students. We then go on to consider the ways Donnie, Sandy, Fred, and Christina try to avoid, or at least minimize, these problems. The intent is *not* to encourage you to spend large amounts of time in seatwork activities, but rather, to provide you with a way of thinking about seatwork so that you can make better decisions about when and how to use it. Throughout the discussion, the two terms—*independent work* and *seatwork*—are used interchangeably.

 PAUSE AND REFLECT

As you have just read, the term *seatwork* has a negative connotation, and the question of whether or not to assign seatwork often arouses debate. What has your experience as a student been with seatwork, and what types of seatwork have you observed in classrooms? What do you think about the contention that seatwork is a "necessary evil"?

WHAT'S WRONG WITH SEATWORK?

As Christina points out, the term *seatwork* conjures up images of bored, passive students doing repetitive, tedious worksheets while teachers sit at their desks calculating grades or reading the newspaper. Consider the following description of a typical seatwork situation. It was observed by Robert Everhart (1983), who spent two years conducting fieldwork in a junior high school. His book, *Reading, Writing and Resistance: Adolescence and Labor in a Junior High School,* is a chronicle of the daily routine experienced by students and, to some extent, by teachers. This scene takes place in Marcy's English class, where students are supposed to be learning about the proper form of business letters.

> *First, Marcy asked the class to turn to the chapter on business letters in their grammar books and read that section. After five minutes Marcy asked the class, "How many have not yet finished?" Initially about one-third of the class raised their hands. Roy, sitting in the rear near where I was sitting, nudged John. John then spoke up, "I'm not finished."*

"I ain't finished either," Roy added, smiling. Needless to say, they both had finished; I had seen them close their books a few minutes earlier and then proceed to trade a Mad *magazine back and forth.*

"Well, I'll give you a few more minutes, but hurry up," said Marcy. Those not finished continued reading while the rest of the class began engaging in different activities: looking out the window, doodling, and pulling pictures from their wallets and looking at them. Roy then pulled a copy of Cycle *magazine from beneath his desk and began leafing through it. After a few minutes Marcy went to the blackboard and began outlining the structure of the business letter.*

"Ok, first thing we do is to place the return address—where, class?"

"On the paper," said one boy slouched in his chair and tapping his pencil.

"All right, comedian, that's obvious. Where else?"

"On the front side of the paper."

"Come on class, get serious! Where do you place the return address? Larry?"

Marcy eventually gets through a description and explanation of the form of the business letter. She then informs students that they will be writing their own business letters, which will be due at the end of the following week. Today, they are to write the initial paragraph:

After about 10 minutes of writing, Marcy asked, "How many are not finished with their paragraph?" About six students raised their hands. "OK, I'll give you a few minutes to finish up. The rest of you, I want you to read your paragraphs to each other because I want you to read them to the class tomorrow and they'd better be clear; if they aren't clear to you now they won't be clear to the class tomorrow."

One of the students at the back of the room seemed somewhat surprised at this. "Hey, you didn't say anything about having to read these in front of the class."

"Yeah, I don't want to read mine in front of the class," added Phil.

Marcy put her hands on her hips and stated emphatically, "Now come on, class, you'll all want to do a good job and this will give you a chance to practice and improve your paragraphs before they're submitted for grades. And you all want to get 'As', I'm sure." There was a chorus of laughs from most of the class and Marcy smiled.

"I don't care," I heard one girl say under her breath.

"Yeah, I don't care either, just so I get this stupid thing done."

After saying that, Don turned to Art and said, "Hey, Art, what you writing your letter on?"

"I am writing the Elephant Rubber Company, telling them that their rubbers were too small."

"Wow," Ron replied.

"Don't think I'll write that letter though. Marcy will have a bird."

"For sure," Art replied.

TABLE 8.1 The Problems with Seatwork

ALL TOO OFTEN:

1. Assignments are not meaningful, educationally useful, or motivating.
2. Assignments are not matched to students' achievement levels.
3. Directions are not clear and thorough.
4. Teachers do not circulate and monitor students' comprehension and behavior.
5. Some students finish early, while others do not finish.

> *The students continued talking to each other, which finally prompted Marcy to get up from her desk and say, "Class, get busy or some of you will be in after school."*

Analysis of this scenario allows us to identify five problems that are frequently associated with seatwork. (These are summarized in Table 8.1.) First, it is clear that *the assignment is not meaningful to students.* Don calls the business letter a "stupid thing," Art jokes about writing to the Elephant Rubber Company, and an unnamed girl mumbles that she doesn't care about getting an A. In Fred's terms, Marcy has given her students the kind of "garbage assignment" that is responsible for seatwork's bad reputation. "Garbage assignments" are not only a waste of precious learning time, they also foster boredom, alienation, and misbehavior. Clearly, if students do not perceive the value of a seatwork assignment, they are unlikely to become invested in it. That's when teachers have to resort to threats about detention or extrinsic incentives like grades. Recall Marcy's words. First she tells her class, "And you all want to get 'As,' I'm sure." Later she warns, "Class, get busy or some of you will be in after school."

Second, it appears that Marcy's assignment *does not match students' varying achievement levels.* (Figure 8.1 depicts Calvin's rather special strategy for dealing

Calvin and Hobbes   by Bill Watterson

Figure 8.1   Calvin's response to seatwork that is too difficult for him.

with seatwork that is too difficult for him.) For some students, the reading assignment seems too easy; they finish reading quickly and fill their time by doodling, looking out the window, and reading magazines. Others seem to find the reading more difficult and need "a few more minutes." Similarly, writing one paragraph in 10 minutes doesn't seem like a particularly challenging assignment for most of Marcy's students, yet six students indicate they are not finished when Marcy checks their progress. (Of course, it's possible that they have just been wasting time.)

Assigning work that does not match students' achievement levels is typical of the behaviors exhibited by the less effective managers studied by Carolyn Evertson and Ed Emmer (1982; see Chapter 4 for a fuller description of this study). You may recall that Evertson and Emmer observed mathematics and English teachers at the junior high level and identified those who were more effective managers and those who were less effective. The observations led Evertson and Emmer to conclude that the more effective teachers had greater awareness of students' entering skills:

> An example of an activity showing low understanding was an assignment in one of the lower achieving English classes to "Write an essay from the perspective of an inanimate object." The problem was compounded by an unclear explanation of the term, perspective. Narratives noted more instances of vocabulary beyond some of the students' comprehension. As a consequence of being more aware of student skills . . . , the more effective teachers' classes had more success in participating in class activities and completing assignments. (p. 496)

A third problem is that Marcy *does not provide her students with clear, complete directions.* At the beginning of the period, Marcy tells the students to read the chapter on business letters, but she says nothing about why they are to read the chapter, how long they have, or whether they should take notes. In other words, she merely tells them to "do it"—without explaining the purpose for reading or suggesting strategies that might be used. Nor does Marcy explain that they will be writing their own letters later in the period. It is only after reviewing the form of the business letter that Marcy instructs her students to write the initial paragraph, and once again, she neglects to tell them what will be coming next—namely, that they will be reading the paragraphs aloud the following day. (Marcy might have made this decision at the last minute, in order to provide an activity for students who finished early.) Not surprisingly, some of the students react with displeasure. One complains, "Hey, you didn't say anything about having to read these in front of the class," while another protests, "Yeah, I don't want to read mine in front of the class."

Marcy's lack of clarity and thoroughness is also reminiscent of the less effective managers studied by Evertson and Emmer (1982). In addition to differing in their awareness of students' entering abilities, more and less effective teachers differed in terms of skill in communicating information. More effective English teachers were clearer in giving directions and stating objectives than less effective teachers. (Interestingly, this difference did not appear in comparisons of more and less effective math teachers.) According to Evertson and Emmer, more effective managers

> were better able to segment complex tasks into step-by-step procedures and to help students understand their tasks, and how to accomplish them. When students knew what to do and had the skills to do it, they were more likely to stay on task. (p. 496)

A fourth problem evident in Marcy's class is her *lack of monitoring.* Although the vignette doesn't explicitly describe what Marcy is doing while her students are reading and writing, the last paragraph does state that Marcy gets up from her desk to admonish students who are talking. Furthermore, Marcy not only has to ask how many students have not yet finished, she also seems unaware that students in the rear of the room are reading *Mad* magazine. These are sure signs that Marcy is not circulating through the room, checking on students' progress, helping them with problems, and providing feedback. If Marcy is not going to provide this supervision and support, she might as well have her students do the assignment at home.

Finally, Marcy does not really plan for the fact that *students work at different paces.* They may *begin* seatwork at the same time, but they never *finish* at the same time. "Ragged" endings can upset a schedule that looked beautiful on paper. Students who cannot complete assignments in the allotted time may have to do the assignment for homework. Students who complete their work earlier than you expected need something to keep them occupied; if they must sit and wait with nothing to do, they may distract students who are still working. In Marcy's class, students who finish earlier than their peers are actually quite well behaved: They read *Mad* and *Cycle* magazines, look out the window, doodle, and look at pictures from their wallets. Nonetheless, they are wasting time that could be spent on more profitable activities.

IMPLICATIONS FOR CLASSROOM PRACTICE

Analysis of Marcy's seatwork sheds light on the special problems associated with this particular subsetting of the classroom. In this section of the chapter, we consider ways to avoid or at least minimize these problems. (These are summarized in the Practical Tips box on page 224.)

Assign Work That Is Meaningful, Useful, and Relevant to Students

Secondary textbooks generally have questions, activities, and exercises at the end of each chapter, and some come with supplemental study guides, workbooks, or activity sheets. Since these materials may not always be meaningful and relevant to students, it is essential that you evaluate the activities you assign. As Fred observes:

> **The typical seatwork assignment is not well thought through. It's mindlessly designed and mindlessly done. "Read and answer the questions on page 287." "Fill in the blank." "Read and outline the chapter." What's *really* scary is when the kids don't even think assignments like that are so bad! That tells me that they're so used to that kind of thing, they don't realize it's a waste of time. But seatwork doesn't *have* to be that way.**

In order to be sure that the independent work they assign is not *"that way,"* Donnie, Christina, Sandy, and Fred carefully evaluate the tasks they give students to complete during class. The Practical Tips box lists some of the questions they ask themselves before they assign independent work.

PRACTICAL TIPS FOR

USING INDEPENDENT WORK EFFECTIVELY

- Assign work that is meaningful, useful, and relevant to students.
  Ask yourself:
  - What is the purpose of the task?
  - Does the task relate to current instruction? Are students likely to see the connection?
  - Are students likely to see the task as something worth doing or something boring and unrewarding?
  - Are the directions unambiguous and easy to follow?
  - Does the task provide students with an opportunity to practice important skills or to apply what they are learning?
  - Does the task provide students with the opportunity to think critically or to engage in problem solving?
  - Does the task require reading and writing, or does it simply ask students to fill in the blank, underline, or circle?
  - Does the task require higher-level responses or does it emphasize low-level, factual recall and "drill and kill" practice of isolated subskills?
  - Is there a reason the task should be done in school (e.g., the need for coaching by the teacher) rather than at home?
  - Will students be able to accomplish the task without assistance? If not, how will assistance be provided?

- Match assignments to students' varying achievement levels.

- Make sure that written and oral directions are clear and thorough.

- Monitor behavior and comprehension.

- Plan for ragged endings.

Many teachers prefer to create their own assignments rather than to rely on commercially prepared materials. In this way, they are better able to connect the tasks with students' backgrounds and experiences, target particular problems that students are having, and provide greater individualization. For example, when Fred wants students to become familiar with the resources in the library, he asks them to do tasks like these:

List three facts on one topic that interests you using the electronic database Facts on File.

Use an almanac to find a country that begins with the first letter of your last name and tell the population of that nation.

Use The New York Times electronic database (Internet or CD-ROM) to identify an important event that occurred on your last birthday.

Locate a biography about a person whose last name begins with the same letter as your first name.

According to Fred, this simple way of individualizing the assignment has a very positive effect on students' motivation. (And there's an added bonus: Students have to do their own work.) Research on "situational interest" (Schraw & Lehman, 2001) suggests that teachers can also enhance interest in tasks by pointing out the relevance of the material, providing students with a greater sense of control (e.g., by providing choice about which problems to do), and giving reasons to persist in a task (i.e., explaining why the task is useful). (See Chapter 7 on motivation for related suggestions.)

Fred acknowledges that he can't always "be creative and wonderful five days a week, week after week," but he always tries to ensure that the independent work he assigns has a valid purpose. It's worth keeping his comments in mind:

> Look, I'm human. . . . There are times when I'll give kids seatwork assignments that are less than wonderful, assignments that I'm not especially proud of. But I really try to make that the exception, not the rule, and to come up with seatwork that's meaningful to kids and educationally useful.

Match the Work to Varying Achievement Levels

Fred also likes to use open-ended assignments that allow students working on a variety of levels to complete the work successfully. For example, when his students read a chapter in their texts, Fred often forgoes the end-of-chapter questions (which often have one correct answer); instead, he may ask students to create their own questions. At other times, he asks a question that is broad enough so that almost everyone in his extremely diverse class is able to respond—in some fashion—to the question, although answers obviously vary in terms of length, substance, and coherence. As I mentioned in Chapter 7, Fred calls this the "slanty rope theory":

> If we set a rope across a room at four feet, some kids can get over it and some can't. But if we slant the rope, then everyone can find their way over at some point. I firmly believe that people don't all want to go over at the lowest level. We can encourage kids to stretch—and once you teach kids to stretch, you've taught something more important than the subject matter.

In the following example (Tomlinson, 1999), we see how a foreign language teacher has created a "slanty rope assignment" that allows her heterogeneous class to pursue the same general topic, but at varying levels of difficulty and sophistication:

> Mrs. Higgins's German 1 class is studying the formation of past-tense verbs. One group of students will work with pattern drills in which much of a German sentence is supplied. However, each sentence uses an English verb, and students must supply the correct form of the past-tense German verb. Mrs. Higgins has ensured that the missing verbs are regular.
>
> A second, more proficient, group has a similar activity. But they will encounter a greater number and complexity of missing words, including a few irregular verbs. Another group of students works with the same sentences as the second group, but virtually all of the sentences are in English and must be translated into German. Two or three students don't need the skill drill at all; they are given a scenario to develop, with instructions about the sorts of grammatical constructions that must be included. (pp. 51–52)

For more about ways of differentiating assignments and responding to the needs of all learners, see Tomlinson (2001).

Make Sure That Written and Oral Directions Are Clear

It is important to check that instructions provided in a text or on a worksheet are clear and precise. If you don't, you may encounter situations like this one, related by a student teacher in a foreign language class:

> *I decided to use this worksheet that listed in random order 10 statements from a short story we had read (e.g., "The gardener reported that the dandelions were growing furiously"). Underneath the list were 10 lines, numbered from 1 through 10, and students were instructed to put the statements or events in sequential order. A lot of the students thought that the numbers (1-10) referred to the order of events, so next to each number, they wrote the number of the statement. (So "1-7" was meant to indicate that the first thing that happened in the story was the seventh item in the list). Other kids figured that the 1 through 10 referred to the number of the statement. When they put "1-7," they meant that the first statement in the list occurred seventh. Needless to say, lots of kids "failed" the assignment! I couldn't understand how it could be, until we went over the papers. Then I realized how confusing it was. I learned a good lesson. Don't assume that everything printed on an "official" worksheet is clear!*

Having had a number of experiences like this one, Christina now makes it a point to rewrite directions she thinks are confusing. For example, one districtwide assignment she gives requires students to read a book and write their reflections in a journal with at least 10 entries. Students are provided with 10 guiding questions, but it's not clear from the directions if students have to answer *one* question or *all* the questions for each journal entry. Actually, they have to do neither. So Christina adds a sentence specifying that students have to address each question *somewhere* in the journal, but not in any specific order and not in every entry.

Sometimes teachers think they don't have to explain orally what students are to do since there are written instructions in the textbook or on the worksheet. It's certainly important for students to read written instructions, but don't assume that they'll do this automatically; this may be a skill you'll have to teach. Consider the lesson learned by this student teacher:

> *These kids don't instinctively read something when it is given to them: They wait to have it explained.... I know that I'm supposed to state all the objectives and explain things carefully, but there are times when I want them . . . to be curious enough to take a look at what's in front of them. I try to pepper my handouts with cartoons and some of my own spectacular drawings just to make them more attractive and engaging. I'm so used to the college mentality—something is passed out and you read it rather than listen to it being explained. I have to remember it's usually the opposite in high school.*

In addition to checking written directions for clarity, make sure your oral directions are clear and complete. Recall that one of the problems with Marcy's letter-writing activity was that she didn't tell students why they were to read the chapter on business letters or how long they would have; nor did she explain that they would be writing their own letters later in the period. Contrast this with the way Donnie introduces a brief seatwork assignment on rearranging equations to solve for different variables. Even though the assignment will take just a few minutes, she explains what students are to do, how much time they will have, and what they will be expected to do when they're finished:

What I need you to do now is turn to page 178. Get out some paper and a pencil or pen. We're going to look at the chapter review, up through #15. I'm going to begin by making an assignment to each person. Problem #1, Ernest; Problem #2, Damika; Problem #3, Latoya; Problem #4, Jerome. [She continues until everyone has been assigned a problem to do.] Now I want you to solve the problem you were assigned. These are just like the homework problems we just reviewed. You're going to be rearranging equations to solve for the different variables. . . . I'll give you approximately two minutes to do this. When we come back, make sure you can give us the answer and explain the problem to the rest of the class.

Marcy also failed to tell students that they would be reading their paragraphs aloud the following day, an omission that upset a number of her students ("Hey, you didn't say anything about having to read these in front of the class."). This is a situation that Christina tries hard to avoid, especially since English class often involves having students write about personal experiences and feelings:

Christina distributes copies of her own personal essay, which deals with her ethnic background. She explains that students should read her essay and then begin to jot down ideas and write a draft of their own personal essay on the topic of identity. They will have a total of 30 minutes. She cautions them to "select something that you will feel OK to share in small groups, and keep in mind that I'll be picking the groups." A girl in the front row nods and comments, "So we should write something we can share with anyone."

When you're presenting directions for seatwork assignments, you also need to make it clear whether or not students can ask peers for assistance. In some classes, teachers encourage students to work collaboratively, while in other classes giving or receiving help is tantamount to cheating (Rizzo, 1989). This latter situation can present a real dilemma for students. On one hand is their need to follow the teacher's directions and to stay out of trouble. On the other hand is their need to complete the assignment successfully and to assist friends who are having difficulty (Bloome & Theodorou, 1988).

Students' understanding and acceptance of the norms for helping peers can also be influenced by culture. Providing assistance may be especially valued by students with cultural roots in collectivist societies (e.g., African, Asian, Hispanic, and Native American). In collectivist cultures, people assume responsibility for one another's welfare, and the focus is on working toward the common good (Cartledge with Milburn, 1996). Thus, students from these cultures may resist teachers' directives to work independently. In contrast, those from individualistic cultures (e.g., English-speaking countries) may value individual effort.

In general, all of our four teachers not only allow, they *encourage* students to help one another. As Donnie puts it, "I can't possibly get around to everybody. The kids would constantly be calling me to come over and help them. For my own sanity, I have to have students help one another. But I think they learn better that way anyway." Christina agrees. When she circulates around the room monitoring students' progress, she'll frequently refer students who are having problems to individuals she's already assisted:

> I do this for a few reasons. First, it's nice for the students I just helped to know that I now consider them to be "experts." Second, I think that having students teach others helps them to remember what I just explained. Third, it saves me having to repeat the same explanations. And finally I think it builds a helping community. But I always try to go back to the kids and check if the helpers were able to explain clearly and if the "helpees" now understand. I don't want kids to think I'm just pushing them off on others because I don't want to be bothered.

It's important to note that all of the teachers work hard to explain what "helping" really means. They take pains to explain to students that simply providing the answer or doing the task for someone else is not helping, and they stress the futility of copying. Donnie says she has "parasites" in her geometry class who don't want to do anything on their own; they just want someone to give them the answer. (This often irritates more diligent students, as Figure 8.2 illustrates.) In order to prevent this from happening, she'll sometimes assign different problems to students sitting next to each other; this allows them to help each other, but not to copy.

Calvin and Hobbes   by Bill Watterson

Figure 8.2   Sometimes students don't like to help classmates who haven't tried to do the assignment on their own.

Source: Calvin and Hobbes © Watterson, Dist. by Universal Press Syndicate.

Although all the teachers firmly believe in the value of peer assistance, there are also times when they do *not* allow students to help one another. In these situations, they are careful to explain that the ground rules are different. Listen to Sandy:

Most of the time, I stress that scientists do not work in isolation, that it's necessary to look at everyone's data and ask, "Did anyone else get these results?" But four or five times a year, I run "quiz labs" where students are *individually* responsible for listening to instructions, carrying out the procedures, and drawing conclusions. This is my way of making certain that every single person knows how to light the Bunsen burner, handle the equipment, etc. These are not discovery or inquiry lessons, but opportunities for students to apply what has been learned in class. During these lab activities, students cannot speak to one another. This is a real departure from regular lab activities, so I have to make it really clear that they are not to consult with one another—that the norms are different.

Monitor Behavior and Comprehension

Observers of classroom life have noted that students' engagement during independent work is often lower than their engagement during teacher-directed activities. Why should this be so? Apparently, even when they do find the activity meaningful and comprehensible, seatwork requires students to pace themselves through assignments. Since there are no external signals such as teachers' questions to push students along (Gump, 1982), they may begin to doodle, pass notes, comb their hair, and sharpen pencils—until the teacher reminds students to get back to work. In fact, research has shown that engagement in seatwork often follows a predictable cycle (deVoss, 1979): Students begin their assignments; attention wanes; the noise level increases; the teacher intervenes; the students return to the assignment. This cycle can repeat several times, until a final spurt when students rush to complete their tasks before the time is over.

In order to avoid the "mad rush" problem, Christina gives students a breakdown of the time that should be spent on each part of an assignment and periodically reminds students where they should be. She also monitors their behavior carefully by circulating around the room. In fact, none of our four teachers sits down while students are working, unless they are having individual conferences. In the following example, also taken from Donnie's lesson on rearranging equations, we see the way she circulates throughout the room while students are working. Notice how she is able to "overlap" (Kounin, 1970)—to monitor the behavior of students doing seatwork while she also works with an individual.

Students are working on the problems Donnie has just assigned. She walks around the room, peering over students' shoulders, commenting, helping, prodding them along. Then she heads over to three students who were absent and are making up the assignment that everyone else did the day before. She checks what they are doing, and helps one girl who is having particular difficulty. While she is working with this student, she periodically

Donnie circulates while students are working so that she can provide immediate feedback and assistance.

looks up and scans the room to monitor the rest of the class. One boy appears to be doing nothing. "Jerome, are you finished with your problem?"

The purpose of circulating is not simply to monitor behavior. Roving around the room allows you to monitor students' *understanding of the assignment.* Recall the distinction between *engaged time* and *productive time* discussed in Chapter 6. Clearly, it's not enough for students to remain busy and on-task. They must also understand what they are supposed to do and carry out their tasks successfully. This requires monitoring. Sandy comments:

 When I give a seatwork assignment, I never sit at my desk doing paperwork. I give an assignment for an instructional reason, not just to keep kids busy while I grade papers. This means that I need to be moving around, seeing what they're doing. For example, at the end of the period, I might say, "Let's try problems 1, 2, and 3." I walk around and help. If I see that students are doing all right, then I know I can have them complete 4 through 6 for homework.

Watching our teachers monitor independent work, I was struck by the very quiet, discreet way they interacted with each student. This kind of discretion appears to have at least two advantages. First, audible comments may disturb everyone's concentration and progress; second, loud, public comments may be embarrassing and may have a negative effect on students' motivation or willingness to ask questions.

Fredric Jones (2000) offers additional advice for giving help to individual students during seatwork: "Be *clear.* Be *brief.* Be *gone*" (p. 54). According to Jones, teachers should give help in 20 seconds or less for each student. Instead of questioning students ("What did we say was the first thing to do?") and providing individual tutoring, teachers should praise something the student has done correctly ("Good job up to here"), give a straightforward prompt ("Follow the model on the chalkboard"), and leave. In this way, teachers can circulate quickly and efficiently and minimize the time that students spend waiting for assistance.

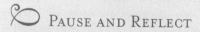 PAUSE AND REFLECT

Consider this comment from a teacher who agrees with Jones's advice to "Be clear. Be brief. Be gone." She states: "We need to get out of the way when students are working independently. If we want students to write, we have to give them time to write, without interrupting with questions and prompts. If we want them to read, we have to allow time for independent reading without telling them what they need to be thinking." This teacher's comments suggest that we sometimes offer *too much assistance* and, in doing so, detract from students' ability to work independently. But how is a balance reached? How do you know when the help you are giving is fostering *dependence* instead of providing just that bit of support that will nudge students to *independence*?

Plan for Ragged Endings

Although it's essential to plan activities for students who finish early, you need to think carefully about the approach that you will take. In Marcy's class, Roy and John both reported that they hadn't finished reading the chapter, when they had. Obviously, they wanted time to read *Mad* rather than move on to a new assignment about business letters. And behavior like this isn't limited to school-smart teenagers; even very young students learn to dawdle if they know that they'll only be given more (uninteresting) work to do when they finish. Jones and Jones (1986) report the following anecdote:

> *During a visit to a second-grade classroom, a student in one of our courses reported observing a child who was spending most of his time staring out the window or doodling on his paper. The observer finally approached the child and asked if she could be of any assistance. Much to her surprise, the child indicated that he understood the work. When asked why he was staring out the window rather than working on his assignment, the boy pointed to a girl several rows away and said, "See her? She does all her work real fast and when she's done she just gets more work." (p. 234)*

In the classrooms of our four teachers, ragged endings are rarely a problem, since class activities are structured so that students rarely finish early. Listen to Sandy:

 Not only do students have to understand what to do and why they're doing it, they need to know what's expected upon completion. If you don't do this, some kids may rush through, thinking I'll finish real fast and then I'll have time to do my homework. If they know they'll have a follow-up related assignment, they keep going. I never make it a closed assignment. I'll say, "Today you're going to do an analysis of knowns. Once you've completed the analysis, formulate the flow chart for your unknowns." I know it usually takes a complete double period to do this. When time is about to run out, I'll say, "If you're not done, do it tonight." If they know at the beginning that it's a homework assignment, they may relax, figure they'll just do it for homework. So I never let them know that they won't be able to finish. If they see that they have a lot to do, they'll say, "Wow, I really need to work." If it's a 10-minute task, they may drag it out. I suggest that teachers predict how long something will take and then tack on a related assignment.

Christina finds that ragged endings are a special challenge when students are doing writing workshop projects:

> Some kids will say "I'm done" after only a few minutes. I tell them they can stop writing if they think they are finished, but they have to move to the next step of the writing process, revision. I give them specific strategies for content revision so they don't get stuck. Individual writing conferences and mini-lessons also help because I give them specific writing options to try out.

CONCLUDING COMMENTS

This chapter has highlighted the pitfalls and problems associated with independent work and has provided suggestions for avoiding, or at least minimizing, these problems. Keep these in mind as you decide on the kinds of activities students will do during seatwork time, the way you will introduce assignments, and the rules and procedures you will establish to guide behavior.

It is important to note that the chapter focused almost exclusively on the situation in which the work is assigned to the entire class while the teacher circulates and assists students in accomplishing the tasks. But this is only one way that seatwork can be used. Another option is to assign independent work to the majority of the class while you work with individuals who need additional help or a more challenging assignment.

This use of seatwork is common at the elementary level. Most of us recall our primary teachers meeting with the "Cardinals," the "Butterflies," or the "Tigers," while the rest of the class worked independently. But independent seatwork combined with small-group instruction is far more unusual at the high school level, where instruction often tends to be conducted in a large group.

Research (Anderson, 1985; Fisher, Filby, Marliave, Cahen, Dishaw, Moore, & Berliner, 1978) suggests that *elementary students spend far too much time doing seatwork assignments that have questionable value, so I am certainly not suggesting that you replicate this situation at the secondary level.* Nonetheless, there are times when it may be appropriate to have the majority of students work on an independent assignment, while you meet with individuals. This format may be particularly useful if you have an extremely heterogeneous class. But take heed: If you are going to be unavailable for circulating and assisting, your assignments need to be even clearer and more meaningful than usual. You also need to hone the skill of overlapping. This is a situation that truly requires you to have "eyes in the back of your head."

SUMMARY

This chapter examined the subsetting known as independent work or seatwork, the situation in which students work individually on a given task at their own desks. Seatwork provides teachers with the opportunity to observe students' performance, to provide support and feedback, to engage in miniconferences with individuals, and to prepare students for homework assignments. But it can also be misused. Too often, seatwork is synonymous with images of bored, passive students doing repetitive, tedious worksheets, while teachers sit at their desks calculating grades or reading the newspaper.

Problems with Seatwork

- The assignment is not meaningful to students.
- The assignment does not match students' varying achievement levels.
- The teacher does not provide students with clear, complete directions.
- The teacher does not monitor what students are doing.
- Students work at different paces, so that some finish early, while others do not finish.

Guidelines for Minimizing the Problems

- Provide assignments that are meaningful, useful, and relevant.
- Match the work to varying achievement levels.
- Make sure written and oral directions are clear.
- Monitor behavior and comprehension.
- Plan for ragged endings.

This chapter focused almost exclusively on the situation in which seatwork is assigned to the entire class, but it may sometimes be appropriate to give an assignment to the majority of the class while you work with individuals who need additional help or a more challenging assignment. This use of seatwork is rare at the secondary level; however, it may be a useful strategy if you need to work with small groups (e.g., if you have an extremely heterogeneous class). But be careful: If you are going to use seatwork this way, you truly need to have "eyes in the back of your head."

ACTIVITIES FOR SKILL BUILDING AND REFLECTION

In Class

1. Select a workbook page or obtain a handout (preferably in your content area), and bring four copies of it to class. In a small group, examine the worksheets, using the following questions as a guide. If you identify problems, suggest a way to improve the worksheet.
   - Are the directions clear?
   - Does the page organization facilitate students' understanding of the task?
   - Does the activity reinforce the intended skill?
   - Is the task meaningful?
   - If there are pictures, are they a help or a distraction?

2. Select a workbook page or obtain a handout (preferably in your content area), and bring four copies of it to class. Working in a small group, examine the pages that students have brought to class. For each page, note the topic, describe the format of the worksheet, identify the skill being practiced or extended, and generate an alternative activity that would accomplish the same goal. An example is provided.

Topic	Description of Worksheet	Skill	Alternative
Who fired the first shot at Lexington and Concord	*Three accounts by individuals who observed or participated in events at Lexington and Concord; students are to determine point of view for each account*	*Identifying point of view and bias*	*Choose two of the following characters (a British officer, an American militiaman, a French reporter, the minister's wife at Lexington, a maid at the inn in Concord) and tell the story of the events at Lexington and Concord from their respective points of view.*

On Your Own

1. Interview two to four middle or high school students to learn their perceptions about seatwork. If possible, select students who vary in terms of achievement level. Include the following questions in your interview:
    *   In what classes is seatwork used most? Least?
    *   To what extent is seatwork used in your academic classes?
    *   Under what circumstances is seatwork useful/useless? Interesting/boring?
    *   What do your teachers generally do when the class is doing seatwork? Are there consistent differences among teachers in this regard?
    *   Are you generally allowed to ask for help from peers or do you have to work alone?

2. Observe a class, preferably in your content area, and note how much time is allocated to independent work during a typical period. During that time, observe three "target" students. Try to select a high-, average-, and low-achieving student. Note what activities each student is required to do during independent work time. (Are the activities the same across achievement levels?) Every two or three minutes, record if the students are on-task or off-task. If possible, ask the students to explain what they are doing and why.

For Your Portfolio

Select a topic in your content area and identify an instructional objective (e.g., "Students will be able to describe the process of respiration"). Then design three independent work activities that all target that objective. Differentiate the activities, so that advanced students, average students, and struggling students can have an assignment well matched to their abilities. In a brief commentary, explain what the objective is and how you are differentiating.

FOR FURTHER READING

Tomlinson, C.A. (2001). *How to differentiate instruction in mixed ability classrooms.* 2nd ed. Alexandria, VA: Association for Supervision and Curriculum Development.

    Tomlinson explains what differentiated instruction is (and isn't), provides a look inside some differentiated classrooms, presents the "how-to's" of planning lessons differentiated by readiness, interest, and learning styles, and discusses the complex issues of grading and record-keeping. An appendix provides a useful summary of instructional and managerial strategies for differentiated, mixed-ability classrooms.

Tomlinson, C.A. (2005). Differentiated instruction. Special theme issue of *Theory Into Practice, 44*(3).

    This issue of TIP examines the concept of differentiated instruction from a variety of perspectives. Authors define the need for differentiated instruction, clarify some of the issues, and provide specific guidance for making classrooms more effective and efficient for all learners in today's schools.

REFERENCES

Anderson, L. (1985). What are students doing when they do all that seatwork? In C. W. Fisher and D. C. Berliner (Eds.), *Perspectives on instructional time.* New York: Longman, pp. 189–202.

Bloome, D., & Theodorou, E. (1988). Analyzing teacher–student and student–student discourse. In J. E. Green & J. O. Harker (Eds.), *Multiple perspective analyses of classroom discourse.* Norwood, NJ: Ablex, pp. 217–248.

Cartledge, G., with Milburn, J. F. (1996). *Cultural diversity and social skills instruction: Understanding ethnic and gender differences.* Champaign, IL: Research Press.

deVoss, G. G. (1979). The structure of major lessons and collective student activity. *Elementary School Journal, 80,* 8–18.

Everhart, R. B. (1983). *Reading, writing, and resistance: Adolescence and labor in a junior high school.* Boston: Routledge and Kegan Paul.

Evertson, C. M., & Emmer, E. T. (1982). Effective management at the beginning of the school year in junior high classes. *Journal of Educational Psychology, 74*(4), 485–498.

Fisher, C. W., Filby, N. N., Marliave, R. S., Cahen, L. S., Dishaw, M. M., Moore, J. E., & Berliner, D. C. (1978). *Teaching behaviors, academic learning time and student achievement. Final report of Phase III-B, Beginning Teacher Evaluation Study.* San Francisco: Far West Laboratory for Educational Research and Development.

Gump, P. V. (1982). School settings and their keeping. In D. L. Duke (Ed.), *Helping teachers manage classrooms.* Alexandria, VA: Association for Supervision and Curriculum Development.

Jones, F. (2000). *Tools for teaching.* Santa Cruz, CA: Fredric H. Jones & Associates.

Jones, V. F., & Jones, L. S. (1986). *Comprehensive classroom management: Creating positive learning environments.* Boston: Allyn and Bacon.

Kounin, J. S. (1970). *Discipline and group management in classrooms.* New York: Holt, Rinehart & Winston.

Kounin, J. S., & Sherman, L. (1979). School environments as behavior settings. *Theory Into Practice, 14,* 145-151.

Rizzo, T. A. (1989). *Friendship development among children in school.* Norwood, NJ: Ablex.

Rosenshine, B. V. (1986). Synthesis of research on explicit teaching. *Educational Leadership, 43*(7), 60-69.

Schraw, G., & Lehman, S. (2001). Situational interest: A review of the literature and directions for future research. *Educational Psychology Review, 31*(1), 23-52.

Tomlinson, C. A. (1999). *The differentiated classroom: Responding to the needs of all learners.* Alexandria, VA: Association for Supervision and Curriculum Development.

Tomlinson, C. A. (2001). How to differentiate instruction in mixed-ability classrooms. 2nd ed. Alexandria, VA: Association for Supervision and Curriculum Development.

MANAGING GROUPWORK

Keep your eyes on your own paper.
Don't talk to the person sitting next to you.
Pay attention to the teacher.
If you need help, raise your hand.
Do your own work.

These are the norms of the traditional classroom, a setting in which students have little opportunity to interact, assist one another, and collaborate on tasks. (See Figure 9.1.) Phrases like these are so much a part of the way we view classrooms that four-year-olds who have never even attended kindergarten use them when playing school.

As these instructions suggest, students in traditional classrooms work either alone or in competition. There are few opportunities for students to interact, to assist one another, or to collaborate on tasks. In some classrooms, helping may even be construed as cheating. This lack of interaction is unfortunate. Letting students work together in pairs or small groups has many advantages. Donnie and Christina alluded to one advantage in Chapter 8: If students can help one another during classwork, they are less likely to "get stuck," to have to sit and wait for the teacher's assistance, and to become uninvolved and disruptive.

237

"This class will stimulate your ideas and thoughts. And remember — no talking."

Figure 9.1   In the traditional classroom, students are rarely allowed to work together. Reprinted with permission.

There are other benefits to groupwork. Working with peers on tasks can enhance students' motivation. Groupwork can also have a positive effect on achievement. In fact, according to a review in the *Harvard Education Letter* (Walters, 2000),

> hundreds of studies over more than three decades show a positive correlation between cooperative learning [a form of groupwork] and achievement. Research has been done in every subject, at all grade levels, in all kinds of schools. And there is widespread consensus that students benefit when they can help one another learn instead of having to work apart from—or against—one another. (pp. 3–4).

One reason for the benefits is that cooperative learning allows students to take an active role in their own learning—to ask questions, to allocate turns for speaking, to evaluate the work of others, to provide encouragement and support, to debate, and to explain—and some of these behaviors have clear academic payoffs. For example, research has consistently demonstrated that providing explanations to peers is beneficial to achievement (Webb & Farivar, 1994); in other words, the more students explain, the more they learn.

Opportunities for interaction also have social payoffs. When students work in heterogeneous groups, they can develop relationships across gender, racial, and ethnic boundaries (Slavin, 1991). Groupwork can also help to integrate individuals with disabilities into the general education classroom (Johnson & Johnson, 1980; Madden & Slavin, 1983). As our school-age population becomes increasingly diverse, fostering positive intergroup relationships grows more and more important.

Given all these benefits, why is there so little groupwork in secondary classrooms? Part of the answer has to do with the teacher's responsibility for keeping order and covering curriculum. In the crowded, complex world of the classroom, it's easier to keep order and cover curriculum when teachers do the talking, and students do the listening. Furthermore, if the school culture equates orderly classrooms with quiet classrooms, teachers may feel uncomfortable when groupwork raises the noise level. Consider this student teacher's journal entry:

> *Every time I read about groupwork it sounds so great I'm ready to use it every day. Then I attempt it in the classroom and I start having second thoughts. I love the learning that comes out of it, but I never feel in control when it is happening. The part that really upsets me is that I really do not mind if the class gets loud. It's the other teachers and the principal I worry about. There have been a few times when I was using cooperative learning and someone has come in to ask if I need any help or they will take it upon themselves to tell my class to be quiet. This really makes me angry. I feel like the only acceptable noise level is no noise at all.*

Finally, like seatwork, groupwork has its own set of challenges and potential pitfalls that can make it difficult for teachers to manage. This chapter examines those special pitfalls. It then discusses ways they can be minimized, drawing on the experiences of our four teachers, as well as the research and scholarly literature on groupwork. In the last section of the chapter, two specific approaches to groupwork are described—Jigsaw and the structural approach to cooperative learning.

THE PITFALLS OF GROUPWORK

Let's begin by considering the experience of Ralph, a student teacher in social studies. During a recent meeting, Ralph recounted his first attempt to use groupwork with his third-period U.S. History I class:

> *We were working on sectional differences—the period from 1800 to 1850, when the Northeast, the West, and the South were like three different countries. I wanted my kids to research the views that each section of the country had on three topics—tariffs, slavery, and the role of the federal government. I didn't want to just lecture, or have them read out of the textbook and then discuss the material, and it seemed like this could be a great cooperative learning activity. My kids haven't had much experience working in groups, but my cooperating teacher is really good about letting me try new things, and he said, "Sure, go ahead and see what happens."*
>
> *I decided to do this over two days. On the first day, I planned to divide the class into the three sections of the country and have each group learn about its section's position on the three topics. I only have 20 kids in this class, so I figured that would be about six or seven kids in each group, which seemed about right. At the end of the first day, they were supposed to pick someone to be their section's spokesman—Daniel*

Webster from the Northeast, John C. Calhoun from the South, and Henry Clay from the West. The second day, these three spokesmen would debate the issues.

So I come into class all fired up about this great thing we're going to do. It didn't seem important to have the groups be absolutely equal in size, and I figured if the kids could choose their own section they'd be more motivated. So I told them they could decide what section of the country they wanted to study. I told them, "If you want to do the Northeast move to this corner, and if you want to do the South move to that corner, etc. Ready, move." Well, it didn't work out. First of all, most of the kids wanted to be the West or the South—there were like nine people in the West and six people in the South and only four people in the Northeast. Plus—I couldn't believe it—the West was all girls (White and Asian American), the South was this really juvenile group of White boys (I just knew they would never get anything done), and the Northeast was my three African American kids and Rick Moore, this White basketball player! And this really quiet, insecure kid just kind of stood there in the middle of the room, not knowing where to go. I had to start asking people to switch and they weren't very happy about that and started making comments about how I didn't know what I was doing and when was Mr. M going to come back and do some "real teaching."

Well, I finally got some of the girls from the West to move into the Northeast group so the sections were about the same size, and I explained what they were going to do. I told them to use their text, and I showed them all the resource materials I had gotten from the library, and told them to use them too. I explained that they were all supposed to help one another research their section's views on tariffs, slavery, and the role of the federal government. Then they were to work together to write a position paper outlining these views and choose someone to be Webster, Calhoun, or Clay for tomorrow's debate. By this time there's only about 25 minutes left, so I tell them to get to work right away. Well, most of them just sat there and stared and kept saying things like, "I don't understand what we're supposed to do." A few kids got up and went back to their desks to get their textbooks and pencils (of course, I had forgotten to tell them to take their books and stuff with them when they moved), and I went around giving out paper, but a lot of the kids just sat there.

I kept going around and trying to get them to work. When I'd come over, they'd begin to jot down notes, but I think they were really just acting like they were working, to get me off their back. Finally, some of the kids in the West and the Northeast began looking up stuff in their texts and taking notes, but they weren't helping each other much. I just could not get them to work together! And some of the kids never did anything—they just sat and let the other kids do it. I even heard comments like, "Let Allison be Clay—she's the smartest one in history." Meanwhile, the guys in the South spent most of the time fooling around and laughing. And they kept putting each other down, saying things like, "He's too dumb to be Calhoun. . . . We don't have any smart kids in this group," and yelling, "Hey Mr. G, we need some smart kids in this group." I kept asking them to be quiet and get to work but they just ignored me.

At the end of the period I told them they'd have to finish looking up their section's views for homework. Then I told them to decide on their spokesman, and of course nobody wanted to do it. In the West, they decided that this one kid who's really conscientious should do it. In the South, they fooled around a lot and then finally this real wise-guy says OK, he'll do it. Well, he was absent the next day, so there was no Calhoun, which they seemed to think was really funny.

All in all, these were two of the worst days of my student teaching experience. After reading all these education theorists who say that co-operative learning is such great stuff, I had been real excited, but now I'm not so sure. Maybe if your class is really motivated to begin with, it would work, but my class is not all that great (the really smart kids are in Honors History), and maybe they just can't work together like this.

 PAUSE AND REFLECT

You have just read Ralph's experiences and thoughts about groupwork. Ralph began with great intentions and optimism. Where did the lesson begin to fall apart? What did he do that contributed to the problems with his lesson? What suggestions might you give to Ralph?

Unfortunately, Ralph's story is not unusual. It illustrates all too vividly what can happen when teachers don't understand the potential problems associated with groupwork and don't work to prevent them from occurring. Let's take a closer look at four of these problems.

First, as Ralph discovered, allowing students to form their own groups often leads to *segregation* among students in terms of gender, race, and ethnicity. Have you ever had lunch in the cafeteria of an ethnically diverse school? One glance is enough to see that members of each ethnic and racial group tend to sit together (Slavin, 1985). It is important to recognize that strong forces operate against the formation of cross-ethnic friendships; left to their own devices, most students will choose to be with those they perceive as similar. Another barrier to friendship exists between students with disabilities and their nondisabled peers (Slavin, 1991). The Individuals with Disabilities Education Act (IDEA) encourages the inclusion of students with disabilities in general education classrooms, but mere physical presence is not enough to ensure that these individuals will be liked, or even accepted.

A second problem of groupwork is the *unequal participation of group members*. Sometimes, this is due to the "freeloader" phenomenon, where one or two students in the group end up doing all the work, while the others sit back and relax. We saw this happen in Ralph's class, when only a few of the students took the research assignment seriously, and one group decided to let Allison, the "smartest" history student, be her group's spokesperson. Although this might be an efficient approach to the task, it's not exactly a fair distribution of responsibility. And those who were freeloading were unlikely to learn anything about sectional differences.

Unequal participation can occur for other, more poignant, reasons as well. In a study of students' perceptions of doing mathematics in a cooperative learning group (King, Luberda, Barry, & Zehnder, 1998), Brett, an average achiever, reported that he often failed to understand the task; consequently, he either withdrew from participation or engaged in distracting, off-task behavior. Similarly, Peter, a low achiever, "was aware that the other students seldom asked for his ideas and if he suggested ideas they never listened to him" (p. 8). In order to save face, he engaged in "silly," "weird" behaviors.

Brett and Peter are good examples of the "discouraged" and "unrecognized" categories in Catherine Mulryan's (1992) typology of passive students (outlined in Table 9.1). It is worth keeping these categories in mind. Although a desire to freeload may be at the root of some students' passivity, it is also possible that

TABLE 9.1 Six Categories of Passive Students

Category	Description	Typical Achievement Level
Discouraged student	The student perceives the group task to be too difficult and thinks it better to leave it to others who understand.	Mostly low achievers
Unrecognized student	The student's initial efforts to participate are ignored or unrecognized by others, and he/she feels that it's best to retire.	Mostly low achievers
Despondent student	The student dislikes or feels uncomfortable with one or more students in the group and does not want to work with them.	High or low achievers
Unmotivated student	The student perceives the tasks as unimportant or "only a game," with no grade being assigned to reward effort expended.	High or low achievers
Bored student	The student thinks the task is uninteresting or boring, often because it is seen as too easy or unchallenging.	Mostly high achievers
Intellectual snob	The student feels that peers are less competent and doesn't want to have to do a lot of explaining. Often ends up working on the task individually.	High achievers

Source: C. Mulryan, 1992.

uninvolved students are feeling discouraged, despondent, unrecognized, bored, or superior.

Just as some individuals may be passive and uninvolved in the group activity, others may take over and dominate the interaction (Cohen, 1994a, 1994b). Frequently, the dominant students are those with high "academic status" in the classroom—those who are recognized by their peers as successful, competent students. At other times the dominant students are those who are popular because they are good athletes or are especially attractive. And sometimes dominance simply reflects the higher status our society accords to those who are White and male. Indeed, research has shown that in heterogeneous groups, males often dominate over females (Webb, 1984), while Whites dominate over African Americans and Hispanics (Cohen, 1972; Rosenholtz & Cohen, 1985).

A third pitfall of groupwork is *lack of accomplishment.* In Ralph's class, a significant amount of instructional time was wasted while students formed groups, and most people didn't get much done even once the groups had formed. A number of students, particularly those in the group doing the South, seemed to view the opportunity to interact as an opportunity to fool around and socialize. (Mulryan, 1992, calls these the "social opportunists.") Their behavior undoubtedly distracted students who were trying to work. Furthermore, the disruption was upsetting to Ralph, who repeatedly asked students to quiet down—without success.

Finally, a fourth problem associated with groupwork is students' *lack of cooperation* with one another. Ralph tells us that the students tended to work alone, and the boys in the "juvenile" group spent a lot of time "putting each other down." Although these kinds of behavior are certainly disappointing, they are not surprising. As we have pointed out, most students have little experience working in cooperative groups, and the norms of the traditional classroom are dramatically different from the norms for successful groupwork (Cohen, 1994a):

> *Ask peers for assistance.*
> *Help one another.*
> *Explain material to other students.*
> *Check that they understand.*
> *Provide support.*
> *Listen to your peers.*
> *Give everyone a chance to talk.*

Students who are used to keeping their eyes on their own papers may find it difficult to follow these new norms. Those who are used to asking the teacher for help may be reluctant to turn to their peers, perhaps because they don't want to appear "dumb." Some may have difficulty giving clear, thorough explanations to their peers. Those who are not "effective speakers" may lack the skills needed to obtain assistance (Wilkinson & Calculator, 1982). Students whose cultural backgrounds have fostered a competitive orientation may have difficulties functioning in cooperative situations. And students who are used to being passive may be unwilling to assume a more active role. As Elizabeth Cohen (1994a) reminds us, it is a mistake to assume that individuals (children *or* adults) know how to work together in a productive, collegial manner.

The next section of this chapter considers some general strategies for managing groupwork. (These are summarized in the Practical Tips box.) Remember, *successful groupwork will not just happen.* If you want your students to work together productively, you must plan the groups and the tasks carefully, teach students the new norms, and provide opportunities for them to practice the behaviors that are required. As Sandy comments:

 Sometimes, when beginning teachers do groupwork, they think, "I'll divide my students into groups and that's it. That's all I have to do." They don't plan the groups and they don't plan the group *work*. That's where they get into trouble. You not only have to think about how you're going to get your kids *into* groups, but what you're going to do after they're *in* the groups. You have to plan it so carefully, and it's not an easy thing to do.

DESIGNING SUCCESSFUL GROUPWORK

Decide on the Type of Group to Use

Students can work together in a variety of ways. Susan Stodolsky (1984) has identified five different types of groupwork: helping permitted, helping obligatory, peer tutoring, cooperative, and completely cooperative. The first three types of groups can be considered "collaborative seatwork" (Cohen, 1994a). All of them involve students assisting one another on individual assignments. In a *helping permitted* group, individuals work on their own tasks, and they are evaluated as individuals; however, they are allowed—but not required—to help one another. *Helping obligatory* situations differ only in that students are now *expected* to offer mutual assistance. In *peer tutoring,* the relationship between the students is not equal: An "expert" is paired with a student who needs help, so assistance flows in only one direction. Peer tutoring is a particularly useful way of meeting the needs of students with disabilities and those who are learning English as a second language.

Cooperative groups differ from these helping situations in that youngsters now share a common goal or end, instead of working on completely individual tasks. In a *simple cooperative group,* some division of responsibilities may occur. For example, a group researching the Civil War might decide that one student will learn about the causes of the war, while another learns about famous battles, and a third learns about important leaders. Tasks are carried out independently, but everyone's assignment has to be coordinated at the end in order to produce the final joint product.

More complex is a *completely cooperative group.* Here, students not only share a common goal, there is little or no division of labor. All members of the group work together to create the group product. This was the type of groupwork that Ralph used when he directed his history students to research their section's views on tariffs, slavery, and the role of the federal government and then develop a position paper. (Of course, his students could have decided to divide up the research assignment, and then coordinate their findings, but Ralph did not direct them to do so.)

PRACTICAL TIPS FOR

DESIGNING AND IMPLEMENTING SUCCESSFUL GROUPWORK

- *Decide on the type of group to use:*
  - *Helping permitted*—students are allowed to assist one another on individual assignments.
  - *Helping obligatory*—students are expected to help one another.
  - *Peer tutoring*—a more skillful peer assists a less skillful peer.
  - *Cooperative*—students share a common goal or end; some division of responsibilities may occur.
  - *Completely cooperative*—students share a common goal and there is little or no division of labor; all members of the group work together to create the group product.

- *Decide on the size of the group:*
  - Partners maximize students' opportunity to participate.
  - Groups of 4–5 are generally recommended, and 6 is the upper limit.

- *Decide on group composition:*
  - Think carefully about achievement level, gender, cultural/linguistic background, race/ethnicity, ableness, and social skills.

- *Structure the task for positive interdependence; have students*
  - Share materials.
  - Work toward a group goal, grade, or reward.
  - Share information.
  - Share talents and multiple abilities.
  - Fulfill different roles (materials person, timekeeper, recorder, facilitator, reporter, etc.).

- *Ensure individual accountability:*
  - Make sure that all group members are held responsible for their contribution to the goal.
  - Assess individual learning.
  - Differentiate responsibilities according to students' individual needs.

- *Teach students to cooperate:*
  - Help them to understand the value of cooperation.
  - Provide group skills training.
  - Provide the chance for them to evaluate their groupwork experiences.

- *Monitor learning, involvement, and cooperative behavior:*
  - Monitor groups and intervene when needed.

It is important to keep these distinctions in mind as you plan groupwork. *Different types of groups are suitable for different types of activities, and they require different kinds of skills.* (See Table 9.2.) In helping situations, for example, students are ultimately responsible for completing individual tasks. Although these students need to know how to ask for help, how to explain and demonstrate (rather than simply providing the right answer), and how to provide support and encouragement, they do not need the more complex skills required in truly cooperative situations where they share a common goal.

TABLE 9.2 Different Types of Groups

Type of Group	Skill Required	Example of an Activity
Helping permitted Helping obligatory	How to ask for help How to explain How to provide support and encouragement	Creating clay sculptures: Students ask each other for assistance and opinions, but everyone completes an individual sculpture
Peer tutoring	How to ask for help How to explain How to provide support and encouragement	Tutor helps tutee to complete a set of chemistry problems

Cooperative group	Divide group task into
	  individual tasks
	Coordinate individual
	  efforts to produce final
	  group product
		Survey on what students do after school: Each group member interviews students at one grade level, then pool figures to make a group graph

Completely cooperative	Take turns Listen to one another Coordinate efforts Share materials Collaborate on a single task Solve conflicts Achieve consensus	Determining political party affiliation: As a group, decide if hypothetical person is Democrat or Republican

As an example of a helping situation, let's consider the following activity that I observed in Christina's class:

 Christina's students are working in small groups, sorting through work in their "collection folders," selecting items to include in their portfolios, and completing "portfolio selection sheets," where they explain why they chose that particular assignment and which criteria it demonstrates. Some of the talk is commentary on progress, not directed to anyone in particular: "I'm going to choose this piece. I finally understood the difference between metaphors and similes." "I love the alliteration in this poem." But there are also requests for assistance and opinions: "Which of these two would you choose?" "How many things are we supposed to select?" "Do you like this one or this one?" "I don't understand what it means here . . ."

In contrast to helping situations, cooperative groups require skills beyond requesting and giving appropriate assistance. Students must be able to develop a plan of action; they must be able to coordinate efforts toward a common goal; they must be able to evaluate the contributions of their peers and give feedback in a constructive way; they must monitor individuals' progress toward the group goal; they must be able to summarize and synthesize individual efforts. Consider the following example, provided by Donnie:

> **In my basic skills class, I work on collecting, analyzing, and depicting data. I have the students work in groups of four. Each group has to create a survey designed to learn what high school kids do after school—for example, how much they play computer games, watch TV, just hang around, play basketball, have an after-school job, do homework. Then, each group has to interview 80 students in the high school, and each person in the group is responsible for interviewing 20 students at one grade level (in other words, one person interviews all freshmen, one interviews all sophomores, and so on). Each person has to collect his or her own information, but then they have to come together to make a group graph showing how people at all four grade levels manage their time. Kids know that they can't complete the project unless everybody does their part, so they really get on each other's case if somebody isn't working.**

Completely cooperative groups with no division of labor present even greater challenges. Not only must students be able to take turns, listen to one another carefully, and coordinate efforts, but they must also be able to collaborate on a single task, reconcile differences, compromise, and reach a consensus. During one visit to Fred's class, I observed a good example of a completely cooperative group activity. The class was divided into groups of four or five to consider profiles of eight hypothetical Americans (e.g., "A union member working in an automobile plant in one of the large factories located in the Industrial Belt that includes Buffalo, Cleveland, Toledo, Detroit, Chicago, and Milwaukee. He is a college graduate"; "A bank executive in a small county seat in Colorado. She is concerned about her career, is unmarried, and is about to buy her own home"). For each profile, students had to determine the probable party affiliation (or lack of one), the kinds of issues that would be important to the individual in a campaign, and whether the individual was likely to be a voter or a nonvoter. Although students were required to carry out individual tasks, they had to coordinate their individual efforts if the groups were to be successful:

> **Fred hands out the worksheet describing the eight hypothetical American voters (or nonvoters). He explains that students will first do the task individually, taking notes for each profile. When everyone is finished, he divides the class into groups of four or five. Fred explains that students are to share their opinions, being sure to provide their reasoning. He encourages the groups to work toward consensus on each hypothetical voter and suggests that a different person serve as recorder for each voter. Each group will be expected to report on their results to the rest of the class.**
> **Students begin to go through the eight profiles, sharing their responses. Fred circulates, asking students to explain their reasoning ("Why do you think he's a Democrat?"), commenting on their responses ("I can't believe how confident you**

people are!"), and checking on group process ("What number are you on? Has everyone had a chance to be a recorder for at least one profile?").

When the groups have finished, Fred announces that Group B will be the first group to report out. The four members of Group B stand in the front of the room. Sandra reports on the group's opinions about the first two profiles: "We think he's a Democrat. He definitely votes. We think he cares about auto safety." The reports continue, with Fred interjecting questions and comments.

Although this activity first required students to think through their responses as individuals, they then had to work together to construct a group report. They had to decide who would be the recorder and reporter for each profile, take turns explaining the reasons for their ideas, listen respectfully to one another, reject ideas without being destructive, and reach consensus on what to report. These are not easy skills to learn—even for adults.

As these three examples illustrate, the more interdependent students are, the more skills they need to cooperate successfully. It's a good idea to use simpler types of groups when you are just starting out. In Ralph's case, we can see that he began with the most complex kind of groupwork. He set up a situation in which students who were not even used to helping one another were expected to cooperate completely.

Decide on the Size of the Group

To some extent, the size of the group you use depends on the task you assign. Pairs are appropriate when foreign language students are preparing a dialogue to role-play, or when home economics students are reviewing weights and measures in preparation for a test. Groups of two maximize students' opportunity to participate. They are also easier for beginning teachers to manage, and teachers of younger or less mature students often prefer pairs over larger groups that require more elaborate social skills. Even with senior high school students, Sandy makes sure to provide students with experiences in pairs before using cooperative groups.

In the following vignette, we see Donnie use pairs of students in a helping situation:

 Donnie is reviewing problems that involve different kinds of angles (supplementary, complementary, and vertical). After going through a number of problems on the board, Donnie announces that students will be doing the next set by themselves. She explains: "Please listen to what you're going to do next. On this assignment, you may confer with one other person. You're going to count off: one, two, three. [The students do so.] If you are a number one, you will start with problem number 19, and then go up by 3s (22, 25, 28, 31, 34, and 37). If you are a number two, your problems will start with 20, and go up by 3s. If you are a number three, your problems will start with 21, and go up by 3s. Pair yourself up with someone who has the same number that you have. Your job is to help one another understand the problems. You have 20 minutes to do these. Please have them ready to be passed in at the end of the period."

In situations where the task is an ambitious one that requires a division of labor (e.g., the survey on what high school students do after school), it makes sense to form groups larger than two. Groups of three are still relatively easy to manage, but you need to make sure that two students don't form a coalition, leaving the third isolated and excluded (Cohen, 1994a).

In general, educators recommend cooperative groups of four or five (Cohen, 1994a), and six is usually the upper limit (Johnson, Johnson, Holubec, & Roy, 1984). Keep in mind that as group size increases, the "resource pool" also increases; in other words, there are more heads to think about the task and more hands to share the work. It is also true, however, that the larger the group, the more difficult it is to develop a plan of action, allocate turns for speaking, share materials, and reach consensus.

Decide on Group Composition

In addition to deciding on the type and size of your groups, you must think carefully about group composition. As I mentioned earlier in this chapter, groupwork can provide opportunities for students to develop relationships with those who are different from themselves. For this reason, educators (e.g., Slavin, 1995) generally advise teachers to form groups that are heterogeneous with respect to gender, ethnicity, race, linguistic background, and ableness. On the other hand, it is important to be sensitive to the fact that trying to achieve heterogeneity can place a burden on students who must be separated from those with whom they feel most comfortable.

Let's consider a concrete example provided by Beth Rubin (2003), who studied two untracked ninth-grade classes in a diverse urban high school. The teachers of these classes were committed to using groupwork so that students could "learn about one another, appreciate differences, and develop the ability to work with others" (p. 553). However, since African American students were a racial minority, constructing groups that reflected the racial makeup of the class led to "one Black kid in each group" (p. 553). Thus, when Tiffany and Christie, two African American students, wanted to be placed in the same group, their teacher said no. Instead, each was assigned to a group with three European American students they did not know well. As Rubin comments, "having one African American student in each group usually meant that that student did not have any close friends in that group" (p. 553). Rachel Lotan (2006) points out another possible consequence of trying to ensure that groups always have an equal number of students from the different ethnic or racial groups represented in the class. According to Lotan, such group assignment can lead students "to interact with their fellow group members as stereotypical representatives of their respective racial or ethnic backrounds rather than as individual persons." (p. 532).

Teachers also need to consider whether small groups will be heterogeneous or homogeneous with respect to achievement level. At times, homogeneous groups can be useful; for example, you may want to form a helping group of several students who are all working on a particular mathematics skill. In general, however, educators recommend the use of groups that are heterogeneous in terms of academic performance (Cohen, 1994a; Slavin, 1995). One reason is that they provide more opportunities for asking questions and receiving explanations.

Just how heterogeneous your groups should be is still not clear. Research by Noreen Webb and her colleagues (1985) has shown that in junior high math groups composed of high-, medium-, and low-achieving students, those of medium ability tend to get left out of the interaction. In fact, Webb (1989) argues that two-level groups (high-medium or medium-low) are most beneficial for all students. In contrast, other proponents of cooperative learning (e.g., Slavin, 1991) recommend that four-person teams consist of a high achiever, a low achiever, and two average achievers.

Another variable you need to consider when deciding on group composition is social skill. After observing a completely cooperative learning activity in Sandy's class, she and I talked about how she had decided on the groups. Her comments emphasized the importance of considering more than ability:

When I form groups, I consider kids' personalities more than their ability, although I do try not to put just one bright kid in a group. (If I do, the others expect that person to tell them what to do.) I think about how they interact with other people and try to think about where they'll feel comfortable and where they'll work best. For example, I try to pair Steven [a student with an emotional disorder] with Jeremy, because Jeremy's unusually patient and mature, and he can deal comfortably with the outrageous things that Steven sometimes says. In the same way, I would never pair Kahlil and Michael. Michael is impulsive—he blurts out the first thing that comes into his mind— while Kahlil is very deliberate and careful. He would retreat into himself and not say a word if I put him in a group with Michael. So I put Kahlil with Laura. Laura is kind of insecure and quiet. But Kahlil draws her out. During today's lesson, he said to her, "What's the matter? Why are you so quiet?" She said, "I'm thinking," and he said, "Well say something—we need to work together." He was really showing good leadership, but he would never have done that with Michael. On the other hand, I was able to put Michael with Nathan. When Michael blurts out, Nathan says, "Wait a minute. Slow down."

As Sandy's comments indicate, groups work better when students' personalities and social skills are taken into consideration. Some students have difficulty working with others—they may be unusually volatile, or angry, or bossy—and it makes sense to distribute them across the groups. On the other hand, some students have unusual leadership abilities; others are particularly adept at resolving conflicts; still others are especially alert to injustice and can help to ensure that everyone in the group has a chance to participate. When forming groups, it generally makes sense to disperse students like these too, so that each group has the benefit of their talents. All four teachers follow this practice; however, Sandy and Donnie occasionally find it useful to put all of the leaders in one group. Donnie explains:

At first, the kids in the other groups say, "Oh, we don't have anybody good in our group. This isn't fair." They sort of sit there aimlessly, wondering what to do. But with encouragement, they begin to get their act together. It doesn't always work, of course, but sometimes this creates a chance for new leaders to emerge.

Teachers develop different systems for assigning students to groups. Some teachers of academic subjects write each student's name on a note card, along with information about achievement and interpersonal relationships (e.g., with whom the student doesn't get along). Then they rank students in terms of achievement level and assign a top-ranked student and a bottom-ranked student to each of the groups (although many teachers try to avoid extremes). Next, the average students are distributed. Having each student's name on a note card allows you to shuffle students around as you try to form equivalent groups that will work well together.

Fred has developed a different system. Like Sandy, he focuses more on social skills and personalities than on academic ability:

First I think about who *can't* be in the same group, and I say, "Okay, he goes in Group 1, and she goes in Group 2, etc." Then I think about who the *nicest* people in the class are—the people who can get along with everybody—and I spread them out too. Then I separate the *loudmouths*— the kids who are not good listeners and who tend to talk a lot. Finally, I think about the kids who need "*special handling*." Maybe somebody who doesn't speak English, or maybe someone who's very sensitive or shy. I think, "Which group will not destroy this person?" and I try to put that kid in a group that will be most supportive.

Trying to create the perfect groups can be a daunting challenge for teachers. Rachel Lotan (2006) suggests another approach—*controlled randomness*—in which teachers make group assignments in the students' presence. Using pocket charts on the wall to display group assignments, teachers shuffle students' names like a deck of cards, and then place the cards in the pockets. After distributing all the cards, teachers review the groups that emerge and make necessary changes. For example, an English language learner might need someone to translate, or two close friends who socialize might need to be separated.

All four teachers use controlled (or uncontrolled) randomness every now and then when they are forming groups. As I mentioned in Chapter 7, I once observed Donnie take a deck of playing cards from her desk, walk toward a student, and ask him to help her shuffle:

"I've never been very good at this. I never learned how." [A few students tease her about her inability to shuffle.] After the cards are shuffled, Donnie moves from student to student, directing each one to "pick a card." As she makes her way around the room, the students and I wonder what she is up to. When everyone has a card, Donnie tells the students to pay close attention. "Now, I need you to find the people with the same number or face card that you have. When you find your partners, choose a table and sit down in a group. Then I'll tell you what you're going to do and pass out the materials." The students get up and walk around the room to find their group members. Once the groups have all formed, Donnie proceeds to give directions for the problem-solving activity they are to do as a group.

After class, Donnie and I talked about this strategy for forming groups:

 This was the first time I ever tried this. My main reason was to get them talking and working with people other than their normal neighbors. They're in seats they chose on the first day, and some of them are very quiet and shy. They don't like to move around or interact with new people. This made them get up and form some new groups.

Finally, there are times when Donnie, Fred, Sandy, and Christina allow their students to form their own groups, but only for certain kinds of tasks, and not until the students have had substantial experience working in various kinds of groups with almost everyone in the class. For example, Christina allows students to form their own groups for long-term assignments that require work to be done at home. As she comments, "It's just too difficult for students to get together with people other than their friends outside of school."

Structure Cooperative Tasks for Positive Interdependence

If you want to ensure that students cooperate on a task, you have to create a situation in which students perceive that they need one another in order to succeed. This is called *positive interdependence,* and it's one of the essential features that transforms a groupwork activity into true cooperative learning (Antil, Jenkins, Wayne, & Vadasy, 1998).

One simple strategy for promoting interdependence is to require group members to *share materials* (Johnson, Johnson, Holubec, & Roy, 1984). If one member of a pair has a page of math problems, for example, and the other member has the answer sheet, they need to coordinate (at least a little) if they are both to complete the problems and check their answers. By itself, however, sharing materials is unlikely to ensure meaningful interaction.

Another way to encourage interdependence is to create a *group goal.* For example, you might have each group produce a single product, such as a report, a science demonstration, a poem, or a skit. When Christina's students studied the play *Antigone,* she had students individually read Henry David Thoreau's essay, "Resistance to Civil Government," and then meet in groups to (1) define civil disobedience in their own words; (2) explain the purpose of civil disobedience; (3) list three to five real-life examples of civil disobedience; and (4) predict how the issue of civil disobedience is important in the play. Christina explained how group members were to discuss each part of the assignment, combine their ideas, and turn in one paper from the whole group. Although requiring a group product increases the likelihood that students will work together, Christina recognizes that this strategy is not foolproof: One person in the group can do all the work while the others remain uninvolved.

A stronger way to stress the importance of collaborating is to give a *group grade or group reward.* For example, suppose you want to encourage students to help one another with the symbols for chemical ions. You can do this by rewarding groups on the basis of the total number of ions correctly supplied by all the members of the group. You can also give bonus points to every group in which all students reach a predetermined level of accomplishment. Some teachers give each group member a number (e.g., one to four) at the beginning of class, and then spin a numbered spinner or toss a die to select the number of the group member whose homework or classwork paper will be graded (Webb & Farivar, 1994). Then everyone in the group receives that score. Such a practice clearly increases the pressure on group members to make sure that everyone's homework or class work is complete and well done.

Another way of promoting collaboration is to structure the task so that students are dependent on one another for *information* (Johnson, Johnson, Holubec, & Roy, 1984). In Donnie's lesson on collecting and displaying information, for example, group members had to pool their individual data on adolescents' after-school activities. Since each student was responsible for collecting data on one grade level, they needed each other in order to construct a graph depicting the activities of freshmen, sophomores, juniors, and seniors.

You can also foster interdependence by creating rich, complex tasks that require *multiple abilities* (e.g., reading, writing, computing, role-playing, building models, spatial problem solving, drawing, creating songs, public speaking). By convincing your students that *every* member of the group is good at *some* of these and that *no* member of the group is good at *all* of them, you can reduce the differences in participation between high- and low-status students and enable those who are often left out to contribute (Cohen, 1994a, 1994b, 1998). Listen to Donnie:

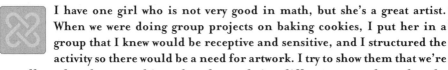 I have one girl who is not very good in math, but she's a great artist. When we were doing group projects on baking cookies, I put her in a group that I knew would be receptive and sensitive, and I structured the activity so there would be a need for artwork. I try to show them that we're not all good at the same things, but that we bring different strengths and weaknesses to the table.

Finally, you can assign *different roles* to group members, requiring each role to be fulfilled if the group is to complete the task. For example, Fred sometimes designates a recorder, a timekeeper, an encourager (to facilitate participation), a taskmaster (to keep people on track), a summarizer (to report out at the end of the group session), and an observer (to monitor group process). At times, the roles that Fred assigns are integral to the activity itself. In a social studies simulation on reconstruction, students form "Presidential Advisory Committees" to advise President Andrew Johnson on a program for the South after the Civil War. Groups have to provide guidance on weighty issues:

 Are the southerners who lately rebelled against us citizens? Shall they have the same rights and privileges as other loyal Americans?

What shall we do with the leaders of the rebellion, especially General Lee and President Davis?

How can I make sure that the South is governed by leaders loyal to the United States?

Are the soldiers who fought against us traitors?

What shall we do about the former slaves? Should they be given citizenship? Should they be allowed to vote? Should we pay former slave owners for the loss of their slave "property?"

Each Presidential Advisory Committee is composed of characters with very different backgrounds and points of view. Here are a few examples:

 The Reverend Harry (Harriet) Stone, 43 years old, deeply religious, attended college in Virginia, not very active in the Abolition Movement. Believed slavery is immoral but felt John Brown took things "too far."

William (Mary) Hardwick, 52, a rich mill owner from Delaware, two sons fought in the war, the youngest was killed in the Wilderness while serving under Grant. Manufactures shirts and has profited from government war contracts, which have been canceled since Lee's surrender at Appomattox. Southern distributors still owe you $40,000 for purchases made before the war began.

Having a variety of roles ensures that everyone has a role to play and that all students have to participate if the group is to succeed.

Ensure Individual Accountability

As I discussed earlier in the chapter, one of the major problems associated with cooperative groupwork is unequal participation. Sometimes individuals refuse to contribute to the group effort, preferring to "freeload." Sometimes more assertive students dominate, making it difficult for others to participate. In either case, lack of participation is a genuine problem. Those who do not actively participate may not learn anything about the academic task; furthermore, the group is not learning the skills of collaboration.

One way to encourage the participation of all group members is to make sure that everyone is held responsible for his or her contribution to the goal and that each student's learning is assessed individually. *Individual accountability* is the second essential feature of cooperative learning—and it is one that teachers most often neglect (Antil, Jenkins, Wayne, & Vadasy, 1998).

There are several ways to establish individual accountability. You can require students to take individual tests on the material and receive individual grades; you can have each student complete an identifiable part of the total group project; or you can call on one or two students from each group to answer a question, explain the group's reasoning, or provide a demonstration. One morning in May, I watched Sandy explain that students were going to be working on understanding the idea of equilibrium. She divided the class into groups of three, explained the task, and reminded students that they needed to work together to discover the operative principle. Before she allowed them to begin work, however, she stressed that a group should not consider itself through until all group members understood, since everyone would eventually be taking an individual quiz. In other words, Sandy made it very clear that every student would be accountable for explaining the process of equilibrium.

Ensuring accountability does not always mean that every student has to perform the same activity or be responsible for the same material. Within a heterogeneous cooperative group, it is sometimes desirable or necessary to differentiate tasks by complexity and quantity (Schniedewind & Davidson, 2000). In other words, students can engage in tasks at different levels of difficulty or learn different amounts of material. The important point is that "every student learns something that he or she doesn't already know" and can "contribute to a common goal" (p. 24). For example, each student in a heterogeneous group might be responsible for reading a segment of a biography of Harriet Tubman (p. 25). Students who are struggling readers might be assigned a relatively short portion of the book and review it with a resource teacher or an aide before the class activity, while more proficient readers read a more demanding section. But all students summarize their reading, report to one another, and are held accountable for knowing about all aspects of Tubman's life. According to Schniedewind and Davidson, students do not appear to feel awkward or resentful about differentiated assignments like these. Indeed, they are well aware of one another's capabilities and seem to "feel more comfortable when teachers acknowledge and engage them in discussion about the tension-producing subject of academic difference" (p. 25). One teacher, for example, explained to her students that differentiated assignments helped her to fulfill her responsibility to challenge each student.

Teach Students to Cooperate

Recently, I read the following entry in a reflective paper written by a student teacher in English:

> *I have tried to use cooperative learning activities as much as possible but I'm not at all sure it's been beneficial. It seems to me that instead of facilitating students' learning—as my education professors claim—these group activities have generally been a waste of time. Students spend more time socializing, goofing off, arguing, and procrastinating than getting anything done. I guess I'm not convinced that cooperative learning can work unless (1) students are mature enough to work without a teacher breathing down their necks and (2) they have the social skills to interact with peers. Given these criteria, I am skeptical about using cooperative learning with freshmen.*

This student teacher has come to understand the fact that students' social skills can make or break a groupwork activity. What he fails to understand, however, is the role of the teacher in teaching these skills. David and Roger Johnson (1989/90), two experts on cooperative learning, warn teachers not to assume that students know how to work together. They write:

> People do not know instinctively how to interact effectively with others. Nor do interpersonal and group skills magically appear when they are needed. Students must be taught these skills and must be motivated to use them. If group members lack the interpersonal and small-group skills to cooperate effectively, cooperative groups will not be productive. (p. 30)

As the classroom teacher, *it is your responsibility to teach students to work together.* This is not a simple process; students do not learn to cooperate in one 45-minute lesson. Indeed, we can think about the process in terms of three stages: learning to value cooperation, developing group skills, and evaluation. Let's consider each of these briefly.

Valuing Cooperation

Before students can work together productively, they must understand the value of cooperation. Sandy introduces cooperative groupwork early in the year by setting up a situation that students are unable to do alone:

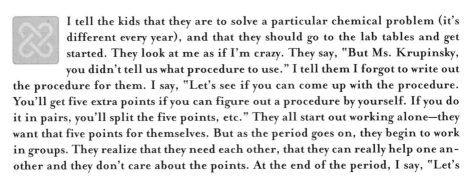 I tell the kids that they are to solve a particular chemical problem (it's different every year), and that they should go to the lab tables and get started. They look at me as if I'm crazy. They say, "But Ms. Krupinsky, you didn't tell us what procedure to use." I tell them I forgot to write out the procedure for them. I say, "Let's see if you can come up with the procedure. You'll get five extra points if you can figure out a procedure by yourself. If you do it in pairs, you'll split the five points, etc." They all start out working alone—they want that five points for themselves. But as the period goes on, they begin to work in groups. They realize that they need each other, that they can really help one another and they don't care about the points. At the end of the period, I say, "Let's

Sandy assists a small group during a lab activity.

talk about what happened here. Why did you start out by yourself?" They tell me, "I wanted the five points, but I had to ask for help because I didn't know enough." We talk about how helpful it is to work together when you're learning something new, and how the points don't matter.

When students are going to work in the same groups over a period of time, it's often helpful to have them engage in a nonacademic activity designed to build a team identity and to foster a sense of group cohesion. For example, when Christina introduces groupwork, the first task that groups have is to write a summary about the group members. Then Christina calls on someone in each group and asks them to tell her what they learned about the members of the group. Another idea is to have each group create a banner or poster displaying a group name and a logo. In order to ensure that everyone participates in creating the banner, each group member can be given a marker of a different color; individuals can only use the marker they have been given, and the banner must contain all the colors.

Group Skills Training

Teaching a group skill is much like teaching students how to balance equations or use a pipette. It requires systematic explanation, modeling, practice, and feedback. *It's simply not enough to state the rules and expect students to understand and remember.* And don't take anything for granted: Even basic guidelines like "don't distract others" and "speak quietly" may need to be taught.

It's helpful to begin by analyzing the groupwork task you have selected in order to determine the specific skills students need to know (Cohen, 1994a). Will students have to explain material? Will they have to listen carefully to one another? Will they have to reach a consensus? Once you have analyzed the task, select one or two key behaviors to teach your students. Resist the temptation to introduce all the required group skills at once; going too far too fast is sure to lead to frustration.

Next, explain to your students that they will be learning a skill necessary for working in groups. *Be sure to define terms, discuss rationales, and provide examples.* Johnson and Johnson (1989/90) suggest that you construct a "T-chart" on which you list the skill and then—with the class—record ideas about what the skill would look like and what it would sound like. Figure 9.2 shows a T-chart for "encouraging participation."

Encouraging Participation	
Looks Like	**Sounds Like**
Make eye contact.	What do YOU think?
Look and nod in person's direction.	We haven't heard from you yet.
Gesture to a person to speak.	Do you agree?
Make sure everyone's chair is in the cluster (no one is physically left out).	Anyone else have something to say?
	I'd like to know what you think?
	Let's go around to see what each person thinks.

Figure 9.2   A T-Chart for Encouraging Participation

Finally, you need to provide opportunities for students to practice the skill and to receive feedback. You might have students role-play; you might pair the skill with a familiar academic task so that students can focus their attention on using the social skill (Carson & Hoyle, 1989/90); or you might have students engage in exercises designed to teach particular skills. (Elizabeth Cohen's book, *Designing Groupwork,* 1994, contains cooperative exercises, such as "Master Designer" and "Guess My Rule," which focus on helping and explaining, and Epstein's "Four-Stage Rocket," designed to improve group discussion skills.)

Donnie sometimes teaches group skills in a more "devious" way. She secretly assigns individuals to act out different roles: the dictator, the nonparticipant, the person who tears down everybody else, and the facilitator who encourages participation and listens well. Students engage in some sort of nonacademic activity—perhaps the task of building a tower with pins and straws—and then debrief, sharing their reactions about the group process. An activity like this serves to heighten students' awareness of group skills—and they have fun at the same time.

Regardless of the type of practice you provide, you need to give students feedback about their performance. Fred has found that it's helpful to designate a "process person" or "observer" for each group. This individual is responsible for keeping track of how well the group is functioning; for example, he or she may monitor how many times each person speaks. At the end of the groupwork session, the process person is able to share specific data that the group can use to evaluate its ability to work together.

Evaluation

In order to learn from their experiences, students need the chance to discuss what happened and to evaluate how successful they were in working together. Ross (1995) demonstrated the power of feedback in a study that audiotaped seventh-grade mathematics students in cooperative learning groups, gave students edited transcripts of their discussions, and trained them in how to interpret them. Students then devised an improvement plan to increase the frequency of requesting help, giving help, and being on task. According to Ross, after the feedback, both the frequency and quality of help seeking and help giving improved. For example, students became more aware of the needs of lower-ability students and felt more obligated to help. Consider the following exchange, recorded before the feedback. Here, Sharon has fallen behind the other members of her group, but they will not wait, and they exclude her from the discussion of the answers:

SHARON: Hey, what about me?

CURTIS: You're not in it.

SHARON: Hey, you guys, what about me? . . . How come you guys won't let me do none?

GWEN: Because you're not even here yet.

SHARON: I'm on number 15.

GWEN: Yeah, I know, but we're on number 16. (p. 135)

In a session recorded after the feedback, group members continue to treat Sharon rather impatiently when she has fallen behind; nonetheless, they are now more willing to wait for her:

> CURTIS: We have to wait for her. We have to wait for her.
>
> GWEN: Come on, Sharon. You know we are waiting.
>
> SHARON: You guys were going ahead and you weren't supposed to.
>
> GWEN: I know; we won't. We won't do the answers.
>
> CURTIS: We won't look at the answers. We'll wait for you. (p. 135)

Obviously, it's impossible to provide this kind of elaborate, detailed feedback on a regular basis. But an extensive evaluation session can be instructive when norms for groupwork are first being established. For example, during one visit to Fred's classroom early in the year, I observed a lesson on U.S. policy toward Afghanistan. Students were working in groups of four or five, trying to reach consensus on a number of politically sensitive questions (e.g., Should the United States maintain a military presence in Afghanistan to train Afghani security and military forces? Should the United States build permanent bases in Afghanistan?) Before students began to work, Fred explained that students were to discuss each question and prepare a report for a special envoy advising the President on Afghanistan. The chairperson of each group was responsible for compiling the report and seeing that all members had an opportunity to participate. Fred made it clear that groups would not be evaluated solely on their reports, but also on how well they worked together—specifically, how quickly they got to work; how involved and engaged they looked; how well group members listened to each other; if members conducted themselves with maturity and decorum; and if all group members had a chance to express their views. During the activity, Fred roamed the room, watching and listening; in addition, the school's media specialist videotaped the entire class.

The following day, Fred spent about half the period evaluating the group activity his students had done. First, Fred talked about how difficult it is to work in groups and told a few "horror" stories about groups in which he had worked. Then he asked students to complete a self-evaluation of their group's interaction. (See Figure 9.3 for one student's evaluation.) Finally, he played the videotape, commenting on the things he had noticed:

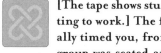

[The tape shows students getting into groups, getting organized, and getting to work.] The first thing I did was watch you getting started. I actually timed you, from the moment you entered class to the time the last group was seated and working. It was less than three minutes. I think that was pretty good. [The camera zooms in on each group.] I also looked at how people were seated. [The tape shows a group where four people are clustered and one person is sitting away.] Your physical placement in the group is very important; if you have someone sitting outside the group, it's a good bet that person's not participating. I also tried to watch the way you took turns participating. Look at this. [William's group is shown on the tape.] William was a very organized

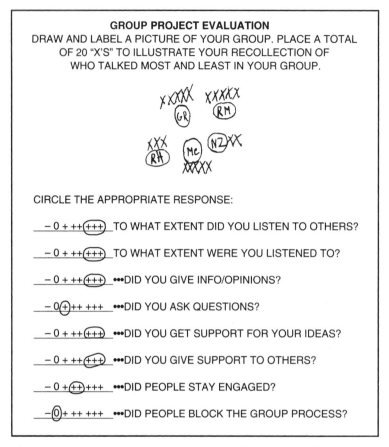

Figure 9.3 **One Student's Evaluation of the Groupwork Activity**

chairperson. He went around to each person, asking "What do you think? What do you think?" It was very orderly, and everyone got a chance to speak. But what's a drawback? A drawback is you might be disengaged when you're not talking. [Camera shows Frank's group.] Now Frank here ran a more free-wheeling group. There was more arguing back and forth. What's a drawback here? [Student responds.] Yeah, someone can easily get left out. Now take a look at Jan's group. Jan really made an effort to draw people in. . . . I also tried to look at whether any people were dominating the discussion. It really ticks people off if you dominate the group. I'll say that again. *It ticks people off.* Now what did you people think about the composition of the groups? [Students comment.] I tried to put one person in each chair's group who I thought the chair could relate to. Instead of separating all the friends, I thought it might make it easier to chair. Did it? What do you think about having friends in the group?

A far simpler approach to evaluation is to ask students to name three things their group did well and one thing the group could do better next time (Johnson

Group rating for younger or less mature students:

1. Did we get to work promptly?
2. Did we stick to the point?
3. Did we work quietly?
4, Did we all contribute?
5. Did we ask for help as soon as we needed it?

What did we accomplish?

Self-rating for younger or less mature students:

1. Was I prepared?
2. Did I follow directions?
3. Did I make good use of my time?
4. Did I work without disturbing other groups?
5. Did I listen to the other people in my group?
6. Did I contribute to my group's task?

My chief contribution to my group was:

Self-rating for older or more mature students:

1. Did I assume the responsibility the group wished?
2. Did I listen alertly?
3. Did I willingly express my own point of view?
4. Did I try to understand the viewpoint of others?
5. Did I attempt to assess the strengths and weaknesses of all opinions expressed?
6. Did I encourage those who seemed reluctant to speak?
7. Did I help maintain a friendly, businesslike atmosphere?
8. Did I keep the discussion moving purposefully?

My greatest contribution to the group was:

Figure 9.4   Checklists for Evaluating Group Skills

Source: Adapted from Stover, L. T., Neubert, G. A., and Lawlor, J. C. (1993). *Creating interactive environments in the secondary school.* New York: National Education Association.

& Johnson, 1989/90). You can also have students consider more specific questions, such as

> Did everyone carry out his or her job?
> Did everyone get a chance to talk?
> Did you listen to one another?
> What did you do if you didn't agree?

Simple checklists, like the ones in Figure 9.4, can be helpful.

After individual groups have talked about their experiences, you might want to have them report to the whole class. You can encourage groups to share and compare their experiences by asking, "Did your group have a similar problem?" "What do you think about the way they solved their problem?" "What do you recommend?"

Instead of using a form or checklist, Christina sometimes has students write letters to members of their group, noting the group's strengths and weaknesses, each member's contributions, and what areas need improvement. Afterwards, students pass the letters around their group, read what everyone has written, and briefly discuss the sentiments that were expressed. They then respond in writing to Christina.

Sometimes this process can be very encouraging for individuals. One very bright senior, for example, was gratified to learn that her less-proficient peers appreciated her patience, encouragement, and explanations. On the other hand, the process can sometimes lead to rancor. During one observation, I saw Christina meet with four students to discuss how they felt about having Nathan—who was now working by himself—rejoin their group. I was curious about what had happened, and after class, Christina explained:

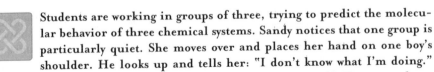

About a week ago, I had the students write letters to their group. Nathan's was really offensive; it was racist, sexist, and vulgar. The other kids were really upset, for good reason. He said it was all a joke, of course, but he got ISS [in-school suspension] for one day. I also removed him from the group for one week, and I told him we would then discuss whether or not he would go back. I know he's afraid to go back to the group. He knows they're mad. He asked me to check out how they feel about having him come back. They wanted to write their responses to me. Two said they don't want him, and two said they don't care. He's really bright and knows the material, but he's always telling everyone how great he is, and distracting everyone, and the kids get annoyed with him. And of course the letter was the last straw. But he's not learning any social skills sitting there by himself. I think I'm going to put him back in the group for a trial period and see what happens.

Obviously, this process can be very sensitive and cause a lot of hard feelings. Things like this don't usually happen, though, because students know that I'm going to collect the letters and that I expect them to give constructive criticism.

Monitor Learning, Involvement, and Cooperative Behavior

During cooperative learning activities, Donnie, Sandy, Christina, and Fred constantly circulate throughout the room, listening, assisting, encouraging, prodding, questioning, and in general, trying to ensure that students are involved, productive, and working collaboratively. For example, during the cooperative learning activity on equilibrium described earlier, Sandy was especially vigilant because she knew that the task was difficult and that students might become frustrated:

Students are working in groups of three, trying to predict the molecular behavior of three chemical systems. Sandy notices that one group is particularly quiet. She moves over and places her hand on one boy's shoulder. He looks up and tells her: "I don't know what I'm doing." Sandy responds: "Why don't you talk to your group members?" He moves closer to the other individuals. As Sandy approaches another group, a girl indicates that she's "got it." Excitedly, she tries to explain the process to her group and to Sandy, but then collapses in confusion. "I'm just babbling," she says. Sandy decides it's time to intervene: "Okay, let's go back to the question. You have to understand what the question is asking first. What's the question?" In another group, a boy doesn't like the idea offered by a teammate: "I don't want to argue, but I don't think that's right." Sandy reaffirms his behavior: "That's okay. You're *supposed* to question one another." At one point, Sandy divides one group and sends its members to temporarily join two adjacent groups. "Mrs. K. says I should ask you my question," one boy says to his new group. While Sandy is working with a group on one side of the room, two groups on the other side begin to fool around. One boy has a bottle of correction fluid that he is tossing into the air with one hand and trying to catch with the other (which is behind his back). Sandy notices the disruption: "Excuse me, I don't think you're done, are you?" One group finally discovers the principle that is involved and erupts in a cheer. A girl in another group expresses frustration: "We're clueless over here and they're cheering over there." A few minutes later, Sandy joins this group to provide some assistance.

After class, during her free period, Sandy reflected on the importance of monitoring cooperative learning activities:

Since this was a difficult activity, I expected that there would be some frustration, so it was really important to keep close tabs on what the groups were doing. You can tell a lot just by watching students' physical positions. If kids' heads are down, or if they're facing away, those are good signs that they're not participating or interacting with other group members. Today, I could tell that Richard was going to try the problem as an individual; he was off by himself—until he got frustrated and joined the other students. But that group never really worked well. I thought that Sylvia would help the group along, but she never got completely involved.

I also try to listen closely to what they're saying to one another in terms of group process. Like Mark—he wasn't sure it was OK to disagree. I was glad I heard that so I could reassure him that he's supposed to do that. What's neat is to see how some kids begin to function as really good group leaders. For example, Sivan is really quiet, but she really listens, and she was able to bring in the other two boys she was working with.

You also have to monitor students' progress in solving the problem and try to prevent them from getting completely off track. Today I could see that one group got stuck; the kids were really in a rut, saying the same words over and over. So I split the group up and sent the kids to explain what they were thinking or to ask their questions to two other groups. Sometimes having them talk to other kids can help to move them forward. In this case, it seemed to work. By interacting with a different group, Roy got out of the rut and then he was able to go back and help the kids in his own group.

Research confirms that teacher monitoring helps to promote a high level of student involvement in group activities (Emmer & Gerwels, 2002). By monitoring, you are able to discern when an intervention into the group's activities is necessary.

Chiu (2004) studied the way that two ninth-grade algebra teachers monitored small group problem-solving activities and the impact of their interventions. He found that teachers typically intervened when students were more off-task than usual or had made little overall progress. In general, teacher interventions were beneficial to the group: Students were more likely to be on-task after an intervention from the teacher than before and were more likely to recognize their errors, develop new ideas, and explain ideas to one another. Unfortunately, such positive effects only persisted for about five minutes; eventually, students' attention wandered to other topics, such as events in their personal lives. Results like these underscore the importance of continuing to monitor students' progress.

Another way of monitoring what groups are actually achieving is to build in "progress checkpoints." For example, after two days of having his students try to rewrite the district's "Human Dignity and Affirmative Action" policies, Fred stopped the groups' activity and asked students to report on what they had accomplished and what problems they were having. Similarly, you can divide large assignments into components that are due every few days (see the section on monitoring student progress in Chapter 6). This allows you to keep track of how well groups are functioning.

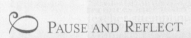

PAUSE AND REFLECT

Now that you've read about managing groupwork, go back to your original suggestions for Ralph. What additional ideas might you offer him? What are some key changes he could make to ensure that his next attempt at cooperative learning will be more successful?

TWO SPECIFIC APPROACHES TO COOPERATIVE LEARNING

Several structured approaches to cooperative learning have been developed to avoid the problems characteristic of groupwork and to encourage norms of effort and mutual support. Designed for use at any grade level and in most school subjects, all of these cooperative learning strategies are characterized by heterogeneous groups working together to achieve a common goal (Slavin, 1985). This section of the chapter briefly examines two of these strategies: Jigsaw and the structural approach to cooperative learning.

Jigsaw

In Jigsaw, one of the earliest cooperative learning methods (Aronson, Blaney, Stephan, Sikes, & Snapp, 1978), heterogeneous teams work on academic material that has been divided into sections. Jigsaw is particularly appropriate for narrative material, such as a social studies chapter, a biography, or a short story. Each team member reads only one section of the material. The teams then disband, and students reassemble in "expert groups" with other people who have been assigned the same section. Working together, they learn the material in these expert groups and then return to their home teams to teach it to their teammates. Since everyone is responsible for learning all the material, successful task completion requires students to listen carefully to their peers. Jigsaw also includes team-building activities and training to improve communication and tutoring skills.

Consider the following example (Hintz, 1995):

> Time constraints in literature classes often negate assigning more than one work
> by a writer. As a result, students are assigned a "typical" work and are expected to
> understand the writer based on only an isolated piece. A jigsawed reading activity
> may be constructed instead. [For example,] several short stories by O. Henry can
> be used. Each member of the small groups is assigned a different short story ("The
> Gift of the Magi" "The Cop and the Anthem," and "After Twenty Years") and is asked
> to consider the writer's style, theme, point of view, and use of literary devices in
> his/her assigned story. After students complete their individual tasks, the small
> groups meet to share information. By combining their knowledge, the groups are
> able to develop an overall profile of O. Henry. Again, "expert" groups of the stu-
> dents who read the same short story may meet first to share ideas and be sure
> everyone has accurate information to provide the small groups. (pp. 306–307)

Jigsaw II (Slavin, 1995) is a modification developed by the researchers at
Johns Hopkins to induce a greater sense of individual accountability. It differs
from the original Jigsaw in that all students on a team read the entire assignment.
Then they are assigned a particular topic on which to become an expert. Jigsaw II
uses individual quizzes to ensure individual accountability, but a team score
(based on individual students' improvement over previous work) also provides a
group goal. Certificates and/or other rewards are given in recognition of successful teams.

The Structural Approach to Cooperative Learning

"Structures" are content-free ways of organizing social interaction among students.
A traditional classroom structure, for example, is the "whole-class question–
answer" situation. In this structure, the teacher asks a question, students raise their
hands to respond, and the teacher calls on one person. If that person answers the
question incorrectly, the other students get a chance to respond and to win the
teacher's praise. Thus, students are often happy if a classmate makes a mistake, and
they may even root for one another's failure.

Spencer Kagan (1989/90) has developed a number of simple cooperative
structures that can be used at a variety of grade levels and in many content areas.
He emphasizes the need for teachers to select the structures that are most appropriate for their specific objectives. Some structures are useful for team building or
for developing communication skills, while others are most suitable for increasing
mastery of factual material or for concept development.

"Numbered Heads Together" is a good example of a structure that is appropriate for checking on students' understanding of content. (It also provides a cooperative alternative to "whole-class question–answer.") In Numbered Heads, students
"number off" within teams (e.g., one through four). When the teacher asks a question, team members "put their heads together" to make sure that everyone on the
team knows the answer. The teacher then calls a number, and students with that
number may raise their hands to answer. This structure promotes interdependence
among team members: If one student knows the answer, everyone's chance of answering correctly increases. At the same time, the structure encourages individual

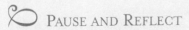

PAUSE AND REFLECT

Teachers sometimes use the terms *groupwork* and *cooperative learning* interchangeably. But although cooperative learning is a form of groupwork, groupwork is not always cooperative learning. It is important to be able to explain to students, parents, and, yes, administrators the type of learning opportunities you will be using in your class. With this in mind, identify the key elements of cooperative learning that set it apart from other groupwork.

accountability: Once the teacher calls a number, students are on their own.

Another structure is "Timed Pair Share," in which students pair up to share their responses to a question posed by the teacher. First Student A talks for a minute, and then Student B has a turn. As Kagan points out, this simultaneous interaction allows all students to respond in the same amount of time that it would have taken for just two students if the teacher had used the more traditional "whole-class question–answer" structure (Walters, 2000).

Some of Kagan's other structures are listed in Table 9.3.

TABLE 9.3 Some of Spencer Kagan's Cooperative Structures

Name	Purpose	Description	Functions
Round-Robin	Team building	Each student in turn shares something with teammates.	Expressing ideas and opinions Getting acquainted
Match Mine	Communication	Students try to match the arrangement of objects on a grid of another student using oral communication only.	Vocabulary building Communication skills Role-taking ability
Three-Step Interview	Concept development	Students interview each other in pairs, first one way, then the other. Students then share information they learned with the group.	Sharing personal information such as hypotheses, reactions to a poem, conclusions from a unit Equal participation Listening
Inside-Outside Circle	Multifunctional	Students stand in pairs in two concentric circles. The inside circle faces out; the outside circle faces in. Students use flash cards or respond to teacher questions as they rotate to each new partner.	Checking for understanding Review Tutoring Sharing Meeting classmates

Source: Adapted from Kagan, S. (1989–1990). The structural approach to cooperative learning. *Educational Leadership, 47*(4), p. 14.

CONCLUDING COMMENTS

Although this chapter is entitled "Managing Groupwork," we have seen that there are actually a number of different groupwork situations, each with its own set of uses, procedures, requirements, and pitfalls. As you plan and implement groupwork in your classroom, it's important to remember these distinctions. Too many teachers think that cooperative learning is putting students into groups and telling them to work together. They select tasks that are inappropriate for the size of the group; they use heterogeneous groups when homogeneous groups would be more suitable (or vice versa); they fail to build in positive interdependence and individual accountability; they fail to appreciate the differences between helping groups and cooperative learning. The following example, taken from O'Donnell and O'Kelly (1994), would be funny—if it weren't true:

> One of our colleagues recently described an example of "cooperative learning" in his son's school. The classroom teacher informed the students that [they] would be using cooperative learning. His son was paired with another student. The two students were required to complete two separate parts of a project but were expected to complete the work outside of class. A grade was assigned to each part of the project and a group grade was given. In this instance, one child received an F as he failed to complete the required part of the project. The other child received an A. The group grade was a C, thus rewarding the student who had failed to complete the work, and punishing the child who had completed his work. In this use of "cooperative learning," there was no opportunity for the students to interact, and the attempt to use a group reward (the group grade) backfired. Although this scenario is not recognizable as cooperative learning to most proponents of cooperation, the classroom teacher described it as such to the students' parents. (p. 322)

This example illustrates the need for teachers to acquire an understanding of the intricacies of groupwork in general and cooperative learning in particular. Hopefully, this chapter has sensitized you to some of the problems that can arise with groupwork and has provided you with some strategies for minimizing these problems. Despite the potential pitfalls, groupwork should be an integral part of middle and high school classrooms. As Sandy puts it:

Having students do cooperative group activities takes a lot longer than just getting up there and telling them the material. But I really believe that this is the best way. When they've worked through the material in a group, they really understand.

Sandy's reflections focus on the academic benefits of groupwork. But as I mentioned at the beginning of the chapter, groupwork has social payoffs as well. It's important to remember that the classroom is not simply a place where students learn academic lessons. It's also a place where students learn *social lessons*—lessons about the value of helping one another, about relationships with students from other racial and ethnic groups, about accepting individuals with disabilities, and about friendship. As a teacher, you will determine the content of these lessons. If planned and implemented well, groupwork can provide students with opportunities to learn lessons of caring, fairness, and self-worth.

SUMMARY

This chapter began by talking about the potential benefits of groupwork and about some of the special challenges it presents. It then suggested strategies for designing successful groupwork. Finally, the chapter described some structured programs of cooperative learning.

Benefits of Groupwork

- Less idle time while waiting for the teacher to help.
- Enhanced motivation.
- Greater achievement.
- More involvement in learning.
- Decreased competition among students.
- Increased interaction across gender, ethnic, and racial lines.
- Improved relationships between disabled students and their nondisabled peers.

Some Common Pitfalls

- Segregation in terms of gender, ethnicity, and race.
- Unequal participation.
- Lack of accomplishment.
- Lack of cooperation among group members.

Challenges of Groupwork

- Maintaining order.
- Achieving accountability for all students.
- Teaching new (cooperative) behavioral norms.
- Creating effective groups.

Designing Successful Groupwork

- Decide on the type of group to use (helping permitted, helping obligatory, peer tutoring, cooperative, completely cooperative).
- Decide on the size of the group.
- Decide on group composition.
- Structure the task for interdependence (e.g., create a group goal or reward).
- Ensure individual accountability.
- Teach students to cooperate.
- Monitor learning, involvement, and cooperative behavior.

Structured Programs of Cooperative Learning

- Jigsaw I and II.
- The structural approach to cooperative learning.

Groupwork offers unique social and academic rewards, but it is important to understand the challenges it presents and not to assume that, just because a task is fun or interesting, the lesson will run smoothly. Remember to plan groupwork carefully, prepare your students thoroughly, and allow yourself time to develop experience as a facilitator of cooperative groups.

ACTIVITIES FOR SKILL BUILDING AND REFLECTION

In Class

1. In small groups that are homogeneous in terms of content area (e.g., math, science, social studies, etc.), choose a topic that you will be teaching and work together to create a completely cooperative activity. As you design the activity, keep in mind the following questions:

   How will you assign students to groups?

   How will you structure the activity to foster positive interdependence?

   What roles will you assign, if any?

   What forms of individual accountability will you build in?

   What are the social skills you need to teach, and how will you teach them?

   How will you monitor the groupwork?

   How will you provide an opportunity for students to evaluate the group process?

2. Consider the following situation: You regularly use small groups that are heterogeneous in terms of achievement because you believe that students can learn from one another. You also believe that learning to work cooperatively and to appreciate differences is an important and valid goal in and of itself. However, the parents of one of your high-achieving students contact you to complain that their son is not being appropriately challenged and is "wasting his time tutoring the slower kids." In a group, discuss what you might say in response.

3. In a group, read the following excerpt from a teacher-authored case on cooperative learning (Shulman, Lotan, & Whitcomb, 1998).

   Period 3 is one of the six eighth-grade social studies classes I teach each day.... [As an experienced proponent of cooperative groups,] I entered into group instruction this year with a good deal of confidence. I met my match with period 3....This is one class in the district that merits a full time Resource Specialist Program teaching aide because we have nine—yes, nine—special education students. We also have 10 sheltered students who have recently left bilingual classes and are now making the transition to full-time English instruction. The makeup of this class creates a disturbing chemistry that is felt within 30 seconds of the starting bell. I usually place them in groups of four or five, then invariably watch in frozen amazement as they torment each other. I persist as I was trained to do, but find myself wondering whether groupwork is appropriate for this uncooperative class of 28 students, skewed with a disproportionate number of emotionally needy individuals ...

   To sum it up, after 42 minutes with period 3, I feel like a giant, emotion-filled ball being slammed from one side of the room to the other....Whether it's beause they lack experience in small group interaction or they lack self-esteem, or some combination of the two, creating a cooperative atmosphere is not something the students of period 3 seem to be able to accomplish.

   At the end of the day I find myself wondering why I don't switch to the more traditional teacher-controlled setting with which these students are more *familiar. Perhaps groupwork is not meant for every class.* "It's okay to give up," *I tell myself. Yet deep down I tell myself,* "It's not okay. I know I need to do something. (pp. 21-23)*

In your group, discuss what that "something" might be.

On Your Own

1. Observe a cooperative learning activity. In what ways has the teacher tried to promote positive interdependence and individual accountability?

2. Consider when you might use each of the following types of groupwork. List an example of an activity from your own content area.

    a. Helping permitted
    b. Helping obligatory
    c. Peer tutoring
    d. Cooperative group
    e. Completely cooperative group

For Your Portfolio

Design a cooperative learning lesson on a topic of your choice. Write a brief commentary describing (a) the social skills that are required in this lesson and how you will teach them; (b) the way(s) in which you built in positive interdependence and individual accountability; and (c) how students will evaluate their group interaction.

FOR FURTHER READING

Lotan, R. (2006). Managing groupwork in the heterogeneous classroom. In C. M. Evertson & C. S. Weinstein (Eds.), *Handbook of classroom management: Research, practice, and contemporary issues.* Mahwah, NJ: Lawrence Erlbaum Associates, Inc.

> This chapter posits that groupwork is not only a useful pedagogical strategy for academically and linguistically heterogeneous classrooms, but that it also has the potential to help teachers build equitable classrooms. Lotan addresses the need to teach social skills, assign specific roles, delegate authority to students, and design interventions to combat unequal participation.

Rubin, B. C. (2003). Unpacking detracking: When progressive pedagogy meets students' social worlds. *American Educational Research Journal, 40*(2), 539-573.

> This article is based on a year-long study of two detracked ninth-grade classes, one in English and one in social studies, in a diverse urban high school. Rubin describes how the teachers used groupwork to facilitate both learning and social interaction across race and class lines and shows how the small groups "often proved to be sites of tension and discomfort where fractures of race and class came to the fore" (p. 541).

Schniedewind, N., & Davidson, E. (2000). Differentiating cooperative learning. *Educational Leadership, 58*(1), 24-27.

> This article provides "guiding tenets" and examples of how to differentiate assignments and responsibilities within heterogeneous cooperative groups.

Slavin, R. E. (1995). *Cooperative learning: Theory, research, and practice.* 2nd ed. Boston: Allyn & Bacon.

This book provides an excellent introduction to cooperative learning methods, describes various approaches (e.g., Student Team Learning methods, Learning Together, Jigsaw, etc.), and summarizes the research on the effects of cooperative learning on achievement and social–emotional outcomes.

ORGANIZATIONAL RESOURCES

Cooperative Learning Center at the University of Minnesota (www.co-operation.org) Co-directed by Roger T. Johnson and David W. Johnson, the CLC is a research and training center focusing on how students should interact with each other as they learn and the skills needed to interact effectively.

The International Association for the Study of Cooperation in Education (IASCE). Established in 1979, IASCE is the only international, nonprofit organization for educators interested in cooperative learning to promote academic achievement and democratic, social processes. The Web site provides an annotated list of Web pages related to cooperative learning (www.iasce.net).

REFERENCES

Antil, L. R., Jenkins, J. R., Wayne, S. K, & Vadasy, P. F. (1998). Cooperative learning: Prevalence, conceptualizations, and the relation between research and practice. *American Educational Research Journal, 35*(3), 419-454.

Aronson, E., Blaney, N., Stephan, C., Sikes, J., & Snapp, M. (1978). *The Jigsaw classroom.* Beverly Hills, CA: Sage.

Carson, L., & Hoyle, S. (1989/90). Teaching social skills: A view from the classroom. *Educational Leadership, 47*(4), p. 31.

Carter, K. (March–April, 1985). Teacher comprehension of classroom processes: An emerging direction in classroom management research. Paper presented at the annual meeting of the American Educational Research Association, Chicago, IL.

Chiu, M. M. (2004). Adapting teacher interventions to student needs during cooperative learning: How to improve student problem solving and time on-task. *American Educational Research Journal, 41*(2), 365-399.

Cohen, E. G. (1972). Interracial interaction disability. *Human Relations, 25,* 9-24.

Cohen, E. G. (1994a). *Designing groupwork: Strategies for the heterogeneous classroom.* 2nd ed. New York: Teacher College Press.

Cohen, E. G. (1994b). Restructuring the classroom: Conditions for productive small groups. *Review of Educational Research, 64*(1), 1-35.

Cohen, E. G. (1998). Making cooperative learning equitable. *Educational Leadership, 56*(1), 18-21.

Edwards, C., & Stout, J. (1989/90). Cooperative learning: The first year. *Educational Leadership, 47*(4), 38-41.

Emmer, E. T., & Gerwels, M. C. (2002). Cooperative learning in elementary classrooms: Teaching practices and lesson characteristics. *The Elementary School Journal, 103*(1), 75–91.

Hintz, J. L. (1995). Putting the pieces together–together. In J. E. Pedersen & A. D. Digby (Eds.), *Secondary schools and cooperative learning: Theories, models, and strategies.* New York: Garland.

Johnson, D. W., & Johnson, R. T. (1980). Integrating handicapped students into the mainstream. *Exceptional Children, 47*(2), 90–98.

Johnson, D. W., & Johnson, R. T. (1989/90). Social skills for successful groupwork. *Educational Leadership, 47*(4), 29–33.

Johnson, D. W., Johnson, R. T., Holubec, E. J., & Roy, P. (1984). *Circles of learning: Cooperation in the classroom.* Alexandria, VA: Association for Supervision and Curriculum Development.

Kagan, S. (1989/90). The structural approach to cooperative learning. *Educational Leadership, 47*(4), 12–15.

King, L., Luberda, H., Barry, K., & Zehnder, S. (1998). A case study of the perceptions of students in a small-group cooperative learning situation. Paper presented at the Annual Conference of the American Education Research Association. San Diego, CA.

Lotan, R. (2006). Managing groupwork in the heterogeneous classroom. In C. M. Evertson & C. S. Weinstein (Eds.), *Handbook of classroom management: Research, practice, and contemporary issues.* Mahwah, NJ: Lawrence Erlbaum Associates, Inc.

Madden, N. A., & Slavin, R. E. (1983). Cooperative learning and social acceptance of mainstreamed academically handicapped students. *Journal of Special Education, 17,* 171–182.

Mulryan, C. M. (1992). Student passivity during cooperative small groups in mathematics. *Journal of Educational Research, 85*(5), 261–273.

O'Donnell, A., & O'Kelly, J. (1994). Learning from peers: Beyond the rhetoric of positive results. *Educational Psychology Review, 6*(4), 321–349.

Rosenholtz, S. J., & Cohen, E. G. (1985). Status in the eye of the beholder. In J. Berger & M. Zelditch, Jr. (Eds.), *Status, rewards, and influence.* San Francisco: Jossey Bass.

Ross, J. A. (1995). Effects of feedback on student behavior in cooperative learning groups in a grade 7 math class. *The Elementary School Journal, 96*(2), 125–143.

Rubin, B. C. (2003). Unpacking detracking: When progressive pedagogy meets students' social worlds. *American Educational Research Journal, 40*(2), 539–573.

Schniedewind, N., & Davidson, E. (2000). Differentiating cooperative learning. *Educational Leadership, 58*(1), 24–27.

Shulman, J. H., Lotan, R. A., & Whitcomb, J. A. (Eds.). (1998). *Groupwork in diverse classrooms: A casebook for educators.* New York: Teachers College Press.

Slavin, R. (1985). An introduction to cooperative learning research. In R. Slavin, S. Sharan, S. Kagan, R. Hertz-Lazarowitz, C. Webb, & R. Schmuck (Eds.), *Learning to cooperate, cooperating to learn.* New York: Plenum Press, pp. 5–15.

Slavin, R. (1991). *Student team learning: A practical guide to cooperative learning.* 3rd ed. Washington, D.C.: National Education Association.

Slavin, R. E. (1995). *Cooperative learning: Theory, research, and practice.* 2nd ed. Boston: Allyn & Bacon.

Stodolsky, S. S. (1984). Frameworks for studying instructional processes in peer work groups. In P. L. Peterson, L. C. Wilkinson, & M. Hallinan (Eds.), *The social context of instruction.* New York: Academic Press, pp. 107–124.

Walters, L. S. (2000). Putting cooperative learning to the test. *Harvard Education Letter, 16*(3), 1-6.

Webb, N. M. (1984). Sex differences in interaction and achievement in cooperative small groups. *Journal of Educational Psychology, 76,* 33-44.

Webb, N. M. (1985). Student interaction and learning in small groups: A research summary. In R. Slavin, S. Sharan, S. Kagan, R. Hertz-Lazarowitz, C. Webb, & R. Schmuck (Eds.), *Learning to cooperate, cooperating to learn.* New York: Plenum Press, pp. 147-172.

Webb, N. M., & Farivar, S. (1994). Promoting helping behavior in cooperative small groups in middle school mathematics. *American Educational Research Journal, 31*(2), 369-395.

Wilkinson, L. C., & Calculator, S. (1982). Effective speakers: Students' use of language to request and obtain information and action in the classroom. In L. C. Wilkinson (Ed.), *Communicating in the classroom.* New York: Academic Press, pp. 85-100.

MANAGING RECITATIONS AND DISCUSSIONS

Much of the talk that occurs between teachers and students is unlike the talk you hear in the "real world." Let's consider just one example (Cazden, 1988). In the real world, if you ask someone for the time, we can assume that you really need to know what time it is and will be grateful for a reply. The conversation would probably go like this:

> *"What time is it?"*
> *"2:30."*
> *"Thank you."*

In contrast, if a teacher asks for the time during a lesson, the dialogue generally sounds like this:

> *"What time is it?"*
> *"2:30."*
> *"Very good."*

Here, the question is not a request for needed information, but a way of finding out what students know. The interaction is more like a quiz show (Roby, 1988) than a true conversation: The teacher asks a question, a student replies, and the teacher evaluates the response (Mehan, 1979). This pattern of interaction (initiation-response-evaluation or I-R-E) is called *recitation,* and several studies (e.g., Stodolsky, 1988) have documented the substantial amount of time that students spend in this subsetting of the classroom.

The recitation has been frequently denounced as a method of instruction. Critics object to the active, dominant role of the teacher and the relatively passive role of the student. They decry the lack of interaction among students. They condemn the fact that recitations often emphasize the recall of factual information and demand little higher-level thinking. (See Figure 10.1 for an example of this kind of recitation.)

An additional criticism focuses on the public evaluation that occurs during recitation. When the teacher calls on a student, everyone can witness and pass

---

Mr. Lowe is conducting a "discussion" about Macbeth in his 12th-grade English class. Students have just finished reading the first act.

MR. LOWE: OK, let's talk about the first act of this play. In the very first scene—which is very brief—three witches are on stage. What's the weather like, Sharon?

SHARON: It's thundering and lightning.

Mr. Lowe: Right. What are the witches talking about, Larry?

LARRY: How they're going to meet Macbeth.

MR. LOWE: Good. When are they going to meet him? Jonathan?

JONATHAN: When the battle's done.

Mr. Lowe: Right. Okay, let's jump to the third scene. The battle's done, and the three witches tell us that "Macbeth doth come." So we meet Macbeth and Banquo, two generals in the King's army. They've just returned from the battle. Who were they fighting? Missy?

MISSY: Cawdor.

MR. LOWE: Very good. Now we know that Cawdor was a traitorous rebel, right? Who was he rebelling against, Tanya?

TANYA: King Duncan.

Mr. Lowe: Good. What country is Duncan king of? Melissa?

MELISSA: Scotland.

MR. LOWE: Yes. Now, when the witches first speak to Macbeth, what do they call him? Eric?

ERIC: Thane of Glamis.

MR. LOWE: Right. That's his own title, so that makes sense. But then what do they call him?

SUSAN: Thane of Cawdor.

MR. LOWE: Right! So we know that Macbeth is going to be named the new thane of Cawdor. What happens to the old thane of Cawdor? Paul?

PAUL: He's killed.

MR. LOWE: Yes, he's put to death.

Figure 10.1   An Example of a Poor Recitation: Macbeth as Quiz Show

judgment on the response. In fact, as Phil Jackson (1968) comments, classmates are sometimes encouraged to "join in the act":

> Sometimes the class as a whole is invited to participate in the evaluation of a student's work, as when the teacher asks, "Who can correct Billy?" or "How many believe that Shirley read that poem with a lot of expression?" (p. 20)

Questions like these exacerbate the "negative interdependence" among students that recitations can generate (Kagan, 1989/90). In other words, if a student is unable to respond to the teacher's question, the other students have a greater chance to be called on and to receive praise; thus, students may actually root for their classmates' failure.

Despite the validity of these criticisms, recitations remain an extremely common feature of middle and high school classrooms. What is there about this instructional strategy that makes it so enduring in the face of other, more highly touted methods (Hoetker & Ahlbrand, 1969)?

I thought hard about this question during one visit to Fred's classroom, and my observation of a recitation session that he conducted provided some clues. Students had just read about the controversy over granting China permanent "most-favored-nation" status, and Fred told them he wanted to hear what they thought about the basic issues described in the reading:

FRED: OK, Ms. Harnett, would you start, please?

HARNETT: I was really confused about this article. . . . I think it was talking about how in China there are a lot of political prisoners . . . and we don't like that . . . so we're trying to get them to change. . . . Oh, I don't know, it was confusing.

FRED: You really understand more than you thought. Let's hear from someone else. Jenny.

JENNY: Well, like the United States doesn't like it that China has all these political prisoners . . . but China says leave us alone, our people are doing OK.

FRED: OK, so China's saying that you have to look at the whole picture. You have to look at it from their perspective. [He calls on a student whose hand is raised.] Philip.

PHILIP: The Chinese are saying we keep talking about the dissidents, but they want to look at everyone. And like there's different ideas about human rights.

FRED: Hmmm. Let's talk about that. Let's talk about what we value as basic human rights in the United States. What are some of our basic human rights?

STUDENT: Equality.

FRED: What does that mean, equality? Come over here, Sally. [She comes up and stands next to him.] Are you my equal? Is she my equal?

STUDENT: Well, she's not as big as you are [laughter], and she's probably not as strong, but she's equal in terms of rights.

FRED: Hmmm. So we're not equal in terms of size or strength. Are we equal economically? [Murmurs of "No . . ."] Probably not. Are we equal in terms of power? You bet we're not. [More laughter.] But we have legal equality; we've got equal rights under the law. What are some of those rights?

Fred leads a whole-class discussion.

STUDENT: Freedom.

FRED: To do what?

STUDENT: To speak . . . freedom of speech.

FRED: OK. What else?

STUDENT: Freedom of religion.

STUDENT: Freedom to vote.

FRED: OK. In the United States, human rights means individual rights. We emphasize personal freedoms—the right of individuals to follow their own religion, to vote for who they want. But in China, the group is the focus of human rights.

Fred's question-and-answer session helped me to identify five very useful functions of classroom recitations. First, the recitation allowed Fred to assess students' comprehension of the reading and to check their background knowledge on the issue of human rights and most-favored-nation status. Second, by asking intellectually demanding questions (e.g., "What do we mean by equality in the United States?"), Fred was able to prod his students to do some critical thinking and to guide them to some fundamental understandings (Good & Brophy, 2000). Third, the recitation permitted Fred to involve students in the presentation of material—what Roby (1988) calls "lecturing in the interrogatory mood." Instead of telling students directly about most-favored-nation status and the debate over human rights, Fred brought out the information by asking questions. Fourth, the recitation provided the chance to interact individually with students, even in the midst of a whole-group lesson. In fact, my notes indicate that Fred made contact with eight different students in just the brief interaction reported here. Finally, through his questions, changes in voice tone, and gestures, Fred was able to maintain a relatively high attention level; in other words, he was able to keep most of his students "with him."

Later, Fred reflected aloud on some other useful functions of recitations:

I'll use recitation a lot at the beginning of the year because it's a good way to get to know kids' names and to see how they handle themselves in class. It's also a tool for building self-confidence in a new class. They have a chance to speak in class, and I can provide them with opportunities for success early in the year. It's generally a pretty nonthreatening activity; since it doesn't ask for as much higher-level thinking as discussions, it's easier. I also try to emphasize that it's *okay not to know,* that we can figure out this stuff together. That's what education *is.*

As we can see, Fred's recitation session was hardly a "quiz show" in which passive students mindlessly recalled low-level, insignificant facts. On the other hand, both the pattern of interaction (I-R-E) and the primary intent (to assess students' understanding of the reading) set it apart from another type of questioning session: the *discussion.* (Table 10.1, adapted from Dillon, 1994, summarizes the differences between recitation and discussion.)

TABLE 10.1 Differences between Recitations and Discussions

Dimension	Recitation	Discussion
1. Predominant speaker	Teacher (2/3 or more)	Students (half or more)
2. Typical exchange	Teacher question; student answer; teacher evaluation (I-R-E)	Mix of statements and questions by mix of teachers and students
3. Pace	Many brief, fast exchanges	Fewer, longer, slower exchanges
4. Primary purpose	To check students' comprehension	To stimulate variety of responses; encourage students to consider different points of view; foster problem solving and critical thinking; examine implications
5. The answer	Predetermined right or wrong; same right answer for all students	No predetermined right or wrong; can have different answers for different students
6. Evaluation	Right/wrong, by teacher only	Agree/disagree, by student and teacher

In order to make the distinction clear, let's consider another example from Fred's class. Here, students had been asked to read brief descriptions of hypothetical voters and determine if they were likely to be Democratic or Republican. (See Chapter 9 for a fuller description of this activity.) In this excerpt from the class, Fred was soliciting students' thoughts about the case of a retired school teacher living in New Jersey and dependent upon Social Security:

FRED: What are the indicators that the retired school teacher is left of center? Jeremy, what do you think?

JEREMY: She's from New Jersey.

FRED: Why would that affect her political views?

JEREMY: Well, New Jersey generally votes Democratic.

STUDENT: [Jumping in.] Wait a minute—what about Christie Whitman? She was a Republican governor.

JEREMY: Yeah, but there's a lot of diversity in NJ, and like, I don't know, but I think people tend to be more liberal.

FRED: Anything else here to indicate she might be liberal?

STUDENT: She's a teacher, so she's well educated.

FRED: Hmmmm . . . why would education be a factor that makes you more liberal?

STUDENT: Well it just seems like the more you know the more you understand about other people.

FRED: What other indicators might make you think that she's liberal?

STUDENT: Since she's a teacher, she probably cares about social issues. So that probably makes her more liberal.

STUDENT: Yeah, but she's older and she's retired. I think that would make her more conservative.

FRED: Let's consider that. Would age tend to make her more conservative?

STUDENT: Yeah. That happens.

FRED: Why? Why would age make her more conservative?

STUDENT: Older people are more set in their ways.

FRED: OK, I tend to be more skeptical because I've been around more. I've been dumped on more. But of course, we've got to remember that these are generalizations. I'm going to bring in an older guy who's a far left liberal and a young guy who's real conservative, just to defy the generalizations. OK, what other indicators are there that she's conservative?

STUDENT: She's living on Social Security, so she's probably real concerned about money.

FRED: So she's concerned about money. Why would that make her conservative?

STUDENT: She might vote against social programs that would cost her.

STUDENT: Yeah, like she'd probably vote against the school budget.

STUDENT: I don't agree with that. As a retired teacher, I can't see that she'd ever vote against a school budget.

Later in the interaction, after Fred and the students had decided that the retired teacher was probably a Democrat (but conservative on issues "close to the pocketbook"), Fred stressed the fact that there could be no right answers in this exercise:

> Are we right? I don't know. All we can make are informed generalizations. If there's a right answer here, it's that there's *no right answer.* But this is not just an exercise in futility that we did. Lots of times in politics, people are given tasks where they are required to make judgments and they don't have enough data to know the right answer. But people can make better judgments—in the absence of complete data—by being more attuned to the indicators. The indicators are useful for making predictions, which is really important in politics. And if it turns out your predictions are right, you're considered a brilliant strategist; if you're wrong, you're fired.

As in the recitation presented earlier, Fred was still very much in charge of this interaction. In fact, we can characterize this as a *teacher-led discussion,* since Fred set the topic, posed the questions, and called on students to speak. Nonetheless, there are some obvious differences. In the discussion, Fred generally initiated the questions and students replied, but he often dispensed with an evaluation of their responses. Thus, the predominant pattern was not I-R-E, but I-R, even I-R-R-R. Furthermore, students occasionally initiated questions of their own, both to Fred and to each other, and sometimes they commented on or evaluated the contributions of their peers. Finally, the purpose of this interaction was not to "go over material" or to "elaborate on a text" (Good & Brophy, 2000). Rather, the teacher-led discussion was intended to stimulate a variety of responses, to encourage students to consider different points of view, to foster problem solving, to examine implications, and to relate material to students' own personal experiences (Good & Brophy, 2000).

Although educational critics frequently decry the use of recitation and promote the use of discussion, both types of interaction have a legitimate place in the secondary classroom—if done well. As Good and Brophy (2000) write: "The operative question about recitation for most teachers is not whether to use it but when and how to use it effectively" (p. 387).

This chapter begins by examining the managerial challenges associated with recitations and teacher-led discussions. Like seatwork and groupwork, these subsettings of the secondary classroom have their own set of potential pitfalls: unequal participation; loss of pace, focus, and involvement; the difficulty of monitoring comprehension; and incompatibility with many students' patterns of communication. Next, we consider what our teachers and the research have to say about minimizing these problems. The final section of the chapter takes a brief look at yet another type of questioning session—the student-centered discussion—and offers some guidelines for managing this third pattern of interaction.

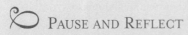

PAUSE AND REFLECT

Even if you are unfamiliar with the term *recitation,* you have most likely participated in many such question-and-answer sessions during your years in school. In contrast, your experiences with student-centered discussions may be far more limited. Reflecting on the differences between these two, consider the appropriateness of both instructional strategies for your own content area. Can you think of instances when a true classroom discussion would be appropriate?

The Pitfalls of Recitations and Teacher-Led Discussions

Unequal Participation

Imagine yourself in front of a class of 25 students. You've just asked a question. A few individuals have their hands up, conveying their desire (or at least their willingness) to be called on. Others are sitting quietly, staring into space, their expressions blank. Still others are slumped down as far as possible in their seats; their posture clearly says, "Don't call on me."

In a situation like this, it's tempting to call on an individual whose hand is raised. After all, you're likely to get the response you want—a very gratifying situation! You also avoid embarrassing students who feel uncomfortable speaking in front of the group or who don't know the answer, and you're able to keep up the pace of the lesson. But selecting only those who volunteer or those who call out may limit the interaction to a handful of students. This can be a problem. Students tend to learn more if they are actively participating. Furthermore, since those who volunteer are often high achievers, calling only on volunteers is likely to give you a distorted picture of how well everyone understands. Finally, restricting your questions to a small number of students can communicate negative attitudes and expectations to the others (Good & Brophy, 2000): "I'm not calling on you because I'm sure you have nothing to contribute." Negative attitudes like this can be communicated even if you have the best of intentions. Listen to Sandy recall a situation in which she made a practice of not calling on a student who seemed painfully shy:

 It was my second year of teaching, but I still remember it clearly. My kids did course evaluations at the end of the year, and one kid said I didn't care about students. I was devastated. I tracked her down and asked her why she thought I didn't care. She said it was because I hadn't required her to participate in class discussions. Here I had been trying to avoid causing her embarrassment. She seemed so afraid to talk, so I left her alone. And she interpreted my behavior as saying I didn't care. That taught me a good lesson!

Losing It All: Pace, Focus, and Involvement

In the early 1960s, a popular television program capitalized on the fact that *Kids Say the Darndest Things.* The title of the show aptly describes what can happen during a recitation or discussion. When you ask your question, you might receive the response you have in mind. You might also get answers that indicate confusion and misunderstanding, ill-timed remarks that have nothing to do with the lesson (e.g., "There's gum on my shoe"), or unexpected comments that momentarily throw you off balance. All of these threaten the smooth flow of a recitation or discussion and can cause it to become sluggish, jerky, or unfocused.

Threats like these require you to make instantaneous decisions about how to proceed. It's not easy. For example, if a student's answer reveals confusion, you need to determine how to provide feedback and assistance without losing the rest of the class. During recitations and discussions, you are frequently confronted with two incompatible needs: the need to stay with one person to enhance that individual's learning and the need to move on to avoid losing both the momentum and the group's attention. Donnie reflects on this common situation:

> There always seems to be one person who doesn't understand! While you're trying to help that student, the rest of the class begins to mumble things like, "Why are we still doing this? We know this stuff already." Of course, they want you to stay with them when *they* don't understand, but they get restless if you spend too long on someone else.

When "kids say the darndest things" during a recitation or discussion, you also need to determine if the comment is genuine or if it is a deliberate ploy to get you sidetracked. Fred has had firsthand experience with this particular hazard:

> I'll have kids try to get me off on a tangent by asking a question that's out of the blue. It's especially true with sharp kids. When that happens, I'll say, "What a great question. It's not what we're dealing with today, but I'd really like to discuss that with you. Is 2:30 okay or how about tomorrow?"

Sometimes, questioning sessions get sluggish because ambiguity in the teacher's question makes it difficult for students to respond. For example, Farrar (1988) analyzed a social studies lesson in which the teacher asked a yes–no question: "Did you read anywhere in the book that Washington's army was destroyed?" When students responded, "No," and "Uh-uh," he rejected their answers. The result was confusion and a momentary breakdown of the recitation. In retrospect, it appears that the teacher was not really expecting a yes or no answer, but wanted a restatement of information that had appeared in the reading. Students responded to his *explicit* question, while he was waiting for the answer to his *implicit* question: "What happened to Washington's army?"

Questioning sessions can also become bogged down if the teacher has not developed a set of verbal or nonverbal signals that communicate to students when they are to raise their hands and when they are to respond chorally. Without clear signals, students are likely to call out when the teacher wants them to raise their hands, or to remain silent and raise their hands when the teacher wants them to call out in a choral response.

Difficulties in Monitoring Students' Comprehension

Recitations and discussions provide an opportunity for teachers to check students' comprehension, but doing so is not always easy. Recently, a fifth-grade teacher talked about a lesson taught by her student teacher, Rebecca. The class had been studying the human body, and halfway through the unit, Rebecca planned to give her students a quiz. On the day of the quiz, she conducted a brief review of the material by firing off a series of questions on the respiratory and circulatory systems. Satisfied with the high percentage of correct answers, Rebecca then asked "Before

I give out the quiz, are there any questions?" When there were none, she added, "So everybody understands?" Again, there was silence. Rebecca told the students to close their books and distributed the quiz papers. That afternoon, she corrected the quiz. The results were an unpleasant shock—a large number of students received Ds and Fs. During a post-lesson conference with her cooperating teacher, she wailed, "How could this happen? They certainly knew the answers during our review session!"

This incident underscores the difficulty of gauging the extent to which all members of a class really understand what is going on. As we mentioned earlier, teachers sometimes get fooled because they call only on volunteers—the students most likely to give the correct answers. In this case, Rebecca's cooperating teacher had kept a "map" of the verbal interaction between teacher and students and was able to share some revealing data: During a 15-minute review, Rebecca had called on only 6 of the 19 children in the class, and all of these had been volunteers. Although this allowed Rebecca to maintain the smooth flow of the interaction, it led her to overestimate the extent of students' mastery. Moreover, as Rebecca's cooperating teacher pointed out to her, questions that try to assess comprehension by asking "Does everyone understand?" are unlikely to be successful. There's no accountability built into questions like this; in other words, they don't require students to demonstrate an understanding of the material. In addition, students who do not understand are often too embarrassed to admit it. (They may not even realize they don't understand!) Clearly, you need to find other ways to assess if your class is "with" you.

Incompatibility with the Communication Patterns That Students Bring to School

Although the I-R-E format of recitations is a staple of schools, it stems from White, middle-class values and represents a way of communicating that is not well matched with the discourse styles of many students from different cultural backgrounds (Arends, 2004). For example, recitation generally follows a "passive-receptive" discourse pattern: Students are expected to listen quietly during teacher presentations and then respond individually to teacher-initiated questions. African American students, however, may be accustomed to a more active, participatory discourse pattern ("call-response"). When they demonstrate their engagement by calling out prompts, comments, and reactions, European American teachers may interpret the behavior as rude and disruptive (Gay, 2000).

Another illustration comes from Susan Philips (1972), who wondered why children on the Warm Springs Indian Reservation in Oregon were so reluctant to participate in classroom recitations. Her analysis of life in this Native American community disclosed a set of behavioral norms that conflict with the way recitations are conducted. As I have noted, recitations permit little student–student interaction, but Warm Springs children are extremely peer oriented. During recitations, the teacher decides who will participate, while Warm Springs traditions allow individuals to decide for themselves if and when to participate in public events. Recitations involve public performance and public evaluation—even if a student has not yet mastered the material—but Warm Springs children are used to testing their skills in private before they choose to demonstrate them in public. Understanding these disparities helps us to see why the children would find recitations unfamiliar and uncomfortable.

More recently, Lubienski (2000) explored students' experiences in her own discussion-intensive seventh-grade mathematics classroom. Committed to the idea that teachers should engage students in the exploration and discussion of mathematical ideas, Lubienski acted as a "facilitator who asked guiding questions instead of an authority figure who told students exactly what to think and do" (p. 398). But this pedagogical approach seemed to have differential effects on her socio-economically diverse group of 18 students. Focusing on the reactions of six European-American female students, Lubienski found that high socioeconomic status (SES) students seemed comfortable with the open nature of the pedagogy; they felt confident to express and defend their own positions and generally perceived the discussions as a useful forum for exchanging ideas. In contrast, lower-SES students said they became confused when conflicting ideas were discussed, seemed afraid to say or believe the "wrong thing," and desired more teacher direction. Lubienski speculates that, although a discussion-intensive approach to mathematics may be well-aligned with middle-class values, it may actually disadvantage lower-SES students.

In addition to cultural and socioeconomic background, gender differences in discourse style may affect students' participation in recitations and discussions. As the linguist Deborah Tannen (1995) notes, boys and girls learn different ways of speaking as they are growing up:

> The research of sociologists, anthropologists, and psychologists observing American children at play has shown that, although both girls and boys find ways of creating rapport and negotiating status, girls tend to learn conversational rituals that focus on the rapport dimension of relationships whereas boys tend to learn rituals that focus on the status dimension. (p. 140)

According to Tannen, females learn to downplay status differences and to stress the ways everyone is the same. They also learn that sounding too sure of themselves will make them unpopular. At the same time, males generally recognize and expect differences in status; in fact, they learn to use language to negotiate their status in the group by displaying their abilities and knowledge. Males in leadership positions give orders, challenge others, and "take center stage by telling stories or jokes" (p. 140). When we consider these very different styles of communication, it is easy to see that the I-R-E pattern of discourse, with its public display of knowledge and its inherent competition, is more compatible with males' communication styles than with those of females (Arends, 2004).

Research on gender and classroom talk has also indicated that "teachers demonstrate a clear bias in favor of male participation in their classes" (Grossman & Grossman, 1994):

> Teachers are more likely to call on a male volunteer when students are asked to recite; this is also true when they call on nonvolunteers. When students recite, teachers are also more likely to listen to and talk to males. They also use more of their

ideas in classroom discussions and respond to them in more helpful ways....This pattern of giving more attention to males is especially clear in science and mathematics classes. (p. 76)

Similarly, *How Schools Shortchange Girls* (1992), a study commissioned by the American Association of University Women (AAUW), reports that males often demand—and receive—more attention from teachers. In one study of 10 high school geometry classes (Becker, 1981), for example, males called out answers to teacher questions twice as frequently as females. The same result was obtained in a study of 30 physical science and 30 chemistry classes (Jones & Wheatley, 1990): Whereas the female students appeared "self-conscious and quiet," the males were "more aggressive in calling out responses and tended to use louder tones of voice when seeking the teacher's attention" (p. 867).

Why would teachers allow male students to dominate classroom interaction by calling out? Morse and Handley (1985) suggest three possible reasons: (1) the behavior is so frequent that teachers come to accept it; (2) teachers expect males to be aggressive; and (3) the call-outs may be perceived by teachers as indicators of interest. Whatever the reasons, Morse and Handley's study of junior high science classes found that the trend toward male dominance became even greater as students moved from seventh to eighth grade.

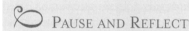 **PAUSE AND REFLECT**

Reflect on your own experiences with respect to communication patterns that students bring to school. Have you noticed any gender differences in communication styles or differences between students from different cultural backgrounds? Has there ever been any explicit discussion of such differences?

STRATEGIES FOR MANAGING RECITATIONS AND TEACHER-LED DISCUSSIONS

Recitations and teacher-led discussions pose formidable challenges to teachers. You need to respond to each individual's learning needs, while maintaining the attention and interest of the group; to distribute participation widely, without dampening the enthusiasm of those who are eager to volunteer; to assess students' understanding without embarrassing those who don't know the answers; to allow students to contribute to the interaction, while remaining "on course."

This section of the chapter considers six strategies for meeting these challenges. As in previous chapters, research on teaching, discussions with the four teachers, and observations of their classes provide the basis for the suggestions. Although there are no foolproof guarantees of success, these strategies can reduce the pitfalls associated with recitations and teacher-led discussions. (The Practical Tips box on page 286 provides a summary of the suggestions.)

Distributing Chances to Participate

Early in the school year, I watched Fred introduce the topics that his Contemporary World Issues class would be studying during the coming year. He explained that

PRACTICAL TIPS FOR

MANAGING RECITATIONS AND TEACHER-LED DISCUSSIONS

- *Distribute chances to participate:*
  Pick names from a cup.
  Check off names on a seating chart.
  Use patterned turn taking.

- *Provide time to think:*
  Extend wait time to three seconds.
  Tell students you don't expect an immediate answer.
  Allow students to write a response.

- *Stimulate and maintain interest:*
  Inject mystery and suspense.
  Inject humor and novelty.
  Challenge students to think.
  Incorporate physical activity.

- *Provide feedback to students:*
  When answer is correct and confident, affirm briefly.
  When answer is correct but hesitant, provide more deliberate affirmation.
  When answer is incorrect but careless, make a simple correction.
  When answer is incorrect but student could get answer with help, prompt or
    backtrack to simpler question.
  If student is unable to respond, don't belabor the issue.

- *Monitor comprehension:*
  Require overt responses (e.g., have students hold up response cards, physically
    display answers with manipulative materials, put thumbs up or down).
  Use a steering group (e.g., observe the performance of a sample of students,
    including low achievers) in order to know when to move on.

- *Support the participation of diverse learners:*
  Be conscious of your pattern of asking questions. Track who you call on, how often
    you call on them, and how you respond to their answers.
  Become familiar with the discourse patterns characteristic of your culturally
    diverse students.
  Consider whether some accommodation to students' discourse style is possible.
  Teach explicitly about the discourse patterns that are expected in school.
  Incorporate "alternative response formats" designed to engage all students rather
    than just one or two.

students would be examining a variety of cultures, looking at how people make a living in each culture.

Okay, let's think about what goes into making a living. Make a list of the five most important elements in our economic system that have a bearing on your own life. I'm going to do this too. [Students begin to write. After a few minutes, Fred continues.] Okay, let's see if we can develop a good answer, a consensus. Let's go around the room and each person give one thing.

In this situation, Fred chose to use a "round-robin" technique, which allowed him to give everyone a chance to participate. Since he didn't have to deliberate each time he called on someone, this strategy also enabled him to keep the pace moving. Watching him, I recalled a study by McDermott (1977) of first-grade reading groups. McDermott found that turn taking in the high-achievement group proceeded efficiently in round-robin fashion, with little time lost between readers. In the low-achievement group, however, the teacher allowed the students to bid for a turn, and so much time was devoted to deciding who would read next that students spent only one-third as much time reading as students in the top group.

Sometimes, teachers prefer to use a pattern that is more subtle than the round-robin, so that students do not know exactly when they will be called on. Donnie uses this approach (described earlier in the section on interaction routines in Chapter 4):

> **Sometimes I'll start in a front corner, and then go diagonally to the back of the room, then across, and down. I find that using a pattern like that helps me to keep track of who I call on, and it helps me make sure I get to everyone. And it's less obvious than just going up and down the rows. This way, kids are not so aware of who I'm going to call on next. So they don't sit there and try to work out the answer to the problem they know they're going to get. Sometimes, they'll try to figure out the pattern, and they'll say, "Wait a minute, you missed me," but it's like a game.**

Instead of a pattern, some teachers use a list of names or a seating chart to keep track of who has spoken. Christina, for example, often records the names of all students who participate during a recitation or discussion, using tick marks to indicate how many times they contribute. When she has the time, she also uses different symbols to indicate types of participation (e.g., responding to a question; asking a question; great idea; adding to something somebody else said). Other teachers use the "popsicle stick system" (described in Chapter 4), pulling sticks labeled with students' names from a can or mug, and placing the sticks on the side after the student has responded.

Whichever system you choose, *the important point is to make sure that the interaction is not dominated by a few volunteers.* Some students are just not comfortable speaking in class and seek to avoid the risk of appearing foolish or stupid. Jones and Gerig (1994) examined verbal interaction between teachers and students in four sixth-grade classrooms. They identified *32 percent of the students as "silent."* During interviews, these students typically described themselves as shy (72 percent) and lacking in self-confidence (50 percent). Karen explained her silence by referring to an incident that happened *four years earlier:*

> *I talk just a little in class. I'm afraid that what I say, someone won't like. When I was in the second grade, we were going to have a Thanksgiving dinner thing and students were going to be Pilgrims. I raised my hand and said I would like to be an Indian and would wear my hair in braids. Nobody said anything, and the teacher just went "Um hum," and it was embarrassing. (p. 177)*

Sometimes, distributing participation is difficult not because students are reluctant to speak and there are too *few* volunteers, but because there are too *many* volunteers. The more teachers stimulate interest in a particular lesson, the more students want to respond. This means greater competition for each turn, and "bidding" for a chance to speak can become loud and unruly.

One useful strategy is to allow several students to answer one question. In the following interaction, we see Christina increase participation by not "grabbing" the first answer and moving on to a new question. She has just focused students' attention on a passage from Edith Wharton's *Ethan Frome,* in which Ethan looks at a cushion his wife Zeena had made for him when they were engaged—"the only piece of needlework he had ever seen her do"—and then flings it across the room.

CHRISTINA: He throws it across the room. What does this suggest about his feelings for her?

STUDENT 1:   I think it shows that he really did hate her.

STUDENT 2:   I think he was fed up, but I don't think he hated her. He had a lot of opportunities to leave her and he didn't.

STUDENT 3:   I think he just felt so guilty. Guilt overpowered the hate. That's why he didn't leave her.

STUDENT 4:   He wouldn't know how to react to the freedom. I think he's afraid to leave.

CHRISTINA: Good point. Is he not leaving because he's used to the farm, or because of Zeena, or because he's afraid to be alone?

STUDENT 5:   Now that you said that, it made me think, maybe it's not Zeena who has the problem. Maybe it's Ethan. And maybe it would happen again with Mattie. . . .

STUDENT 6:   Yeah. He needs someone to rely on. First he relied on Zeena and his parents. Now she's getting sicker, and he can't rely on her, so he's turning to Mattie.

STUDENT 7:   But if he relied on her when he needed it, why can't she rely on him now that she needs it?

STUDENT 8:   He could slip something into her drink and get rid of her and marry Mattie.

STUDENT 9:   I don't think he hates her enough. He's just fed up with her.

During one visit to Donnie's class, I watched her distribute participation widely by specifying that each student should give only one possible answer to the problem:

DONNIE: Today we start a new adventure—equations with two variables. Our answers are going to be ordered pairs. I'm going to put this up here, $x + y = 3$. [She writes the equation on the board.] Now, if I ask you to give me all the possible answers, what would you say? [There are lots of hands up.] Okay, give me one, Shameika.

SHAMEIKA: (0, 3).

DONNIE: [She writes that on the board.] Okay, give me another. Sharif.

SHARIF: (1, 2).
DONNIE: Another. Tayeisha.
TAYEISHA: (2, 1).

Another strategy is to have each student write a response and share it with one or two neighbors. This allows everyone to participate actively. You might then ask some of the groups to report on what they discussed.

One final thought: While you're thinking about ways to distribute participation, keep in mind the suggestions made in Chapter 2 for counteracting the action zone phenomenon: (1) move around the room whenever possible; (2) establish eye contact with students seated farther away from you; (3) direct comments to students seated in the rear and on the sides; and (4) periodically change students' seats so that all students have an opportunity to be up front.

Providing Time to Think without Losing the Pace

Envision this scenario: You've just asked a well-formulated, carefully worded, higher-level question designed to stimulate critical thinking and problem solving. And you're met with total silence. Your face begins to feel flushed, and your heart beats a little faster. What to do now?

One reason silence is so uncomfortable is that it's hard to interpret: Are students thinking about the question? Are they asleep? Are they so muddled they're unable to respond? Silence is also troubling to teachers because it can threaten the pace and momentum of the lesson. Even a few seconds of silence can seem like eternity. This helps to explain why many teachers wait less than *one second* before calling on a student (Rowe, 1974). Yet research demonstrates that if you extend *"wait time"* to three or four seconds, you can increase the quality of students' answers and promote participation. Extending wait time is also helpful to students with learning disabilities, who tend to process information more slowly than their peers.

Sometimes it's helpful to tell students that you don't expect an immediate answer. This legitimates the silence and gives students an opportunity to formulate their responses. During a visit to Fred's class, I saw him indicate that he wanted everyone to think for a while before responding:

 We're been talking about how you can use indicators to decide if a person will be a liberal or conservative, a Republican or a Democrat, and some people came to me after school and said they thought that maybe I was encouraging you all to make stereotypes. I'm really glad they brought that up. You should not do an assignment in an unthinking, unquestioning way. So let's talk about this. First, these people obviously thought it was bad to stereotype people. Why? Why is it bad to stereotype people? *Before you answer, think.* [There's a long pause. Fred finally calls on a student to respond.]

Allowing students to write an answer to your question is another way of providing them with time to think. Written responses also help to maintain students' engagement, since everyone has to construct a response. In addition, students who are uncomfortable speaking extemporaneously can read from their written papers. In the following example, we see Sandy use this strategy:

 Sandy is introducing the concept of chemical equilibrium. She has drawn a diagram on the board showing the relative concentrations of A + B and C + D over time. She asks, "Where is equilibrium established? At Time 1, Time 2, or Time 3? Jot it down and write a sentence explaining why you chose T1, T2, or T3." She walks around the room, looking at students' papers. With a little laugh, she comments: "I see a lot of correct answers, and then the word *because*."

During our conversation about her lesson, Sandy recalled an incident that underscored the value of having all students write a response to a question:

 I had this girl in my honors class, who came to see me about the second week of school. She was obviously upset about how she was doing; she wanted to drop the class. She started to cry. "Everyone is so much smarter than I am." I asked her how she had come to that conclusion, and it was clear that she was equating response time with ability. I find that a lot of the girls do that. She says, "I'm just in the middle of figuring it out, and the other kids are already answering." She says, "I like it when you ask us to write our answers down first. But when I have to respond orally I'm intimidated."

Once you have selected someone to respond, it's also important to protect their opportunity to respond before allowing anyone else (you included) to jump into the interaction. Watch the way Donnie deals with this situation during a lesson on linear measurement:

 DONNIE: Okay, so how are you going to figure this out? (Pause) Eugene.
EUGENE: You have to know how many inches are in a mile.
DONNIE: And how are you going to figure that out? [Eugene is silent, but Ebony is waving her hand.]
EBONY: Ooh, ooh, Miss, I know, I know how to do it.
DONNIE: [very softly] Wait a minute, Ebony, give him a chance. Let him think.

Stimulating and Maintaining Interest

In previous chapters, we have discussed Kounin's classic study (1970) of the differences between orderly and disorderly classrooms. One finding of that study was that students are more involved in work and less disruptive when teachers attempt to involve nonreciting individuals in the recitation task, maintain their attention, and keep them "on their toes." Kounin called this behavior "group alerting." Observations of our four teachers reveal that they frequently use group-alerting strategies to stimulate attention and to maintain the pace of the lesson. For example, watch how Christina tries to generate interest in "parenthetical documentation"—a lesson that has the potential to be really deadly:

Today we're going to be talking about the next step in doing the research paper—how to cite sources in the body of the paper using MLA format. It's called parenthetical documentation. Now some of you have been asking why you have to learn this. Well, here's an example of a paper using parenthetical documentation. [She puts an excerpt from a paper on the overhead.] This is an excerpt from a 60-page paper [she waves it in the air] written by a friend of mine who works for a sales corporation. The paper doesn't have anything to do with literary analysis; it's a profitability analysis of one of my friend's $2.5 million clients. She's not in English, but we went to high school together, and we learned how to do this there, just like you're learning how to do it now. This is a skill that you'll use in lots of different situations, not just writing a literary analysis for English 10R.

Students' interest can also be stimulated and maintained if you inject some humor or novelty into the recitation itself. During a lesson on the difference between third-person limited narration and third-person omniscient narration, Christina uses Michaela, a student in the class, as an example:

CHRISTINA: Let's say that Michaela comes into the room, goes to her seat, does her journal entry, and then does her group task. We don't know anything at all about how she's feeling inside. That's an example of third-person, limited narration. All we know is what the narrator can see. Now, here's another version: Michaela comes into the room feeling tired, but then she sees the journal topic on the board and gets really excited. She enjoys writing her journal entry, and then enthusiastically moves to her group task. What would that be?

STUDENT: A fairy tale! [Everyone laughs.]

Challenges to students can also be a way of encouraging students to think and to pay attention. Here are a few examples:

FRED: Please listen to this now . . . most Americans don't understand this at all; they don't have a clue. I want you to understand this.

DONNIE: You need to fix this in your minds because we're going to use this later. . . . Now this is not really a trick question, but you'll have to think.

SANDY: This usually isn't covered in a first-year chemistry course. As a matter of fact, it's a problem that I asked on my honors chemistry test. But I know you guys can do it. I have confidence that you can do it. Just take it apart, step by step.

These challenges are reminiscent of the behavior of "Teacher X," one of the subjects in Hermine Marshall's (1987) study of three teachers' motivational strategies.

Marshall found that Teacher X frequently used statements designed to challenge students to think:"I'm going to trick you," "Get your brain started . . .You're going to think," "Get your mind started," "Look bright-eyed and bushy-tailed" (stated, according to Marshall,"with enthusiasm and a touch of humor").This frequent use of statements to stimulate and maintain student attention was in sharp contrast to the typical statements made by the other two teachers in the study (e.g.,"The test will be on Thursday" or "Open your books to page 382"). In fact,Teacher Y and Teacher Z *never* used the strategy of alerting students to pay attention, and they rarely challenged students to think. The vast majority of their directives were attempts to *return* students to the task *after* attention and interest had waned.

Another way of engaging students is to make room for personal knowledge and experience. Bracha Alpert (1991) studied students' behavior during classroom recitations and discussions in three high school English classrooms. She found that in two classrooms, students tended to be resistant:They mumbled, refused to answer, and argued. In the third classroom, no signs of student resistance were apparent; instead, students in this class actively participated in discussions. Alpert concluded that the resistance was created by the teachers' tendency to emphasize factual, formal, academic knowledge, without any attempt to relate students' personal life experiences to what was being taught. She provides some examples of this approach:"What's the significance of the dream [in the poem]?" "What is the tone of the poem?" or "What's being implied [by the author] in that scene?"In sharp contrast, the third teacher encouraged students to relate their personal experiences to the literary works they read. For example, when discussing why the literary character is so angry, he asked students to think of things that made them angry. He also asked them questions that promoted their involvement with the literary works—for example,"Do you feel sorry for any of the characters?" "Do you want Eliza to marry Freddy?"

Although it may be easier to do this in subjects like English and social studies, observations indicate that Sandy and Donnie also try to relate topics to students' own personal experiences. For example, when Sandy is introducing acids and bases, she'll begin by inviting students to tell her everything they already know about the topic. Her invitation usually leads to a discussion about fish tanks and pools, and once, they talked about what could happen if a child for whom you were babysitting drank Drano (a base) and why you couldn't use vinegar (an acid) to neutralize it! Similarly, when Donnie teaches about circles in geometry, she talks in terms of bicycles; each spoke of the tire is a radius, and the place where the chain touches the gear is the point of tangency.

Providing Feedback without Losing the Pace

As we discussed in Chapter 7, the Beginning Teacher Evaluation Study (Fisher, Berliner, Filby, Marliave, Cahan, & Dishaw, 1980) documented the importance of providing feedback to students:

> When more frequent feedback is offered, students pay attention more and learn more. Academic feedback was more strongly and consistently related to achievement than any of the other teaching behaviors. (p. 27)

Donnie challenges students to think during a lesson on triangles.

But how can you provide appropriate feedback while maintaining the pace and momentum of your lesson? Barak Rosenshine (1986) reviewed the research on effective teaching and developed a set of guidelines that may be helpful. According to Rosenshine, when students give correct, confident answers, you can simply ask another question or provide a brief verbal or nonverbal indication that they are correct. If students are correct but hesitant, however, a more deliberate affirmation is necessary. You might also explain *why* the answer is correct ("Yes, that's correct, because . . . ") in order to reinforce the material.

When students provide an incorrect answer, the feedback process is trickier. If you think the individual has made a careless error, you can make a simple correction and move on. If you decide that the student can arrive at the correct answer with a little help, you can provide hints or prompts. Sometimes it's useful to backtrack to a simpler question that you think the individual can answer, and then work up to your original question step by step. Watch Sandy:

Students are stuck on the question: "Given the following balanced equation, what volume of hydrogen gas can be produced from the decomposition of two moles of H_2O?" Their faces are blank, and there's absolute silence. Sandy asks: "Well, what is the volume of one mole of *any* gas at STP [standard temperature and pressure]?" All hands shoot up. Sandy calls on a student to respond. "22.4 liters." Sandy continues: "Do you know the relationship between moles of H_2O and moles of hydrogen gas produced?" Again, there are lots of hands, and a student replies: "It's a one-to-one relationship. The equation shows you that." Suddenly there is a lot of hand-waving, and students begin to call out, "Ooh, I see." "Oh, I got it." With a smile, Sandy motions for them to calm down and wait: "Okay, hold on, let's go back to the original question. Given the following balanced equation, what volume of hydrogen gas can be produced from the decomposition of two moles of H_2O?"

There are times when students are simply unable to respond to your question. When that happens, there's little point in belaboring the issue by providing prompts or cues; this will only make the recitation or discussion sluggish. Donnie sometimes allows students in this situation to "pass." This practice not only helps to maintain the pace, it also allows students to "save face." Meanwhile, she makes a mental note that she needs to reteach the material to the individuals having difficulty.

Donnie is reviewing homework problems on the Pythagorean theorem. "Okay, moving on to number 14." She moves over to Edward and looks as though she's going to call on him. He signals that he doesn't want to answer that question. "Don't call on you? Okay. I'll come back." She moves away and calls on someone else.

The most problematic situation for teachers is when students' answers are clearly incorrect. Saying "No, that's not right" can be uncomfortable, yet students deserve to have accurate feedback. As Sandy emphasizes: "It's really important to be clear about what's correct and what's not. The students have to know that the teacher will not leave them thinking the wrong thing." Rather than directly correcting students, however, Sandy prefers to help them discover their own errors:

I have difficulty saying "Your answer is wrong," but I usually don't have to. I can ask them to explain their reasoning. Or I can take the part of the answer that is correct and work with it. I can ask a question about their response. "How does the graph show that?" "So you're saying it would have to be like this . . ." I like students to find their *own* mistakes and correct them.

Similarly, Fred will tell students: "That answer doesn't make sense to me. How did you figure it out?" Sometimes, he compliments students on making a "really good mistake": "I love mistakes. That's how we all learn."

Monitoring Comprehension

A simple way to determine how well your students understand the material is to have them respond overtly to your questions. For example, you can ask them to put their thumbs up or down to indicate agreement or disagreement with a particular statement. You can also have them physically display answers with materials or write down responses. Watch Donnie in this lesson on the properties of circles:

Donnie tells her students to take out a piece of unlined paper, a compass, a ruler, and a pencil. She tells the students: "Now I want to check on your ability to apply the terms that we've been going over, not just regurgitate the definitions. I will repeat the directions two or three times.... Draw a circle with a radius of two inches. [She pauses to give the students the chance to do so.] Call the center of the circle point *P*. . . . From the center, going due south, draw radius *PA*. Label it. . . . The next thing you're going to do is draw a chord, but listen, the chord you're going to draw is going to bisect *PA* and go in an east-west direction." As students work, Donnie circulates, checking on how individual students are doing.

Another way of checking on students' understanding is to observe a "steering group." This is a sample of students whose performance is used as an indicator that the class is "with you" and that it's all right to move on to a new topic (Lundgren, 1972). Be careful, however, about choosing students for the steering group. If you select only high achievers, their performance may lead you to overestimate the comprehension of the class as a whole.

During one discussion with Donnie, she explained that a boy in her algebra class was a key member of her steering group:

I have this one boy who's average in ability. He generally sits in the back of the room, and when he doesn't understand, he gets a certain look on his face. I can tell he's confused. But when he *does* understand, the "light goes on." When I see the light is on with him, I can be sure most of the other kids understand.

Supporting the Participation of Diverse Learners

By understanding and appreciating the fact that students' home patterns of discourse may be mismatched with the discourse pattern used in recitation, you are better able to ensure that all students in your class—regardless of cultural background or gender—will have equitable opportunities to participate. Although there are no simple solutions, several guidelines may be useful. (These are summarized in the Practical Tips box on managing recitations.) First, teachers need to be conscious of their patterns of asking questions, using wait time, and providing praise (Arends, 2004). This means tracking which students you call on, how often you call on them, and how you respond to their answers. (Since it is difficult to monitor your own questioning patterns, it's helpful to have someone do this for you.) Second, it is essential to become familiar with the discourse patterns characteristic of your culturally diverse students (Arends, 2004). Before assuming that children are being disrespectful by calling out, for example, it's a good idea to ask whether this behavior could represent a culturally learned style of discourse that is appropriate and normal in settings outside of school. Third, consider whether some accommodation to students' discourse style is possible. For example, during recitations and discussions, "Mr. Appleby," a White, middle-class teacher of 17 low-achieving, predominantly Black students, encouraged his students to call out answers and make comments and did not expect them to raise their hands and speak one at a time. Observing this, Dillon (1989) reports:

> Appleby also allowed his students to interact with each other and with him, in the way they spoke to peers and adults in their family/community. In other words, within these lessons, Appleby allowed the interactions in his classrooms to be culturally congruent. . . . For example, students often talked sarcastically, interrupted Appleby, or overlapped the speech of other students as they presented their ideas. (p. 245)

Despite this "permissiveness," Dillon observed no disrespect. Students recognized that Appleby had high academic and behavioral expectations, and they met them. As LaVonne commented, "Students obey Appleby's wishes—we act crazy but we calm ourselves down and don't go overboard" (p. 244).

Although accommodation to students' discourse patterns may be possible and appropriate at times, some educators (e.g., Delpit, 1995) argue that teachers need to be explicit about the discourse patterns that are expected (and usually implicit) in school. Indeed, the explicit teaching of this knowledge is considered a teacher's "moral responsibility," since it enables individuals to participate fully in the classroom community and the larger society (Gallego, Cole, & Laboratory of Comparative Human Cognition, 2001, p. 979). Thus, a fourth guideline emphasizes the need to provide explicit instruction on the discourse pattern of recitations (I-R-E) and to allow students to practice these communication skills.

In addition to monitoring and supporting the participation of learners from diverse cultural backgrounds, it is also important to be sensitive to gender differences in participation and use strategies to ensure that both males and females have opportunities to participate. Sandy is one science teacher who does not allow the boys to "grab the floor":

> **I find that the boys are often faster at responding than the girls. Boys will call out the answers even if they're not sure, while the girls will sit and think before they give an answer. I really have to stay aware of that and make sure that the girls get an opportunity to respond.**

The following vignette illustrates one strategy that Sandy uses to ensure that girls have the opportunity to participate:

SANDY: **Listen really carefully. [She writes an equation on the board. Pointing to the equation, she turns to the class and continues.] A student was asked to produce 30 grams of O_2 gas. How many grams of $KClO_3$ must the student use to do this? [There is no response.] Can I say that if the student needs to produce 30 grams of O_2 gas she would need to start with 30 grams of $KClO_3$?**

STUDENTS: **[in chorus] No-o-o.**

SANDY: Why not? [Students raise their hands. A few boys start to call out.] Wait, raise your hand. [She calls on a girl who has not raised her hand.] Janice.

JANICE: Because oxygen is different. [Several boys start to call out again. Sandy shakes her head to indicate that they should wait.]

SANDY: Okay, Janice. Because O_2 is a different chemical, but what is the relationship between moles of O_2 and moles of $KClO_3$?

JANICE: [She shrugs. Again, boys start to call out.]

SANDY: Look back at the board. Does the equation reveal anything to you about the relationship?

JANICE: [Her eyes light up.] It's a two-to-three ratio.

SANDY: Super!

Finally, teachers can incorporate "alternative response formats" designed to engage all students rather than just one or two (Walsh & Sattes, 2005). Some we've already mentioned—such as choral responses, overt responses (e.g., "thumbs up" or "thumbs down"), and work samples (e.g., students individually solve a problem). While these all require students to answer individually, others allow students to work cooperatively before responding to the teacher's question; recall "Numbered Heads Together" and "Timed Pair Share" described in the chapter on groupwork. These more active, participatory response formats may be more comfortable for students who find the traditional pattern of question-response-evaluation to be unfamiliar or intimidating.

 PAUSE AND REFLECT

Think about the strategies for managing recitations described in the previous section. What are five of the most important things you will want to keep in mind as you plan a recitation?

MODERATING STUDENT-CENTERED DISCUSSIONS

In both the recitation and the teacher-led discussion, the teacher is in charge, determining the content, the participants, and the pacing. In contrast, the *student-centered discussion* provides an opportunity for students to interact directly with one another, while the teacher acts as a facilitator or moderator.

Consider this example observed in Fred's Institute for Legal and Political Education (IPLE) class. The topic was budget deficits, and Hope had just asked a key question: "Why can't the government just print more money to pay off a debt?" Fred noted that this was an important question, and he attempted to provide an explanation. Hope wasn't convinced. Other students joined in:

SUSAN: I think I got it now. You know how they say that everyone can't be a millionaire. There's got to be some poor people? It's like that.

JOHN: Yeah, like when I play Monopoly. I buy every property, so I go into bankruptcy. So I take out a loan, and I'm ruining the game because I'm not playing with the money I'm supposed to have. It's like cheating.

LORIE: Yeah, that money doesn't really exist.

HOPE: What do you mean? If the government prints the money, it does exist. [A number of students begin talking at the same time.]

FRED: Hold on. Stuart, then Roy, then Alicia.

STUART: The money's worth a lot because there's only a little. If there were a lot, it would only be worth a little.

HOPE: I still don't understand. So what, if it's only worth a little.

ROY: Pretend there's this gold block sitting in Fort Knox and it's worth $10, but there's only one $10 bill. Now if we make up 10 $10 bills, each will only be worth $1.

HOPE: So what? I can still use it to buy stuff. [A few students start to jump in, but Fred intervenes.]

FRED: Alicia hasn't had her chance to talk.

ALICIA: I think I got it now. Let me try. There's this diamond, and we both want it. . . . [She continues to explain, but Hope is still confused.]

FRED: Let's see if I can help out here. . . .

As we can see from this excerpt, Fred essentially stays out of the interaction, except for making sure that students have an opportunity to speak when the interaction gets excited. In contrast to the recitation, or even many teacher-led discussions, students speak directly to one another. They comment on one another's contributions, they question, they disagree, and they explain.

Providing opportunities for student–student discussions means that teachers have to give up their role as *leader* and assume the role of *facilitator*. This can be difficult for teachers who are used to dominating or at least directing the conversation. But acting as a facilitator rather than a leader does not mean abdicating responsibility for guiding the interaction. This became very clear during a conversation with Fred, when he described some of the problems that he tries to anticipate and avoid:

First of all, a discussion like this can be an opportunity for some kids to show how smart they are and to get airtime, so it's important to watch out that kids don't pontificate and monopolize. Second, you have to listen carefully and ask yourself, "Where is this going?" I often have an end goal in mind, and I try to make sure that the discussion doesn't get too far afield. Occasionally, I'll jump in and say something like, "I think we're losing the focus here" or "I think you're arguing over semantics." Also, a lot of times kids state opinions as fact, and I think it's important not to let them get away with that. I'll interject and ask them to provide supporting evidence. Or I'll ask for clarification: "Is that what you meant to say?"

Because student-centered discussions can be so difficult for both students and teachers, Christina has developed a strategy she calls "Post-it Note discussions." When students read an assigned text, they choose a passage that especially interests them—it can be a few words, a few pages, or anything in between. They place a Post-it Note near the passage they've chosen, and write responses to questions that Christina constructed (e.g., Why did you choose this passage? What does it mean? What does it tell you about the rest of the text? What issues are raised here?) Then they take a second Post-it Note and write a question for discussion. The following exchange is from a Post-it Note discussion on *Ethan Frome:*

STUDENT 1: My passage is on page 95, beginning with "His impulses . . . " [Students turn to page 95, and she reads the paragraph aloud, while everyone follows along.] I chose this passage because I think it's the most important in the chapter. It shows how Ethan is finally deciding to tell Zeena how he feels, but then he begins to change his mind and he's thinking he can't do it. My question is, why do you think Ethan is having such a hard time about leaving Zeena?

STUDENT 2: I think he feels it's wrong to leave her because she's sick and she's relying on him.

STUDENT 3: I also think he's worried about the money, but it wouldn't stop him.

STUDENT 4: But I do think it would stop him. He can't even afford the train ticket to leave her.

STUDENT 3: But in the next sentence, he says he's sure he's going to get work.

STUDENT 5: He's worried he won't be able to support Mattie.

STUDENT 6: He wants to leave but he's afraid of change. . . .

As we can see, the students' role is to pose the discussion questions and to call on classmates to respond—not a role to which students are accustomed. During the previous discussion, in fact, a girl asked her question and then seemed paralyzed in the face of her peers' raised hands. When she turned to Christina for assistance, Christina quietly reminded her, "You're in charge, Renata." The girl laughed, "I'm not used to this!"

Being "in charge" is certainly an unfamiliar role for students, but one that students gradually learn to assume with the Post-it Note strategy. After class, Christina shared her thoughts on the importance of having students take responsibility for class discussions:

During my field experiences and student teaching, I often saw class "discussions," where the teachers did almost all the talking. I worried that I wouldn't be able to run an effective discussion because even the most experienced and talented teachers I observed were struggling to involve their students. It seemed like it would be torture to stand in front of a class and get no response. So I started thinking about how I could get students to take more responsibility for the discussion. I always write in the margins of my books when a passage interests me, but obviously kids can't do that with the school's books. So I hit upon the idea of Post-it Notes. I think it's working pretty well, and students' reactions have been overwhelmingly positive. This way, students really "own" the discussion. They talk about what interests them, rather than just what *I* think is important. They have to prepare for the discussion by putting their thoughts into writing, and that almost always makes it a better discussion. And all the students *have* to participate, at least to read their passage and ask their question. I think the students really like it too. The hardest part is being quiet. I purposely sit on the outside of the group, so I'm less likely to dominate, but I still have to remind myself a lot to stay out of it as much as possible.

When you're learning to lead a discussion, keep in mind three basic suggestions (Gall & Gillett, 1981). First, it may be wise to *limit the size of the group*. It's difficult to have a student-centered discussion with a large number of participants. Fred's IPLE class has only 12 students, so group size wasn't too much of a problem here, but in a class like Christina's, opportunities to speak are more limited. In his larger classes, Fred sometimes uses the "fishbowl" method, in which five or six students carry on the discussion in the middle of the room, while the rest of the class sits in a large circle around them and acts as observers and recorders. Another solution is to divide the class into small discussion groups of five, with one student in each group acting as a discussion leader.

Second, *arrange students so they can make eye contact*. It's difficult to speak directly to someone if all you can see is the back of a head. If at all possible, students should move their desks into an arrangement that allows them to be face-to-face.

Finally, *prepare students for participating in a student-centered discussion by explicitly teaching the prerequisite skills*:

- Talk to each other, not just to the moderator.
- Don't monopolize.
- Ask others what they think.
- Don't engage in personal attack.
- Listen to others' ideas.
- Acknowledge others' ideas.
- Question irrelevant remarks.
- Ask for clarification.
- Ask for reasons for others' opinions.
- Give reasons for your opinions.

James Dillon (1994) also provides some extremely helpful guidelines for preparing and conducting discussions. (See the Practical Tips box on page 302.) Note that Dillon advises against asking questions during a student-centered discussion for fear of turning the discussion into a recitation. Although his concern is well-founded, other discussion experts believe that questions can be an appropriate and effective way to keep conversation going. In fact, Brookfield and Preskill (1999) identify several kinds of questions that are especially helpful in maintaining momentum:

Questions that ask for more evidence:
   How do you know that?
   What data is that claim based on?

What does the author say that supports your argument?

Where did you find that view expressed in the text?

What evidence would you give to someone who doubted your interpretation?

Questions that ask for clarification:

Can you put that another way?

What do you mean by that?

What's an example of what you are talking about?

Can you explain the term you just used?

Linking or extension questions:

Is there any connection between what you've just said and what Rajiv was saying a moment ago?

How does your comment fit in with Neng's earlier comment?

How does your observation relate to what the group decided last week?

Does your idea challenge or support what we seem to be saying?

Hypothetical questions:

What might have happened if Joey hadn't missed the school bus?

In the video we just saw, how might the story have turned out if Arnold had caught the ball?

If the author had wanted the teacher to be a more sympathetic figure, how might he have changed this conversation?

Cause-and-effect questions:

What is likely to be the effect of the name calling?

How might the rumor affect the school play?

Summary and synthesis questions:

What are the one or two most important ideas that emerged from this discussion?

What remains unresolved or contentious about this topic?

What do you understand better as a result of today's discussion?

Based on our discussion today, what do we need to talk about next time if we're to understand this issue better?

What key word or concept best captures our discussion today?

CONCLUDING COMMENTS

This chapter has focused on three different patterns of verbal interaction: recitations, teacher-led discussions, and student-centered discussions. It's important not to get them confused—to think that you're leading a discussion when you're actually conducting a recitation.

Teachers often say that they use discussion a great deal, when in fact they are conducting recitations. For example, in a provocative article entitled "What Teachers Do When They Say They're Having Discussions of Content Area Reading Assignments," Alvermann, O'Brien, and Dillon (1990) found that although 24 middle school teachers reported using discussion, only seven could actually be observed

PRACTICAL TIPS FOR

MODERATING STUDENT-CENTERED DISCUSSIONS

- Carefully formulate the discussion question (making sure that it is not in a form that invites a yes/no or either/or answer), along with subsidiary questions, embedded questions, follow-up questions, and related questions.

- Create a question outline, identifying at least three subquestions and at least four alternative answers to the main question.

- Present the discussion question to the class, writing it on the chalkboard or on an overhead transparency or on paper distributed to the class. After reading the question aloud, go on to give the sense of the question, identifying terms, explaining the relevance of the question, connecting it to a previous discussion or class activity, etc. End with an invitation to the class to begin addressing the question.

- Initially, help the class focus on the question, rather than giving answers to it. For example, invite the class to tell what they know about the question, what it means to them.

- DO NOT COMMENT AFTER THE FIRST STUDENT'S CONTRIBUTION. (If you do, the interaction will quickly become I-R-E.) In addition, do not ask, "What does someone else think about that?" (If you do, you invite statements of difference or opposition to the first position, and your discussion turns into a debate.)

- In general, do not ask questions beyond the first question. Use instead nonquestion alternatives: statements (the thoughts that occurred to you in relation to what the speaker has just said; reflective statements that basically restate the speaker's contribution; statements indicating interest in hearing further about what the speaker has just said; statements indicating the relationship between what the speaker has just said and what a previous speaker has said); signals (sounds or words indicating interest in what the speaker has said); even silence. (Dillon acknowledges that deliberate silence is the hardest of all for teachers to do. To help teachers remain quiet, he recommends silently singing "Baa, baa, black sheep" after each student's contribution.)

- Facilitate the discussion by
  - Locating: "Where are we now? What are we saying?"
  - Summarizing: "What have we accomplished? agreed on?"
  - Opening: "What shall we do next?"
  - Tracking: "We seem a little off track here. How can we all get back on the same line of thought?"
  - Pacing: "Just a minute, I wonder whether we're not moving a little too fast here. Let's take a closer look at this idea...."

- When it is time to end the discussion, help students to summarize the discussion and identify the remaining questions.

doing so; the others were using recitation or lecture interspersed with questions. These findings are consistent with observations of 1,000 elementary and secondary classrooms across the country, in which discussion was seen only 4 to 7 percent of the time (Goodlad, 1984). More than 20 years later, the amount of discussion does not appear to have changed: A recent study of 64 English/language arts classes in 19 middle and high schools found that discussion occurred for only 1.7 minutes per 60 minutes of class time—or 3.8 percent of the time (Applebee, Langer, Nystrand, & Gamoran, 2003). It is clear that real discussion is very rarely used in classrooms. As Sandy comments:

A lot of beginning teachers get these two mixed up. They've been told they're supposed to ask a lot of questions, so they do, but often the questions are yes/no questions or questions that elicit short answers without a lot of depth: What do all atoms have in common? How many protons are in this atom? In discussions, the majority of the questions are critical thought questions, and the response time is longer. You're trying to develop an idea or draw a conclusion. You're not just reviewing; you're working toward a conceptual goal.

Also keep in mind the criticisms that have been leveled against recitations, and reflect on how frequently you dominate the verbal interaction in your classroom. Ask yourself whether you also provide opportunities for student-centered discussion, during which you serve as a facilitator (rather than a questioner) and encourage direct student–student interaction. Reflect on the level of thinking that you require from students. The classroom recitation can serve a number of useful functions, but *overuse* suggests that your curriculum consists largely of names, dates, facts, and algorithms (Cazden, 1988).

Summary

This chapter began by examining some of the major criticisms of recitation, as well as the useful functions it can serve. It then distinguished recitations from teacher-led discussions and considered the potential pitfalls of these two subsettings. Next, the chapter suggested a number of strategies for using recitations and teacher-led discussions successfully in your classroom. Finally, we looked at two examples of a student-centered discussion and briefly considered a number of guidelines for managing this type of verbal interaction.

Characteristic Pattern of a Recitation

- I-R-E (teacher initiation, student response, teacher evaluation).
- Quick pace.
- Used to review material, to elaborate on a text.

Criticisms of Recitation

- Gives the teacher a dominant role, the student a passive one.
- Discourages interaction among students.
- Emphasizes recall over higher-level thinking skills.
- Promotes public evaluation, which can lead to negative interdependence.

Five Functions of Recitation

- Provides opportunity to check on students' comprehension.
- Offers an opportunity to push students to construct more complete responses.
- Involves students in presentation of material.
- Allows for contact with individuals in a group setting.
- Helps to maintain attention level.

Characteristics of a Teacher-Led Discussion

- I-R (or even I-R-R-R).
- Student-initiated questions.
- Student comments on contributions of peers.
- Slower pace.
- Intended to stimulate thinking, to foster problem solving, to examine implications.

Four Pitfalls of Recitations and Teacher-Led Discussions

- Unequal participation.
- Losing the pace and focus.
- Difficulty in monitoring comprehension.
- Incompatibility with discourse patterns that students bring to school.

Strategies for Successful Use of Recitations and Teacher-Led Discussions

- Distribute chances for participation.
    Use some type of patterned turn taking.
    Ensure that interaction is not dominated by a few volunteers.
- Provide time to think about answers before responding.
- Stimulate and maintain interest by
    Injecting mystery/suspense elements into your questions.
    Using humor, novelty.
    Making room for personal knowledge and experience.
- Provide feedback without losing the pace.
- Monitor comprehension by requiring overt responses and by observing a steering group.
- Support the participation of diverse learners.

Moderating Student-Centered Discussions

- Act as facilitator rather than questioner.
- Ensure that some students don't monopolize.
- Make sure the discussion stays on track.
- Ask students to provide supporting evidence for opinions.
- Limit group size.
- Arrange students so they have eye contact.
- Teach discussion skills.

When planning your lessons, think about the extent to which you use recitations, teacher-led discussions, and student-centered discussions in your classroom. Think about the level of the questions that you ask: Are all of your questions low-level, factual questions that can be answered with a word or two, or are your questions designed to stimulate thinking and problem solving? Ask yourself if you consistently dominate the interaction, or if you also provide opportunities for real discussion among students.

ACTIVITIES FOR SKILL BUILDING AND REFLECTION

In Class

1. Your colleague has asked you to help him figure out why his students are not paying attention in class. He would like you to observe him and offer feedback. What follows is a session you observed. In a small group, identify the trouble spots of his lesson and provide three specific suggestions for improvement. Use what you know about distributing participation, stimulating and maintaining interest, and monitoring comprehension.

> MR. B.: Who remembers what photosynthesis is? [No response.] Do you remember yesterday when we looked at green plants and we discussed how a plant makes its own food? [Mr. B. notices that Thea is nodding.] Thea, do you remember about photosynthesis?
>
> THEA: Yeah.
>
> MR. B.: Well, can you tell the class about it?
>
> THEA: It has something to do with light and chlorophyll.
>
> MR. B.: Good. Tom, can you add to this? [Tom was drawing in his notebook.]
>
> TOM: No.
>
> MR. B.: Tom, Thea told us that photosynthesis had to do with light and chlorophyll. Do you recall our discussion from yesterday when we defined photosynthesis?
>
> TOM: Sort of.
>
> MR. B.: What do you mean? Didn't you write down the definition with the rest of the class? Look in your notebook and tell me the definition. [Tom starts to page through his notebook. Many of the students have begun to whisper and snicker. Some are looking in their notebooks.] How many of you have found the page where we defined photosynthesis? [Seven students raise their hands.] Good. Would somebody read to me that definition? Thea.
>
> THEA: Photosynthesis is the process of forming sugars and starches in plants from water and carbon dioxide when sunlight acts upon chlorophyll.
>
> MR. B.: Excellent. Does everyone understand? [A few students nod.] Good. Tomorrow we will be having a quiz about plants and photosynthesis. Tom, will you be ready for the quiz?
>
> TOM: Sure, Mr. B.
>
> MR. B.: Okay, now let's all turn to page 135 in our science texts and read about the uses of plants.

2. Monitoring students' comprehension is sometimes problematic. In a small group, consider three of the following topics (or think of one in your own content area) and suggest two different ways a teacher could elicit overt participation in order to determine student understanding.
   a. Main characters and their traits.
   b. Characteristics of parallelograms.
   c. Symbols for chemical ions.
   d. Foreign language vocabulary words.

e.   Longitude and latitude.

f.   Types of clouds.

g.   Fat content of various products.

On Your Own

1.   Visit a classroom and observe a recitation. On a seating chart, map the verbal interaction by placing a check in the "seat" of each student who participates. Analyze your results and draw conclusions about how widely and fairly participation is distributed in this class.

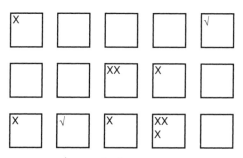

√ = question/comment
X = response to a question

2.   We know that recitations and discussions are often confused. Observe and record 10 minutes of a class "discussion." Then, using the following checklist, see if the verbal interaction actually meets the criteria for a discussion or if it is more like a recitation.

- Students are the predominant speakers.
- The verbal interaction pattern is not I-R-E, but a mix of statements and questions by a mix of teacher and students.
- The pace is longer and slower.
- The primary purpose is to stimulate a variety of responses, to encourage students to consider different points of view, to foster problem solving, and the like.
- Evaluation consists of agree/disagree, rather than right/wrong.

For Your Portfolio

Create two lesson plans, one that includes a recitation and one that includes a student-centered discussion. In sequence, list the questions that you will use for each. In a brief commentary, explain how these lessons differ from one another and why the chosen teaching strategy is appropriate for the content of the lesson.

FOR FURTHER READING

Brookfield, S. D., & Preskill, S. (2005). *Discussion as a way of teaching: Tools and techniques for democratic classrooms.* 2nd ed. San Francisco: Jossey-Bass.

This book offers a wealth of practical information on how to plan, conduct, and assess classroom discussions. The authors describe strategies for starting discussions and maintaining their momentum. A chapter on discussion in culturally diverse classrooms provides valuable information on eliciting diverse views and voices.

Gambrell, L. B., & Almasi, J. F. (Eds.) (1996). *Lively discussions! Fostering engaged reading.* Newark, DE: International Reading Association.

    The first chapter of this book contrasts recitation and discussion and clearly explains the difference between the two in terms of the teachers' and students' roles. Other chapters offer practical strategies that teachers can use to foster discussions that promote literacy development. The book presents many examples of children collaboratively constructing meaning and considering alternative interpretations of a text in order to arrive at new understandings.

Walsh, J. A., & Sattes, B. D. (2005). *Quality questioning: Research-based pracice to engage every learner.* Thousand Oaks, CA: Corwin Press.

    Based on the authors' QUILT framework (Questioning and Understanding to Improve Learning and Thinking), this book discusses preparing questions, presenting questions, prompting student responses, processing student responses, teaching students to generate questions, and reflecting on questioning practice. Walsh and Sattes suggest strategies to engage all students in the teacher's questions and prompt students to generate their own questions.

REFERENCES

The AAUW Report: How schools shortchange girls. (1992). Washington, D.C.: The AAUW Educational Foundation and National Education Association.

Alvermann, D., O'Brien, D., & Dillon, D. (1990). What teachers do when they say they're having discussions of content area reading assignments. *Reading Research Quarterly, 25,* 296–322.

Alpert, B. (1991). Students' resistance in the classroom. *Anthropology and Education Quarterly, 22,* 350–366.

Applebee, A. N., Langer, J. A., Nystrand, M., & Gamoran, A. (2003). Discussion-based approaches to developing understanding: Classroom instruction and student performance in middle and high school English. *American Educational Research Journal, 40*(3), 685–730.

Arends, R. I. (2004). *Learning to teach.* 6th ed. New York: McGraw-Hill.

Becker, J. R. (1981). Differential treatment of females and males in mathematics classes. *Journal for Research in Mathematics Education, 12*(1), 40–53.

Brookfield, S. D., & Preskill, S. (1999). *Discussion as a way of teaching: Tools and techniques for democratic classrooms.* San Francisco: Jossey-Bass.

Carter, K. (March–April 1985). Teacher comprehension of classroom processes: An emerging direction in classroom management research. Paper presented at the annual meeting of the American Educational Research Association, Chicago.

Cazden, C. B. (1988). *Classroom discourse: The language of teaching and learning.* Portsmouth, NH: Heinemann.

Delpit, L. (1995). *Other people's children: Cultural conflict in the classroom.* New York: The New Press.

Dillon, D. R. (1989). Showing them that I want them to learn and that I care about who they are: A microethnography of the social organization of a secondary low-track English-reading classroom. *American Educational Research Journal, 26*(2), 227–259.

Dillon, J. T. (1994). *Using discussion in classrooms.* Philadelphia: Open University Press.

Farrar, M. T. (1988). A sociolinguistic analysis of discussion. In J. T. Dillon (Ed.), *Questioning and discussion—A multidisciplinary study.* Norwood, NJ: Ablex.

Fisher, C. W., Berliner, D. C., Filby, N. N., Marliave, R., Cahen, L. S., & Dishaw, M. M. (1980). Teaching behaviors, academic learning time, and student achievement: An overview. In C. Denham & A. Lieberman (Eds.), *Time to learn.* Washington, D.C.: U.S. Department of Education.

Gall, M. D., & Gillett, M. (1981). The discussion method in classroom teaching. *Theory Into Practice, 19,* 98–103.

Gallego, M. A., Cole, M., & The Laboratory of Comparative Human Cognition (2001). Classroom cultures and cultures in the classroom. In V. Richardson (Ed.), *Handbook of research on teaching.* 4th ed. Washington, D.C.: American Educational Research Association.

Gay, G. (2000). *Culturally responsive teaching: Theory, research, and practice.* New York: Teachers College Press.

Good, T., & Brophy, J. E. (2000). *Looking in classrooms.* 8th ed. New York: Addison Wesley Longman.

Goodlad, J. (1984). *A place called school.* New York: McGraw-Hill.

Grossman, H., & Grossman, S. H. (1994). *Gender issues in education.* Boston: Allyn and Bacon.

Hoetker, J., & Ahlbrand, W. P., Jr. (1969). The persistence of the recitation. *American Educational Research Journal, 6,* 145–167.

Jackson, P. W. (1968). *Life in classrooms.* New York: Holt, Rinehart and Winston.

Jones, M. G., & Gerig, T. M. (1994). Silent sixth-grade students: Characteristics, achievement, and teacher expectations. *The Elementary School Journal, 95*(2), 169–182.

Jones, M. G., & Wheatley, J. (1990). Gender differences in teacher–student interactions in science classrooms. *Journal of Research in Science Teaching, 27,* 861–874.

Kagan, S. (1989/90). The structural approach to cooperative learning. *Educational Leadership, 47*(4), 12–15.

Kounin, J. S. (1970). *Discipline and group management in classrooms.* New York: Holt, Rinehart & Winston.

Lubienski, S. T. (2000). A clash of social class cultures? Students' experiences in a discussion-intensive seventh grade mathematics classroom. *The Elementary School Journal, 100*(4), 377–403.

Lundgren, U. (1972). *Frame factors and the teaching process.* Stockholm: Almqvist and Wiksell.

Marshall, H. H. (1987). Motivational strategies of three fifth-grade teachers. *The Elementary School Journal, 88*(2), 135–150.

McDermott, R. P. (1977). Social relations as contexts for learning in school. *Harvard Educational Review, 47,* 198–213.

Mehan, H. (1979). *Learning lessons: Social organization in a classroom.* Cambridge, MA: Harvard University Press.

Morse, L. W., & Handley, H. M. (1985). Listening to adolescents: Gender differences in science classroom interaction. In L. C. Wilkinson & C. B. Marrett (Eds.), *Gender influences in classroom interaction.* Orlando, FL: Academic Press.

Philips, S. (1972). Participant structures and communicative competence: Warm Springs children in community and classroom. In C. Cazden, V. John, & D. Hymes (Eds.), *Functions of language in the classroom.* New York: Teachers College Press.

Roby, T. W. (1988). Models of discussion. In J. T. Dillon (Ed.), *Questioning and discussion— A multidisciplinary study.* Norwood, NJ: Ablex, pp. 163-191.

Rosenshine, B. V. (1986). Synthesis of research on explicit teaching. *Educational Leadership, 43*(7), 60-69.

Rowe, M. B. (1974). Wait-time and rewards as instructional variables, their influence on language, logic, and fate control: Part 1: Wait time. *Journal of Research in Science Teaching, 11,* 291-308.

Stodolsky, S. S. (1988). *The subject matters: Classroom activity in math and social studies.* Chicago: University of Chicago Press.

Tannen, D. (1995). The power of talk: Who gets heard and why. *Harvard Business Review, 73*(5), 138-148.

Walsh, J. A., & Satates, B. D. (2005). *Quality questioning: Research-based practice to engage every learner.* Thousand Oaks, CA: Corwin Press.

PART IV

Coping with the Challenges

PROTECTING AND RESTORING ORDER

Not too long ago, I read an entry in the journal of a student teacher whose fourth- and fifth-period English classes were giving her a hard time. It was the middle of November, and Sharon was feeling frustrated by the disrespectful and disruptive behavior of her students. "They just won't sit still long enough to hear directions," she wrote. "I am spending more and more time on telling people to 'Shhh.' I don't understand why they are so rude, and I just don't know what to do."

As I read more, it became clear that this student teacher's problem was not due to an absence of clear rules and routines or to boring, tedious instruction:

> *On the first day that I took over, we reviewed the rules my cooperating teacher had established (just like you suggested!): Come to class on time,*

don't call out, treat each other with respect, etc. They were really cooperative; I thought this was going to be great, but I guess they were just "psyching me out." Now they argue with me all the time. I say "quiet" and they say, "But I was just telling him . . ." I say, "Put the newspaper/comic book/photo album away," and they say "Just let me look, I have to see . . ." There doesn't seem much else to do except repeat myself. Sometimes it works, sometimes it doesn't. . . . I'm really at my wit's end. If I can't gain some control, there's obviously no way I can teach anything. Sometimes I think I'd be better off if I just forgot about trying to have interesting discussions, projects, small groups, etc., and just gave out worksheets every day, lectured, and didn't allow any talking. That's a far cry from the kind of classroom I wanted to have. I wanted to respect my students, to treat them like adults, but I found I can't. I've always gotten along great with kids, but not now. All these kids seem to understand is discipline referrals and detention.

This student teacher had learned a sad fact of classroom life: Having clear, reasonable rules and routines doesn't automatically mean that everyone will follow them. At the beginning of the school year, students work hard at "figuring out the teacher"—determining teachers' expectations and requirements, the amount of socializing they will tolerate, and how far they can be pushed. Most students will pursue their agendas within the limits the teacher sets, but they need to know those limits. This underscores the importance of communicating your behavioral expectations to students (the topic of Chapter 4)—and then *enforcing those expectations.* In other words, just as it's part of the students' role to push, it's part of the teacher's role to communicate that students can't push too far. Listen to Donnie:

New teachers should not be fooled by the good behavior that students exhibit at the very beginning of school. I usually find that on the first day of school, everyone is really subdued. They're checking you out. It isn't until the second week that they really start testing. That's when the problems are going to start, and you have to make sure you hold students to the expectations you set.

In this chapter, we consider ways of responding to the problems that you may encounter—from minor, nondisruptive infractions to chronic, more serious misbehaviors.

PRINCIPLES FOR DEALING WITH INAPPROPRIATE BEHAVIOR

There is little research on the relative effectiveness of disciplinary strategies (see Emmer & Aussiker, 1990), but five principles guide our discussion. (See Table 11.1.) First, *disciplinary strategies must be consistent with the goal of creating a safe, caring classroom environment.* You need to achieve order, but you also need to choose strategies that support your relationship with students, help them to

TABLE 11.1 Principles for Dealing with Inappropriate Behavior

1. Disciplinary strategies must be consistent with the goal of creating a safe, caring classroom environment.
2. Keep the instructional program going with a minimum of disruption.
3. Whether or not a particular action constitutes misbehavior depends on the context in which it occurs.
4. Match the severity of the disciplinary strategy with the misbehavior you are trying to eliminate.
5. Be "culturally responsive," because differences in norms, values, and styles of communication can have a direct effect on students' behavior.

become self-regulating, and allow them to save face in front of their peers. Curwin and Mendler (1988), authors of *Discipline with Dignity,* put it this way:

> Students will protect their dignity at all costs, even with their lives if pushed hard enough. In the game of chicken, with two cars racing at top speed toward a cliff, the loser is the one who steps on the brake. Nothing explains this bizarre reasoning better than the need for peer approval and dignity. (p. 27)

In order to protect students' dignity, it is important to avoid power struggles that cause students to feel humiliated and ridiculed. (Remember our discussion of "when school was awful" in Chapter 3.) Fred, Donnie, Sandy, and Christina all make a real effort to speak with misbehaving students calmly and quietly. They don't bring up past sins. They take care to separate the youngster's *character* from the specific *misbehavior;* instead of attacking the student as a person ("You're lazy"), they talk about what the student has done ("You have not handed in the last two homework assignments"). When more than a brief intervention is necessary, they try to meet with students privately.

During the first week of school, I witnessed a good example of disciplining with dignity in Sandy's classroom. Even though it was early in the school year, some students had already begun to test Sandy's adherence to the rules she had distributed a few days earlier:

Sandy stands by the door, greeting students as they come in. The bell rings; Sandy begins to close the door, when William breathlessly rushes up. "You're late," she tells him quietly. "Does that mean I have to come after school?" he asks. "I'll talk to you later," she replies and moves to the front of the room to begin the lesson.

Later in the period, students are working in small groups on a lab experiment. Sandy circulates through the room, helping students with the procedure. She goes over to William and pulls him aside. She speaks softly:

"You owe me 10 minutes. Today or tomorrow?"

"What's today?"

"Tuesday."

"Uh-oh." William looks worried.

"Is it better for you to come tomorrow?" Sandy asks.

"Yeah—but will you remind me?"

"I certainly will," she says with a rueful smile. Sandy goes over to her desk, makes a note in her grade book, and then continues circulating. A few minutes later, she stands beside William again, helping him with a problem and encouraging his progress.

In this vignette, we see how Sandy tried to avoid embarrassing William by speaking with him privately; how she demonstrated concern for William by offering him a choice about when to come for detention; how she avoided accusations, blame, and character assassination; and how she showed William that she held no grudge by helping with the lab a few minutes later. In short, the vignette demonstrates the way a teacher can communicate clear expectations for appropriate behavior while preserving a student's dignity.

Another way of disciplining with dignity is to structure opportunities for students to assume some responsibility for regulating their own behavior. In Chapter 3, I talked about the importance of sharing responsibility and decision-making authority. This chapter continues that theme by discussing strategies that involve students in solving the problems that arise in classrooms.

The second principle for dealing with misbehavior is that it is essential to *keep the instructional program going with a minimum of disruption.* Achieving this goal requires a delicate balancing act. On one hand, you cannot allow inappropriate behavior to interrupt the teaching–learning process. On the other hand, you must realize that disciplinary strategies themselves can be disruptive. As Doyle comments, interventions are "inherently risky" because they call attention to misbehavior and can actually pull students away from a lesson (1986, p. 421). In order to avoid this situation, you must try to anticipate potential problems and head them off; if you decide that a disciplinary intervention *is* necessary, you need to be as unobtrusive as possible.

Watching the four teachers in action, it is clear that they recognize the importance of protecting the instructional program. In the following incident, Christina sizes up a potentially disruptive situation and is able to maintain the flow of her lesson:

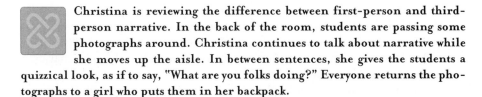 Christina is reviewing the difference between first-person and third-person narrative. In the back of the room, students are passing some photographs around. Christina continues to talk about narrative while she moves up the aisle. In between sentences, she gives the students a quizzical look, as if to say, "What are you folks doing?" Everyone returns the photographs to a girl who puts them in her backpack.

The third principle is that *whether or not a particular action constitutes misbehavior depends on the context in which it occurs* (Doyle, 1986). There are obvious exceptions to this notion—punching another person and stealing property are obvious violations that always require a teacher response. But other behaviors are not so clear-cut. For example, in some classes, wearing a hat, sitting on your desk, chewing gum, and talking to neighbors are all misbehaviors, while in other classes these are perfectly acceptable. What constitutes misbehavior is often a function of a particular teacher's tolerance level or the standards set by a particular school. Even within a class, the definition of misbehavior is dependent upon the context. A teacher may decide that talking out of turn is acceptable during a class discussion, as long as students' comments contribute to the lesson and the situation doesn't turn into a free-for-all; at other times, this same teacher may feel that a more structured lesson is needed.

When determining a course of action, you need to ask yourself, "Is this behavior disrupting or benefiting the ongoing instructional activity? Is it hurtful to other students? Does it violate established rules?" If the answer to these questions is no, disciplinary interventions may not be necessary.

"I've got no control today," Fred announces with a grin. A glance around the room seems to confirm his assessment. Some students are sitting on their desks; others are standing in the aisles, leaning over other students who are writing. In the back of the room, four students are turned around in their seats and are having an animated discussion. One girl is standing by Fred's desk, loudly debating with a girl seated nearby. Just about everyone is talking. After a few moments, the topic of all this heated conversation becomes clear. Because of severe winter storms, the school district has exceeded the normal allotment of snow days. In order to meet the state mandate for 180 days of school, the board of education must now decide whether to eliminate spring break or extend the school year. Fred has seized the opportunity to teach a lesson on political activism. His students are to think about the issue, consider whether there should be a waiver from the 180-day mandate, and write to their state legislators. Today's assignment is to construct the first draft of the letter. After class, Fred thinks about the atmosphere in the class: "I know I could have exerted a lot more control over the situation. I could have told them to sit quietly, to jot down ideas, and then silently write a first draft. But what would I have gained?"

The fourth principle emphasizes the importance of *making sure the severity of the disciplinary strategy matches the misbehavior you are trying to eliminate.* Research (e.g., Pittman, 1985) has indicated that some teachers think about misbehavior in terms of three categories: *minor misbehaviors* (noisiness, socializing, daydreaming); *more serious misbehaviors* (arguing, failing to respond to a group directive); and *never tolerated misbehaviors* (stealing, intentionally hurting someone, destroying property). They also consider whether the misbehavior is part of a pattern or an isolated event.

When deciding how to respond to a problem, it is useful to think in terms of these categories and to select a response that is congruent with the seriousness of the misbehavior. This is easier said than done, of course. When misbehavior occurs, teachers have little time to assess its seriousness, decide if it's part of a pattern, and select an appropriate response. And too often, the situation is ambiguous: Since misbehavior often occurs when the teacher is looking somewhere else, it may not be absolutely clear who is doing what to whom. Nonetheless, you don't want to ignore or react mildly to misbehavior that warrants a more severe response; nor do you want to overreact to behavior that is relatively minor.

Finally, the fifth principle stresses *the need to be "culturally responsive," because differences in norms, values, and styles of communication can have a direct effect on students' behavior.* A good example of being culturally responsive comes from Cindy Ballenger's *Teaching Other People's Children* (1999). Ballenger, European American and an experienced preschool teacher, expected to have little difficulty with her class of 4-year-old Haitian children. To her surprise, however, her usual repertoire of management strategies failed to create a respectful, orderly environment. Since her colleagues—all Haitian—were experiencing no difficulty with classroom management, Ballenger had to conclude that the problem "did not reside in the children" (p. 32). She began to explore her own beliefs and practices with respect to children's behavior and to visit other teachers' classrooms to examine their "control statements." Eventually, Ballenger was able to identify several key differences between her own style of discourse and that of her Haitian colleagues. While the Haitian teachers stressed the fact that they cared for the children and had their best interests at heart (e.g., "The adults here like you, they want you to be good children"), Ballenger frequently referred to children's internal states (e.g., "You must be angry"). Moreover, she tended to stress the logical consequences of children's behavior (e.g., "If you don't listen, you won't know what to do"), while the Haitian teachers articulated the values and responsibilities of group membership and stressed less immediate consequences, such as bringing shame to one's family. Once Ballenger had identified these differences in control statements, she made a deliberate effort to adopt some of the Haitian discourse style. Order in her classroom improved significantly.

As this vignette suggests, being culturally responsive means reflecting on the kinds of behaviors you judge to be problematic and considering how these might be related to race and ethnicity. For example, Gail Thompson (2004), an African American educator whose research focuses on the schooling experiences of students of color, notes that African American children are often socialized to talk loudly at home—a behavior that gets them into trouble at school. Listen to the mother of an eighth-grader who was starting to be labeled as a discipline problem at school for this reason:

> She's a loud person. My husband is a loud person, and when they get to explain themselves, they get loud. Their voices go up. Then, the teachers think she's being disrespectful. She's gotten a referral for that once. Actually, she's just starting to have problems. (Thompson, 2004, p. 98)

Similarly, African American youngsters tend to be more intense and confrontational than European-American youngsters; they are more likely to challenge school personnel since they see leadership as a function of strength and forcefulness (rather than as a function of position and credentials); and they may jump into heated discussion instead of waiting for their "turn" (Irvine, 1990). Teachers who subscribe to the dominant culture are likely to see these behavioral patterns as examples of rudeness and disruptiveness, to respond with anger, and to invoke punitive measures. Alternatively, teachers who view the behaviors as reflections of cultural norms are better able to remain calm and nondefensive and to consider a variety of more constructive options (e.g., discussing classroom norms and the need for turn taking in large groups). Indeed, they may actually come to see the benefits of allowing intensity and passion to be expressed in the classroom and broaden their definition of what is acceptable student behavior.

In addition, culturally responsive classroom managers examine the ways that race and ethnicity influence the use of disciplinary consequences. Research conducted over 25 years repeatedly shows that African American youngsters, particularly males, are disproportionately referred for behavior problems compared to their majority counterparts (Skiba & Rausch, 2006). In fact, recent analyses (Raffaele Mendez & Knoff, 2003) have found out-of-school suspension rates for African American elementary school students that are between four and seven times greater than for European Americans.

What accounts for this disproportionality? One obvious explanation is that Black students violate class and school norms more often than their White peers. If this is the case, then disproportionate punishment is an appropriate response to inappropriate behavior, rather than an indicator of bias. Research on student behavior, race, and discipline, however, has yielded no evidence to support this explanation. In fact, studies suggest that African American students tend to receive harsher punishments for less severe behaviors (Skiba & Rausch, 2006). In addition, it appears that White students are referred to the office more frequently for "objective" offenses, such as vandalism, leaving without permission, and obscene language, while Black students are referred more often for "subjective" offenses—disrespect, excessive noise, and threat (Skiba, Michael, Nardo, and Peterson, 2002). In sum, it does not appear that racial disparities in school discipline are due to higher rates of misbehavior on the part of African American students. Instead, the evidence indicates that African American students are sent to the office and given punitive disciplinary consequences for less serious or more subjective reasons (Skiba & Rausch, 2006).

The implication is clear: In order to be a culturally responsive classroom manager, teachers need to acknowledge their biases and values and think about how these affect their interactions with students. As Weinstein, Curran, and Tomlinson-Clarke (2003) suggest, teachers need to ask themselves hard questions:

> "Am I more patient and encouraging with some? Am I more likely to reprimand others? Do I expect African American and Latino children to be disruptive? Do I use hair style and dress to form stereotypical judgments of my students' character and academic potential? When students violate norms, do I recommend suspension for students of color and parent conferences for students who are European American?" (p. 275)

 PAUSE AND REFLECT

Before reading about specific disciplinary interventions, think back to your own years as a student in elementary and high school. What disciplinary strategies did your most effective teachers use? What strategies did your least effective teachers use?

With these five principles in mind—preserving a safe, caring classroom environment; protecting the instructional program; considering the context; selecting a disciplinary strategy that matches the misbehavior; and being culturally responsive—we turn now to specific ways of responding to inappropriate behavior.

DEALING WITH MINOR MISBEHAVIOR

As I mentioned in Chapter 4, Jacob Kounin's (1970) classic study of orderly and disorderly classrooms gave research support to the belief that successful classroom managers have eyes in the back of their heads. Kounin found that effective managers knew what was going on all over the room; moreover, *their students knew they knew,* because the teachers were able to spot minor problems and "nip them in the bud." Kounin called this ability *"with-it-ness,"* a term that has since become widely used in discussions of classroom management.

How do "with-it" teachers deal with minor misbehavior? How do they succeed in nipping problems in the bud? This section discusses both nonverbal and verbal interventions and then considers the times when it may be better to do nothing at all. (Suggestions are summarized in the Practical Tips box.)

Nonverbal Interventions

A while back, an 11-year-old I know announced that she could be a successful teacher. When I asked why she was so confident, she replied: "I know how to make *the look.*" She proceeded to demonstrate: her eyebrows slanted downward, her forehead creased, and her lips flattened into a straight line. She definitely had "the look" down pat.

The "teacher look" is a good example of an unobtrusive, nonverbal intervention. Making eye contact, using hand signals (e.g., thumbs down; pointing to what the individual should be doing), and moving closer to the misbehaving student are other nonverbal ways of communicating with-it-ness. Nonverbal interventions all convey the message, "I see what you're doing, and I don't like it," but since they are

---

PRACTICAL TIPS FOR

DEALING WITH MINOR MISBEHAVIOR

- Use a nonverbal intervention such as:
    Facial expressions.
    Eye contact.
    Hand signals.
    Proximity.

- Use a nondirect verbal intervention:
    State the student's name.
    Incorporate the name into the lesson.
    Call on the student to participate.
    Use gentle humor.
    Use an I-message.

- Use a direct verbal intervention:
    Give a succinct command.
    Remind students about a rule.
    Give a choice between behaving appropriately or receiving penalty.

- Ignore the misbehavior (but only if it is minor and fleeting).

less directive than verbal commands, they encourage students to assume responsibility for getting back on task. Watch Donnie:

Donnie is at the board demonstrating how to construct congruent segments and congruent angles. Students are supposed to be following along, constructing congruent segments with rulers and compasses. Instead of working, two boys sit twirling their rulers on their pencils. Donnie notices what they are doing, but continues with her explanation. While she's talking, she gives the two boys a long, hard stare. They put down the rulers and get to work.

Nonverbal strategies are most appropriate for behaviors that are minor but persistent: frequent or sustained whispering, staring into space, calling out, putting on makeup, and passing notes. The obvious advantage of using nonverbal cues is that you can deal with misbehaviors like these without distracting other students. In short, nonverbal interventions enable you to protect and continue your lesson with minimum disruption.

A nonverbal cue is sometimes all that's needed to stop a misbehavior and get a student back "on task." In fact, a study of six middle school teachers (Lasley, Lasley, & Ward, 1989) found that the *most successful responses to misbehavior were nonverbal.* These strategies stopped misbehavior 79 percent of the time; among the three "more effective managers," the success rate was even higher—an amazing 95 percent.

Verbal Interventions

Sometimes you find yourself in situations where it's just not possible to use a nonverbal cue. Perhaps you can't catch the student's eye, or you're working with a small group, and it would be too disruptive to get up and walk across the room to the misbehaving individual. Other times, you're able to use a nonverbal cue, but it's unsuccessful in stopping the misbehavior.

In cases like this, you might use a *nondirective verbal intervention.* These allow you to prompt the appropriate behavior, while leaving the responsibility for figuring out what to do with the misbehaving student. For example, *simply saying the student's name* might be enough to get the student back on task. Sometimes it's possible to *incorporate the student's name* into the ongoing instruction:

Shaheed is slouching down in his seat and appears inattentive. As Fred talks about respect for the elderly in China, he moves closer to him. "Let's say Shaheed was my son, and I beat him up because he was getting a failing grade in class. What happens to me?" Shaheed sits up and "tunes in."

If the misbehavior occurs while a group discussion or recitation is going on, *you can call on the student to answer a question.* Consider the following example:

The class is going over homework on isosceles triangles. As Donnie calls on students to do the problems, she walks through the room. "OK, we need someone to do number 14." Hands begin to go up. Donnie notices

a girl in the back of the room who is gazing off into space. "Dominica, please do number 14." Dominica "comes back" from wherever she was, looks at the book, and answers correctly. Donnie smiles, "Good!"

Calling on a student allows you to communicate that you know what's going on and to capture the student's attention—without even citing the misbehavior. But keep in mind what we said earlier about preserving students' dignity. If you are obviously trying to "catch" students and to embarrass them, the strategy may well backfire by creating resentment (Good & Brophy, 1994). One way to avoid this problem is to alert the student that you will be calling on him or her to answer the *next question:* "Sharon, what's the answer to number 18? Taysha, the next one's yours."

The *use of humor* can provide another "gentle" way of reminding students to correct their behavior. Used well, humor can show them that you are able to understand the funny sides of classroom life. But you must be careful that the humor is not tinged with sarcasm that can hurt students' feelings.

It's near the end of the year, and Fred's students obviously have a case of "senioritis." They have just entered the room, and Fred is trying to get them to settle down. "Ladies and gentlemen, I know it's almost the end of the year, but could we make believe we're students now?"

An *"I-message"* is another way of verbally prompting appropriate behavior without giving a direct command. I-messages generally contain three parts. First, the teacher *describes the unacceptable behavior in a nonblaming, nonjudgmental way.* This phrase often begins with "when": "When people talk while I'm giving directions . . ." The second part describes the *tangible effect on the teacher:* "I have to repeat the directions and that wastes time . . . " Finally, the third part of the message states the *teacher's feelings* about the tangible effect: "and I get frustrated." Consider these examples of I-messages:

> "When you come to class without your supplies, I can't start the lesson on time, and I get really irritated."
> "When you leave your book bag in the middle of the aisle, I can trip over it, and I'm afraid I'll break a leg."

Although I-messages ideally contain all three parts in the recommended sequence, I-messages in any order, or even with one part missing, can still be effective (Gordon, 1974). I've witnessed the four teachers use "abbreviated" I-messages. For example, Fred communicates how strongly he feels about paying attention when he tells his class: "If you pass notes while I'm lecturing, I'll become suicidal." To a student who called him by his first name, he says, "I really feel uncomfortable when you call me by my first name in school."

There are several benefits to using this approach. In contrast to typical "you-messages" (e.g., "You are being rude," "You ought to know better," "You're acting like a baby"), I-messages minimize negative evaluations of the student. They make it easier to avoid using extreme (and usually inaccurate) words like *always* and *never* (as in "You *always* forget to do your homework" or "You're *never* prepared for class"). For these reasons, they foster and preserve a positive relationship between people. Since I-messages leave decisions about changing behavior up to students, this approach is also likely to promote a sense of responsibility and autonomy. In addition, I-messages show students that their behavior has consequences and that teachers are people with genuine feelings. Unlike you-messages, I-messages don't make students defensive and stubborn; thus, they may be more willing to change their behavior.

Most of us are not used to speaking this way, so I-messages can seem awkward and artificial. With practice, however, using I-messages can become natural. I once heard a four-year-old girl (whose parents had consistently used I-messages at home) tell her nursery school peer: "When you poke me with that pencil, it really hurts, and I feel bad 'cause I think you don't want to be my friend."

In addition to these nondirective approaches, there are also *more directive strategies* that you can try. Indeed, these may be particularly appropriate for African American students and students from working-class families. Lisa Delpit, African American author of *Other People's Children: Cultural Conflict in the Classroom* (1995), observes that framing directives as questions (e.g., "Would you like to sit down now?") is a particularly mainstream, middle-class (and female) way of speaking, designed to foster a more egalitarian and nonauthoritarian climate. According to Delpit,

> Many kids will not respond to that structure because commands are not couched as questions in their home culture. Rather than asking questions, some teachers need to learn to say, "Put the scissors away" and "Sit down now" or "Please sit down now." (Valentine, 1998, p. 17)

As Delpit suggests, the most straightforward approach is to *direct students to the task at hand* ("Get to work on that math problem"; "Your group should be discussing the first three pages"). You can also *remind the student about the rule* or behavioral expectation that is being violated (e.g., "When someone is talking, everyone else is supposed to be listening"). Sometimes, if inappropriate behavior is fairly widespread, it's useful to review rules with the entire group. This is often true after a holiday, a weekend, or a vacation.

Another strategy is to *give students a choice between behaving appropriately or receiving a penalty* for continued inappropriate behavior (e.g., "If you can't handle working in your group, you'll have to return to your seats"; "You either choose to raise your hand instead of calling out, or you will be choosing not to participate in our discussion"). Statements like these not only warn students that a penalty will be invoked if the inappropriate behavior continues, they also emphasize that students have real choices about how to behave and that penalties are not imposed without reason. In the following example, we see how Fred embellishes this strategy with a little humor:

The bell rings; Fred moves to the front of the room and tries to get his students' attention. They continue talking. "Ladies and gentlemen, if you want a zero for life, talk now. If you don't, listen." Students laugh and settle down.

Deliberately Ignoring the Misbehavior

If misbehavior is extremely brief and unobtrusive, the best course of action may be *inaction*. For example, during a discussion a student may be so eager to comment that she forgets to raise her hand; or someone becomes momentarily distracted and inattentive; or two boys quietly exchange a comment while you're giving directions. In cases like these, an intervention can be more disruptive than the students' behavior.

One risk of ignoring minor misbehavior is that students may conclude you're unaware of what's going on. Suspecting that you're not "with-it," they may decide to see how much they can get away with, and then problems are sure to escalate. You need to monitor your class carefully to make sure this doesn't happen.

Another problem is that occasional ignoring can turn into full-fledged "blindness." This was vividly demonstrated in a study of a student teacher named Heleen (Créton, Wubbels, & Hooymayers, 1989). When Heleen was lecturing, her students frequently became noisy and inattentive. In response, Heleen talked more loudly and looked more at the chalkboard, turning her back on her students. She did not allow herself to see or hear the disorder—perhaps because it was too threatening and she didn't know how to handle it. Unfortunately, Heleen's students seemed to interpret her "blindness" as an indication that noise was allowed, and they became even more disorderly. Heleen eventually recognized the importance of "seeing" and responding to slight disturbances, in order to prevent them from escalating.

DEALING WITH MORE SERIOUS MISBEHAVIOR: USING PENALTIES

Sometimes, nonverbal cues or verbal reminders are not enough to convince students that you're serious about the behavioral expectations that you've established. And sometimes misbehavior is just too serious to use these kinds of low-level responses. In cases like these, it may be necessary to impose a penalty in order to enforce your expectations for appropriate behavior.

In some cases, teachers discuss penalties when they teach rules and procedures, so students understand the consequences of violating a rule from the very beginning. We saw Sandy do this with her students in Chapter 4, when she laid out the penalties for coming late to class. This practice prevents unpleasant "surprises," and hopefully minimizes protests of blissful ignorance—"But you didn't *tell* me that would happen!"

Selecting Penalties

It's often difficult for beginning teachers to decide on appropriate penalties. One student teacher in social studies recently vented his frustration in this way:

> *These two kids come to class every day and sit and do absolutely nothing. They don't create a big disturbance, and they're not really nasty or belligerent; they just won't do any work. They prefer to sit there and talk, and draw cartoons, and goof off. I keep telling them they're getting a zero for each day they just sit, and that they're going to fail for the marking*

period, but they just don't care. I've told them I'm going to call their parents, but they just laugh. I don't want to send them to the disciplinarian's office, because my cooperating teacher says I could get a reputation as a teacher who can't control the class, and I'd really like to get a job in this district. So I'm really at a loss. These kids are really smart, and I hate to see them fail. But what can I do?

During one meeting, I posed this question to all four teachers and learned about the types of penalties that they typically use. The question brought a variety of responses, but one theme emerged clearly. In Fred's words:

It's important to remember that the goal of a penalty is not to hurt kids, but to help them change their behavior. It's not to put kids down; it's to bring them up. If kids see that, then they'll accept the penalty. But if the behavior doesn't change, it's not a good penalty, no matter what it is.

With this idea in mind, let's consider the seven categories into which these teachers' penalties generally fall.

Mandatory Private Conferences

When students do not respond to nonverbal cues or verbal reminders, our teachers generally call a private conference, often after school or during a free period. During these conferences, they express their disappointment in the student's behavior. We normally don't think of this as a penalty, but since students in these classes really like their teachers, they feel bad when their teachers are upset. In serious, almost sorrowful tones, our teachers express their disappointment and surprise at the inappropriate behavior and direct students to think about the consequences of their actions. Sometimes, they will negotiate a plan for change, trying to get the students to take responsibility for their behavior. For example, when a student in Sandy's class failed a test, she held a private conference with him after school. Sandy shares this account of their meeting:

We talked about how he had been doing in class, and what had happened in this particular exam. It turned out that he had gone clubbing until 11:30 the night before the test. I told him, 'Well, that was your choice, and this was the outcome. What do you think? Do you like this outcome?' Obviously he didn't. We agreed that the next time there was a test, he wouldn't stay out late the night before and see if it makes a difference. I really think it's important to approach teenagers this way—to put the responsibility back on them whenever possible.

Loss of Privileges

Sometimes, students lose the right to sit wherever they like, particularly if their behavior is having a negative impact on other students. Other privileges that can be taken away include working with a friend, free time, chewing gum, freely moving around the room, and joining in a class popcorn party.

Isolation from the Group

All four teachers will move students to an isolated or secluded area of the room if they are unable to work productively, but they try to be positive rather than negative about the move. Fred will signal a student to move to a place that's "less distracting." When Sandy covered a seventh-grade class, she sometimes had to tell a student, "Come with me. Let's go to the back of the class and see what you can do back here where you can concentrate better. This will be your own private office." This strategy can be particularly effective with students who suffer from attention deficit/hyperactivity disorder (ADHD). These students have trouble dealing with the distraction and stimulation of the typical classroom environment; moving temporarily to a secluded area of the room can provide a much needed opportunity to refocus.

Exclusion from Class

All four teachers believe that "kicking kids out" is a strategy that should be reserved for major disruption. As Donnie points out, "Some students *want* to get out; they'll provoke a teacher just so they can leave the room. I know teachers who throw kids out all the time, but what's the point? Kids can't learn if they're in the office."

Despite their preference for handling problems within the room, the teachers recognize that there are times when this is just not possible. Sandy remembers how she sent a student to the "time-out" room when his behavior was so infuriating that she couldn't discuss it calmly: "I was so mad, I knew I was losing it. I was yelling, and the kid was yelling. So it was better for him to be out of the room. But 10 minutes later, I called and told him to come back. By then we had both cooled down and we were able to talk." Sandy has also worked out a system with another teacher so that she can send a student to his classroom if necessary. In the other room, the student must sit quietly and do chemistry work, ignored by both teacher and students.

Fred also sends students to the office if their behavior is really out of control. He recalls one student who was severely disturbed:

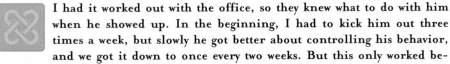

I had it worked out with the office, so they knew what to do with him when he showed up. In the beginning, I had to kick him out three times a week, but slowly he got better about controlling his behavior, and we got it down to once every two weeks. But this only worked because class was a good place to be. He had friends there, we laughed every day, he got to do good stuff. If he hadn't liked it—and me—getting to leave would have been a reward.

Detention

For routine violations of rules (e.g., coming late to class), Donnie, Sandy, and Fred use regular school detention as a penalty. However, they are cautious about using this for "big" problems. As Sandy puts it, "If students are disrespectful, or really having problems controlling themselves, I prefer to talk privately with them. What's going to be learned from 45 minutes of detention?"

Written Reflections on the Problem

Sometimes, a situation is so complex that it warrants serious reflection in writing. Fred recalls this incident:

 My senior honors class was supposed to do a short research paper on China. When I began to grade the papers, it seemed to me that a lot of the citations were suspicious. I did some checking and found that some students had simply lifted material from the Web and made up the references. I went into class and told them how serious this was, and how they would all get zeros for their papers if they couldn't validate their references. But I gave them a way out: they could write a letter to me explaining what they had done and why, and they had to make 'reparation' by doing two additional research papers with valid citations. The letters were really revealing. A lot of these kids were absolutely clueless about why it's important to reference accurately. One kid came in and thanked me for making a big deal about this. He said he really didn't know that what he was doing was dishonest.

Contacting Parents

Donnie, Sandy, Christina, and Fred all contact parents or guardians if a student shows a pattern of consistent misbehavior. For example, when a student in Sandy's class repeatedly "forgot" to do his homework, Sandy told him she would be calling his parents to discuss the problem. She tried to make it clear that she was calling not in anger but out of serious concern. She also wanted to convey the idea that "between all of us, maybe we can help you get it together."

These penalties illustrate the ways Christina, Donnie, Fred, and Sandy choose to deal with problems when they have a degree of flexibility. In addition, there are times when they are required to follow school policies mandating particular responses to specific misbehaviors. Consider the example of cutting class. In Christina's school, two instances of cutting a class result in no credit earned for that course. In Fred's school, one cut requires parental notification and a warning letter; two cuts result in "student/counselor contact" and "administrator/parent contact," a possible conference, and a warning letter. The third cut requires removal from class with a grade of AW (administrative withdrawal) and placement in study hall.

It's also important to note that under the federal education legislation, *No Child Left Behind,* schools must have a plan for keeping schools safe and drug free. These plans must include discipline policies that prohibit disorderly conduct, the illegal possession of weapons, and the illegal use, possession, distribution, and sale of tobacco, alcohol, and other drugs. As a result, almost all schools now have *"zero tolerance"* policies with predetermined consequences for such offenses. Zero tolerance may also be applied to other problems, like bullying and threatening. Such policies usually result in automatic suspension or expulsion, although there may still be wide variation in severity. Be sure to familiarize yourself with the zero tolerance policies in your school.

If you have students with disabilities in your classes, it's also essential that you consult with a special educator or a member of the child study team about appropriate intervention strategies. Serious behavior problems require a team effort, and parents, special education teachers, psychologists, social workers, and administrators can all provide valuable insights and suggestions. Also be aware that the Individuals with Disabilities Education Act (recently reauthorized as IDEA 2004) includes several stipulations about the rights of students with disabilities with respect to disciplinary procedures. For example, if the problematic behavior is "caused by" or has a "direct and substantial relationship" to the child's disability, removing the student for more than 10 school days may not be allowed.

Selecting Penalties That Are Logical Consequences

Whenever possible, penalties should be *logically related to the misbehavior* (Curwin & Mendler, 1988; Dreikurs, Grunwald, & Pepper, 1982). For example, when a student in Christina's class failed to work constructively in his small group, he had to work by himself until he indicated a readiness to cooperate. Similarly, if students make a mess in the home economics kitchen, a logical penalty would be to make them clean it up. If an individual forgets her book and can't do the assignment, she must borrow someone's book and do the assignment during free period. A student who hands in a carelessly done paper has to rewrite it.

Dreikurs, Grunwald, and Pepper (1982) distinguish logical consequences like these from traditional punishments, which bear no relationship to the misbehavior involved. An example of such a traditional punishment would be to have students write "I will not come late to class" 50 times. Here are some other examples of punishments that are unrelated to the offense:

- A student continually whispers to her neighbor. Instead of isolating the student (a logical consequence), the teacher makes her do an additional homework assignment.
- A student forgets to get his parent's permission to go on a field trip. Instead of having the student write a letter home to parents about the need to sign the permission slip (a logical consequence), the teacher gives him detention.
- A student continually calls out during a whole-class discussion. Instead of having him make a cue-card to post on his desk ("I won't call out") or not allowing him to participate in the discussion, the teacher gives him an F for the day.

According to Dreikurs and his colleagues, punishment is likely to be seen as an arbitrary exercise of power by a dictatorial teacher. Sometimes, youngsters do not even associate the punishment with the misbehavior, but rather with the punisher. Instead of teaching students about the unpleasant results of their inappropriate behavior, unrelated punishments teach students only to make certain they don't get caught the next time around!

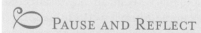 PAUSE AND REFLECT

Review the various penalties that our four teachers generally use when dealing with inappropriate behavior. Which ones would you be most inclined to implement? Are there any with which you disagree?

Imposing Penalties

It's frustrating when students misbehave, and sometimes we let our frustration color the way we impose penalties. I've seen teachers scream at students from across the room, lecture students on their history of misbehavior, insinuate that they come from terrible homes, and attack their personalities. Clearly, behavior like this destroys students' dignity and ruins the possibility of a good relationship. How can you avoid creating a situation like this?

First, if you're feeling really angry at a student, *delay the discussion*. You can simply say to the individual, "Sit there and think about what happened. I'll talk to you in a few minutes." During one observation in Fred's room, it was clear that he was becoming really annoyed at two students who were talking while he was introducing a film the class was about to watch. Twice during his comments he turned and told them to stop talking, but their conversation would begin again. I watched with curiosity to see if he would do anything further, but he continued the lesson. At the end of the period, however, he promptly went over and quietly spoke with the two offending students. Later, he reflected on their conversation:

> I told them I couldn't talk while they were talking, that it distracted me and made me really mad—especially since I was talking about Gandhi, who's one of my favorite guys. They apologized; they said they had been talking about some of the ideas that had come up in class. I told them I was really glad they were so excited, but they had to share their thoughts with the whole class, or wait until after class to talk. I think they got the message. Talking with them after class had three advantages: It allowed me to continue with my lesson, it gave me a chance to calm down, and it made it possible to talk to them privately.

As Fred's comments point out, by delaying discussion, you have a chance to calm down and to think about what you want to say. You'll also be more able to separate the student's character from the student's behavior. Your message must be: "*You're* okay, but your *behavior* is unacceptable."

Second, it's a good idea to *impose penalties privately, calmly, and quietly*. Despite the temptation to yell and scream, the softer your voice and the closer you stand, the more effective you tend to be (Bear, 1998). Remember, students are very concerned about saving face in front of their peers. Public sanction may have the advantage of "making an example" out of one student's misbehavior, but it has the disadvantage of creating resentment and embarrassment. Numerous studies (e.g., Turco & Elliott, 1986) have found that students view public reprimand as the *least acceptable method* of dealing with problems. Furthermore, the ability to be firm without using threats and public humiliation appears to be particularly important for students who are already disaffected or alienated from school. Schlosser (1992), for example, interviewed 31 "marginal" junior high school students judged to be at risk of school failure. Students considered teachers to be uncaring and unfair adversaries if they "engaged in public acts intended to convey an impression of authority: making examples of specific students, sending students from the room, and ordering compliance" (p. 135).

Our four teachers agree. Sandy observes:

> Let's say you've just given back some paper you graded. A student looks at
> his or her paper, crumples it up, and throws it on the floor. If you yell,
> "Pick that paper up," you've created a confrontational situation. It's a
> lot better to go over and talk privately and calmly. If you say something
> like, "If you have a problem with your grade, we can talk about it," then the kid
> doesn't lose face. It's really important not to back students into a corner; if you
> do, they'll come out fighting and create an even bigger problem than before.

Finally, after imposing a penalty, it's a good idea to get back to the student and
reestablish a positive relationship. At the beginning of this chapter, we saw how
Sandy made a point of helping William with his lab experiment after giving him detention. Similarly, complimenting a student's work or patting a back communicates
that there are no hard feelings.

The Issue of Consistency

As Emmer, Evertson, and Worsham (2000) note, "The dictum 'be consistent' has
been repeated more frequently than the pledge of allegiance" (p. 134). Beginning
teachers are taught that if they do not consistently enforce the rules, students will
become confused, will begin to test the limits, and misbehavior will escalate.

There is research evidence to support this emphasis on consistency. Recall
Evertson and Emmer's (1982) study of effective classroom management on the junior high level (discussed in Chapter 4). This study showed that more successful
managers responded in a consistent, predictable fashion, often invoking the rules
or procedures in order to stop the disruptive behavior. In contrast, the ineffective
managers were more likely to act inconsistently: Sometimes they ignored the behavior; sometimes they invoked a prestated consequence (e.g., detention); sometimes they warned students of penalties, but then didn't act on their warnings. In-
evitably, behavior problems increased in frequency and severity.

Although the importance of being consistent is obvious, teachers sometimes
feel trapped by the need for consistency. (See the discussion in Chapter 3 about
being fair.) When a normally conscientious student forgets a homework assignment, it seems unreasonable to send the same note home to parents that you
would send if a student repeatedly missed assignments. In order to get out of this
bind, it's desirable to develop a *hierarchy of consequences* that can be invoked if
rules are violated. Some teachers develop a graduated list of generic consequences that can be applied to all misbehaviors. Consider the following hierarchy
as an example:

First violation:	Verbal warning
Second violation:	Name is written down
Third time:	Private conference with teacher
Fourth time:	Call parents

Another approach is to develop a graduated list of consequences for individual
classroom rules. Sandy used this approach when she developed her graduated list

of consequences for coming late (see Chapter 4), and she makes sure to enforce the consequences no matter who is involved. She tells us:

> Kids have got to see that you're fair. If my best student walks through that door late, I have to give the same detention that I'd give to my worst student. If I don't give detention, the kids will see that and think to themselves, "She's playing favorites. She's letting him get away with coming late." That's the end of my relationship with them.

Although all four teachers are absolutely consistent when dealing with straightforward behaviors like coming late, they consider these the "little problems." With the "big things," they prefer to talk privately with students and to develop a plan of action that is tailored to the individual student. By holding mandatory private conferences, the four teachers can show students they are consistent in terms of enforcing class rules and dealing with problem behavior, but they can remain flexible with respect to the solution.

Penalizing the Group for Individual Misbehavior

Sometimes teachers impose a consequence on the whole class even if only one or two individuals have been misbehaving. The hope is that other students will be angry at receiving a penalty when they weren't misbehaving and will exert pressure on their peers to behave. Our four teachers are unanimous in their negative response to this practice. Donnie observes, "If you even attempt to do this, students will be furious. You'll alienate the whole class." And Fred puts it this way: "I do this when I'm teaching about the causes of revolutions. It's a great way to foment a rebellion!"

DEALING WITH CHRONIC MISBEHAVIOR

Some students with persistent behavior problems fail to respond to the routine strategies we have described so far: nonverbal cues, verbal reminders, and penalties. What additional strategies are available? In this section, we consider three different approaches. First, we examine a *problem-solving strategy,* which views inappropriate behavior as a conflict to be resolved through discussion and negotiation. Next, we take a look at *four self-management approaches based on principles of behavior modification*—namely, self-monitoring, self-evaluation, self-instruction, and contingency contracting. Finally, we discuss an unconventional strategy called "*reframing,*" in which teachers formulate a positive interpretation of problem behavior and then act in ways that are consistent with that interpretation (Molnar & Lindquist, 1989).

Resolving Conflicts through Problem Solving

Most teachers think in terms of winning or losing when they think about classroom conflicts. According to Thomas Gordon, author of *T.E.T.—Teacher Effectiveness Training,*

> This win–lose orientation seems to be at the core of the knotty issue of discipline in schools. Teachers feel that they have only two approaches to choose from: They

can be strict or lenient, tough or soft, authoritarian or permissive. They see the teacher–student relationship as a power struggle, a contest, a fight.... When conflicts arise, as they always do, most teachers try to resolve them so that they win, or at least don't lose. This obviously means that students end up losing, or at least not winning. (1974, p. 183)

A third alternative is a "no-lose" problem-solving method of conflict resolution (Gordon, 1974) consisting of six steps. In Step 1, the teacher and the student (or students) *define the problem.* In Step 2, everyone *brainstorms possible solutions.* As in all brainstorming activities, suggestions are not evaluated at this stage. In Step 3, the *solutions are evaluated:* "Now let's take a look at all the solutions that have been proposed and decide which we like and which we don't like. Do you have some preferences?" It is important that you state your own opinions and preferences. Do not permit a solution to stand if it is not really acceptable to you. In Step 4, you and the students involved *decide on the solution that you will try.* If more than one student is involved, it is tempting to vote on the solution, but that's probably not a good idea. Voting always produces winners and losers unless the vote is unanimous, so some people leave the discussion feeling dissatisfied. Instead, try to work for consensus.

Once you have decided which solution to try, you move to Step 5 and *determine how to implement the decision:* who will do what by when. Finally, in Step 6, *the solution is evaluated.* You may want to call everybody together again and ask, "Are you still satisfied with our solution?" It is important that everyone realize that decisions are not chiseled in granite and that they can be discarded in search of a better solution to the problem.

During one meeting, Donnie explained how she used problem solving when some of her students were not sitting in their assigned places during assemblies:

 Whenever there's an assembly program, we're supposed to walk together to the auditorium and sit together. But it's crowded in the halls on the way to the auditorium, and everyone "loses" kids; someone has darted here or there, joined another class, faded into the crowd. By the time we get to the auditorium, the kids are scattered all over. They sit with other classes, and they act up. The teachers don't really know who they are, and sometimes the kids even give wrong names when the teachers ask. The behavior in assembly programs can be really bad. I decided this was a problem that we had to deal with before another assembly program was held.

I told the class that I felt this was a problem, and they agreed. Then I explained that we were going to brainstorm solutions. Boy, these kids can really be hard on each other! They came up with about eight different solutions:

Kick the offenders out of the assemblies.
Don't let past offenders go to assemblies at all.
Suspension.
Kids have to get permission to sit with another class.
Bring your friend to sit with you and your class (your friend would have to have special permission from his/her teacher).
Invite parents to assemblies (kids would act better).
Take attendance once you get to the assembly.
Have a buddy system.

The next day, we talked about each of these possible solutions, focusing on how they would affect everyone. I told them I didn't like the one about kicking people out of the assemblies because assembly programs were part of their education. I also explained that teachers don't have the right to suspend students, and if we chose that one, we'd have to get the disciplinarian involved. The kids said they could live with getting permission, and they also liked the buddy system. They said buddies should also have the responsibility of telling the person next to them to stop if he or she was disruptive. So we agreed to try those two. We also agreed that I would use the "teacher look" technique if I saw kids acting up and then write up a referral to the disciplinarian if they didn't stop.

We haven't had an assembly program yet, so I don't know how this is going to work, but I think it was good to get the kids involved in trying to solve the problem. Maybe they'll be more interested in trying to improve the situation.

Approaches Based on Principles of Behavior Modification

Behavior modification programs involve the systematic use of reinforcement to strengthen desired behavior. Probably more research has focused on the effectiveness of behavior modification than any other classroom management approach, and dozens of books on behavior modification techniques are available for teachers (e.g., Alberto & Troutman, 2006; Zirpoli, 2005).

More recently, however, educators have come to view full-blown behavior modification approaches as ill-suited for most regular classroom teachers. First of all, a single teacher working with a class of 25 or 30 students cannot possibly keep track of—let alone systematically reinforce—all the desirable behaviors each student exhibits (Brophy, 1983). Secondly, in order to extinguish inappropriate behavior that is maintained by teacher attention, behavior modification calls for teachers to ignore the behavior. Although this is effective in one-to-one situations, ignoring misbehavior in the crowded, public environment of the classroom can cause problems to escalate (an issue that was discussed earlier). This is even more likely to occur if teachers forget that ignoring is not a behavior management strategy by itself, but must be paired with attention for positive and appropriate behaviors. Finally, traditional behavior modification techniques emphasize external control by the teacher, rather than trying to foster internal control by the student.

For all of these reasons, educators recommend behavioral approaches that involve the student in *self-management:* self-monitoring, self-evaluation, self-instruction, and contingency contracting. Self-management strategies have been reported to be effective with children from preschool through secondary school, with and without identified disabilities, and for a wide variety of problem behaviors, both academic and social (Shapiro, DuPaul & Bradley-Klug, 1998; Smith & Sugai, 2000). The goal of self-management is to help students learn to regulate their own behavior. The perception of control is crucial in this process: When we feel in control, we are much more likely to accept responsibility for our actions.

The next section of the chapter describes the behavioral approaches that rely on self-management. In the next chapter, I summarize *functional behavioral assessment,* another approach based on behavioral principles.

Self-Monitoring

Some students may not realize how often they're out of their seats or how frequently they sit daydreaming instead of focusing on their work. Others may be unaware of how often they call out during class discussions or how many times they make nasty comments to other members of their small group. Youngsters like this may benefit from a self-monitoring program, in which they learn to observe and record a targeted behavior during a designated period of time. Interestingly, self-monitoring can have positive effects even when students are *inaccurate* (Graziano & Mooney, 1984).

Before beginning a self-monitoring program, you need to make sure that students can identify the behaviors targeted for change. For example, some students may not be able to accurately describe all the component parts of "working independently." You may have to model, explicitly noting that "When I work independently, I am sitting down (without tilting back in my chair), I am looking at the paper on my desk, and I am holding my pencil in my hand."

Students then learn how to observe and record their own behavior. Recording can be done in two ways. The first approach has individuals tally each time they engage in the targeted behavior. For example, students can learn to chart the number of math problems they complete during an in-class assignment, the number of times they blurt out irrelevant comments during a discussion, or the number of times they raise their hand to speak. For middle school children, the tally sheet might contain pictures of the appropriate and inappropriate behaviors. (See the "countoon" suggested by Jones and Jones, 2001, in Figure 11.1.) In the second approach, individuals observe and record the targeted behavior at regular intervals. At the designated time, for instance, students can mark a recording sheet with a

Figure 11.1   An Example of a "Countoon"

Source: Vernon F. Jones and Louise S. Jones, *Comprehensive classroom management: Creating communities of support and solving problems,* 6th ed. Copyright 2001 by Allyn and Bacon. Reprinted with permission.

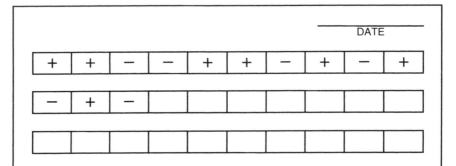

At the top of the page are several rows of squares. At different times during the period (whenever you think of it but don't fill them all in at the same time) put down a "+" if you were studying, a "-" if you weren't. If, for example, you were ready to mark a square, you would ask yourself if—for the last few minutes—you had been studying and then you would put down a "+" if you had been or a "-" if you hadn't been studying.

Figure 11.2   The Recording Sheet Used by Liza

"1" or a "2," depending on whether they are engaged in appropriate or inappropriate behavior.

These two approaches are well-illustrated in an early study conducted by Broden, Hall, and Mitts (1971). In the first part of the study, Liza, an eighth-grade girl who had difficulty paying attention in history class, was directed to record her "study" or "on-task" behavior on the sheet shown in Figure 11.2. Before Liza began recording her behavior, she was on task only about 30 percent of the time. During the self-recording phases, Liza averaged on-task rates of 76 percent to 89 percent.

The second part of the study involved Stu, an eighth-grade boy whose math teacher wanted to find a way "to shut Stu up" (p. 195). According to the teacher, Stu continually talked out in class, disturbing both the teacher and the other students. Having Stu record his talking-out behavior on the simple form shown in Figure 11.3 led to a decrease in his calling out, although the self-monitoring seemed to lose its effectiveness after a while (possibly because the teacher never acknowledged Stu's improved behavior).

There has been some debate about whether self-management can be helpful for students diagnosed with ADHD, since "the lack of self-management skills can be viewed as a core deficit among individuals with this disorder" (Shapiro, DuPaul, & Bradley-Klug, 1998). Recent research, however, supports the use of these strategies. For example, Barry and Messer (2003) investigated the practicality and efficacy of self-monitoring for five middle school students with ADHD. According to their teacher, all five boys had limited attention spans, rarely completed in-class assignments, frequently wandered around the room, and engaged in loud, disruptive behavior. Students were taught to ask themselves a series of questions written on a data-collection sheet: "Was I in my seat or where I needed to be to complete my class work? Was I paying attention by working on the assignment or listening to the teacher? Did I complete my assignments? Did I play or fight with my classmates in

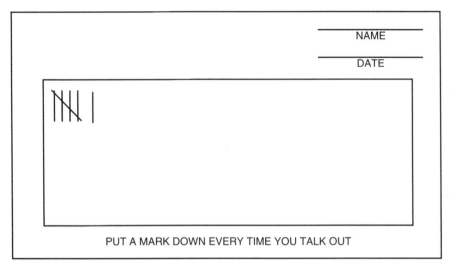

NAME

DATE

PUT A MARK DOWN EVERY TIME YOU TALK OUT

Figure 11.3   The Recording Sheet Used by Stu

the classroom? Did I talk loudly or make noise in class?" In individual conferences, the teacher went over each question and asked the student to describe an example of his behavior that would indicate occurrence or nonoccurrence. The teacher also modeled the on-task behaviors that were described and had the students practice recording data. Initially, the boys had to respond to the questions every 15 minutes, but this interval was gradually increased. Goals were set (e.g., 75 percent or more 15-minute intervals on task), and students earned simple reinforcers from the teacher such as snacks and increased computer time. Barry and Messer report that the use of self-monitoring was effective in increasing students' on-task behaviors and academic performance and decreasing disruptive behaviors. Moreover, the intervention was relatively easy to implement. The teacher's initial meeting with each student took only about 20 minutes; although some additional time was spent checking for accuracy and providing feedback to students, this time was gained back as students' behavior and academic work improved.

Self-Evaluation

This self-management approach goes beyond simple self-monitoring by requiring individuals to judge the quality or acceptability of their behavior (Hughes, Ruhl, & Misra, 1989). Sometimes self-evaluation is linked with reinforcement, so that an improvement in behavior brings points or rewards.

A study by Smith, Young, West, Morgan, and Rhode (1988) provides a good example of how these strategies can be used to reduce off-task, disruptive behavior. The study involved four students (ages 13 to 15) who spent half of each day in a special education resource room; three students were classified as behaviorally disordered, and one was classified as learning disabled. All four students were taught to rate how well they followed the resource room rules using a simple scale that went from zero ("unacceptable") to five ("excellent"). Ratings were converted to points that could be exchanged for snacks, school supplies, or magazines at the end of each class period. Since bonus points were earned when students' ratings closely matched their teacher's ratings, the students were rewarded not only for behaving well but also for rating themselves accurately.

By tracking students' behavior over time, the investigators were able to show that the self-evaluation procedures were extremely effective in decreasing students' inappropriate behavior in the resource room. Darren, for example, went from an average of 71 percent off-task, disruptive behavior to 17 percent. Sadly, the results weren't as impressive when self-evaluation was tried in the general education classes, where the teachers were less consistent in doing the ratings.

This study raises the question of whether self-evaluation strategies are feasible for use in inclusive general education classrooms where teachers are responsible for large numbers of students and often have little training in behavior management. In this regard, a study by Mitchem, Young, West, and Benyo (2001) is encouraging. The study took place in three seventh-grade inclusive language arts classrooms all taught by the same teacher; there were 31 students in the second-period class, and 33 each in the fourth- and seventh-period classes. From the three classes, 10 students were identified as target students based on a history of referrals for disruptive and/or off-task behavior, poor social skills, and poor grades. Using lesson plans and materials provided by the investigators, the teacher taught all students procedures for a ClassWide Peer-Assisted Self-Management (CWPASM) program, in which students evaluated their behavior using a rating system based on the school's citizenship grades: "H" (honors), "S" (satisfactory), "N" (needs improvement), and "U" (unsatisfactory). Training required from two to three periods, depending on the class. The teacher also assigned every student a partner based on her knowledge of students' personalities and preferences. During the implementation of the CWPASM program, students rated their own behavior and that of their partner every 10 minutes. Partners then compared their ratings and earned points for perfect or near-perfect ratings. The initial 10-minute interval was later lengthened to 20 minutes; eventually students did the ratings just once at the end of the period. The CWPASM program had an immediate and marked effect on both the classes as a whole and the 10 target students. The researchers write:

> Before CWPASM was introduced, it was rare to see the entire group on task at the same time for even one minute during the entire period. The teacher spent a substantial portion of the class period managing students, redirecting them to get on task, and repeating instructions. After CWPASM was introduced, group on-task behavior across all target classes increased from near zero levels to almost 80 percent. In practical terms, this meant that all students were on task at the same time for approximately 32 minutes of the 40-minute observation. Group on-task behavior continued to increase the longer the intervention was in effect.

Recently, Fred decided to try a self-evaluation procedure with a boy in his Contemporary World Issues class. Daniel was in serious danger of failing the course; although he was not disruptive, Daniel was consistently inattentive and rarely completed assignments. Fred and Daniel discussed self-evaluation, and Daniel was enthusiastic about trying it. Together, they designed a simple sheet, which they agreed

```
                    WHAT DID YOU DO IN CLASS?

1. How well did you behave?
        Were you attentive?
        Did you complete assignments?
        Did you contribute to class discussion?
        Did you think?
        Did you learn something?

2. What score would be accurate?        1      2     3     4
                                     (Excellent)        (Poor)


Monday:

Tuesday:

Wednesday:

Thursday:

Friday:
```

Figure 11.4   Daniel's Self-Evaluation Form

that Fred would keep and give to Daniel to fill out at the end of each class period. As you can see from Figure 11.4, the form requires Daniel to describe and evaluate his behavior. Fred describes how the self-evaluation procedure worked out:

> We did it faithfully for three weeks, and it really worked. Sometimes I forgot to give Daniel the self-evaluation sheet at the end of the period, and he actually reminded me. I took that as a sign of his commitment.
>
> His behavior really improved; he started paying attention and completing assignments for the first time all year. At the end of three weeks, Daniel was out for several days. When he got back, we didn't pick it up again, and I didn't push it. He was doing what he was supposed to be doing, without any monitoring.

Self-Instruction

The third self-management approach is self-instruction, in which students learn to give themselves silent directions about how to behave. Most self-instruction strategies are based on Meichenbaum's (1977) five-step process of cognitive behavior modification: (1) an adult performs a task while talking aloud about it, carefully describing each part; (2) the student performs the task while the adult talks aloud (overt, external guidance); (3) the student performs the task while talking aloud to self (overt self-guidance); (4) the student performs the task while whispering (faded, overt self-guidance); (5) the student performs the task while thinking the directions (covert, self-instruction). This approach has been used to teach impulsive students to approach tasks more deliberately, to help social isolates initiate peer activity, to teach aggressive students to control their anger, and to teach defeated students to try problem solving instead of giving up (Brophy, 1983).

There is evidence that even seriously emotionally disturbed adolescents can learn to engage in self-instruction. In a study conducted in a self-contained special education class (Ninness, Fuerst, Rutherford, & Glenn, 1991), three teenage males who displayed high rates of off-task and inappropriate behaviors (running, fighting, fondling, spitting, throwing objects, jumping, or inappropriate language) were given formal instruction in social skills and self-management for one hour a day. Students were taught to raise their hands to ask questions, to avoid distractions of other students, and to talk politely to teachers and students. While others played the role of distractors, students rehearsed overt statements such as "I'm not going to let him or her bother me. I'm going to keep doing my work," and they practiced avoiding eye contact with those who annoyed them. In addition, students were taught to evaluate their own on-task and socially appropriate behavior, using a scale ranging from one to four. A bonus point was awarded on any occasion in which a student's self-assessment was within one point of the teacher's assessment.

After five weeks, the training in social skills and self-management was discontinued, and a series of experimental conditions was begun. In one condition ("instructed"), students were left alone for 20 minutes in the classroom with instructions to assess and record their behavior. In a similar condition ("instructed under provocation"), students were told to self-manage while others deliberately tried to provoke and distract them. Two other conditions investigated students' behavior when the teacher left the room without giving explicit instructions to self-manage ("uninstructed" and "uninstructed under provocation").

The results of the study demonstrated that training in self-management can dramatically improve students' behavior. Prior to the training, off-task and socially inappropriate behavior in the classroom averaged 92 percent, 95 percent, and 76 percent for Subjects 1, 2, and 3, respectively. All three subjects improved substantially during the course of the five-week self-management training—and all three demonstrated *near-zero off-task or socially inappropriate behavior during the experimental situations.*

Before we leave the discussion of self-monitoring, self-evaluation, and self-instruction, it is important to note that these strategies hold particular promise for students with disabilities in general education settings. Only a handful of studies have been conducted in inclusive secondary classrooms, but they indicate that students with disabilities can be taught to use self-management to improve both their social and academic performance (McDougall, 1998). On the other hand, this training requires time and expertise that general education teachers may not have. If you decide to try one of these self-management strategies, you should consult with your school's psychologist, a counselor, or a special education teacher.

Contingency Contracting

A contingency or behavior contract is an agreement between a teacher and an individual student that specifies what the student must do to earn a particular reward. Contingency contracts are negotiated with students; both parties must agree on the behaviors students must exhibit, the period of time involved, and the rewards that will result. To be most effective, contracts should be written and signed.

Date _____

After discussion between Mr. Schroeder (social studies teacher) and Justin Mayer (student), the following decisions were reached:

During the next marking period, I, Justin Mayer, agree:

1. To be on time for U. S. History I, with book, notebook, and writing utensil.

2. To complete all homework assignments and to turn them in on time.

3. To meet with Mr. Schroeder after school on Thursdays to check on the progress of my quarterly project.

4. To sit on the other side of the room from Sam Holloway.

5. To pay attention during class.

If I meet these conditions, I will pass this class with a C or better for this marking period.

Student _____

Teacher _____

Parent _____

Figure 11.5   An Example of a Contract

And, of course, there should be an opportunity for review and renegotiation if the contract is not working. An example of a typical contract appears in Figure 11.5.

Using an Ecosystemic Approach: Changing Problem Behavior by Reframing

We often explain problem behavior by focusing on the characteristics of individual students (e.g., "He's insolent and sarcastic because he comes from a broken home"; "She never participates in class because she's so shy"). These explanations may have some validity, but they are unlikely to help us bring about positive change. Since we cannot alter a student's home environment or basic personality, we may conclude there is nothing we can do and fail to consider ways in which the social context of the classroom is contributing to the problem.

On the other hand, if we take an *ecosystemic perspective,* we recognize that problem behaviors are part of a stable pattern of interpersonal interactions. In other words, the classroom constitutes an *ecosystem,* in which every individual's behavior influences and is influenced by everyone else's behavior. According to Alex Molnar and Barbara Lindquist (1989), this is a more optimistic way of approaching problems, because it means that we can influence problem behaviors by making changes to the ecosystem. As they put it, "when you want something to change, you must change something" (p. 10).

Given the fact that behaviors can have multiple interpretations, Molnar and Lindquist suggest that a powerful way to change the ecosystem is to formulate an *alternative, positive interpretation of the problem behavior and to act in ways that are consistent with the new interpretation*. This technique is called *reframing*. Let's look at a few examples adapted from Molnar and Lindquist's book, *Changing Problem Behavior in Schools* (1989).

Problem behavior:	Brian continually blurts out answers during discussions.
Standard interpretation:	Brian is trying to get attention.
Standard response:	Teacher ignores Brian as long as possible, but eventually chastises him.
Alternative interpretation:	Brian is so intensely engaged in the discussion he forgets to raise his hand.
Problem behavior:	Shandra never participates in class discussions. She also takes a long time to get started on written classroom assignments, so she makes little progress by the end of class.
Standard interpretation:	Since Shandra is capable of doing the work, she is simply being resistant and lazy.
Standard response:	Teacher talks with Shandra about the importance of participating and doing classwork. When that doesn't work, teacher has conference with parents. Teacher also tries giving Shandra special attention for participation.
Alternative interpretation:	Shandra needs to think carefully before participating in discussions or doing written work. She wants to get all her thoughts together before speaking or writing. (Shandra is not resistant or lazy; she is careful and deliberate.)

Not all teachers will find these alternative interpretations plausible, but that doesn't matter. What *does* matter is that you generate an interpretation that is plausible to *you*. Then the *alternative frame can suggest alternative responses*. Reframing helps you to get "unstuck" from routine, unproductive ways of dealing with problem behavior and to consider fresh approaches that change the social context or ecosystem of the classroom. The following account was written by a student teacher who tried reframing:

Ruben is a sophomore in my English 2 class. He loves to be the center of attention. He is constantly disrupting the class by talking over me during a lesson. He also shouts across the room to his friend Oscar.... In addition, Ruben does not do any class work or homework on his own....

My initial reaction to Ruben's behavior was that of frustration. I thought he wanted to irritate me and the only way he knew how was to disrupt the entire class.... I tried several techniques to change his behavior. I started by separating Ruben from his friends, specifically Oscar, and putting his desk in the middle of a group of [other] students ... but it only made matters worse. He started talking ... to the students around him and now the yelling across the room got louder. Ruben would also copy the other students' work and hand it in. The second thing I did was to try to talk to him. I explained that I thought he was an intelligent boy, and that he should use his energy toward his success and stop disrupting me as well as the other students. I also told Ruben that I thought it was rude and he promised he would change. But within a few days, he went back to his old behavior. The third approach I took was reprimanding him. I gave Ruben detention and this made him behave for about 40 minutes of the class, but then his behavior reverted. I finally called in his mother, but once again his [good] behavior did not last. In the end I found myself frustrated and angry with him. I began to yell at him whenever he was out of control.

Ruben was taking too much of my class time and attention, and I was exhausted by the end of third period.... I decided to view this problem from a different perspective. I [reframed it this way]: Ruben performs better in class when he voices his opinion and demonstrates his understanding.... Since he likes and is good at using his speaking skills, I assigned him [the job of] classroom manager. As classroom manager, Ruben was able to walk around class checking homework assignments [and] taking attendance.... He was [also] allowed to open the journal topic discussion and have students share their journal entries for the first 10 minutes of class. He conducted the class in an organized fashion and he was able to interact with his fellow classmates....

Allowing Ruben to walk around the room and take responsibility for certain tasks gave him the chance to speak to his friend Oscar on the other side of the room as well as others. It also gave him a chance to voice his own opinion and thoughts, so the yelling mostly ceased to exist.... [I also think] that he wants to set a good example to his classmates and he does not want to be rude to me because he sees me as a companion who has given him the opportunity to utilize his skills.... His class work and homework have improved drastically. Ruben now wants to resign as classroom manager and he would like to choose the next one for the new marking period.

Wow! It really worked! I won't deny the fact that I thought the entire method ... was impossible. I was in need of a change for all of my students' sake and I was desperate. I am glad that I did try it because ... it made me realize that a problem behavior can change and [a student] can become an asset to my classroom setting. The change has not only improved my relationship with Ruben, but with the entire class.

In accordance with an ecosystemic perspective, this student teacher first recognizes her interpretation of Ruben's problem behavior: *He is trying to irritate her and disrupt the class, and he does not want to learn literature.* She also recognizes that this interpretation has led to unproductive responses. She and Ruben are in a rut, and a different approach is obviously needed. Although she is skeptical, she tries to reframe the situation. She formulates an alternative, positive interpretation of the behavior that she finds plausible: *Ruben needs to voice his opinion and demonstrate his understanding.* She then acts in ways that are consistent with the new interpretation: *She gives him a job that allows him to express his views, interact with peers, and use his understanding to conduct the class.* This leads to a decrease in both yelling and interruption. In short, by changing her own behavior to reflect the new interpretation, this student teacher has changed the ecosystem of the classroom, bringing about a positive change in Ruben's behavior.

Dealing with Thorny Problems

Every year, student teachers from extremely different placements return to their seminars with similar tales of behavior that they find especially vexing or troublesome. It's impossible to generate recipes for dealing with these problems, since every instance is unique in terms of key players, circumstances, and history. Nonetheless, it is helpful to reflect on ways to deal with them *before* they occur and to hear some of the thinking that guides the actions of our four teachers. In this section of the chapter, we will consider three behaviors that keep teachers awake at night wondering what to do.

Defiance

Some years ago, Claire came to seminar looking shaken and upset. When I inquired what was wrong, she shared this story:

> *My ninth-graders were really rowdy today. I'm not sure what was going on, but they just wouldn't stop talking and laughing and calling out. One boy in particular, Jamal, was really annoying me. He wouldn't stay in his seat; he kept going to the back corner of the room where his buddies sit. I kept telling him to sit down, and he'd slowly saunter over to his desk. But then a few minutes later, I'd see he was up again. Finally, I got so mad, I just yelled across the room, "Jamal, I've had it with you. Get out! Go to the office!" And he looked at me and in this real slow, mocking voice he said, "Make me." I just froze. This kid is more than six feet tall and really strong. He towers over me. I had no idea what to do. Finally, I said something stupid like, "I'm not going to make you, but you just better sit down." Then I just ignored him for the rest of the period. I felt like a complete jerk, and he knew it.*

Claire's interaction with Jamal was traumatic for her and unfortunate for him, but it gave our seminar group an opportunity to examine ways of dealing with defiance. As we pondered alternative strategies, it became obvious that *the best course of action would have been to avoid the situation in the first place.* For example, after she had repeatedly told him to sit down without success, she might have approached him and quietly, but firmly, let him know that he had the choice of getting to work or facing one of the consequences for inappropriate behavior (e.g., "Jamal, here are your choices. You can sit down and begin working or you can go to Ms. Rosen's classroom

PRACTICAL TIPS FOR

HANDLING DEFIANCE

- **Don't lose your cool.** Stay in control of yourself. Even though your first inclination may be to shout back, don't. (It may help to take a few deep breaths and to use self-talk: "I can handle this calmly. I'm going to speak quietly.")

- **Direct the rest of the class to work on something.** (e.g., "Everyone do the next three problems" or "Start reading the next section").

- **Move the student away from peers.** Talk to the student in an area where you can have more privacy. This eliminates the need for the student to worry about saving face.

- **Stand a few feet away from the student (i.e., don't get "in his face").** A student who is feeling angry and defiant may interpret closing in on him as an aggressive act (Wolfgang, 1999).

- **Acknowledge the student's feelings.** "I can see that you're really angry…"

- **Avoid a power struggle.** Do not use assertions like "I'm the boss in here and I'm telling you to …"

- **Offer a choice.** In Jamal's case, the confrontation was no longer about doing the work, but about going to the office. So the choices should focus on this issue: "Jamal, I can see that you're really upset, and we'll have to talk later. But meanwhile, here are the choices. You can go to the office, or I'll have to send for someone to come and get you."

for time out"; "Jamal, you can sit down and begin working now or you can work on it after school"). Unfortunately, by shouting across the room, Claire created a public power struggle. She backed Jamal into a corner with no "graceful exit," and Jamal was forced to challenge her if he wanted to save face with his peers.

Having said that, we still need to consider Claire's options once Jamal defied her order to get out. When I recounted this episode to our four teachers, they gave several suggestions for dealing with defiance. (These are listed in the Practical Tips box.)

Interestingly, as the teachers and I discussed ways of responding to defiance, I began to understand that this was not a major problem for any of them. When Sandy commented that she could "count on one hand the cases of insubordination" she had encountered in a lifetime of teaching, the others nodded in agreement. So I asked why they thought that students in their classes were rarely defiant. The teachers were unanimous in their response: They don't allow minor problems to escalate into major ones. Donnie put it this way:

I sometimes see students in the office, and I ask them, "Why are you down here?" They'll tell me, "I was thrown out for chewing gum." But you know that couldn't be the whole story. It probably started out with gum chewing, but escalated into a real power struggle. And for what? We need to make sure that we don't blow up situations way out of proportion.

And Fred had one last suggestion for new teachers: "If defiance is *not* a rare thing in your classroom, then it's time to think seriously about what you're doing with those kids. Some examination of your own practice is clearly in order." (See Chapter 13 for a related discussion of defusing potentially explosive situations.)

Failure to Do Homework

When students consistently fail to do homework assignments, you need to consider just how valuable those assignments are and if you have communicated that value to students. Fred comments:

I am convinced that if teachers were evaluated on the basis of the amount and quality of their homework assignments, students would have much less homework and would do more of it! I never give homework assignments unless I can explain the reason to my students. Having students understand the importance of doing a particular task at home cuts down dramatically on the number of missing assignments.

In a similar vein, Sandy tells her students "there's a reason for every assignment I give":

I tell them, "I will not insult your intelligence by giving you garbage assignments that waste your time. Every assignment is necessary for what we're currently working on; you have to do it to meet with success."

It's also important to reflect on how much homework you're assigning, if it's too difficult for students to complete independently, and whether the time allotted is sufficient. Recall that in Chapter 3, Christina talked about an instance when students had been disgruntled by the amount and difficulty of the homework she had assigned: "They kept saying it was like college work and . . . they were only 15!" Together, Christina and her students forged an agreement that was mutually satisfactory. Some due dates were postponed, in-class time was provided so that students could work in groups on some of the work, and Christina made sure she was available for help after school.

The Practical Tips box lists some additional strategies that can help increase the likelihood of students completing homework.

Despite your best efforts, some students will still not turn in homework. In this case, you need to meet individually to discuss the problem, generate possible solutions, and decide on an action plan. This might include contacting parents and asking for their cooperation and assistance, writing a contingency contract, or assigning a "homework buddy" to help the student remember and complete homework. Listen to Fred:

Many teachers have hard and fast rules about homework, with serious consequences if homework is not turned in on time. But I've come to believe that this kind of rigidity often does more harm than good. I try to work individually with kids who seem to be "irresponsible" with regard to homework. Together, we develop a plan for improving in this area.

PRACTICAL TIPS FOR

INCREASING THE LIKELIHOOD THAT STUDENTS WILL DO THEIR HOMEWORK

- **Review, collect, or grade assignments.** If you assign homework and then fail to check that students have done it, you're conveying the message that the homework just wasn't that important. Not all homework has to be graded, or even collected, but it's wise to check that students have done it and to record that fact in your grade book.

- **Give "homework quizzes."** Since Donnie finds that getting some students to do homework is a "constant struggle," she gives students a daily quiz with one or two problems that are just like those assigned the night before for homework. In addition, she gives a "homework quiz" every week or two. She selects five problems that were previously given for homework and allows students to refer to their homework papers, but not their books.

- **Require a "product" in addition to reading.** When Christina assigned 17 pages of *The Martian Chronicles* for homework, she discovered that fully one-half of the class had not done the reading—despite the fact that she had warned them about having a quiz. According to Christina, "students just don't count reading as homework." She has learned that they are far more likely to do the reading if she also has them do something *with* it (e.g., use Post-it notes to mark your three favorite passages; list 10 words or phrases the author uses to give clues about the protagonist's character; generate three questions about the reading to ask your classmates).

- **Accept no excuses.** Sandy warns new teachers: "There are valid reasons for not doing homework. But if you start judging what's valid and what's not, that leads to a host of problems. My students know that I don't accept late homework. Period. If they don't have it, they come in and do it after school, because it's necessary for going on. But they get no credit for it."

- **Provide in-school support.** Sometimes, students' home circumstances may interfere with doing homework. They may be in the midst of a family crisis. They may be living in an abusive situation. They may have after-school jobs or other responsibilities that leave little time for schoolwork. Donnie shares this incident: "Just last week I was visiting a friend in the hospital and ran into one of my students—a girl who often dozed off in class and frequently didn't have her homework. It turned out that she worked at the hospital every day from 3:00 to 11:00! This explained a lot! She's got a full-time job in addition to going to high school." In situations like this, you might work with the student to develop a plan for getting homework done in school. Perhaps the student can do her homework during lunch or during a study hall. (If lunch is 40 minutes, a student can eat in 20 minutes and still have time to get started on homework.) Perhaps she can stop by your room before or after school for 15 minutes.

Cheating

A number of studies suggest that cheating is more prevalent than we like to think. A 2004 national survey conducted by the Josephson Institute of Ethics asked nearly 25,000 high school students about their behavior during the last 12 months. Nearly two-thirds (62 percent) reported that they had cheated on a test, 35 percent said they'd copied an Internet document, and 83 percent admitted they'd copied a classmate's homework. Despite these admissions, 92 percent said they were "satisfied with my own ethics and character," and 74 percent agreed with the statement, "When it comes to doing what is right I am better than most people I know." And cheating isn't confined to students who aren't doing well in school: In the 1998 Survey of High Achievers conducted by *Who's Who Among American High School Students,* four out of five high-achieving teenagers admitted having cheated in some way (Ditman, 2000).

Obviously, cell phones, e-mail, and online searches make it easier than ever before to distribute information to friends and to plagiarize. Web sites offer research papers for sale or give them away; often the papers are not well written and contain spelling and grammatical errors—a fact that can actually help students avoid suspicion (Ditman, 2000).

Once again, it's better to prevent the problem than to deal with it after the fact. This means finding ways to *diminish the temptation to cheat.* A study by Anderman, Griesinger, and Westerfield (1998) indicates that students are more likely to report cheating when they perceive the teacher as emphasizing performance over mastery (i.e., when it's more important to get an A on a test than to really learn the material). Similarly, students report more cheating when the teacher relies on extrinsic incentives to stimulate motivation (e.g., giving homework passes to students who get As on a test) rather than trying to foster genuine interest in academic tasks. In light of this research, you need to make sure that the work you assign and the tests you give are fair and worthwhile and that you use the information they provide to help students master the material (Savage, 1999). You can also help students avoid the temptation to cheat by not basing students' grades on one or two "high-stakes" tasks (Savage, 1999). Although students may complain about frequent testing or assignments, they are less likely to cheat if they know that no one task will determine success or failure in the course.

At the beginning of the year, our four teachers also take the time to define cheating and to discuss how they feel about it. As I mentioned in Chapter 4, Sandy elaborates on the distinction between helping one another with homework and cheating. She emphasizes the act that cheating is "the ultimate disrespectful behavior," talks about the numerous behaviors that constitute cheating, gives students strategies for resisting peer pressure to cheat, and reviews the school's academic integrity policy, which students and parents have to sign. Similarly, Fred gives what he calls his "cheating sermonette": "Listen, you can lie and cheat and you may not be caught.... But if you don't cheat, you will be admirable."

In addition to reducing temptation, you can also take a number of simple precautions to *minimize opportunity.* When giving tests, for example, it's helpful to circulate throughout the room, use new tests each year, and create different forms of the same test for students seated in different rows. (With the help of a computer program, Donnie actually makes up four different forms for each test she administers.) I recently heard about a teacher who let four students take a makeup test out in the hallway. Not only was the test the same as the one the rest of the class had taken two days before (and which these students had heard about), the four students were allowed to sit together—unsupervised—to complete the test. Even the most ethical of students would find it hard to resist an opportunity like this!

If you are assigning papers, make sure that you give realistic deadlines, provide enough preparation so that students feel comfortable, and require links with class work and textbooks (Ditman, 2000). Make it clear to students that you know about Web sites that offer papers for sale or for free; also make it clear that you know how to detect plagiarism by using a search engine like Google to search for words and phrases that don't sound like student writing. (You might even demonstrate!)

Christina has students turn in bits and pieces of their research papers all along the way (e.g. note cards, an outline, the first paragraph, a first draft), making it far more difficult for students to use a research paper obtained from a Web site.

Obviously, despite all your precautions, incidents of cheating will occur. It then becomes necessary to confront the students involved. The Practical Tips box lists some suggestions for handling those encounters.

 PAUSE AND REFLECT

Before reading the next section, consider the following scenario: A student in one of your classes comes to school wearing a T-shirt with a picture of President Bush above the caption, "International Terrorist." You tell him to turn the shirt inside out or to cover it with a jacket because it's inappropriate for school and because other students think it is disrespectful. Are you acting within your rights—or are you violating your student's freedom of expression? Reflect, and then read on.

 PRACTICAL TIPS FOR

DEALING WITH CHEATING

- **Talk privately.** Once again, avoid creating a situation where the student may be publicly humiliated. This is likely to lead to a series of accusations and denials that get more and more heated.

- **Present your reasons for suspecting cheating.** Lay out your evidence calmly and firmly, even sorrowfully. (One "electronic" hint: If you suspect plagiarism, you might get help from www.plagiarism.org.)

- **Express concern.** Make it clear that you do not expect this kind of behavior from this student. Try to find out why students cheated (e.g., Were they simply unprepared? Are they under a lot of pressure to excel?)

- **Explain consequences.** A common response to cheating is to give the student a low grade or a zero on the assignment or test. This seems like a sensible solution at first glance, but it confounds the act of cheating with the student's mastery of the content (Cangelosi, 1993). In other words, a person looking at the teacher's grade book would be unable to tell if the low grade meant the student had violated the test-taking procedures or if it indicated a failure to learn the material. I prefer using a logical consequence; namely, having the student redo the assignment or test under more carefully controlled conditions. But some schools have predetermined consequences for cheating, such as detention and parental notification. If so, you need to follow your school's policy.

- **Discuss the consequences for subsequent cheating.** Alert the student to the consequences for additional cheating incidents. Emphasize that you are available for assistance if cheating was the result of academic difficulties (i.e., there is no need to cheat because of problems with the material). If the student is under pressure at home to succeed, you may want to talk with parents. If students have no appropriate place to study at home, you might explore alternatives (e.g., studying at school or the public library).

WHEN DISCIPLINE VIOLATES STUDENTS' CONSTITUTIONAL RIGHTS

Before leaving the topic of disciplinary interventions, it's important to examine two types of situations in which well-meaning teachers may unknowingly violate students' constitutional rights. The first situation involves students' *freedom of expression.* Consider the case of Tim Gies, a sophomore at a Michigan high school when the United States was preparing to go to war in Iraq. Passionately antiwar and anti-Bush, Gies painted symbols and slogans onto T-shirts and sweatshirts. School administrators repeatedly told him to remove the clothing, but Gies refused; as a result, he was suspended for weeks at a time and eventually threatened with expulsion. That's when he called the local American Civil Liberties Union (ACLU), which notified the school that it was infringing on Gies's First Amendment rights (Juarez, 2005). In April 2005, right before graduation, administrators rescinded their prohibition on his antiwar clothing.

Conflicts like this occur on all points of the political spectrum. In 2001 Elliot Chambers, a high school student in Minnesota, wore a T-shirt to school bearing the slogan "Straight pride." The principal prohibited him from wearing the shirt, and Chambers's parents filed a lawsuit on his behalf. A federal judge ruled in their favor. And in 2005 Daniel Goergen's Minnesota high school refused to allow him to wear his sweatshirt with the words "Abortion is homicide." When a Christian law center warned of legal action, the school retreated (Juarez, 2005).

According to David Schimmel (2006), an expert on law and education, "despite decades of judicial decisions reaffirming the free speech rights of students, teachers and administrators continue to restrict controversial expression that they think might be offensive" (p. 1007). More than 30 years ago, the U.S. Supreme Court ruled that the First Amendment applies to public schools and that a student's right to freedom of expression "does not stop at the schoolhouse gate" (*Tinker v. Des Moines,* 1969, p. 506; cited by Schimmel, 2006). In that groundbreaking case, schools in Des Moines, Iowa, fearing disruption, had forbidden students to wear black armbands protesting the Vietnam War. The Court rejected the schools' argument, concluding that schools cannot prohibit expression just "to avoid the discomfort and unpleasantness that always accompany an unpopular viewpoint" (p. 509). Although subsequent Supreme Court decisions have narrowed *Tinker,* the basic principle remains intact, "that is, a student's nondisruptive personal expression that occurs in school is protected by the First Amendment even if the ideas are unpopular and controversial" (Schimmel, 2006, p. 1006). Given these judicial rulings, you need to be careful about disciplining students for controversial expression. The Court acknowledged that schools can prohibit student expression that causes "substantial disruption or interferes with the rights of others" (Schimmel, 2006), but this judgment is not easy to make. Without question, you need to consult with a school administrator or the district's legal counsel before taking disciplinary action.

Search and seizure is another area in which educators' actions sometimes conflict with students' constitutional rights. For example, suppose you suspect that a student is in possession of drugs or alcohol in school (e.g., in a purse or back-pack). Do you have the right to search the student's belongings or not? The answer derives from a landmark case (*New Jersey v. T.L.O.,* 1985), in which the United States Supreme Court ruled that a school official may properly conduct a search of a student "when there are reasonable grounds for suspecting that the search will turn up evidence that the student has violated or is violating either the law or the rules of the school" (Fischer, Schimmel, & Kelly, 1999). In other words, students in school have fewer protections than are normally afforded to citizens under the stricter "probable cause" standard (Stefkovich & Miller, 1998). Nonetheless, search-ing a student's belongings is best left to an administrator who is aware of the sub-tleties of the law.

Although the Supreme Court ruling in *T.L.O.* was issued more than 20 years ago, some teachers still engage in unconstitutional disciplinary interventions, as il-lustrated by the following 2003 decision described by Schimmel (2006). Ms. Apley, a third-grade teacher in Ohio, discovered that $10 was missing from her desk. She asked Shaneequa Watkins and two other students to open their book bags, empty their pockets, and turn down the waistband of their pants, but she didn't find any-thing. The teacher then took Shaneequa to a supply closet; there the girl was re-quired to pull out her pants and underwear so Ms. Apley could look down them for the money.

In the subsequent lawsuit (*Watkins v. Millenium School,* 2003), the court ruled that the school's interest in maintaining order and instilling moral values did not outweigh Shaneequa Watkins's privacy interest. They wrote that "a reasonable teacher should have known that students have Fourth Amendment rights against unreasonable search and seizure" and that requiring a student to expose the private areas of her body without individualized suspicion is clearly unreasonable (p. 902; cited in Schimmel, 2006, p. 1009).

Keep these judicial rulings in mind if you suspect that a student has stolen and hidden money or is in possession of drugs or alcohol. Given the difficulty of deter-mining what constitutes "reasonable grounds," it's best to bring that person to the appropriate school official rather than undertake a search by yourself.

CONCLUDING COMMENTS

In a study of the ways that teachers cope with problem students, Brophy and Rohrkemper (1981) found that a basic distinction between more effective and less effective teachers was their *willingness to take responsibility.* More effective teachers used a wide variety of strategies: Some used behavioral approaches—negotiating contracts, providing rewards, praising desirable behavior—while oth-ers tried to build positive relationships, provide encouragement, and foster self-esteem. Regardless, effective teachers were willing to assume the responsibility for managing youngsters' behavior. In sharp contrast, *less effective teachers tended to disclaim responsibility and to refer problems to other school personnel* (e.g., the principal, guidance counselor, etc.).

Clearly, our four teachers are willing to take responsibility for the behavior of their students. They recognize that they are accountable for what happens in their classrooms. Furthermore, they are willing to admit when they have contributed to problems that occur. Listen to Christina:

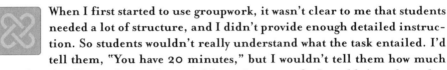

> When I first started to use groupwork, it wasn't clear to me that students needed a lot of structure, and I didn't provide enough detailed instruction. So students wouldn't really understand what the task entailed. I'd tell them, "You have 20 minutes," but I wouldn't tell them how much time they should spend on each part of the assignment. Or I wouldn't explain what each person in the group was supposed to do.... When I would realize the groupwork was falling apart, I'd say, "This is what you should be doing now." I'd add the instructions I should have given at the beginning!

I agree with Christina, Sandy, Donnie, and Fred that teachers need to assume responsibility for students' behavior problems, and I hope that this chapter will help you to feel more competent in this area. This doesn't mean that you have to go it alone. As Donnie observes: "Teachers have to recognize that there are kids you can't help by yourself. Then it's important to seek out the special services that are available and try to get assistance." We turn to this topic in Chapter 12.

SUMMARY

Inappropriate behavior threatens order by interrupting the flow of classroom activity. This chapter discussed ways of responding to a variety of problems—from minor, nondisruptive infractions to chronic, more serious misbehaviors.

Guidelines for Dealing with Misbehavior

- Use disciplinary strategies that preserve the dignity of the student.
  Separate the student's character from the specific misbehavior.
  Encourage students to take responsibility for regulating their own behavior.
- Try to keep the instructional program going with a minimum of disruption.
- Consider the context of students' actions. Behavior that is acceptable in one context may be unacceptable in another.
- Match your disciplinary strategy to the misbehavior.
- Be culturally responsive, because differences in norms, values, and styles of communication can have a direct effect on students' behavior.

Strategies for Dealing with Minor Misbehavior

- Nonverbal interventions.
- Verbal interventions:
  Direct student to the task at hand.
  State student's name.

      Remind student of rule.

      Call on student.

      Use gentle humor.

      Use an I-message.

- Ignoring misbehavior that is fleeting.

Strategies for Dealing with More Serious Misbehavior

- Plan penalties ahead of time.
- Choose penalties that are logically related to misbehavior.
- Impose penalties calmly and quietly.
- Reestablish a positive relationship with the student as quickly as possible.
- Develop a range of alternative consequences.

Strategies for Dealing with Chronic Misbehavior

- Problem-solving process:
    Step 1: Define the problem.
    Step 2: Brainstorm possible solutions.
    Step 3: Evaluate solutions.
    Step 4: Decide on a solution to try.
    Step 5: Determine how to implement the decision.
    Step 6: Evaluate the solution.
- Behavior modification approaches:
    Self-monitoring.
    Self-evaluation.
    Self-instruction.
    Contingency contracting.
- An ecosystemic approach:
    Recognize your current interpretation of the problem.
    Formulate an alternative, positive interpretation (reframe the situation).
    Act in ways that are consistent with the new interpretation.

Dealing with Thorny Problems

      Defiance.

      Failure to do homework.

      Cheating.

When Discipline Violates Students' Constitutional Rights

- The First Amendment protects students' freedom of expression, unless it causes substantial disruption or interferes with the rights of others.
- The Fourth Amendment protects students from unreasonable search and seizure; however, school searches are permitted if they are based on "reasonable suspicion" that the student violated the law or school rules.

    Effective teachers are willing to take responsibility for managing students' behavior. Work on developing a system for dealing with misbehavior that suits your personality and your teaching style. You may have a student whose problems are too severe for you to deal with. If so, it is your responsibility to get this student outside help.

ACTIVITIES FOR SKILL BUILDING AND REFLECTION

In Class

1. When a misbehavior occurs, there usually isn't much time for careful consideration of logical consequences. I've listed a few typical misbehaviors for your practice. In a small group, think of two logical consequences for each example.

    a. As part of a small group, Lou monopolizes the discussion and tells everyone what to do in an authoritarian manner.

    b. At the end of the year, Arianna returns her book with ripped pages and the cover missing.

    c. Shemeika yells out answers throughout your class discussion, even though you have instructed students to raise their hands.

    d. Whenever you're not looking, Tom practices juggling with three small bean bags he has brought to school.

    e. Instead of working on the class activity, Tanya examines the contents of her cosmetic kit.

2. In a small group, discuss what would you do in the following situation. You are reviewing homework from the night before. You call on James to do number 5. He slumps in his seat and fidgets with the chain around his neck. You tell him the class is waiting for his answer to number 5. Finally he mutters, "I didn't do the f_____ homework."

On Your Own

1. Beginning teachers sometimes overreact to misbehavior or take no action at all because they simply don't know what to do or say. First, read the examples. Then consider the situations that follow and devise a nonverbal intervention, a verbal cue, and an I-message.

Example	Nonverbal	Verbal	I-Message
A student writes on the desk	Hand the student an eraser.	"We use paper to write on."	"When you write on the desk, the custodian complains to me and I get embarrassed."
A student makes a big show of looking through her book bag for her homework, distracting other students and delaying the start of the lesson.	Give the "look".	"We're ready to begin."	"When you take so long to get your things out, I can't begin the lesson, and I get very frustrated about the lost time."

   a.   A student is copying from another student's paper.

   b.   A student takes another student's notebook.

   c.   A student sharpens his pencil during your presentation.

   d.   A student calls out instead of raising her hand.

2.   Try reframing a problem behavior according to an ecosystemic approach. First, think of a problem you are currently having or observing. What is your current interpretation of the behavior? How do you typically respond to the behavior? Next, consider some positive alternative interpretations of the behavior. Based on one of the explanations, how might you respond differently?

For Your Portfolio

Develop a behavior modification plan (such as self-monitoring or a contingency contract) to deal with the following problems:

   a.   Arthur is a seventh-grader who exhibits aggressive behavior. Hardly a day goes by that another student hasn't come to you complaining of Arthur's pushing, teasing, or name-calling. You've talked to his parents, but they are at a loss about what to do.

   b.   Cynthia, an eleventh-grader, rarely completes her work. She daydreams, socializes with others, misunderstands directions, and gets upset when you speak to her about her incomplete work. The problem seems to be getting worse.

FOR FURTHER READING

Bear, G. G. (1998). School discipline in the United States: Prevention, correction, and long-term social development. *School Psychology Review, 27*(1), 724–742.

   This article reviews strategies used by highly effective classroom teachers to achieve the short-term goal of order and the long-term goal of self-discipline. Bear argues that effective teachers can be characterized by an authoritative style that combines strategies for preventing behavior problems, operant learning strategies for short-term management, and decision-making and social problem-solving strategies to achieve the long-term goal of self-discipline.

Gordon, T. (1974). *T.E.T.—Teacher Effectiveness Training.* New York: Peter H. Wyden.

   Gordon contends that both authoritarian and permissive approaches to dealing with young people in schools are destructive, "win–lose," power-based approaches. Instead, he advocates a "no-lose" approach to solving problems that protects the teacher–student relationship and promotes communication and caring. He explains the concept of "problem-ownership" so that teachers can respond in appropriate ways.

Obidah, J. E., & Teel, K. M. (2001). *Because of the kids: Facing racial and cultural differences in schools.* New York: Teachers College Press.

   Jennifer Obidah is Black; Karen Mannhein Teel is White. Together, they conducted a three-year study to explore the impact of racial and cultural differences on Karen's relationship with her primarily African American middle school students. In the process, the two teachers also had to learn to communicate with each other across racial and cultural boundaries. This book describes the challenges they faced as they tried to generate specific ways that Karen could more effectively educate her African American students.

Thompson, G. L. (2004). *Through ebony eyes: What teachers need to know but are afraid to ask about African American students.* San Francisco: Jossey-Bass.

Written in lively, conversational language, this book provides information and strategies to help teachers increase their effectiveness with African American students. Thompson talks about why some African American students misbehave in class and how teachers often unwittingly contribute to their misbehavior.

References

Alberto, P. A., & Troutman, A. C. (2006). *Applied behavior analysis for teachers.* 7th ed. Upper Saddle River, NJ: Pearson Prentice Hall.

Anderman, E. M., Griesinger, T., & Westerfield, G. (1998). Motivation and cheating during early adolescence. *Journal of Educational Psychology, 90*(1), 84–93.

Barry, L., & Messer, J. J. (2003). A practical application of self-management for students diagnosed with attention-deficit/hyperactivity disorder. *Journal of Positive Behavior Interventions, 5*(4), 238–248.

Bear, G. G. (1998). School discipline in the United States: Prevention, Correction, and long-term social development. *School Psychology Review, 27*(1), 724–742.

Broden, M., Hall, R.V., & Mitts, B. (1971). The effect of self-recording on the classroom behavior of two eighth-grade students. *Journal of Applied Behavior Analysis, 4,* 191–199.

Brophy, J. E. (1983). Classroom organization and management. *The Elementary School Journal, 83*(4), 265–285.

Brophy, J., & Rohrkemper, M. (1981). The influence of problem ownership on teachers' perceptions of and strategies for coping with problem students. *Journal of Educational Psychology, 73,* 295–311.

Cangelosi, J. S. (1993). *Classroom management strategies: Gaining and maintaining students' cooperation.* 2nd ed. New York: Longman.

Créton, H. A., Wubbels, T., & Hooymayers, H. P. (1989). Escalated disorderly situations in the classroom and the improvement of these situations. *Teaching & Teacher Education, 5*(3), 205–215.

Curwin, R. L., & Mendler, A. N. (1988). *Discipline with dignity.* Alexandria VA: Association for Supervision and Curriculum Development.

Delpit, L. (1995). *Other people's children: Cultural conflict in the classroom.* New York: The New Press.

Ditman, O. (July/August 2000). Online term-paper mills produce a new crop of cheaters. *Harvard Education Letter, 16*(4), 6–7.

Doyle, W. (1986). Classroom organization and management. In M. C. Wittrock (Ed.), *Handbook of research on teaching.* New York: Macmillan, pp. 392–431.

Doyle, W. (1990). Classroom management techniques. In O. C. Moles (Ed.), *Student discipline strategies: Research and practice.* Albany, NY: SUNY Press.

Dreikurs, R., Grunwald, B. B., & Pepper, F. C. (1982). *Maintaining sanity in the classroom: Classroom management techniques.* 2nd ed. New York: Harper & Row.

Emmer, E.T., & Aussiker, A. (1990). School and classroom discipline programs: How well do they work? In O. C. Moles (Ed.), *Student discipline strategies.* New York: SUNY Press, pp. 129–165.

Emmer, E. T., Evertson, C., & Worsham, M. E., (2000). *Classroom management for secondary teachers.* 5th ed. Boston: Allyn and Bacon.

Epanchin, B. C., Townsend, B., & Stoddard, K. (1994). *Constructive classroom management: Strategies for creating positive learning environments.* Pacific Grove, CA: Brooks/Cole.

Evertson, C. M. (1989). Classroom organization and management. In M. C. Reynolds (Ed.), *Knowledge base for the beginning teacher.* New York: Pergamon Press, pp. 59-70.

Evertson, C. M., & Emmer, E. T. (1982). Effective management at the beginning of the school year in junior high classes. *Journal of Educational Psychology, 74*(4), 485-498.

Fischer, L., Schimmel, D., & Kelly, C. (1999). *Teachers and the law.* 5th ed. New York: Longman.

Good, J. E., & Brophy, T. L. (1994). *Looking in classrooms.* 6th ed. New York: Harper Collins.

Gordon, T. (1974). *T.E.T.—Teacher Effectiveness Training.* New York: Peter H. Wyden.

Graziano, A. M., & Mooney, K. C. (1984). *Children and behavior therapy.* New York: Aldine.

Hughes, C. A., Ruhl, K. L. & Misra, A. (1989). Disordered students in school settings: A promise unfulfilled? *Behavioral Disorders, 14,* 250-262.

Irvine, J. J. (1990). *Black students and school failure: Policies, practices, and prescriptions.* New York: Greenwood.

Janney, R., & Snell, M. E. (2000). *Behavioral support.* Baltimore: Paul Brookes.

Johnston, R. C. (November 24, 1999) Decatur furor sparks wider policy debate. *Education Week, 19*(13), pp. 1, 12.

Jones, V. F., & Jones, L. S. (2001). *Comprehensive classroom management: Creating communities of support and solving problems.* 6th ed. Boston: Allyn and Bacon.

Josephson Institute of Ethics (2004). 2004 report card: The ethics of American Youth. Downloaded from http://josephsoninstitute.org/Survey2004/.

Juarez, V. (Oct. 4, 2005). They dress to express. *Newsweek.* Downloaded from http://www.msnbc.msn.com/id/6098629/site/newsweek.

Kounin, J. S. (1970). *Discipline and group management in classrooms.* New York: Holt, Rinehart and Winston.

Lasley, T. J., Lasley, J. O., & Ward, S. H. (1989). Activities and desists used by more and less effective classroom managers. Paper presented at the annual meeting of the American Educational Research Association, San Francisco.

McDougall, D. (1998). Research on self-management techniques used by students with disabilities in general education settings: A descriptive review. *Remedial and Special Education, 19*(5), 310-320.

Meichenbaum, D. (1977). *Cognitive behavior modification.* New York: Plenum.

Mitchem, K. J., Young, K. R., West, R. P., & Benyo, J. (2001). CWPASM: A classwide peer-assisted self-management program for general education classrooms. *Education & Treatment of Children, 24*(2), 111-140.

Molnar, A., & Lindquist, B. (1989). *Changing problem behavior in schools.* San Francisco: Jossey-Bass.

National Center for Educational Statistics. (1998). *Violence and discipline problems in U.S. public schools: 1996-97, NCES 98-030.* Washington, D.C.: U.S. Department of Education, Office of Educational Research and Improvement.

Ninness, H. A. C., Fuerst, J., Rutherford, R. D., & Glenn, S. S. (1991). Effects of self-management training and reinforcement on the transfer of improved conduct in the absence of supervision. *Journal of Applied Behavior Analysis, 24*(3), 499-508.

Pittman, S. I. (1985). A cognitive ethnography and quantification of a first-grade teacher's selection routines for classroom management. *The Elementary School Journal, 85*(4), 541–558.

Raffaele-Mendez, L. M., & Knoff, H. M. (2003). Who gets suspended from school and why: A demographic analysis of schools and disciplinary infractions in a large school district. *Education and Treatment of Children, 26,* 30–51.

Richard, A. (September 8, 1999). As students return, focus is on security. *Education Week, 19*(1), 1, 14–15.

Sack, J. L. (June 7, 2000). ADHD student's expulsion voided. *Education Week,* p. 4.

Savage, T. V. (1999). *Teaching self-control through management and discipline.* 2nd ed. Boston: Allyn and Bacon.

Schimmel, D. (2006). Classroom management, discipline, and the law: Clarifying confusions about students' rights and teachers' authority. In C. M. Evertson & C. S. Weinstein (Eds.), *Handbook of classroom management: Research, practice, and contemporary issues.* Mahwah, NJ: Lawrence Erlbaum Associates, Inc.

Schlosser, L. K. (1992). Teacher distance and student disengagement: School lives on the margin. *Journal of Teacher Education, 43*(2), 128–140.

Shapiro, E. S., DuPaul, G. J., & Bradley-Klug, K. L. (1998). Self-management as a strategy to improve the classroom behavior of adolescents with ADHD. *Journal of Learning Disabilities, 31*(6), 545–555.

Skiba, R. J., Michael, R. S., Nardo, A. C., & Peterson, R. (2002). The color of discipline: Sources of racial and gender disproportionality in school punishment. *Urban Review, 34,* 317–342.

Skiba, R. J., & Rausch, M. K. (2006). Zero tolerance, suspension, and expulsion: Questions of equity and effectiveness. In C. M. Evertson & C. S. Weinstein (Eds.), *Handbook of classroom management: Research, practice, and contemporary issues.* Mahwah, NJ: Lawrence Erlbaum.

Smith, B. W., & Sugai, G. (2000). A self-management functional assessment-based behavior support plan for a middle school student with EBD. *Journal of Positive Behavior Interventions, 2*(4), 208–217.

Smith, D. J., Young, K. R., West, R. P., Morgan, D. P., & Rhode, G. (1988). Reducing the disruptive behavior of junior high school students: A classroom self-management procedure. *Behavioral Disorders, 18,* 231–239.

Stefkovich, J. A., & Miller, J. A. (April 13, 1998). Law enforcement officers in public schools: Student citizens in safe havens? Paper presented at the conference of the American Educational Research Association, San Diego, California.

Turco, T. L., & Elliott, S. N. (1986). Assessment of students' acceptability ratings of teacher-initiated interventions for classroom misbehavior. *Journal of School Psychology, 24,* 277–283.

Valentine, G. (Fall 1998). Lessons from home (an interview with Lisa Delpit). *Teaching Tolerance, 7*(2), 15–19.

Weinstein, C. S., Curran, M., & Tomlinson-Clarke, S. (2003). Culturally responsive classroom management: Awareness into action. *Theory Into Practice, 42*(4), 269–276.

Wolfgang, C. H. (1999). *Solving discipline problems: Methods and models for today's teachers.* 4th ed. Boston: Allyn and Bacon.

Zirpoli, T. J. (2005). *Behavior management: Applications for teachers.* 4th ed. Upper Saddle River, NJ: Pearson Education, Inc.

HELPING STUDENTS WITH SPECIAL NEEDS

Teaching in today's classrooms is more challenging than ever before. Part of the challenge stems from the fact that about half of the nation's children with disabilities are now educated in general education classrooms with their nondisabled peers (Soodak & McCarthy, 2006). Increasing immigration means that more and more students come from a wide range of cultural and linguistic backgrounds, and many of these students are learning English for the first time. In addition, too many young people are growing up in circumstances that delay their development, create physical, emotional, and psychological problems, and jeopardize their futures. (For a chilling picture of the plight of America's children, see Figure 12.1.)

Although the term *special needs* is typically used to refer to children and adolescents with disabilities, those who are learning English as a second language and those who are troubled also have special needs that must be addressed. How can you help *all* the students with special needs who may be in your classroom? One

357

1 in 2 never completes a single year of college.
1 in 2 will live in a single-parent family at some point in childhood.
1 in 3 is born to unmarried parents.
1 in 3 is behind a year or more in school.
1 in 4 lives with only one parent.
1 in 5 is born to a mother who did not graduate from high school.
1 in 5 was born poor.
1 in 6 is born to a mother who did not receive prenatal care in the first three months of pregnancy.
1 in 7 never graduates from high school.
1 in 8 has no health insurance
1 in 9 is born to a teenage mother.
1 in 12 has a disability.
1 in 13 was born with low birthweight.
1 in 13 will be arrested at least once before age 17.
1 in 35 lives with grandparents (or other relative but neither parent).
1 in 60 sees his or her parents divorce in any year.
1 in 83 will be in state or federal prison before age 20.
1 in 146 will die before their first birthday.
1 in 1,339 will be killed by guns before age 20.

Figure 12.1   Key Facts about American Children
Source: Adapted from Children's Defense Fund, 2004.

answer is to be informed about the various special services that are available and to know how to obtain access to those services. Maynard Reynolds, a leading special educator, writes:

> It is too much to ask that a beginning teacher know about all of the problems he or she will encounter in teaching; but it is not too much to ask that the beginning teacher recognize needs for support and assistance when challenging problems arise, and to understand that it is a sign of professionalism to seek help when needed rather than a sign of weakness. (Reynolds, 1989, p. 138)

Seeking help does *not* mean that you are "off the hook." *Teachers are responsible for all the students in their classes, including those with special needs.* This may mean communicating and collaborating with special support personnel in order to provide students with appropriate educational experiences. It also means working with special-needs individuals when they are in your room—not putting them in the back and ignoring them—like the teacher in this journal entry written by one of my student teachers:

> *There's a boy in my classroom who goes to a resource room every day for reading and math. When he's in the classroom, he sits in a back corner, basically doing nothing. My cooperating teacher gives him some worksheets to do, but doesn't even really monitor to see if he does them. He never includes him in any of the class's activities. Sometimes the boy wanders around the room, looking at what the other kids are doing, and I get the feeling he'd like to do the lesson too, but my teacher*

doesn't make any attempt to involve him. When I asked about the boy, my teacher told me he can't do anything for the child, that his learning disabilities are just too great. He said he doesn't have the necessary expertise to help him—that he's not a special educator. So he just lets him sit. It makes me want to cry.

This chapter begins by examining ways of helping students with disabilities and attention-deficit/hyperactivity disorder, the most commonly diagnosed behavior disorder among children in the United States (Coles, 2000). The chapter then turns to strategies for supporting individuals who are English-language learners. The final section of the chapter discusses the needs of students who are troubled—namely, those who suffer from the problems associated with substance abuse, child abuse and neglect, and eating disorders.

 PAUSE AND REFLECT

What do you think about the inclusion of students with disabilities in the general education classroom? Do your views depend on the kind of disability (e.g., physical, emotional, cognitive)? What are your specific concerns, if any, about teaching in inclusive classrooms?

HELPING STUDENTS WITH DISABILITIES AND ADHD

Matthew is a student in Sandy's last period class who has been identified as emotionally disturbed. Although he's very quiet, he erupts angrily when provoked and is prone to violent outbursts. Sandy says that you can tell something is boiling just beneath the surface. She makes sure to place him in groups with students who are cooperative and supportive; even so, he frequently gets tense and frustrated with group members who he thinks are "wasting his time." According to Sandy, "Matthew is really bright, and when students are quibbling over something he thinks is silly (like how to write down an answer), he'll get a funny look on his face and turn his back on the other group members. It's almost as if he's trying to block out whatever's bothering him. When I see that look, I know to get over there and intervene." Sandy has carefully reviewed Matthew's individualized education program (IEP), but it's the close communication with his case manager and the school psychologist that has allowed her to gain a deeper understanding of Matthew's behavior. As she puts it, "Matthew's having a successful year in chemistry—and that's due to the fact that many people are helping *me* to help *him*."

Matthew's presence in Sandy's classroom is a direct result of the Individuals with Disabilities Education Act (IDEA), federal legislation mandating a "free appropriate public education" for all children with disabilities. According to the IDEA, disability is defined as mental retardation, a hearing impairment including deafness, a speech or language impairment, a visual impairment including blindness, serious emotional disturbance, an orthopedic impairment, autism, traumatic brain injury, other health impairment (e.g., limited strength or vitality due to chronic or acute health problems such as asthma or diabetes), a specific learning disability, deaf-blindness, or multiple disabilities.

Sometimes called the "mainstreaming law," the IDEA requires *students with disabilities to be educated with their nondisabled peers to the maximum extent appropriate, with the supplementary aids and services needed to help them achieve.* The general education, mainstream class needs to be considered as the "*least restrictive environment.*" However, the law also requires schools to have available a *continuum of alternative placements* (e.g., part-time placement in a special education classroom; full time placement in a special education classroom; placement in a special school; placement in a residential school) if the nature or severity of a child's disability precludes the possibility of a satisfactory education in the general education setting.

In recent years, increasing numbers of educators have rejected the notion of a continuum of *placements;* they argue that it is far preferable to provide a continuum of *services* in the general education setting. Advocates of this position, often referred to as *inclusion,* contend that the general classroom benefits students with disabilities academically because they are held to higher expectations and are exposed to more stimulating content. Furthermore, they benefit socially, since they can make friends with children from their own neighborhoods and can observe peers behaving in a socially appropriate manner. (Table 12.1 lists the assumptions that underlie arguments about inclusion.) Mara Sapon-Shevin is a proponent of full inclusion:

> The idea is that these [inclusive] schools would be restructured so that they are supportive, nurturing communities that really meet the needs of all the children within them: rich in resources and support for both students and teachers....As far as a rationale, we should not have to defend inclusion—we should make others defend exclusion. There's very little evidence that some children need segregated settings in which to be educated.... [W]e know that the world is an inclusive community. There are lots of people in it who vary not only in terms of disabilities, but in race, class, gender, and religious background. It's very important for children to have the opportunity to learn and grow within communities that represent the kind of world they'll live in when they finish school. (O'Neil, 1994/95, p. 7)

On the other side of the debate are educators who argue that it is essential to maintain a continuum of placements (e.g., Zigmond, Jenkins, Fuchs, Deno, & Fuchs, 1995; Zigmond, et al., 1995). Jim Kauffman reflects this point of view:

> I'm convinced that we must maintain the alternative of moving kids to other places when that appears necessary in the judgment of teachers and parents.... Sure, we ought to meet special needs in a regular class when that's possible. But there isn't anything wrong with meeting special needs outside the regular class if that is required. In fact, the law and best practice say we must consider both possibilities. (O'Neil, 1994/95, p. 7)

Critics of inclusion also worry that financially desperate school districts will use it to reduce special education costs and "dump" children and adolescents with disabilities in regular classrooms without support. Not surprisingly, many regular classroom teachers share this view. Indeed, they often resist inclusion, afraid that they lack the expertise to meet students' special needs and worried about the time and effort that those with disabilities take away from other students (Semmel, et al.,

TABLE 12.1 The Inclusion Argument

Proponents of Full Inclusion	Opponents of Full Inclusion
1. Labeling and segregation are inherently bad.	1. Labeling is not bad if the labels indicate real differences; it's the only way to ensure that funds go to the neediest children.
2. Students with disabilities aren't different from nondisabled students in any meaningful way; everyone is unique.	2. Students with disabilities are different from nondisabled children, precisely because of their disabilities.
3. Students with disabilities can best be served in regular classrooms because	3. Some children with disabilities may be best served in regular classrooms, but some may be better served in separate special educational programs because
teachers have lower expectations when all students in a class have disabilities.	special education teachers have appropriate expectations for their students.
they benefit academically because they are held to higher expectations and are exposed to more stimulating curriculum.	they benefit academically because teachers are specially trained, can implement an appropriate curriculum, and can give more individualized attention.
virtually all regular teachers can teach disabled students and are willing to do so.	regular education teachers don't want children with disabilities in their classes and don't consider themselves prepared to serve them.
students with disabilities can make friends with children in their neighborhoods and model appropriate behavior of nondisabled peers.	students with disabilities are often isolated and rejected by their nondisabled peers; they need the social acceptance and camaraderie of peers with similar disabilities.
4. Special education is too costly, fragmented, and inefficient.	4. Opponents of special education just want to save money at the expense of needy students.
5. Many students in special education are not actually disabled, but are placed there because of faculty evaluations.	5. Most children in special education belong there; evaluations are generally reliable.
6. Nondisabled students benefit from having children with disabilities in their classes because they learn to accept and respect differences.	6. Nondisabled students suffer from having children with disabilities in their classes because the teacher has to spend too much time working with the disabled students.

Source: Adapted from Webb, 1994, p. 4.

1991). On the other hand, inclusion advocates point out that including children and adolescents with disabilities in the regular classroom does not mean placing unreasonable demands on teachers. A good program that is based on students' Individualized Education Programs (IEPs) should provide the supports necessary to make it work: aides, special services personnel, interpreters, planning time, administrative assistance, special materials, and equipment.

The next sections of the chapter summarize the characteristics of students with learning disabilities, emotional and behavior disorders, autism and Asperger Syndrome, and ADHD. I then discuss a variety of general strategies that may be useful as you work to achieve a classroom that is truly inclusive.

Learning Disabilities

More students are identified as having "specific learning disabilities" than any other type of disability. Of the 10 percent of school-age children identified as having disabilities, just over 50 percent of this group (or 5 percent of the total school-age population) is diagnosed as LD, and the number has been increasing dramatically (Vaughn, Bos, & Schumm, 2003). According to Henley, Ramsey, and Algozzine (2002), "In almost every public school classroom, there is at least one student identified as learning disabled, and probably several more" (p. 136).

It is difficult to get a satisfactory definition of LD because there are many types of learning disabilities and children diagnosed with LD are a heterogeneous group. The IDEA defines learning disabilities as a "disorder in one or more of the basic psychological processes involved in understanding or in using language, spoken or written," which results in learning problems that are not explained by some other disability (such as mental retardation). A diagnosis of LD is made when there is a "severe discrepancy" between intellectual ability and academic performance in one or more of seven areas: oral expression, listening comprehension, written expression, basic reading skills, reading comprehension, mathematics calculation, and mathematics reasoning. The discrepancy criterion is a source of concern to many parents and educators, since children have to struggle for several years before the disparity between achievement and ability is severe enough to allow diagnosis. As Vaughn, Bos, and Schumm (2003) point out, this means that most students with LD do not qualify for services until late second or third grade—a practice that seems to set these children up for failure. These educators suggest that one alternative might be to intervene early to provide small-group, intensive instruction in the needed academic areas. If this early intervention fails to benefit the child, then he or she may qualify as having a specific learning disability.

Although it is difficult to list a set of characteristics that adequately describe all students with LD, Table 12.2 presents some signs that may indicate a learning disability. If a student displays a number of these problems, then teachers should consider the possibility of a learning disability and seek advice from special services personnel.

Reviews of research indicate that three teaching strategies are particularly powerful in promoting the academic success of students with LD (Vaughn, Gersten, & Chard, 2000). First, teachers need to match tasks to the student's abilities and skills, sequencing examples and problems to allow high levels of student success. Second, small group instruction with no more than six students appears to be especially beneficial. Finally, students with LD need to learn self-questioning strategies (i.e., to ask themselves questions while reading or working on a mathematics

TABLE 12.2 Possible Indicators of a Learning Disability

When a child has a learning disability, he or she

- May have trouble learning the alphabet, rhyming words, or connecting letters to their sounds.
- May have trouble blending sounds into words.
- May make many mistakes when reading aloud, and repeat and pause often.
- May not understand what he or she reads.
- May confuse similar letters and words, such as *b* and *d, was* and *saw.*
- May have real trouble with spelling.
- May have very messy handwriting.
- May have difficulty with fine motor activities.
- May have trouble remembering the sounds that letters make or hearing slight differences between words.
- May have trouble understanding and following directions.
- May have trouble organizing what he or she wants to say or not be able to think of the word he or she needs for writing or conversation.
- May confuse math symbols and misread numbers.
- May not be able to retell a story in order.
- May not know where to begin a task or how to go on from there.

Source: Adapted from Fact Sheet 7 of the National Dissemination Center for Children with Disabilities (2004).

problem). Teachers can model this by thinking aloud about text being read or mathematics problems to be solved. As Vaughn, Gersten, and Chard (2000) point out, these instructional practices are hardly revolutionary; unfortunately, they are too rarely implemented in classrooms.

Emotional and Behavioral Disorders

The terms *emotional disturbance* and *behavioral disorder* are often used interchangeably. While the IDEA uses the term *emotional disturbance,* many professionals prefer the term *behavioral disorder,* which they feel is less stigmatizing (Vaugh, Bos, & Schumm, 2003).

IDEA defines an "emotional disturbance" as a condition characterized by one or more of the following: an inability to learn that cannot be explained by intellectual, sensory, or health factors; an inability to build or maintain satisfactory interpersonal relationships with peers and teachers; inappropriate types of behavior or feeling under normal circumstances; a general pervasive mood of unhappiness or depression; or a tendency to develop physical symptoms or fears associated with personal or school problems. As you can see, like the term *learning disabilities,* the term *emotional disturbance* actually encompasses a variety of conditions, from conduct disorders to depression.

When teachers are asked to talk about "problem students," they tend to speak about those who are disruptive, aggressive, and defiant and whose behaviors interfere with others—students whose behavioral disorders are *externalizing* (Vaughn, Bos, & Schumm, 2003). Students like these have a "conduct disorder" (CD), characterized by a "repetitive and persistent pattern of behavior in which the basic rights of others or major age-appropriate societal norms or rules are violated" (American Psychiatric Association, 2000). It's easy to identify students who display this kind of behavior, but what do you do about it?

First, it's essential to be *proactive*. Too often, teachers react only to the student's negative behaviors, but students with CD must be taught how to behave more appropriately. This means monitoring students' behavior closely so that you can prompt, recognize, and reward acceptable behaviors (i.e., "catch 'em being good") and anticipate and head off unacceptable behavior. Second, students with CD can benefit from *direct teaching of appropriate social behavior,* with rewards provided for the display of these behaviors, as well as a response-cost procedure in which points (or tokens) are lost for inappropriate behavior (Ostrander, 2004). Third, *exploring the intent or purpose of the unacceptable behavior* may reveal what a student needs in order to behave more appropriately and to learn, such as getting help with a difficult or frustrating assignment. (This is discussed further in the section on Functional Behavioral Assessment.) Some additional suggestions are listed in the Practical Tips box. Also refer to the section on defiance in Chapter 11 and the section on deescalating potentially explosive situations in Chapter 13.

PRACTICAL TIPS FOR

HELPING STUDENTS WITH CONDUCT DISORDER

- Make sure your classroom environment is organized, predictable, and structured.
- Plan and implement activities to promote a sense of community (see Chapter 3).
- Actively work on establishing positive relationships; provide consistent, positive attention and decrease negative comments.
- Closely monitor behavior and acknowledge and reward positive behavior.
- Directly teach social skills (e.g., anger management skills).
- Provide structured choices ("Would you prefer to do your math or your writing first?" "Do you want to do this alone or work in a group?").
- Have a plan for removing the student if he/she has an outburst.
- Learn to anticipate and de-escalate problem situations (see Chapter 13).
- Use self-management approaches (see Chapter 11) such as self-monitoring, self-evaluation, and self-instruction.
- Develop and implement contingency contracts (see Chapter 11).
- Make sure that instruction is appropriate for student's level of ability, because frustration and academic failure can exacerbate student's emotional/behavioral problems.

TABLE 12.3 Indicators of Early-Onset Depression

- Indecision, lack of concentration, or forgetfulness
- Change in personality, such as increased anger, irritability, moodiness, agitation, or whining
- Change in sleep patterns and appetite
- Loss of energy
- Lack of enthusiasm or motivation
- Loss of interest in personal appearance and hygiene
- Hopelessness, helplessness, and sadness
- Frequent physical complaints such as headaches and stomachaches
- Thoughts of suicide or death
- Low self-esteem, frequently expressed through self-blame and self-criticism
- Withdrawal from friends and activities once enjoyed
- Poor school performance

Children and adolescents with emotional disturbance may also show a pattern of *internalizing* behaviors, such as shyness, withdrawal, anxiety, and depression (Vaughn, Bos, & Schumm, 2003). Consider the following journal entry written by a student teacher I know:

I'm really worried about one of my kids. She's unbelievably shy and withdrawn. It took me a long time to even notice her. She never partici-pates in class discussions, never raises her hand, and never volunteers for anything. When I call on her, she looks down and doesn't answer, or her answer is so soft that I can't hear her. I've watched her during lunchtime in the cafeteria, and she doesn't seem to have any friends. The other kids aren't mean to her—they act like she doesn't even exist— and that's sort of the way I feel too!

Students like this, who act sad, reserved, withdrawn, or irritable, may actually be suffering from depression. Table 12.3 lists the signs that suggest depression in children and adolescents.

In "Too Sad to Learn," Steven Schlozman (2001), a clinical instructor in psy-chiatry at Harvard, suggests that teachers consult with a guidance counselor or school psychologist if they are concerned that a youngster is depressed. Certainly, classroom behavior that is dangerous or journals, drawings, or essays that suggest suicidal or homicidal thoughts warrant a formal referral. In addition, teachers need to understand that depressed students frequently feel as though they have little to contribute. To counter these feelings, you need to communicate respect and confidence in the student's abilities, minimize the possibility of embarrass-ment (e.g., by calling on depressed students to answer questions that have no clearly correct answer), and encourage them to assist younger or less able stu-dents. Most importantly, you need to forge a connection with the depressed stu-dent. As Schlozman writes, "Studies have shown that adults who suffered from de-pression when they were younger often recall a specific teacher as central to their recovery" (p. 81).

Pervasive Developmental Disorders:
Autism and Asperger Syndrome

Autism and Asperger Syndrome are two "pervasive developmental disorders" (PDDs), a cluster of disorders characterized by marked impairments in the development of social interaction and communication skills. Biological and neurological in origin, autism and Asperger Syndrome (AS) are generally evident by three to five years of age (Hagin, 2004). Just how frequently PDDs occur is not entirely clear. Studies suggest a rate of about 1 in 200 for PDDs as a whole (Vaughn, Bos, & Schumm, 2003), while estimates for autism alone range from 2 to 6 in 1,000 (Strock, 2004). In any case, the prevalence of PDDs appears to be increasing dramatically. For example, Vaughn, Bos, and Schumm (2003) report that between 1993 and 1998, there was an increase of 244 percent in identified cases of autism. Why this should be happening is unclear. Some educators hypothesize that the increase is due to better assessment measures, changes in diagnostic criteria, and growing awareness of PDDs among parents and professionals, rather than an actual rise in incidence (Hagin, 2004).

Children and adolescents with autism often display a lack of responsiveness and unawareness of social situations; for example, they may make little or no eye contact, show little awareness of social situations, and exhibit a lack of interest in sharing enjoyable activities with other people. In addition, they may have little or no spoken language; those who do develop language may use it idiosyncratically (e.g., repeating sentences said to them, a condition known as "echolalia"). Finally, individuals with autism often exhibit restricted, repetitive patterns of behavior (e.g., body rocking or hand flapping; inflexible adherence to routines or rituals) and a consuming preoccupation with specific topics (e.g., train schedules). Hypersensitivity to sensory input such as noise, lights, and touch is also common. Autism is four times more common in boys than in girls (National Dissemination Center for Children with Disabilities, 2003).

There is ongoing debate about whether Asperger Syndrome (AS) is an independent diagnostic category or a mild form of autism (Myles, Gagnon, Moyer, & Trautman, 2004). In fact, the Individuals with Disabilities Education Act (IDEA) does not recognize AS as a specific disability category, so that youngsters with Asperger Syndrome are often served under the diagnostic labels of autism, behavior disorders, or learning disabilities. Like autism, AS is characterized by marked impairment in social interaction; however, individuals with AS often desire interaction—they just lack the skills and knowledge needed to initiate and respond appropriately in social situations. For example, they often demonstrate an inability to understand the perspectives of others and have difficulty understanding nonverbal social cues. Although individuals with AS have no clinically significant delay in cognition and do not have delayed language development, they have difficulty understanding the subtleties of language, like irony and humor (National Dissemination Center, 2003) and their voice quality may be flat, stilted, and "robotic." They also have a restricted range of interests or obsessions, often developing an exhaustive knowledge of one topic (e.g., monsters, numbers, or movies) on which they give long-winded lectures. In addition, children and adolescents with AS tend to have poor motor skills and to be clumsy and uncoordinated. Like those with autism, individuals with AS show an "apparently inflexible adherence to specific, nonfunctional routines or rituals" (American Psychiatric Association, 2000, p. 84).

It is important to note that manifestations of autism and AS can range from mild to severe. Thus, two children with the same diagnosis may function very differently and require different kinds and amounts of support. Although there are no cures for PDDs, educational interventions can be effective in bringing about improvements. Students with autism can benefit from augmentative and alternative communication systems. For example, they can learn to point to a picture on a communication board to indicate preferences for academic work. Students with PDD can also benefit from direct instruction in social skills and in reading social cues. Since students with autism and AS adhere rigidly to routines, it's also essential that you create and follow a consistent classroom schedule. If a change in the schedule is necessary, you need to provide plenty of warning. See the Practical Tips box for additional suggestions on helping students with AS; also refer to Kline and Silver (2004) for a comprehensive discussion.

Practical Tips for

HELPING STUDENTS WITH ASPERGER SYNDROME

- *Establish a "home base,"* a safe area in which a student can calm down, away from the overstimulation of the classroom (e.g., a counselor's office, a resource room, the nurse's office). Home base should *not* be used for time-out or punishment.

- *Use "priming" to familiarize students with academic material prior to its use in school.* Priming can reduce the stress associated with new tasks and increase success. A typical priming session lasts 10 to 15 minutes and is held in a quiet space the evening or morning before the materials are to be used.

- *Modify the environment:*
  Seat the student in an area free of distraction.
  Keep the student's space free of unnecessary materials.
  Use checklists to help the student be organized.
  Provide opportunities for the student to move around.

- *Modify instruction:*
  Since fine motor skills can make handwriting difficult, let the student type or record responses.
  Since verbal information can be difficult to process, use visual supports whenever possible.
  Color code assignments.
  Provide the student with a skeletal outline of the main ideas.
  Schedule short, frequent conferences with the student to check for comprehension.
  Break assignments into shorter tasks.
  Allow the student to use a computer or calculator.

Source: Myles, Gagnon, Moyer, & Trautman, 2004.

Attention-Deficit/Hyperactivity Disorder

Although teachers often find it particularly challenging to work with students who have attention-deficit/hyperactivity disorder (ADHD), this condition is *not* included in the IDEA's definition of children with disabilities. For this reason, students with ADHD are not eligible for services under IDEA unless they fall into other disability categories (e.g., learning disabilities, serious emotional disturbance, other health impairment). They may, however, be able to receive special services under Section 504 of the Rehabilitation Act of 1973. Section 504 prohibits discrimination on the basis of disability by recipients of federal funds and requires that public schools receiving federal funding address the needs of children with disabilities. As defined in Section 504, a person with a disability is any person who has a physical or mental impairment substantially limiting a major life activity such as learning. Thus, students with ADHD may fit within that definition.

No diagnostic test for ADHD is currently available, but Table 12.4 lists the criteria for identifying an individual as having ADHD. As the table notes, four conditions must be met for a positive diagnosis: (1) Six or more symptoms must be present; (2) the symptoms have to have persisted for at least six months; (3) the symptoms had to have appeared before seven years of age; and (4) the symptoms must result in impaired functioning in at least two settings. Keep in mind that any one of the behaviors can be normal. It is when an individual frequently displays a large number of these behaviors at a developmentally inappropriate age that the possibility of ADHD should be considered.

It is estimated that 3 percent to 5 percent of school-age children in the United States have ADHD, with far more boys than girls affected (Wodrich, 2000). The reason for the disparity is not clear. Some researchers believe the explanation lies in brain biochemistry or structure; others point to the way boys are socialized, which may make it harder to sit quietly and attend. Still others suggest subtle discrimination on the part of elementary teachers, who are predominantly women (Wodrich, 2000).

Students with ADHD often have difficulties in school. They may be underproductive or disorganized, failing to complete their work, or even losing it. They may also have problems with memory, language, visual perception, and fine motor control, which interfere with academic achievement. Indeed, as many as 35 percent of children and adolescents with ADHD may have learning disabilities, compared with 3 percent of all children (Wodrich, 2000). Finally—and not surprisingly—individuals with ADHD may have problems meeting behavioral expectations and getting along with their peers.

To help students with ADHD, your classroom needs to be predictable, secure, and structured. Behavioral expectations must be clear, and consequences must be fair and consistent. The Practical Tips box on page 371 offers some more specific suggestions.

 PAUSE AND REFLECT

In recent years, dramatic increases in the number of children who have been diagnosed and treated for ADHD have stirred debate not only about the possibility of overdiagnosis, but even whether the disorder really exists. Skeptics criticize teachers for wanting to suppress children's natural enthusiasm and energy, parents for failing to provide appropriate guidance and discipline, and physicians for overmedicating. What do you think about this?

TABLE 12.4 DSM-IV Definition of Attention-Deficit/Hyperactivity Disorder

A. Either (1) or (2):

(1) Six (or more) of the following symptoms of inattention have persisted for at least 6 months to a degree that is maladaptive and inconsistent with developmental level:

Inattention

(a) Often fails to give close attention to details or makes careless mistakes in schoolwork, work, or other activities.

(b) Often has difficulty sustaining attention in tasks or play activities.

(c) Often does not seem to listen when spoken to directly.

(d) Often does not follow through on instructions and fails to finish schoolwork, chores, or duties in the workplace (not due to oppositional behavior or failure to understand instructions).

(e) Often has difficulty organizing tasks and activities.

(f) Often avoids, dislikes, or is reluctant to engage in tasks that require sustained mental effort (such as schoolwork or homework).

(g) Often loses things necessary for tasks or activities (e.g., toys, school assignments, pencils, books, tools).

(h) Is often easily distracted by extraneous stimuli.

(i) Is often forgetful in daily activities.

(2) Six (or more) of the following symptoms of hyperactivity-impulsivity have persisted for at least 6 months to a degree that is maladaptive and inconsistent with developmental level:

Hyperactivity

(a) Often fidgets with hands or feet or squirms in seat.

(b) Often leaves seat in classroom or in other situations in which remaining seated is expected.

(c) Often runs about or climbs excessively in situations in which it is inappropriate (in adolescents or adults, may be limited to subjective feelings of restlessness).

(d) Often has difficulty playing or engaging in leisure activities quietly.

(e) Is often "on the go" or often acts as if "driven by a motor."

(f) Often talks excessively.

Impulsivity

(g) Often blurts out answers before questions have been completed.

(h) Often has difficulty awaiting turn.

(i) Often interrupts or intrudes on others (e.g., butts into conversations or games).

B. Some hyperactive-impulsive symptoms that caused impairment were present before age 7 years.

C. Some impairment from the symptoms is present in two or more settings (e.g., at school [or work] and at home).

D. There must be clear evidence of clinically significant impairment in social, academic, or occupational functioning.

E. The symptoms do not occur exclusively during the course of a Pervasive Developmental Disorder, Schizophrenia, or other Psychotic Disorder and are not better accounted for by another mental disorder (e.g., Mood Disorder, Anxiety Disorder, Dissociative Disorder, or a Personality Disorder).

(continued)

TABLE 12.4 (*continued*)

Code based on type:

Attention-deficit/hyperactivity disorder, combined type: If both Criteria A1 and A2 are met for the past 6 months.

Attention-deficit/hyperactivity disorder, predominantly inattentive type: If Criterion A1 is met but Criterion A2 is not met for the past 6 months.

Attention-deficit/hyperactivity disorder, predominantly hyperactive-impulsive type: If Criterion A2 is met but Criterion A1 is not met for the past 6 months.

Source: American Psychiatric Association (APA). (1994). *Diagnostic and statistical manual of mental disorders* (4th ed., pp. 83–85). Washington, D.C.: Author. Reprinted with permission from the *Diagnostic and Statistical Manual of Mental Disorders,* 4th ed.

General Strategies for Helping Students with Disabilities and ADHD

Tony Valenti is a ninth-grade world history teacher responsible for six classes a day, each with approximately 35 students. Covering the textbook is Tony's major concern:

> *I have 38 chapters to cover in 36 weeks. We really have only 30 weeks, when you consider pep rallies and things like that. My biggest problem is trying to fit everything in. My assistant principal, who supervises curriuum and instruction, would like me to teach study skills and to make adaptations for kids who can't read, but frankly I don't see how to cram it into an already impossible schedule. (Vaughn, Bos, & Schumm, 2003, p. 436).*

Tony's position illustrates the special challenges of implementing inclusion on the secondary level. Secondary teachers generally feel pressure to "cover the curriculum"—pressure that has been heightened in this age of high-stakes testing. In addition, they expect students to have independent study skills and to possess the prior knowledge required to master new material, something that may not be true of students with disabilities (Mastropieri & Scruggs, 2001).

Despite these special challenges, research indicates that inclusion on the secondary level can be successful in terms of academic and social outcomes (Wallace, Anderson, Bartholomay, & Hupp, 2002; Mastropieri & Scruggs, 2001). The following section of the chapter delineates some of the ways to enhance the likelihood of such success.

Become Familiar with the Student's IEP or 504 Plan

The IDEA requires that an individualized education program (IEP) be developed for each student with a disability. IEPs are developed by a team comprised of a representative of the local education agency (e.g., an administrator who can commit school district resources), one of the student's general education teachers, the

Practical Tips for

HELPING STUDENTS WITH ADHD

- Provide structure, routine, predictability, and consistency.
- Make sure that behavioral expectations are clear.
- Tape a copy of the schedule on their desks.
- Seat them close to you, among attentive, well-focused students (the second row is better than the first).
- Make frequent eye contact.
- Make sure their desks are free of distractions (provide cardboard dividers to block out distractions).
- Provide a quiet work area or a "private office" to which students can move for better concentration.
- Provide headphones to block out noise during seatwork or other times that require concentration.
- Provide opportunities to move around in legitimate ways (e.g., exercise breaks, doing errands).
- Use physical contact to focus attention (e.g., a hand on a shoulder).
- Develop private signals to help focus attention.
- Ease transitions by providing cues and warnings.
- Use positive reinforcement and behavior modification techniques.
- Modify assignments:
    Cut the written workload.
    Break the assignment into manageable parts.
- Limit the amount of homework.
- Allow more time on assignments or tests.
- Assist with organization (e.g., assignment pads; checklists; color-coded notebooks for different subjects; accordion folders for loose papers).
- Try to give students at least one task each day that they can do successfully.
- Try to call on students when they are paying attention; use their first names before calling on them.
- Provide extra sets of books to keep at home so that students are not overwhelmed after an absence and to prevent problems caused by forgetting books.
- Provide access to a computer, along with keyboard and word-processing instruction; do not remove access to the computer as a penalty.
- DO NOT PUNISH; DO NOT ASSUME STUDENTS ARE LAZY; DO NOT GIVE UP.

Source: Adapted from Rief, 1993; and CHADD Facts, 1993.

special education teacher who will have primary responsibility for implementing the IEP, parents or guardians, a person who can interpret the instructional implications of the evaluation results, the student (when appropriate), and other individuals at the discretion of the parent or school.

Similarly, a student who is eligible for special services under Section 504 of the Rehabilitation Act will have a "504 plan" outlining the accommodations and services needed to ensure that the student receives an appropriate education. Like the IEP, a 504 plan is developed by a team, although composition is not specified by law.

Unfortunately, at the middle and high school levels, general education teachers often do not participate in the IEP or 504 process; sometimes they do not even know which students in their classrooms have been identified as having special needs (Schumm & Vaughn, 1992). Moreover, obtaining access to students' IEPs and 504s is not always easy. Policies and procedures vary from school to school. Sandy reports that by the second day of school, her mailbox is filled with the IEPs and 504s of students in her classes, and she has to sign a form indicating that she's received them. In contrast, Christina never gets copies; instead, a special educator or the school nurse shows her the documents. However you're told, our teachers emphasize the fact that implementation is your responsibility. As Sandy comments: "Teachers need to realize that 504s and IEPs are not optional. You can't ignore them. And if no one shows you any IEPs or 504s (as sometimes happens), it's your responsibility to track them down and read them."

It's also important to reexamine IEPs every marking period and make sure that you are monitoring the progress of students with disabilities. In this regard, it's helpful to keep a folder of relevant work samples to document progress (Vaughn, Bos, & Schumm, 2003).

Create an Accepting Climate

Secondary teachers often display a less positive attitude toward inclusion than their elementary-level counterparts (Scruggs & Mastropieri, 1996). This is unfortunate, since the success of inclusion largely depends on a teacher's ability and willingness to create a positive atmosphere that is accepting of individual differences (Mastropieri & Scruggs, 2001). You can promote a positive climate by making it clear that all students are accepted, valued members of the class, establishing norms that emphasize belonging and respect, and implementing group activities that foster interaction between students with disabilities and their nondisabled peers (Soodak & McCarthy, 2006). Refer back to Chapter 3 for specific ideas.

Coordinate and Collaborate with Special Education Teachers and Paraprofessionals

As inclusion has become more widespread, so too has the practice of having content specialists co-teach with special educators in the general education classroom. Co-teaching, also known as collaborative teaching or cooperative teaching, can take a variety of forms (Dieker, 2001). For example, in the "lead and support" model, one teacher takes responsibility for instruction while the other offers assistance and support to individuals or small groups. In "parallel teaching," teachers jointly plan instruction, but each delivers it to half the class, and in "team teaching," both teachers share the planning and instruction of students.

Although co-teaching can be very effective, it also poses challenges for both parties. Some of these difficulties stem from inadequate school supports (e.g., lack of common preparation time), personality conflicts, and a lack of clarity about roles and responsibilities in co-taught classrooms (Murray, 2004). None of our four teachers works in a co-teaching arrangement, but they have seen situations that are less than ideal. Christina comments:

> Regular ed teachers sometimes have a problem working with special ed teachers; they are very "territorial" and treat the special educator like an aide. They don't do collaborative planning; they just say, "Here's what we're doing." But sometimes the problem is the other way around. You have a regular ed teacher who really wants to collaborate with the special ed teacher, but the special ed teacher wants to sit in the back of the room and only help a couple of kids.

In order to avoid these problems, it is essential to discuss the roles that each teacher will have in the general education classroom. The Practical Tips box lists strategies for co-teaching at the secondary level.

Even if you are not in a co-teaching situation, it's important to communicate regularly with special services personnel. For example, you can ask a special educator for suggestions about enhancing the learning of students with disabilities; you might also ask the special educator to demonstrate lessons or to come in and help you instruct students with special needs. You should also inform the special education teacher if you are concerned about a student's progress.

Practical Tips for

CO-TEACHING IN SECONDARY CLASSROOMS

- **Begin slowly.** Discuss your respective understandings of co-teaching; examine various models.

- **Involve an administrator.** Discuss the kinds of administrative support that are needed (especially with respect to common planning time). Find out if such support will be forthcoming.

- **Get to know your partner.** Discuss your expectations with respect to roles and responsibilities regarding
    Planning whole class instruction
    Planning modifications for individual students
    Conducting instruction
    Grading
    Parental contact
    Discipline

- **Create a workable schedule.** Decide how often co-teaching will occur (daily, a few times a week, for a specific unit). Decide on the model that will be used. Think about how to ensure that both teachers are actively involved and that neither feels over- or underutilized. Arrange for common planning time.

Source: Adapted from Murawski & Dieker, 2004.

When approaching special services personnel, it's important to have specific information about the student and about the interventions and accommodations you've already tried. Complaints like "He's driving me crazy," "She constantly demands attention," or "He just can't hack it in my class" are not helpful. The more detailed your information can be, the more likely you are to receive assistance. Here are some of our teachers' suggestions about the kinds of information to bring:

- An overall description of the student (both strengths and weaknesses).
- If the student exhibits problem behavior, a detailed description of the inappropriate behavior:

   When does the student exhibit the behavior?

   How frequently does the student exhibit the behavior?

   What antecedent events set off the behavior?

   What is the duration of the behavior?

   What is the reaction of other students in the class?

- If the student is having academic problems, a detailed description of the student's academic difficulties (with work samples to support your description).
- Efforts on your part to correct or deal with the problem.
- How you'd like to be helped or what type of help you believe the student needs.

Like co-teaching, the use of paraprofessionals or teaching assistants has become an increasingly popular method of supporting students with disabilities in general education classrooms. In fact, in many schools, having a paraprofessional accompany a student with disabilities to class is the "primary or exclusive" way in which inclusion is accomplished (Giangreco & Doyle, 2002, p. 2). Paraprofessionals can play a valuable, vital role in inclusive classrooms, but too often, they become the student's actual instructor, while the teacher becomes the delegator (Giangreco & Doyle, 2002). When this happens, we have a situation in which those who are least qualified to teach are responsible for instructing the students who present the most complex challenges.

If you have paraprofessionals in your classes, it is critical that you remain engaged with the students who have disabilities and not turn their education over to someone who may be uncomfortable and unknowledgeable about the subject matter. You also need to discuss explicitly what your respective roles and responsibilities will be with respect to instruction and behavior management. Paraprofessionals can provide support by carrying out a variety of noninstructional activities (e.g., preparing materials, taking attendance) as well as instructional tasks (e.g., assisting students during independent work, providing additional practice opportunities to reinforce previously taught material), but they should not have primary responsibility for a student's learning. It is also desirable to have paraprofessionals interact with *all* students, not just those with disabilities.

Examine Your Classroom Environment for Possible Mismatch

It's important to remember that problems do not always reside exclusively within a student. Sometimes problems are the result of a discrepancy between a student's needs and the classroom environment. A fourth-grade teacher I know shares this example of an obvious mismatch:

> I have a boy in my class who's 5'6" and weighs about 200 pounds. He's constantly picking up his desk with his knees and dropping it on the floor. It's disturbing and disruptive, but I can't blame him. I've had a request in for months for a bigger desk, but so far nothing has happened. Meanwhile, he's always fumbling and bumping into things and knocking things over. It's easy to get frustrated with him—he's got lots of other problems too—but it's clear that one contributing factor is that the physical setting is just too small for him!

As this story illustrates, we sometimes think of a child as disabled, when actually the problem is the result of a *disabling situation* (Gearheart, Weishahn, & Gearheart, 1992). For example, since individuals with ADHD are easily distracted, you need to arrange the classroom environment so that distractions are minimized.

In sum, before concluding that "the entire problem is the kid," examine your classroom situation and reflect on ways the environment may be contributing to the student's difficulties. Here are some questions that our teachers ask themselves:

- Where is the student sitting? Is the seat near a source of distraction? Is it too far from the teacher?

- Is sitting in groups too difficult for the student to handle? Should I move the student to a pair or to individual seating?

- What type of academic work am I providing? Are assignments too mechanical? too dry? too long? Do they require too much independence? Do I ever allow choice?

- How do I speak with the student? How do I praise the student? *Do* I praise the student?

- What rules and routines have I set up and are they contrary to the student's ability to comply? Am I expecting quiet behavior too long? Am I setting the student up for failure?

- Am I allowing an appropriate amount of time for completing assignments? For transitions?

Use Peer Tutoring, Peer Assistance, and Cooperative Learning

Successful inclusion programs make effective use of peers. Students can serve as *tutors* on academic tasks, *buddies* who assist with difficult activities, or *advocates* who watch out for the welfare of those with special needs (Gearheart, Weishahn, & Gearheart, 1992). For example, Peer Buddies is a structured program of peer support in which a nondisabled high school student is paired with a student with disabilities for at least one period each day. The Buddies support their partners in a variety of ways and in a variety of settings. They may accompany them to a school pep rally, introduce them to other general education students during lunch, help them complete a lab project in a science class, or teach them to set tables at a restaurant serving as a job training site. (See Table 12.5 for additional ways that peers can provide supports.) Copeland and her colleagues (2002) found that general and special educators involved in a Peer Buddies program reported both

TABLE 12.5 Ways That Peers Can Support Classmates with Disabilities

- Teach classroom routines (e.g., where to put homework, what to do when you first get to class)
- Read a test and record answers
- Read or record selections from a textbook, paraphrasing as needed
- Take notes during a teacher lecture and spend time discussing the notes and answering questions at the end of the period
- Help a classmate fulfill an assigned role during cooperative learning activities
- Facilitate conversation with other general education students during free time
- Keep track of assignments when students are absent
- Provide tutoring in a specific skill
- Provide assistance with organization (e.g., recording assignments, finding the relevant place in the textbook, organizing notebooks)

Note: Although peers can support classmates with disabilities, it is important to make sure that every student has an opportunity to be the tutor or supporter; in other words, students with disabilities should not always be relegated to the position of "helpee."

Source: Adapted from Copeland, McCall, Williams, Guth, Carter, Fowler, Presley, & Hughes, 2002.

academic and social benefits; in particular, students who received support from peers seemed more independent, more self-confident, and more willing to participate in everyday high school activities.

As I stressed in Chapter 9, research has also demonstrated that cooperative learning can promote positive social relationships between students with disabilities and their peers. The use of cooperative learning can help to minimize the problem of students with special needs being isolated and rejected *socially,* even though they are included *physically* in the regular classroom. Unfortunately, research indicates that cooperative learning is not always this successful. O'Connor and Jenkins (1996) observed 22 children with mild disabilities and 12 average-performing children in grades three through six. They classified only 40 percent of the disabled students as successfully participating in cooperative groups. Successful participation depended on the selection of suitable partners, careful monitoring, the teaching of cooperative behaviors, and the establishment of a cooperative ethic. (See Chapter 9 on Managing Groupwork.)

Use a Variety of Instructional Strategies

Diverse classrooms demand diverse teaching approaches. It is unlikely that a steady diet of traditional instruction—whole-group teacher presentation, recitation, independent seatwork—will be successful when classrooms contain individuals who vary in academic ability and have a range of disabilities. The use of cooperative learning is one instructional alternative. There are others: group problem solving, role-playing, debates, writing and reading workshop, computer-assisted instruction, hands-on, activity-based instruction.

With this in mind, our teachers try to plan curriculum units that allow for a wide range of activities, from writing reports, to making charts and graphs, to hands-on experiments, to creating raps. The intention is to provide all students with the chance to work in ways that are comfortable for them, while also providing opportunities to "stretch." (See the discussion of multiple intelligences in Chapter 7.)

Remember the Principles of Effective Management

Although you may feel you lack the skills needed to teach students who are especially low-achieving or those who have mild academic disabilities, research indicates that the teaching behaviors associated with outstanding achievement gains for these students are similar to the behaviors that are effective with *all* students (Slavin, 1989). In fact, effective teaching behaviors include many of the strategies we've discussed in earlier chapters:

- Providing feedback to students.
- Providing specific, informative praise.
- Providing learning tasks that students can accomplish with a high rate of success.
- Using classroom time efficiently, minimizing transitional or noninstructional time.
- Limiting the use of punishment.
- Maintaining high engagement rates.
- Focusing on preventive management strategies, rather than disciplinary interventions.
- Creating a supportive, nonthreatening learning environment.

Conduct a Functional Behavioral Assessment for Students Who Display Challenging Behavior

Functional behavioral assessment (FBA) is a process for gathering information about causal relationships between environmental events and a student's inappropriate behavior in order to determine the *function or purpose* of that behavior. FBA procedures have historically been used in cases of severe behavior disorders, and in fact, IDEA 2004 mandates schools to conduct FBAs of a student with disabilities if he or she is to be removed more than 10 consecutive school days or if the removal constitutes a change in placement. In recent years, however, FBA has also been widely recommended for use in general education classrooms with typically developing students and those with mild disabilities (Robinson & Ricord Griesemer, 2006).

   FBA is based on the premise that behavior occurs for one of two reasons. It either enables the student to obtain something that he or she desires (e.g., the teacher's attention) or it enables the student to avoid something that he or she finds unpleasant (e.g., doing math). In other words, the behavior happens for a reason (Kerr & Nelson, 2006), although the student may not be conscious of this.

   FBA is comprised of several steps. First, it is necessary to *describe the problem behavior* in precise, measurable, observable terms so that two or more persons could agree on the occurrence. This means that instead of saying that "Michael is aggressive," you need to say, "Michael curses at other kids, puts his foot out to trip people, and throws his books on the floor when angry." In the second step, *information is collected regarding the environmental events that occur before and after the student's behavior.* This is generally referred to as an A-B-C assessment, where A represents the antecedents of the behavior, B represents the behavior, and C represents the consequences. (Figure 12.2 shows a sample ABC recording sheet.) Since it's generally not feasible to collect this information while you're teaching, you will probably have to arrange for someone else (e.g., a collaborating teacher, a teaching assistant, a school counselor) to do the assessment while you provide instruction (or vice versa). It's also essential to conduct observations across several days, so that you can be confident you are getting a representative sample of the student's behavior. Finally, make sure to observe times when the target behavior typically occurs and times when it typically does *not* occur. If you carry out this step carefully, you should then be able to answer the following questions (Kerr & Nelson, 2006):

Does the behavior occur in the presence of certain persons?
During what activities is the behavior more likely to occur?
During what activities is the behavior less likely to occur?
What happens to the student following the behavior?
How do others respond to the behavior?
Does the surrounding environment change in any way following the behavior?

Student _Ronald_   Date _10/11_

Observer _Mr. Green_   Time _9:15_

Setting/Activity _Spanish Class_

Target behavior(s) _Noncompliance/Aggression_

Time	Antecedents (What happened before the behavior?)	Behavior (What did the student do?)	Consequences (What happened after the behavior?)
9:15	Teacher tells class to get into pairs to create a role play about eating in a restaurant and not having money to pay the bill.	Ronald sits slumped in seat. He ignores the students who ask if he wants to be their partner.	Teacher tells Ronald to work with Lauren. He continues to sit slumped in seat. Ignores both teacher & Lauren.
9:17	Teacher goes over to Ronald; quietly tells him to start role play activity *now*.	Ronald says he doesn't want to do the "stupid" role play.	Teacher tells Ronald that he either does the role play or gets a zero for the day. She walks away. Ronald continues to ignore Lauren.
9:20	Lauren tells teacher that Ronald still won't participate. Teacher tells Ronald he's getting a zero for the day.	Ronald throws books on the floor, yells at teacher: "Who cares about a f ___ zero?!" and walks toward the door.	Teacher follows Ronald; tells him to go with her out into the hallway where they can talk.

Figure 12.2   A Sample ABC Recording Sheet

In the third step of the FBA, *hypotheses are developed about the purpose of the behavior;* in other words, this is when you try to figure out what the student stands to gain. For example, let's assume that as a result of gathering information in step 2, it has become clear that Justin, a student in a middle school English/language arts class, is disruptive only during writing workshop (the antecedent), when he annoys the students sitting nearby by uttering silly comments, making noises, and dropping books on the floor (the behavior). In response to this behavior, the teacher repeatedly tells him to "settle down and get to work" (one consequence). When this doesn't bring about a positive change, the teacher tells him to take a seat in the back of the room and think about how students are supposed to behave during writing workshop (another consequence). On the basis of this information, we can hypothesize that Justin's behavior enables him to avoid something he seems to find aversive—namely, writing workshop.

The fourth step is to *test the hypotheses you have developed* by creating a behavior intervention plan (BIP). This involves modifying some aspect of the environment and observing the effect. In Justin's case, since the writing task appears to be frustrating, the teacher might provide him with additional support such as his own personal dictionary, allow him to seek assistance from a "writing buddy," and provide encouragement and additional instructional guidance as needed. In addition, the teacher might stop responding to the inappropriate behavior and instead respond to appropriate behavior with smiles and praise. If *monitoring* (the fifth step) shows the BIP is successful (i.e., the inappropriate behavior ceases), then the FBA is done. If the inappropriate behavior continues, you need to go back to the third step and develop some new hypotheses. Remember, however, that long-standing behavior does not change overnight; you may need to follow the plan for two or three weeks before deciding whether it is making a difference (Friend & Bursuck, 2002).

Although FBA is an extremely useful tool, it is not simple, and identifying the underlying function of a behavior may require the assistance of well-trained observers (Landrum & Kauffman, 2006). Therefore, teachers need to consult with special services personnel.

HELPING STUDENTS WHO ARE ENGLISH-LANGUAGE LEARNERS

The past two decades have seen a significant increase in the language minority population of the United States. According to the census conducted in 2000 (Shin with Bruno, 2003), 47 million people or 18 percent of the general population aged five and over speak a language other than English at home. This is up from 14 percent in 1990 and 11 percent in 1980. California has the largest percentage of language-minority speakers (39 percent), followed by New Mexico (37 percent), Texas (31 percent), New York (28 percent), Hawaii (27 percent), Arizona, and New Jersey (each about 26 percent). The 2000 census also indicates that Spanish is the non–English language spoken most frequently at home, followed by Chinese, French, German, Tagalog, Vietnamese, Italian, Korean, Russian, Polish, and Arabic.

The growth in the language-minority population is reflected in public school enrollments. It has been estimated that in the 2003–2004 school year, almost 5 million English-language learners (ELLs) were enrolled in public schools (pre-K to 12th grade). This represents more than 10 percent of the total school enrollment, and a 40.7 percent increase from 1993 to 1994 (Padolsky, 2005).

Before considering ways that you can provide the special help these students may need, let's talk a bit about terminology. Language-minority students are frequently referred to as "Limited English Proficient" (or LEP); however, this term emphasizes language *deficiency* rather than the very real potential to become bilingual or multilingual, which is certainly a strength. Given the importance of conveying respect and appreciation for students' native languages, as well as their native language facility, I prefer to use the term "English-language learner" (ELL) in the following discussion.

Federal legislation provides funding and encouragement for programs to assist ELLs; however, there are no federally mandated programs like those provided for students who have disabilities. In fact, a landmark statement supporting the rights of ELLs comes not from the legislature, but from a Supreme Court case, *Lau v. Nichols* (1974), in which a group of Chinese-speaking students sued the San Francisco Unified School District for providing them with an education they could not understand. The Court found for the plaintiffs, stating:

> [T]here is no equality of treatment merely by providing students with the same facilities, textbooks, teachers, and curriculum: for students who do not understand English are effectively foreclosed from any meaningful education. Basic English skills are at the very core of what these public schools teach. Imposition of a requirement that, before a child can effectively participate in the education program he must already have acquired those basic skills is to make a mockery of public education. We know that those who do not understand English are certain to find their classroom experiences wholly incomprehensible and in no way meaningful. (p. 27)

As a result of *Lau,* a number of states enacted legislation requiring services for ELLs, but laws change constantly and vary substantially from state to state. The state in which you teach may mandate such services or merely permit them; it may even prohibit them! Despite the variability, state laws generally call for the identification and assessment of ELLs and describe options for special services. One option is a *bilingual education program,* which teaches students in their native language as well as in English, thus allowing them to learn academic subjects while they're learning English. In some states, if there is a given number of ELLs in a district, speaking a common native language at approximately the same grade level, the district is required to provide bilingual programs.

 PAUSE AND REFLECT

Bilingual education programs are extremely controversial, and in some states, laws have been passed restricting bilingual education and substituting programs that stress the use of English. Even the parents of some English-language learners oppose bilingual education, contending that they hinder children's learning of English. At the same time, scholars in bilingual education stress the importance of receiving instruction in a child's first language to build on their existing literacy skills. What do *you* think about this issue?

When English-language learners come from many different language backgrounds, bilingual education programs are impractical. In this case, schools typically place students in regular English-only classrooms and pull them out for instruction from a specially trained teacher in *English as a Second Language.* Since the focus is on learning English, students with different native languages can be in the same room.

In general education, English-only classrooms, ELLs will undoubtedly have problems if they are expected to "sink or swim," and if teachers are unwilling to make any modifications. ELLs may be able to function admirably, however, if you implement some of the environmental supports used in "sheltered instruction" or "Specially Designed Academic Instruction in English" (SDAIE). A comprehensive model of SDAIE includes five components (Diaz-Rico & Weed, 2002). First—and critical—is the *teacher's attitude;* unless the teacher is open and willing to learn from students, SDAIE cannot be successful. The second component is *content,* meaning that lessons must have both subject matter and language objectives and lessons must be planned and implemented with language in mind. Third is an emphasis on *comprehensibility;* lessons must include explicit strategies that aid in students' understanding (e.g., modeling, frequent comprehension checks, adjustment in use of language). Fourth, *connections* refers to the importance of connecting curriculum to students' background and experiences. The final component is *interaction:* Students in a sheltered English classroom have frequent opportunities to work together, to clarify concepts in their native language, and to represent learning in a variety of ways. (See Diaz-Rico & Weed, 2002, for additional information on these five components.)

Having a number of English-language learners in your class will add to the cultural richness and global understanding of your students. It may also be a source of stress, especially for new teachers. Questions are likely to arise about how to meet the needs of your ELLs while not shortchanging the rest of the class; however, incorporating some sheltered English strategies into your teaching and following the suggestions listed in the Practical Tips box on page 382 should benefit *everyone.*

HELPING STUDENTS WHO ARE TROUBLED

During one meeting, the teachers talked about how they try to be alert to problems their students might be experiencing. Sandy told us how she tries to distinguish between problems that warrant immediate action and those that do not, and how she collects additional information:

I watch for changes in students' behavior. If I see anything that looks like drug abuse, I report it immediately. If it doesn't seem like a drug problem, I generally approach the student and ask what's going on. If the kid seems depressed, I'll say something like, "Hey, you seem a little down today. Are you having a problem? Do you want to talk?" We all have bad days, and adolescents have wide swings of mood; it's the nature of the beast. A day or two of strange behavior doesn't necessarily mean there's a big problem. Adolescents aren't very good at masking their emotions, and most of the time they're upset

PRACTICAL TIPS FOR

HELPING ENGLISH-LANGUAGE LEARNERS

- Provide a safe, welcoming environment for language risk taking.
- Increase time and opportunities for meaningful talk.
- Find ways for students to participate in group activties, giving them roles that are less dependent on language use (e.g., have them draw pictures or serve as timekeepers).
- Encourage English speaking while honoring students' first language and culture.
- Encourage children to tell about their culture. View ethnic and linguistic diversity within a classroom not as a problem, but as an asset from which both teachers and students can profit.
- Build on and utilize students' background knowledge and personal interests.
- Encourage students to write about topics of their choice and for real-world purposes.
- Encourage parents to develop and maintain their primary language at home.
- Learn and use some second language yourself with students.
- Emphasize collaborative over individual work.
- Emphasize doing rather than telling.
- Enunciate clearly, with your mouth in direct view of the students.
- Use gestures and body language to accompany your verbal messages to students.
- Make the language of the text comprehensible by interpreting it in simple, everyday language.
- Offer periodic summaries.
- Paraphrase questions and statements to allow for different levels of proficiency. Use synonyms to clarify the meaning of unknown words.
- Control vocabulary and sentence structure (e.g., if you use idioms like "It's raining cats and dogs," explain what they mean).
- Ask questions that require different degrees of English proficiency in responding (e.g., nonverbal signals to communicate agreement or disagreement, yes–no, single-word, or short answers).
- When students respond to your questions, focus on the content, rather than on the form of the response.
- Use objects, video, pictures, movement to increase comprehensibility.
- Apply Specially Designed Academic Instruction in English (SDAIE) strategies across the curriculum. Often known as "sheltered instruction," SDAIE focuses on core curriculum content and uses a rich variety of techniques and materials such as artifacts, visuals, video, storyboarding, movement, role-plays, and collaborative learning.
- Think aloud and model a variety of reading comprehension strategies (e.g., making connections, predicting, inferring).
- Use a variety of reading supports such as text tours and picture walks (to preview material), graphic organizers (story maps, character analyses), and text signposts (chapter headings, bold print).
- Use a variety of writing supports, such as group composing, graphic organizers, and drawing-based texts.

Sources: Cary, 2000; Romero, Mercado, & Vazquez-Faria, 1987.

because they had a fight with their mother, or the dog had to be put to sleep, or their boyfriend or girlfriend broke up with them. But if a kid is acting weird or seems depressed for longer than a few days, I check with other teachers to find out if they're seeing anything unusual too. If they've also noticed problems, I go to the principal or the vice-principal; often they know if something is going on at home. If there appears to be a real problem, I'll report it.

As Sandy's comments illustrate, *you need to be alert to the indicators of potential problems.* As an adult immersed in adolescent culture, you will probably develop a good idea of what typical teenage behavior is like. This allows you to detect deviations or changes in a student's behavior that might signal the presence of a problem. In *Teacher as Counselor: Developing the Helping Skills You Need* (1993), Jeffrey and Ellen Kottler suggest that you learn to ask yourself a series of questions when you notice atypical behavior:

- What is unusual about this student's behavior?
- Is there a pattern to what I have observed?
- What additional information do I need to make an informed judgment?
- Whom might I contact to collect this background information?
- What are the risks of waiting longer to figure out what is going on?
- Does this student seem to be in any imminent danger?
- Whom can I consult about this case?

Substance Abuse

In order to deal with problems rooted in drugs and alcohol, many schools have established student assistance programs (SAPs) and have hired full-time student assistance counselors (SACs). Note that the initials "SA" do *not* stand for substance abuse. The wording is deliberate. Although SAPs focus on identifying and helping students at risk for alcohol and other drug problems, they generally adopt a broad-based approach. There are two good reasons for this strategy. First, drug problems usually occur in conjunction with other problems—depression, abuse, academic difficulties, family problems, pregnancy (Gonet, 1994). Second, it's less stigmatizing to go to a student assistance counselor than a substance abuse counselor. Shirley Sexton, the SAC in Christina's school, emphasizes this point: "It's really important not to be known as the 'drug lady.' I try to make it clear that I'm available to talk about all kinds of problems that kids may be experiencing—from bereavement to divorce to communication problems with parents."

With respect to alcohol and drugs, SACs can provide help to students who are the *children of alcoholics/addicts (COAs) and students who are themselves substance abusers.* Let's turn first to the problems of COAs and consider the cases of Amanda and Eric (adapted from Powell, Zehm, & Kottler, 1995).

Amanda's father is an alcoholic who becomes aggressive and abusive when he drinks. At age 13, Amanda is her mother's primary source of support and works hard to make her family appear normal. She has assumed many adult responsibilities that would normally be carried out by the father of a household. At school, she is a very successful student; her teachers describe her as superdependable and motivated. They don't realize that she is filled with feelings of inadequacy and confusion, that her behavior is prompted by a compulsive need to be perfect. Nor do they notice that in between classes and at lunchtime Amanda spends most of her time alone. Amanda avoids forming friendships because she is afraid of revealing the family secret.

Eric is a ninth grader whose teacher describes him as sullen, disrespectful, and obstructive. He frequently fights with other students and has been suspended several times for antisocial behavior. His mother claims not to understand his behavior; she reports that Eric never acts this way at home and implies that his teachers are the cause of his perpetual negative attitude. Yet he often has violent outbursts at home. At the core of Eric's behavior is anger: He is enraged by the rejection he feels from his alcoholic father and feels resentful that his mother spends so much time wallowing in self-pity. He soothes his pain by planning ways to leave home when he's old enough to drop out of school. He is on the verge of jumping into his own life of addiction.

Substance abuse touches secondary classrooms every time youngsters like Amanda and Eric enter the room—and their presence is not a rare occurrence. It is estimated that one in every four students sitting in a classroom comes from a family in which one or both parents are addicted to drugs or alcohol (Powell, Zehm, & Kottler, 1995). When these youngsters are angry and disruptive like Eric, it is relatively easy to recognize that a problem exists; it is far more difficult when students are compliant perfectionists like Amanda.

Leslie Lillian, a student assistance counselor in Fred's district, stresses that COAs can exhibit a wide variety of behaviors (see Table 12.6):

Some children become perfectionists and peacemakers. They want to prevent situations that might evoke their parents' anger because their parents' responses are so unpredictable. It's as if they think to themselves, "I'm not going to disturb anything; I'm not going to do anything wrong; I'll try and keep the peace, so that no one will be angry. Some children become class clowns; maybe they've found that making people laugh breaks the tension, or maybe they're seeking attention. Others become very angry; they may begin to lie, or steal, or cheat. Some become sad and melancholy; everything about them says, "Nurture me." We see a whole spectrum of reactions—and it's the same spectrum of behaviors that we see in kids from violent homes.

It's important to understand that for COAs, family life revolves around the addiction. Rules are arbitrary and irrational; boundaries between parents and children are blurred; and life is marked by unpredictability and inconsistency. Leslie comments:

These kids never know what they're going home to. One day, they may bring a paper home from school that's gotten a low grade, and the parent might say, "That's OK, just do it over." Another day, they might get beaten up for bringing home a paper like that.

TABLE 12.6 Characteristics of Children of Alcoholics/Addicts

- Difficulty in creating and maintaining trusting relationships, often leading to isolation
- Low self-esteem
- Self-doubt
- Difficulty in being spontaneous and open, caused by a need to be in control and to minimize the risk of being surprised
- Denial and repression because of the need to collaborate with other family members in keeping "the secret"
- General feelings of guilt about areas for which the child had no responsibility
- Uncertainty about his/her own feelings and desires caused by shifting parental roles
- Seeing things in an "all or nothing" context, which sometimes manifests itself in a perfectionist fear of failure
- Poor impulse control, which may result in acting-out behavior, probably caused by lack of parental guidance, love, and discipline
- Potential for depression, phobias, panic reactions, and hyperactivity
- Preoccupation with the family
- Abuse of alcohol and/or drugs

Source: Adapted from Towers, 1989.

Sadly, it's often difficult for COAs to reach out for help. In a chemically dependent family, everyone works to maintain the family secret. Tonia Moore, a student assistance counselor in Sandy's district, finds that COAs move back and forth between "wanting to report the lies and wanting to believe the lies":

A while back I worked with a sister and brother; the girl was in elementary school and the boy was in high school. Their mother was an alcoholic, and she would tell them if they did well on their report cards, she would stop drinking. They'd go to church and pray for that; they'd even dream about it. I would tell them, "Don't count on it. It's not that easy for your mom to stop drinking, even though she wants to." But they wanted to believe it would happen. *They really tried to improve their grades, and they did, and she still didn't stop. They were heartbroken.*

Sometimes, she'd come to back-to-school night, and you could tell she'd been drinking. The boy would put his arm around her and try to keep her from making a scene. And then the next day, he'd come in to see me, all embarrassed, and apologize for her behavior. He'd say she wasn't feeling well, that she had the flu, even though he knew that I knew she was an alcoholic. He'd participate in the secret, *he'd try to cover up, even as he confided in me. Children of substance abusers have such a tremendous need* to have things be normal.

One of the most frustrating aspects of working with COAs is the realization that you do not have the power to change the child's home life. Instead, you must concentrate on what you *are* able to do during the time the student is in your classroom. Many of the strategies are not different from those I have espoused for all

PRACTICAL TIPS FOR

HELPING CHILDREN OF ALCOHOLICS/ADDICTS

- *Be observant.* Watch your students not just for academic or behavior problems, but also for the more subtle signs of addiction and emotional distress. Remember that COAs can be overachieving, cooperative, and quiet as well as disruptive and angry.

- *Set boundaries that are enforced consistently.* When chaos exists at home, some sense of order is crucial at school.

- *Be flexible.* Although it is necessary to set boundaries, classroom rules that are too rigid and unyielding may invite students to act out.

- *Make addiction a focus of discussion.* Find a way to deal with this subject. Incorporate addiction into literacy instruction (e.g., through adolescent literature, writing), science, social studies, etc.

- *Make it clear you are available.* Communicate that you are eager and open to talk to children. Reach out to the troubled student in a gentle, caring way. "I notice you are having some difficulty. I just want you to know that I care about you. Call me any time you are ready to talk. And if you would rather speak to someone else, let me find you someone you can trust."

- *Develop a referral network.* Find out what services are available to help and refer the student for appropriate professional care.

- *Accept what you can do little about.* You can't make people stop drinking or taking drugs.

Source: Adapted from Powell, Zehm, & Kottler, 1995.

students. (See the Practical Tips box.) For example, it is essential that you establish clear, consistent rules and work to create a climate of trust and caring.

In addition to using these strategies, you should find out if your school has student assistance counselors or other special services personnel who can provide help. Find out if support groups for COAs are available. For example, Tonia runs groups at school, sometimes alone and sometimes with the guidance counselor. Tonia speaks about the benefits that joining such a group can bring:

> *There's such a sense of relief. The comments are always the same: "I thought I was the only one." "I didn't know anyone else was going through this stuff." The shame is so great, even at a very young age, and the need to keep it all a secret is so hard. There's instant camaraderie.*
>
> *We'll often start off by asking, "On a scale from 1 to 10, how are you feeling today?" That allows us to get a sense of the group and to learn quickly who's in the middle of a crisis. Then we'll ask them to share something positive that happened this week and something negative that happened. We'll ask who needs group time. We do activities that help to build self-esteem. We do role-playing to get at feelings—being disappointed, being unsafe, being embarrassed, being angry that you can never make plans, that you can never say, "My mother will be there," or even "I'll be there."*

Unfortunately, COAs may be reluctant to join such groups. Shirley Sexton (the SAC in Christina's school) has recently started three groups at the high school, one on bereavement, one on divorce and separation, and one for COAs. Although students immediately signed up for the first two groups, thus far she's gotten little response to the third. Shirley is not surprised. "It'll take some time," she explains. "Talking about your parents' alcoholism or addiction is a touchy issue."

A second way that substance abuse can affect middle and high school classrooms is when students themselves abuse drugs and alcohol. Up-to-date information on adolescent drug and alcohol use comes from an annual study sponsored by the National Institute on Drug Abuse (Johnston, O'Malley, Bachman, & Schulenberg, 2005), which surveys 50,000 students in grades 8, 10, and 12 located in about 400 schools nationwide. Results from the 2004 study show that the proportion of eighth-, tenth-, and twelfth-grade students who reported using any illicit drug in the prior 12 months continued a gradual decline that began in 1996 for eighth-graders and in 2001 for tenth- and twelfth-graders. Indeed, among the nation's eighth-graders, there has now been a one-third decline in annual use of illicit drugs (from 23.6 percent in 1996 to 15.2 percent in 2004). Specific drugs showing some decline in use are marijuana (still the "drug of choice"), ecstasy, amphetamines, and methamphetamine. The decrease in ecstasy use is particularly important, since ecstasy had been increasing sharply in recent years. On the other hand, use of inhalants (e.g., glues, aerosols, butane, paint thinner, and nail polish remover) increased this year after a decline in their use since 1995 when the Partnership for a Drug-Free America conducted an anti-inhalant media campaign. With respect to alcohol, there has been a decline in all measures of drinking at all three grade levels since 2001. However, in 2004, among the twelfth-graders, drinking and drunkenness did not continue to decline. In fact, most drinking measures showed some increase in use.

To a large extent, SACs rely on teachers to refer students who might be having problems with alcohol and other drugs or who might be at risk for such problems. But teachers may be particularly reluctant to make referrals about suspected drug use. Several different reasons for this reluctance emerged during my conversations with teachers and counselors. First, some teachers think drug use is just not all that serious. According to Carol Lowinger, the SAC in Fred's school,

> *Some teachers have a tendency to minimize the situation—especially if it involves alcohol or pot. They just don't consider pot to be a "real" drug. They think, "Oh, all kids do this; it's not that big a deal."*

In addition, Carol speculates that some teachers feel it's not their role to get involved, while others want to play the role of confidante:

> *Sometimes, teachers are overwhelmed by all the responsibilities of teaching. They feel like they have more than enough to do without getting involved in students' personal problems. They tell themselves, "It's not my role to report this; I'm here to teach." But other times, teachers don't refer because they want to try to help the kid themselves. You know, a lot of teachers really like the role of mediator, caretaker, trusted*

confidante. They like *the fact that a student is confiding in them about a problem, and sometimes they make a pact of confidentiality with the student: "You can tell me your secret. I won't tell anybody." But if the kid is in serious trouble, that can be a problem. First of all, they don't really have the training to help the way a counselor could. Second, they might be sending a message to the kid that it's not okay to go to a counselor or a mental health professional—and that's* not *a message we want to send. We want kids to see that we all need a variety of people in our lives, people who can help us in many different ways. We don't want kids to think that one person is all they need, and if they have the teacher they don't need to go to anybody else. Third, they could actually be serving as a "professional enabler"—they're allowing the kid to continue behavior that could be self-destructive. That's not helpful to the kid. What you've got to do is say to the kid, "I care too much about you to allow this to continue. We've got to get help for you."*

Another reason for teachers' reluctance to refer is the belief that they are "turning kids in" when they would rather "give the kid a break" (Newsam, 1992). Sandy herself comments on this attitude:

Some teachers are afraid to report suspected drug use because they don't want to create a hassle *for the kid*. They don't want to get the kid in trouble. They may also be afraid that reporting kids will ruin their relationship with students. But I haven't found that to be the case. Sometimes, the kid will come back and say, "Why did you do that?" But I say, "This is too big for us. We need more help." Sometimes, I'll even have kids come to tell me about a problem with a friend. They know I'll find help. *That's what they want.*

Finally, teachers may be reluctant to report suspected drug use because they are unsure about the indicators. Tonia is very sensitive to this problem:

Teachers tell me, "I have no idea what substance abuse looks like. It wasn't a part of my training. I wouldn't know when to refer a student." I tell them, that's okay. You can't tell substance abuse just by looking. There has to be a chemical screening. But you can see changes in behavior. You know enough about kids to know when somebody's behavior has changed, or if their behavior is different from all the other kids. You don't need to know *the student is using; you just need to* suspect *that there may be drug use or a problem related to drug use.*

What are the behaviors that might lead you to suspect drug use and to make a referral? Figure 12.3 shows the behavior checklist used at Fred's high school. Many schools use forms that are very similar to this one. Keeping your school's behavior checklist handy can help you stay alert to the possibility that students are using drugs or living with addiction in their families.

**STUDENT ASSISTANCE PROGRAM
BEHAVIOR CHECKLIST**

The goal of the Student Assistance Program is to help students who may be experiencing problems in their lives. These problems can be manifested in school through any combination of behaviors. The following is a list of typical behaviors students having problems may exhibit. While most students engage in many of the behaviors at one time or another, the student who may be having trouble will show a combination or pattern of these behaviors.

Student: _____   Grade: _____

Staff
Member: _____   Date: _____

Academic Performance
____Drop in grades
____Decrease in participation
____Inconsistent work
____Works below potential
____Compulsive overachievement
    (preoccupied w/school success)

School Attendance
____Change in attendance
____Absenteeism
____Tardiness
____Class cutting
____Frequent visits to nurse
____Frequent visits to counselor
____Frequent restroom visits
____Frequent requests for hall passes

Social Problems
____Family problems
____Runs away
____Job problems
____Peer problems
____Constantly borrowing money
____Relationship problems

Physical Symptoms
____Staggering/stumbling
____Incoherent
____Smelling of alcohol/marijuana
____Vomiting/nausea

____Glassy, bloodshot eyes/dark
____Poor coordination
____Slurred speech
____Deteriorating physical
    appearance
____Sleeping in class
____Physical injuries
____Frequent physical complaints
____Dramatic change in musculature

Extracurricular Activities
____Lack of participation
____Possession of drugs/alcohol
____Involvement in thefts and
    assaults
____Vandalism
____Talking about involvement in
    illegal activities
____Possession of paraphernalia
____Increasing noninvolvement
____Decrease in motivation
____Dropping out, missing practice(s)
____Not fulfilling responsibilities
____Performance changes

Disruptive Behavior
____Defiance of rules
____Irresponsibility, blaming, lying,
    fighting
____Cheating

Figure 12.3   The Referral Form Used in Fred's District

_____Sudden outburst, verbal abuse
_____Obscene language, gesture
_____Attention-getting behavior
_____Frequently in wrong area
_____Extreme negativism
_____Hyperactivity, nervousness
_____Lack of motivation, apathy
_____Problem with authority figures

_____Defensive
_____Withdrawn/difficulty relating
_____Unrealistic goals
_____Sexual behavior in public
_____Seeking adult advice without a
    specific problem
_____Rigid obedience
_____Constantly seeks approval

Atypical Behavior
_____Difficulty in accepting mistakes
_____Boasts about alcohol or drug use,
    "partying bravado"
_____Erratic behavior
_____Change of friends
_____Overly sensitive
_____Disoriented
_____Inappropriate responses
_____Depression

Other
_____Students talking about alcohol or
    other drugs
_____Having beeper
_____Bragging about sexual exploits
_____Mentions concerns about
    significant other's alcohol or other
    drug use, gambling
_____Staff knowledge of addiction in
    family

Additional Comments:

_____

Figure 12.3   (*continued*)

It's important to distinguish between situations in which a pattern of behavior problems suggests possible *drug use outside of school* and situations in which a student appears to be *under the influence of drugs during school, at school functions,* or *on school property.* When you see students who might be "under the influence," you cannot wait to fill out a behavior checklist; you need to alert the appropriate personnel as soon as you possibly can. Fred shares this experience:

A few years ago, I had this really bright kid in my first-period class. He was a star football player; he could have gone to college anywhere. But then he got into drugs. I remember one day in particular when he came into class high. I didn't realize it at first, because he just sat down quietly and everything seemed okay. But then he got up to sharpen his pencil, and I could see that he was walking funny. He was actually *leaning* to one side. It looked like he was going to fall over. I never saw anyone walk like that. I gave the rest of the class an assignment and asked him to come with me out into the hall. I tried to be really discreet; I didn't want everyone watching and talking about him. I planned to call the assistant principal, but the principal happened to be walking by just at that minute, so he took him to the nurse.

Tonia Moore explains one of the reasons for immediately alerting the appropriate personnel if you suspect a student is under the influence:

It used to be that teachers would come to me at the end of the day and say, "I was really worried about X today. I think he was really on something."

That's no good. I need to know at the time. *After all, that student could fall down the stairs, or the student could leave the building during lunchtime and get killed crossing the street.* We have to deal with the problem immediately. *It can really be a matter of life and death.*

Make sure you know to whom you're supposed to refer students who appear to be under the influence of drugs. In Fred's and Christina's schools, teachers call an administrator, who comes to the classroom and accompanies the student to the nurse. In Sandy's school, teachers send students to the nurse, who then contacts the student assistance counselor. In Donnie's school, teachers call a security guard who takes the student to the nurse.

Since you cannot be sure that a student is using drugs just by looking, it's important not to be accusatory when you talk with the student. Sandy describes how she usually handles this situation:

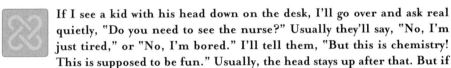

If I see a kid with his head down on the desk, I'll go over and ask real quietly, "Do you need to see the nurse?" Usually they'll say, "No, I'm just tired," or "No, I'm bored." I'll tell them, "But this is chemistry! This is supposed to be fun." Usually, the head stays up after that. But if the head goes back down, I'll say, "I think you need to see the nurse. You don't seem to be feeling well." I'm not confrontational, and I try to show the kid that I'm acting out of concern. Sometimes I'm wrong, and it turns out that the kid just stayed up until 4:00 A.M. doing a term paper. That's fine. It's better to err on the side of caution.

Making a referral can be difficult, but you need to remember that turning away and remaining silent can send the message that you condone the behavior—or that you don't care enough to do anything.

Abuse and Neglect

During one conversation with Donnie, she emphasized the difficulty of detecting abuse and neglect among older students:

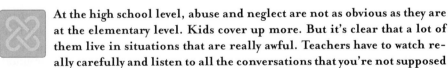

At the high school level, abuse and neglect are not as obvious as they are at the elementary level. Kids cover up more. But it's clear that a lot of them live in situations that are really awful. Teachers have to watch really carefully and listen to all the conversations that you're not supposed to hear. That way you can learn about what's going on in kids' lives and in the community.

As Donnie points out, abuse of adolescents is often well hidden. Furthermore, adolescents just don't seem as vulnerable as younger children: They may have as much strength or weight as adults; they seem able to run away from abusive situations; and they appear to have more access to potential help outside the family. For these reasons, it's easy to think that abuse and neglect are not problems at the high school level. But adolescents still need protection. During one meeting, Christina recalled a girl who had worn a short-sleeved shirt in December when temperatures were in the 20s:

 It was as if she was saying, "Please look at my arm." I did—and saw she had bruises all over it. As a new teacher, I was a little nervous about handling this the right way, so I went to consult with a more experienced teacher. We spoke with one of the school counselors, who took the student to the nurse.

It's also important to realize that girls are not the only victims of abuse. Consider this tale, shared by Donnie:

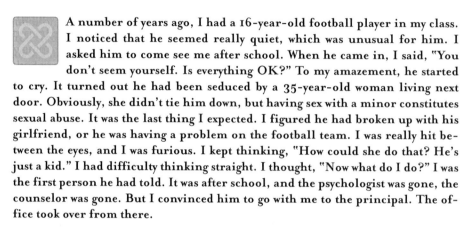 A number of years ago, I had a 16-year-old football player in my class. I noticed that he seemed really quiet, which was unusual for him. I asked him to come see me after school. When he came in, I said, "You don't seem yourself. Is everything OK?" To my amazement, he started to cry. It turned out he had been seduced by a 35-year-old woman living next door. Obviously, she didn't tie him down, but having sex with a minor constitutes sexual abuse. It was the last thing I expected. I figured he had broken up with his girlfriend, or he was having a problem on the football team. I was really hit between the eyes, and I was furious. I kept thinking, "How could she do that? He's just a kid." I had difficulty thinking straight. I thought, "Now what do I do?" I was the first person he had told. It was after school, and the psychologist was gone, the counselor was gone. But I convinced him to go with me to the principal. The office took over from there.

The National Child Abuse and Neglect Data System reports that approximately 900,000 children were victims of maltreatment in 2004 (U.S. Department of Health and Human Services, 2006). In order to protect these youth, most states have laws requiring educators to report suspected abuse to the state's "child protective service." Although definitions of abuse vary, states generally include nonaccidental injury, neglect, sexual abuse, and emotional maltreatment. It is essential that you become familiar with the physical and behavioral indicators of these problems. (See Table 12.7.)

Teachers are often reluctant to file a report unless they have absolute proof of abuse. They worry about invading the family's privacy and causing unnecessary embarrassment to everyone involved. Nonetheless, it's important to keep in mind that *no state requires the reporter to have absolute proof before reporting.* What most states do require is "reason to believe" or "reasonable cause to believe or suspect" that abuse has occurred (Fischer, Schimmel, & Kelly, 1999). If you are uncertain whether abuse is occurring, but have reasonable cause, you should err in favor of the youngster and file a report. Waiting for proof can be dangerous; it may also be illegal. If a child is later harmed, and it becomes clear that you failed to report suspected abuse, both you and your school district may be subject to both civil and criminal liability (Michaelis, 1993). Also keep in mind that every state provides immunity from any civil suit or criminal prosecution that might result from the

TABLE 12.7 Physical and Behavioral Indicators of Child Abuse and Neglect

Type of Child Abuse or Neglect	Physical Indicators	Behavioral Indicators
Physical abuse	Unexplained bruises and welts: —on face, lips, mouth —on torso, back, buttocks, thighs —in various stages of healing —clustered, forming regular patterns —reflecting shape of article used to inflict (electric cord, belt buckle) —on several different surface areas —regularly appear after absence, weekend, or vacation Unexplained burns: —cigar, cigarette burns, especially on soles, palms, back, or buttocks —immersion burns (sock-like, glove-like, doughnut shaped on buttocks or genitalia) —patterned like electric burner, iron, etc. —rope burns on arms, legs, neck, or torso Unexplained fractures: —to skull, nose, facial structure —in various stages of healing —multiple or spiral fractures Unexplained lacerations or abrasions: —to mouth, lips, gums, eyes —to external genitalia	Wary of adult contact Apprehensive when other children cry Behavioral extremes: —aggressiveness —withdrawal Frightened of parents Afraid to go home Reports injury by parents
Physical neglect	Consistent hunger, poor hygiene, inappropriate dress Consistent lack of supervision, especially in dangerous activities or long periods Constant fatigue or listlessness Unattended physical problems or medical needs Abandonment	Begging, stealing food Extended stays at school (early arrival and late departure) Constantly falling asleep in class Alcohol or drug abuse Delinquency (e.g., thefts) States there is no caretaker
Sexual abuse	Difficulty in walking or sitting Torn, stained, or bloody underclothing Pain or itching in genital area Bruises or bleeding in external genitalia, vaginal, or anal areas Venereal disease, especially in preteens Pregnancy	Unwilling to change for gym or participate in PE Withdrawal, fantasy or infantile behavior Bizarre, sophisticated, or unusual sexual behavior or knowledge Poor peer relationships Delinquent or runaway Reports sexual assault by caretaker

(continued)

TABLE 12.7   Physical and Behavioral Indicators of Child Abuse and Neglect (*continued*)

Type of Child Abuse or Neglect	Physical Indicators	Behavioral Indicators
Emotional maltreatment	Habit disorders (sucking, biting, rocking, etc.) Conduct disorders (antisocial, destructive, etc.) Neurotic traits (sleep disorders, speech disorders, inhibition of play) Psychoneurotic reactions (hysteria, obsession, compulsion, phobias, hypochondria)	Behavior extremes: —compliant, passive —aggressive, demanding Overly adaptive behavior: —inappropriately adult —inappropriately infantile Developmental lags (physical, mental, emotional) Attempted suicide

Source: Child Abuse and Neglect: A Professional's Guide to Identification, Reporting, Investigation, and Treatment. Trenton, NJ: Governor's Task Force on Child Abuse and Neglect, October 1988.

reporting of suspected child abuse or neglect—as long as you have acted "in good faith" (Fischer, Schimmel, & Kelly, 1999).

It's essential that you learn about the reporting procedures in your state *before* you are faced with a situation of suspected child abuse. Some states explicitly name the school personnel who are required to file the report. Other states have more general provisions that require reporting by "any person" who works with children; this would clearly include teachers, nurses, therapists, and counselors (Fischer, Schimmel, & Kelly, 1999). States also vary with respect to the form and content of reports required. Most states require an oral report, followed by a more detailed written report, and some states also have a 24-hour, toll-free hotline. Generally, you should be prepared to provide the student's name and address; the nature and extent of injury or condition observed; and your own name and address (Fischer, Schimmel, & Kelly, 1999).

The variation among states underscores the importance of becoming familiar with the procedures and resources in your own school. The best way to do this is to speak with people who can provide guidance and direction—experienced teachers, the principal, the school nurse, and student assistance counselors.

Eating Disorders

During a visit to one of Fred's honors classes in late April, I was shocked by the emaciated appearance of one of his female students, Sara. Her eyes and cheeks were sunken in, and her arms looked like twigs. I couldn't take my eyes off her. After class, Fred shared the story:

 This kid is a straight A student—she'll probably be valedictorian or salutatorian of her class. Everything she does is perfect. I don't think she's ever gotten less than 100 on any test or assignment I've given. And she's a fantastic soccer player. As a matter of fact, she's being

recruited by a number of schools that want her to play soccer. To me, it looks like she couldn't even kick the ball. But I know that she practices every day, and she runs too.

A couple of Sara's friends have come to talk with me after school—they're worried about her too. They say that she insists she's fat and that she hardly eats. She seems to be particularly obsessed about not eating anything with fat in it—no pizza, no cheese, no cakes or cookies, and of course no meat of any kind. Apparently, all they ever see her eat is bagels and lettuce!

I've talked with Sara—I've told her that I'm really worried about her, but she insists that she's fine and that everyone's overreacting. I've also reported the situation to the school psychologist and the SAC [student assistance counselor], and I know that they've called Sara's parents. I even called her parents myself. But her parents don't acknowledge that there's a problem. It's just so sad, but what else can we do?

Given our society's obsession about thinness, it's not surprising that teenage girls often become concerned about body image. But Sara's intense preoccupation with losing weight goes way beyond ordinary concern. Sara seems to suffer from anorexia nervosa, an eating disorder that generally begins during adolescence and primarily afflicts White females, although it's increasing among Black females and does occur among males (Brodey, 2005; Gonet, 1994). Anorexic adolescents literally starve themselves; even so, they continue to feel fat and may actually perceive that they are becoming heavier. Sara's involvement in running and soccer is also typical; in an attempt to lose weight more quickly, anorexics may combine excessive physical exercise with dieting.

Another eating disorder is bulimia nervosa, in which individuals starve themselves, then binge (often on high-calorie or high-sugar foods), and finally purge themselves (by inducing vomiting). Individuals with bulimia may be underweight, overweight, or average, but they share an intense fear of gaining weight. They may also feel that they have lost control over their lives; thus, they seek to control their eating and their weight (Gonet, 1994).

Of the two eating disorders, bulimia is more common, while anorexia is more severe and can actually be fatal. But both are long-term illnesses that require treatment; they will not go away by themselves. This means that you need to be alert to the signs of eating disorders and report your concern to the appropriate person in your school. Too often, teachers overlook eating disorders since concern about weight is a "normal pathology" in our society. Furthermore, the young women who most frequently suffer from eating disorders are often high-achieving, compliant, perfectionist students who cause no problems in class. Naomi Wolf, author of *The Beauty Myth* (1991), recalls how no one in her school tried to intervene when she was an anorexic teenager:

> There were many starving girls in my junior high school, and every one was a teacher's paragon. We were allowed to come and go, racking up gold stars, as our hair fell out in fistfuls and the pads flattened behind the sockets of our eyes. . . . An alien voice took mine over. I have never been so soft-spoken. It lost expression and timbre and sank to a monotone, a dull murmur the opposite of strident. My

teachers approved of me. They saw nothing wrong with what I was doing, and I could swear they looked straight at me. My school had stopped dissecting alley-cats, since it was considered inhumane. [But] there was no interference in my self-directed science experiment: to find out just how little food could keep a human body alive. (p. 202)

TALKING WITH STUDENTS WHO HAVE PROBLEMS

As I've stressed earlier, it is not your job to be a school counselor, therapist, or confidante for all your students. You have neither the time nor the training to serve in those roles. Nonetheless, there will be instances in which students will reach out to you for understanding. A student might confide her fears about being pregnant; another might tell you about his alcoholic parents; still another might want to talk about her feelings of inadequacy and isolation. What will you do? As I've already indicated, in many cases, the appropriate response is to put the student in touch with a special service provider who has the expertise needed to intervene. Listen to Sandy:

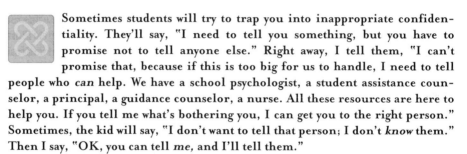

Sometimes students will try to trap you into inappropriate confidentiality. They'll say, "I need to tell you something, but you have to promise not to tell anyone else." Right away, I tell them, "I can't promise that, because if this is too big for us to handle, I need to tell people who *can* help. We have a school psychologist, a student assistance counselor, a principal, a guidance counselor, a nurse. All these resources are here to help you. If you tell me what's bothering you, I can get you to the right person." Sometimes, the kid will say, "I don't want to tell that person; I don't *know* them." Then I say, "OK, you can tell *me,* and I'll tell them."

In addition to getting professional help for a student with a serious problem, you can also be helpful by developing the communication skills discussed in Chapter 3—attending and acknowledging, active listening, open-ended questioning, and problem solving. Remember, listening attentively to students and showing you care can be powerful ways of helping students who are hurting.

CONCLUDING COMMENTS

The problems that students bring to school can seem overwhelming, especially for beginning teachers who are still learning the basics. And in fact, there may be students whose problems are so great, you really cannot help a whole lot. As Fred reminds us,

There's failure in this business. Some problems transcend the classroom, and there's only so much an individual teacher or the school can do. Sometimes you just have to say, "I tried. Now I need to let go."

"Letting go" means recognizing that you may not be able to change a student's life; it *doesn't* mean abandoning your responsibility for making that student's time in school as productive and meaningful as possible. Carol Lowinger, the SAC at Fred's school, believes that, to some extent, teachers need to treat troubled students "like everyone else":

> *Sometimes teachers think, "These kids are going through a hard time; I'll give them a break." But out of this sense of caring, they give kids breaks they shouldn't get. Kids need to be held accountable. They have to learn to live in the real world where you can't hide behind your problems. You have to learn to cope, and you* mustn't *learn "I don't have to cope." I'm not saying that we shouldn't give them some leeway if their problems are really great; obviously, we need to be flexible and supportive. But they still need to be responsible for their current behavior. If we always bail kids out, we're enabling. That's not helpful—and it's even dangerous.*

When students have serious problems, it's more important than ever to create a classroom that is safe, orderly, and humane. You may not be able to change youngsters' relationships with their families, but you can still work to establish positive teacher–student relationships. You may not be able to provide students with control over unstable, chaotic home lives, but you can allow them opportunities to make decisions and to have some control over their time in school. You may not be able to do anything about the violence that permeates the neighborhoods in which they live, but you can structure classroom situations to foster cooperation and group cohesiveness. In Fred's words, "You can show them you care enough about them not to let them slough off. You can still keep teaching."

SUMMARY

Today's classrooms are more challenging than ever before. Students come from a wide range of cultural and linguistic backgrounds, and many are learning English as a second language. Students with disabilities are frequently educated alongside their nondisabled peers. A greater number of young people are growing up in circumstances that put them at risk for physical, emotional, and psychological problems.

This chapter reflects the belief that teachers are responsible for all the students in the class—not just the ones who are easy to teach. It began by examining ways of helping students with learning disabilities, emotional/behavioral disorders, autism and Asperger syndrome, and ADHD. Then the chapter considered strategies for supporting children who are English-language learners. Finally, it discussed the needs of individuals who are troubled—those who suffer from the problems associated with substance abuse, child abuse and neglect, and eating disorders.

Inclusion Classes May Contain Students with a Variety of Disabilities

- A diagnosis of LD is made when there is a "severe discrepancy" between intellectual ability and academic performance in one or more of seven areas: oral expression, listening comprehension, written expression, basic reading skills, reading comprehension, mathematics calculation, and mathematics reasoning.

- Emotional/behavioral disorders can be externalizing (e.g., conduct disorder) or internalizing (e.g., depression).
- Autism and Asperger Syndrome are two "pervasive developmental disorders," a cluster of disorders characterized by marked impairments in the development of social interaction and communication skills.
- ADHD is not included as a disability in the IDEA; however, individuals may receive services under Section 504 of the Rehabilitation Act of 1973. ADHD is characterized by inattention, hyperactivity, and impulsivity.

Helping Students with Disabilities and ADHD

- Become familiar with students' IEPs or 504 plans.
- Create an accepting climate.
- Coordinate with special education teachers and paraprofessionals.
- Examine your classroom environment for possible mismatch.
- Use peer tutoring and peer assistance.
- Use a variety of instructional strategies.
- Remember the principles of effective management.
- Conduct a Functional Behavioral Assessment if students display challenging behavior.

Helping Students Who Are English-Language Learners

- Provide a safe environment for language risk taking.
- Avoid idioms and complex sentences.
- Ask questions that allow for different levels of proficiency in responding.
- Encourage English speaking while honoring students' first language.
- Offer periodic summaries and paraphrases.
- Emphasize collaborative over individual work.
- Emphasize process over product.
- Apply SDAIE strategies across the curriculum.
- Encourage students to write about topics of their choice and for real-world purposes.

Helping Students Who Are Troubled

- Substance abuse:
  - Students may be children of alcoholics/addicts (COAs) and/or may be abusing drugs and alcohol themselves.
  - COAs can benefit from support groups.
  - Teachers must be watchful for students who may be abusing drugs and alcohol and refer students to the SAC or other appropriate persons.
  - Distinguish between situations in which drugs are being used outside of school and situations in which students are under the influence during school.
- Abuse and neglect:
  - Educators are required to report suspected abuse and neglect to the state's child protective service.
  - No state requires the reporter to have absolute proof before reporting.
  - Most states require "reason to believe" or "reasonable cause to believe or suspect."
- Eating disorders:
  - Students who suffer from eating disorders are often high-achieving, compliant, and perfectionist students who cause no problems in class.

Sometimes the problems that students bring to school can be overwhelming, especially for beginning teachers who are still learning the basics. And in fact, there may be students whose problems are so great, you just cannot help. Nonetheless, you can still try to create a classroom environment that is safe, orderly, and humane. You can show students you care by holding them accountable for their behavior and by continuing to teach.

ACTIVITIES FOR SKILL BUILDING AND REFLECTION

In Class

1. In a small group, read the following scenario and discuss the questions that are listed below.

    Joanne Wilson's second-period English class has 28 students. One has been identified with learning disabilities, and he struggles with the novels the class is reading, as well as the writing assignments. In addition, two students are recent immigrants with very limited English, and one student has ADHD. Although he is supposed to be on medication, he sometimes skips a dose; on days like that, he "bounces off the walls" and accomplishes very little in terms of academic work. Ms. Wilson is very concerned about these students' academic progress, and she doesn't know where to turn. An in-class support (ICS) teacher provides some assistance two days a week, but they have no planning time and so she functions more like an aide than a real teacher. Ms. Wilson is also painfully aware of the fact that the class is not a cohesive community; although there is no obvious disrespect, the other students generally ignore the students with special needs and are reluctant to work with them in cooperative groups.

    Questions:
    a. What strategies could Ms. Wilson use to help create a more inclusive, more accepting climate?
    b. For each student with special needs (i.e., the student with LD, the two ELLs, and the student with ADHD), think of one strategy that Ms. Wilson could use to enhance his or her academic progress.
    c. What kinds of help could Ms. Wilson ask for from the ICS teacher?

2. Working together in a small group, imagine that you are a general education teacher working in a co-teaching arrangement with a special education teacher. Generate a list of issues that you would want to discuss before beginning to teach together. In particular, consider what expectations you have with respect to planning and delivering instruction and with respect to classroom management. Then assume the role of the special education teacher and repeat the process.

On Your Own

1. In the school where you are observing or teaching, interview the principal or the director of special services to learn about the district's policies and procedures for supporting students with disabilities. Are any students with severe disabilities being educated in the general education classroom? If so, what kind of special supports are being provided for those individuals? Interview a teacher about his/her attitudes toward including a student with special needs who would have previously been educated in a special education classroom or sent to a special school.

2. In the school where you are observing or teaching, interview the principal or an ESL teacher about the district's policies and programs for supporting ELLs. How many languages are represented in the school? Interview a teacher in an English-only classroom who has English-language learners in his/her classroom. How does the teacher provide supports for English-language learners?

3. In the school where you are observing or teaching, interview the student assistance counselor, a guidance counselor, or the director of special services to determine the policies for reporting drug abuse. Get copies of the referral forms that are used and compare them with the form shown in this chapter.

For Your Portfolio

Reporting suspected abuse and neglect varies from state to state. Find out the policies used in your state. Also find out if your school has particular policies and procedures you are to follow. In particular, get answers to the following questions and compile your findings into a set of guidelines that you keep in your portfolio.

Who is required to report abuse and neglect?

When should you report child abuse? (When you have reasonable cause to suspect? Reasonable cause to believe?)

To what state agency do you report?

What information must be included in the report?

Do you have to give your name when reporting?

For Further Reading

Cary, S. (2000). *Working with second language learners: Answers to teachers' top ten questions.* Portsmouth, NH: Heinemann.

This book addresses teachers' "top ten" questions, chosen with four criteria in mind: veracity (meaning that they were asked by real teachers teaching real kids), frequency, relevancy, and difficulty (they needed to be challenging). Questions include: How do I assess a student's English? How do I find useful information on a student's cultural background? How do I make my spoken language more understandable? How do I get my reluctant speakers to speak English?

Kline, F. M., & Silver, L. B. (Eds.) (2004). *The educator's guide to mental health issues in the classroom.* Baltimore: Paul H. Brookes Publishing Co.

This book is dedicated to "general education classroom teachers who are charged with serving ALL students!" It is designed to serve as a reference for educators who work with students who have mental health issues and who need to collaborate with mental health workers. Chapters address biologically based disorders (e.g., ADHD), biologically based and/or psychologically based disorders (e.g., substance abuse), and behavioral disorders (e.g., oppositional defiant disorder).

Snell, M. E., & Janney, R. (2000). *Social relationships and peer support.* Baltimore: Paul H. Brookes Publishing Co.

This book is part of a series of reader-friendly teachers' guides to inclusive practices. This one focuses on ways of facilitating positive peer relationships in an inclusive classroom. Topics include creating a positive atmosphere, establishing peer support programs, teaching social skills, and building friendship groups.

Soodak, L. C., & McCarthy, M. R. (2006). Classroom management in inclusive settings. In C. M. Evertson & C. S. Weinstein (Eds.), *Handbook of classroom management: Research, practice, and contemporary issues.* Mahwah, NJ: Lawrence Erlbaum Associates, Inc.
This chapter reviews research-based practices that promote positive academic, social, and behavioral outcomes for students in inclusive classrooms. Practices include teacher-directed strategies (such as building classroom community and establishing programs that foster acceptance and friendship), peer-mediated strategies (such as cooperative learning and peer-tutoring), and self-directed strategies (such as self-monitoring). The authors stress the role of teachers in creating classrooms in which all students have greater access to the general education curriculum.

ORGANIZATIONAL RESOURCES

CHADD (Children and Adults with Attention-Deficit/Hyperactivity Disorder), 8181 Professional Place, Suite 150, Landover, MD 20785 (www.chadd.org). CHADD is a non-profit organization serving children and adults with ADHD. It runs the National Resource Center on ADHD, a national clearinghouse for evidence-based information about ADHD (800-233-4050).

The Council for Exceptional Children, 1110 North Glebe Rd., Suite 300, Arlington, VA 22201 (phone: 703-620-3660; www.cec.sped.org). CEC is the largest international professional organization dedicated to improving educational outcomes for students with disabilities and those who are gifted. The Web site for CEC's Information Center on Disabilities and Gifted Education provides fact sheets, answers to frequently asked questions, and links to laws and other online resources (www.ericec.org).

CREDE (Center for Research on Education, Diversity, and Excellence), 1640 Tolman Hall, University of California, Berkeley, CA 94720-1670 (phone: 510-643-9024; www.crede.org). CREDE is a federally funded research and development center focused on improving the education of students whose ability to reach their potential is challenged by language or cultural barriers, race, geographic location, or poverty. It offers a wide range of multimedia products.

National Dissemination Center for Children with Disabilities. U.S. Dept. of Education, Office of Special Education Programs, P. O. Box 1492, Washington, DC 20013-1492 (http://www.nichcy.org).

TASH, 29 W. Susquehanna Ave., Suite 210, Baltimore, MD 21204 (410-828-8274; www.tash.org). TASH is dedicated to "equity, opportunity and inclusion for people with disabilities."

REFERENCES

American Psychiatric Association (2000). *Diagnostic and statistical manual of mental disorders.* 4th ed., text rev. Washington, D.C.

Brodey, D. (Sept. 20, 2005). Blacks join the eating-disorder mainstream. *New York Times,* Section F, 5.

Cary, S. (2000). *Working with second language learners: Answers to teachers' top ten questions.* Portsmouth, NH: Heinemann.

CHADD (1993). *Attention deficit disorders: an educator's guide (CHADD Facts #5).* Plantation, FL: Childen and Adults with Attention Deficit Disorders.

Children's Defense Fund (2001). *The state of America's children yearbook 2001.* Washington, D.C.: Children's Defense Fund.

Coles, A. D. (September 8, 1999). Teenage drug use continues to slide. *Education Week,* 10.

Coles, A. D. (June 14, 2000). Lately, teens less likely to engage in risky behaviors. *Education Week,* 6.

Copeland, S. R., McCall, J., Williams, C. R., Guth, C., Carter, E. W., Fowler, S. E., Presley, J. A., & Hughes, C. (2002). High school peer buddies: A win–win situation. *Teaching Exceptional Children, 35*(1), 16–21.

Diaz-Rico, L. T., & Weed, K. Z. (2004). *The crosscultural, language, and academic development handbook. A complete K-12 reference guide.* 2nd ed. Boston: Allyn and Bacon.

Dieker, L. A. (2001). What are the characteristics of "effective" middle and high school co-taught teams for students with disabilities? *Preventing School Failure, 46*(1), 14–23.

Fischer, L., Schimmel, D., & Kelly, C. (1999). *Teachers and the law.* New York: Longman.

Friend, M., & Bursuck, W. D. (2002). *Including students with special needs: A practical guide for classroom teachers.* Boston: Allyn and Bacon.

Gearheart, B. R., Weishahn, M. W., & Gearheart, C. J. (1992). *The exceptional student in the regular classroom.* 5th ed. New York: Macmillan.

Giangreco, M. F., & Doyle, M. B. (2002). Students with disabilities and paraprofessional supports: Benefits, balance, and band-aids. *Focus on Exceptional Children, 34*(7), 1–12.

Gonet, M. M. (1994). *Counseling the adolescent substance abuser: School-based intervention and prevention.* Thousand Oaks, CA: Sage Publications.

Henley, M., Ramsey, R. S., & Algozzine, R. F. (2002). *Characteristics of and strategies for teaching students with mild disabilities.* 4th ed. Boston: Allyn and Bacon.

Johnston, L. D., O'Malley, P. M., Bachman, J. G., & Schulenberg, J. E. (2005). *Monitoring the future: National results on adolescent drug use: Overview of key findings, 2004.* Bethesda, MD: National Institute on Drug Abuse.

Kerr, M. M., & Nelson, C. M. (2006). *Strategies for addressing behavior problems in the classroom.* 5th ed. Upper Saddle River, NJ: Pearson Prentice Hall.

Kottler, J. A., & Kottler, E. (1993). *Teacher as counselor: Developing the helping skills you need.* Newbury Park, CA: Corwin Press.

Landrum, T. J., & Kauffman, J. M. (2006). Behavioral approaches to classroom management. In C. M. Evertson & C. S. Weinstein (Eds.), *Handbook of classroom management: Research, practice, and contemporary issues.* Mahwah, NJ: Lawrence Erlbaum Associates, Inc.

Mastropieri, M. A., & Scruggs, T. E. (2001). Promoting inclusion in secondary classrooms. *Learning Disability Quarterly, 24,* 265–274.

Michaelis, K. L. (1993). *Reporting child abuse: A guide to mandatory requirements for school personnel.* Newbury Park, CA: Corwin Press.

Murawski, W. W., & Dieker, L. A. (2004). Tips and strategies for co-teaching at the secondary level. *Teaching Exceptional Children, 36*(5), 52–58.

Murray, C. (2004). Clarifying collaborative roles in urban high schools: General educators' perspectives. *Teaching Exceptional Children, 36*(5), 44–51.

Myles, B. S., Gagnon, E., Moyer, S. A., & Trautman, M. L. (2004). Asperger syndrome. In F. M. Kline & L. B. Silver (Eds.), *The educator's guide to mental health issues in the classroom.* Baltimore: Paul H. Brookes Publishing Co.

National Dissemination Center for Children with Disabilities (2003). Pervasive developmental disorders. Fact Sheet 20. (Downloaded from www.nichcy.org/pubs/factshe/fs20txt.htm.)

National School Safety Center (1990). *School safety check book.* Malibu, CA: Pepperdine University Press.

Newsam, B. S. (1992). *Complete student assistance program handbook.* West Nyack, NY: The Center for Applied Research in Education.

O'Connor, R. E., & Jenkins, J. R. (1996). Cooperative learning as an inclusion strategy: A closer look. *Exceptionality, 6*(1), 9-51.

O'Neil, J. (1994/95). Can inclusion work? A conversation with Jim Kauffman and Mara Sapon-Shevin. *Educational Leadership, 52*(4), 7-11.

Ostrander, R. (2004). Oppositional defiant disorder and conduct disorder. In F. M. Kline & L. B. Silver (Eds.), *The educator's guide to mental health issues in the classroom.* Baltimore: Paul H. Brookes Publishing Co.

Padolsky, D. (2005). NCELA FAQ No. 1: How many school-aged English language learners (ELLs) are there in the United States? Washington, D.C.: National Clearinghouse for English Language Acquisition. (Available online at www.ncela.gwu.edu/expert/faq/01/eps.htm.)

Parkay, F. W., & Stanford, B. H. (1992). *Becoming a teacher.* 2nd ed. Boston: Allyn and Bacon.

Portner, J., & Galley, M. (May 31, 2000). More students are abusing Ritalin, DEA official testifies. *Education Week, 8.*

Portner, J. (April 12, 2000a). Complex set of ills spurs rising teen suicide rate. *Education Week, 1,* 22-31.

Portner, J. (April 12, 2000b). Suicide: Many schools fall short on prevention. *Education Week, 1,* 20-22.

Powell, R. R., Zehm, S. J., & Kottler, J. A. (1995). *Classrooms under the influence: Addicted families/addicted students.* Thousand Oaks, CA: Corwin Press.

Remafedi, G. (1994). *Death by denial.* Boston: Alyson Publications.

Reynolds, M. C. (1989). Students with special needs. In M. C. Reynolds (Ed.), *Knowledge base for the beginning teacher.* Oxford, England: Pergamon Press.

Robinson, S., & Ricord Griesemer, S. M. (2006). Helping individual students with problem behavior. In C. M. Evertson & C. S. Weinstein (Eds.), *Handbook of classroom management: Research, practice, and contemporary issues.* Mahwah, NJ: Lawrence Erlbaum Associates, Inc.

Romero, M., Mercado, C., & Vazquez-Faria, J. A. (1987). Students of limited English proficiency. In V. Richardson-Koehler (Ed.), *Educators' handbook: A research perspective.* New York: Longman.

Sandham, J. L. (May 24, 2000). Cranked up. *Education Week, 36-41.*

Schlozman, S. C. (2001). Too sad to learn? *Educational Leadership, 59*(1), 80-81.

Schumm, J. S., & Vaughn, S. (1992). Planning for mainstreamed special education students: Perceptions of general classroom teachers. *Exceptionality, 3,* 81-98.

Scruggs, T. E., & Mastropieri, M. A. (1996). Teacher perceptions of mainstreaming/inclusion, 1958-1995: A research synthesis. *Exceptional Children, 63,* 59-74.

Semmel, M. I., Abernathy, T. V., Butera, G., & Lesar, S. (1991). Teacher perceptions of the regular education initiative. *Exceptional Children, 58,* 9–24.

Shin, H. B., with Bruno, R. (2003). Language use and English-speaking ability: 2000. Washington, D.C.: U. S. Census Bureau. (Downloaded from www.census.gov/prod/2003pubs/c2kbr-29.pdf.)

Slavin, R. E. (1989). Students at risk of school failure: The problems and its dimensions. In R. E. Slavin, N. L. Karweit, & N. A. Madden (Eds.), *Effective programs for students at risk.* Boston: Allyn and Bacon, 3–19.

Soodak, L. C., & McCarthy, M. R. (2006). Classroom management in inclusive settings. In C. M. Evertson & C. S. Weinstein (Eds.), *Handbook of classroom management: Research, practice, and contemporary issues.* Mahwah, NJ: Lawrence Erlbaum Associates, Inc.

Stefkovich, J. A., & Miller, J. A. (April 13, 1998). Law enforcement officers in public schools: Student citizens in safe havens? Paper presented at the conference of the American Educational Research Association, San Diego, California.

Towers, R. L. (1989). *Children of alcoholics/addicts.* Washington D.C.: National Education Association.

Underwood, M. M., & Dunne-Maxim, K. (1993). *Managing sudden violent loss in the schools.* Piscataway, NJ: Governor's Advisory Council on Youth Suicide Prevention.

U.S. Department of Health and Human Services, Administration on Children, Youth, and Families. (2006). *Child Maltreatment 2004.* Washington, D.C.: U.S. Government Printing Office. (Available online at http://www.acf.hhs.gov/programs/cb/stats_research/index.htm#can.)

Vaughn, S., Bos, C. S., & Schumm, J. S. (2003). *Teaching exceptional, diverse, and at-risk students in the general education classroom.* Boston: Allyn and Bacon.

Vaughn, S., Gersten, R., & Chard, D. J. (2000). The underlying message in LD intervention research: Findings from research syntheses. *Exceptional Children, 67*(1), 99–114.

Wallace, T., Anderson, A. R., Bartholomay, T., & Hupp, S. (2002). An ecobehavioral examination of high school classrooms that include students with disabilities. *Exceptional Children, 68*(3), 345–359.

Wodrich, D. L. (2000). *Attention-deficit/hyperactivity disorder: What every parent wants to know.* 2nd ed. Baltimore, MD: Paul Brookes Publishing Co.

Wolf, N. (1991). *The beauty myth: How images of beauty are used against women.* New York: Anchor Books, Doubleday.

Zigmond, N., Jenkins, J., Fuchs, D., Deno, S., & Fuchs, L. S. (1995). When students fail to achieve satisfactorily: A reply to McLeskey and Waldron. *Phi Delta Kappan, 77*(4), 303–306.

Zigmond, N., Jenkins, J., Fuchs, L., Deno, S., Fuchs, D., Baker, J., Jenkins, L., & Couthino, M. (1995). Special education in restructured schools: Findings from three multi-year studies. *Phi Delta Kappan, 76*(7), 533–540.

PREVENTING AND RESPONDING TO VIOLENCE

By the year 2000 all schools in America will be free of drugs and violence and the unauthorized presence of firearms and alcohol, and offer a disciplined environment that is conducive to learning. (*Goals 2000: Educate America Act,* 1994)

In the late 1990s, a series of school shootings in Mississippi, Kentucky, Arkansas, Pennsylvania, Tennessee, and Oregon made it clear that this laudable national goal, adopted by Congress and signed by President Clinton, was certainly out of reach. But nothing prepared the country for the events of April 20, 1999. On that day, two seniors at Columbine High School in Littleton, Colorado, shot and killed 12 students and a teacher before turning their guns on themselves. Overnight, the topic of school violence catapulted to the front page. Copycat shootings, bomb scares, and threats of violence created unprecedented terror and upheaval during the final weeks of the school year. Parents agonized about sending their children to school. Politicians, policy makers, and pundits talked about youth violence as a "national epidemic" and speculated on the causes. School officials across the country worried that "their schools could become the next Columbine High" and increased security measures (Drummond & Portner, 1999). Five years later the country was jolted again when a high school student went on a shooting rampage on the Red Lake Indian Reservation in northern Minnesota, killing his grandparents, five fellow students, a teacher, a security guard, and himself.

But just how widespread is school violence? Were Columbine and Red Lake symptomatic of a growing epidemic, or horrible but isolated incidents? Let's look at some facts and figures.

How Much Violence Is There?

Information on the frequency and severity of school violence comes from the U.S. Departments of Education and Justice (DeVoe, Peter, Kaufman, Miller, Noonan, Snyder, & Baum, 2004). The data show that from 1992 to 2002 crime in the nation's schools actually decreased by 50 percent—from 48 violent incidents per 100,000 students to 24 violent incidents (Butterfield, 2004), and students from age 12 to age 18 were more likely to experience a serious violent crime away from school than at school. From 1993 to 2003, the percentage of high school students who said they had been in a fight on school property declined from 16 percent to 13 percent. Similarly, the percentage of students who reported carrying a weapon such as a gun, knife, or club on school property within the previous 30 days also declined, from 12 percent to 6 percent.

It is hard to believe numbers like these when we read headlines about murderous rampages and see television news clips of students fleeing from schools under siege. Indeed, after the Red Lake shootings, a Gallup/CNN poll reported that close to three-quarters of the American public believed such school shootings were likely to happen in their communities, and 60 percent did not think events like these could be prevented (Astor & Benbenishty, 2005). Moreover, despite the decreasing percentages, in 2002, 88,000 students from ages 12–18 were victims of serious violent crimes at school (DeVoe et al, 2004), and an additional 1.1 million students said they had been victims of theft at school (Butterfield, 2004). Bullying, the presence of gangs, drinking, and drug abuse still remain serious problems. Clearly, teachers and administrators must work to decrease students' fears and anxiety, as well as actual incidents of school violence. But what can actually be done?

 Pause and Reflect

With the issue of school violence so prevalent in the media, anxiety around this issue is normal for all teachers, but for novice teachers in particular. What are your fears associated with school violence? Talk to teachers in your building about the procedures in place to deal with issues of violence. Are there standard procedures in place? Knowing what to do in a crisis situation will not only ease anxieties but may make a significant difference in the outcome.

Improving Security Systems

In the wake of Columbine, school officials all across the country reexamined their safety and security measures. Schools installed metal detectors and surveillance cameras, stationed police officers in high schools, introduced photo identification cards, practiced "lock-downs" and safety drills, and required clear plastic backpacks or banned them completely. Although enhanced security is a logical reaction to the threat of violent crime, studies suggest that measures like these may actually make students feel *less* safe and may not reduce incidents of violent crime (Barton, Coley,

& Wenglinsky, 1998; Portner, 2000). Furthermore, some educators worry that security measures create a negative environment, turning schools into prisonlike, oppressive institutions (Astor, Meyer, & Behre, 1999; Berreth & Berman, 1997; Noguera, 1995).

It is clear that enhanced security systems alone will not solve the problem of school violence, nor will they allay students' fears and anxieties. Creating safer schools—and schools that *feel* safer—requires a collaborative effort to reach out to students (especially those on the margins), build a climate of tolerance, and recognize the early warning signs of potential violence. This chapter examines some of the ways that individual teachers can contribute to this effort.

STRATEGIES FOR PREVENTING VIOLENCE

Building Supportive School Communities

Although we talked about creating safer, more caring classrooms in Chapter 3, it's important to revisit this topic in relationship to violence prevention. Numerous educators argue that violence prevention has to focus on the creation of more humane environments in which students are known and feel supported (Astor, Meyer, & Behre, 1999; Noguera, 1995). Indeed, Richard Riley, President Clinton's Secretary of Education, has suggested that schools look beyond traditional security issues to find better solutions for students who need help: "We need to make sure that in every community, in school, every child is connected to at least one responsible, caring adult" (Richard, 1999). The superintendent of Sandy's district echoes this sentiment:

> *A safe school is one that is responsive to students, where the staff knows the kids, where you can get help for troubled kids right away. . . . We don't talk much about metal detectors or security measures here. Our approach to violence prevention emphasizes connecting to kids and addressing their social-emotional needs. We try hard to make sure that one group isn't elevated over another. . . . and to respect differences among kids.*

Creating a supportive school community is not easy, especially in large high schools, where feelings of anonymity, alienation, and apathy are leading causes of problems. Following the suggestions in Chapter 3 should help to build a sense of community in the classes you teach. In addition, a number of useful suggestions come from *Responding to Hate at School* (1999) published by Teaching Tolerance, a project of the Southern Poverty Law Center. (See Organizational Resources.)

Be Alert to Signs of Hate

According to a report from the Southern Poverty Law Center (2004), the number of hate crimes by youngsters has risen sharply since 9/11:

> [A] disproportionate number of assaults on Muslim-Americans were committed by teenagers. The same appears to be true for attacks against sexual and gender minorities, Hispanics and the homeless. And hate activity is no longer the province of white boys, though they are still the main offenders. Not only are more Hispanic

and African American kids getting involved in hate, but more girls as well. . . . [Furthermore,] in another demographic shift, the bulk of hate activity now bubbles up in the suburbs—among reasonably well-off youth. (p. 1)

As a teacher, you need to take note if book reports, essays, or journal entries convey messages of hate or violence, and report your concerns to the principal, a school counselor, or the district's affirmative action officer. Be aware of online hate sites and recruitment by hate groups. (The Southern Poverty Law Center's Intelligence Project can help you stay informed about this.) Help students recognize hate literature containing swastikas, derogatory references to race or ethnicity, and caricatures of racial/ethnic groups, and discuss what students can do if they find or someone gives them a hate flier. At Halloween time, discourage costumes that involve negative stereotyping (e.g., "Gypsy" costumes or "homeless person" outfits) or organizations that promote hate (e.g., Ku Klux Klan robes).

Examine the Ways Your School Recognizes Student Achievement

Traditions that contribute to a sense of superiority among some students may lead to feelings of frustration or inadequacy in others. Are athletes disciplined less severely for offenses? Are their achievements highlighted more than the achievements of other students? Do honors students and student leaders enjoy special privileges? Take action to avoid institutionalized favoritism. Find ways to recognize and celebrate different kinds of achievement.

Curb Peer Harassment and Bullying

We already touched on peer harassment in Chapter 3, but this problem clearly warrants further discussion. Every day, students suffer teasing, name calling, ridicule, humiliation, ostracism, and even physical injury at the hands of their peers. The problem is substantial: In a large-scale, national study of 15,686 students in grades 6 through 10 (Nansel, Overpeck, Pilla, Ruan, Simons-Morton, & Scheidt, 2001), about 30 percent of the sample reported moderate or frequent involvement in bullying—as a bully (13 percent), one who was bullied (10.6 percent), or both (6.3 percent). Also frightening is the fact that peer harassment is quasi-acceptable (Hoover & Oliver, 1996). Bullies can be popular, and their behavior is often dismissed as normal. When the bullies are males, for example, it is not uncommon to hear adults dismiss their behavior by reminding us that "boys will be boys."

According to Dan Olweus (2003), an internationally known researcher and developer of the Olweus Bullying Prevention Program, bullying also entails an imbalance in strength or power, which means that victims have difficulty defending themselves. Moreover, much bullying is "proactive"; in other words, it often occurs without provocation from the victim. There are also gender differences in the frequency and nature of bullying: Boys bully other students more often than girls do, and their bullying tends to be physical. Girls typically use more subtle, "relational" bullying, such as excluding someone from the group and spreading rumors.

Teasing is the most frequent bullying behavior at all ages, but it can be difficult for students to draw the line between playful exchanges and hurtful harassment. Hoover and Oliver (1996) suggest that whether an exchange represents teasing or

DO:	**DON'T:**
1. Be careful of others' feelings.	1. Tease someone you don't know well.
2. Use humor gently and carefully.	2. [If you are a boy] tease girls about sex.
3. Ask whether teasing about a certain topic hurts someone's feelings.	3. Tease about a person's body.
4. Accept teasing from others if you tease.	4. Tease about a person's family members.
5. Tell others if teasing about a certain topic hurts your feelings.	5. Tease about a topic when a student has asked you not to.
6. Know the difference between friendly gentle teasing and hurtful ridicule or harassment.	6. Tease someone who seems agitated or who you know is having a bad day.
7. Try to read others' "body language" to see if their feelings are hurt—even when they don't tell you.	7. Be thin-skinned about teasing that is meant in a friendly way.
8. Help a weaker student when he or she is being ridiculed.	8. Swallow your feelings about teasing—tell someone in a direct and clear way what is bothering you.

Figure 13.1   Teasing Dos and Don'ts

Source: Reprinted, with permission, from *The Bullying Prevention Handbook: A Guide for Principals, Teachers, and Counselors* by John H. Hoover and Ronald Oliver. Copyright 1996 by the National Educational Service, 304 W. Kirkwood Ave., Suite 2, Bloomington, IN 47404, 800-733-6786, www.nesonline.com

friendly banter may have to do with the social level or popularity of the individuals involved. If a higher-status student mocks a lower-status student, the exchange is likely to be seen as an attack. Teasing someone of the same status is more likely to be interpreted as playful. Figure 13.1 contains some "Teasing Dos and Don'ts" that may help your students understand when teasing is acceptable and when it is not.

During one discussion with Christina, she related a story that illustrated the pain that "friendly" teasing can cause.

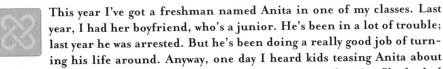

This year I've got a freshman named Anita in one of my classes. Last year, I had her boyfriend, who's a junior. He's been in a lot of trouble; last year he was arrested. But he's been doing a really good job of turning his life around. Anyway, one day I heard kids teasing Anita about him. They'd ask if he was on house arrest, or if he was in jail again. She looked unhappy about it, but she didn't say anything to me. After class, I told her that I had heard what the kids were saying, and I asked how she felt about it. She indicated that she didn't like it, but she didn't want to make a "big deal." She said she didn't want to get them in trouble. I offered to talk to the other kids—without indicating that I had spoken with her. I told her I'd make it clear that she hadn't asked me to intervene. The next day, I took the kids aside—there were two boys specifically—and said I had overheard them saying these things to Anita, and that I didn't think it was appropriate. They said they were "only teasing." I told them, "But teasing can hurt." I said that from the expression on Anita's face, it was clear that she didn't think it was funny. They looked surprised—as if they just hadn't given it any thought before. They promised to stop it, and they did.

In an effort to curb peer harassment, you need to be alert to hurtful comments about race and ethnicity, body size, disabilities, sexual orientation, unfashionable or eccentric dress, use of languages other than English, and socioeconomic status. Barone (1997) reports that counselors, teachers, and administrators tend to underestimate the amount of bullying that exists in their schools. In a survey administered to eighth-graders and school staff, Barone found that almost 60 percent of students reported having "been bothered by a bully or bullies" in middle school. In contrast, staff members believed that only 16 percent of the students had been victims of bullies.

Teachers also need to make it clear that disrespectful speech and slurs—even when used in a joking manner—are absolutely unacceptable. This means intervening if you hear a student use a hateful epithet (e.g., "That word hurts people, so you may not use it in this classroom" or "Disrespectful words are never acceptable in this school" or even "Watch your language, please!"). According to Stephen Wessler (2000/2001), a former prosecutor of school hate crimes, intervention "breaks the pattern of escalation from language to more focused harassment to threats and, finally to violence" (p. 31). If you stay silent, students are likely to think you condone the degrading language. You're also serving as a poor role model for students, modeling passivity instead of the courage, skills, and empathy to speak up. Some schools encourage students to speak up by having them sign an antibullying pledge. (See Figure 13.2.)

In the last few years, peer harassment has expanded from school grounds to cyberspace, as "cyber-bullies" use e-mail, cell phone and pager text messages, instant messaging, Web logs, and online voting booths to pursue their victims. For example, when eighth-grader Amanda Marcuson reported the fact that some of her

---

We, the students of the _____ school district, agree to join together to stop bullying.

BY SIGNING THIS PLEDGE I AGREE TO:

- Treat others respectfully.
- Try to include those who are left out.
- Refuse to bully others.
- Refuse to watch, laugh or join in when someone is being bullied.
- Tell an adult.
- Help those who are being bullied.

Signed by

_____

Date

_____

Figure 13.2   Antibullying Pledge
Source: Harrison, 2005.

classmates had stolen her makeup, she was immediately hounded by instant messages that began by calling her a tattletale and a liar and escalated to "increasingly ugly epithets" (Harmon, 2005). When 16-year-old Denise broke up with her boyfriend, he retaliated by posting her e-mail address and cell phone number on sex-oriented Web sites and blogs. For months, Denise was besieged with messages and calls that were embarrassing and frightening (Strom & Strom, 2005). And when a middle school student decided to do a survey on the top five "hated kids" in the sixth grade, he set up a Web site where students could vote (Lisante, 2005). Fortunately, the parents of one "winner" reported the survey to the principal, which prompted an in-school program on the damage that cyber-bullying can cause.

Online harassment is less visible to adults than "off-line" harassment, and adults who are unfamiliar and uncomfortable with the new technologies may have no sense of the nature or magnitude of the problem. At the same time, cyber-bullying can be vastly more humiliating to victims. Rumors, ridicule, embarrassing pictures, and hateful comments can be circulated among a huge number of peers with just a few clicks, and home no longer provides a safe haven from the taunting. Furthermore, youngsters may say things online they would never say in person, mainly because of the feeling of anonymity and the distance from the victim. As one student comments, "Over the Internet you don't really see their face or they don't see yours, and you don't have to look in their eyes and see they're hurt" (Leishman, 2002, cited in Shariff, 2004). Cyber-bullying also seems to have a particular appeal for girls, who prefer "relational aggression" rather than physical harassment and often try to avoid direct confrontation (Harmon, 2004).

It's important to note that harassment waged on the Internet and away from school grounds raises complex legal issues. Clear legal standards have yet to be developed, but in 1997 the Supreme Court ruled that speech on the Internet (just like speech in print) is entitled to the highest degree of protection under the First Amendment (Haynes, Chaltain, Ferguson Jr., Hudson Jr., & Thomas, 2003). Therefore, even if you are outraged by the content of Internet communications that are brought to your attention, you need to be prudent and seek advice from a school administrator before taking disciplinary action. On the other hand, regardless of the legal technicalities, you can always treat incidents of cyber-bullying as an opportunity for teaching. Is there a way to organize an activity, program, or discussion about free speech? About bullying? These activities are always worthwhile and as long as you do not "name names" but keep the discussions general, there are no legal concerns. Some additional strategies for dealing with cyber-bullying appear in the Practical Tips box on page 412.

Teaching Social–Emotional Skills and Conflict Resolution

Concerns about safety and order have led to a raft of violence prevention programs such as conflict resolution training, peer mediation, and social problem solving. These programs emphasize anger management and impulse control; effective communication skills; social perspective taking (i.e., understanding that others can have a different and equally valid perspective on the same situation); resisting peer pressure; and prejudice, sexism, and racism (Dusenbury, Falco, Lake, Brannigan, &

PRACTICAL TIPS FOR

DEALING WITH CYBER-BULLYING

- Develop an explicit policy for acceptable in-school use of the Internet and include it in the school handbook (or your class rules). The policy should spell out what constitutes cyber-bullying and list consequences.

- Make sure that children and young people are aware that bullying will be dealt with seriously.

- Ensure that parents/guardians who express cyber-bullying concerns are taken seriously.

- Explain to students that they
    Should never share or give out personal information, PIN numbers, phone numbers, etc.
    Should not delete messages; they do not have to read them, but they should show them to an adult they trust. Messages can be used to take action against cyber-bullies.
    Should not open a message from someone they don't know.
    Should *never* reply to the message.
    Can block the sender's message if they are being bullied through e-mail or instant messaging.
    Can forward the messages to their Internet Service Provider.
    Should tell an adult.
    Should show the message to the police if it contains physical threats.
    Should speak out against cyber-bullying.
    Should never send messages when they are angry.
    Should never send messages they wouldn't want others to see.

- Make parents aware of the fact that all of the major Internet Service Providers offer some form of parental controls. For example, AOL has developed "AOL Guardian," which reports with whom youngsters exchange messages and what Web sites they visit and monitors chat rooms for children 13 and under.

- Encourage parents to keep computers in a public room in the house.

- Invite members of the local police department to come to school to speak with parents and students about proper Internet use.

- Make sure ethics is included in any computer instruction given at your school.

Source: Adapted from Keith & Martin, 2005; Lisante, 2005; and the National Crime Prevention Council, 2003, at www.mcgruff.org.

Bosworth, 1997). All programs also teach students a series of steps for dealing constructively with conflicts. These generally consist of strategies for cooling down, expressing feelings (in the form of I-messages), generating solutions, evaluating consequences, selecting the best action, and implementing the plan. All of our teachers work in districts that have implemented some kind of program to address these social–emotional skills.

There is great diversity in approaches, but generally the programs fall into two categories: those that train the entire student body in social–emotional skills and conflict resolution strategies and those that train a particular cadre of students to mediate disputes among their peers (Johnson & Johnson, 1996). An example of a program that targets the entire student body is Johnson and Johnson's *Teaching Students to be Peacemakers* (1995). The program spans Grades 1 through 12; each year all students learn increasingly sophisticated negotiation and mediation procedures. Research conducted by Johnson and Johnson indicates that students trained in the peacemaker program are able to apply the negotiation and mediation procedures to a variety of conflicts—both in and out of the classroom. In addition, training results in fewer discipline problems that have to be managed by the teacher and the principal (Bodine & Crawford, 1998).

In a peer mediation program, selected students guide disputants through the problem-solving process. The advantage of using peers as mediators rather than adults is that students can frame disputes in a way that is age appropriate. Generally working in pairs, mediators explain the ground rules for mediation, provide an opportunity for disputants to identify the problem from their differing perspectives, explain how they feel, brainstorm solutions, evaluate the advantages and disadvantages of each proposed solution, and select a course of action. These steps can be seen in the example of a peer mediation that appears in Figure 13.3.

Peer mediation programs are becoming increasingly popular in schools across the country. Sandy's school has had a peer mediation program for many years, and Tonia Moore, the student assistance counselor, believes that it has definitely helped to reduce incidents of violence:

> *Before we had peer mediation, we had lots of kids getting suspended for fighting; now we rarely have fights. Kids will tell the peer mediators when something is brewing, and they can prevent the problem from erupting into a physical fight. Peer mediation gives kids a structure they may not have developed yet for dealing with emotional issues. Sometimes, kids will mock the structure—they tell me, "All we do in peer mediation is hear our own words repeated back to us." But they still go; they still use it. We have to recognize that settling problems this way is a very new approach for some kids; this may be the first time they've ever done anything like this. It's a real life change for them.*

Thus far, anecdotal evidence supports Tonia's conviction that peer mediation programs can substantially reduce violent incidents. Some researchers contend that peer mediation actually has more impact on the *mediators* than on the disputants, since they acquire valuable conflict resolution skills and earn the respect of their peers (Bodine & Crawford, 1998; Miller, 1994). If this is so, it means that high-risk students—not just the "good kids"—must be trained and used as mediators.

In schools with ethnic and racial diversity, it's extremely important to sensitize peer mediators to cultural differences (Hyman, 1997). For example, African American, Italian, and Eastern European cultures encourage emotional expressiveness, and this frequently involves the dramatic use of hands and body language. On the other hand, English and Scandinavian cultures value the control of overt emotionality. Thus, an innocuous interaction can turn into an angry exchange if students from these different backgrounds misread cues. Consider an argument

Trouble in the Classroom

Situation: Jimmy has been sitting in front of Eduardo all year in math class. Eduardo has this habit of tapping his foot on Jimmy's chair. It's been driving Jimmy crazy.

Jimmy: You jerk! Why don't you stop bothering me?

Eduardo: Who are you calling a jerk? I don't know what you are talking about.

Jimmy: If you touch my chair one more time, I'm going to let you have it.

Eduardo: I'll touch your chair all I want. See if I care.

The boys start pushing and the teacher asks them if they would like to go to mediation.

The boys agree.

▶ **Step 1   Introductions and Ground Rules**
Mediator 1:
Our names are _____ and _____ and we are student mediators. We are not here to punish you or tell you what to do. We are here to help you solve your conflict. What are your names? (Write them on the form.) Thank you for coming. Everything you say here is CONFIDENTIAL, except if it involves drugs, weapons, or abuse. Then, we'll have to report it to our advisor or stop the mediation.

Mediator 2:
There are five rules you must agree to before we begin. They are:
1. Be willing to solve the problem.   2. Tell the truth.
3. Listen without interrupting.   4. Be respectful: no name calling or fighting.
          5. Take responsibility for carrying out your agreement.
Do you agree to the rules? (Be sure the students agree.)

▶ **Step 2   Telling the Story**
(Each person tells his/her side of the story. Mediator chooses the person who begins.)

Mediator 1:   Jimmy, tell us what happened.

Jimmy: I was minding my own business when this creep starts hitting my chair.

Mediator 1:   No name calling, please.

Jimmy: Okay. Like I said, I was sitting in my chair when he started hitting it, like he always does, just to bother me. I'm not going to take it anymore.

Mediator 1:   You said that you were sitting in your chair when Eduardo started hitting it. How do you feel about this situation?

Figure 13.3   Peer Mediation Script
Source: Reprinted with permission from Grace Contrino Abrams Peace Education Foundation Inc., 1992

Jimmy:	I feel angry because he's doing this all the time. He does it just to get me mad.
Mediator 1:	You feel angry because he does it all the time just to get you mad.
Mediator 2:	Eduardo, tell us what happened.
Eduardo:	I always tap my foot. I do it to keep myself awake. It's just a nervous habit. You can ask anybody, I always tap my foot.
Mediator 2:	You said that you always tap your foot to keep yourself awake and it's a habit. How do you feel about what happened?
Eduardo:	I feel upset because I really didn't mean to start a fight. He's too picky.
Mediator 2:	You feel upset because you didn't mean to start a fight and you also think that Jimmy is too picky. Is there any other information that we need to know? (If yes, ask each one to speak following the same rules. If no, continue to Step 3.)

▶ **Step 3**   **Searching For Solutions**

One mediator asks questions, the other writes the suggested solutions on paper. This is not the time for choosing—only thinking.

Mediator 1:	You both listened to each other's side of the story. How do you think this conflict can be solved? What could you do to solve this conflict? We're going to write down all your ideas. Later, you'll pick the idea or ideas you like best.
Jimmy:	I could apologize for calling Eduardo a creep.
Eduardo:	I could tap my foot on my bookbag, instead of his chair so it won't make a noise.
Jimmy:	I could ask the teacher to move my seat to the front of the room.
Eduardo:	We could exchange seats with each other.
Mediator 1:	Any more ideas? (If none, go to Step 4.)

▶ **Step 4**   **Choosing the Solution**

Mediator 2:	Let's go over the suggestions you both made. Which ones do you think will solve this conflict?
Jimmy:	I'll apologize for calling you a creep. I got mad and the words just came out.
Eduardo:	I'll apologize for tapping on your chair. I didn't know that it was bothering you. I will tap on my bookbag from now on.
Jimmy:	It sounds good to me.
Mediator 2:	Is this conflict solved? (If they both say "yes" have them fill out their section of the Mediation Report Form. If not, go back to Step 3.)

Figure 13.3 *(cont.)*

▶ **Step 5**	**In The Future**
Mediator 1:	What do you think you could do differently to prevent this from happening again?
Jimmy:	I'm going to try to tell people what is bothering me before I explode.
Eduardo:	I'm going to try to be more aware of bothering other people.
▶ **Step 6**	**Choosing**
Mediator 2:	Jimmy and Eduardo, congratulations for solving your conflict. To keep rumors from spreading, please tell your friends that the conflict has been resolved: Thank you for coming to mediation.

Figure 13.3 (*cont.*)

between Salim, who comes from Lebanon, and Jim, whose family heritage is British and German:

> SALIM: Jim, why did you laugh in class when I was reading that part from Romeo and Juliet out loud?
>
> JIM: I don't know. Something was funny.
>
> SALIM: What was funny? (Salim wonders if Jim was laughing at him. His voice becomes louder as he uses his hands to help express himself.)
>
> JIM: Listen, I have to get to my next class. I'll talk to you later. (Jim begins to get uncomfortable about Salim's raised voice and hand waving.)
>
> SALIM: Just tell me what was funny. (Salim now feels he is being ignored. He steps in front of Jim, who has turned to walk away.)
>
> JIM: Why are you waving your fist at me? I told you I don't have time now. Now get out of my way. You better not try anything! (Salim's hand waving and attempt to get Jim's attention was misinterpreted.)
>
> SALIM: I am not waving my fist. I just want to know why you laughed.
>
> JIM: I wasn't laughing at you. I was laughing about what those words meant. This is ridiculous. I'm not going to stand here and argue about such a silly thing.
>
> SALIM: What words were so funny? (Salim will forget the matter if he believes he wasn't insulted.)
>
> JIM: I don't have time for this. (Jim turns to walk away. This action is a direct insult to Salim. It means he is being treated with contempt, when all he asked for were the words that were funny. He would actually like to know what he missed.) (Hyman, 1997, p. 255)

Hyman suggests that Jim's immediate response might have been adequate for someone he knew well or who was not part of a culture in which any possible insult is treated seriously:

> Salim, who does not believe in violence, had no intention of becoming aggressive, but he was worried that he did not understand if there was something funny in the

text he was reading. However, Jim's initial response made him wonder if Jim were laughing at him. Salim's hand waving and animated body language are typical in his culture, but to Jim, they suggest real danger. (p. 255)

Obviously, peer mediation is not an option when the conflict involves drugs, alcohol, theft, or violence, since these are criminal actions. But mediation *can* help to resolve disputes involving behavior such as gossiping, name calling, racial putdowns, and bullying, as well as conflicts over property (e.g., borrowing a book and losing it). Even then, mediation must be voluntary and confidential. In cases where school rules have been violated, mediation should not substitute for disciplinary action; rather, it can be offered as an opportunity to solve problems and "clear the air."

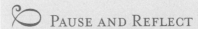

PAUSE AND REFLECT

With pressure to cover the curriculum and the specter of high-stakes testing, teachers are loathe to "sacrifice" academic learning time to teach social-emotional skills like social problem solving and conflict resolution. How do you feel about this dilemma? If you think that social-emotional learning (SEL) is critical, can you think of ways of integrating SEL into your curriculum?

Knowing the Early Warning Signs of Potential for Violence

In 1998, at the request of President Clinton, the U. S. Department of Education and the Department of Justice published a guide to assist schools in developing comprehensive violence prevention plans (Dwyer, Osher, & Warger, 1998). The guide contains a list of "early warning signs" that can alert teachers and other school staff to students' potential for violence, as well as signs that violence is imminent. These appear in Tables 13.1 and 13.2.

TABLE 13.1 Early Warning Signs of Potential for Violence

- Social withdrawal.
- Excessive feelings of isolation and being alone.
- Excessive feelings of rejection.
- Being a victim of violence.
- Feelings of being picked on and persecuted.
- Low school interest and poor academic performance.
- Expression of violence in writings and drawings.
- Uncontrolled anger.
- Patterns of impulsive and chronic hitting, intimidating, and bullying behaviors.
- History of discipline problems.
- Past history of violent and aggressive behavior.
- Intolerance for differences and prejudicial attitudes.
- Drug use and alcohol use.
- Affiliation with gangs.
- Inappropriate access to, possession of, and use of firearms.
- Serious threats of violence.

TABLE 13.2 Imminent Signs of Violence

- Serious physical fighting with peers or family members.
- Severe destruction of property.
- Severe rage for seemingly minor reasons.
- Detailed threats of lethal violence.
- Possession and/or use of firearms and other weapons.
- Other self-injurious behaviors or threats of suicide.

It's important to remember that the early warning signs are not an infallible predictor that a child or youth will commit a violent act toward self or others (Dwyer, Osher, & Warger, 1998). Also keep in mind that potentially violent students typically exhibit multiple warning signs. Thus, be careful about overreacting to single signs, words, or actions, and don't be biased by a student's race, socioeconomic status, academic ability, or physical appearance. Lindy Mandy, a counselor in Fred's school, acknowledges the tension between needing to identify students who may pose a risk for violence and *social profiling:*

> *We have kids who wear the gothic look, and after Columbine, we wanted to reach out to them. But you have to be so careful about stereotyping, thinking that everyone who dresses in gothic must be potentially violent or alienated. It really made us think about our process. At what point does identifying kids who might be violent become social profiling?*

The difficulty of distinguishing between a real threat to safety and harmless student expression is underscored by a 2000 federal court ruling in the state of Washington (Walsh, 2000). In this case, a high school junior submitted a poem to his English teacher about a lonely student who roamed his high school with a pounding heart. The poem contained this passage:

As I approached the classroom door,
I drew my gun and threw open the door.
Bang, Bang, Bang-Bang.
When it was all over, 28 were dead,
and all I remember was not felling [sic] any remorce [sic],
for I felt, I was, cleansing my soul.

The student's teacher alerted administrators, and the poem was reviewed by a psychologist, who determined that the student was unlikely to cause harm to himself or others. Nonetheless, the district decided to expel him on an emergency basis. After the student was examined by a psychiatrist, the district rescinded the expulsion, and the student completed his junior year. The boy's parents then sued the district, claiming that the school had violated his First Amendment right to free speech and asking that the expulsion be removed from their son's record. On February 24, 2000, a federal district judge ruled for the family, maintaining that the district had overreacted in expelling the student. She suggested that there were less restrictive ways the district could have ensured the safety of students and school personnel, such as imposing a temporary suspension pending psychiatric examination.

Stories like this can discourage teachers from reporting essays or artwork that contain threatening messages or behavior that suggests a potential for violence. But it's better to alert school officials about what you have learned than to ignore indicators and be sorry later. Find out what the reporting procedures are in your school: Do you report your concerns to the principal? The school nurse? A counselor? Do you notify parents? Remember that parental involvement and consent are required before personally identifiable information is shared with agencies outside the school (except in case of emergencies or suspicion of abuse). The Family Educational Rights and Privacy Act (FERPA), a federal law that addresses the privacy of educational records, must be observed in all referrals to community agencies (Dwyer, Osher, & Warger, 1998).

In addition to knowing the early warning signs, teachers can help prevent violence by being observant in hallways, cafeterias, stairwells, and locker rooms—"unowned" spaces where violence is most likely to erupt (Astor, Meyer, & Behre, 1999). Chester Quarles, a criminologist who specializes in crime prevention, suggests that teachers attempt to make eye contact whenever they pass students in the halls:

> The subliminal message being exchanged is that "I know who is here and I know who you are. I can remember your features. I can identify you." The influence of careful observation is a strong criminal deterrent for everyone that you observe. . . . Observant teachers . . . can decrease the probability that any of the people they encounter will commit a delinquent act against another that day. (1989, pp. 12–13)

Being Attentive to Whispers and Rumors

The high-profile school shootings that we have witnessed in the last decade are what the Secret Service calls *targeted violence*—incidents in which the attacker selects a particular target prior to the violent attack. As part of the Safe School Initiative of the U.S. Secret Service and the U.S. Department of Education, researchers studied 37 school shootings involving 41 attackers who were current or recent students at the school (Vosekuil, Fein, Reddy, Borum, & Modzelski, 2002). Here are some of their findings:

> Incidents of targeted violence at school are rarely sudden or impulsive. Typically, the attacker *planned* the attack in advance.
>
> In most of the cases, other people knew about the attack before it occurred. In over three-quarters of the cases, at least one person knew; in nearly two-thirds, more than one person knew. Some peers knew details of the attack, while others just knew that something "big" or "bad" was going to happen in school on a particular day.
>
> Most attackers engaged in some behavior prior to the incident that caused others concern or indicated a need for help.

These findings contradict the common perception that students who commit targeted acts of violence have simply "snapped." Nor are they loners who keep their plans to themselves. This means that school staff must be attentive to whispers that something is afoot and impress upon students the need to report rumors of potential violence. As Tonia Moore puts it, "You have to have your radar out all the time."

De-escalating Potentially Explosive Situations

Explosive situations often begin benignly. You make a reasonable request ("Would you join the group over there?") or give an ordinary directive ("Get started on the questions at the end of this section"). But the student is feeling angry—maybe he has just been taunted and humiliated in the hallway; maybe her mother has just grounded her for a month; maybe the teacher in the previous class has ridiculed an answer. The anger may have nothing to do with you at all, but it finds its outlet in your class. In a hostile mood, the student fails to comply immediately and may even respond defiantly. Unfortunately, at this point, teachers often contribute to the escalation of a conflict by becoming angry and impatient. They issue an ultimatum: "Do what I say or else." And now teacher and student are combatants in a potentially explosive situation neither of them wanted.

Let's consider an example (adapted from Walker, Colvin, & Ramsey, 1995) of a teacher–student interaction that begins innocuously enough, but quickly escalates into an explosive situation:

 Students are working on a set of math problems the teacher has assigned. Michael sits slouched in his seat staring at the floor, an angry expression on his face. The teacher sees that Michael is not doing his math and calls over to him from the back of the room where she is working with other students.

TEACHER: Michael, why aren't you working on the assignment?

MICHAEL: I finished it.

TEACHER: Well, let me see it then. [She walks over to Michael's desk and sees that he has four problems completed.] Good. You've done 4 but you need to do 10.

MICHAEL: Nobody told me that!

TEACHER: Michael, I went over the assignment very clearly and asked if there were any questions about what to do!

MICHAEL: I don't remember that.

TEACHER: Look at the board. I wrote it there. See, page 163, numbers 11–20.

MICHAEL: I didn't see it. Anyway, I hate this boring stuff.

TEACHER: OK, that's enough. No more arguments. Page 163, 11 through 20. Now.

MICHAEL: It's dumb. I'm not going to do it.

TEACHER: Yes you are, mister.

MICHAEL: Yeah? Make me.

TEACHER: If you don't do it now, you're going to the office.

MICHAEL: F———you!

TEACHER: That's enough!

MICHAEL: You want math? Here it is! [He throws the math book across the room.]

At first glance, it appears that the teacher is being remarkably patient and reasonable in the face of Michael's stubbornness, defiance, and abuse. On closer examination, however, we can detect a chain of successive escalating interactions, in which Michael's behavior moves from questioning and challenging the teacher to defiance and abuse, and for which the teacher is also responsible (Walker, Colvin, & Ramsey, 1995). Could the teacher have broken this chain earlier? The probable answer is yes.

First, the teacher should have been sensitive to Michael's angry facial expression and the fact that he was slouching down in his seat. Facial expression, flushing, squinty eyes, clenched fists, rigid body posture, pacing and stomping—these all suggest an impending eruption (Hyman, 1997). Second, teachers can usually avoid defiant situations if they do not corner a student, do not argue, do not engage in a power struggle ("I'm the boss in this classroom, and I'm telling you to …") and do not embarrass the student in front of peers. The Practical Tips box summarizes specific recommendations.

With this background, let's go back to Michael and see how the teacher might have dealt with the situation to prevent it from escalating.

PRACTICAL TIPS FOR

MANAGING POTENTIALLY EXPLOSIVE SITUATIONS

- *Move slowly and deliberately toward the problem situation.*
- *Speak privately, quietly, and calmly.* Do not threaten. Be as matter-of-fact as possible.
- *Be as still as possible.* Avoid pointing or gesturing.
- *Keep a reasonable distance.* Do not crowd the student. Do not "get in the student's face."
- *Speak respectfully.* Use the student's name.
- *Establish eye-level position.*
- *Be brief.* Avoid long-winded statements or nagging.
- *Stay with the agenda.* Stay focused on the problem at hand. Do not get sidetracked. Deal with less severe problems later.
- *Avoid power struggles.* Do not get drawn into "I won't, you will" arguments.
- *Inform the student of the expected behavior and the negative consequence as a choice or decision for the student to make.* Then withdraw from the student and allow some time for the student to decide. ("Michael, you need to return to your desk, or I will have to send for the principal. You have a few seconds to decide." The teacher then moves away, perhaps attending to other students. If Michael does not choose the appropriate behavior, deliver the negative consequence. "You are choosing to have me call the principal.") Follow through with the consequence.

Source: Adapted from Walker, Colvin, & Ramsey, 1995.

Students are working on a set of math problems the teacher has assigned. Michael sits slouched in his seat staring at the floor, an angry expression on his face. The teacher notices Michael's posture and realizes that he is feeling upset about something. She goes over, bends down so that she is on eye-level with Michael, and speaks very quietly.

TEACHER: Are you doing OK, Michael? You look upset. [Teacher demonstrates empathy.]

MICHAEL: I'm OK.

TEACHER: Well, good, but if you'd like to talk later, let me know. [Teacher invites further communication.] Meanwhile, you need to get going on this assignment.

MICHAEL: I already did it.

TEACHER: Oh, good. Let me see how you did. [She checks the paper.] OK, you've done the first four, and they're fine. Now do the next four problems and let me see them when you're done. [She walks away, giving the student space.]

Being Alert for the Presence of Gang Activity

A report issued by the U. S. Departments of Education and Justice (Chandler, Chapman, Rand, & Taylor, 1998) found that the presence of gangs in schools nearly doubled between 1989 and 1995, when approximately one-third of the 10,000 students surveyed (aged 12 to 19) reported gang presence. Since gang presence is strongly linked to the presence of guns, drugs, and violence (Howell & Lynch, 2000), teachers need to be alert to the presence of gang activity in schools.

It's not easy to identify a gang, since teenagers frequently "run in packs" and try to look and act just like everyone else. But Kenneth Trump, coordinator of the Youth Gang Unit of the Cleveland Public Schools, reminds us that the key to gang activity is negative behavior:

> Kids who sit together in the lunch room don't constitute a gang. But when groups start assaulting other students or creating an atmosphere of fear and intimidation, they become a gang. In short, groups of students reach gang status when their behavior, either individually or collectively, is disruptive, antisocial, or criminal. (1993, p. 40).

In order to determine the extent to which gangs are present in your school, you need to be familiar with the indicators summarized in Table 13.3. In addition, you may find it helpful to use a gang assessment tool developed by the National School Safety Center (1992; see Figure 13.4). Each "yes" response earns the indicated number of points. The total score is an assessment of the severity of the problem and can suggest the possible need for school security measures: 0-15 points indicate no significant gang problem; 20-40 points, emerging gang problem; 45-60 points, a significant gang problem that must be addressed; 65 points or higher, acute gang problem that requires urgent attention and intervention.

TABLE 13.3 Signs of Gang Presence

Gathering or hanging out:	Gang members may establish territory (e.g., in the lunch room, on playing fields, and in bleachers). Once these areas are claimed, other students will stay away.
Nonverbal and verbal signs:	Gang members often have special ways of signaling one another and conveying messages: "Flashing"—the use of finger and hand signs. "Monikers"—nicknames emphasizing a member's particular attribute (e.g., "Shooter" uses a gun well; "Lil Man" is short).
Graffiti:	Signs, symbols, and nicknames on notebooks, papers, clothing, and walls; graffiti advertises the gang and its members and may contain challenging messages to other gangs; when graffiti is crossed out, that constitutes a direct challenge from a rival gang.
Stance and walk:	Unique ways of standing and walking that set them apart: "Standing duck-footed"—feet are pointed outward. "Holding up the wall"—leaning back with one hand in the pocket and one foot against a wall.
Symbols:	Tattoos, earrings, colors, scarves, bandannas, shoelaces, caps, belts (change over time).

Source: Adapted from Lal, Lal, & Achilles, 1993.

According to Donnie, gang activity in her city was intense about five years ago, when adolescents were divided into "uptown" and "downtown" gangs:

> What you saw was that the kids who lived in the projects stayed together and kept up a feud with the kids on the other side of town. They'd fight about drugs, about somebody from one side of town going out with a girl from the other side of town, about somebody "ratting" on somebody else. Whenever there was a gang fight over the weekend or at night, the kids would all come in buzzing the next day. One year, a kid got killed in a gang fight, and there was a tremendous amount of tension that spilled over into the school. It would simmer down, and then every year, there'd be a big memorial to him that would rekindle all the trouble. But it seems as if the main kids who were involved have moved on. Things have been a lot quieter the last few years.

As Donnie's comment suggests, gangs consist of the "main kids" and those who are on the periphery. In fact, Lal, Lal, and Achilles (1993) suggest that there are at least four types of gang members. *Hard core* members, "in for life and ready to die," determine the character of the gang and are most likely to be involved in illegal behavior. *Affiliates* constitute the "homeboys" or the basic membership. *Peripheral* members exist in a "gray area," dressing like a member, flashing signs, and engaging

1. Do you have graffiti on or near your campus? (5)

2. Do you have crossed-out graffiti on or near your campus? (10)

3. Do your students wear colors, jewelry, clothing, flash hand signals or display other behavior that may be gang-related? (10)

4. Are drugs available near your school? (5)

5. Has there been a significant increase in the number of physical confrontations or stare-downs within the past 12 months in or around your school? (5)

6. Is there an increasing presence of weapons in your community? (10)

7. Are beepers, pagers, or cellular phones used by your students? (10)

8. Have you had a drive-by shooting at or around your school? (15)

9. Have you had a "show-by" display of weapons at or around your school? (10)

10. Is the truancy rate of your school increasing? (5)

11. Are there increasing numbers of racial incidents occurring in your community or school? (5)

12. Is there a history of gangs in your community? (10)

13. Is there an increasing presence of "informal social groups" with unusual names—for example, "Woodland Heights Posse," "Rip Off and Rule," "Females Simply Chillin'" or "Kappa Phi Nasty"? (15)

Figure 13.4 Gang Assessment Tool

Source: Reprinted with permission from *School Safety Update, March 1992, p. 8.* Copyright 1992 by the National School Safety Center, Westlake Village, CA.

in minor activities. *Wannabes* are sometimes viewed as "posers" or "pretenders" who are experimenting with gang behavior. In addition, *homegirls,* relatives and girlfriends, are sometimes "appendages" to male gangs (Verdugo, 1997), although they have recently begun forming their own gangs. Knowing about the types of gang members can help you to identify the leadership of a gang, focus your efforts on the core individuals, and avoid exaggerating the extent of the problem (Verdugo, 1997).

Asking Students to Contribute to Violence Prevention Efforts

It is critical to learn what students' views are with respect to violence and violence prevention strategies—and to include not just the "good ones," but also "the toughies, the gangbangers, the disruptive, the withdrawn, and the unmotivated" (Curwin, 1995, p. 75). Encourage students to organize their own antiviolence events. Solicit their perceptions of the school's high-conflict areas (e.g., hallways, cafeterias, restrooms) and their ideas about how to make these safer. Invite students to develop an antibullying campaign.

A good example of the way students can become meaningfully involved is the Health Informed Teens' Own Program on Sexuality (HITOPS) that Tonia Moore helps to run at Sandy's high school. Together with the health teacher, Tonia runs sessions for juniors who have volunteered to become student experts on health and sexuality issues (e.g., pregnancy prevention, postponing sexual involvement, sexual harassment, homophobia). The students then conduct lessons for their peers. According to Tonia, the hardest issue for students to grasp was sexual harassment:

They kept dismissing it as teasing or flirting. They'd say, "But it's only in fun." It was really hard for them to understand that what counted was not how it was intended, *but how it was* received. *It took time, but they finally got it, and they've done a really good job of communicating the message. Kids will listen a lot more closely to what their peers say than to what adults say.*

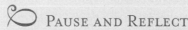

PAUSE AND REFLECT

Imagine an incident of aggressive behavior occurring in your classroom (e.g., a student explodes in anger and throws a book at another student). Think about the steps you would take to stop the aggression from escalating and to restore calm. What words would you use? Then, continue on to the next section and see how Sandy handled an outburst that occurred in her classroom.

RESPONDING TO VIOLENCE

Coping with Aggressive Behavior

Despite your best efforts at prevention, there are times when students erupt in hostile, aggressive behavior. A girl screams profanities and knocks a pile of dictionaries to the floor. A boy explodes in anger and throws a chair across the room. Someone yells, "I'll kill you," and hurls a notebook at another student. In situations like this—every teacher's nightmare—it's easy to lose self-control and lash out. As Fred puts it,

The *normal* reaction is to become angry and aggressive and to get in the kid's face. But *teachers can't react normally.* That will only make things worse, and your responsibility is *to make things better.*

In order to "make things better," you need to think carefully about what you will do to defuse the aggression and protect yourself and your students. Let's consider an episode that occurred in Sandy's classroom.

As usual, I was standing at the doorway as the kids were coming into the classroom. I noticed Robert come in without his backpack or any books. That didn't look right, and I watched him cross the room and go over to Daniel, who was sitting at his desk. Robert picked up the desk and the leg of Daniel's chair and overturned them, cursing and screaming the whole time. I ran over. The first thing I said was "Daniel, don't raise your hands." He was on the floor on his back, and Robert was standing over him screaming. I kept saying, "Robert, look at me, look at me, look at me." Finally, he made eye contact. Then I said, "You need to come with me." We began to walk toward the door, but he turned back and started cursing again. Very quietly and firmly I told him, "You need to come with me now." He followed me to the door, and as I reached the door I picked up the phone and called the office and said there was a problem and to send someone up. Then we stepped out into the hallway. Robert was angry and was going to leave, and I asked him to please stop and talk to me about what was going on, what was bothering him. I didn't yell, I didn't say, "How could you do something so stupid?" (even though that's what I felt like saying). I said, "Obviously you're upset about something. Tell me about it." It turns out that these two were friends, but Robert found out that Daniel was sleeping with his [Robert's] girl-friend. I heard a lot I didn't really want to hear, but it kept him occupied until the vice-principal came up.

Once the vice-principal took Robert, I got Daniel out into the hallway and asked him if he was OK, and if he needed to go to the nurse, or needed to be out of the classroom. He said no, he was OK. I told him, "You were very smart for not raising your hands against Robert." He returned to his seat, and all the kids started saying, "Daniel, are you OK?" and crowding around him. I told them, "Robert's in the office. Daniel's OK. Let's get started on chemistry." At the end of the period, the office called for Daniel to go to the peer mediation room to have the dispute mediated.

In addition to going to peer mediation, Robert was suspended for three days. But the day he was suspended, he came back after school hours (something he wasn't supposed to do) to apologize for his language. I accepted his apology, but I said that there were other ways to handle the situation and to express anger. It was a very low key discussion. I didn't make light of what had happened, but I told him I was glad he realized the danger of the situation.

After the suspension, Daniel came to me before homeroom to say he was feeling frightened about coming to class that day. It was going to be his first meeting with Robert, and Robert sits right in front of him. I said that I had already changed *both* their seats. I told him, "Don't worry, I'll be watching." When they came in, I told them each "You have a new seat," and showed them where to sit. There was no problem from that point on.

Analysis of Sandy's response to Robert's outburst reveals some important guidelines for dealing with aggression in the classroom. Let's examine her behavior more closely and consider the lessons to be learned.

1. Although Sandy admits that she wanted to respond with anger ("What is wrong with you?!"), she remained outwardly calm and in control. By doing so, she was able to *prevent the situation from escalating.* She lowered the level of emotion in the class and decreased the chance of becoming a victim herself. She then directed Daniel not to raise his hands against Robert. This prevented Robert's aggressive actions from escalating into a full-scale physical fight. Next, she issued quiet, firm, repetitive instructions for Robert to look at her. This created a lull in the altercation, during which she was able to separate the two boys ("You need to come with me"). Since Daniel was lying on the floor under the desk, it was easier for her to have Robert move away. In other cases, however, it may be advisable to remove the targets of the aggression. You can direct them to go to a nearby teacher's classroom, preferably with a friend, since they are bound to be angry and upset ("Take Scott and go to Ms. Thomson's room so we can get this sorted out") or have them move to a far corner of the room, out of the aggressor's line of sight.

2. Sandy's next action was to report that there was a problem in her room and *to summon help.* Never send angry, aggressive students to the office alone: You cannot be certain they will actually get there, nor do you know what they will

do on the way. If you do not have a telephone or intercom, quietly instruct a responsible student to go for assistance.

Who should be summoned will vary, so it's important for you to check on the procedures in your own school. Fred would call one of the two SROs—security resource officers—who patrol the hallways. Christina and Sandy would call the main office. Donnie would contact one of the security guards.

3. While Sandy waited for someone from the office to provide assistance, she spoke privately and quietly with Robert in an attempt to *defuse the aggression.* She did not rebuke or threaten punishment. Instead, she acknowledged his anger and showed her willingness to listen.

    Again, it's critical that you resist the temptation to "react normally" and lash out at the student. You need to speak slowly and softly and to minimize threat by not invading the student's space and keeping your hands by your side. Allow the student to relate facts and feelings, even if it involves profanity, and use active listening ("So you were really furious when you found out what was happening . . . "). Do not disagree or argue.

    If, despite your efforts to restore calm, the student's aggression escalates, it is best to move away unless you are trained in physical restraint techniques. Even then, don't use restraint unless you are strong enough and there are no other options. As Hyman (1997) emphasizes, "The last thing you ever want to do is to physically engage an enraged student who may be out of control" (p. 251).

4. When Robert came to see Sandy after school, he gave her the opportunity to discuss what had happened, to reinforce alternative ways to handle anger, and to accept his apology. He also gave her the chance to *reestablish a positive relationship.* Fred emphasizes how important this is:

    Suspending a violent kid isn't the end of the situation. At some point, the kid is going to come back, and then it's your job to rebuild the relationship. You need to reassure them that they're still a member of the class. You need to tell them, "OK, you messed up. But I'm on your side. You can learn from this."

5. Once Robert was on his way to the office and Daniel was back in his seat, Sandy scanned the room in order to *determine how the other students were feeling* and what to do next. She decided that her best course of action was to provide them with the basic facts ("Robert is in the office. Daniel's OK.") and to begin the lesson ("Let's get started on chemistry"). She certainly did not want to explore with her class the reasons behind Robert's aggressive actions.

Sometimes, however, your students may be so upset and frightened that it's impossible to continue working. Tonia Moore suggests that it's important to allow them to express their feelings:

If the students are upset, you have to give them the opportunity to talk about what happened and to acknowledge their fear. You don't want to pretend nothing happened and then send them on to the next class all churned up inside.

PRACTICAL TIPS FOR

RESPONDING EFFECTIVELY TO PHYSICAL FIGHTS

- *Quickly appraise the situation.* Is this a verbal altercation? Is there physical contact? Does anyone have a weapon?

- *Send a responsible student for help.* Send for the nearest teacher and for the principal or vice principal. Once other people are there to help, it's easier—and safer—to get the situation under control.

- *Tell students to stop.* Often, students don't want to continue the fight, and they'll respond to a short, clear, firm command. If you know the combatants' names, use them.

- *Disperse other students.* There's no need for an audience, and you don't want onlookers to become part of the fray. If you're in the hallway, direct students to be on their way. If you're in the classroom, send your students to the library or to some other safe place.

- *Do not intervene physically*—unless the age, size, and number of combatants indicates that it's safe to do so, there are three or four people to help, or you have learned physical restraint.

Responding Effectively to Physical Fights

Physical fights are more likely to occur in hallways and cafeterias than in classrooms. But what do you do if you're on the scene when a fight erupts? I asked the teachers that question one evening, as we talked about the problem of violence in schools. They were unanimous in their response, listed in the Practical Tips box. As we discussed the issue of fighting in school, the teachers repeatedly stressed the fact that fights are fast. They can erupt quickly—so you don't have a lot of time to think through a response—and they're usually over in less than 30 seconds (although that can seem like a lifetime). There was also amazing unanimity among the teachers on the issue of fights among girls versus boys. As Donnie put it: "Teachers shouldn't think that fighting is only going to happen among boys. Girls fight too— and girl fights are terrible. Girls kick, pull earrings, bite, scratch, and when you try to stop it, they turn on *you*."

It's important to remember that you must report violent acts. Every school system needs to have a violent incident reporting system that requires you to report what happened, when and where it happened, who was involved, and what action was taken (Blauvelt, 1990).

CONCLUDING COMMENTS

Resnick, Ireland, and Borowsky (2004) recently set out to identify factors that predict whether adolescents will commit acts of violence. Using data from the National Longitudinal Study of Adolescent Health, the largest study ever conducted of teenagers in the United States, these researchers identified several factors that make violence more likely, such as carrying a weapon, experiencing problems at school, and using alcohol and marijuana. They also identified factors that decrease the likelihood of involvement in violence. Of particular relevance to this chapter is their finding that *feeling connected to school is a key protective factor;* in other words, both males and females are less likely to perpetrate violence when they feel part of the school community.

Installing metal detectors and state-of-the-art security systems can only go so far in creating a more peaceful school. The challenge for teachers and administrators is to reach out to young people and help them feel connected. In the final analysis, it is the presence of caring adults that holds the greatest promise for preventing school violence.

SUMMARY

In the late 1990s, a series of horrific school shootings catapulted the topic of school violence to the front page. Politicians, policy makers, and pundits talked about youth violence as a national epidemic. Although data on the frequency and severity of school violence indicate a decrease, students, teachers, and parents are fearful, and the perception that violence is increasing is widespread.

School officials have tried to counter the problem of school violence by installing metal detectors and sophisticated security systems, but it is clear that these will not solve all the problems. This chapter presented a variety of strategies for preventing and responding to violence.

Prevention Strategies

- Build supportive school communities:
    Be alert to signs of hate.
    Examine the ways your school recognizes student achievement.
    Curb peer harassment.
- Teach social–emotional skills and conflict resolution.
- Know the early warning signs of potential for violence.
- Be attentive to whispers and rumors.
- De-escalate potentially explosive situations.
- Be alert for the presence of gang activity.
- Ask students to contribute to violence prevention efforts.

Responding to Violence

- Cope with aggressive behavior:
    Prevent escalation.
    Summon help.
    Defuse the aggression.
    Reestablish a positive relationship with the aggressor.
    Determine how the other students are feeling.
- Respond effectively to physical fights:
    Quickly appraise the situation.
    Send a responsible student for help.
    Tell the students to stop.
    Disperse onlookers.
    Do not intervene physically unless it is safe.

Metal detectors and security systems can only go so far. It's essential to build connections with students. In the final analysis, it is the presence of caring adults that holds the greatest promise for preventing violence.

Activities for Skill Building and Reflection

In Class

Consider the following situations. In small groups, discuss what you would do in each case.

a. As students enter your classroom, you overhear a girl teasing Annamarie about the boy Annamarie's dating. They go to their seats, but the taunts continue. Suddenly, Annamarie stands up, turns to the girl, and shouts, "You shut up, bitch. Just shut up, or I'll get you!"

b. Your students are taking a brief quiz on the homework. Those who have finished already are reading. As you circulate throughout the room, collecting the finished papers, you notice that James is looking at a catalog of weapons. He makes no attempt to conceal it.

c. Jesse comes to your first period class wearing a T-shirt with a Celtic cross surrounded by the words "White Pride World Wide."

d. You ask Taysha where her textbook is. She mutters something under her breath. When you tell her you didn't hear what she said, she shouts, "I left the f——— book in my locker!"

On Your Own

1. Interview an experienced teacher, the student assistance counselor, the school nurse, or a guidance counselor about the school's efforts to prevent violence. Find out answers to the following questions:

    If you think a student exhibits some of the early warning signs of potential for violence, to whom do you report?

    Is there an official form to file?

    Do you contact parents?

    Are school personnel aware of gang activity?

    What are the indicators of gang membership and gang activity?

2. Find out if the school where you are observing or teaching has a peer mediation program. If so, find answers to the following questions:

    How are students selected to be peer mediators?

    Who schedules peer mediation sessions?

    What is the procedure for requesting peer mediation?

    Can a teacher insist/suggest that two students go to peer mediation?

For Your Portfolio

Using the antibullying pledge in Figure 13.2 as a model, develop an antibullying pledge for your own students. Write a brief commentary explaining how you would introduce the pledge to your students and how you would reinforce it.

FOR FURTHER READING

Creating caring schools (2003).Theme issue of *Educational Leadership, 60(6)*.

   This entire issue of *Educational Leadership* is devoted to the topic of creating caring schools. Topics include bullying, teasing, creating community, social–emotional learning programs, student-led class meetings, collaborative learning, racial and ethnic tolerance.

Espelage, D. L., & Swearer, S. M. (Eds.) (2004). *Bullying in American schools:A social-ecological perspective on prevention and intervention.* Mahwah, NJ: Lawrence Erlbaum Associates, Inc.

   Espelage and Swearer argue that bullying is not just a matter of a "few bad kids" who make life miserable for other people. Rather, bullying has to be understood across family, peer, school, and community contexts, and interventions have to target the multiple environments that youngsters inhabit. Part III of this book examines "classroom characteristics associated with bullying." Chapters address teachers' attitudes toward bullying, the influence of peers and teachers on bullying among young children, and classroom ecologies that support or discourage bullying.

Teaching Tolerance is a magazine that is mailed twice a year at no charge to educators. It is published by the Southern Poverty Law Center, a nonprofit legal and educational foundation. (See listing below.) The magazine provides a wealth of information and resources on all aspects of promoting tolerance and respect and eliminating bias, oppression, and bullying (www.teachingtolerance.org).

ORGANIZATIONAL RESOURCES

The Anti-Defamation League (ADL), 823 United Nations Plaza, New York, NY 10017 (www.adl.org; 212-885-7800). Dedicated to combating hate crime and promoting intergroup cooperation and understanding.

Drug Strategies, 1575 Eye Street, NW, Suite 210,Washington, DC 20005 (www.drugstrategies.org; 202-289-9070). Publishes a guide on conflict resolution and violence prevention curricula.

National Educational Service, 1252 Loessch Rd., Bloomington, IN 47401 (www.nesonline.com; 1-800-733-6786). Provides a variety of resources and materials for understanding, preventing, and reducing violence in schools.

National School Safety Center, 141 Duesenberg Dr., Suite 11,Westlake Village, CA 91362 (www.nssc1.org; 805-373-9977). Resource for school safety information, training, and violence prevention.

The Safe and Drug Free Schools Web site for the U.S. Department of Education (www.ed.gov/offices/OESE/SDFS/news.html). Provides reports and articles on school safety and school violence.

The Southern Poverty Law Center, 400 Washington Avenue, Montgomery,AL 36104 (www.teachingtolerance.org).The Teaching Tolerance project provides teachers at all levels with ideas and free resources for building community, fighting bias, and celebrating diversity.

REFERENCES

Astor, R. A., & Benbenishty, R. (July 27, 2005). Zero tolerance for zero knowledge. *Education Week.* (Downloaded from www.edweek.org/ew/articles/2005.)

Astor, R. A., Meyer, H. A., & Behre, W. J. (1999). Unowned places and times: Maps and interviews about violence in high schools. *American Educational Research Journal, 36*(1), 3–42.

Barone, F. J. (1997). Bullying in school: It doesn't have to happen. *Phi Delta Kappan, 79,* 80–82.

Barton, P. E., Coley, R. J., & Wenglinsky, H. (1998). *Order in the classroom: Violence, discipline, and student achievement.* Princeton, NJ: Educational Testing Service.

Berreth, D., & Berman, S. (1997). The moral dimensions of schools. *Educational Leadership, 54*(8), 24–26.

Blauvelt, P. D. (1990). School security: "Who you gonna call?" *School Safety Newsjournal,* Fall, 4–8.

Bodine, R. J., & Crawford, D. K. (1998). *The handbook of conflict resolution education: A guide to building quality programs in schools.* San Francisco: Jossey-Bass.

Brener, N. D., Simon, T. R., Krug, E. G., & Lowry, R. (1999). Recent trends in violence-related behaviors among high school students in the United States. *Journal of the American Medical Association, 282,* 440–446.

Butterfield, F. (November 30, 2004). Crime in schools fell sharply over the 10 years ended '02. *The New York Times,* p. A21.

Chandler, K. A., Chapman, C. D., Rand, M. R., & Taylor, B. M. (1998). *Students' reports of school crime: 1989 and 1995.* Washington, D.C.: U. S. Department of Education, Office of Educational Research and Improvement, National Center for Education Statistics, and U. S. Department of Justice, Office of Justice Programs, Bureau of Justice Statistics.

Curwin, R. L. (1995). A humane approach to reducing violence in schools. *Educational Leadership, 52*(5), 72–75.

DeVoe, J. F., Peter, K., Kaufman, P., Miller, A., Noonan, M., Snyder, T. D., & Baum, K. (2004). *Indicators of school crime and safety: 2004* (NCESs 2005-002/NCJ 205290). U. S. Departments of Education and Justice. Washington, D.C.: U. S. Government Printing Office. (Can be downloaded from the World Wide Web at http://nces.ed.gov.)

Drummond, S., & Portner, J. (May 26, 1999). Arrests top 350 in threats, bomb scares. *Education Week,* pp. 1, 12–13.

Dwyer, K., Osher, D., & Warger, C. (1998). *Early warning, timely response: A guide to safe schools.* Washington, D.C.: U.S. Department of Education.

Dusenbury, L., Falco, M., Lake, A., Brannigan, R., & Bosworth, K. (1997). Nine critical elements of promising violence prevention programs. *Journal of School Health, 67*(10), 409–414.

Glassner, B. (August 13, 1999). School violence: The fears, the facts. *The New York Times,* p. A21.

Harmon, A. (August 26, 2004). Internet gives teenage bullies weapons to wound from afar. *The New York Times,* pp. A1, A23.

Haynes, C. C., Chaltain, S., Ferguson Jr., J. E., Hudson Jr., D. L., & Thomas. O. (2003). *The first amendment in schools.* Alexandria, VA: Association of Supervision and Curriculum Development.

Hoover, J., & Oliver, R. (1996). *The bullying prevention handbook: A guide for teachers, principals and counselors.* Bloomington, IN: National Educational Service.

Howell, J. C., & Lynch, J. P. (2000). *Youth gangs in schools.* Washington, D.C.: Office of Juvenile Justice and Delinquency Prevention, U. S. Department of Justice. (Available online at www.ncjrs.org/html/ojjdp/jjbul2000_8_2/contents.html.)

Hyman, I. A. (1997). *School discipline and school violence: The teacher variance approach.* Boston: Allyn and Bacon.

Johnson, D. W., & Johnson, R. T. (1995). *Teaching students to be peacemakers.* 3rd ed. Edina, MN: Interaction Book Co.

Johnson, D. W., & Johnson, R. T. (1996). Reducing school violence through conflict resolution training. *NASSP Bulletin, 80*(579), 11-18.

Keith, S., & Martin, M. E. (2005). Cyber-bullying: Creating a culture of respect in a cyber world. *Reclaiming children and youth, 13*(4), 224-228.

Lal, S. R., Lal, D., & Achilles, C. M. (1993). *Handbook on gangs in schools: Strategies to reduce gang-related activities.* Newbury Park, CA: Corwin Press.

Leishman, J. (2002). Cyberbullying: The Internet is the latest weapon in a bully's arsenal. Toronto: CBC News. Available at: http://cbc/ca/news/national/news/cyberbullying/index.html.

Lisante, J. E. (June 6, 2005). Cyber bullying: No muscles needed. Published on Connect for Kids (http://www.connectforkids.org).

Miller, E. (1994). Peer mediation catches on, but some adults don't. *Harvard Education Letter, 10*(3), 8.

Nansel, T. R., Overpeck, M., Pilla, R. S., Ruan, W. J., Simons-Morton, B., & Scheidt, P. (2001). Bullying behaviors among US youth: Prevalence and association with psychosocial adjustment. *Journal of the American Medical Association, 285*(16), 2094-2100.

Noguera, P. A. (1995). Preventing and producing violence: A critical analysis of responses to school violence. *Harvard Educational Review, 65*(2), 189-212.

Olweus, D. (2003). A profile of bullying at school. *Educational Leadership, 60*(6), 12-17.

Portner, J. (April 12, 2000). School violence down, report says, but worry high. *Education Week,* 3.

Quarles, C. L. (1989). *School violence: A survival guide for school staff, with emphasis on robbery, rape, and hostage taking.* Washington D.C.: National Education Association.

Remboldt, C. (1998). Making violence unacceptable. *Educational Leadership, 56*(1), 32-38.

Resnick, M. D., Ireland, M., & Borowsky, I. (2004). Youth violence perpetration: What protects? What predicts? Findings from the National Longitudinal Study of Adolescent Health. *Journal of Adolescent Health, 35*(5), 424.e1-424.e10. (Available online at www.allaboutkids.umn.edu/cfahad/JAHViolence.pdf.)

Richard, A. (September 8, 1999). As students return, focus is on security. *Education Week,* 1, 14-15.

Shariff, S. (2004). Keeping schools out of court: Legally defensible models of leadership. *The Educational Forum, 68,* 222-232.

Southern Poverty Law Center (September 2004). Hate among youth becomes widespread. *SPLC Report, 34*(3), p. 1.

Stephens, R. D. (1994). Planning for safer and better schools: School violence prevention and intervention strategies. *School Psychology Review, 23*(2), 204–215.

Strom, P. S., & Strom, R. D. (2005). Cyberbullying by adolescents: A preliminary assessment. *The Educational Forum, 70*(1), 21–36.

Trump, K. (1993). Tell teen gangs: School's out. *American School Board Journal, 180*(7), 39–42.

U.S. Department of Education (February/March 2001). Studies report declining rate of school violence. *Community Update, 85,* 1–2.

Verdugo, R. (1997). *Youth gangs: Findings and solutions for schools, communities, and families.* Washington, D.C.: National Education Association.

Vossekuil, B., Fein, R., Reddy, M., Borum, R., & Modzeleski, W. (2002). *The final report and findings of the Safe School Initiative: Implications for the prevention of school attacks in the United States.* Washington, D.C.: U. S. Secret Service and the U. S. Department of Education. (Available on the Web at www.secretservice.gov/ntac/ssi_final_report.pdf.)

Walker, H. M., Colvin, G., Ramsey, E. (1995). *Antisocial behavior in school: Strategies and best practices.* Pacific Grove, CA: Brooks/Cole.

Walsh, M. (March 8, 2000). Law update: A fine line between dangerous and harmless student expression. *Education Week,* 14.

Wessler, S. L. (2000/2001). Sticks and stones. *Educational Leadership, 58*(4), 28–33.

Name Index

SUBJECT INDEX

Note: Page numbers in *italic* type indicate figures or tables.